Children's
Book
Review
Index

ISSN 0147-5681

Children's Book Review Index

Volume 24, 1998

Beverly Baer
Charles B. Montney
Editors

GALE

DETROIT • LONDON

Managing Editor: Debra Kirby
Project Editors: Beverly Baer, Charles B. Montney
Editors: Shelly Dickey, Dana Ferguson, Lydia Fink, Kelly Sprague,
Associate Editors: Paula Cutcher-Jackson, Nancy Franklin, William H. Harmer,
Sharon M. McGilvray, Kathleen Meek
Assistant Editors: Ellice Engdahl, Robert Franzino, Prindle LaBarge
Intern: Noah Schusterbauer

Research Manager: Victoria B. Cariappa

Production Director: Mary Beth Trimper
External Production Assistants: Deborah Milliken
Product Design Manager: Cynthia Baldwin
Desktop Publisher: Gary Leach

Manager, Data Entry Services: Eleanor Allison
Data Entry Coordinators: Janine Whitney
Data Entry Associates: Maleka Imrana, Arlene Ann Kevonian, Nancy Sheridan,
Angela Simpson, Shanitta L. Watkins, Constance J. Wells

Manager, Technical Support Services: Theresa Rocklin
Senior Programmer/Analyst: Piotr Luczycki
Program Design: Donald G. Dillaman

While every effort has been made to ensure the reliability of the information presented in this publication, Gale does not guarantee the accuracy of the data contained herein. Gale accepts no payment for listing; and inclusion in the publication of any organization, agency, institution, publication, service, or individual does not imply endorsement of the publisher. Errors brought to the attention of the publisher and verified to the satisfaction of the publisher will be corrected in future editions.

Library of Congress Catalog Card Number 75-27408
ISBN 0-7876-2435-7
ISSN 0147-5681

Printed in the United States of America

10 9 8 7 6 5 4 3 2 1

Contents

Introduction

Children's Book Review Index (*CBRI*) is a master key providing access to reviews of thousands of children's books and periodicals. Reviews of audio books or electronic media are cited if they are presentations of previously published books. The citations in *CBRI* are extracted from *Book Review Index* (*BRI*), which currently indexes more than 600 publications. The list of journals in which reviews of children's books appear includes those devoted to children's literature, such as *Horn Book Magazine* and *School Library Journal*; reviewing media that cover many types of books, like *Booklist*, *Kirkus Reviews* and the *Times Literary Supplement*; and many other periodicals that occasionally carry reviews of children's books.

Children's Book Review Index Now Provides Online Review Citations

CBRI now indexes online book review citations, thereby enhancing its already extensive indexing of print journals. Newly indexed sources from the World Wide Web include: *CM: Canadian Review of Materials*; *First Monday: Peer-Reviewed Journal on the Internet*; *H-Net: Humanities and Social Science Online*; *Rettig on Reference*, James Rettig's review column appearing on Gale's web site; and *Teaching English as a Second or Foreign Language*. All online sources indexed are included in the Publications Indexed section.

Highlights

- **Comprehensive**—*CBRI* includes citations to all books, periodicals, books-on-tape, and book-related electronic media appearing in *BRI* in the past year that at least one reviewer recommended for children ages ten and younger.

- **Accurate**—Each entry is double-checked for accuracy.

- **Easy-to-Use**—Entries are arranged by author's name, or by title if there is no primary author, in a single alphabetical sequence with citations listed in an easy-to-read format. A Title Index aids readers who do not have complete author information, and the Illustrator Index allows *CBRI* users to find additional works by their favorite artist or photographer.

Form and Content of Entries

[1] **Naylor, Phyllis Reynolds**
[2] *Saving Shiloh* [3](*Illus. by Barry Moser*)
[4] y [5] CCB-B – [6] v51 – S '97 – [7] p20+ [8] [51-250]

[1] Author or Editor of work being reviewed
[2] Title of work being reviewed
[3] Illustrator (if applicable)
[4] Age or Type code (see explanation below)
[5] Abbreviation of reviewing periodical title (see Publications Indexed for complete list of abbreviations)
[6] Volume number and date or issue number
[7] Page on which review appears (see explanation of page number designations below)
[8] Approximate number of words in the review. Ranges used are 1-50, 51-250, 251-500, and 500+.

Works published in several editions over the years may have the name of the editor, translator, or publisher added in parentheses after the title to clarify which version is under review. For audio books, the last name of the reader or performer may appear in parentheses following the title.

Explanation of Letter Codes Some entries in *CBRI* include age and/or type codes that help define the kind of work being reviewed.

- **Age codes:** Age designations are determined by the reviewer or publisher. A "y" identifies books for young adults ages eleven and older. This code appears with some *CBRI* entries when a book has been considered appropriate for children by at least one reviewer and for young adults by others. It identifies the specific reviews that recommend a book for readers ages eleven and up. All other citations are for reviews that recommend a book for readers ages 10 and younger.

- **Type codes:** A "p" identifies a review of a periodical; "r" identifies a review of a reference work.

Page Number Designations:

"R" before a page number in a citation indicates that the page number appears as a roman numeral in the periodical.

"*" (an asterisk) following a page number indicates a page within a special section of a periodical that was not numbered sequentially with the main section.

"+" (plus sign) following the page number indicates a review that continues on a succeeding page(s).

"ONL" instead of a page number: indicates that the review appears in an online publication and, as such, does not have a page number. To locate these reviews, consult the source site's searching instructions.

Arrangement of Entries

A user searching for a particular entry in the author or title indexes should note the following guidelines.

● Roman and arabic numerals file in numerical order before the letter A. For example, the title *50 Fun Games for Kids* would file at the beginning of the Title Index; *Fifty Paper Planes* would file in the F's.

● Acronyms and initialisms file as single words unless periods or spaces divide the letters. Letters following a period or space file as new words. Users should note that variant forms of initialisms would file separately under this arrangement. For example, U.S.A. would appear near the beginning of the U section, while USA would file just before the word "Use."

● Corporate (group-name) authors and titles with no author are interfiled with authors in the main (Author) entry section.

Indexes Aid Search for Reviews

The Illustrator and Title Indexes, which follow the main Author section, allow the user to find citations by way of the title or the name of the illustrator. These indexes are useful when the name of the author is unknown or when the reader is looking for additional works by a favorite artist, information that is often difficult to find. Listings in these indexes refer the user back to the review citations found in the main Author section.

CBRI Available in Electronic Formats

Diskette/Magnetic Tape: *CBRI* is available for licensing on magnetic tape or diskette in a fielded format. Either the complete database or a custom selection of entries may be ordered. The database is available for internal data processing and nonpublishing only. For more information, call 800-877-GALE.

Online: *CBRI* entries are also available on DIALOG as part of *Book Review Index* (File 137).

Comments and Suggestions Are Welcome

The editors welcome comments or suggestions on the scope and coverage of *CBRI*. Please address correspondence to:

Editors, *Children's Book Review Index*
The Gale Group
27500 Drake Rd.
Farmington Hills, MI 48331-3535
Phone: 248-699-GALE
Toll-free: 800-347-GALE
Fax: 248-699-8067

Publications Indexed

The periodical abbreviations used in *Children's Book Review Index* citations are arranged here alphabetically in letter-by-letter sequence. The full periodical title appears to the right of the abbreviation. The following information is also provided for each publication: frequency, ISSN, subscription address, and URL if the source is available online.

A

A Anth: *American Anthropologist*
Quarterly ISSN 0002-7294
American Anthropological Association
4350 N. Fairfax Dr., Ste.640
Arlington, VA 22203-1621

A Art: *American Artist*
Monthly ISSN 0002-7375
P.O. Box 1944
Marion, OH 43305-1944

AB: *AB Bookman's Weekly*
Weekly ISSN 0001-0340
P.O. Box AB
Clifton, NJ 07015
http://www.abbookman.com/

ABR: *American Book Review*
Bimonthly ISSN 0149-9408
Unit for Contemporary Literature
Campus Box 4241
Illinois St. Univ.
Normal, IL 61790-4241

Advocate: *Advocate*
Biweekly ISSN 0001-8996
P.O. Box 541
Mount Morris, IL 61054-0541
http://www.advocate.com/

Aethlon: *Aethlon: The Journal of Sport Literature*
Biannual ISSN 1048-3756
Department of English
East Tennessee State University
Box 70683
Johnson City, TN 37614-0683

Afterimage: *Afterimage*
10 issues/year ISSN 0300-7472
31 Prince St.
Rochester, NY 14607
http://www2.rpa.net/~vsw/

AH: *American Heritage*
8 issues/year ISSN 0002-8738
American Heritage Subscription Dept.
P.O. Box 5022
Harlan, IA 51593-0522
http://www.forbes.com/ah/

AJA: *American Journal of Archaeology*
Quarterly ISSN 0002-9114
Archaeological Institute of America
Boston University
656 Beacon St.
Boston, MA 02215-2010
http://classics.lsa.umich.edu/AJA.html

AL: *American Literature*
Quarterly ISSN 0002-9831
Duke University Press
Box 90660
Duke University
Durham, NC 27708-0660

A Lib: *American Libraries*
Monthly ISSN 0002-9769
Subscription Services
American Library Association
50 E. Huron St.
Chicago, IL 60611

Am: *America*
Weekly ISSN 0002-7049
America Press, Inc.
106 W. 56th St.
New York, NY 10019

Am MT: *American Music Teacher*
Bimonthly ISSN 0003-0112
The Carew Tower
441 Vine St., Suite 505
Cincinnati, OH 45202-2814

Am Sci: *American Scientist*
Bimonthly ISSN 0003-0996
Sigma Xi
P.O. Box 13975
Research Triangle Park, NC 27709
http://www.amsci.org/amsci/

Am Spect: *American Spectator*
Monthly ISSN 0148-8414
P.O. Box 1978
Marion, OH 43305-1978
http://www.spectator.org/

Analog: *Analog Science Fiction and Fact*
Monthly ISSN 1059-2113
P.O. Box 54625
Boulder, CO 80328-4625

Ant & CM: *Antiques & Collecting Magazine*
Monthly ISSN 1084-0818
1006 S. Michigan Ave.
Chicago, IL 60605

Ant R: *Antioch Review*
Quarterly ISSN 0003-5769
Subscriptions
P.O. Box 148
Yellow Springs, OH 45387
http://www.elibrary.com/

APH: *Air Power History*
Quarterly ISSN 1044-016X
George C. Marshall Library
Virginia Military Institute
Lexington, VA 24450
http://www.aon.af.mil/historic.htm

Apo: *Apollo*
Monthly ISSN 0003-6356
c/o Speedimpex USA Inc.
35-02 48th Ave.
L.I.C., NY 11101-2421

ARBA: *American Reference Books Annual*
Annual ISSN 0065-9959
Libraries Unlimited, Inc.
P.O. Box 6633
Englewood, CO 80155-6633

Arch: *Archaeology*
Bimonthly ISSN 0003-8113
Subscription Service
P.O. Box 420423
Palm Coast, FL 32142-0427
http://www.he.net/~archaeol/

Arm Det: *Armchair Detective*
Quarterly ISSN 0004-217Z
P.O. Box 929
Bound Brook, NJ 08805-0929

A & S Sm: *Air & Space/Smithsonian*
Bimonthly ISSN 0886-2257
P.O. Box 420113
Palm Coast, FL 32142-0113
http://www.airspacemag.com/

ASBYP: *Appraisal: Science Books for Young People*
Quarterly ISSN 0003-7052
605 Commonwealth Ave.
Boston, MA 02215

Astron: *Astronomy*
Monthly ISSN 0091-6358
21027 Crossroads Circle
P.O. Box 1612
Waukesha, WI 53187-1612
http://www.kalmbach.com/

Atl: *Atlantic Monthly*
Monthly ISSN 0276-9077
Atlantic Subscription Processing Center
Box 52661
Boulder, CO 80322
http://www.theatlantic.com/

Aud: *Audubon*
Bimonthly ISSN 0097-7136
National Audubon Society
P.O. Box 52529
Boulder, CO 80322-2529

Aust Bk R: *Australian Book Review*
10 issues/year ISSN 0155-2864
Box 2320
Richmond South 3121, Australia
http://www.vicnet.au/~abr/

B

BAS: *Bulletin of the Atomic Scientists*
6 issues/year ISSN 0096-3402
6042 S. Kimbark Ave.
Chicago, IL 60637
http://neog.com/atomic/

Belles Let: *Belles Lettres*
3 issues/year ISSN 0884-2957
Karen T. Jenkins
P.O. Box 372068
Satellite Beach, FL 32937-0068

B Ent: *Black Enterprise*
Monthly ISSN 0006-4165
Circulation Center
P.O. Box 3009
Harlan, IA 51537-4100
http://www.blackenterprise.com/

BIC: *Books in Canada*
9 issues/year ISSN 0045-2564
Canadian Review of Books Ltd.
Circulation Dept.
50 St. Clair Ave. East
Toronto, ON, Canada M4T 1M9

Bkbird: *Bookbird*
Quarterly ISSN 0006-7377
Subscriptions
P.O. Box 807
Highland Park, IL 60035-0807

Bks Keeps: *Books for Keeps*
Bimonthly ISSN 0143-909X
6 Brightfield Rd., Lee
London SE12 8QF, England

BL: *Booklist*
22 issues/year ISSN 0006-7385
434 W. Downer
Aurora, IL 60506
http://www.ala.org/booklist/

Bloom Rev: *Bloomsbury Review*
Bimonthly ISSN 0276-1564
1762 Emerson St.
Denver, CO 80218-1012

Bl S: *Black Scholar*
Quarterly ISSN 0006-4246
P.O. Box 2869
Oakland, CA 94618

Books: *Books Magazine*
Bimonthly ISSN 0006-7423
43 Museum St.
London WC1A 1LY, England

Boston R: *Boston Review*
Bimonthly ISSN 0734-2306
E53-407
30 Wadsworth St.
M.I.T.
Cambridge, MA 02139
http://www-polisci.mit.edu/bostonreview/

B Rpt: *Book Report*
5 issues/year ISSN 0731-4388
Linworth Publishing, Inc.
480 East Wilson Bridge Rd., Suite L
Worthington, OH 43085-2372

BSA-P: *Bibliographical Society of America.*
Papers
Quarterly ISSN 0006-128X
P.O. Box 397
Grand Central Station
New York, NY 10163-0397

Bus W: *Business Week*
Weekly ISSN 0007-7135
P.O. Box 430
Hightstown, NJ 08520
http://www.businessweek.com/

BW: *Book World*
Weekly ISSN 0006-7369
Washington Post
1150 15th St. N.W.
Washington, DC 20071

BWatch: *Bookwatch*
Monthly ISSN 0896-6521
James A Cox
278 Orchard Dr.
Oregon, WI 53575
http://www.execpc.com/~mbr/bookwatch/

C

Callaloo: *Callaloo*
Quarterly ISSN 0161-2492
Johns Hopkins University Press
Journals Publishing Division
2715 N. Charles St.
Baltimore, MD 21218-4319
http://muse.jhu.edu/journals/callaloo/

Can CL: *Canadian Children's Literature*
Quarterly ISSN 0319-0080
Depts. of English and French
University of Guelph
Guelph, ON, Canada N1G 2W1
http://www.uoguelph.ca/englit/ccl/

Can Lit: *Canadian Literature*
Quarterly ISSN 0008-4360
Circulation Manager, Canadian Literature
#167-1855 West Mall
University of British Columbia
Vancouver, BC, Canada V6T 1Z2
http://www.swifty.com/cdn_lit/

CAY: *Come-All-Ye*
Quarterly ISSN 0736-6132
P.O. Box 494
Hatboro, PA 19040-0494

CBR: *Computer Book Review*
Quarterly ISSN 0737-0334
P.O. Box 61067
Honolulu, HI 96839
http://www.BostonBookReview.com/cbr/

CBRS: *Children's Book Review Service*
Monthly ISSN 0090-7987
220 Berkeley Place
Brooklyn, NY 11217

CC: *Christian Century*
Weekly ISSN 0009-5281
Subscription Service
407 S. Dearborn St.
Chicago, IL 60605-1150

CCB-B: *Center for Children's Books.*
Bulletin
11 issues/year ISSN 0008-9036
The Bulletin of the Center for Children's
Books
University of Illinois Press
1325 S. Oak
Champaign, IL 61820
http://edfu.lis.uiuc.edu/puboff/bccb/

CG: *Canadian Geographic*
Bimonthly ISSN 0706-2168
Box 1182
Lewiston, NY 14092-8182
http://www.cangeo.ca/

Ch Bk News: *Children's Book News*
Quarterly ISSN 0075-9938
Canadian Children's Book Centre
35 Spadina Rd.
Toronto, ON, Canada M5R 2S9
http://www.lglobal.com/~ccbc/

Ch BWatch: *Children's Bookwatch*
Monthly ISSN 0896-4521
James A. Cox
278 Orchard Drive
Oregon, WI 53575
http://www.execpc.com/~mbr/bookwatch/

Child Lit: *Children's Literature*
Annual ISSN 0092-8208
Yale University Press
P.O. Box 209040
New Haven, CT 06520-9040

ChLAQ: *Children's Literature Association*
Quarterly
Quarterly ISSN 0885-0429
ChLA
P.O. Box 138
Battle Creek, MI 49016

Choice: *Choice*
11 issues/year ISSN 0009-4978
100 Riverview Center
Middletown, CT 06457
http://www.ala.org/acrl/choice/

Ch Today: *Christianity Today*
14 issues/year ISSN 0009-5753
P.O. Box 11618
Des Moines, IA 50340-1618
http://www.christianity.net/ct/

Class Out: *Classical Outlook*
Quarterly ISSN 0009-8361
Business Manager
American Classical League
Miami University
Oxford, OH 45056
http://www.classics.uga.edu/journals.html

CLW: *Catholic Library World*
Bimonthly ISSN 0008-820X
Catholic Library Association
5005 Jamieson Ave.
St. Louis, MO 63109

CML: *Classical and Modern Literature*
Quarterly ISSN 0197-2227
CML, Inc.
P.O. Box 629
Terre Haute, IN 47808-0629

Col Lit: *College Literature*
3 issues/year ISSN 0093-3139
Editor, College Literature
SSC2/474
West Chester University
West Chester, PA 19383

Comw: *Commonweal*
Biweekly ISSN 0010-3330
Commonweal Foundation
475 Riverdrive Dr., Room 405
New York, NY 10115
http://www.commonwealmagazine.org/

Cont Ed: *Contemporary Education*
Quarterly ISSN 0010-7476
School of Education
Indiana State University
Terre Haute, IN 47809

CP: *Contemporary Psychology*
Monthly ISSN 0010-7549
750 First St. NE
Washington, DC 20002-4242

CR: *Contemporary Review*
Monthly ISSN 0010-7565
Mercury Airfreight International Ltd., Inc.
2323 Randolph Ave.
Avenel, NJ 07001

Cres: *Cresset*
9 issues/year ISSN 0011-1198
#10 Huegli Hall
Valparaiso University
651 S. College Ave.
Valparaiso, IN 46383

Critm: *Criticism*
Quarterly ISSN 0011-1589
Wayne State University Press
Leonard N. Simons Bldg.
4809 Woodward Ave.
Detroit, MI 48201-1309

CRL: *College & Research Libraries*
Bimonthly ISSN 0010-0870
Subscription Dept.
c/o Choice Magazine
100 Riverview Center
Middletown, CT 06457-3445

CSM: *Christian Science Monitor*
Daily ISSN 0882-7729
P.O. Box 37308
Boone, IA 50037-0308
http://www.csmonitor.com/

Cur R: *Curriculum Review*
9 issues/year ISSN 0147-2453
c/o W D & S Publishing
20 Highland Ave. Ste. 4
Metuchen, NJ 08840
http://www.ragan.com/

CW: *Classical World*
Bimonthly ISSN 0009-8418
Classical Assn. of the Atlantic States
Dept. of Classics
Duquesne University
Pittsburgh, PA 15282-1704

D

Dance: *Dance Magazine*
Monthly ISSN 0011-6009
P.O. Box 5068
Brentwood, TN 37024-9725
http://www.dancemagazine.com/

Dog Fan: *Dog Fancy*
Monthly ISSN 0892-6522
P.O. Box 53264
Boulder, CO 80328-3264
http://www.dogfancy.com/

E

Econ: *Economist*
Weekly ISSN 0013-0613
P.O. Box 58524
Boulder, CO 80328-8524
http://www.economist.com/

EJ: *English Journal*
8 issues/year ISSN 0013-8274
NCTE
1111 W. Kenyon Road
Urbana, IL 61801-1096

EL: *Educational Leadership*
8 issues/year ISSN 0013-1784
Membership Dept.
1250 N. Pitt St.
Alexandria, VA 22314-1453
http://www.asco.org/

Emerg Lib: *Emergency Librarian*
5 issues/year ISSN 0315-8888
Transborder Mail
Box 6016
Federal Way, WA 98063-6016

Ent W: *Entertainment Weekly*
Weekly ISSN 1049-0434
P.O. Box 30608
Tampa, FL 33630-0608
http://www.PathFinder.com/ew/

Esq: *Esquire*
Monthly ISSN 0194-9535
P.O. Box 7146
Red Oak, IA 51591

Essence: *Essence*
Monthly ISSN 0014-0880
P.O. Box 53400
Boulder, CO 80322-3400

Ext: *Extrapolation*
Quarterly ISSN 0014-5483
Journals Dept.
Kent State University Press
Kent, OH 44242

F

Fam Relat: *Family Relations*
Quarterly ISSN 0197-6664
National Council on Family Relations
3989 Central Ave. NE, Suite 550
Minneapolis, MN 55421
http://www.iog.wayne.edu/FR/
homepage.html

Fic Int: *Fiction International*
Semiannual ISSN 0092-1912
San Diego State University Press
San Diego State University
San Diego, CA 92182

FIR: *Films in Review*
Bimonthly ISSN 0015-1688
P.O. Box 970
Wantagh, NY 11793

Five Owls: *Five Owls*
5 issues/year ISSN 0892-6735
Hamline Univ. Crossroads Ctr. MS-C1924
1536 Hewitt Ave.
St. Paul, MN 55104

Fortune: *Fortune*
Biweekly ISSN 0015-8259
P.O. Box 30604
Tampa, FL 33630-0604
http://fortune.com/

FQ: *Film Quarterly*
Quarterly ISSN 0015-1386
University of California Press
Journals Dept.
2120 Berkeley Way
Berkeley, CA 94720

FR: *French Review*
Bimonthly ISSN 0016-111X
Mailcode 4510
Dept. of Modern Languages
Southern Illinois University
Carbondale, IL 62901-4510

Fut: *Futurist*
Bimonthly ISSN 0016-3317
7910 Woodmont Ave., Ste. 450
Bethesda, MD 20814
http://www.wfs.org/wfs/

G

Ga R: *Georgia Review*
Quarterly ISSN 0016-8386
University of Georgia
Athens, GA 30602-9009

Ger Q: *German Quarterly*
Quarterly ISSN 0016-8831
American Association of Teachers of German
112 Haddontowne Court, #104
Cherry Hill, NJ 08034-3668

GJ: *Geographical Journal*
3 issues/year ISSN 0016-7398
Royal Geographical Society
1 Kensington Gore
London SW7 2AR, England

H

HB: *Horn Book Magazine*
Bimonthly ISSN 0018-5078
Circulation Dept.
11 Beacon St., Ste. 1000
Boston, MA 02108

HB Guide: *Horn Book Guide*
Semiannual ISSN 1044-405X
The Horn Book, Inc.
Circulation Dept.
11 Beacon St., Ste. 1000
Boston, MA 02108

HE: *Human Events*
Weekly ISSN 0018-7194
Subscription Services Dept.
7811 Montrose Rd.
Potomac, MD 20854

HER: *Harvard Educational Review*
Quarterly ISSN 0017-8055
Gutman Library, Ste. 349
6 Appian Way
Cambridge, MA 02138-3752
http://hugse1.harvard.edu/~hepg/her.html

Hisp: *Hispania*
Quarterly ISSN 0018-2133
AATSP
Frasier Hall - Room 8
University of Northern Colorado
Greeley, CO 80639

HMR: *Hungry Mind Review*
Quarterly ISSN 0887-5499
1648 Grand Ave.
St. Paul, MN 55105
http://www.BostonBookReview.com/hmr/

Hort: *Horticulture*
10 issues/year ISSN 0018-5329
Subscription Service
P.O. Box 53880
Boulder, CO 80322

HR: *Hudson Review*
Quarterly ISSN 0018-702X
684 Park Ave.
New York, NY 10021

HT: *History Today*
Monthly ISSN 0018-2753
M.A.I. Ltd.
2323 Randolph Ave.
Avenel, NJ 07001

I

ILN: *Illustrated London News*
6 issues/year ISSN 0019-2422
Orient-Express Magazine
c/o Mercury Airfreight International, Ltd.
2323 Randolph Ave.
Avenel, NJ 07001

ILS: *Irish Literary Supplement*
Semiannual ISSN 0733-3390
Irish Studies
114 Paula Blvd.
Selden, NY 11784

Inc.: *Inc.*
Monthly ISSN 0162-8968
P.O. Box 54129
Boulder, CO 80322-4129
http://www.inc.com/

Inst: *Instructor*
8 issues/year ISSN 1049-5851
P.O. Box 53896
Boulder, CO 80322-3896
http://www.scholastic.com/instructor/

J

JAF: *Journal of American Folklore*
Quarterly ISSN 0021-8715
American Folklore Society
4350 North Fairfax Drive, Ste. 640
Arlington, VA 20035

JAL: *Journal of Academic Librarianship*
Bimonthly ISSN 0099-1333
JAI Press
55 Old Post Rd., No. 2
P.O. Box 1678
Greenwich, CT 06836-1678
gopher://ukoln.bath.ac.uk:7070/11/
BUBL_Main_Menu/E

J Am St: *Journal of American Studies*
3 issues/year ISSN 0021-8758
Cambridge University Press
Journals Dept.
40 W. 20th St.
New York, NY 10011-4211
http://www.cup.org/

J Bl St: *Journal of Black Studies*
Bimonthly ISSN 0021-9347
Sage Publications, Inc.
2455 Teller Rd.
Thousand Oaks, CA 91320

JEGP: *Journal of English and Germanic Philology*
Quarterly ISSN 0363-6941
University of Illinois Press
1325 S. Oak St.
Champaign, IL 61820

JEL: *Journal of Economic Literature*
Quarterly ISSN 0022-0515
2014 Broadway, Ste. 305
Nashville, TN 37203

JNE: *Journal of Negro Education*
Quarterly ISSN 0022-2984
Circulation Dept.
P.O. Box 311
Howard University
Washington, DC 20059

JOYS: *Journal of Youth Services in Libraries*
Quarterly ISSN 0894-2498
American Library Association
Subscription Dept.
50 E. Huron St.
Chicago, IL 60611
http://scholar.lib.vt.edu/ejournals/JYSL/
jysl.html

JPC: *Journal of Popular Culture*
Quarterly ISSN 0022-3840
Popular Press
Bowling Green State University
Bowling Green, OH 43403

JPE: *Journal of Political Economy*
Bimonthly ISSN 0022-3808
University of Chicago Press
5720 S. Woodlawn Ave.
Chicago, IL 60637

JSH: *Journal of Southern History*
Quarterly ISSN 0022-4642
Dept. of History
University of Georgia
Athens, GA 30602

J Urban H: *Journal of Urban History*
6 issues/year ISSN 0096-1442
Sage Publications, Inc.
2455 Teller Rd.
Thousand Oaks, CA 91320

K

Kliatt: *Kliatt Young Adult Paperback Book Guide*
6 issues/year ISSN 1065-8602
33 Bay State Road
Wellesley, MA 02181

KR: *Kirkus Reviews*
Semi-Monthly ISSN 0042-6598
200 Park Ave. S.
New York, NY 10003

L

LA: *Language Arts*
8 issues/year ISSN 0360-9170
NCTE
1111 W. Kenyon Rd.
Urbana, IL 61801-1096

Lam Bk Rpt: *Lambda Book Report*
Bimonthly ISSN 1048-9487
Lambda Rising, Inc.
1625 Connecticut Avenue, NW
Washington, DC 20009-1013

LAR: *Library Association Record*
Monthly ISSN 0024-2195
World Wide Subscription Service Ltd.
Unit 4 Gibbs Reed Farm
Ticehurst, East Sussex TN5 7HE, England
http://www.la-hq.org.uk/

LATBR: *Los Angeles Times Book Review*
Weekly ISSN 0458-3035
Los Angeles Times, Inc.
Times Mirror Square
Los Angeles, CA 90053

Learning: *Learning*
6 issues/year ISSN 0090-3167
P.O. Box 54293
Boulder, CO 80322-4293
http://www.theeducationcenter.com/

LJ: *Library Journal*
20 issues/year ISSN 0363-0277
P.O. Box 59690
Boulder, CO 80322-9690

Lon R Bks: *London Review of Books*
24 issues/year ISSN 0260-9592
P.O. Box 1953
Marion, OH 43305-1953

LT: *Library Talk*
5 issues/year ISSN 1043-237X
Linworth Publishing
480 East Wilson Bridge Rd., Suite L
Worthington, OH 43085-2373

M

Mac: *Maclean's*
Weekly ISSN 0024-9262
P.O. Box 1600
Postal Station A
Toronto, ON, Canada M5W 2B8
http://www.enews.com/magazines/
macleans/

Magpies: *Magpies*
5 issues/year ISSN 0817-0088
Subscription
P.O. Box 563
Hamilton, Queensland 4007, Australia

MailboxT: *Mailbox Teacher*
4/year ISSN 1098-5670
P.O. Box 54293
Boulder, CO 80328-4293
http://www.themailboxteacher.com

Meanjin: *Meanjin*
Quarterly ISSN 0025-6293
99 Barry Street
Carlton, Victoria 3053, Australia

M Ed J: *Music Educators Journal*
6 issues/year ISSN 0027-4321
1806 Robert Fulton Drive
Reston, VA 20191-4348

MEJ: *Middle East Journal*
Quarterly ISSN 0026-3141
Circulation Dept.
Middle East Journal
1761 N Street NW
Washington, DC 20036-2882
http://www.mideasti.org/mej/

Meridian: *Meridian*
Semiannual ISSN 1040-7421
Subscription Manager
Map Collection
University of Arizona Library
Tucson, AZ 85721

MFSF: *Magazine of Fantasy and Science Fiction*
11 issues/year ISSN 1095-8258
143 Cream Hill Rd.
West Cornwall, CT 06796
http://www.enews.com/magazines/fsf/

MLJ: *Modern Language Journal*
Quarterly ISSN 0026-7902
Journal Division
University of Wisconsin Press
2537 Daniels St.
Madison, WI 53718

MLR: *Modern Language Review*
Quarterly ISSN 0026-7937
Modern Humanities Research Association
King's College London, Strand
London WC2R 2LS, England

MQR: *Michigan Quarterly Review*
Quarterly ISSN 0026-2420
3032 Rackham Bldg.
915 E. Washington St.
Ann Arbor, MI 48109-1070

Ms: *Ms.*
Bimonthly ISSN 0047-8318
P.O. Box 5299
Harlan, IA 51593
http://www.womweb.com/msnet.htm

N

Nat: *Nation*
Weekly ISSN 0027-8378
P.O. Box 37072
Boone, IA 50037
http://www.thenation.com/

Nat Peop: *Native Peoples*
Quarterly ISSN 0895-7606
P.O. Box 36820
Phoenix, AZ 85067-6820
http://www.nativepeoples.com/

Nat R: *National Review*
Biweekly ISSN 0028-0038
Circulation Dept.
P.O. Box 668
Mt. Morris, IL 61054-0668
http://www.nationnalreview.com/

Nature: *Nature*
Weekly ISSN 0028-0836
345 Park Ave. S. 10th Fl.
New York, NY 10010-1707
http://www.nature.com/

New Ad: *New Advocate*
Quarterly ISSN 0895-1381
480 Washington Street
Norwood, MA 02062

New Age: *New Age Journal*
Bimonthly ISSN 0746-3618
P.O. Box 53275
Boulder, CO 80321-3275
http://www.newage.com/home/newage/

New R: *New Republic*
Weekly ISSN 0028-6583
Subscription Service Dept.
P.O. Box 37298
Boone, IA 50037-0298
http://www.thenewrepublic.com/

New Sci: *New Scientist*
Weekly ISSN 0262-4079
c/o M.A.I.L. America
2323 Randolph Ave.
Avenel, NJ 07001
http://www.nsplus.com/

NGSQ: *National Genealogical Society Quarterly*
Quarterly ISSN 0027-934X
4527 17th St. N.
Arlington, VA 22207-2399

NH: *Natural History*
Monthly ISSN 0028-0712
P.O. Box 5000
Harlan, IA 51537-5000
http://www.tkandf.co.uk/

Nine-C Lit: *Nineteenth-Century Literature*
Quarterly ISSN 0891-9356
Periodicals Dept.
University of California Press
2120 Berkeley Way
Berkeley, CA 94720
http://library.berkeley.edu:8080/ucalpress/journals/

Notes: *Notes (Music Library Association)*
Quarterly ISSN 0027-4380
P.O. Box 487
Canton, MA 02021

NP: *National Parks*
Bimonthly ISSN 0276-8186
1776 Mass. Ave. N.W.
Washington, DC 20036
http://www.ncpa.org/home/ncpa/np/
npmag.html

NS: *New Statesman*
Weekly ISSN 0954-2361
C & C Mailers International Inc.
900 Lincoln Boulevard
P.O. Box 177
Middlesex, NJ 08846

NW: *Newsweek*
Weekly ISSN 0028-9604
P.O. Box 59968
Boulder, CO 80328-9968

NY: *New Yorker*
Weekly ISSN 0028-792X
Box 56447
Boulder, CO 80328-6447
http://www.enews.com/magazines/
new_yorker/

NYRB: *New York Review of Books*
20 issues/year ISSN 0028-7504
Subscription Service Dept.
P.O. Box 420384
Palm Coast, FL 32142-0384
http://www.nybooks.com/

NYTBR: *New York Times Book Review*
Weekly ISSN 0028-7806
P.O. Box 3009
South Hackensack, NJ 07606-3009

NYTLa: *New York Times (Late Ed.)*
Daily ISSN 0362-4331
P.O. Box 3009
South Hackensack, NJ 07606-1009
http://www.nytimes.com/

O

Obs: *Observer (London)*
Weekly ISSN 0029-7712
Observer, Ltd.
Chelsea Bridge House,
Queenstown Rd.,
London SW8 4NN, England
http://www.guardian.co.uk/observer/

OnIssues: *On the Issues*
Quarterly ISSN 0895-6014
The Progressive Women's Quarterly
P.O. Box 3000, Dept. OTI
Denville, NJ 07834
http://www.echonyl.com/onissues/

P

Pac A: *Pacific Affairs*
Quarterly ISSN 0030-851X
University of British Columbia
Vancouver, BC, Canada V6T 1Z2

Par: *Parents Magazine*
Monthly ISSN 0195-0967
P.O. Box 3042
Harlan, IA 51537-0207

Parabola: *Parabola*
Quarterly ISSN 0362-1596
P.O. Box 3000
Denville, NJ 07834
http://www.parabola.org/

Parnassus: *Parnassus: Poetry in Review*
Semiannual ISSN 0048-3028
205 W. 89th St. #8F
New York, NY 10024

Pet PM: *Petersen's Photographic Magazine*
Monthly ISSN 0199-4913
Subscriber Services
P.O. Box 56495
Boulder, CO 80322-6495

Poet: *Poetry*
Monthly ISSN 0032-2032
60 W. Walton St.
Chicago, IL 60610

Poetics T: *Poetics Today*
Quarterly ISSN 0333-5372
Duke University Press
Box 90660
Durham, NC 27708-0660
http://www.duke.edu/web/dupress/

PQ: *Philological Quarterly*
Quarterly ISSN 0031-7977
Publication Order Dept.
University of Iowa
100 Oakdale Campus M1050H
Iowa City, IA 52242-5000

Prog: *Progressive*
Monthly ISSN 0033-0736
P.O. Box 421
Mount Morris, IL 61054-0421
http://www.progressive.org/

Prog Arch: *Progressive Architecture*
Monthly ISSN 0033-0752
Reinhold Publishing
1100 Superior Ave.
Cleveland, OH 44114-2543

PS: *Prairie Schooner*
Quarterly ISSN 0032-6682
201 Andrews Hall
University of Nebraska
Lincoln, NE 68588-0334

PT: *Psychology Today*
Bi-monthly ISSN 0033-3107
P.O. Box 55046
Boulder, CO 80322-5046

Pub Hist: *Public Historian*
Quarterly ISSN 0272-3433
University of California Press
Berkeley, CA 94720

PW: *Publishers Weekly*
Weekly ISSN 0000-0019
P.O. Box 6457
Torrance, CA 90504
http://www.bookwire.com/

Q

Queens Q: *Queen's Quarterly*
Quarterly ISSN 0033-6041
Queen's University
Kingston, ON, Canada K7L 3N6
http://info.queensu.ca/quarterly/

Quill & Q: *Quill & Quire*
Monthly ISSN 0033-6491
Customer Service
35 Riviera Dr., Unit 17
Markham, ON, Canada L3R 8N4

R

Rapport: *Rapport: The Modern Guide to Books, Music & More*
Bimonthly ISSN 1061-6861
Rapport Publishing Co., Inc.
5265 Fountain Ave.
Los Angeles, CA 90029

Rel St Rev: *Religious Studies Review*
Quarterly ISSN 0319-485X
CSSR Executive Office
Valparaiso University
Valparaiso, IN 46383
http://www.cssr.org/

Roundup M: *Roundup Magazine*
Bimonthly ISSN 1081-2229
James Crutchfield
1012 Fair St.
Franklin, TN 37064-2718
http://www.imt.net/~gedison/wwa.html

R&R Bk N: *Reference & Research Book News*
8 times/year ISSN 0887-3763
5739 NE Sumner St.
Portland, OR 97218
http://www.amazon.com/

RR: *Review for Religious*
Bimonthly ISSN 0034-639X
P.O. Box 6070
Duluth, MN 55806

RSR: *Reference Services Review*
Quarterly ISSN 0090-7324
Pierian Press
P.O. Box 1808
Ann Arbor, MI 48106

RT: *Reading Teacher*
8 issues/year ISSN 0034-0561
International Reading Association
P.O. Box 8139
Newark, DE 19714-8139

S

SA: *Scientific American*
Monthly ISSN 0036-8733
P.O. Box 3187
Harlan, IA 51537

SB: *Science Books & Films*
9 issues/year ISSN 0098-342X
P.O. Box 3000, Dept. SBF
Denville, NJ 07834

Sch Arts: *School Arts*
9 issues/year ISSN 0036-6463
50 Portland St.
Worcester, MA 01608

Sch Lib: *School Librarian*
Quarterly ISSN 0036-6595
School Library Association
Liden Library, Barrington Close
Liden, Swindon SN3 6HF, England

Sci: *Science*
Weekly ISSN 0036-8075
P.O. Box 1811
Danbury, CT 06813-1811
http://www.sciencemag.org/

SciTech: *SciTech Book News*
10 issues/year ISSN 0196-6006
Book News, Inc.
5739 NE Sumner St.
Portland, OR 97218

SE: *Social Education*
7 issues/year ISSN 0037-7724
3501 Newark St., N.W.
Washington, DC 20016-3167
http://www.ncss.org/howe/ncss/

Sea H: *Sea History*
Quarterly ISSN 0146-9312
5 John Walsh Blvd.
P.O. Box 68
Peekskill, NY 10566

SEP: *Saturday Evening Post*
Bimonthly ISSN 0048-9239
Subscription Offices
P.O. Box 420235
Palm Coast, FL 32142-0235
http://www.satevepost.org/

Ser R: *Serials Review*
Quarterly ISSN 0098-7913
Pierian Press
P.O. Box 1808
Ann Arbor, MI 48106

Sew R: *Sewanee Review*
Quarterly ISSN 0037-3052
Sewanee, TN 37383-1000
http://www.sewanee.edu/sreview/
home.html

SF Chr: *Science Fiction Chronicle*
Monthly ISSN 0195-5365
P.O. Box 22730
Brooklyn, NY 11202-0056

SFS: *Science-Fiction Studies*
3 issues/year ISSN 0091-7729
East College
DePauw University
Greencastle, IN 46135

Sierra: *Sierra*
Bimonthly ISSN 0161-7362
Sierra Club Member Services
P.O. Box 52968
Boulder, CO 80322-2968
http://www.sierraclub.org/

Signs: *Signs: Journal of Women in Culture and Society*
Quarterly ISSN 0097-9740
University of Chicago Press
Journals Division
P.O. Box 37005
Chicago, IL 60637

Si & So: *Sight and Sound*
Monthly ISSN 0037-4806
c/o Mercury Airfreight International Ltd., Inc.
2323 Randolph Ave.
Avenel, NJ 07001

S Liv: *Southern Living*
Monthly ISSN 0038-4305
Customer Service
P.O. Box 830119
Birmingham, AL 35283
http://southern-living.com/

SLJ: *School Library Journal*
Monthly ISSN 0362-8930
P.O. Box 57559
Boulder, CO 80322-7559
http://www.slj.com/

SLMQ: *School Library Media Quarterly*
Quarterly ISSN 0278-4823
Subscription Dept.
American Library Association
50 E. Huron St.
Chicago, IL 60611

Smith: *Smithsonian*
Monthly ISSN 0037-7333
P.O. Box 420312
Palm Coast, FL 32142-0312

Sm Pr R: *Small Press Review*
Monthly ISSN 0037-7228
Dustbooks
P.O. Box 100
Paradise, CA 95967
http://www.dustbooks.com/

South CR: *South Carolina Review*
Semiannual ISSN 0038-3163
Dept. of English
Strode Tower, Box 341503
Clemson University
Clemson, SC 29634-1503

South R: *Southern Review*
Quarterly ISSN 0038-4534
43 Allen Hall
Louisiana State University
Baton Rouge, LA 70803-5005

Spec: *Spectator*
Weekly ISSN 0038-6952
c/o Mercury Airfreight International LTD
2323 Randolph Ave.
Avenel, NJ 07001

SS: *Social Studies*
Bimonthly ISSN 0037-7996
Heldref Publications
1319 Eighteenth St., N.W.
Washington, DC 20036-1802
http://www.heldref.org/

SSF: *Studies in Short Fiction*
Quarterly ISSN 0039-3789
Newberry College
Newberry, SC 29108

S&T: *Sky & Telescope*
Monthly ISSN 0037-6604
P.O. Box 9111
Belmont, MA 02178-9111
http://www.skypup.com/

SWR: *Southwest Review*
Quarterly ISSN 0038-4712
307 Fondren Library West
Southern Methodist University
Dallas, TX 75275

T

T&C: *Technology and Culture*
Quarterly ISSN 0040-165X
University of Chicago Press
P.O. Box 37005
Chicago, IL 60637
http://hfm.umd.umich.edu/TC/index.html

Teach Mus: *Teaching Music*
Monthly ISSN 1069-7446
1806 Robert Fulton Drive
Reston, VA 22091-4348

TES: *Times Educational Supplement*
Weekly ISSN 0040-7887
P.O. Box 3000
Denville, NJ 07834

Tikkun: *Tikkun*
Bimonthly ISSN 0887-9982
P.O. Box 460926
Escondido, CA 92046

Time: *Time*
Weekly ISSN 0040-781X
Time
P.O. Box 30601
Tampa, FL 33630-0601
http://www.pathfinder.com/time/

TLS: *Times Literary Supplement*
Weekly ISSN 0040-7895
P. O. Box 3000
Denville, NJ 07834

TPR: *Threepenny Review*
Quarterly ISSN 0275-1410
P.O. Box 9131
Berkeley, CA 94709

Trib Bks: *Tribune Books (Chicago)*
Weekly
Mail Subscription Div.
777 W. Chicago Ave.
Chicago, IL 60610

TSWL: *Tulsa Studies in Women's*
Literature
Semiannual ISSN 0732-7730
600 S. College
Tulsa, OK 74104-3189
http://www.utulsa.edu/tswl/tswlhome.html

U

Univ Bkmn: *University Bookman*
Quarterly ISSN 0041-9265
F.M. Kirby Campus
3901 Centerville Rd.
P.O. Box 4431
Wilmington, DE 19807-0431

Utne R: *Utne Reader*
Bimonthly ISSN 8750-0256
Box 7460
Red Oak, IA 51591-0460
http://www.utne.com/

V

VLS: *Village Voice Literary Supplement*
10 issues/year ISSN 0887-8633
P.O. Box 3000, Dept. VLS
Denville, NJ 07834-9891

VOYA: *Voice of Youth Advocates*
Bimonthly ISSN 0160-4201
Scarecrow Press, Inc.
4720A Boston Way
Lanham, MD 20706

VQR: *Virginia Quarterly Review*
Quarterly ISSN 0042-675X
Business Manager
1 W. Range
Charlottesville, VA 22903

VS: *Victorian Studies*
Quarterly ISSN 0042-5222
Journals Division
Indiana University Press
601 N. Morton
Bloomington, IN 47404-3797
http://www.indiana.edu/~iupress/

VV: *Village Voice*
Weekly ISSN 0042-6180
P.O. Box 3000
Denville, NJ 07834
http://www.villagevoice.com/

W

WAL: *Western American Literature*
Quarterly ISSN 0043-3462
Utah State University
Logan, UT 84322-3200

Wash M: *Washington Monthly*
10 issues/year ISSN 0043-0633
Box 587
Mount Morris, IL 61054
http://www.enews.com/magazines/
wash_month/

WER: *Whole Earth Review*
Quarterly ISSN 0749-5056
P.O. Box 3000
Denville, NJ 07834

WHQ: *Western Historical Quarterly*
Quarterly ISSN 0043-3810
Utah State University
Logan, UT 84322-0740

W&I: *World & I*
Monthly ISSN 0887-9346
3400 New York Ave., N.E.
Washington, DC 20002
http://www.worldandi.com/

Wil Q: *Wilson Quarterly*
Quarterly ISSN 0363-3276
Subscriber Service
P.O. Box 420406
Palm Coast, FL 32142-0406

WLT: *World Literature Today*
Quarterly ISSN 0196-3570
630 Parrington Oval
University of Oklahoma
Norman, OK 73069

Wom R Bks: *Women's Review of Books*
  11 issues/yr. ISSN 0738-1433
  Wellesley College
  Center for Research on Women
  Wellesley, MA 02181
  http://www.wellesley.edy/WCW/CRW/
  WROB/welcome.html

Workbook: *Workbook*
  Quarterly ISSN 0195-4636
  Southwest Research and Information
  Center
  P.O. Box 4524
  Albuquerque, NM 87106

Y

Yacht: *Yachting*
  Monthly ISSN 0043-9940
  P.O. Box 56349
  Boulder, CO 80322-6349
  http://www.yachtingmag.com/

A

The 12 Circus Rings. Electronic Media Version
BL - v94 - D 1 '97 - p649 [51-250]

100 Greatest. Vols. 1-12
r   R&R Bk N - v12 - N '97 - p1 [51-250]
r   SLJ - v43 - N '97 - p139 [51-250]

101 Amazing Things to Do with Your Computer
Books - v11 - O '97 - p21 [51-250]
TES - O 10 '97 - p39U [251-500]
TES - N 7 '97 - p10* [51-250]

Aardema, Verna
Anansi Does the Impossible! (Illus. by Lisa Desimini)
BL - v94 - D 1 '97 - p638 [51-250]
CCB-B - v51 - Ja '98 - p152 [51-250]
Ch BWatch - v7 - N '97 - p3 [1-50]
Inst - v107 - Ag '97 - p20+ [1-50]
SLJ - v43 - S '97 - p198+ [51-250]

Borreguita and the Coyote (Illus. by Petra Mathers)
PW - v245 - F 2 '98 - p92 [1-50]
SLJ - v43 - N '97 - p40 [1-50]

This for That (Illus. by Victoria Chess)
Ch BWatch - v7 - Mr '97 - p7 [1-50]
Emerg Lib - v24 - My '97 - p57 [1-50]
HB Guide - v8 - Fall '97 - p331 [51-250]
NYTBR - v102 - O 12 '97 - p26 [501+]
SLJ - v43 - D '97 - p104 [51-250]

Aaron, Moses
Crow Puzzles
Magpies - v12 - My '97 - p32 [51-250]

Aaseng, Nathan
1930-1939
ASBYP - v29 - Sum '96 - p64+ [51-250]

1940-1949
ASBYP - v29 - Sum '96 - p64+ [51-250]

American Dinosaur Hunters
SB - v32 - D '96 - p276 [51-250]

Poisonous Creatures
y   BL - v94 - Mr 15 '98 - p1224 [1-50]
Ch BWatch - v8 - Ja '98 - p6 [1-50]
y   VOYA - v21 - Ap '98 - p39 [1-50]

Treacherous Traitors
Ch BWatch - v7 - N '97 - p6 [1-50]
SLJ - v44 - F '98 - p110 [51-250]

Yearbooks in Science 1920-1929
ASBYP - v29 - Sum '96 - p64+ [51-250]

You Are the Corporate Executive
Ch BWatch - v7 - Je '97 - p5 [51-250]
y   HB Guide - v8 - Fall '97 - p323 [51-250]
y   SLJ - v43 - Je '97 - p130 [51-250]

You Are the Juror
Ch BWatch - v7 - N '97 - p6 [1-50]
y   SLJ - v44 - Ja '98 - p116+ [251-500]
y   VOYA - v20 - F '98 - p397 [51-250]

You Are the Senator
Ch BWatch - v7 - Je '97 - p5 [51-250]
y   HB Guide - v8 - Fall '97 - p323 [51-250]
y   SLJ - v43 - Ag '97 - p160 [51-250]
y   VOYA - v20 - Ag '97 - p198 [51-250]

Aborio, Portia
Pig Out!
   Ch BWatch - v7 - Jl '97 - p5 [1-50]

Academic American Encyclopedia. Vols. 1-21
   r   BL - v94 - S 15 '97 - p251+ [501+]

Acheson, Alison
Thunder Ice
   CBRA - '96 - p462 [51-250]

Acierno, Maria
Children of Flight Pedro Pan
   Ch BWatch - v7 - Mr '97 - p2 [51-250]

Ackerman, Diane
Bats: Shadows in the Night (Illus. by Merlin Tuttle)
   BL - v94 - O 1 '97 - p320 [51-250]
   CCB-B - v51 - S '97 - p4+ [51-250]
   Ch BWatch - v7 - S '97 - p6 [51-250]

Ackerman, Ned
Spirit Horse
   CCB-B - v51 - Mr '98 - p234 [51-250]
   KR - v66 - Ja 1 '98 - p52 [51-250]
   SLJ - v44 - Ap '98 - p128 [51-250]

Acton, Thomas
Romanichal Gypsies
   Bks Keeps - S '97 - p29 [51-250]
   Sch Lib - v45 - Ag '97 - p162 [51-250]

Ada, Alma Flor
The Christmas Tree (Illus. by Terry Ybanez)
   KR - v65 - D 15 '97 - p1832 [51-250]
   PW - v244 - O 6 '97 - p54 [51-250]

Gathering the Sun (Illus. by Simon Silva)
   ABR - v19 - N '97 - p12+ [501+]
   CBRS - v25 - Spr '97 - p138 [51-250]
   CCB-B - v50 - Je '97 - p348+ [51-250]
   Ch BWatch - v7 - My '97 - p2 [1-50]

Jordi's Star (Illus. by Susan Gaber)
   RT - v51 - O '97 - p150 [51-250]

La Lagartija Y El Sol
   SLJ - v43 - Ag '97 - p180 [51-250]

The Lizard and the Sun (Illus. by Felipe Davalos)
   BL - v94 - D 15 '97 - p698 [51-250]
   CCB-B - v51 - O '97 - p40 [51-250]
   KR - v65 - Jl 1 '97 - p1026 [51-250]

The Malachite Palace (Illus. by Leonid Gore)
   CCB-B - v51 - Mr '98 - p234+ [51-250]

Adams, Georgie
A Year Full of Stories (Illus. by Selina Young)
   Bks Keeps - N '97 - p6 [51-250]
   KR - v65 - O 15 '97 - p1578 [51-250]
   PW - v244 - N 10 '97 - p76 [51-250]
   SLJ - v43 - N '97 - p104 [51-250]
   TES - O 31 '97 - p16* [51-250]
   TES - N 7 '97 - p5* [51-250]

Adams, Lisa K
Dealing with Lying
   SLJ - v44 - Mr '98 - p191 [51-250]

Dealing with Teasing
   SLJ - v44 - Ap '98 - p112 [51-250]

Adams, Richard, 1920-
Watership Down
   y   BL - v94 - D 15 '97 - p695 [1-50]
      NYTBR - v102 - N 16 '97 - p26 [1-50]

Adams, Richard Crittenden
Ideas for Science Projects. Rev. Ed.
   y   BL - v94 - D 1 '97 - p621 [51-250]
      SLJ - v43 - D '97 - p132+ [51-250]

Adams, Simon
20th Century: A Visual History
   r   TES - Jl 4 '97 - p11* [501+]

Addabbo, Carole
Dina the Deaf Dinosaur (Illus. by Valentine)
   Ch BWatch - v7 - D '97 - p5 [51-250]

Adeleke, Tunde
Songhay
   Cur R - v36 - Mr '97 - p12+ [51-250]

Adinolfi, JoAnn
Tina's Diner (Illus. by JoAnn Adinolfi)
> CBRS - v25 - Ag '97 - p158 [51-250]
> HB Guide - v8 - Fall '97 - p257 [51-250]
> SLJ - v43 - Je '97 - p78 [51-250]

Adler, C S
Her Blue Straw Hat
> BL - v94 - S 1 '97 - p121 [51-250]
> CCB-B - v51 - S '97 - p5 [51-250]
> PW - v244 - Je 23 '97 - p92+ [51-250]
> SLJ - v43 - S '97 - p210 [51-250]

More than a Horse
> Ch BWatch - v7 - O '97 - p2 [51-250]
> HB Guide - v8 - Fall '97 - p295 [51-250]
> SLJ - v43 - Ap '97 - p134 [51-250]

Adler, David A
Cam Jansen and the Scary Snake Mystery (Illus. by Susanna Natti)
> SLJ - v43 - D '97 - p81 [51-250]

Chanukah in Chelm (Illus. by Kevin O'Malley)
> BL - v94 - S 1 '97 - p137 [51-250]
> CBRS - v26 - N '97 - p30+ [51-250]
> CCB-B - v51 - D '97 - p116 [51-250]
> Ch BWatch - v8 - Ja '98 - p8 [1-50]
> HB - v73 - S '97 - p584 [251-500]
> NYTBR - v102 - D 7 '97 - p66 [1-50]
> PW - v244 - O 6 '97 - p52 [51-250]

Easy Math Puzzles (Illus. by Cynthia Fisher)
> HB Guide - v8 - Fall '97 - p340 [51-250]
> SLJ - v43 - Je '97 - p104 [51-250]

Hiding from the Nazis (Illus. by Karen Ritz)
> BL - v94 - N 1 '97 - p463 [51-250]
> CCB-B - v51 - Ja '98 - p153 [51-250]
> KR - v65 - O 15 '97 - p1578 [51-250]
> PW - v244 - O 20 '97 - p76 [51-250]
> SLJ - v44 - F '98 - p94 [51-250]

Hilde and Eli (Illus. by Karen Ritz)
> SS - v88 - My '97 - p139+ [501+]

Lou Gehrig: The Luckiest Man (Illus. by Terry Widener)
> BL - v94 - Mr 15 '98 - p1219 [1-50]
> HB - v73 - Jl '97 - p471+ [51-250]

> HB Guide - v8 - Fall '97 - p368 [51-250]
> Inst - v107 - O '97 - p48+ [51-250]
> NYTBR - v102 - Je 8 '97 - p27 [1-50]
> NYTLa - v147 - D 4 '97 - pE8 [51-250]
> SLJ - v43 - My '97 - p118 [51-250]

Magic Money
> BL - v93 - Ag '97 - p1908 [51-250]

A Picture Book of Amelia Earhart (Illus. by Jeff Fisher)
> KR - v66 - Mr 1 '98 - p334 [51-250]
> SLJ - v44 - Ap '98 - p112 [51-250]

A Picture Book of Louis Braille (Illus. by John Wallner)
> HB Guide - v8 - Fall '97 - p378 [51-250]
> Inst - v107 - O '97 - p24+ [51-250]
> SLJ - v43 - Je '97 - p104+ [51-250]

A Picture Book of Rosa Parks. Book and Audio Version
> Ch BWatch - v7 - My '97 - p5 [1-50]
> SLJ - v43 - Jl '97 - p58 [51-250]

A Picture Book of Thomas Alva Edison (Illus. by John Wallner)
> ASBYP - v29 - Fall '96 - p7 [251-500]

A Picture Book of Thurgood Marshall (Illus. by Robert Casilla)
> SLJ - v44 - Ja '98 - p96 [51-250]

Young Cam Jansen and the Lost Tooth (Illus. by Susanna Natti)
> HB Guide - v8 - Fall '97 - p286 [51-250]
> SLJ - v43 - Jl '97 - p60 [51-250]

Adler, Naomi
Play Me a Story (Illus. by Greta Cencetti)
> KR - v66 - Ja 15 '98 - p108 [51-250]
> SLJ - v44 - Ap '98 - p112 [51-250]

Adlerman, Daniel
Africa Calling, Nighttime Falling (Illus. by Kimberly M Adlerman)
> RT - v51 - N '97 - p256 [51-250]

Adoff, Arnold
I Am the Darker Brother. Rev. Ed. (Illus. by Benny Andrews)
> y   BL - v94 - Mr 15 '98 - p1225 [1-50]

y   Ch BWatch - v7 - Je '97 - p7 [1-50]
y   HB Guide - v8 - Fall '97 - p374 [51-250]
     SLJ - v43 - My '97 - p141 [51-250]
y   VOYA - v20 - Je '97 - p130 [251-500]
y   VOYA - v21 - Ap '98 - p39 [1-50]

Love Letters (Illus. by Lisa Desimini)
     HB Guide - v8 - Fall '97 - p375 [51-250]
     PW - v244 - N 3 '97 - p59 [1-50]
     SLJ - v43 - D '97 - p23 [1-50]

Adshead, Paul
Around the World with Phineas Frog
     Cur R - v37 - D '97 - p12 [51-250]

Adventures with Nicholas (Illus. by Chris L Demarest). Book and Audio Version
     SLJ - v43 - Je '97 - p69 [51-250]

Aesop's Fables (Illus. by Jacob Lawrence)
     NYTBR - v103 - Mr 15 '98 - p23 [1-50]
     PW - v244 - Ag 25 '97 - p74 [51-250]

Agard, John
Another Day on Your Foot and I Would Have Died (Illus. by Colin McNaughton)
     Bks Keeps - My '97 - p24+ [51-250]

Grandfather's Old Bruk-a-Down Car (Illus. by Kevin Dean)
     Bks Keeps - S '97 - p25 [51-250]

Agbami, Akulah
Gloria's Gramophone
     Bks Keeps - My '97 - p24 [51-250]

Agee, Jon
Dmitri the Astronaut
     PW - v245 - Mr 23 '98 - p102 [1-50]

The Return of Freddy LeGrand (Illus. by Jon Agee)
     SLJ - v43 - Jl '97 - p34 [1-50]
     SLJ - v43 - N '97 - p40 [1-50]
     SLJ - v44 - Mr '98 - p119 [1-50]

Ahlberg, Allan
Janet's Last Book
     TES - D 5 '97 - p17* [1-50]

Master Track's Train (Illus. by Andre Amstutz)
     Bks Keeps - S '97 - p21 [51-250]
     Magpies - v12 - Jl '97 - p29 [51-250]
     Sch Lib - v45 - Ag '97 - p135 [51-250]
     TES - N 14 '97 - p14* [51-250]

Miss Dirt the Dustman's Daughter (Illus. by Tony Ross)
     Magpies - v12 - My '97 - p31 [51-250]

Monkey Do! (Illus. by Andre Amstutz)
     CCB-B - v51 - Ap '98 - p272+ [51-250]

Mrs. Vole the Vet (Illus. by Emma Chichester Clark)
     Magpies - v12 - My '97 - p31 [51-250]

Ms. Cliff the Climber (Illus. by Fritz Wegner)
     TES - N 14 '97 - p14* [51-250]

The Mysteries of Zigomar (Illus. by John Lawrence)
     BL - v94 - D 1 '97 - p616 [51-250]
     KR - v65 - Ag 15 '97 - p1302 [51-250]
     Obs - D 7 '97 - p17* [1-50]
     PW - v244 - O 13 '97 - p75 [51-250]
     SLJ - v43 - N '97 - p76 [51-250]
     Spec - v279 - D 6 '97 - p44 [1-50]
     TES - N 7 '97 - p2* [1-50]
     TES - Ja 2 '98 - p23* [501+]

Ahlberg, Janet
The Jolly Postman
     Bks Keeps - N '97 - p4 [51-250]

Peek-a-Boo!
     PW - v244 - Ag 25 '97 - p73 [1-50]

Peepo!
     Bks Keeps - N '97 - p4 [51-250]
     Bks Keeps - N '97 - p19 [51-250]

Ahmad, Nyla
CyberSurfer: The OWL Internet Guide for Kids
     CBRA - '96 - p534+ [51-250]

Aiken, Joan
*Fog Hounds, Wind Cat, Sea Mice
(Illus. by Peter Bailey)*
Bks Keeps - Jl '97 - p24 [51-250]
Sch Lib - v45 - Ag '97 - p135 [51-250]

A Handful of Gold
NS - v126 - D 5 '97 - p65 [1-50]

Ainsworth, Ken
Carly's Stories (Illus. by Ruth Ohi)
Can CL - v23 - Fall '97 - p69+ [501+]

Aitken, Gillian
Spotlight on Blends. Bks. 1-2
TES - N 14 '97 - p12* [51-250]

Ajmera, Maya
Children from Australia to Zimbabwe
BL - v94 - Ja 1 '98 - p796 [51-250]
KR - v65 - Je 1 '97 - p870 [51-250]
PW - v244 - Jl 28 '97 - p76 [51-250]
SLJ - v43 - Jl '97 - p79+ [51-250]

Alameida, Roy Kakulu
Stories of Old Hawai'i
Ch BWatch - v7 - S '97 - p2 [51-250]

Alarcon, Francisco X
*Laughing Tomatoes and Other Spring
Poems (Illus. by Maya Christina
Gonzalez)*
BL - v93 - Je 1 '97 - p1707+ [51-250]
CCB-B - v50 - Je '97 - p349 [51-250]
HB Guide - v8 - Fall '97 - p338 [51-250]
HMR - Sum '97 - p26+ [51-250]
SLJ - v43 - My '97 - p118 [51-250]

Alarcon, Karen Beaumont
*Louella Mae, She's Run Away! (Illus.
by Rosanne Litzinger)*
BL - v93 - Je 1 '97 - p1714+ [51-250]
HB Guide - v8 - Fall '97 - p248 [51-250]
NYTBR - v102 - Jl 20 '97 - p22 [1-50]
SLJ - v43 - My '97 - p92 [51-250]

Albee, Sarah
*6 Wild Adventures (Illus. by Eric
Brace)*
PW - v244 - Ag 18 '97 - p94 [51-250]

The Curious Little Lamb
PW - v244 - D 1 '97 - p55 [1-50]

I Can Do It! (Illus. by Larry DiFiori)
SLJ - v44 - F '98 - p78 [51-250]

Spotty Can't Sleep!
PW - v244 - D 1 '97 - p55 [1-50]

Albert, Burton
*Journey of the Nightly Jaguar (Illus.
by Robert Roth)*
SE - v61 - Ap '97 - p5* [1-50]

Albert, Toni
*The Incredible Coral Reef (Illus. by
Ada Hanlon)*
Ch BWatch - v7 - Je '97 - p2 [51-250]

*The Remarkable Rainforest (Illus. by
Ada Hanlon)*
Ch BWatch - v7 - Je '97 - p2 [51-250]

Alberts, Nancy Markham
*Elizabeth's Beauty (Illus. by Pat
Skiles)*
CBRS - v25 - Jl '97 - p151 [51-250]
CLW - v68 - D '97 - p85 [51-250]

Alborough, Jez
*Watch Out! Big Bro's Coming! (Illus.
by Jez Alborough)*
BL - v94 - S 1 '97 - p131 [51-250]
CCB-B - v51 - S '97 - p5 [51-250]
HB Guide - v8 - Fall '97 - p257 [51-250]
Magpies - v12 - My '97 - p26 [51-250]
Sch Lib - v45 - Ag '97 - p129 [51-250]
SLJ - v43 - Ag '97 - p128 [51-250]

Alcantara, Ricardo
Sinbarba Y Las Gaviotas
BL - v93 - Ag '97 - p1913 [1-50]

Sinbarba Y Los Fantasmas
BL - v93 - Ag '97 - p1913 [1-50]
SLJ - v44 - F '98 - p130 [51-250]

Alcock, Vivien
The Cuckoo Sister
PW - v244 - Ag 4 '97 - p77 [1-50]

The Red-Eared Ghosts
> HB Guide - v8 - Fall '97 - p295 [51-250]
> NYTBR - v102 - Jl 20 '97 - p22 [1-50]
> SLJ - v43 - Ap '97 - p134 [51-250]
> y VOYA - v20 - O '97 - p250 [251-500]

The Silver Egg (Illus. by Ivan Bates)
> Magpies - v12 - My '97 - p30 [1-50]
> Sch Lib - v45 - Ag '97 - p135 [51-250]

Stranger at the Window
> PW - v245 - Mr 16 '98 - p64+ [51-250]

Alcott, Louisa May
Little Women (Illus. by James Prunier)
> SLJ - v43 - D '97 - p120 [51-250]

Aldana, Patricia
Jade and Iron (Illus. by Luis Garay)
> CBRA - '96 - p502+ [51-250]

Aldape, Virginia Totorica
David, Donny, and Darren
> BL - v94 - Mr 15 '98 - p1236 [51-250]

Alderson, Sue Ann
Pond Seasons (Illus. by Ann Blades)
> Quill & Q - v63 - Ap '97 - p37 [51-250]

Alderton, David
Birds (Illus. by L R Galante)
> SLJ - v44 - F '98 - p110 [51-250]

Plants (Illus. by Ivan Stalio)
> SLJ - v44 - F '98 - p110 [51-250]

Aldrich, Bess Streeter
A Lantern in Her Hand
> CSM - v90 - F 24 '98 - p16 [1-50]
> y Legacy - v14 - 2 '97 - p160+ [501+]
> y VOYA - v21 - Ap '98 - p42 [1-50]

Alexander, Lloyd
The Cat Who Wished to Be a Man. Audio Version
> SLJ - v44 - Mr '98 - p157 [51-250]

The Fortune-Tellers (Illus. by Trina Schart Hyman)
> PW - v244 - S 22 '97 - p83 [1-50]
> SLJ - v43 - N '97 - p40 [1-50]

The House Gobbaleen (Illus. by Diane Goode)
> SLJ - v43 - N '97 - p40 [1-50]

The Iron Ring
> y BL - v94 - Mr 15 '98 - p1211 [1-50]
> BL - v94 - Mr 15 '98 - p1224 [1-50]
> y CBRS - v25 - Jl '97 - p153 [51-250]
> y CCB-B - v50 - Jl '97 - p386 [51-250]
> HB - v73 - Jl '97 - p447+ [51-250]
> HB Guide - v8 - Fall '97 - p295 [51-250]
> y MFSF - v94 - F '98 - p51 [51-250]
> Par Ch - Awards '97 - p6 [51-250]
> SLJ - v43 - My '97 - p128 [51-250]
> y VOYA - v20 - O '97 - p250 [51-250]
> y VOYA - v20 - F '98 - p363 [51-250]
> y VOYA - v21 - Ap '98 - p11 [1-50]
> y VOYA - v21 - Ap '98 - p36 [1-50]

The Remarkable Journey of Prince Jen
> SLJ - v43 - Jl '97 - p34 [1-50]

The Wizard in the Tree (Illus. by Laszlo Kubinyi)
> PW - v245 - Ja 5 '98 - p69 [1-50]

Alexander, Pat
The Lion First Bible (Illus. by Leon Baxter)
> Sch Lib - v45 - Ag '97 - p149 [51-250]

Song of the Morning (Illus. by Robin Lawrie)
> Sch Lib - v45 - Ag '97 - p135 [51-250]

Alexander, Sally Hobart
On My Own
> Ch BWatch - v7 - Jl '97 - p1 [51-250]
> y CLW - v68 - D '97 - p80 [51-250]
> y HB Guide - v8 - Fall '97 - p326 [51-250]
> y SLJ - v43 - Je '97 - p130 [51-250]

Alfonsi, Alice
Godzilla vs. Gigan and the Smog Monster
> SF Chr - v18 - Je '97 - p42 [1-50]

Alford, Jan
I Can't Believe I Have to Do This
> BL - v94 - O 15 '97 - p404 [51-250]
> CBRS - v26 - F '98 - p79 [51-250]
> KR - v65 - Ag 15 '97 - p1302 [51-250]

SLJ - v43 - S '97 - p210 [51-250]

Ali, Hemlata Farida
Storyteller: A Collection of 17 Stories for Children (Illus. by Hemlata Farida Ali)
CBRA - '96 - p431 [51-250]

Aliki
My Visit to the Zoo (Illus. by Aliki)
HB - v73 - S '97 - p589 [51-250]
KR - v65 - Ag 15 '97 - p1302 [51-250]
NH - v106 - D '97 - p9 [51-250]
PW - v244 - Ag 11 '97 - p402 [51-250]

Allaire, Francois
Hockey Goaltending for Young Players
Quill & Q - v63 - D '97 - p39 [251-500]

Allan, Nicholas
The Bird (Illus. by Nicholas Allan)
KR - v65 - D 1 '97 - p1772 [51-250]
Obs - Jl 20 '97 - p18* [51-250]
Sch Lib - v45 - Ag '97 - p129 [51-250]
TES - O 17 '97 - p12* [51-250]

Heaven
HB Guide - v8 - Fall '97 - p257 [51-250]

Jesus' Christmas Party
PW - v244 - O 6 '97 - p58 [1-50]

A Pig's Book of Manners
Bks Keeps - S '97 - p23 [51-250]

Stories from Hilltop Hospital
Sch Lib - v45 - N '97 - p184 [51-250]

Allan, Ted
Dr. Ah Chu and Jonah's Egg (Illus. by Philippe Germain)
CBRA - '96 - p462+ [51-250]

Allard, Harry
There's a Party at Mona's Tonight (Illus. by James Marshall)
PW - v244 - Je 2 '97 - p73 [1-50]

Allen, Ashley
We Are All Related
Quill & Q - v63 - D '97 - p39 [51-250]

Allen, Jonathan
Chicken Licken--A Wickedly Funny Flap Book
Bks Keeps - My '97 - p20 [51-250]

Fowl Play
Magpies - v12 - My '97 - p5 [51-250]

Wake Up, Sleeping Beauty (Illus. by Jonathan Allen)
KR - v65 - O 1 '97 - p1528 [51-250]
Par - v73 - F '98 - p186 [51-250]

Wolf Academy (Illus. by Jonathan Allen)
Bks Keeps - N '97 - p21+ [51-250]
Books - v11 - Je '97 - p21 [1-50]
Sch Lib - v45 - N '97 - p184 [51-250]

Allen, Judy
Anthology for the Earth
y   CCB-B - v51 - Ap '98 - p273 [51-250]
New Sci - v157 - Mr 14 '98 - p49 [1-50]
PW - v245 - Mr 23 '98 - p100 [51-250]
SLJ - v44 - Ap '98 - p141 [51-250]

The Most Brilliant Trick Ever (Illus. by Scoular Anderson)
Sch Lib - v45 - N '97 - p190 [51-250]

Allen, Nicholas
The Happy Princess
Obs - D 7 '97 - p17* [51-250]

Allen, Pamela
The Bear's Lunch (Illus. by Pamela Allen)
Aust Bk R - S '97 - p64+ [51-250]
Magpies - v12 - S '97 - p26 [51-250]

Allen, Paula Gunn
As Long as the Rivers Flow
RT - v51 - D '97 - p335 [51-250]
y   VOYA - v20 - Ap '97 - p50 [251-500]
y   VOYA - v20 - Ag '97 - p163 [51-250]

Aller, Susan Bivin
Emma and the Night Dogs (Illus. by Marni Backer)
BL - v94 - S 15 '97 - p239 [51-250]
CBRS - v25 - My '97 - p114 [51-250]
CCB-B - v50 - Jl '97 - p387 [51-250]
CLW - v68 - D '97 - p84 [51-250]

HB Guide - v8 - Fall '97 - p257 [51-250]

SLJ - v43 - My '97 - p92 [51-250]

Allman, Barbara
Her Piano Sang (Illus. by Shelly O Haas)

HB Guide - v8 - Fall '97 - p378 [51-250]

Alma, Ann
Under Emily's Sky

CM:CanRev - v4 - Ap 24 '98 - pONL [501+]

Quill & Q - v63 - N '97 - p45 [251-500]

Almagor, Gila
Under the Domim Tree

RT - v51 - F '98 - p430 [51-250]

Alonso, Manuel L
Tiempo De Nubes Negras (Illus. by Jesus Gaban)

SLJ - v43 - N '97 - p136 [51-250]

Alphin, Elaine Marie
Toasters (Illus. by Elaine Marie Alphin)

KR - v66 - Ap 15 '98 - p576 [51-250]

Vacuum Cleaners

BL - v94 - Ja 1 '98 - p796 [51-250]

Ch BWatch - v7 - D '97 - p8 [1-50]

KR - v65 - N 1 '97 - p1640 [51-250]

Alter, Judy
Amusement Parks, Roller Coasters, Ferris Wheels, and Cotton Candy

BL - v94 - D 15 '97 - p692 [51-250]

Beauty Pageants

BL - v94 - D 1 '97 - p616 [51-250]

CCB-B - v51 - O '97 - p41 [51-250]

HB Guide - v8 - Fall '97 - p366 [51-250]

SLJ - v43 - S '97 - p228 [51-250]

Callie Shaw, Stable Boy

SLJ - v43 - Ag '97 - p154 [51-250]

Meet Me at the Fair

BL - v94 - D 15 '97 - p692 [51-250]

SLJ - v44 - Ap '98 - p112 [51-250]

Wild West Shows

BL - v94 - O 1 '97 - p320 [51-250]

HB Guide - v8 - Fall '97 - p393 [51-250]

SLJ - v43 - Ag '97 - p144+ [51-250]

Althea
Being Friends (Illus. by Conny Jude)

Bks Keeps - S '97 - p26 [51-250]

Sch Lib - v45 - Ag '97 - p149 [51-250]

Feeling Angry (Illus. by Conny Jude)

Bks Keeps - S '97 - p26 [51-250]

Sch Lib - v45 - Ag '97 - p149 [51-250]

Feeling Shy (Illus. by Conny Jude)

Bks Keeps - S '97 - p26 [51-250]

Sch Lib - v45 - Ag '97 - p149 [51-250]

Telling the Truth (Illus. by Conny Jude)

Bks Keeps - S '97 - p26 [51-250]

Sch Lib - v45 - Ag '97 - p149 [51-250]

Altman, Linda Jacobs
Amelia's Road (Illus. by Enrique O Sanchez)

ECEJ - v25 - Fall '97 - p45 [1-50]

The California Gold Rush in American History

SLJ - v44 - Mr '98 - p226 [51-250]

The Decade That Roared

Ch BWatch - v7 - D '97 - p7 [1-50]

y   SLJ - v44 - Ja '98 - p117+ [251-500]

Forever Outsiders

y   BL - v94 - O 15 '97 - p396 [51-250]

r   CCB-B - v51 - Ja '98 - p162+ [51-250]

y   KR - v65 - S 15 '97 - p1452 [51-250]

yr   SLJ - v44 - F '98 - p134 [51-250]

Amazing Facts
New Sci - v156 - O 4 '97 - p45 [1-50]

Sch Lib - v45 - N '97 - p204 [51-250]

American Heritage: The History of the United States for Young People. Electronic Media Version
r   SLJ - v43 - S '97 - p148 [51-250]

The American Horticultural Society Pruning and Training
SB - v32 - D '96 - p266 [251-500]

American Kennel Club

The Complete Dog Book for Kids
R&R Bk N - v12 - Ag '97 - p174 [1-50]

Amery, Heather

Chasmosaurus (Illus. by Tony Gibbons)
ASBYP - v29 - Sum '96 - p51+ [501+]

Green, Tamara, Muttaburrasaurus (Illus. by Tony Gibbons)
ASBYP - v29 - Sum '96 - p51+ [501+]

Oviraptor (Illus. by Tony Gibbons)
ASBYP - v29 - Sum '96 - p51+ [501+]

Psittacosaurus (Illus. by Tony Gibbons)
ASBYP - v29 - Sum '96 - p51+ [501+]

Spinosaurus (Illus. by Tony Gibbons)
ASBYP - v29 - Sum '96 - p51+ [501+]

Vulcanodon (Illus. by Tony Gibbons)
ASBYP - v29 - Sum '96 - p51+ [501+]

Ammon, Richard

An Amish Christmas (Illus. by Pamela Patrick)
RT - v51 - N '97 - p255+ [51-250]

Amo, Montserrat Del

Mao Tiang Pelos Tiesos (Illus. by Fatima Garcia)
SLJ - v44 - F '98 - p130 [51-250]

Amoore, Susannah

Motley the Cat
TES - D 5 '97 - p17* [51-250]

Amos, Janine

Honest (Illus. by Gwen Green)
Bks Keeps - My '97 - p22+ [51-250]

Kind (Illus. by Gwen Green)
Bks Keeps - My '97 - p22 [51-250]

Reliable (Illus. by Gwen Green)
Bks Keeps - My '97 - p22+ [51-250]

Amphibians and Reptiles. Book and Electronic Media Version

SLJ - v43 - D '97 - p56+ [51-250]

Anastasio, Dina

Fly Trap (Illus. by Jeff Spackman)
HB Guide - v8 - Fall '97 - p288 [51-250]

Anaya, Rudolfo

The Farolitos of Christmas (Illus. by Edward Gonzales)
PW - v244 - O 6 '97 - p58 [1-50]

Maya's Children (Illus. by Maria Baca)
CBRS - v25 - Ag '97 - p164 [51-250]
CCB-B - v50 - Jl '97 - p387 [51-250]
Ch BWatch - v7 - Je '97 - p6 [1-50]
HB Guide - v8 - Fall '97 - p257 [51-250]
SLJ - v43 - Je '97 - p78 [51-250]

Ancona, George

Fiesta Fireworks (Illus. by George Ancona)
SLJ - v44 - Mr '98 - p191 [51-250]

Mayeros: A Yucatec Maya Family (Illus. by George Ancona)
HB Guide - v8 - Fall '97 - p398 [51-250]
SLJ - v43 - Je '97 - p105 [51-250]

The Pinatas Maker
ECEJ - v25 - Fall '97 - p45 [1-50]

Andersen, Hans Christian

The Emperor's New Clothes (Illus. by Angela Barrett)
BL - v94 - D 15 '97 - p701 [51-250]
HB - v73 - N '97 - p688+ [251-500]
KR - v65 - Ag 1 '97 - p1218 [51-250]
Magpies - v12 - Jl '97 - p30 [51-250]
NYTBR - v102 - N 16 '97 - p57 [501+]
PW - v244 - Jl 7 '97 - p68 [51-250]
SLJ - v43 - N '97 - p76 [51-250]
TES - S 5 '97 - p8* [501+]
TES - D 26 '97 - p14 [1-50]

The Swan's Stories (Illus. by Chris Riddell)
Bks Keeps - N '97 - p6 [51-250]
BL - v94 - D 15 '97 - p696 [51-250]
Books - v11 - Ag '97 - p15 [51-250]
Ch BWatch - v7 - S '97 - p1 [1-50]
HB - v73 - N '97 - p688+ [251-500]
KR - v65 - Jl 15 '97 - p1106 [51-250]
NYTBR - v102 - N 16 '97 - p57 [501+]

Obs - Jl 20 '97 - p18* [251-500]
PW - v244 - Ag 4 '97 - p76 [51-250]
Sch Lib - v45 - N '97 - p190 [51-250]
SLJ - v43 - S '97 - p210 [51-250]
TES - S 5 '97 - p8* [501+]

Thumbelina (Illus. by Arlene Graston)
Ch BWatch - v7 - N '97 - p3 [1-50]
Ch BWatch - v8 - Ja '98 - p2 [1-50]
KR - v65 - S 15 '97 - p1464 [51-250]
NYTBR - v102 - N 16 '97 - p57 [501+]
PW - v244 - O 6 '97 - p82 [51-250]
SLJ - v43 - S '97 - p172 [51-250]

Anderson, C W
*Blaze and the Gray Spotted Pony
(Illus. by C W Anderson)*
Par Ch - Awards '97 - p8 [51-250]

Anderson, Dave
The Story of Basketball. Rev. Ed.
BL - v94 - Ja 1 '98 - p796 [51-250]
y   Ch BWatch - v7 - D '97 - p4 [1-50]

The Story of Football
BL - v94 - Ja 1 '98 - p796 [51-250]
y   Ch BWatch - v7 - D '97 - p4 [1-50]

Anderson, Janet S
Going through the Gate
BL - v94 - F 15 '98 - p1010 [51-250]
CBRS - v26 - F '98 - p79+ [51-250]
KR - v65 - Jl 15 '97 - p1106 [51-250]
PW - v244 - O 13 '97 - p76 [51-250]
SLJ - v43 - N '97 - p114 [51-250]

Sunflower Sal (Illus. by Elizabeth Johns)
BL - v94 - O 1 '97 - p335 [51-250]
CCB-B - v51 - O '97 - p41 [51-250]
KR - v65 - Ag 1 '97 - p1218 [51-250]
SLJ - v43 - S '97 - p172 [51-250]

Anderson, Joan
*Batboy: An Inside Look at Spring
Training (Illus. by Matthew
Cavanaugh)*
RT - v51 - O '97 - p141 [1-50]

Anderson, Laurie Halse
Ndito Runs (Illus. by Anita Van Der Merwe)
RT - v51 - F '98 - p431 [51-250]

Anderson, Lena
Tick-Tock (Illus. by Lena Anderson)
KR - v66 - F 1 '98 - p192 [51-250]
PW - v245 - Ja 19 '98 - p376 [51-250]

Anderson, Margaret J
Carl Linnaeus: Father of Classification
BL - v94 - D 1 '97 - p625 [51-250]
y   KR - v65 - Jl 1 '97 - p1026 [51-250]
SLJ - v43 - S '97 - p228 [51-250]

Isaac Newton: The Greatest Scientist of All Time
ASBYP - v29 - Fall '96 - p47+ [501+]

Anderson, Margaret Jean
Children of Summer (Illus. by Marie LeGlatin Keis)
y   Am Sci - v85 - N '97 - p561 [1-50]
CCB-B - v50 - Je '97 - p349+ [51-250]
Ch BWatch - v7 - S '97 - p8 [1-50]
HB - v73 - Jl '97 - p448 [51-250]
HB Guide - v8 - Fall '97 - p295 [51-250]
SLJ - v43 - S '97 - p210 [51-250]

Anderson, Mary Elizabeth
Link across America
Ch BWatch - v7 - Je '97 - p2 [51-250]

Anderson, Peggy Perry
Out to Lunch (Illus. by Peggy Perry Anderson)
KR - v66 - Mr 15 '98 - p398 [51-250]
SLJ - v44 - Ap '98 - p91 [51-250]

Anderson, Peter
A Grand Canyon Journey
HB Guide - v8 - Fall '97 - p342 [51-250]
SLJ - v43 - Ag '97 - p160 [51-250]

Anderson, Scoular
Puzzling Day in the Land of the Pharaohs
Emerg Lib - v24 - My '97 - p51 [51-250]

Anderson, Susan
Flowers for Mommy (Illus. by Susan Anderson)
  Ch BWatch - v7 - O '97 - p5 [51-250]

Anderson, William, 1952-
Pioneer Girl (Illus. by Dan Andreasen)
  KR - v65 - N 15 '97 - p1704 [51-250]
  PW - v244 - D 8 '97 - p72 [51-250]
  SLJ - v44 - Mr '98 - p191 [51-250]

Andreae, Giles
The Lion Who Wanted to Love (Illus. by David Wojtowycz)
  Sch Lib - v45 - N '97 - p184 [51-250]

Rumble in the Jungle (Illus. by David Wojtowycz)
  CBRS - v26 - S '97 - p1 [1-50]
  CCB-B - v51 - O '97 - p41+ [51-250]
  SLJ - v43 - N '97 - p76 [51-250]

Andrews, Jan
Keri
    BIC - v26 - O '97 - p35 [501+]
  y CBRA - '96 - p463 [51-250]
  y JAAL - v40 - O '96 - p157+ [51-250]

Very Last First Time (Illus. by Ian Wallace)
  PW - v245 - F 2 '98 - p92 [1-50]

Andrews, Sylvia
Rattlebone Rock (Illus. by Jennifer Plecas)
  PW - v244 - O 6 '97 - p50 [1-50]

Andryszewski, Tricia
The March on Washington
  BL - v94 - F 15 '98 - p998 [1-50]

Anema, Durlynn
Harriet Chalmers Adams: Explorer and Adventurer
    Ch BWatch - v7 - Jl '97 - p4 [51-250]
  y HB Guide - v8 - Fall '97 - p378 [51-250]
  y SLJ - v43 - Ap '97 - p142+ [51-250]
  y VOYA - v20 - O '97 - p256 [251-500]

Angelo, Sandra McFall
The Easy Way to Draw Animals
  Ch BWatch - v7 - D '97 - p4 [1-50]

Angelou, Maya
Kofi and His Magic (Illus. by Margaret Courtney-Clarke)
  Ch BWatch - v7 - Ap '97 - p6 [1-50]
  HB Guide - v8 - Fall '97 - p392 [51-250]
  HMR - Sum '97 - p28 [1-50]

Anglund, Joan Walsh
Little Angels' Book of Christmas
  Ch BWatch - v7 - D '97 - p2 [1-50]

Angus, Monica
Lost Lagoon (Illus. by Vivian Kuhn)
  CBRA - '96 - p431+ [51-250]

Anholt, Catherine
A Kiss Like This
  BW - v27 - D 7 '97 - p21 [51-250]

Sun Snow Stars Sky
  SB - v33 - O '97 - p195 [1-50]

Anholt, Laurence
Billy and the Big New School (Illus. by Catherine Anholt)
  Bks Keeps - Jl '97 - p20 [51-250]
  Sch Lib - v45 - Ag '97 - p129 [51-250]

Daft Jack and the Bean Stack (Illus. by Arthur Robins)
  TES - Jl 11 '97 - p14* [51-250]

Degas and the Little Dancer
  Emerg Lib - v25 - N '97 - p59+ [51-250]

The Forgotten Forest
  New Sci - v154 - Je 28 '97 - p44 [51-250]

The Rather Small Turnip (Illus. by Arthur Robins)
  TES - Jl 11 '97 - p14* [51-250]

Animal Ark Series
  Bks Keeps - My '97 - p7 [501+]

Animal Friends (Balloon)
  PW - v244 - N 10 '97 - p76 [1-50]

Animals (Fit-a-Shape)
  Magpies - v12 - Mr '97 - p29 [51-250]

Anozie, Frederick
Khoekhoe
  Ch BWatch - v8 - Ja '98 - p7 [51-250]

Ansary, Mir Tamim
Dolls
  SLJ - v43 - Jl '97 - p80 [51-250]

Insects
  SLJ - v43 - Ag '97 - p145 [51-250]

Model Cars
  SLJ - v43 - Jl '97 - p80 [51-250]

Natural Objects
  SLJ - v43 - Ag '97 - p145 [51-250]

Stamps
  SLJ - v43 - Jl '97 - p80 [51-250]

Ansley, Frank
Trucks at Work
  PW - v244 - N 3 '97 - p87 [51-250]

Antillano, Laura
Una Vaca Querida (Illus. by Ana Ochoa)
  SLJ - v43 - N '97 - p136 [51-250]

Antle, Nancy
Ordinary Albert (Illus. by Pamela Allen)
  Magpies - v12 - My '97 - p27 [51-250]

Staying Cool (Illus. by E B Lewis)
  Am Vis - v12 - D '97 - p34 [1-50]
  BL - v93 - Je 1 '97 - p1715 [51-250]
  CBRS - v26 - D '97 - p37 [51-250]
  CCB-B - v51 - S '97 - p5+ [51-250]
  KR - v65 - Je 15 '97 - p946 [51-250]
  PW - v244 - Je 2 '97 - p71 [51-250]
  SLJ - v43 - Ag '97 - p128 [51-250]

Antoine, Heloise
Curious Kids Go on Vacation (Illus. by Ingrid Godon)
  HB Guide - v8 - Fall '97 - p248 [51-250]
  RT - v51 - F '98 - p431 [51-250]

Aoki, Hisako
Santa's Favorite Story (Illus. by Ivan Gantschev)
  PW - v244 - O 6 '97 - p59 [1-50]

Apel, Lorelei
Dealing with Weapons at School and at Home
  SLJ - v43 - S '97 - p199 [51-250]

Appelbaum, Diana Karter
Cocoa Ice (Illus. by Holly Meade)
  BL - v94 - N 1 '97 - p466 [51-250]
  CBRS - v26 - Ja '98 - p54 [51-250]
  CCB-B - v51 - Mr '98 - p235 [51-250]
  KR - v65 - Ag 1 '97 - p1218 [51-250]
  SLJ - v44 - Ja '98 - p80 [51-250]

Appelt, Kathi
Bat Jamboree
  TCMath - v4 - O '97 - p122 [51-250]

Elephants Aloft (Illus. by Keith Baker)
  PW - v244 - Jl 21 '97 - p203 [1-50]

I See the Moon (Illus. by Debra Reid Jenkins)
  HB Guide - v8 - Fall '97 - p375 [51-250]

Applegate, Katherine
Animorphs Series
  HB - v74 - Ja '98 - p53+ [501+]

The Message
  SLJ - v43 - Je '97 - p114 [51-250]

Apps, Roy
The Genius Academy
  TES - My 16 '97 - p14* [51-250]

Melvin and the Deadheads
  Magpies - v12 - S '97 - p32 [51-250]
  TES - N 7 '97 - p7* [1-50]

Arbuckle, Kathy
Bible Praises for Preschoolers
  PW - v244 - O 27 '97 - p71 [51-250]

Bible Wisdom for Preschoolers
  PW - v244 - O 27 '97 - p71 [51-250]

Arbuckle, Scott
*Zeb, the Cow's on the Roof Again!
and Other Tales of Early Texas
Dwellings (Illus. by Scott Arbuckle)*
    SLJ - v43 - Ap '97 - p134 [51-250]

Archer, Chris
Alien Blood
    BL - v94 - D 15 '97 - p696+ [51-250]
y SLJ - v44 - Mr '98 - p208 [51-250]

Alien Terror
    BL - v94 - D 15 '97 - p696+ [51-250]
    PW - v244 - O 6 '97 - p84 [51-250]
y SLJ - v44 - Mr '98 - p208 [51-250]

Archibald, Erika F
A Sudanese Family
    Bloom Rev - v17 - S '97 - p23 [51-250]
    Ch BWatch - v7 - My '97 - p6 [1-50]
    SLJ - v43 - Jl '97 - p99 [51-250]

Ardley, Neil
101 Great Science Experiments
r JOYS - v11 - Fall '97 - p75 [1-50]

Armbruster, Ann
Floods
    SB - v33 - Je '97 - p143 [51-250]

Lake Erie
    HB Guide - v8 - Fall '97 - p393 [51-250]

Lake Huron
    HB Guide - v8 - Fall '97 - p393 [51-250]

Lake Michigan
    HB Guide - v8 - Fall '97 - p393 [51-250]

Lake Ontario
    HB Guide - v8 - Fall '97 - p393 [51-250]
    SLJ - v43 - Ap '97 - p119 [51-250]

Lake Superior
    HB Guide - v8 - Fall '97 - p393 [51-250]

St. Lawrence Seaway
    HB Guide - v8 - Fall '97 - p393 [51-250]
    SLJ - v43 - Ap '97 - p119 [51-250]

Armitage, Ronda
*Flora and the Strawberry Red
Birthday Party (Illus. by David
Armitage)*
    Magpies - v12 - S '97 - p28 [51-250]

The Lighthouse Keeper's Cat
    Bks Keeps - S '97 - p21 [51-250]

Arms Law
    Ch BWatch - v7 - Ap '97 - p8 [51-250]

Armstrong, Carole
Women of the Bible
y BL - v94 - Mr 1 '98 - p1123 [51-250]
    HB - v74 - Mr '98 - p231+ [51-250]
    KR - v66 - Ja 1 '98 - p52 [51-250]
    PW - v245 - F 23 '98 - p66 [51-250]
    SLJ - v44 - Mr '98 - p228 [51-250]

Armstrong, Jennifer
*Chin Yu Min and the Ginger Cat
(Illus. by Mary GrandPre)*
    ECEJ - v25 - Fall '97 - p45 [1-50]

*Foolish Gretel (Illus. by Donna
Diamond)*
    SLJ - v43 - D '97 - p81 [51-250]

Mary Mehan Awake
y BL - v94 - D 1 '97 - p615 [51-250]
y CCB-B - v51 - D '97 - p116+ [51-250]
    HB - v73 - N '97 - p675+ [251-500]
y SLJ - v44 - Ja '98 - p108 [51-250]

*Sunshine, Moonshine (Illus. by Lucia
Washburn)*
    SLJ - v43 - Ag '97 - p128 [51-250]

Armstrong, Robb
*Drew and the Bub Daddy Showdown
(Illus. by Robb Armstrong)*
    RT - v51 - O '97 - p137 [1-50]

*Drew and the Homeboy Question
(Illus. by Robb Armstrong)*
    CCB-B - v51 - S '97 - p6 [51-250]
    HB Guide - v8 - Fall '97 - p295 [51-250]
    SLJ - v43 - Jl '97 - p90 [51-250]

Armstrong, William H
Trueno
    SLJ - v43 - My '97 - p152 [51-250]

Arnold, Caroline

African Animals
> HB Guide - v8 - Fall '97 - p344 [51-250]
> SB - Ag '97 - p162 [1-50]

The Ancient Cliff Dwellings of Mesa Verde
> JOYS - v10 - Sum '97 - p426 [1-50]

Bobcats (Illus. by Richard Hewett)
> SLJ - v44 - Mr '98 - p191+ [51-250]

Hawk Highway in the Sky (Illus. by Robert Kruidenier)
> Am Sci - v85 - N '97 - p556 [51-250]
> BL - v93 - Je 1 '97 - p1687 [51-250]
> HB Guide - v8 - Fall '97 - p351 [51-250]
> SB - v33 - Ag '97 - p162 [1-50]
> SLJ - v43 - Je '97 - p130 [51-250]

Stone Age Farmers Beside the Sea (Illus. by Arthur P Arnold)
> HB Guide - v8 - Fall '97 - p387 [51-250]
> SLJ - v43 - Jl '97 - p99 [51-250]

Stories in Stone (Illus. by Richard Hewett)
> SE - v61 - Ap '97 - p10* [1-50]

Arnold, Elizabeth

Gold and Silver Water
> TES - N 7 '97 - p8* [1-50]

Arnold, Katya

Duck, Duck, Goose? (Illus. by Katya Arnold)
> CBRS - v25 - Jl '97 - p146 [51-250]
> CCB-B - v51 - S '97 - p6 [51-250]
> Ch BWatch - v7 - O '97 - p6 [1-50]
> HB - v73 - S '97 - p553+ [51-250]
> HB Guide - v8 - Fall '97 - p258 [51-250]
> SLJ - v43 - S '97 - p172 [51-250]

Katya's Book of Mushrooms (Illus. by Katya Arnold)
> AB - v100 - N 17 '97 - p1270 [51-250]
> HB Guide - v8 - Fall '97 - p348 [51-250]
> SLJ - v43 - Ap '97 - p143 [51-250]

Meow! (Illus. by Katya Arnold)
> KR - v66 - Ap 1 '98 - p492 [51-250]

Arnold, Nick

Blood, Bones and Body Bits
> New Sci - v154 - Je 7 '97 - p48 [51-250]

Volcano, Earthquake, and Hurricane
> HB Guide - v8 - Fall '97 - p342 [51-250]
> SB - v33 - O '97 - p208+ [51-250]

Arnold, Tedd

Green Wilma
> PW - v244 - D 22 '97 - p61 [1-50]

Help! I'm Falling Apart (Illus. by Tedd Arnold)
> Magpies - v12 - S '97 - p31 [51-250]

Parts (Illus. by Tedd Arnold)
> BL - v93 - Ag '97 - p1904 [51-250]
> CBRS - v26 - Ja '98 - p49 [51-250]
> CCB-B - v51 - O '97 - p42 [51-250]
> KR - v65 - Jl 15 '97 - p1106 [51-250]
> PW - v244 - Ag 4 '97 - p73+ [51-250]

The Signmaker's Assistant
> PW - v244 - Je 2 '97 - p73 [1-50]

Arnosky, Jim

All about Alligators (Illus. by Jim Arnosky)
> SLJ - v43 - My '97 - p56 [1-50]

All about Deer (Illus. by Jim Arnosky)
> Emerg Lib - v24 - My '97 - p57 [1-50]

All about Rattlesnakes (Illus. by Jim Arnosky)
> BL - v94 - D 1 '97 - p625 [51-250]
> HB - v73 - S '97 - p589+ [51-250]

Bird Watcher
> Am Sci - v85 - N '97 - p559 [51-250]

Bring 'Em Back Alive! (Illus. by Jim Arnosky)
> SLJ - v43 - Je '97 - p130 [51-250]

Crinkleroot's Guide to Knowing Animal Habitats (Illus. by Jim Arnosky)
> BL - v93 - Je 1 '97 - p1708 [51-250]
> HB Guide - v8 - Fall '97 - p344 [51-250]
> KR - v65 - My 15 '97 - p796 [51-250]
> SLJ - v43 - Je '97 - p105 [51-250]

Crinkleroot's Guide to Knowing Butterflies and Moths
Inst - v106 - Ap '97 - p4* [1-50]
SB - v33 - Ag '97 - p162 [1-50]

Little Lions (Illus. by Jim Arnosky)
BL - v94 - Mr 1 '98 - p1139 [51-250]
KR - v65 - D 1 '97 - p1772 [51-250]
PW - v245 - Ja 12 '98 - p58 [51-250]
SLJ - v44 - Mr '98 - p166 [51-250]

Rabbits and Raindrops
Ch BWatch - v7 - Mr '97 - p7 [1-50]
HB Guide - v8 - Fall '97 - p258 [51-250]

Watching Water Birds (Illus. by Jim Arnosky)
BL - v94 - O 1 '97 - p334 [51-250]
HB - v74 - Ja '98 - p88+ [51-250]
KR - v65 - S 1 '97 - p1384 [51-250]
PW - v244 - O 27 '97 - p79 [51-250]
SLJ - v43 - D '97 - p23 [1-50]

Aronson, Billy
Eclipses: Nature's Blackouts
SB - v33 - Ap '97 - p83 [51-250]
SB - v33 - Ag '97 - p162 [1-50]

The Truth behind Shooting Stars
SB - v33 - Ap '97 - p83 [51-250]

Artell, Mike
Starry Skies
SB - v34 - Ap '98 - p79 [51-250]

Arthur, Joe
The Story of Thurgood Marshall
Ch BWatch - v7 - Mr '97 - p4+ [1-50]

Arthy, Judith
The Children of Mirrabooka
y   Aust Bk R - Ap '97 - p62 [501+]
Magpies - v12 - My '97 - p36+ [251-500]

Artiles Perez, Emma
El Alma En Una Nube (Illus. by Alejandro Campos Garcia)
Bkbird - v35 - Sum '97 - p57 [1-50]

Asbjornsen, Peter Christen
Three Billy Goats Gruff (Illus. by Glen Rounds)
SLJ - v43 - N '97 - p40 [1-50]

Asbury, Kelly
Bonnie's Blue House (Illus. by Kelly Asbury)
CBRS - v25 - Spr '97 - p133 [1-50]
HB Guide - v8 - Fall '97 - p258 [1-50]
NYTBR - v102 - Ag 17 '97 - p19 [1-50]
SLJ - v43 - Je '97 - p78 [51-250]

Rusty's Red Vacation (Illus. by Kelly Asbury)
CBRS - v25 - Spr '97 - p133 [1-50]
HB Guide - v8 - Fall '97 - p258 [1-50]
SLJ - v43 - Je '97 - p78 [51-250]

Yolanda's Yellow School (Illus. by Kelly Asbury)
CBRS - v25 - Spr '97 - p133 [1-50]
HB Guide - v8 - Fall '97 - p258 [1-50]
SLJ - v43 - Je '97 - p78 [51-250]

Asch, Frank
Barnyard Lullaby (Illus. by Frank Asch)
BL - v94 - Ja 1 '98 - p798 [51-250]
CCB-B - v51 - Mr '98 - p235 [51-250]
KR - v65 - D 1 '97 - p1772 [51-250]
PW - v244 - D 22 '97 - p58 [51-250]
SLJ - v44 - F '98 - p78 [51-250]

Cactus Poems (Illus. by Ted Levin)
BL - v94 - Mr 15 '98 - p1238 [51-250]
PW - v245 - Mr 9 '98 - p70 [51-250]

I Can Blink like an Owl
PW - v244 - O 27 '97 - p78 [1-50]

I Can Roar like a Lion
PW - v244 - O 27 '97 - p78 [1-50]

Moonbear's Pet (Illus. by Frank Asch)
BL - v93 - Je 1 '97 - p1715 [51-250]
CCB-B - v50 - Jl '97 - p387+ [51-250]
HB Guide - v8 - Fall '97 - p258 [51-250]
SLJ - v43 - Je '97 - p78 [51-250]

One Man Show (Illus. by Jan Asch)
SLJ - v43 - S '97 - p199 [51-250]

Sawgrass Poems (Illus. by Ted Levin)
SB - v33 - Ag '97 - p162 [1-50]
SB - v33 - O '97 - p195 [1-50]

Up River (Illus. by Ted Levin)
SB - v33 - O '97 - p195 [51-250]

Ash, Rhiannon
Roman Colosseum (Illus. by Mike Bell)
Ch BWatch - v8 - Ja '98 - p6 [1-50]
SLJ - v44 - Ap '98 - p112+ [51-250]

Ash, Russell
The World in One Day
Obs - D 7 '97 - p18* [51-250]
PW - v244 - O 20 '97 - p78 [51-250]

Ashabranner, Brent
The Lion's Whiskers and Other Ethiopian Tales (Illus. by Helen Siegl)
BL - v94 - O 1 '97 - p320 [51-250]
HB Guide - v8 - Fall '97 - p331 [51-250]
SLJ - v43 - My '97 - p141 [51-250]

Our Beckoning Borders
SE - v61 - Ap '97 - p4* [1-50]

To Seek a Better World (Illus. by Paul Conklin)
HB Guide - v8 - Fall '97 - p322 [51-250]
SLJ - v43 - My '97 - p141 [51-250]

Asher, Sandy
But That's Another Story
RT - v51 - N '97 - p252 [51-250]

Ashley, Allen
We Are All Related
BL - v93 - Ag '97 - p1897 [51-250]

We Are All Related (Illus. by James Jardine)
CBRA - '96 - p523 [51-250]

Ashley, Bernard
Cleversticks (Illus. by Derek Brazell)
ECEJ - v25 - Fall '97 - p45 [1-50]

Roller Madonnas (Illus. by Kim Harley)
Bks Keeps - S '97 - p25 [51-250]
Sch Lib - v45 - Ag '97 - p135 [51-250]
TES - Jl 4 '97 - p10* [501+]

Ashley, Chris
Wasim in the Deep End (Illus. by Sascha Lipscomb)
Bks Keeps - N '97 - p2 [51-250]
Sch Lib - v45 - N '97 - p190 [51-250]

Ashley, Mike
The Mammoth Book of Fairy Tales
y   BL - v94 - O 15 '97 - p389 [51-250]
     CAY - v18 - Fall '97 - p2 [51-250]
y   Kliatt - v32 - Mr '98 - p16 [251-500]
     KR - v65 - S 1 '97 - p1338 [51-250]
     LJ - v122 - S 1 '97 - p182 [51-250]

Ashton, Jay
Keeping Cats
Bks Keeps - My '97 - p23 [51-250]
Magpies - v12 - My '97 - p32 [51-250]

Killing the Demons
TES - Ja 2 '98 - p22* [51-250]

Ashworth, Liz
Teach the Bairns to Bake
Sch Lib - v45 - N '97 - p203 [51-250]

Asikinack, Bill
Exploration into North America
SB - v32 - D '96 - p277 [51-250]

Asimov, Janet
Norby and the Terrified Taxi
BL - v94 - Ja 1 '98 - p809 [51-250]
KR - v65 - N 1 '97 - p1640 [51-250]
y   SLJ - v43 - D '97 - p120 [51-250]

Atkin, S Beth
Voices from the Streets (Illus. by S Beth Atkin)
y   HMR - Sum '97 - p29 [1-50]
y   JAAL - v41 - O '97 - p166 [51-250]
     SE - v61 - Ap '97 - p4* [1-50]
y   SE - v61 - S '97 - p270 [51-250]

Atkins, Jeannine
Get Set! Swim! (Illus. by Hector Viveros Lee)
KR - v66 - Ap 1 '98 - p492 [51-250]

Atxaga, Bernardo
Shola Y Los Jabalies (Illus. by Mikel Valverde)
SLJ - v44 - F '98 - p130 [51-250]

Auch, Mary Jane
Bantam of the Opera (Illus. by Mary Jane Auch)
BL - v94 - O 1 '97 - p335 [51-250]
CBRS - v26 - S '97 - p1 [51-250]
Ch BWatch - v7 - O '97 - p6 [1-50]
Inst - v107 - N '97 - p22 [51-250]
PW - v244 - Jl 28 '97 - p74 [51-250]

Eggs Mark the Spot (Illus. by Mary Jane Auch)
Inst - v106 - Ap '97 - p25 [1-50]
Inst - v106 - My '97 - p18 [51-250]

Eggs Mark the Spot. Book and Audio Version
Ch BWatch - v7 - My '97 - p5 [1-50]
SLJ - v43 - N '97 - p68 [51-250]

I Was a Third Grade Science Project (Illus. by Herm Auch)
BL - v94 - Mr 15 '98 - p1243 [51-250]
KR - v66 - Mr 1 '98 - p334 [51-250]
PW - v245 - Mr 23 '98 - p100 [51-250]

Journey to Nowhere
CBRS - v25 - Je '97 - p128 [51-250]
CCB-B - v50 - Je '97 - p350 [51-250]
HB - v73 - Jl '97 - p449 [51-250]
HB Guide - v8 - Fall '97 - p296 [51-250]
NYTBR - v102 - Ag 31 '97 - p13 [1-50]
SLJ - v43 - My '97 - p128 [51-250]

Auerbach, Margaret
A Spider in the Library
Bkbird - v35 - Spr '97 - p50 [51-250]

Auerbacher, Inge
Beyond the Yellow Star to America (Moore). Audio Version
y   BL - v94 - D 15 '97 - p711 [1-50]
SLJ - v43 - S '97 - p164+ [51-250]

Aura, Alejandro
The Other Side (Illus. by Julia Gukova)
Bkbird - v34 - Win '96 - p55 [51-250]

Aveling, Ann
Trouble on Wheels
Can CL - v23 - Fall '97 - p73+ [501+]

Avi
The Barn
BL - v93 - Je 1 '97 - p1700 [1-50]

The Escape from Home
y   Kliatt - v32 - Ja '98 - p6 [51-250]
y   Sch Lib - v45 - N '97 - p211 [51-250]
TES - S 12 '97 - p8* [251-500]

Finding Providence (Illus. by James Watling)
HB Guide - v8 - Fall '97 - p288 [51-250]

Lord Kirkle's Money
y   Sch Lib - v45 - N '97 - p211 [51-250]
TES - S 12 '97 - p8* [251-500]

Poppy
BL - v94 - D 15 '97 - p695 [1-50]

Tom, Babette, and Simon
PW - v244 - Ag 18 '97 - p95 [1-50]

The True Confessions of Charlotte Doyle
HB - v74 - Ja '98 - p26+ [501+]
SLJ - v43 - Jl '97 - p34 [51-250]
SLJ - v43 - S '97 - p130 [51-250]

What Do Fish Have to Do with Anything? and Other Stories (Illus. by Tracy Mitchell)
CCB-B - v51 - O '97 - p42 [51-250]
HB - v73 - N '97 - p676 [51-250]
KR - v65 - N 1 '97 - p1640 [51-250]
PW - v244 - O 27 '97 - p77 [51-250]
SLJ - v43 - D '97 - p120 [51-250]
y   VOYA - v21 - Ap '98 - p44 [51-250]

Who Was That Masked Man, Anyway?
SLJ - v44 - Mr '98 - p119 [1-50]

Awan, Shaila
The Burrow Book (Illus. by Richard Orr)
Emerg Lib - v25 - Ja '98 - p51 [51-250]

Away in a Manger (Illus. by Ruth Hills)
PW - v244 - O 6 '97 - p57 [1-50]

Away in a Manger (Little Angels Series) (Illus. by Laura Rader)
Ch BWatch - v7 - N '97 - p6 [1-50]

Axelrod, Amy
Pigs Go to Market (Illus. by Sharon McGinley-Nally)
PW - v244 - O 6 '97 - p49 [51-250]
SLJ - v43 - S '97 - p172 [51-250]

Pigs in the Pantry (Illus. by Sharon McGinley-Nally)
Ch BWatch - v7 - O '97 - p6 [1-50]
HB Guide - v8 - Fall '97 - p258 [51-250]
NYTBR - v102 - N 16 '97 - p38 [51-250]
SLJ - v43 - Ap '97 - p90 [51-250]

Aye, Nila
Orchard's Little Blue Book of Nursery Rhymes
KR - v66 - Ja 1 '98 - p52 [51-250]
PW - v245 - Mr 9 '98 - p70 [51-250]
TES - N 7 '97 - p2* [1-50]

Orchard's Little Green Book of Nursery Rhymes
PW - v245 - Mr 9 '98 - p70 [51-250]

Orchard's Little Red Book of Nursery Rhymes
PW - v245 - Mr 9 '98 - p70 [51-250]

Orchard's Little Yellow Book of Nursery Rhymes
PW - v245 - Mr 9 '98 - p70 [51-250]

Ayer, Eleanor H
Colorado
Ch BWatch - v7 - My '97 - p7 [51-250]
HB Guide - v8 - Fall '97 - p394 [51-250]
SLJ - v43 - Ag '97 - p160+ [51-250]

A Firestorm Unleashed January 1942 to June 1943
y   BL - v94 - O 15 '97 - p396 [51-250]
CCB-B - v51 - Ja '98 - p162+ [51-250]
yr   SLJ - v44 - F '98 - p134 [51-250]

From the Ashes May 1945 and After
y   BL - v94 - O 15 '97 - p396 [51-250]
CCB-B - v51 - Ja '98 - p162+ [51-250]
yr   SLJ - v44 - F '98 - p134 [51-250]

Inferno: July 1943 to April 1945
CCB-B - v51 - Ja '98 - p162+ [51-250]
yr   SLJ - v44 - F '98 - p134 [51-250]

Aylesworth, Jim
The Folks in the Valley (Illus. by Stefano Vitale)
PW - v245 - F 16 '98 - p213 [1-50]

The Gingerbread Man (Illus. by Barbara McClintock)
KR - v66 - Ja 1 '98 - p52 [51-250]
PW - v245 - Ja 26 '98 - p90 [51-250]
SLJ - v44 - Ap '98 - p113 [51-250]

Teddy Bear Tears (Illus. by Jo Ellen McAllister-Stammen)
CBRS - v25 - My '97 - p109 [51-250]
Ch BWatch - v7 - Jl '97 - p7 [1-50]
HB Guide - v8 - Fall '97 - p248 [51-250]
Par - v72 - S '97 - p205 [51-250]
SLJ - v43 - Je '97 - p78+ [51-250]

Through the Night (Illus. by Pamela Patrick)
KR - v66 - Ja 15 '98 - p108 [51-250]
SLJ - v44 - Ap '98 - p91 [51-250]

Ayres, Katherine
Family Tree
PW - v244 - D 15 '97 - p60 [1-50]

Ayres, Pam
The Nubbler
Bks Keeps - Jl '97 - p24 [51-250]
Magpies - v12 - S '97 - p32 [51-250]
Sch Lib - v45 - Ag '97 - p135 [51-250]

B

Babbitt, Natalie
*Knee Knock Rise (Toren). Audio
Version*
y Kliatt - v31 - Jl '97 - p47 [51-250]
  SLJ - v43 - Ap '97 - p82 [51-250]

**Babes in Toyland (Illus. by Erin
McGonigle Brammer)**
  KR - v65 - O 15 '97 - p1578 [51-250]
  PW - v244 - O 20 '97 - p78 [51-250]

Baby Animals (Balloon)
  PW - v244 - N 10 '97 - p76 [1-50]

Baby Tweety's Flying Machine
  Ch BWatch - v7 - Jl '97 - p2 [1-50]

Babybug
p Par Ch - Awards '97 - p27 [1-50]

**Baby's Bedtime (Illus. by Jonathan
Langley)**
  Bks Keeps - Jl '97 - p18 [51-250]

Baby's First Prayers
  PW - v245 - Mr 23 '98 - p95+ [51-250]

**Baby's World--At Home (Illus. by
Geoff Dann)**
  CM:CanRev - v4 - Ja 2 '98 - pONL
  [251-500]

**Baby's World--Outdoors (Illus. by
Geoff Dann)**
  CM:CanRev - v4 - Ja 2 '98 - pONL
  [251-500]

Bachrach, Deborah
The Resistance
  SLJ - v44 - F '98 - p111 [51-250]

Bagert, Brod
*The Gooch Machine (Illus. by Tim
Ellis)*
  CLW - v68 - S '97 - p66 [51-250]
  HB Guide - v8 - Fall '97 - p375 [1-50]
  SLJ - v43 - Ap '97 - p119+ [51-250]

Baggette, Susan
*Jonathan Goes to the Doctor (Illus. by
William Moriarty)*
  PW - v245 - F 9 '98 - p97 [51-250]

*Jonathan Goes to the Grocery Store
(Illus. by William Moriarty)*
  PW - v245 - F 9 '98 - p97 [51-250]

*Jonathan Goes to the Library (Illus.
by William Moriarty)*
  PW - v245 - F 9 '98 - p97 [51-250]

Baicker-McKee, Carol
*Mapped Out! (Illus. by Traci O'Very
Covey)*
  SLJ - v44 - Ja '98 - p108 [51-250]

Bailer, Darice
*The Last Rail (Illus. by Bill
Farnsworth). Book and Audio Version*
  SLJ - v43 - Je '97 - p70+ [51-250]

*Wanted: A Few Bold Riders. Book and
Audio Version*
  SLJ - v44 - Ja '98 - p70+ [251-500]

Bailey, Debbie
Grandma (Illus. by Susan Huszar)
  Can CL - v23 - Fall '97 - p92 [51-250]

Grandpa (Illus. by Susan Huszar)
  Can CL - v23 - Fall '97 - p92 [51-250]

Bailey, Linda
Gordon Loggins and the Three Bears
(Illus. by Tracy Walker)
  CBRS - v26 - S '97 - p1 [1-50]
  CCB-B - v51 - D '97 - p117 [51-250]
  CM:CanRev - v4 - N 14 '97 - pONL
  [251-500]
  PW - v244 - N 10 '97 - p73 [51-250]
  Quill & Q - v63 - Jl '97 - p51 [251-500]

How Can a Frozen Detective Stay Hot
on the Trail?
  CBRA - '96 - p463 [51-250]

Petula, Who Wouldn't Take a Bath
(Illus. by Jackie Snider)
  CBRA - '96 - p432 [51-250]

What's a Daring Detective like Me
Doing in the Doghouse?
  CM:CanRev - v4 - Ja 16 '98 - pONL
  [251-500]
  Quill & Q - v63 - Ag '97 - p38 [51-250]
  SLJ - v44 - Ja '98 - p108 [51-250]

Who's Got Gertie? and How Can We
Get Her Back!
  Can CL - v23 - Fall '97 - p73+ [501+]

Baillie, Allan
The Last Shot
  y   Aust Bk R - Ap '97 - p63 [501+]
       Magpies - v12 - My '97 - p37 [51-250]

Wreck!
  Aust Bk R - N '97 - p59 [501+]

Baillie, Marilyn
Side by Side (Illus. by Romi Caron)
  Ch Bk News - v20 - Spr '97 - p31 [51-
  250]
  SLJ - v43 - Jl '97 - p80 [51-250]

Wild Talk (Illus. by Romi Caron)
  CBRA - '96 - p527 [51-250]

Baird, Alison
The Dragon's Egg (Illus. by Frances
Tyrrell)
  Can CL - v23 - Sum '97 - p54+ [501+]

Baiul, Oksana
Oksana: My Own Story
  HB Guide - v8 - Fall '97 - p368 [51-
  250]
  SLJ - v43 - My '97 - p142 [51-250]

Baker, Alan
Mouse's Halloween (Illus. by Alan
Baker)
  PW - v244 - O 6 '97 - p48 [51-250]
  SLJ - v44 - F '98 - p78 [51-250]

Baker, Barbara
Digby and Kate and the Beautiful Day
(Illus. by Marsha Winborn)
  KR - v65 - D 1 '97 - p1772 [51-250]
  SLJ - v44 - Mr '98 - p166 [51-250]

Baker, Christopher W
Let There Be Life!
  BL - v94 - Ja 1 '98 - p800 [51-250]
  KR - v65 - My 15 '97 - p796 [51-250]

Baker, Karen Lee
Seneca (Illus. by Karen Lee Baker)
  CBRS - v25 - Je '97 - p121 [51-250]
  HB Guide - v8 - Fall '97 - p258 [1-50]
  SLJ - v43 - Ap '97 - p90 [51-250]

Baker, Keith, 1953-
Cat Tricks (Illus. by Keith Baker)
  BL - v94 - D 15 '97 - p701 [51-250]
  KR - v65 - Jl 15 '97 - p1106+ [51-250]
  PW - v244 - Jl 28 '97 - p74 [51-250]
  SLJ - v43 - D '97 - p81 [51-250]

Baker, Lucy
Life in the Rain Forests
  AB - v100 - N 17 '97 - p1269 [51-250]

Baker, Rosalie F
Ancient Greeks
  y   BL - v93 - Ag '97 - p1889 [51-250]
  yr   BL - v94 - S 15 '97 - p262 [251-500]
  y   Ch BWatch - v7 - O '97 - p7 [51-250]
       KR - v65 - My 15 '97 - p796 [51-250]

y   SLJ - v43 - S '97 - p228 [51-250]

Bakken, Edna
Alberta. Rev. Ed.
    CBRA - '96 - p512+ [501+]

Balan, Bruce
In Search of Scum
    Ch BWatch - v7 - Je '97 - p3 [51-250]

A Picture's Worth
    Ch BWatch - v7 - Je '97 - p3+ [51-250]

Balcavage, Dynise
Ludwig Van Beethoven: Composer
y   HB Guide - v8 - Fall '97 - p378 [51-250]
    SLJ - v43 - Jl '97 - p99+ [51-250]

Balcker, Terence
Dream Team
    TES - Ap 18 '97 - p12* [51-250]

Balgassi, Haemi
Peacebound Trains (Illus. by Chris K Soentpiet)
    RT - v51 - D '97 - p309 [51-250]
    RT - v51 - D '97 - p332 [51-250]
    SE - v61 - Ap '97 - p6* [1-50]

Tae's Sonata
    BL - v94 - O 15 '97 - p404 [51-250]
    CBRS - v26 - D '97 - p45 [51-250]
y   CCB-B - v51 - N '97 - p80 [51-250]
    KR - v65 - Jl 1 '97 - p1026 [51-250]
    PW - v244 - Je 30 '97 - p76 [51-250]
    SLJ - v43 - S '97 - p210 [51-250]

Balkwill, Fran
Amazing Schemes within Your Genes (Illus. by Mic Rolph)
    SB - v33 - Ap '97 - p67 [1-50]

Cells Are Us (Illus. by Mic Rolph)
    SB - v33 - Ap '97 - p67 [1-50]

The Egg and Sperm Race
    Bks Keeps - My '97 - p27 [51-250]

Ball, Duncan
Selby Speaks (Illus. by M K Brown)
    SLJ - v43 - Jl '97 - p60 [51-250]

Ballard, Carol
The Heart and Circulatory System
y   HB Guide - v8 - Fall '97 - p355 [51-250]
    SB - v33 - Ag '97 - p180 [51-250]
    SLJ - v43 - Ag '97 - p162 [51-250]

The Skeleton and Muscular System
y   SB - v34 - Ap '98 - p76+ [51-250]
    SLJ - v44 - F '98 - p111 [51-250]

The Stomach and Digestive System
y   HB Guide - v8 - Fall '97 - p355 [51-250]
    SB - v33 - Ag '97 - p180 [51-250]
    SLJ - v43 - Ag '97 - p162 [51-250]

Ballard, Robert D
Exploring the Titanic
    BL - v94 - Mr 15 '98 - p1244 [51-250]

Ballard, Robin
When I Am a Sister (Illus. by Robin Ballard)
    BL - v94 - Mr 1 '98 - p1139 [51-250]
    SLJ - v44 - Ap '98 - p91 [51-250]

Bancroft, Henrietta
Animals in Winter. Rev. Ed. (Illus. by Helen Davie)
    HB Guide - v8 - Fall '97 - p344 [51-250]
    SB - v33 - Ag '97 - p187 [1-50]

Bang, Molly
Chattanooga Sludge
y   JAAL - v40 - Ap '97 - p586 [51-250]
    SB - v33 - Ag '97 - p162+ [1-50]

Common Ground (Illus. by Molly Bang)
    BL - v94 - O 1 '97 - p330 [51-250]
    CBRS - v26 - N '97 - p31 [1-50]
    CCB-B - v51 - D '97 - p117+ [51-250]
    HB - v73 - N '97 - p692+ [51-250]
    KR - v65 - Ag 15 '97 - p1302+ [51-250]
    PW - v244 - S 22 '97 - p81 [51-250]

Goose
    Inst - v106 - My '97 - p19 [51-250]
    RT - v51 - O '97 - p152 [51-250]

21

Banim, Lisa
The Hessian's Secret Diary (Illus. by James Watling)
    Cur R - v36 - Mr '97 - p12 [51-250]
    HB Guide - v8 - Fall '97 - p296 [51-250]
    SLJ - v43 - Ap '97 - p90 [51-250]

Banks, Kate
And If the Moon Could Talk (Illus. by Georg Hallensleben)
    BL - v94 - F 15 '98 - p1012 [51-250]
    CCB-B - v51 - Ap '98 - p273+ [51-250]
    HB - v74 - Mr '98 - p209+ [501+]
    KR - v66 - Ja 15 '98 - p109 [51-250]
    PW - v245 - Ja 19 '98 - p376 [51-250]
    SLJ - v44 - F '98 - p78 [51-250]

Baboon (Illus. by Georg Hallensleben)
    BL - v94 - Ja 1 '98 - p735 [1-50]
    HB Guide - v8 - Fall '97 - p248 [51-250]
    NYTBR - v102 - O 26 '97 - p47 [1-50]

Spider Spider (Illus. by Georg Hallensleben)
    RT - v51 - S '97 - p57 [51-250]

Banks, Lynne Reid
Angela and Diabola
    Bks Keeps - S '97 - p11 [501+]
    CBRS - v25 - Spr '97 - p140+ [51-250]
 y HB Guide - v8 - Fall '97 - p311 [51-250]
    NYTBR - v102 - Ag 3 '97 - p14 [1-50]
    SLJ - v43 - Jl '97 - p90 [51-250]
    TES - S 19 '97 - p13* [501+]

The Farthest-Away Mountain (Banks). Audio Version
    SF Chr - v19 - O '97 - p44 [51-250]
    SLJ - v43 - Jl '97 - p56 [51-250]

Harry the Poisonous Centipede (Illus. by Tony Ross)
    BL - v94 - S 15 '97 - p234 [51-250]
    CBRS - v26 - S '97 - p7 [51-250]
    Inst - v107 - N '97 - p19 [51-250]
    KR - v65 - Je 15 '97 - p946 [51-250]
    SLJ - v43 - S '97 - p172 [51-250]

I, Houdini (Banks). Audio Version
    SLJ - v43 - Ap '97 - p82 [51-250]

The Indian in the Cupboard
    NYTBR - v102 - N 16 '97 - p26 [1-50]

Banks, Martin
Conserving Rain Forests
    BL - v94 - D 1 '97 - p628 [1-50]

Banks, Sara Harrell
Under the Shadow of Wings
    HB Guide - v8 - Fall '97 - p296 [51-250]
    SLJ - v43 - Je '97 - p114 [51-250]

Banks, William, 1946-
The Black Muslims
    SLJ - v43 - My '97 - p142 [51-250]

Bannatyne-Cugnet, Jo
Estelle and the Self-Esteem Machine (Illus. by Leslie Bell)
    Can CL - v23 - Fall '97 - p69+ [501+]

A Prairie Year (Illus. by Yvette Moore)
    Can CL - v23 - Sum '97 - p68+ [501+]

Bannerman, Helen
The Story of Little Babaji (Illus. by Fred Marcellino)
    Obs - D 7 '97 - p17* [51-250]
    SE - v61 - Ap '97 - p5* [1-50]

Bansemer, Roger
Rachael's Splendifilous Adventure (Illus. by Roger Bansemer)
    Ch BWatch - v7 - Ap '97 - p6 [1-50]
    Ch BWatch - v7 - N '97 - p3 [1-50]

Banyai, Istvan
Re-Zoom (Illus. by Istvan Banyai)
    NY - v73 - O 6 '97 - p116 [51-250]

REM--Rapid Eye Movement (Illus. by Istvan Banyai)
    HB Guide - v8 - Fall '97 - p296 [51-250]
    NW - v130 - D 1 '97 - p78 [1-50]
    NY - v73 - O 6 '97 - p116 [51-250]
 r Par - v72 - D '97 - p204 [1-50]
    SLJ - v43 - Je '97 - p79 [51-250]

Zoom (Illus. by Istvan Banyai)
    NY - v73 - O 6 '97 - p116 [51-250]

Bany-Winters, Lisa
On Stage (Illus. by Sean O'Neill)
    PW - v244 - N 24 '97 - p76 [51-250]
    SLJ - v44 - Mr '98 - p192 [51-250]

Barasch, Lynne
Old Friends (Illus. by Lynne Barasch)
    KR - v66 - Ja 15 '98 - p109 [51-250]
    PW - v245 - F 16 '98 - p211 [51-250]
    SLJ - v44 - Ap '98 - p91 [51-250]

Barber, Antonia
Catkin (Illus. by P J Lynch)
    Bkbird - v35 - Sum '97 - p58 [1-50]

Noah and the Ark (Illus. by Ian Beck)
    NS - v126 - D 5 '97 - p62 [1-50]
    Sch Lib - v45 - N '97 - p184 [51-250]
    TES - O 17 '97 - p12* [51-250]
    TES - N 7 '97 - p11* [51-250]

Barber, Barbara
Allie's Basketball Dream
    Par - v72 - My '97 - p92 [1-50]

Barber, Nicola
The Search for Gold
    Sch Lib - v45 - Ag '97 - p149 [51-250]
    TES - O 31 '97 - p17* [501+]

The Search for Lost Cities
    SLJ - v44 - Ja '98 - p118 [51-250]
    TES - O 31 '97 - p17* [501+]

The Search for Sunken Treasure
    TES - O 31 '97 - p17* [501+]

Bardi, Piero
*The Atlas of the Classical World
(Illus. by Matteo Chesi)*
  r   KR - v65 - D 15 '97 - p1832 [51-250]
  yr PW - v245 - F 2 '98 - p92 [51-250]
  r   SLJ - v44 - Mr '98 - p228 [51-250]

Bare, Colleen Stanley
*Sammy, Dog Detective (Illus. by
Colleen Stanley Bare)*
    BL - v94 - Ja 1 '98 - p817 [51-250]
    CCB-B - v51 - Mr '98 - p236 [51-250]
    KR - v65 - D 1 '97 - p1772 [51-250]
    SLJ - v44 - Ja '98 - p96 [51-250]

*Toby: The Tabby Kitten (Illus. by
Colleen Stanley Bare)*
    ASBYP - v29 - Sum '96 - p4 [51-250]

Barker, Cicely Mary
*The Complete Book of the Flower
Fairies*
    TES - D 26 '97 - p22 [51-250]

Barker, George
*Dibby Dubby Dhu (Illus. by Sara
Fanelli)*
    Bks Keeps - Jl '97 - p25+ [51-250]
  y Obs - Jl 27 '97 - p16* [1-50]
    Sch Lib - v45 - Ag '97 - p156 [51-250]
    TES - N 7 '97 - p2* [1-50]

Barkhouse, Joyce
*Smallest Rabbit (Illus. by Barbara
Martin)*
    CBRA - '96 - p432 [51-250]

Barklem, Jill
*Brambly Hedge Spring and Summer
Stories (Moffat). Audio Version*
    TES - D 19 '97 - p23 [51-250]

Barlas, Robert
Canada
    Ch BWatch - v7 - O '97 - p4+ [51-250]

Barlow, Steve
Erik Bloodaxe, Viking Warrior
    Sch Lib - v45 - Ag '97 - p149 [51-250]

Henry VIII's Executioner
    Sch Lib - v45 - Ag '97 - p149 [51-250]

*The Lost Diary of Erik Bloodaxe
(Tompkinson). Book and Audio
Version*
    TES - D 19 '97 - p23 [51-250]

A Tale of Two Cities
    Sch Lib - v45 - Ag '97 - p156 [51-250]

Barmeir, Jim
The Brain
    ASBYP - v29 - Fall '96 - p60+ [501+]

Barner, Bob
Which Way to the Revolution? (Illus. by Bob Barner)
    KR - v66 - Mr 1 '98 - p334 [51-250]

Barnes, Johnny Ray
Bad Circuits
    Ch BWatch - v7 - Ap '97 - p4 [51-250]

Frozen Dinners
    Ch BWatch - v7 - Ap '97 - p4 [51-250]

Knightmare
    Ch BWatch - v7 - Ap '97 - p4 [1-50]

The Midnight Game
    Ch BWatch - v7 - Ap '97 - p4 [51-250]

A Place to Hide
    Ch BWatch - v7 - Ap '97 - p4 [1-50]

Barnes, Joyce Annette
Promise Me the Moon
    HB Guide - v8 - Fall '97 - p296 [51-250]
  y VOYA - v20 - O '97 - p241 [51-250]

Barnhart, Robert K
The World Book Dictionary. 1996 Ed., Vols. 1-2
  r BL - v93 - Je 1 '97 - p1748 [51-250]

Baron, Alan
Little Pig's Bouncy Ball
    Bks Keeps - Jl '97 - p21 [51-250]

Red Fox and the Baby Bunnies
    Ch BWatch - v7 - My '97 - p3 [1-50]
    HB Guide - v8 - Fall '97 - p248 [51-250]

Baron, Deborah G
Asian American Chronology
  r Inst - v107 - N '97 - p8 [51-250]

Baron, Marcie
Your Own ABC (Illus. by June Bradford)
    CBRA - '96 - p432+ [51-250]

Barracca, Debra
Las Aventuras De Maxi, El Perro Taxista (Illus. by Mark Buehner)
    HB Guide - v8 - Fall '97 - p338 [51-250]
    SLJ - v43 - My '97 - p152 [51-250]

Barraclough, John
Mohandas Gandhi
    BL - v94 - Mr 15 '98 - p1245 [51-250]

Barrett, Judi
Pickles to Pittsburgh (Illus. by Ron Barrett)
    CBRS - v26 - N '97 - p25 [51-250]
    CCB-B - v51 - D '97 - p118 [51-250]
    Ch BWatch - v8 - Ja '98 - p2+ [51-250]
    KR - v65 - S 1 '97 - p1384 [51-250]
    SLJ - v43 - N '97 - p76 [51-250]

Things That Are Most in the World (Illus. by John Nickle)
    KR - v66 - Ja 15 '98 - p109 [51-250]
    PW - v245 - Ja 19 '98 - p377 [51-250]

Barrett, Tracy
Tennessee
    Ch BWatch - v8 - Ja '98 - p7 [1-50]

Virginia
    SLJ - v43 - Je '97 - p130 [51-250]

Barrie, J M
Peter Pan (Illus. by George Buchanan)
    HB Guide - v8 - Fall '97 - p288 [51-250]

Peter Pan and Wendy (Illus. by Michael Foreman)
    TES - N 7 '97 - p11* [1-50]

Barron, T A
The Lost Years of Merlin
  y BL - v94 - N 1 '97 - p475 [1-50]
  y BWatch - v18 - Je '97 - p7 [51-250]
    Ch BWatch - v7 - Mr '97 - p2 [51-250]

The Seven Songs of Merlin
  y BL - v94 - S 1 '97 - p105 [51-250]
    KR - v65 - Ag 1 '97 - p1218 [51-250]
    PW - v244 - Jl 21 '97 - p202 [51-250]
  y SLJ - v43 - S '97 - p210+ [51-250]

Barrow, Allison
The Artist's Model
    Inst - v106 - Ap '97 - p27 [1-50]

Barry, David, 1949-
*The Rajah's Rice (Illus. by Donna
Perrone)*
    SB - v33 - O '97 - p195 [51-250]

Bartlett, Alison
Cat among the Cabbages
    Books - v10 - S '96 - p24 [51-250]
    HB Guide - v8 - Fall '97 - p248 [51-
    250]

Eric the Reindeer
    Sch Lib - v45 - Ag '97 - p129 [51-250]

Bartlett, T C
*Tuba Lessons (Illus. by Monique
Felix)*
    BL - v94 - N 1 '97 - p477 [51-250]
    CBRS - v26 - Ja '98 - p49 [51-250]
    KR - v65 - S 1 '97 - p1384 [51-250]
    PW - v244 - N 3 '97 - p85 [51-250]
    SLJ - v43 - N '97 - p76 [51-250]

Bartoletti, Susan Campbell
*Dancing with Dziadziu (Illus. by
Annika Nelson)*
    HB Guide - v8 - Fall '97 - p258 [51-
    250]
    SLJ - v43 - My '97 - p92 [51-250]

Growing Up in Coal Country
    y   BL - v94 - Mr 15 '98 - p1210 [1-50]
        HB Guide - v8 - Fall '97 - p394 [51-
        250]
        SE - v61 - Ap '97 - p10* [1-50]
    y   VOYA - v20 - Je '97 - p84 [51-250]
    y   VOYA - v21 - Ap '98 - p36 [1-50]

Barton, Byron
I Want to Bean Astronaut
    PW - v244 - S 22 '97 - p82 [1-50]

*The Little Red Hen (Illus. by Byron
Barton)*
    HB Guide - v8 - Fall '97 - p331 [51-
    250]

Machines at Work
    PW - v244 - S 22 '97 - p82 [1-50]

*The Three Bears (Illus. by Byron
Barton)*
    HB Guide - v8 - Fall '97 - p331 [51-
    250]

Barton, Carol
Summer Visitors
    Sch Lib - v45 - Ag '97 - p135 [51-250]

Barton, Geoff
Voices of the Great War
    Sch Lib - v45 - N '97 - p208 [51-250]

Bartone, Elisa
American Too (Illus. by Ted Lewin)
    SE - v61 - Ap '97 - p9* [1-50]

*American Too (Caruso). Audio
Version*
    BL - v94 - S 15 '97 - p250 [51-250]

Base, Graeme
Animalia
    PW - v244 - D 15 '97 - p60 [51-250]

The Eleventh Hour
    PW - v244 - S 22 '97 - p83 [1-50]

*Lewis Carroll's Jabberwocky (Illus. by
Graeme Base)*
    Magpies - v12 - Mr '97 - p20+ [501+]

Bash, Barbara
Ancient Ones (Illus. by Barbara Bash)
    SLJ - v43 - My '97 - p56 [1-50]

*In the Heart of the Village (Illus. by
Barbara Bash)*
    RT - v51 - D '97 - p312 [51-250]
    SE - v61 - Ap '97 - p6* [1-50]

*Shadows of Night (Illus. by Barbara
Bash)*
    ASBYP - v29 - Sum '96 - p4+ [251-
    500]
    SLJ - v43 - My '97 - p56 [1-50]

***The Basic Oxford Picture
Dictionary***
    r   Ch BWatch - v7 - Mr '97 - p1 [51-250]

Bassede, Francine
George's Store at the Shore (Illus. by Francine Bassede)
> BL - v94 - F 15 '98 - p1016+ [51-250]
> KR - v66 - Ja 1 '98 - p53 [51-250]
> PW - v244 - D 22 '97 - p58 [51-250]
> SLJ - v44 - Ap '98 - p91 [51-250]

Bassis, Volodymyr
Ukraine
> Ch BWatch - v7 - Je '97 - p5 [51-250]
> HB Guide - v8 - Fall '97 - p390 [51-250]

Bastyra, Judy
Fun Food (Illus. by Michael Michaels)
> SLJ - v44 - Ap '98 - p113 [51-250]

Bateman, Teresa
Leprechaun Gold (Illus. by Rosanne Litzinger)
> KR - v66 - Mr 15 '98 - p398 [51-250]

The Ring of Truth (Illus. by Omar Rayyan)
> HB Guide - v8 - Fall '97 - p258 [51-250]
> Inst - v107 - S '97 - p22 [1-50]
> SLJ - v43 - My '97 - p92 [51-250]

Bates, Dianne
Big Bad Bruce (Illus. by Phoebe Middleton)
> CBRS - v25 - Spr '97 - p133 [51-250]

Grandma Cadbury's Water World (Illus. by Julie Kingston)
> Magpies - v12 - Jl '97 - p32 [51-250]

Bateson-Hill, Margaret
Lao Lao of Dragon Mountain (Illus. by Francesca Pelizzoli)
> Ch BWatch - v7 - Ap '97 - p6 [51-250]

Bath, Linda H
Peggy Goes Cod Fishing (Illus. by Brett Gosling)
> CBRA - '96 - p527+ [51-250]

Peggy's Scrawny Green Lobster (Illus. by Brett Gosling)
> CBRA - '96 - p527+ [51-250]

Batten, Mary
Shark Attack Almanac (Illus. by Carol Lyon)
> SLJ - v43 - Ag '97 - p162 [51-250]

Battle-Lavert, G
Off to School (Illus. by Gershom Griffith)
> ECEJ - v25 - Fall '97 - p45 [1-50]

Bauer, Joan
Sticks
> y   JAAL - v40 - O '96 - p153 [51-250]
> PW - v244 - Ag 11 '97 - p403 [1-50]

Bauer, Marion Dane
Alison's Fierce and Ugly Halloween (Illus. by Laurie Spencer)
> BL - v94 - S 1 '97 - p137 [51-250]
> KR - v65 - S 15 '97 - p1452 [51-250]
> PW - v244 - O 6 '97 - p50 [1-50]

Alison's Puppy (Illus. by Laurie Spencer)
> SLJ - v43 - Ag '97 - p128 [51-250]

If You Were Born a Kitten (Illus. by Jo Ellen McAllister-Stammen)
> BL - v94 - O 15 '97 - p407 [51-250]
> CBRS - v26 - F '98 - p73 [1-50]
> CCB-B - v51 - Ja '98 - p153 [51-250]
> Ch BWatch - v8 - Ja '98 - p3 [51-250]
> KR - v65 - S 1 '97 - p1385 [51-250]
> Par - v72 - D '97 - p204 [1-50]
> PW - v244 - O 6 '97 - p82 [51-250]
> SLJ - v43 - N '97 - p104+ [51-250]

A Question of Trust
> SLJ - v44 - Ja '98 - p42 [1-50]

Turtle Dreams (Illus. by Diane Dawson Hearn)
> SLJ - v44 - Ja '98 - p80 [51-250]

Baum, L Frank
The Scarecrow of Oz (Illus. by John R Neill)
> HB Guide - v8 - Fall '97 - p296 [51-250]

The Wizard of Oz (Illus. by Lisbeth Zwerger)
> RT - v51 - S '97 - p58 [51-250]

Der Zauberer Von Oz (Illus. by Lisbeth Zwerger)
Bkbird - v35 - Fall '97 - p50 [1-50]

Bauman, David
Disney's Hercules: Zero to Hero
Ch BWatch - v7 - D '97 - p2 [51-250]

Baumgart, Klaus
Laura's Star
CBRS - v26 - F '98 - p73 [51-250]

Bawden, Nina
Granny the Pag
Bks Keeps - Jl '97 - p25 [51-250]
Emerg Lib - v25 - Ja '98 - p46 [51-250]
PW - v245 - Ja 19 '98 - p380 [1-50]

Baxter, Lesley
Oliver Twist (Illus. by Christian Birmingham)
Bks Keeps - Jl '97 - p4+ [51-250]

Baxter, Nicola
The Enormous Turnip (Illus. by Peter Stevenson)
HB Guide - v8 - Fall '97 - p331 [51-250]

Our Wonderful Earth
Sch Lib - v45 - N '97 - p203 [51-250]

Parallel Universe (Illus. by Mike Taylor)
SLJ - v44 - F '98 - p111+ [51-250]

Rain, Wind and Storm
Sch Lib - v45 - N '97 - p203 [51-250]

Rapunzel (Illus. by Martin Aitchison)
HB Guide - v8 - Fall '97 - p331 [51-250]

Baxter, Stephen
Gulliverzone
Books - v11 - Ag '97 - p15 [51-250]

Baylor, Byrd
The Other Way to Listen
PW - v244 - D 15 '97 - p60 [1-50]

Bazilian, Barbara
The Red Shoes
BL - v94 - N 1 '97 - p477+ [51-250]
Ch BWatch - v7 - S '97 - p3 [51-250]
Ch BWatch - v7 - O '97 - p6 [1-50]
NYTBR - v102 - N 16 '97 - p57 [501+]
PW - v244 - O 20 '97 - p77+ [1-50]

Bea, Holly
Where Does God Live? (Illus. by Kim Howard)
HB Guide - v8 - Fall '97 - p258 [1-50]
SLJ - v43 - My '97 - p92 [51-250]

Beadle, Cosette
Star Track Reading and Spelling
TES - N 14 '97 - p12* [51-250]

Beaglehole, Helen
Strange Company
Magpies - v12 - Jl '97 - p7* [51-250]

Beames, Margaret
Archway Arrow
Magpies - v12 - Mr '97 - p2* [1-50]

The Shearwater Bell
Magpies - v12 - S '97 - p7* [51-250]

Beard, Darleen Bailey
The Flimflam Man (Illus. by Eileen Christelow)
BL - v94 - F 15 '98 - p1010 [51-250]
HB - v74 - Mr '98 - p218+ [51-250]
KR - v66 - Ja 1 '98 - p53 [51-250]
PW - v245 - F 2 '98 - p90+ [51-250]
SLJ - v44 - Mr '98 - p166 [251-500]

Beaton, Clare
Colors (Illus. by Clare Beaton)
Ch BWatch - v7 - S '97 - p4 [1-50]

Beatty, Monica Driscoll
My Sister Rose Has Diabetes (Illus. by Kathy Parkinson)
SLJ - v44 - Ap '98 - p51 [51-250]

Bechard, Margaret
My Mom Married the Principal
BL - v94 - Mr 1 '98 - p1132 [51-250]
CCB-B - v51 - Ap '98 - p274 [51-250]
y   Kliatt - v32 - Mr '98 - p5 [51-250]

27

KR - v66 - F 1 '98 - p192 [51-250]
SLJ - v44 - Mr '98 - p208 [51-250]
y   VOYA - v20 - F '98 - p384 [51-250]

Beck, Ian
The Ugly Duckling (Illus. by Ian Beck)
Spec - v279 - D 6 '97 - p43 [1-50]

Beck, Jennifer
The Bantam and the Soldier (Illus. by Robyn Belton)
Magpies - v12 - Mr '97 - p2* [1-50]
Magpies - v12 - Mr '97 - p31 [51-250]

Beckett, Mary
Hannah, or Pink Balloons
Bkbird - v35 - Sum '97 - p58 [51-250]

Beckett, Wendy
The Duke and the Peasant
BL - v93 - Ag '97 - p1893 [51-250]
PW - v244 - Je 2 '97 - p73 [1-50]

Bedard, Michael
The Divide (Illus. by Emily Arnold McCully)
BL - v94 - O 1 '97 - p334 [51-250]
BW - v27 - D 7 '97 - p21 [51-250]
CBRS - v26 - F '98 - p73 [51-250]
Ch BWatch - v8 - Ja '98 - p2 [1-50]
CM:CanRev - v4 - O 31 '97 - pONL [251-500]
KR - v65 - S 15 '97 - p1452 [51-250]
PW - v244 - S 22 '97 - p80 [51-250]
Quill & Q - v63 - S '97 - p72 [251-500]
SLJ - v43 - S '97 - p199+ [51-250]

Glass Town (Illus. by Laura Fernandez)
BL - v93 - Ag '97 - p1897+ [51-250]
CBRS - v26 - O '97 - p19 [51-250]
CCB-B - v51 - Ja '98 - p154 [51-250]
HB - v73 - N '97 - p707+ [501+]
PW - v244 - Ag 4 '97 - p75 [51-250]
Quill & Q - v63 - O '97 - p41+ [251-500]

Bedell, Sean
I Wish I Had an Elegant Elephant (Illus. by Susie Tyner-Keating)
CBRA - '96 - p433 [51-250]

Bednarczyk, Angela
Happy Birthday (Illus. by Emma Illiffe)
TES - My 2 '97 - p16* [251-500]

Opposites: A Beginner's Book of Signs (Illus. by Emma Illiffe)
TES - My 2 '97 - p16* [251-500]

Bedwell, Randall
General Lee and Santa Claus
Bloom Rev - v17 - N '97 - p33 [51-250]

Beeke, Jemma
The Brand New Creature
Sch Lib - v45 - Ag '97 - p129 [51-250]

Beeler, Cecil Freeman
Boys in the Well
Can CL - v22 - Win '96 - p118+ [501+]
CBRA - '96 - p464 [51-250]

Behan, Brendan
The King of Ireland's Son (Illus. by P J Lynch)
HB Guide - v8 - Fall '97 - p331 [51-250]
SLJ - v43 - Je '97 - p105+ [51-250]

Behm, Barbara
Extinct Animals of the Islands
Ch BWatch - v7 - Jl '97 - p3+ [51-250]

Extinct Animals of the Northern Continents
Ch BWatch - v7 - Jl '97 - p3+ [51-250]

Extinct Animals of the Southern Continents
Ch BWatch - v7 - Jl '97 - p3+ [51-250]

Extinct Wildlife
Ch BWatch - v7 - Jl '97 - p3+ [51-250]

Behrens, June
Missions of the Central Coast
SLJ - v43 - Jl '97 - p100 [51-250]

Bell, Krista
Pidge (Illus. by Ann James)
Aust Bk R - v279 - My '97 - p62+ [501+]
Magpies - v12 - My '97 - p30 [51-250]

Bell, Lili
The Sea Maidens of Japan (Illus. by Erin McGonigle Brammer)
> BL - v93 - Je 1 '97 - p1715 [51-250]
> HB Guide - v8 - Fall '97 - p258 [51-250]
> SLJ - v43 - Je '97 - p79 [51-250]

Bell, Mary Hayley
Whistle down the Wind
> Books - v11 - Ag '97 - p15 [51-250]

Bell, Simon M
Insects and Spiders (Illus. by Simon M Bell)
> PW - v244 - Je 16 '97 - p61 [51-250]

Snakes and Lizards (Illus. by Simon M Bell)
> PW - v244 - Je 16 '97 - p61 [51-250]
> Quill & Q - v63 - My '97 - p41 [251-500]

Bell, Tony
Mathematics Now!. Bk. 1
> TES - O 3 '97 - pR15 [501+]

Bell, William
River, My Friend (Illus. by Ken Campbell)
> CBRA - '96 - p433 [51-250]

Beller, Susan Provost
Never Were Men So Brave
> y   BL - v94 - F 15 '98 - p993 [51-250]
> CCB-B - v51 - Mr '98 - p236 [51-250]
> KR - v65 - D 1 '97 - p1773 [51-250]
> PW - v244 - D 8 '97 - p74 [51-250]
> SLJ - v44 - F '98 - p112 [51-250]

Bellingham, Brenda
Lilly to the Rescue (Illus. by Kathy Kaulbach)
> CM:CanRev - v4 - S 19 '97 - pONL [251-500]

Belton, Sandra
Ernestine and Amanda, members of the C.L.U.B.
> SLJ - v43 - N '97 - p114 [51-250]

Ernestine and Amanda, Summer Camp Ready or Not!
> BL - v93 - Ag '97 - p1900 [51-250]

Ernestine and Amanda Summer Camp, Ready or Not!
> CCB-B - v51 - S '97 - p6+ [51-250]

Ernestine and Amanda: Summer Camp, Ready or Not!
> HB Guide - v8 - Fall '97 - p296 [51-250]

Ernestine and Amanda, Summer Camp Ready or Not!
> KR - v65 - My 15 '97 - p796+ [51-250]
> SLJ - v43 - Ag '97 - p154 [51-250]

From Miss Ida's Porch (Illus. by Floyd Cooper)
> PW - v245 - Ja 12 '98 - p61 [1-50]

Bemelmans, Ludwig
Madeline. Book and Audio Version
> Ch BWatch - v7 - My '97 - p5 [1-50]
> SLJ - v43 - D '97 - p69 [51-250]

Bender, Lionel
Heat and Drought
> Sch Lib - v45 - N '97 - p203 [51-250]

Bender, Robert
The A to Z Beastly Jamboree (Illus. by Robert Bender)
> RT - v51 - S '97 - p52 [51-250]

Bendick, Jeanne
Markets: From Barter to Bar Codes
> BL - v94 - S 1 '97 - p108 [51-250]
> HB Guide - v8 - Fall '97 - p329 [51-250]
> SLJ - v44 - Ja '98 - p118 [51-250]

Benenfeld, Rikki
I Go to School (Illus. by Rikki Benenfeld)
> PW - v244 - D 22 '97 - p55 [51-250]

Ben-Ezer, Ehud
Hosni the Dreamer (Illus. by Uri Shulevitz)
> BL - v94 - N 1 '97 - p478 [51-250]
> CBRS - v26 - D '97 - p37 [51-250]

Ch BWatch - v8 - Ja '98 - p2 [51-250]
HB - v73 - S '97 - p585 [51-250]
NYTBR - v102 - N 16 '97 - p42 [501+]
NYTLa - v147 - D 4 '97 - pE8 [1-50]
PW - v244 - Je 30 '97 - p75 [51-250]
SLJ - v43 - D '97 - p81 [51-250]

Benge, Janet
George Washington Carver, What Do You See? (Illus. by Kennon James)
SLJ - v43 - Ag '97 - p145 [51-250]

Benjamin, A H
A Duck So Small (Illus. by Elisabeth Holstien)
PW - v245 - Mr 23 '98 - p97 [51-250]

Benjamin, Alan
Hanukkah Chubby Board Book and Dreidels (Illus. by Ellen Appleby)
PW - v244 - O 6 '97 - p53 [1-50]

Bennett, Paul, 1954-
Eating
Sch Lib - v45 - N '97 - p203 [51-250]

Bennett, William J
The Children's Book of Virtue
Par - v72 - My '97 - p92 [1-50]

Benoit, Margaret
Who Killed Olive Souffle?
CBRS - v26 - O '97 - p22 [51-250]
y   CCB-B - v51 - D '97 - p118 [51-250]
y   KR - v65 - S 1 '97 - p1385 [51-250]
y   SLJ - v43 - N '97 - p114 [51-250]

Benson, Michael
Crashes and Collisions
SLJ - v44 - F '98 - p112 [51-250]

Bentley, Dawn
My First Flashlight (Illus. by Jeff Cummins)
PW - v244 - Ag 18 '97 - p94 [1-50]

Bentley, Joan
Simple Science Experiments (Illus. by Barbara Lorseyedi)
SB - v33 - Je '97 - p141 [51-250]

Bentley, Judith
Dear Friend
y   HB Guide - v8 - Fall '97 - p394 [51-250]
SLJ - v43 - Je '97 - p130+ [51-250]
y   VOYA - v20 - D '97 - p329 [51-250]

Bentley, Nancy
Putting on a Play (Illus. by Katy Keck Arnsteen)
HB Guide - v8 - Fall '97 - p366 [51-250]

Benton, Amanda
Silent Stranger
y   BL - v94 - O 15 '97 - p397 [51-250]
CBRS - v26 - Win '98 - p68 [51-250]
KR - v65 - O 1 '97 - p1528 [51-250]
SLJ - v43 - D '97 - p120 [51-250]

Benton, Michael
Picture Poems
Sch Lib - v45 - N '97 - p208 [51-250]
TES - S 19 '97 - pR7 [251-500]

Berendes, Mary
Mexico
SLJ - v44 - F '98 - p94 [51-250]

Berenstain, Stan
The Berenstain Bears' Christmas Tree
PW - v244 - O 6 '97 - p58 [1-50]

The Berenstain Bears' Moving Day
Par - v72 - Je '97 - p126 [1-50]

The Berenstain Bears' Thanksgiving
PW - v244 - O 6 '97 - p52 [1-50]

Berenstains' A Book
PW - v244 - D 8 '97 - p74 [1-50]

Berenstains' B Book
PW - v244 - D 8 '97 - p74 [1-50]

Berenstains' C Book
PW - v244 - D 8 '97 - p74 [1-50]

Inside Outside Upside Down
PW - v244 - Ag 4 '97 - p77 [51-250]

Old Hat New Hat
PW - v244 - Ag 4 '97 - p77 [51-250]

Berenzy, Alix
A Frog Prince (Illus. by Alix Berenzy)
SLJ - v43 - N '97 - p40 [1-50]

Beresford, Elizabeth
Lizzy Fights On
TES - Ap 18 '97 - p12* [51-250]

Berg, Adriane
The Totally Awesome Money Book for Kids and Their Parents
Ch BWatch - v7 - S '97 - p1 [51-250]

Berg, Elizabeth
Mexico
Ch BWatch - v7 - O '97 - p4+ [51-250]
Emerg Lib - v24 - My '97 - p57 [1-50]

Berg, Lois Anne
An Eritrean Family
Bloom Rev - v17 - S '97 - p23 [51-250]
Ch BWatch - v7 - My '97 - p6 [1-50]
SLJ - v43 - Ag '97 - p162 [51-250]

Bergen, Lara
Washington Irving's Rip Van Winkle (Illus. by Donald Cook)
SLJ - v44 - F '98 - p78 [51-250]

Berger, Barbara Helen
A Lot of Otters (Illus. by Barbara Helen Berger)
CBRS - v26 - O '97 - p13 [1-50]
CCB-B - v51 - Ja '98 - p154 [51-250]
Ch BWatch - v7 - N '97 - p5 [1-50]
KR - v65 - Jl 1 '97 - p1026+ [51-250]
SLJ - v43 - S '97 - p172 [51-250]
SLJ - v43 - D '97 - p23 [1-50]

Berger, Melvin
Amazing Sharks
ASBYP - v29 - Sum '96 - p57+ [501+]

Amazing Water
SB - v33 - Ap '97 - p84 [51-250]

Animal Senses
ASBYP - v29 - Sum '96 - p57+ [501+]

Can Kids Save the Earth?
ASBYP - v29 - Sum '96 - p57+ [501+]

Digging for Dinosaurs
ASBYP - v29 - Sum '96 - p57+ [501+]

The Human Body
SB - v33 - Je '97 - p141 [51-250]

Life in a Coral Reef
ASBYP - v29 - Sum '96 - p57+ [501+]

Life on the African Savannah
ASBYP - v29 - Sum '96 - p57+ [501+]

The Native Americans Told Us
ASBYP - v29 - Sum '96 - p57+ [501+]

The Restless Earth
ASBYP - v29 - Sum '96 - p57+ [501+]

Those Fabulous Frogs
ASBYP - v29 - Sum '96 - p57+ [501+]

Bergman, Mara
Bears, Bears, Everywhere! (Illus. by Helen Craig)
Sch Lib - v45 - N '97 - p184 [51-250]

Berliner, Don
Aviation: Reaching for the Sky
y   HB Guide - v8 - Fall '97 - p357 [51-250]
SLJ - v43 - Jl '97 - p100 [51-250]

Berman, Matt
What Else Should I Read?. Vol. 2
r   SLMQ - v25 - Win '97 - p116 [51-250]

Berman, Ruth
Peacocks (Illus. by Richard Hewett)
ASBYP - v29 - Fall '96 - p43+ [251-500]

Bernard, Patricia
Duffy: Everyone's Dog (Illus. by Cathy Netherwood)
Aust Bk R - Jl '97 - p62+ [501+]
Magpies - v12 - My '97 - p28 [251-500]

The Outcast
Magpies - v12 - My '97 - p37 [51-250]

Bernhard, Emery
Prairie Dogs (Illus. by Durga Bernhard)
BL - v94 - D 1 '97 - p632+ [51-250]
HB - v73 - N '97 - p693+ [51-250]

SLJ - v43 - D '97 - p104+ [51-250]

Berocay, Roy
Pateando Lunas
  Bkbird - v35 - Sum '97 - p22 [51-250]

Berquist, Paul
Saguaro Cactus
  HB Guide - v8 - Fall '97 - p344 [51-250]
  SB - v33 - N '97 - p243 [251-500]
  SLJ - v43 - S '97 - p200 [51-250]

Berry, James
Classic Poems to Read Aloud (Illus. by James Mayhew)
  Bks Keeps - N '97 - p5 [51-250]

Everywhere Faces Everywhere (Illus. by Reynold Ruffins)
  HB - v73 - Jl '97 - p469+ [51-250]
  HB Guide - v8 - Fall '97 - p375 [51-250]
  HMR - Sum '97 - p34+ [501+]
 y SLJ - v43 - Je '97 - p131 [51-250]
 y VOYA - v20 - O '97 - p258 [51-250]

First Palm Trees (Illus. by Greg Couch)
  BL - v94 - D 15 '97 - p698 [51-250]
  KR - v65 - N 15 '97 - p1704 [51-250]
  NYTBR - v103 - Mr 15 '98 - p23 [51-250]
  PW - v244 - N 24 '97 - p73+ [51-250]
  SLJ - v43 - D '97 - p105 [51-250]

We Couldn't Provide Fish Thumbs (Illus. by Colin McNaughton)
  Bks Keeps - My '97 - p24+ [51-250]

Berry, Steve
The Boy Who Wouldn't Speak (Illus. by Deirdre Betteridge)
  Can CL - v23 - Sum '97 - p65+ [501+]

Bertrand, Diane Gonzales
Sip, Slurp, Soup (Illus. by Alex Pardo DeLange)
  SLJ - v43 - Ag '97 - p128 [51-250]

Best, Cari
Red Light, Green Light, Mama and Me (Illus. by Niki Daly)
  ECEJ - v25 - Fall '97 - p45 [1-50]

Top Banana (Illus. by Erika Oller)
  HB Guide - v8 - Fall '97 - p258+ [51-250]
  SLJ - v43 - Ap '97 - p90 [51-250]

Best, Elizabeth
Peter and the Polar Bear (Illus. by Steven Woolman)
  Sch Lib - v45 - Ag '97 - p129 [51-250]

Best, Ysola
Kombumerri--Saltwater People
  Magpies - v12 - Jl '97 - p41+ [501+]

Bett, Brian
Planet Ocean (Illus. by Mic Rolph)
  Bks Keeps - N '97 - p25 [51-250]
  New Sci - v154 - Je 28 '97 - p44 [51-250]
  TES - N 7 '97 - p10* [51-250]

Bevan, Clare
Lucky Numbers
  TES - N 14 '97 - p14* [51-250]

Bevan, Finn
Fabulous Beasts (Illus. by Diana Mayo)
  Sch Lib - v45 - N '97 - p203 [51-250]
  TES - O 31 '97 - p17* [501+]

Mighty Mountains (Illus. by Diana Mayo)
  Sch Lib - v45 - N '97 - p203 [51-250]
  TES - O 31 '97 - p17* [501+]

Sacred Skies (Illus. by Diana Mayo)
  TES - O 31 '97 - p17* [501+]

The Waters of Life (Illus. by Diana Mayo)
  TES - O 31 '97 - p17* [501+]

Bial, Raymond
Amish Home
  ECEJ - v25 - Fall '97 - p45 [1-50]

Cajun Home (Illus. by Raymond Bial)
  BL - v94 - Mr 15 '98 - p1236+ [51-250]
  KR - v66 - F 15 '98 - p264 [51-250]

The Fresh Grave and Other Ghostly Stories
  SLJ - v43 - D '97 - p120+ [51-250]

Mist over the Mountains (Illus. by Raymond Bial)

    CCB-B - v50 - Je '97 - p350 [51-250]
    HB Guide - v8 - Fall '97 - p394 [51-250]
    SLJ - v43 - My '97 - p142 [51-250]

The Strength of These Arms (Illus. by Raymond Bial)

    BL - v94 - S 15 '97 - p224 [51-250]
    CCB-B - v51 - O '97 - p43 [51-250]
    SLJ - v43 - N '97 - p125 [51-250]

Where Lincoln Walked (Illus. by Raymond Bial)

    BL - v94 - Mr 1 '98 - p1125 [51-250]
    KR - v65 - N 15 '97 - p1704 [51-250]
    PW - v244 - D 15 '97 - p59+ [51-250]
    SLJ - v44 - F '98 - p94+ [51-250]

With Needle and Thread

    RT - v51 - D '97 - p330+ [51-250]

Biale, Rachel

We are Moving

    Par - v72 - Je '97 - p126 [1-50]

Bianchi, John

The Lab Rats of Doctor Eclair (Illus. by John Bianchi)

    SLJ - v43 - Ag '97 - p128 [51-250]

Welcome Back to Pokeweed Public School

    CBRA - '96 - p433 [51-250]

Bible Companion (DK)

    Ch BWatch - v7 - Je '97 - p4 [1-50]

Bible. English. New International. Selections. 1997

The Illustrated Family Bible (Illus. by Peter Dennis)

    Bks Keeps - S '97 - p28 [51-250]
    BWatch - v18 - My '97 - p6 [51-250]
    CLW - v68 - D '97 - p71+ [251-500]
    Sch Lib - v45 - Ag '97 - p150 [51-250]
    TES - D 5 '97 - pR4 [251-500]

Bible. N.T. English. Authorized. Selections. 1996

Stories from the New Testament

y   BL - v94 - O 1 '97 - p321+ [51-250]
    PW - v244 - O 27 '97 - p71 [51-250]

Bible. N.T. Luke I, 26-II, 16. Authorized. Selections. 1997

Visions of Christmas

    CM:CanRev - v4 - D 12 '97 - pONL [51-250]
    PW - v244 - O 6 '97 - p53 [51-250]

Bible. O.T. Genesis. English. Young. 1995

Genesis

    HB Guide - v8 - Fall '97 - p320 [51-250]

Bible. O.T. Psalms. English. Le Tord. Selections. 1997

Sing a New Song (Illus. by Bijou Le Tord)

    HB Guide - v8 - Fall '97 - p319 [51-250]
    PW - v244 - N 3 '97 - p57 [1-50]

Biebow, Natascha

Eleanora (Illus. by Britta Teckentrup)

    ASBYP - v29 - Sum '96 - p5 [251-500]

Bierhorst, John

The Dancing Fox (Illus. by Mary K Okheena)

    CCB-B - v50 - Jl '97 - p388 [51-250]
    HB Guide - v8 - Fall '97 - p331 [51-250]
    NYTBR - v102 - N 16 '97 - p30 [501+]
    SLJ - v43 - Je '97 - p131 [51-250]
y   VOYA - v20 - F '98 - p364 [51-250]

Bierman, Valerie

Best of Friends

    Bks Keeps - My '97 - p25 [51-250]

Biesty, Stephen

Stephen Biesty's Cross-Sections: Man-of-War (Illus. by Stephen Biesty)

    Bks Keeps - N '97 - p7 [51-250]

Stephen Biesty's Incredible Everything (Illus. by Stephen Biesty)

y   BL - v94 - Mr 15 '98 - p1225 [1-50]
    Emerg Lib - v25 - Ja '98 - p52 [51-250]
    Learning - v26 - N '97 - p28 [1-50]
    SLJ - v44 - Ja '98 - p128 [51-250]
    TES - N 7 '97 - p10* [51-250]
    TES - D 26 '97 - p23 [251-500]
y   VOYA - v20 - F '98 - p404 [251-500]

y   VOYA - v21 - Ap '98 - p40 [1-50]

*Stephen Biesty's Incredible Explosions
(Illus. by Stephen Biesty)*
> ASBYP - v29 - Fall '96 - p25+ [251-
> 500]
> Books - v10 - S '96 - p24 [51-250]
> Ch BWatch - v7 - Jl '97 - p8 [1-50]

Biffi, Inos
*The Way of the Cross (Illus. by
Franco Vignezia)*
> CLW - v68 - S '97 - p48+ [251-500]

Bikes, Cars, Trucks and Trains
> BL - v94 - D 15 '97 - p700 [1-50]

Billingsley, Franny
Well Wished
> BL - v93 - Je 1 '97 - p1694 [51-250]
> CBRS - v25 - Je '97 - p128 [51-250]
> HB Guide - v8 - Fall '97 - p296 [51-
> 250]
> SLJ - v43 - My '97 - p128 [51-250]
> SLJ - v43 - D '97 - p23 [1-50]
> Trib Bks - Je 8 '97 - p7 [51-250]

Binch, Caroline
*Gregory Cool (Illus. by Caroline
Binch)*
> SLJ - v43 - Jl '97 - p34 [1-50]

*Since Dad Left (Illus. by Caroline
Binch)*
> PW - v245 - Ja 5 '98 - p67 [51-250]

Bingham, Caroline, 1962-
Monster Machines
> r   PW - v245 - Mr 16 '98 - p67 [51-250]

Bingham, Jane
The Usborne Illustrated Thesaurus
> r   Sch Lib - v45 - Ag '97 - p149 [51-250]

Biography Today Sport Series. Vol. 1-
> r   BL - v94 - S 1 '97 - p157 [51-250]

Biography Today Sports Series. Vol. 2
> r   BL - v94 - Mr 15 '98 - p1258 [1-50]

Birchman, David F
*A Green Horn Blowing (Illus. by
Thomas B Allen)*
> BL - v94 - S 15 '97 - p239 [51-250]
> CBRS - v26 - Ja '98 - p54+ [51-250]
> PW - v244 - O 6 '97 - p83 [51-250]
> SLJ - v43 - N '97 - p76+ [51-250]

Birchmore, Daniel A
*Harry, the Happy Snake of Happy
Hollow (Illus. by Gail Lucas)*
> CBRS - v25 - My '97 - p109 [1-50]
> Ch BWatch - v7 - Ap '97 - p1 [51-250]
> SLJ - v44 - F '98 - p78 [51-250]

*The Reluctant Santa (Illus. by Gail
Lucas)*
> CBRS - v26 - N '97 - p25 [51-250]

*The Rock (Illus. by Nancy Carol
Willis)*
> Bloom Rev - v17 - Jl '97 - p21 [51-250]
> Ch BWatch - v7 - Mr '97 - p1 [51-250]
> SLJ - v43 - D '97 - p81 [51-250]

*The White Curtain (Illus. by Gail
Lucas)*
> Bloom Rev - v17 - My '97 - p27 [51-
> 250]
> Ch BWatch - v7 - Ap '97 - p1 [51-250]
> SLJ - v44 - F '98 - p78 [51-250]

Birds of the Countryside
> New Sci - v154 - Ap 26 '97 - p46 [51-
> 250]

Birdsel, Sandra
*The Town That Floated Away (Illus.
by Helen Flook)*
> Quill & Q - v63 - Ag '97 - p39 [251-
> 500]

Birdseye, Debbie Holsclaw
*Under Our Skin (Illus. by Robert
Crum)*
> BL - v94 - D 15 '97 - p692 [51-250]
> y   PW - v244 - N 3 '97 - p87 [1-50]
> SLJ - v44 - Ap '98 - p141 [51-250]

Birdseye, Tom
*Soap! Soap! Don't Forget the Soap!
(Stechschulte). Audio Version*
> BL - v94 - S 15 '97 - p250 [51-250]

Birney, Betty
Let's Play Hide and Seek! (Illus. by Dara Goldman)
 HB Guide - v8 - Fall '97 - p249 [1-50]

Biro, Val
Hansel and Gretel
 Sch Lib - v45 - Ag '97 - p129 [51-250]

Birt, Hazel
Flikka and the Prince Edward Island Mystery (Illus. by Hazel Birt)
 CBRA - '96 - p464 [51-250]

Bishop, Gavin
Little Rabbit and the Sea (Illus. by Gavin Bishop)
 Ch BWatch - v8 - Ja '98 - p3 [1-50]
 PW - v244 - O 20 '97 - p74 [51-250]
 SLJ - v43 - D '97 - p81 [51-250]

Maui and the Sun (Illus. by Gavin Bishop)
 Magpies - v12 - Mr '97 - p2* [1-50]

Bishop, Nic
The Secrets of Animal Flight (Illus. by Nic Bishop)
 CCB-B - v50 - Je '97 - p350+ [51-250]
 HB Guide - v8 - Fall '97 - p344 [51-250]
 SLJ - v43 - Ap '97 - p120 [51-250]
 SLJ - v43 - D '97 - p23 [1-50]

Bissell, Robert
The Dream Road and Other Tales from Hidden Hills (Some Involving Rabbits)
 AB - v100 - N 17 '97 - p1264 [51-250]
 Ch BWatch - v7 - N '97 - p3 [51-250]
 Ch BWatch - v7 - N '97 - p4 [51-250]

Bittingers, Gayle
Teaching Snacks
 Ch BWatch - v7 - S '97 - p5 [1-50]

Bitton-Jackson, Livia
I Have Lived a Thousand Years
 y   BL - v94 - Mr 15 '98 - p1210 [1-50]
    BW - v27 - Je 8 '97 - p8 [501+]
 y   HB - v73 - Jl '97 - p472+ [51-250]

 y   HB Guide - v8 - Fall '97 - p389 [51-250]
 y   NYTBR - v102 - Ag 3 '97 - p14 [1-50]
 y   SLJ - v43 - My '97 - p142+ [51-250]
 y   VOYA - v20 - Je '97 - p124 [51-250]
 y   VOYA - v20 - F '98 - p363 [51-250]
 y   VOYA - v21 - Ap '98 - p36 [1-50]

Bjarkman, Peter C
Sports Great Dominique Wilkins
 CLW - v68 - S '97 - p69 [51-250]

Bjork, Christina
Linnea in Monet's Garden (Moore). Audio Version
 BL - v94 - F 15 '98 - p1027 [51-250]
 SLJ - v44 - Mr '98 - p158 [51-250]

Black, Thom
55 Waverly Street (Illus. by Mary Chambers)
 KR - v66 - F 1 '98 - p192 [51-250]

Blacker, Terence
Ms. Wiz Supermodel (Illus. by Tony Ross)
 Books - v11 - Ag '97 - p15 [1-50]
 Sch Lib - v45 - N '97 - p190 [51-250]
 TES - O 31 '97 - p8* [51-250]

On the Wing
 TES - Ap 18 '97 - p12* [51-250]

Pride and Penalties
 TES - Ap 18 '97 - p12* [51-250]

Shooting Star
 TES - Ap 18 '97 - p12* [51-250]

Blacklock, Dyan
Crab Bait
 Magpies - v12 - Mr '97 - p32 [251-500]
 TES - N 7 '97 - p7* [1-50]

Nudes and Nikes
 Magpies - v12 - S '97 - p42 [51-250]

Pankration
 y   Aust Bk R - Ap '97 - p62 [501+]
    Magpies - v12 - My '97 - p32+ [51-250]

Blackman, Malorie
A.N.T.I.D.O.T.E.
 Bks Keeps - My '97 - p24 [51-250]

Magic Betsey (Illus. by Lis Toft)
Bks Keeps - My '97 - p22 [51-250]
TES - Jl 11 '97 - p14* [51-250]

Pig-Heart Boy
NS - v126 - D 5 '97 - p64 [51-250]
y   Obs - D 7 '97 - p17* [51-250]
y   TES - N 7 '97 - p12* [51-250]

Space Race (Illus. by Colin Mier)
Sch Lib - v45 - N '97 - p190 [51-250]

Blackman, Steven
Planes and Flight
SB - v32 - D '96 - p257 [1-50]

Blackstone, Stella
Baby Rock, Baby Roll (Illus. by Denise Fernando)
BL - v94 - S 1 '97 - p131 [51-250]
CBRS - v26 - N '97 - p25 [1-50]
PW - v244 - Je 30 '97 - p75 [51-250]

Blackwood, Gary L
The Shakespeare Stealer
KR - v66 - Ap 15 '98 - p576 [51-250]

Blades, Ann
Back to the Cabin (Illus. by Ann Blades)
BL - v93 - Je 1 '97 - p1715+ [51-250]
CBRA - '96 - p434 [51-250]

Blair, Margaret Whitman
Brothers at War
BL - v93 - Ag '97 - p1900 [51-250]

Blake, Quentin
Clown (Illus. by Quentin Blake)
SE - v61 - Ap '97 - p4* [1-50]

Mrs. Armitage and the Big Wave (Illus. by Quentin Blake)
Bks Keeps - N '97 - p22 [51-250]
KR - v66 - Mr 1 '98 - p335 [51-250]
Magpies - v12 - Jl '97 - p26 [51-250]
Obs - Jl 20 '97 - p18* [51-250]
PW - v245 - Mr 16 '98 - p62+ [51-250]
Sch Lib - v45 - N '97 - p184 [51-250]

The Penguin Book of Nonsense Verse (Illus. by Quentin Blake)
Comw - v124 - D 5 '97 - p14 [1-50]

y   Kliatt - v31 - S '97 - p25+ [51-250]

The Quentin Blake Book of Nonsense Stories
Magpies - v12 - Mr '97 - p8 [51-250]

Blake, Robert J
Akiak: A Tale from the Iditarod (Illus. by Robert J Blake)
BL - v94 - S 1 '97 - p131 [51-250]
CCB-B - v51 - O '97 - p43 [251-500]
Ch BWatch - v7 - N '97 - p5 [1-50]
KR - v65 - Jl 15 '97 - p1107 [51-250]
PW - v244 - Ag 25 '97 - p72 [51-250]
SLJ - v43 - S '97 - p172+ [51-250]
SLJ - v43 - D '97 - p23 [1-50]
SLJ - v44 - Mr '98 - p119 [1-50]

Blakeslee, Ann R
A Different Kind of Hero
BL - v94 - S 1 '97 - p121+ [51-250]
CBRS - v26 - N '97 - p33 [51-250]
CCB-B - v51 - N '97 - p80+ [51-250]
KR - v65 - S 1 '97 - p1385 [51-250]
SLJ - v44 - Ja '98 - p108 [51-250]

Blakey, J
Ashley and the Soapy Suds Flying Club
CBRA - '96 - p464 [51-250]

Blankman, Lynn
Green-Eyed Ghost
SLJ - v44 - Ja '98 - p108+ [51-250]

Blashfield, Jean F
Mines and Minie Balls
BL - v94 - Ja 1 '98 - p800 [51-250]

Women at the Front
BL - v94 - Ja 1 '98 - p800 [51-250]

Blathwayt, Benedict
Little Red Train to the Rescue (Illus. by Benedict Blathwayt)
Sch Lib - v45 - Ag '97 - p129 [51-250]
TES - Jl 25 '97 - p29 [51-250]

The Runaway Train
TES - Jl 25 '97 - p29 [51-250]

Blazek, Sarah Kirwan

*A Leprechaun's St. Patrick's Day
(Illus. by James Rice)*
> HB Guide - v8 - Fall '97 - p259 [51-250]

Bledsoe, Lucy Jane

Tracks in the Snow
> BL - v93 - Ag '97 - p1900 [51-250]
> Par Ch - Awards '97 - p6 [51-250]
> SLJ - v43 - Jl '97 - p90 [51-250]

Bleifeld, Maurice

*Adventures with Biology (Illus. by
Jacob Katari)*
> BL - v94 - D 1 '97 - p625 [51-250]
> SB - v34 - Ap '98 - p80 [51-250]
> y   SLJ - v44 - F '98 - p112 [51-250]

Bliss, Corinne Demas

*Electra and the Charlotte Russe (Illus.
by Michael Garland)*
> CBRS - v26 - D '97 - p42 [51-250]
> KR - v65 - S 15 '97 - p1452 [51-250]

Bloom, Valerie

*Fruits: A Caribbean Counting Poem
(Illus. by David Axtell)*
> AB - v100 - N 17 '97 - p1268 [51-250]
> Bks Keeps - Jl '97 - p20+ [51-250]
> Ch BWatch - v7 - Je '97 - p6 [1-50]
> HB Guide - v8 - Fall '97 - p375 [51-250]
> Sch Lib - v45 - Ag '97 - p129 [51-250]
> SLJ - v43 - Jl '97 - p80 [51-250]
> TES - Je 13 '97 - pR7 [51-250]
> TES - N 7 '97 - p5* [1-50]

Blos, Joan W

Bedtime! (Illus. by Stephen Lambert)
> CCB-B - v51 - Ap '98 - p274 [51-250]
> KR - v66 - F 1 '98 - p192 [51-250]

*Nellie Bly's Monkey (Illus. by
Catherine Stock)*
> RT - v51 - O '97 - p150 [51-250]

*One Very Best Valentine's Day (Illus.
by Emily Arnold McCully)*
> PW - v245 - Ja 5 '98 - p69 [1-50]

Blue, Rose

Colin Powell: Straight to the Top
> BL - v94 - S 15 '97 - p224+ [51-250]
> HB Guide - v8 - Fall '97 - p378 [51-250]
> SLJ - v44 - Ja '98 - p119 [51-250]

Good Yontif (Illus. by Lynne Feldman)
> Ch BWatch - v7 - My '97 - p4+ [1-50]
> HB Guide - v8 - Fall '97 - p320 [51-250]

Blum, Raymond

*Mathamusements (Illus. by Jeff
Sinclair)*
> SLJ - v43 - N '97 - p125 [51-250]

Blume, Judy

*Are You There, God? It's Me,
Margaret*
> NYTBR - v102 - N 16 '97 - p26 [1-50]

*Are You There God? It's Me,
Margaret (Hamilton). Audio Version*
> SLJ - v44 - F '98 - p72 [51-250]
> SLJ - v44 - Ap '98 - p38 [1-50]

*Otherwise Known as Sheila the Great
(Blume). Audio Version*
> SLJ - v43 - Jl '97 - p56 [51-250]

Blumenthal, Deborah

*The Chocolate-Covered Cookie
Tantrum (Illus. by Harvey Stevenson)*
> Magpies - v12 - My '97 - p26+ [251-500]

Bluthenthal, Diana Cain

*Matilda the Moocher (Illus. by Diana
Cain Bluthenthal)*
> CBRS - v25 - My '97 - p109 [51-250]
> HB Guide - v8 - Fall '97 - p259 [51-250]
> SLJ - v43 - My '97 - p92 [51-250]

Blyton, Enid

Best Stories for Eight-Year-Olds
> Books - v11 - Je '97 - p21 [51-250]

Best Stories for Five-Year-Olds
> Books - v11 - Je '97 - p21 [51-250]

Best Stories for Seven-Year-Olds
> Books - v11 - Je '97 - p21 [51-250]

Best Stories for Six-Year-Olds
Books - v11 - Je '97 - p21 [51-250]

Bo, Arno
Chirpy, the Girl of the Sun
Sch Lib - v45 - Ag '97 - p135 [51-250]

Boada, Francesc
El Gato Con Botas (Illus. by Jose Luis Merino)
SLJ - v44 - F '98 - p130 [51-250]

Boardman, Alan
Eureka Stockade (Illus. by Roland Harvey)
Magpies - v12 - Mr '97 - p24 [51-250]

The First Fleet (Illus. by Roland Harvey)
Magpies - v12 - Mr '97 - p24 [51-250]

Boase, Petra
T-Shirt Fun
CM:CanRev - v4 - F 27 '98 - pONL [51-250]

Boats and Ships (Editions Gallimard Jeunesse)
r   SE - v61 - Ap '97 - p12* [1-50]

Bochak, John
The Gamemaster (Illus. by Grayce Bochak)
LA - v73 - N '96 - p528 [51-250]

Bock, Hal
David Robinson
Ch BWatch - v7 - S '97 - p8 [1-50]
HB Guide - v8 - Fall '97 - p368 [51-250]

Bodanis, David
The Secret Family
y   BL - v93 - Ag '97 - p1864 [51-250]
y   BL - v94 - D 1 '97 - p624 [1-50]
y   BL - v94 - Ja 1 '98 - p731 [1-50]
Ent W - Ag 22 '97 - p128 [51-250]
Esq - v128 - Jl '97 - p28 [1-50]
KR - v65 - Je 15 '97 - p922+ [251-500]
LJ - v122 - Jl '97 - p118 [51-250]
New Sci - v156 - O 18 '97 - p52 [1-50]
PW - v244 - Je 16 '97 - p52 [51-250]

Bode, Janet
Food Fight
BL - v93 - Je 1 '97 - p1690 [51-250]
HB Guide - v8 - Fall '97 - p355 [51-250]
y   JAAL - v41 - F '98 - p408 [51-250]
KR - v65 - My 15 '97 - p797 [51-250]
y   Nat - v265 - N 3 '97 - p54+ [501+]
SLJ - v43 - Ag '97 - p162+ [51-250]
y   VOYA - v20 - Ag '97 - p198+ [251-500]

Bodger, Joan
Clever-Lazy
CM:CanRev - v4 - Mr 27 '98 - pONL [501+]

Bodkin, Odds
The Evergreens (Bodkin). Audio Version
Ch BWatch - v7 - My '97 - p5 [1-50]

Boehm, Arlene
A Cheerful Note for Jack
HB Guide - v8 - Fall '97 - p259 [1-50]

Boelts, Maribeth
A Kid's Guide to Staying Safe around Water
SLJ - v44 - Ap '98 - p113 [51-250]

Little Bunny's Cool Tool Set (Illus. by Kathy Parkinson)
BL - v94 - S 15 '97 - p239 [51-250]
Ch BWatch - v7 - N '97 - p4 [1-50]

Bofane, In Koli
The Lion Is No Longer King (Illus. by Lev)
KR - v65 - N 1 '97 - p1641 [51-250]
PW - v244 - N 24 '97 - p72+ [51-250]
SLJ - v44 - Ja '98 - p80 [51-250]

Bogacki, Tomasz
Cat and Mouse (Illus. by Tomasz Bogacki)
Obs - D 7 '97 - p17* [51-250]
RT - v51 - F '98 - p428 [51-250]
TES - N 7 '97 - p4* [1-50]

Cat and Mouse in the Rain (Illus. by Tomasz Bogacki)
KR - v65 - Je 15 '97 - p946 [51-250]

SLJ - v43 - Ag '97 - p128 [51-250]

I Hate You! I Like You! (Illus. by Tomasz Bogacki)
HB Guide - v8 - Fall '97 - p259 [51-250]
NYTBR - v103 - Mr 15 '98 - p23 [501+]

The Story of a Blue Bird (Illus. by Tomasz Bogacki)
KR - v66 - Ja 1 '98 - p53+ [51-250]
PW - v245 - Ja 5 '98 - p66 [51-250]
SLJ - v44 - Mr '98 - p166 [51-250]

Bogan, Paulette
Spike (Illus. by Paulette Bogan)
KR - v65 - D 1 '97 - p1773 [51-250]
PW - v245 - Ja 5 '98 - p66 [51-250]
SLJ - v44 - Mr '98 - p166 [51-250]

Bogart, Jo Ellen
Gifts (Illus. by Barbara Reid)
Emerg Lib - v25 - Ja '98 - p45+ [51-250]

Jeremiah Learns to Read (Illus. by Laura Fernandez)
CM:CanRev - v4 - Ja 16 '98 - pONL [251-500]
Quill & Q - v64 - Ja '98 - p37 [251-500]

Boggs, Cary
W.D. the Wonder Dog (Illus. by Annora Spence)
BL - v94 - Mr 1 '98 - p1139 [51-250]
KR - v66 - F 1 '98 - p192+ [51-250]

Bogot, Howard I
Seven Animal Stories for Children (Illus. by Harry Araten)
SLJ - v43 - D '97 - p105 [51-250]

Bohdal, Susi
1,2,3 What Do You See? (Illus. by Susi Bodal)
HB Guide - v8 - Fall '97 - p249 [51-250]

1,2,3 What Do You See? (Illus. by Susi Bohdal)
BL - v93 - Ag '97 - p1904+ [51-250]
Bloom Rev - v17 - My '97 - p27 [51-250]

CBRS - v25 - Je '97 - p121 [1-50]
RT - v51 - F '98 - p426 [51-250]

Bohlmeijer, Arno
Something Very Sorry
PW - v244 - N 24 '97 - p76 [1-50]
RT - v51 - O '97 - p142 [1-50]

Boitano, Brian
Boitano's Edge
BL - v94 - F 15 '98 - p1001 [51-250]
CCB-B - v51 - Mr '98 - p236+ [51-250]
PW - v244 - D 8 '97 - p73+ [251-500]
SLJ - v44 - Ap '98 - p141+ [51-250]
y　VOYA - v21 - Ap '98 - p64+ [51-250]

Bolaane, Maitseo
Batswana
Ch BWatch - v8 - Ja '98 - p7 [51-250]

Bolden, Tonya
And Not Afraid to Dare
y　BL - v94 - F 15 '98 - p993 [51-250]
　KR - v66 - Ja 1 '98 - p54 [51-250]
y　SLJ - v44 - Mr '98 - p228+ [51-250]

Through Loona's Door
Am Vis - v12 - D '97 - p34 [1-50]

Bolton, Michael
The Secret of the Lost Kingdom (Illus. by David Jermann)
PW - v244 - N 24 '97 - p72 [51-250]

Bomberger, Jane
Benny Gets a Bully-Ache
Ch BWatch - v7 - N '97 - p2 [51-250]

Benny's Coloring Book from A to Z
Ch BWatch - v7 - N '97 - p2 [51-250]

Bond, Adrienne Moore
Sugarcane House and Other Stories about Mr. Fat (Illus. by Leuyen Pham)
y　Am Vis - v12 - D '97 - p36 [1-50]
　BL - v94 - D 1 '97 - p635+ [51-250]
　CBRS - v26 - D '97 - p45 [51-250]
　CCB-B - v51 - D '97 - p119 [51-250]
　HB - v73 - N '97 - p676+ [251-500]
　SLJ - v44 - Ja '98 - p80 [51-250]

Bond, Michael
Paddington Bear and the Christmas Surprise (Illus. by R W Alley)
> BL - v94 - S 15 '97 - p239 [51-250]
> PW - v244 - O 6 '97 - p58+ [1-50]

Bond, Nancy
The Love of Friends
> y CCB-B - v51 - Ja '98 - p154+ [51-250]
>   Ch BWatch - v8 - Ja '98 - p4 [51-250]
> y KR - v65 - S 15 '97 - p1453 [51-250]
> y PW - v244 - Ag 11 '97 - p403 [51-250]
> y VOYA - v20 - D '97 - p313 [251-500]

Bond, Royce
The Case of the Smelly Armpit (Illus. by Gus Gordon)
> Magpies - v12 - S '97 - p41 [51-250]

Bond, Ruskin
Angry River
> Bkbird - v34 - Win '96 - p33 [51-250]

Cherry Tree (Illus. by Allan Eitzen)
> ECEJ - v25 - Fall '97 - p45 [1-50]

Island of Trees
> Bkbird - v34 - Win '96 - p33 [1-50]

Bonechillers. Audio Version
> TES - D 19 '97 - p23 [51-250]

Bonicatto, Marsha
Christmas Song of the North (Illus. by Karlyn Holman)
> Ch BWatch - v7 - D '97 - p1 [51-250]
> PW - v244 - O 6 '97 - p58 [1-50]

Bonners, Susan
Hunter in the Snow (Illus. by Susan Bonners)
> SLJ - v43 - My '97 - p56 [1-50]

The Silver Balloon (Illus. by Susan Bonners)
> BL - v94 - S 15 '97 - p234 [51-250]
> CBRS - v26 - O '97 - p19 [51-250]
> CCB-B - v51 - N '97 - p81 [51-250]
> PW - v244 - S 1 '97 - p105 [51-250]

Bonnet, Robert L
Science Fair Projects: Energy (Illus. by Alex Pang)
> BL - v94 - Mr 1 '98 - p1125+ [51-250]

Science Fair Projects: Flight, Space and Astronomy (Illus. by Frances Zweifel)
> SLJ - v44 - F '98 - p112 [51-250]

Science Fair Projects: The Environment (Illus. by Frances Zweifel)
> ASBYP - v29 - Fall '96 - p8+ [251-500]
> ASBYP - v29 - Sum '96 - p5+ [251-500]
> SLJ - v43 - Ap '97 - p144 [51-250]

Bonney, Barbara
Soccer: Attacking
> SLJ - v44 - Mr '98 - p192 [51-250]

Soccer: Defending
> SLJ - v44 - Mr '98 - p192 [51-250]

Soccer: Equipment
> SLJ - v44 - Mr '98 - p192 [51-250]

Soccer: Rules of the Game
> SLJ - v44 - Mr '98 - p192 [51-250]

Soccer: Skills
> SLJ - v44 - Mr '98 - p192 [51-250]

Soccer: The Fundamentals
> SLJ - v44 - Mr '98 - p192 [51-250]

Bonsall, Joseph S
Molly (Illus. by Erin Marie Mauterer)
> SLJ - v43 - D '97 - p81 [51-250]

Bonson, Richard
Disaster! (Illus. by Richard Bonson)
> NS - v126 - D 5 '97 - p62 [1-50]
> PW - v244 - O 6 '97 - p85 [51-250]
> TES - N 7 '97 - p9* [51-250]
> y VOYA - v21 - Ap '98 - p72 [51-250]

Bontemps, Arna Wendell
The Pasteboard Bandit (Illus. by Peggy Turley)
> y Am Vis - v12 - D '97 - p36 [1-50]
>   BL - v94 - Ja 1 '98 - p821 [51-250]
>   CBRS - v26 - D '97 - p42 [1-50]
>   HB - v73 - N '97 - p677 [51-250]

y KR - v65 - N 1 '97 - p1641 [51-250]
 PW - v244 - N 10 '97 - p74 [51-250]
 SLJ - v44 - Ja '98 - p111 [51-250]

Bonvillain, Nancy
Native American Medicine
 SB - v33 - D '97 - p277 [51-250]

Booker, Jean
Ellen's Secret
 Can CL - v22 - Win '96 - p111+ [501+]

Boon, Debbie
My Gran (Illus. by Debbie Boon)
 KR - v66 - Mr 1 '98 - p335 [51-250]
 Sch Lib - v45 - N '97 - p184 [51-250]

Booth, David
The Dust Bowl (Illus. by Karen Reczuch)
 Beav - v77 - Je '97 - p44 [51-250]
 BL - v94 - S 1 '97 - p131 [51-250]
 Can CL - v22 - Win '96 - p121+ [501+]
 CBRA - '96 - p434 [51-250]
 CBRS - v26 - Ja '98 - p55 [51-250]
 CCB-B - v51 - O '97 - p43+ [51-250]
 KR - v65 - Ag 15 '97 - p1303 [51-250]
 SLJ - v43 - D '97 - p81+ [51-250]

Booth, Martin
Music on the Bamboo Radio
 Bks Keeps - S '97 - p28 [51-250]
 FEER - v160 - Ag 7 '97 - p58 [251-500]
y Sch Lib - v45 - Ag '97 - p157 [51-250]
 TES - v43 - Ag 15 '97 - p23 [251-500]

War Dog
y BL - v94 - N 1 '97 - p461 [51-250]
y CBRS - v26 - Ja '98 - p57 [51-250]
 CCB-B - v51 - N '97 - p81 [51-250]
 KR - v65 - O 1 '97 - p1528 [51-250]
y PW - v244 - O 27 '97 - p77 [51-250]
y VOYA - v20 - F '98 - p384 [51-250]

Booth, Zilpha
Finding a Friend
 Ch BWatch - v7 - N '97 - p3 [1-50]

Borden, Louise
Good-Bye, Charles Lindbergh (Illus. by Thomas B Allen)
 BL - v94 - Mr 1 '98 - p1129 [51-250]

 KR - v66 - F 1 '98 - p193 [51-250]
 SLJ - v44 - Mr '98 - p166 [51-250]

The Little Ships (Illus. by Michael Foreman)
 HB Guide - v8 - Fall '97 - p296 [51-250]
 NYTBR - v102 - My 18 '97 - p25 [501+]
 Par Ch - Awards '97 - p4 [51-250]
 SLJ - v43 - Ap '97 - p90 [51-250]
 TES - N 7 '97 - p6* [51-250]

Thanksgiving Is... (Illus. by Steve Bjorkman)
 SLJ - v44 - Mr '98 - p192 [51-250]

Bornoff, Nicholas
Japan
 Ch BWatch - v7 - D '97 - p7 [51-250]
 HB Guide - v8 - Fall '97 - p391 [51-250]
 SLJ - v43 - Ag '97 - p163 [51-250]

Bornstein, Ruth
That's How It Is When We Draw (Illus. by Ruth Bornstein)
 KR - v65 - Je 15 '97 - p946 [51-250]
 SLJ - v43 - S '97 - p173 [51-250]

Borntrager, Mary Christner
Annie
 SLJ - v43 - Ag '97 - p154 [51-250]

Borton, Lady
Junk Pile! (Illus. by Kimberly Bulcken Root)
 CBRS - v25 - Je '97 - p126 [51-250]
 HB Guide - v8 - Fall '97 - p259 [51-250]
 SLJ - v43 - Ap '97 - p90+ [51-250]

Bortz, Fred
Martian Fossils on Earth?
 BL - v94 - Ja 1 '98 - p800 [51-250]
 CCB-B - v51 - Ap '98 - p274+ [51-250]
y SB - v34 - Ap '98 - p75 [51-250]
y SLJ - v44 - Mr '98 - p229 [51-250]

Bos, Burny
Ollie the Elephant (Illus. by Hans De Beer)
 Bloom Rev - v17 - N '97 - p31+ [51-250]

PW - v244 - O 27 '97 - p79 [1-50]

Bosak, Susan V
Something to Remember Me By (Illus. by Laurie McGaw)
> BL - v94 - N 1 '97 - p478 [51-250]
> KR - v65 - Ag 15 '97 - p1303 [51-250]
> SLJ - v43 - D '97 - p87 [51-250]

Bossley, Michele Martin
The Perfect Gymnast
> CBRA - '96 - p465 [51-250]

Water Fight!
> BIC - v26 - S '97 - p32+ [501+]
> CBRA - '96 - p465+ [251-500]

Bottigheimer, Ruth B
The Bible for Children
> Bkbird - v34 - Win '96 - p62 [1-50]
> TES - O 17 '97 - p12* [51-250]

Bottner, Barbara
Bootsie Barker, Ballerina (Illus. by G Brian Karas)
> HB Guide - v8 - Fall '97 - p286 [51-250]
> Learning - v26 - S '97 - p45 [1-50]
> SLJ - v43 - Je '97 - p79 [51-250]

Bouchard, Dave
The Elders Are Watching (Illus. by Roy Henry Vickers)
> CM:CanRev - v4 - Mr 13 '98 - pONL [51-250]

The Great Race (Illus. by Huang-Zhong Yang)
> CBRS - v26 - Ja '98 - p55 [51-250]
> CM:CanRev - v4 - N 28 '97 - pONL [51-250]
> SLJ - v44 - Ja '98 - p96+ [51-250]

If Sarah Will Take Me (Illus. by Robb Terrence Dunfield)
> SLJ - v43 - Ag '97 - p163+ [51-250]

If You're Not from the Prairie... (Illus. by Henry Ripplinger)
> Can CL - v23 - Sum '97 - p68+ [501+]

Prairie Born (Illus. by Peter Shostak)
> CM:CanRev - v4 - N 28 '97 - pONL [251-500]
> PW - v244 - D 22 '97 - p58 [51-250]

Voices from the Wild (Illus. by Ron Parker)
> CBRA - '96 - p528 [51-250]

Boulais, Sue
Tommy Nunez
> Ch BWatch - v7 - O '97 - p5 [51-250]
> SLJ - v43 - D '97 - p133 [51-250]

Boulton, Jane
Only Opal (Illus. by Barbara Cooney)
> PW - v244 - Je 23 '97 - p93 [51-250]

Bourgeau, Vincent
I'm Sick of It! A Fishy Melodrama (Illus. by Vincent Bourgeau)
> Ch BWatch - v7 - Jl '97 - p2 [1-50]
> SLJ - v43 - Je '97 - p79 [51-250]

I'm Sick of It! A Mouse's Reality Check (Illus. by Vincent Bourgeau)
> Ch BWatch - v7 - Jl '97 - p2 [1-50]
> SLJ - v43 - Je '97 - p79 [51-250]

Bourgeois, Paulette
Franklin Has a Sleepover (Illus. by Brenda Clark)
> CBRA - '96 - p434+ [51-250]

Franklin Rides a Bike (Illus. by Brenda Clark)
> SLJ - v43 - D '97 - p87 [51-250]

Franklin's Bad Day (Illus. by Brenda Clark)
> CBRA - '96 - p435 [251-500]
> SLJ - v43 - My '97 - p93 [51-250]

Franklin's Halloween (Illus. by Brenda Clark)
> CBRA - '96 - p435 [51-250]

Franklin's New Friend (Illus. by Brenda Clark)
> SLJ - v43 - D '97 - p87 [51-250]

Franklin's School Play (Illus. by Brenda Clark)
> CBRA - '96 - p435 [251-500]

Garbage Collectors (Illus. by Kim LaFave)
> KR - v66 - Ap 1 '98 - p492 [51-250]

The Moon (Illus. by Bill Slavin)
> CBRS - v26 - O '97 - p19+ [51-250]
> PW - v244 - S 1 '97 - p106 [1-50]
> SLJ - v43 - S '97 - p200 [51-250]

The Sun (Illus. by Bill Slavin)
> BL - v94 - S 1 '97 - p108 [51-250]
> CBRS - v26 - O '97 - p19+ [51-250]
> PW - v244 - S 1 '97 - p106 [1-50]
> SLJ - v43 - S '97 - p200 [51-250]

Bourke, Linda
Eye Count
> LA - v73 - N '96 - p523+ [51-250]

Boutan, Mila
Gauguin
> Emerg Lib - v25 - N '97 - p60 [51-250]

Monet
> Emerg Lib - v25 - N '97 - p60 [51-250]

Bow, Patricia
The Spiral Maze
> CM:CanRev - v4 - Ap 10 '98 - pONL [501+]
> Quill & Q - v63 - Jl '97 - p49 [251-500]

Bowdish, Lynea
Living with My Stepfather Is Like Living with a Moose (Illus. by Blanche Sims)
> HB Guide - v8 - Fall '97 - p288 [51-250]
> SLJ - v43 - Ap '97 - p91 [51-250]

Bowen, Andy Russell
The Back of Beyond (Illus. by Ralph L Ramstad)
> BL - v94 - S 1 '97 - p109 [51-250]
> SLJ - v44 - Mr '98 - p192 [51-250]

A Head Full of Notions (Illus. by Lisa Harvey)
> HB Guide - v8 - Fall '97 - p378 [51-250]
> SB - v33 - Je '97 - p146 [251-500]

Bowen, Fred
Full Court Fever (Illus. by Ann Barrow)
> PW - v245 - Mr 16 '98 - p67 [1-50]

The Golden Glove
> BW - v27 - My 4 '97 - p16 [501+]

The Kid Coach
> BW - v27 - My 4 '97 - p16 [501+]

Playoff Dreams (Illus. by Ann Barrow)
> BL - v94 - N 1 '97 - p469 [51-250]
> SLJ - v44 - Mr '98 - p166+ [51-250]

T.J.'S Secret Pitch
> BW - v27 - My 4 '97 - p16 [51-250]

Bowers, Vivien
Crime Science (Illus. by Martha Newbigging)
> BL - v94 - D 1 '97 - p625 [51-250]
> Quill & Q - v63 - N '97 - p48 [251-500]
> Quill & Q - v64 - F '98 - p42 [51-250]

Bowkett, Stephen
Dreamcastle
> Books - v11 - Ag '97 - p15 [51-250]

Bowles, Colin
Surfing Mr. Petrovic
> y   Aust Bk R - S '97 - p61+ [501+]
> Magpies - v12 - S '97 - p32 [51-250]

Bowman, Crystal
If Peas Could Taste Like Candy and Other Funny Poems for Kids (Illus. by Lynn Jeffrey)
> PW - v245 - F 23 '98 - p68 [1-50]

Ivan and the Dynamos
> HB Guide - v8 - Fall '97 - p296 [51-250]
> SLJ - v43 - S '97 - p213 [51-250]

Bowring, Jane
You Little Monster (Illus. by Loui Silvestro)
> Magpies - v12 - S '97 - p31 [51-250]

Boyd, Aaron
Tiger Woods
> SLJ - v43 - Ag '97 - p164 [51-250]
> y   VOYA - v20 - O '97 - p255+ [251-500]

Boyd, Lizi
Lulu Crow's Garden (Illus. by Lizi Boyd)
KR - v66 - Mr 15 '98 - p398 [51-250]

Boyer, Catherine
The Image of Jonathan Plum
Sch Lib - v45 - N '97 - p190 [51-250]

Boyes, Vivien
The Druid's Head
Sch Lib - v45 - N '97 - p190 [51-250]

Boynton, Sandra
Snoozers: 7 Short Short Bedtime Stories for Lively Little Kids (Illus. by Sandra Boynton)
CCB-B - v51 - Mr '98 - p237 [51-250]

Bradbury, Judy
One Carton of Oops! (Illus. by Cathy Trachok)
CBRS - v25 - Ag '97 - p158 [51-250]

Bradby, Marie
More than Anything Else (Illus. by Chris K Soentpiet)
ECEJ - v25 - Fall '97 - p46 [1-50]

Bradford, Karleen
More Animal Heroes
CBRA - '96 - p528 [51-250]

There Will Be Wolves
RT - v51 - D '97 - p333 [51-250]
y   SE - v61 - Ap '97 - p7* [1-50]
y   VOYA - v20 - Ap '97 - p27 [251-500]

Write Now!. Rev. Ed.
CBRA - '96 - p515 [51-250]

Bradley, Christine
Freedom of Movement
TES - O 17 '97 - pR7 [51-250]

Bradley, Kimberly Brubaker
Ruthie's Gift (Illus. by David Kramer)
BL - v94 - Ja 1 '98 - p809 [51-250]
KR - v65 - D 15 '97 - p1833 [51-250]
PW - v244 - D 22 '97 - p59 [51-250]
SLJ - v44 - F '98 - p78+ [51-250]

Bradman, Tony
Billy and the Baby (Illus. by Lynn Breeze)
Bks Keeps - My '97 - p20 [51-250]

Dilly and the Cup Final
TES - N 14 '97 - p14* [51-250]

Dilly and the Goody Goody (Illus. by Susan Hellard)
Magpies - v12 - My '97 - p31 [51-250]

The Magnificent Mummies (Illus. by Martin Chatterton)
Bks Keeps - S '97 - p24 [51-250]
Sch Lib - v45 - Ag '97 - p136 [51-250]

Michael (Illus. by Tony Ross)
Bks Keeps - S '97 - p21+ [51-250]

Terrific! I'm a Tarantula (Illus. by Clive Scruton)
Books - v11 - D '97 - p21 [1-50]

Braine, S
Drumbeat, Heartbeat
ECEJ - v25 - Fall '97 - p46 [1-50]

Branch, Muriel Miller
Juneteenth: Freedom Day (Illus. by Willis Branch)
BL - v94 - F 15 '98 - p1001 [51-250]
KR - v66 - Ja 1 '98 - p54 [51-250]

Pennies to Dollars
BL - v94 - N 1 '97 - p463 [51-250]
y   Kliatt - v32 - Ja '98 - p22 [251-500]

Brandenberg, Alexa
Chop, Simmer, Season (Illus. by Alexa Brandenberg)
CBRS - v25 - Spr '97 - p133 [1-50]
HB Guide - v8 - Fall '97 - p249 [51-250]
SLJ - v43 - My '97 - p93 [51-250]

Brandenburg, Jim
To the Top of the World (Illus. by Jim Brandenburg)
JOYS - v10 - Sum '97 - p427 [1-50]
SLJ - v43 - My '97 - p56 [1-50]
y   VOYA - v21 - Ap '98 - p42 [1-50]

Brandis, Marianne
*Rebellion: A Novel of Upper Canada
(Illus. by G Brender A Brandis)*
y   Can CL - v22 - Win '96 - p105+ [501+]
     CBRA - '96 - p467 [51-250]

Branford, Henrietta
Fire, Bed, and Bone
     BL - v94 - Mr 15 '98 - p1240 [51-250]
     PW - v245 - F 16 '98 - p212 [51-250]
     TES - N 7 '97 - p7* [51-250]
     TES - D 12 '97 - p40 [251-500]

Branley, Franklyn Mansfield
*Day Light, Night Light (Illus. by
Stacey Schuett)*
     BL - v94 - D 1 '97 - p633 [51-250]
     KR - v65 - N 15 '97 - p1704 [51-250]
     SLJ - v44 - F '98 - p95 [51-250]

*Down Comes the Rain (Illus. by James
Graham Hale)*
     BL - v94 - S 1 '97 - p127 [51-250]

*Floating in Space (Illus. by True
Kelley)*
     BL - v94 - D 1 '97 - p633 [51-250]
     CCB-B - v51 - Ap '98 - p275 [51-250]
     KR - v65 - N 15 '97 - p1704+ [51-250]
     SLJ - v44 - F '98 - p95 [51-250]

The Sun and the Solar System
     SB - v33 - Ag '97 - p187 [1-50]

*What Makes a Magnet (Illus. by True
Kelley)*
     SB - v33 - Ag '97 - p187 [1-50]

Branzei, Sylvia
*Grossology Begins at Home (Illus. by
Jack Keely)*
y   BL - v94 - Mr 15 '98 - p1224 [1-50]
     PW - v244 - O 27 '97 - p79 [51-250]
y   VOYA - v21 - Ap '98 - p39 [1-50]

*Grossology: The Science of Really
Gross Things. Electronic Media
Version*
     PW - v244 - O 13 '97 - p77 [51-250]
     PW - v244 - D 22 '97 - p61 [1-50]

Bratton, Heidi
*Imagine: A Story about the Beginning
(Illus. by Heidi Bratton)*
     PW - v244 - Ag 25 '97 - p66 [51-250]
     SLJ - v44 - Ja '98 - p97 [51-250]

Spirit! (Illus. by Heidi Bratton)
     PW - v244 - Ag 25 '97 - p66 [51-250]
     SLJ - v44 - Ja '98 - p97 [51-250]

*Where Is God? (Illus. by Heidi
Bratton)*
     PW - v244 - Ag 25 '97 - p66 [51-250]
     SLJ - v44 - Ja '98 - p97 [51-250]

Yes, I Can! (Illus. by Heidi Bratton)
     PW - v244 - Ag 25 '97 - p66 [51-250]
     SLJ - v44 - Ja '98 - p97 [51-250]

Bray, Rosemary L
*Martin Luther King (Illus. by Malcah
Zeldis)*
     BL - v94 - F 15 '98 - p998 [1-50]

Braz, Julio Emilio
Kinder Im Dunkeln
     Bkbird - v35 - Fall '97 - p50 [1-50]

Breathed, Berkeley
*Red Ranger Came Calling (Illus. by
Berkeley Breathed)*
     PW - v244 - O 6 '97 - p59 [1-50]

Breckler, Rosemary
*Sweet Dried Apples (Illus. by Deborah
Kogan Ray)*
     RT - v51 - D '97 - p310 [51-250]
     SE - v61 - Ap '97 - p6* [1-50]

Bredeson, Carmen
The Battle of the Alamo
     SLJ - v43 - Ap '97 - p144 [51-250]

Gus Grissom: A Space Biography
     KR - v65 - D 1 '97 - p1773 [51-250]

Texas
     SLJ - v43 - Je '97 - p130 [51-250]

Brennan, Herbie
*Letters from a Mouse (Illus. by Louise
Voce)*
     Bks Keeps - Jl '97 - p22 [51-250]

Magpies - v12 - My '97 - p33 [51-250]
Sch Lib - v45 - Ag '97 - p136 [51-250]

Brennan, J H
Blood Brother
Bks Keeps - Jl '97 - p26 [51-250]

Brennan, Linda Crotta
Flannel Kisses (Illus. by Mari Takabayashi)
BL - v94 - O 15 '97 - p411 [51-250]
CBRS - v26 - Ja '98 - p49 [51-250]
KR - v65 - Jl 15 '97 - p1107 [51-250]
PW - v244 - Ag 25 '97 - p71 [51-250]
SLJ - v43 - S '97 - p173 [51-250]

Brenner, Barbara
Chibi: A True Story from Japan (Illus. by June Otani)
RT - v51 - F '98 - p430+ [51-250]

Thinking about Ants (Illus. by Carol Schwartz)
BL - v93 - Je 1 '97 - p1708 [51-250]
HB Guide - v8 - Fall '97 - p349 [51-250]

The Tremendous Tree Book (Illus. by Fred Brenner)
PW - v245 - F 9 '98 - p98 [1-50]

Breslin, Theresa
Across the Roman Wall (Illus. by Michael Charlton)
Bks Keeps - N '97 - p24 [51-250]

Blair the Winner (Illus. by Ken Cox)
Bks Keeps - Jl '97 - p22 [51-250]
Sch Lib - v45 - Ag '97 - p136 [51-250]
TES - Jl 11 '97 - p14* [51-250]

Name Games
TES - N 14 '97 - p14* [51-250]

Brett, Jan
The Hat (Illus. by Jan Brett)
BL - v94 - S 1 '97 - p116 [51-250]
CBRS - v26 - O '97 - p13 [51-250]
Ch BWatch - v8 - Ja '98 - p3 [1-50]
KR - v65 - Jl 1 '97 - p1027 [51-250]
NYTBR - v103 - F 15 '98 - p25 [51-250]
PW - v244 - Je 2 '97 - p71 [51-250]
SLJ - v43 - S '97 - p173 [51-250]

Brewster, Hugh
Anastasia's Album (Illus. by Peter Christopher)
CBRA - '96 - p505 [51-250]
Ch Bk News - v20 - Sum '97 - p29 [51-250]
CR - v270 - Je '97 - p327+ [501+]
RT - v51 - D '97 - p328 [51-250]
SE - v61 - Ap '97 - p3* [1-50]

Brian, Gleeson
Koi and the Kola Nuts (Gobbege). Audio Version
BL - v94 - N 1 '97 - p494 [51-250]

Brian, Janeen
Dog Star (Illus. by Ann James)
Magpies - v12 - My '97 - p30+ [51-250]

Bridwell, Norman
Clifford the Big Red Dog Board Book
PW - v244 - Ag 25 '97 - p73 [1-50]

Clifford's Peek-and-Seek Animal Riddles
Ch BWatch - v7 - S '97 - p4 [1-50]
HB Guide - v8 - Fall '97 - p249 [51-250]

What Time Is It, Clifford?
PW - v245 - Mr 16 '98 - p67 [1-50]

Brierly, Anthony
Explorers of the Ancient World
CLW - v68 - D '97 - p86 [51-250]

Briggs, Raymond
Father Christmas
PW - v244 - O 6 '97 - p58 [1-50]

The Snowman Storybook (Illus. by Raymond Briggs)
PW - v244 - O 6 '97 - p59 [1-50]

Briggs, Stephen
Johnny and the Dead
Sch Lib - v45 - Ag '97 - p156 [51-250]

Briggs-Bunting, Jane
Laddie of the Light
Ch BWatch - v7 - Jl '97 - p6 [51-250]

Bright Ideas (Illus. by Susan Synarski)
PW - v244 - S 22 '97 - p82 [1-50]

Brighton, Catherine
My Napoleon (Illus. by Catherine Brighton)
HB Guide - v8 - Fall '97 - p259 [51-250]
SLJ - v43 - Je '97 - p79 [51-250]

Brill, Marlene Targ
Diary of a Drummer Boy (Illus. by Michael Garland)
BL - v94 - Mr 1 '98 - p1132+ [51-250]
KR - v66 - F 1 '98 - p193 [51-250]

Indiana
Ch BWatch - v7 - My '97 - p7 [51-250]
HB Guide - v8 - Fall '97 - p394 [51-250]
SLJ - v43 - Ag '97 - p160+ [51-250]

Brillhart, Julie
When Daddy Took Us Camping (Illus. by Julie Brillhart)
HB Guide - v8 - Fall '97 - p259 [51-250]
SLJ - v43 - My '97 - p93 [51-250]

Brillon, Gilles
Discovering the Heavens (Illus. by Evelyne Arcouette)
CBRA - '96 - p528 [51-250]

Brimner, Larry Dane
Bobsledding and the Luge
SLJ - v44 - F '98 - p95 [51-250]

Country Bear's Surprise (Illus. by Ruth Tietjen Councell)
PW - v244 - S 29 '97 - p91 [1-50]

E-Mail
HB Guide - v8 - Fall '97 - p317 [51-250]
SB - v33 - D '97 - p272 [51-250]
SLJ - v43 - N '97 - p105 [51-250]

Merry Christmas, Old Armadillo (Illus. by Dominic Catalano)
PW - v244 - O 6 '97 - p59 [1-50]

Mountain Biking
BL - v94 - S 1 '97 - p109 [51-250]

HB Guide - v8 - Fall '97 - p368 [51-250]
SLJ - v43 - Ag '97 - p164 [51-250]

Polar Mammals
HB Guide - v8 - Fall '97 - p352 [51-250]
SB - v33 - Ag '97 - p178 [251-500]
SLJ - v43 - Ap '97 - p120 [51-250]

Rock Climbing
BL - v93 - Je 1 '97 - p1687 [51-250]
HB Guide - v8 - Fall '97 - p368 [51-250]

Snowboarding
BL - v94 - N 1 '97 - p463 [51-250]
SLJ - v44 - F '98 - p112 [51-250]

Speed Skating
BL - v94 - Ja 1 '98 - p800+ [51-250]
SLJ - v44 - F '98 - p95 [51-250]

The Winter Olympics
BL - v94 - Ja 1 '98 - p800+ [51-250]
SLJ - v44 - F '98 - p95 [51-250]

The World Wide Web
HB Guide - v8 - Fall '97 - p317 [51-250]
SB - v33 - D '97 - p272 [51-250]
SLJ - v44 - Ja '98 - p97 [51-250]

Brink, Carol Ryrie
Caddie Woodlawn
CSM - v90 - F 24 '98 - p16 [1-50]

Brinster, Richard
Jeff Gordon
Ch BWatch - v7 - S '97 - p8 [1-50]
HB Guide - v8 - Fall '97 - p368 [51-250]

Brisson, Pat
Hot Fudge Hero (Illus. by Diana Cain Bluthenthal)
CBRS - v25 - Spr '97 - p139 [51-250]
CCB-B - v50 - Je '97 - p351 [51-250]
HB - v73 - Jl '97 - p450+ [51-250]
HB Guide - v8 - Fall '97 - p288 [51-250]
SLJ - v43 - Jl '97 - p60 [51-250]

The Summer My Father Was Ten (Illus. by Andrea Shine)
KR - v66 - F 1 '98 - p193 [51-250]
SLJ - v44 - Ap '98 - p91 [51-250]

Britt, Grant
Charlie Sifford
    BL - v94 - F 15 '98 - p1001 [51-250]

Brittan, Dolly
The People of Thailand
    SLJ - v44 - Mr '98 - p192+ [51-250]

Broda, Ron
3-D Paper Crafts (Illus. by Wally Randall)
    Ch Bk News - v20 - Sum '97 - p28 [51-250]
    CM:CanRev - v4 - N 28 '97 - pONL [51-250]
    Quill & Q - v63 - My '97 - p41+ [251-500]

Brokering, Herbert
Angels Love Children
    PW - v244 - Je 2 '97 - p66 [1-50]

Brook, Donna
The Journey of English (Illus. by Jean Day Zallinger)
    KR - v66 - Ap 1 '98 - p493 [51-250]

Brooke, Agnes-Mary
The Owl, the Two and the Medlar
    Magpies - v12 - S '97 - p6* [251-500]

Brooks, Alan
Frogs Jump (Illus. by Steven Kellogg)
    RT - v51 - S '97 - p58 [51-250]
    RT - v51 - O '97 - p131 [1-50]

Brooks, Bruce
Boot
    SLJ - v44 - Mr '98 - p208+ [51-250]

Cody
    SLJ - v43 - D '97 - p123 [51-250]

NBA by the Numbers
    CM:CanRev - v4 - O 31 '97 - pONL [251-500]
    HB Guide - v8 - Fall '97 - p368 [51-250]

Shark
    KR - v66 - Ap 1 '98 - p493 [51-250]

What Hearts (McDonough). Audio Version
    y   Kliatt - v32 - Ja '98 - p46 [51-250]
         SLJ - v43 - N '97 - p70 [51-250]

Woodsie (Illus. by Erik Butler)
    BL - v94 - Ja 1 '98 - p809+ [51-250]
    KR - v65 - O 1 '97 - p1528 [51-250]
    PW - v244 - S 1 '97 - p105 [51-250]
    SLJ - v43 - D '97 - p123 [51-250]

Zip
    BL - v94 - Ja 1 '98 - p809+ [51-250]
    SLJ - v43 - D '97 - p123 [51-250]

Brooks, Martha
I Met a Bully on the Hill
    CBRA - '96 - p496 [51-250]

Brooks, Susan
The Geography of the Earth
    ASBYP - v29 - Fall '96 - p9 [501+]

Brooksbank, Angela
I've Lost My Yellow Zebra
    TES - Je 27 '97 - p12* [51-250]

Broome, Errol
Quicksilver (Illus. by Anna Pignataro)
    Magpies - v12 - Jl '97 - p32 [51-250]

What a Goat!
    Magpies - v12 - Mr '97 - p31 [51-250]

Brouillet, Chrystine
The Chinese Puzzle (Illus. by Nathalie Gagnon)
    CBRA - '96 - p467 [51-250]
    TES - Ag 1 '97 - p25 [251-500]

The Enchanted Horses (Illus. by Nathalie Gagnon)
    CBRA - '96 - p467 [51-250]
    TES - Ag 1 '97 - p25 [251-500]

No Orchids for Andrea! (Illus. by Nathalie Gagnon)
    CBRA - '96 - p467 [51-250]

Brousseau, Linda
Marina's Star
    CM:CanRev - v4 - Ja 2 '98 - pONL [251-500]

Brouwer, Sigmund
Thunderbird Spirit
    CBRA - '96 - p467+ [51-250]

Winter Hawk Star
    CBRA - '96 - p468 [51-250]

Brower, Pauline
Missions of the Inland Valleys
    HB Guide - v8 - Fall '97 - p394 [51-250]

Brown, Alan, 1950, Jan., 1-
Christian Church
    Sch Lib - v45 - N '97 - p206 [51-250]

The Windhover (Illus. by Christian Birmingham)
    BL - v94 - N 1 '97 - p478 [51-250]
    Books - v11 - Je '97 - p21 [1-50]
    CBRS - v26 - F '98 - p73 [51-250]
    KR - v65 - S 15 '97 - p1453 [51-250]
    SLJ - v44 - Ja '98 - p80 [51-250]

Brown, Andrew
Amazing Sea Creatures
    Ch BWatch - v7 - Ap '97 - p4 [1-50]
    HB Guide - v8 - Fall '97 - p344 [51-250]
    SLJ - v43 - Ag '97 - p145 [51-250]

Armored Animals
    Ch BWatch - v7 - Ap '97 - p4 [1-50]
    HB Guide - v8 - Fall '97 - p344 [51-250]
    SLJ - v43 - Jl '97 - p80 [51-250]

Baby Animals
    Ch BWatch - v7 - Ap '97 - p4 [1-50]
    HB Guide - v8 - Fall '97 - p344 [51-250]
    SLJ - v43 - Jl '97 - p80 [51-250]

Dangerous Animals
    Ch BWatch - v7 - Ap '97 - p4 [1-50]
    HB Guide - v8 - Fall '97 - p344 [51-250]
    SLJ - v43 - Ag '97 - p145 [51-250]

Brown, Calef
Polkabats and Octopus Slacks (Illus. by Calef Brown)
    BL - v94 - Mr 15 '98 - p1243 [51-250]
    PW - v245 - Mr 9 '98 - p67 [51-250]

Brown, Cinita
The Black Kettle Ride (Illus. by Jean Lirley Huff)
    SLJ - v43 - Ag '97 - p128+ [51-250]

Brown, Don
Alice Ramsey's Grand Adventure (Illus. by Don Brown)
    BL - v94 - S 15 '97 - p236+ [51-250]
    CCB-B - v51 - O '97 - p44 [251-500]
    HB - v73 - N '97 - p694 [51-250]
    KR - v65 - Jl 1 '97 - p1027 [51-250]
    PW - v244 - Ag 25 '97 - p71 [51-250]
    SLJ - v43 - S '97 - p200 [51-250]
    SLJ - v43 - D '97 - p23+ [1-50]
    SLJ - v44 - Mr '98 - p119 [1-50]

Brown, Ernest Douglas
Lozi
    Ch BWatch - v8 - Ja '98 - p7 [51-250]

Brown, Fern G
American Indian Science
    BL - v94 - S 1 '97 - p109 [51-250]

Brown, Judith Gwyn
Bless All Creatures Here Below (Illus. by Judith Gwyn Brown)
    CLW - v68 - D '97 - p83 [51-250]

Brown, Karen
Kids Are Cookin' (Illus. by Laurel Aiello)
    BL - v93 - Je 1 '97 - p1687+ [51-250]
    Ch BWatch - v7 - Je '97 - p2 [51-250]
    SLJ - v43 - Jl '97 - p80 [51-250]

Brown, Ken
Mucky Pup (Illus. by Ken Brown)
    BL - v94 - D 15 '97 - p701+ [51-250]
    Books - v11 - Je '97 - p21 [1-50]
    Sch Lib - v45 - Ag '97 - p129 [51-250]
    SLJ - v43 - D '97 - p87 [51-250]

Brown, Laurene Krasny
Rex and Lilly Schooltime (Illus. by Marc Brown)
    HB Guide - v8 - Fall '97 - p286 [51-250]

Visiting a Museum
    Inst - v106 - My '97 - p4* [1-50]

What's the Big Secret? (Illus. by Marc Brown)

> BL - v94 - O 1 '97 - p326 [51-250]
> CBRS - v26 - O '97 - p13 [51-250]
> CCB-B - v51 - N '97 - p82 [51-250]
> HB - v74 - Ja '98 - p89+ [51-250]
> KR - v65 - Ag 1 '97 - p1219 [51-250]
> PW - v244 - Jl 7 '97 - p67 [51-250]
> SLJ - v44 - Mr '98 - p193 [51-250]

When Dinosaurs Die (Illus. by Marc Brown)

> SE - v61 - Ap '97 - p4* [1-50]

Brown, Marc

Arthur Babysits

> HB Guide - v8 - Fall '97 - p249 [1-50]

Arthur Writes a Story (Illus. by Marc Brown)

> RT - v51 - O '97 - p132 [1-50]

Arthur's Chicken Pox

> Books - v11 - D '97 - p21 [51-250]

Arthur's Computer Disaster (Illus. by Marc Brown)

> BL - v94 - S 15 '97 - p239 [51-250]
> HB - v73 - N '97 - p668 [51-250]
> PW - v244 - Ag 25 '97 - p73+ [1-50]

Arthur's Family Vacation (Brown) (Illus. by Marc Brown). Book and Audio Version

> SLJ - v43 - Ap '97 - p82 [51-250]

Arthur's First Sleepover

> Books - v11 - D '97 - p21 [51-250]

Arthur's Halloween (Brown) (Illus. by Marc Brown). Book and Audio Version

> SLJ - v43 - Ap '97 - p82 [51-250]

Arthur's New Puppy

> HB Guide - v8 - Fall '97 - p249 [1-50]

Arthur's Nose (Illus. by Marc Brown)

> NYTBR - v102 - N 16 '97 - p26 [1-50]

Arthur's Reading Race. Electronic Media Version

> BL - v94 - D 1 '97 - p646+ [51-250]
> BW - v27 - D 7 '97 - p23 [51-250]
> Emerg Lib - v25 - N '97 - p48 [51-250]

Arthur's Really Helpful Word Book (Illus. by Marc Brown)

> Emerg Lib - v25 - N '97 - p54 [1-50]
> SLJ - v43 - N '97 - p78 [51-250]

D.W. All Wet (Illus. by Marc Brown)

> PW - v244 - Jl 7 '97 - p70 [1-50]

D.W. Flips (Illus. by Marc Brown)

> PW - v244 - Jl 7 '97 - p70 [51-250]

Brown, Margaret Wise

Goodnight Moon (Illus. by Clement Hurd)

> NYTBR - v102 - N 16 '97 - p25 [1-50]

The Quiet Noisy Book (Illus. by Leonard Weisgard)

> Comw - v124 - D 5 '97 - p14 [51-250]

Brown, Margot

Our World, Our Rights

> TES - O 17 '97 - pR6 [51-250]

Brown, Roberta Simpson

Scared in School

> SLJ - v44 - Ja '98 - p111 [51-250]

Brown, Ruth

Baba (Illus. by Ruth Brown)

> Bks Keeps - S '97 - p20 [51-250]
> Sch Lib - v45 - Ag '97 - p129+ [51-250]
> TES - Jl 18 '97 - p35 [1-50]

Cry Baby (Illus. by Ruth Brown)

> SLJ - v44 - F '98 - p79 [51-250]

Toad

> Ch BWatch - v7 - Mr '97 - p7 [1-50]
> HB Guide - v8 - Fall '97 - p259 [51-250]
> SB - v33 - Ag '97 - p163 [1-50]

Brown, Sterling

First Lady of the Air

> SLJ - v44 - Ap '98 - p142 [51-250]

Brown, Tricia

Konnichiwa! I Am a Japanese-American Girl (Illus. by Kazuyoshi Arai)

> SE - v61 - Ap '97 - p217 [51-250]

Brown, Virginia Pounds
Cochula's Journey

HB Guide - v8 - Fall '97 - p297 [51-250]

y   VOYA - v20 - Je '97 - p108 [251-500]

Browne, Anthony
Changes

Bks Keeps - Jl '97 - p20 [51-250]

Willy the Dreamer (Illus. by Anthony Browne)

Bks Keeps - N '97 - p4 [51-250]
Magpies - v12 - S '97 - p24 [501+]
NS - v126 - D 5 '97 - p62 [51-250]
PW - v245 - F 2 '98 - p89+ [51-250]
TES - N 14 '97 - p8* [51-250]

Willy the Wizard (Illus. by Anthony Browne)

SLJ - v44 - Mr '98 - p119 [1-50]

Browne, Eileen
Handa's Surprise

Bks Keeps - N '97 - p21 [51-250]

La Sorpresa De Nandi (Illus. by Eileen Browne)

SLJ - v44 - F '98 - p130 [51-250]

Browne, Philippa-Alys
Elephants and Emus and Other Animal Rhymes

Magpies - v12 - S '97 - p28 [51-250]

Kangaroos Have Joeys

SB - v33 - Ag '97 - p163 [1-50]

Brownlie, Alison
Jamaica

Bks Keeps - N '97 - p25 [51-250]
Sch Lib - v45 - N '97 - p203 [51-250]

Senegal

H-Net - Ap '98 - pONL [501+]

Brown-Neathway, Maxine
Tummy Talks

CBRA - '96 - p525+ [51-250]

Brownridge, William Roy
The Final Game (Illus. by William Roy Brownridge)

BL - v94 - Mr 1 '98 - p1139+ [51-250]

CM:CanRev - v4 - O 17 '97 - pONL [251-500]
NYTBR - v103 - F 15 '98 - p26 [251-500]
Quill & Q - v63 - O '97 - p38+ [251-500]

The Moccasin Goalie

Can CL - v23 - Sum '97 - p61+ [501+]

Bruchac, Joseph
The Arrow over the Door (Illus. by James Watling)

BL - v94 - F 15 '98 - p1007 [251-500]
CCB-B - v51 - Ap '98 - p275 [51-250]
KR - v65 - D 15 '97 - p1833 [51-250]
PW - v245 - Mr 9 '98 - p68 [51-250]
SLJ - v44 - Ap '98 - p128 [51-250]

Between Earth and Sky (Illus. by Thomas Locker)

RT - v51 - D '97 - p307 [51-250]
SE - v61 - Ap '97 - p5* [1-50]

Children of the Longhouse

RT - v51 - S '97 - p56 [51-250]
SE - v61 - Ap '97 - p9* [1-50]

Dog People (Illus. by Murv Jacob)

Ch BWatch - v7 - Mr '97 - p3 [51-250]

Eagle Song (Illus. by Dan Andreasen)

CBRS - v25 - Je '97 - p126 [51-250]
HB Guide - v8 - Fall '97 - p297 [51-250]

Four Ancestors (Illus. by S S Burrus)

Emerg Lib - v24 - My '97 - p57 [1-50]

Lasting Echoes (Illus. by Paul Morin)

y   BL - v94 - D 15 '97 - p688 [51-250]
y   CCB-B - v51 - Mr '98 - p237+ [51-250]
     HB - v74 - Ja '98 - p90 [51-250]
y   KR - v65 - N 1 '97 - p1641 [51-250]
     PW - v244 - N 24 '97 - p75 [51-250]
     SLJ - v44 - Mr '98 - p229 [51-250]

Many Nations (Illus. by Robert F Goetzl)

BL - v94 - S 15 '97 - p237 [51-250]
SLJ - v43 - D '97 - p105+ [51-250]

The Native Stories from Keepers of the Animals (Illus. by John Kahionhes Fadden)

Can Lit - Aut '97 - p118+ [501+]

Tell Me a Tale

y   CBRS - v25 - Je '97 - p129 [51-250]

HB Guide - v8 - Fall '97 - p366 [51-250]

SLJ - v43 - Ag '97 - p164 [51-250]

Brueghel, Jan
Where's the Bear?
TES - D 5 '97 - p18* [51-250]

Bruna, Dick
Miffy Goes Outside
PW - v244 - O 27 '97 - p78 [1-50]

Miffy Likes to...
PW - v244 - O 27 '97 - p78 [1-50]

Brunelli, Roberto
A Family Treasury of Bible Stories (Illus. by Mikhail Fiodorov)
BL - v94 - O 1 '97 - p321+ [51-250]
Ch BWatch - v8 - Ja '98 - p1 [1-50]
y   PW - v244 - N 10 '97 - p70 [51-250]
SLJ - v44 - F '98 - p95+ [51-250]

Bruno, Leonard C
Science and Technology Breakthroughs. Vols. 1-2
r   BL - v94 - Mr 1 '98 - p1171 [251-500]

Bryan, Ashley
Ashley Bryan's ABC of African American Poetry (Illus. by Ashley Bryan)
BL - v94 - S 1 '97 - p128 [51-250]
CBRS - v26 - S '97 - p7 [51-250]
NYTBR - v103 - F 15 '98 - p25 [1-50]
Par Ch - Awards '97 - p7 [51-250]
PW - v244 - Jl 28 '97 - p77 [51-250]
SLJ - v43 - S '97 - p200 [51-250]

Bryan, Jenny
The History of Health and Medicine
Ch BWatch - v7 - Ap '97 - p8 [51-250]

Bryant, Bonnie
Horse Wise
JOYS - v10 - Spr '97 - p261 [1-50]

Bryant-Mole, Karen
Autumn
SLJ - v43 - D '97 - p106 [51-250]

Blue
ASBYP - v29 - Fall '96 - p49+ [251-500]

Clothes
BL - v94 - O 15 '97 - p407 [51-250]

Flowers
ASBYP - v29 - Fall '96 - p64+ [251-500]

Food
BL - v94 - O 15 '97 - p407 [51-250]
SLJ - v43 - D '97 - p106 [51-250]

Homes Discovered through Art and Technology
TES - Je 13 '97 - p16* [51-250]

Insects
ASBYP - v29 - Fall '96 - p64+ [251-500]

Myself Discovered through Art and Technology
TES - Je 13 '97 - p16* [51-250]

Rojo (Illus. by Jean Wheeler)
SLJ - v43 - My '97 - p152 [51-250]

Soil
ASBYP - v29 - Fall '96 - p64+ [251-500]

Spring
SLJ - v43 - D '97 - p106 [51-250]

Summer
SLJ - v43 - D '97 - p106 [51-250]

Texture
ASBYP - v29 - Fall '96 - p49+ [251-500]

Toys
SLJ - v43 - D '97 - p106 [51-250]

Toys Discovered through Art and Technology
TES - Je 13 '97 - p16* [51-250]

Trees
ASBYP - v29 - Fall '96 - p64+ [251-500]

Water Discovered through Art and Technology
TES - Je 13 '97 - p16* [51-250]

Winter
SLJ - v43 - D '97 - p106 [51-250]

Brynjolson, Rhian
Foster Baby (Illus. by Rhian Brynjolson)
> CBRA - '96 - p435+ [51-250]
> Ch Bk News - v20 - Spr '97 - p29+ [51-250]

Buchanan, Jane
Gratefully Yours
> BL - v94 - O 15 '97 - p404+ [51-250]
> CBRS - v26 - F '98 - p80 [51-250]
> CCB-B - v51 - N '97 - p82 [51-250]
> KR - v65 - O 15 '97 - p1579 [51-250]
> PW - v244 - O 27 '97 - p76 [51-250]
> SLJ - v43 - D '97 - p123 [51-250]

Buchberg, Wendy
Quilting Activities across the Curriculum
> SB - v33 - Je '97 - p141 [251-500]

Buchignani, Walter
Tell No One Who You Are
> TES - Ag 29 '97 - p28 [51-250]

Buck, Gisela
Fuzzy the Duckling
> ASBYP - v29 - Fall '96 - p62+ [251-500]

Mitzi, Molly and Max the Kittens
> ASBYP - v29 - Fall '96 - p62+ [251-500]

Pete the Puppy
> ASBYP - v29 - Fall '96 - p62+ [251-500]

Sallie the Shrew
> ASBYP - v29 - Fall '96 - p62+ [251-500]

Buck, Nola
Oh, Cats! (Illus. by Nadine Bernard Westcott)
> HB Guide - v8 - Fall '97 - p249 [51-250]

Santa's Short Suit Shrunk and Other Christmas Tongue Twisters (Illus. by Sue Truesdell)
> BL - v94 - S 15 '97 - p237 [51-250]
> CCB-B - v51 - D '97 - p119 [51-250]
> HB - v73 - N '97 - p695 [51-250]
> PW - v244 - O 6 '97 - p57+ [1-50]

Buckley, Helen Elizabeth
Grandfather and I (Illus. by Jan Ormerod)
> Bks Keeps - My '97 - p20 [51-250]
> Magpies - v12 - Jl '97 - p28 [51-250]

Grandmother and I (Illus. by Jan Ormerod)
> Bks Keeps - My '97 - p20 [51-250]
> Magpies - v12 - Jl '97 - p28 [51-250]

Moonlight Kite (Illus. by Elise Primavera)
> HB Guide - v8 - Fall '97 - p259 [51-250]

Buck-Murray, Marian
The Mash and Smash Cookbook (Illus. by Ralph Butler)
> BL - v94 - Ja 1 '98 - p802 [51-250]
> PW - v244 - S 22 '97 - p83 [51-250]
> SLJ - v44 - F '98 - p96 [51-250]

Buehner, Caralyn
Fanny's Dream (Illus. by Mark Buehner)
> Inst - v107 - Ag '97 - p23 [51-250]

I Did It, I'm Sorry (Illus. by Mark Buehner)
> KR - v66 - Ap 15 '98 - p576 [51-250]

It's a Spoon, Not a Shovel (Illus. by Mark Buehner)
> LA - v73 - N '96 - p524+ [51-250]

Buell, Janet
Bog Bodies
> Ch BWatch - v8 - Ja '98 - p6 [1-50]
> SLJ - v44 - Mr '98 - p229+ [51-250]

Ice Maiden of the Andes
> Ch BWatch - v8 - Ja '98 - p6 [1-50]
> SLJ - v44 - Mr '98 - p229+ [51-250]

Buetter, Barbara MacDonald
Simple Puppets from Everyday Materials (Illus. by George Buetter)
> CBRA - '96 - p517 [51-250]

Buettner, Dan
*Africatrek: A Journey by Bicycle
through Africa (Illus. by Dan
Buettner)*
    BL - v94 - S 15 '97 - p218 [51-250]
    SLJ - v43 - Ag '97 - p164 [51-250]
  y VOYA - v21 - Ap '98 - p66 [51-250]

Bulla, Dale
*Traditional Stories for Children of All
Ages (Bulla). Audio Version*
    SLJ - v43 - Je '97 - p69 [51-250]

Bulldozer (Box Cars)
    PW - v245 - Mr 23 '98 - p102 [1-50]

Buller, Jon
Space Mall
    HB Guide - v8 - Fall '97 - p288 [51-250]

Bulloch, Ivan
I Wish I Were...a Princess
    CBRS - v26 - S '97 - p1 [1-50]

Bunny (DK)
    Ch BWatch - v7 - Je '97 - p4 [1-50]

Bunting, Eve
*The Blue and the Gray (Illus. by Ned
Bittinger)*
    Emerg Lib - v24 - My '97 - p66 [51-250]
    RT - v51 - N '97 - p240 [51-250]
    RT - v51 - D '97 - p334 [51-250]

Dandelions (Illus. by Greg Shed)
    SLJ - v43 - Jl '97 - p34 [1-50]

*The Day the Whale Came (Illus. by
Scott Menchin)*
    KR - v66 - Mr 1 '98 - p335 [51-250]
    PW - v245 - F 23 '98 - p76+ [51-250]

*A Day's Work (Illus. by Ronald
Himler)*
    Par - v72 - My '97 - p92 [1-50]
    Par Ch - Awards '97 - p9 [51-250]

December (Illus. by David Diaz)
    BL - v94 - S 1 '97 - p138 [251-500]
    CBRS - v26 - N '97 - p31 [51-250]
    CCB-B - v51 - D '97 - p119+ [51-250]
    KR - v65 - O 15 '97 - p1579 [51-250]

    PW - v244 - O 6 '97 - p57 [51-250]

Ducky (Illus. by David Wisniewski)
    BL - v93 - Ag '97 - p1905 [51-250]
    CBRS - v26 - O '97 - p13 [1-50]
    CCB-B - v51 - Ja '98 - p155+ [51-250]
    HB - v73 - N '97 - p668 [51-250]
    KR - v65 - Ag 1 '97 - p1219 [51-250]
    SLJ - v43 - S '97 - p173 [51-250]

*Flower Garden (Illus. by Kathryn
Hewitt)*
    ECEJ - v25 - Fall '97 - p46 [1-50]

*Fly Away Home (Illus. by Ronald
Himler)*
    ECEJ - v25 - Fall '97 - p46 [1-50]

Going Home (Illus. by David Diaz)
    NYTBR - v102 - My 11 '97 - p24 [501+]

*I Am the Mummy Heb-Nefert (Illus. by
David Christiana)*
    CBRS - v25 - My '97 - p114 [51-250]
    Ch BWatch - v7 - Ap '97 - p6 [1-50]
    HB Guide - v8 - Fall '97 - p297 [51-250]
    Magpies - v12 - My '97 - p41 [251-500]
    NYTBR - v102 - Ag 17 '97 - p19 [501+]
    SLJ - v43 - Ag '97 - p154 [51-250]

*I Don't Want to Go to Camp (Illus. by
Maryann Cocca-Leffler)*
    RT - v51 - O '97 - p151 [51-250]

*Moonstick: The Seasons of the Sioux
(Illus. by John Sandford)*
    BL - v94 - S 1 '97 - p132 [51-250]
    CBRS - v26 - D '97 - p43 [51-250]
    Ch BWatch - v7 - N '97 - p5 [1-50]
    KR - v65 - Jl 15 '97 - p1108 [51-250]

*My Backpack (Illus. by Maryann
Cocca-Leffler)*
    CBRS - v25 - Je '97 - p121 [51-250]
    HB Guide - v8 - Fall '97 - p260 [51-250]
    SLJ - v44 - Ap '98 - p91 [51-250]

*On Call Back Mountain (Illus. by
Barry Moser)*
    Ch BWatch - v7 - My '97 - p4 [1-50]
    Emerg Lib - v25 - N '97 - p55 [1-50]
    HB Guide - v8 - Fall '97 - p260 [51-250]

The Pumpkin Fair (Illus. by Eileen Christelow)

BL - v94 - N 1 '97 - p478+ [51-250]
KR - v65 - Je 15 '97 - p947 [51-250]
PW - v244 - My 26 '97 - p84 [51-250]
SLJ - v43 - S '97 - p173 [51-250]

Secret Place (Illus. by Ted Rand)

RT - v51 - O '97 - p152 [51-250]
SB - v33 - Ag '97 - p163 [1-50]

So Far from the Sea (Illus. by Chris K Soentpiet)

KR - v66 - Ap 15 '98 - p576 [51-250]

SOS Titanic

y   BL - v94 - Mr 15 '98 - p1244 [51-250]
y   JAAL - v40 - O '96 - p151+ [51-250]
    SE - v61 - Ap '97 - p7* [1-50]

Train to Somewhere (Illus. by Ronald Himler)

Emerg Lib - v24 - My '97 - p66 [51-250]

Trouble on the T-Ball Team (Illus. by Irene Trivas)

HB Guide - v8 - Fall '97 - p260 [51-250]
SLJ - v43 - My '97 - p93 [51-250]

Twinnies (Illus. by Nancy Carpenter)

BL - v94 - S 15 '97 - p240 [51-250]
CBRS - v26 - Ja '98 - p55 [51-250]
PW - v244 - Jl 21 '97 - p201+ [51-250]

The Wall (Ramirez). Audio Version

BL - v94 - S 15 '97 - p250 [51-250]

Your Move (Illus. by James Ransome)

BL - v94 - F 15 '98 - p1010 [51-250]
PW - v245 - F 23 '98 - p77 [51-250]

Bunting, Jane
My Little ABC Board Book

PW - v245 - Mr 23 '98 - p102 [1-50]

Burandt, Harriet
Tales from the Homeplace

CBRS - v25 - Je '97 - p129 [1-50]
y   CCB-B - v50 - Jl '97 - p388 [51-250]
    HB Guide - v8 - Fall '97 - p297 [51-250]
    SLJ - v43 - Ap '97 - p134 [51-250]
y   VOYA - v20 - D '97 - p314 [251-500]

Burby, Liza N
Family Violence

Ch BWatch - v8 - Ja '98 - p7 [1-50]

Burdett, Lois
Macbeth for Kids

CBRA - '96 - p496 [51-250]

A Midsummer Night's Dream for Kids

SLJ - v44 - F '98 - p96 [51-250]

Burgess, Melvin
An Angel for May

BL - v93 - Ag '97 - p1892 [1-50]

The Earth Giant (Illus. by Melvin Burgess)

BL - v94 - O 1 '97 - p328 [51-250]
KR - v65 - O 1 '97 - p1529 [51-250]

Junk

y   Bks Keeps - My '97 - p27 [51-250]
y   NS - v126 - D 5 '97 - p64 [51-250]
y   Obs - Jl 27 '97 - p15*+ [51-250]
    TES - My 2 '97 - p8* [1-50]
y   TES - N 7 '97 - p13* [1-50]

Kite

TES - D 12 '97 - p40 [51-250]

Burke, Patrick
Eastern Europe

Bks Keeps - S '97 - p28 [51-250]
Emerg Lib - v25 - N '97 - p54 [1-50]
HB Guide - v8 - Fall '97 - p390 [51-250]
Magpies - v12 - Jl '97 - p42 [251-500]
SLJ - v43 - Ag '97 - p164 [51-250]

Burke, Timothy
Tugboats in Action

HB Guide - v8 - Fall '97 - p357 [51-250]

Burke-Weiner, Kimberly
Penny Wishes

Ch BWatch - v7 - Ap '97 - p6 [1-50]

Burks, Brian
Walks Alone

y   KR - v66 - Mr 1 '98 - p336 [51-250]
    SLJ - v44 - Ap '98 - p128 [51-250]

Burleigh, Robert

Black Whiteness (Illus. by Walter Lyon Krudop)

    BL - v94 - Ja 1 '98 - p798 [51-250]
    HB - v74 - Mr '98 - p232+ [251-500]
    KR - v65 - D 1 '97 - p1773 [51-250]
    NYTBR - v103 - F 15 '98 - p25 [501+]
    PW - v244 - D 15 '97 - p58+ [51-250]
    SLJ - v44 - Mr '98 - p193 [51-250]

Hoops (Illus. by Stephen T Johnson)

    Am Vis - v12 - D '97 - p34 [1-50]
    BL - v94 - Ja 1 '98 - p734 [51-250]
    BL - v94 - Mr 15 '98 - p1224 [1-50]
    CBRS - v26 - F '98 - p78 [1-50]
    KR - v65 - S 1 '97 - p1385 [51-250]
    PW - v244 - O 6 '97 - p83 [51-250]
    SLJ - v43 - N '97 - p105 [51-250]
    SLJ - v43 - D '97 - p24 [1-50]
    SLJ - v44 - Mr '98 - p119 [1-50]

Who Said That? (Illus. by David Catrow)

    AB - v100 - N 17 '97 - p1271 [51-250]
    CBRS - v25 - Spr '97 - p141 [51-250]
    HB Guide - v8 - Fall '97 - p395 [51-250]
    SLJ - v43 - My '97 - p143 [51-250]

Burnard, Damon

Pork and Beef's Great Adventure (Illus. by Damon Burnard)

    BL - v94 - Mr 1 '98 - p1134 [51-250]
    PW - v245 - Mr 23 '98 - p99 [51-250]
    SLJ - v44 - Ap '98 - p91+ [51-250]

Burnett, Frances Hodgson

The Secret Garden

    Bks Keeps - My '97 - p28 [501+]
    TES - N 14 '97 - p11* [51-250]

The Secret Garden (McCaddon). Audio Version

    BL - v94 - F 15 '98 - p1026 [51-250]

The Secret Garden Book and Charm (Illus. by Tasha Tudor)

    PW - v244 - O 20 '97 - p78 [1-50]

Burnie, David

Concise Encyclopedia of the Human Body

  r ASBYP - v29 - Sum '96 - p6 [51-250]

Insects and Spiders

    KR - v65 - Jl 1 '97 - p1027 [51-250]

Microlife

    Emerg Lib - v25 - Ja '98 - p52 [1-50]

Seashore

    CLW - v68 - S '97 - p63 [1-50]
    Par Ch - Awards '97 - p9+ [51-250]

Burningham, John

Cloudland (Illus. by John Burningham)

    Bks Keeps - Jl '97 - p6+ [501+]
    Magpies - v12 - Mr '97 - p30 [51-250]

Get Off Our Train

    TES - N 14 '97 - p11* [51-250]

Burns, Diane L

Frogs, Toads and Turtles

    BL - v93 - Ag '97 - p1893 [51-250]

Burns, Marilyn

Spaghetti and Meatballs for All! (Illus. by Debbie Tilley)

    CCB-B - v51 - D '97 - p120 [51-250]
    PW - v244 - Jl 28 '97 - p75 [51-250]
    SLJ - v43 - S '97 - p173+ [51-250]

Burns, Peggy

Engineers

    TES - S 19 '97 - p16* [51-250]

Explorers

    TES - S 19 '97 - p16* [51-250]

Inventors

    TES - S 19 '97 - p16* [51-250]

Burr, Claudia

Broken Shields

    BL - v94 - D 1 '97 - p617 [51-250]
    CBRS - v26 - O '97 - p23 [51-250]
    HB - v73 - N '97 - p697+ [51-250]
    SLJ - v44 - Ja '98 - p120 [51-250]

Burrell, Roy E C

Oxford Children's Ancient History (Illus. by Peter Connolly)

  y NS - v126 - D 5 '97 - p66 [1-50]
    Spec - v279 - D 6 '97 - p44 [1-50]
    TES - D 26 '97 - p23 [251-500]

Burton, Eric
Going Places. Bks. 1-2
   TESL-EJ - v2 - Je '97 - pONL [501+]

Burton, John
Jungles and Rainforests
   Emerg Lib - v25 - N '97 - p55 [1-50]

Burton, Katherine
One Gray Mouse (Illus. by Kim Fernandes)
   CBRS - v26 - N '97 - p25+ [1-50]
   KR - v65 - Ag 1 '97 - p1219 [51-250]
   PW - v244 - S 1 '97 - p107 [1-50]
   SLJ - v43 - D '97 - p87 [51-250]

Burton, Virginia Lee
Calico the Wonder Horse
   PW - v244 - Jl 28 '97 - p76 [51-250]

Maybelle the Cable Car
   HB Guide - v8 - Fall '97 - p260 [51-250]

Bush, Karen
Handy Hints for Horse Persons (Illus. by Clare Corwin)
   Spec - v279 - D 6 '97 - p44 [51-250]

Busy (Machines)
   Ch BWatch - v7 - Je '97 - p4 [1-50]

Butcher, Kristin
The Runaways
   BIC - v26 - O '97 - p35 [501+]
   CM:CanRev - v4 - O 31 '97 - pONL [251-500]
   KR - v66 - Mr 15 '98 - p399 [51-250]
   Quill & Q - v63 - Ag '97 - p40 [251-500]
   SLJ - v44 - Ap '98 - p128 [51-250]

Butcher, Nancy
Princess Ballerina
   Ch BWatch - v8 - Ja '98 - p5 [1-50]

Butler, Daphne
Caring for Young
   ASBYP - v29 - Sum '96 - p56+ [501+]

Finding Shelter
   ASBYP - v29 - Sum '96 - p56+ [501+]

Fire Burns
   ASBYP - v29 - Sum '96 - p61+ [251-500]

Flowers Grow
   ASBYP - v29 - Sum '96 - p61+ [251-500]

Food Cooks
   ASBYP - v29 - Sum '96 - p61+ [251-500]

Gathering Food
   ASBYP - v29 - Sum '96 - p56+ [501+]

Getting Around
   ASBYP - v29 - Sum '96 - p56+ [501+]

People Talk
   ASBYP - v29 - Sum '96 - p61+ [251-500]

Rain Falls
   ASBYP - v29 - Sum '96 - p61+ [251-500]

Volcanoes Erupt
   ASBYP - v29 - Sum '96 - p61+ [251-500]

Wheels Turn
   ASBYP - v29 - Sum '96 - p61+ [251-500]

Wind Blows
   ASBYP - v29 - Sum '96 - p61+ [251-500]

Butler, Dori Hillestad
The Great Tooth Fairy (Illus. by Jack Lindstrom)
   HB Guide - v8 - Fall '97 - p260 [51-250]

Butler, Geoff
The Killick: A Newfoundland Story
   Can CL - v22 - Win '96 - p121+ [501+]

Butler, Jerry
A Drawing in the Sand (Illus. by Jerry Butler)
   HMR - Fall '97 - p37 [501+]

Butterfield, Moira
Big and Bulky (Illus. by Wayne Ford)
   Bks Keeps - S '97 - p24 [51-250]

Big, Rough, and Wrinkly (Illus. by Wayne Ford)

> HB Guide - v8 - Fall '97 - p353 [51-250]
> SB - v33 - Je '97 - p144 [51-250]

Brown, Fierce, and Furry (Illus. by Wayne Ford)

> Bks Keeps - S '97 - p24 [51-250]
> HB Guide - v8 - Fall '97 - p353 [51-250]
> SB - v33 - Je '97 - p144 [51-250]
> SLJ - v43 - Jl '97 - p80 [51-250]

Colourful and Bright (Illus. by Wayne Ford)

> Bks Keeps - S '97 - p24 [51-250]

Fast, Strong, and Striped (Illus. by Wayne Ford)

> HB Guide - v8 - Fall '97 - p353 [51-250]
> SLJ - v43 - Jl '97 - p80 [51-250]

Hansel and Gretel (Illus. by Frances Cony)

> SLJ - v44 - F '98 - p96 [51-250]

Little Red Riding Hood (Illus. by Frances Cony)

> SLJ - v44 - Mr '98 - p193+ [51-250]

Puss-in-Boots (Illus. by Sue Cony)

> SLJ - v44 - Mr '98 - p193+ [51-250]

Quick, Quiet, and Feathered (Illus. by Wayne Ford)

> HB Guide - v8 - Fall '97 - p351 [1-50]

Scaly and Snappy (Illus. by Wayne Ford)

> Bks Keeps - S '97 - p24 [51-250]

Sleeping Beauty (Illus. by Sue Cony)

> SLJ - v44 - F '98 - p96 [51-250]

Strong and Stripy (Illus. by Wayne Ford)

> Bks Keeps - S '97 - p24 [51-250]

Swift and Silent (Illus. by Wayne Ford)

> Bks Keeps - S '97 - p24 [51-250]

Butterworth, Nick
The Badger's Bath (Briers) (Illus. by Nick Butterworth). Book and Audio Version

> TES - N 7 '97 - p13* [1-50]

The Hedgehog's Balloon (Briers). Book and Audio Version

> TES - N 7 '97 - p13* [1-50]

Percy's Friends (Briers) (Illus. by Nick Butterworth). Book and Audio Version

> TES - N 7 '97 - p13* [1-50]

Thud

> Obs - D 7 '97 - p17* [51-250]

The Treasure Hunt (Briers). Book and Audio Version

> TES - N 7 '97 - p13* [1-50]

Butts, Nancy
The Door in the Lake

> y   KR - v66 - Ap 15 '98 - p577 [51-250]
> PW - v245 - Mr 23 '98 - p100+ [51-250]

Buxton, Jane
Donkey Dust

> Magpies - v12 - Jl '97 - p7*+ [51-250]

Byars, Betsy Cromer
Ant Plays Bear (Illus. by Marc Simont)

> BL - v94 - S 1 '97 - p116 [51-250]
> BL - v94 - Ja 1 '98 - p735 [1-50]
> CCB-B - v51 - S '97 - p7 [51-250]
> HB - v73 - Jl '97 - p451+ [51-250]
> KR - v65 - My 15 '97 - p797 [51-250]
> Par - v72 - D '97 - p204 [1-50]
> SLJ - v43 - Je '97 - p79 [51-250]

Bingo Brown, Gypsy Lover

> SLJ - v44 - Ja '98 - p42 [1-50]

Dead Letter

> RT - v51 - O '97 - p141 [1-50]

Death's Door

> CCB-B - v50 - Je '97 - p351 [51-250]
> HB Guide - v8 - Fall '97 - p297 [51-250]
> SLJ - v43 - Je '97 - p114 [51-250]

Disappearing Acts
>   BL - v94 - Mr 1 '98 - p1134 [51-250]
>   KR - v66 - Ja 1 '98 - p54+ [51-250]
>   SLJ - v44 - Mr '98 - p211 [51-250]

The Golly Sisters Ride Again (Illus. by Sue Truesdell)
>   BL - v93 - Je 1 '97 - p1700 [1-50]

The Golly Sisters Ride Again (Critt). Audio Version
>   BL - v94 - F 15 '98 - p1027 [51-250]

Tarot Says Beware (Fairman). Audio Version
> y   Kliatt - v31 - Jl '97 - p52 [51-250]
>   SLJ - v43 - Ap '97 - p83 [51-250]

Tornado (Illus. by Doron Ben-Ami)
>   RT - v51 - O '97 - p139 [1-50]
>   RT - v51 - N '97 - p244 [51-250]
>   RT - v51 - N '97 - p254 [51-250]

The TV Kid
>   PW - v245 - Ja 19 '98 - p380 [1-50]

Bydlinski, Georg
The Shadow Jumper and the Monster
>   CBRA - '96 - p468 [51-250]

Byman, Jeremy
Madam Secretary
> y   BL - v94 - D 15 '97 - p688 [51-250]
>   SLJ - v44 - Ap '98 - p142 [51-250]

C

Caboodle: The Interactive Kids' Magazine. Electronic Media Version

p   SLMQ - v25 - Win '97 - p119 [51-250]

Cabrera, Jane

Cat's Colors (Illus. by Jane Cabrera)
> BL - v94 - Ja 1 '98 - p735 [1-50]
> CBRS - v25 - Ag '97 - p158 [1-50]
> CCB-B - v50 - Jl '97 - p388+ [51-250]
> HB Guide - v8 - Fall '97 - p260 [51-250]
> SLJ - v43 - My '97 - p93 [51-250]

Cat's Colours (Illus. by Jane Cabrera)
> Books - v11 - Je '97 - p21 [51-250]
> Sch Lib - v45 - Ag '97 - p130 [51-250]

Cadnum, Michael

The Lost and Found House (Illus. by Steve Johnson)
> BL - v94 - D 1 '97 - p639 [51-250]
> CBRS - v26 - F '98 - p73+ [51-250]
> CCB-B - v51 - O '97 - p45 [51-250]
> KR - v65 - S 1 '97 - p1386 [51-250]
> NYTBR - v102 - N 9 '97 - p24 [1-50]
> PW - v244 - O 13 '97 - p74 [51-250]
> SLJ - v43 - N '97 - p78 [51-250]

Caduto, Michael J

The Crimson Elf (Illus. by Tom Sarmo)
> AB - v100 - N 17 '97 - p1264 [51-250]
> BL - v93 - Ag '97 - p1893 [51-250]
> HB Guide - v8 - Fall '97 - p331 [51-250]
> SLJ - v43 - Ag '97 - p145+ [51-250]

Earth Tales from around the World (Illus. by Adelaide Murphy Tyrol)
> AB - v100 - N 17 '97 - p1264 [51-250]
> CAY - v18 - Win '97 - p2 [51-250]
> PW - v244 - O 27 '97 - p79 [1-50]
> VOYA - v21 - Ap '98 - p80+ [51-250]

Keepers of the Animals
> Ch BWatch - v7 - Jl '97 - p7 [51-250]

Caffrey, Jaye Andras

First Star I See (Illus. by Tracy L Kane)
> Ch BWatch - v7 - Ap '97 - p4 [51-250]
> SLJ - v43 - Ap '97 - p91 [51-250]

Cain, Sheridan

Why So Sad, Brown Rabbit? (Illus. by Jo Kelly)
> BL - v94 - Ja 1 '98 - p822 [51-250]
> KR - v65 - N 15 '97 - p1705 [51-250]
> PW - v245 - Ja 19 '98 - p377 [51-250]
> SLJ - v44 - F '98 - p79 [51-250]

Caldwell, Chris

Alsek's ABC Adventure (Illus. by Chris Caldwell)
> CBRA - '96 - p436 [51-250]

Caldwell, Norm

Lunch Box Notes
> Ch BWatch - v8 - Ja '98 - p1 [51-250]

Calhoun, B B

Bite Makes Right (Illus. by Daniel Mark Duffy)
> SB - v33 - O '97 - p195 [51-250]

The Competition (Illus. by Daniel Mark Duffy)
ASBYP - v29 - Sum '96 - p46 [51-250]

Fair Play (Illus. by Daniel Mark Duffy)
SB - v33 - O '97 - p195 [1-50]

On the Right Track (Illus. by Daniel Mark Duffy)
SB - v33 - O '97 - p195 [1-50]

Out of Place (Illus. by Daniel Mark Duffy)
SB - v33 - O '97 - p195 [1-50]

The Raptor's Claw (Illus. by Danny O'Leary)
ASBYP - v29 - Sum '96 - p46 [51-250]

Calhoun, Mary
Flood (Illus. by Erick Ingraham)
Ch BWatch - v7 - My '97 - p2 [1-50]
HB Guide - v8 - Fall '97 - p260 [51-250]
SB - v33 - Ag '97 - p163 [1-50]
SLJ - v43 - My '97 - p93 [51-250]

Call of Cthulhu: Dreamlands. 4th Ed.
r   Ch BWatch - v7 - Jl '97 - p5 [1-50]

Calmenson, Stephanie
Engine, Engine, Number Nine (Illus. by Paul Meisel)
CBRS - v25 - Je '97 - p121 [51-250]
HB Guide - v8 - Fall '97 - p260 [51-250]
SLJ - v43 - Jl '97 - p60 [51-250]

Rockin' Reptiles (Illus. by Lynn Munsinger)
HB Guide - v8 - Fall '97 - p289 [51-250]
SLJ - v43 - Ap '97 - p91 [51-250]

Rosie: A Visiting Dog's Story
JOYS - v10 - Sum '97 - p427 [1-50]

Calvert, Frankie
The Sea Serpent
Bks Keeps - S '97 - p28 [51-250]
y   Sch Lib - v45 - Ag '97 - p157 [51-250]
TES - O 10 '97 - p8* [51-250]

Calvert, Patricia
Great Lives: The American Frontier
BL - v94 - F 15 '98 - p1001+ [51-250]
y   KR - v65 - N 1 '97 - p1642 [51-250]
SLJ - v44 - Ja '98 - p120 [251-500]

Sooner
KR - v66 - Mr 15 '98 - p400 [51-250]

Calvert, Samantha
We're Talking about Vegetarianism
Sch Lib - v45 - Ag '97 - p149 [51-250]
y   TES - D 26 '97 - p23 [501+]

Cameron, Ann
El Jugar Mas Bonito Del Mundo (Illus. by Thomas B Allen)
BL - v93 - Ag '97 - p1913 [1-50]

More Stories Huey Tells (Illus. by Lis Toft)
CCB-B - v50 - Jl '97 - p389 [51-250]
HB - v73 - Jl '97 - p452+ [51-250]
HB Guide - v8 - Fall '97 - p289 [51-250]
Inst - v107 - S '97 - p21 [51-250]
NYTBR - v102 - Ag 31 '97 - p13 [1-50]
SLJ - v43 - Je '97 - p85 [51-250]

The Secret Life of Amanda K. Woods
KR - v66 - Mr 1 '98 - p336 [51-250]
PW - v245 - Mr 23 '98 - p101 [51-250]

Camp, Carole Ann
Invitations to Cells
SB - v33 - Ap '97 - p67 [51-250]

Invitations to Evolving
SB - v33 - Ap '97 - p67 [51-250]

Invitations to Heredity
SB - v33 - Ap '97 - p67 [51-250]

Sally Ride: First American Woman in Space
y   BL - v94 - Ja 1 '98 - p788 [51-250]
SLJ - v43 - D '97 - p133+ [51-250]

Camp, Lindsay
Billy and the Barglebogle (Illus. by Peter Utton)
Bks Keeps - Jl '97 - p19 [51-250]

Campbell, Ann

The New York Public Library Amazing Space (Illus. by Jessica Wolk-Stanley)

r   New Sci - v156 - O 4 '97 - p45 [1-50]
      SB - v33 - Ag '97 - p177 [51-250]
      SLJ - v43 - Jl '97 - p100 [51-250]
      S&T - v94 - N '97 - p74+ [501+]

The New York Public Library Incredible Earth (Illus. by Jessica Wolk-Stanley)

r   Magpies - v12 - Mr '97 - p43+ [51-250]

Campbell, Eric

Elephant Gold

      Magpies - v12 - S '97 - p33 [251-500]

Campbell, Jim

Cal Ripken, Jr.

      Ch BWatch - v7 - Je '97 - p2 [1-50]
      HB Guide - v8 - Fall '97 - p368 [51-250]

Campbell, Joanna

A Horse Called Wonder

      JOYS - v10 - Spr '97 - p261 [1-50]

Campbell, Judith

Relationships (Illus. by Teco G Rodrigues)

      CBRA - '96 - p526 [51-250]

Campbell, Peter A

Launch Day (Illus. by Peter A Campbell)

      ASBYP - v29 - Sum '96 - p6+ [251-500]

Campbell, Rod

Little Bird (Illus. by Rod Campbell)

      Bks Keeps - Jl '97 - p19 [51-250]

Campling, Annie

And the Stars Were Gold

      TES - Ja 9 '98 - p17* [251-500]

Cann, Kate

Living in the World (Illus. by Derek Matthews)

      SLJ - v44 - Ja '98 - p120 [51-250]

Cannon, Janell

Stellaluna. Electronic Media Version

      Emerg Lib - v25 - N '97 - p48 [51-250]
      Par - v72 - Je '97 - p194 [51-250]

Stellaluna: A Pop-up Book and Mobile (Illus. by Janell Cannon)

      Ch BWatch - v7 - O '97 - p1 [1-50]
      NYTBR - v102 - N 16 '97 - p26 [1-50]
      PW - v244 - S 1 '97 - p107 [1-50]

Verdi (Illus. by Janell Cannon)

      CBRS - v25 - Je '97 - p126 [51-250]
      CCB-B - v50 - Je '97 - p351+ [51-250]
      Ch BWatch - v7 - Ap '97 - p6 [1-50]
      HB Guide - v8 - Fall '97 - p289 [51-250]
      Inst - v107 - N '97 - p22+ [51-250]
      Magpies - v12 - S '97 - p28 [51-250]
      NY - v73 - O 6 '97 - p116 [51-250]
      NYTBR - v102 - Je 1 '97 - p36 [1-50]
      NYTLa - v147 - D 4 '97 - pE8 [51-250]
      SB - v33 - Ag '97 - p163 [1-50]
      Sch Lib - v45 - N '97 - p184 [51-250]
      SLJ - v43 - My '97 - p93+ [51-250]
      TES - O 3 '97 - p9* [501+]

Capucilli, Alyssa

Biscuit Finds a Friend (Illus. by Pat Schories)

      HB Guide - v8 - Fall '97 - p249 [51-250]
      SLJ - v43 - Je '97 - p85 [51-250]

Caras, Roger A

A Most Dangerous Journey (Illus. by Roger A Caras)

      ASBYP - v29 - Sum '96 - p7+ [251-500]

Carbone, Elisa Lynn

Starting School with an Enemy

      CCB-B - v51 - Ap '98 - p276+ [51-250]

Career Discovery Encyclopedia. 3rd Ed., Vols. 1-6

yr   BL - v93 - Ag '97 - p1923+ [501+]
r   Ch BWatch - v7 - Je '97 - p8 [51-250]

Carey, Peter

American Dreams (Illus. by Gregory Rogers)

      Magpies - v12 - My '97 - p37 [251-500]

The Big Bazoohley (Illus. by Abira Ali)

    Can CL - v23 - Sum '97 - p79+ [501+]

Carle, Eric

Catch the Ball (Illus. by Eric Carle)

    PW - v245 - F 16 '98 - p213 [1-50]

Flora and Tiger (Illus. by Eric Carle)

    BL - v94 - D 15 '97 - p692 [51-250]
    CBRS - v26 - D '97 - p43 [51-250]
    CCB-B - v51 - Ja '98 - p156 [51-250]
    Ch BWatch - v8 - Ja '98 - p2 [1-50]
    NYTBR - v102 - N 23 '97 - p32 [1-50]
    PW - v244 - S 22 '97 - p82 [51-250]
    SLJ - v44 - F '98 - p113 [51-250]

From Head to Toe (Illus. by Eric Carle)

    CCB-B - v50 - Je '97 - p352 [51-250]
    HB Guide - v8 - Fall '97 - p355 [1-50]
    Par - v72 - D '97 - p201 [1-50]
    SLJ - v43 - Ap '97 - p120 [51-250]

Hello, Red Fox (Illus. by Eric Carle)

    KR - v66 - F 1 '98 - p194 [51-250]
    PW - v245 - Ja 26 '98 - p91 [51-250]

A House for Hermit Crab (Illus. by Eric Carle)

    Books - v11 - Je '97 - p21 [51-250]
    Magpies - v12 - Jl '97 - p26+ [51-250]
    Sch Lib - v45 - Ag '97 - p130 [51-250]

Let's Paint a Rainbow (Illus. by Eric Carle)

    PW - v245 - F 16 '98 - p213 [1-50]

Little Cloud

    Sch Lib - v45 - N '97 - p184 [51-250]

Papa, Please Get the Moon for Me

    Magpies - v12 - Mr '97 - p26 [51-250]

The Secret Birthday

    PW - v245 - F 16 '98 - p213 [1-50]

Today Is Monday (Illus. by Eric Carle)

    PW - v244 - Je 30 '97 - p77 [1-50]

The Very Hungry Caterpillar (Illus. by Eric Carle)

    Inst - v106 - Ap '97 - p4* [1-50]
    NYTBR - v102 - N 16 '97 - p26 [1-50]

The Very Quiet Cricket (Illus. by Eric Carle)

    Bks Keeps - N '97 - p5+ [51-250]
    HB Guide - v8 - Fall '97 - p249 [51-250]

What's for Lunch (Illus. by Eric Carle)

    PW - v245 - F 16 '98 - p213 [1-50]

Carlson, Laurie

Boss of the Plains (Illus. by Holly Meade)

    BL - v94 - Mr 1 '98 - p1138 [51-250]
    KR - v66 - Ja 15 '98 - p109 [51-250]
    SLJ - v44 - Ap '98 - p113 [51-250]

Colonial Kids

    BL - v94 - F 15 '98 - p1002 [51-250]
    PW - v244 - N 24 '97 - p76 [1-50]
    SLJ - v44 - Mr '98 - p194 [51-250]

Carlson, Lori M

Sol A Sol (Illus. by Emily Lisker)

    PW - v245 - Mr 23 '98 - p98 [51-250]
    SLJ - v44 - Mr '98 - p194 [51-250]

Carlson, Nancy L

ABC, I Like Me! (Illus. by Nancy L Carlson)

    Ch BWatch - v7 - Je '97 - p6 [1-50]
    HB Guide - v8 - Fall '97 - p260 [51-250]
    SLJ - v43 - Je '97 - p85 [51-250]

I Like Me! (Weeks) (Illus. by Nancy L Carlson). Book and Audio Version

    SLJ - v43 - My '97 - p87 [51-250]

Me Gusto Como Soy! (Illus. by Nancy L Carlson)

    BL - v94 - D 15 '97 - p707 [1-50]

Carlstrom, Nancy White

Baby-O (Illus. by Sucie Stevenson)

    ECEJ - v25 - Fall '97 - p46 [1-50]

Does God Know How to Tie Shoes?. Book and Audio Version

    Ch BWatch - v7 - Mr '97 - p7 [51-250]

Guess Who's Coming, Jesse Bear (Illus. by Bruce Degen)

    BL - v94 - F 15 '98 - p1018 [51-250]
    KR - v66 - F 1 '98 - p194 [51-250]

PW - v245 - F 23 '98 - p78 [1-50]
SLJ - v44 - Ap '98 - p97 [51-250]

It's about Time, Jesse Bear (Illus. by Bruce Degen)
PW - v245 - Mr 9 '98 - p70 [1-50]

Midnight Dance of the Snowshoe Hare (Illus. by Ken Kuroi)
PW - v245 - Mr 9 '98 - p70 [1-50]

Raven and River (Illus. by Jon Van Zyle)
CCB-B - v50 - Je '97 - p352 [51-250]
Ch BWatch - v7 - My '97 - p3 [1-50]
HB Guide - v8 - Fall '97 - p261 [51-250]
KR - v65 - Ap 15 '97 - p638 [51-250]
SLJ - v43 - Ap '97 - p91 [51-250]

Carmichael, Claire
Doctor Death
Magpies - v12 - S '97 - p32+ [51-250]

Carmichael, Clay
Used-Up Bear (Illus. by Clay Carmichael)
KR - v66 - Mr 15 '98 - p400 [51-250]

Carmody, Isobelle
Greylands
Aust Bk R - O '97 - p58+ [501+]

Carnell, Suzanne
A Treasury of Pet Stories (Illus. by Michael Reid)
BL - v93 - Ag '97 - p1902 [51-250]
SLJ - v43 - D '97 - p87 [51-250]

Carney, Margaret
At Grandpa's Sugar Bush (Illus. by Janet Wilson)
KR - v66 - Mr 1 '98 - p336 [51-250]
SLJ - v44 - Ap '98 - p114 [51-250]

Carolan, Trevor
Big Whiskers Saves the Cove (Illus. by Jim Collins)
CBRA - '96 - p436 [51-250]

Carpenter, Angelica Shirley
Robert Louis Stevenson: Finding Treasure Island
y   Ch BWatch - v7 - O '97 - p5 [51-250]
SLJ - v43 - D '97 - p134 [51-250]

Carpenter, Humphrey
More Shakespeare without the Boring Bits
Bks Keeps - My '97 - p27 [51-250]
TES - My 9 '97 - p10 [251-500]

Music
Sch Lib - v45 - Ag '97 - p149 [51-250]

The Puffin Book of Classic Children's Stories (Illus. by Diz Wallis)
Magpies - v12 - Mr '97 - p8+ [251-500]

Carpenter, Zelma V
People and Plants
ASBYP - v29 - Sum '96 - p8 [51-250]

Carpenter-Davis, Sandra
Bounce Me, Tickle Me, Hug Me (Illus. by Trevor Black)
Quill & Q - v64 - Ja '98 - p36+ [251-500]

Carreiro, Carolyn
Hand-Print Animal Art (Illus. by Carolyn Carreiro)
CCB-B - v51 - Mr '98 - p238 [51-250]
Ch BWatch - v8 - Ja '98 - p6 [1-50]
SLJ - v44 - Ap '98 - p114 [51-250]

Carreno, Mada
La Pulga Cecilia (Illus. by Khitish Chatterjee)
SLJ - v43 - N '97 - p136 [51-250]

Carrick, Carol
Melanie (Illus. by Alisher Dianov)
RT - v51 - O '97 - p151+ [51-250]

Carrier, Roch
The Basketball Player (Illus. by Sheldon Cohen)
y   BIC - v26 - Ap '97 - p34+ [501+]
CBRA - '96 - p436+ [51-250]

The Hockey Sweater (Illus. by Sheldon Cohen)

Ch Bk News - v20 - Spr '97 - p34 [251-500]

Carrillo, Louis
Edward James Olmos

HB Guide - v8 - Fall '97 - p379 [51-250]

Carroll, Jane
Jade McKade (Illus. by Virginia Barrett)

Magpies - v12 - My '97 - p30+ [51-250]

Carrow, Robert
Put a Fan in Your Hat! (Illus. by Rick Brown)

Ch BWatch - v7 - S '97 - p4 [1-50]
y   SB - v33 - O '97 - p206 [51-250]
SLJ - v43 - My '97 - p143 [51-250]

Turn on the Lights--from Bed! (Illus. by Rick Brown)

Ch BWatch - v7 - S '97 - p4 [1-50]
SLJ - v43 - Jl '97 - p100 [51-250]

Carter, Alden R
Big Brother Dustin (Illus. by Dan Young)

BL - v93 - Ag '97 - p1905 [51-250]
HB Guide - v8 - Fall '97 - p249 [51-250]
SLJ - v43 - Je '97 - p85 [51-250]

Carter, David A
Alpha Bugs

Par - v72 - Je '97 - p189 [1-50]

Bugs in Space

PW - v244 - S 29 '97 - p91 [1-50]

If You're Happy and You Know It, Clap Your Hands

HB Guide - v8 - Fall '97 - p365 [51-250]
Learning - v26 - S '97 - p45 [1-50]

Carter, Dorothy
Bye, Mis' Lela (Illus. by Harvey Stevenson)

BL - v94 - F 15 '98 - p1018 [51-250]
KR - v66 - Ja 1 '98 - p55 [51-250]
SLJ - v44 - Mr '98 - p168 [51-250]

Carter, Jimmy
Talking Peace. Rev. Ed.

SE - v61 - S '97 - p270 [1-50]

Carter, Penny
A Big Trip for the Morrisons (Illus. by Penny Carter)

BL - v93 - Je 1 '97 - p1716 [51-250]
HB Guide - v8 - Fall '97 - p261 [51-250]
KR - v65 - My 15 '97 - p798 [51-250]
SLJ - v43 - Ag '97 - p129 [51-250]

Cartlidge, Michelle
The Mice of Mousehole (Illus. by Michelle Cartlidge)

Books - v11 - Je '97 - p21 [1-50]
HB Guide - v8 - Fall '97 - p249 [51-250]

Carusone, Al
Teacher's Pet

Ch BWatch - v8 - Ja '98 - p5 [1-50]

Cary, Alice
Katherine Paterson

SLJ - v43 - Jl '97 - p100 [51-250]

Casanova, Mary
Wolf Shadows

BL - v94 - O 1 '97 - p328 [51-250]

Cascone, A G
Ghost Knight

Ch BWatch - v7 - Jl '97 - p5 [1-50]

It Came from the Deep

Ch BWatch - v7 - Mr '97 - p3 [51-250]

Caseley, Judith
Dorothy's Darkest Days (Illus. by Judith Caseley)

BL - v93 - Ag '97 - p1900 [51-250]
CCB-B - v51 - S '97 - p7 [51-250]
y   Ch BWatch - v8 - Ja '98 - p4 [1-50]
KR - v65 - Je 15 '97 - p947 [51-250]
SLJ - v43 - Ag '97 - p129 [51-250]

Jorah's Journal (Illus. by Judith Caseley)

HB Guide - v8 - Fall '97 - p289 [51-250]
NYTBR - v102 - S 28 '97 - p28 [1-50]

SLJ - v43 - Je '97 - p85 [51-250]

Caserta, Carmen
The Dog Ate My Homework (Illus. by Megan Jeffery)
Ch BWatch - v7 - S '97 - p3 [51-250]

Casey, Moe
The Most Excellent Book of Dress Up (Illus. by Rob Shone)
Ch BWatch - v7 - My '97 - p7 [51-250]
HB Guide - v8 - Fall '97 - p362 [51-250]
SLJ - v43 - Ag '97 - p164+ [51-250]

Casey, Patricia
Animals in the City
Sch Lib - v45 - N '97 - p184 [51-250]
TES - N 7 '97 - p5* [1-50]

Beep! Beep! Oink! Oink! Animals in the City (Illus. by Patricia Casey)
PW - v244 - Ag 25 '97 - p71 [51-250]
SLJ - v43 - N '97 - p78 [51-250]

Casey, Susan
Women Invent
y   Kliatt - v32 - Ja '98 - p30 [51-250]
PW - v244 - N 17 '97 - p63 [51-250]

Cassidy, Anne
Spider Pie (Illus. by Bee Willey)
Bks Keeps - S '97 - p25 [51-250]

Cassidy, John
Devil Sticks for the Complete Klutz
PW - v244 - Je 23 '97 - p93 [51-250]

Zap Science
PW - v244 - O 6 '97 - p84 [51-250]

Casteneda, Omar
Abuela's Weave
Emerg Lib - v25 - Ja '98 - p45 [51-250]

Castle, Caroline
Phoebe and the Monster Maze (Illus. by Susie Jenkin-Pearce)
KR - v65 - N 1 '97 - p1642 [51-250]

Castor, Harriet
Ballet Stories (Illus. by Sally Holmes)
SLJ - v44 - Ja '98 - p111 [51-250]

Queen Victoria
TES - S 19 '97 - p16* [51-250]

Wolfgang Amadeus Mozart
TES - S 19 '97 - p16* [51-250]

Caswell, Brian
Only the Heart
y   Aust Bk R - Ag '97 - p56+ [501+]
Magpies - v12 - Jl '97 - p36 [51-250]

Relax Max!
Aust Bk R - Ap '97 - p63 [501+]

Cate, Dick
Bernard's Magic
TES - N 7 '97 - p8* [1-50]

Cather, Willa
O Pioneers
AL - v69 - S '97 - p657 [1-50]
CSM - v90 - F 24 '98 - p16 [1-50]

Catling, Patrick Skene
The Chocolate Touch II (Illus. by Philip Hopman)
Sch Lib - v45 - N '97 - p190 [51-250]

Caudill, Rebecca
A Certain Small Shepherd (Illus. by William Pene Du Bois)
PW - v244 - O 6 '97 - p59 [1-50]

Caughey, Ellen
My Bible for Preschoolers
Ch BWatch - v7 - Mr '97 - p7 [51-250]

Caughill, Michael
Disney's Hercules: The Heart of a Hero (Illus. by Gita Lloyd)
Ch BWatch - v7 - D '97 - p2 [51-250]

Causley, Charles
Quack! Said the Billy-Goat (Illus. by Barbara Firth)
Bks Keeps - Jl '97 - p20 [51-250]

Selected Poems for Children (Illus. by John Lawrence)
Spec - v279 - D 6 '97 - p44 [1-50]
TES - S 12 '97 - p7* [501+]
TES - N 7 '97 - p2* [51-250]
TLS - D 26 '97 - p23 [501+]

Cave, Kathryn
My Journey through Art
Inst - v106 - My '97 - p4* [1-50]

Something Else (Illus. by Chris Riddell)
TES - Ap 18 '97 - p12* [1-50]

Cazet, Denys
Born in the Gravy
ECEJ - v25 - Fall '97 - p46 [1-50]

Night Lights (Illus. by Denys Cazet)
HB Guide - v8 - Fall '97 - p376 [1-50]
SLJ - v43 - My '97 - p99 [51-250]

CDs, Super Glue, and Salsa Series 2. Vols. 1-2
r   SLJ - v43 - Ag '97 - p182 [51-250]

Cech, John
My Grandmother's Journey (Illus. by Sharon McGinley-Nally)
PW - v245 - Ja 26 '98 - p93 [1-50]

Cecil, Laura
The Frog Princess (Illus. by Emma Chichester Clark)
SLJ - v43 - N '97 - p40 [1-50]

Ceng, Yangqing
Yuanyuan De Facai Meng (Illus. by Zonghui Liu)
Bkbird - v34 - Win '96 - p55 [51-250]

Cerasini, Marc
Diana: Queen of Hearts
BL - v94 - D 1 '97 - p617 [51-250]

The Twelve Labors of Hercules (Illus. by Isidre Mones)
SLJ - v44 - F '98 - p96 [51-250]

Cerullo, Mary M
The Octopus: Phantom of the Sea (Illus. by Jeffrey L Rotman)
Ch BWatch - v7 - Ap '97 - p3 [1-50]
Emerg Lib - v25 - Ja '98 - p57 [51-250]
HB Guide - v8 - Fall '97 - p349 [51-250]
SB - v33 - D '97 - p275 [51-250]
SLJ - v43 - D '97 - p24 [1-50]
SLJ - v43 - D '97 - p134 [51-250]

Sharks: Challengers of the Deep (Illus. by Jeffrey L Rotman)
SLJ - v43 - My '97 - p56 [1-50]

Cha, Dia
Dia's Story Cloth (Illus. by Chu Cha)
PW - v245 - Mr 16 '98 - p67 [1-50]
SE - v61 - Ap '97 - p9* [1-50]

Chadwick, Bruce
John Madden
Ch BWatch - v7 - Je '97 - p2 [1-50]
HB Guide - v8 - Fall '97 - p369 [51-250]

Chaikin, Miriam
Clouds of Glory (Illus. by David Frampton)
KR - v66 - F 15 '98 - p264 [51-250]
PW - v245 - F 23 '98 - p67 [51-250]
SLJ - v44 - Ap '98 - p142 [51-250]

Chalk, Gary
Gary Chalk's Hide and Seek in History
Ch BWatch - v7 - O '97 - p7 [1-50]
HB Guide - v8 - Fall '97 - p386 [51-250]
Sch Lib - v45 - Ag '97 - p130 [51-250]
SLJ - v43 - D '97 - p106+ [51-250]

Challoner, Jack
Flight
SB - v32 - D '96 - p257 [1-50]

Chalmers, Aldie
In-Line Skating
SLJ - v44 - Mr '98 - p230 [51-250]

Chambers, Catherine

Africa

>Sch Lib - v45 - Ag '97 - p153+ [51-250]
>
>SLJ - v43 - Jl '97 - p100+ [51-250]

All Saints, All Souls, and Halloween

>Ch BWatch - v7 - O '97 - p5 [51-250]
>
>HB Guide - v8 - Fall '97 - p329 [51-250]

Bark

>ASBYP - v29 - Fall '96 - p69 [501+]

Chinese New Year

>Emerg Lib - v25 - N '97 - p54 [1-50]
>
>HB Guide - v8 - Fall '97 - p329 [51-250]

Christmas

>HB Guide - v8 - Fall '97 - p320 [51-250]

Grasses

>ASBYP - v29 - Fall '96 - p69 [501+]

The History of Emigration from Africa

>Bks Keeps - My '97 - p26 [51-250]
>
>HB Guide - v8 - Fall '97 - p392 [51-250]
>
>TES - S 19 '97 - p16* [501+]

Nuts

>ASBYP - v29 - Fall '96 - p69 [501+]

Shells

>ASBYP - v29 - Fall '96 - p69 [501+]

Stones

>ASBYP - v29 - Fall '96 - p69 [501+]

Wood

>ASBYP - v29 - Fall '96 - p69 [501+]

Chambers, Veronica

Amistad Rising (Illus. by Paul Lee)

>BL - v94 - F 15 '98 - p1003 [51-250]
>
>KR - v66 - Mr 1 '98 - p336+ [51-250]
>
>PW - v245 - Mr 16 '98 - p64 [51-250]
>
>SLJ - v44 - Ap '98 - p97 [51-250]

Chan, Arlene

Spirit of the Dragon

>Ch Bk News - v20 - Sum '97 - p30 [51-250]
>
>CM:CanRev - v4 - O 31 '97 - pONL [251-500]

Chan, Barbara

Kid Pix around the World

>TESL-EJ - v2 - Ja '97 - pONL [501+]

Chan, Gillian

Golden Girl and Other Stories

>y   BL - v94 - S 15 '97 - p220 [51-250]
>
>y   Can CL - v22 - Win '96 - p106+ [501+]
>
>CBRS - v26 - N '97 - p33 [51-250]
>
>y   CCB-B - v51 - Ja '98 - p156 [51-250]
>
>y   KR - v65 - Ag 1 '97 - p1219 [51-250]
>
>y   SLJ - v43 - N '97 - p114 [51-250]

Chancellor, Deborah

Travelling on Land

>Sch Lib - v45 - N '97 - p203 [51-250]

Chandler, Clare

Carnival

>Sch Lib - v45 - Ag '97 - p149 [51-250]

Chandler, Gary

Alternative Energy Sources

>ASBYP - v29 - Fall '96 - p55+ [501+]
>
>SB - v32 - D '96 - p271 [51-250]
>
>SB - v33 - Ag '97 - p163 [1-50]

Environmental Causes

>SLJ - v44 - Ja '98 - p120+ [251-500]

Guardians of Wildlife

>ASBYP - v29 - Fall '96 - p55+ [501+]
>
>SB - v32 - D '96 - p271 [51-250]
>
>SB - v33 - Ag '97 - p163 [1-50]
>
>SLJ - v43 - Ap '97 - p146 [51-250]

Kids Who Make a Difference

>ASBYP - v29 - Fall '96 - p55+ [501+]
>
>SB - v32 - D '96 - p271+ [51-250]
>
>SB - v33 - Ag '97 - p163 [1-50]
>
>SLJ - v43 - Ap '97 - p146 [51-250]

Natural Foods and Products

>ASBYP - v29 - Fall '96 - p55+ [501+]
>
>SB - v33 - Ag '97 - p163 [1-50]

Protecting Our Air, Land, and Water

>SB - v32 - D '96 - p272 [51-250]
>
>SB - v33 - Ag '97 - p163 [1-50]

Recycling

>ASBYP - v29 - Fall '96 - p55+ [501+]
>
>SB - v32 - D '96 - p272 [51-250]
>
>SB - v33 - Ag '97 - p163 [1-50]
>
>SLJ - v43 - Ap '97 - p146 [51-250]

Chang, Margaret
The Beggar's Magic (Illus. by David Johnson)
> BL - v94 - O 15 '97 - p407+ [51-250]
> CCB-B - v51 - O '97 - p45 [51-250]
> HB - v73 - N '97 - p690 [51-250]
> KR - v65 - Jl 15 '97 - p1108 [51-250]
> SLJ - v43 - D '97 - p107 [51-250]

Chang, Monica
The Mouse Bride (Illus. by Lesley Liu)
> RT - v51 - F '98 - p424 [51-250]

Channing, William Henry
My Symphony (Illus. by Mary Engelbreit)
> AB - v100 - N 17 '97 - p1267 [1-50]
> PW - v244 - N 24 '97 - p72 [51-250]

Chapman, Gillian
Autumn
> Sch Lib - v45 - Ag '97 - p150 [51-250]
> SLJ - v44 - Mr '98 - p194 [51-250]

The Aztecs
> SLJ - v44 - Ap '98 - p142 [51-250]

The Egyptians
> SLJ - v44 - Ap '98 - p142 [51-250]

Exploring Time
> ASBYP - v29 - Sum '96 - p8+ [251-500]

Winter
> Sch Lib - v45 - Ag '97 - p150 [51-250]
> SLJ - v44 - Mr '98 - p194 [51-250]

Chapman, Victoria
Junior Environmental Activities on File
> r   SLJ - v44 - F '98 - p134+ [51-250]

Chappell, Ruth Paterson
The Mysterious Tail of a Charleston Cat (Illus. by Dean Wroth)
> HB Guide - v8 - Fall '97 - p289 [51-250]

Charles, Faustin
A Caribbean Counting Book (Illus. by Roberta Arenson)
> RT - v51 - F '98 - p427 [51-250]

Charles, Veronika Martenova
Necklace of Stars (Illus. by Veronika Martenova Charles)
> BIC - v26 - Ap '97 - p36+ [501+]
> CBRA - '96 - p437 [51-250]

Charlip, Remy
Arm in Arm
> BL - v94 - S 1 '97 - p128 [51-250]
> Ch BWatch - v7 - S '97 - p3 [1-50]
> PW - v244 - Jl 28 '97 - p76 [51-250]

Chartier, Normand
Gertie's Not Alone
> Ch BWatch - v7 - Mr '97 - p6 [51-250]

Chase, Edith Newlin
Secret Dawn (Illus. by Yolaine Lefebvre)
> Can CL - v23 - Sum '97 - p65+ [501+]
> CBRA - '96 - p496 [51-250]

Chats Peles (Group of Artists)
Long Live Music! (Illus. by Chats Peles (Group of Artists))
> RT - v51 - F '98 - p426 [51-250]

Chatterton, Martin
The Utterly Nutty History of Football
> Books - v11 - O '97 - p21 [1-50]

Chausse, Sylvia
The Egg and I (Illus. by Francois Crozat)
> RT - v51 - F '98 - p426 [51-250]

Cheong, Colin
China
> Ch BWatch - v7 - O '97 - p4+ [51-250]

Cherry, Lynne
The Armadillo from Amarillo (Illus. by Lynne Cherry)
> SB - v33 - O '97 - p195+ [1-50]

The Dragon and the Unicorn. Book and Audio Version
> Ch BWatch - v7 - S '97 - p2 [51-250]

Flute's Journey (Illus. by Lynne Cherry)

> Am Sci - v85 - N '97 - p559 [51-250]
> Ch BWatch - v7 - Ap '97 - p6 [1-50]
> HB Guide - v8 - Fall '97 - p351 [51-250]
> SB - v33 - Ag '97 - p163 [1-50]
> SLJ - v43 - Jl '97 - p80+ [51-250]

The Great Kapok Tree

> BL - v94 - D 1 '97 - p628 [1-50]

Grizzly Bear

> PW - v245 - Mr 23 '98 - p101 [1-50]

Orangutan

> PW - v245 - Mr 23 '98 - p101 [1-50]

Seal

> PW - v245 - Mr 23 '98 - p101 [1-50]

Snow Leopard

> PW - v245 - Mr 23 '98 - p101 [1-50]

Chessen, Sherri
The Gorp's Gift (Illus. by Dale Duncan Johnson)

> Bloom Rev - v17 - Mr '97 - p20 [1-50]

Chester, Jonathan
Splash! A Penguin Counting Book (Illus. by Jonathan Chester)

> KR - v65 - O 1 '97 - p1535+ [51-250]
> PW - v244 - O 27 '97 - p79 [1-50]
> SLJ - v44 - Ja '98 - p103 [51-250]

Chiarelli, Brunetto
Atlas De Pueblos Y Culturas (Illus. by Paola Ravaglia)

> r   BL - v94 - D 15 '97 - p717 [51-250]

The Atlas of World Cultures (Illus. by Paola Ravaglia)

> r   Ch BWatch - v7 - O '97 - p1 [1-50]
> r   KR - v65 - Ag 1 '97 - p1220 [51-250]

The People Atlas

> r   Sch Lib - v45 - N '97 - p203 [51-250]

Chichester Clark, Emma
Little Miss Muffet Counts to Ten (Illus. by Emma Chichester Clark)

> Bks Keeps - Jl '97 - p20 [51-250]
> Sch Lib - v45 - Ag '97 - p130 [51-250]
> TES - Je 13 '97 - pR7 [51-250]

> TES - N 7 '97 - p5* [1-50]

Little Miss Muffet's Count-Along Surprise (Illus. by Emma Chichester Clark)

> BL - v94 - D 15 '97 - p702 [51-250]
> CBRS - v26 - F '98 - p74 [51-250]
> KR - v65 - S 15 '97 - p1454 [51-250]
> PW - v244 - N 3 '97 - p83 [51-250]

Chick (Covent Garden Books)

> Ch BWatch - v7 - Je '97 - p4 [1-50]

Chicoine, Stephen
A Liberian Family (Illus. by Stephen Chicoine)

> Ch BWatch - v7 - N '97 - p6 [51-250]
> SLJ - v44 - F '98 - p96+ [51-250]

Spain: Bridge between Continents

> Ch BWatch - v7 - My '97 - p7 [1-50]
> HB Guide - v8 - Fall '97 - p390 [51-250]
> SLJ - v44 - Ja '98 - p97+ [51-250]

Children's School of Science (Woods Hole, Mass.)
The Big Book of Nature Projects (Illus. by Len Rubenstein)

> CBRS - v25 - Jl '97 - p154 [51-250]
> SLJ - v44 - Ja '98 - p98 [51-250]

Chin-Lee, Cynthia
A Is for Asia (Illus. by Yumi Heo)

> HB Guide - v8 - Fall '97 - p391 [51-250]
> SLJ - v43 - Ap '97 - p120 [51-250]

Chinn, Karen
Sam and the Lucky Money (Illus. by Cornelius Van Wright)

> Bloom Rev - v17 - N '97 - p32+ [51-250]
> ECEJ - v25 - Fall '97 - p46 [1-50]

Chiu, Esther
The Lobster and the Sea

> Ch BWatch - v8 - Ja '98 - p2 [1-50]

Chocolate, Deborah M Newton
Kente Colors (Illus. by John Ward)

> RT - v51 - N '97 - p251+ [51-250]

The Piano Man (Illus. by Eric Velasquez)

    BL - v94 - F 15 '98 - p1018 [51-250]
    HB - v74 - Mr '98 - p211 [51-250]
    KR - v65 - D 15 '97 - p1833 [51-250]
    PW - v244 - N 24 '97 - p73 [51-250]
    SLJ - v44 - F '98 - p79 [51-250]

Chodzin, Sherab

The Wisdom of the Crows and Other Buddhist Tales (Illus. by Marie Cameron)

    KR - v66 - Ja 1 '98 - p55 [51-250]
y   SLJ - v44 - Ap '98 - p143 [51-250]

Choi, Sook Nyul

The Best Older Sister (Illus. by Cornelius Van Wright)

    HB Guide - v8 - Fall '97 - p289 [51-250]
    SLJ - v43 - Je '97 - p85 [51-250]

Halmoni and the Picnic (Illus. by Karen Dugan)

    ECEJ - v25 - Fall '97 - p46 [1-50]

Yunmi and Halmoni's Trip (Illus. by Karen Dugan)

    BL - v94 - S 15 '97 - p240 [51-250]

Choi, Yangsook

The Sun Girl and the Moon Boy (Illus. by Yangsook Choi)

    BL - v94 - D 15 '97 - p698 [51-250]
    Ch BWatch - v8 - Ja '98 - p2 [1-50]
    PW - v244 - N 3 '97 - p84+ [51-250]
    SLJ - v44 - Ap '98 - p114 [51-250]

Choldenko, Gennifer

Moonstruck: The True Story of the Cow Who Jumped over the Moon (Illus. by Paul Yalowitz)

    CBRS - v25 - My '97 - p109 [51-250]
   ' HB Guide - v8 - Fall '97 - p261 [51-250]
    NYTBR - v102 - Je 1 '97 - p36 [1-50]
    SLJ - v43 - Ap '97 - p91 [51-250]

Chorao, Kay

Jumpety-Bumpety Hop (Illus. by Kay Chorao)

    Bloom Rev - v17 - N '97 - p33 [51-250]
    HB - v73 - N '97 - p692 [51-250]

    KR - v65 - S 15 '97 - p1454 [51-250]
    PW - v244 - Ag 18 '97 - p95 [51-250]
    SLJ - v43 - N '97 - p105 [51-250]

Little Farm by the Sea (Illus. by Kay Chorao)

    HB - v74 - Mr '98 - p211 [51-250]

Mother Goose Magic (Illus. by Kay Chorao)

    PW - v244 - N 3 '97 - p87 [1-50]

Number One Number Fun

    TCMath - v4 - S '97 - p52+ [51-250]

Choyce, Lesley

Falling through the Cracks

    CBRA - '96 - p469 [51-250]

Go for It, Carrie (Illus. by Mark Thurman)

    CM:CanRev - v4 - S 19 '97 - pONL [251-500]

Chrisp, Peter

The Colosseum, How It Was Built and How It Was Used

    Magpies - v12 - Mr '97 - p42 [51-250]

Great Journeys

    HB Guide - v8 - Fall '97 - p385 [51-250]

Mapping the Unknown

    ASBYP - v29 - Fall '96 - p63+ [501+]
    HB Guide - v8 - Fall '97 - p341 [51-250]

The Parthenon

    Magpies - v12 - Mr '97 - p42 [51-250]

Christelow, Eileen

Not until Christmas, Walter! (Illus. by Eileen Christelow)

    BL - v94 - S 1 '97 - p137+ [51-250]
    CCB-B - v51 - D '97 - p120+ [51-250]
    KR - v65 - Jl 15 '97 - p1108 [51-250]
    PW - v244 - O 6 '97 - p56 [51-250]

What Do Authors Do?

    PW - v244 - Ag 4 '97 - p77 [1-50]

Christensen, Bonnie

Rebus Riot

    CBRS - v25 - Spr '97 - p133 [1-50]
    HB Guide - v8 - Fall '97 - p376 [51-250]

Christenson, Evelyn
What Happens When Children Pray (Illus. by Joy Dunn Keenan)
Ch BWatch - v7 - D '97 - p5 [51-250]

Christian, Mary Blount
The Mystery of the Fallen Tree (Illus. by Joe Boddy)
SB - v33 - O '97 - p218 [51-250]

The Mystery of the Message in the Sky
SB - v33 - O '97 - p218 [51-250]

The Mystery of the Polluted Stream
SB - v33 - O '97 - p218 [51-250]

The Toady and Dr. Miracle (Illus. by Christine Jenny)
HB Guide - v8 - Fall '97 - p289 [51-250]
SLJ - v43 - S '97 - p179 [51-250]

Who'd Believe John Colter?
JOYS - v10 - Sum '97 - p427 [51-250]

Christian, Peggy
Chocolate, a Glacier Grizzly (Illus. by Carol Cottone-Kolthoff)
KR - v65 - N 1 '97 - p1642 [51-250]
SLJ - v43 - N '97 - p105+ [51-250]

Christian, Spencer
Can It Really Rain Frogs?
KR - v65 - Jl 15 '97 - p1108+ [51-250]
PW - v244 - Jl 21 '97 - p203 [51-250]
SB - v33 - D '97 - p273+ [51-250]
SLJ - v44 - Ap '98 - p4792 [51-250]

Shake, Rattle, and Roll
New Sci - v157 - Ja 31 '98 - p45 [51-250]
PW - v244 - Jl 21 '97 - p203 [51-250]
SB - v33 - D '97 - p273+ [51-250]

What Makes the Grand Canyon Grand?
KR - v66 - Ja 15 '98 - p110 [51-250]
SLJ - v44 - Ap '98 - p143 [51-250]

Christiansen, Candace
The Mitten Tree (Illus. by Elaine Greenstein)
BL - v94 - O 15 '97 - p411+ [51-250]
CCB-B - v51 - N '97 - p82+ [51-250]
PW - v244 - Ag 11 '97 - p402 [51-250]

SLJ - v44 - F '98 - p79 [51-250]

Christmas Buttons
Ch BWatch - v7 - D '97 - p1 [51-250]

Christopher, Matt
Baseball Turnaround
BL - v93 - Je 1 '97 - p1702 [51-250]
HB Guide - v8 - Fall '97 - p297 [51-250]
SLJ - v43 - Ag '97 - p154 [51-250]

Football Jokes and Riddles
BL - v94 - O 15 '97 - p399 [51-250]

In the Huddle with...Steve Young (Davidson). Audio Version
SLJ - v44 - Ap '98 - p86 [51-250]

On the Court with...Andre Agassi
SLJ - v43 - D '97 - p107 [51-250]

On the Court with...Grant Hill
SLJ - v43 - Je '97 - p132 [51-250]

On the Court with...Michael Jordan
SLJ - v43 - Je '97 - p132 [51-250]

Penalty Shot
HB Guide - v8 - Fall '97 - p297 [51-250]

Snowboard Maverick
KR - v65 - N 15 '97 - p1705 [51-250]
SLJ - v44 - Mr '98 - p211 [51-250]

Soccer Scoop
BL - v94 - F 15 '98 - p1010 [51-250]
KR - v65 - N 15 '97 - p1705 [51-250]

Stranger in Right Field (Illus. by Bert Dodson)
BL - v94 - S 1 '97 - p124 [51-250]
HB Guide - v8 - Fall '97 - p290 [51-250]

Churchill, Vicki
Butterfly Kiss (Illus. by Charles Fuge)
Sch Lib - v45 - N '97 - p184+ [51-250]

Chwast, Seymour
Mr. Merlin and the Turtle (Illus. by Seymour Chwast)
RT - v51 - O '97 - p131 [1-50]

Cibula, Matt
What's Up with You, Taquandra Fu?
(Illus. by Brian Strassburg)
PW - v245 - Ja 12 '98 - p59 [51-250]
SLJ - v44 - Ap '98 - p97 [51-250]

Citra, Becky
School Campout (Illus. by Susan Gardos)
CBRA - '96 - p469 [51-250]

Civardi, Anne
The Kingfisher First Encyclopedia
r   Books - v10 - S '96 - p24 [1-50]
r   SB - v32 - D '96 - p271 [51-250]

Clancy, Dorothy
Buckskin, the Brave (Illus. by Gerard Blommaert)
CBRA - '96 - p469+ [51-250]

Clare, John D
Growing Up in the People's Century
Books - v10 - S '96 - p24 [51-250]

Clark, Ann Nolan
Secret of the Andes (Illus. by Jean Charlot)
NYTBR - v102 - N 16 '97 - p25 [1-50]

Clark, Catherine Anthony
The Golden Pine Cone (Illus. by Greta Guzek)
Can CL - v23 - Sum '97 - p92 [501+]

Clark, Clara Gillow
Willie and the Rattlesnake King
BL - v94 - D 1 '97 - p636 [51-250]
SLJ - v43 - N '97 - p114+ [51-250]

Clark, Eliza
Butterflies and Bottlecaps (Illus. by Vladyana Krykorka)
CBRA - '96 - p437 [51-250]

Clark, Margaret
A Treasury of Dragon Stories (Illus. by Mark Robertson)
SLJ - v44 - Ja '98 - p80 [51-250]

Clark, Margaret Goff
Save the Florida Key Deer
BL - v94 - Mr 1 '98 - p1126 [51-250]
KR - v65 - D 1 '97 - p1773+ [51-250]
SLJ - v44 - F '98 - p113 [51-250]

Clarke, Gillian
The Whispering Room (Illus. by Justin Todd)
RT - v51 - O '97 - p139 [1-50]

Clarke, Gus
Nothing but Trouble
Bks Keeps - S '97 - p20 [51-250]
Sch Lib - v45 - N '97 - p185 [51-250]

Clarke-Giles, Telene
Rock and Roll Clyde! (Illus. by Marjorie Scott)
Sch Lib - v45 - Ag '97 - p130 [51-250]

Clay, Rebecca
Space Travel and Exploration
SLJ - v44 - Ja '98 - p121 [51-250]

Stars and Galaxies
Ch BWatch - v7 - My '97 - p8 [1-50]
SLJ - v43 - Je '97 - p132 [51-250]

Clayton, Iris
Wiradjuri of the Rivers and Plains
Magpies - v12 - Jl '97 - p41+ [501+]

Cleary, Beverly
The Growing-Up Feet (Illus. by DyAnne DiSalvo-Ryan)
PW - v244 - Ag 4 '97 - p77 [1-50]

Henry and Beezus (Roberts). Audio Version
SLJ - v43 - Jl '97 - p56 [51-250]

The Hullabaloo ABC (Illus. by Ted Rand)
KR - v66 - Ap 1 '98 - p504 [51-250]
PW - v245 - F 16 '98 - p210 [51-250]

Ramona the Pest
NYTBR - v102 - N 16 '97 - p25 [1-50]

Cleary, Brian P
Give Me Bach My Schubert (Illus. by Rick Dupre)
> RT - v51 - O '97 - p137 [1-50]

Clement, Rod
Grandad's Teeth (Illus. by Rod Clement)
> Magpies - v12 - My '97 - p5 [51-250]

Grandpa's Teeth (Illus. by Rod Clement)
> BL - v94 - F 15 '98 - p1018+ [51-250]
> KR - v65 - D 1 '97 - p1774 [51-250]
> PW - v244 - D 22 '97 - p58+ [51-250]
> SLJ - v44 - Mr '98 - p168 [51-250]

Just Another Ordinary Day (Illus. by Rod Clement)
> CBRS - v25 - Je '97 - p122 [1-50]
> CCB-B - v50 - Jl '97 - p389+ [51-250]
> Ch BWatch - v7 - Je '97 - p7 [1-50]
> HB Guide - v8 - Fall '97 - p261 [51-250]
> Inst - v107 - S '97 - p22 [51-250]
> KR - v65 - Ap 15 '97 - p652 [51-250]
> SLJ - v43 - Je '97 - p85 [51-250]

Clements, Andrew
Double Trouble in Walla Walla (Illus. by Sal Murdocca)
> CBRS - v26 - D '97 - p37 [1-50]
> PW - v244 - O 13 '97 - p74 [51-250]
> SLJ - v44 - Ja '98 - p81 [51-250]

Frindle (Illus. by Brian Selznick)
> PW - v245 - F 9 '98 - p98 [1-50]

Temple Cat (Illus. by Kate Kiesler)
> H-Net - D '97 - pONL [501+]

Things That Go Eek on Halloween (Illus. by George Ulrich)
> PW - v244 - O 6 '97 - p50 [1-50]

Clements, Gillian
The Picture History of Great Inventors
> r   JOYS - v11 - Fall '97 - p75 [1-50]

Clever Kids Science: Ages 5-7
> ASBYP - v29 - Sum '96 - p45 [501+]

Clever Kids Science: Ages 8-10
> ASBYP - v29 - Sum '96 - p45 [501+]

Clifford, Eth
Family for Sale
> RT - v51 - N '97 - p253+ [51-250]

Flatfoot Fox and the Case of the Missing Schoolhouse (Illus. by Brian Lies)
> HB Guide - v8 - Fall '97 - p290 [51-250]
> SLJ - v43 - Ap '97 - p91 [51-250]

Clifford, N J
Incredible Earth
> SB - v33 - Ap '97 - p84 [51-250]
> SB - v33 - Ag '97 - p187 [1-50]

Climo, Shirley
The Korean Cinderella (Illus. by Ruth Heller)
> ECEJ - v25 - Fall '97 - p46 [1-50]

A Treasury of Mermaids (Illus. by Jean Tseng)
> Ch BWatch - v7 - N '97 - p5 [1-50]
> KR - v65 - O 1 '97 - p1529 [51-250]
> PW - v244 - S 22 '97 - p83 [51-250]

A Treasury of Princesses (Illus. by Ruth Sanderson)
> NYTBR - v102 - Ap 27 '97 - p29 [1-50]

Clise, Michele Durkson
Stop the Violence Please
> SE - v61 - S '97 - p270 [1-50]

Clothes (First Words Series)
> Ch BWatch - v7 - Je '97 - p4 [1-50]
> SLJ - v43 - Ap '97 - p120+ [51-250]

Clouse, Nancy L
Perugino's Path
> PW - v244 - N 3 '97 - p83 [51-250]

Coan, Peter M
Ellis Island Interviews
> CAY - v18 - Win '97 - p3 [51-250]
> KR - v65 - N 15 '97 - p1705 [51-250]
> y   PW - v244 - O 6 '97 - p71 [1-50]

Coatsworth, Elizabeth
Song of the Camels (Illus. by Anna Vojtech)
> Ch BWatch - v7 - D '97 - p1 [1-50]

KR - v65 - O 15 '97 - p1579 [51-250]
PW - v244 - O 6 '97 - p56 [51-250]

Cobb, Vicki
Don't Try This at Home! (Illus. by True Kelley)
CCB-B - v51 - Ap '98 - p277 [51-250]

Why Can't I Live Forever? and Other Not Such Dumb Questions about Life (Illus. by Mena Dolobowsky)
HB Guide - v8 - Fall '97 - p344+ [51-250]
SLJ - v43 - My '97 - p118 [51-250]

Coburn, Brian
Adventures in Cranberry Forest (Illus. by Susan Little)
CBRA - '96 - p437 [51-250]

Coburn, Walt
Stirrup High
Roundup M - v5 - O '97 - p25 [51-250]

Cocca-Leffler, Maryann
Clams All Year (Illus. by Maryann Cocca-Leffler)
RT - v51 - O '97 - p151 [51-250]

Missing: One Stuffed Rabbit
BL - v94 - Mr 15 '98 - p1246 [51-250]

Cochrane, Patricia A
Purely Rosie Pearl
PW - v244 - Ag 11 '97 - p403 [1-50]
SE - v61 - Ap '97 - p10* [1-50]

Cockett, Stephen
The Birds Keep on Singing
Sch Lib - v45 - Ag '97 - p156 [51-250]

Cocks, Nancy
Fearless Fergie (Illus. by Michael Leveille)
CBRA - '96 - p438 [251-500]

Fergie Feels Left Out (Illus. by Michael Leveille)
CBRA - '96 - p438 [251-500]

Fergie Goes Moose Hunting (Illus. by Michael Leveille)
CBRA - '96 - p438 [251-500]

Fergie Hogs the Lily Pad (Illus. by Michael Leveille)
CBRA - '96 - p438 [251-500]

Cody, Tod
The Cowboy's Handbook
SE - v61 - Ap '97 - p10* [1-50]

Coerr, Eleanor
Sadako Y Las Mil Grullas De Papel (Illus. by Ronald Himler)
SLJ - v43 - My '97 - p152 [51-250]

Coffey, Maria
A Cat in a Kayak (Illus. by Eugenie Fernandes)
Quill & Q - v64 - F '98 - p47 [251-500]

Cohen, Barbara
Molly's Pilgrim (Moore). Audio Version
BL - v94 - F 15 '98 - p1027 [51-250]

Cohen, Caron Lee
Crookjaw (Illus. by Linda Bronson)
CBRS - v26 - Win '98 - p61 [51-250]
CCB-B - v51 - O '97 - p46 [51-250]
KR - v65 - Je 15 '97 - p947 [51-250]
PW - v244 - Ag 25 '97 - p70+ [51-250]
SLJ - v43 - S '97 - p179 [51-250]

How Many Fish? (Illus. by S D Schindler)
KR - v65 - D 1 '97 - p1774 [51-250]
SLJ - v44 - F '98 - p79 [51-250]

Cohen, Daniel, 1936-
Dangerous Ghosts
SLJ - v43 - Ap '97 - p146 [51-250]

Ghosts of the Deep
JOYS - v10 - Sum '97 - p427 [1-50]

Raising the Dead
BL - v94 - O 1 '97 - p320+ [51-250]
SLJ - v43 - N '97 - p126 [51-250]

Werewolves
RT - v51 - O '97 - p143 [1-50]
RT - v51 - N '97 - p252 [51-250]

Cohen, Joel H
Norman Rockwell: America's Best-Loved Illustrator
> BL - v94 - N 1 '97 - p463 [51-250]
> HB Guide - v8 - Fall '97 - p363 [51-250]
> SLJ - v43 - Ag '97 - p165 [51-250]

Superstars of Women's Gymnastics
> Ch BWatch - v7 - S '97 - p8 [1-50]
> HB Guide - v8 - Fall '97 - p369 [51-250]
> y VOYA - v20 - O '97 - p260 [251-500]

Cohn, Amy L
From Sea to Shining Sea
> JOYS - v11 - Fall '97 - p77 [51-250]
> SLJ - v43 - N '97 - p40 [1-50]

Cohn, Arlen
Eric VanNoodle (Illus. by Rosemary Petruzzi)
> CBRS - v26 - N '97 - p31 [51-250]
> Ch BWatch - v7 - D '97 - p5 [51-250]

Cohn, Janice
The Christmas Menorahs
> SE - v61 - S '97 - p270 [1-50]

Colbert, Jan
Dear Dr. King
> BL - v94 - F 15 '98 - p1002 [51-250]
> PW - v245 - Mr 16 '98 - p66 [251-500]

Colbert, Nancy A
Lou Henry Hoover: The Duty to Serve
> BL - v94 - F 15 '98 - p1002 [51-250]
> y KR - v65 - O 15 '97 - p1579 [51-250]
> SLJ - v44 - Mr '98 - p230 [51-250]

Coldwell, Michael
Camp All-Star
> BIC - v26 - S '97 - p32+ [501+]
> CBRA - '96 - p465+ [251-500]

Fast Break
> CBRA - '96 - p465 [51-250]

Cole, Alison
Colour
> Magpies - v12 - S '97 - p6+ [51-250]

Cole, Babette
The Bad Good Manners Book
> Bks Keeps - S '97 - p23 [51-250]

Drop Dead (Illus. by Babette Cole)
> Bks Keeps - Jl '97 - p6+ [501+]
> Books - v10 - S '96 - p24 [51-250]
> Ch BWatch - v7 - My '97 - p2 [1-50]
> HB Guide - v8 - Fall '97 - p261 [51-250]
> SLJ - v43 - Jl '97 - p60 [51-250]

Two of Everything
> Books - v11 - O '97 - p21 [51-250]
> Obs - D 7 '97 - p17* [51-250]
> TES - N 7 '97 - p4* [251-500]

The Un-Wedding (Illus. by Babette Cole)
> KR - v66 - Ap 1 '98 - p493 [51-250]

Cole, Barbara Hancock
Texas Star (Illus. by Barbara Minton)
> ECEJ - v25 - Fall '97 - p46 [1-50]

Cole, Brock
The Facts Speak for Themselves
> y BL - v94 - O 1 '97 - p318 [501+]
> y BL - v94 - Ja 1 '98 - p733 [1-50]
> y BL - v94 - Mr 15 '98 - p1225 [1-50]
> y CBRS - v26 - D '97 - p45 [51-250]
> y CCB-B - v51 - O '97 - p46+ [251-500]
> y HB - v73 - N '97 - p678+ [251-500]
> y KR - v65 - O 15 '97 - p1580 [51-250]
> y NYTBR - v102 - N 16 '97 - p39 [501+]
> y NYTBR - v102 - D 7 '97 - p78 [1-50]
> y PW - v244 - S 1 '97 - p105+ [51-250]
> PW - v244 - N 3 '97 - p59 [51-250]
> y SLJ - v43 - D '97 - p24 [1-50]
> y VOYA - v20 - D '97 - p315+ [251-500]
> y VOYA - v21 - Ap '98 - p40 [1-50]

Cole, Henry
I Took a Walk (Illus. by Henry Cole)
> CCB-B - v51 - Mr '98 - p238 [51-250]
> KR - v66 - F 15 '98 - p264 [51-250]
> PW - v245 - Mr 16 '98 - p63 [51-250]

Jack's Garden
> SB - v33 - Ag '97 - p180 [51-250]
> SB - v33 - O '97 - p218 [51-250]

Cole, Joanna
The Anyday Book (Illus. by Alan Tiegreen)
> BL - v93 - Ag '97 - p1893 [51-250]
> PW - v244 - Jl 28 '97 - p77 [51-250]

I'm a Big Brother (Illus. by Maxie Chambliss)
> HB Guide - v8 - Fall '97 - p250 [51-250]
> SLJ - v43 - Ap '97 - p91+ [51-250]

I'm a Big Sister (Illus. by Maxie Chambliss)
> HB Guide - v8 - Fall '97 - p250 [51-250]
> SLJ - v43 - Ap '97 - p91+ [51-250]

The Magic School Bus and the Electric Field Trip (Illus. by Bruce Degen)
> BL - v94 - O 15 '97 - p408 [51-250]
> HB - v74 - Ja '98 - p90 [51-250]
> KR - v65 - S 15 '97 - p1454 [51-250]
> PW - v244 - S 22 '97 - p83 [51-250]
> SLJ - v43 - N '97 - p106 [51-250]

The Magic School Bus at the Waterworks (Illus. by Bruce Degen)
> NYTBR - v102 - N 16 '97 - p26 [1-50]

The Magic School Bus Blows Its Top (Illus. by Bruce Degen)
> RT - v51 - O '97 - p138 [1-50]

The Magic School Bus Inside a Beehive (Illus. by Bruce Degen)
> RT - v51 - N '97 - p256 [51-250]

The New Baby at Your House. Rev. Ed. (Illus. by Margaret Miller)
> BL - v94 - Mr 1 '98 - p1138 [51-250]
> SLJ - v44 - Ap '98 - p114 [51-250]

On the Bus with Joanna Cole
> Inst - v106 - Ap '97 - p27 [1-50]

Cole, Melanie
Mariah Carey
> Ch BWatch - v7 - O '97 - p5 [51-250]
> SLJ - v44 - F '98 - p114 [51-250]

Cole, Ron
Bats!
> SB - v33 - Je '97 - p144 [51-250]

Remarkable Rocks
> SB - v33 - Ap '97 - p84 [51-250]

Stephen Hawking: Solving the Mysteries of the Universe
> HB Guide - v8 - Fall '97 - p379 [51-250]

Coleman, Evelyn
To Be a Drum (Illus. by Aminah Brenda Lynn Robinson)
> BL - v94 - F 15 '98 - p1019 [51-250]
> KR - v66 - F 15 '98 - p264 [51-250]
> PW - v245 - Mr 23 '98 - p99 [51-250]

White Socks Only (Illus. by Tyrone Geter)
> BL - v94 - F 15 '98 - p999 [1-50]

Coleman, Michael
Escape Key
> BL - v94 - Mr 1 '98 - p1134 [51-250]

Fizzy in the Spotlight (Illus. by Philippe Dupasquier)
> Sch Lib - v45 - N '97 - p201 [51-250]

Net Bandits
> BL - v94 - Mr 1 '98 - p1134 [51-250]
> Books - v10 - S '96 - p24 [51-250]
> PW - v244 - O 13 '97 - p75 [51-250]

Weirdo's War
> TES - v135 - My 2 '97 - p8* [1-50]

Coles, Robert
The Story of Ruby Bridges (Illus. by George Ford)
> BL - v94 - F 15 '98 - p998 [1-50]

Collard, Sneed B
Animal Dads (Illus. by Steve Jenkins)
> CBRS - v25 - Spr '97 - p134 [51-250]
> HB Guide - v8 - Fall '97 - p345 [51-250]
> Inst - v107 - N '97 - p18 [51-250]
> KR - v65 - Ap 15 '97 - p638 [51-250]
> NYTBR - v102 - S 14 '97 - p30 [501+]
> SLJ - v43 - Je '97 - p106 [51-250]

Colle, Gisela
The Star Tree (Illus. by Gisela Colle)
> BL - v94 - S 1 '97 - p138 [51-250]
> CBRS - v26 - Ja '98 - p49+ [51-250]
> NYTBR - v102 - D 21 '97 - p18 [1-50]

PW - v244 - O 6 '97 - p56 [51-250]

Collier, James Lincoln
Jazz: An American Saga
    CCB-B - v51 - Ja '98 - p156+ [51-250]
y   SLJ - v44 - Ja '98 - p121 [51-250]
y   VOYA - v21 - Ap '98 - p66 [51-250]

Collier, Mary Jo
The King's Giraffe (Illus. by Stephane Poulin)
    SE - v61 - Ap '97 - p7* [1-50]

Collier, Sandra L
Wake Up to Your Dreams (Illus. by Ray Boudreau)
    CBRA - '96 - p526+ [51-250]

Collington, Peter
The Angel and the Soldier Boy (Illus. by Peter Collington)
    TES - D 5 '97 - p18* [501+]

The Coming of the Surfman (Illus. by Peter Collington)
    TES - D 5 '97 - p18* [501+]

Little Pickle (Illus. by Peter Collington)
    TES - D 5 '97 - p18* [501+]

On Christmas Eve (Illus. by Peter Collington)
    TES - D 5 '97 - p18* [501+]

A Small Miracle (Illus. by Peter Collington)
    BL - v94 - O 15 '97 - p402 [51-250]
    CCB-B - v51 - Ja '98 - p157 [51-250]
    Emerg Lib - v25 - Ja '98 - p52 [51-250]
    HB - v73 - N '97 - p668+ [251-500]
    NYTBR - v102 - D 7 '97 - p66 [1-50]
    PW - v244 - O 6 '97 - p53 [51-250]
    TES - N 7 '97 - p11* [1-50]
    TES - D 5 '97 - p18* [501+]

The Tooth Fairy (Illus. by Peter Collington)
    TES - D 5 '97 - p18* [501+]

Collins, Carolyn
My Little House Christmas Crafts Book (Illus. by Mary Collier)
    PW - v244 - O 6 '97 - p57 [51-250]

Collins, Carolyn Strom
The World of Little House
    CSM - v90 - F 24 '98 - p16 [1-50]

Collins, Heather
Eensy Weensy Spider
    PW - v244 - O 27 '97 - p78 [1-50]

Hickory Dickory Dock
    PW - v244 - O 27 '97 - p78 [1-50]

One, Two, Buckle My Shoe
    PW - v244 - O 27 '97 - p78 [1-50]

This Little Piggy
    PW - v244 - O 27 '97 - p78 [1-50]

Collins, Judy
My Father (Illus. by Jane Dyer)
    PW - v244 - Je 16 '97 - p61 [1-50]

Collins, Ross
The Sea Hole
    Magpies - v12 - S '97 - p30+ [51-250]

Collins Pocket School Dictionary
r   TES - S 19 '97 - p19* [501+]

Collinson, Roger
Butterfingers
    Bks Keeps - Jl '97 - p25 [51-250]
    TES - My 16 '97 - p14* [51-250]
    TES - N 7 '97 - p7* [51-250]

Collodi, Carlo
Pinocchio (Sessions). Book and Audio Version
    TES - D 19 '97 - p23 [51-250]

Colman, Penny
Corpses, Coffins, and Crypts
y   BL - v94 - N 1 '97 - p466 [51-250]
y   BL - v94 - Ja 1 '98 - p733 [1-50]
    HB - v74 - Ja '98 - p91 [51-250]
    PW - v244 - N 3 '97 - p60 [1-50]
    PW - v244 - N 3 '97 - p86 [51-250]
y   SLJ - v43 - D '97 - p134 [51-250]

Rosie the Riveter
y   JAAL - v41 - N '97 - p214 [51-250]
    PW - v245 - F 9 '98 - p98 [51-250]

Colombo, Luann
Creatures (Illus. by Peter Georgeson)
PW - v244 - Je 16 '97 - p61 [51-250]

Germs (Illus. by Peter Georgeson)
PW - v244 - Je 16 '97 - p61 [51-250]

Colors (Fit-a-Shape)
Magpies - v12 - Mr '97 - p29 [51-250]

Colors (Star Bright) (Illus. by Bill Thomas)
PW - v244 - D 15 '97 - p60 [51-250]

Colours, an Australian Board Book
Magpies - v12 - Mr '97 - p29 [51-250]

Come All Ye Faithful (Illus. by Laura Rader)
Ch BWatch - v7 - N '97 - p6 [1-50]

Comissiong, Lynette
Mind Me Good Now! (Illus. by Marie Lafrance)
BL - v94 - Ja 1 '98 - p818 [51-250]
CM:CanRev - v4 - N 28 '97 - pONL [251-500]
Quill & Q - v63 - S '97 - p73 [251-500]

Compton's Encyclopedia 97. Vols. 1-26
r   BL - v94 - S 15 '97 - p254+ [251-500]

Conan, Sally Anne
God's Best Gift (Illus. by Kathy Rogers)
PW - v245 - Ja 26 '98 - p86 [51-250]

Condy, Roy
Shark Attacks and Spider Snacks (Illus. by Roy Condy)
Can CL - v23 - Fall '97 - p94+ [51-250]
CBRA - '96 - p528+ [51-250]

Cone, Molly
Come Back, Salmon
JOYS - v10 - Sum '97 - p427 [51-250]

Squishy, Misty, Damp and Muddy
ASBYP - v29 - Fall '96 - p10 [251-500]
RT - v51 - N '97 - p257 [51-250]

Conford, Ellen
Crush: Stories
y   BL - v94 - Ja 1 '98 - p794 [51-250]
y   CCB-B - v51 - Mr '98 - p238+ [51-250]
     HB - v74 - Mr '98 - p220 [51-250]
y   KR - v65 - N 15 '97 - p1706 [51-250]
y   PW - v244 - D 1 '97 - p54 [51-250]
     SLJ - v44 - Ja '98 - p111 [51-250]

The Frog Princess of Pelham
CCB-B - v50 - Jl '97 - p390 [51-250]
HB Guide - v8 - Fall '97 - p297 [51-250]
KR - v65 - Ap 15 '97 - p638 [51-250]
Par Ch - Awards '97 - p6 [51-250]
SLJ - v43 - Je '97 - p114 [51-250]

Conlon-McKenna, Marita
Fields of Home (Illus. by Donald Teskey)
CCB-B - v50 - Jl '97 - p390 [51-250]
HB Guide - v8 - Fall '97 - p298 [51-250]
SLJ - v43 - Je '97 - p114 [51-250]

No Goodbye
Magpies - v12 - Mr '97 - p32+ [251-500]

Connelly, Bernardine
Follow the Drinking Gourd (Illus. by Yvonne Buchanan)
SLJ - v44 - Mr '98 - p211 [251-500]

Connolly, Margaret
It Isn't Easy (Illus. by Rosita Manahan)
Sch Lib - v45 - N '97 - p185 [51-250]

Connolly, Peter
The Cavalryman
Bks Keeps - N '97 - p26 [51-250]

The Legionary
Bks Keeps - N '97 - p26 [51-250]

Pompeii
Bks Keeps - N '97 - p26 [51-250]

The Roman Fort
Bks Keeps - N '97 - p26 [51-250]

Connor, Nikki

Cardboard Boxes (Illus. by Sarah-Jane Neaves)

> Sch Lib - v45 - Ag '97 - p130 [51-250]
> SLJ - v43 - Ag '97 - p146 [51-250]

Cardboard Tubes (Illus. by Sarah-Jane Neaves)

> HB Guide - v8 - Fall '97 - p362 [51-250]
> Sch Lib - v45 - Ag '97 - p130 [51-250]
> SLJ - v43 - Ag '97 - p146 [51-250]

Plastic Bottles (Illus. by Sarah-Jane Neaves)

> HB Guide - v8 - Fall '97 - p362 [51-250]
> Sch Lib - v45 - Ag '97 - p130 [51-250]
> SLJ - v43 - Ag '97 - p146 [51-250]

Plastic Cups (Illus. by Sarah-Jane Neaves)

> Sch Lib - v45 - Ag '97 - p130 [51-250]
> SLJ - v43 - Ag '97 - p146 [51-250]

Conrad, Pam

Animal Lullabies (Illus. by Richard Cowdrey)

> BL - v94 - S 1 '97 - p128 [51-250]
> CBRS - v26 - N '97 - p26 [1-50]
> Ch BWatch - v7 - N '97 - p5 [1-50]
> KR - v65 - S 15 '97 - p1454 [51-250]
> PW - v244 - O 20 '97 - p74 [51-250]
> SLJ - v44 - Ja '98 - p98 [51-250]

Call Me Ahnighito (Illus. by Richard Egielski)

> SLJ - v43 - Jl '97 - p34 [1-50]

The Rooster's Gift (Illus. by Eric Beddows)

> CBRA -   '96 - p438 [51-250]
> y   JAAL - v40 - Ap '97 - p584+ [51-250]

This Mess (Illus. by Elizabeth Sayles)

> KR - v66 - Mr 15 '98 - p400 [51-250]
> SLJ - v44 - Ap '98 - p97 [51-250]

The Tub Grandfather (Illus. by Richard Egielski)

> Par Ch - Awards '97 - p8 [51-250]

The Tub People (Salley). Book and Audio Version

> SLJ - v43 - My '97 - p88 [51-250]

Converse All Star Baseball

> SLJ - v44 - Ja '98 - p121 [51-250]

Converse All Star Soccer

> SLJ - v44 - Ja '98 - p121 [51-250]

Cook, James G

The Thomas Edison Book of Easy and Incredible Experiments

> SB - v32 - D '96 - p259 [1-50]

Cook, Nick

Roller Coasters

> KR - v66 - Ap 1 '98 - p493+ [51-250]

Cooke, Trish

So Much (Illus. by Helen Oxenbury)

> ECEJ - v25 - Fall '97 - p46 [1-50]
> PW - v244 - O 6 '97 - p85 [1-50]

Cookson, Paul

Tongue Twisters and Tonsil Twizzlers (Illus. by Jane Eccles)

> Bks Keeps - My '97 - p25 [51-250]

Cooling, Wendy

Aliens to Earth

> Sch Lib - v45 - Ag '97 - p136 [51-250]

Bad Dreams

> Sch Lib - v45 - Ag '97 - p136 [51-250]

Go for Goal

> Sch Lib - v45 - Ag '97 - p136 [51-250]

On the Run

> Sch Lib - v45 - Ag '97 - p136 [51-250]

Spine Chillers

> Sch Lib - v45 - Ag '97 - p136 [51-250]

Stars in Your Eyes

> Sch Lib - v45 - Ag '97 - p136 [51-250]

Time Watch

> Sch Lib - v45 - Ag '97 - p136 [51-250]

Top Secret

> Sch Lib - v45 - Ag '97 - p136 [51-250]

Weird and Wonderful

> Sch Lib - v45 - Ag '97 - p136 [51-250]

Wild and Free

> Sch Lib - v45 - Ag '97 - p136 [51-250]

Coombs, Karen Mueller
Jackie Robinson: Baseball's Civil Rights Legend
>   BL - v93 - Je 1 '97 - p1689 [51-250]
> y   HB Guide - v8 - Fall '97 - p369 [51-250]

Cooney, Barbara
Eleanor (Illus. by Barbara Cooney)
>   Inst - v106 - My '97 - p20 [1-50]
>   RT - v51 - N '97 - p240 [51-250]
>   RT - v51 - D '97 - p335 [51-250]
>   SE - v61 - Ap '97 - p3* [1-50]

Eleanor. Hattie and the Wild Waves (Cooney). Audio Version
>   SLJ - v43 - D '97 - p73 [51-250]

Cooney, Caroline B
The Terrorist
> y   BL - v94 - Mr 15 '98 - p1225 [1-50]
> y   CBRS - v26 - S '97 - p10 [1-50]
> y   CCB-B - v51 - O '97 - p47 [51-250]
> y   JAAL - v41 - D '97 - p322 [51-250]
> y   KR - v65 - Je 1 '97 - p870 [51-250]
> y   PW - v244 - Jl 28 '97 - p75 [51-250]
>   SLJ - v43 - S '97 - p213 [51-250]
> y   VOYA - v20 - O '97 - p242 [51-250]
> y   VOYA - v21 - Ap '98 - p40 [1-50]

Cooney, Helen
Underwater Animals
>   SB - v33 - Je '97 - p145 [51-250]

Cooper, Alison
A Punishment to Fit the Crime?
>   Bks Keeps - My '97 - p26+ [51-250]
>   HB Guide - v8 - Fall '97 - p327 [51-250]

Cooper, Ann C
Along the Seashore (Illus. by Dorothy Emerling)
>   Bloom Rev - v17 - Jl '97 - p21 [51-250]
>   KR - v65 - My 15 '97 - p798 [51-250]
>   SLJ - v43 - Ag '97 - p146 [51-250]

Cooper, Elisha
Ballpark (Illus. by Elisha Cooper)
>   CCB-B - v51 - Mr '98 - p239 [51-250]
>   KR - v66 - F 15 '98 - p265 [51-250]
>   PW - v245 - Ja 19 '98 - p378 [51-250]
>   SLJ - v44 - Mr '98 - p194 [51-250]

Country Fair (Illus. by Elisha Cooper)
>   BL - v94 - S 15 '97 - p240+ [51-250]
>   CBRS - v26 - S '97 - p1+ [51-250]
>   CCB-B - v51 - S '97 - p8 [51-250]
>   HB - v73 - S '97 - p554 [51-250]
>   KR - v65 - Je 15 '97 - p947+ [51-250]
>   PW - v244 - My 26 '97 - p85 [51-250]
>   SLJ - v43 - S '97 - p179 [51-250]

Cooper, Floyd
Cumbayah (Illus. by Floyd Cooper)
>   BL - v94 - F 15 '98 - p1014 [51-250]
>   PW - v245 - Mr 23 '98 - p94+ [51-250]

Mandela: From the Life of the South African Statesman (Illus. by Floyd Cooper)
>   Bl S - v27 - Spr '97 - p76 [1-50]
> y   JAAL - v40 - Ap '97 - p587+ [251-500]
>   RT - v51 - D '97 - p334 [51-250]
>   SE - v61 - Ap '97 - p3* [1-50]
> y   SE - v61 - S '97 - p270 [1-50]

Cooper, Helen, 1963-
The Baby Who Wouldn't Go to Bed (Illus. by Helen Cooper)
>   NS - v126 - D 5 '97 - p62 [1-50]
>   TES - N 7 '97 - p4* [1-50]

The Boy Who Wouldn't Go to Bed (Illus. by Helen Cooper)
>   BL - v93 - Ag '97 - p1898 [51-250]
>   CCB-B - v51 - S '97 - p8 [51-250]
>   Ch BWatch - v7 - Jl '97 - p6 [1-50]
>   HB Guide - v8 - Fall '97 - p261 [51-250]
>   KR - v65 - My 15 '97 - p798 [51-250]
>   SLJ - v43 - Jl '97 - p60 [51-250]

Cooper, Ilene
The Dead Sea Scrolls (Illus. by John Thompson)
>   Ch BWatch - v7 - O '97 - p7 [1-50]
>   HB - v73 - S '97 - p590+ [51-250]
>   HB Guide - v8 - Fall '97 - p387 [51-250]
> y   SLJ - v43 - Je '97 - p133 [51-250]

I'll See You in My Dreams
> y   BL - v93 - Je 1 '97 - p1682 [1-50]
>   CCB-B - v51 - S '97 - p8+ [51-250]
> y   JAAL - v41 - F '98 - p410 [51-250]
>   KR - v65 - Je 1 '97 - p870 [51-250]
>   PW - v244 - Je 2 '97 - p72 [51-250]
>   SLJ - v43 - Ag '97 - p154 [51-250]

The New, Improved Gretchen
Hubbard
>   BL - v94 - Ja 1 '98 - p795 [1-50]

Queen of the Sixth Grade
>   BL - v94 - S 1 '97 - p119 [1-50]

Cooper, Melrose
I Got a Family (Illus. by Dale
Gottlieb)
>   PW - v244 - O 20 '97 - p78 [1-50]

Pets! (Illus. by Yumi Heo)
>   KR - v66 - F 15 '98 - p265 [51-250]
>   PW - v245 - Ja 19 '98 - p377 [51-250]
>   SLJ - v44 - Ap '98 - p97 [51-250]

Cooper, Stephen R
The Great Pyramid (Illus. by Carolyn
Croll)
>   TES - D 5 '97 - p18* [51-250]

Cooper, Susan
The Boggart and the Monster
>   HB Guide - v8 - Fall '97 - p298 [51-250]
>   NYTBR - v102 - My 18 '97 - p29 [501+]
>   SLJ - v43 - My '97 - p131 [51-250]

The Boggart and the Monster
(Rintoul). Audio Version
>   SLJ - v44 - Ap '98 - p38 [1-50]

The Dark Is Rising
>   TES - Ja 2 '98 - p22* [1-50]

Copage, Eric V
A Kwanzaa Fable (Daniel). Audio
Version
> y   Kliatt - v32 - Ja '98 - p44 [51-250]
>   SLJ - v43 - D '97 - p70 [51-250]

Corbell, Jean-Claude
The Oxford Children's Visual
Dictionary
> r   Magpies - v12 - My '97 - p23 [251-500]

Corbet-Singleton, Paul
The Face
>   Aust Bk R - Je '97 - p58+ [501+]
>   Magpies - v12 - Jl '97 - p36 [51-250]

Corbett, Grahame
Fantastic Animals
>   Ch BWatch - v7 - D '97 - p4 [1-50]
>   SLJ - v44 - F '98 - p116 [51-250]

Corbishley, Mike
The World of Architectural Wonders
(Illus. by Mike Foster)
> r   BL - v93 - Je 1 '97 - p1689+ [51-250]
> r   Class Out - v75 - Fall '97 - p29 [51-250]
> r   HB Guide - v8 - Fall '97 - p363 [51-250]
> r   SLJ - v43 - Jl '97 - p81 [51-250]

The Young Oxford History of Britain
and Ireland
> r   Magpies - v12 - My '97 - p43 [251-500]
> y   SLJ - v43 - Jl '97 - p109 [51-250]
> r   VOYA - v20 - Ag '97 - p212 [501+]

Corbridge, Fiona
Thank You God
>   Bloom Rev - v17 - N '97 - p31 [51-250]

Cordova, Amy
Abuelita's Heart (Illus. by Amy
Cordova)
>   BL - v93 - Ag '97 - p1905 [51-250]
>   CBRS - v26 - Win '98 - p61 [51-250]
>   SLJ - v43 - S '97 - p179 [51-250]

Coren, Michael
The Man Who Created Narnia
>   Can CL - v23 - Fall '97 - p90+ [501+]

Corentin, Philippe
Papa! (Illus. by Philippe Corentin)
>   CBRS - v25 - Ag '97 - p158 [51-250]
>   CCB-B - v51 - S '97 - p9 [51-250]
>   Ch BWatch - v7 - S '97 - p3 [1-50]
>   HB Guide - v8 - Fall '97 - p261 [51-250]
>   KR - v65 - Je 1 '97 - p870 [51-250]
>   PW - v244 - My 26 '97 - p84 [51-250]
>   SLJ - v43 - S '97 - p179 [51-250]

Cormier, Robert
The Chocolate War
> y   BL - v94 - S 1 '97 - p119 [1-50]
>   NYTBR - v102 - N 16 '97 - p26 [1-50]

Cornish, Jane
Emily's Wonderful Pie (Illus. by Sue Hitchcock-Pratt)
>Magpies - v12 - My '97 - p6* [51-250]

Corpi, Lucha
Where Fireflies Dance (Illus. by Mira Reisberg)
>BL - v94 - Ja 1 '98 - p822 [51-250]
>CCB-B - v51 - O '97 - p47 [51-250]
>Ch BWatch - v7 - O '97 - p6 [1-50]
>KR - v65 - Jl 15 '97 - p1109 [51-250]
>SLJ - v43 - D '97 - p87 [51-250]

Corrain, Lucia
The Art of the Renaissance (Illus. by L R Galante)
>y   BL - v94 - Mr 1 '98 - p1123 [51-250]
>Ch BWatch - v7 - N '97 - p6 [1-50]
>y   HMR - Win '97 - p46 [51-250]
>SLJ - v44 - F '98 - p114 [51-250]

Corrin, Ruth
Get Real Paddy Manson (Illus. by Fifi Colston)
>Magpies - v12 - Mr '97 - p7* [251-500]

Cosby, Bill
The Best Way to Play (Illus. by Varnette P Honeywood)
>Am Vis - v12 - D '97 - p34 [51-250]
>BL - v94 - F 15 '98 - p1010+ [51-250]
>CBRS - v26 - O '97 - p20 [51-250]
>CCB-B - v51 - D '97 - p121+ [51-250]
>CM:CanRev - v4 - Ja 16 '98 - pONL [251-500]
>Par - v72 - D '97 - p204 [1-50]
>SLJ - v43 - D '97 - p87+ [51-250]

The Meanest Thing to Say (Illus. by Varnette P Honeywood)
>Am Vis - v12 - D '97 - p34 [51-250]
>BL - v94 - F 15 '98 - p1010+ [51-250]
>CBRS - v26 - O '97 - p20 [51-250]
>CCB-B - v51 - D '97 - p121+ [51-250]
>CM:CanRev - v4 - Ja 16 '98 - pONL [251-500]
>Par - v72 - D '97 - p204 [1-50]
>SLJ - v43 - D '97 - p87+ [51-250]

Shipwreck Saturday (Illus. by Varnette P Honeywood)
>PW - v245 - F 23 '98 - p78 [1-50]

The Treasure Hunt (Illus. by Varnette P Honeywood)
>BL - v94 - F 15 '98 - p1010+ [51-250]
>CBRS - v26 - O '97 - p20 [51-250]
>CCB-B - v51 - D '97 - p121+ [51-250]
>CM:CanRev - v4 - Ja 16 '98 - pONL [251-500]
>KR - v65 - S 15 '97 - p1455 [51-250]
>Par - v72 - D '97 - p204 [1-50]
>SLJ - v43 - D '97 - p87+ [51-250]

Costain, Meredith
Rock Raps
>Magpies - v12 - S '97 - p42+ [51-250]

Cote, Nancy
Flip-Flops (Illus. by Nancy Cote)
>KR - v66 - Mr 1 '98 - p337 [51-250]

Cotler, Amy
My Little House Cookbook and Apron (Illus. by Holly Jones)
>PW - v245 - F 16 '98 - p213 [51-250]

Couper, Heather
Big Bang (Illus. by Luciano Corbella)
>BL - v93 - Je 1 '97 - p1690 [51-250]
>Ch BWatch - v7 - Jl '97 - p8 [1-50]
>y   CLW - v68 - D '97 - p82 [51-250]
>y   HB Guide - v8 - Fall '97 - p341 [51-250]
>Magpies - v12 - S '97 - p44 [51-250]
>New Sci - v156 - O 18 '97 - p53 [51-250]
>Obs - Jl 20 '97 - p18* [51-250]
>SB - v33 - Ag '97 - p163 [1-50]
>y   Sch Lib - v45 - Ag '97 - p163 [51-250]
>y   SLJ - v43 - Ag '97 - p165 [51-250]
>TES - N 7 '97 - p9* [1-50]
>TES - N 7 '97 - p13* [501+]

Black Holes (Illus. by Luciano Corbella)
>ASBYP - v29 - Fall '96 - p10+ [251-500]
>y   VOYA - v20 - Ap '97 - p51+ [251-500]

Coursen, Valerie
Mordant's Wish (Illus. by Valerie Coursen)
>BL - v94 - S 1 '97 - p132 [51-250]
>Bloom Rev - v17 - N '97 - p32 [51-250]
>CBRS - v26 - F '98 - p74 [51-250]
>CCB-B - v51 - O '97 - p48 [51-250]

KR - v65 - Jl 1 '97 - p1028 [51-250]
PW - v244 - My 26 '97 - p85 [51-250]
SLJ - v43 - S '97 - p179 [51-250]

Courtney, Vincent
Virtual Fred (Illus. by Eric Brace)
SLJ - v43 - Ap '97 - p97 [51-250]

Cousins, Lucy
Count with Maisy (Illus. by Lucy Cousins)
HB - v73 - Jl '97 - p442+ [51-250]
HB Guide - v8 - Fall '97 - p250 [51-250]

Maisy's Colors
HB Guide - v8 - Fall '97 - p250 [1-50]

Maisy's House
Bkbird - v35 - Sum '97 - p56 [51-250]

Noah's Ark
HB Guide - v8 - Fall '97 - p250 [1-50]
TES - O 17 '97 - p12* [51-250]

Couture, Susan Arkin
The Biggest Horse I Ever Did See (Illus. by Claire Ewart)
HB Guide - v8 - Fall '97 - p261 [51-250]

Covault, R
Pablo and Pimienta (Illus. by Francisco Mora)
ECEJ - v25 - Fall '97 - p46 [1-50]

Covey, Stephen R
Disney's Beauty and the Beast
Ch BWatch - v7 - D '97 - p2 [51-250]

Coville, Bruce
Bruce Coville's Book of Monsters. Audio Version
SLJ - v43 - Ap '97 - p80 [51-250]

Into the Land of the Unicorns
BL - v94 - N 1 '97 - p475 [1-50]

The Lapsnatcher (Illus. by Marissa Moss)
BL - v93 - Je 1 '97 - p1716 [51-250]
HB Guide - v8 - Fall '97 - p262 [51-250]
SLJ - v43 - Jl '97 - p60 [51-250]

The Skull of Truth (Illus. by Gary A Lippincott)
BL - v94 - O 1 '97 - p328 [51-250]
Ch BWatch - v7 - N '97 - p2 [1-50]
PW - v244 - Ag 11 '97 - p402 [51-250]
SLJ - v43 - D '97 - p24 [1-50]

The Skull of Truth (Coville). Audio Version
SLJ - v44 - Ap '98 - p39 [1-50]

William Shakespeare's A Midsummer Night's Dream (Illus. by Dennis Nolan)
Bks Keeps - S '97 - p24 [51-250]
RT - v51 - D '97 - p332 [51-250]
Sch Lib - v45 - Ag '97 - p136 [51-250]
TES - D 26 '97 - p22 [51-250]

William Shakespeare's Macbeth (Illus. by Gary Kelley)
BL - v94 - N 1 '97 - p464 [51-250]
y   BL - v94 - Mr 15 '98 - p1224 [1-50]
CCB-B - v51 - Ja '98 - p177 [51-250]
KR - v65 - O 1 '97 - p1530 [51-250]
SLJ - v43 - D '97 - p134+ [51-250]
y   VOYA - v21 - Ap '98 - p39 [1-50]

Cowan, Catherine
My Life with the Wave (Illus. by Mark Buehner)
BL - v94 - Mr 15 '98 - p1219 [1-50]
BW - v27 - D 7 '97 - p21 [51-250]
CBRS - v26 - O '97 - p20 [51-250]
CCB-B - v51 - O '97 - p48 [51-250]
HB - v73 - S '97 - p555+ [51-250]
Inst - v107 - Ja '98 - p31 [51-250]
KR - v65 - Je 15 '97 - p955 [51-250]
NYTBR - v102 - N 9 '97 - p24 [501+]
PW - v244 - N 3 '97 - p59 [1-50]
SLJ - v43 - Ag '97 - p129 [51-250]
SLJ - v43 - D '97 - p24 [1-50]

Cowcher, Helen
Jaguar (Illus. by Helen Cowcher)
BL - v94 - O 15 '97 - p412 [51-250]
KR - v65 - Jl 1 '97 - p1028 [51-250]
NYTBR - v102 - N 23 '97 - p32 [1-50]
Sch Lib - v45 - N '97 - p185 [51-250]
SLJ - v43 - Ag '97 - p129 [51-250]

Cowen-Fletcher, Jane
Baby Angels (Illus. by Jane Cowen-Fletcher)
> ECEJ - v24 - Sum '97 - p252 [51-250]
> PW - v245 - Ja 12 '98 - p61 [1-50]

Cowley, Joy
Gracias, the Thanksgiving Turkey (Illus. by Joe Cowley)
> SE - v61 - Ap '97 - p13* [1-50]

The Great Bamboozle (Illus. by Philip Webb)
> Magpies - v12 - Jl '97 - p7* [51-250]

Nicketty-Nacketty, Noo-Noo-Noo (Illus. by Tracey Moroney)
> Magpies - v12 - Mr '97 - p2* [1-50]
> Magpies - v12 - My '97 - p26 [51-250]

Singing Down the Rain (Illus. by Jan Spivey Gilchrist)
> CBRS - v26 - D '97 - p37 [51-250]
> CCB-B - v51 - Ja '98 - p157 [51-250]
> KR - v65 - S 15 '97 - p1455 [51-250]
> PW - v244 - N 3 '97 - p85 [51-250]

Cox, Clinton
Fiery Vision
> CBRS - v25 - My '97 - p118 [51-250]
> y　CCB-B - v50 - Jl '97 - p390+ [51-250]

Cox, Judy
Now We Can Have a Wedding! (Illus. by DyAnne DiSalvo-Ryan)
> BL - v94 - F 15 '98 - p1019 [51-250]
> KR - v66 - F 15 '98 - p265 [51-250]
> PW - v245 - F 9 '98 - p94+ [51-250]
> SLJ - v44 - Mr '98 - p168 [51-250]

Cox, Phil Roxbee
Whatever Happened to Professor Potts?
> Emerg Lib - v24 - My '97 - p51 [51-250]

Cox, Steve
Big Machines in Town (Illus. by Steve Cox)
> Bks Keeps - S '97 - p21 [51-250]

Big Machines on the Farm (Illus. by Steve Cox)
> Bks Keeps - S '97 - p21 [51-250]

Coxe, Molly
Big Egg
> HB Guide - v8 - Fall '97 - p286 [51-250]

Coxon, Michele
Look Out, Lion Cub!
> Sch Lib - v45 - Ag '97 - p130 [51-250]

Coyne, Rachel
Daughter, Have I Told You? (Illus. by Virginia Halstead)
> KR - v66 - Mr 15 '98 - p400+ [51-250]
> PW - v245 - F 2 '98 - p88 [51-250]

Crabtree, Judith
A Strange and Powerful Magic
> Aust Bk R - v279 - My '97 - p62+ [501+]

Craddock, Sonia
Rosemary for Remembrance (Illus. by Daniel Shelton)
> BIC - v26 - Je '97 - p34+ [501+]
> CBRA - '96 - p470 [51-250]

Craft, Marie Charlotte
Cupid and Psyche (Illus. by Kinuko Craft)
> RT - v51 - D '97 - p332 [51-250]

Craig, Claire
Explorers and Traders
> ASBYP - v29 - Fall '96 - p57 [251-500]
> SB - v32 - D '96 - p277 [51-250]

Incredible Creatures
> SB - v33 - Je '97 - p145 [51-250]

Craighead, Charles
The Eagle and the River
> JOYS - v10 - Sum '97 - p427 [1-50]

Cranston, Patty
Superstars on Ice
> CBRA - '96 - p523 [51-250]

Cray, Jordan
Gemini7
> PW - v244 - Ag 25 '97 - p72 [51-250]
> y SLJ - v44 - Ja '98 - p111 [51-250]

Crayola Kids
> p LA - v73 - N '96 - p537+ [501+]

Creagh, Carson
Reptiles
> ASBYP - v29 - Fall '96 - p57+ [501+]

Crebbin, June
Into the Castle (Illus. by John Bendall-Brunello)
> Bks Keeps - Jl '97 - p19 [51-250]

The Train Ride (Illus. by Stephen Lambert)
> Bks Keeps - N '97 - p21 [51-250]

Creech, Sharon
Chasing Redbird
> y BL - v94 - Mr 15 '98 - p1214 [1-50]
> y Books - v11 - O '97 - p21 [1-50]
> y BW - v27 - My 4 '97 - p16 [51-250]
> HB Guide - v8 - Fall '97 - p298 [51-250]
> y Sch Lib - v45 - Ag '97 - p157 [51-250]
> SLJ - v43 - Ap '97 - p137 [51-250]
> y SLJ - v44 - Ja '98 - p41 [251-500]
> y TES - N 7 '97 - p12* [51-250]
> y VOYA - v21 - Ap '98 - p36 [1-50]

Pleasing the Ghost
> PW - v244 - S 1 '97 - p107 [1-50]

Walk Two Moons (Harper). Audio Version
> BL - v94 - F 15 '98 - p1027 [51-250]
> y Kliatt - v32 - Ja '98 - p46 [51-250]
> PW - v244 - D 8 '97 - p29 [51-250]

Creith, Elizabeth
Erik the Viking Sheep (Illus. by Linda Hendry)
> CM:CanRev - v4 - Ja 16 '98 - pONL [251-500]
> Quill & Q - v63 - S '97 - p73 [51-250]

Crespi, Francesca
Ding Dong! Merrily on High (Illus. by Francesca Crespi)
> CM:CanRev - v4 - F 13 '98 - pONL [51-250]

Make a Joyful Noise
> PW - v244 - O 6 '97 - p57 [1-50]

Cresswell, Helen
Bag of Bones
> Bks Keeps - Jl '97 - p24 [51-250]
> TES - Ja 2 '98 - p22* [1-50]

The Sea Piper (Illus. by Jason Cockcroft)
> Books - v11 - D '97 - p21 [51-250]
> Sch Lib - v45 - N '97 - p190 [51-250]
> TES - S 19 '97 - p13* [501+]

Sophie and the Sea Wolf (Illus. by Jason Cockcroft)
> Spec - v279 - D 6 '97 - p43 [51-250]
> TES - N 7 '97 - p6* [251-500]

Crew, Gary
Bright Star (Illus. by Anne Spudvilas)
> BL - v94 - O 15 '97 - p412 [51-250]
> Ch BWatch - v7 - N '97 - p4 [1-50]
> Ch BWatch - v7 - D '97 - p6 [51-250]
> KR - v65 - O 1 '97 - p1530 [251-500]
> SLJ - v44 - F '98 - p79 [51-250]

First Light (Illus. by Peter Gouldthorpe)
> Ch BWatch - v7 - S '97 - p3 [51-250]

Tagged (Illus. by Steven Woolman)
> Aust Bk R - D '97 - p64+ [501+]

The Watertower (Illus. by Steven Woolman)
> KR - v66 - Ja 1 '98 - p55+ [51-250]
> PW - v245 - Ja 19 '98 - p378 [51-250]
> SLJ - v44 - Mr '98 - p168 [51-250]

Crew, Linda
Long Time Passing
> y KR - v65 - Ag 1 '97 - p1220 [51-250]
> PW - v244 - Jl 21 '97 - p202 [51-250]
> y VOYA - v21 - Ap '98 - p44 [51-250]

Crewe, Sabrina
The Alligator (Illus. by Jim Chanell)
> SB - v34 - Ap '98 - p80+ [51-250]

The Bear (Illus. by Robert Morton)
ASBYP - v29 - Fall '96 - p53+ [251-500]
SLJ - v43 - Ap '97 - p121 [51-250]

The Beaver (Illus. by Andrew Pepworth)
SB - v34 - Ap '98 - p80+ [51-250]

The Bee (Illus. by Stuart Lafford)
ASBYP - v29 - Fall '96 - p53+ [251-500]
SLJ - v43 - Ap '97 - p121 [51-250]

The Buffalo (Illus. by Robert Morton)
SB - v34 - Ap '98 - p80+ [51-250]

The Butterfly
ASBYP - v29 - Fall '96 - p53+ [251-500]

The Chimpanzee
ASBYP - v29 - Fall '96 - p53+ [251-500]

The Frog
ASBYP - v29 - Fall '96 - p53+ [251-500]

Hills and Mountains (Illus. by Andrew Farmer)
HB Guide - v8 - Fall '97 - p385 [51-250]
Sch Lib - v45 - Ag '97 - p150 [51-250]

The Kangaroo
ASBYP - v29 - Fall '96 - p53+ [251-500]

The Ladybug
ASBYP - v29 - Fall '96 - p53+ [251-500]

Maps and Globes (Illus. by Raymond Turvey)
HB Guide - v8 - Fall '97 - p385 [51-250]
Sch Lib - v45 - Ag '97 - p150 [51-250]

The Prairie Dog
ASBYP - v29 - Fall '96 - p53+ [251-500]

The Salmon
ASBYP - v29 - Fall '96 - p53+ [251-500]

The Snake
ASBYP - v29 - Fall '96 - p53+ [251-500]

The Spider (Illus. by Stuart Lafford)
SB - v34 - Ap '98 - p80+ [51-250]

The Swallow
ASBYP - v29 - Fall '96 - p53+ [251-500]

The Whale
ASBYP - v29 - Fall '96 - p53+ [251-500]

Crews, Donald
Bigmama's
PW - v245 - Ja 26 '98 - p93 [1-50]

Night at the Fair (Illus. by Donald Crews)
BL - v94 - Mr 1 '98 - p1140 [51-250]
KR - v66 - Ap 1 '98 - p494 [51-250]
PW - v245 - F 16 '98 - p210 [51-250]
SLJ - v44 - Ap '98 - p97+ [51-250]

Truck (Illus. by Donald Crews)
PW - v244 - Ag 25 '97 - p73 [1-50]

Crews, Nina
I'll Catch the Moon
RT - v51 - D '97 - p332 [51-250]

Snowball (Illus. by Nina Crews)
BL - v94 - D 1 '97 - p640 [51-250]
CCB-B - v51 - D '97 - p122 [51-250]
KR - v65 - O 1 '97 - p1530 [251-500]
NYTBR - v103 - Ja 4 '98 - p20 [1-50]
PW - v244 - N 10 '97 - p73 [51-250]
SLJ - v43 - S '97 - p179 [51-250]

Crichton, Michael
The Lost World
Books - v11 - Ag '97 - p15 [51-250]

Lost World
Books - v11 - Ag '97 - p15 [51-250]

Cricket
p   Par Ch - Awards '97 - p27 [1-50]

Crisfield, D W
Louisville Slugger Book of Great Hitters
r   PW - v245 - Mr 16 '98 - p67 [51-250]
r   SLJ - v44 - Ap '98 - p143 [51-250]

Cristaldi, Kathryn
Princess Lulu Goes to Camp (Illus. by Heather Harms Maione)
　　BL - v93 - Ag '97 - p1908+ [51-250]
　　HB Guide - v8 - Fall '97 - p286 [51-250]
　　SLJ - v43 - D '97 - p88 [51-250]

Croasdale, Laurine
Trivia Man
　　Magpies - v12 - S '97 - p33 [51-250]

Croll, Carolyn
Redoute: The Man Who Painted Flowers (Illus. by Carolyn Croll)
　　RT - v51 - S '97 - p53 [51-250]

Crompton, Richmal
William in Trouble
　　Books - v11 - D '97 - p21 [1-50]

William the Explorer
　　Books - v11 - D '97 - p21 [1-50]

Cronin, Gaynell Bordes
The Best of Holy Days and Holidays (Illus. by Chris Larson)
　　CLW - v68 - D '97 - p72 [51-250]

Crook, Connie Brummel
Maple Moon (Illus. by Scott Cameron)
　　Quill & Q - v64 - Ja '98 - p38 [251-500]
　　SLJ - v44 - Ap '98 - p98 [51-250]

Crook, Marion
Riding Scared
　　BIC - v26 - S '97 - p32+ [501+]
　　CBRA - '96 - p465+ [251-500]

Cross, Gillian
The Demon Headmaster Strikes Again
　　Magpies - v12 - Mr '97 - p33 [51-250]

The Demon Headmaster Takes Over
　　Books - v11 - D '97 - p21 [1-50]

The Great American Elephant Chase
　　SLJ - v43 - S '97 - p130 [1-50]

The Iron Way
　　TES - O 10 '97 - p8* [51-250]

Pictures in the Dark
　　Magpies - v12 - My '97 - p37+ [51-250]

Crossley-Holland, Kevin
The Old Stories (Illus. by John Lawrence)
　　Bks Keeps - N '97 - p24 [51-250]
　　TES - S 5 '97 - p8* [251-500]

Poems from East Anglia
　　y　Obs - O 26 '97 - p15* [51-250]
　　Sch Lib - v45 - N '97 - p208 [51-250]

Croteau, Marie-Danielle
Fred and the Stinky Cheese (Illus. by Bruno St.-Aubin)
　　BIC - v26 - My '97 - p35+ [501+]
　　CBRA - '96 - p470 [51-250]

Crowe, Anna
Skating Out of the House
　　Sch Lib - v45 - N '97 - p208+ [51-250]

Crowe, Carole
Sharp Horns on the Moon
　　KR - v66 - F 1 '98 - p194 [51-250]
　　SLJ - v44 - Mr '98 - p211 [51-250]

Crowther, Robert
Dump Trucks and Diggers (Illus. by Robert Crowther)
　　Magpies - v12 - Mr '97 - p20+ [501+]

My Pop-Up Surprise 123 (Illus. by Robert Crowther)
　　Magpies - v12 - Mr '97 - p20+ [501+]
　　Par - v72 - D '97 - p202 [1-50]
　　PW - v244 - S 1 '97 - p106 [51-250]
　　SLJ - v43 - Ag '97 - p129+ [51-250]

My Pop-Up Surprise ABC (Illus. by Robert Crowther)
　　KR - v65 - Jl 1 '97 - p1028 [51-250]
　　Magpies - v12 - Mr '97 - p20+ [51-250]
　　Par - v72 - D '97 - p202 [1-50]
　　PW - v244 - S 1 '97 - p106 [51-250]
　　SLJ - v43 - Ag '97 - p129+ [51-250]

Robert Crowther's Pop-Up Olympics (Illus. by Robert Crowther)
　　RT - v51 - O '97 - p138 [1-50]

Tractors and Trucks (Illus. by Robert Crowther)

Magpies - v12 - Mr '97 - p20+ [501+]

Crozat, Francois
I Am a Little Kangaroo

HB Guide - v8 - Fall '97 - p250 [51-250]

Cruise, Robin
The Top-Secret Journal of Fiona Claire Jardin

KR - v66 - Mr 15 '98 - p401 [51-250]
SLJ - v44 - Ap '98 - p128+ [51-250]

Cruz, Barbara C
Ruben Blades: Salsa Singer and Social Activist

SLJ - v44 - Ja '98 - p122 [51-250]
y   VOYA - v20 - F '98 - p399 [251-500]

Cuetara, Mittie
Terrible Teresa and Other Very Short Stories (Illus. by Mittie Cuetara)

BL - v94 - O 15 '97 - p412+ [51-250]
CBRS - v26 - F '98 - p74 [51-250]
KR - v65 - Ag 1 '97 - p1220 [51-250]
NYTBR - v103 - F 15 '98 - p26 [51-250]
PW - v244 - Ag 18 '97 - p91 [51-250]
SLJ - v43 - N '97 - p78+ [51-250]

Cullen, Lynn
Stink Bomb

PW - v245 - Ja 19 '98 - p378 [51-250]
SLJ - v44 - Mr '98 - p211 [51-250]

Cumbaa, Stephen
The Neanderthal Book and Skeleton (Illus. by Kim LaFave)

Quill & Q - v64 - F '98 - p45 [251-500]

Cumming, David
Coasts

HB Guide - v8 - Fall '97 - p345 [51-250]

Cummings, Pat
My Aunt Came Back (Illus. by Pat Cummings)

KR - v66 - F 1 '98 - p194 [51-250]
PW - v245 - Ja 26 '98 - p93 [1-50]

Cummings, Phil
Angel

Magpies - v12 - S '97 - p33 [51-250]

Cummings, Priscilla
Autumn Journey

KR - v65 - Je 1 '97 - p871 [51-250]
PW - v244 - Ag 11 '97 - p402 [51-250]

Cundiff, Alice
Charlie Keeps His Promise and Other Animal Stories (Illus. by Cynthia Post)

CBRA - '96 - p470+ [51-250]

Cunliffe, John
Postman Pat and the Hole in the Road (Barrie). Book and Audio Version

TES - N 7 '97 - p13* [51-250]

Curious Creatures. Electronic Media Version

SLJ - v44 - F '98 - p54 [251-500]

Curlee, Lynn
Into the Ice (Illus. by Lynn Curlee)

BW - v28 - Mr 1 '98 - p11 [51-250]
KR - v66 - Mr 1 '98 - p337 [51-250]

Currey, Anna
Barnaby's Surprise (Illus. by Anna Currey)

Sch Lib - v45 - N '97 - p185 [51-250]

Currie, Stephen
Adoption

y   HB Guide - v8 - Fall '97 - p327 [51-250]
SLJ - v43 - Ap '97 - p146+ [51-250]

We Have Marched Together

CCB-B - v50 - Je '97 - p353 [51-250]
HB Guide - v8 - Fall '97 - p323 [51-250]
SLJ - v43 - Jl '97 - p101+ [51-250]

Curry, Barbara K
Sweet Words so Brave (Illus. by Jerry Butler)

SLJ - v43 - Ap '97 - p121+ [51-250]

Curry, Jane Louise
Robin Hood and His Merry Men
BL - v94 - Mr 1 '98 - p1125 [51-250]

Curry, Jennifer
*Hands Off Our Hens! (Illus. by
Christine Pilsworth)*
Bks Keeps - Jl '97 - p23 [51-250]

Young Hippo Magic
NS - v126 - D 5 '97 - p63 [1-50]

Curti, Anna
My Very First Nature Craft Book
HB Guide - v8 - Fall '97 - p362 [51-250]

Curtis, Christopher Paul
The Watsons Go to Birmingham--1963
BL - v94 - F 15 '98 - p999 [1-50]
Ch BWatch - v8 - Ja '98 - p4 [51-250]
CM:CanRev - v4 - Ja 16 '98 - pONL [251-500]
y JAAL - v41 - N '97 - p215 [51-250]
y Kliatt - v32 - Ja '98 - p8 [51-250]
PW - v244 - O 27 '97 - p79 [51-250]
Sch Lib - v45 - N '97 - p211 [251-500]
TES - v43 - Ag 15 '97 - p23 [251-500]
y TES - N 7 '97 - p13* [51-250]
y TES - D 26 '97 - p14 [51-250]

Curtis, Jamie Lee
*Tell Me Again about the Night I Was
Born (Illus. by Laura Cornell)*
ECEJ - v24 - Sum '97 - p250 [51-250]
Obs - D 7 '97 - p17* [51-250]
RT - v51 - D '97 - p330 [51-250]

Curtis, Munzee
*When the Big Dog Barks (Illus. by
Susan Avishai)*
HB Guide - v8 - Fall '97 - p250 [51-250]
SLJ - v43 - Ap '97 - p97 [51-250]

Curtis, Patricia
Animals You Never Even Heard Of
BL - v94 - S 1 '97 - p109+ [51-250]
Ch BWatch - v7 - Jl '97 - p3 [51-250]
HB Guide - v8 - Fall '97 - p345 [51-250]
KR - v65 - Je 1 '97 - p871 [51-250]
SLJ - v43 - S '97 - p201 [51-250]

Curtis, Rebecca S
Charlotte Avery on Isle Royale
Ch BWatch - v7 - Je '97 - p3 [51-250]

Cushman, Doug
*Mouse and Mole and the All Weather
Train Ride (Illus. by Doug Cushman)*
ASBYP - v29 - Sum '96 - p10 [251-500]

*Mouse and Mole and the Year-Round
Garden (Illus. by Doug Cushman)*
SB - v33 - O '97 - p218 [51-250]

Cushman, Karen
The Ballad of Lucy Whipple
BL - v93 - Je 1 '97 - p1700+ [1-50]
Learning - v26 - Ag '97 - p26 [51-250]
RT - v51 - O '97 - p149 [51-250]
y RT - v51 - N '97 - p244 [51-250]
y Sch Lib - v45 - N '97 - p211 [51-250]
y SE - v61 - Ap '97 - p10* [1-50]
SLJ - v43 - S '97 - p130 [1-50]
TES - Ag 29 '97 - p28 [51-250]
y TES - N 7 '97 - p12* [51-250]

*The Ballad of Lucy Whipple (Moore).
Audio Version*
y BL - v94 - D 15 '97 - p711 [1-50]
HB - v73 - N '97 - p701+ [251-500]
y Kliatt - v32 - Ja '98 - p40 [51-250]
SLJ - v44 - Ap '98 - p38 [1-50]

Catherine, Called Birdy
HB - v74 - Ja '98 - p26+ [501+]
y SLJ - v43 - S '97 - p130 [1-50]
y VOYA - v21 - Ap '98 - p43 [1-50]

The Midwife's Apprentice
Bks Keeps - Jl '97 - p25 [51-250]
y Sch Lib - v45 - Ag '97 - p157 [51-250]
y TES - Jl 4 '97 - p11* [251-500]

Cutler, Jane
*Darcy and Gran Don't Like Babies
(Illus. by Susannah Ryan)*
SLJ - v44 - Ja '98 - p42 [1-50]

Spaceman
HB Guide - v8 - Fall '97 - p298 [51-250]
SLJ - v43 - My '97 - p131 [51-250]

Cwiklik, Robert
Bill Clinton: President of the 90s

BL - v94 - S 15 '97 - p224+ [51-250]
Ch BWatch - v7 - S '97 - p7 [51-250]
HB Guide - v8 - Fall '97 - p379 [51-250]
SLJ - v43 - Jl '97 - p102 [51-250]

Cyrus, Kurt
Tangle Town (Illus. by Kurt Cyrus)

CBRS - v25 - Je '97 - p122 [51-250]
HB Guide - v8 - Fall '97 - p262 [51-250]
Inst - v107 - S '97 - p22 [1-50]
NYTBR - v102 - Jl 20 '97 - p22 [1-50]

Czernecki, Stefan
The Cricket's Cage (Illus. by Stefan Czernecki)

CBRA - '96 - p501 [51-250]
CBRS - v25 - Jl '97 - p146 [1-50]
CCB-B - v50 - Je '97 - p353 [51-250]
CM:CanRev - v4 - S 5 '97 - pONL [51-250]
HB Guide - v8 - Fall '97 - p332 [51-250]
SLJ - v43 - Je '97 - p106 [51-250]

D

Dabcovich, Lydia
The Polar Bear Son (Illus. by Lydia Dabcovich)
> CBRS - v25 - My '97 - p110 [51-250]
> HB Guide - v8 - Fall '97 - p332 [51-250]
> SLJ - v43 - Je '97 - p106 [51-250]

Dadey, Debbie
Mrs. Jeepers Is Missing! (Illus. by John Steven Gurney)
> RT - v51 - O '97 - p134 [1-50]

Shooting Star (Illus. by Scott Goto)
> CBRS - v25 - My '97 - p110 [1-50]
> CCB-B - v50 - Je '97 - p353+ [51-250]
> HB Guide - v8 - Fall '97 - p369 [51-250]
> Inst - v107 - O '97 - p24 [51-250]
> SLJ - v43 - Ap '97 - p122 [51-250]

Dahab, Farida Elizabeth
Hurley and the Bone (Illus. by George Molina-Sy)
> Ch BWatch - v7 - Mr '97 - p6 [51-250]

Dahl, Roald
Charlie and the Chocolate Factory (Illus. by Joseph Schindelman)
> Bks Keeps - Jl '97 - p28 [501+]
> NYTBR - v102 - N 16 '97 - p26 [1-50]

Matilda (Hanley). Audio Version
> TES - D 19 '97 - p23 [51-250]

The Roald Dahl Treasury (Illus. by Quentin Blake)
> Bks Keeps - N '97 - p6 [51-250]
> BL - v94 - D 1 '97 - p617 [51-250]
> BW - v27 - O 5 '97 - p11 [251-500]

> Ch BWatch - v8 - Ja '98 - p3 [51-250]
> NW - v130 - D 1 '97 - p78 [51-250]
> Obs - O 5 '97 - p15* [501+]
> Obs - D 7 '97 - p18* [251-500]
> PW - v244 - S 22 '97 - p82 [51-250]
> TES - N 21 '97 - p8* [51-250]

Dakos, Kalli
Get Out of the Alphabet, Number 2! (Illus. by Jenny Graham)
> CBRS - v26 - S '97 - p2 [51-250]
> PW - v244 - Jl 28 '97 - p77 [51-250]

The Goof Who Invented Homework and Other School Poems (Illus. by Denise Brunkus)
> RT - v51 - O '97 - p137 [1-50]

Dale, Mitzi
What's Tuesday
> Ch Bk News - v20 - Sum '97 - p30 [51-250]

Dale, Penny
Big Brother, Little Brother (Illus. by Penny Dale)
> BL - v94 - S 15 '97 - p242 [51-250]
> Ch BWatch - v7 - N '97 - p3 [1-50]
> SLJ - v43 - N '97 - p79 [51-250]

D'Alelio, Jane
I Know That Building
> SB - v32 - D '96 - p259 [1-50]

Daley, Michael J
Nuclear Power
> y   BL - v94 - N 1 '97 - p459 [51-250]
> y   SB - v33 - D '97 - p267+ [251-500]
> SLJ - v44 - Ja '98 - p122 [51-250]

Dalgish, Gerard M
Random House Webster's Dictionary of American English
r   BL - v93 - Je 1 '97 - p1749+ [51-250]
r   SLJ - v43 - My '97 - p156 [51-250]

Dalton, Annie
Tilly Beany Saves the World (Illus. by Lesley Harker)
Sch Lib - v45 - N '97 - p190+ [51-250]

Dalton, Sheila
Doggerel (Illus. by Kim LaFave)
CBRA - '96 - p496+ [51-250]

Daly, Audrey
Spelling and Grammar (Illus. by David Till)
Sch Lib - v45 - N '97 - p203 [51-250]

D'Amico, Joan
The Math Chef (Illus. by Tina Cash-Walsh)
New Sci - v156 - N 22 '97 - p62 [51-250]
SB - v33 - Ag '97 - p177 [51-250]

The Science Chef Travels around the World (Illus. by Tina Cash-Walsh)
ASBYP - v29 - Fall '96 - p11+ [251-500]

Dana, Barbara
Zucchini Out West (Illus. by Lynette Hemmant)
HB Guide - v8 - Fall '97 - p298 [51-250]
KR - v65 - My 15 '97 - p798 [51-250]
SLJ - v43 - Jl '97 - p60+ [51-250]

Danes, Emma
Music Theory for Beginners
Ch BWatch - v7 - Ap '97 - p1 [1-50]

Dangerous Animals
HB Guide - v8 - Fall '97 - p345 [51-250]

Dann, Penny
The Secret Fairy Handbook
Bks Keeps - N '97 - p4 [51-250]
Books - v11 - Ag '97 - p15 [51-250]

TES - D 26 '97 - p22 [51-250]

D'Antonio, Nancy
Our Baby from China (Illus. by Nancy D'Antonio)
CBRS - v25 - Je '97 - p122 [1-50]
HB Guide - v8 - Fall '97 - p321 [51-250]
SLJ - v43 - Je '97 - p106+ [51-250]

Danziger, Paula
The Amber Brown Collection (Witt). Audio Version
BL - v94 - F 15 '98 - p1026+ [51-250]
PW - v244 - Jl 28 '97 - p29 [51-250]
SLJ - v43 - N '97 - p67+ [51-250]

Amber Brown Sees Red (Illus. by Tony Ross)
HB Guide - v8 - Fall '97 - p298 [51-250]
PW - v245 - F 16 '98 - p213 [1-50]
SLJ - v43 - Jl '97 - p61 [51-250]

Amber Brown Wants Extra Credit
Books - v10 - S '96 - p24 [51-250]

Forever Amber Brown (Illus. by Tony Ross)
Bks Keeps - S '97 - p25+ [51-250]
TES - Je 20 '97 - p12* [501+]

P.S. Longer Letter Later
PW - v245 - F 16 '98 - p212 [51-250]

Darian-Smith, Kate
Australia and Oceania
HB Guide - v8 - Fall '97 - p400 [51-250]
Magpies - v12 - Mr '97 - p40+ [251-500]
SLJ - v44 - F '98 - p97 [51-250]

Dark, Daniel
Lightfoot: Adventure in Stonescrow
Aust Bk R - Ag '97 - p61+ [501+]

Darling, Christina
Mirror (Illus. by Alexandra Day)
BW - v27 - My 4 '97 - p16 [51-250]
CBRS - v25 - My '97 - p115 [51-250]
CCB-B - v50 - Jl '97 - p391 [51-250]

Darling, Kathy
ABC Dogs (Illus. by Tara Darling)
    BL - v94 - O 15 '97 - p408 [51-250]
    PW - v244 - O 27 '97 - p79 [51-250]

Amazon ABC (Illus. by Tara Darling)
    ASBYP - v29 - Fall '96 - p12 [251-500]
    BL - v94 - D 1 '97 - p628 [1-50]

Chameleons: On Location (Illus. by Tara Darling)
    HB Guide - v8 - Fall '97 - p350 [51-250]
    SLJ - v43 - Ap '97 - p148 [51-250]

Desert Babies (Illus. by Tara Darling)
    HB Guide - v8 - Fall '97 - p345 [51-250]

Komodo Dragon (Illus. by Tara Darling)
    HB Guide - v8 - Fall '97 - p351 [51-250]
    SB - v33 - Ag '97 - p163 [1-50]
    SLJ - v43 - Ap '97 - p148 [51-250]

Seashore Babies (Illus. by Tara Darling)
    HB Guide - v8 - Fall '97 - p345 [51-250]

Dartez, Cecilia Casrill
Jenny Giraffe's Mardi Gras Ride (Illus. by Andy Green)
    HB Guide - v8 - Fall '97 - p262 [51-250]

Dash, Joan
We Shall Not Be Moved
    y   Kliatt - v32 - Mr '98 - p32 [51-250]
         PW - v245 - Ja 19 '98 - p380 [1-50]
         SE - v61 - Ap '97 - p11* [1-50]
    y   VOYA - v20 - Ag '97 - p163 [51-250]

D'Ath, Justin
Infamous
    Aust Bk R - Ag '97 - p61+ [501+]

Datnow, Claire
Edwin Hubble: Discoverer of Galaxies
    BL - v94 - D 1 '97 - p630 [51-250]
    SLJ - v44 - Mr '98 - p230+ [51-250]
    y   VOYA - v20 - D '97 - p330+ [251-500]

D'Aulaire, Ingri
D'Aulaires' Book of Greek Myths (Illus. by Ingri D'Aulaire)
    NYTBR - v102 - N 16 '97 - p26 [1-50]

Davenier, Christine
Leon and Albertine (Illus. by Christine Davenier)
    CCB-B - v51 - Mr '98 - p239 [51-250]
    KR - v66 - Ja 1 '98 - p56 [51-250]
    PW - v245 - Ja 5 '98 - p66+ [51-250]
    SLJ - v44 - Mr '98 - p168 [51-250]

Davidson, Margaret
The Story of Jackie Robinson, Bravest Man in Baseball (Illus. by Floyd Cooper)
    Ch BWatch - v7 - Mr '97 - p4 [1-50]

Davies, Gill
I'm Scared (Illus. by Susi Adams)
    PW - v244 - O 6 '97 - p50 [1-50]

Surprise Spell (Illus. by Gerry Hawksley)
    PW - v244 - O 6 '97 - p50 [1-50]

What's That Noise (Illus. by Kate Davies)
    PW - v244 - O 6 '97 - p50 [1-50]

Whizzer Bat (Illus. by Gerry Hawksley)
    PW - v244 - O 6 '97 - p50 [1-50]

Davies, Kay
Rain (Illus. by Robert Pickett)
    ASBYP - v29 - Sum '96 - p59+ [501+]

Snow and Ice
    ASBYP - v29 - Sum '96 - p59+ [501+]

Sun
    ASBYP - v29 - Sum '96 - p59+ [501+]

Wind
    ASBYP - v29 - Sum '96 - p59+ [501+]

Davies, Nicola
Big Blue Whale (Illus. by Nick Maland)
    Bks Keeps - N '97 - p23 [51-250]
    BL - v94 - S 1 '97 - p128 [51-250]
    CBRS - v25 - Ag '97 - p164 [51-250]

CCB-B - v51 - O '97 - p48+ [251-500]
Ch BWatch - v7 - Jl '97 - p3 [51-250]
HB Guide - v8 - Fall '97 - p353 [51-250]
KR - v65 - Je 1 '97 - p871+ [51-250]
Magpies - v12 - My '97 - p41+ [51-250]
NYTLa - v147 - D 4 '97 - pE8 [51-250]
Obs - Jl 20 '97 - p18* [51-250]
Sch Lib - v45 - N '97 - p185 [51-250]
SLJ - v43 - Jl '97 - p81+ [51-250]

Davies, Sally J K
Why Did We Have to Move Here?
(Illus. by Sally J K Davies)
BL - v94 - D 15 '97 - p702 [51-250]
KR - v65 - N 1 '97 - p1642 [51-250]

Davis, Amanda
Extraterrestrials: Is There Life in Outer Space?
SLJ - v44 - Ap '98 - p114+ [51-250]

Davis, Aubrey
Bone Button Borscht (Illus. by Dusan Petricic)
BL - v94 - N 1 '97 - p480 [51-250]
CCB-B - v51 - N '97 - p83 [251-500]
NYTBR - v103 - F 15 '98 - p25 [51-250]
SLJ - v43 - N '97 - p106 [51-250]

The Enormous Potato (Illus. by Dusan Petricic)
Quill & Q - v63 - Jl '97 - p50+ [251-500]

Sody Salleratus (Illus. by Alan Daniel)
BL - v94 - Mr 15 '98 - p1246 [51-250]
CBRA - '96 - p438+ [51-250]
PW - v245 - F 2 '98 - p88 [51-250]
SLJ - v44 - Ap '98 - p115 [51-250]

Davis, Gary W
Coral Reef
HB Guide - v8 - Fall '97 - p344 [51-250]

Davis, Meredith
Up and Away! (Illus. by Ken Dubrowski)
SLJ - v44 - Ja '98 - p98 [51-250]

Davis, Wendy
Douglas Fir
HB Guide - v8 - Fall '97 - p344 [51-250]

From Metal to Music (Illus. by Wendy Davis)
BL - v94 - O 15 '97 - p408+ [51-250]
HB Guide - v8 - Fall '97 - p357 [51-250]
SB - v33 - N '97 - p244 [251-500]

Davis, Wendy M
Closing the Borders
TES - O 17 '97 - pR7 [51-250]

Davol, Marguerite W
Batwings and the Curtain of Night (Illus. by Mary GrandPre)
HB Guide - v8 - Fall '97 - p262 [51-250]
SLJ - v43 - Ap '97 - p97 [51-250]

The Paper Dragon (Illus. by Robert Sabuda)
BL - v94 - O 15 '97 - p402 [51-250]
BL - v94 - Mr 15 '98 - p1219 [1-50]
CBRS - v26 - Win '98 - p66 [51-250]
HB - v74 - Ja '98 - p63+ [51-250]
Inst - v107 - Ja '98 - p28+ [51-250]
KR - v65 - S 1 '97 - p1386 [51-250]
PW - v244 - S 29 '97 - p89 [51-250]
SLJ - v43 - N '97 - p79+ [51-250]

DaVolls, Andy
Tano and Binti (Illus. by Andy DaVolls)
SB - v33 - Ap '97 - p91 [51-250]

Dawe, Maxine
NewFindBook: The Great Newfoundland and Labrador Puzzle Book
CBRA - '96 - p523+ [51-250]

Dawson, Blair
Mary Margaret's Tree (Illus. by Blair Dawson)
CBRA - '96 - p439 [51-250]

Dawson, Mildred Leinweber
Beauty Lab
Cur R - v36 - Mr '97 - p12 [51-250]

y   HB Guide - v8 - Fall '97 - p355 [51-250]
y   SB - v33 - Ag '97 - p175 [51-250]

Day, Alexandra

Carl's Birthday
PW - v244 - S 29 '97 - p91 [1-50]

The Christmas We Moved to the Barn (Illus. by Alexandra Day)
BL - v94 - S 1 '97 - p138 [51-250]
CBRS - v26 - N '97 - p26 [51-250]
KR - v65 - S 1 '97 - p1386 [51-250]
PW - v244 - O 6 '97 - p54 [51-250]

Good Dog, Carl
PW - v244 - Jl 7 '97 - p70 [1-50]

Mirror
Bloom Rev - v17 - S '97 - p23 [51-250]
Ch BWatch - v7 - Je '97 - p6 [1-50]
HB Guide - v8 - Fall '97 - p262 [51-250]

Day, Malcolm

The World of Castles and Forts
CLW - v68 - S '97 - p63 [51-250]
HB Guide - v8 - Fall '97 - p323 [51-250]

Day, Trevor

The Incredible Journey to the Centre of the Atom. The Incredible Journey to the Edge of the Universe
New Sci - v154 - Je 7 '97 - p48 [51-250]

The Incredible Journey to the Edge of the Universe. The Incredible Journey to the Centre of the Atom
Magpies - v12 - My '97 - p42 [251-500]

Light
BL - v94 - Mr 15 '98 - p1237 [51-250]

Day-Bivins, Pat

The Rabbit and the Promise Sign (Illus. by Donna Brooks)
PW - v245 - Ja 26 '98 - p86 [51-250]

Deall, Alanna

Kensani's Kite
Bkbird - v34 - Win '96 - p55 [51-250]

De Anda, Diane

The Ice Dove and Other Stories
BL - v94 - O 1 '97 - p328+ [51-250]
CBRS - v26 - D '97 - p43 [1-50]

Deane, Bill

Top 10 Baseball Home Run Hitters
BL - v94 - S 15 '97 - p225 [51-250]

De Angelis, Gina

The Black Cowboys
BL - v94 - F 15 '98 - p1002 [51-250]

Deary, Terry

The Groovy Greeks (Illus. by Martin Brown)
Books - v11 - D '97 - p21 [51-250]

The Rotten Romans (Illus. by Martin Brown)
Books - v11 - D '97 - p21 [51-250]

De Beer, Hans

Little Polar Bear
PW - v244 - S 1 '97 - p107 [1-50]

Debnam, Rosemary

Runaway Fred (Illus. by Claudio Munoz)
Bks Keeps - S '97 - p24 [51-250]

DeCesare, Angelo

Anthony the Perfect Monster (Illus. by Angelo DeCesare)
RT - v51 - O '97 - p130 [1-50]

Deck the Halls (Illus. by Ruth Hills)

PW - v244 - O 6 '97 - p57 [1-50]

DeClements, Barthe

Double Trouble
PW - v244 - D 1 '97 - p55 [1-50]

Liar, Liar
PW - v245 - F 9 '98 - p96 [51-250]

Dedieu, Thierry
The Boy Who Ate Words (Illus. by Thierry Dedieu)
>   HB Guide - v8 - Fall '97 - p290 [51-250]
>   KR - v65 - Ap 15 '97 - p638 [51-250]
>   SLJ - v43 - Jl '97 - p90 [51-250]

Dee, Catherine
The Girls' Guide to Life (Illus. by Cynthia Jabar)
>   CCB-B - v50 - Jl '97 - p391 [51-250]
>   HB - v73 - Jl '97 - p473+ [51-250]
> y   Kliatt - v31 - Jl '97 - p26 [51-250]
>   KR - v65 - Ap 15 '97 - p639 [51-250]
>   Ms - v8 - Jl '97 - p90 [1-50]
> y   VOYA - v20 - Ag '97 - p200 [251-500]

Dee, M M
The Adventures of Jason Jackrabbit (Illus. by Donna Newsome)
>   Ch BWatch - v7 - S '97 - p6 [51-250]

Deedy, Carmen Agra
The Secret of Old Zeb (Illus. by Michael P White)
>   PW - v244 - S 1 '97 - p105 [51-250]
>   SLJ - v44 - Mr '98 - p168+ [51-250]

Deem, James M
Bodies from the Bog
>   SLJ - v44 - Ap '98 - p144 [51-250]

How to Make a Mummy Talk (Illus. by True Kelley)
>   PW - v244 - Jl 7 '97 - p70 [1-50]

DeFelice, Cynthia
The Apprenticeship of Lucas Whitaker
>   PW - v245 - Mr 9 '98 - p70 [1-50]
>   SE - v61 - Ap '97 - p10* [1-50]
>   SLJ - v43 - S '97 - p130 [1-50]

The Apprenticeship of Lucas Whitaker (McDonough). Audio Version
>   HB - v73 - N '97 - p703+ [51-250]
>   SLJ - v43 - S '97 - p166 [51-250]

Casey in the Bath (Illus. by Chris L Demarest)
>   RT - v51 - O '97 - p133 [1-50]

Clever Crow (Illus. by S D Schindler)
>   KR - v66 - F 1 '98 - p195 [51-250]

The Ghost of Fossil Glen
>   BL - v94 - Mr 15 '98 - p1243 [51-250]
>   CCB-B - v51 - Mr '98 - p240 [51-250]
>   KR - v66 - F 1 '98 - p195 [51-250]

Weasel
>   SLJ - v43 - S '97 - p130 [1-50]

Willy's Silly Grandma (Illus. by Shelley Jackson)
>   CCB-B - v50 - Je '97 - p354 [51-250]
>   HB Guide - v8 - Fall '97 - p290 [51-250]
>   SLJ - v43 - Ap '97 - p97 [51-250]

DeFord, Diane
The Day Miss Francie Got Skunked (Illus. by Brian Hoskin)
>   Ch BWatch - v8 - Ja '98 - p1 [51-250]

Degen, Bruce
Sailaway Home (Illus. by Bruce Degen)
>   RT - v51 - O '97 - p136 [1-50]

DeGroat, Diane
Roses Are Pink, Your Feet Really Stink (Illus. by Diane DeGroat)
>   RT - v51 - O '97 - p135+ [1-50]

Delafosse, Claude
Construction (Illus. by Philippe Biard)
>   HB Guide - v8 - Fall '97 - p357 [51-250]

Landscapes
>   Emerg Lib - v25 - N '97 - p60 [51-250]

Delainey, Gary
So, This Is Canada! (Illus. by Gerry Rasmussen)
>   CBRA - '96 - p513 [51-250]

De La Mare, Walter
The Lord Fish (Illus. by Patrick Benson)
>   Ch BWatch - v7 - N '97 - p4 [1-50]

Delaney, A
Pearl's First Prize Plant (Illus. by A Delaney)
>   CBRS - v25 - Jl '97 - p146+ [51-250]

HB Guide - v8 - Fall '97 - p262 [51-250]

SLJ - v43 - Jl '97 - p61 [51-250]

Del Prado, Dana
Terror Below! (Illus. by Stephen Marchesi)
Ch BWatch - v7 - Jl '97 - p5 [1-50]

Delton, Judy
Camp Ghost-Away (Moore). Audio Version
SLJ - v44 - F '98 - p72 [51-250]

Halloween Helpers (Illus. by Alan Tiegreen)
SLJ - v44 - Ja '98 - p81 [51-250]

Pee Wee Scouts (Illus. by Alan Tiegreen)
PW - v244 - O 6 '97 - p50 [1-50]

DeLuise, Dom
Dom DeLuise's Hansel and Gretel (Illus. by Christopher Santoro)
Ch BWatch - v7 - O '97 - p6 [1-50]
PW - v244 - N 10 '97 - p73 [51-250]
SLJ - v43 - D '97 - p109 [51-250]

Dem Bones (Illus. by Bob Barner)
Ch BWatch - v7 - Ap '97 - p8 [1-50]
Learning - v26 - S '97 - p45 [1-50]
SB - v33 - Ag '97 - p163 [1-50]

DeMarco, Neil
The Children's Atlas of World History
r   TES - S 19 '97 - p16* [51-250]

Demarest, Chris L
All Aboard!
Par - v72 - D '97 - p201 [1-50]
PW - v244 - O 27 '97 - p78 [51-250]

Demi
Buddha (Illus. by Demi)
SE - v61 - Ap '97 - p3* [1-50]

Buddha Stories (Illus. by Demi)
Ch BWatch - v7 - Jl '97 - p6 [1-50]
HB Guide - v8 - Fall '97 - p318 [51-250]
SLJ - v43 - Je '97 - p107 [51-250]

The Dalai Lama: A Biography of the Tibetan Spiritual and Political Leader (Illus. by Demi)
BL - v94 - Mr 15 '98 - p1240 [51-250]
CCB-B - v51 - Ap '98 - p277 [51-250]
HB - v74 - Mr '98 - p233 [51-250]
SLJ - v44 - Mr '98 - p194 [51-250]

The Dragon's Tale (Illus. by Demi)
SE - v61 - Ap '97 - p5* [1-50]

The Empty Pot
ECEJ - v25 - Fall '97 - p46 [1-50]

Happy New Year! (Illus. by Demi)
BL - v94 - F 15 '98 - p1014 [51-250]
SLJ - v44 - Mr '98 - p194 [51-250]

One Grain of Rice (Illus. by Demi)
BL - v94 - Ja 1 '98 - p734 [1-50]
Ch BWatch - v7 - My '97 - p3 [1-50]
Emerg Lib - v25 - N '97 - p55 [1-50]
HB Guide - v8 - Fall '97 - p332 [51-250]
HMR - Win '97 - p46 [51-250]
Inst - v107 - Ag '97 - p22 [51-250]
NY - v73 - O 6 '97 - p115 [1-50]
SLJ - v43 - D '97 - p24 [1-50]

Demuth, Patricia
Achoo! All about Colds (Illus. by Maggie Smith)
BL - v93 - Ag '97 - p1909 [51-250]
HB Guide - v8 - Fall '97 - p355 [51-250]
SLJ - v43 - D '97 - p107+ [51-250]

Johnny Appleseed (Illus. by Michael Montgomery)
SLJ - v43 - Ap '97 - p122 [51-250]

Denchfield, Nick
Charlie the Chicken (Illus. by Ant Parker)
Bks Keeps - N '97 - p19 [51-250]
Books - v11 - Je '97 - p21 [1-50]
Magpies - v12 - S '97 - p28+ [51-250]
TES - N 7 '97 - p5* [1-50]

The Complete Castle
Books - v10 - S '96 - p24 [1-50]

Denenberg, Barry
An American Hero
y   Kliatt - v32 - Mr '98 - p32 [51-250]
PW - v245 - Ja 12 '98 - p61 [1-50]

RT - v51 - D '97 - p335 [51-250]
y   VOYA - v20 - Ag '97 - p163 [51-250]

So Far from Home
BL - v94 - D 15 '97 - p697 [51-250]

Denham, Joyce
*A Child's Book of Celtic Prayers
(Illus. by Helen Cann)*
PW - v245 - Mr 23 '98 - p95 [51-250]

Denim, Sue
*The Dumb Bunnies (Illus. by Dav
Pilkey)*
PW - v245 - Mr 16 '98 - p67 [1-50]

*The Dumb Bunnies' Easter (Illus. by
Dav Pilkey)*
PW - v245 - Mr 16 '98 - p67 [1-50]

*The Dumb Bunnies Go to the Zoo
(Illus. by Dav Pilkey)*
Ch BWatch - v7 - My '97 - p3 [1-50]
CM:CanRev - v4 - N 14 '97 - pONL
[251-500]
HB Guide - v8 - Fall '97 - p262 [51-
250]

Denzel, Justin
Return to the Painted Cave
BL - v94 - N 1 '97 - p469 [51-250]
KR - v65 - Jl 1 '97 - p1028+ [51-250]
SLJ - v43 - N '97 - p117 [51-250]

De Paola, Tomie
The Art Lesson
Inst - v106 - My '97 - p4* [1-50]

*The Baby Sister (Illus. by Tomie De
Paola)*
ECEJ - v24 - Sum '97 - p252 [51-250]
RT - v51 - D '97 - p330 [51-250]

*Bill and Pete to the Rescue (Illus. by
Tomie De Paola)*
KR - v66 - Ap 1 '98 - p494 [51-250]

*Charlie Needs a Cloak (Illus. by
Tomie De Paola)*
Bkbird - v35 - Spr '97 - p34+ [501+]

*Days of the Blackbird (Illus. by Tomie
De Paola)*
Ch BWatch - v7 - Mr '97 - p7 [1-50]
HB Guide - v8 - Fall '97 - p290 [51-
250]

*Nana Upstairs and Nana Downstairs
(Illus. by Tomie De Paola)*
BL - v94 - F 15 '98 - p1020 [51-250]
PW - v245 - Ja 5 '98 - p69 [1-50]

*Strega Nona (Illus. by Tomie De
Paola)*
PW - v244 - O 20 '97 - p78 [1-50]

*Strega Nona, Her Story (Illus. by
Tomie De Paola)*
Emerg Lib - v25 - Ja '98 - p46 [51-250]
RT - v51 - O '97 - p148 [51-250]

Tom
PW - v244 - Je 23 '97 - p93 [1-50]

*Tomie's Little Mother Goose (Illus. by
Tomie De Paola)*
HB Guide - v8 - Fall '97 - p337 [51-
250]

De Regniers, Beatrice Schenk
*What Can You Do with a Shoe? (Illus.
by Maurice Sendak)*
BW - v27 - O 5 '97 - p11 [51-250]
PW - v244 - Ag 18 '97 - p94 [51-250]

DeRolf, Shane
*The Crayon Box That Talked (Illus. by
Michael Letzig)*
PW - v244 - N 10 '97 - p72 [51-250]
SLJ - v44 - F '98 - p79+ [51-250]

DeRubertis, Barbara
Janey Crane. Book and Audio Version
SLJ - v43 - D '97 - p70 [51-250]

Joey Goat. Book and Audio Version
SLJ - v43 - D '97 - p70 [51-250]

Suzy Mule. Book and Audio Version
SLJ - v43 - D '97 - p70 [51-250]

Tiny Tiger. Book and Audio Version
SLJ - v43 - D '97 - p70 [51-250]

Zeely Zebra. Book and Audio Version
SLJ - v43 - D '97 - p70 [51-250]

Desimini, Lisa
All Year Round
BL - v94 - D 15 '97 - p702 [51-250]
CBRS - v26 - D '97 - p37+ [51-250]
PW - v244 - O 13 '97 - p73 [51-250]

Deuker, Carl
*Heart of a Champion (Longenhagen).
Audio Version*
    SLJ - v44 - Mr '98 - p157 [51-250]

Devaney, John
Right from the Horse's Mouth
    JOYS - v10 - Spr '97 - p261 [1-50]

Devonshire, Hilary
Flight
    SB - v32 - D '96 - p257 [1-50]

Dewan, Ted
*The Sorcerer's Apprentice (Illus. by
Ted Dewan)*
    KR - v65 - D 1 '97 - p1774 [51-250]
    PW - v245 - Ja 12 '98 - p59 [51-250]
    Sch Lib - v45 - N '97 - p185 [51-250]
    SLJ - v44 - F '98 - p97 [51-250]
    TES - O 3 '97 - p9* [501+]
    TES - N 7 '97 - p11* [51-250]

*The Sorcerer's Apprentice (Dewan).
Audio Version*
    TES - O 3 '97 - p9* [501+]

Top Secret
    CBRS - v25 - Je '97 - p122 [1-50]
    Ch BWatch - v7 - My '97 - p4 [1-50]
    HB Guide - v8 - Fall '97 - p262 [51-250]

Dewey, Jennifer Owings
*Bedbugs in Our House (Illus. by
Jennifer Owings Dewey)*
    BL - v94 - Ja 1 '98 - p802 [51-250]

*Faces Only a Mother Could Love
(Illus. by Jennifer Owings Dewey)*
    ASBYP - v29 - Fall '96 - p12+ [251-500]

*Poison Dart Frogs (Illus. by Jennifer
Owings Dewey)*
    BL - v94 - Mr 1 '98 - p1138 [51-250]
    CCB-B - v51 - Ap '98 - p278 [51-250]
    HB - v74 - Mr '98 - p233+ [51-250]
    KR - v66 - F 1 '98 - p195 [51-250]
    SLJ - v44 - Ap '98 - p115 [51-250]

*Rattlesnake Dance (Illus. by Jennifer
Owings Dewey)*
    CBRS - v25 - Je '97 - p129 [51-250]
    Emerg Lib - v25 - Ja '98 - p52 [1-50]

    HB Guide - v8 - Fall '97 - p351 [51-250]
    NH - v106 - D '97 - p9+ [51-250]
    SLJ - v43 - Ap '97 - p122 [51-250]

*Stories on Stone (Illus. by Jennifer
Owings Dewey)*
    Am Sci - v85 - N '97 - p560 [51-250]
    SE - v61 - Ap '97 - p10* [1-50]

*Wildlife Rescue (Illus. by Don
MacCarter)*
    SLJ - v43 - My '97 - p56 [1-50]

Dexter, Catherine
I Dream of Murder
  y BL - v93 - Je 1 '97 - p1684 [51-250]
    HB Guide - v8 - Fall '97 - p298 [51-250]
    KR - v65 - Ap 15 '97 - p639 [51-250]
    SLJ - v43 - My '97 - p131+ [51-250]

Dhanjal, Beryl
What Do We Know about Sikhism?
    HB Guide - v8 - Fall '97 - p318+ [51-250]
  y VOYA - v20 - Ap '97 - p52 [251-500]

Dheensaw, Cleve
Celebrate the Spirit
    CBRA - '96 - p524 [51-250]

Diagram Group
European History on File
  r BL - v94 - Ja 1 '98 - p856+ [501+]
  r R&R Bk N - v12 - Ag '97 - p16 [51-250]

Nations of Africa
  r Ch BWatch - v7 - My '97 - p1 [1-50]
  r Ch BWatch - v7 - Je '97 - p5 [51-250]
    Ch BWatch - v7 - D '97 - p7 [1-50]

Peoples of Central Africa
    Ch BWatch - v7 - Je '97 - p5 [51-250]
    Ch BWatch - v7 - D '97 - p7 [1-50]
  y SLJ - v44 - F '98 - p121+ [51-250]

Peoples of East Africa
    Ch BWatch - v7 - Je '97 - p5 [51-250]
    Ch BWatch - v7 - D '97 - p7 [1-50]

Peoples of North Africa
    Ch BWatch - v7 - Je '97 - p5 [51-250]
    Ch BWatch - v7 - D '97 - p7 [1-50]
  y SLJ - v44 - F '98 - p121+ [51-250]

Peoples of Southern Africa
> Ch BWatch - v7 - Je '97 - p5 [51-250]
> Ch BWatch - v7 - D '97 - p7 [1-50]

Peoples of West Africa
> Ch BWatch - v7 - Je '97 - p5 [51-250]
> Ch BWatch - v7 - D '97 - p7 [1-50]

Diakite, Baba Wague

The Hunterman and the Crocodile (Illus. by Baba Wague Diakite)
> BL - v94 - Mr 15 '98 - p1219 [1-50]
> HB Guide - v8 - Fall '97 - p332 [51-250]
> NY - v73 - O 6 '97 - p115 [1-50]
> NYTBR - v102 - O 12 '97 - p26 [501+]

Diaz, Gloria Cecilia

La Bruja De La Montana (Illus. by Emilio Urberuaga)
> SLJ - v43 - Ag '97 - p180 [51-250]

El Sol De Los Venados
> Bkbird - v35 - Sum '97 - p23 [51-250]
> SLJ - v43 - My '97 - p152 [51-250]

El Valle De Los Cocuyos (Illus. by Francisco Melendez)
> SLJ - v43 - Ag '97 - p180 [51-250]

Diccionario Escolar De La Lengua Espanola

> r   BL - v94 - D 15 '97 - p717 [51-250]

Dickens, Charles

A Christmas Carol (Illus. by Everett Shinn)
> LJ - v122 - N 1 '97 - p121 [51-250]

A Christmas Carol (Illus. by Andrew Wheatcroft)
> LJ - v122 - N 1 '97 - p121 [51-250]
> PW - v244 - O 6 '97 - p58 [1-50]
> PW - v244 - O 6 '97 - p58 [1-50]

Great Expectations (Schofield). Audio Version
> Sch Lib - v45 - N '97 - p209 [51-250]

Oliver Twist
> NS - v126 - My '97 - p129 [51-250]

Oliver Twist (Illus. by Christian Birmingham)
> SLJ - v43 - My '97 - p132 [51-250]

Oliver Twist (Illus. by John Holder)
> HB Guide - v8 - Fall '97 - p288 [51-250]

A Tale of Two Cities (Acclaim)
> LATBR - Mr 2 '97 - p13 [501+]

Dickinson, Joan D

Bill Gates: Billionaire Computer Genius
> CLW - v68 - D '97 - p79+ [51-250]
> SLJ - v43 - D '97 - p135 [51-250]
> y   VOYA - v20 - F '98 - p399+ [251-500]

Dickinson, Peter

Chuck and Danielle (Sachs). Audio Version
> SLJ - v44 - Mr '98 - p157 [51-250]

Dicks, Terrance

Harvey Goes to School (Illus. by Susan Hellard)
> Bks Keeps - My '97 - p22 [51-250]

True Horror Stories
> BW - v27 - S 7 '97 - p11 [251-500]

Diehn, Gwen

Nature Crafts for Kids
> CAY - v18 - Win '97 - p11 [51-250]

Dijs, Carla

The Boy Who Cried Wolf (Illus. by Carla Dijs)
> PW - v244 - O 27 '97 - p79 [1-50]

The Lion and the Mouse (Illus. by Carla Dijs)
> PW - v244 - O 27 '97 - p79 [1-50]

The Little Red Hen (Illus. by Carla Dijs)
> PW - v244 - O 27 '97 - p79 [1-50]

The Tortoise and the Hare
> PW - v244 - O 27 '97 - p79 [1-50]

Dille, Ed

The Online Gaming Starter Kit
> r   Ch BWatch - v7 - O '97 - p8 [51-250]

Diller, Harriett
Big Band Sound (Illus. by Andrea Shine)
RT - v51 - S '97 - p58 [51-250]

The Faraway Drawer (Illus. by Andrea Shine)
RT - v51 - D '97 - p330 [51-250]

Dils, Tracey E
Anabelle's Awful Waffle (Illus. by John Jones)
Ch BWatch - v7 - S '97 - p3 [51-250]

Dinan, Carolyn
Goodnight, Monster
Bks Keeps - My '97 - p21 [51-250]
TES - N 14 '97 - p14* [51-250]

The Seal Singer
TES - Jl 11 '97 - p14* [51-250]

Dineen, Jacqueline
Electricity
ASBYP - v29 - Sum '96 - p60+ [251-500]

Oil, Gas and Coal
ASBYP - v29 - Sum '96 - p60+ [251-500]

Renewable Energy
ASBYP - v29 - Sum '96 - p60+ [251-500]

Saving Energy
ASBYP - v29 - Sum '96 - p60+ [251-500]

Tables, Facts and Figures (Illus. by John Dillow)
Sch Lib - v45 - N '97 - p203 [51-250]

Ding, Jing Jing
Story of the Three Buddhist Monks (Illus. by Nelson Daboud)
CBRA - '96 - p501+ [51-250]

Dionetti, Michelle
Coal Mine Peaches (Illus. by Anita Riggio)
ECEJ - v25 - Fall '97 - p46 [1-50]

Painting the Wind (Illus. by Kevin Hawkes)
Emerg Lib - v25 - N '97 - p59 [51-250]
Magpies - v12 - Mr '97 - p23+ [251-500]
RT - v51 - N '97 - p243 [51-250]

Dipper, Frances
The New Book of Treasure under the Ocean
Ch BWatch - v8 - Ja '98 - p6 [1-50]

The Ocean Deep
ASBYP - v29 - Fall '96 - p56+ [251-500]

Disney's Animated Storybook: 101 Dalmations. Electronic Media Version
BL - v93 - Je 1 '97 - p1730 [51-250]

Disney's Animated Storybook: The Hunchback of Notre Dame. Electronic Media Version
BL - v93 - Je 1 '97 - p1730 [51-250]

Dispezio, Michael A
Critical Thinking Puzzles
Ch BWatch - v7 - Jl '97 - p4 [1-50]

Diviny, Sean
Snow Inside the House (Illus. by Joe Rocco)
KR - v65 - D 1 '97 - p1774 [51-250]
PW - v244 - D 15 '97 - p57 [51-250]

Dixon, Andy
Dragon Quest (Illus. by Nick Harris)
Sch Lib - v45 - Ag '97 - p136 [51-250]

Dixon, Dougal
Dougal Dixon's Dinosaurs Updated
PW - v245 - F 23 '98 - p78 [1-50]

Djali's Day Out (Little Play a Sound)
Ch BWatch - v7 - Ap '97 - p2 [1-50]

Djandilnga, Elizabeth
Yolngu of the Island Galiwin'ku
Magpies - v12 - Jl '97 - p41+ [501+]

DK Concise World Atlas
r   CLW - v68 - S '97 - p62+ [51-250]

DK Pocket Encyclopedia
r   Ch BWatch - v7 - Jl '97 - p8 [51-250]

DK Publishing, Inc.
DK World Atlas
r   BL - v94 - N 1 '97 - p508+ [251-500]
r   Choice - v35 - Ja '98 - p788 [51-250]
r   LJ - v122 - N 15 '97 - p50 [51-250]
r   Rettig - O '97 - pONL [51-250]

Dobson, David
Can We Save Them? (Illus. by James M Needham)
    HB Guide - v8 - Fall '97 - p345 [51-250]
    SB - v33 - Je '97 - p145 [51-250]
    SLJ - v43 - Jl '97 - p82 [51-250]

Dobson, Mary
Roman Aromas
    Bks Keeps - Jl '97 - p24 [51-250]
    Ch BWatch - v7 - Je '97 - p1 [51-250]
    Magpies - v12 - Jl '97 - p44 [51-250]
    Sch Lib - v45 - Ag '97 - p150 [51-250]

Tudor Odours
    Bks Keeps - Jl '97 - p24 [51-250]
    Ch BWatch - v7 - Je '97 - p1 [51-250]
    Magpies - v12 - Jl '97 - p44 [51-250]
    Sch Lib - v45 - Ag '97 - p150 [51-250]

Victorian Vapours
    Bks Keeps - Jl '97 - p24 [51-250]
    Ch BWatch - v7 - Je '97 - p1 [51-250]
    Magpies - v12 - Jl '97 - p44 [51-250]
    Sch Lib - v45 - Ag '97 - p150 [51-250]

Dodd, Lynley
Hairy Maclary,
    Magpies - v12 - S '97 - p27 [51-250]
    TES - N 7 '97 - p5* [51-250]

Schnitzel Von Krumm Forget-Me-Not (Illus. by Lynley Dodd)
    Magpies - v12 - Mr '97 - p*2 [1-50]

Sniff-Snuff-Snap
    Magpies - v12 - Jl '97 - p28 [51-250]

Dodds, Dayle Ann
Sing, Sophie! (Illus. by Rosanne Litzinger)
    CBRS - v25 - Ag '97 - p159 [1-50]
    CCB-B - v50 - Jl '97 - p392 [51-250]
    Ch BWatch - v7 - My '97 - p3 [1-50]
    HB Guide - v8 - Fall '97 - p262 [51-250]
    Inst - v107 - Ja '98 - p26 [1-50]
    Magpies - v12 - My '97 - p26 [51-250]
    Par - v72 - S '97 - p205+ [51-250]
    Sch Lib - v45 - Ag '97 - p130 [51-250]
    SLJ - v43 - Je '97 - p86 [51-250]
    TES - My 30 '97 - p8* [501+]

Doherty, Berlie
Daughter of the Sea (Illus. by Sian Bailey)
y   BL - v94 - O 1 '97 - p319 [51-250]
    CBRS - v26 - D '97 - p46 [51-250]
    CCB-B - v51 - D '97 - p122 [51-250]
    HB - v73 - N '97 - p679+ [251-500]
y   KR - v65 - S 1 '97 - p1386+ [51-250]
    Magpies - v12 - Mr '97 - p18+ [501+]
y   PW - v244 - Ag 25 '97 - p73 [51-250]
    SLJ - v43 - S '97 - p213+ [51-250]
    TES - N 7 '97 - p7* [1-50]
y   VOYA - v21 - Ap '98 - p12 [1-50]
y   VOYA - v21 - Ap '98 - p54 [51-250]

The Snake-Stone
    Bks Keeps - My '97 - p25 [51-250]
y   JAAL - v40 - O '96 - p153 [51-250]
    PW - v245 - Mr 9 '98 - p70 [1-50]
y   SE - v61 - Ap '97 - p14* [1-50]
    TES - Je 6 '97 - p8* [51-250]
y   VOYA - v20 - Je '97 - p84 [51-250]

Doherty, Craig A
The Alaska Pipeline
    SLJ - v44 - Ap '98 - p144 [51-250]

The Empire State Building (Illus. by Lewis W Hine)
    KR - v65 - S 15 '97 - p1455 [51-250]
    SLJ - v44 - Ja '98 - p122 [51-250]

The Statue of Liberty
    Ch BWatch - v7 - Je '97 - p2 [51-250]
    SLMQ - v25 - Win '97 - p117 [1-50]

Doherty, Gillian
Windows 95 for Beginners
    Ch BWatch - v7 - S '97 - p3 [51-250]
    Sch Lib - v45 - Ag '97 - p156 [51-250]

Doherty, Paul
The Cool Hot Rod and Other
Electrifying Experiments on Energy
and Matter
    ASBYP - v29 - Fall '96 - p44+ [251-500]

The Spinning Blackboard and Other
Dynamic Experiments on Force and
Motion
    ASBYP - v29 - Fall '96 - p44+ [251-500]

Dolan, Edward F
The American Civil War
    BL - v94 - Mr 1 '98 - p1126 [51-250]
    SLJ - v44 - Mr '98 - p231 [51-250]

Dolan, Penny
The Ghost of Able Mabel (Illus. by
Philip Hopman)
    Bks Keeps - Jl '97 - p23 [51-250]

Dolan, Terrance
The Santee Sioux Indians
    HB Guide - v8 - Fall '97 - p398 [51-250]

Dolin, Nick
Basketball Stars
    BL - v93 - Ag '97 - p1893 [51-250]

Dolphin, Laurie
Magical Objects from around the
World
    PW - v244 - N 24 '97 - p76 [51-250]

Our Journey from Tibet (Illus. by
Nancy Jo Johnson)
    BL - v93 - Ag '97 - p1893+ [51-250]
    CCB-B - v51 - Ja '98 - p158 [51-250]
    KR - v65 - Jl 1 '97 - p1029 [51-250]
    SLJ - v43 - Ag '97 - p146+ [51-250]

Dolphin Log
  p Par Ch - Awards '97 - p27 [1-50]

Dommermuth-Costa, Carol
Agatha Christie: Writer of Mystery
  y Ch BWatch - v7 - S '97 - p7 [1-50]
  y Cur R - v37 - N '97 - p12 [51-250]
  y HB Guide - v8 - Fall '97 - p379 [51-250]

    SLJ - v43 - Ag '97 - p165+ [51-250]
  y VOYA - v21 - Ap '98 - p66 [51-250]

Doney, Meryl
Papercraft
    SLJ - v43 - D '97 - p136 [51-250]

Donigan, Linda
Alligators Always Dress for Dinner
    HMR - Win '97 - p46 [51-250]

Donkin, Andrew
The Footprints Mystery
    Sch Lib - v45 - Ag '97 - p136 [51-250]

Donnelly, Jane
Fearsome Hunters (Illus. by Peter
Anderson)
    ASBYP - v29 - Fall '96 - p39+ [501+]

Mighty Giants
    ASBYP - v29 - Fall '96 - p39+ [501+]

Donnelly, Judy
The Titanic: Lost...and Found (Illus.
by Keith Kohler)
    BL - v94 - Mr 15 '98 - p1244 [51-250]

Donoghue, Emma
Kissing the Witch
    ABR - v19 - N '97 - p6+ [501+]
  y BL - v93 - Je 1 '97 - p1684 [51-250]
  y CBRS - v25 - My '97 - p118 [51-250]
  y Emerg Lib - v25 - N '97 - p51 [51-250]
  y JAAL - v41 - S '97 - p80+ [51-250]
  y NYTBR - v102 - S 28 '97 - p28 [501+]
  y NYTBR - v102 - D 7 '97 - p80 [1-50]
  y SLJ - v43 - Je '97 - p117 [51-250]
  y TES - My 16 '97 - p9* [501+]
  y TLS - Je 27 '97 - p23 [501+]
  y VOYA - v20 - Ag '97 - p192 [251-500]
  y VOYA - v21 - Ap '98 - p12 [1-50]

Donovan, Mary Lee
Won't You Come and Play with Me?
(Illus. by Cynthia Jabar)
    KR - v66 - F 15 '98 - p265 [51-250]
    PW - v245 - F 9 '98 - p94 [51-250]

Dorling Kindersley Children's
Picture Encyclopedia
  r Obs - Jl 20 '97 - p18* [51-250]

The Dorling Kindersley Science Encyclopedia. 2nd Ed., Rev. and Updated

r   Books - v11 - Ag '97 - p15 [51-250]

Dorris, Michael
Morning Girl

SLJ - v43 - S '97 - p130 [1-50]
SLJ - v44 - Ja '98 - p42 [1-50]

Sees behind Trees

y   Kliatt - v32 - Mr '98 - p8 [51-250]
RT - v51 - O '97 - p149 [51-250]
RT - v51 - N '97 - p244 [51-250]
SLJ - v43 - Jl '97 - p34 [1-50]

Tainos (Illus. by Vivi Escriva)

SLJ - v43 - My '97 - p152+ [51-250]

The Window

y   BL - v94 - S 15 '97 - p220 [51-250]
y   BL - v94 - Mr 15 '98 - p1214 [1-50]
CCB-B - v51 - Ja '98 - p158 [51-250]
HB - v73 - N '97 - p666+ [501+]
y   JAAL - v41 - F '98 - p409 [51-250]
y   KR - v65 - S 15 '97 - p1455 [51-250]
NYTBR - v103 - F 15 '98 - p26 [251-500]
y   PW - v244 - Ag 18 '97 - p94 [51-250]
SLJ - v43 - N '97 - p117 [51-250]
y   VOYA - v20 - F '98 - p364 [51-250]
y   VOYA - v21 - Ap '98 - p37 [1-50]

Dorros, Arthur
Abuela (Illus. by Elisa Kleven)

ECEJ - v25 - Fall '97 - p46 [1-50]

Rain Forest Secrets

BL - v94 - D 1 '97 - p628 [1-50]

Tonight Is Carnaval

ECEJ - v25 - Fall '97 - p46 [1-50]

A Tree Is Growing (Illus. by S D Schindler)

CCB-B - v50 - Je '97 - p355 [51-250]
HB Guide - v8 - Fall '97 - p348 [51-250]
NYTBR - v102 - N 9 '97 - p24 [1-50]

Dorson, Mercedes
Tales from the Rain Forest

BL - v94 - F 15 '98 - p1002 [51-250]
CBRS - v26 - Win '98 - p69 [51-250]
HB - v74 - Mr '98 - p225 [51-250]
PW - v244 - O 27 '97 - p77+ [51-250]

Dotlich, Rebecca Kai
Lemonade Sun and Other Summer Poems (Illus. by Jan Spivey Gilchrist)

BL - v94 - F 15 '98 - p1014 [51-250]
KR - v66 - F 1 '98 - p195 [51-250]
PW - v245 - F 2 '98 - p92 [51-250]
SLJ - v44 - Mr '98 - p194 [51-250]

Doty, Jean Slaughter
The Monday Horses

JOYS - v10 - Spr '97 - p262 [1-50]

Doucet, Sharon Arms
Why Lapin's Ears Are Long and Other Tales from the Louisiana Bayou (Illus. by David Catrow)

BL - v93 - Ag '97 - p1894 [51-250]
CBRS - v26 - S '97 - p8 [51-250]
CCB-B - v51 - O '97 - p49 [51-250]
Ch BWatch - v7 - N '97 - p4 [1-50]
HB - v73 - S '97 - p586 [51-250]
Inst - v107 - N '97 - p19+ [51-250]
KR - v65 - Jl 1 '97 - p1038 [51-250]
PW - v244 - O 20 '97 - p76 [51-250]
SLJ - v43 - S '97 - p201 [51-250]

Douglas, Kirk
The Broken Mirror (Illus. by Jenny Vasilyev)

BL - v94 - O 1 '97 - p322+ [51-250]
CBRS - v26 - S '97 - p10 [51-250]
CCB-B - v51 - O '97 - p49+ [251-500]
PW - v244 - Jl 7 '97 - p68 [51-250]
SLJ - v43 - S '97 - p216 [51-250]
y   VOYA - v20 - F '98 - p384 [251-500]

Douzou, Olivier
The Wolf's Lunch (Illus. by Olivier Douzou)

KR - v65 - N 1 '97 - p1643 [51-250]
PW - v244 - N 3 '97 - p87 [1-50]
SLJ - v44 - Ap '98 - p98 [51-250]

Dow, Lesley
Incredible Plants

Bks Keeps - Jl '97 - p26 [51-250]
BL - v93 - Je 1 '97 - p1692 [51-250]
HB Guide - v8 - Fall '97 - p349 [51-250]
Sch Lib - v45 - Ag '97 - p163 [51-250]
SLJ - v43 - Jl '97 - p100 [51-250]

Insects and Spiders
  Magpies - v12 - S '97 - p43 [51-250]

Dowling, Paul
The Night Journey
  HB Guide - v8 - Fall '97 - p262 [51-250]

Downes, Belinda
Every Little Angel's Handbook (Illus. by Belinda Downes)
  BL - v94 - D 1 '97 - p640 [51-250]
  KR - v65 - O 1 '97 - p1530 [51-250]
  PW - v244 - O 20 '97 - p78 [51-250]
  SLJ - v43 - D '97 - p88 [51-250]

Downey, Lynn
Sing, Henrietta! Sing! (Illus. by Tony Sansevero)
  HB Guide - v8 - Fall '97 - p263 [51-250]
  SLJ - v43 - Jl '97 - p61 [51-250]

Downie, Mary Alice
Snow Paws (Illus. by Kathryn Naylor)
  Can CL - v23 - Sum '97 - p59+ [501+]
  CBRA - '96 - p439+ [51-250]

Downing, Julie
Baby Jesus (Illus. by Julie Downing)
  PW - v244 - Ag 25 '97 - p66 [51-250]

Jonah and the Whale (Illus. by Julie Downing)
  PW - v244 - Ag 25 '97 - p66 [51-250]

Joseph's Colorful Coat (Illus. by Julie Downing)
  PW - v244 - Ag 25 '97 - p66 [51-250]

Noah's Ark (Illus. by Julie Downing)
  PW - v244 - Ag 25 '97 - p66 [51-250]

Dowswell, Paul
Tales of Real Haunting
  Books - v11 - Je '97 - p21 [51-250]

Doyle, Arthur Conan, Sir
The Sherlock Holmes Collection (Rathbone). Audio Version
  Sch Lib - v45 - N '97 - p209 [51-250]

Doyle, Brian
Uncle Ronald
  y   BIC - v26 - Je '97 - p34 [501+]
       CBRA - '96 - p471 [51-250]
  y   HB Guide - v8 - Fall '97 - p312 [51-250]
  y   SLJ - v43 - My '97 - p132 [51-250]

Doyle, Charlotte
You Can't Catch Me (Illus. by Rosanne Litzinger)
  KR - v66 - F 15 '98 - p265 [51-250]

Draanen, Wendelin Van
How I Survived Being a Girl
  HB Guide - v8 - Fall '97 - p310 [51-250]

Dragonfly
  p   Par Ch - Awards '97 - p27 [1-50]

Dragonwagon, Crescent
Alligators and Others All Year Long (Illus. by Jose Aruego)
  PW - v244 - N 17 '97 - p63 [1-50]

Bat in the Dining Room (Illus. by S D Schindler)
  BL - v94 - O 1 '97 - p335+ [51-250]
  CBRS - v26 - S '97 - p2 [1-50]
  CCB-B - v51 - D '97 - p123 [51-250]
  KR - v65 - S 1 '97 - p1387 [51-250]
  PW - v244 - Ag 4 '97 - p74+ [51-250]
  SLJ - v43 - S '97 - p179 [51-250]

Brass Button (Illus. by Susan Paradise)
  BL - v93 - Je 1 '97 - p1716 [51-250]
  CBRS - v25 - Jl '97 - p146+ [51-250]
  HB Guide - v8 - Fall '97 - p290 [51-250]
  SLJ - v43 - Je '97 - p86 [51-250]

Drake, Jane
Forestry (Illus. by Pat Cupples)
  CBRA - '96 - p535 [51-250]

The Kids Campfire Book (Illus. by Heather Collins)
  BL - v94 - Mr 15 '98 - p1237 [51-250]
  CBRA - '96 - p524 [51-250]
  SLJ - v44 - Ap '98 - p144 [51-250]

Dramer, Kim
China
- BL - v94 - O 15 '97 - p399 [51-250]
- HB Guide - v8 - Fall '97 - p369 [51-250]

Draper, Sharon M
Forged by Fire
- y   BL - v94 - Mr 15 '98 - p1214 [1-50]
- y   BL - v94 - Mr 15 '98 - p1225 [1-50]
- y   CCB-B - v50 - Je '97 - p355 [51-250]
- y   HB Guide - v8 - Fall '97 - p312 [51-250]
-     Par Ch - Awards '97 - p6 [51-250]
-     PW - v245 - Ja 12 '98 - p61 [1-50]
- y   VOYA - v20 - Je '97 - p108+ [251-500]
- y   VOYA - v21 - Ap '98 - p37 [1-50]
- y   VOYA - v21 - Ap '98 - p40 [1-50]

Ziggy and the Black Dinosaurs
- Ch BWatch - v7 - N '97 - p2 [51-250]

Drawson, Blair
Flying Dimitri (Illus. by Blair Drawson)
- BL - v94 - D 15 '97 - p702 [51-250]
- CBRS - v26 - Win '98 - p61 [51-250]
- CM:CanRev - v4 - Mr 13 '98 - pONL [51-250]
- KR - v65 - Ag 1 '97 - p1220 [51-250]
- PW - v244 - O 13 '97 - p73 [51-250]
- SLJ - v44 - Ap '98 - p98 [51-250]

Drescher, Henrik
The Boy Who Ate Around (Illus. by Henrik Drescher)
- Par Ch - Awards '97 - p8 [51-250]

Drillsma, Barbara
What's inside the Human Body?
- Ch BWatch - v7 - D '97 - p2 [1-50]
- SLJ - v44 - Mr '98 - p231 [51-250]
- y   VOYA - v21 - Ap '98 - p68 [51-250]

Drimmer, Frederick
Incredible People
- BL - v93 - Je 1 '97 - p1690 [51-250]
- CCB-B - v50 - Jl '97 - p392 [51-250]
- y   HB Guide - v8 - Fall '97 - p383 [51-250]
- SLJ - v43 - My '97 - p143+ [51-250]
- y   VOYA - v20 - Ag '97 - p200 [251-500]

Driscoll, Laura
The Bravest Cat! (Illus. by DyAnne DiSalvo-Ryan)
- SLJ - v44 - F '98 - p97+ [51-250]

D-Rok
Barnaby and the Sea (Illus. by D-Rok)
- Ch BWatch - v7 - Ap '97 - p6 [51-250]

Drost, Joost
Bubblegum Guy
- Sch Lib - v45 - Ag '97 - p136 [51-250]
- TES - Je 20 '97 - p12* [501+]

Drummond, Allan
Moby Dick (Illus. by Allan Drummond)
- Books - v11 - Je '97 - p21 [51-250]
- Books - v11 - Ag '97 - p15 [1-50]
- NY - v73 - O 6 '97 - p117 [51-250]
- NYTBR - v103 - F 1 '98 - p24 [501+]
- Sch Lib - v45 - N '97 - p191 [51-250]

Drury, Maxine
To Dance, to Dream
- BW - v27 - D 7 '97 - p20 [1-50]

Duane, Diane
A Wizard Abroad
- y   BL - v94 - O 1 '97 - p319 [51-250]
- SLJ - v43 - S '97 - p216 [51-250]

Du Bois, William Pene
The Twenty-One Balloons (McDonough). Audio Version
- SLJ - v44 - Ap '98 - p82 [51-250]

Dubosarsky, Ursula
The White Guinea-Pig
- TES - N 7 '97 - p7* [1-50]

DuBosque, D C
Draw Cars
- BWatch - v18 - D '97 - p2 [1-50]

Draw Dinosaurs
- BL - v94 - D 15 '97 - p692 [51-250]
- Ch BWatch - v7 - O '97 - p4 [51-250]

Dubovoy, Sina
Civil Rights Leaders
  Ch BWatch - v7 - Je '97 - p5 [1-50]
y HB Guide - v8 - Fall '97 - p383 [51-250]

Dubowski, Cathy East
Pirate School (Illus. by Mark Dubowski)
  SLJ - v43 - Ap '97 - p97 [51-250]

Dubrovin, Vivian
Storytelling Adventures (Illus. by Bobbi Shupe)
  SLJ - v43 - My '97 - p144 [51-250]

Duchesne, Christiane
Who's Afraid of the Dark? (Illus. by Doris Barrette)
  CBRA - '96 - p440 [51-250]

Dudley, Karen
Alligators and Crocodiles (Illus. by Warren Clark)
  CM:CanRev - v4 - D 12 '97 - pONL [51-250]

Bald Eagles (Illus. by Warren Clark)
  CM:CanRev - v4 - D 12 '97 - pONL [51-250]

Elephants (Illus. by Warren Clark)
  CBRA - '96 - p529 [51-250]
  HB Guide - v8 - Fall '97 - p353 [51-250]

Giant Pandas (Illus. by Warren Clark)
  BIC - v26 - S '97 - p33+ [251-500]
  CBRA - '96 - p529 [51-250]
  HB Guide - v8 - Fall '97 - p353 [51-250]
  Quill & Q - v63 - My '97 - p42 [51-250]
  SB - v33 - O '97 - p209+ [51-250]
  SLJ - v43 - Ag '97 - p147 [51-250]

Great African Americans in Government
  Ch BWatch - v7 - Je '97 - p4 [51-250]
  HB Guide - v8 - Fall '97 - p384 [51-250]
  SLJ - v44 - Ja '98 - p122+ [51-250]

Whooping Cranes (Illus. by Warren Clark)
  BIC - v26 - S '97 - p33+ [251-500]

  CBRA - '96 - p529 [51-250]
  HB Guide - v8 - Fall '97 - p352 [51-250]

Wolves (Illus. by Warren Clark)
  BIC - v26 - S '97 - p33+ [251-500]
  CBRA - '96 - p529 [51-250]
  SB - v33 - O '97 - p209+ [51-250]
  SLJ - v43 - Ag '97 - p147 [51-250]

Dueck, Adele
Anywhere but Here
  CBRA - '96 - p471 [51-250]

Duey, Kathleen
Blizzard: Estes Park, Colorado 1886
  SLJ - v44 - Mr '98 - p211+ [51-250]

Earthquake
  CCB-B - v51 - Ap '98 - p278 [51-250]
  PW - v244 - D 15 '97 - p59 [51-250]
  SLJ - v44 - Mr '98 - p212 [51-250]

Ellen Elizabeth Hawkins
  SLJ - v43 - Ag '97 - p157 [51-250]

Evie Peach
  BL - v94 - F 15 '98 - p1011 [51-250]
  SLJ - v44 - Mr '98 - p212 [51-250]

Willow Chase
  SLJ - v43 - Ap '97 - p137 [51-250]

Duffey, Betsy
Buster and the Black Hole
  TES - N 7 '97 - p7* [1-50]

The Camp Knock Knock Mystery (Illus. by Fiona Dunbar)
  KR - v65 - Je 15 '97 - p948 [51-250]

Hey, New Kid! (Illus. by Ellen Thompson)
  Inst - v106 - My '97 - p21 [1-50]

Virtual Cody (Illus. by Ellen Thompson)
  BL - v93 - Je 1 '97 - p1702 [51-250]
  CCB-B - v50 - Je '97 - p355+ [51-250]
  HB - v73 - Jl '97 - p453+ [51-250]
  HB Guide - v8 - Fall '97 - p298 [51-250]
  KR - v65 - My 15 '97 - p799 [51-250]
  SLJ - v43 - Jl '97 - p61 [51-250]

Duffy, Carol Ann
*I Wouldn't Thank You for a Valentine
(Illus. by Trisha Rafferty)*
     PW - v244 - D 1 '97 - p55 [1-50]

Duffyall, Dee Dee
*Forest Tracks (Illus. by Janet
Marshall)*
     LA - v73 - N '96 - p524 [51-250]

Dugan, Barbara
*Loop the Loop (Illus. by James
Stevenson)*
     SLJ - v44 - Mr '98 - p119+ [1-50]

Dugan, Michael
*Wombats Can't Fly (Illus. by Jane
Burrell)*
     Magpies - v12 - Mr '97 - p28 [51-250]

Duggleby, John
Artist in Overalls
     Emerg Lib - v25 - N '97 - p59 [51-250]

Duke, Kate
Archaeologists Dig for Clues
     HB Guide - v8 - Fall '97 - p387 [51-250]
     SB - v33 - Je '97 - p146 [251-500]
     SB - v33 - Ag '97 - p187 [1-50]

Aunt Isabel Tells a Good One
     Inst - v107 - S '97 - p24 [1-50]
y   JAAL - v40 - My '97 - p669 [51-250]

*One Guinea Pig Is Not Enough (Illus.
by Kate Duke)*
     CCB-B - v51 - Mr '98 - p240 [51-250]
     KR - v65 - D 15 '97 - p1833 [51-250]
     PW - v245 - F 2 '98 - p88 [51-250]
     SLJ - v44 - Mr '98 - p179 [51-250]

Dump Truck (Box Cars)
     PW - v245 - Mr 23 '98 - p102 [1-50]

Dunbar, Joyce
This Is the Star (Illus. by Gary Blythe)
     Books - v10 - S '96 - p24 [1-50]

Duncan, Alice Faye
*The National Civil Rights Museum
Celebrates Everyday People*
     BL - v94 - F 15 '98 - p998 [1-50]

Duncan, Beverly K
Explore the Wild
     RT - v51 - N '97 - p253 [51-250]

Duncan, Dayton
People of the West
     BL - v93 - Je 1 '97 - p1700 [1-50]
y   VOYA - v20 - Je '97 - p84+ [51-250]

*The West: An Illustrated History for
Children*
     SE - v61 - Ap '97 - p11* [51-250]

Duncan, Lois
*The Magic of Spider Woman (Illus. by
Shonto Begay)*
     RT - v51 - N '97 - p250+ [51-250]

A Dune Buggy Ride with Baby Taz
     Ch BWatch - v7 - Jl '97 - p2 [1-50]

Dunlop, Eileen
The Ghost by the Sea
     Ch BWatch - v7 - Mr '97 - p2 [51-250]
     HB Guide - v8 - Fall '97 - p298 [51-250]

Tales of St. Patrick
     Bks Keeps - S '97 - p26 [51-250]

Dunmore, Helen
Allie's Apples (Illus. by Simone Lia)
     Sch Lib - v45 - N '97 - p191 [51-250]

Dunn, Andrew
*The Children's Atlas of Scientific
Discoveries and Inventions*
r   Ch BWatch - v7 - N '97 - p6 [1-50]
r   SB - v34 - Ap '98 - p79 [51-250]

Dunn, Sonja
*Beauty and the Beast Rap (Illus. by
Susan Darrach)*
     Can CL - v23 - Sum '97 - p94 [51-250]

Dunphy, Madeleine
*Here Is the Tropical Rain Forest
(Illus. by Michael Rothman)*
    BL - v94 - D 1 '97 - p628 [1-50]

Here Is the Wetland
    SB - v33 - Ag '97 - p163 [1-50]

Dunrea, Olivier
*The Trow-Wife's Treasure (Illus. by
Olivier Dunrea)*
    KR - v66 - Ja 1 '98 - p56 [51-250]
    PW - v245 - F 9 '98 - p95 [51-250]
    SLJ - v44 - Ap '98 - p98 [51-250]

Dunwoodie, Helen
Solo Act
    Bks Keeps - Jl '97 - p25 [51-250]
 y   Sch Lib - v45 - N '97 - p211 [51-250]

Dupasquier, Philippe
My Busy Day
    HB Guide - v8 - Fall '97 - p250 [51-250]

Duplacey, James
The Leafs vs. the Canadiens
    CBRA - '96 - p524 [51-250]

Dupre, Ben
*Oxford Children's Encyclopedia. New
Ed., Vols. 1-9*
 r   Bks Keeps - N '97 - p6+ [51-250]
 r   Magpies - v12 - My '97 - p44 [501+]

Durrant, Lynda
The Beaded Moccasins
    BL - v94 - Mr 15 '98 - p1233+ [51-250]

Dussling, Jennifer
Bug Off! (Illus. by Amy Wummer)
    SLJ - v44 - F '98 - p85 [51-250]

*The Bunny Slipper Mystery (Illus. by
Joe Ewers)*
    HB Guide - v8 - Fall '97 - p287 [51-250]

DuTemples, Leslie
Tigers (Illus. by Lynn M Stone)
    ASBYP - v29 - Fall '96 - p43+ [251-500]

Dutta, Swapna
Juneli's First Term
    Bkbird - v34 - Win '96 - p34 [51-250]

Duvall, Jill
*Chef Ki Is Serving Dinner! (Illus. by
Lili Duvall)*
    HB Guide - v8 - Fall '97 - p322 [51-250]

*Meet Rory Hohenstein, a Professional
Dancer (Illus. by Lili Duvall)*
    HB Guide - v8 - Fall '97 - p322 [51-250]
    SLJ - v43 - Jl '97 - p82 [51-250]

*Mr. Duvall Reports the News (Illus. by
Lili Duvall)*
    HB Guide - v8 - Fall '97 - p322 [51-250]

*Ms. Moja Makes Beautiful Clothes
(Illus. by Lili Duvall)*
    HB Guide - v8 - Fall '97 - p322 [51-250]

*Who Keeps the Water Clean? Ms.
Schindler! (Illus. by Lili Duvall)*
    HB Guide - v8 - Fall '97 - p322 [51-250]
    SB - v33 - O '97 - p212 [51-250]
    SLJ - v43 - Jl '97 - p82 [51-250]

Dwyer, Jacqueline
Godzilla on Monster Island
    SF Chr - v18 - Je '97 - p42 [1-50]

Dwyer, Mindy
*Aurora: A Tale of the Northern Lights
(Illus. by Mindy Dwyer)*
    Ch BWatch - v7 - D '97 - p5 [51-250]
    PW - v244 - N 3 '97 - p84 [51-250]
    SLJ - v44 - F '98 - p98 [51-250]

*Coyote in Love (Illus. by Mindy
Dwyer)*
    CM:CanRev - v4 - O 17 '97 - pONL [251-500]
    HB Guide - v8 - Fall '97 - p332 [51-250]
    SLJ - v43 - Jl '97 - p82 [51-250]

Dykstra, Mary
Annabelle's Wish
    Ch BWatch - v7 - D '97 - p2 [51-250]

Dyrbye, Helen
No More Time for Paisley (Illus. by
Paula Martyr)
TES - Jl 11 '97 - p14* [51-250]

E

Eagle, Kin
Hey, Diddle Diddle (Illus. by Rob Gilbert)
    CBRS - v25 - My '97 - p110 [51-250]
    HB Guide - v8 - Fall '97 - p337 [51-250]
    SLJ - v43 - Jl '97 - p61 [51-250]

Eagle Walking Turtle
Full Moon Stories (Illus. by Eagle Walking Turtle)
    BL - v93 - Je 1 '97 - p1690 [51-250]
    CBRS - v25 - Ag '97 - p166 [1-50]
    SLJ - v43 - Jl '97 - p61 [51-250]

Early, Margaret
Robin Hood (Illus. by Margaret Early)
    BL - v94 - Mr 1 '98 - p1125 [51-250]

Romeo and Juliet (Illus. by Margaret Early)
    KR - v66 - Ap 15 '98 - p577 [51-250]

Earth's Natural Resources CD-ROM. Electronic Media Version
    r   SB - v33 - Je '97 - p151 [251-500]

Easley, Mary Ann
I Am the Ice Worm
    RT - v51 - N '97 - p255 [51-250]

Eason, Cassandra
Benjamin's First Book
    PW - v244 - N 10 '97 - p76 [51-250]

East, Jacqueline
I Won't Eat That!
    Sch Lib - v45 - N '97 - p185 [51-250]

I'm Scared of the Dark
    Sch Lib - v45 - N '97 - p185 [51-250]

Eastman, P D
The Cat in the Hat Beginner Book Dictionary (Illus. by P D Eastman)
    r   JOYS - v11 - Fall '97 - p75 [1-50]

Go, Dog, Go!
    PW - v244 - Ag 4 '97 - p77 [51-250]

Eaton, Deborah
No One Told the Aardvark (Illus. by Jim Spence)
    HB Guide - v8 - Fall '97 - p345 [51-250]
    SLJ - v43 - Je '97 - p86 [51-250]

Eccleshare, Julia
Time for a Tale (Illus. by Rowan Barnes-Murphy)
    Bks Keeps - My '97 - p21 [51-250]

Eckert, Allan W
Return to Hawk's Hill
    KR - v66 - Mr 15 '98 - p401 [51-250]

Eco, Umberto
The Three Astronauts
    Emerg Lib - v24 - My '97 - p9+ [1-50]

Edelman, Marian Wright
Stand for Children (Illus. by Adrienne Yorinks)
    PW - v245 - Mr 16 '98 - p62 [51-250]

Edens, Cooper
Nicholi (Illus. by A Scott Banfill)
> BL - v94 - S 1 '97 - p138 [51-250]
> Ch BWatch - v7 - D '97 - p2 [1-50]
> KR - v65 - S 1 '97 - p1387 [51-250]
> PW - v244 - O 6 '97 - p55 [51-250]

Editorial Cartoons by Kids 1997
> Ch BWatch - v7 - Jl '97 - p1 [51-250]

Edmonds, Alex
Acid Rain
> Ch BWatch - v7 - My '97 - p7 [1-50]
> HB Guide - v8 - Fall '97 - p328 [51-250]
> SB - v33 - Ag '97 - p163 [1-50]
> SLJ - v43 - Ag '97 - p147 [51-250]

A Closer Look at the Greenhouse
> Ch BWatch - v7 - N '97 - p6 [1-50]

The Ozone Hole
> Ch BWatch - v7 - My '97 - p7 [1-50]
> HB Guide - v8 - Fall '97 - p328 [51-250]
> SB - v33 - Ag '97 - p163 [1-50]
> SLJ - v43 - Ag '97 - p147 [51-250]

Eduar, Gilles
Jooka Saves the Day (Illus. by Gilles Eduar)
> BL - v94 - D 1 '97 - p640 [51-250]
> Bloom Rev - v17 - N '97 - p32 [51-250]
> CBRS - v26 - F '98 - p74 [51-250]
> CCB-B - v51 - O '97 - p50 [51-250]
> HB - v73 - S '97 - p556 [51-250]
> KR - v65 - Jl 1 '97 - p1029 [51-250]
> PW - v244 - Je 16 '97 - p58 [51-250]
> SLJ - v43 - S '97 - p180 [51-250]

Edwards, Elwyn Hartley
Saddlery. Rev. Ed.
> r   JOYS - v10 - Spr '97 - p262 [1-50]

Edwards, Elywn Hartley
The Ultimate Horse Book
> r   JOYS - v10 - Spr '97 - p260 [1-50]

Edwards, Frank B
Melody Mooner Takes Lessons (Illus. by John Bianchi)
> CBRA - '96 - p440 [51-250]
> CLW - v68 - S '97 - p64 [51-250]

Edwards, Pamela Duncan
Barefoot: Escape on the Underground Railroad (Illus. by Henry Cole)
> Ch BWatch - v7 - S '97 - p1 [1-50]
> Emerg Lib - v24 - My '97 - p64 [51-250]
> HB Guide - v8 - Fall '97 - p263 [51-250]
> JAAL - v41 - D '97 - p323 [51-250]
> Learning - v26 - Ag '97 - p22+ [51-250]

Dinorella: A Prehistoric Fairy Tale (Illus. by Henry Cole)
> BL - v94 - N 1 '97 - p480 [51-250]
> CCB-B - v51 - D '97 - p123 [51-250]
> Inst - v107 - Ja '98 - p28 [51-250]
> KR - v65 - Ag 15 '97 - p1304 [51-250]
> PW - v244 - Ag 18 '97 - p92 [51-250]
> SLJ - v43 - N '97 - p80 [51-250]

The Grumpy Morning (Illus. by Darcia Labrosse)
> KR - v66 - Mr 15 '98 - p402 [51-250]

Livingstone Mouse (Illus. by Henry Cole)
> Inst - v106 - My '97 - p19 [1-50]
> RT - v51 - O '97 - p148 [51-250]

Warthogs in the Kitchen (Illus. by Henry Cole)
> KR - v66 - Ap 15 '98 - p577 [51-250]

Edwards, Richard, 1949-
Fly with the Birds (Illus. by Satoshi Kitamura)
> Magpies - v12 - My '97 - p22+ [251-500]

You're Safe Now, Waterdog (Illus. by Sophy Williams)
> CBRS - v25 - Jl '97 - p147 [51-250]
> CCB-B - v50 - Jl '97 - p392+ [51-250]
> HB Guide - v8 - Fall '97 - p263 [51-250]
> SLJ - v43 - Jl '97 - p67 [51-250]

Egan, Lorraine Hopping
Inventors and Inventions
> SB - v34 - Ap '98 - p82 [51-250]

Egan, Robert
From Wheat to Pasta (Illus. by Robert Egan)
> HB Guide - v8 - Fall '97 - p357 [51-250]

SB - v33 - N '97 - p244+ [51-250]
SLJ - v43 - S '97 - p201 [51-250]

Egan, Ted
The Drover's Boy (Illus. by Robert Ingpen)
Aust Bk R - D '97 - p64+ [501+]

Egan, Terry
The Good Guys of Baseball
HB Guide - v8 - Fall '97 - p369 [51-250]
SLJ - v43 - My '97 - p144 [51-250]

Egan, Tim
Burnt Toast on Davenport Street (Illus. by Tim Egan)
CCB-B - v51 - S '97 - p9+ [51-250]
HB Guide - v8 - Fall '97 - p263 [51-250]
Inst - v107 - S '97 - p24 [51-250]
SLJ - v43 - My '97 - p99 [51-250]
SLJ - v43 - D '97 - p24 [1-50]

Distant Feathers (Illus. by Tim Egan)
BL - v94 - Mr 15 '98 - p1246+ [51-250]
KR - v66 - F 15 '98 - p266 [51-250]

Egielski, Richard
The Gingerbread Boy (Illus. by Richard Egielski)
BL - v94 - O 15 '97 - p409 [51-250]
BW - v27 - N 2 '97 - p6 [51-250]
CBRS - v26 - O '97 - p13+ [1-50]
HB - v73 - S '97 - p587 [51-250]
KR - v65 - S 1 '97 - p1387 [51-250]
NYTBR - v103 - Ja 4 '98 - p20 [1-50]
PW - v244 - S 22 '97 - p79 [51-250]
SLJ - v43 - S '97 - p180 [51-250]
SLJ - v43 - D '97 - p24 [1-50]

Ehlert, Lois
Color Farm
HB Guide - v8 - Fall '97 - p250 [51-250]
Par - v72 - Je '97 - p189 [1-50]

Color Zoo
HB Guide - v8 - Fall '97 - p250 [51-250]
Par - v72 - Je '97 - p189 [1-50]
Par - v72 - Je '97 - p189 [1-50]

Cuckoo: A Mexican Folktale (Illus. by Lois Ehlert)
BL - v94 - Ja 1 '98 - p735 [1-50]
CCB-B - v50 - Je '97 - p356 [51-250]

Hands (Illus. by Lois Ehlert)
BL - v94 - Ja 1 '98 - p735 [1-50]
CCB-B - v51 - Ja '98 - p158+ [51-250]
HB - v73 - S '97 - p556+ [51-250]
KR - v65 - Jl 15 '97 - p1109 [51-250]
PW - v244 - Je 30 '97 - p76 [51-250]
SLJ - v43 - D '97 - p88 [51-250]

Moon Rope
ECEJ - v25 - Fall '97 - p46 [1-50]

Ehrlich, Amy
Parents in the Pigpen, Pigs in the Tub (Illus. by Steven Kellogg)
PW - v244 - D 22 '97 - p61 [1-50]

When I Was Your Age
HMR - Sum '97 - p29 [51-250]
y   JAAL - v40 - O '96 - p151 [51-250]

Eisenberg, Lisa
The Story of Sitting Bull (Illus. by David Rickman)
Ch BWatch - v7 - Mr '97 - p4 [1-50]

Ekker, Ernst A
Franz Schubert—Ein Musikalisches Bilderbuch (Illus. by Doris Eisenburger)
Bkbird - v35 - Spr '97 - p48 [51-250]

Ekman, Fam
Dagbok Forsvunnet
Bkbird - v34 - Win '96 - p55 [51-250]

Elboz, Stephen
Ghostlands
Magpies - v12 - My '97 - p33 [51-250]

Eldin, Peter
The Best-Ever Book of Magic
TES - D 5 '97 - p17* [1-50]

The Most Excellent Book of How to Do Card Tricks
Ch BWatch - v7 - My '97 - p7 [51-250]

Eldridge, Jim
*Captain Hawk and the Stone of
Destiny (Illus. by Janek Matysiak)*
Bks Keeps - S '97 - p25 [51-250]
Sch Lib - v45 - Ag '97 - p146 [51-250]
TES - Jl 4 '97 - p10* [501+]

El Droubie, Riadh
My Muslim Life
Bks Keeps - My '97 - p24 [51-250]

Electric Library. Electronic Media Version
r   SLJ - v44 - Ja '98 - p54 [501+]

Elgar, Rebecca
*Jack: Happy Birthday (Illus. by
Rebecca Elgar)*
KR - v66 - Mr 1 '98 - p337 [51-250]

Elish, Dan
Vermont
HB Guide - v8 - Fall '97 - p394 [51-250]
SLJ - v43 - Ag '97 - p160+ [51-250]

Ellen, Laura
*Clever Letters (Illus. by Valerie
Coursen)*
PW - v244 - S 22 '97 - p82 [1-50]

Elliott, Donald
Frogs and the Ballet
BW - v27 - D 7 '97 - p20 [1-50]

Elliott, Michele
Be Smart, Stay Safe
Bks Keeps - Jl '97 - p23+ [51-250]

Beat the Bullies
Bks Keeps - Jl '97 - p23+ [51-250]

Elliott, W Peter
The Magic Sleigh Bell
CBRA - '96 - p471+ [51-250]

Ellis, Kathryn
The Acting Bug
CBRA - '96 - p472 [51-250]

A Stroke of Luck
CBRA - '96 - p465 [51-250]

Ellis, Sarah
Back of Beyond
y   BIC - v26 - Je '97 - p33 [501+]
y   BL - v94 - Ja 1 '98 - p794 [51-250]
     CBRA - '96 - p472 [51-250]
y   CBRS - v26 - Ja '98 - p57 [51-250]
y   CCB-B - v51 - N '97 - p83+ [51-250]
     HB - v73 - N '97 - p680 [51-250]
y   KR - v65 - O 1 '97 - p1531 [51-250]
y   SLJ - v43 - N '97 - p117 [51-250]
y   SLJ - v43 - D '97 - p24 [1-50]
y   VOYA - v20 - D '97 - p324 [251-500]
y   VOYA - v21 - Ap '98 - p12 [1-50]

Ellis, Veronica Freeman
Wynton Marsalis
HB Guide - v8 - Fall '97 - p379 [51-250]
SLJ - v44 - F '98 - p114 [51-250]

Ellsworth, Mary Ellen
*Gertrude Chandler Warner and the
Boxcar Children (Illus. by Marie
DeJohn)*
BL - v93 - Ag '97 - p1894 [51-250]
HB - v73 - Jl '97 - p474+ [51-250]
HB Guide - v8 - Fall '97 - p379 [51-250]
KR - v65 - Ap 15 '97 - p639 [51-250]
SLJ - v43 - Jl '97 - p82 [51-250]

Ellwand, David
*Emma's Elephant and Other Favorite
Animal Friends (Illus. by David
Ellwand)*
CBRS - v26 - S '97 - p3 [51-250]
KR - v65 - Je 1 '97 - p872 [51-250]
Par - v72 - D '97 - p201 [1-50]
SLJ - v43 - Ag '97 - p135 [51-250]

Elmer, Robert
Follow the Star
SLJ - v44 - F '98 - p106 [51-250]

Touch the Sky
SLJ - v43 - Ag '97 - p157 [51-250]

Else, Barbara
Skitterfoot Leaper
Magpies - v12 - My '97 - p6* [251-500]

Elsom, Derek
Weather Explained
>BL - v94 - Mr 1 '98 - p1126 [51-250]
>SLJ - v44 - F '98 - p115 [51-250]

Elste, Joan
True Blue (Illus. by DyAnne DiSalvo-Ryan)
>RT - v51 - O '97 - p136 [1-50]

Elya, Susan Middleton
Say Hola to Spanish, Otra Vez (Again!) (Illus. by Loretta Lopez)
>KR - v65 - N 1 '97 - p1643 [51-250]
>PW - v244 - O 27 '97 - p75 [51-250]
>SLJ - v44 - Ja '98 - p98 [51-250]

Emberley, Barbara
Drummer Hoff (Illus. by Ed Emberley)
>HB Guide - v8 - Fall '97 - p250 [51-250]

Emberley, Ed
Glad Monster, Sad Monster (Illus. by Ed Emberley)
>CCB-B - v51 - O '97 - p63 [51-250]
>KR - v65 - Ag 15 '97 - p1309 [51-250]
>PW - v244 - S 1 '97 - p107 [1-50]

Emberley, Rebecca
My Mother's Secret Life (Illus. by Rebecca Emberley)
>KR - v66 - Mr 15 '98 - p402 [51-250]
>SLJ - v44 - Ap '98 - p98 [51-250]

Three Cool Kids
>ECEJ - v25 - Fall '97 - p41 [51-250]

Emerson, Charlotte
Jo's Troubled Heart
>PW - v245 - F 9 '98 - p97 [1-50]

Emmond, Ken
Manitoba. Rev. Ed.
>CBRA - '96 - p512+ [501+]

Emory, Jerry
Dirty, Rotten, Dead
>Am Sci - v85 - N '97 - p559 [1-50]

Encarta 97 Encyclopedia. Deluxe Ed. Electronic Media Version
>r   Emerg Lib - v24 - My '97 - p53 [51-250]

Encarta 97 World Atlas. Electronic Media Version
>r   Emerg Lib - v24 - My '97 - p53 [51-250]

The Encyclopedia of North American Indians. Vols. 1-11
>yr   BL - v94 - S 1 '97 - p164 [251-500]
>yr   Choice - v35 - S '97 - p106 [51-250]
>yr   R&R Bk N - v12 - My '97 - p31+ [51-250]
>r   SLJ - v43 - Ag '97 - p184 [51-250]

Ende, Michael
The Neverending Story
>PW - v244 - Jl 7 '97 - p70 [1-50]

Enderle, Judith Ross
Dear Timothy Tibbitts (Illus. by Carolyn Ewing)
>CBRS - v26 - O '97 - p14 [51-250]
>SLJ - v43 - S '97 - p180 [51-250]

Six Sandy Sheep (Illus. by John O'Brien)
>HB Guide - v8 - Fall '97 - p263 [51-250]
>SLJ - v43 - Jl '97 - p67 [51-250]

What's the Matter with Kelly Beans? (Illus. by Blanche Sims)
>Emerg Lib - v24 - My '97 - p67 [1-50]

Where Are You, Little Zack? (Illus. by Brian Floca)
>HB Guide - v8 - Fall '97 - p263 [1-50]
>SLJ - v43 - Ap '97 - p98 [51-250]

Engel, Diana
Holding On (Illus. by Diana Engel)
>BL - v94 - S 15 '97 - p234 [51-250]
>CCB-B - v51 - N '97 - p84 [51-250]
>SLJ - v43 - N '97 - p117 [51-250]

Engelbert, Phillis
Astronomy and Space. Vols. 1-3
>r   SLJ - v43 - My '97 - p158 [51-250]
>yr   SLMQ - v25 - Spr '97 - p183 [1-50]
>yr   VOYA - v20 - Ag '97 - p213 [51-250]

The Complete Weather Resource.
Vols. 1-3
  r   BL - v94 - D 1 '97 - p652 [251-500]

Engfer, LeeAnne
My Pet Cats (Illus. by Andy King)
  SLJ - v44 - Mr '98 - p194+ [51-250]

My Pet Hamster and Gerbils (Illus. by Andy King)
  SLJ - v44 - Mr '98 - p194+ [51-250]

England, Linda
3 Kids Dreamin' (Illus. by Dena Schutzer)
  HB Guide - v8 - Fall '97 - p263 [51-250]
  KR - v65 - Ap 15 '97 - p639 [51-250]
  SLJ - v43 - Je '97 - p86 [51-250]

The Old Cotton Blues (Illus. by Teresa Flavin)
  BL - v94 - F 15 '98 - p1019 [51-250]
  KR - v66 - F 1 '98 - p195+ [51-250]

Engle, Marty M
Deadly Delivery
  Ch BWatch - v7 - Ap '97 - p4 [1-50]

Driven to Death
  Ch BWatch - v7 - Ap '97 - p4 [1-50]

Fly the Unfriendly Skies
  Ch BWatch - v7 - Ap '97 - p4 [1-50]

The Last One In
  Ch BWatch - v7 - Ap '97 - p4 [1-50]

No Substitutions
  Ch BWatch - v7 - Ap '97 - p4 [1-50]

English, June
Transportation: Automobiles to Zeppelins
  r   JOYS - v11 - Fall '97 - p76 [1-50]

English, Karen
Just Right Stew (Illus. by Anna Rich)
  BL - v94 - F 15 '98 - p1019 [51-250]
  KR - v66 - F 1 '98 - p196 [51-250]
  PW - v245 - Ja 12 '98 - p59 [51-250]
  SLJ - v44 - Mr '98 - p179 [51-250]

Neeny Coming, Neeny Going (Illus. by Synthia Saint James)
  Afr Am R - v31 - Fall '97 - p556+ [501+]

English Dictionary, A to Z
  r   Ch BWatch - v7 - Jl '97 - p8 [51-250]
  r   TES - My 2 '97 - pR2 [501+]

Ennew, Judith
The Exploitation of Children
  TES - O 17 '97 - pR7 [51-250]

Enright, Elizabeth
Spider-Web for Two
  PW - v244 - N 24 '97 - p76 [1-50]

Then There Were Five (Illus. by Elizabeth Enright)
  PW - v244 - N 24 '97 - p76 [1-50]

Ensor, Eloise
Good Golly Miss Molly and the 4th of July Parade
  Ch BWatch - v7 - S '97 - p6 [51-250]
  Ch BWatch - v7 - O '97 - p1 [51-250]

Epstein, Rachel
Anne Frank
  BL - v94 - D 1 '97 - p617+ [51-250]
  SLJ - v43 - N '97 - p126 [51-250]

Erdrich, Louise
Grandmother's Pigeon (Illus. by Jim LaMarche)
  ECEJ - v25 - Fall '97 - p42 [51-250]
  Emerg Lib - v25 - Ja '98 - p46 [51-250]
  LA - v73 - N '96 - p527 [51-250]

Erickson, John R
The Case of the Vampire Vacuum Sweeper (Illus. by Gerald L Holmes)
  PW - v244 - N 10 '97 - p76 [1-50]

The Original Adventures of Hank the Cowdog (Illus. by Gerald L Holmes)
  PW - v244 - N 10 '97 - p76 [1-50]

Erickson, Jon
Glacial Geology
  ASBYP - v29 - Fall '96 - p42 [251-500]

Undersea Landforms and Life Forms
ASBYP - v29 - Fall '96 - p42 [251-500]

Erickson, Paul
Daily Life on a Southern Plantation 1853
PW - v245 - F 2 '98 - p92 [51-250]

Erlbach, Arlene
Happy Birthday, Everywhere! (Illus. by Sharon Lane Holm)
BL - v94 - D 1 '97 - p618 [51-250]
CBRS - v26 - Win '98 - p66 [1-50]
SLJ - v44 - F '98 - p98 [51-250]

Sidewalk Games around the World (Illus. by Sharon Lane Holm)
CBRS - v25 - My '97 - p115 [51-250]
HB Guide - v8 - Fall '97 - p367 [51-250]
SLJ - v43 - My '97 - p118+ [51-250]

Teddy Bears
BL - v94 - Ja 1 '98 - p796 [51-250]
Ch BWatch - v7 - D '97 - p8 [1-50]

Erlbruch, Wolf
Mrs. Meyer the Bird (Illus. by Wolf Erlbruch)
CBRS - v25 - Spr '97 - p134 [1-50]
HB Guide - v8 - Fall '97 - p263 [51-250]
NYTBR - v102 - O 12 '97 - p26 [1-50]
SLJ - v43 - Ap '97 - p98 [51-250]

Ernest, Kate Elizabeth
Tricky Tricky Twins (Illus. by David Mitchell)
Bks Keeps - S '97 - p23 [51-250]

Ernst, Barbara
Song of the Kalahari (Illus. by Barbara Ernst)
SLJ - v43 - Jl '97 - p67 [51-250]

Ernst, Carl H
Snakes in Question (Illus. by Molly Dwyer Griffin)
AB - v99 - Je 23 '97 - p2029 [51-250]
r   BioSci - v47 - O '97 - p624+ [501+]
yr   BL - v94 - D 1 '97 - p624 [1-50]
BW - v27 - Ap 27 '97 - p8 [251-500]
Choice - v34 - Je '97 - p1688+ [51-250]

y   Nature - v387 - Je 5 '97 - p568 [501+]
y   SB - v33 - Je '97 - p139 [251-500]

Ernst, Lisa Campbell
Bubba and Trixie (Illus. by Lisa Campbell Ernst)
BL - v93 - Ag '97 - p1905 [51-250]
CBRS - v26 - O '97 - p14 [51-250]
CCB-B - v51 - O '97 - p50 [51-250]
Inst - v107 - N '97 - p23 [1-50]
PW - v244 - Je 23 '97 - p92 [51-250]
SLJ - v43 - N '97 - p80 [51-250]

The Letters Are Lost (Illus. by Lisa Campbell Ernst)
LA - v73 - N '96 - p528 [51-250]
RT - v51 - O '97 - p131 [1-50]

Erricker, Clive
Buddhist Festivals
SLJ - v43 - D '97 - p136 [51-250]

Erya, Susan Middleton
Say Hola to Spanish (Illus. by Loretta Lopez)
r   Inst - v106 - My '97 - p21 [1-50]

Esbensen, Barbara Juster
Dance with Me (Illus. by Megan Lloyd)
Inst - v106 - Ap '97 - p25 [1-50]

Echoes for the Eye (Illus. by Helen Davie)
RT - v51 - N '97 - p242+ [51-250]

Echoes for the Eye (Illus. by Helen K Davie)
LA - v73 - N '96 - p523 [51-250]

Swift as the Wind (Illus. by Jean Cassels)
RT - v51 - N '97 - p254 [51-250]
SB - v33 - Ag '97 - p163 [1-50]

Escardo I Bas, Merce
Los Tres Cerditos (Illus. by Joan Pere)
SLJ - v44 - F '98 - p130 [51-250]

Esmeralda's Merry Chase (Little Play a Sound)
Ch BWatch - v7 - Ap '97 - p2 [1-50]

Espino Ortega, Jose Manuel
Barco De Suenos (Illus. by Rosa Salgado)
Bkbird - v35 - Fall '97 - p50 [1-50]

Ethan, Eric
Boas, Pythons and Anacondas
ASBYP - v29 - Sum '96 - p49 [251-500]

Camaros
PW - v245 - Ja 26 '98 - p93 [51-250]

Cobras
ASBYP - v29 - Sum '96 - p49 [251-500]
PW - v245 - Ja 26 '98 - p93 [51-250]

Copperheads
ASBYP - v29 - Sum '96 - p49 [251-500]

Corvettes
PW - v245 - Ja 26 '98 - p93 [51-250]

Cottonmouths
ASBYP - v29 - Sum '96 - p49 [251-500]

Firebirds
PW - v245 - Ja 26 '98 - p93 [51-250]

GTOs
PW - v245 - Ja 26 '98 - p93 [51-250]

Mustangs
PW - v245 - Ja 26 '98 - p93 [51-250]

Rattlesnakes
ASBYP - v29 - Sum '96 - p49 [251-500]

Vipers
ASBYP - v29 - Sum '96 - p49 [251-500]

Europe on File. Vols. 1-2
r   BL - v94 - Ja 1 '98 - p856+ [501+]

Evans, Dilys
Weird Pet Poems (Illus. by Jacqueline Rogers)
BL - v94 - S 15 '97 - p238 [51-250]
CCB-B - v51 - Ja '98 - p159 [51-250]
KR - v65 - S 15 '97 - p1456 [51-250]
NYTBR - v102 - N 16 '97 - p36 [501+]
SLJ - v43 - N '97 - p106 [51-250]

Evans, Douglas
So What Do You Do?
BL - v94 - N 1 '97 - p469+ [51-250]
CBRS - v26 - Ja '98 - p57 [51-250]
CCB-B - v51 - Mr '98 - p240+ [51-250]
KR - v65 - O 15 '97 - p1580 [51-250]
PW - v244 - N 3 '97 - p86 [51-250]
SLJ - v44 - Ja '98 - p111+ [251-500]
y   VOYA - v20 - F '98 - p384 [251-500]

Evans, Gregory
Owl in the House (Illus. by Peter Bailey)
Bks Keeps - S '97 - p24 [51-250]
Sch Lib - v45 - Ag '97 - p136 [51-250]

Evans, Karen L B
You Must Remember This
CBRS - v25 - Spr '97 - p141 [51-250]
CCB-B - v50 - Je '97 - p356 [51-250]
HB Guide - v8 - Fall '97 - p298 [51-250]

Evans, Lezlie
If I Were the Wind (Illus. by Victoria Lisi)
BL - v93 - Ag '97 - p1905 [51-250]
HB Guide - v8 - Fall '97 - p264 [51-250]
SLJ - v43 - Je '97 - p86 [51-250]

Snow Dance (Illus. by Cynthia Jabar)
BL - v94 - O 1 '97 - p336 [51-250]
CCB-B - v51 - D '97 - p123+ [51-250]
KR - v65 - S 1 '97 - p1387 [51-250]
SLJ - v43 - D '97 - p88 [51-250]

The Eventful History of Three Blind Mice (Illus. by Winslow Homer)
Sch Lib - v45 - Ag '97 - p145 [51-250]

Everitt, Betsy
Up the Ladder, down the Slide (Illus. by Betsy Everitt)
KR - v66 - Ap 1 '98 - p504 [51-250]

Eversole, Robyn
Flood Fish (Illus. by Sheldon Greenberg)
LA - v73 - N '96 - p527 [51-250]
SB - v33 - O '97 - p218 [51-250]

Evetts-Secker, Josephine
Father and Daughter Tales (Illus. by Helen Cann)

Can CL - v23 - Fall '97 - p61+ [501+]
Emerg Lib - v25 - N '97 - p54 [1-50]
Quill & Q - v63 - Ag '97 - p38 [251-500]

Mother and Daughter Tales (Illus. by Helen Cann)

Can CL - v23 - Fall '97 - p61+ [501+]
CM:CanRev - v4 - N 14 '97 - pONL [251-500]

Evslin, Bernard
Hercules (Sorbo). Audio Version

BL - v94 - F 15 '98 - p1025 [51-250]

Ewing, Lynne
Drive-By

PW - v245 - F 16 '98 - p213 [1-50]

Explorers and Adventurers (Child's First Library of Learning)

HB Guide - v8 - Fall '97 - p385 [51-250]

Exploring with Power Polygons

SLMQ - v25 - Spr '97 - p179+ [51-250]
TCMath - v4 - N '97 - p189 [51-250]

Eyewitness Children's Encyclopedia. Electronic Media Version

r   Emerg Lib - v25 - Ja '98 - p47 [51-250]
r   SLJ - v44 - F '98 - p52 [251-500]

Eyewitness Encyclopedia of Science 2.0. Electronic Media Version

r   Emerg Lib - v25 - N '97 - p48 [51-250]
r   Sch Lib - v45 - Ag '97 - p140 [251-500]
r   TES - My 23 '97 - p19* [51-250]

Eyvindson, Peter
Red Parka Mary (Illus. by Rhian Brynjolson)

CBRA - '96 - p440 [51-250]
Ch Bk News - v20 - Sum '97 - p28 [51-250]

Ezra, Mark
The Frightened Little Owl (Illus. by Gavin Rowe)

BL - v93 - Je 1 '97 - p1716+ [51-250]
Ch BWatch - v7 - Je '97 - p6 [1-50]
PW - v244 - Je 16 '97 - p61 [51-250]
SLJ - v43 - Jl '97 - p67 [51-250]

The Hungry Otter (Illus. by Gavin Rowe)

PW - v244 - Je 16 '97 - p61 [51-250]
SLJ - v43 - Ap '97 - p98 [51-250]

F

Fabrick, Harriett
Furello (Illus. by Harriett Fabrick)
SLJ - v44 - Ja '98 - p112 [51-250]

Facklam, Margery
The Biggest Bug Book (Illus. by Paul Facklam)
SLJ - v43 - My '97 - p56 [1-50]

Tracking Dinosaurs in the Gobi
y   Ch BWatch - v8 - Ja '98 - p6 [51-250]
SLJ - v44 - F '98 - p115 [51-250]

What Does the Crow Know? (Illus. by Pamela Johnson)
SLJ - v43 - My '97 - p56 [1-50]

Facts about Britain 1945 to 1995. Electronic Media Version
r   Sch Lib - v45 - Ag '97 - p141 [251-500]

Fain, Moira
Snow Day
Ch BWatch - v7 - Mr '97 - p7 [51-250]

Falk, John H
Bubble Monster and Other Science Fun (Illus. by Charles C Somerville)
SLJ - v43 - Ap '97 - p122 [51-250]

Fallen, Anne-Catherine
USA from Space
BL - v94 - Mr 1 '98 - p1126 [51-250]
KR - v65 - D 1 '97 - p1774+ [51-250]
PW - v244 - D 8 '97 - p74 [51-250]
SLJ - v43 - D '97 - p136 [51-250]

Falloon, Jane
Thumbelina (Illus. by Emma Chichester Clark)
HB Guide - v8 - Fall '97 - p264 [51-250]
SLJ - v43 - Je '97 - p78 [51-250]

Falwell, Cathryn
Feast for Ten
ECEJ - v25 - Fall '97 - p46 [1-50]

P.J. and Puppy
HB Guide - v8 - Fall '97 - p250 [51-250]

Family Encyclopedia
r   BL - v94 - F 15 '98 - p1036 [51-250]
r   PW - v244 - O 13 '97 - p77 [51-250]

Fanelli, Sara
Wolf (Illus. by Sara Fanelli)
Bks Keeps - My '97 - p22 [51-250]
CBRS - v25 - Jl '97 - p147 [1-50]
HB Guide - v8 - Fall '97 - p264 [51-250]
Sch Lib - v45 - Ag '97 - p136+ [51-250]
SLJ - v43 - Jl '97 - p67 [51-250]

Fang, Linda
The Ch'i-Lin Purse (Illus. by Jeanne M Lee)
PW - v244 - S 1 '97 - p107 [1-50]

Fang, Su Chen
Happy Birthday to You (Illus. by Gui Fong Chang)
AB - v100 - N 17 '97 - p1268 [51-250]
HB Guide - v8 - Fall '97 - p264 [51-250]

Farber, Norma
*The Boy Who Longed for a Lift (Illus.
by Brian Selznick)*
> CBRS - v25 - Jl '97 - p147 [51-250]
> HB Guide - v8 - Fall '97 - p250+ [51-250]
> SLJ - v43 - Je '97 - p86+ [51-250]

*I Swim an Ocean in My Sleep (Illus.
by Elivia Savadier)*
> HB Guide - v8 - Fall '97 - p264 [51-250]
> SLJ - v43 - Ap '97 - p100 [51-250]

*Without Wings, Mother, How Can I
Fly? (Illus. by Keiko Narahashi)*
> BL - v94 - Mr 15 '98 - p1247 [51-250]
> KR - v66 - F 15 '98 - p266 [51-250]
> PW - v245 - Mr 9 '98 - p67 [51-250]

Farjeon, Eleanor
*Elsie Piddock Skips in Her Sleep
(Illus. by Charlotte Voake)*
> Ch BWatch - v7 - N '97 - p4 [1-50]
> KR - v65 - S 15 '97 - p1456 [51-250]

*Morning Has Broken (Illus. by Tim
Ladwig)*
> Bloom Rev - v17 - Mr '97 - p20 [51-250]

Farley, Carol J
*Mr. Pak Buys a Story (Illus. by Benrei
Huang)*
> CBRS - v25 - Spr '97 - p134 [1-50]
> HB - v73 - Jl '97 - p466+ [51-250]
> HB Guide - v8 - Fall '97 - p332 [51-250]
> Inst - v107 - S '97 - p22 [51-250]
> SLJ - v43 - Ap '97 - p122+ [51-250]

Farley, Steven
The Black Stallion's Steeplechaser
> SLJ - v44 - F '98 - p106 [51-250]

Farley, Walter
The Horse Tamer
> JOYS - v10 - Spr '97 - p262 [1-50]

Farman, John
Egyptians (Illus. by John Farman)
> Books - v11 - Ag '97 - p15 [51-250]

Tudors (Illus. by John Farman)
> Books - v11 - Ag '97 - p15 [51-250]

Victorians (Illus. by John Farman)
> Books - v11 - Ag '97 - p15 [51-250]

Vikings (Illus. by John Farman)
> Books - v11 - Ag '97 - p15 [51-250]

Farmer, Nancy
A Girl Named Disaster
> y   Bks Keeps - S '97 - p30 [51-250]
> y   BW - v27 - My 4 '97 - p16 [51-250]
> y   Emerg Lib - v24 - My '97 - p56 [51-250]
> y   HMR - Sum '97 - p29 [51-250]
> y   Kliatt - v32 - Mr '98 - p10 [51-250]
>   PW - v245 - F 16 '98 - p213 [1-50]
>   RT - v51 - D '97 - p334 [51-250]
> y   SLJ - v43 - Jl '97 - p34 [1-50]
> y   TES - N 7 '97 - p12* [51-250]
> y   VOYA - v20 - Je '97 - p85 [51-250]

Farmer, Patti
*To Tell the Truth (Illus. by Stephen
Taylor)*
> CLW - v68 - D '97 - p83 [51-250]
> Quill & Q - v63 - Ag '97 - p38 [251-500]

*What's He Doing Now? (Illus. by
Janet Wilson)*
> CBRA - '96 - p441 [51-250]

Farmyard Animals (Balloon)
> PW - v244 - N 10 '97 - p76 [1-50]

Farndon, John
Pockets Encyclopedia
> r   CLW - v68 - D '97 - p82+ [51-250]

Royal Castle
> Sch Lib - v45 - Ag '97 - p150 [51-250]

Farrell, Mame
Bradley and the Billboard
> CCB-B - v51 - Ap '98 - p278+ [51-250]
> KR - v66 - Ap 15 '98 - p578 [51-250]

Farrer, Vashti
Ned's Kang-U-Roo
> Aust Bk R - S '97 - p63 [501+]
> Magpies - v12 - S '97 - p37+ [251-500]

Farris, Katherine
You Asked?
   CBRA - '96 - p538+ [51-250]

Farris, Pamela J
Young Mouse and Elephant (Illus. by Valeri Gorbachev)
   RT - v51 - N '97 - p250 [51-250]

Faulkner, Keith
Bertie's Big Blue Binoculars (Illus. by Jo Davies)
   Bloom Rev - v17 - My '97 - p27 [51-250]

Gizmos Galore (Illus. by Jonathan Lambert)
   PW - v244 - N 24 '97 - p76+ [1-50]

Jazzy Jewelry
   PW - v244 - N 24 '97 - p76 [1-50]

The Long-Nosed Pig (Illus. by Jonathan Lambert)
   BL - v94 - D 15 '97 - p700 [1-50]
   KR - v66 - Ja 15 '98 - p110 [51-250]

Web Willy in Cyberspace (Illus. by Piers Baker)
   KR - v66 - Ap 15 '98 - p578 [51-250]

The Wide-Mouthed Frog (Illus. by Jonathan Lambert)
   RT - v51 - O '97 - p132 [1-50]

Fawcett, Melissa Jayne
Makiawisug: The Gift of the Little People (Illus. by David Wagner)
   BL - v94 - S 15 '97 - p234+ [51-250]

Feder, Jane
Table, Chair, Bear
   ECEJ - v25 - Fall '97 - p46 [1-50]

Feelings, Tom
The Middle Passage (Illus. by Tom Feelings)
   Bkbird - v34 - Win '96 - p56 [51-250]
  y JAAL - v41 - N '97 - p212 [51-250]

Feelings and Manners
   HB Guide - v8 - Fall '97 - p361 [51-250]
   SB - v33 - O '97 - p207 [51-250]

Feeney, Josephine
The Dadhunters
   Bks Keeps - My '97 - p24 [51-250]

Truth, Lies and Homework
   Bks Keeps - My '97 - p25 [51-250]

Fehr, Kristin Smith
Monica Seles: Returning Champion
   Ch BWatch - v7 - S '97 - p8 [1-50]

Feiffer, Jules
I Lost My Bear (Illus. by Jules Feiffer)
   HB - v74 - Mr '98 - p212 [251-500]
   KR - v66 - Mr 15 '98 - p402 [51-250]
   PW - v245 - Ja 26 '98 - p91 [51-250]
   SLJ - v44 - Mr '98 - p179 [51-250]

Meanwhile... (Illus. by Jules Feiffer)
   BL - v94 - D 1 '97 - p636 [51-250]
   CBRS - v26 - O '97 - p14 [1-50]
   HB - v73 - S '97 - p557 [51-250]
   KR - v65 - Jl 15 '97 - p1110 [51-250]
   NYTBR - v103 - Mr 15 '98 - p24 [51-250]
   Par - v72 - D '97 - p204+ [1-50]
   SLJ - v43 - S '97 - p180 [51-250]

Felder, Deborah
Ride of Courage (Illus. by Sandy Rabinowitz)
   PW - v244 - N 17 '97 - p63 [1-50]

Felstead, Cathie
What Am I? Seashore (Illus. by Cathie Felstead)
   TES - Je 13 '97 - pR7 [51-250]

Felwell, John
Butterflies and Moths
   CLW - v68 - S '97 - p63 [51-250]

Ferber, Elizabeth
Diabetes
   SB - v33 - Ap '97 - p86 [51-250]

Ferguson, Alane
Secrets
   CBRS - v25 - Jl '97 - p154 [1-50]
   CCB-B - v50 - Jl '97 - p393 [51-250]
   HB Guide - v8 - Fall '97 - p299 [51-250]
  y KR - v65 - My 15 '97 - p799 [51-250]

SLJ - v43 - Jl '97 - p93 [51-250]

Ferguson, Dwayne J
Case of the Missing Ankh
SLJ - v43 - S '97 - p180+ [51-250]

Ferguson, John
Grampa's Cat (Illus. by Velma Genaille)
CBRA - '96 - p441 [51-250]

Ferguson, Neil, 1947-
English Weather
Books - v10 - S '96 - p24 [51-250]

Fernandes, Eugenie
Little Toby and the Big Hair (Illus. by Kim Fernandes)
Quill & Q - v63 - My '97 - p43 [251-500]

The Tree That Grew to the Moon (Fernandes). Book and Audio Version
Quill & Q - v63 - Ap '97 - p38 [51-250]

Fernandes, Kim
Christmas Crafts with Crayola Model Magic (Illus. by Wally Randall)
CM:CanRev - v4 - D 12 '97 - pONL [251-500]

Gifts to Make with Crayola Model Magic (Illus. by Wally Randall)
CBRA - '96 - p517 [51-250]

Ferraro, Christine
Elmo Saves Christmas (Illus. by Ellen Appleby)
PW - v244 - O 6 '97 - p58 [1-50]

Ferrell, Nancy Warren
The Battle of the Little Bighorn in American History
Ch BWatch - v7 - S '97 - p2 [51-250]
y   CLW - v68 - S '97 - p70 [51-250]

Feth, Monika
Die Blauen Und Die Grauen Tage
Bkbird - v35 - Spr '97 - p48 [51-250]

Feuerman, Ruchama King
The Marvelous Mix-Up and Other Tales of Reb Shalom (Illus. by Vitaliy Romanenko)
Ch BWatch - v7 - N '97 - p2 [51-250]

Fewell, Anne
Merrywinkle: The Adventures of Santa's Big Brother
Ch BWatch - v7 - D '97 - p1 [51-250]

Fiarotta, Noel
Great Experiments with H2O
BL - v94 - D 1 '97 - p630 [51-250]

Water Science, Water Fun
SLJ - v43 - Ap '97 - p123 [51-250]

Field, Dorothy
In the Street of the Temple Cloth Printers (Illus. by Dorothy Field)
CBRA - '96 - p518 [51-250]

Field, Rachel
Prayer for a Child (Illus. by Elizabeth Orton Jones)
HB Guide - v8 - Fall '97 - p251 [51-250]

Fields, Terri
Danger in the Desert
CBRS - v25 - Je '97 - p126 [51-250]
SLJ - v43 - N '97 - p117+ [51-250]

Fifth-Grade Frankenstein
SLJ - v43 - Ap '97 - p137 [51-250]

Fienberg, Anna
Tashi (Illus. by Kim Gamble)
Cur R - v36 - Mr '97 - p12 [51-250]

Tashi and the Genie (Illus. by Kim Gamble)
Magpies - v12 - S '97 - p29+ [51-250]

Tashi and the Giants (Illus. by Kim Gamble)
Cur R - v36 - Mr '97 - p12 [51-250]

Fietzek, Petra
Bald Geht's Mir Wieder Gut (Illus. by Ruth Scholte Van Mast)
Bkbird - v35 - Spr '97 - p49 [51-250]

Figley, Marty Rhodes
Noah's Wife (Illus. by Anita Riggio)
PW - v245 - F 23 '98 - p67 [51-250]
The Story of Lydia
Ch BWatch - v7 - Mr '97 - p8 [51-250]

Filipovic, Zlata
Zlata's Diary
Bks Keeps - My '97 - p4+ [501+]

Find Your Way to the Lost World
Books - v11 - Ag '97 - p15 [51-250]

Findon, Joanne
Auld Lang Syne (Illus. by Ted Nasmith)
PW - v244 - D 15 '97 - p58 [51-250]
Quill & Q - v63 - D '97 - p37 [251-500]
SLJ - v44 - Mr '98 - p195 [51-250]

Fine, Anne
Care of Henry (Illus. by Paul Howard)
Emerg Lib - v25 - Ja '98 - p45 [51-250]
Magpies - v12 - Mr '97 - p30 [51-250]
TES - Ap 18 '97 - p12* [51-250]

Flour Babies
Sch Lib - v45 - Ag '97 - p156 [51-250]

Jennifer's Diary
TES - N 14 '97 - p14* [51-250]

Step by Wicked Step
PW - v244 - Je 30 '97 - p77 [1-50]
RT - v51 - D '97 - p331 [51-250]
y   TES - Je 27 '97 - pR6 [251-500]

The Tulip Touch
BL - v94 - S 15 '97 - p230 [51-250]
BL - v94 - Ja 1 '98 - p734 [51-250]
BL - v94 - Mr 15 '98 - p1224 [1-50]
y   Books - v11 - Ag '97 - p15 [51-250]
CBRS - v26 - S '97 - p10 [51-250]
CCB-B - v51 - S '97 - p3+ [501+]
y   HB - v73 - S '97 - p568+ [251-500]
y   KR - v65 - Jl 15 '97 - p1110 [51-250]
y   Magpies - v12 - Mr '97 - p36 [251-500]
y   NYTBR - v103 - F 15 '98 - p26 [251-500]
PW - v244 - Jl 7 '97 - p68 [51-250]
y   SLJ - v43 - S '97 - p216 [51-250]
y   SLJ - v43 - D '97 - p24 [1-50]
TES - My 2 '97 - p8* [1-50]

Finkelstein, Norman H
With Heroic Truth
y   BL - v93 - Je 1 '97 - p1671 [51-250]
y   CCB-B - v50 - Je '97 - p357 [51-250]
y   HB Guide - v8 - Fall '97 - p380 [51-250]
KR - v65 - Ap 15 '97 - p640 [51-250]
y   SLJ - v43 - Jl '97 - p102 [51-250]
TV Q - v29 - 2 '97 - p92 [251-500]

Finlayson, Reggie
Colin Powell
y   Ch BWatch - v7 - Ap '97 - p5 [1-50]
HB Guide - v8 - Fall '97 - p380 [51-250]
SLJ - v43 - Ap '97 - p149 [51-250]
y   VOYA - v20 - Je '97 - p128 [251-500]

Finney, Fred
Viking Longboat (Illus. by Mike Bell)
Am Sci - v85 - N '97 - p558 [51-250]
Ch BWatch - v7 - My '97 - p7 [1-50]
HB Guide - v8 - Fall '97 - p387 [51-250]
SLJ - v43 - Ag '97 - p166 [51-250]

Fire Engine (Box Cars)
PW - v245 - Mr 23 '98 - p102 [1-50]

The First Noel (Angel Wings) (Illus. by Laura Rader)
Ch BWatch - v7 - N '97 - p6 [1-50]

Fischel, Emma
Captain Scott
TES - S 19 '97 - p16* [51-250]
Florence Nightingale
TES - S 19 '97 - p16* [51-250]

Fisher, Aileen
The Story of Easter (Illus. by Stefano Vitale)
HB Guide - v8 - Fall '97 - p320 [51-250]
PW - v245 - F 23 '98 - p68 [1-50]

Fisher, Leonard Everett
Anasazi (Illus. by Leonard Everett Fisher)
BL - v94 - N 1 '97 - p464 [51-250]
KR - v65 - S 1 '97 - p1388 [51-250]
SLJ - v43 - D '97 - p108 [51-250]

The Gods and Goddesses of Ancient Egypt (Illus. by Leonard Everett Fisher)
> BL - v94 - D 1 '97 - p618 [51-250]
> PW - v244 - S 22 '97 - p82 [51-250]
> SLJ - v43 - N '97 - p106 [51-250]

The Jetty Chronicles
> BL - v94 - O 15 '97 - p397 [51-250]
> CBRS - v26 - Ja '98 - p58 [51-250]
> y KR - v65 - S 15 '97 - p1456 [51-250]
> SLJ - v43 - D '97 - p123 [51-250]
> y VOYA - v20 - F '98 - p384+ [251-500]

Fisher, Lilian M
Brave Bessie Flying Free
> Ch BWatch - v7 - O '97 - p5 [1-50]

Fisher, Robert
Games for Thinking
> TES - O 3 '97 - p12* [501+]

Poems for Thinking
> TES - O 3 '97 - p12* [501+]

Fisher, Teresa
France
> HB Guide - v8 - Fall '97 - p390 [51-250]
> SB - v33 - Ag '97 - p180 [51-250]
> SLJ - v43 - Ag '97 - p166 [51-250]

Fishman, Cathy
On Passover (Illus. by Melanie W Hall)
> CBRS - v25 - Jl '97 - p147 [51-250]
> Ch BWatch - v7 - Jl '97 - p7 [1-50]
> HB Guide - v8 - Fall '97 - p321 [51-250]
> SLJ - v43 - Ap '97 - p100 [51-250]

On Rosh Hashanah and Yom Kippur (Illus. by Melanie W Hall)
> BL - v94 - O 1 '97 - p322+ [51-250]
> NYTBR - v102 - S 28 '97 - p28 [1-50]

Fison, Josie
Roald Dahl's Revolting Recipes (Illus. by Quentin Blake)
> NYTBR - v102 - N 16 '97 - p38 [51-250]
> PW - v244 - Ag 18 '97 - p95 [1-50]

Fitch, Sheree
If You Could Wear My Sneakers! (Illus. by Darcia Labrosse)
> BIC - v26 - S '97 - p33 [51-250]
> Ch Bk News - v20 - Spr '97 - p29 [51-250]
> CM:CanRev - v4 - N 28 '97 - pONL [251-500]
> Quill & Q - v63 - Ap '97 - p37 [51-250]

There's a Mouse in My House! (Illus. by Leslie Elizabeth Watts)
> CM:CanRev - v30 - Ja 30 '98 - pONL [51-250]
> Quill & Q - v63 - D '97 - p36 [251-500]

Fitzgerald, Karen
The Story of Iron
> BL - v94 - S 1 '97 - p113 [51-250]
> HB Guide - v8 - Fall '97 - p342 [51-250]
> SB - v33 - O '97 - p208 [51-250]

The Story of Nitrogen
> BL - v94 - S 1 '97 - p113 [51-250]
> HB Guide - v8 - Fall '97 - p342 [51-250]
> SB - v33 - O '97 - p208 [51-250]

Fitz-Gibbon, Sally
The Patchwork House (Illus. by Dean Griffiths)
> CBRA - '96 - p441 [51-250]

Fitzpatrick, Marie-Louise
The Long March (Illus. by Marie-Louise Fitzpatrick)
> KR - v66 - Ap 15 '98 - p578 [51-250]

Fitzsimons, Cecilia
Animal Habitats (Illus. by Adam Hook)
> ASBYP - v29 - Fall '96 - p59+ [251-500]

Creatures of the Past (Illus. by Chris Forsey)
> ASBYP - v29 - Fall '96 - p59+ [251-500]

Water Life (Illus. by Helen Ward)
> ASBYP - v29 - Fall '96 - p59+ [251-500]

Flack, Marjorie
La Historia De Ping (Illus. by Kurt Wiese)
   HB Guide - v8 - Fall '97 - p338 [1-50]

Flanagan, Alice K
Ask Nurse Pfaff, She'll Help You! (Illus. by Christine Osinski)
   SB - v34 - Ap '98 - p79 [51-250]

A Day in Court with Mrs. Trinh (Illus. by Christine Osinski)
   SB - v34 - Ap '98 - p79 [51-250]
   SLJ - v44 - Ja '98 - p98+ [51-250]

Dr. Kanner, Dentist with a Smile (Illus. by Christine Osinski)
   SB - v34 - Ap '98 - p82 [51-250]
   SLJ - v44 - Ja '98 - p98+ [51-250]

Ms. Murphy Fights Fires (Illus. by Christine Osinski)
   SLJ - v44 - Ja '98 - p98 [51-250]

Fleetwood-Morrow, Jane
Fabulous Doll Fashions (Illus. by William Kimber)
   CBRA - '96 - p518 [51-250]

Fantastic Jewelry (Illus. by William Kimber)
   CBRA - '96 - p518 [51-250]

Fleischman, Paul
Bull Run
   SLJ - v43 - S '97 - p130 [1-50]
y VOYA - v21 - Ap '98 - p43 [1-50]

Dateline: Troy
   LA - v73 - N '96 - p523 [51-250]
y VOYA - v20 - Je '97 - p85 [51-250]
y VOYA - v20 - Ag '97 - p164 [51-250]

Seedfolks (Illus. by Judy Pedersen)
y BL - v94 - Mr 15 '98 - p1214 [1-50]
y BL - v94 - Mr 15 '98 - p1225 [1-50]
   CBRS - v25 - My '97 - p118 [51-250]
y CCB-B - v50 - Jl '97 - p393+ [51-250]
   HB Guide - v8 - Fall '97 - p299 [51-250]
y JAAL - v41 - D '97 - p321 [51-250]
   Learning - v26 - Ag '97 - p26 [51-250]
   PW - v244 - N 3 '97 - p59 [51-250]
   SLJ - v43 - My '97 - p132 [51-250]
   SLJ - v43 - D '97 - p25 [1-50]

y VOYA - v20 - Je '97 - p109 [51-250]
y VOYA - v21 - Ap '98 - p37 [1-50]
y VOYA - v21 - Ap '98 - p40 [1-50]

Time Train (Illus. by Claire Ewart)
   SLJ - v43 - Jl '97 - p34+ [1-50]

Fleischman, Sid
The 13th Floor (Illus. by Peter Sis)
   Ch BWatch - v7 - Je '97 - p7 [1-50]
   Emerg Lib - v25 - N '97 - p47 [51-250]

The Abracadabra Kid
   RT - v51 - D '97 - p328 [51-250]
y VOYA - v20 - Ap '97 - p52+ [51-250]
y VOYA - v20 - Je '97 - p85 [51-250]

Chancy and the Grand Rascal
   HB Guide - v8 - Fall '97 - p299 [51-250]

The Ghost on Saturday Night (Illus. by Laura Cornell)
   HB Guide - v8 - Fall '97 - p290 [51-250]

Jim Ugly (Illus. by Jos. A Smith)
   BL - v93 - Je 1 '97 - p1701 [1-50]

Mr. Mysterious and Company (Illus. by Eric Von Schmidt)
   HB Guide - v8 - Fall '97 - p299 [51-250]

Fleischner, Jennifer
The Dred Scott Case
   HB Guide - v8 - Fall '97 - p324 [51-250]
   SLJ - v43 - Ap '97 - p149 [51-250]

I Was Born a Slave (Illus. by Melanie K Reim)
   BL - v94 - S 15 '97 - p225 [51-250]
y CBRS - v26 - O '97 - p22 [51-250]
   CCB-B - v51 - D '97 - p124 [51-250]
y Ch BWatch - v7 - D '97 - p6 [51-250]
   KR - v65 - S 1 '97 - p1388 [51-250]
   SLJ - v44 - Ja '98 - p123 [51-250]

Fleisher, Paul
Coral Reef
   Ch BWatch - v7 - D '97 - p7 [1-50]
   SLJ - v44 - Ap '98 - p115 [51-250]

Life Cycles of a Dozen Diverse Creatures
   Am Sci - v85 - N '97 - p557 [51-250]

SB - v33 - Ag '97 - p163 [1-50]

Oak Tree
BL - v94 - F 15 '98 - p1002 [51-250]
Ch BWatch - v7 - D '97 - p7 [1-50]

Our Oceans (Illus. by Patricia Keeler)
ASBYP - v29 - Sum '96 - p12+ [251-500]

Saguaro Cactus
Ch BWatch - v7 - D '97 - p7 [1-50]

Tide Pool
BL - v94 - F 15 '98 - p1002 [51-250]
Ch BWatch - v7 - D '97 - p7 [1-50]
SLJ - v44 - Ap '98 - p115 [51-250]

Fleming, Candace
Gabriella's Song (Illus. by Giselle Potter)
BL - v94 - D 1 '97 - p640 [51-250]
BL - v94 - Mr 15 '98 - p1219 [1-50]
CBRS - v26 - F '98 - p75 [51-250]
KR - v65 - Ag 15 '97 - p1304 [51-250]
NYTBR - v103 - Mr 15 '98 - p23 [1-50]
PW - v244 - Ag 11 '97 - p400+ [51-250]
PW - v244 - N 3 '97 - p59 [51-250]
SLJ - v43 - N '97 - p80 [51-250]

The Hatmaker's Sign (Illus. by Robert Andrew Parker)
BL - v94 - F 15 '98 - p1010 [51-250]
HB - v74 - Mr '98 - p212+ [251-500]
KR - v66 - Ja 15 '98 - p110 [51-250]
PW - v245 - F 9 '98 - p95 [51-250]
SLJ - v44 - Ap '98 - p98 [51-250]

Fleming, Denise
Count!
HB Guide - v8 - Fall '97 - p251 [51-250]

Time to Sleep (Illus. by Denise Fleming)
BL - v94 - O 1 '97 - p336 [51-250]
CBRS - v26 - O '97 - p14 [51-250]
CCB-B - v51 - D '97 - p124 [51-250]
Emerg Lib - v25 - Ja '98 - p52 [1-50]
Inst - v107 - N '97 - p18 [1-50]
KR - v65 - Ag 1 '97 - p1221 [51-250]
NYTBR - v103 - Ja 4 '98 - p20 [1-50]
Par - v73 - F '98 - p185 [1-50]
PW - v244 - Ag 11 '97 - p400 [51-250]
SLJ - v43 - N '97 - p80 [51-250]

Where Once There Was a Wood
ASBYP - v29 - Fall '96 - p14+ [251-500]
SB - v33 - Ag '97 - p163 [1-50]

Fleming, Fergus
Greek Gazette
Books - v11 - Ag '97 - p15 [51-250]

Fleming, Sibley
How to Rock Your Baby (Illus. by John Amoss)
Bloom Rev - v17 - Jl '97 - p21 [51-250]
HB Guide - v8 - Fall '97 - p264 [51-250]
SLJ - v43 - Ap '97 - p100 [51-250]

Fleming, Virginia
Be Good to Eddie Lee (Illus. by Floyd Cooper)
PW - v244 - Je 30 '97 - p77 [1-50]

Fletcher, Ralph
Buried Alive (Illus. by Andrew Moore)
RT - v51 - O '97 - p141 [1-50]

Ordinary Things (Illus. by Walter Lyon Krudop)
y   BL - v94 - Mr 15 '98 - p1224 [1-50]
y   HB Guide - v8 - Fall '97 - p376 [51-250]
     SLJ - v43 - My '97 - p144 [51-250]
y   VOYA - v21 - Ap '98 - p39 [1-50]

Room Enough for Love
PW - v245 - F 2 '98 - p91+ [51-250]

Spider Boy
BL - v93 - Je 1 '97 - p1702 [51-250]
HB - v73 - Jl '97 - p454+ [51-250]
HB Guide - v8 - Fall '97 - p299 [51-250]
SLJ - v43 - Jl '97 - p93 [51-250]

Twilight Comes Twice (Illus. by Kate Kiesler)
BL - v94 - O 15 '97 - p414 [51-250]
CBRS - v26 - Ja '98 - p50 [51-250]
KR - v65 - S 1 '97 - p1388 [51-250]
PW - v244 - O 27 '97 - p75 [51-250]

Flint, David
Great Britain
SLJ - v43 - Ag '97 - p166 [51-250]

South Africa
SLJ - v43 - Ag '97 - p166 [51-250]

Flint, Helen
Not Just Babysitting (Illus. by Nathalie Gagnon)
y   Bks Keeps - N '97 - p27 [51-250]
y   Sch Lib - v45 - N '97 - p211 [51-250]
     TES - Ag 1 '97 - p25 [251-500]
     TES - N 7 '97 - p7* [1-50]

Floca, Brian
The Frightful Story of Harry Walfish
HB Guide - v8 - Fall '97 - p264 [51-250]

Flood, Nancy Bo
I'll Go to School If... (Illus. by Ronnie Walter Shipman)
BL - v93 - Je 1 '97 - p1717 [51-250]
CBRS - v26 - S '97 - p3 [51-250]

Florian, Douglas
Beast Feast
Inst - v107 - N '97 - p18 [1-50]

In the Swim (Illus. by Douglas Florian)
HB - v73 - Jl '97 - p470+ [51-250]
HB Guide - v8 - Fall '97 - p376 [51-250]
NYTBR - v102 - O 12 '97 - p26 [1-50]
SLJ - v43 - My '97 - p119 [51-250]

Insectlopedia (Illus. by Douglas Florian)
BL - v94 - Mr 15 '98 - p1240 [51-250]
KR - v66 - F 15 '98 - p266 [51-250]
PW - v245 - Mr 9 '98 - p69+ [51-250]
SLJ - v44 - Ap '98 - p115+ [51-250]

The Flower Fairies Sticker Activity Book
TES - D 26 '97 - p22 [51-250]

Flynn, Kieran
Haunted Cleats
PW - v244 - N 17 '97 - p62 [51-250]

Foggo, Cheryl
One Thing That's True
BL - v94 - F 15 '98 - p1011 [51-250]

CM:CanRev - v4 - O 31 '97 - pONL [251-500]
y   KR - v66 - Mr 15 '98 - p402 [51-250]
y   Quill & Q - v63 - Ag '97 - p39 [251-500]
y   SLJ - v44 - Ap '98 - p131 [51-250]

Foley, Erin
Costa Rica
HB Guide - v8 - Fall '97 - p400 [51-250]

Puerto Rico
Ch BWatch - v7 - O '97 - p4+ [51-250]
SLJ - v44 - Ja '98 - p99 [51-250]

Fonseka, Kulasena
Somapura Weerayo (Illus. by Kusum Mangalika)
Bkird - v35 - Fall '97 - p52 [51-250]

Food (First Words Series)
Ch BWatch - v7 - Je '97 - p4 [1-50]

Food (First Words Series)
SLJ - v43 - Ap '97 - p120+ [51-250]

Ford, Barbara
The Most Wonderful Movie in the World
RT - v51 - D '97 - p328 [51-250]

Ford, Juwanda G
K Is for Kwanzaa (Illus. by Ken Wilson-Max)
BL - v94 - S 1 '97 - p138 [51-250]
CBRS - v26 - N '97 - p26 [51-250]
KR - v65 - N 1 '97 - p1643 [51-250]
PW - v244 - O 6 '97 - p53 [1-50]

Ford, Miela
Watch Us Play (Illus. by Miela Ford)
KR - v66 - F 15 '98 - p276 [51-250]

What Color Was the Sky Today? (Illus. by Sally Noll)
CBRS - v25 - Spr '97 - p134 [51-250]
HB Guide - v8 - Fall '97 - p251 [51-250]

Foreman, Mark
Mark Foreman's Great Race (Illus. by Mark Foreman)
    SLJ - v43 - Jl '97 - p67 [51-250]

Foreman, Michael
After the War Was Over (Illus. by Michael Foreman)
    Bks Keeps - Jl '97 - p24 [51-250]

Angel and the Box of Time (Illus. by Michael Foreman)
    TES - N 7 '97 - p5* [1-50]

The Little Reindeer (Illus. by Michael Foreman)
    BL - v94 - S 1 '97 - p138+ [51-250]
    CBRS - v26 - D '97 - p38 [51-250]
    CCB-B - v51 - D '97 - p124+ [51-250]
    KR - v65 - S 15 '97 - p1456 [51-250]
    NYTBR - v102 - D 21 '97 - p18 [1-50]
    PW - v244 - O 6 '97 - p55+ [51-250]

Look! Look! (Illus. by Michael Foreman)
    Sch Lib - v45 - Ag '97 - p130 [51-250]

Seal Surfer (Illus. by Michael Foreman)
    CBRS - v25 - Spr '97 - p139 [51-250]
    HB Guide - v8 - Fall '97 - p264 [51-250]
    SLJ - v43 - D '97 - p25 [1-50]
    SLJ - v44 - Mr '98 - p120 [1-50]

Forest, Heather
A Big Quiet House (Illus. by Susan Greenstein)
    RT - v51 - N '97 - p253 [51-250]

The Woman Who Flummoxed the Fairies (Illus. by Susan Graber)
    ECEJ - v25 - Fall '97 - p46 [1-50]

Forman, Michael H
Arctic Tundra
    HB Guide - v8 - Fall '97 - p344 [51-250]
    SLJ - v43 - S '97 - p201+ [51-250]

From Wax to Crayon
    HB Guide - v8 - Fall '97 - p357 [51-250]

Formby, Caroline
Tristan's Temper Tantrum (Illus. by Caroline Formby)
    Cur R - v37 - D '97 - p12 [51-250]

Formiguera, Pere
Se llama Cuerpo
    Bkbird - v35 - Sum '97 - p56 [51-250]

Forrestal, Elaine
Someone like Me
  y Aust Bk R - v279 - My '97 - p60+ [501+]
    Magpies - v12 - Mr '97 - p33 [51-250]
    TES - N 7 '97 - p8* [1-50]

Forrester, Sandra
My Home Is over Jordan
  y Am Vis - v12 - D '97 - p36 [1-50]
  y BL - v94 - O 1 '97 - p319 [51-250]
    CCB-B - v51 - D '97 - p125 [51-250]
    KR - v65 - O 15 '97 - p1580 [51-250]
    PW - v244 - O 20 '97 - p77 [51-250]
    SLJ - v43 - D '97 - p123 [51-250]

Forsyth, Adrian
How Monkeys Make Chocolate
    BL - v94 - D 1 '97 - p628 [1-50]
    Can CL - v23 - Fall '97 - p95 [51-250]

Forsyth, Chris
Face Off
    CBRA - '96 - p465+ [251-500]

Forth, Melissa Deal
The Heavenly Seven (Illus. by Robert J Schwalb)
    HB Guide - v8 - Fall '97 - p299 [51-250]

Fortunato, Frank
Sports Great Alonzo Mourning
    CLW - v68 - S '97 - p69 [51-250]
    HB Guide - v8 - Fall '97 - p369 [51-250]
  y VOYA - v20 - Je '97 - p129 [251-500]

Forward, Toby
Making Faces (Illus. by James Marsh)
    Sch Lib - v45 - N '97 - p191 [51-250]

Fosberg, John
Cookie Shapes (Illus. by John Fosberg)
> SLJ - v43 - D '97 - p88 [51-250]

Ice Cream Colors (Illus. by John Fosberg)
> SLJ - v43 - D '97 - p88 [51-250]

Foster, Genevieve
George Washington's World. Expanded Ed.
> Ch BWatch - v7 - O '97 - p8 [1-50]
> SLJ - v44 - Mr '98 - p231+ [51-250]

Foster, Joanna
The Magpie's Nest (Illus. by Julie Downing)
> ASBYP - v29 - Sum '96 - p13 [251-500]
> SB - v33 - O '97 - p218 [1-50]

Foster, John
Action Rhymes (Illus. by Carol Thompson)
> Magpies - v12 - My '97 - p29 [51-250]
> PW - v245 - Mr 9 '98 - p70 [1-50]

Chanting Rhymes (Illus. by Carol Thompson)
> Magpies - v12 - My '97 - p29 [51-250]
> PW - v245 - Mr 9 '98 - p70 [1-50]

Counting Rhymes (Illus. by Carol Thompson)
> PW - v245 - Mr 9 '98 - p70 [51-250]

Excuses, Excuses
> Sch Lib - v45 - N '97 - p209 [51-250]
> TES - S 12 '97 - p15U [51-250]
> TES - N 7 '97 - p2* [1-50]

Finger Rhymes (Illus. by Carol Thompson)
> Magpies - v12 - My '97 - p29 [51-250]
> PW - v245 - Mr 9 '98 - p70 [1-50]

First Verses (Illus. by Carol Thompson)
> NS - v126 - D 5 '97 - p63 [1-50]
> SLJ - v44 - Ap '98 - p116 [51-250]
> TES - O 31 '97 - p16* [51-250]

Magic Poems (Illus. by Korky Paul)
> NS - v126 - D 5 '97 - p63 [1-50]

Spaceways
> Sch Lib - v45 - N '97 - p209 [51-250]
> TES - S 12 '97 - p15U [51-250]

Foster, Karen Sharp
Good Night My Little Chicks (Illus. by Karen Sharp Foster)
> KR - v65 - O 15 '97 - p1581 [51-250]
> SLJ - v43 - N '97 - p81 [51-250]

Foster, Leila Merrell
Benjamin Franklin: Founding Father and Inventor
> SLJ - v43 - N '97 - p126 [51-250]

Foster, Scarlett Ryan
Secret of the Viking Dagger
> Ch BWatch - v7 - Mr '97 - p3 [51-250]

Foster-Morgan, Kathleen
Sunflower Mountain (Illus. by Faye Loverock)
> CBRA - '96 - p441+ [51-250]

Fowler, Allan
The Dewey Decimal System
> HB Guide - v8 - Fall '97 - p317 [51-250]
> SLJ - v43 - Ap '97 - p123 [51-250]

Energy from the Sun
> SB - v34 - Ap '98 - p78 [51-250]

Icebergs, Ice Caps, and Glaciers
> BL - v94 - D 1 '97 - p633 [51-250]

It Could Still Be a Desert
> HB Guide - v8 - Fall '97 - p346 [51-250]
> SB - v33 - N '97 - p241 [51-250]

It Could Still Be a Robot
> BL - v94 - D 1 '97 - p633 [51-250]

It Could Still Be Coral
> SB - v33 - Je '97 - p143 [51-250]

Let's Talk about Tongues
> HB Guide - v8 - Fall '97 - p346 [51-250]

Life in a Tidepool
> SB - v33 - Je '97 - p143+ [51-250]

Squirrels and Chipmunks
HB Guide - v8 - Fall '97 - p353 [51-250]

They Could Still Be Mountains
HB Guide - v8 - Fall '97 - p346 [51-250]
SB - v33 - N '97 - p241 [51-250]

The Top and Bottom of the World
HB Guide - v8 - Fall '97 - p400 [51-250]
SB - v33 - D '97 - p277 [51-250]

Where Land Meets Sea
HB Guide - v8 - Fall '97 - p346 [51-250]

Fowler, Mark
Codes and Ciphers
Emerg Lib - v24 - My '97 - p50 [51-250]

Fowler, Thurley
A Brat Called Annie (Illus. by Mark Payne)
Magpies - v12 - My '97 - p33 [51-250]

Fox, Allan
Amazing Facts about Australian Landscapes (Illus. by Steve Parish)
Magpies - v12 - Jl '97 - p43 [51-250]

Fox, Mary Virginia
Edwin Hubble: American Astronomer
y   BL - v94 - D 1 '97 - p621 [51-250]
SLJ - v43 - N '97 - p127 [51-250]

Lasers
ASBYP - v29 - Sum '96 - p50+ [251-500]

Rockets
ASBYP - v29 - Sum '96 - p50+ [251-500]

Fox, Mem
A Bedtime Story (Illus. by Elivia Savadier)
NYTBR - v102 - My 18 '97 - p23+ [501+]

Boo to a Goose (Illus. by David Miller)
CCB-B - v51 - Mr '98 - p241 [51-250]
KR - v65 - D 15 '97 - p1834 [51-250]

SLJ - v44 - Mr '98 - p179 [51-250]

Sophie (Illus. by Aminah Brenda Lynn Robinson)
Par Ch - Awards '97 - p8 [51-250]
PW - v244 - S 1 '97 - p107 [1-50]

The Straight Line Wonder (Illus. by Marc Rosenthal)
BL - v94 - O 15 '97 - p414 [51-250]
CBRS - v26 - D '97 - p38 [51-250]
KR - v65 - S 1 '97 - p1388 [51-250]
PW - v244 - Ag 18 '97 - p93 [51-250]
SLJ - v44 - Ja '98 - p81 [51-250]

Time for Bed (Illus. by Jane Dyer)
PW - v244 - Jl 7 '97 - p70 [1-50]

Whoever You Are (Illus. by Leslie Staub)
BL - v94 - O 1 '97 - p334 [51-250]
CBRS - v26 - N '97 - p26 [1-50]
KR - v65 - S 15 '97 - p1457 [51-250]
PW - v244 - N 3 '97 - p84 [51-250]

Zoo-Looking (Illus. by Candace Whitman)
AB - v100 - N 17 '97 - p1268 [51-250]

Fox, Paula
A Likely Place (Illus. by Edward Ardizzone)
CBRS - v25 - Jl '97 - p151 [51-250]
HB Guide - v8 - Fall '97 - p291 [51-250]

Radiance Descending
BL - v94 - S 1 '97 - p124 [51-250]
CBRS - v26 - N '97 - p33+ [51-250]
CCB-B - v51 - N '97 - p84 [51-250]
HB - v73 - S '97 - p569+ [51-250]
y   KR - v65 - S 1 '97 - p1389 [51-250]
PW - v244 - Jl 21 '97 - p202 [51-250]
SLJ - v43 - S '97 - p216 [51-250]
y   VOYA - v20 - F '98 - p385 [251-500]

Foy, Don
Israel
Ch BWatch - v7 - O '97 - p4+ [51-250]

Frabetti, Carlo
Ulrico Y Las Puertas Que Hablan (Illus. by Araceli Sanz)
BL - v93 - Ag '97 - p1913 [1-50]

Fradin, Dennis B
*Louis Braille: The Blind Boy Who
Wanted to Read (Illus. by Robert
Sauber)*
　　SLJ - v43 - Jl '97 - p82 [51-250]

*Maria De Sautuola: The Bulls in the
Cave (Illus. by Ed Martinez)*
　　BL - v93 - Je 1 '97 - p1690 [51-250]
　　SLJ - v43 - Jl '97 - p82 [51-250]

The Planet Hunters
　　BL - v94 - D 1 '97 - p621 [51-250]
y　　BL - v94 - Mr 15 '98 - p1211 [1-50]
　　HMR - Win '97 - p46 [51-250]
　　PW - v244 - O 6 '97 - p84+ [51-250]
　　SLJ - v44 - Ja '98 - p123 [51-250]
y　　VOYA - v21 - Ap '98 - p37 [1-50]

Searching for Alien Life
　　Ch BWatch - v8 - Ja '98 - p6 [1-50]
　　SLJ - v44 - Ja '98 - p123 [51-250]

Francis, Leslie J
The Song
　　Ch BWatch - v7 - S '97 - p1 [51-250]

Francis, Neil
*Paper Airplanes and Other Super
Flyers (Illus. by June Bradford)*
　　CBRA - '96 - p518+ [51-250]

Frank, Anne
*The Diary of a Young Girl: The
Definitive Edition*
　　CR - v271 - Ag '97 - p112 [51-250]
　　Magpies - v12 - Jl '97 - p12 [501+]

Frank, Steven
Dennis Rodman
　　SLJ - v44 - Ap '98 - p144 [51-250]

Franklin, Kristine L
*Iguana Beach (Illus. by Lori
Lohstoeter)*
　　HB Guide - v8 - Fall '97 - p264+ [51-250]
　　SLJ - v43 - Ag '97 - p135 [51-250]
　　Trib Bks - Je 8 '97 - p7 [51-250]

Lone Wolf
y　　CBRS - v25 - Je '97 - p129+ [51-250]
　　HB Guide - v8 - Fall '97 - p299 [51-250]

Magpies - v12 - My '97 - p33+ [251-500]
　　SLJ - v43 - Je '97 - p117 [51-250]
　　SLJ - v43 - D '97 - p25 [1-50]

Out of the Dump
　　RT - v51 - F '98 - p431+ [51-250]
　　SE - v61 - Ap '97 - p6* [1-50]

*The Wolfhound (Illus. by Kris
Waldherr)*
　　Par Ch - Awards '97 - p7 [1-50]

Fraser, Andrew F
*Newfoundland Pony Tales (Illus. by
Cliff George)*
　　CBRA - '96 - p472+ [51-250]

Fraser, Mary Ann
*A Mission for the People (Illus. by
Mary Ann Fraser)*
　　KR - v66 - Mr 15 '98 - p403 [51-250]
　　SLJ - v44 - Ap '98 - p116 [51-250]

Frasier, Debra
*Out of the Ocean (Illus. by Debra
Frasier)*
　　KR - v66 - Mr 1 '98 - p337 [51-250]
　　PW - v245 - F 16 '98 - p209 [51-250]

Frazier, Deneen
Internet for Kids. 2nd Ed.
　　FMon - v1 - S 2 '96 - pONL [51-250]

Freedman, Florence B
Two Tickets to Freedom
　　TES - My 2 '97 - p8* [501+]
y　　TES - N 7 '97 - p13* [51-250]

Freedman, Russell
Buffalo Hunt
　　BL - v93 - Je 1 '97 - p1700 [1-50]

*The Life and Death of Crazy Horse
(Illus. by Amos Bad Heart Bull)*
y　　BL - v93 - Je 1 '97 - p1700 [1-50]
y　　HMR - Sum '97 - p29 [1-50]
y　　RT - v51 - N '97 - p245 [51-250]
　　RT - v51 - D '97 - p310 [51-250]
y　　SE - v61 - Ap '97 - p3* [1-50]
y　　VOYA - v20 - Je '97 - p85 [51-250]
y　　VOYA - v20 - Ag '97 - p164 [51-250]
y　　RT - v51 - N '97 - p255 [51-250]

Martha Graham: A Dancer's Life
    KR - v66 - Ap 15 '98 - p578 [51-250]

Out of Darkness (Illus. by Kate Kiesler)
   y Ch BWatch - v7 - S '97 - p7 [51-250]
      HB Guide - v8 - Fall '97 - p380 [51-250]
      NYTBR - v102 - O 12 '97 - p26 [1-50]

The Wright Brothers
    JOYS - v10 - Sum '97 - p427+ [51-250]

Freeman, David
The Nutcracker (Illus. by Joanna Isles)
    KR - v65 - Je 1 '97 - p872 [51-250]
    PW - v244 - O 6 '97 - p58 [1-50]

Freeman, Don
Corduroy (Illus. by Don Freeman)
    NYTBR - v102 - N 16 '97 - p26 [1-50]

Freeman, Marcia
Push and Pull
    SB - v33 - D '97 - p273 [501+]

Freeman, Marcia S
Catfish and Spaghetti (Illus. by Rose Stock)
    Ch BWatch - v7 - O '97 - p2 [1-50]

Listen to This
    Ch BWatch - v7 - Je '97 - p1 [1-50]

Freeman, Martha
The Year My Parents Ruined My Life
   y BL - v94 - D 1 '97 - p615 [51-250]
      CBRS - v26 - Ja '98 - p58 [1-50]
      KR - v65 - O 1 '97 - p1531 [51-250]
      SLJ - v43 - D '97 - p123+ [51-250]

Freeman, Pamela
Nanna (Illus. by Greg Somers)
    Magpies - v12 - S '97 - p31 [51-250]

Fremon, David K
The Great Depression in American History
   y CLW - v68 - D '97 - p87 [51-250]
      HB Guide - v8 - Fall '97 - p395 [51-250]

French, Fiona
King of Another Country (Illus. by Fiona French)
    Magpies - v12 - Jl '97 - p28 [51-250]

Lord of the Animals (Illus. by Fiona French)
    Bks Keeps - My '97 - p21 [51-250]
    BL - v93 - Je 1 '97 - p1708 [51-250]
    CBRS - v25 - My '97 - p115 [51-250]
    CCB-B - v50 - Je '97 - p357 [51-250]
    CM:CanRev - v4 - S 19 '97 - pONL [51-250]
    HB Guide - v8 - Fall '97 - p332 [51-250]
    Sch Lib - v45 - Ag '97 - p130 [51-250]
    SLJ - v43 - S '97 - p202 [51-250]

French, Jackie
The Book of Unicorns
    Magpies - v12 - My '97 - p34 [51-250]

Dancing with Ben Hall and Other Yarns
    Magpies - v12 - Jl '97 - p32 [51-250]

Somewhere around the Corner
    BL - v93 - Ag '97 - p1892 [1-50]

There's an Echidna at the Bottom of My Garden (Illus. by David Stanley)
    Magpies - v12 - S '97 - p31 [51-250]

French, Vivian
Aesop's Funky Fables (Illus. by Korky Paul)
    PW - v245 - F 9 '98 - p95+ [51-250]

Christmas Mouse (Illus. by Chris Fisher)
    PW - v244 - O 6 '97 - p58 [1-50]

A Christmas Star Called Hannah (Illus. by Anne Yvonne Gilbert)
    BL - v94 - N 1 '97 - p480 [51-250]
    Ch BWatch - v7 - O '97 - p4 [1-50]
    PW - v244 - O 6 '97 - p55 [51-250]

Kelly and the Crime Club (Illus. by Lesley Harker)
    Sch Lib - v45 - Ag '97 - p145 [51-250]

Oh No, Anna! (Illus. by Alex Ayliffe)
    Magpies - v12 - Jl '97 - p26 [51-250]
    SLJ - v43 - D '97 - p88 [51-250]

Peter and the Ghost (Illus. by Lesley Harker)
> Sch Lib - v45 - Ag '97 - p145 [51-250]

Frere, Jane
Sticky Little Fingers (Illus. by Bettina Paterson)
> Magpies - v12 - Mr '97 - p42+ [251-500]

Friedhoffer, Bob
Physics Lab in a Hardware Store (Illus. by Joe Hosking)
> y   SB - v32 - D '96 - p269 [51-250]
>   SB - v33 - Ag '97 - p163 [1-50]
> y   SLJ - v43 - My '97 - p144 [51-250]

Physics Lab in a Housewares Store (Illus. by Joe Hosking)
> New Sci - v156 - N 22 '97 - p62 [51-250]
> y   SB - v32 - D '96 - p269 [51-250]

Friedrich, Elizabeth
Leah's Pony (Illus. by Michael Garland)
> Inst - v107 - O '97 - p48 [1-50]
> RT - v51 - O '97 - p138 [1-50]
> RT - v51 - N '97 - p243 [51-250]
> SE - v61 - Ap '97 - p10* [1-50]

Friends in High Places (Little Play a Sound)
> Ch BWatch - v7 - Ap '97 - p2 [1-50]

Friesen, Peter
A Sheep Tale
> CBRA - '96 - p442 [51-250]

Frith, Margaret
Mermaid Island (Illus. by Julie Durrell)
> SLJ - v44 - F '98 - p85 [51-250]

Froese, Deborah L
The Wise Washerman (Illus. by Wang Kui)
> Can CL - v23 - Fall '97 - p65+ [251-500]
> CBRA - '96 - p502 [51-250]

Frogs (Illus. by Daniel Moignot)
> Ch BWatch - v7 - Ap '97 - p4 [1-50]
> HB Guide - v8 - Fall '97 - p351 [51-250]

Frolick, Gloria Kupchenko
Anna Veryha
> Can CL - v22 - Win '96 - p109+ [501+]

Fry, Ron
How to Study (Butler). Audio Version
> Ch BWatch - v7 - S '97 - p2 [1-50]

Fryatt, Evelyn Howe
Candy Making for Beginners (Illus. by Jerry Grajewski)
> CBRA - '96 - p519 [51-250]

Frydenborg, Kay
They Dreamed of Horses
> JOYS - v10 - Spr '97 - p260 [1-50]

Fuchshuber, Annegert
Carly
> Ch BWatch - v7 - D '97 - p5 [51-250]

Two Peas in a Pod (Illus. by Annegert Fuchshuber)
> KR - v66 - Mr 1 '98 - p338 [51-250]

Funke, Cornelia
Gespensterjager Im Feuerspuk (Illus. by Cornelia Funke)
> Bkbird - v35 - Spr '97 - p49 [1-50]

Funston, Sylvia
Animal Smarts (Illus. by Pat Stevens)
> Quill & Q - v63 - N '97 - p47+ [251-500]
> SLJ - v44 - Ap '98 - p144 [51-250]

Scary Science (Illus. by Dusan Petricic)
> CBRA - '96 - p535 [51-250]

Furlong, Monica
Robin's Country
> BL - v94 - Mr 1 '98 - p1125 [51-250]

G

Gaarder, Jostein
Hello? Is Anybody There? (Illus. by Sally Gardner)
Books - v11 - D '97 - p21 [51-250]
NS - v126 - D 5 '97 - p64+ [51-250]

Gabriel, Richard P
Patterns of Software
SB - v32 - D '96 - p260 [51-250]

Gaetz, Dayle Campbell
The Golden Rose
CBRA - '96 - p473 [51-250]
y   Kliatt - v31 - Jl '97 - p8 [51-250]

The Mystery of Eagle Lake (Illus. by Isabelle Langevin)
CBRA - '96 - p473 [51-250]

Night of the Aliens
CBRA - '96 - p473 [51-250]

Gaffington, Urslan
Silver Berries and Christmas Magic (Illus. by Steven Morris)
Ch BWatch - v7 - D '97 - p1 [51-250]

Gaffney, Timothy
Grandpa Takes Me to the Moon (Illus. by Barry Root)
SB - v33 - Ag '97 - p163 [1-50]

Gage, Simon
Light and Illusion
ASBYP - v29 - Sum '96 - p43+ [501+]

Gail, Judy
Day of the Moon Shadow (Illus. by Kimberly Louise Shaw)
ASBYP - v29 - Sum '96 - p13+ [251-500]

Gaiman, Neil
The Day I Swapped My Dad for Two Goldfish (Illus. by Dave McKean)
Bloom Rev - v17 - Jl '97 - p21 [51-250]
NW - v130 - D 1 '97 - p77 [1-50]

Gal, Laszlo
Merlin's Castle (Illus. by Laszlo Gal)
Can CL - v23 - Fall '97 - p85+ [501+]
CBRA - '96 - p442 [51-250]

The Parrot (Illus. by Laszlo Gal)
BL - v94 - S 15 '97 - p237 [51-250]
CBRS - v26 - D '97 - p38 [51-250]
CM:CanRev - v4 - N 14 '97 - pONL [251-500]
Quill & Q - v63 - Ag '97 - p37 [251-500]

Galan, Mark
There's Still Time
BL - v94 - D 15 '97 - p692 [51-250]
CBRS - v26 - N '97 - p34 [51-250]
HB - v74 - Ja '98 - p91+ [51-250]

Galdone, Paul
Los Tres Chivitos Gruff
BL - v94 - D 15 '97 - p707 [1-50]

Gallagher, Debbie
The Kimberley
SLJ - v43 - N '97 - p127 [51-250]

Gallant, Roy A

Geysers: When Earth Roars

    BL - v94 - D 1 '97 - p630 [51-250]

    SLJ - v44 - Ja '98 - p123 [51-250]

Sand on the Move

    BL - v94 - D 1 '97 - p630 [51-250]

    SB - v34 - Ap '98 - p79 [51-250]

    SLJ - v44 - Ja '98 - p123+ [51-250]

Gallimard Jeunesse

Bees (Illus. by Ute Fuhr)

    Ch BWatch - v7 - Ap '97 - p4 [1-50]

    HB Guide - v8 - Fall '97 - p349 [51-250]

Butterflies (Illus. by Heliadore)

    Ch BWatch - v7 - Ap '97 - p4 [1-50]

    HB Guide - v8 - Fall '97 - p349 [51-250]

Galloway, Priscilla

Daedalus and the Minotaur (Illus. by Normand Cousineau)

    BL - v94 - Ja 1 '98 - p802+ [51-250]

    CM:CanRev - v4 - Mr 13 '98 - pONL [251-500]

    Quill & Q - v64 - F '98 - p51 [251-500]

    SLJ - v44 - F '98 - p115 [51-250]

Gamble, Kim

Amazing Faces

    Ch BWatch - v7 - D '97 - p4 [1-50]

    Sch Lib - v45 - N '97 - p204 [51-250]

    SLJ - v44 - F '98 - p116 [51-250]

Gambrell, Jamey

Telephone (Illus. by Vladimir Radunsky)

    Comw - v124 - D 5 '97 - p14 [1-50]

Gamlin, Linda

Trees

    CLW - v68 - S '97 - p63 [51-250]

Gammell, Stephen

Is That You, Winter? (Illus. by Stephen Gammell)

    BL - v94 - S 1 '97 - p132 [51-250]

    CBRS - v26 - N '97 - p26 [1-50]

    KR - v65 - O 1 '97 - p1531 [51-250]

    NYTBR - v103 - F 15 '98 - p26 [251-500]

    PW - v244 - Ag 11 '97 - p401 [51-250]

Gan, Geraldine

Communication

    HB Guide - v8 - Fall '97 - p357 [51-250]

  y SB - v33 - D '97 - p268 [51-250]

    SLJ - v43 - S '97 - p229+ [51-250]

Ganeri, Anita

Bizarre Beasts and Other Oddities of Nature

    Magpies - v12 - Mr '97 - p42 [51-250]

Buddhism

    Sch Lib - v45 - Ag '97 - p150 [51-250]

Buddhist

    HB Guide - v8 - Fall '97 - p319 [51-250]

Creature Features (Illus. by Steve Fricker)

    Magpies - v12 - Jl '97 - p43 [51-250]

Descubre Por Tu Mismo Los Secretos Del Cuerpo Humano

  r BL - v94 - D 15 '97 - p717 [1-50]

Forests

    HB Guide - v8 - Fall '97 - p345 [51-250]

Funny Bones (Illus. by Steve Fricker)

    HB Guide - v8 - Fall '97 - p355 [51-250]

Hindu Mandir

    Sch Lib - v45 - N '97 - p206 [51-250]

The Hunt for Food (Illus. by Graham Austin)

    BL - v94 - D 1 '97 - p630 [51-250]

    CBRS - v26 - D '97 - p43 [1-50]

    SLJ - v44 - Ja '98 - p99 [51-250]

Inside the Body

    SB - v33 - Ag '97 - p163 [1-50]

The Kingfisher First Science Encyclopedia

  r SB - v34 - Ap '98 - p78 [51-250]

  r SLJ - v43 - N '97 - p140 [51-250]

Out of the Ark (Illus. by Jackie Morris)

    SE - v61 - Ap '97 - p15* [1-50]

Plants (Illus. by B Watson)

    ASBYP - v29 - Sum '96 - p63+ [501+]

Religions Explained
    Ch BWatch - v7 - O '97 - p7 [1-50]
r   HB Guide - v8 - Fall '97 - p319 [51-250]
    SLJ - v43 - Je '97 - p134 [51-250]
y   VOYA - v20 - O '97 - p258 [251-500]

The Search for Tombs
    Sch Lib - v45 - Ag '97 - p149 [51-250]
    SLJ - v44 - F '98 - p116 [51-250]
    TES - O 31 '97 - p17* [501+]

The Story of Numbers and Counting
    HB Guide - v8 - Fall '97 - p340+ [51-250]
y   VOYA - v20 - Je '97 - p129+ [251-500]

The Story of Time and Clocks
    Ch BWatch - v7 - S '97 - p4 [1-50]
    KR - v65 - Je 15 '97 - p948 [51-250]
    SLJ - v43 - N '97 - p106+ [51-250]

The Story of Weights and Measures
    Ch BWatch - v7 - S '97 - p4 [1-50]
    SLJ - v43 - N '97 - p106+ [51-250]

The Story of Writing and Printing
    HB Guide - v8 - Fall '97 - p357 [51-250]
y   VOYA - v20 - Je '97 - p129+ [251-500]

Gann, Marjorie
New Brunswick. Rev. Ed.
    CBRA - '96 - p512+ [501+]

Gannett, Ruth Stiles
My Father's Dragon (Illus. by Ruth Chrisman Gannett)
    NYTBR - v102 - N 16 '97 - p25 [1-50]

Three Tales of My Father's Dragon (Illus. by Ruth Chrisman Gannett)
    PW - v244 - N 24 '97 - p75 [51-250]

Three Tales of My Father's Dragon (Sevra). Audio Version
    BL - v94 - F 15 '98 - p1027 [51-250]
    SLJ - v43 - N '97 - p69+ [51-250]

Gans, Roma
How Do Birds Find Their Way? (Illus. by Paul Mirocha)
    ASBYP - v29 - Fall '96 - p52+ [501+]
    SB - v33 - Ag '97 - p187 [1-50]

Let's Go Rock Collecting (Illus. by Holly Keller)
    HB Guide - v8 - Fall '97 - p342 [51-250]
    SLJ - v43 - Ag '97 - p147 [51-250]

Gantos, Jack
Heads or Tails (Longenhagen). Audio Version
    SLJ - v44 - Ap '98 - p82 [51-250]

Jack's Black Book
y   BL - v94 - O 15 '97 - p397 [51-250]
    CCB-B - v51 - D '97 - p125+ [51-250]
    CM:CanRev - v4 - Ja 16 '98 - pONL [251-500]
    HB - v74 - Ja '98 - p70 [51-250]
y   KR - v65 - Ag 1 '97 - p1221 [51-250]
    PW - v244 - Ag 25 '97 - p74 [1-50]

Rotten Ralph's Rotten Romance (Illus. by Nicole Rubel)
    HB Guide - v8 - Fall '97 - p265 [51-250]

Gantschev, Ivan
El Lago De La Luna
    HB Guide - v8 - Fall '97 - p338 [51-250]

Moon Lake (Illus. by Ivan Gantschev)
    Bloom Rev - v17 - Mr '97 - p20 [51-250]

Where the Moon Lives (Illus. by Ivan Gantschev)
    KR - v66 - Mr 15 '98 - p403 [51-250]

Garay, Luis
The Long Road (Illus. by Luis Garay)
    BL - v94 - N 1 '97 - p480+ [51-250]
    CM:CanRev - v4 - Ja 2 '98 - pONL [51-250]
    Quill & Q - v63 - N '97 - p46 [251-500]
    SLJ - v44 - Ja '98 - p81 [51-250]

Pedrito's Day (Illus. by Luis Garay)
    BIC - v26 - O '97 - p34 [501+]
    Ch Bk News - v20 - Sum '97 - p28 [51-250]
    HB Guide - v8 - Fall '97 - p265 [51-250]
    SLJ - v43 - Ap '97 - p100+ [51-250]

Garcia, Eulalia
Baby Birds (Illus. by Gabriel Casadevall)
    Ch BWatch - v7 - Jl '97 - p4 [1-50]

Giant Squid (Illus. by Gabriel Casadevall)
    Ch BWatch - v7 - Jl '97 - p4 [1-50]

Jellyfish: Animals with a Deadly Touch (Illus. by Gabriel Casadevall)
    Ch BWatch - v7 - Jl '97 - p4 [1-50]

Gardella, Tricia
Casey's New Hat (Illus. by Margot Apple)
    HB Guide - v8 - Fall '97 - p265 [51-250]
    SLJ - v43 - Ap '97 - p102 [51-250]

Garden (First Words Series)
    Ch BWatch - v7 - Je '97 - p4 [1-50]
    SLJ - v43 - Ap '97 - p120+ [51-250]

Gardener, Martin
Classic Brainteasers (Illus. by Jeff Sinclair)
    ASBYP - v29 - Sum '96 - p14+ [251-500]

Gardiner, Tony
The Mathematical Olympiad Handbook
    TES - O 3 '97 - pR15 [251-500]

More Mathematical Challenges
    TES - O 3 '97 - pR15 [251-500]

Gardner, Robert
Experiments with Balloons
    ASBYP - v29 - Sum '96 - p49+ [501+]

Experiments with Bubbles
    ASBYP - v29 - Sum '96 - p49+ [501+]

Experiments with Light and Mirrors
    ASBYP - v29 - Sum '96 - p49+ [501+]

Experiments with Motion
    ASBYP - v29 - Sum '96 - p49+ [501+]

Science Project Ideas about Air
    SLJ - v44 - Ap '98 - p144+ [51-250]

Science Project Ideas about Animal Behavior (Illus. by Jacob Katari)
    SLJ - v44 - F '98 - p116 [51-250]

Science Project Ideas about Rain
    SB - v33 - N '97 - p241+ [51-250]
    SLJ - v44 - Ja '98 - p124 [51-250]
y   VOYA - v20 - D '97 - p333 [51-250]

Science Project Ideas about the Moon
    BL - v94 - D 1 '97 - p630 [51-250]

Science Project Ideas about the Sun
    SLJ - v44 - Ja '98 - p124 [51-250]

Science Project Ideas about Trees (Illus. by Jacob Katari)
    BL - v94 - D 1 '97 - p630 [51-250]
    SB - v34 - Ap '98 - p80 [51-250]
    SLJ - v44 - F '98 - p116 [51-250]

Where on Earth Am I?
y   SB - v33 - Ap '97 - p78 [51-250]
    SB - v33 - Ag '97 - p163 [1-50]

Gardner, Rosalind
Under My Bed There Lives a Tiger (Illus. by Betty Brownlie)
    Magpies - v12 - Mr '97 - p6* [51-250]

Gardner, Sally
The Orion Book of Princesses
    TES - N 7 '97 - p5* [51-250]

Garfield, Leon
Fair's Fair
    TES - N 14 '97 - p11* [51-250]

Garg, Samidha
Racism
y   HB Guide - v8 - Fall '97 - p327 [51-250]
    TES - O 17 '97 - pR7 [51-250]

Garlake, Theresa
The Rich-Poor Divide
    TES - O 17 '97 - pR7 [51-250]

Garland, Michael
Dinner at Magritte's
    Inst - v106 - Ap '97 - p26 [1-50]

The Mouse before Christmas (Illus. by Michael Garland)
> BL - v94 - O 15 '97 - p414 [51-250]
> Ch BWatch - v7 - D '97 - p2 [1-50]
> PW - v244 - O 6 '97 - p54 [51-250]

Garland, Sarah
Seeing Red (Illus. by Tony Ross)
> Ch BWatch - v7 - Mr '97 - p6 [51-250]

Tex the Cowboy (Illus. by Sarah Garland)
> Bks Keeps - S '97 - p24 [51-250]

Garland, Sherry
The Last Rainmaker
> CBRS - v25 - Jl '97 - p154 [51-250]
> y HB Guide - v8 - Fall '97 - p313 [51-250]
> y Kliatt - v31 - S '97 - p10 [51-250]
> KR - v65 - My 15 '97 - p799+ [51-250]
> SLJ - v43 - Je '97 - p117 [51-250]
> y VOYA - v20 - Ag '97 - p183+ [251-500]

The Lotus Seed (Illus. by Tatsuro Kiuchi)
> y BL - v93 - Je 1 '97 - p1675 [1-50]
> ECEJ - v25 - Fall '97 - p47 [1-50]

Garlick, Jackie
Mama Bessie's Nest (Illus. by Jackie Garlick)
> CBRA - '96 - p442+ [51-250]

Garner, Alan
Elidor (Green). Audio Version
> y Kliatt - v31 - Jl '97 - p44 [51-250]
> SLJ - v43 - S '97 - p164+ [51-250]

The Little Red Hen (Illus. by Norman Messenger)
> BL - v94 - N 1 '97 - p476 [51-250]
> CCB-B - v51 - D '97 - p126 [51-250]
> SLJ - v43 - D '97 - p88 [51-250]

The Owl Service
> TES - Ja 2 '98 - p22* [51-250]

Garrett, Leslie
Superkids: Young Heroes in Action
> Quill & Q - v63 - Je '97 - p62 [251-500]

Garwood, Val
The World of the Pirate (Illus. by Richard Berridge)
> KR - v65 - D 1 '97 - p1775 [51-250]
> SLJ - v44 - Ja '98 - p124 [51-250]

Gaskin, Chris
Picture Book Magic
> Magpies - v12 - Mr '97 - p2* [1-50]

Gatehouse, John
Eric's Elephant Goes Camping (Illus. by Sue Cony)
> TES - Jl 11 '97 - p14* [51-250]

Gates, Phil
The History News: Medicine (Illus. by Vanessa Card)
> y BL - v94 - Mr 15 '98 - p1224 [1-50]
> Ch BWatch - v7 - D '97 - p7+ [1-50]
> KR - v65 - N 1 '97 - p1643 [51-250]
> Magpies - v12 - S '97 - p43 [51-250]
> PW - v244 - N 3 '97 - p87 [51-250]
> SLJ - v44 - Ja '98 - p124 [51-250]
> y VOYA - v21 - Ap '98 - p39 [1-50]

Medicine News: Medecine
> Obs - D 7 '97 - p18* [1-50]

Gato, Sam E
Disney's The Hunchback of Notre Dame (Quasimado) (Illus. by DiCicco Digital Arts)
> Ch BWatch - v7 - Ap '97 - p2 [1-50]

Gatti, Anne
The Magic Flute (Illus. by Peter Malone)
> KR - v65 - N 15 '97 - p1706 [51-250]
> PW - v244 - N 24 '97 - p74 [51-250]
> SLJ - v44 - Ja '98 - p124 [51-250]

Gatti, Will
The Drowning Pool
> Sch Lib - v45 - N '97 - p211+ [51-250]
> TES - O 10 '97 - p8* [51-250]

Gauch, Patricia Lee
Christina Katerina and Fats and the Great Neighborhood War (Illus. by Stacey Schuett)

    CCB-B - v50 - Je '97 - p357+ [51-250]
    Ch BWatch - v7 - My '97 - p4 [1-50]
    HB Guide - v8 - Fall '97 - p265 [51-250]

Tanya and the Magic Wardrobe (Illus. by Satomi Ichikawa)

    BL - v94 - N 1 '97 - p481 [51-250]
    Ch BWatch - v8 - Ja '98 - p2 [1-50]
    PW - v244 - O 20 '97 - p78 [1-50]

Gauthier, Gail
A Year with Butch and Spike

    KR - v66 - Mr 1 '98 - p338 [51-250]
    PW - v245 - Mr 9 '98 - p68+ [51-250]

Gauthier, Gilles
Good for You, Mikey Mite! (Illus. by Pierre-Andre Derome)

    BIC - v26 - My '97 - p35+ [501+]
    CBRA - '96 - p474 [51-250]

Gavin, Jamila
Children Just like Me (Illus. by Amanda Hall)

    CCB-B - v51 - S '97 - p10 [51-250]

Our Favorite Stories (Illus. by Amanda Hall)

    Bks Keeps - N '97 - p21 [51-250]
    CBRS - v25 - Ag '97 - p164 [51-250]
    HB Guide - v8 - Fall '97 - p332 [51-250]
    Sch Lib - v45 - Ag '97 - p145 [51-250]
    TES - Ag 22 '97 - p25 [51-250]

Gay, Marie-Louise
Fat Charlie's Circus (Illus. by Marie-Louise Gay)

    HB Guide - v8 - Fall '97 - p265 [51-250]
    SLJ - v43 - Je '97 - p88 [51-250]

Rumpelstiltskin (Illus. by Marie-Louise Gay)

    CM:CanRev - v4 - N 28 '97 - pONL [251-500]
    PW - v244 - Jl 28 '97 - p74 [51-250]
    Quill & Q - v63 - Ag '97 - p38 [251-500]
    SLJ - v43 - N '97 - p107 [51-250]

Geddes, Angella
The Scarecrows of Necum Teuch (Illus. by John Davis)

    CBRA - '96 - p474+ [51-250]

Gee, Maurice
The Fat Man

    y   BL - v94 - D 15 '97 - p693 [51-250]
    y   CCB-B - v51 - D '97 - p126 [51-250]
    y   HB - v74 - Ja '98 - p70+ [51-250]
    y   KR - v65 - O 15 '97 - p1581 [51-250]
    y   PW - v244 - O 27 '97 - p77 [51-250]
          PW - v244 - N 3 '97 - p59 [51-250]
    y   SLJ - v43 - N '97 - p118 [51-250]
    y   SLJ - v43 - D '97 - p25 [1-50]
    y   VOYA - v20 - D '97 - p316 [51-250]

The Halfmen of O

    Magpies - v12 - S '97 - p8* [501+]

Motherstone

    Magpies - v12 - S '97 - p8* [501+]

The Priests of Ferris

    Magpies - v12 - S '97 - p8* [501+]

Under the Mountain

    Magpies - v12 - S '97 - p8* [501+]

Geeslin, Campell
In Rosa's Mexico (Illus. by Andrea Arroyo)

    NYTBR - v102 - My 11 '97 - p24 [501+]

Geisert, Arthur
The Etcher's Studio (Illus. by Arthur Geisert)

    ABR - v19 - N '97 - p12+ [501+]
    CBRS - v25 - My '97 - p110 [51-250]
    CCB-B - v50 - Je '97 - p358 [51-250]
    HB Guide - v8 - Fall '97 - p265 [51-250]
    Learning - v26 - S '97 - p45 [1-50]
    Magpies - v12 - S '97 - p7+ [51-250]
    PW - v244 - N 3 '97 - p59 [51-250]
    SLJ - v43 - Ap '97 - p102 [51-250]

Roman Numerals I to MM

    RT - v51 - S '97 - p52+ [51-250]

Geisert, Bonnie
Prairie Town (Illus. by Arthur Geisert)

    KR - v66 - Mr 1 '98 - p338 [51-250]
    PW - v245 - Mr 23 '98 - p98 [51-250]

SLJ - v44 - Ap '98 - p116 [51-250]

Geissler, Carol
Why, Nana? (Illus. by Linda McClelland)
Magpies - v12 - S '97 - p5* [51-250]

Gellman, Marc
Always Wear Clean Underwear! and Other Ways Parents Say I Love You (Illus. by Debbie Tilley)
BL - v94 - O 1 '97 - p321+ [51-250]
NYTBR - v103 - Mr 15 '98 - p24 [51-250]
PW - v244 - Ag 18 '97 - p94 [51-250]
SLJ - v43 - N '97 - p127 [51-250]

How Do You Spell God? (Illus. by Jos. A Smith)
PW - v245 - Mr 23 '98 - p95 [1-50]

Gelman, Rita Golden
I Went to the Zoo (Kovalski) (Illus. by Maryann Kovalski). Book and Audio Version
Quill & Q - v63 - Ap '97 - p38 [51-250]

Queen Esther Saves Her People (Illus. by Frane Lessac)
BL - v94 - Mr 1 '98 - p1138 [51-250]
CCB-B - v51 - Mr '98 - p241 [251-500]
PW - v244 - D 22 '97 - p54 [51-250]
SLJ - v44 - F '98 - p98 [51-250]

Gentieu, Penny
Wow! Babies
Par - v72 - D '97 - p201 [1-50]
PW - v244 - Jl 28 '97 - p77 [1-50]

Gentile, Petrina
Big Trucks, Big Wheels
Ch BWatch - v7 - N '97 - p1 [1-50]
HB Guide - v8 - Fall '97 - p357 [51-250]

Geography of the World
r   Par Ch - Awards '97 - p29 [51-250]

George, Jean Craighead
Acorn Pancakes, Dandelion Salad and 38 Other Wild Recipes (Illus. by Paul Mirocha)
ASBYP - v29 - Sum '96 - p15 [251-500]

Arctic Son (Illus. by Wendell Minor)
BL - v94 - S 1 '97 - p132+ [51-250]
Ch BWatch - v7 - N '97 - p4 [1-50]
Emerg Lib - v25 - N '97 - p54 [1-50]
PW - v244 - Jl 21 '97 - p200 [51-250]
SLJ - v43 - N '97 - p81+ [51-250]

The Case of the Missing Cutthroats
LA - v73 - N '96 - p526 [51-250]

Julie's Wolf Pack (Illus. by Wendell Minor)
BL - v94 - S 1 '97 - p124+ [51-250]
CBRS - v26 - S '97 - p10+ [51-250]
CCB-B - v51 - O '97 - p51 [51-250]
Ch BWatch - v7 - O '97 - p2 [1-50]
HB - v74 - Ja '98 - p71 [251-500]
KR - v65 - Je 15 '97 - p949 [51-250]
NYTBR - v102 - N 16 '97 - p58+ [501+]
Par - v72 - D '97 - p206 [1-50]
PW - v244 - Jl 7 '97 - p69 [51-250]
SLJ - v43 - S '97 - p216+ [51-250]

Look to the North (Illus. by Lucia Washburn)
HB Guide - v8 - Fall '97 - p265 [51-250]
NYTBR - v102 - N 16 '97 - p58+ [501+]
Par Ch - Awards '97 - p5 [51-250]
SB - v33 - Ag '97 - p163 [1-50]
SB - v33 - N '97 - p245 [51-250]
SLJ - v43 - Ap '97 - p123+ [51-250]

One Day in the Tropical Rain Forest
BL - v94 - D 1 '97 - p628 [1-50]

The Tarantula in My Purse
RT - v51 - D '97 - p330 [51-250]

George, Kristine O'Connell
The Great Frog Race and Other Poems (Illus. by Kate Kiesler)
CCB-B - v50 - Je '97 - p358 [51-250]
Ch BWatch - v7 - My '97 - p4 [1-50]
HB Guide - v8 - Fall '97 - p376 [51-250]
SLJ - v43 - Ap '97 - p124 [51-250]
SLJ - v43 - D '97 - p25 [1-50]

George, Linda
Golden Age of Islam
Ch BWatch - v8 - Ja '98 - p7 [51-250]

George, Michael
Antarctica
Ch BWatch - v7 - Mr '94 - p8 [51-250]

Cells
Ch BWatch - v7 - '92 - p8 [51-250]

Coral Reef
Ch BWatch - v7 - '92 - p8 [51-250]

Galaxies
Ch BWatch - v7 - '92 - p8 [51-250]

Glaciers
Ch BWatch - v7 - '91 - p8 [51-250]

Life
Ch BWatch - v7 - '94 - p8 [51-250]

Mars
Ch BWatch - v7 - '92 - p8 [51-250]
SLJ - v44 - F '98 - p98 [51-250]

The Moon
Ch BWatch - v7 - '92 - p8 [51-250]

Rain Forest
BL - v94 - D 1 '97 - p628 [1-50]
Ch BWatch - v7 - '92 - p8 [51-250]

Sequoias
Ch BWatch - v7 - '92 - p8 [51-250]

Space Exploration
Ch BWatch - v7 - '92 - p8 [51-250]

Stars
Ch BWatch - v7 - '91 - p8 [51-250]

The Sun
Ch BWatch - v7 - '91 - p8 [51-250]

Tundra
Ch BWatch - v7 - '94 - p8 [51-250]

Volcanoes
Ch BWatch - v7 - '92 - p8 [51-250]

Geras, Adele
From Lullaby to Lullaby (Illus. by Kathryn Brown)
Ch BWatch - v7 - My '97 - p3 [51-250]
HB Guide - v8 - Fall '97 - p265 [51-250]
SLJ - v43 - Jl '97 - p67+ [51-250]

Gerber, Carole
Hush! A Gaelic Lullaby (Illus. by Marty Husted)
CBRS - v26 - O '97 - p15 [1-50]
Ch BWatch - v7 - O '97 - p6 [1-50]
SLJ - v44 - Ja '98 - p99+ [51-250]

Geringer, Laura
Hercules the Strong Man (Illus. by Peter Bollinger)
RT - v51 - O '97 - p141+ [1-50]

Ulysses the Soldier King (Illus. by Peter Bollinger)
RT - v51 - O '97 - p143 [1-50]

Gerrard, Roy
Sir Cedric Rides Again
PW - v245 - Mr 23 '98 - p102 [1-50]

Wagons West! (Illus. by Roy Gerrard)
RT - v51 - O '97 - p136 [1-50]
RT - v51 - O '97 - p149 [51-250]
SLJ - v43 - Jl '97 - p35 [1-50]

Gershator, David
Palampam Day (Illus. by Enrique O Sanchez)
BL - v93 - Ag '97 - p1905+ [51-250]
CBRS - v26 - Ja '98 - p50 [51-250]
SLJ - v43 - S '97 - p182 [51-250]

Gershator, Phillis
Greetings, Sun (Illus. by Synthia Saint James)
BL - v94 - Mr 15 '98 - p1247 [51-250]
CCB-B - v51 - Ap '98 - p279 [51-250]
KR - v66 - F 1 '98 - p196 [51-250]

Gerstein, Mordicai
Jonah and the Two Great Fish (Illus. by Mordicai Gerstein)
BL - v94 - O 1 '97 - p322+ [51-250]
CCB-B - v51 - N '97 - p84+ [51-250]
NYTBR - v103 - F 1 '98 - p24 [1-50]
SLJ - v43 - Ag '97 - p147+ [51-250]

Getz, David
Floating Home (Illus. by Michael Rex)
AB - v100 - N 17 '97 - p1268+ [51-250]
HB Guide - v8 - Fall '97 - p265 [1-50]
NYTBR - v103 - Ja 4 '98 - p20 [501+]

SLJ - v43 - My '97 - p99 [51-250]

Life on Mars (Illus. by Peter McCarty)
AB - v100 - N 17 '97 - p1269 [51-250]
CCB-B - v51 - S '97 - p10+ [51-250]
HB Guide - v8 - Fall '97 - p360 [51-250]
SLJ - v43 - Je '97 - p107 [51-250]

Ghigna, Charles
Riddle Rhymes (Illus. by Julia Gorton)
LA - v73 - N '96 - p528 [51-250]

Gibbons, Faye
Hook Moon Night (Illus. by Ronald Himler)
BL - v94 - N 1 '97 - p470 [51-250]
CBRS - v26 - Ja '98 - p58 [1-50]
CCB-B - v51 - N '97 - p85 [51-250]
KR - v65 - Je 15 '97 - p949 [51-250]
PW - v244 - O 6 '97 - p50 [1-50]

Gibbons, Gail
Cats (Illus. by Gail Gibbons)
RT - v51 - N '97 - p254 [51-250]

Click! A Book about Cameras and Taking Pictures (Illus. by Gail Gibbons)
Emerg Lib - v25 - Ja '98 - p57 [51-250]
HB Guide - v8 - Fall '97 - p363 [51-250]
SLJ - v43 - My '97 - p119 [51-250]

Dogs (Illus. by Gail Gibbons)
RT - v51 - N '97 - p254 [51-250]

Gulls--Gulls--Gulls (Illus. by Gail Gibbons)
BL - v94 - S 1 '97 - p113 [51-250]
Emerg Lib - v25 - N '97 - p54+ [1-50]
KR - v65 - S 15 '97 - p1457 [51-250]
SLJ - v43 - S '97 - p202 [51-250]

The Honey Makers (Illus. by Gail Gibbons)
HB Guide - v8 - Fall '97 - p350 [51-250]
SB - v33 - Ag '97 - p163 [1-50]
SLJ - v43 - My '97 - p119 [51-250]

Marshes and Swamps (Illus. by Gail Gibbons)
BL - v94 - Mr 15 '98 - p1245 [51-250]
CCB-B - v51 - Ap '98 - p279 [51-250]

Monarch Butterfly
Inst - v106 - Ap '97 - p4* [1-50]

The Moon Book (Illus. by Gail Gibbons)
CCB-B - v50 - Jl '97 - p394 [51-250]
HB Guide - v8 - Fall '97 - p341 [51-250]
SLJ - v43 - Ap '97 - p124 [51-250]

Nature's Green Umbrella
BL - v94 - D 1 '97 - p628 [1-50]

Paper, Paper Everywhere
PW - v244 - My 19 '97 - p77 [1-50]

Sea Turtles (Illus. by Gail Gibbons)
ASBYP - v29 - Sum '96 - p15+ [251-500]

Soaring with the Wind (Illus. by Gail Gibbons)
SLJ - v44 - Ap '98 - p116 [51-250]

Yippee-Yay! A Book about Cowboys and Cowgirls (Illus. by Gail Gibbons)
SLJ - v44 - Mr '98 - p195 [51-250]

Giberga, Jane Sughrue
Friends to Die For
y   BL - v94 - Mr 15 '98 - p1225 [1-50]
    CBRS - v26 - S '97 - p11 [51-250]
y   KR - v65 - My 15 '97 - p800 [51-250]
y   PW - v244 - My 19 '97 - p77 [51-250]
y   VOYA - v20 - D '97 - p316 [51-250]
y   VOYA - v21 - Ap '98 - p40 [1-50]

Giblin, James Cross
Charles A. Lindbergh: A Human Hero
y   BL - v94 - S 15 '97 - p230 [51-250]
y   BL - v94 - Ja 1 '98 - p733 [1-50]
y   BL - v94 - Mr 15 '98 - p1211 [1-50]
    BL - v94 - Mr 15 '98 - p1224 [1-50]
    CBRS - v26 - N '97 - p34 [51-250]
y   Ch BWatch - v7 - D '97 - p6 [1-50]
    HB - v73 - N '97 - p695+ [51-250]
    NYTBR - v103 - Mr 15 '98 - p24 [51-250]
    PW - v244 - O 27 '97 - p78 [51-250]
    PW - v244 - N 3 '97 - p60 [51-250]
    SLJ - v43 - N '97 - p128 [51-250]
    SLJ - v43 - D '97 - p25 [1-50]
y   VOYA - v20 - F '98 - p364 [51-250]
y   VOYA - v21 - Ap '98 - p37 [1-50]

George Washington: A Picture Book Biography (Illus. by Michael Dooling)
PW - v245 - Ja 12 '98 - p61 [1-50]

When Plague Strikes (Illus. by David Frampton)
y   Kliatt - v31 - S '97 - p37+ [51-250]
    PW - v244 - My 19 '97 - p77 [1-50]

Gibson, Gary
Making Shapes
ASBYP - v29 - Sum '96 - p58+ [501+]

Making Things Change
ASBYP - v29 - Sum '96 - p58+ [501+]

Pushing and Pulling
ASBYP - v29 - Sum '96 - p58+ [501+]

Science for Fun Experiments
SB - v33 - Ag '97 - p163 [1-50]

Understanding Electricity
ASBYP - v29 - Sum '96 - p58+ [501+]

Gibson, Kathleen
Rocking Chair Love (Illus. by Jo Dose). Book and Audio Version
Ch BWatch - v7 - Jl '97 - p1 [51-250]

Gibson, Ray
What Shall I Grow?
Ch BWatch - v7 - O '97 - p4 [1-50]

Giff, Patricia Reilly
A Glass Slipper for Rosie (Illus. by Julie Durrell)
BL - v94 - O 1 '97 - p329 [51-250]
SLJ - v43 - D '97 - p90 [51-250]

Lily's Crossing
BL - v94 - Mr 15 '98 - p1219 [1-50]
HB Guide - v8 - Fall '97 - p299 [51-250]
NYTBR - v102 - My 18 '97 - p24 [501+]
RT - v51 - F '98 - p427 [51-250]

Lily's Crossing (Moore). Audio Version
SLJ - v44 - Mr '98 - p158 [51-250]
SLJ - v44 - Ap '98 - p38 [1-50]

Not-So-Perfect Rosie (Illus. by Julie Durrell)
HB Guide - v8 - Fall '97 - p299 [51-250]

Rosie's Big City Ballet
BL - v94 - F 15 '98 - p1011 [51-250]

Starring Rosie (Illus. by Julie Durrell)
HB Guide - v8 - Fall '97 - p299 [51-250]

Gilbert, Adrian
Arms and Armor (Illus. by James Field)
r   SLJ - v44 - Ap '98 - p145 [51-250]

Arms and Armour
r   Sch Lib - v45 - N '97 - p206 [51-250]

Gilbert, Barbara Snow
Stone Water
Ch BWatch - v7 - Mr '97 - p2 [51-250]
y   VOYA - v20 - Ap '97 - p28+ [251-500]

Gilchrist, Jan Spivey
Madelia (Illus. by Jan Spivey Gilchrist)
BL - v94 - O 1 '97 - p322+ [51-250]
CBRS - v26 - Win '98 - p62 [51-250]
KR - v65 - Ag 15 '97 - p1304 [51-250]
PW - v244 - N 3 '97 - p84 [51-250]
SLJ - v43 - D '97 - p90 [51-250]

Giles, Gail
Breath of the Dragon (Illus. by June Otani)
CBRS - v25 - My '97 - p118+ [51-250]
HB Guide - v8 - Fall '97 - p300 [51-250]
SLJ - v43 - Je '97 - p117 [51-250]

Gilierlain, G
Reverend Thomas' False Teeth (Illus. by Dena Schutzer)
ECEJ - v25 - Fall '97 - p47 [1-50]

Gill, Janie Spaht
Circles (Illus. by Lori Anderson Wing)
SLJ - v44 - Ja '98 - p81 [51-250]

Gator's Out, Said the Trout (Illus. by Bob Reese)
SLJ - v44 - Ja '98 - p81 [51-250]

Monster Stew (Illus. by Bob Reese)
SLJ - v44 - Ja '98 - p81 [51-250]

Pigouts (Illus. by Bob Reese)
SLJ - v44 - Ja '98 - p81 [51-250]

Socks (Illus. by Elizabeth Lambson)
SLJ - v44 - Ja '98 - p81 [51-250]

Gillette, J Lynett
Dinosaur Ghosts (Illus. by Douglas Henderson)
CCB-B - v50 - Jl '97 - p394 [51-250]
HB - v73 - Jl '97 - p475 [51-250]
HB Guide - v8 - Fall '97 - p343 [51-250]
SB - v33 - N '97 - p243 [51-250]
SLJ - v43 - Ap '97 - p149 [51-250]
SLJ - v43 - D '97 - p25 [1-50]

Gillmor, Don
The Fabulous Song (Illus. by Marie-Louise Gay)
Can CL - v23 - Sum '97 - p57+ [251-500]
CBRA - '96 - p443 [51-250]
KR - v66 - Mr 1 '98 - p338+ [51-250]
PW - v245 - Mr 16 '98 - p63 [51-250]

Gilman, Phoebe
The Gypsy Princess
Ch BWatch - v7 - My '97 - p4 [1-50]
HB Guide - v8 - Fall '97 - p266 [51-250]

Jillian Jiggs to the Rescue (Illus. by Phoebe Gilman)
Can CL - v23 - Fall '97 - p69+ [501+]

Gilmore, Rachna
A Friend like Zilla (Illus. by Alice Priestley)
Can CL - v23 - Sum '97 - p54+ [501+]

Lights for Gita (Illus. by Alice Priestley)
Can CL - v23 - Fall '97 - p69+ [501+]

Roses for Gita (Illus. by Alice Priestley)
BIC - v26 - My '97 - p34 [501+]
CBRA - '96 - p443 [51-250]

Gilmour, Nancy
Mystery on Grandma's Farm (Illus. by Muriel E Newton-White)
CBRA - '96 - p475 [51-250]

Gilson, Jamie
Bug in a Rug (Illus. by Diane De Groat)
KR - v66 - Ap 15 '98 - p579 [51-250]

Can't Catch Me, I'm the Gingerbread Man (Illus. by Jamie Gilson)
PW - v244 - S 1 '97 - p107 [1-50]

Wagon Train 911 (Woodman). Audio Version
SLJ - v43 - N '97 - p70 [51-250]

Ginsburg, Mirra
Clay Boy (Illus. by Jos. A Smith)
CCB-B - v50 - Jl '97 - p394+ [51-250]
HB Guide - v8 - Fall '97 - p332 [51-250]
Inst - v107 - Ag '97 - p20 [51-250]
SLJ - v43 - My '97 - p119 [51-250]

Girling, Brough
Nark the Mysterious Crocodile (Illus. by Chris Smedley)
TES - Jl 11 '97 - p14* [51-250]

Gisbert, Joan Manuel
La Aventura Inmortal De Max Urkhaus (Illus. by Joan Manuel Gisbert)
JAAL - v40 - Ap '97 - p591 [51-250]

Givens, Steven J
Tornado Warning
SLJ - v43 - D '97 - p124 [51-250]

Givens, Terryl
Dragon Scales and Willow Leaves (Illus. by Andrew Portwood)
BL - v94 - O 15 '97 - p414+ [51-250]
CBRS - v26 - F '98 - p75 [1-50]
Ch BWatch - v8 - Ja '98 - p2+ [1-50]
KR - v65 - O 1 '97 - p1531+ [51-250]
PW - v244 - O 20 '97 - p75 [51-250]
SLJ - v43 - D '97 - p90 [51-250]

Gjersvik, Marianne Haug
Green Fun
BL - v93 - Ag '97 - p1894 [51-250]
SB - v33 - N '97 - p242 [51-250]

Glaser, Linda
Beautiful Bats (Illus. by Sharon Lane Holm)
CBRS - v26 - F '98 - p79 [51-250]
Ch BWatch - v7 - N '97 - p6 [1-50]
SLJ - v43 - D '97 - p108 [51-250]

The Borrowed Hanukkah Latkes (Illus. by Nancy Cote)
BL - v94 - S 1 '97 - p139 [51-250]
PW - v244 - O 6 '97 - p52 [51-250]

Compost! Growing Gardens from Your Garbage (Illus. by Anca Hariton)
ASBYP - v29 - Fall '96 - p15+ [501+]
SB - v33 - Ag '97 - p163 [1-50]

Glass, Andrew
A Right Fine Life (Illus. by Andrew Glass)
CCB-B - v51 - Ja '98 - p160 [51-250]
SLJ - v44 - F '98 - p85 [51-250]

The Sweetwater Run (Illus. by Andrew Glass)
Emerg Lib - v24 - My '97 - p66 [51-250]

Glass, Tom
Even a Little Is Something (Illus. by Elena Gerard)
HB - v74 - Ja '98 - p72 [51-250]
KR - v65 - N 15 '97 - p1706 [51-250]
PW - v244 - D 8 '97 - p73 [251-500]
SLJ - v44 - F '98 - p106 [51-250]

Glassman, Miriam
Box Top Dreams
CCB-B - v51 - Mr '98 - p241+ [51-250]
KR - v65 - D 15 '97 - p1834 [51-250]
PW - v244 - D 8 '97 - p73 [251-500]
SLJ - v44 - Mr '98 - p212 [51-250]

Glaze, Dave
Who Took Henry and Mr. Z?
CBRA - '96 - p475 [51-250]

Gleeson, Brian
Anansi (Washington). Book and Audio Version
BL - v94 - N 1 '97 - p494 [51-250]

Gleeson, Libby
Hannah Plus One (Illus. by Ann James)
Sch Lib - v45 - Ag '97 - p145 [51-250]

Queen of the Universe (Illus. by David Cox)
Magpies - v12 - My '97 - p30+ [51-250]

Gleitzman, Morris
Belly Flop
TES - N 7 '97 - p7* [51-250]

Water Wings
Bks Keeps - S '97 - p27 [51-250]
Books - v11 - Je '97 - p21 [51-250]
TES - N 7 '97 - p7* [51-250]

Glen, Maggie
The Midnight Doll (Illus. by Maggie Glen)
SLJ - v43 - My '97 - p99 [51-250]

Glenchur, Paul
Quincy's Clubhouse (Illus. by Melody Sarecky)
SLJ - v43 - Ap '97 - p102+ [51-250]

Glenn, Mel
Who Killed Mr. Chippendale?
RT - v51 - O '97 - p143 [1-50]
y RT - v51 - N '97 - p246 [51-250]

Glenn, Patricia Brown
Discover America's Favorite Architects
ASBYP - v29 - Fall '96 - p16+ [251-500]

Gliori, Debi
Mr. Bear Says a Spoonful for You
PW - v244 - N 3 '97 - p87 [1-50]

Mr. Bear Says Goodnight
PW - v244 - N 3 '97 - p87 [1-50]

Mr. Bear Says I Love You
PW - v244 - N 3 '97 - p87 [1-50]

Mr. Bear Says Peek-a-boo
> PW - v244 - N 3 '97 - p87 [1-50]

The Snow Lambs
> Inst - v106 - My '97 - p20 [1-50]

Glossop, Jennifer

Presenting Triceratops (Illus. by Ely Kish)
> CBRA - '96 - p529+ [51-250]

Tattoo You! (Illus. by Barbara Klunder)
> CBRA - '96 - p519 [51-250]

Velociraptor (Illus. by Ely Kish)
> Quill & Q - v63 - Je '97 - p63 [251-500]

Glover, David

The Young Oxford Book of the Human Being
> Magpies - v12 - Jl '97 - p43+ [251-500]
> PW - v244 - D 15 '97 - p60 [51-250]
> y   SLJ - v44 - Ap '98 - p145 [501+]
> y   VOYA - v21 - Ap '98 - p68 [51-250]

Goble, Paul

Death of the Iron Horse
> BL - v93 - Je 1 '97 - p1701 [1-50]

Dream Wolf
> PW - v244 - My 19 '97 - p77 [1-50]

The Legend of the White Buffalo Woman (Illus. by Paul Goble)
> BL - v94 - Mr 15 '98 - p1237+ [51-250]
> KR - v66 - Mr 15 '98 - p403 [51-250]

Love Flute
> PW - v244 - N 17 '97 - p63 [1-50]

Remaking the Earth (Illus. by Paul Goble)
> SE - v61 - Ap '97 - p5* [1-50]

The Return of the Buffaloes (Illus. by Paul Goble)
> SE - v61 - Ap '97 - p5* [1-50]

Godden, Rumer

Premlata and the Festival of Lights (Illus. by Ian Andrew)
> Ch BWatch - v7 - My '97 - p2 [1-50]
> HB Guide - v8 - Fall '97 - p300 [51-250]

> HMR - Sum '97 - p30 [501+]
> SLJ - v43 - My '97 - p132+ [51-250]

Goddesses, Heroes, and Shamans
> BL - v94 - O 1 '97 - p326 [51-250]
> Ch BWatch - v7 - Ap '97 - p3 [51-250]

Godfrey, Martyn

Baseball Crazy
> CBRA - '96 - p475+ [51-250]

Do You Want Fries with That?
> CBRA - '96 - p476 [51-250]

Why Just Me?
> CBRA - '96 - p505 [51-250]

Godkin, Celia

Ladybug Garden
> CBRA - '96 - p530 [51-250]

Sea Otter Inlet (Illus. by Celia Godkin)
> Quill & Q - v64 - F '98 - p44+ [501+]

Godwin, Jane

Dreaming of Antarctica (Illus. by Terry Denton)
> Aust Bk R - Jl '97 - p62+ [501+]
> Magpies - v12 - Mr '97 - p22 [51-250]

Godwin, Laura

Forest (Illus. by Stacey Schuett)
> KR - v66 - Ap 1 '98 - p494 [51-250]

Goffin, Josse

The Amazing ABC Book
> PW - v244 - D 15 '97 - p60 [51-250]

Gogerty, Clare

Conflict in Art
> Ch BWatch - v7 - Ap '97 - p8 [1-50]

Gold, Alison Leslie

Memories of Anne Frank
> BL - v94 - S 1 '97 - p113 [51-250]
> CBRS - v26 - N '97 - p34 [51-250]
> y   CCB-B - v51 - N '97 - p85 [51-250]
> PW - v244 - Jl 7 '97 - p69+ [51-250]
> SLJ - v43 - N '97 - p128 [51-250]

Gold, Carolyn J
Dragonfly Secret
> HB Guide - v8 - Fall '97 - p300 [51-250]
> SLJ - v43 - Jl '97 - p68 [51-250]

Gold, Kari Jenson
Patterns Everywhere
> TCMath - v4 - S '97 - p51+ [51-250]

Short, Tall, Big or Small?
> TCMath - v4 - S '97 - p51+ [51-250]

Gold, Susan Dudley
Arms Control
> y BL - v94 - S 1 '97 - p70+ [51-250]
>   Ch BWatch - v7 - My '97 - p8 [1-50]
> y SLJ - v43 - D '97 - p137 [51-250]

Human Rights
> y BL - v94 - S 1 '97 - p70+ [51-250]
>   Ch BWatch - v7 - My '97 - p8 [1-50]
> y SLJ - v43 - Jl '97 - p104 [51-250]

Goldenberg, Janet
Weird but True (Illus. by Phoebe Gloeckner)
> KR - v65 - Je 15 '97 - p949 [51-250]

Goldilocks and the Three Bears (Illus. by Peter Stevenson)
> PW - v244 - S 1 '97 - p106 [51-250]

Goldin, Barbara Diamond
The Girl Who Lived with the Bears (Illus. by Andrew Plewes)
> CBRS - v25 - Je '97 - p126+ [51-250]
> CCB-B - v50 - Jl '97 - p395 [51-250]
> Ch BWatch - v7 - Ap '97 - p6 [1-50]
> HB Guide - v8 - Fall '97 - p332 [51-250]
> Inst - v107 - Ag '97 - p22 [1-50]
> Quill & Q - v63 - My '97 - p43+ [251-500]
> SLJ - v43 - Ap '97 - p124+ [51-250]

While the Candles Burn (Illus. by Elaine Greenstein)
> RT - v51 - N '97 - p255 [51-250]

Goldman, Martin S
Richard M. Nixon: The Complex President
> KR - v65 - N 15 '97 - p1707 [51-250]

Goldsack, Gaby
Little Reindeer's Present
> Ch BWatch - v7 - N '97 - p6 [51-250]

Goldsmith, Howard
Sleepy Little Owl (Illus. by Denny Bond)
> CBRS - v26 - F '98 - p75 [51-250]
> SLJ - v44 - F '98 - p85 [51-250]

The Twiddle Twins' Music Box Mystery (Illus. by Charles Jordan)
> SLJ - v43 - D '97 - p90 [51-250]

Goldstein, Margaret J
Eyeglasses
> BL - v94 - Ja 1 '98 - p796 [51-250]
> Ch BWatch - v7 - D '97 - p8 [1-50]
> KR - v65 - N 1 '97 - p1643+ [51-250]

Golembe, Carla
Dog Magic (Illus. by Carla Golembe)
> BL - v94 - N 1 '97 - p481 [51-250]
> CBRS - v26 - Win '98 - p62 [51-250]
> KR - v65 - Jl 15 '97 - p1110 [51-250]
> SLJ - v43 - S '97 - p182 [51-250]

Golenbock, Peter, 1946-
Teammates (Illus. by Paul Bacon)
> ECEJ - v25 - Fall '97 - p47 [1-50]
> Inst - v107 - O '97 - p49 [1-50]

Gollub, Matthew
Los Veinticinco Gatos Mixtecos (Illus. by Leovigildo Martinez)
> SLJ - v43 - N '97 - p136 [51-250]

Golsack, Gaby
Kitten's Spell (Illus. by Caroline Jayne Church)
> PW - v244 - O 6 '97 - p49+ [1-50]

Pumpkin Ted (Illus. by Caroline Jayne Church)
> PW - v244 - O 6 '97 - p49+ [1-50]

Gomi, Taro
Todos Hacemos Caca
> BL - v94 - D 15 '97 - p707 [1-50]

Gonzalez, Lucia M
Senor Cat's Romance and Other Favorite Stories from Latin America (Illus. by Lulu Delacre)
    Ch BWatch - v7 - My '97 - p3 [1-50]
    HB Guide - v8 - Fall '97 - p333 [51-250]

Gonzalez-Granat, Olga
Check-It-Out: Calculator Cash Register Activity Book
    TCMath - v4 - N '97 - p186+ [51-250]

Goobie, Beth
I'm Not Convinced
  y CM:CanRev - v4 - O 17 '97 - pONL [251-500]
    Quill & Q - v63 - Ap '97 - p37+ [251-500]

Goodall, Jane
With Love (Illus. by Alan Marks)
    PW - v245 - Mr 9 '98 - p69 [51-250]

Goode, Diane
Diane Goode's American Christmas (Illus. by Diane Goode)
    PW - v244 - O 6 '97 - p59 [1-50]

Diane Goode's Book of Giants and Little People (Illus. by Diane Goode)
    BL - v94 - S 15 '97 - p237 [51-250]
    KR - v65 - Ag 1 '97 - p1221 [51-250]
    PW - v244 - Jl 28 '97 - p73 [51-250]
    SLJ - v43 - N '97 - p107 [51-250]

Mama's Perfect Present (Illus. by Diane Goode)
    Sch Lib - v45 - Ag '97 - p130+ [51-250]

Goodhart, Pippa
Bed Time
    Sch Lib - v45 - N '97 - p185 [51-250]

Ginny's Egg (Illus. by Aafke Brouwer)
    Bks Keeps - My '97 - p23 [251-500]

The Lie Spider (Illus. by Rian Hughes)
    Sch Lib - v45 - N '97 - p191 [51-250]

Morning Time
    Sch Lib - v45 - N '97 - p185 [51-250]

Noah Makes a Boat (Illus. by Bernard Lodge)
    BL - v94 - O 1 '97 - p323 [51-250]
    CBRS - v26 - Ja '98 - p50 [51-250]
    HB - v73 - S '97 - p557+ [51-250]
    KR - v65 - Jl 15 '97 - p1110+ [51-250]
    NYTBR - v103 - F 15 '98 - p25 [1-50]
    PW - v244 - Ag 25 '97 - p65+ [51-250]
    SLJ - v43 - S '97 - p182 [51-250]
    TES - O 17 '97 - p12* [51-250]

Pest Friends (Illus. by Louise Armour-Chudu)
    Sch Lib - v45 - N '97 - p191 [51-250]
    TES - N 14 '97 - p14* [51-250]

Play Time
    Sch Lib - v45 - N '97 - p185 [51-250]

Row, Row, Row Your Boat (Illus. by Stephen Lambert)
    Bks Keeps - N '97 - p19 [51-250]
    SLJ - v43 - D '97 - p90 [51-250]

Shopping Time
    Sch Lib - v45 - N '97 - p185 [51-250]

Goodkey, Janine Lynn
Help! I'm Bored
    CBRA - '96 - p524+ [51-250]

Goodman, Joan Elizabeth
Hope's Crossing
    KR - v66 - Ap 15 '98 - p579 [51-250]

Goodman, Michael
Chicago Bears
    HB Guide - v8 - Fall '97 - p370 [51-250]

Goodman, Susan E
Bats, Bugs, and Biodiversity
    BL - v94 - D 1 '97 - p628 [51-250]
  y JOYS - v10 - Sum '97 - p428 [51-250]

Stones, Bones, and Petroglyphs (Illus. by Michael J Doolittle)
  y HB - v74 - Mr '98 - p234 [251-500]
    KR - v66 - Ja 15 '98 - p110+ [51-250]
    SLJ - v44 - Ap '98 - p145+ [51-250]

Goodnough, David
Pablo Casals: Cellist for the World
    CLW - v68 - D '97 - p80 [51-250]

Goodwin, Peter
Landslides, Slumps, and Creep
   BL - v94 - N 1 '97 - p464 [51-250]
   SB - v34 - Ap '98 - p79+ [51-250]
   SLJ - v44 - Ja '98 - p124 [51-250]

Goor, Ron
Insect Metamorphosis (Illus. by Ron Goor)
   SLJ - v43 - My '97 - p56 [1-50]

Gorbachev, Valeri
Nicky and the Big, Bad Wolves (Illus. by Valeri Gorbachev)
   KR - v66 - Mr 15 '98 - p403 [51-250]

Gordon, Dan, 1947-
Davin
   CBRS - v25 - Spr '97 - p141+ [51-250]
   CCB-B - v50 - Jl '97 - p395 [51-250]
   HB Guide - v8 - Fall '97 - p300 [51-250]

Gordon, Henry
Henry Gordon's Magic Show (Illus. by Jane Kurisu)
   CBRA - '96 - p516+ [51-250]

Gordon, Lynn
Lights Out (Illus. by Val Martino)
   PW - v244 - O 6 '97 - p50 [1-50]

The Witch's Revenge (Illus. by Val Martino)
   SLJ - v44 - Ja '98 - p81 [51-250]

Gordon, Maria
Fun with Materials (Illus. by Mike Gordon)
   SLJ - v43 - Ap '97 - p126 [51-250]

Rocks and Soil (Illus. by Mike Gordon)
   SLJ - v43 - Ap '97 - p126 [51-250]

Gorrell, Gena K
North Star to Freedom
   y   Can CL - v22 - Win '96 - p100 [251-500]
   y   CBRA - '96 - p505+ [51-250]
       Ch BWatch - v7 - Mr '97 - p5 [51-250]
       HB Guide - v8 - Fall '97 - p395 [51-250]

   y   VOYA - v20 - F '98 - p364 [51-250]

Goscinny
Asterix on Top!
   TES - N 7 '97 - p16* [51-250]

Goss, Linda
The Frog Who Wanted to Be a Singer (Illus. by Cynthia Jabar)
   Inst - v106 - Ap '97 - p24 [51-250]
   RT - v51 - N '97 - p254 [51-250]

Gosselin, Kim
Smoking Stinks! (Illus. by Thom Buttner)
   Ch BWatch - v7 - O '97 - p5 [51-250]
   PW - v244 - N 24 '97 - p74 [51-250]
   SLJ - v44 - Ja '98 - p100 [51-250]

Gott, Robert
New South Wales
   Magpies - v12 - Jl '97 - p42 [251-500]

Northern Territory
   Magpies - v12 - Jl '97 - p42 [251-500]

South Australia
   Magpies - v12 - Jl '97 - p42 [251-500]

Victoria
   Magpies - v12 - Jl '97 - p42 [251-500]

Gottlieb, Dale
Busy Little Hands Books (Illus. by Dale Gottlieb)
   PW - v245 - Ja 26 '98 - p93 [51-250]

Ms. Sneed's Guide to Hygiene (Illus. by Dale Gottlieb)
   KR - v65 - N 15 '97 - p1707 [51-250]
   PW - v244 - N 24 '97 - p76 [51-250]
   SLJ - v44 - Ja '98 - p100 [51-250]

Gould, Roberta
Making Cool Crafts and Awesome Art (Illus. by Roberta Gould)
   PW - v245 - F 2 '98 - p92 [51-250]
   SLJ - v44 - Ap '98 - p116 [51-250]

Goulden, Shirley
The Royal Book of Ballet
   BW - v27 - D 7 '97 - p20 [1-50]

Gourley, Catherine
Sharks! True Stories and Legends
    SB - v33 - Ap '97 - p85 [51-250]

Wheels of Time
    CCB-B - v51 - Ja '98 - p160 [51-250]

Gowar, Mick
Jack and Me and the Ball (Illus. by Lesley Harker)
    Sch Lib - v45 - N '97 - p185+ [51-250]

Jack and Me and the Pizza (Illus. by Lesley Harker)
    Sch Lib - v45 - N '97 - p185+ [51-250]

Jack and Me and the Snowman (Illus. by Lesley Harker)
    Sch Lib - v45 - N '97 - p185+ [51-250]

Jack and Me at the Seaside (Illus. by Lesley Harker)
    Sch Lib - v45 - N '97 - p185+ [51-250]

Gowell, Elizabeth Tayntor
Sea Jellies
    SLJ - v43 - My '97 - p56+ [1-50]

Goyallon, Jerome
Drawing Prehistoric Animals (Illus. by Jerome Goyallon)
    SLJ - v43 - My '97 - p145 [51-250]

Grace, Catherine O'Neill
I Want to Be--an Engineer (Illus. by Peter Menzel)
    SLJ - v43 - D '97 - p112+ [51-250]

Graff, Nancy Price
In the Hush of the Evening (Illus. by G Brian Karas)
    BL - v94 - Mr 15 '98 - p1247+ [51-250]

Graham, Amanda
Smart Dad
    Magpies - v12 - My '97 - p30+ [51-250]

Graham, Bob
Greetings from Sandy Beach (Illus. by Bob Graham)
    Bks Keeps - My '97 - p21 [51-250]

Queenie, One of the Family (Illus. by Bob Graham)
    BL - v94 - Ja 1 '98 - p798 [51-250]
    CBRS - v26 - D '97 - p38 [51-250]
    HB - v74 - Ja '98 - p64+ [51-250]
    KR - v65 - O 1 '97 - p1532 [51-250]
    PW - v244 - O 6 '97 - p83 [51-250]
    SLJ - v43 - N '97 - p82 [51-250]

Queenie the Bantam (Illus. by Bob Graham)
    Bks Keeps - N '97 - p20 [51-250]
    Magpies - v12 - S '97 - p27 [51-250]

Graham, Ian, 1953-
Fakes and Forgeries
    Emerg Lib - v24 - My '97 - p50 [51-250]

How Things Work
    ASBYP - v29 - '96 - p57+ [501+]

Photography and Film (Illus. by Nicholas Hewetson)
    SLJ - v44 - F '98 - p116 [51-250]

Graham, Julie
My Dad Never Had a Paper Route (Illus. by Beverley Boomer)
    CBRA - '96 - p443+ [51-250]

Grahame, Kenneth
The River Bank and Other Stories from The Wind in the Willows (Illus. by Inga Moore)
    HMR - Sum '97 - p29 [51-250]

The Wind in the Willows. Audio Version
    PW - v244 - D 8 '97 - p29 [51-250]

Gralla, Preston
Online Kids
    Am Sci - v85 - N '97 - p556 [51-250]
    FMon - v1 - S 2 '96 - pONL [51-250]

Granados, Antonio
El Rey Que Se Equivoco De Cuento (Illus. by Alain Espinosa)
    SLJ - v43 - Ag '97 - p180 [51-250]

Granfield, Linda
1984: The Year I Was Born (Illus. by Bill Slavin)
CBRA - '96 - p506 [51-250]

Amazing Grace (Illus. by Janet Wilson)
Can CL - v23 - Fall '97 - p89+ [501+]
Ch Bk News - v20 - Spr '97 - p33 [251-500]
CM:CanRev - v4 - S 19 '97 - pONL [251-500]
HB Guide - v8 - Fall '97 - p319 [51-250]
PW - v244 - Je 2 '97 - p66 [51-250]
Quill & Q - v63 - My '97 - p41 [251-500]
Quill & Q - v64 - F '98 - p42 [51-250]
SLJ - v43 - Ag '97 - p167 [51-250]

Circus
Quill & Q - v64 - Ja '98 - p36 [251-500]

Circus: An Album
BL - v94 - Mr 1 '98 - p1126 [51-250]
CCB-B - v51 - Ap '98 - p280 [51-250]
KR - v66 - Ja 15 '98 - p111 [51-250]
PW - v245 - Ja 26 '98 - p92+ [51-250]
SLJ - v44 - Mr '98 - p232 [51-250]

In Flanders Fields (Illus. by Janet Wilson)
y   BL - v93 - Je 1 '97 - p1675 [1-50]
y   Can CL - v22 - Win '96 - p99 [251-500]
    RT - v51 - N '97 - p243 [51-250]

Postcards Talk (Illus. by Mark Thurman)
Quill & Q - v64 - F '98 - p46 [251-500]

Silent Night (Illus. by Nelly Hofer)
CM:CanRev - v4 - Ja 2 '98 - pONL [251-500]
NYTBR - v102 - D 7 '97 - p66 [1-50]
PW - v244 - O 6 '97 - p54 [51-250]
Quill & Q - v63 - Jl '97 - p48 [51-250]
Quill & Q - v63 - D '97 - p36 [251-500]

Grant, Larry
One in a Million (Illus. by Reggie Byers)
BL - v94 - O 15 '97 - p417 [1-50]

Gravelle, Karen
Growing Up in a Holler in the Mountains
BL - v94 - Ja 1 '98 - p804 [51-250]
SLJ - v44 - Mr '98 - p232 [51-250]

Growing Up Where the Partridge Drums Its Wings
BL - v94 - Ja 1 '98 - p804 [51-250]
SLJ - v44 - Mr '98 - p232 [51-250]

Graves, Bonnie
Mystery of the Tooth Gremlin (Illus. by Paige Billin-Frye)
SLJ - v43 - Ag '97 - p135 [51-250]

Gravett, Christopher
The Knight's Handbook
Ch BWatch - v7 - S '97 - p7 [1-50]
HB Guide - v8 - Fall '97 - p388 [51-250]
SLJ - v43 - My '97 - p145 [51-250]

The World of the Medieval Knight (Illus. by Brett Breckon)
Ch BWatch - v7 - S '97 - p1 [51-250]
HB Guide - v8 - Fall '97 - p388 [51-250]
Magpies - v12 - Mr '97 - p41 [51-250]

Gray, Keith
Creepers
CBRS - v26 - N '97 - p34 [51-250]
y   CCB-B - v51 - Ja '98 - p160+ [51-250]
y   HB - v73 - S '97 - p570+ [51-250]
KR - v65 - S 15 '97 - p1457 [51-250]

From Blood Two Brothers
y   Sch Lib - v45 - Ag '97 - p158 [51-250]
TES - Je 20 '97 - p7* [501+]

Gray, Libba Moore
Is There Room on the Feather Bed? (Illus. by Nadine Bernard Westcott)
HB Guide - v8 - Fall '97 - p266 [51-250]
SLJ - v43 - Ap '97 - p104 [51-250]

Little Lil and the Swing-Singing Sax (Illus. by Lisa Cohen)
Inst - v106 - Ap '97 - p24 [1-50]
Learning - v26 - S '97 - p45 [1-50]

Gray, Luli
Falcon's Egg
　　PW - v244 - Ag 25 '97 - p74 [1-50]

Gray, Nigel
Running Away from Home (Illus. by Gregory Rogers)
　　Magpies - v12 - Jl '97 - p28 [51-250]

Greeley, Ronald
The NASA Atlas of the Solar System
　yr　BL - v93 - Ag '97 - p1928+ [251-500]
　yr　BL - v94 - Ja 1 '98 - p738 [1-50]
　r　Choice - v34 - Jl '97 - p1822+ [51-250]
　r　LJ - v122 - My 15 '97 - p72 [51-250]
　r　Sci - v276 - My 23 '97 - p1210 [1-50]
　r　SLJ - v43 - Ag '97 - p184 [51-250]
　r　S&T - v94 - Jl '97 - p68 [51-250]
　r　TLS - D 5 '97 - p10 [1-50]

Green, Jen
Dealing with Racism
　　Sch Lib - v45 - Ag '97 - p150 [51-250]

Exploring the Polar Regions (Illus. by David Antram)
　　Ch BWatch - v7 - D '97 - p2 [1-50]
　　SLJ - v44 - Ap '98 - p146 [51-250]

Green, John F, 1943-
The Curse of Jonathan Matthew
　　Quill & Q - v63 - Je '97 - p64 [251-500]

Green, Richard G
Sing, like a Hermit Thrush
　　CBRA - '96 - p476 [51-250]

Green, Robert
King George III
　　SLJ - v44 - Ja '98 - p124 [51-250]

Queen Elizabeth I
　　SLJ - v44 - Ja '98 - p124+ [51-250]

Queen Elizabeth II
　　BL - v94 - D 1 '97 - p618 [51-250]
　　SLJ - v43 - D '97 - p137+ [51-250]

Green, Sheila
God and Me (Illus. by Alison R Grapes)
　　CBRA - '96 - p497 [51-250]

Greenaway, Kate
The Pied Piper of Hamelin (Illus. by Kate Greenaway)
　　AB - v100 - N 17 '97 - p1266+ [51-250]

Greenaway, Theresa
Powerful Beasts of the Wild
　　BL - v93 - Je 1 '97 - p1708 [51-250]
　　Ch BWatch - v7 - Jl '97 - p8 [1-50]
　　HB Guide - v8 - Fall '97 - p346 [51-250]
　　Sch Lib - v45 - N '97 - p204 [51-250]
　　SLJ - v43 - Jl '97 - p82+ [51-250]

The Really Fearsome Blood-Loving Vampire Bat and Other Creatures with Strange Eating Habits
　　SB - v33 - Ag '97 - p185 [1-50]

The Really Fearsome Bloodloving Vampire Bat and Other Creatures with Curious Eating Habits
　　Magpies - v12 - Mr '97 - p42 [51-250]

The Really Hairy Scary Spider and Other Creatures with Lots of Legs
　　Magpies - v12 - Mr '97 - p42 [51-250]
　　SB - v33 - Ag '97 - p185 [1-50]

The Really Horrible Horned Toad and Other Cold, Clammy Creatures
　　SB - v33 - Ag '97 - p185 [1-50]

The Really Horrible Horny Toad and Other Cold, Clammy Creatures
　　Magpies - v12 - Mr '97 - p42 [51-250]

The Really Wicked Droning Wasp and Other Things That Bite and Sting
　　Magpies - v12 - Mr '97 - p42 [51-250]
　　SB - v33 - Ag '97 - p185 [1-50]

Weird Creatures of the Wild
　　BL - v93 - Je 1 '97 - p1708 [51-250]
　　Ch BWatch - v7 - Jl '97 - p8 [1-50]
　　HB Guide - v8 - Fall '97 - p346 [51-250]
　　SB - v33 - Ag '97 - p185 [1-50]
　　SLJ - v43 - Jl '97 - p82+ [51-250]

Greenberg, David T
Bugs! (Illus. by Lynn Munsinger)
　　BL - v94 - S 1 '97 - p128+ [51-250]
　　CBRS - v26 - N '97 - p27 [51-250]
　　CCB-B - v51 - N '97 - p86 [51-250]

HB - v74 - Ja '98 - p86 [51-250]
PW - v244 - Jl 21 '97 - p201 [51-250]
SLJ - v43 - S '97 - p202 [51-250]

Greenberg, Jan

Chuck Close, Up Close
BL - v94 - Mr 15 '98 - p1242 [51-250]
y KR - v66 - Ja 15 '98 - p111 [51-250]
PW - v245 - Mr 9 '98 - p69 [51-250]
SLJ - v44 - Mr '98 - p232+ [51-250]

Greenberg, Keith Elliot

An Armenian Family (Illus. by Carol Halebian)
Ch BWatch - v7 - N '97 - p6 [51-250]
SLJ - v44 - F '98 - p96+ [51-250]

Daredevil Specialist
SLMQ - v25 - Win '97 - p117 [1-50]

Disease Detective (Illus. by Leita Cowart)
SLJ - v44 - Ja '98 - p100 [51-250]

A Haitian Family (Illus. by Carol Halebian)
BL - v94 - Mr 1 '98 - p1126+ [51-250]
Ch BWatch - v8 - Ja '98 - p6 [51-250]
KR - v65 - D 15 '97 - p1834 [51-250]

Storm Chaser
SLJ - v43 - D '97 - p138 [51-250]

Greenblat, Rodney Alan

Thunder Bunny
HB Guide - v8 - Fall '97 - p266 [51-250]

Greenburg, Dan

Dr. Jekyll, Orthodontist (Illus. by Jack E Davis)
HB Guide - v8 - Fall '97 - p291 [51-250]

A Ghost Named Wanda (Illus. by Jack E Davis)
HB Guide - v8 - Fall '97 - p291 [51-250]

Great-Grandpa's in the Litter Box (Illus. by Jack E Davis)
HB Guide - v8 - Fall '97 - p291 [51-250]

I'm Out of My Body--Please Leave a Message (Illus. by Jack E Davis)
HB Guide - v8 - Fall '97 - p291 [51-250]

My Son, the Time Traveler (Illus. by Jack E Davis)
HB Guide - v8 - Fall '97 - p291 [51-250]

Never Trust a Cat Who Wears Earrings (Illus. by Jack E Davis)
HB Guide - v8 - Fall '97 - p291 [51-250]

Through the Medicine Cabinet (Illus. by Jack E Davis)
HB Guide - v8 - Fall '97 - p291 [51-250]

Zap! I'm a Mind Reader (Illus. by Jack E Davis)
HB Guide - v8 - Fall '97 - p291 [51-250]

Greene, Carol

Astronauts Work in Space
SLJ - v44 - Ap '98 - p116 [51-250]

At the Animal Hospital (Illus. by Phil Martin)
SLJ - v44 - F '98 - p98 [51-250]

At the Fire Station (Illus. by Phil Martin)
SLJ - v44 - Ap '98 - p116+ [51-250]

Firefighters Fight Fires
SLJ - v43 - Ap '97 - p126 [51-250]

Teachers Help Us Learn (Illus. by Phil Martin)
SLJ - v44 - Ap '98 - p116 [51-250]

Veterinarians Help Animals
SLJ - v43 - Ap '97 - p126 [51-250]

Greene, Gracie

Tjarany Roughtail
Magpies - v12 - Jl '97 - p40 [51-250]

Greene, Jacqueline D

Marie: Mystery at the Paris Ballet, Paris 1775 (Illus. by Lyn Durham)
SLJ - v43 - Ag '97 - p135 [51-250]

Marie: Summer in the Country, Paris 1775 (Illus. by Lyn Durham)
> SLJ - v44 - Ap '98 - p131 [51-250]

Greene, Rhonda Gowler
Barnyard Song (Illus. by Robert Bender)
> BL - v93 - Ag '97 - p1906 [51-250]
> CBRS - v26 - S '97 - p3 [51-250]
> CCB-B - v51 - O '97 - p51 [51-250]
> SLJ - v43 - S '97 - p182 [51-250]
> SLJ - v43 - D '97 - p25 [1-50]

When a Line Bends...a Shape Begins (Illus. by James Kaczman)
> CBRS - v26 - F '98 - p75 [1-50]
> CCB-B - v51 - Ja '98 - p161 [51-250]
> KR - v65 - Jl 1 '97 - p1029 [51-250]
> PW - v244 - S 1 '97 - p104 [51-250]

Greene, Stephanie
Owen Foote, Soccer Star (Illus. by Martha Weston)
> BL - v94 - Mr 15 '98 - p1243+ [51-250]
> KR - v66 - F 15 '98 - p266 [51-250]
> PW - v245 - F 16 '98 - p211 [51-250]

Greenfield, Eloise
Africa Dream
> Inst - v107 - N '97 - p14 [1-50]

For the Love of the Game (Illus. by Jan Spivey Gilchrist)
> HB Guide - v8 - Fall '97 - p376 [51-250]

Kia Tanisha
> HB Guide - v8 - Fall '97 - p251 [51-250]

Kia Tanisha Drives Her Car (Illus. by Jan Spivey Gilchrist)
> HB Guide - v8 - Fall '97 - p251 [51-250]

Greenfield, Monica
Waiting for Christmas (Illus. by Jan Spivey Gilchrist)
> RT - v51 - N '97 - p256 [51-250]

Greenlaw, M Jean
Welcome to the Stock Show
> BL - v94 - S 15 '97 - p225+ [51-250]
> CCB-B - v51 - O '97 - p51+ [51-250]

SLJ - v43 - S '97 - p230 [51-250]

Greenstein, Elaine
Mattie's Hats Won't Wear That!
> BL - v94 - D 15 '97 - p702 [51-250]

Greenwald, Sheila
Rosy Cole: She Grows and Graduates (Illus. by Sheila Greenwald)
> BL - v94 - N 1 '97 - p470 [51-250]
> CCB-B - v51 - N '97 - p86 [51-250]
> Ch BWatch - v7 - O '97 - p3 [1-50]
> KR - v65 - O 15 '97 - p1581 [51-250]
> SLJ - v43 - N '97 - p82 [51-250]

Greenway, Shirley
Two's Company (Illus. by Oxford Scientific Films)
> HB Guide - v8 - Fall '97 - p337 [51-250]
> SLJ - v43 - My '97 - p119+ [51-250]

Greenwood, Barbara
The Kids Book of Canada (Illus. by Jock MacRae)
> r   CM:CanRev - v4 - N 14 '97 - pONL [51-250]
> r   PW - v245 - Mr 16 '98 - p67 [51-250]
> r   Quill & Q - v63 - S '97 - p71+ [251-500]
> r   Quill & Q - v64 - F '98 - p42 [51-250]

Pioneer Crafts (Illus. by Heather Collins)
> BL - v94 - S 15 '97 - p228 [51-250]
> Ch Bk News - v20 - Spr '97 - p32 [51-250]
> SLJ - v43 - S '97 - p230 [51-250]

Greenwood, Ted
After Dusk (Illus. by Ann James)
> Aust Bk R - N '97 - p62+ [501+]

Greer, Colin
A Call to Character
> Par - v72 - My '97 - p92 [1-50]

Greer, Gery
Billy the Ghost and Me (Illus. by Roger Roth)
> HB Guide - v8 - Fall '97 - p287 [51-250]

Gregory, Kristiana
Across the Wide and Lonesome Prairies
> HB Guide - v8 - Fall '97 - p300 [51-250]

Orphan Runaways
> BL - v94 - F 15 '98 - p1011 [51-250]
> CCB-B - v51 - Mr '98 - p242 [51-250]
> SLJ - v44 - Mr '98 - p212 [51-250]

Gregory, Nan
How Smudge Came (Illus. by Ron Lightburn)
> Can CL - v23 - Sum '97 - p61+ [501+]
> Ch Bk News - v20 - Spr '97 - p34 [251-500]
> Magpies - v12 - Jl '97 - p18 [501+]

Gregory, Valiska
Kate's Giants (Illus. by Virginia Austin)
> PW - v244 - Je 2 '97 - p73 [1-50]

Grejniec, Michael
Buenos Dias, Buenas Noches
> BL - v94 - D 15 '97 - p707 [51-250]

Gretz, Susanna
The Nut Map
> Magpies - v12 - My '97 - p31 [51-250]

Grier, Ella
Seven Days of Kwanzaa (Illus. by John Ward)
> PW - v244 - O 6 '97 - p53 [51-250]

Griffin, Adele
Rainy Season
> HB Guide - v8 - Fall '97 - p300 [51-250]

Sons of Liberty (Illus. by Peter McCarty)
> BL - v94 - S 15 '97 - p235 [51-250]
> y BL - v94 - Mr 15 '98 - p1214 [1-50]
> HB - v74 - Ja '98 - p72+ [251-500]
> KR - v65 - Ag 15 '97 - p1305 [51-250]
> y SLJ - v43 - N '97 - p118 [51-250]
> y VOYA - v21 - Ap '98 - p37 [1-50]

Split Just Right
> BL - v93 - Je 1 '97 - p1702+ [51-250]
> CBRS - v25 - Ag '97 - p166 [51-250]

> y CCB-B - v51 - S '97 - p11 [51-250]
> HB - v73 - Jl '97 - p455 [51-250]
> HB Guide - v8 - Fall '97 - p300+ [51-250]
> Par Ch - Awards '97 - p7 [51-250]
> SLJ - v43 - Je '97 - p117 [51-250]

Griffin, Peni R
Switching Well
> BL - v93 - Ag '97 - p1892 [1-50]
> SLJ - v43 - S '97 - p131 [51-250]

Griffith, Helen V
Alex and the Cat (Illus. by Sonja Lamut)
> BL - v94 - O 15 '97 - p406 [51-250]
> CCB-B - v51 - D '97 - p126+ [51-250]

Dinosaur Habitat (Illus. by Sonja Lamut)
> BL - v94 - Mr 15 '98 - p1245 [51-250]
> KR - v66 - Mr 15 '98 - p403+ [51-250]
> PW - v245 - Mr 9 '98 - p68 [51-250]

Griffiths, Andy
Just Tricking (Illus. by Terry Denton)
> Magpies - v12 - S '97 - p33+ [51-250]

Grigg, Neil S
Water Resources Management
> SB - v32 - D '96 - p262 [51-250]

Grimes, Nikki
Come Sunday (Illus. by Michael Bryant)
> SLJ - v43 - Je '97 - p107+ [51-250]

It's Raining Laughter (Illus. by Myles C Pinkney)
> BL - v94 - O 1 '97 - p334 [51-250]
> CBRS - v26 - Ja '98 - p55+ [51-250]
> CCB-B - v51 - Ja '98 - p161 [51-250]
> SLJ - v43 - D '97 - p90 [51-250]

Wild, Wild Hair (Illus. by George Ford)
> SLJ - v43 - Ap '97 - p104 [51-250]

Grimm, Jacob
The Brave Little Tailor (Illus. by Sergei Goloshapov)
> Bloom Rev - v17 - Mr '97 - p20 [51-250]

HB Guide - v8 - Fall '97 - p333 [51-250]

SLJ - v43 - Jl '97 - p83 [51-250]

The Brothers Grimm: Popular Folk Tales (Illus. by Michael Foreman)

Bks Keeps - My '97 - p23 [51-250]

SLJ - v44 - Ja '98 - p125 [51-250]

Snow White and Rose Red (Illus. by Gennady Spirin)

PW - v244 - O 13 '97 - p77 [1-50]

Grimm's Grimmest (Illus. by Tracy Dockray)

AB - v100 - N 17 '97 - p1260 [251-500]

Grindley, Sally

Breaking the Spell (Illus. by Susan Field)

BL - v94 - Ja 1 '98 - p812 [51-250]

NS - v126 - D 5 '97 - p65 [1-50]

PW - v244 - Ag 4 '97 - p76 [51-250]

SLJ - v43 - D '97 - p90 [51-250]

Kitten Tales (Illus. by Kate Simpson)

Sch Lib - v45 - N '97 - p186 [51-250]

Peter's Place (Illus. by Michael Foreman)

RT - v51 - O '97 - p135 [1-50]

SE - v61 - Ap '97 - p8* [1-50]

There's a Monster Who Eats Books in Our House (Illus. by Arthur Robins)

Sch Lib - v45 - Ag '97 - p131 [51-250]

What Are Friends For? (Illus. by Penny Dann)

KR - v66 - Ap 1 '98 - p495 [51-250]

Why Is the Sky Blue? (Illus. by Susan Varley)

CCB-B - v50 - Je '97 - p359 [51-250]

HB Guide - v8 - Fall '97 - p266 [1-50]

SLJ - v43 - Je '97 - p88 [51-250]

Grisewood, John

The Kingfisher Illustrated Junior Dictionary

r   BL - v94 - D 1 '97 - p650+ [501+]

r   PW - v244 - Ag 18 '97 - p95 [51-250]

r   SLJ - v44 - F '98 - p139 [51-250]

Grolier Educational (Firm)

Maps of the World. Vols. 1-10

yr   BL - v94 - O 1 '97 - p355 [251-500]

r   LJ - v122 - S 1 '97 - p175 [51-250]

r   SLJ - v43 - N '97 - p139 [51-250]

The Grolier Library of Women's Biographies. Vols. 1-10

r   BL - v94 - Mr 15 '98 - p1261+ [251-500]

Grolier Multimedia Encyclopedia 1997. Electronic Media Version

yr   Kliatt - v31 - Jl '97 - p38 [51-250]

r   SLJ - v44 - Ja '98 - p56 [251-500]

Grolier Multimedia Encyclopedia 1998. Deluxe Ed. Electronic Media Version

r   LJ - v122 - N 15 '97 - p83 [51-250]

Grolier Multimedia Encyclopedia 1998. Electronic Media Version

r   BL - v94 - Ja 1 '98 - p844 [501+]

r   Emerg Lib - v25 - Ja '98 - p48 [51-250]

Groner, Judyth

Make Your Own Megillah (Illus. by Katherine Janus Kahn)

PW - v245 - F 23 '98 - p68 [1-50]

Groom Your Room (Illus. by Michael Walker)

PW - v244 - S 22 '97 - p82 [51-250]

SLJ - v44 - Mr '98 - p233 [51-250]

Groover, Bobbi

Fun in the Yellow Pages

Ch BWatch - v7 - N '97 - p2 [51-250]

y   SLJ - v44 - Ja '98 - p112 [51-250]

Gross, Gay Merrill

Paper Creations

Bloom Rev - v17 - N '97 - p25 [51-250]

Grossenbacher, Brian

Tying Flies

Ch BWatch - v7 - Je '97 - p4 [51-250]

Grossman, Bill
The Bear Whose Bones Were Jezebel Jones (Illus. by Jonathan Allen)
KR - v65 - Je 15 '97 - p949 [51-250]
PW - v244 - Jl 21 '97 - p201 [51-250]
SLJ - v43 - D '97 - p90+ [51-250]

My Little Sister Ate One Hare (Illus. by Kevin Hawkes)
RT - v51 - O '97 - p131 [1-50]

Grove, Vicki
Reaching Dustin
CCB-B - v51 - Mr '98 - p242+ [51-250]
HB - v74 - Mr '98 - p220 [251-500]
y   KR - v66 - Mr 1 '98 - p339 [51-250]

Grover, Max
Max's Wacky Taxi Day (Illus. by Max Grover)
KR - v65 - Ag 1 '97 - p1221 [51-250]

Grupper, Jonathan
Destination: Rain Forest
BL - v94 - N 1 '97 - p464 [51-250]
BL - v94 - D 1 '97 - p628+ [51-250]

Gryski, Camilla
Let's Play (Illus. by Dusan Petricic)
KR - v66 - Ap 1 '98 - p495 [51-250]

Guarino, Deborah
Is Your Mama a Llama? (Illus. by Steven Kellogg)
PW - v244 - Jl 7 '97 - p70 [1-50]

Guiberson, Brenda Z
Into the Sea (Illus. by Alix Berenzy)
SB - v33 - Ag '97 - p185 [1-50]
SLJ - v43 - My '97 - p57 [1-50]

Spoonbill Swamp (Illus. by Megan Lloyd)
SLJ - v43 - My '97 - p57 [1-50]

Teddy Roosevelt's Elk (Illus. by Patrick O'Brien)
BL - v94 - S 15 '97 - p237 [51-250]
CCB-B - v51 - O '97 - p52 [51-250]

Guillet, Jean-Pierre
The Magdalen Islands Mystery (Illus. by Huguette Marquis)
Can CL - v23 - Sum '97 - p56+ [51-250]

Guintero, Aramis
Los Suenos (Illus. by Rita Gutierrez Varela)
Bkbird - v35 - Sum '97 - p57 [1-50]

Gukova, Julia
The Mole's Daughter (Illus. by Julia Gukova)
Quill & Q - v64 - F '98 - p46+ [251-500]

Gunning, Monica
Under the Breadfruit Tree (Illus. by Fabricio Vanden Broeck)
SLJ - v44 - Ap '98 - p146 [251-250]
BL - v94 - F 15 '98 - p1002 [51-250]
KR - v66 - F 1 '98 - p196 [51-250]
PW - v245 - Mr 9 '98 - p70 [51-250]

Gunson, Christopher
Over on the Farm (Illus. by Christopher Gunson)
CBRS - v25 - My '97 - p110 [1-50]
Ch BWatch - v7 - My '97 - p4 [1-50]
HB Guide - v8 - Fall '97 - p251 [1-50]

Gunther, Richard
Bit Scream
Magpies - v12 - Jl '97 - p7* [51-250]

Gutelle, Andrew
9 Puzzle Mysteries (Illus. by Eric Brace)
PW - v244 - Ag 18 '97 - p94 [51-250]

Gutfreund, Geraldine Marshall
1970-1979
ASBYP - v29 - Sum '96 - p64+ [51-250]

Guthrie, Donna W
The Secret Admirer (Illus. by Tony Sansevero)
HB Guide - v8 - Fall '97 - p266 [51-250]

Gutman, Bill

Alonzo Mourning: Center of Attention
>Ch BWatch - v7 - Ap '97 - p5 [1-50]
>HB Guide - v8 - Fall '97 - p370 [51-250]

Anfernee Hardaway: Super Guard
>Ch BWatch - v7 - Ap '97 - p5 [1-50]
>HB Guide - v8 - Fall '97 - p370 [51-250]

Be Aware of Danger
>ASBYP - v29 - Fall '96 - p45+ [501+]

Becoming Best Friends with Your Hamster, Guinea Pig, or Rabbit (Illus. by Anne Canevari Green)
>BL - v93 - Ag '97 - p1894 [51-250]
>CCB-B - v50 - Je '97 - p359 [51-250]
>HB Guide - v8 - Fall '97 - p354 [51-250]
>SLJ - v43 - Jl '97 - p105 [51-250]

Becoming Your Cat's Best Friend (Illus. by Anne Canevari Green)
>BL - v93 - Ag '97 - p1894 [51-250]
>CCB-B - v50 - Je '97 - p359 [51-250]
>HB Guide - v8 - Fall '97 - p354 [51-250]
>SLJ - v43 - Jl '97 - p105 [51-250]

Grant Hill: Basketball's High Flier
>Ch BWatch - v7 - Ap '97 - p5 [1-50]

Harmful to Your Health
>ASBYP - v29 - Fall '96 - p45+ [501+]

Hazards at Home
>ASBYP - v29 - Fall '96 - p45+ [501+]

Recreation Can Be Risky
>ASBYP - v29 - Fall '96 - p45+ [501+]

Steve Young: NFL Passing Wizard
>Ch BWatch - v7 - Ap '97 - p5 [1-50]

Gutman, Dan

Honus and Me
>HB Guide - v8 - Fall '97 - p301 [51-250]
>SLJ - v43 - Je '97 - p117+ [51-250]

The Million Dollar Shot
>BL - v94 - O 1 '97 - p329 [51-250]
>SLJ - v43 - D '97 - p124 [51-250]

Guy, Ginger Foglesong

Fiesta! (Illus. by Rene King Moreno)
>HB Guide - v8 - Fall '97 - p338 [51-250]

Guy, Jonathan

Hawkwood
>SLJ - v43 - Jl '97 - p93 [51-250]

Gwynne, Fred

Easy to See Why
>PW - v244 - Je 2 '97 - p73 [1-50]

H

Haarhoff, Dorian
Desert December (Illus. by Leon Vermeulen)
    BL - v93 - Je 1 '97 - p1724 [1-50]
    JOYS - v11 - Win '98 - p141 [1-50]

Haas, Dan
You Can Call Me Worm
y   BL - v94 - O 15 '97 - p397 [51-250]
    CBRS - v26 - Win '98 - p69 [51-250]
    CCB-B - v51 - Ja '98 - p161+ [51-250]
    KR - v65 - O 15 '97 - p1582 [51-250]
    SLJ - v43 - N '97 - p118 [51-250]
y   VOYA - v20 - F '98 - p386 [251-500]

Haas, David
Dear God...Prayers for Children
    CLW - v68 - D '97 - p72 [51-250]

Haas, Irene
A Summertime Song (Illus. by Irene Haas)
    BW - v27 - My 4 '97 - p15 [51-250]
    CBRS - v25 - Spr '97 - p134 [51-250]
    CCB-B - v51 - S '97 - p12 [51-250]
    Ch BWatch - v7 - My '97 - p3 [51-250]
    HB Guide - v8 - Fall '97 - p266 [51-250]
    NYTBR - v102 - Je 1 '97 - p36 [501+]
    PW - v244 - N 3 '97 - p59 [1-50]
    SLJ - v43 - Je '97 - p88 [51-250]

Haas, Jessie
Fire! My Parents' Story
    CCB-B - v51 - Mr '98 - p243 [51-250]

Keeping Barney
    JOYS - v10 - Spr '97 - p260 [1-50]

Safe Horse, Safe Rider
    JOYS - v10 - Spr '97 - p260 [1-50]

Sugaring (Illus. by Jos. A Smith)
    SE - v61 - Ap '97 - p8* [1-50]

Westminster West
    CBRS - v25 - My '97 - p119 [51-250]
y   HB Guide - v8 - Fall '97 - p313 [51-250]
    SLJ - v43 - My '97 - p133 [51-250]

Working Trot
    JOYS - v10 - Spr '97 - p260 [1-50]

Hacker, Carlotta
Great African Americans in History
    BL - v94 - S 15 '97 - p228 [51-250]
    Ch BWatch - v7 - Je '97 - p4 [51-250]
    HB Guide - v8 - Fall '97 - p384 [51-250]
    SLJ - v44 - Ja '98 - p122+ [51-250]

Great African Americans in Jazz
    Ch BWatch - v7 - Je '97 - p4 [51-250]
    HB Guide - v8 - Fall '97 - p384 [51-250]

Great African Americans in the Arts
    Ch BWatch - v7 - Je '97 - p4 [51-250]
    HB Guide - v8 - Fall '97 - p384 [51-250]
    SLJ - v43 - D '97 - p138 [51-250]

Hadden, Gerry
Teenage Refugees from Guatemala Speak Out
    SLJ - v44 - Ja '98 - p125 [51-250]

Teenage Refugees from Mexico Speak Out
    SLJ - v44 - Ja '98 - p125 [51-250]

Haddon, Mark
The Sea of Tranquillity (Illus. by Christian Birmingham)
> RT - v51 - O '97 - p139 [1-50]
> SB - v33 - Ag '97 - p185 [1-50]

Haffner, Margaret
Fearless Jake (Illus. by Mark Thurman)
> Can CL - v23 - Sum '97 - p65+ [501+]

Hafner, Marylin
Mommies Don't Get Sick!
> PW - v244 - Je 16 '97 - p61 [1-50]

A Year with Molly and Emmett (Illus. by Marylin Hafner)
> HB Guide - v8 - Fall '97 - p266 [51-250]
> KR - v65 - Je 1 '97 - p872 [51-250]
> NYTBR - v102 - Je 1 '97 - p36 [1-50]
> Sch Lib - v45 - N '97 - p186 [51-250]
> SLJ - v43 - Je '97 - p88 [51-250]

Haggarty, Holly
Dream Dad
> BIC - v26 - Je '97 - p34+ [501+]
> CBRA - '96 - p476+ [51-250]
> CM:CanRev - v4 - Ja 16 '98 - pONL [251-500]

Hague, Kathleen
Calendarbears: A Book of Months (Illus. by Michael Hague)
> Ch BWatch - v7 - Je '97 - p6 [1-50]
> HB Guide - v8 - Fall '97 - p266 [51-250]
> SLJ - v43 - Jl '97 - p68 [51-250]

Hague, Michael
The Perfect Present (Illus. by Michael Hague)
> RT - v51 - O '97 - p135 [1-50]

Teddy Bear, Teddy Bear (Illus. by Michael Hague)
> HB Guide - v8 - Fall '97 - p337 [51-250]

Hahn, Mary Downing
As Ever, Gordy
> KR - v66 - Ap 15 '98 - p580 [51-250]

The Gentleman Outlaw and Me, Eli
> Ch BWatch - v7 - Ap '97 - p4 [51-250]
> y   Kliatt - v32 - Ja '98 - p8+ [51-250]

Stepping on the Cracks
> SLJ - v43 - S '97 - p131 [1-50]

Halam, Ann
The Powerhouse
> Books - v11 - Je '97 - p21 [51-250]
> Books - v11 - Ag '97 - p15 [51-250]
> y   Sch Lib - v45 - N '97 - p212 [51-250]

Haley, Gail E
Two Bad Boys (Illus. by Gail E Haley)
> RT - v51 - N '97 - p255 [51-250]

Hall, Donald, 1928-
The Milkman's Boy (Illus. by Greg Shed)
> BL - v94 - S 1 '97 - p125 [51-250]
> CBRS - v26 - O '97 - p15 [51-250]
> Ch BWatch - v7 - O '97 - p6 [1-50]
> KR - v65 - Jl 15 '97 - p1111 [51-250]
> SLJ - v43 - S '97 - p182 [51-250]

Old Home Day (Illus. by Emily Arnold McCully)
> RT - v51 - D '97 - p330 [51-250]

When Willard Met Babe Ruth (Illus. by Barry Moser)
> Inst - v107 - O '97 - p49 [1-50]
> RT - v51 - S '97 - p55 [51-250]

Hall, Katy
Bunny Riddles (Illus. by Nicole Rubel)
> HB Guide - v8 - Fall '97 - p367 [51-250]
> Inst - v107 - N '97 - p22 [1-50]

Chickie Riddles (Illus. by Thor Wickstrom)
> HB Guide - v8 - Fall '97 - p367 [51-250]
> Inst - v107 - N '97 - p22 [1-50]

Mummy Riddles (Illus. by Nicole Rubel)
> BL - v93 - Ag '97 - p1909 [51-250]
> SLJ - v43 - N '97 - p107 [51-250]

Sheepish Riddles (Illus. by R W Alley)
> RT - v51 - S '97 - p52 [51-250]

Hall, Kirsten
Noah's Ark (Illus. by Brooke Scudder)
PW - v244 - N 24 '97 - p76 [51-250]

Hall, Willis
The Vampire Vanishes (Glover). Audio Version
BL - v93 - Je 1 '97 - p1733 [51-250]

Hall, Zoe
Apple Pie Tree (Illus. by Shari Halpern)
Emerg Lib - v24 - My '97 - p57 [1-50]

The Surprise Garden (Illus. by Shari Halpern)
BL - v94 - Ja 1 '98 - p822 [51-250]
CCB-B - v51 - Mr '98 - p243+ [51-250]
KR - v65 - D 15 '97 - p1834 [51-250]
PW - v244 - D 22 '97 - p59 [51-250]
SLJ - v44 - Mr '98 - p179 [51-250]

Halley, Linda P
Snail (Illus. by Charles Fuge)
PW - v245 - F 23 '98 - p78 [1-50]

Halligan, Marion
The Midwife's Daughters (Illus. by David Mackintosh)
Aust Bk R - S '97 - p64 [251-500]
Magpies - v12 - S '97 - p22+ [501+]

Halliwell, Sarah
The 17th Century
SLJ - v44 - F '98 - p117 [51-250]

The 18th Century
SLJ - v44 - F '98 - p117 [51-250]

The Renaissance: Artists and Writers
y   BL - v94 - D 15 '97 - p688+ [51-250]
SLJ - v44 - Ja '98 - p125 [51-250]

Halls, Kelly Milner
Dino-Trekking (Illus. by Rick Spears)
ASBYP - v29 - Sum '96 - p17 [251-500]

Hamilton, Jake
Special Effects
KR - v66 - Ap 15 '98 - p580 [51-250]

Hamilton, Maggie
Mister Eternity
y   Aust Bk R - Je '97 - p56+ [501+]
Magpies - v12 - Jl '97 - p33 [51-250]

Hamilton, Morse
Belching Hill (Illus. by Forest Rogers)
CBRS - v25 - Spr '97 - p135 [51-250]
HB Guide - v8 - Fall '97 - p333 [51-250]
SLJ - v43 - Ap '97 - p126 [51-250]

Hamilton, Virginia
The Bells of Christmas (Illus. by Lambert Davis)
PW - v244 - O 6 '97 - p59 [1-50]

Her Stories (Illus. by Leo Dillon)
y   BL - v94 - Mr 15 '98 - p1235 [1-50]
SLJ - v43 - N '97 - p40 [1-50]

Primos
SLJ - v43 - Ag '97 - p180 [51-250]

A Ring of Tricksters (Illus. by Barry Moser)
BL - v94 - Ja 1 '98 - p802 [51-250]
CCB-B - v51 - N '97 - p86+ [51-250]
HB - v74 - Ja '98 - p83 [51-250]
KR - v65 - N 15 '97 - p1707 [51-250]
NW - v130 - D 1 '97 - p76 [51-250]
PW - v244 - N 3 '97 - p59 [1-50]
PW - v244 - N 3 '97 - p83 [51-250]
SLJ - v43 - N '97 - p107 [51-250]

Zeely (Thigpen). Audio Version
SLJ - v44 - Ap '98 - p39 [1-50]
SLJ - v44 - Ap '98 - p82+ [51-250]

Hamley, Dennis
The Ghosts Who Waited
Sch Lib - v45 - N '97 - p191 [51-250]

Hamm, Diane Johnston
Daughter of Suqua
BL - v94 - S 1 '97 - p125 [51-250]
HB Guide - v8 - Fall '97 - p301 [51-250]

Hammond, Elaine Breault
Beyond the Waterfall
Quill & Q - v64 - Ja '98 - p39 [51-250]

The Secret under the Whirlpool (Illus. by Mary Montgomery)
    CBRA - '96 - p477 [51-250]

Hamner, Earl
Lassie: A Christmas Story (Illus. by Kevin Burke)
    PW - v244 - O 6 '97 - p58 [1-50]

Hampton, Wilborn
Kennedy Assassinated!
    BL - v94 - S 15 '97 - p230 [51-250]
    BL - v94 - Ja 1 '98 - p734 [1-50]
y   BL - v94 - Mr 15 '98 - p1225 [1-50]
    CCB-B - v51 - O '97 - p52+ [51-250]
    HB - v74 - Ja '98 - p92 [51-250]
    NYTBR - v102 - N 16 '97 - p28 [501+]
    NYTBR - v102 - D 7 '97 - p80 [1-50]
    PW - v244 - Jl 28 '97 - p75 [51-250]
    PW - v244 - N 3 '97 - p60 [51-250]
y   VOYA - v21 - Ap '98 - p39 [1-50]

Han, Suzanne Crowder
The Rabbit's Escape (Illus. by Yumi Heo)
    SLJ - v43 - N '97 - p40+ [1-50]

Hancock, Lyn
Northwest Territories. Rev. Ed.
    CBRA - '96 - p512+ [501+]

Hancock, Pat
1985: The Year I Was Born (Illus. by Bill Slavin)
    CBRA - '96 - p506 [51-250]

Handford, Martin
Where's Wally?
    TES - N 21 '97 - p12* [251-500]

Where's Wally in Hollywood?
    TES - N 21 '97 - p12* [251-500]

Where's Wally Now?
    TES - N 21 '97 - p12* [251-500]

Where's Wally: The Fantastic Journey
    TES - N 21 '97 - p12* [251-500]

Where's Wally: The Wonder Book
    TES - N 21 '97 - p12* [251-500]

Hanel, Wolfram
The Gold at the End of the Rainbow (Illus. by Loek Koopmans)
    CBRS - v25 - Spr '97 - p135 [51-250]
    HB Guide - v8 - Fall '97 - p266 [51-250]
    SLJ - v43 - Jl '97 - p68 [51-250]

Old Mahony and the Bear Family (Illus. by Jean-Pierre Corderoc'h)
    BL - v94 - S 15 '97 - p235 [51-250]
    HB Guide - v8 - Fall '97 - p291 [51-250]
    Sch Lib - v45 - Ag '97 - p145 [51-250]
    SLJ - v43 - Jl '97 - p68 [51-250]

The Other Side of the Bridge
    TES - Ap 18 '97 - p12* [51-250]

Haney, Michael
Blue
    PW - v244 - N 10 '97 - p76 [51-250]

Hanly, Sheila
The Big Book of Animals
    Ch BWatch - v7 - Jl '97 - p8 [1-50]
    SB - v33 - Ag '97 - p185 [1-50]
    Sch Lib - v45 - N '97 - p186 [51-250]

Hannaford, Priscilla
Animal Homes
    Sch Lib - v45 - N '97 - p204 [51-250]

Our Planet
    Sch Lib - v45 - Ag '97 - p152 [51-250]

Hansen, Brooks
Caesar's Antlers (Illus. by Brooks Hansen)
    BL - v94 - O 1 '97 - p329 [51-250]
    CBRS - v26 - D '97 - p46 [51-250]
    HB - v74 - Ja '98 - p73 [51-250]
    KR - v65 - Ag 15 '97 - p1305 [51-250]
    PW - v244 - O 13 '97 - p76 [51-250]
    SLJ - v43 - N '97 - p118 [51-250]

Hansen, Joyce
Breaking Ground, Breaking Silence
    KR - v66 - Mr 15 '98 - p404 [51-250]

I Thought My Soul Would Rise and Fly
    BL - v94 - D 15 '97 - p697 [51-250]
    SLJ - v43 - N '97 - p118 [51-250]

Hansen, Ole Steen
Vietnam
Ch BWatch - v7 - S '97 - p7 [51-250]

Hanson, Mary Elizabeth
Snug (Illus. by Cheryl Munro Taylor)
SLJ - v44 - Ap '98 - p100 [51-250]

Hanson, Regina
The Face at the Window (Illus. by Linda Saport)
Am Vis - v12 - D '97 - p33 [1-50]
BL - v93 - Je 1 '97 - p1717 [51-250]
CBRS - v25 - My '97 - p115 [51-250]
HB Guide - v8 - Fall '97 - p267 [51-250]
SLJ - v43 - Je '97 - p88+ [51-250]

Hanze
Yann and the Whale (Illus. by Hanze)
HB Guide - v8 - Fall '97 - p265 [51-250]
SLJ - v43 - Je '97 - p88 [51-250]

Hao, Kuang-Ts'
Emperor and the Nightingale (Illus. by Shih-Ming Chang)
RT - v51 - F '98 - p424 [51-250]

Hao, Kuang-Ts'ai
The Giant and the Spring (Illus. by Eva Wang)
RT - v51 - F '98 - p428 [51-250]

Seven Magic Brothers (Illus. by Eva Wang)
RT - v51 - F '98 - p424 [51-250]

Harawira, Wena
Te Kawa O Te Marae
Magpies - v12 - Mr '97 - p7* [51-250]

Harber, Frances
The Brothers' Promise (Illus. by Thor Wickstrom)
BL - v94 - Mr 15 '98 - p1248 [51-250]
CCB-B - v51 - Ap '98 - p280 [51-250]
KR - v66 - F 15 '98 - p267 [51-250]

Harbison, Elizabeth M
Loaves of Fun (Illus. by John Harbison)
SLJ - v43 - S '97 - p230 [51-250]

Harcombe, Dale
Chasing after the Wind
y   Aust Bk R - Je '97 - p59+ [501+]
Magpies - v12 - Jl '97 - p33 [51-250]

Hardcastle, Michael
Matthew's Goals (Illus. by Pauline Hazelwood)
TES - Jl 4 '97 - p10* [501+]

Matthew's Goals (Illus. by Bob Moulder)
Bks Keeps - S '97 - p25 [51-250]
Sch Lib - v45 - Ag '97 - p135 [51-250]

The Price of Football
Books - v11 - D '97 - p21 [51-250]

Harder, Dan
Colliding with Chris (Illus. by Kevin O'Malley)
KR - v66 - Mr 15 '98 - p404 [51-250]
PW - v245 - Mr 23 '98 - p98 [51-250]

Hardin, Wes
Henry Ford Museum
HB Guide - v8 - Fall '97 - p358 [51-250]
New Sci - v154 - Ap 12 '97 - p44 [51-250]

Harding, Donal
The Leaving Summer
LA - v73 - N '96 - p526 [51-250]

Hardman, Ric Lynden
Sunshine Rider
y   BL - v94 - F 15 '98 - p1007 [251-500]
y   PW - v244 - D 15 '97 - p59 [51-250]
SLJ - v44 - F '98 - p106 [51-250]
y   VOYA - v21 - Ap '98 - p46 [51-250]

Hardy, Tad
Lost Cat (Illus. by David Goldin)
RT - v51 - O '97 - p131 [1-50]

Haring, Keith
Keith Haring: I Wish I Didn't Have to Sleep
> PW - v244 - Je 2 '97 - p73 [1-50]

Harkonen, Reijo
The Grandchildren of the Vikings (Illus. by Matti A Pitkanen)
> SE - v61 - Ap '97 - p7* [1-50]

Harlan, Judith
Girl Talk (Illus. by Debbie Palen)
> BL - v94 - D 1 '97 - p620 [51-250]
> KR - v65 - O 15 '97 - p1582 [51-250]
> PW - v244 - N 24 '97 - p76 [51-250]
> y VOYA - v20 - F '98 - p400+ [251-500]

Harlem School of the Arts
The Sweet and Sour Animal Book
> PW - v244 - O 13 '97 - p77 [1-50]

Harley, Bill
Sitting Down to Eat (Illus. by Kitty Harvill)
> SE - v61 - Ap '97 - p14* [1-50]

Harms, John
The Saving of Valiant Blue Heron (Illus. by Robin Lee Makowski)
> SLJ - v44 - Mr '98 - p179 [51-250]

Harness, Cheryl
Abe Lincoln Goes to Washington 1837-1865 (Illus. by Cheryl Harness)
> HB Guide - v8 - Fall '97 - p395 [51-250]
> Inst - v107 - O '97 - p25 [1-50]

Ghosts of the White House (Illus. by Cheryl Harness)
> BL - v94 - Mr 1 '98 - p1128 [51-250]
> CCB-B - v51 - Mr '98 - p244 [251-500]
> KR - v65 - D 1 '97 - p1775 [51-250]
> PW - v244 - D 15 '97 - p58 [51-250]
> SLJ - v44 - Ap '98 - p117 [51-250]

They're Off!
> Ch BWatch - v7 - Mr '97 - p5 [1-50]

Young Abe Lincoln (Illus. by Cheryl Harness)
> Inst - v107 - O '97 - p25 [1-50]
> SE - v61 - Ap '97 - p4* [1-50]

Young Teddy Roosevelt (Illus. by Cheryl Harness)
> BL - v94 - Mr 15 '98 - p1238 [51-250]
> CCB-B - v51 - Ap '98 - p280+ [51-250]

Harper, Jo
The Legend of Mexicatl (Illus. by Robert Casilla)
> KR - v66 - Ap 1 '98 - p495 [51-250]

Harper, Piers
Snakes and Ladders and Hundreds of Mice (Illus. by Piers Harper)
> KR - v65 - N 15 '97 - p1707 [51-250]
> TES - N 21 '97 - p12* [51-250]

Turtle Quest
> HB Guide - v8 - Fall '97 - p267 [51-250]

Harper, Suzanne
Clouds: From Mare's Tails to Thunderheads
> HB Guide - v8 - Fall '97 - p342 [51-250]

Lightning: Sheets, Streaks, Beads, and Balls
> HB Guide - v8 - Fall '97 - p342 [51-250]

Harrah, Madge
My Brother, My Enemy
> CBRS - v25 - Spr '97 - p142 [51-250]
> CCB-B - v50 - Jl '97 - p396 [51-250]
> HB Guide - v8 - Fall '97 - p301 [51-250]
> y SLJ - v43 - Jl '97 - p93+ [51-250]
> y VOYA - v20 - O '97 - p244 [51-250]

Harris, Christine
Pitt Man
> Magpies - v12 - Mr '97 - p33 [51-250]

Harris, Dorothy Joan
Cameron and Me (Illus. by Marilyn Mets)
> BIC - v26 - My '97 - p36+ [501+]
> CBRS - v25 - Ag '97 - p159 [51-250]
> CLW - v68 - S '97 - p66 [51-250]

Harris, Jerry
Cake Decorating
Ch BWatch - v7 - Je '97 - p4 [51-250]

Harris, Jim
Jack and the Giant (Illus. by Jim Harris)
CBRS - v26 - D '97 - p39 [1-50]
Ch BWatch - v8 - Ja '98 - p2 [1-50]
PW - v244 - S 1 '97 - p104 [51-250]
SLJ - v44 - F '98 - p98 [51-250]

Harris, Joel Chandler
Brer Rabbit and the Wonderful Tar Baby (Lover) (Illus. by Henrik Drescher). Book and Audio Version
Ch BWatch - v7 - D '97 - p4 [51-250]

Harris, Laurie Lanzen
Biography Today: Profiles of People of Interest to Young Readers. Vol. 2
r   SLJ - v43 - Ag '97 - p184+ [51-250]

Harris, Lurie Lanzen
Biography Today: Artists Series. Vol. 1
r   SLMQ - v25 - Win '97 - p116 [1-50]

Harris, Pamela
Hot, Cold, Shy, Bold (Illus. by Pamela Harris)
BL - v94 - Mr 15 '98 - p1245 [51-250]
KR - v66 - F 15 '98 - p267 [51-250]

Harris, Peter
Mouse Creeps (Illus. by Reg Cartwright)
Bks Keeps - My '97 - p21 [51-250]
BL - v93 - Je 1 '97 - p1717 [51-250]
CBRS - v25 - Ag '97 - p159 [51-250]
Ch BWatch - v7 - Jl '97 - p6+ [1-50]
HB Guide - v8 - Fall '97 - p267 [51-250]
Sch Lib - v45 - Ag '97 - p131 [51-250]
SLJ - v43 - Je '97 - p90 [51-250]

Harris, Richard, 1942-
The Sun and Other Stars (Illus. by Dennis Davidson)
ASBYP - v29 - Fall '96 - p48+ [501+]

Harris, Robie H
Happy Birth Day! (Illus. by Michael Emberley)
ECEJ - v24 - Sum '97 - p250 [1-50]

It's Perfectly Normal (Illus. by Michael Emberley)
r   JOYS - v11 - Fall '97 - p77 [1-50]

Harrison, Barbara, 1936-
A Ripple of Hope
BL - v93 - Je 1 '97 - p1692 [51-250]
y   CCB-B - v50 - Jl '97 - p396+ [51-250]
y   Ch BWatch - v7 - S '97 - p8 [51-250]
y   KR - v65 - Je 1 '97 - p872+ [51-250]
y   SLJ - v43 - Ag '97 - p167+ [51-250]

Harrison, David L
The Animals' Song (Illus. by Chris L Demarest)
CCB-B - v50 - Je '97 - p359+ [51-250]
CLW - v68 - S '97 - p64 [51-250]
HB Guide - v8 - Fall '97 - p267 [51-250]

A Thousand Cousins (Illus. by Betsy Lewin)
RT - v51 - O '97 - p139 [1-50]

Harrison, George H
Backyard Bird Watching for Kids
BL - v94 - D 1 '97 - p630 [51-250]
KR - v65 - My 15 '97 - p800 [51-250]

Harrison, Joanna
When Mom Turned into a Monster
HB Guide - v8 - Fall '97 - p267 [51-250]

Harrison, Michael
It's My Life
y   BL - v94 - Mr 1 '98 - p1124 [51-250]
CCB-B - v51 - Mr '98 - p244 [51-250]
y   KR - v66 - Ap 1 '98 - p495+ [51-250]
y   SLJ - v44 - Ap '98 - p132 [51-250]

The New Oxford Treasury of Children's Poems
BL - v94 - Ja 1 '98 - p804 [51-250]
PW - v244 - O 6 '97 - p85 [1-50]
SLJ - v43 - N '97 - p107+ [51-250]

The Oxford Treasury of Classic Poems
y   HB Guide - v8 - Fall '97 - p374 [51-250]
     TES - N 7 '97 - p2* [1-50]

Harrison, Peter

An Introduction to Claude Monet
     Magpies - v12 - S '97 - p6 [51-250]

An Introduction to Vincent Van Gogh
     Magpies - v12 - S '97 - p6 [51-250]

Harrison, Troon

Aaron's Awful Allergies (Illus. by Eugenie Fernandes)
     CBRA - '96 - p444 [51-250]
     SLJ - v44 - Mr '98 - p179+ [51-250]

Don't Dig So Deep, Nicholas
     Ch Bk News - v20 - Spr '97 - p30 [51-250]

Lavender Moon (Illus. by Eugenie Fernandes)
     CM:CanRev - v4 - D 12 '97 - pONL [251-500]
     Quill & Q - v63 - O '97 - p41 [251-500]
     SLJ - v44 - Ja '98 - p81+ [51-250]

Harsham, Edward

Fantastic Lateral Thinking Puzzles (Illus. by Myron Miller)
     Ch BWatch - v7 - Jl '97 - p5 [1-50]

Harshman, Marc

Moving Days
     Par - v72 - Je '97 - p126 [1-50]

Hart, Avery

Boredom Busters
     Ch BWatch - v8 - Ja '98 - p6 [1-50]

Pyramids! 50 Hands-On Activities to Experience Ancient Egypt (Illus. by Michael Kline)
     Ch BWatch - v7 - O '97 - p7 [51-250]
     Cur R - v37 - N '97 - p12 [51-250]
     PW - v244 - S 22 '97 - p82 [51-250]

Hartas, Leo

Haunted Castle (Illus. by Leo Hartas)
     PW - v244 - O 6 '97 - p49 [51-250]
     SLJ - v44 - Ja '98 - p112 [51-250]
     TES - N 21 '97 - p12* [51-250]

Harter, Debbie

Walking through the Jungle (Illus. by Debbie Harter)
     CBRS - v26 - F '98 - p75 [1-50]
     KR - v65 - Je 15 '97 - p950 [51-250]
     Sch Lib - v45 - N '97 - p186 [51-250]

Hartman, Bob

The Lion Storyteller Bible
     Ch BWatch - v7 - Mr '97 - p8 [51-250]

Hartmann, Wendy

The Dinosaurs Are Back and It's All Your Fault, Edward! (Illus. by Niki Daly)
     BL - v93 - Je 1 '97 - p1717 [51-250]
     CBRS - v25 - Spr '97 - p135 [51-250]
     HB Guide - v8 - Fall '97 - p267 [51-250]
     SLJ - v43 - Je '97 - p90 [51-250]

Hartry, Nancy

Hold On, McGinty (Illus. by Don Kilby)
     Ch Bk News - v20 - Sum '97 - p27 [51-250]
     Quill & Q - v64 - Ja '98 - p37 [251-500]

Hartz, Paula

Native American Religions
     Ch BWatch - v7 - O '97 - p7+ [1-50]

Shinto
     Ch BWatch - v7 - O '97 - p7 [1-50]

Harvey, Brett

Cassie's Journey (Illus. by Deborah Kogan Ray)
     BL - v93 - Je 1 '97 - p1701 [1-50]

Harvey, Diane Kelsay

Melody's Mystery
     Inst - v106 - Ap '97 - p4* [1-50]

Harvey, Gill

Usborne Soccer School
     Books - v11 - Je '97 - p21 [51-250]

Harvey, Miles
Italy
>   HB Guide - v8 - Fall '97 - p370 [51-250]

Harvey, Roland
Burke and Wills (Illus. by Roland Harvey)
>   Magpies - v12 - Mr '97 - p24 [51-250]

Haskins, James
African American Entrepreneurs
> y   BL - v94 - F 15 '98 - p995 [51-250]
>   KR - v66 - Ja 15 '98 - p111 [51-250]
>   PW - v245 - F 2 '98 - p92 [51-250]

African Beginnings (Illus. by Floyd Cooper)
>   BL - v94 - F 15 '98 - p1002 [51-250]
>   CCB-B - v51 - Ap '98 - p281 [51-250]
>   KR - v66 - Ja 15 '98 - p112 [51-250]
>   PW - v244 - D 22 '97 - p60 [251-500]

Bayard Rustin: Behind the Scenes of the Civil Rights Movement
>   BL - v94 - F 15 '98 - p998 [1-50]
> y   HB Guide - v8 - Fall '97 - p324 [51-250]
> y   SLJ - v43 - Ap '97 - p149+ [51-250]
> y   VOYA - v20 - F '98 - p402 [501+]

Black, Blue and Gray
>   BL - v94 - F 15 '98 - p1003 [51-250]
>   KR - v65 - D 1 '97 - p1775 [51-250]
>   PW - v244 - D 8 '97 - p74 [51-250]
> y   SLJ - v44 - Mr '98 - p233+ [51-250]

Freedom Rides
>   BL - v94 - F 15 '98 - p998 [1-50]

Separate but Not Equal
> y   BL - v94 - F 15 '98 - p995 [51-250]
>   KR - v65 - N 15 '97 - p1708 [51-250]
>   SLJ - v44 - F '98 - p117+ [51-250]

Haslam, Andrew
Maps
>   Sch Lib - v45 - Ag '97 - p152 [51-250]

Rivers
>   Sch Lib - v45 - Ag '97 - p152 [51-250]

Hasler, Eveline
The Giantess (Illus. by Renate Seelig)
>   BL - v94 - D 1 '97 - p640+ [51-250]

>   Ch BWatch - v7 - N '97 - p4 [1-50]
>   KR - v65 - O 1 '97 - p1532+ [51-250]
>   PW - v244 - O 13 '97 - p73+ [51-250]
>   SLJ - v43 - D '97 - p92 [51-250]

Hassett, John
Charles of the Wild (Illus. by John Hassett)
>   HB Guide - v8 - Fall '97 - p267 [51-250]
>   SLJ - v43 - My '97 - p99 [51-250]

Hassig, Susan M
Somalia
>   HB Guide - v8 - Fall '97 - p392 [51-250]
>   SLJ - v43 - Jl '97 - p106 [51-250]

Hastings, Chris
The Zoo Garden (Illus. by Janet Hamlin)
>   HB Guide - v8 - Fall '97 - p360 [51-250]

Hastings, Selina
The Illustrated Jewish Bible for Children (Illus. by Eric Thomas)
>   CLW - v68 - D '97 - p84 [251-500]
>   SLJ - v44 - F '98 - p100 [51-250]

Hatchett, Clint
The Glow-in-the-Dark Night Sky Book
>   Par - v72 - Ag '97 - p170 [1-50]

Hathorn, Libby
The Climb
>   Sch Lib - v45 - N '97 - p212 [51-250]

Sky Sash So Blue (Illus. by Benny Andrews)
>   BL - v94 - F 15 '98 - p1019 [51-250]

Hatrick, Gloria
Masks
>   Ch BWatch - v7 - My '97 - p5 [51-250]

Hatt, Christine
Slavery from Africa to the Americas
>   Bks Keeps - S '97 - p29 [51-250]

Hauff, Wilhelm
Little Long-Nose (Illus. by Laura Stoddart)
    Ch BWatch - v7 - N '97 - p3 [1-50]
    KR - v65 - S 15 '97 - p1457 [51-250]

Haughian, Sheree
The Private Journal of Day Applepenny Prisoner
    CM:CanRev - v4 - N 14 '97 - pONL [251-500]

Haughton, Emma
A Right to Smoke?
    Bks Keeps - My '97 - p26+ [51-250]
    BL - v93 - Je 1 '97 - p1690 [51-250]
    HB Guide - v8 - Fall '97 - p327 [51-250]
    SB - v33 - Ag '97 - p176 [51-250]
    SB - v33 - N '97 - p226 [51-250]
    SLJ - v43 - My '97 - p145+ [51-250]

Rights in the Home
    Bks Keeps - S '97 - p29 [51-250]
    TES - O 17 '97 - pR7 [51-250]

Hauser, Jill Frankel
Super Science Concoctions (Illus. by Michael Kline)
    SLJ - v43 - Ap '97 - p126 [51-250]

Hausherr, Rosmarie
Celebrating Families
    HB Guide - v8 - Fall '97 - p321 [51-250]

Hausman, Gerald
Eagle Boy (Illus. by Cara Moser)
    SE - v61 - Ap '97 - p5* [1-50]

Night Flight
    RT - v51 - O '97 - p151 [51-250]

Hautzig, Deborah
A Little Princess
    Ch BWatch - v7 - S '97 - p4 [51-250]

Havard, Christian
The Wolf
    ASBYP - v29 - Fall '96 - p39 [251-500]

Haven, Kendall
Great Moments in Science
    ASBYP - v29 - Fall '96 - p17 [251-500]

Havens, John C
Government and Politics
    Ch BWatch - v7 - Ap '97 - p5 [51-250]
    r HB Guide - v8 - Fall '97 - p324 [51-250]

Havill, Juanita
Jamaica's Find
    Par - v72 - My '97 - p92 [1-50]

Hawcock, David
The Amazing Pull-Out Pop-Up Body in a Book
    BL - v94 - D 15 '97 - p700 [1-50]
    Obs - D 7 '97 - p18* [51-250]
    PW - v244 - S 29 '97 - p91 [51-250]
    SB - v34 - Ap '98 - p82 [51-250]

Hawkes, Nigel
The Fantastic Cutaway Book of Spacecraft
    ASBYP - v29 - Sum '96 - p17+ [251-500]

The Universe
    ASBYP - v29 - Sum '96 - p18 [251-500]

Hawkins, Colin
Aliens
    Books - v11 - Ag '97 - p15 [1-50]

Baby Boo!
    Magpies - v12 - Mr '97 - p29 [51-250]

Busy ABC
    Magpies - v12 - Mr '97 - p29 [51-250]

Hawkins, Joyce
Concise Oxford School Dictionary
    r Sch Lib - v45 - N '97 - p205 [51-250]
    r TES - S 19 '97 - p19* [501+]

Hawkins, Peter
The Halifax Explosion (Illus. by Michael Dixon)
    p BIC - v26 - My '97 - p35 [251-500]

Haworth-Attard, Barbara
Dark of the Moon
> CBRA - '96 - p477+ [51-250]

Home Child
> CBRA - '96 - p478 [51-250]
> y   VOYA - v20 - Ag '97 - p184 [251-500]

The Three Wishbells
> CBRA - '96 - p478 [51-250]

Truth Singer
> CBRA - '96 - p478 [51-250]
> y   VOYA - v20 - Ap '97 - p42 [251-500]

Hawthorn, Libby
The Wonder Thing (Illus. by Peter Gouldthorpe)
> LA - v73 - N '96 - p522 [51-250]

Hawthorne, Nathaniel
A Wonder Book for Girls and Boys (Illus. by Walter Crane)
> HB Guide - v8 - Fall '97 - p333 [51-250]
> Nine-C Lit - v52 - Je '97 - p131 [51-250]

Hayes, Ann
Onstage and Backstage (Illus. by Karmen Thompson)
> BL - v94 - N 1 '97 - p476 [51-250]
> KR - v65 - S 1 '97 - p1389 [51-250]
> PW - v244 - O 13 '97 - p73 [51-250]
> SLJ - v43 - N '97 - p82 [51-250]

Hayes, Geoffrey
House of the Horrible Ghosts
> HB Guide - v8 - Fall '97 - p291 [51-250]

Hayes, Rosemary
The Silver Fox
> Magpies - v12 - Jl '97 - p33 [51-250]

Hayes, Sarah
A Bad Start for Santa Claus (Illus. by Jamie Charteris)
> PW - v244 - O 6 '97 - p58 [1-50]

The Candlewick Book of Fairy Tales (Illus. by P J Lynch)
> PW - v244 - O 6 '97 - p85 [1-50]

This Is the Bear and the Scary Night (Illus. by Helen Craig)
> Bks Keeps - N '97 - p21 [51-250]

Hayles, Karen
The Star That Fell (Illus. by Cliff Wright). Book and Audio Version
> TES - N 7 '97 - p13* [51-250]

Haynes, David, 1955-
Business as Usual (Illus. by David Zinn)
> CBRS - v26 - Win '98 - p69 [51-250]
> CBRS - v26 - S '97 - p11 [1-50]
> KR - v65 - Je 15 '97 - p950 [51-250]
> PW - v244 - Je 23 '97 - p93 [51-250]
> SLJ - v44 - Mr '98 - p212 [51-250]

Business as Usual. The Gumma Wars
> BL - v94 - O 15 '97 - p406 [51-250]

The Gumma Wars (Illus. by David Zinn)
> CBRS - v26 - Win '98 - p69 [51-250]
> CBRS - v26 - S '97 - p11 [1-50]

Haynes, Max
In the Driver's Seat (Illus. by Max Haynes)
> CBRS - v26 - Win '98 - p62 [51-250]
> KR - v65 - O 1 '97 - p1533 [51-250]
> PW - v244 - O 27 '97 - p74 [51-250]

Hazelaar, Cor
Zoo Dreams
> CBRS - v25 - Spr '97 - p135 [51-250]
> HB Guide - v8 - Fall '97 - p251 [51-250]

Hazell, Rebecca
The Barefoot Book of Heroes
> Bks Keeps - My '97 - p25 [51-250]
> HT - v47 - Ap '97 - p56 [1-50]
> Sch Lib - v45 - Ag '97 - p152 [51-250]

The Barefoot Book of Heroines
> Bks Keeps - My '97 - p25 [51-250]

Heroes: Great Men through the Ages (Illus. by Rebecca Hazell)
> HB Guide - v8 - Fall '97 - p384 [51-250]
> SLJ - v43 - Je '97 - p135+ [51-250]

Hazen, Barbara Shook

Digby (Illus. by Barbara J Phillips-Duke)

> HB Guide - v8 - Fall '97 - p287 [51-250]

The New Dog (Illus. by R W Alley)

> BL - v93 - Ag '97 - p1906 [51-250]
> KR - v65 - Je 15 '97 - p950 [51-250]
> SLJ - v43 - D '97 - p92 [51-250]

What Does Amy Want?

> PW - v244 - D 1 '97 - p55 [1-50]

Heal, Gillian

Grandpa Bear's Fantastic Scarf (Illus. by Gillian Heal)

> Bloom Rev - v17 - My '97 - p27 [51-250]
> Ch BWatch - v7 - Je '97 - p6 [1-50]
> HB Guide - v8 - Fall '97 - p267 [51-250]
> SLJ - v43 - Jl '97 - p68 [51-250]

Heaney, Seamus

The School Bag

> y   Bks Keeps - S '97 - p30 [51-250]
> Spec - v278 - Mr 29 '97 - p34+ [501+]
> TES - N 7 '97 - p2* [51-250]

Heap, Sue

Cowboy Baby (Illus. by Sue Heap)

> BL - v94 - Mr 1 '98 - p1140 [51-250]
> Books - v11 - D '97 - p21 [51-250]

Hearn, Diane Dawson

Anna in the Garden (Illus. by Diane Dawson Hearn)

> SB - v33 - O '97 - p218 [51-250]

Hearne, Betsy

Seven Brave Women (Illus. by Bethanne Andersen)

> BL - v93 - Je 1 '97 - p1694 [51-250]
> BL - v94 - Ja 1 '98 - p735 [1-50]
> CBRS - v26 - S '97 - p8 [51-250]
> CCB-B - v51 - O '97 - p53 [1-50]
> Emerg Lib - v25 - N '97 - p55 [1-50]
> HB - v73 - S '97 - p558+ [51-250]
> KR - v65 - Je 15 '97 - p950+ [51-250]
> NYTBR - v102 - N 16 '97 - p52+ [501+]
> NYTBR - v102 - D 7 '97 - p80 [1-50]
> PW - v244 - My 19 '97 - p76 [51-250]

> SLJ - v43 - S '97 - p182+ [51-250]

Heatwole, Marsha

Primary Cats (Illus. by Marsha Heatwole)

> Ch BWatch - v7 - D '97 - p2 [51-250]
> SLJ - v44 - F '98 - p85 [51-250]

Hebert, Marie-Francine

Un Crocodile Dans La Baignoire (Illus. by Philippe Germain)

> Can CL - v22 - Win '96 - p125+ [501+]

Poppy's Whale (Illus. by Philippe Germain)

> CBRA - '96 - p478+ [51-250]

Heckman, Philip

Waking Upside Down (Illus. by Dwight Been)

> RT - v51 - O '97 - p139 [1-50]

Hedderwick, Mairi

Katie Morag and the Grand Concert (Illus. by Mairi Hedderwick)

> Bks Keeps - N '97 - p20 [51-250]
> Obs - Jl 20 '97 - p18* [51-250]
> Sch Lib - v45 - N '97 - p186 [51-250]
> TES - D 5 '97 - p17* [51-250]

Katie Morag and the New Pier (Illus. by Mairi Hedderwick)

> Bks Keeps - N '97 - p20 [51-250]

Katie Morag and the Two Grandmothers (Illus. by Mairi Hedderwick)

> Bks Keeps - N '97 - p20 [51-250]

Katie Morag and the Wedding (Illus. by Mairi Hedderwick)

> Bks Keeps - N '97 - p20 [51-250]

Katie Morag Delivers the Mail (Illus. by Mairi Hedderwick)

> Bks Keeps - N '97 - p20 [51-250]

Oh No, Peedie Peebles! (Illus. by Mairi Hedderwick)

> Bks Keeps - N '97 - p20 [51-250]

Hedlund, Carey
Night Fell at Harry's Farm (Illus. by Carey Hedlund)
BL - v93 - Je 1 '97 - p1718 [51-250]
CBRS - v25 - Jl '97 - p147+ [51-250]
CCB-B - v50 - Jl '97 - p398 [51-250]
HB Guide - v8 - Fall '97 - p267 [51-250]
PW - v244 - My 19 '97 - p75 [51-250]
SLJ - v43 - My '97 - p99 [51-250]

Hegedus, Umar
Muslim Mosque
Sch Lib - v45 - N '97 - p206 [51-250]

Hehner, Barbara
The Ultimate Science Kit
Quill & Q - v63 - N '97 - p46+ [251-500]

Heidbreder, Robert
Eenie Meenie Manitoba (Illus. by Scot Ritchie)
CBRA - '96 - p497+ [51-250]

Heide, Florence Parry
Tio Armando (Illus. by Ann Grifalconi)
KR - v66 - Mr 1 '98 - p339 [51-250]

Heidenreich, Elke
Nero Corleone (Illus. by Quint Buchholz)
BL - v94 - S 15 '97 - p235 [51-250]
CCB-B - v51 - D '97 - p127+ [51-250]
KR - v65 - Ag 15 '97 - p1306 [51-250]
SLJ - v43 - D '97 - p92 [51-250]

Heifetz, Milton D
A Walk through the Heavens
y Am Sci - v85 - N '97 - p561 [1-50]
r SB - v33 - Ap '97 - p83 [51-250]

Heiligman, Deborah
From Caterpillar to Butterfly (Illus. by Bari Weissman)
ASBYP - v29 - Fall '96 - p52 [501+]
RT - v51 - O '97 - p152 [51-250]

In Search of Human Beginnings (Illus. by Janet Hamlin)
ASBYP - v29 - Sum '96 - p18 [251-500]

On the Move (Illus. by Lizzy Rockwell)
ASBYP - v29 - Fall '96 - p52 [501+]

Heinemann, Sue
The New York Public Library Amazing Women in American History
KR - v66 - Ja 15 '98 - p112 [51-250]
PW - v245 - F 2 '98 - p92 [51-250]

Heinemann English Dictionary
r TES - S 19 '97 - p19* [501+]

Heinrichs, Ann
China
BL - v94 - S 15 '97 - p228 [51-250]
HB Guide - v8 - Fall '97 - p391 [51-250]
SLJ - v43 - N '97 - p108 [51-250]

Japan
HB Guide - v8 - Fall '97 - p391 [51-250]
SLJ - v43 - N '97 - p108 [51-250]

Mexico
SLJ - v43 - N '97 - p108 [51-250]

South Africa
BL - v94 - S 15 '97 - p228 [51-250]

Heinrichs, Sally
What Sort of Day?
Magpies - v12 - Mr '97 - p27+ [51-250]

Heinz, Brian
Kayuktuk: An Arctic Quest (Illus. by Jon Van Zyle)
NH - v106 - D '97 - p8+ [51-250]

The Monsters' Test (Illus. by Sal Murdocca)
RT - v51 - O '97 - p134 [1-50]

Helldorfer, M C
Gather Up, Gather In (Illus. by Judy Pedersen)
PW - v245 - Ja 26 '98 - p93 [1-50]
SB - v33 - O '97 - p218 [51-250]

Harmonica Night (Illus. by Alexi Natchev)

     CBRS - v25 - Ag '97 - p159 [1-50]
     HB Guide - v8 - Fall '97 - p267 [51-250]
     SLJ - v43 - Je '97 - p90 [51-250]

Heller, Nicholas

The Giant (Illus. by Jos. A Smith)

     CBRS - v26 - D '97 - p43+ [51-250]
     KR - v65 - O 15 '97 - p1582 [51-250]
     PW - v244 - O 27 '97 - p75+ [51-250]

This Little Piggy (Illus. by Sonja Lamut)

     CBRS - v25 - My '97 - p111 [51-250]
     Ch BWatch - v7 - My '97 - p3 [1-50]
     HB Guide - v8 - Fall '97 - p268 [51-250]
     SLJ - v43 - My '97 - p99+ [51-250]

Heller, Ruth

Color

     Inst - v106 - Ap '97 - p27 [1-50]

Mine, All Mine (Illus. by Ruth Heller)

     CCB-B - v51 - Mr '98 - p244+ [51-250]
     HB - v74 - Mr '98 - p234+ [51-250]
     SLJ - v44 - F '98 - p100 [51-250]

Hellman, Hal

Beyond Your Senses

y   BL - v93 - Je 1 '97 - p1671+ [51-250]
y   CCB-B - v50 - Jl '97 - p397 [51-250]
y   KR - v65 - My 15 '97 - p800+ [51-250]
     SLJ - v43 - S '97 - p230 [51-250]

Hellweg, Paul

The American Heritage Children's Thesaurus

r   BL - v94 - D 1 '97 - p650+ [501+]
r   SLJ - v44 - F '98 - p136 [51-250]

Helmer, Marilyn

The Boy, the Dollar and the Wonderful Hat (Illus. by San Murata)

     Can CL - v23 - Sum '97 - p65+ [501+]

Helprin, Mark

A City in Winter (Illus. by Chris Van Allsburg)

     Magpies - v12 - Mr '97 - p32 [51-250]

The Veil of Snows (Illus. by Chris Van Allsburg)

     Bloom Rev - v17 - N '97 - p31 [51-250]
     BW - v27 - D 7 '97 - p22 [51-250]
y   KR - v65 - S 1 '97 - p1389 [51-250]
     NYTBR - v103 - Ja 4 '98 - p20 [51-250]
     PW - v244 - S 29 '97 - p90 [51-250]
     SLJ - v43 - N '97 - p118+ [51-250]

Henderson, Aileen Kilgore

The Monkey Thief

     BL - v94 - N 1 '97 - p470 [51-250]
     CBRS - v26 - F '98 - p80 [51-250]
     SLJ - v43 - D '97 - p124 [51-250]

Henderson, Kathy

The Market Guide for Young Writers

r   Bloom Rev - v17 - N '97 - p30 [51-250]

Hendra, Sue

Tie Your Shoes?

     Ch BWatch - v7 - O '97 - p3 [1-50]

Hendry, Diana

Harvey Angell and the Ghost Child

y   TES - O 24 '97 - p7* [51-250]
     TES - N 7 '97 - p7* [1-50]

Hendry, Frances Mary

Chandra

     Bkbird - v34 - Win '96 - p56 [51-250]
     Bks Keeps - S '97 - p28 [51-250]
     TES - Ja 2 '98 - p22* [51-250]

Heneghan, James

The Case of the Blue Raccoon

     CBRA - '96 - p479 [51-250]

Wish Me Luck

     BL - v93 - Je 1 '97 - p1703 [51-250]
     HB - v73 - S '97 - p571 [51-250]
     HB Guide - v8 - Fall '97 - p301 [51-250]
y   JAAL - v41 - F '98 - p411 [51-250]
y   Quill & Q - v63 - Ag '97 - p39 [251-500]
     Quill & Q - v64 - F '98 - p42 [51-250]
     SLJ - v43 - Je '97 - p118 [51-250]

Henkes, Kevin

Bailey Goes Camping (Illus. by Kevin Henkes)

> Par Ch - Awards '97 - p8 [51-250]

The Biggest Boy (Illus. by Nancy Tafuri)

> TCMath - v3 - Ja '97 - p254 [51-250]

Chester's Way

> PW - v244 - Ag 25 '97 - p74 [1-50]

Lilly's Purple Plastic Purse (Illus. by Kevin Henkes)

> Emerg Lib - v24 - My '97 - p67 [1-50]
> HMR - Sum '97 - p28 [1-50]
> Inst - v106 - My '97 - p19 [1-50]
> NYTBR - v102 - N 16 '97 - p26 [1-50]
> RT - v51 - O '97 - p134 [1-50]
> RT - v51 - O '97 - p153 [51-250]

Sun and Spoon

> BL - v93 - Ag '97 - p1900 [51-250]
> BL - v94 - Mr 15 '98 - p1219 [1-50]
> CBRS - v26 - O '97 - p22 [51-250]
> CCB-B - v51 - D '97 - p128 [51-250]
> HB - v73 - S '97 - p571+ [51-250]
> y   JAAL - v41 - D '97 - p322 [51-250]
> KR - v65 - Je 1 '97 - p873 [51-250]
> NYTBR - v102 - N 16 '97 - p47 [501+]
> Par - v72 - D '97 - p206 [1-50]
> PW - v244 - Je 16 '97 - p60 [51-250]
> PW - v244 - N 3 '97 - p59+ [1-50]
> SLJ - v43 - Jl '97 - p94 [51-250]
> SLJ - v43 - D '97 - p25 [1-50]

Hennessy, B G

Corduroy's Birthday (Illus. by Lisa McCue)

> HB Guide - v8 - Fall '97 - p251 [51-250]

Henriques, Pegotty

Dressage for the Young Rider

> JOYS - v10 - Spr '97 - p261 [1-50]

Henry, Ernest

Not More Poems to Shout Out Loud (Illus. by Paul Daviz)

> Sch Lib - v45 - N '97 - p209 [51-250]

Henry, Maeve

A Gift for a Gift

> TES - Ja 2 '98 - p22* [51-250]

Midwinter

> Bks Keeps - My '97 - p25 [51-250]

Henry, Marguerite

Brighty of the Grand Canyon

> JOYS - v10 - Spr '97 - p262 [1-50]

Justin Morgan Had a Horse (McDonough). Audio Version

> SLJ - v43 - D '97 - p69+ [51-250]

Misty of Chincoteague (Illus. by Wesley Dennis)

> JOYS - v10 - Spr '97 - p260 [1-50]
> NYTBR - v102 - N 16 '97 - p25 [1-50]

White Stallion of Lipizza

> JOYS - v10 - Spr '97 - p261 [1-50]

Henry, O

The Gift of the Magi and Other Stories (Illus. by Michael Dooling)

> y   BL - v94 - O 15 '97 - p397 [51-250]
>   BW - v27 - S 7 '97 - p11 [251-500]
> y   Ch BWatch - v8 - Ja '98 - p8 [1-50]

Henry, Sandi

Cut-Paper Play! (Illus. by Norma Jean Jourdenais)

> Ch BWatch - v8 - Ja '98 - p6 [1-50]
> SLJ - v43 - S '97 - p202 [51-250]

Hepplewhite, Peter

Livingstone and the Victorian Explorers

> Sch Lib - v45 - N '97 - p204 [51-250]

Hepworth, Cathi

Bug Off! (Illus. by Cathi Hepworth)

> KR - v66 - Ap 15 '98 - p580 [51-250]

Herbst, Judith

The Mystery of UFOs (Illus. by Greg Clarke)

> BL - v94 - D '97 - p620 [51-250]
> CCB-B - v51 - D '97 - p128 [51-250]
> HB - v73 - N '97 - p696 [51-250]
> KR - v65 - N 1 '97 - p1644 [51-250]
> PW - v244 - N 17 '97 - p62 [51-250]
> SLJ - v43 - N '97 - p108 [51-250]

Herck, Alice
*The Enchanted Gardening Book (Illus.
by Linda Graves)*

> Ch BWatch - v7 - My '97 - p1 [51-250]
> HB Guide - v8 - Fall '97 - p360 [51-250]
> SLJ - v43 - My '97 - p120 [51-250]

Hercules Sticker Story Booklet

> Books - v11 - D '97 - p21 [1-50]

Herge
The Adventures of Tintin. Vol. 6

> HB Guide - v8 - Fall '97 - p301 [51-250]

Herman, Gail
*Storm Chasers (Illus. by Larry
Schwinger)*

> SLJ - v43 - N '97 - p108 [51-250]

Hermann, Spring
Geronimo: Apache Freedom Fighter

> CLW - v68 - S '97 - p68 [51-250]
> HB Guide - v8 - Fall '97 - p399 [51-250]
> y   SLJ - v43 - Je '97 - p138 [51-250]

Hermes, Jules
*Children of Guatemala (Illus. by Jules
Hermes)*

> BL - v94 - Mr 15 '98 - p1238 [51-250]
> KR - v65 - D 1 '97 - p1776 [51-250]
> SLJ - v44 - Mr '98 - p195 [51-250]

Hermes, Patricia
Mama, Let's Dance

> SLJ - v44 - Ja '98 - p42 [1-50]

Herron, Carolivia
Nappy Hair

> NW - v130 - D 1 '97 - p78 [1-50]

Hershenhorn, Esther
*There Goes Lowell's Party! (Illus. by
Jacqueline Rogers)*

> BL - v94 - Mr 15 '98 - p1248 [51-250]
> CCB-B - v51 - Ap '98 - p282 [51-250]
> KR - v66 - Mr 1 '98 - p339 [51-250]
> SLJ - v44 - Mr '98 - p180 [51-250]

Hesketh, Phoebe
A Box of Silver Birch

> Sch Lib - v45 - N '97 - p209 [51-250]

Hesse, Karen
Letters from Rifka

> SLJ - v43 - Jl '97 - p35 [1-50]
> SLJ - v43 - S '97 - p131 [1-50]

The Music of Dolphins

> y   Kliatt - v32 - Mr '98 - p19 [51-250]
> PW - v245 - F 2 '98 - p92 [1-50]
> RT - v51 - D '97 - p330 [51-250]
> y   VOYA - v20 - Je '97 - p85 [51-250]

Out of the Dust

> y   BL - v94 - O 1 '97 - p330 [51-250]
> y   BL - v94 - Ja 1 '98 - p733 [1-50]
> y   BL - v94 - Mr 15 '98 - p1214+ [1-50]
> BL - v94 - Mr 15 '98 - p1224 [1-50]
> CBRS - v26 - N '97 - p34+ [51-250]
> y   CCB-B - v51 - D '97 - p128+ [51-250]
> HB - v74 - Ja '98 - p73+ [51-250]
> KR - v65 - S 15 '97 - p1458 [51-250]
> y   NYTBR - v103 - F 1 '98 - p24 [51-250]
> y   PW - v244 - Ag 25 '97 - p72+ [51-250]
> PW - v244 - N 3 '97 - p60 [51-250]
> SLJ - v43 - S '97 - p217 [51-250]
> SLJ - v43 - D '97 - p25 [1-50]
> y   VOYA - v20 - F '98 - p364 [51-250]
> y   VOYA - v21 - Ap '98 - p37 [1-50]
> y   VOYA - v21 - Ap '98 - p46 [51-250]

Hest, Amy
*The Babies Are Coming! (Illus. by
Chloe Cheese)*

> BL - v94 - N 1 '97 - p481+ [51-250]
> PW - v244 - S 22 '97 - p79 [51-250]
> SLJ - v44 - Ja '98 - p87 [51-250]

*Gabby Growing Up (Illus. by Amy
Schwartz)*

> BL - v94 - Ja 1 '98 - p822+ [51-250]
> KR - v66 - Ja 1 '98 - p56 [51-250]
> NYTBR - v103 - F 15 '98 - p25 [51-250]
> PW - v244 - D 1 '97 - p53 [51-250]
> SLJ - v44 - Mr '98 - p180 [51-250]

*In the Rain with Baby Duck (Illus. by
Jill Barton)*

> Bks Keeps - Jl '97 - p20 [51-250]

*Jamaica Louise James (Illus. by Sheila
White Samton)*

> Inst - v106 - Ap '97 - p26 [51-250]

Magpies - v12 - S '97 - p7 [51-250]

When Jessie Came across the Sea
(Illus. by P J Lynch)
  Books - v11 - O '97 - p21 [51-250]
  CCB-B - v51 - Mr '98 - p245 [251-500]
  Ch BWatch - v8 - Ja '98 - p3 [51-250]
  NS - v126 - D 5 '97 - p62 [51-250]
  NYTBR - v102 - N 23 '97 - p32 [1-50]
  Par Ch - Awards '97 - p4 [51-250]
  PW - v244 - O 27 '97 - p76 [51-250]
  SLJ - v43 - N '97 - p82+ [51-250]

You're the Boss, Baby Duck! *(Illus. by Jill Barton)*
  BL - v94 - S 1 '97 - p133 [51-250]
  HB - v74 - Ja '98 - p65 [51-250]
  Magpies - v12 - Jl '97 - p27+ [501+]
  Par - v73 - F '98 - p185+ [51-250]
  PW - v244 - Ag 25 '97 - p73 [1-50]
  Sch Lib - v45 - N '97 - p186 [51-250]

Hewetson, Sarah
Silly Heads (Illus. by Sarah Hewetson)
  Magpies - v12 - Mr '97 - p20+ [501+]

Hewitt, Sally
The Clothes We Wear
  HB Guide - v8 - Fall '97 - p329 [51-250]

The Homes We Live In
  HB Guide - v8 - Fall '97 - p363 [51-250]

Measuring
  ASBYP - v29 - Fall '96 - p67+ [501+]

Numbers
  ASBYP - v29 - Fall '96 - p67+ [501+]

Puzzles
  ASBYP - v29 - Fall '96 - p67+ [501+]

Shapes
  ASBYP - v29 - Fall '96 - p67+ [501+]

Sorting and Sets
  ASBYP - v29 - Fall '96 - p67+ [501+]

The Things We Use
  HB Guide - v8 - Fall '97 - p358 [51-250]

Time
  ASBYP - v29 - Fall '96 - p67+ [501+]

The Toys We Play With
  HB Guide - v8 - Fall '97 - p367 [51-250]

Heyer, Carol
The Sleeping Beauty in the Wood
  HB Guide - v8 - Fall '97 - p333 [51-250]

Heyer, Marilee
The Girl, the Fish and the Crown
  PW - v244 - Je 30 '97 - p77 [1-50]

Heynen, Jim
Being Youngest
  y BL - v94 - O 15 '97 - p397 [51-250]
     CCB-B - v51 - D '97 - p129 [51-250]
     HB - v74 - Ja '98 - p74 [51-250]
     KR - v65 - S 15 '97 - p1458 [51-250]
  y SLJ - v43 - N '97 - p119 [51-250]
  y VOYA - v21 - Ap '98 - p46+ [51-250]

Hiatt, Fred
If I Were Queen of the World (Illus. by Mark Graham)
  CCB-B - v50 - Je '97 - p360 [51-250]
  HB Guide - v8 - Fall '97 - p268 [51-250]
  NYTBR - v102 - S 14 '97 - p30 [1-50]
  SLJ - v43 - My '97 - p100 [51-250]

Hickman, Pamela
Animal Senses (Illus. by Pat Stephens)
  Quill & Q - v64 - F '98 - p45+ [501+]

At the Seashore (Illus. by Twila Robar-DeCoste)
  CBRA - '96 - p530 [51-250]

Hungry Animals (Illus. by Heather Collins)
  BIC - v26 - S '97 - p34+ [251-500]
  Ch Bk News - v20 - Spr '97 - p30 [51-250]

The Jumbo Book of Nature Science (Illus. by Judie Shore)
  CBRA - '96 - p530+ [51-250]

The Kids Canadian Bug Book (Illus. by Heather Collins)
  CBRA - '96 - p531 [251-500]

The Kids Canadian Plant Book (Illus. by Heather Collins)
  CBRA - '96 - p531 [251-500]

A New Butterfly (Illus. by Heather Collins)
  BIC - v26 - S '97 - p34+ [251-500]
  Ch Bk News - v20 - Spr '97 - p30 [51-250]

The Night Book (Illus. by Suzanne Mogensen)
  CBRA - '96 - p531 [51-250]

A Seed Grows (Illus. by Heather Collins)
  BIC - v26 - S '97 - p34+ [251-500]
  Ch Bk News - v20 - Spr '97 - p30 [51-250]
  KR - v65 - Jl 15 '97 - p1111 [251-250]

Hickox, Rebecca
The Golden Sandal (Illus. by Will Hillenbrand)
  HB - v74 - Mr '98 - p226 [251-500]
  KR - v66 - F 15 '98 - p267 [51-250]
  PW - v245 - Ja 26 '98 - p91 [51-250]
  SLJ - v44 - Ap '98 - p117+ [51-250]

Per and the Dala Horse (Illus. by Yvonne Gilbert)
  PW - v244 - O 6 '97 - p85 [1-50]

Zorro and Quwi (Illus. by Kim Howard)
  CBRS - v25 - My '97 - p111 [1-50]
  HB Guide - v8 - Fall '97 - p333 [51-250]

Hicks, John V, 1907-
Renovated Rhymes (Illus. by VictoR GAD)
  Ch Bk News - v20 - Spr '97 - p33 [251-500]

Hicks, Peter
The Hidden Past
  HB Guide - v8 - Fall '97 - p388 [51-250]

High, Linda Oatman
Beekeepers (Illus. by Doug Chayka)
  CCB-B - v51 - Ap '98 - p282 [51-250]
  KR - v66 - F 1 '98 - p197 [51-250]
  PW - v245 - F 2 '98 - p90 [51-250]

A Christmas Star (Illus. by Ronald Himler)
  BL - v94 - S 1 '97 - p139 [51-250]
  CBRS - v26 - S '97 - p9 [51-250]
  KR - v65 - Ag 15 '97 - p1306 [51-250]
  NYTBR - v102 - D 7 '97 - p66 [501+]
  PW - v244 - O 6 '97 - p55 [51-250]

A Stone's Throw from Paradise
  BL - v93 - Je 1 '97 - p1703 [51-250]
  HB Guide - v8 - Fall '97 - p301 [51-250]
y SLJ - v43 - D '97 - p124+ [51-250]

The Highlights Big Book of Science Secrets
  SB - v33 - Ag '97 - p185 [1-50]

Highlights for Children, Inc.
The Timbertoes 1 2 3 Counting Book (Illus. by Judith Hunt)
  CLW - v68 - S '97 - p66 [51-250]
  HB Guide - v8 - Fall '97 - p254 [51-250]
  SLJ - v43 - Jl '97 - p67 [51-250]

The Timbertoes A B C Alphabet Book (Illus. by Judith Hunt)
  HB Guide - v8 - Fall '97 - p254 [51-250]
  SLJ - v43 - Jl '97 - p67 [51-250]

Hightower, Paul
Galileo: Astronomer and Physicist
  CLW - v68 - S '97 - p68 [51-250]
  HB Guide - v8 - Fall '97 - p380 [51-250]

Hightower, Susan
Twelve Snails to One Lizard (Illus. by Matt Novak)
  CBRS - v25 - Spr '97 - p135+ [51-250]
  HB Guide - v8 - Fall '97 - p268 [51-250]
  SLJ - v43 - My '97 - p100 [51-250]

Hildick, E W
The Purloined Corn Popper
  BL - v94 - Ja 1 '98 - p812 [51-250]
  SLJ - v44 - F '98 - p106 [51-250]

The Serial Sneak Thief
  BL - v94 - Ja 1 '98 - p812 [51-250]
  SLJ - v44 - F '98 - p106+ [51-250]

Hill, Anthony
The Burnt Stick (Illus. by Mark Sofilas)
LA - v73 - N '96 - p527 [51-250]

Hill, Cherry
From the Center of the Ring
JOYS - v10 - Spr '97 - p262 [1-50]

Hill, David J
Cold Comfort
Magpies - v12 - Mr '97 - p2* [1-50]

Fat, Four-Eyed and Useless
Magpies - v12 - S '97 - p6* [51-250]

Second Best
Magpies - v12 - Mr '97 - p33+ [251-500]

Hill, Douglas
The Dragon Charmer
TES - S 19 '97 - p13* [501+]

Witches and Magic-Makers (Illus. by Alex Wilson)
HB Guide - v8 - Fall '97 - p318 [51-250]
y SLJ - v43 - Ag '97 - p168 [51-250]

Hill, Eric
Where's Spot? (Illus. by Eric Hill)
NYTBR - v102 - N 16 '97 - p26 [1-50]

Hill, Lee Sullivan
Bridges Connect
BL - v94 - S 15 '97 - p237 [51-250]
HB Guide - v8 - Fall '97 - p358 [51-250]
SLJ - v43 - Jl '97 - p83 [51-250]

Canals Are Water Roads
BL - v94 - S 15 '97 - p237 [51-250]
Ch BWatch - v7 - My '97 - p6 [1-50]
SLJ - v43 - Jl '97 - p83+ [51-250]

Dams Give Us Power
BL - v94 - S 15 '97 - p237 [51-250]
Bloom Rev - v17 - N '97 - p32 [51-250]
Ch BWatch - v7 - My '97 - p6 [1-50]
SLJ - v43 - Jl '97 - p83+ [51-250]

Farms Feed the World
Ch BWatch - v7 - D '97 - p8 [1-50]

Parks Are to Share
Ch BWatch - v7 - D '97 - p8 [1-50]
KR - v65 - N 1 '97 - p1644 [51-250]

Roads Take Us Home
BL - v94 - S 15 '97 - p237 [51-250]
HB Guide - v8 - Fall '97 - p358 [51-250]
SLJ - v43 - Jl '97 - p83 [51-250]

Schools Help Us Learn
KR - v66 - Ap 15 '98 - p581 [51-250]

Towers Reach High
BL - v94 - S 15 '97 - p237 [51-250]
Ch BWatch - v7 - My '97 - p6 [1-50]
KR - v65 - Ap 15 '97 - p640 [51-250]
SLJ - v43 - Jl '97 - p83+ [51-250]

Hill, Susan
The Random House Book of Ghost Stories (Illus. by Angela Barrett)
HB Guide - v8 - Fall '97 - p373 [51-250]

Hill, William
The Magic Bicycle
BL - v94 - Ja 1 '98 - p812 [51-250]
SLJ - v44 - Mr '98 - p212+ [51-250]

Hiller, Margaret
The Sky Is Not So Far Away (Illus. by Thomas Werner)
RT - v51 - N '97 - p252 [51-250]

Himmelman, John
Honest Tulio (Illus. by John Himmelman)
BL - v93 - Je 1 '97 - p1718 [51-250]
HB Guide - v8 - Fall '97 - p268 [51-250]
SLJ - v43 - Jl '97 - p68+ [51-250]

Hinds, Kathryn
The Incas
Ch BWatch - v8 - Ja '98 - p7 [51-250]

The Vikings
Ch BWatch - v8 - Ja '98 - p7 [51-250]

Hines, Anna Grossnickle
Miss Emma's Wild Garden (Illus. by Anna Grossnickle Hines)
HB Guide - v8 - Fall '97 - p268 [1-50]

SLJ - v43 - My '97 - p100 [51-250]

Hines-Stephens, Sarah

Bean (Illus. by Anna Grossnickle Hines)
> PW - v245 - Mr 23 '98 - p101 [51-250]

Bean's Games (Illus. by Anna Grossnickle Hines)
> PW - v245 - Mr 23 '98 - p101 [51-250]

Bean's Night (Illus. by Anna Grossnickle Hines)
> PW - v245 - Mr 23 '98 - p101 [51-250]

Hinton, S E

The Outsiders
> y   Ch BWatch - v7 - S '97 - p5 [51-250]
> NYTBR - v102 - N 16 '97 - p26 [1-50]

The Puppy Sister (Illus. by Jacqueline Rogers)
> PW - v244 - Jl 28 '97 - p77 [1-50]

Hirschi, Ron

Dance with Me (Illus. by Thomas D Mangelsen)
> ASBYP - v29 - Sum '96 - p19 [251-500]

Faces in the Forest (Illus. by Thomas D Mangelsen)
> BL - v94 - S 15 '97 - p237+ [51-250]
> SLJ - v44 - Mr '98 - p195+ [51-250]

Faces in the Mountains (Illus. by Thomas D Mangelsen)
> BL - v94 - S 15 '97 - p237+ [51-250]
> SLJ - v44 - Mr '98 - p195+ [51-250]

People of Salmon and Cedar (Illus. by Deborah Cooper)
> SE - v61 - Ap '97 - p9* [1-50]

Hirshberg, Dan

John Elway
> Ch BWatch - v7 - My '97 - p7 [1-50]
> HB Guide - v8 - Fall '97 - p369 [51-250]

Lawrence Taylor
> Ch BWatch - v7 - N '97 - p7 [1-50]

Hirst, Mike

Freedom of Belief
> Bks Keeps - S '97 - p29 [51-250]
> BL - v94 - Ja 1 '98 - p804+ [51-250]
> y   Sch Lib - v45 - N '97 - p218 [51-250]
> TES - O 17 '97 - pR7 [51-250]

Scotland
> SLJ - v44 - F '98 - p118 [51-250]

Hiscock, Bruce

The Big Rivers (Illus. by Bruce Hiscock)
> BL - v93 - Je 1 '97 - p1690+ [51-250]
> CCB-B - v51 - S '97 - p12 [51-250]
> HB Guide - v8 - Fall '97 - p342 [51-250]
> KR - v65 - Je 1 '97 - p873 [51-250]
> NYTBR - v102 - Jl 20 '97 - p22 [1-50]
> SLJ - v43 - Jl '97 - p84 [51-250]

Hissey, Jane

Hoot (Illus. by Jane Hissey)
> BL - v93 - Je 1 '97 - p1718 [51-250]
> HB Guide - v8 - Fall '97 - p268 [51-250]
> SLJ - v43 - Jl '97 - p69 [51-250]

The History of Printmaking (Voyages of Discovery)
> BL - v94 - D 15 '97 - p700 [1-50]

Ho, Minfong

Brother Rabbit (Illus. by Jennifer Hewitson)
> CBRS - v25 - Jl '97 - p148 [51-250]
> Ch BWatch - v7 - Je '97 - p7 [1-50]
> HB Guide - v8 - Fall '97 - p333 [51-250]
> Inst - v107 - Ag '97 - p21 [51-250]
> SLJ - v43 - My '97 - p120 [51-250]

Hush! A Thai Lullaby (Illus. by Holly Meade)
> HMR - Sum '97 - p28 [1-50]
> RT - v51 - N '97 - p250 [51-250]

Hoban, Julia

Busby (Hoban). Book and Audio Version
> SLJ - v43 - Je '97 - p69 [51-250]

Hoban, Lillian

Big Little Lion
> HB Guide - v8 - Fall '97 - p251 [51-250]

Big Little Otter
> HB Guide - v8 - Fall '97 - p251 [51-250]

Silly Tilly's Valentine (Illus. by Lillian Hoban)
> KR - v65 - N 15 '97 - p1708 [51-250]
> SLJ - v44 - F '98 - p85 [51-250]

Hoban, Russell

A Bargain for Frances (Illus. by Lillian Hoban)
> Par - v73 - F '98 - p185 [1-50]

A Birthday for Frances
> Par - v72 - My '97 - p92 [1-50]

The Last of the Wallendas and Other Poems (Illus. by Patrick Benson)
> NS - v126 - D 5 '97 - p63 [1-50]
> TES - N 7 '97 - p2* [51-250]
> TES - Ja 2 '98 - p23* [501+]

La Nueva Hermanita De Francisca (Illus. by Lillian Hoban)
> SLJ - v43 - Ag '97 - p180 [51-250]

The Trokeville Way
> y   BW - v27 - Jl 6 '97 - p11 [251-500]
> y   Kliatt - v32 - Ja '98 - p16 [51-250]
> y   Magpies - v12 - Mr '97 - p37 [51-250]
>   NYTBR - v102 - Ap 27 '97 - p29 [1-50]
>   PW - v244 - D 1 '97 - p55 [1-50]

Hoban, Tana

Construction Zone
> HB Guide - v8 - Fall '97 - p358 [51-250]

Just Look (Illus. by Tana Hoban)
> LA - v73 - N '96 - p522 [51-250]
> RT - v51 - N '97 - p252+ [51-250]

Look Book (Illus. by Tana Hoban)
> HB - v73 - S '97 - p591 [51-250]
> SLJ - v43 - Ag '97 - p135 [51-250]

So Many Circles, So Many Squares (Illus. by Tana Hoban)
> BL - v94 - Mr 1 '98 - p1138 [51-250]
> KR - v66 - F 15 '98 - p267 [51-250]
> SLJ - v44 - Mr '98 - p196 [51-250]

Hobbie, Holly

Toot and Puddle (Illus. by Holly Hobbie)
> CBRS - v26 - D '97 - p39 [51-250]
> Ch BWatch - v7 - N '97 - p4 [1-50]
> KR - v65 - O 1 '97 - p1533 [51-250]
> SLJ - v43 - D '97 - p92+ [51-250]

Hobbs, Leigh

Old Tom Goes to Mars (Illus. by Leigh Hobbs)
> Magpies - v12 - Mr '97 - p30+ [51-250]

Hobbs, Will

Beardream (Illus. by Jill Kastner)
> HB Guide - v8 - Fall '97 - p268 [51-250]
> JAAL - v41 - S '97 - p83 [51-250]
> SLJ - v43 - Ap '97 - p104 [51-250]

Far North
> y   Kliatt - v32 - Ja '98 - p9 [51-250]
>   PW - v244 - Ag 25 '97 - p74 [1-50]
> y   SE - v61 - Ap '97 - p13* [1-50]
> y   VOYA - v20 - Je '97 - p85 [51-250]

Ghost Canoe
> HB Guide - v8 - Fall '97 - p301 [1-50]
> y   SLJ - v43 - Ap '97 - p137+ [51-250]
> y   VOYA - v20 - Ag '97 - p184 [251-500]
> y   VOYA - v20 - F '98 - p364+ [51-250]

Hoberman, Mary Ann

The Llama Who Had No Pajama (Illus. by Betty Fraser)
> HB - v74 - Mr '98 - p228 [51-250]
> PW - v245 - Mr 23 '98 - p97+ [51-250]
> SLJ - v44 - Ap '98 - p118 [51-250]

Miss Mary Mack (Illus. by Nadine Bernard Westcott)
> BL - v94 - Mr 15 '98 - p1245+ [51-250]

One of Each (Illus. by Marjorie Priceman)
> BL - v94 - N 1 '97 - p466 [51-250]
> BL - v94 - Ja 1 '98 - p735 [1-50]
> CBRS - v26 - O '97 - p15 [51-250]
> CCB-B - v51 - O '97 - p53 [51-250]
> Emerg Lib - v25 - Ja '98 - p52 [51-250]
> KR - v65 - Ag 1 '97 - p1222 [51-250]
> PW - v244 - Ag 4 '97 - p74 [51-250]
> PW - v244 - N 3 '97 - p59 [51-250]
> SLJ - v43 - S '97 - p183 [51-250]
> SLJ - v43 - D '97 - p25 [1-50]

The Seven Silly Eaters (Illus. by Marla Frazee)
> Ch BWatch - v7 - Je '97 - p7 [1-50]
> HB Guide - v8 - Fall '97 - p268 [51-250]
> NW - v130 - D 1 '97 - p78 [51-250]
> NYTBR - v102 - Jl 6 '97 - p16 [501+]

Hockey Superstars 1996-1997
> CBRA - '96 - p525 [51-250]

Hodge, Deborah
Bears: Polar Bears, Black Bears and Grizzly Bears (Illus. by Pat Stephens)
> BL - v94 - S 15 '97 - p238 [51-250]
> CBRA - '96 - p531+ [51-250]
> CBRS - v26 - Win '98 - p69+ [51-250]
> SLJ - v43 - S '97 - p202+ [51-250]

Simple Machines (Illus. by Ray Boudreau)
> CBRA - '96 - p536 [51-250]

Whales: Killer Whales, Blue Whales and More (Illus. by Pat Stephens)
> CBRS - v26 - Win '98 - p69+ [51-250]
> SLJ - v43 - N '97 - p108+ [51-250]

Wild Cats (Illus. by Nancy Gray Ogle)
> BL - v94 - S 15 '97 - p238 [51-250]
> CBRA - '96 - p531+ [51-250]
> CBRS - v26 - Win '98 - p69+ [51-250]
> SB - v33 - D '97 - p275 [51-250]
> SLJ - v43 - S '97 - p202+ [51-250]

Wild Dogs (Illus. by Pat Stephens)
> CBRS - v26 - Win '98 - p69+ [51-250]
> SB - v33 - D '97 - p275 [251-500]
> SLJ - v43 - N '97 - p108+ [51-250]

Hodge, Susie
Ancient Egyptian Art
> SLJ - v44 - Ap '98 - p146 [51-250]

Prehistoric Art
> SLJ - v44 - Ap '98 - p146 [51-250]

Hodges, Margaret
Silent Night (Illus. by Tim Ladwig)
> BL - v94 - S 1 '97 - p141 [51-250]
> CCB-B - v51 - D '97 - p129+ [51-250]
> Ch BWatch - v7 - D '97 - p1 [1-50]

The True Tale of Johnny Appleseed (Illus. by Kimberly Bulcken Root)
> CCB-B - v51 - S '97 - p12 [51-250]
> HB Guide - v8 - Fall '97 - p380 [51-250]
> Inst - v107 - O '97 - p24 [1-50]
> SLJ - v43 - S '97 - p203 [51-250]

Hodges, Susan
Healthy Snacks
> Ch BWatch - v7 - S '97 - p5 [1-50]

Multicultural Snacks
> Ch BWatch - v7 - S '97 - p5 [1-50]

Hoestlandt, Jo
Star of Fear, Star of Hope (Illus. by Johanna Kang)
> y   Emerg Lib - v24 - My '97 - p10 [1-50]
> SS - v88 - My '97 - p139+ [501+]

Hoff, Carol
Johnny Texas
> Ch BWatch - v7 - Jl '97 - p2 [51-250]

Hoff, Syd
Danny and the Dinosaur Go to Camp (Illus. by Syd Hoff)
> RT - v51 - O '97 - p133 [1-50]

Where's Prancer? (Illus. by Syd Hoff)
> BL - v94 - S 1 '97 - p139 [51-250]
> PW - v244 - O 6 '97 - p58 [1-50]

Hoffman, Alice
Fireflies (Illus. by Wayne McLoughlin)
> Ch BWatch - v7 - N '97 - p4 [1-50]
> KR - v65 - S 1 '97 - p1390 [51-250]
> SLJ - v43 - N '97 - p83 [51-250]

Hoffman, Mary
Amazing Grace (Illus. by Caroline Binch)
> ECEJ - v25 - Fall '97 - p47 [1-50]
> Par - v72 - My '97 - p92 [1-50]
> TES - N 14 '97 - p11* [51-250]

An Angel Just like Me (Illus. by Cornelius Van Wright)
> Am Vis - v12 - D '97 - p33 [1-50]
> BL - v94 - N 1 '97 - p482 [51-250]
> CCB-B - v51 - Mr '98 - p245+ [51-250]
> NYTBR - v102 - D 7 '97 - p66 [501+]

Sch Lib - v45 - N '97 - p186 [51-250]
SLJ - v43 - D '97 - p93 [51-250]
TES - D 5 '97 - p17* [51-250]

Boundless Grace (Illus. by Caroline Binch)
ECEJ - v25 - Fall '97 - p47 [1-50]

A First Bible Story Book (Illus. by Julie Downing)
Bks Keeps - S '97 - p23+ [251-500]
Sch Lib - v45 - Ag '97 - p152 [51-250]
TES - O 17 '97 - p12* [51-250]

Grace and Family (Illus. by Caroline Binch)
CM:CanRev - v4 - D 12 '97 - pONL [51-250]

Henry's Baby (Illus. by Susan Winter)
SB - v33 - O '97 - p218 [51-250]

Quantum Squeak
TES - Jl 11 '97 - p14* [51-250]

Special Powers
Bks Keeps - My '97 - p25 [51-250]

Hoffman, Mary Ann
Counseling Clients with HIV Disease
SB - v32 - D '96 - p262 [251-500]

Hoffmann, E T A
Nutcracker (Illus. by Roberto Innocenti)
HB Guide - v8 - Fall '97 - p301 [51-250]
TES - D 5 '97 - p17* [51-250]

Hogrogian, Nonny
Un Buen Dia
BL - v94 - D 15 '97 - p707 [51-250]

Holbrook, Sara
Am I Naturally This Crazy?
CLW - v68 - D '97 - p83+ [51-250]
SLJ - v43 - Ap '97 - p126 [51-250]

I Never Said I Wasn't Difficult?
CLW - v68 - D '97 - p83+ [51-250]

Which Way to the Dragon!
CLW - v68 - D '97 - p83+ [51-250]
SLJ - v43 - Ap '97 - p126 [51-250]

Holden, Robert
The Pied Piper of Hamelin (Illus. by Drahos Zak)
Aust Bk R - D '97 - p64+ [501+]
BL - v94 - Mr 1 '98 - p1129 [51-250]
KR - v66 - Mr 1 '98 - p339+ [51-250]

Holeman, Linda
Frankie on the Run (Illus. by Heather Collins)
Can CL - v23 - Fall '97 - p63+ [501+]

Promise Song
BL - v93 - Je 1 '97 - p1703 [51-250]
y   Ch Bk News - v20 - Spr '97 - p32+ [251-500]
y   CM:CanRev - v4 - F 13 '98 - pONL [501+]
y   Quill & Q - v64 - F '98 - p42 [51-250]

Holland, Gini
Airplanes
ASBYP - v29 - Sum '96 - p50+ [251-500]

Diego Rivera (Illus. by Gary Rees)
HB Guide - v8 - Fall '97 - p363 [51-250]

The Empire State Building
Sch Lib - v45 - Ag '97 - p153 [51-250]

Johnny Appleseed (Illus. by Kim Palmer)
HB Guide - v8 - Fall '97 - p380 [1-50]

Nelson Mandela (Illus. by Mike White)
HB Guide - v8 - Fall '97 - p380 [1-50]
SLJ - v44 - F '98 - p100 [51-250]

Photography
ASBYP - v29 - Sum '96 - p50+ [251-500]

Rosa Parks (Illus. by David Price)
SLJ - v44 - F '98 - p100 [51-250]

Sandra Day O'Connor (Illus. by Gary Rees)
HB Guide - v8 - Fall '97 - p380 [1-50]

Telephones
ASBYP - v29 - Sum '96 - p50+ [251-500]

Wilma Mankiller (Illus. by Mike White)
HB Guide - v8 - Fall '97 - p380 [1-50]

Holland, Julia
Through the Doorway
　　Magpies - v12 - My '97 - p34 [51-250]

Holleyman, Sonia
The Creepy Crawly Collection
　　Books - v10 - S '96 - p24 [51-250]

Little Space Scout's Space Case
　　CM:CanRev - v4 - Ap 24 '98 - pONL
　　[51-250]

Holling, Holling C
*Minn of the Mississippi (Illus. by
Holling C Holling)*
　　NYTBR - v102 - N 16 '97 - p25 [1-50]

Holloway, Tracey
*The Ikho of Laos (Illus. by Helen
Groome)*
　　Magpies - v12 - Mr '97 - p40 [251-500]

Holman, Felice
Real (Illus. by Robin Moore)
　y　BL - v94 - O 1 '97 - p319+ [51-250]
　　CBRS - v26 - Win '98 - p70 [51-250]
　　CCB-B - v51 - D '97 - p130 [51-250]
　　KR - v65 - S 1 '97 - p1390 [51-250]
　　PW - v244 - O 6 '97 - p84 [51-250]
　　SLJ - v43 - N '97 - p119+ [51-250]
　y　VOYA - v20 - F '98 - p386 [251-500]

Holmes, Barbara Ware
*My Sister the Sausage Roll (Illus. by
Karen Lee Schmidt)*
　　CCB-B - v50 - Jl '97 - p398 [51-250]
　　KR - v65 - Ap 15 '97 - p640 [51-250]
　　SLJ - v43 - Ag '97 - p135+ [51-250]

Holsonback, Anita
*Monkey See, Monkey Do (Illus. by Leo
Timmers)*
　　CBRS - v26 - D '97 - p44 [51-250]
　　SLJ - v44 - Ja '98 - p87 [51-250]

Holtzman, Caren
No Fair! (Illus. by Joan Holub)
　　SLJ - v43 - N '97 - p83+ [51-250]

Holub, Joan
Boo Who
　　PW - v244 - O 6 '97 - p50 [1-50]

Pen Pals (Illus. by Joan Holub)
　　CCB-B - v51 - D '97 - p130 [51-250]
　　SLJ - v44 - F '98 - p85 [51-250]

Holub, Josef
The Robber and Me
　　BL - v94 - O 15 '97 - p406 [51-250]
　　BL - v94 - Mr 15 '98 - p1224 [1-50]
　　CBRS - v26 - N '97 - p35 [51-250]
　y　KR - v65 - O 15 '97 - p1582 [51-250]
　　NYTBR - v103 - F 1 '98 - p24 [51-250]
　　PW - v244 - O 27 '97 - p76 [51-250]
　　PW - v244 - N 3 '97 - p60 [51-250]
　　SLJ - v43 - D '97 - p26 [1-50]
　　SLJ - v43 - D '97 - p125 [51-250]
　y　VOYA - v20 - F '98 - p386 [251-500]

Holyoke, Nancy
*Oops! The Manners Guide for Girls
(Illus. by Debbie Tilley)*
　　PW - v244 - S 22 '97 - p82 [1-50]
　　SLJ - v44 - Mr '98 - p234 [51-250]

Holzwarth, Werner
*Vom Kleinen Maulwurf, Der Wissen
Wollte, Wer Ihm Auf Den Kopf
Gemacht Hat (Illus. by Wolf Erlbruch)*
　　Bkbird - v35 - Spr '97 - p49 [51-250]

Homan, Beulah
Growing Up (Illus. by Jane Stryker)
　　CBRA - '96 - p479 [51-250]

Honey, Elizabeth
45 and 47 Stella Street
　　TES - Ag 1 '97 - p25 [251-500]

Don't Pat the Wombat!
　　Sch Lib - v45 - N '97 - p191 [51-250]
　　TES - Ag 1 '97 - p25 [251-500]

Honeycutt, Natalie
Granville Jones: Commando
　　KR - v66 - F 15 '98 - p267+ [51-250]
　　PW - v245 - F 9 '98 - p96 [51-250]

Twilight in Grace Falls
　　CCB-B - v50 - Je '97 - p360+ [51-250]
　　HB - v73 - Jl '97 - p455+ [51-250]
　　HB Guide - v8 - Fall '97 - p302 [51-
　　250]
　y　SLJ - v43 - My '97 - p133+ [51-250]
　y　VOYA - v20 - Ag '97 - p185 [251-500]

Hong, L
The Empress and the Silkworm
ECEJ - v25 - Fall '97 - p47 [1-50]

Hoobler, Dorothy
Florence Robinson (Illus. by Robert Sauber)
HB Guide - v8 - Fall '97 - p302 [51-250]
SLJ - v43 - Ag '97 - p136 [51-250]

Julie Meyer (Illus. by Robert Gantt Steele)
BL - v93 - Je 1 '97 - p1703 [51-250]
HB Guide - v8 - Fall '97 - p302 [51-250]
SLJ - v43 - Ag '97 - p136 [51-250]

Priscilla Foster (Illus. by Robert Gantt Steele)
BL - v93 - Ag '97 - p1900+ [51-250]
HB Guide - v8 - Fall '97 - p302 [51-250]
SLJ - v43 - Ag '97 - p136 [51-250]

Sally Bradford (Illus. by Robert Gantt Steele)
BL - v93 - Je 1 '97 - p1703 [51-250]
HB Guide - v8 - Fall '97 - p302 [51-250]
SLJ - v43 - Ag '97 - p136 [51-250]

The Scandinavian American Family Album
AB - v100 - Jl 28 '97 - p151 [51-250]
HB Guide - v8 - Fall '97 - p322 [51-250]

Hood, Alison
The Wolf Watchers (Illus. by Andy DaVolls)
Sch Lib - v45 - Ag '97 - p152 [51-250]

Hood, Susan
Farmer Jed's Busy Year (Illus. by Alfred Ortiz)
PW - v244 - D 1 '97 - p55 [1-50]

Firefighter Sam Finds a Friend (Illus. by Alfred Ortiz)
PW - v244 - D 1 '97 - p55 [1-50]

If I Went on Safari (Illus. by Francese Rigol)
PW - v244 - D 1 '97 - p55 [1-50]

Hook, Brendan
Harry the Honkerzoid (Illus. by Jeff Hook)
Magpies - v12 - Jl '97 - p31 [51-250]

Hooks, William
Feed Me!
Ch BWatch - v7 - My '97 - p6 [1-50]

Peach Boy
Ch BWatch - v7 - My '97 - p6 [1-50]

Hooper, Caroline
Nursery Rhyme Songbook
Ch BWatch - v7 - O '97 - p4 [1-50]

Hooper, Mary
The Lost Treasure (Illus. by Lesley Bisseker)
Bks Keeps - My '97 - p22 [51-250]

Poppy's Secret (Illus. by Lesley Bisseker)
Bks Keeps - My '97 - p22 [51-250]

Hooper, Meredith
A Cow, a Bee, a Cookie, and Me (Illus. by Alison Bartlett)
BL - v93 - Je 1 '97 - p1718 [51-250]
CCB-B - v51 - S '97 - p13 [51-250]

Honey Biscuits (Illus. by Alison Bartlett)
TES - Je 13 '97 - pR7 [51-250]

The Pebble in My Pocket (Illus. by Chris Coady)
Bks Keeps - Jl '97 - p22 [51-250]
CM:CanRev - v4 - N 28 '97 - pONL [51-250]
New Sci - v155 - Ag 23 '97 - p44 [51-250]

Hooper, Nigel
Learn to Play Electric Guitar
Ch BWatch - v7 - O '97 - p4 [1-50]

Hoopes, Lyn Littlefield
Condor Magic (Illus. by Peter Stone)
KR - v65 - N 1 '97 - p1644 [51-250]
PW - v244 - N 17 '97 - p62 [51-250]

Hopcraft, Xan
How It Was with Dooms (Illus. by Xan Hopcraft)
>CBRS - v25 - My '97 - p115+ [51-250]
>CCB-B - v50 - Je '97 - p361 [51-250]
>HB Guide - v8 - Fall '97 - p353 [51-250]
>NH - v106 - D '97 - p9 [51-250]
>SLJ - v43 - Ap '97 - p126+ [51-250]

Hopkins, Lee Bennett
All God's Children (Illus. by Amanda Schaffer)
>PW - v245 - F 23 '98 - p66+ [51-250]
>SLJ - v44 - Mr '98 - p196 [51-250]

Marvelous Math (Illus. by Karen Barbour)
>CBRS - v26 - S '97 - p8 [1-50]
>CCB-B - v51 - S '97 - p13+ [51-250]
>Emerg Lib - v25 - Ja '98 - p56 [51-250]
>Par Ch - Awards '97 - p5 [51-250]
>PW - v244 - Jl 28 '97 - p76 [51-250]

Opening Days (Illus. by Scott Medlock)
>RT - v51 - O '97 - p138 [1-50]

Song and Dance (Illus. by Cheryl Munro Taylor)
>HB Guide - v8 - Fall '97 - p374 [1-50]
>Inst - v106 - Ap '97 - p25 [1-50]
>SLJ - v43 - Je '97 - p108 [51-250]

Weather (Illus. by Melanie W Hall)
>SB - v33 - O '97 - p218 [1-50]

Hopkins, Liz
Platform Maths 1-3
>TES - O 3 '97 - pR12 [251-500]

Hopkinson, Deborah
Birdie's Lighthouse (Illus. by Kimberly Bulcken Root)
>SLJ - v43 - Je '97 - p90+ [51-250]
>BL - v93 - Je 1 '97 - p1718+ [51-250]
>CCB-B - v51 - S '97 - p14 [51-250]
>Ch BWatch - v7 - My '97 - p3 [51-250]
>HB - v73 - Jl '97 - p443 [51-250]
>HB Guide - v8 - Fall '97 - p291 [51-250]
>Par Ch - Awards '97 - p4 [1-50]

Horenstein, Henry
Baseball in the Barrios (Illus. by Henry Horenstein)
>HB - v73 - Jl '97 - p475+ [51-250]
>HB Guide - v8 - Fall '97 - p370 [51-250]
>NYTBR - v102 - Je 8 '97 - p27 [1-50]
>SLJ - v43 - Je '97 - p138 [51-250]

Beisbol En Los Barrios (Illus. by Henry Horenstein)
>SLJ - v43 - Ag '97 - p180+ [51-250]

Horgan, Dorothy
Charlie's Eye
>Bks Keeps - My '97 - p23 [51-250]
>TES - N 7 '97 - p8* [51-250]

Horn, Sandra Ann
The Silkie (Illus. by Stephanie Hawken)
>Sch Lib - v45 - Ag '97 - p145 [51-250]
>TES - Je 20 '97 - p12* [501+]

Horne, Constance
Nykola and Granny
>Bkbird - v34 - Win '96 - p25+ [501+]

Trapped by Coal
>Bkbird - v34 - Win '96 - p25+ [501+]
>Can CL - v22 - Win '96 - p116+ [501+]

Horniman, Joanne
Billygoat Goes Wild (Illus. by Robert Roennfeldt)
>Magpies - v12 - Mr '97 - p28 [51-250]

Horowitz, Ruth
Mommy's Lap (Illus. by Henri Sorensen)
>ECEJ - v24 - Sum '97 - p251+ [51-250]

Horrocks, Anita
Breath of a Ghost
>CBRA - '96 - p479+ [51-250]

Horse Illustrated: The Magazine for Responsible Horse Owners
>p JOYS - v10 - Spr '97 - p263 [1-50]

Horsepower: Magazine for Young Horse Lovers

p   JOYS - v10 - Spr '97 - p263 [1-50]

Horsfall, Jacqueline
Play Lightly on the Earth
   Ch BWatch - v7 - N '97 - p5 [51-250]

Horvath, Betty
Sir Galahad, Mr. Longfellow, and Me
   KR - v66 - Mr 15 '98 - p404 [51-250]

Hough, Libby
If Somebody Lived Next Door (Illus. by Laura McGee Kvasnosky)
   BL - v93 - Je 1 '97 - p1719 [51-250]
   CBRS - v25 - Ag '97 - p159 [51-250]
   HB Guide - v8 - Fall '97 - p268 [51-250]
   KR - v65 - Je 1 '97 - p873 [51-250]
   SLJ - v43 - Jl '97 - p69 [51-250]

Houghton, Diane R
The Wishing Star
   Ch BWatch - v7 - D '97 - p6 [51-250]

Houk, Randy
Chessie, the Travelin' Man (Illus. by Paula Bartlett)
   SLJ - v43 - N '97 - p105+ [51-250]

Houston, Gloria
Littlejim's Dreams (Illus. by Thomas B Allen)
   HB Guide - v8 - Fall '97 - p302 [51-250]
   SLJ - v43 - Jl '97 - p94 [51-250]

Howard, Annabelle
The Great Wonder. Book and Audio Version
   SLJ - v43 - D '97 - p73 [51-250]

Howard, Arthur
When I Was Five (Illus. by Arthur Howard)
   RT - v51 - O '97 - p132 [1-50]

Howard, Elizabeth Fitzgerald
What's in Aunt Mary's Room? (Illus. by Cedric Lucas)
   RT - v51 - N '97 - p253 [51-250]

Howard, Ellen
The Big Seed (Illus. by Lillian Hoban)
   SB - v33 - O '97 - p218 [51-250]
The Log Cabin Quilt (Illus. by Ronald Himler)
   RT - v51 - D '97 - p331 [51-250]

Howard, John
Dinosaurs (Illus. by Christopher Santoro)
   ASBYP - v29 - Fall '96 - p48+ [501+]

Howard, Milly
The Case of the Dognapped Cat (Illus. by Bruce Day)
   BL - v94 - Ja 1 '98 - p812+ [51-250]

Howarth, Lesley
Fort Biscuit
   TES - Ap 18 '97 - p12* [51-250]

MapHead: The Return
y   CCB-B - v51 - Mr '98 - p246 [51-250]
   HB - v74 - Ja '98 - p74+ [51-250]
y   KR - v65 - O 15 '97 - p1583 [51-250]
   SLJ - v44 - Ja '98 - p112 [251-500]
y   VOYA - v21 - Ap '98 - p55+ [51-250]

The Pits
   HB Guide - v8 - Fall '97 - p302 [51-250]

Howe, James
Nighty-Nightmare (Illus. by Leslie Morrill)
   PW - v244 - Jl 21 '97 - p203 [1-50]
   PW - v244 - Ag 18 '97 - p95 [1-50]

Pinky and Rex (Moore). Audio Version
   SLJ - v44 - Ap '98 - p82 [51-250]

Pinky and Rex and the Mean Old Witch (Moore). Audio Version
   SLJ - v44 - Ap '98 - p82 [51-250]

Pinky and Rex and the New Neighbors (Illus. by Melissa Sweet)
   HB Guide - v8 - Fall '97 - p291 [51-250]

SLJ - v43 - Je '97 - p92 [51-250]

*Pinky and Rex and the School Play
(Illus. by Melissa Sweet)*
KR - v66 - Ja 15 '98 - p112 [51-250]

*Pinky and Rex and the Spelling Bee
(Moore). Audio Version*
SLJ - v44 - Ap '98 - p82 [51-250]

*Pinky and Rex Get Married (Moore).
Audio Version*
SLJ - v44 - Ap '98 - p82 [51-250]

*Pinky and Rex Go to Camp (Moore).
Audio Version*
SLJ - v44 - Ap '98 - p82 [51-250]

Howe, John
The Knight with the Lion
Magpies - v12 - My '97 - p34 [251-500]

Howker, Janni
The Nature of the Beast
TES - Ja 2 '98 - p22* [51-250]

*Walk with a Wolf (Illus. by Sarah
Fox-Davies)*
BL - v94 - Mr 15 '98 - p1248 [51-250]
PW - v245 - F 9 '98 - p95 [51-250]
SLJ - v44 - Ap '98 - p100 [51-250]
TES - N 7 '97 - p6* [251-500]

Howlin, Patricia
Autism: Preparing for Adulthood
TES - N 7 '97 - p8* [251-500]

Hoyt-Goldsmith, Diane
*Buffalo Days (Illus. by Lawrence
Migdale)*
BL - v94 - N 1 '97 - p467 [51-250]
KR - v65 - S 15 '97 - p1458 [51-250]
SLJ - v43 - D '97 - p26 [1-50]
SLJ - v43 - D '97 - p109 [51-250]

*Celebrating Hanukkah (Illus. by
Lawrence Migdale)*
Inst - v107 - N '97 - p14 [1-50]
RT - v51 - N '97 - p255 [51-250]

*Day of the Dead (Illus. by Lawrence
Migdale)*
ECEJ - v25 - Fall '97 - p47 [1-50]

*Lacrosse: The National Game of the
Iroquois (Illus. by Lawrence Migdale)*
KR - v66 - Ap 15 '98 - p581 [51-250]

*Migrant Worker (Illus. by Lawrence
Migdale)*
SE - v61 - Ap '97 - p6* [1-50]

*Potlatch: A Tsimshian Celebration
(Illus. by Lawrence Migdale)*
HB Guide - v8 - Fall '97 - p329 [51-
250]
SLJ - v43 - Je '97 - p138 [51-250]

Hru, Dakari
*Joshua's Masai Mask (Illus. by Anna
Rich)*
ECEJ - v25 - Fall '97 - p47 [1-50]

*The Magic Moonberry Jump Ropes
(Illus. by E B Lewis)*
RT - v51 - N '97 - p253 [51-250]

Hubbard, Kate
Help Yourself to Safety
SE - v61 - S '97 - p271 [1-50]

Hubbard, Patricia
*My Crayons Talk (Illus. by G Brian
Karas)*
Inst - v106 - Ap '97 - p26 [1-50]
RT - v51 - O '97 - p131 [1-50]

Huck, Charlotte S
*Toads and Diamonds (Illus. by Anita
Lobel)*
RT - v51 - S '97 - p54 [51-250]

Hucko, Bruce
A Rainbow at Night
HB Guide - v8 - Fall '97 - p364 [51-
250]

Huddleston, Ruth
Time for Bed (Illus. by Tony Linsell)
RT - v51 - O '97 - p131 [1-50]

Hudson, Jan
Sweetgrass
y   BL - v93 - Je 1 '97 - p1701 [1-50]
SLJ - v43 - S '97 - p131 [51-250]

Hudson, Wade
In Praise of Our Fathers and Our Mothers
y   HB Guide - v8 - Fall '97 - p373 [51-250]
     SLJ - v43 - Je '97 - p138 [51-250]

Huff, Ronald
Gangs in America
     BWatch - v18 - Ap '97 - p5 [1-50]

Hughes, Carol
Jack Black and the Ship of Thieves
     Sch Lib - v45 - N '97 - p191 [51-250]
     TES - N 7 '97 - p7* [51-250]
     TES - D 12 '97 - p40 [51-250]

Toots and the Upside-Down House
     BL - v94 - S 1 '97 - p125 [51-250]
     Books - v10 - S '96 - p24 [51-250]
     HB Guide - v8 - Fall '97 - p302 [51-250]
     PW - v244 - My 19 '97 - p76 [51-250]

Hughes, Frieda
The Tall Story (Illus. by Chris Riddell)
     Sch Lib - v45 - N '97 - p191 [51-250]

Hughes, Langston
Black Misery
     Afr Am R - v30 - Sum '96 - p328 [51-250]
     Am Vis - v12 - D '97 - p33 [1-50]

The Sweet and Sour Animal Book (Illus. by Harlem School of the Arts)
     AB - v100 - N 17 '97 - p1267+ [251-500]

Hughes, Monica
A Handful of Seeds (Illus. by Luis Garay)
     SE - v61 - Ap '97 - p6* [1-50]

Un Punado De Semillas (Illus. by Luis Garay)
     Ch BWatch - v7 - Jl '97 - p5 [1-50]

The Seven Magpies
     CBRA - '96 - p480 [51-250]
y   JAAL - v40 - My '97 - p676 [251-500]

Hughes, Shirley
Alfie and the Birthday Surprise (Illus. by Shirley Hughes)
     BL - v94 - Mr 1 '98 - p1141 [51-250]
     CCB-B - v51 - Mr '98 - p246+ [51-250]
     KR - v66 - F 15 '98 - p268 [51-250]
     PW - v245 - Mr 16 '98 - p67 [51-250]
     SLJ - v44 - Mr '98 - p180 [51-250]
     Spec - v279 - D 6 '97 - p43 [51-250]
     TES - N 7 '97 - p5* [51-250]

Alfie's Alphabet
     TES - D 5 '97 - p17* [1-50]

All about Alfie
     Ch BWatch - v8 - Ja '98 - p3 [1-50]
     PW - v244 - Ag 25 '97 - p74 [1-50]

Being Together (Illus. by Shirley Hughes)
     Obs - Jl 20 '97 - p18* [1-50]
     PW - v244 - Ag 4 '97 - p76+ [1-50]
     SLJ - v44 - F '98 - p85+ [1-50]

Enchantment in the Garden (Illus. by Shirley Hughes)
     CBRS - v25 - Je '97 - p127 [51-250]
     CCB-B - v50 - Jl '97 - p399 [51-250]
     Ch BWatch - v7 - My '97 - p2 [1-50]
     HB Guide - v8 - Fall '97 - p291 [51-250]
     SLJ - v43 - My '97 - p100 [51-250]

Playing (Illus. by Shirley Hughes)
     PW - v244 - Ag 4 '97 - p76+ [1-50]
     SLJ - v44 - F '98 - p85+ [1-50]

Tales of Trotter Street
     Ch BWatch - v7 - My '97 - p3 [1-50]
     ECEJ - v25 - Fall '97 - p41+ [51-250]
     HB Guide - v8 - Fall '97 - p269 [1-50]

Hughes, Ted
Iron Man (Hughes). Audio Version
     Bks Keeps - N '97 - p5 [51-250]

Shaggy and Spotty (Illus. by David Lucas)
     Books - v11 - O '97 - p21 [1-50]
     Obs - D 7 '97 - p17* [51-250]
     TES - N 7 '97 - p5* [51-250]

Hugo, Victor
The Hunchback of Notre Dame (Illus. by Bill Slavin)
     CBRA - '96 - p444 [51-250]

Hull, Robert
Stargazer
NS - v126 - D 5 '97 - p63 [51-250]

Hulpach, Vladimir
Ahaiyute and Cloud Eater (Illus. by Marek Zawadzki)
SE - v61 - Ap '97 - p5* [1-50]

The Human Machine
ASBYP - v29 - Sum '96 - p65+ [501+]

Humphrey, Paul
Weather
HB Guide - v8 - Fall '97 - p342 [51-250]
Sch Lib - v45 - Ag '97 - p150 [51-250]

Humphries, Tudor
Hiding (Illus. by Tudor Humphries)
BL - v94 - D 1 '97 - p641 [51-250]
CBRS - v26 - F '98 - p76 [51-250]
Ch BWatch - v7 - N '97 - p5 [1-50]
KR - v65 - Ag 1 '97 - p1222 [51-250]
Obs - Jl 20 '97 - p18* [51-250]
SLJ - v44 - Mr '98 - p180 [51-250]

The Hunchback of Notre Dame (Play a Sound)
Ch BWatch - v7 - Ap '97 - p2 [1-50]

Hundal, Nancy
I Heard My Mother Call My Name (Illus. by Laura Fernandez)
Can CL - v23 - Fall '97 - p67+ [501+]

November Boots (Illus. by Marilyn Mets)
Can CL - v23 - Fall '97 - p67+ [501+]

Snow Story (Illus. by Kasia Charko)
Quill & Q - v63 - O '97 - p39 [251-500]

The Hungry Pig
PW - v245 - F 9 '98 - p97 [1-50]

Hunter, Anne
Possum and the Peeper (Illus. by Anne Hunter)
KR - v66 - Mr 15 '98 - p404 [51-250]
PW - v245 - F 23 '98 - p76 [51-250]
SLJ - v44 - Mr '98 - p180 [51-250]

Hunter, Bernice Thurman
Amy's Promise
Can CL - v22 - Win '96 - p108+ [501+]
Emerg Lib - v25 - Ja '98 - p45 [51-250]

Hunter, Eirlys
The Robber and the Millionaire
Magpies - v12 - Mr '97 - p2* [1-50]

Hunter, Ryan Ann
Cross a Bridge (Illus. by Edward Miller)
KR - v66 - F 15 '98 - p268 [51-250]
SLJ - v44 - Mr '98 - p196 [51-250]

Hunter, Sally M
Four Seasons of Corn (Illus. by Joe Allen)
HB Guide - v8 - Fall '97 - p329 [51-250]

Hunter, Sara Hoagland
The Unbreakable Code (Illus. by Julia Miner)
ECEJ - v25 - Fall '97 - p47 [1-50]

Hunter, Shaun
Great African Americans in the Olympics
Ch BWatch - v7 - Je '97 - p4 [51-250]
HB Guide - v8 - Fall '97 - p370 [51-250]

Hurd, Thacher
Art Dog (Illus. by Thacher Hurd)
Inst - v106 - Ap '97 - p25 [51-250]
Inst - v106 - My '97 - p18+ [1-50]
RT - v51 - O '97 - p132 [1-50]

Zoom City (Illus. by Thacher Hurd)
KR - v66 - F 1 '98 - p197 [51-250]
PW - v245 - Ja 26 '98 - p93 [1-50]

Hurst, Mike
The History of Emigration from Scotland
TES - S 19 '97 - p16* [501+]

Hurwitz, Jane
Choosing a Career in Animal Care
SLJ - v43 - Ag '97 - p168 [51-250]

Hurwitz, Johanna
Ever-Clever Elisa (Illus. by Lillian Hoban)
> HB - v73 - S '97 - p572 [51-250]
> KR - v65 - Je 15 '97 - p951 [51-250]
> SLJ - v43 - N '97 - p84 [51-250]

Faraway Summer (Illus. by Mary Azarian)
> BL - v94 - Mr 1 '98 - p1134 [51-250]
> KR - v66 - Ap 15 '98 - p582 [51-250]

Spring Break (Illus. by Karen Dugan)
> HB Guide - v8 - Fall '97 - p302 [51-250]
> SLJ - v43 - My '97 - p100 [51-250]

Hush, Little Baby (Illus. by Shari Halpern)
> BL - v94 - O 15 '97 - p409 [51-250]
> KR - v65 - O 1 '97 - p1532 [51-250]
> PW - v244 - N 3 '97 - p83+ [51-250]
> SLJ - v44 - Ja '98 - p100+ [51-250]

Hussein, Ikram
Teenage Refugees from Somalia Speak Out
> SLJ - v43 - D '97 - p138 [51-250]

Huszar, Karen
Meet Matt and Roxy (Illus. by Susan Huszar)
> CBRA - '96 - p444+ [51-250]
> HB Guide - v8 - Fall '97 - p269 [51-250]

Hutchins, H J
The Prince of Tarn (Illus. by Ruth Ohi)
> BIC - v26 - O '97 - p34 [251-500]
> BL - v94 - F 15 '98 - p1011 [51-250]
> Quill & Q - v63 - Je '97 - p64 [251-500]
> SLJ - v44 - F '98 - p109 [51-250]

Shoot for the Moon, Robyn (Illus. by Yvonne Cathcart)
> CM:CanRev - v4 - O 31 '97 - pONL [251-500]
> Quill & Q - v63 - Jl '97 - p50 [51-250]

Yancy and Bear (Illus. by Ruth Ohi)
> CBRA - '96 - p445 [51-250]

Hutchins, Pat
Shrinking Mouse (Illus. by Pat Hutchins)
> Ch BWatch - v7 - My '97 - p2 [1-50]
> HB Guide - v8 - Fall '97 - p252 [51-250]
> SLJ - v43 - Ap '97 - p106 [51-250]

Three-Star Billy
> Bks Keeps - My '97 - p20 [51-250]

Titch and Daisy (Illus. by Pat Hutchins)
> Magpies - v12 - Mr '97 - p26 [51-250]

Hutchinson, J Gribbin
The Christmas Wish
> CBRS - v26 - N '97 - p35 [51-250]
> Ch BWatch - v7 - D '97 - p2 [1-50]
> KR - v65 - O 15 '97 - p1583 [51-250]
> PW - v244 - O 6 '97 - p57 [51-250]

The Hutchinson Treasury of Teddy Bear Tales
> Obs - D 7 '97 - p18* [1-50]

Huth, Holly Young
I'm in the Sky and I Can't Come Back (Illus. by Anna Pignataro)
> Magpies - v12 - Jl '97 - p24 [501+]

Hutton, Warwick
Theseus and the Minotaur (Illus. by Warwick Hutton)
> SLJ - v43 - Jl '97 - p35 [1-50]

Huynh, Quang Nhuong
Water Buffalo Days (Illus. by Jean Tseng)
> CCB-B - v51 - Ja '98 - p163 [51-250]
> HB - v74 - Ja '98 - p75 [51-250]
> KR - v65 - N 1 '97 - p1644 [51-250]
> NYTBR - v102 - N 23 '97 - p32 [1-50]
> PW - v244 - N 3 '97 - p85+ [51-250]
> SLJ - v44 - F '98 - p100 [51-250]

Hwang, Jean
Eye Spy a Panda!
> Ch BWatch - v7 - S '97 - p4 [1-50]

Eye Spy a Puppy!
> Ch BWatch - v7 - S '97 - p4 [1-50]

Hyde, Margaret O
The Disease Book (Illus. by Bari Weissman)
> BL - v94 - S 15 '97 - p228 [51-250]
> SLJ - v43 - N '97 - p128 [51-250]

Know about Smoking. 3rd Ed.
> ASBYP - v29 - Sum '96 - p19+ [501+]

Hyppolite, Joanne
Ola Shakes It Up (Illus. by Warren Chang)
> BL - v94 - F 15 '98 - p1011+ [51-250]
> HB - v74 - Mr '98 - p221+ [51-250]
> KR - v65 - D 1 '97 - p1776 [51-250]
> PW - v245 - Ja 5 '98 - p68 [51-250]
> SLJ - v44 - F '98 - p109 [51-250]

I

Ibbotson, Eva
The Secret of Platform 13 (Illus. by Sue Porter)

    BL - v94 - F 15 '98 - p1011 [51-250]
    BW - v28 - Mr 1 '98 - p11 [51-250]
    KR - v66 - Ja 1 '98 - p57 [51-250]
    PW - v245 - F 23 '98 - p77 [51-250]
    SLJ - v44 - Mr '98 - p214 [51-250]

Iguchi, Brian
The Young Snowboarder

    SLJ - v44 - F '98 - p118 [51-250]

Igus, Toyomi
I See the Rhythm (Illus. by Michele Wood)

    BL - v94 - F 15 '98 - p1003 [51-250]
    KR - v66 - Ap 15 '98 - p582 [51-250]
    PW - v245 - Mr 23 '98 - p100 [251-500]

Ikram, Salima
Egyptology (Illus. by Riham El Sherbini)

    KR - v66 - Ap 15 '98 - p582 [51-250]

I'm Going to the Doctor (Illus. by Maxie Chambliss)

    BL - v94 - D 15 '97 - p700 [1-50]

Impey, Rose
Potbelly and the Haunted House (Illus. by Keith Brunton)

    TES - Jl 11 '97 - p14* [51-250]

Potbelly in Love (Illus. by Keith Brunton)

    TES - Jl 11 '97 - p14* [51-250]

Potbelly Needs a Job (Illus. by Keith Brunton)

    TES - Jl 11 '97 - p14* [51-250]

Potbelly's Lost His Bike (Illus. by Keith Brunton)

    TES - Jl 11 '97 - p14* [51-250]

In Daddy's Arms I Am Tall (Illus. by Javaka Steptoe)

    Am Vis - v12 - D '97 - p34 [1-50]
    BL - v94 - F 15 '98 - p1007 [51-250]
    BL - v94 - Mr 15 '98 - p1224 [1-50]
    HB - v74 - Ja '98 - p87 [51-250]
    KR - v65 - N 15 '97 - p1713 [51-250]
    PW - v244 - O 27 '97 - p74+ [51-250]
    SLJ - v44 - F '98 - p118 [51-250]

Inches, Alison
The Thanksgiving Monster (Illus. by Richard Brown)

    PW - v244 - O 6 '97 - p52 [1-50]

Ingman, Bruce
Lost Property (Illus. by Bruce Ingman)

    KR - v66 - F 15 '98 - p268 [51-250]
    PW - v245 - Mr 16 '98 - p63 [51-250]
    SLJ - v44 - Ap '98 - p100 [51-250]

Ingram, Anne
Fantastic Plastic (Illus. by Mark David)

    Magpies - v12 - Jl '97 - p43 [51-250]

Inkpen, Mick
Bear (Illus. by Mick Inkpen)

    NS - v126 - D 5 '97 - p62 [1-50]

Everyone Hide from Wibbly Pig (Illus. by Mick Inkpen)

    Bks Keeps - N '97 - p19 [51-250]
    Books - v11 - Je '97 - p21 [51-250]
    Magpies - v12 - S '97 - p28+ [51-250]
    Par - v72 - D '97 - p202 [1-50]
    Sch Lib - v45 - N '97 - p186 [51-250]
    SLJ - v43 - D '97 - p93+ [51-250]

Kipper's Snowy Day (French). Book and Audio Version

    TES - D 19 '97 - p23 [51-250]

Nothing (Illus. by Mick Inkpen)

    BL - v94 - Mr 15 '98 - p1248+ [51-250]
    CCB-B - v51 - Mr '98 - p247 [51-250]
    KR - v66 - Ja 15 '98 - p112 [51-250]
    PW - v245 - Ja 19 '98 - p376+ [51-250]

Innocenti, Roberto

Rose Blanche

    Emerg Lib - v24 - My '97 - p9+ [1-50]
y   Emerg Lib - v24 - My '97 - p10 [1-50]
y   JAAL - v40 - My '97 - p670 [51-250]

Inserra, Rose

The Kalahari

    SLJ - v43 - N '97 - p127 [51-250]

Interactive Science Encyclopedia on CD-ROM. Electronic Media Version

r   LJ - v123 - Ja '98 - p157+ [51-250]

Intrater, Roberta Grobel

Peek-a-Boo! (Illus. by Roberta Grobel Intrater)

    PW - v244 - O 27 '97 - p78 [1-50]
    SLJ - v44 - F '98 - p86 [51-250]

Smile! (Illus. by Roberta Grobel Intrater)

    PW - v244 - O 27 '97 - p78 [1-50]
    SLJ - v44 - F '98 - p86 [51-250]

Ireland, Karen

Wonderful Nature, Wonderful You (Illus. by Christopher Canyon)

    CLW - v68 - S '97 - p66 [51-250]

Ironside, Virginia

The Huge Bag of Worries (Illus. by Frank Rodgers)

    Bks Keeps - N '97 - p16 [51-250]

Irvine, Joan

How to Make Holiday Pop-Ups

    SLMQ - v25 - Spr '97 - p185 [1-50]

Isaac, John

Rwanda: Fierce Clashes in Central Africa

    SLJ - v43 - Je '97 - p107 [51-250]
    SLMQ - v25 - Win '97 - p114 [1-50]

Isaacs, Anne

Swamp Angel (Illus. by Paul O Zelinsky)

    SLJ - v43 - N '97 - p41 [1-50]

Treehouse Tales (Illus. by Lloyd Bloom)

    BL - v94 - S 15 '97 - p235 [51-250]
    CBRS - v25 - Ag '97 - p164 [1-50]
    CCB-B - v51 - O '97 - p54 [51-250]
    HB - v73 - S '97 - p572+ [51-250]
    KR - v65 - Je 1 '97 - p874 [51-250]
    NYTBR - v102 - Je 22 '97 - p22 [1-50]
    PW - v244 - My 26 '97 - p86 [51-250]
    SLJ - v43 - Jl '97 - p69 [51-250]

Isaacson, Michael

My School Is Cool (Illus. by Damon Taylor)

    Ch BWatch - v7 - D '97 - p2 [51-250]

Isaacson, Philip M

A Short Walk around the Pyramids and through the World of Art

    SLJ - v43 - Jl '97 - p35 [1-50]

Isadora, Rachel

At the Crossroads (Illus. by Rachel Isadora)

    BL - v93 - Je 1 '97 - p1724 [1-50]
    ECEJ - v25 - Fall '97 - p47 [1-50]
    JOYS - v11 - Win '98 - p141 [51-250]

Isadora Dances (Illus. by Rachel Isadora)

    BL - v94 - Mr 15 '98 - p1246 [51-250]
    BW - v28 - Mr 1 '98 - p11 [51-250]

KR - v66 - Ja 15 '98 - p113 [51-250]
SLJ - v44 - Mr '98 - p196 [51-250]

Lili Backstage (Illus. by Rachel Isadora)

Ch BWatch - v7 - My '97 - p4 [51-250]
HB - v73 - Jl '97 - p443 [51-250]
HB Guide - v8 - Fall '97 - p269 [51-250]
SLJ - v43 - Je '97 - p92 [51-250]

The Little Mermaid (Illus. by Rachel Isadora)

KR - v66 - Ap 15 '98 - p582 [51-250]

Max

BW - v27 - D 7 '97 - p20 [1-50]

A South African Night (Illus. by Rachel Isadora)

BL - v94 - F 15 '98 - p1019+ [51-250]
CCB-B - v51 - Ap '98 - p282+ [51-250]
KR - v66 - Ap 1 '98 - p496 [51-250]
PW - v245 - Mr 9 '98 - p68 [51-250]

Young Mozart (Illus. by Rachel Isadora)

CBRS - v25 - Je '97 - p127 [51-250]
CCB-B - v51 - S '97 - p14 [51-250]
HB Guide - v8 - Fall '97 - p365 [51-250]
NYTBR - v102 - Jl 20 '97 - p22 [1-50]
SLJ - v43 - Jl '97 - p84 [51-250]

Isau, Ralf

Die Traume Von Jonathan Jabbok (Illus. by Claudia Seeger)

Bkbird - v35 - Spr '97 - p49 [51-250]

Isherwood, Shirley

The Band over the Hill (Illus. by Reg Cartwright)

KR - v65 - N 1 '97 - p1645 [51-250]
SLJ - v44 - Ja '98 - p87 [251-500]
TES - My 30 '97 - p8* [501+]

Israel, Fred L

The Presidents. Vols. 1-8

r   BL - v93 - Ag '97 - p1930 [501+]
yr SLJ - v43 - Ag '97 - p186 [51-250]

Ito, Tom

Abraham Lincoln

y   Ch BWatch - v7 - Jl '97 - p7 [51-250]

y   HB Guide - v8 - Fall '97 - p381 [51-250]
SLJ - v43 - My '97 - p146 [51-250]

Izcoa, Carmen Rivera

Mediopollito (Illus. by Nivea Ortiz Montanez)

SLJ - v43 - N '97 - p136 [51-250]

J

J. Paul Getty Museum
A Is for Artist
> BL - v94 - O 15 '97 - p407 [51-250]
> TES - D 5 '97 - p18* [51-250]

Jackson, Alison
I Know an Old Lady Who Swallowed a Pie (Illus. by Judith Byron Schachner)
> BL - v94 - S 1 '97 - p139 [51-250]
> CBRS - v26 - F '98 - p76 [51-250]
> CCB-B - v51 - N '97 - p87 [51-250]
> NYTBR - v102 - N 16 '97 - p56 [501+]
> PW - v244 - O 6 '97 - p52 [51-250]
> SLJ - v43 - N '97 - p84 [51-250]

Jackson, Chris
Edmund for Short (Illus. by Chris Jackson)
> Quill & Q - v64 - F '98 - p46 [251-500]

Jackson, Dave
The Drummer Boy's Battle (Illus. by Julian Jackson)
> SLJ - v43 - Jl '97 - p94 [51-250]

Jackson, Donna M
The Bone Detectives (Illus. by Charlie Fellenbaum)
> RT - v51 - N '97 - p252 [51-250]
> SE - v61 - Ap '97 - p4* [51-250]

Jackson, Ellen
The Book of Slime (Illus. by Jan Davey Ellis)
> Am Sci - v85 - N '97 - p558 [51-250]
> HB Guide - v8 - Fall '97 - p355 [51-250]

> SB - v33 - Ag '97 - p186 [1-50]
> SLJ - v43 - Je '97 - p108 [51-250]

Cinder Edna (Illus. by Kevin O'Malley)
> Inst - v107 - Ag '97 - p23 [1-50]

Here Come the Brides (Illus. by Carol Heyer)
> KR - v66 - Ap 1 '98 - p496 [51-250]
> SLJ - v44 - Ap '98 - p118 [51-250]

Jackson, Jean
Thorndike and Nelson (Illus. by Vera Rosenberry)
> BL - v94 - O 1 '97 - p336 [51-250]
> CBRS - v26 - S '97 - p3 [1-50]
> PW - v244 - Je 30 '97 - p75 [51-250]
> SLJ - v43 - S '97 - p183+ [51-250]

Jackson, Nancy, 1951-
Photographers: History and Culture through the Camera
> SLJ - v43 - Jl '97 - p106 [51-250]

Jackson, Shelley
The Old Woman and the Wave (Illus. by Shelley Jackson)
> CCB-B - v51 - Mr '98 - p247 [51-250]
> KR - v66 - Ja 15 '98 - p113 [51-250]
> PW - v245 - Ja 19 '98 - p377 [51-250]
> SLJ - v44 - Mr '98 - p180 [51-250]

Jackson, Tandi
Racing Clouds (Illus. by Nicki Wise)
> Magpies - v12 - Mr '97 - p7* [51-250]

Jacobs, Francine
Follow That Trash!
>Ch BWatch - v7 - S '97 - p4 [1-50]

The Tainos: The People Who Welcomed Columbus
>JOYS - v10 - Sum '97 - p428 [1-50]

Jacobs, Paul Samuel
James Printer
>CBRS - v25 - Je '97 - p130 [51-250]
>Ch BWatch - v7 - O '97 - p3 [51-250]
>HB Guide - v8 - Fall '97 - p303 [51-250]
>y SLJ - v43 - Je '97 - p120 [51-250]

Jacques, Brian
The Long Patrol
>BL - v94 - D 15 '97 - p694 [51-250]
>Books - v11 - Ag '97 - p15 [51-250]
>CCB-B - v51 - Ap '98 - p283 [51-250]
>HB - v74 - Mr '98 - p222 [251-500]
>y KR - v65 - D 15 '97 - p1835 [51-250]
>y PW - v244 - D 1 '97 - p54 [51-250]
>y SLJ - v44 - Ja '98 - p112 [251-500]
>TES - Ag 8 '97 - p23 [251-500]
>TES - N 7 '97 - p7* [51-250]

Pearls of Lutra (Illus. by Allan Curless)
>BL - v94 - N 1 '97 - p475 [1-50]
>Ch BWatch - v7 - Ap '97 - p4 [1-50]
>y HB Guide - v8 - Fall '97 - p314 [51-250]
>Learning - v26 - Ag '97 - p26 [51-250]
>y VOYA - v20 - Je '97 - p118 [251-500]

Redwall
>NYTBR - v102 - N 16 '97 - p26 [1-50]

Redwall (Jacques). Audio Version
>BL - v94 - F 15 '98 - p1026+ [51-250]
>y Kliatt - v32 - Mr '98 - p51 [51-250]
>SLJ - v44 - Ap '98 - p39 [1-50]

Jafa, Manorama
Gandhi: The Man of Peace (Illus. by Deepak Harichandan)
>Bkbird - v35 - Sum '97 - p57+ [51-250]

Jaffe, Nina
The Mysterious Visitor (Illus. by Elivia Savadier)
>CCB-B - v50 - Je '97 - p361+ [51-250]
>SLJ - v43 - Je '97 - p108 [51-250]

Older Brother, Younger Brother (Illus. by Wenhai Ma)
>PW - v244 - Je 23 '97 - p93 [1-50]

A Voice for the People
>y BL - v94 - N 1 '97 - p459 [51-250]
>y CCB-B - v51 - S '97 - p14+ [51-250]
>HB - v73 - N '97 - p697 [51-250]
>NYTBR - v102 - Je 22 '97 - p22 [51-250]
>y SLJ - v43 - D '97 - p138+ [51-250]

Jaffrey, Madhur
Robi Dobi (Illus. by Amanda Hall)
>Ch BWatch - v7 - O '97 - p7 [1-50]
>HB - v73 - Jl '97 - p456+ [51-250]
>KR - v65 - Ag 1 '97 - p1222 [51-250]
>NYTBR - v103 - Ja 4 '98 - p20 [1-50]
>Par Ch - Awards '97 - p4 [1-50]
>PW - v244 - Je 16 '97 - p59 [51-250]
>SLJ - v43 - S '97 - p184 [51-250]
>TES - My 16 '97 - p14* [501+]
>TES - N 7 '97 - p8* [51-250]

Jahn-Clough, Lisa
1 2 3 Yippie (Illus. by Lisa Jahn-Clough)
>BL - v94 - Mr 15 '98 - p1249 [51-250]
>KR - v66 - Mr 15 '98 - p405 [51-250]
>PW - v245 - Mr 23 '98 - p102 [1-50]

ABC Yummy (Illus. by Lisa Jahn-Clough)
>HB Guide - v8 - Fall '97 - p269 [51-250]
>SLJ - v43 - Je '97 - p92+ [51-250]

Jam, Teddy
The Charlotte Stories (Illus. by Harvey Chan)
>Can CL - v23 - Fall '97 - p69+ [501+]

The Fishing Summer (Illus. by Ange Zhang)
>ABR - v19 - N '97 - p12+ [501+]
>BL - v94 - S 15 '97 - p242 [51-250]
>Ch Bk News - v20 - Sum '97 - p27 [51-250]
>CM:CanRev - v4 - O 3 '97 - pONL [251-500]
>Quill & Q - v63 - Jl '97 - p50 [251-500]
>SLJ - v44 - F '98 - p86 [51-250]

Jacob's Best Sisters (Illus. by Joanne Fitzgerald)

    Can CL - v23 - Sum '97 - p59+ [501+]
    CBRA - '96 - p445 [51-250]
    CBRS - v25 - My '97 - p111 [51-250]
    Ch BWatch - v7 - Je '97 - p7 [1-50]
    SLJ - v43 - Ap '97 - p106 [51-250]

James, Ann
Making Pictures

    Magpies - v12 - S '97 - p7 [51-250]

James, Betsy
Flashlight (Illus. by Stacey Schuett)

    BL - v94 - D 15 '97 - p703 [51-250]
    KR - v65 - N 15 '97 - p1708 [51-250]
    PW - v244 - N 17 '97 - p61 [51-250]
    SLJ - v44 - Ja '98 - p87 [51-250]

James, Brant
Mike Piazza

    Ch BWatch - v7 - Je '97 - p2 [1-50]
    HB Guide - v8 - Fall '97 - p368 [51-250]

James, JoAnne
Three Quest Plays

    CBRA - '96 - p498 [51-250]

James, John
How We Know about the Romans

    BL - v94 - D 15 '97 - p692 [51-250]
    Class Out - v75 - Fall '97 - p28 [51-250]

James, Louise
The Vikings

    BL - v94 - D 15 '97 - p692 [51-250]

James, Simon
Leon and Bob (Illus. by Simon James)

    CBRS - v25 - Jl '97 - p148 [1-50]
    HB Guide - v8 - Fall '97 - p269 [51-250]
    NYTBR - v102 - N 9 '97 - p24 [1-50]
    NYTBR - v102 - D 7 '97 - p80 [1-50]
    NYTLa - v147 - D 4 '97 - pE8 [1-50]
    Sch Lib - v45 - Ag '97 - p131 [51-250]
    SLJ - v43 - Ap '97 - p106+ [51-250]

James, Vincent
My Favourite Monsters

    Books - v10 - S '96 - p24 [51-250]

Jameson, Neil
Sports and Games

    HB Guide - v8 - Fall '97 - p372 [51-250]

Sports and Games (Illus. by Christer Eriksson)

    Bks Keeps - Jl '97 - p26 [51-250]
  y Magpies - v12 - Mr '97 - p44 [51-250]
  y Sch Lib - v45 - Ag '97 - p163 [51-250]

Jameson, W C
Buried Treasures of New England

    LJ - v122 - Je 1 '97 - p126 [51-250]

Buried Treasures of the Atlantic Coast

    LJ - v122 - Je 1 '97 - p126 [51-250]

Buried Treasures of the Great Plains

    LJ - v122 - Je 1 '97 - p126 [51-250]
    SLJ - v43 - Jl '97 - p106 [51-250]

Jamieson, Marshall
Beginnings: From the First Nations to the Great Migration

    CBRA - '96 - p506+ [51-250]

Jane, Pamela
The Big Monkey Mix-Up (Illus. by Cathy Bobak)

    SLJ - v44 - Ja '98 - p87+ [251-500]

Halloween Hide-and-Seek (Illus. by Julie Durrell)

    PW - v244 - O 6 '97 - p50 [1-50]
    SLJ - v43 - D '97 - p94 [51-250]

Noelle of the Nutcracker (Illus. by Jan Brett)

    PW - v244 - O 6 '97 - p59 [1-50]

Janeczko, Paul B
Home on the Range (Illus. by Bernie Fuchs)

    BL - v94 - O 15 '97 - p400 [51-250]
    CCB-B - v51 - N '97 - p87+ [51-250]
    KR - v65 - S 1 '97 - p1390 [51-250]
    PW - v244 - O 6 '97 - p85 [1-50]
    SLJ - v43 - D '97 - p139 [51-250]

That Sweet Diamond (Illus. by Carole Katchen)
> KR - v66 - Ja 15 '98 - p113 [51-250]
> PW - v245 - Mr 16 '98 - p64 [51-250]
> SLJ - v44 - Ap '98 - p118 [51-250]

Jango-Cohen, Judith
The School Bus Adventure
> PW - v244 - D 1 '97 - p55 [1-50]

Janisch, Heinz
Noah's Ark (Illus. by Lisbeth Zwerger)
> BL - v94 - O 1 '97 - p323 [51-250]
> BL - v94 - Mr 15 '98 - p1224 [1-50]
> Bloom Rev - v17 - N '97 - p32 [51-250]
> CCB-B - v51 - D '97 - p115+ [501+]
> HB - v74 - Mr '98 - p213+ [51-250]
> KR - v65 - S 1 '97 - p1390 [51-250]
> NW - v130 - D 1 '97 - p77 [1-50]
> NYTBR - v102 - N 9 '97 - p24 [1-50]
> SLJ - v43 - N '97 - p84 [51-250]
> TES - D 5 '97 - p18* [51-250]

Janover, Caroline
Zipper, the Kid with ADHD (Illus. by Rick Powell)
> SLJ - v44 - Mr '98 - p214 [51-250]

Janovitz, Marilyn
Bowl Patrol
> RT - v51 - O '97 - p148 [51-250]

Cuidado, Pajarito!
> BL - v94 - D 15 '97 - p707 [51-250]

What Could Be Keeping Santa?
> BL - v94 - O 1 '97 - p336 [51-250]
> CBRS - v26 - N '97 - p27 [1-50]
> PW - v244 - O 6 '97 - p54 [51-250]

Janulewicz, Mike
Yikes! Your Body, Up Close!
> BL - v94 - S 1 '97 - p114 [51-250]
> y   BL - v94 - Mr 15 '98 - p1225 [1-50]
> CBRS - v26 - O '97 - p20 [51-250]
> CCB-B - v51 - S '97 - p15 [51-250]
> KR - v65 - Jl 1 '97 - p1030 [51-250]
> PW - v244 - Jl 21 '97 - p202+ [51-250]
> Sch Lib - v45 - N '97 - p204+ [51-250]
> SLJ - v43 - D '97 - p109+ [51-250]
> y   VOYA - v21 - Ap '98 - p39 [1-50]

Jarman, Julia
Little Mouse Grandma (Illus. by Alex De Wolf)
> TES - Jl 11 '97 - p14* [51-250]
> Bks Keeps - S '97 - p23 [51-250]

More Jessame Stories (Illus. by Duncan Smith)
> Sch Lib - v45 - N '97 - p192 [51-250]

Jarrett, Clare
Catherine and the Lion
> HB Guide - v8 - Fall '97 - p269 [51-250]

Jarvis, Robin
The Deptford Histories
> Books - v10 - S '96 - p25 [51-250]

Jefferis, David
Aircraft
> r   TES - My 2 '97 - pR2 [501+]

Aircraft (DK)
> r   Ch BWatch - v7 - Je '97 - p4 [1-50]

Jeng, Trio Jan
Sing'n Learn Chinese. Book and Audio Version
> Ch BWatch - v7 - S '97 - p6+ [51-250]

Jenike, David
A Walk through a Rain Forest
> BL - v94 - D 1 '97 - p629 [1-50]

Jenkins, Martin
Chameleons Are Cool (Illus. by Sue Shields)
> PW - v245 - Ja 26 '98 - p91 [51-250]

Fly Traps! (Illus. by David Parkins)
> RT - v51 - O '97 - p137 [1-50]

Jenkins, Priscilla Belz
A Safe Home for Manatees (Illus. by Martin Classen)
> BL - v94 - D 1 '97 - p633 [51-250]

Jenkins, Sandy
My Book about Me
> Ch BWatch - v7 - Jl '97 - p8 [1-50]

Jenkins, Steve
Big and Little (Illus. by Steve Jenkins)
  Magpies - v12 - My '97 - p28 [51-250]

Biggest, Strongest, Fastest
  LA - v73 - N '96 - p527+ [51-250]

What Do You Do When Something Wants to Eat You? (Illus. by Steve Jenkins)
  BL - v94 - D 1 '97 - p633 [51-250]
  BL - v94 - Ja 1 '98 - p735 [1-50]
  CCB-B - v51 - D '97 - p131 [51-250]
  Inst - v107 - N '97 - p18 [1-50]
  KR - v65 - S 15 '97 - p1458 [51-250]
  PW - v244 - N 10 '97 - p73 [51-250]
  SLJ - v43 - N '97 - p109 [51-250]

Jennings, Dana Andrew
Me, Dad and Number 6 (Illus. by Goro Sasaki)
  HB Guide - v8 - Fall '97 - p269 [51-250]
  KR - v65 - Ap 15 '97 - p640+ [51-250]
  SLJ - v43 - Ap '97 - p108 [51-250]

Jennings, Elizabeth
A Spell of Words
  Bks Keeps - My '97 - p26 [51-250]

Jennings, Linda
Easy Peasy! (Illus. by Tanya Linch)
  HB Guide - v8 - Fall '97 - p252 [51-250]
  SLJ - v43 - My '97 - p100+ [51-250]

Kitty's Fishy Dinner (Illus. by Tanya Linch)
  Bks Keeps - My '97 - p20 [51-250]

Penny and Pup (Illus. by Jane Chapman)
  CBRS - v26 - D '97 - p39 [1-50]
  Sch Lib - v45 - N '97 - p186 [51-250]

Jennings, Paul
Unreal! (Mitchley). Audio Version
  BL - v93 - Je 1 '97 - p1733 [51-250]

Jennings, Terry
101 Amazing Optical Illusions (Illus. by Alex Pang)
  BL - v94 - S 15 '97 - p228 [51-250]
  SLJ - v43 - Ag '97 - p168 [51-250]

Jenoff, Marvyne
The Emperor's Body (Illus. by Miles Lowry)
  CBRA - '96 - p186+ [51-250]

Jensen, Nancy
Make It a Merry Christmas! (Illus. by Dorothy Stott)
  PW - v244 - O 6 '97 - p57 [1-50]

Jeram, Anita
Contrary Mary
  Bks Keeps - Jl '97 - p21 [51-250]

I Don't Care! Said the Bear
  Bks Keeps - Jl '97 - p21 [51-250]

Jessup, Harley
What's Alice Up To? (Illus. by Harley Jessup)
  BL - v94 - S 15 '97 - p242 [51-250]
  CBRS - v26 - F '98 - p76 [1-50]
  KR - v65 - O 1 '97 - p1533 [51-250]
  PW - v244 - N 3 '97 - p83 [51-250]

Jewell, Nancy
Silly Times with Two Silly Trolls (Illus. by Lisa Thiesing)
  RT - v51 - O '97 - p136 [1-50]

Jewett, Sarah Orne
A White Heron (Illus. by Wendy Anderson Halperin)
  Ch BWatch - v7 - N '97 - p3+ [1-50]

Jiang, Ji-Li
Red Scarf Girl
  y   BL - v94 - O 1 '97 - p331 [51-250]
  y   BL - v94 - Ja 1 '98 - p733 [51-250]
  y   BL - v94 - Mr 15 '98 - p1211 [1-50]
      BL - v94 - Mr 15 '98 - p1224 [1-50]
      CBRS - v26 - Win '98 - p70 [51-250]
      Ch BWatch - v7 - D '97 - p3 [1-50]
      HB - v74 - Ja '98 - p76 [51-250]
  y   KR - v65 - S 1 '97 - p1391 [51-250]
      PW - v244 - Jl 28 '97 - p75+ [51-250]
  y   PW - v244 - N 3 '97 - p60 [51-250]
      SLJ - v43 - D '97 - p139 [51-250]
  y   VOYA - v20 - F '98 - p365 [51-250]
  y   VOYA - v21 - Ap '98 - p37 [1-50]

Jimenez, Francisco
The Circuit: Stories from the Life of a Migrant Child
> BL - v94 - D 1 '97 - p619 [51-250]
> BL - v94 - Ja 1 '98 - p734 [1-50]
> y   Kliatt - v32 - Mr '98 - p24 [51-250]

Jimenez, Juan Ramon
Platero Y Yo (Illus. by Antonio Frasconi)
> RT - v51 - F '98 - p429 [51-250]

Jocelyn, Marthe
The Invisible Day (Illus. by Abby Carter)
> BL - v94 - Ja 1 '98 - p813 [51-250]
> CBRS - v26 - Ja '98 - p56 [1-50]
> CM:CanRev - v4 - Mr 27 '98 - pONL [251-500]
> Learning - v26 - N '97 - p29 [51-250]
> PW - v244 - O 27 '97 - p76 [51-250]
> Quill & Q - v64 - Ja '98 - p38 [51-250]
> SLJ - v44 - Mr '98 - p180+ [51-250]

Joerg, Donna
When Dawn Stole the Dark (Illus. by Judith Ann Benedict)
> PW - v244 - Jl 28 '97 - p74 [51-250]
> SLJ - v44 - Ja '98 - p88 [51-250]

Johansen, Hanna
Dinosaur with an Attitude
> Ch BWatch - v7 - S '97 - p5 [51-250]

Johnson, Allen, Jr.
A Breeze in the Willows (Illus. by Roger Mitchell)
> HB Guide - v8 - Fall '97 - p376 [51-250]

Johnson, Angela
Daddy Calls Me Man (Illus. by Rhonda Mitchell)
> BL - v94 - O 15 '97 - p415 [51-250]
> KR - v65 - Jl 15 '97 - p1112 [51-250]

The Rolling Store (Illus. by Peter Catalanotto)
> HB Guide - v8 - Fall '97 - p269 [51-250]
> SLJ - v43 - Ap '97 - p108 [51-250]

Shoes Like Miss Alice's (Illus. by Ken Page)
> ECEJ - v25 - Fall '97 - p47 [1-50]

Songs of Faith
> BL - v94 - F 15 '98 - p1008 [51-250]
> HB - v74 - Mr '98 - p222+ [251-500]
> y   Kliatt - v32 - Mr '98 - p5 [51-250]
> KR - v65 - D 15 '97 - p1835 [51-250]
> PW - v245 - Ja 12 '98 - p60 [51-250]
> SLJ - v44 - Mr '98 - p214 [51-250]

When I Am Old with You (Illus. by David Soman)
> ECEJ - v25 - Fall '97 - p47 [1-50]

Johnson, Anne
A Student's Guide to African American Genealogy
> Ch BWatch - v7 - Je '97 - p8 [51-250]

Johnson, Arden
The Lost Tooth Club (Illus. by Arden Johnson)
> KR - v66 - Mr 1 '98 - p340 [51-250]
> PW - v245 - Mr 23 '98 - p99 [51-250]

Johnson, Crockett
Harold and the Purple Crayon (Illus. by Crockett Johnson)
> NYTBR - v102 - N 16 '97 - p26 [1-50]

Johnson, David, 1951-
The Bremen Town Musicians (Illus. by David Johnson)
> SLJ - v43 - D '97 - p108+ [51-250]

Oh, That Nuzzle! (Illus. by Tom Brannon)
> SLJ - v44 - Ja '98 - p88 [51-250]

Johnson, David A
Old Mother Hubbard (Illus. by David A Johnson)
> HB - v74 - Mr '98 - p229 [51-250]
> KR - v66 - Ja 15 '98 - p113 [51-250]
> PW - v245 - Mr 23 '98 - p97 [51-250]
> SLJ - v44 - Mr '98 - p196 [51-250]

Johnson, Debra A
I Dreamed I Was a Koala (Illus. by Stephanie Kranz)
> SB - v33 - O '97 - p218 [51-250]

I Dreamed I Was a Toucan (Illus. by Stephanie Kranz)
SB - v33 - O '97 - p218 [51-250]

Johnson, Diana F
Princesa and Friskie... (Illus. by Ernesto Lopez)
PW - v244 - D 15 '97 - p57+ [51-250]

Johnson, Dinah
All around Town (Illus. by Richard Samuel Roberts)
BL - v94 - F 15 '98 - p1014 [51-250]
CCB-B - v51 - Ap '98 - p283+ [51-250]
HB - v74 - Mr '98 - p235+ [251-500]
KR - v66 - Ja 15 '98 - p114 [51-250]
PW - v245 - Ja 12 '98 - p60 [51-250]
SLJ - v44 - Mr '98 - p196 [51-250]

Johnson, Dolores
The Children's Book of Kwanzaa
PW - v244 - O 6 '97 - p53 [51-250]

She Dared to Fly
ASBYP - v29 - Fall '96 - p18 [251-500]
SLJ - v43 - Ag '97 - p168+ [51-250]

Johnson, Jinny
Simon and Schuster Children's Guide to Insects and Spiders
r	CBRS - v25 - Spr '97 - p142+ [51-250]
	HB Guide - v8 - Fall '97 - p350 [51-250]
r	Inst - v107 - N '97 - p19 [1-50]
	SLJ - v43 - N '97 - p128+ [51-250]

What Makes the World Go Round?
SLJ - v43 - Jl '97 - p106 [51-250]

Johnson, Mark
Alice: The Musical. Book and Audio Version
TES - O 3 '97 - p12* [51-250]

Johnson, Paul Brett
Farmers' Market (Illus. by Paul Brett Johnson)
HB Guide - v8 - Fall '97 - p269 [51-250]
SLJ - v43 - Je '97 - p94 [51-250]

Lost (Illus. by Paul Brett Johnson)
RT - v51 - O '97 - p151 [51-250]

A Perfect Pork Stew (Illus. by Paul Brett Johnson)
BL - v94 - Mr 15 '98 - p1249 [51-250]
CCB-B - v51 - Ap '98 - p284 [51-250]
KR - v66 - Ja 1 '98 - p57 [51-250]
PW - v245 - F 23 '98 - p76 [51-250]
SLJ - v44 - Ap '98 - p100+ [51-250]

Johnson, Pete
My Friend's a Werewolf
Bks Keeps - Jl '97 - p26 [51-250]
Sch Lib - v45 - Ag '97 - p146 [51-250]

Johnson, Rebecca L
Braving the Frozen Frontier
HB Guide - v8 - Fall '97 - p400 [51-250]
SB - v33 - Je '97 - p145+ [51-250]

Johnson, Sam
A Resection of Time
Ch BWatch - v7 - Ap '97 - p7 [51-250]

Johnson, Scott
Hide and Seek
SLJ - v43 - My '97 - p134 [51-250]

Johnson, Sue
Starting Gardening
Ch BWatch - v7 - O '97 - p4 [1-50]

Johnson, Sylvia A
Ferrets
Ch BWatch - v7 - Jl '97 - p3 [1-50]
KR - v65 - Je 1 '97 - p874 [51-250]
SLJ - v43 - Ag '97 - p148 [51-250]

Tomatoes, Potatoes, Corn, and Beans
CCB-B - v50 - Jl '97 - p399 [51-250]
y	HB Guide - v8 - Fall '97 - p361 [51-250]
y	SLJ - v43 - My '97 - p146 [51-250]
y	VOYA - v20 - D '97 - p334+ [251-500]

Johnson-Feelings, Dianne
The Best of the Brownies' Book
BW - v27 - D 7 '97 - p22 [51-250]
y	SE - v61 - Ap '97 - p11* [1-50]

Johnston, Andrea
Girls Speak Out
HB Guide - v8 - Fall '97 - p317 [51-250]

Johnston, Basil
*The Star Man and Other Tales (Illus.
by Ken Syrette)*
CM:CanRev - v4 - O 3 '97 - pONL
[251-500]

Johnston, Ginny
Slippery Babies
SLJ - v43 - My '97 - p57 [1-50]

Johnston, Julie
Hero of Lesser Causes
SLJ - v44 - Ja '98 - p42 [1-50]

Johnston, Marianne
Dealing with Insults
SLJ - v43 - S '97 - p199 [51-250]

Let's Talk about Going to the Hospital
SLJ - v44 - Ap '98 - p118 [51-250]

Johnston, Norma
Lotta's Progress
CBRS - v25 - Ag '97 - p166+ [51-250]
HB Guide - v8 - Fall '97 - p303 [51-
250]
SLJ - v43 - S '97 - p218 [51-250]

Johnston, Tony
*The Chizzywink and the
Alamagoozlum (Illus. by Robert
Bender)*
KR - v66 - Ap 15 '98 - p583 [51-250]

*Day of the Dead (Illus. by Jeanette
Winter)*
BL - v94 - S 15 '97 - p242 [51-250]
CCB-B - v51 - O '97 - p54 [51-250]
KR - v65 - Ag 1 '97 - p1223 [51-250]
NY - v73 - O 6 '97 - p114+ [51-250]
NYTBR - v102 - O 26 '97 - p47 [1-50]
PW - v244 - S 1 '97 - p103 [51-250]
SLJ - v43 - S '97 - p184 [51-250]

Fishing Sunday (Illus. by Barry Root)
ECEJ - v25 - Fall '97 - p47 [1-50]
RT - v51 - N '97 - p255 [51-250]

*The Magic Maguey (Illus. by Elisa
Kleven)*
NYTBR - v102 - My 11 '97 - p24
[501+]

My Mexico (Illus. by F John Sierra)
RT - v51 - F '98 - p427 [51-250]

SE - v61 - Ap '97 - p12* [1-50]

*Sparky and Eddie: The First Day of
School (Illus. by Susannah Ryan)*
BL - v93 - Ag '97 - p1910 [51-250]
CCB-B - v51 - N '97 - p88 [51-250]
SLJ - v43 - S '97 - p184 [51-250]

*Sparky and Eddie: Wild, Wild Rodeo!
(Illus. by Susannah Ryan)*
KR - v66 - Ja 1 '98 - p57 [51-250]

The Wagon (Illus. by James Ransome)
RT - v51 - N '97 - p242 [51-250]
RT - v51 - D '97 - p334 [51-250]
SE - v61 - Ap '97 - p8* [1-50]

*We Love the Dirt (Illus. by Alexa
Brandenberg)*
SLJ - v43 - N '97 - p84+ [51-250]

Johnstone, Michael
The History News: Explorers
Ch BWatch - v7 - D '97 - p7+ [1-50]
KR - v65 - N 1 '97 - p1645 [51-250]
Magpies - v12 - S '97 - p43 [51-250]
Obs - D 7 '97 - p18* [1-50]
PW - v244 - N 3 '97 - p87 [51-250]
SLJ - v44 - Ja '98 - p124 [51-250]

*The Jolly Post Office. Electronic
Media Version*
BL - v94 - D 1 '97 - p648+ [51-250]
BW - v27 - D 7 '97 - p23 [51-250]

Joly, Dominique
*How Does Your Garden Grow? (Illus.
by Nathalie Locoste)*
SLJ - v43 - My '97 - p120 [51-250]

Joly, Fanny
*Mr. Fine, Porcupine (Illus. by Remi
Saillard)*
BL - v94 - D 1 '97 - p641 [51-250]
CBRS - v26 - N '97 - p27 [51-250]
Ch BWatch - v8 - Ja '98 - p2 [1-50]
KR - v65 - N 1 '97 - p1645 [51-250]
PW - v244 - N 10 '97 - p72 [51-250]
SLJ - v44 - F '98 - p86 [51-250]

Jonas, Ann
*Watch William Walk (Illus. by Ann
Jonas)*
CBRS - v25 - Jl '97 - p148 [1-50]

HB - v73 - Jl '97 - p444 [51-250]
HB Guide - v8 - Fall '97 - p269 [51-250]
KR - v65 - Ap 15 '97 - p641 [51-250]
NYTBR - v102 - Ag 17 '97 - p19 [1-50]
SLJ - v43 - Ap '97 - p112 [51-250]

Jonell, Lynne
I Need a Snake (Illus. by Petra Mathers)
KR - v66 - Ap 15 '98 - p583 [51-250]

Mommy Go Away! (Illus. by Petra Mathers)
BL - v94 - O 15 '97 - p415 [51-250]
CBRS - v26 - F '98 - p76 [51-250]
CCB-B - v51 - D '97 - p131 [51-250]
HB - v73 - S '97 - p559+ [251-500]
KR - v65 - Ag 15 '97 - p1306 [51-250]
NYTBR - v103 - Mr 15 '98 - p23 [501+]
PW - v244 - S 22 '97 - p79 [51-250]
SLJ - v43 - D '97 - p94 [51-250]

Jones, Allan Frewin
Anna's Birthday Adventure (Illus. by Judy Brown)
Sch Lib - v45 - N '97 - p191 [51-250]

Jones, Betty
A Child's Seasonal Treasury
KR - v65 - Je 1 '97 - p874 [51-250]

Jones, Carol
The Lion and the Mouse (Illus. by Carol Jones)
Magpies - v12 - Jl '97 - p31 [51-250]
SLJ - v43 - N '97 - p85 [51-250]

Jones, Charlotte Foltz
Fingerprints and Talking Bones (Illus. by David G Klein)
BL - v93 - Je 1 '97 - p1692 [51-250]
BW - v27 - S 7 '97 - p11 [251-500]
CCB-B - v50 - Je '97 - p362 [51-250]
HB Guide - v8 - Fall '97 - p327 [51-250]
KR - v65 - My 15 '97 - p801 [51-250]
SLJ - v43 - Ag '97 - p169 [51-250]

Mistakes That Worked
JOYS - v10 - Sum '97 - p428 [1-50]

Jones, J Sydney
Frankie
BL - v94 - D 15 '97 - p697 [51-250]
CBRS - v26 - Ja '98 - p58 [51-250]
KR - v65 - O 15 '97 - p1583 [51-250]
SLJ - v43 - N '97 - p120 [51-250]

Jones, Jennifer Berry
Heetunka's Harvest (Illus. by Shannon Keegan)
ECEJ - v25 - Fall '97 - p47 [1-50]

Jones, Jenny
The Carver
Bks Keeps - S '97 - p28 [51-250]

Jones, K Maurice
Spike Lee and the African American Filmmakers
Ch BWatch - v7 - Je '97 - p4 [51-250]
y   VOYA - v20 - Je '97 - p132 [251-500]

Jones, Sally Lloyd
Child's First Bible
PW - v245 - Mr 23 '98 - p95+ [51-250]

Jones, Terry
The Knight and the Squire (Illus. by Michael Foreman)
Spec - v279 - D 6 '97 - p44 [51-250]

Jones, Tim Wynne
The Flight of Burl Crow
Magpies - v12 - Jl '97 - p39 [51-250]

Joosse, Barbara M
Ghost Trap (Illus. by Sue Truesdell)
KR - v66 - Ap 15 '98 - p583 [51-250]

I Love You the Purplest (Illus. by Mary Whyte)
SLJ - v43 - My '97 - p102 [51-250]

Mama, Do You Love Me? (Illus. by Barbara Lavallee)
ECEJ - v25 - Fall '97 - p47 [1-50]

Nugget and Darling (Illus. by Sue Truesdell)
HB Guide - v8 - Fall '97 - p269 [51-250]
SLJ - v43 - Ap '97 - p112 [51-250]

Jordan, Jennifer
Albert Goes to Town (Illus. by Shannon McNeill)
> CBRS - v26 - D '97 - p39 [51-250]
> KR - v65 - N 1 '97 - p1645 [51-250]
> PW - v244 - N 17 '97 - p60 [51-250]
> SLJ - v44 - Ja '98 - p88 [51-250]

Jordan, Martin
Amazon Alphabet (Illus. by Martin Jordan)
> RT - v51 - N '97 - p240 [51-250]

Jorgensen, Gail
Gotcha! (Illus. by Kerry Argent)
> CBRS - v25 - My '97 - p111 [51-250]
> Ch BWatch - v7 - My '97 - p3 [1-50]
> HB Guide - v8 - Fall '97 - p270 [51-250]

Jortberg, Charles A
The Internet
> BL - v93 - Je 1 '97 - p1692 [51-250]

Virtual Reality and Beyond
> BL - v93 - Je 1 '97 - p1692 [51-250]

Joseph, Vivienne
The Penguins' Day Out (Illus. by Ruth Paul)
> Magpies - v12 - Jl '97 - p7* [51-250]

Josephova, Ekaterina
Drakonche To Polly (Illus. by Nadeszda Stefanova)
> Bkbird - v35 - Sum '97 - p56 [1-50]

Joy to the World (Illus. by Laura Rader)
> Ch BWatch - v7 - N '97 - p6 [1-50]

Joyce, William
Bently and Egg
> Magpies - v12 - Jl '97 - p30 [51-250]

Buddy (Illus. by William Joyce)
> BL - v93 - Ag '97 - p1901 [51-250]
> BW - v27 - Jl 6 '97 - p11 [251-500]
> CBRS - v25 - Ag '97 - p165 [51-250]
> CCB-B - v51 - S '97 - p15 [51-250]
> HB Guide - v8 - Fall '97 - p292 [51-250]
> PW - v244 - Je 23 '97 - p93 [51-250]

> SLJ - v43 - Ag '97 - p136 [51-250]

The Leaf Men and the Brave Good Bugs
> Magpies - v12 - Mr '97 - p29 [51-250]

The World of William Joyce Scrapbook (Illus. by Philip Gould)
> BL - v94 - Ja 1 '98 - p805 [51-250]
> BW - v27 - D 7 '97 - p19+ [501+]
> CBRS - v26 - Ja '98 - p56 [51-250]
> PW - v244 - O 20 '97 - p78 [51-250]
> SLJ - v44 - F '98 - p100 [51-250]

Judson, Karen
Ronald Reagan
> BL - v93 - Ag '97 - p1894+ [51-250]
> y CLW - v68 - S '97 - p67 [51-250]
> HB Guide - v8 - Fall '97 - p395 [51-250]

Julio, Susan
Great Map Mysteries
> SB - v33 - N '97 - p245 [51-250]

Jung, Sung-Hoon
South Korea
> HB Guide - v8 - Fall '97 - p392 [51-250]

Jungman, Ann
Monster in Love (Illus. by Jan Smith)
> TES - Jl 11 '97 - p14* [51-250]

Monster in Trouble (Illus. by Jan Smith)
> TES - Jl 11 '97 - p14* [51-250]

There's a Troll at the Bottom of Our Street (Illus. by Doffy Weir)
> Bks Keeps - N '97 - p23 [51-250]

Junior Chronicle of the 20th Century
> r   BL - v94 - O 1 '97 - p356 [1-50]
> r   HMR - Win '97 - p46 [51-250]
> r   PW - v244 - Ag 18 '97 - p95 [51-250]
> r   SLJ - v44 - Ja '98 - p117 [51-250]
> r   Spec - v279 - D 6 '97 - p44 [1-50]
> r   TES - N 7 '97 - p9* [1-50]
> r   TES - N 7 '97 - p13* [501+]
> yr VOYA - v20 - F '98 - p407 [51-250]

Jurenka, Nancy Allen
Cultivating a Child's Imagination through Gardening
    SB - v33 - Ap '97 - p82 [51-250]

Jurmain, Suzanne
Freedom's Sons
    BL - v94 - F 15 '98 - p1003 [51-250]
    SLJ - v44 - Ap '98 - p147 [51-250]

Just about Horses
p   JOYS - v10 - Spr '97 - p262+ [1-50]
p   JOYS - v10 - Spr '97 - p263 [1-50]

Just Look 'n' Learn Spanish Picture Dictionary (Illus. by Daniel J Hochstatter)
r   BL - v94 - D 15 '97 - p717 [51-250]

Juster, Norton
The Phantom Tollbooth (Illus. by Jules Feiffer)
    NYTBR - v102 - N 16 '97 - p26 [1-50]
    TES - Ja 2 '98 - p22* [51-250]

K

Kachur, Wanda Gilberts
The Nautilus
SLJ - v43 - S '97 - p218 [51-250]

Kadodwala, Dilip
Holi
BL - v93 - Je 1 '97 - p1692 [51-250]
Emerg Lib - v25 - N '97 - p55 [1-50]
HB Guide - v8 - Fall '97 - p320 [51-250]

Kagda, Falaq
Algeria
Ch BWatch - v7 - Je '97 - p5 [51-250]
HB Guide - v8 - Fall '97 - p392 [51-250]
India
Ch BWatch - v7 - O '97 - p4+ [51-250]
Kenya
Ch BWatch - v7 - O '97 - p4+ [51-250]
H-Net - Mr '98 - pONL [501+]

Kagda, Sakina
Lithuania
Ch BWatch - v7 - Je '97 - p5 [51-250]
HB Guide - v8 - Fall '97 - p390 [51-250]

Kahl, Jonathan D
Hazy Skies
BL - v94 - Mr 15 '98 - p1238 [51-250]

Kahukiwa, Robyn
Kehua (Illus. by Robyn Kahukiwa)
Magpies - v12 - Mr '97 - p6*+ [51-250]

Kajpust, Melissa
The Peacock's Pride (Illus. by Jo'Anne Kelly)
BL - v94 - Ja 1 '98 - p818 [51-250]
CM:CanRev - v4 - S 19 '97 - pONL [251-500]

Kalbacken, Joan
Badgers
SLJ - v43 - Ap '97 - p127 [51-250]

Kallen, Stuart
Quincy Jones
Ch BWatch - v7 - S '97 - p7 [1-50]

Kallen, Stuart A
Exploring the Origins of the Universe
Ch BWatch - v7 - My '97 - p8 [1-50]
SLJ - v43 - Je '97 - p132 [51-250]

Kalman, Bobbie
19th Century Girls and Women
Ch BWatch - v7 - S '97 - p1 [1-50]
HB Guide - v8 - Fall '97 - p330 [51-250]
Quill & Q - v63 - My '97 - p42 [51-250]
SLJ - v43 - Ag '97 - p148 [51-250]

Celebrating the Powwow
HB Guide - v8 - Fall '97 - p330 [51-250]
SLJ - v44 - Ja '98 - p101 [51-250]

The General Store (Illus. by Barbara Bedell)
CBRA - '96 - p507 [51-250]
HB Guide - v8 - Fall '97 - p330 [51-250]
SLJ - v43 - Jl '97 - p84 [51-250]

The Wonders of Me from A to Z
SB - v34 - Ap '98 - p78+ [51-250]

Kamerman, Sylvia E
Great American Events on Stage
SLJ - v43 - My '97 - p146 [51-250]

Thirty Plays from Favorite Stories
SLJ - v43 - D '97 - p110 [51-250]

Kamida, Vicki
Night Mare
BL - v94 - N 1 '97 - p470+ [51-250]
CCB-B - v51 - O '97 - p55 [51-250]
KR - v65 - Ag 15 '97 - p1306+ [51-250]
SLJ - v43 - N '97 - p120 [51-250]

Kandel, Bethany
Trevor's Story
BL - v94 - Mr 15 '98 - p1236 [51-250]

Kaplan, Elizabeth
Taiga
SB - v32 - D '96 - p275 [51-250]

Karas, G Brian
The Windy Day (Illus. by G Brian Karas)
HB - v74 - Mr '98 - p214+ [251-500]

Karas, Phyllis
For Lucky's Sake
BL - v94 - O 1 '97 - p329 [51-250]

Karim, Roberta
This Is a Hospital, Not a Zoo! (Illus. by Sue Truesdell)
BL - v94 - Mr 1 '98 - p1140 [51-250]
KR - v66 - Mr 15 '98 - p405 [51-250]

Karlin, Nurit
I See, You Saw (Illus. by Nurit Karlin)
HB Guide - v8 - Fall '97 - p252 [51-250]
SLJ - v43 - Jl '97 - p69+ [51-250]

Karon, Jan
Miss Fannie's Hat (Illus. by Toni Goffe)
PW - v245 - F 23 '98 - p66 [51-250]

Karr, Kathleen
The Great Turkey Walk
KR - v66 - Mr 15 '98 - p405 [51-250]
SLJ - v44 - Mr '98 - p214 [51-250]

Spy in the Sky (Illus. by Thomas F Yezerski)
SLJ - v43 - Ag '97 - p136 [51-250]

Karrebaek, Dorte
Pigen Der Var God Til Mange Ting (Illus. by Dorte Karrebaek)
Bkbird - v35 - Fall '97 - p51 [51-250]

Kaschula, Russell
Xhosa
Ch BWatch - v8 - Ja '98 - p7 [51-250]

Kasoff, Jerry
Baseball Just for Kids
SLJ - v43 - Ap '97 - p127 [51-250]

Kasperson, James
Little Brother Moose (Illus. by Karlyn Holman)
SB - v33 - O '97 - p218 [51-250]

Kassirer, Sue
Joseph and His Coat of Many Colors (Illus. by Danuta Jarecka)
BL - v93 - Ag '97 - p1909 [51-250]

Kastner, Jill
Barnyard Big Top (Illus. by Jill Kastner)
BL - v94 - N 1 '97 - p482 [51-250]
KR - v65 - S 1 '97 - p1391 [51-250]
PW - v244 - N 3 '97 - p84 [51-250]
SLJ - v43 - N '97 - p85 [51-250]

Kasza, Keiko
Don't Laugh, Joe! (Illus. by Keiko Kasza)
BL - v93 - Ag '97 - p1906 [51-250]
CBRS - v25 - Ag '97 - p160 [1-50]
Ch BWatch - v7 - Je '97 - p6 [1-50]
HB Guide - v8 - Fall '97 - p270 [51-250]
SLJ - v43 - Je '97 - p94 [51-250]

Katz, Bobbi
Could We Be Friends? (Illus. by Joung Un Kim)
    CBRS - v25 - Je '97 - p127 [1-50]
    HB Guide - v8 - Fall '97 - p376 [51-250]
    SLJ - v43 - Jl '97 - p84 [51-250]
Truck Talk
    HB Guide - v8 - Fall '97 - p358 [51-250]

Katz, Fred E
Birthday Cake and I Scream
    Ch BWatch - v7 - Mr '97 - p2 [51-250]
Hospitals Make Me Sick
    Ch BWatch - v7 - N '97 - p2 [51-250]

Katz, Karen
Over the Moon (Illus. by Karen Katz)
    BL - v94 - S 1 '97 - p133 [51-250]
    CBRS - v26 - O '97 - p15 [51-250]
    KR - v65 - Jl 1 '97 - p1030 [51-250]
    NYTBR - v102 - Jl 6 '97 - p16 [1-50]
    PW - v244 - Ag 4 '97 - p73 [51-250]
    SLJ - v43 - S '97 - p184 [51-250]

Katz, Rosalyn B
Start Playing Chess
    Ch BWatch - v7 - Jl '97 - p4 [1-50]

Katz, William Loren
Breaking the Chains
    PW - v245 - Ja 12 '98 - p61 [1-50]

Kay, Geraldine
The Dragon Upstairs (Illus. by Colin King)
    Bks Keeps - S '97 - p25 [51-250]

Kaye, Geraldine
Comfort Herself
    Bks Keeps - Jl '97 - p25 [51-250]

Kaye, Rosalind Charney
Brainteasers from Jewish Folklore
    PW - v244 - D 8 '97 - p74 [1-50]

Kazimiroff, Theodore
The Last Algonquin
    PW - v244 - D 1 '97 - p55 [1-50]

Kazunas, Charnan
The Internet for Kids
    HB Guide - v8 - Fall '97 - p317 [51-250]
    SB - v33 - D '97 - p272 [51-250]
Personal Computers
    HB Guide - v8 - Fall '97 - p317 [51-250]
    SB - v33 - N '97 - p240 [51-250]
    SLJ - v44 - Ja '98 - p97 [51-250]

Keane, Christoper
Prince of the Stable (Mike). Book and Audio Version
    SLJ - v43 - S '97 - p165 [51-250]

Keats, Ezra Jack
The Snowy Day (Illus. by Ezra Jack Keats)
    NYTBR - v102 - N 16 '97 - p26 [1-50]

Keck, Katy
Deborah (Illus. by Katy Keck)
    CLW - v68 - D '97 - p69 [51-250]
Jonah, the Whale and the Vine (Illus. by Katy Keck)
    CLW - v68 - D '97 - p69 [51-250]
Joshua, God's General (Illus. by Katy Keck)
    CLW - v68 - D '97 - p69 [51-250]
Moses (Illus. by Katy Keck)
    CLW - v68 - D '97 - p69 [51-250]

Keenan, Sheila
Scholastic Encyclopedia of Women in the United States
    r   SE - v61 - Ap '97 - p11* [1-50]

Keens-Douglas, Richardo
Grandpa's Visit (Illus. by Frances Clancy)
    CBRA - '96 - p445+ [51-250]

Keeshan, Bob
Itty Bitty Kitty (Illus. by Jane Maday)
    Ch BWatch - v7 - Je '97 - p3 [51-250]
    HB Guide - v8 - Fall '97 - p270 [51-250]

Keeshig-Tobias, Lenore
*Emma and the Trees (Illus. by Polly
Keeshig-Tobias)*
    CBRA - '96 - p446 [51-250]

Kehret, Peg
The Blizzard Disaster
    KR - v66 - Ap 15 '98 - p583 [51-250]

Earthquake Terror
    RT - v51 - O '97 - p141 [1-50]

*The Ghost Followed Us Home
(Montbertrand). Audio Version*
    SLJ - v43 - N '97 - p68 [51-250]

Searching for Candlestick Park
    BL - v93 - Ag '97 - p1901 [51-250]
    CBRS - v26 - F '98 - p80 [51-250]
    CCB-B - v51 - N '97 - p88+ [51-250]
    KR - v65 - Je 1 '97 - p874 [51-250]
    SLJ - v43 - S '97 - p218 [51-250]

Small Steps
    SB - v33 - Ag '97 - p176 [51-250]

Keillor, Garrison
*Cat, You Better Come Home (Illus. by
Steve Johnson)*
    PW - v244 - Jl 28 '97 - p77 [1-50]

*The Old Man Who Loved Cheese
(Illus. by Anne Wilsdorf)*
    RT - v51 - O '97 - p135 [1-50]

The Sandy Bottom Orchestra
    Books - v11 - Je '97 - p21 [51-250]
y   Sch Lib - v45 - N '97 - p213 [51-250]
y   TES - Jl 4 '97 - p7* [251-500]
y   TES - N 7 '97 - p12*+ [51-250]
    TLS - S 5 '97 - p23 [251-500]

Keith, Lois
A Different Life
    TES - My 23 '97 - p7* [501+]

Kelleher, Victor
*Where the Whales Sing (Illus. by
Vivienne Goodman)*
    TES - O 10 '97 - p8* [51-250]
    TES - N 7 '97 - p7* [51-250]

Keller, Ellen
*Flashlight Games (Illus. by Abby
Carter)*
    Ch BWatch - v8 - Ja '98 - p4 [51-250]

Jump Rope Rhymes
    Ch BWatch - v7 - Mr '97 - p4 [51-250]

Sidewalk Chalk Games
    Ch BWatch - v7 - Mr '97 - p4 [51-250]

Keller, Holly
*Angela's Top-Secret Computer Club
(Illus. by Holly Keller)*
    CCB-B - v51 - Mr '98 - p247+ [51-250]

Brave Horace (Illus. by Holly Keller)
    BL - v94 - Mr 1 '98 - p1140 [51-250]
    KR - v66 - F 15 '98 - p269 [51-250]
    PW - v245 - Mr 23 '98 - p98+ [51-250]
    SLJ - v44 - Ap '98 - p102 [51-250]

Grandfather's Dream
    ECEJ - v25 - Fall '97 - p47 [1-50]

I Am Angela (Illus. by Holly Keller)
    HB Guide - v8 - Fall '97 - p292 [51-
250]
    SLJ - v43 - My '97 - p102 [51-250]

*Merry Christmas, Geraldine (Illus. by
Holly Keller)*
    BL - v94 - S 1 '97 - p139 [51-250]
    KR - v65 - O 1 '97 - p1533 [51-250]

Keller, James
*The Traveler: A Magical Journey
(Illus. by Daniel Page Schallau)*
    CBRS - v26 - F '98 - p76+ [51-250]
    Ch BWatch - v7 - N '97 - p4 [51-250]

Kellerhals-Stewart, Heather
*My Brother's Train (Illus. by Paul
Zwolak)*
    CBRS - v26 - Win '98 - p62 [51-250]
    CCB-B - v51 - O '97 - p55 [51-250]
    CM:CanRev - v4 - N 28 '97 - pONL
[251-500]
    Quill & Q - v64 - F '98 - p48 [251-500]

Kellogg, Steven
La Bruja De Navidad
    HB Guide - v8 - Fall '97 - p338 [51-
250]

I Was Born about 10,000 Years Ago (Illus. by Steven Kellogg)

RT - v51 - D '97 - p331 [51-250]

The Mysterious Tadpole Book and Toy Package

PW - v244 - Ag 11 '97 - p403 [1-50]

The Three Little Pigs (Illus. by Steven Kellogg)

BL - v93 - Ag '97 - p1898 [51-250]
BW - v27 - N 2 '97 - p6 [251-500]
KR - v65 - Jl 1 '97 - p1030 [51-250]
Par - v73 - F '98 - p186 [51-250]
SLJ - v43 - S '97 - p203 [51-250]

Kelly, Emery J
Paper Airplanes

BL - v94 - D 1 '97 - p620 [51-250]
Emerg Lib - v25 - Ja '98 - p57 [51-250]
SLJ - v44 - F '98 - p118 [51-250]

Kelly, Geoff
Stuck with Baby (Illus. by Geoff Kelly)

Bloom Rev - v17 - My '97 - p27 [51-250]

Kelly, J
Clyde Drexler

Ch BWatch - v7 - S '97 - p8 [1-50]

Superstars of Women's Basketball

Ch BWatch - v7 - S '97 - p8 [1-50]
HB Guide - v8 - Fall '97 - p369 [51-250]
SLJ - v44 - Ap '98 - p147 [51-250]

Kelly, Jo'Anne
Terrific Stencils and Stamps (Illus. by Teddy Cameron Long)

CBRA - '96 - p519 [51-250]

Kelly, Joanne, 1934-
The Beverly Cleary Handbook

SLMQ - v25 - Win '97 - p118 [51-250]

Kemp, Gene
Rebel Rebel

TES - N 21 '97 - p8* [51-250]

Kenda, Margaret
Geography Wizardry for Kids

SB - v33 - D '97 - p277 [51-250]

Kendall, Martha E
Susan B. Anthony: Voice for Women's Voting Rights

CLW - v68 - S '97 - p67+ [51-250]
y   HB Guide - v8 - Fall '97 - p378 [51-250]
y   SLJ - v43 - Ag '97 - p170 [51-250]

Kennedy, Dorothy
Make Things Fly (Illus. by Sasha Meret)

HB - v74 - Mr '98 - p229 [51-250]
KR - v66 - F 1 '98 - p197 [51-250]
PW - v245 - Mr 9 '98 - p70 [1-50]

Kennedy, Jimmy
Teddy Bear's Picnic

Ch BWatch - v7 - Je '97 - p6 [1-50]

Kennedy, Kim
Mr. Bumble (Illus. by Doug Kennedy)

Ch BWatch - v7 - N '97 - p4 [1-50]
KR - v65 - Ag 1 '97 - p1223 [51-250]
NYTBR - v103 - Mr 15 '98 - p23 [51-250]
PW - v244 - Ag 11 '97 - p401+ [51-250]
SLJ - v43 - S '97 - p184 [51-250]

Kennedy, Richard
Hans Christian Andersen's The Snow Queen (Illus. by Edward S Gazsi)

HB Guide - v8 - Fall '97 - p367 [51-250]

Kennedy, X J
The Eagle as Wide as the World

KR - v65 - Ag 15 '97 - p1307 [51-250]
PW - v244 - Je 30 '97 - p76 [51-250]
SLJ - v43 - D '97 - p125+ [51-250]

Talking like the Rain (Illus. by Jane Dyer)

Comw - v124 - D 5 '97 - p14+ [1-50]

Uncle Switch (Illus. by John O'Brien)

HB Guide - v8 - Fall '97 - p376 [51-250]
SLJ - v43 - Ap '97 - p127 [51-250]

Kennemore, Tim
Alice's Birthday Pig (Illus. by Alex De Wolf)

Bks Keeps - S '97 - p25 [51-250]

Alice's World Record (Illus. by Alex De Wolf)

    Bks Keeps - S '97 - p25 [51-250]
    TES - Jl 11 '97 - p14* [51-250]

Kent, Deborah

Amsterdam

    HB Guide - v8 - Fall '97 - p391 [51-250]
    SLJ - v44 - F '98 - p119 [51-250]

Dublin

    HB Guide - v8 - Fall '97 - p391 [51-250]

New York City

    HB Guide - v8 - Fall '97 - p395 [51-250]

Thurgood Marshall and the Supreme Court

    Ch BWatch - v7 - O '97 - p8 [1-50]
    HB Guide - v8 - Fall '97 - p325 [51-250]

Kent, Peter

Go to Jail! (Illus. by Peter Kent)

    KR - v66 - Mr 1 '98 - p340 [51-250]

Quest for the West

    BL - v94 - D 1 '97 - p636+ [51-250]
    CBRS - v26 - F '98 - p80 [51-250]
    Magpies - v12 - S '97 - p43 [51-250]
    Sch Lib - v45 - N '97 - p205 [51-250]

Kentley, Eric

Discover the Titanic

    Obs - D 7 '97 - p18* [1-50]

Kerby, Mona

Robert E. Lee: Southern Hero of the Civil War

    BL - v94 - O 1 '97 - p326 [51-250]
    CLW - v68 - D '97 - p81 [51-250]
y   SLJ - v43 - S '97 - p231 [51-250]

Kerins, Tony

The Brave Ones

    Bks Keeps - Jl '97 - p21 [51-250]

Kern, Noris

I Love You with All My Heart (Illus. by Noris Kern)

    KR - v66 - Ap 1 '98 - p496 [51-250]

Kerr, Bob

Mechanical Harry (Illus. by Bob Kerr)

    Magpies - v12 - Mr '97 - p2* [51-250]

Kerr, Daisy

Knights and Armor (Illus. by Mark Bergin)

    SLJ - v43 - Jl '97 - p84 [51-250]

Medieval Town (Illus. by Gerald Wood)

    SLJ - v43 - Jl '97 - p84 [51-250]

Kerr, Judith

When Hitler Stole Pink Rabbit

    PW - v244 - D 1 '97 - p55 [1-50]

Kerr, M E

Deliver Us from Evie

    Bks Keeps - My '97 - p4+ [501+]

Kerr, Rita

The Texas Cowboy

    Roundup M - v5 - D '97 - p27 [1-50]

Kerrod, Robin

Facts on File Wildlife Atlas

r   BL - v94 - Mr 15 '98 - p1260 [251-500]

Machines (Illus. by Robin Kerrod)

    ASBYP - v29 - Fall '96 - p51+ [251-500]

Matter and Materials (Illus. by Terry Hadler)

    ASBYP - v29 - Fall '96 - p51+ [251-500]

The Night Sky (Illus. by Terry Hadler)

    ASBYP - v29 - Fall '96 - p51+ [251-500]

Kertes, Joseph

The Gift (Illus. by Peter Perko)

    Can CL - v23 - Fall '97 - p82+ [501+]

The Red Corduroy Shirt (Illus. by Peter Perko)

    BIC - v26 - N '97 - p39 [501+]

Kerven, Rosalind

Enchanted Kingdom

    TES - N 7 '97 - p10* [1-50]

Id-Ul-Fitr

> BL - v93 - Je 1 '97 - p1692 [51-250]
> Emerg Lib - v25 - N '97 - p55 [1-50]
> HB Guide - v8 - Fall '97 - p320 [51-250]

Ramadan and Id-Ul-Fitr

> Bks Keeps - N '97 - p24 [51-250]

Keselman, Gabriela
El Regalo (Illus. by Pep Montserrat)

> BL - v93 - Ag '97 - p1913 [51-250]

Kessler, Brad
Moses in Egypt (Illus. by Phil Huling)

> SLJ - v43 - D '97 - p110 [51-250]

Kessler, Cristina
Konte Chameleon, Fine, Fine, Fine!
(Illus. by Christian Epanya)

> BL - v94 - O 1 '97 - p336 [51-250]
> CBRS - v26 - Ja '98 - p50 [51-250]
> KR - v65 - Jl 15 '97 - p1112 [51-250]

Konte Chameleon, Fine, Fine, Fine
(Illus. by Christian Epanya)

> SLJ - v43 - S '97 - p184 [51-250]

Kessler, Deirdre
Prince Edward Island. Rev. Ed.

> CBRA - '96 - p512+ [501+]

Kessler, James
Distinguished African American
Scientists of the 20th Century

> r   ASBYP - v29 - Fall '96 - p19 [251-500]

Ketteman, Helen
Bubba the Cowboy Prince (Illus. by
James Warhola)

> BL - v94 - D 1 '97 - p641+ [51-250]
> CCB-B - v51 - D '97 - p131 [51-250]
> Inst - v107 - Ja '98 - p28 [1-50]
> KR - v65 - N 1 '97 - p1646 [51-250]
> PW - v244 - N 17 '97 - p61 [51-250]

Heat Wave! (Illus. by Scott Goto)

> KR - v65 - D 1 '97 - p1776 [51-250]
> PW - v244 - D 15 '97 - p58 [51-250]
> SLJ - v44 - Mr '98 - p182 [51-250]

I Remember Papa (Illus. by Greg
Shed)

> BL - v94 - Mr 15 '98 - p1249+ [51-250]

> KR - v66 - Ja 15 '98 - p114 [51-250]

Khalsa, Dayal Kaur
Tales of a Gambling Grandma (Illus.
by Dayal Kaur Khalsa)

> Ch Bk News - v20 - Spr '97 - p35 [251-500]

Khan, Eaniqa
Pakistan

> Bks Keeps - N '97 - p25 [51-250]

Khanduri, Kamini
Great History Search

> Emerg Lib - v24 - My '97 - p50 [51-250]

The Great World Tour

> TES - Ag 22 '97 - p25 [51-250]

Kharms, Daniil
First, Second (Illus. by Marc
Rosenthal)

> RT - v51 - F '98 - p427 [51-250]

Kherdian, David
The Rose's Smile (Illus. by Stefano
Vitale)

> BL - v94 - S 1 '97 - p114 [51-250]
> CBRS - v26 - O '97 - p15+ [51-250]
> CCB-B - v51 - N '97 - p89 [51-250]
> Ch BWatch - v8 - Ja '98 - p2 [1-50]
> PW - v244 - Je 23 '97 - p91 [51-250]
> SLJ - v43 - N '97 - p109 [51-250]

Kidd, Richard
Almost Famous Daisy!

> Inst - v106 - Ap '97 - p27 [1-50]

Monsieur Thermidor (Illus. by Lindsey
Kidd)

> PW - v245 - F 2 '98 - p89 [51-250]
> Sch Lib - v45 - N '97 - p186 [51-250]
> TES - N 7 '97 - p5* [1-50]

Kids Discover

> p   LA - v73 - N '96 - p535+ [501+]
> p   Par Ch - Awards '97 - p27 [1-50]

Kids on the Web

> p   SLJ - v43 - Je '97 - p43 [51-250]

Kids Review Kids' Books
r   Inst - v107 - N '97 - p8 [51-250]

Kightly, Charles
Barley Hall
Bks Keeps - S '97 - p27 [51-250]
Sch Lib - v45 - Ag '97 - p155 [51-250]

Kilworth, Garry
The Gargoyle (Illus. by Dan Williams)
Sch Lib - v45 - N '97 - p192 [51-250]
TES - Ja 2 '98 - p22* [1-50]

The Welkin Weasels
TES - Ag 8 '97 - p23 [251-500]
y   TES - N 7 '97 - p7* [51-250]

Kim, Bo-Kyang
Sing 'n Learn Korean. Book and Audio Version
Ch BWatch - v7 - S '97 - p6+ [51-250]

Kimble, Gregory A
Portraits of Pioneers in Psychology. Vol. 2
SB - v32 - D '96 - p261 [51-250]

Kimmel, Elizabeth Cody
In the Stone Circle
CCB-B - v51 - Mr '98 - p248 [51-250]
y   KR - v66 - Ap 15 '98 - p583+ [51-250]
PW - v245 - F 23 '98 - p77 [51-250]
SLJ - v44 - Ap '98 - p132 [51-250]

Kimmel, Eric A
Be Not Far from Me (Illus. by David Diaz)
PW - v245 - Mr 23 '98 - p95 [51-250]

I Took My Frog to the Library. Book and Audio Version
Ch BWatch - v7 - My '97 - p5 [1-50]

The Magic Dreidels (Illus. by Katya Krenina)
PW - v244 - O 6 '97 - p53 [1-50]
RT - v51 - N '97 - p255 [51-250]

Rimonah of the Flashing Sword (Illus. by Omar Rayyan)
ECEJ - v25 - Fall '97 - p47 [1-50]

Sirko and the Wolf (Illus. by Robert Sauber)
BL - v94 - S 15 '97 - p238 [51-250]
Emerg Lib - v25 - N '97 - p55 [1-50]
SLJ - v43 - N '97 - p109 [51-250]

Squash It! (Illus. by Robert Rayevsky)
BL - v93 - Je 1 '97 - p1692 [51-250]
CBRS - v25 - Ag '97 - p160 [51-250]
HB - v73 - Jl '97 - p467+ [51-250]
HB Guide - v8 - Fall '97 - p334 [51-250]
KR - v65 - My 15 '97 - p801 [51-250]
NYTBR - v102 - Jl 20 '97 - p22 [1-50]
SLJ - v43 - Jl '97 - p85 [51-250]

The Tale of Aladdin and the Wonderful Lamp (Illus. by Ju-Hong Chen)
ECEJ - v25 - Fall '97 - p47 [1-50]

The Tale of Ali Baba and the Forty Thieves (Illus. by Will Hillenbrand)
RT - v51 - D '97 - p332 [51-250]

Ten Suns (Illus. by Yongsheng Xuan)
KR - v66 - Ap 1 '98 - p496+ [51-250]

The Three Princes (Illus. by Leonard Everett Fisher)
ECEJ - v25 - Fall '97 - p47 [1-50]

Kindersley, Barnabas
Celebrations!
PW - v244 - S 29 '97 - p91 [51-250]
Quill & Q - v63 - D '97 - p39 [1-50]
SLJ - v44 - Ja '98 - p101+ [51-250]
TES - N 7 '97 - p7* [501+]

Kindl, Patrice
Owl in Love
BL - v94 - N 1 '97 - p475 [1-50]

The Woman in the Wall
y   BL - v94 - Mr 15 '98 - p1216 [1-50]
y   BW - v27 - My 4 '97 - p16 [51-250]
y   HB - v73 - Jl '97 - p458+ [51-250]
y   HB Guide - v8 - Fall '97 - p314 [51-250]
    SLJ - v43 - Ap '97 - p138 [51-250]
y   SLJ - v44 - Ja '98 - p40 [251-500]
y   VOYA - v20 - Ag '97 - p186 [251-500]
y   VOYA - v20 - F '98 - p365 [51-250]
y   VOYA - v21 - Ap '98 - p37 [1-50]

Kindley, Jeff
Scamper's Year (Illus. by Laura Rader)
>   SLJ - v43 - Ag '97 - p136 [51-250]

King, Casey
Oh, Freedom! (Illus. by Joe Brooks)
>   BL - v94 - F 15 '98 - p998 [1-50]
>   Ch BWatch - v7 - Ap '97 - p1 [1-50]
>   CLW - v68 - S '97 - p69+ [51-250]
>   HB Guide - v8 - Fall '97 - p325 [51-250]
>   PW - v244 - D 8 '97 - p74 [1-50]
>   SLJ - v43 - Je '97 - p139+ [51-250]
> y VOYA - v20 - F '98 - p365 [51-250]
> y VOYA - v20 - F '98 - p402 [501+]

King, Celia
Seven Great Explorations
>   CBRA - '96 - p507 [51-250]

King, David C
Colonial Days
>   PW - v245 - Ja 19 '98 - p380 [51-250]

Egypt: Ancient Traditions, Modern Hopes
>   Ch BWatch - v7 - My '97 - p7 [1-50]
>   HB Guide - v8 - Fall '97 - p393 [51-250]
>   SLJ - v44 - Ja '98 - p97+ [51-250]

First Facts about American Heroes
>   SE - v61 - Ap '97 - p3* [1-50]

Freedom of Assembly
>   Ch BWatch - v7 - Je '97 - p4 [51-250]
>   HB Guide - v8 - Fall '97 - p325 [51-250]

Italy: Gem of the Mediterranean
>   Ch BWatch - v8 - Ja '98 - p7 [1-50]

Kenya: One Nation, Many Cultures
>   Ch BWatch - v8 - Ja '98 - p7 [1-50]

Lexington and Concord
>   SLJ - v44 - Ja '98 - p125 [51-250]

Peru: Lost Cities, Found Hopes
>   Ch BWatch - v8 - Ja '98 - p7 [1-50]

Pioneer Days (Illus. by Bobbie Moore)
>   PW - v244 - Jl 28 '97 - p77 [51-250]
>   SLJ - v44 - F '98 - p119 [51-250]

The Right to Speak Out
>   HB Guide - v8 - Fall '97 - p325 [51-250]

King, John, 1939-
A Family from Iraq
>   SLJ - v44 - F '98 - p100 [51-250]

King, Martin Luther, Jr.
I Have a Dream
>   BL - v94 - F 15 '98 - p1008 [51-250]
> y BL - v94 - Mr 15 '98 - p1225 [1-50]
>   CBRS - v26 - D '97 - p44 [51-250]
>   KR - v65 - N 15 '97 - p1708 [51-250]
>   PW - v244 - N 10 '97 - p72 [51-250]
>   SLJ - v43 - N '97 - p109 [51-250]
> y VOYA - v21 - Ap '98 - p39 [1-50]

King, Penny
Myths and Legends (Illus. by Lindy Norton)
>   PW - v244 - N 24 '97 - p76 [51-250]
>   SLJ - v44 - Ap '98 - p147+ [51-250]

Out of This World
>   SLJ - v43 - D '97 - p110 [51-250]

Secrets of the Sea
>   SLJ - v43 - D '97 - p110 [51-250]

Spooky Things
>   SLJ - v43 - D '97 - p110 [51-250]

Sports and Games (Illus. by Lindy Norton)
>   PW - v244 - N 24 '97 - p76 [51-250]
>   SLJ - v44 - Ap '98 - p147+ [51-250]

King, Stephen Michael
Do You Love Me, Dad?
>   Bks Keeps - N '97 - p22 [51-250]
>   Sch Lib - v45 - N '97 - p187 [51-250]

A Special Kind of Love
>   RT - v51 - D '97 - p330 [51-250]

The Kingfisher Beano Book of Amazing Facts
> r Books - v11 - Je '97 - p21 [51-250]
>   Books - v11 - Ag '97 - p15 [51-250]

King-Smith, Dick

All Because of Jackson (Illus. by John Eastwood)
Bks Keeps - My '97 - p22 [51-250]

Babe and Other Stories (Illus. by Michael Terry)
Magpies - v12 - S '97 - p34 [51-250]

Godhanger (Illus. by Andrew Davidson)
Magpies - v12 - Mr '97 - p34 [251-500]
NS - v126 - D 5 '97 - p64 [51-250]

Harry's Mad (Illus. by Jill Bennett)
PW - v244 - Je 30 '97 - p77 [1-50]

The Invisible Dog (Illus. by Paul Howard)
Bks Keeps - My '97 - p23 [51-250]

The Jolly Witch (Illus. by Frank Rodgers)
Bks Keeps - N '97 - p21 [51-250]

Martin's Mice (Illus. by Jez Alborough)
PW - v245 - Mr 9 '98 - p70 [1-50]

A Mouse Called Wolf (Illus. by Jon Goodell)
BL - v94 - O 1 '97 - p329 [51-250]
Ch BWatch - v7 - D '97 - p4 [1-50]
Inst - v107 - N '97 - p22 [51-250]
PW - v244 - Je 30 '97 - p77 [1-50]
SLJ - v43 - D '97 - p94 [51-250]

A Mouse Called Wolf (Illus. by Alex De Wolf)
Bks Keeps - N '97 - p24 [51-250]
Obs - Jl 27 '97 - p16* [51-250]
Sch Lib - v45 - N '97 - p192 [51-250]
Spec - v279 - D 6 '97 - p43 [51-250]
TES - S 19 '97 - p13* [501+]

Mr. Ape (Illus. by Roger Roth)
PW - v245 - Mr 16 '98 - p64 [51-250]

Puppy Love (Illus. by Anita Jeram)
BL - v94 - D 15 '97 - p698+ [51-250]
BW - v27 - D 7 '97 - p21 [51-250]
CBRS - v26 - Ja 1 '98 - p50 [51-250]
Ch BWatch - v7 - N '97 - p3 [1-50]
KR - v65 - O 1 '97 - p1534 [51-250]
PW - v244 - N 3 '97 - p84 [51-250]
SLJ - v43 - N '97 - p109 [51-250]

The Sheep-Pig
TES - N 14 '97 - p11* [51-250]

The Sheep-Pig (Thorne). Audio Version
SLJ - v43 - Ap '97 - p82+ [51-250]

Smasher (Illus. by Richard Bernal)
BL - v94 - Ja 1 '98 - p813 [51-250]

The Spotty Pig (Illus. by Mary Wormell)
Ch BWatch - v7 - My '97 - p3 [1-50]
HB Guide - v8 - Fall '97 - p270 [51-250]
SLJ - v43 - My '97 - p102 [51-250]
TES - My 30 '97 - p8* [501+]

The Stray
TES - S 19 '97 - p13* [501+]

The Stray (Illus. by Wayne Parmenter)
PW - v245 - Mr 16 '98 - p67 [1-50]

The Stray (Whitfield). Audio Version
BL - v94 - F 15 '98 - p1027 [51-250]
y   Kliatt - v31 - N '97 - p45 [51-250]

Three Terrible Trins (Illus. by Mark Teague)
BL - v94 - N 1 '97 - p475 [1-50]

Kinsey-Warnock, Natalie

As Long as There Are Mountains
BL - v93 - Ag '97 - p1901 [51-250]
CCB-B - v51 - N '97 - p89 [51-250]
KR - v65 - Je 1 '97 - p875 [51-250]
SLJ - v43 - Ag '97 - p157 [51-250]
y   VOYA - v21 - Ap '98 - p47 [51-250]

The Bear Who Heard Crying (Illus. by Ted Rand)
ECEJ - v25 - Fall '97 - p48 [1-50]

The Fiddler of the Northern Lights (Illus. by Leslie W Bowman)
SE - v61 - Ap '97 - p5* [1-50]

In the Language of Loons
y   CCB-B - v51 - Ap '98 - p284+ [51-250]
KR - v65 - D 1 '97 - p1776+ [51-250]
SLJ - v44 - Mr '98 - p214 [51-250]

The Summer of Stanley (Illus. by Donald Gates)
CBRS - v25 - Ag '97 - p160 [51-250]
HB Guide - v8 - Fall '97 - p270 [1-50]
SLJ - v43 - Je '97 - p94 [51-250]

Sweet Memories Still (Illus. by Laurie Harden)
> HB Guide - v8 - Fall '97 - p303 [51-250]

Wilderness Cat (Illus. by Mark Graham)
> ECEJ - v25 - Fall '97 - p47 [1-50]

Kipling, Rudyard
Rikki Tikki Tavi (Illus. by Danuta Mayer)
> Ch BWatch - v7 - N '97 - p4 [1-50]

Kiralfy, Bob
The Most Excellent Book of How to Be a Cheerleader (Illus. by Roger Vlitos)
> SLJ - v44 - Mr '98 - p234 [51-250]

Kirk, Daniel
Bigger (Illus. by Daniel Kirk)
> KR - v66 - Mr 15 '98 - p406 [51-250]

Breakfast at the Liberty Diner (Illus. by Daniel Kirk)
> BL - v94 - N 1 '97 - p482 [51-250]
> KR - v65 - Ag 15 '97 - p1307 [51-250]
> PW - v244 - O 27 '97 - p74 [51-250]
> SLJ - v43 - N '97 - p85+ [51-250]

Trash Trucks!
> CBRS - v25 - Ag '97 - p160 [51-250]
> HB Guide - v8 - Fall '97 - p270 [51-250]

Kirk, David
Miss Spider's New Car (Illus. by David Kirk)
> BL - v94 - N 1 '97 - p482+ [51-250]
> KR - v65 - S 15 '97 - p1459 [51-250]
> NY - v73 - O 6 '97 - p115+ [51-250]
> SLJ - v44 - Ja '98 - p88 [51-250]

Miss Spider's Tea Party (Illus. by David Kirk)
> HB Guide - v8 - Fall '97 - p252 [51-250]

Kirkpatrick, Katherine
Keeping the Good Light
> Ch BWatch - v7 - Je '97 - p7 [1-50]

Kirkwood, Jon
Cutaway Fire Fighters
> Ch BWatch - v8 - Ja '98 - p6 [1-50]

The Fantastic Book of Car Racing (Illus. by Peter Harper)
> Ch BWatch - v7 - My '97 - p7 [1-50]
> HB Guide - v8 - Fall '97 - p370+ [51-250]
> SLJ - v43 - Ag '97 - p170 [51-250]

Fire Fighters (Illus. by Simon Tegg)
> PW - v244 - O 13 '97 - p76+ [51-250]

Giant Buildings
> Ch BWatch - v8 - Ja '98 - p6 [1-50]

Trucks (Illus. by Simon Tegg)
> Ch BWatch - v8 - Ja '98 - p6 [1-50]
> PW - v244 - O 13 '97 - p76+ [51-250]

Kirtland, Mark
Why Do We Do That?
> SLJ - v43 - Ag '97 - p170 [51-250]

Kirwan, Anna
Juliet: Midsummer at Greenchapel, England 1340 (Illus. by Lynne Marshall)
> SLJ - v44 - Ap '98 - p131 [51-250]

Juliet: Rescue at Marlehead Manor, England 1340 (Illus. by Lynne Marshall)
> SLJ - v43 - Ag '97 - p135 [51-250]

Kitamura, Satoshi
Bath-Time Boots (Illus. by Satoshi Kitamura)
> KR - v66 - Ja 1 '98 - p58 [51-250]
> PW - v245 - Mr 23 '98 - p101 [1-50]

A Friend for Boots
> PW - v245 - Mr 23 '98 - p101 [1-50]

Goldfish Hide-and-Seek (Illus. by Satoshi Kitamura)
> CBRS - v26 - Win '98 - p62+ [1-50]
> KR - v65 - Je 15 '97 - p951 [51-250]
> Sch Lib - v45 - N '97 - p187 [51-250]

Sheep in Wolves' Clothing (McDonough). Audio Version
> SLJ - v43 - N '97 - p69 [51-250]

Kitchen (First Words Series)
  Ch BWatch - v7 - Je '97 - p4 [1-50]

Kite, L Patricia
Blood-Feeding Bugs and Beasts
  ASBYP - v29 - Fall '96 - p20+ [501+]
  SB - v33 - Ag '97 - p186 [1-50]

Dandelion Adventures (Illus. by Anca Hariton)
  BL - v94 - Mr 15 '98 - p1246 [51-250]
  KR - v66 - F 1 '98 - p202 [51-250]

Kittinger, Jo S
Dead Log Alive!
  SB - v33 - Ag '97 - p186 [1-50]
  SLJ - v43 - My '97 - p146 [51-250]

A Look at Rocks
  BL - v94 - D 1 '97 - p630 [51-250]
  SB - v34 - Ap '98 - p80 [51-250]
  SLJ - v44 - Ja '98 - p126 [51-250]

Klare, Roger
Gregor Mendel: Father of Genetics
  BL - v94 - D 1 '97 - p625 [51-250]
  KR - v65 - Jl 15 '97 - p1112 [51-250]
  SLJ - v43 - D '97 - p139+ [51-250]
y   VOYA - v20 - D '97 - p330+ [251-500]

Klass, David
Screen Test
y   BL - v94 - D 1 '97 - p615+ [51-250]
  CBRS - v26 - Win '98 - p70+ [51-250]
y   CCB-B - v51 - Mr '98 - p248+ [51-250]
y   KR - v65 - Jl 15 '97 - p1112+ [51-250]
y   PW - v244 - S 29 '97 - p90 [51-250]

Klass, Sheila Solomon
A Shooting Star
  HB Guide - v8 - Fall '97 - p303 [51-250]
  SLJ - v43 - My '97 - p135 [51-250]

The Uncivil War
y   BL - v94 - F 15 '98 - p1000 [51-250]
  KR - v66 - Ap 1 '98 - p497 [51-250]
  PW - v244 - D 22 '97 - p60 [51-250]
  SLJ - v44 - Ap '98 - p132 [51-250]

Klein, James
Gold Rush! (Illus. by Michael Rohani)
  KR - v66 - F 15 '98 - p269 [51-250]

Kleinbaum, N H
Story of Dr. Dolittle (Illus. by Hugh Lofting)
  Ch BWatch - v7 - Je '97 - p7 [1-50]

Voyages of Dr. Dolittle (Illus. by Hugh Lofting)
  Ch BWatch - v7 - Je '97 - p7 [1-50]

Kleven, Elisa
The Puddle Pail (Illus. by Elisa Kleven)
  BL - v93 - Je 1 '97 - p1719 [51-250]
  HB Guide - v8 - Fall '97 - p270 [51-250]
  KR - v65 - Je 1 '97 - p875 [51-250]
  SLJ - v43 - Je '97 - p94 [51-250]
  SLJ - v43 - D '97 - p26 [1-50]

Viva! Una Pinata!
  HB Guide - v8 - Fall '97 - p338 [51-250]

Kline, Suzy
Horrible Harry and the Ant Invasion (Heller). Audio Version
  BL - v94 - F 15 '98 - p1027 [51-250]

Horrible Harry and the Drop of Doom
  BL - v94 - F 15 '98 - p1012 [51-250]

Horrible Harry and the Purple People (Illus. by Frank Remkiewicz)
  KR - v65 - Je 1 '97 - p875+ [51-250]
  SLJ - v43 - S '97 - p184 [51-250]

Horrible Harry's Secret (Heller). Audio Version
  SLJ - v44 - Mr '98 - p157 [51-250]

Marvin and the Mean Words (Illus. by Blanche Sims)
  HB Guide - v8 - Fall '97 - p292 [51-250]
  KR - v65 - Ap 15 '97 - p641 [51-250]
  SLJ - v43 - My '97 - p102 [51-250]

Klinting, Lars
Bruno the Baker
  BL - v94 - Ja 1 '98 - p824 [51-250]
  PW - v244 - Ag 25 '97 - p73 [1-50]

Bruno the Carpenter (Illus. by Lars Klinting)
  RT - v51 - F '98 - p429 [51-250]

Bruno the Tailor (Illus. by Lars Klinting)
RT - v51 - F '98 - p430 [51-250]

Klise, Kate
Regarding the Fountain (Illus. by M Sarah Klise)
KR - v65 - D 15 '97 - p1835+ [51-250]
PW - v245 - Ja 12 '98 - p60 [51-250]

Klum, Mattias
Exploring the Rain Forest (Illus. by Mattias Klum)
BL - v94 - Mr 1 '98 - p1128 [51-250]
KR - v65 - D 15 '97 - p1837 [51-250]
SLJ - v44 - F '98 - p103 [51-250]

Knapp, Brian J
Elements. Vols. 1-15 (Illus. by David Woodroffe)
yr   SB - v33 - Ap '97 - p78+ [501+]
r   SLJ - v43 - My '97 - p160 [51-250]

Knapp, Ron
Andre Agassi: Star Tennis Player
CLW - v68 - S '97 - p68+ [51-250]
HB Guide - v8 - Fall '97 - p371 [51-250]
y   SLJ - v43 - Ag '97 - p170+ [51-250]

Chris Webber: Star Forward
CLW - v68 - S '97 - p68 [51-250]
HB Guide - v8 - Fall '97 - p371 [51-250]

Mummies
RT - v51 - O '97 - p138 [1-50]

Kneidel, Sally Stenhouse
Creepy Crawlies and the Scientific Method
Inst - v107 - S '97 - p8 [1-50]

Kniedel, Sally
Slugs, Bugs, and Salamanders
AB - v100 - N 17 '97 - p1269+ [51-250]

Knight, Bertram T
From Cow to Ice Cream (Illus. by Bertram T Knight)
BL - v94 - O 15 '97 - p408+ [51-250]

HB Guide - v8 - Fall '97 - p357 [51-250]
SB - v33 - N '97 - p245 [51-250]
SLJ - v43 - S '97 - p201 [51-250]

From Mud to House
BL - v94 - F 15 '98 - p1003+ [51-250]

Knight, Dawn
Mischief, Mad Mary, and Me (Illus. by Jared T Williams)
CBRS - v25 - Jl '97 - p151+ [51-250]
CCB-B - v51 - S '97 - p15+ [51-250]
HB Guide - v8 - Fall '97 - p303 [51-250]
SLJ - v43 - My '97 - p102 [51-250]

Knight, Khadijah
Islamic Festivals
SLJ - v43 - D '97 - p140 [51-250]

Knight, Margy Burns
Talking Walls (Illus. by Anne Sibley O'Brien)
SE - v61 - Ap '97 - p7* [1-50]

Talking Walls (Knight). Audio Version
PW - v245 - F 9 '98 - p26 [51-250]

Knister
Hexe Lilli Zaubert Hausaufgaben (Illus. by Birgit Rieger)
Bkbird - v35 - Spr '97 - p49 [51-250]

Knowles, Sheena
Edwina the Emu (Illus. by Rod Clement)
Magpies - v12 - Jl '97 - p28 [51-250]
SLJ - v43 - S '97 - p185 [51-250]

Knowlton, Jack
Mapas Y Globos Terraqueos (Illus. by Harriet Barton)
SLJ - v43 - My '97 - p154 [51-250]

Koertge, Ron
The Heart of the City
CCB-B - v51 - Ap '98 - p285 [51-250]
KR - v66 - F 15 '98 - p269 [51-250]
SLJ - v44 - Mr '98 - p214+ [51-250]

Koh, Frances M
Korean Games (Illus. by Tony Letourneau)
    SLJ - v44 - F '98 - p100 [51-250]

Kohl, Mary Ann F
Cooking Art (Illus. by Ronni Roseman-Hall)
    CBRS - v26 - S '97 - p8 [51-250]
    Ch BWatch - v7 - Jl '97 - p2 [51-250]

Koja, Stephan
Claude Monet: The Magician of Colour
    PW - v244 - Je 2 '97 - p73 [1-50]
    SLJ - v44 - Ja '98 - p102 [51-250]

Kolar, Bob
Stomp, Stomp! (Illus. by Bob Kolar)
    KR - v65 - S 1 '97 - p1391 [51-250]

Kolatch, Alfred J
Let's Celebrate Our Jewish Holidays (Illus. by Alex Bloch)
    SLJ - v43 - D '97 - p110+ [51-250]

Koller, Jackie French
No Such Thing (Illus. by Betsy Lewin)
    CLW - v68 - S '97 - p64+ [51-250]
    HB Guide - v8 - Fall '97 - p270 [51-250]
    SLJ - v43 - Je '97 - p95 [51-250]

Komaiko, Leah
Annie Bananie (Illus. by Abby Carter)
    HB Guide - v8 - Fall '97 - p292 [51-250]

Annie Bananie and the People's Court (Illus. by Abby Carter)
    SLJ - v44 - Ap '98 - p102 [51-250]

Annie Bananie--Best Friends to the End (Illus. by Abby Carter)
    Par - v73 - F '98 - p185 [1-50]
    SLJ - v43 - My '97 - p102 [51-250]

Annie Bananie--Best Friends to the End (Moore). Audio Version
    SLJ - v44 - Mr '98 - p156 [51-250]

Konigsburg, E L
From the Mixed-Up Files of Mrs. Basil E. Frankwiler (Illus. by E L Konigsburg)
    NYTBR - v102 - N 16 '97 - p26 [1-50]

The View from Saturday
y   ABR - v19 - N '97 - p11+ [501+]
    PW - v245 - F 2 '98 - p92 [1-50]
    RT - v51 - O '97 - p153 [51-250]
y   VOYA - v20 - F '98 - p365 [51-250]

The View from Saturday (Adamson). Audio Version
    BL - v94 - F 15 '98 - p1027 [51-250]
    PW - v244 - N 10 '97 - p30 [51-250]
    SLJ - v44 - Mr '98 - p158 [51-250]
    SLJ - v44 - Ap '98 - p39 [1-50]

Kooharian, David
Sammy's Story (Illus. by David Kooharian)
    CBRS - v26 - S '97 - p3 [1-50]
    CCB-B - v51 - O '97 - p55+ [251-500]
    KR - v65 - Ag 15 '97 - p1307 [51-250]
    PW - v244 - Ag 18 '97 - p92+ [51-250]
    SLJ - v43 - S '97 - p185 [51-250]

Kopper, Lisa
Daisy Is a Mommy
    HB Guide - v8 - Fall '97 - p252 [51-250]

Daisy Is a Mummy (Illus. by Lisa Kopper)
    Magpies - v12 - Mr '97 - p26 [51-250]

My Pony Ride
    Bks Keeps - S '97 - p20+ [51-250]

Koralek, Jenny
Keeping Secrets (Illus. by Steve Cox)
    Bks Keeps - S '97 - p24 [51-250]
    Sch Lib - v45 - Ag '97 - p146 [51-250]

Korman, Gordon
The Chicken Doesn't Skate
    CBRA - '96 - p480 [51-250]

The Last-Place Sports Poems of Jeremy Bloom
    CBRA - '96 - p498 [51-250]
    SLJ - v43 - Ap '97 - p112 [51-250]

Liar, Liar, Pants on Fire (Illus. by
JoAnn Adinolfi)
> CBRS - v26 - D '97 - p44 [51-250]
> CM:CanRev - v4 - Ap 24 '98 - pONL
> [51-250]
> KR - v65 - Je 1 '97 - p876 [51-250]
> Quill & Q - v63 - N '97 - p44+ [251-
> 500]
> SLJ - v43 - S '97 - p185 [51-250]

Koscielniak, Bruce
Hear, Hear, Mr. Shakespeare (Illus.
by Bruce Koscielniak)
> KR - v66 - Mr 15 '98 - p406 [51-250]

Koslow, Philip
Building a New World
> Ch BWatch - v7 - O '97 - p7 [1-50]
> HB Guide - v8 - Fall '97 - p395 [51-
> 250]

Lords of the Savanna
> Ch BWatch - v7 - O '97 - p7 [1-50]
> y   SLJ - v44 - Ja '98 - p126 [251-500]

Senegambia: Land of the Lion
> Ch BWatch - v7 - Mr '97 - p5 [1-50]
> HB Guide - v8 - Fall '97 - p393 [51-
> 250]
> y   SLJ - v43 - Ap '97 - p150 [51-250]

Kosman, Miriam R
Red, Blue, and Yellow Yarn (Illus. by
Valeri Gorbachev)
> HB Guide - v8 - Fall '97 - p270 [51-
> 250]

Kostenevich, A G
Henri Matisse
> HMR - Win '97 - p46 [51-250]
> y   KR - v65 - N 1 '97 - p1646 [51-250]
> PW - v244 - D 22 '97 - p61 [1-50]

Kovacs, Deborah
Beneath Blue Waters (Illus. by Larry
Madin)
> SB - v33 - Ap '97 - p85 [51-250]

Kovalski, Maryann
Brenda and Edward (Illus. by
Maryann Kovalski)
> BL - v94 - O 15 '97 - p415 [51-250]
> KR - v65 - Ag 1 '97 - p1223 [51-250]
> SLJ - v43 - S '97 - p185 [51-250]

Kowalski, Kathiann M
Hazardous Waste Sites
> SB - v33 - Ap '97 - p82 [251-500]

Kraan, Hanna
The Wicked Witch Is at It Again!
(Illus. by Annemarie Van Haeringen)
> BL - v94 - S 15 '97 - p235 [51-250]
> HB Guide - v8 - Fall '97 - p303 [51-
> 250]
> KR - v65 - My 15 '97 - p802 [51-250]
> SLJ - v43 - Jl '97 - p70 [51-250]

Kramer, Barbara
Neil Armstrong: The First Man on the
Moon
> SLJ - v43 - D '97 - p133+ [51-250]

Kramer, Stephen
Theodoric's Rainbow (Illus. by Daniel
Mark Duffy)
> ASBYP - v29 - Sum '96 - p21+ [251-
> 500]

Kramer, Stephen P
Eye of the Storm (Illus. by Warren
Faidley)
> y   BL - v94 - Mr 15 '98 - p1225 [1-50]
> CBRS - v25 - My '97 - p119 [51-250]
> HB Guide - v8 - Fall '97 - p364 [51-
> 250]
> y   VOYA - v21 - Ap '98 - p39 [1-50]

Kranendonk, Anke
Just a Minute! (Illus. by Jung-Hee
Spetter)
> KR - v66 - Ap 15 '98 - p584 [51-250]

Krasno, Rena
Kneeling Carabao and Dancing
Giants (Illus. by Ileana C Lee)
> BL - v94 - D 1 '97 - p620 [51-250]
> Ch BWatch - v7 - Jl '97 - p2 [51-250]
> KR - v65 - S 15 '97 - p1459 [51-250]

Kratholm, Julie
Goldilocks and the Three Bears (Illus.
by Kendra Dew)
> SLJ - v44 - Ja '98 - p88 [51-250]

Kraus, Robert

Leo the Late Bloomer (Illus. by Jose Aruego)
> PW - v245 - F 16 '98 - p213 [1-50]

Little Louie the Baby Bloomer (Illus. by Jose Aruego)
> BL - v94 - Mr 15 '98 - p1250 [51-250]

Kraus, Scott

The Search for the Right Whale
> SLJ - v43 - My '97 - p57 [1-50]

Krauss, Ronnie

Take a Look, It's in a Book (Illus. by Christopher Hornsby)
> Ch BWatch - v7 - S '97 - p4 [51-250]
> HB Guide - v8 - Fall '97 - p367 [51-250]
> SLJ - v43 - Je '97 - p109 [51-250]

Krehbiel, Randy

Little Bighorn
> SLJ - v44 - Ja '98 - p125 [51-250]

Krensky, Stephen

Breaking into Print (Illus. by Bonnie Christensen)
> RT - v51 - O '97 - p148+ [51-250]
> SE - v61 - Ap '97 - p6* [1-50]

Kress, Camille

Tot Shabbat (Illus. by Camille Kress)
> SLJ - v43 - S '97 - p185 [51-250]

Kress, Stephen W

Project Puffin
> BL - v93 - Ag '97 - p1895 [51-250]
> CCB-B - v50 - Jl '97 - p400 [51-250]

Krishnaswami, Uma

The Broken Tusk (Illus. by Maniam Selven)
> SLJ - v43 - Jl '97 - p107 [51-250]
> SLMQ - v25 - Spr '97 - p184 [1-50]

Krohn, Katherine E

Marcia Clark, Voice for the Victims
> y Ch BWatch - v7 - Ap '97 - p5 [1-50]
> Emerg Lib - v24 - My '97 - p67 [1-50]
> HB Guide - v8 - Fall '97 - p325 [51-250]

Kroll, S

Mary Mclean and the St. Patrick's Day Parade (Illus. by Michael Dooling)
> ECEJ - v25 - Fall '97 - p48 [1-50]

Kroll, Steven

Pony Express! (Illus. by Dan Andreasen)
> Emerg Lib - v24 - My '97 - p64+ [51-250]
> SE - v61 - Ap '97 - p10* [1-50]

Kroll, Virginia

Africa Brothers and Sisters (Illus. by Vanessa French)
> PW - v245 - Ja 12 '98 - p61 [1-50]

Faraway Drums (Illus. by Floyd Cooper)
> BL - v94 - F 15 '98 - p1008 [51-250]

Kroll, Virginia L

Butterfly Boy (Illus. by Gerardo Suzan)
> BL - v94 - N 1 '97 - p483 [51-250]
> CBRS - v25 - Jl '97 - p148 [1-50]
> CCB-B - v51 - S '97 - p16 [51-250]
> Ch BWatch - v7 - Je '97 - p3 [51-250]
> HB Guide - v8 - Fall '97 - p271 [51-250]
> SLJ - v43 - Je '97 - p95+ [51-250]

Hands! (Illus. by Cathryn Falwell)
> BL - v94 - S 15 '97 - p238 [51-250]
> SLJ - v43 - D '97 - p94 [51-250]

Masai and I (Illus. by Nancy Carpenter)
> ECEJ - v25 - Fall '97 - p48 [1-50]

Kroninger, Stephen

If I Crossed the Road (Illus. by Stephen Kroninger)
> BL - v94 - D 15 '97 - p703 [51-250]
> CBRS - v26 - F '98 - p77 [51-250]
> KR - v65 - O 1 '97 - p1534 [51-250]
> PW - v244 - S 22 '97 - p80 [51-250]
> SLJ - v43 - D '97 - p94+ [51-250]

Krueger, Richard

The Dinosaurs (Illus. by Ted Finger)
> ASBYP - v29 - Fall '96 - p61+ [501+]

Krull, Kathleen

Lives of the Athletes (Illus. by Kathryn Hewitt)

> CCB-B - v50 - Je '97 - p363 [51-250]
> HB Guide - v8 - Fall '97 - p371 [51-250]
> SLJ - v43 - My '97 - p146+ [51-250]

Wilma Unlimited (Illus. by David Diaz)

> Inst - v106 - My '97 - p20 [51-250]
> Inst - v107 - O '97 - p49 [1-50]
> SLJ - v44 - Mr '98 - p120 [1-50]

Wish You Were Here (Illus. by Amy Schwartz)

> BL - v93 - Je 1 '97 - p1692+ [51-250]
> Emerg Lib - v25 - Ja '98 - p57 [51-250]
> HB Guide - v8 - Fall '97 - p395 [51-250]
> KR - v65 - My 15 '97 - p802 [51-250]
> PW - v244 - My 19 '97 - p77 [51-250]
> SLJ - v43 - Je '97 - p109 [51-250]

Krupinski, Loretta

Bluewater Journal

> SB - v33 - O '97 - p218+ [51-250]

Into the Woods (Illus. by Loretta Krupinski)

> HB Guide - v8 - Fall '97 - p346 [51-250]
> KR - v65 - Ap 15 '97 - p641 [51-250]
> SLJ - v43 - My '97 - p120 [51-250]

Kruusval, Catarina

Beach Day (Illus. by Catarina Kruusval)

> CBRS - v25 - Jl '97 - p148+ [1-50]
> HB Guide - v8 - Fall '97 - p271 [1-50]
> SLJ - v43 - D '97 - p95 [51-250]

Birthday Flowers (Illus. by Catarina Kruusval)

> CBRS - v25 - Jl '97 - p148+ [1-50]
> HB Guide - v8 - Fall '97 - p271 [1-50]
> RT - v51 - F '98 - p429 [51-250]

Kuch, K D

The Babysitter's Handbook (Illus. by J J Smith-Moore)

> y   Kliatt - v31 - Jl '97 - p26 [51-250]
> SLJ - v43 - Jl '97 - p107 [51-250]

Kuchling, Gerald

Yakkinn the Swamp Tortoise (Illus. by Guundie Kuchling)

> Magpies - v12 - My '97 - p42 [51-250]

Kudler, David

The Seven Gods of Luck (Illus. by Linda Finch)

> BL - v94 - D 15 '97 - p703+ [51-250]
> CBRS - v26 - Win '98 - p63 [51-250]
> CCB-B - v51 - O '97 - p56 [51-250]
> KR - v65 - Jl 1 '97 - p1031 [51-250]
> NYTBR - v103 - F 1 '98 - p24 [1-50]

Kudlinski, Kathleen V

Shannon: The Schoolmarm Mysteries, San Francisco 1880 (Illus. by Bill Farnsworth)

> SLJ - v44 - Ap '98 - p102 [51-250]

Kulling, Monica

Edgar Badger's Balloon Day (Illus. by Carol O'Malia)

> SLJ - v44 - Ja '98 - p88 [51-250]

Marmee's Surprise (Illus. by Diane Paterson)

> SLJ - v43 - D '97 - p95 [51-250]

Kunhardt, Edith

Honest Abe (Illus. by Malcah Zeldis)

> PW - v245 - Ja 26 '98 - p93 [1-50]

Kunstler, James Howard

Johnny Appleseed (Keillor) (Illus. by Stan Olson). Book and Audio Version

> Ch BWatch - v7 - D '97 - p4 [51-250]

Kurelek, William

A Prairie Boy's Summer (Illus. by William Kurelek)

> Ch Bk News - v20 - Spr '97 - p34 [251-500]

A Prairie Boy's Winter (Illus. by William Kurelek)

> Ch Bk News - v20 - Spr '97 - p34 [251-500]

Kurt, Kemal
The Five Fingers and the Moon (Illus. by Aljoscha Blau)
BL - v94 - O 15 '97 - p415+ [51-250]
KR - v65 - Ag 1 '97 - p1224 [51-250]
PW - v244 - S 1 '97 - p104+ [51-250]

Kurtis-Kleinman, Eileen
When Aunt Lena Did the Rhumba (Illus. by Diane Greenseid)
CBRS - v25 - Ag '97 - p160 [51-250]
CCB-B - v51 - S '97 - p16+ [51-250]
HB Guide - v8 - Fall '97 - p271 [51-250]
NYTBR - v102 - S 14 '97 - p30 [1-50]
SLJ - v43 - Je '97 - p96 [51-250]

Kurts, Charles
These Are the Voyages
BL - v94 - D 15 '97 - p700 [1-50]

Kurtz, Jane
Fire on the Mountain (Illus. by E B Lewis)
PW - v245 - Ja 19 '98 - p380 [1-50]

Miro in the Kingdom of the Sun (Illus. by David Frampton)
RT - v51 - N '97 - p250 [51-250]

Only a Pigeon (Illus. by E B Lewis)
BL - v93 - Je 1 '97 - p1719 [51-250]
CBRS - v25 - Jl '97 - p152 [51-250]
CCB-B - v50 - Jl '97 - p400+ [51-250]
HB Guide - v8 - Fall '97 - p271 [51-250]
KR - v65 - My 15 '97 - p802 [51-250]
Par Ch - Awards '97 - p4 [51-250]
SLJ - v43 - Je '97 - p96 [51-250]

Trouble (Illus. by Durga Bernhard)
HB Guide - v8 - Fall '97 - p334 [51-250]
Inst - v107 - Ag '97 - p21 [1-50]
SLJ - v43 - Ap '97 - p127+ [51-250]

Kushner, Lawrence
The Book of Miracles (Illus. by Lawrence Kushner)
PW - v245 - Ja 26 '98 - p87 [51-250]

Kuskin, Karla
City Dog
PW - v245 - F 16 '98 - p213 [1-50]

The Upstairs Cat (Illus. by Howard Fine)
CBRS - v26 - N '97 - p27 [1-50]
Ch BWatch - v7 - N '97 - p4 [1-50]
PW - v244 - O 13 '97 - p74 [51-250]
SLJ - v43 - D '97 - p95+ [51-250]

Kusugak, Michael
My Arctic 1,2,3 (Illus. by Vladyana Krykorka)
CBRA - '96 - p446 [51-250]
SLJ - v43 - My '97 - p120+ [51-250]
TES - Je 13 '97 - pR7 [51-250]

Kutschbach, Doris
The Blue Rider
PW - v244 - Je 2 '97 - p73 [1-50]
SLJ - v44 - Ja '98 - p102 [51-250]

Kvasnosky, Laura McGee
Zelda and Ivy (Illus. by Laura McGee Kvasnosky)
CCB-B - v51 - Ap '98 - p285 [51-250]

Kwan, Michelle
Michelle Kwan, Heart of a Champion
y   BL - v94 - Mr 15 '98 - p1225 [1-50]
       PW - v244 - N 10 '97 - p75 [51-250]
       SLJ - v43 - N '97 - p130 [51-250]
y   VOYA - v21 - Ap '98 - p39 [1-50]
y   VOYA - v21 - Ap '98 - p68 [51-250]

Kwei, Eleanor
Winnie-the-Pooh's Giant Lift-the-Flap-Book
PW - v244 - N 10 '97 - p76 [51-250]

Kyte, Kathy S
Play It Safe
SE - v61 - S '97 - p271 [1-50]

L

Lace, William W
The Dallas Cowboys Football Team
    BL - v94 - O 15 '97 - p400 [51-250]

Lachner, Dorothea
Look Out, Cinder! (Illus. by Eugen Sopko)
    RT - v51 - F '98 - p427+ [51-250]

Meredith, the Witch Who Wasn't (Illus. by Christa Unzner)
    BL - v94 - S 1 '97 - p133 [51-250]
    KR - v65 - Ag 1 '97 - p1224 [51-250]
    NYTBR - v102 - O 26 '97 - p47 [501+]
    SLJ - v43 - N '97 - p91 [51-250]
    TES - O 31 '97 - p8* [51-250]

Lachtman, Ofelia Dumas
Call Me Consuelo
    HB Guide - v8 - Fall '97 - p303 [51-250]
    SLJ - v43 - Jl '97 - p94 [51-250]

Leticia's Secret
    SLJ - v44 - Ja '98 - p114 [51-250]

Lade, Roger
The Most Excellent Book of How to Be a Puppeteer
    Ch BWatch - v7 - My '97 - p7 [51-250]

Ladwig, Tim
Psalm Twenty-Three (Illus. by Tim Ladwig)
    BL - v94 - O 1 '97 - p324 [51-250]

Lady Kaguya's Secret (Illus. by Jirina Marton)
    BL - v94 - Ja 1 '98 - p805 [51-250]

    CBRS - v26 - Win '98 - p67 [51-250]
    Ch Bk News - v20 - Sum '97 - p27 [51-250]
    PW - v244 - D 8 '97 - p72 [51-250]
    Quill & Q - v63 - S '97 - p74 [251-500]
    SLJ - v44 - F '98 - p100+ [51-250]

The Ladybird Guide to the Presidents of the United States
    HB Guide - v8 - Fall '97 - p396 [51-250]

The Ladybird Thesaurus
    r Sch Lib - v45 - N '97 - p205 [51-250]

Ladybug
    p Par Ch - Awards '97 - p27 [1-50]

Lafferty, Peter
Everyday Things (Illus. by B Watson)
    ASBYP - v29 - Sum '96 - p63+ [501+]

Heat and Cold (Illus. by Terry Hadler)
    ASBYP - v29 - Fall '96 - p51+ [251-500]

A History of Inventions
    Bks Keeps - S '97 - p29 [51-250]
    New Sci - v154 - Je 28 '97 - p44 [51-250]
    Sch Lib - v45 - Ag '97 - p152 [51-250]

Light and Sound (Illus. by Peter Lafferty)
    ASBYP - v29 - Fall '96 - p51+ [251-500]

Radio and Television (Illus. by David Antram)
    SLJ - v44 - F '98 - p116 [51-250]

La Fontaine, Jean De
Fables of La Fontaine (Illus. by Marc Chagall)
> Bloom Rev - v17 - N '97 - p24 [51-250]
> BW - v27 - D 7 '97 - p22 [51-250]

Laird, Elizabeth
Kiss the Dust
> Bks Keeps - My '97 - p4+ [501+]

The Listener
> TES - Jl 4 '97 - p10* [501+]

The Listener (Illus. by Pauline Hazelwood)
> Bks Keeps - S '97 - p25 [51-250]
> Sch Lib - v45 - Ag '97 - p146 [51-250]
> TES - N 7 '97 - p8* [1-50]

Secret Friends
> TES - My 2 '97 - p8* [1-50]

Lakin, Patricia
Creativity: Around the World
> Ch BWatch - v7 - Mr '97 - p1 [51-250]

Lalli, Judy
I Like Being Me (Illus. by Douglas L Mason-Fry)
> SLJ - v44 - Mr '98 - p196+ [51-250]

Lamb (Snapshot)
> Ch BWatch - v7 - Je '97 - p4 [1-50]

Lamb, Nancy
One April Morning (Illus. by Floyd Cooper)
> LA - v73 - N '96 - p525 [51-250]
> SE - v61 - Ap '97 - p4* [1-50]
> y SE - v61 - S '97 - p271 [1-50]

Lambert, David
The Kingfisher Young People's Book of Oceans
> Ch BWatch - v7 - D '97 - p3 [1-50]
> SLJ - v44 - Mr '98 - p234 [51-250]

The Mediterranean Sea
> Ch BWatch - v7 - D '97 - p7 [1-50]
> HB Guide - v8 - Fall '97 - p385 [51-250]

The Pacific Ocean
> ASBYP - v29 - Fall '96 - p64 [251-500]

> HB Guide - v8 - Fall '97 - p385 [51-250]

Lambier, Doug
Genesis for Kids (Illus. by Ken Save)
> BL - v94 - O 1 '97 - p322+ [51-250]
> PW - v244 - Jl 28 '97 - p69 [51-250]

Lamm, C Drew
Sea Lion Roars. Book and Audio Version
> SLJ - v43 - N '97 - p72 [51-250]

Lamond, Margrete
Plagues and Pestilence
> Magpies - v12 - Jl '97 - p44 [51-250]

Lampton, Christopher
Home Page
> HB Guide - v8 - Fall '97 - p317 [51-250]
> SLJ - v44 - F '98 - p119 [51-250]

The World Wide Web
> HB Guide - v8 - Fall '97 - p317 [51-250]
> SLJ - v44 - F '98 - p119 [51-250]

Lamstein, Sarah Marwil
Annie's Shabbat (Illus. by Cecily Lang)
> BL - v94 - O 1 '97 - p324 [51-250]
> PW - v244 - Ag 25 '97 - p66 [51-250]
> SLJ - v43 - D '97 - p111 [51-250]

Landau, Elaine
The Assyrians
> CBRS - v26 - Ja '98 - p58+ [51-250]
> SLJ - v44 - Mr '98 - p234+ [51-250]

The Babylonians
> BL - v94 - Ja 1 '98 - p805 [51-250]
> CBRS - v26 - Ja '98 - p58+ [51-250]
> SLJ - v44 - Mr '98 - p234+ [51-250]

Bill Clinton and His Presidency
> BL - v94 - S 15 '97 - p228 [51-250]
> HB Guide - v8 - Fall '97 - p381 [51-250]
> SLJ - v43 - S '97 - p232 [51-250]

The Curse of Tutankhamen
> SB - v32 - D '96 - p277 [51-250]

Desert Mammals
> HB Guide - v8 - Fall '97 - p352 [51-250]

ESP
> SB - v32 - D '96 - p271 [51-250]

Ghosts
> ASBYP - v29 - Sum '96 - p54 [251-500]

Grassland Mammals
> HB Guide - v8 - Fall '97 - p352 [51-250]

Joined at Birth
> BL - v94 - S 15 '97 - p228 [51-250]
> HB Guide - v8 - Fall '97 - p356 [51-250]
> SLJ - v43 - Ag '97 - p171 [51-250]

Mountain Mammals
> HB Guide - v8 - Fall '97 - p352 [51-250]
> SLJ - v43 - Ap '97 - p120 [51-250]

Near-Death Experiences
> ASBYP - v29 - Sum '96 - p54 [251-500]

Ocean Mammals
> HB Guide - v8 - Fall '97 - p352 [51-250]
> SB - v33 - Ag '97 - p178+ [251-500]

The Shawnee
> HB Guide - v8 - Fall '97 - p399 [51-250]

Short Stature
> BL - v94 - S 15 '97 - p228 [51-250]
> HB Guide - v8 - Fall '97 - p356 [51-250]
> SLJ - v43 - Ag '97 - p171 [51-250]

Standing Tall
> HB Guide - v8 - Fall '97 - p356 [51-250]
> SLJ - v43 - Jl '97 - p107+ [51-250]

The Sumerians
> BL - v94 - Ja 1 '98 - p805 [51-250]
> CBRS - v26 - Ja '98 - p58+ [51-250]
> SLJ - v44 - Mr '98 - p234+ [51-250]

Temperate Forest Mammals
> HB Guide - v8 - Fall '97 - p352 [51-250]
> SLJ - v43 - Ap '97 - p120 [51-250]

Tropical Forest Mammals
> BL - v94 - D 1 '97 - p629 [1-50]

> HB Guide - v8 - Fall '97 - p352 [51-250]
> SB - v33 - Ag '97 - p178+ [251-500]
> SLJ - v43 - Ap '97 - p120 [51-250]

Tropical Rain Forests around the World
> BL - v94 - D 1 '97 - p629 [1-50]

UFOs
> ASBYP - v29 - Sum '96 - p54 [251-500]

Landon, Lucinda
Meg Mackintosh and the Mystery at the Soccer Match (Illus. by Lucinda Landon)
> SLJ - v44 - Mr '98 - p182 [51-250]

Landstrom, Olof
Boo and Baa at Sea (Illus. by Olof Landstrom)
> HB Guide - v8 - Fall '97 - p252 [51-250]
> RT - v51 - F '98 - p428+ [51-250]
> SLJ - v43 - Jl '97 - p70 [51-250]

Boo and Baa on a Cleaning Spree (Illus. by Olof Landstrom)
> HB Guide - v8 - Fall '97 - p252 [51-250]
> SLJ - v43 - Jl '97 - p70 [51-250]

Lane, Brian
The Investigation of Murder
> Ch BWatch - v7 - My '97 - p7 [1-50]

Langille, Carole Glasser
Where the Wind Sleeps (Illus. by Tom Ward)
> CBRA - '96 - p498 [51-250]

Langley, Andrew
Alexander the Great (Illus. by Alan Marks)
> Sch Lib - v45 - N '97 - p205 [51-250]
> TES - S 19 '97 - p16* [51-250]

Amelia Earhart (Illus. by Alan Marks)
> Sch Lib - v45 - N '97 - p205 [51-250]
> TES - S 19 '97 - p16* [51-250]

The Roman News
> Bks Keeps - My '97 - p26 [51-250]
> NYTBR - v102 - Ap 27 '97 - p29 [1-50]

RT - v51 - O '97 - p150+ [51-250]

The Search for Riches
HB Guide - v8 - Fall '97 - p386 [51-250]

Langlois, Florence
The Extraordinary Gift (Illus. by Florence Langlois)
HB Guide - v8 - Fall '97 - p271 [51-250]
NYTBR - v102 - My 18 '97 - p23+ [501+]
SLJ - v43 - Je '97 - p96 [51-250]

Langreuter, Jutta
Little Bear Brushes His Teeth (Illus. by Vera Sobat)
CBRS - v25 - Je '97 - p122 [51-250]
HB Guide - v8 - Fall '97 - p252 [51-250]
SLJ - v43 - Jl '97 - p70 [51-250]

Little Bear Goes to Kindergarten (Illus. by Vera Sobat)
CBRS - v25 - Je''97 - p122 [51-250]
HB Guide - v8 - Fall '97 - p252 [51-250]
SLJ - v43 - Ap '97 - p112 [51-250]

Langsen, Richard C
When Someone in the Family Drinks Too Much (Illus. by Nicole Rubel)
RT - v51 - O '97 - p139 [1-50]

Lankford, Mary D
Dominoes around the World (Illus. by Karen Dugan)
BL - v94 - Mr 15 '98 - p1238 [51-250]
SLJ - v44 - Ap '98 - p118+ [51-250]

Lansdown, Andrew
Dragonfox
Magpies - v12 - My '97 - p34+ [251-500]

Lansky, Bruce
Newfangled Fairy Tales. Bk. 1
BL - v94 - Mr 1 '98 - p1134 [51-250]
PW - v244 - D 22 '97 - p59+ [51-250]

No More Homework! No More Tests! (Illus. by Stephen Carpenter)
BL - v94 - S 15 '97 - p233 [51-250]
Inst - v107 - N '97 - p8 [51-250]

Lansky, Vicki
It's Not Your Fault, Koko Bear
Ch BWatch - v8 - Ja '98 - p1 [51-250]

Lantz, Francess
Stepsister from the Planet Weird
PW - v244 - N 10 '97 - p74 [51-250]
SLJ - v44 - F '98 - p109 [51-250]

La Pierre, Yvette
Mapping a Changing World
BW - v27 - Jl 6 '97 - p11 [251-500]

La Prise, Larry
The Hokey Pokey (Illus. by Sheila Hamanaka)
HB Guide - v8 - Fall '97 - p365 [51-250]
Learning - v26 - S '97 - p45 [1-50]

Lasenby, Jack
The Battle of Pook Island
Magpies - v12 - Mr '97 - p1*+ [51-250]
Magpies - v12 - Mr '97 - p7* [501+]

Laser, Michael
The Rain (Illus. by Jeffrey Greene)
CCB-B - v50 - Je '97 - p363+ [51-250]
HB Guide - v8 - Fall '97 - p271 [51-250]
SB - v33 - Ag '97 - p186 [1-50]
SLJ - v43 - My '97 - p102+ [51-250]

Lasky, Kathryn
Alice Rose and Sam
y   KR - v66 - Mr 1 '98 - p341 [51-250]
PW - v245 - F 16 '98 - p212 [51-250]

A Brilliant Streak (Illus. by Barry Moser)
KR - v66 - Ap 1 '98 - p497 [51-250]
PW - v245 - Mr 16 '98 - p66 [51-250]
SLJ - v44 - Ap '98 - p148 [51-250]

Hercules: The Man, the Myth, the Hero (Illus. by Mark Hess)
BL - v93 - Je 1 '97 - p1696 [51-250]
HB Guide - v8 - Fall '97 - p334 [51-250]
PW - v244 - My 26 '97 - p85 [51-250]
SLJ - v43 - Jl '97 - p108 [51-250]

*Marven of the Great North Woods
(Illus. by Kevin Hawkes)*

    BL - v94 - D 15 '97 - p702 [51-250]
    BL - v94 - Mr 15 '98 - p1219 [1-50]
    CBRS - v26 - Ja '98 - p56 [51-250]
    HB - v73 - N '97 - p670 [51-250]
    Inst - v107 - O '97 - p26 [51-250]
    KR - v65 - S 1 '97 - p1391 [51-250]
    NYTBR - v102 - N 16 '97 - p46 [501+]
    Par Ch - Awards '97 - p5 [51-250]
    PW - v244 - O 6 '97 - p83 [51-250]

*The Most Beautiful Roof in the World
(Illus. by Christopher G Knight)*

    BL - v94 - D 1 '97 - p629 [1-50]
    BL - v94 - Ja 1 '98 - p734 [1-50]
    HB Guide - v8 - Fall '97 - p346 [51-250]
    HMR - Sum '97 - p31+ [501+]
    SB - v33 - Ag '97 - p186 [1-50]
    SB - v33 - D '97 - p274 [251-500]
    SLJ - v43 - Ap '97 - p150 [51-250]

True North

y   RT - v51 - N '97 - p246 [51-250]
    SE - v61 - Ap '97 - p8* [1-50]
y   VOYA - v20 - Ap '97 - p30 [251-500]

Lattimore, Deborah Nourse

*Cinderhazel: The Cinderella of
Halloween (Illus. by Deborah Nourse
Lattimore)*

    BL - v94 - S 1 '97 - p139 [51-250]
    CBRS - v26 - Win '98 - p66 [51-250]
    CCB-B - v51 - N '97 - p90 [51-250]
    KR - v65 - O 1 '97 - p1534 [51-250]
    PW - v244 - O 6 '97 - p49 [51-250]

*The Fool and the Phoenix (Illus. by
Deborah Nourse Lattimore)*

    BL - v93 - Ag '97 - p1901 [51-250]
    KR - v65 - Je 15 '97 - p951 [51-250]
    SLJ - v43 - S '97 - p185+ [51-250]

Laube, Sigrid

Wenn Jakob Unterm Kirschbaum Sitzt

    Bkbird - v35 - Fall '97 - p50 [51-250]

Lauber, Patricia

Hurricanes: Earth's Mightiest Storms

    RT - v51 - S '97 - p56 [51-250]
y   VOYA - v20 - Ag '97 - p164+ [51-250]

*Living with Dinosaurs (Illus. by
Douglas Henderson)*

    SLJ - v43 - My '97 - p57 [1-50]

Painters of the Caves

    KR - v66 - F 15 '98 - p269 [51-250]
    SLJ - v44 - Mr '98 - p235 [51-250]

Summer of Fire

    JOYS - v10 - Sum '97 - p428 [1-50]

*The True-or-False Book of Cats (Illus.
by Rosalyn Schanzer)*

    BL - v94 - F 15 '98 - p1005 [51-250]
    PW - v245 - Mr 23 '98 - p102 [1-50]

Lauren, Jill

Succeeding with LD

    BL - v93 - Je 1 '97 - p1693 [51-250]
    SLJ - v43 - Jl '97 - p108 [51-250]
y   VOYA - v20 - Ag '97 - p203+ [251-500]

Lavender, David

*Snowbound: The Tragic Story of the
Donner Party*

    JOYS - v10 - Sum '97 - p428 [1-50]
    LA - v73 - N '96 - p526 [51-250]
y   VOYA - v20 - Ag '97 - p165 [51-250]

Lavies, Bianca

*Compost Critters (Illus. by Bianca
Lavies)*

    SLJ - v43 - My '97 - p57 [1-50]

A Gathering of Garter Snakes

    JOYS - v10 - Sum '97 - p428 [51-250]

Lavis, Steve

*Cock-a-Doodle-Doo: A Farmyard
Counting Book*

    CBRS - v25 - Je '97 - p123 [51-250]
    HB Guide - v8 - Fall '97 - p252 [51-250]

Jump! (Illus. by Steve Lavis)

    BL - v94 - Ja 1 '98 - p824 [51-250]
    KR - v66 - Ja 1 '98 - p58 [51-250]

Noisy Farm Animals

    Bks Keeps - N '97 - p19 [51-250]

Lawlor, Laurie
Addie's Forever Friend (Illus. by Helen Cogancherry)
    KR - v65 - O 1 '97 - p1534 [51-250]
    SLJ - v44 - F '98 - p86 [51-250]

The Biggest Pest on Eighth Avenue (Illus. by Cynthia Fisher)
    PW - v244 - N 10 '97 - p73+ [51-250]
    SLJ - v44 - Mr '98 - p182 [51-250]

Where Will This Shoe Take You?
    Ch BWatch - v7 - Jl '97 - p1 [1-50]
    HMR - Sum '97 - p49 [51-250]
y SE - v61 - Ap '97 - p8* [1-50]
    SLJ - v43 - My '97 - p148 [51-250]
y VOYA - v20 - Je '97 - p134 [251-500]

The Worst Kid Who Ever Lived on Eighth Avenue (Illus. by Cynthia Fisher)
    KR - v66 - F 15 '98 - p270 [51-250]
    SLJ - v44 - Ap '98 - p102 [51-250]

Lawlor, Veronica
I Was Dreaming to Come to America
    PW - v244 - Jl 7 '97 - p70 [1-50]

Lawrence, Jacob
Harriet and the Promised Land (Dee) (Illus. by Jacob Lawrence). Book and Audio Version
    SLJ - v44 - Ap '98 - p38 [1-50]

Lawson, Julie
Cougar Cove (Illus. by David Powell)
    CBRA - '96 - p480+ [51-250]

Emma and the Silk Train (Illus. by Paul Mombourquette)
    CM:CanRev - v4 - O 3 '97 - pONL [251-500]
    Quill & Q - v63 - Jl '97 - p50 [51-250]

Too Many Suns (Illus. by Martin Springett)
    CBRA - '96 - p446 [51-250]
    Ch BWatch - v7 - Je '97 - p3 [51-250]
    CLW - v68 - D '97 - p81 [51-250]
    Trib Bks - Je 8 '97 - p7 [51-250]

Whatever You Do, Don't Go Near That Canoe! (Illus. by Werner Zimmermann)
    CBRA - '96 - p447 [51-250]

White Jade Tiger
    Bkbird - v34 - Win '96 - p25+ [501+]

Layton, George
The Swap
    BL - v94 - O 1 '97 - p329 [51-250]
    CBRS - v26 - Win '98 - p71 [51-250]
y CCB-B - v51 - O '97 - p56+ [51-250]
    KR - v65 - Ag 15 '97 - p1308 [51-250]
    SLJ - v43 - S '97 - p218+ [51-250]

The Swap and Other Stories
    Books - v11 - Je '97 - p21 [51-250]
    Sch Lib - v45 - Ag '97 - p146 [51-250]
    TES - My 16 '97 - p14* [251-500]

The Swap and Other Stories (Layton). Audio Version
    Bks Keeps - S '97 - p27+ [51-250]

Lear, Edward
A Book of Nonsense (Illus. by Edward Lear)
    Comw - v124 - D 5 '97 - p14 [51-250]

Nonsense Songs (Illus. by Bee Willey)
    HB Guide - v8 - Fall '97 - p376 [1-50]
    SLJ - v43 - Je '97 - p109 [51-250]

Leavey, Peggy Dymond
A Circle in Time
    CM:CanRev - v4 - F 27 '98 - pONL [251-500]
    Quill & Q - v63 - O '97 - p36+ [251-500]

Leavy, Una
Goodbye Pappa (Illus. by Jennifer Eachus)
    Bks Keeps - Jl '97 - p6+ [501+]

Irish Fairy Tales and Legends (Illus. by Susan Field)
    KR - v65 - N 15 '97 - p1708 [51-250]
    PW - v244 - D 8 '97 - p74 [51-250]
    SLJ - v44 - F '98 - p102 [51-250]

Leblanc, Anne
Benjamin's First Word Book
    PW - v244 - N 10 '97 - p76 [51-250]

Benjamin's Toys
    PW - v244 - N 10 '97 - p76 [51-250]

Shopping with Benjamin
PW - v244 - N 10 '97 - p76 [51-250]

What's the Time? (Illus. by Hamlet Group)
KR - v65 - N 15 '97 - p1709 [51-250]
PW - v244 - N 10 '97 - p76 [1-50]

Leblanc, Louise
Maddie in Hospital
BIC - v26 - My '97 - p35+ [501+]

Maddie in Hospital (Illus. by Marie-Louise Gay)
CBRA - '96 - p481 [51-250]

LeBox, Annette
Miss Rafferty's Rainbow Socks (Illus. by Heather Holbrook)
CBRA - '96 - p447 [51-250]

The Princess Who Danced with Cranes (Illus. by Kasia Charko)
Quill & Q - v63 - My '97 - p42 [251-500]

Leder, Jane Mersky
A Russion Jewish Family
SE - v61 - Ap '97 - p9* [51-250]

Lee, Cynthia Chin
A Is for Asia (Illus. by Yumi Heo)
Emerg Lib - v25 - Ja '98 - p56+ [51-250]

Lee, Dennis, 1939-
Dinosaur Dinner with a Slice of Alligator Pie (Illus. by Debbie Tilley)
CCB-B - v50 - Je '97 - p364 [51-250]
Ch BWatch - v7 - My '97 - p2 [1-50]
HB Guide - v8 - Fall '97 - p377 [51-250]
SLJ - v43 - Ap '97 - p128 [51-250]

Lee, Hector Viveros
Yo Tenia Un Hipopotamo (Illus. by Hector Viveros Lee)
SLJ - v43 - Ag '97 - p181 [51-250]

Lee, Huy Voun
In the Park (Illus. by Huy Voun Lee)
KR - v66 - F 15 '98 - p270 [51-250]

Lee, Kathleen
Illegal Immigration
Ch BWatch - v8 - Ja '98 - p7 [1-50]

Lee, Milly
Nim and the War Effort (Illus. by Yangsook Choi)
BL - v94 - Mr 15 '98 - p1219 [1-50]
Ch BWatch - v7 - My '97 - p3 [1-50]
CLW - v68 - D '97 - p82 [51-250]
HB Guide - v8 - Fall '97 - p303 [51-250]
NYTBR - v102 - O 12 '97 - p26 [51-250]
NYTLa - v147 - D 4 '97 - pE8 [51-250]

Leedy, Loreen
2 X 2 = BOO!
TCMath - v4 - O '97 - p122 [51-250]

Measuring Penny (Illus. by Loreen Leedy)
KR - v66 - F 15 '98 - p270 [51-250]
PW - v245 - Mr 16 '98 - p63+ [51-250]
SLJ - v44 - Ap '98 - p119 [51-250]

Mission--Addition (Illus. by Loreen Leedy)
BL - v94 - O 15 '97 - p409 [51-250]
KR - v65 - Ag 1 '97 - p1224 [51-250]
PW - v244 - Jl 28 '97 - p76 [51-250]
SLJ - v43 - Ag '97 - p148 [51-250]

Leeson, Christine
Davy's Scary Journey (Illus. by Tim Warnes)
CBRS - v25 - Ag '97 - p161 [51-250]
Magpies - v12 - Jl '97 - p27 [51-250]
Sch Lib - v45 - N '97 - p187 [51-250]
SLJ - v43 - N '97 - p91 [51-250]

Leeson, Robert
Smart Girls Forever (Illus. by Axel Scheffler)
Bks Keeps - My '97 - p23 [51-250]
TES - Ap 18 '97 - p12* [51-250]

Legg, Gerald
From Caterpillar to Butterfly (Illus. by Carolyn Scrace)
SLJ - v44 - Mr '98 - p197 [51-250]

From Egg to Chicken (Illus. by Carolyn Scrace)
SLJ - v44 - Mr '98 - p197 [51-250]

From Seed to Sunflower (Illus. by Carolyn Scrace)
SLJ - v44 - Mr '98 - p197 [51-250]

Leitch, Patricia
Mystery Horse
SLJ - v43 - My '97 - p136 [51-250]

Show Jumper Wanted
SLJ - v43 - My '97 - p136 [51-250]

Le Jars, David
My Animal Friends
AB - v100 - N 17 '97 - p1268 [1-50]

Lelooska
Echoes of the Elders (Illus. by Lelooska)
y   BL - v94 - D 15 '97 - p690 [51-250]
　　 BL - v94 - Mr 15 '98 - p1224 [1-50]
　　 CBRS - v26 - Ja '98 - p59 [51-250]
　　 CCB-B - v51 - D '97 - p136 [51-250]
　　 HB - v73 - N '97 - p690+ [51-250]
　　 KR - v65 - O 15 '97 - p1583+ [51-250]
　　 NYTBR - v102 - N 9 '97 - p24 [1-50]
　　 PW - v244 - Ag 4 '97 - p73 [51-250]
　　 SLJ - v43 - N '97 - p105 [51-250]
　　 TES - Ja 9 '98 - p17* [501+]

Lember, Barbara Hirsch
The Shell Book (Illus. by Barbara Hirsch Lember)
HB Guide - v8 - Fall '97 - p350 [51-250]
SLJ - v43 - Ap '97 - p128 [51-250]

LeMieux, Anne C
Dare to Be, M.E.! (Illus. by Marcy Dunn Ramsey)
BL - v93 - Je 1 '97 - p1703 [51-250]
CBRS - v25 - Ag '97 - p167 [51-250]
HB Guide - v8 - Fall '97 - p304 [51-250]
KR - v65 - My 15 '97 - p802+ [51-250]
PW - v244 - Je 2 '97 - p73 [1-50]
SLJ - v43 - Jl '97 - p94+ [51-250]

The Fairy Lair
SLJ - v44 - Ap '98 - p132+ [51-250]

Lenagh, Cecilia
The Cleaning Witch (Illus. by Serena Feneziani)
Bks Keeps - Jl '97 - p23 [51-250]

L'Engle, Madeleine
A Swiftly Tilting Planet (L'Engle). Audio Version
SLJ - v43 - Je '97 - p69 [51-250]

A Wrinkle in Time
NYTBR - v102 - N 16 '97 - p26 [1-50]

Lennon, Jessie
And I Always Been Moving! (Illus. by Doreen Brown)
Magpies - v12 - My '97 - p20+ [251-500]

Leon, Georgina Lazaro
El Flamboyan Amarillo (Illus. by Myrna Oliver)
SLJ - v43 - N '97 - p136 [51-250]

Leon, Vicki
Outrageous Women of Ancient Times (Illus. by Lisa M Brown)
BL - v94 - N 1 '97 - p464 [51-250]
PW - v244 - N 24 '97 - p76 [51-250]
SLJ - v43 - D '97 - p140 [51-250]

Outrageous Women of the Middle Ages
y   KR - v66 - Mr 15 '98 - p406 [51-250]
　　 PW - v245 - Mr 16 '98 - p67 [51-250]

Lepthien, Emilie U
Giraffes
SLJ - v43 - Je '97 - p109+ [51-250]

Grizzlies
SLJ - v43 - Ap '97 - p127 [51-250]

Llamas
SLJ - v43 - Je '97 - p109+ [51-250]

Sea Turtles
SLJ - v43 - Je '97 - p110 [51-250]

Walruses
SLJ - v43 - Je '97 - p110 [51-250]

Lerman, Rory S
Charlie's Checklist (Illus. by Alison Bartlett)

> Bks Keeps - My '97 - p20 [51-250]
> BL - v93 - Je 1 '97 - p1719+ [51-250]
> CCB-B - v50 - Je '97 - p364 [51-250]
> HB Guide - v8 - Fall '97 - p271 [51-250]
> SLJ - v43 - My '97 - p104 [51-250]

Lerner, Carol
Backyard Birds of Summer

> ASBYP - v29 - Fall '96 - p21 [251-500]
> RT - v51 - O '97 - p152 [51-250]

My Backyard Garden (Illus. by Carol Lerner)

> BL - v94 - Mr 15 '98 - p1238 [51-250]
> KR - v66 - F 15 '98 - p270 [51-250]
> SLJ - v44 - Ap '98 - p149 [51-250]

Lerner, Harriet
What's So Terrible about Swallowing an Apple Seed? (Illus. by Catharine O'Neill)

> RT - v51 - O '97 - p146 [1-50]

Lerner Publications Company. Geography Dept.
Italy--in Pictures

> Ch BWatch - v7 - Mr '97 - p5 [51-250]
> HB Guide - v8 - Fall '97 - p391 [51-250]

Laos--in Pictures

> Cur R - v36 - Mr '97 - p13 [51-250]

Libya--in Pictures

> Cur R - v36 - Mr '97 - p13 [51-250]

Leroe, E W
Monster Vision

> SLJ - v43 - My '97 - p136 [51-250]

Nasty the Snowman

> SLJ - v43 - My '97 - p136 [51-250]

Pizza Zombies

> SLJ - v43 - My '97 - p136 [51-250]

Revenge of the Hairy Horror

> SLJ - v43 - My '97 - p136 [51-250]

Leslie, Amanda
Let's Look Inside the Red Can

> HB Guide - v8 - Fall '97 - p253 [51-250]

Let's Look Inside the Yellow Truck

> HB Guide - v8 - Fall '97 - p253 [51-250]

Lessem, Don
Bigger than T. Rex

> SLJ - v43 - D '97 - p140 [51-250]

Inside the Amazing Amazon

> BL - v94 - D 1 '97 - p629 [1-50]

Ornithomimids: The Fastest Dinosaur (Illus. by Donna Braginetz)

> ASBYP - v29 - Fall '96 - p66+ [501+]

Supergiants! The Biggest Dinosaurs (Illus. by David Peters)

> Ch BWatch - v8 - Ja '98 - p8 [1-50]
> PW - v244 - S 1 '97 - p106 [1-50]
> SLJ - v43 - S '97 - p232+ [51-250]

Troodon: The Smartest Dinosaur (Illus. by Donna Braginetz)

> ASBYP - v29 - Fall '96 - p66+ [501+]

Utahraptor: The Deadliest Dinosaur (Illus. by Donna Braginetz)

> RT - v51 - O '97 - p139 [1-50]

Lesser, Carolyn
Great Crystal Bear (Illus. by William Noonan)

> ASBYP - v29 - Fall '96 - p21+ [251-500]
> SE - v61 - Ap '97 - p7* [1-50]

Storm on the Desert (Illus. by Ted Rand)

> HB Guide - v8 - Fall '97 - p346 [51-250]
> KR - v65 - Ap 15 '97 - p642 [51-250]
> NH - v106 - D '97 - p10 [51-250]
> SLJ - v43 - My '97 - p121 [51-250]

Lester, Alison
Alice and Aldo (Illus. by Alison Lester)

> BL - v94 - Mr 1 '98 - p1140+ [51-250]
> KR - v66 - Mr 1 '98 - p341 [51-250]
> PW - v245 - F 16 '98 - p210 [51-250]
> TES - Je 27 '97 - p12* [51-250]

The Quicksand Pony (Illus. by Alison Lester)
Aust Bk R - D '97 - p60+ [501+]

When Frank Was Four
TES - N 14 '97 - p14* [51-250]

Lester, Helen
Author: A True Story (Illus. by Helen Lester)
HB Guide - v8 - Fall '97 - p73 [51-250]
Inst - v107 - S '97 - p20 [51-250]
NYTBR - v102 - Ag 3 '97 - p14 [501+]
SLJ - v43 - My '97 - p121 [51-250]
SLJ - v43 - D '97 - p26 [1-50]

Lester, Julius
From Slave Ship to Freedom Road (Illus. by Rod Brown)
BL - v94 - F 15 '98 - p1009 [251-500]
KR - v65 - N 15 '97 - p1709 [51-250]
PW - v244 - D 1 '97 - p54+ [251-500]
SLJ - v44 - F '98 - p119+ [51-250]

John Henry (Illus. by Jerry Pinkney)
ECEJ - v25 - Fall '97 - p48 [1-50]

Sam and the Tigers (Illus. by Jerry Pinkney)
JAAL - v41 - O '97 - p161 [51-250]
Magpies - v12 - Mr '97 - p27 [251-500]
SE - v61 - Ap '97 - p5* [1-50]
SLJ - v43 - N '97 - p41 [1-50]

Lesynski, Loris
Boy Soup or When Giant Caught Cold
CBRA - '96 - p447 [51-250]

Ogre Fun (Illus. by Loris Lesynski)
Quill & Q - v63 - S '97 - p73 [251-500]

Leten, Mats
Kaj, Smukke Kaj
Bkbird - v35 - Fall '97 - p51 [51-250]

Let's Talk about Me!
PW - v244 - O 13 '97 - p77 [51-250]

Leuck, Laura
My Baby Brother Has Ten Tiny Toes (Illus. by Clara Vulliamy)
HB Guide - v8 - Fall '97 - p253 [51-250]

Leuzzi, Linda
Industry and Business
Ch BWatch - v7 - Ap '97 - p5 [51-250]
r HB Guide - v8 - Fall '97 - p324 [51-250]

Leverich, Kathleen
Daisy (Illus. by Lynne Woodcock Cravath)
SLJ - v43 - Ap '97 - p112+ [51-250]

Violet (Illus. by Lynne Woodcock Cravath)
SLJ - v43 - Ap '97 - p112+ [51-250]

Levert, Mireille
Little Red Riding Hood (Illus. by Mireille Levert)
Ch BWatch - v7 - Mr '97 - p6 [51-250]

Molly's Bath (Illus. by Mireille Levert)
Can CL - v23 - Sum '97 - p95 [251-500]
Ch Bk News - v20 - Spr '97 - p30+ [51-250]
Quill & Q - v63 - Ap '97 - p38 [51-250]

Molly's Breakfast (Illus. by Mireille Levert)
Can CL - v23 - Sum '97 - p95 [251-500]
Ch Bk News - v20 - Spr '97 - p30+ [51-250]
Quill & Q - v63 - Ap '97 - p38 [51-250]

Molly's Clothes (Illus. by Mireille Levert)
Can CL - v23 - Sum '97 - p95 [251-500]
Ch Bk News - v20 - Spr '97 - p30+ [51-250]
Quill & Q - v63 - Ap '97 - p38 [51-250]

Molly's Toys (Illus. by Mireille Levert)
Can CL - v23 - Sum '97 - p95 [251-500]
Ch Bk News - v20 - Spr '97 - p30+ [51-250]
Quill & Q - v63 - Ap '97 - p38 [51-250]

LeVert, Suzanne
Louisiana
Ch BWatch - v7 - My '97 - p7 [51-250]
HB Guide - v8 - Fall '97 - p394 [51-250]
SLJ - v43 - Jl '97 - p108 [51-250]

Levete, Sarah
*Loneliness and Making Friends (Illus.
by Christopher O'Neill)*
     Bks Keeps - My '97 - p21 [51-250]

Levin, Betty
Island Bound
     CBRS - v26 - N '97 - p35 [51-250]
     CCB-B - v51 - N '97 - p90+ [51-250]
     KR - v65 - Je 15 '97 - p951+ [51-250]

Levine, Abby
*This Is the Pumpkin (Illus. by Paige
Billin-Frye)*
     BL - v94 - S 1 '97 - p140 [51-250]
     PW - v244 - O 6 '97 - p48 [51-250]
     SLJ - v43 - S '97 - p186 [51-250]

Levine, Arthur A
*Pearl Moscowitz's Last Stand (Illus.
by Robert Roth)*
 y   BL - v93 - Je 1 '97 - p1675 [1-50]
     ECEJ - v25 - Fall '97 - p48 [1-50]

Levine, Ellen
A Fence Away from Freedom
     SE - v61 - Ap '97 - p216+ [51-250]
 y   SE - v61 - S '97 - p271 [1-50]

Levine, Gail Carson
Ella Enchanted
     BL - v94 - Ja 1 '98 - p734 [1-50]
 y   BL - v94 - Mr 15 '98 - p1218 [1-50]
     BL - v94 - Mr 15 '98 - p1219 [1-50]
 y   BL - v94 - Mr 15 '98 - p1226 [1-50]
     CBRS - v25 - Je '97 - p130 [1-50]
     HB Guide - v8 - Fall '97 - p304 [51-250]
 y   JAAL - v41 - O '97 - p158 [51-250]
     Learning - v26 - Ag '97 - p26 [51-250]
     NYTBR - v102 - Jl 6 '97 - p16 [51-250]
     PW - v244 - N 3 '97 - p60 [1-50]
     SLJ - v43 - Ap '97 - p138 [51-250]
     SLJ - v43 - D '97 - p26 [1-50]
 y   VOYA - v20 - Ag '97 - p194 [251-500]
 y   VOYA - v20 - F '98 - p365 [51-250]
 y   VOYA - v21 - Ap '98 - p38 [1-50]
 y   VOYA - v21 - Ap '98 - p40 [1-50]

Levine, Shar
*The Microscope Book (Illus. by David
Sovka)*
     SLJ - v43 - Jl '97 - p108 [51-250]

*Science around the World (Illus. by
Laurel Aiello)*
     ASBYP - v29 - Fall '96 - p22 [251-500]
     CBRA - '96 - p536 [51-250]

Wormworld (Illus. by Louise Phillips)
     Quill & Q - v63 - Ag '97 - p38 [251-500]

Levinson, Nancy Smiler
*She's Been Working on the Railroad
(Illus. by Shirley Burman)*
     BL - v94 - S 15 '97 - p228+ [51-250]
     CCB-B - v51 - Ja '98 - p163+ [51-250]
     KR - v65 - O 1 '97 - p1534+ [51-250]
 y   SLJ - v43 - D '97 - p140 [51-250]
 y   VOYA - v20 - D '97 - p334 [251-500]

Levitin, Sonia
Adam's War
     SE - v61 - S '97 - p271 [1-50]

*Boom Town (Illus. by Cat Bowman
Smith)*
     BL - v94 - F 15 '98 - p1020 [51-250]
     HB - v74 - Mr '98 - p215 [251-500]
     KR - v66 - Ja 15 '98 - p114 [51-250]
     PW - v245 - F 16 '98 - p210+ [51-250]
     SLJ - v44 - Mr '98 - p182 [51-250]

*Nine for California (Illus. by Cat
Bowman Smith)*
     CLW - v68 - S '97 - p65 [51-250]
     NYTBR - v102 - Ap 27 '97 - p29 [1-50]

*A Piece of Home (Illus. by Juan
Wijngaard)*
     RT - v51 - D '97 - p331 [51-250]

Levoy, Myron
Alan and Naomi
     BL - v94 - O 1 '97 - p323 [1-50]

Levy, David H, 1948-
Stars and Planets
     ASBYP - v29 - Fall '96 - p57+ [501+]
     Par - v72 - Ag '97 - p170 [1-50]

Levy, Elizabeth
Cleo and the Coyote (Illus. by Diana Bryer)
    RT - v51 - O '97 - p133 [1-50]

My Life as a Fifth-Grade Comedian
    BL - v93 - Ag '97 - p1901+ [51-250]
    CCB-B - v51 - Ja '98 - p164 [251-500]
    KR - v65 - Je 15 '97 - p952 [51-250]
    Learning - v26 - N '97 - p29 [51-250]
    PW - v244 - Je 23 '97 - p92 [51-250]
    SLJ - v43 - S '97 - p219 [51-250]

Something Queer in the Wild West (Illus. by Mordicai Gerstein)
    HB Guide - v8 - Fall '97 - p292 [51-250]
    SLJ - v43 - My '97 - p104 [51-250]

Wolfman Sam (Illus. by Bill Basso)
    SLJ - v43 - Ap '97 - p113 [51-250]

Levy, Marilyn
Run for Your Life
  y JAAL - v40 - O '96 - p151 [51-250]
  y Kliatt - v32 - Ja '98 - p10 [51-250]
    RT - v51 - N '97 - p254 [51-250]

Levy, Matthys
Earthquake Games (Illus. by Christina C Blatt)
    BL - v94 - S 1 '97 - p114+ [51-250]
    SLJ - v43 - D '97 - p140 [51-250]

Levy, Patricia
Sudan
    HB Guide - v8 - Fall '97 - p392 [51-250]
    SLJ - v43 - Jl '97 - p106 [51-250]

Lewin, Betsy
Booby Hatch (Illus. by Betsy Lewin)
    SLJ - v43 - My '97 - p57 [1-50]

Chubbo's Pool
    SB - v33 - Ag '97 - p186 [1-50]

What's the Matter, Habibi? (Illus. by Betsy Lewin)
    BL - v94 - S 15 '97 - p242 [51-250]
    CCB-B - v51 - S '97 - p17 [51-250]
    PW - v244 - Je 2 '97 - p70 [51-250]
    SLJ - v43 - S '97 - p186 [51-250]

Lewin, Hugh
Jafta: The Homecoming (Illus. by Lisa Kopper)
    BL - v93 - Je 1 '97 - p1724 [1-50]
    JOYS - v11 - Win '98 - p141 [1-50]

Lewin, Ted
Amazon Boy
    ECEJ - v25 - Fall '97 - p48 [1-50]

Fair! (Illus. by Ted Lewin)
    KR - v65 - Jl 1 '97 - p1031 [51-250]
    SLJ - v43 - Jl '97 - p85 [51-250]

I Was a Teenage Professional Wrestler (Illus. by Ted Lewin)
    JOYS - v10 - Sum '97 - p428+ [1-50]
  y SLJ - v44 - Mr '98 - p120 [1-50]

Market! (Illus. by Ted Lewin)
    RT - v51 - D '97 - p311 [51-250]
    SE - v61 - Ap '97 - p7* [1-50]

The Storytellers (Illus. by Ted Lewin)
    CCB-B - v51 - Ap '98 - p286 [51-250]
    PW - v245 - F 16 '98 - p211 [51-250]
    SLJ - v44 - Ap '98 - p102+ [51-250]

Lewington, Anna
Antonio's Rain Forest
    BL - v94 - D 1 '97 - p629 [1-50]

Mexico
    Ch BWatch - v7 - S '97 - p7 [51-250]

Lewington, Anna, 1950-
Atlas of Rain Forests
  r Ch BWatch - v7 - S '97 - p7 [51-250]
  r HB Guide - v8 - Fall '97 - p347 [51-250]
  yr SLJ - v43 - Ag '97 - p171 [51-250]

Lewis, Amanda
Lettering: Make Your Own Cards, Signs, Gifts and More (Illus. by Esperanca Melo)
    BL - v94 - O 15 '97 - p400+ [51-250]
    CBRA - '96 - p519+ [51-250]
    SLJ - v44 - Ja '98 - p126 [51-250]

Lewis, C S
The Chronicles of Narnia (Illus. by Pauline Baynes)
    NYTBR - v102 - N 16 '97 - p25 [1-50]

Edmund and the White Witch (Illus. by Deborah Maze)
  Ch BWatch - v7 - N '97 - p5 [51-250]
  PW - v244 - Ag 4 '97 - p77 [1-50]

The Horse and His Boy
  BL - v94 - D 15 '97 - p695 [1-50]

The Lion, the Witch and the Wardrobe (Illus. by Pauline Baynes)
  PW - v244 - Ag 4 '97 - p77 [1-50]

Lucy Steps through the Wardrobe (Illus. by Deborah Maze)
  Ch BWatch - v7 - N '97 - p5 [1-50]
  PW - v244 - Ag 4 '97 - p77 [1-50]

The Narnia Journal
  PW - v244 - Ag 4 '97 - p77 [1-50]

Lewis, Diana
Magical Chango (Illus. by Katherine Rose Slocum)
  Ch BWatch - v7 - O '97 - p1 [51-250]

Lewis, J D
Journeys in Art
  Ch BWatch - v7 - Ap '97 - p8 [1-50]

Lewis, J Patrick
The Boat of Many Rooms (Illus. by Reg Cartwright)
  HB Guide - v8 - Fall '97 - p271 [51-250]
  PW - v244 - N 3 '97 - p57 [51-250]

The La-Di-Da Hare (Illus. by Diana Cain Bluthenthal)
  CBRS - v25 - Je '97 - p127 [51-250]
  Ch BWatch - v7 - Jl '97 - p7 [1-50]
  HB Guide - v8 - Fall '97 - p272 [51-250]
  SLJ - v43 - My '97 - p104 [51-250]

Long Was the Winter Road They Traveled (Illus. by Drew Bairley)
  BL - v94 - O 1 '97 - p323+ [51-250]
  NYTBR - v102 - D 7 '97 - p66 [1-50]
  PW - v244 - O 6 '97 - p56 [51-250]

Lewis, Kim
The Last Train (Illus. by Kim Lewis)
  TES - Jl 25 '97 - p29 [51-250]

Lewis, Paul Owen
Frog Girl (Illus. by Paul Owen Lewis)
  AB - v100 - N 17 '97 - p1262+ [51-250]
  BL - v94 - N 1 '97 - p476+ [51-250]
  Bloom Rev - v17 - N '97 - p33 [51-250]
  Ch BWatch - v7 - D '97 - p2 [1-50]
  KR - v65 - O 1 '97 - p1535 [51-250]
  SLJ - v43 - N '97 - p91 [51-250]

Lewis, Rob
Grandpa Comes to Stay (Illus. by Rob Lewis)
  SLJ - v43 - Ag '97 - p137 [51-250]

Hide-and-Seek with Grandpa (Illus. by Rob Lewis)
  SLJ - v43 - Ag '97 - p137 [51-250]
  TES - Jl 11 '97 - p14* [51-250]

Lewis, Shari
Lamb Chop's Special Chanukah
  Teach Mus - v5 - O '97 - p47 [1-50]

Lewis, Thomas P
La Montana De Fuego (Illus. by Joan Sandin)
  BL - v94 - D 15 '97 - p707 [51-250]

L'Hommedieu, Arthur John
From Plant to Blue Jeans
  BL - v94 - F 15 '98 - p1003+ [51-250]

Liatsos, Sandra Olson
Bicycle Riding and Other Poems (Illus. by Karen Dugan)
  HB Guide - v8 - Fall '97 - p377 [51-250]
  KR - v65 - My 15 '97 - p803 [51-250]
  SLJ - v43 - My '97 - p121 [51-250]

Libura, Krystyna
What the Aztecs Told Us
  BL - v94 - D 1 '97 - p617 [51-250]
  CBRS - v26 - O '97 - p23 [51-250]
  HB - v73 - N '97 - p697+ [51-250]
  SLJ - v43 - D '97 - p111 [51-250]

Lidgold, Carole M
The Adventures of Inch Worm Willie
  CBRA - '96 - p447+ [51-250]

Lidz, Jane

Zak: The One-of-a-Kind Dog (Illus. by Jane Lidz)

KR - v65 - N 15 '97 - p1709 [51-250]
PW - v244 - N 17 '97 - p60 [51-250]
SLJ - v44 - Mr '98 - p182 [51-250]

Lied, Kate

Potato: A Tale from the Great Depression (Illus. by Lisa Campbell Ernst)

CBRS - v25 - Spr '97 - p139 [51-250]
HB Guide - v8 - Fall '97 - p272 [1-50]
Inst - v107 - O '97 - p27+ [51-250]
SLJ - v43 - Jl '97 - p70 [51-250]

Lies, Betty Bonham

My Ticket to Tomorrow

AB - v100 - N 17 '97 - p1270+ [51-250]

Lillegard, Dee

The Poombah of Badoombah (Illus. by Kevin Hawkes)

KR - v66 - Ap 1 '98 - p497 [51-250]

Tortoise Brings the Mail (Illus. by Jillian Lund)

CBRS - v25 - Spr '97 - p136 [51-250]
ECEJ - v25 - Fall '97 - p41 [51-250]
HB Guide - v8 - Fall '97 - p272 [51-250]
KR - v65 - Ap 15 '97 - p642 [51-250]
SLJ - v43 - My '97 - p104 [51-250]

The Wild Bunch

Ch BWatch - v7 - N '97 - p5 [1-50]

Lilly, Melinda

Shapes for Lunch (Illus. by Charles Reasoner)

PW - v244 - S 22 '97 - p82 [51-250]

Lincoln, Margaret

Face Painting (Illus. by Rob Shone)

Ch BWatch - v7 - My '97 - p7 [51-250]
HB Guide - v8 - Fall '97 - p362 [51-250]
SLJ - v43 - Ag '97 - p164+ [51-250]

Lincoln, Margarette

The Pirate's Handbook

Emerg Lib - v25 - N '97 - p47 [51-250]

Lindahn, Val

Olde Missus Milliwhistle's Book of Beneficial Beasties

Ch BWatch - v7 - Je '97 - p6 [1-50]
Ch BWatch - v7 - Jl '97 - p5+ [51-250]

Lindbergh, Reeve

The Awful Aardvarks Go to School (Illus. by Tracey Campbell Pearson)

BL - v94 - O 15 '97 - p402 [51-250]
Ch BWatch - v7 - O '97 - p6 [1-50]
KR - v65 - S 15 '97 - p1459 [51-250]
PW - v244 - Ag 25 '97 - p70 [51-250]
SLJ - v43 - D '97 - p96 [51-250]

The Circle of Days (Illus. by Cathie Felstead)

CCB-B - v51 - Ap '98 - p286 [51-250]
PW - v245 - Mr 23 '98 - p95 [51-250]
SLJ - v44 - Ap '98 - p119 [51-250]

Nobody Owns the Sky (Illus. by Pamela Paparone)

Magpies - v12 - Mr '97 - p23 [51-250]
PW - v245 - Ja 19 '98 - p380 [1-50]
RT - v51 - S '97 - p57+ [51-250]
SE - v61 - Ap '97 - p3* [1-50]

North Country Spring (Illus. by Liz Sivertson)

CBRS - v25 - My '97 - p111 [51-250]
HB Guide - v8 - Fall '97 - p272 [1-50]
NYTBR - v102 - My 11 '97 - p24 [1-50]
SLJ - v43 - Ap '97 - p113 [51-250]

Linden, Ann Marie

One Smiling Grandma (Illus. by Lynne Russell)

ECEJ - v25 - Fall '97 - p48 [1-50]

Lindgren, Astrid

The Adventures of Pippi Longstocking (Illus. by Michael Chesworth)

Bloom Rev - v17 - N '97 - p32 [51-250]
Ch BWatch - v7 - My '97 - p5 [1-50]
PW - v244 - O 13 '97 - p77 [51-250]

Pippi Goes on Board

Ch BWatch - v7 - My '97 - p5 [1-50]

Pippi in the South Seas

Ch BWatch - v7 - My '97 - p5 [1-50]

Pippi Longstocking (Illus. by Louis S Glanzman)
    NYTBR - v102 - N 16 '97 - p25 [1-50]

Lindgren, Barbro
Rosa Moves to Town
    Ch BWatch - v7 - Je '97 - p7 [1-50]

Lindop, Edmund
Panama and the United States
    BL - v93 - Ag '97 - p1895 [51-250]
    Ch BWatch - v7 - My '97 - p7 [1-50]
y   SLJ - v43 - Jl '97 - p108 [51-250]

Lindop, Laurie
Champions of Equality
y   BL - v94 - S 1 '97 - p71 [51-250]
    Ch BWatch - v7 - Je '97 - p5 [1-50]
y   SLJ - v43 - S '97 - p233 [51-250]

Scientists and Doctors
    Ch BWatch - v7 - Je '97 - p5 [1-50]
y   SB - v33 - N '97 - p239 [51-250]
y   SLJ - v43 - S '97 - p233 [51-250]

Lindsay, Janice
The Milly Stories
y   KR - v66 - F 1 '98 - p198 [51-250]
    SLJ - v44 - Ap '98 - p134 [51-250]

Lines, Patricia
A Friend for Cyril (Illus. by Rae Whitesell)
    CBRA - '96 - p448 [51-250]

Ling, Bettina
Maya Lin
    HB Guide - v8 - Fall '97 - p364 [51-250]

Ling, Mary
The Pirate Cook Book (Illus. by Dave King)
    Ch BWatch - v7 - Jl '97 - p8 [1-50]
    HB Guide - v8 - Fall '97 - p361 [51-250]
    NYTBR - v102 - N 16 '97 - p38 [51-250]
    SLJ - v43 - Jl '97 - p85 [51-250]

The Snake Book (Illus. by Frank Greenaway)
    CBRS - v25 - Je '97 - p128 [51-250]

Ch BWatch - v7 - Jl '97 - p8 [1-50]
CLW - v68 - S '97 - p65+ [51-250]
HB Guide - v8 - Fall '97 - p351 [51-250]
New Sci - v155 - Ag 23 '97 - p44 [51-250]
NW - v130 - D 1 '97 - p78 [1-50]
SB - v33 - Ag '97 - p187 [1-50]
Sch Lib - v45 - N '97 - p205 [51-250]
SLJ - v43 - S '97 - p203+ [51-250]

Lionel
Peekaboo Babies
    BL - v94 - D 15 '97 - p700 [1-50]
    HB Guide - v8 - Fall '97 - p253 [51-250]

Lionni, Leo
A Color of His Own (Illus. by Leo Lionni)
    PW - v244 - Ag 25 '97 - p74 [1-50]

Frederick's Fables
    PW - v244 - Ag 25 '97 - p74 [1-50]

Matthew's Dream
    Inst - v106 - My '97 - p4* [1-50]

Lipinski, Tara
Tara Lipinski: Triumph on Ice
    BL - v94 - Ja 1 '98 - p805+ [51-250]
    CCB-B - v51 - Mr '98 - p249 [51-250]
    PW - v244 - N 10 '97 - p75 [51-250]
    SLJ - v44 - Ap '98 - p148 [51-250]

Lippert, Meg
Finist the Falcon (Mike). Book and Audio Version
    SLJ - v43 - S '97 - p165 [51-250]

Lipsyte, Robert
One Fat Summer
    BL - v94 - Ja 1 '98 - p795 [1-50]

Lisandrelli, Elaine Slivinski
Bob Dole: Legendary Senator
    CLW - v68 - D '97 - p79+ [51-250]

Lishak, Antony
Baby Bear Comes Home (Illus. by Ian Newsham)
    Magpies - v12 - My '97 - p31 [51-250]

Lisson, Deborah
A Place of Safety
Magpies - v12 - Mr '97 - p34 [51-250]

Lister, Jan
Animal Tails
CBRA - '96 - p481 [51-250]

Captain Blackheart's Gold
CBRA - '96 - p481+ [51-250]

Cousin Clash
CBRA - '96 - p482 [51-250]

Pussywillows and Other Things. 3rd Ed.
CBRA - '96 - p498+ [51-250]

Time-Travel Runaway
CBRA - '96 - p482 [51-250]

The Young Lion and the Castle Curse
CBRA - '96 - p482 [51-250]

Lister, Robin
The Story of King Arthur (Illus. by Alan Baker)
CLW - v68 - D '97 - p85+ [51-250]

Little, Jean
Bats about Baseball (Illus. by Kim LaFave)
Can CL - v23 - Fall '97 - p66+ [251-500]

The Belonging Place
y   BIC - v26 - Je '97 - p33+ [251-500]
     CBRS - v26 - Ja '98 - p59 [51-250]
     CCB-B - v51 - Ja '98 - p164+ [51-250]
y   Ch Bk News - v20 - Sum '97 - p26 [501+]
     KR - v65 - N 1 '97 - p1646 [51-250]
     Quill & Q - v63 - My '97 - p40 [251-500]
     SLJ - v43 - N '97 - p120 [51-250]

Gruntle Piggle Takes Off (Illus. by Johnny Wales)
     Can CL - v23 - Fall '97 - p63+ [501+]
     CBRA - '96 - p448 [51-250]
     CBRS - v25 - Ag '97 - p161 [1-50]
     Ch BWatch - v7 - Mr '97 - p6 [51-250]
     HB Guide - v8 - Fall '97 - p272 [51-250]
     Magpies - v12 - Jl '97 - p30 [51-250]
     SLJ - v43 - Je '97 - p96+ [51-250]

Jenny and the Hanukkah Queen (Illus. by Suzanne Mogensen)
Can CL - v23 - Fall '97 - p85+ [501+]

Spring Begins in March
CBRA - '96 - p482 [51-250]

Little, Kimberley Griffiths
Breakaway
BL - v94 - O 1 '97 - p329 [51-250]
SLJ - v43 - D '97 - p126 [51-250]

Little, Mimi Otey
Yoshiko and the Foreigner (Illus. by Mimi Otey Little)
SE - v61 - Ap '97 - p6* [1-50]

Little Red Riding Hood (Illus. by Peter Stevenson)
PW - v244 - S 1 '97 - p106 [51-250]

Littlefield, Holly
Colors of Japan (Illus. by Helen Byers)
SLJ - v44 - Ja '98 - p102 [51-250]

Littlesugar, Amy
Jonkonnu (Illus. by Ian Schoenherr)
BL - v94 - Ja 1 '98 - p824 [51-250]
CCB-B - v51 - Ja '98 - p165 [51-250]
KR - v65 - D 15 '97 - p1836 [51-250]
PW - v244 - D 8 '97 - p71 [251-500]
SLJ - v44 - F '98 - p86 [51-250]

Marie in Fourth Position (Illus. by Ian Schoenherr)
Inst - v106 - Ap '97 - p24+ [51-250]
RT - v51 - N '97 - p241 [51-250]

A Portrait of Spotted Deer's Grandfather (Illus. by Marlowe DeChristopher)
BL - v94 - Ja 1 '98 - p813 [51-250]
KR - v65 - Ag 15 '97 - p1308 [51-250]
PW - v244 - Ag 25 '97 - p72 [51-250]
SLJ - v43 - S '97 - p186 [51-250]

Litvinoff, Miles
The Atlas of Earthcare
r   New Sci - v154 - Je 7 '97 - p48 [51-250]

Lively, Penelope
Staying with Grandpa (Illus. by Paul Howard)
> Bks Keeps - My '97 - p22 [51-250]
> TES - Jl 11 '97 - p14* [51-250]

Livesey, Robert
The Railways (Illus. by A G Smith)
> Quill & Q - v63 - D '97 - p38 [251-500]

The Living World (World Book)
> ASBYP - v29 - Sum '96 - p65+ [501+]

Livingston, Myra Cohn
Cricket Never Does (Illus. by Kees De Kiefte)
> BW - v27 - My 4 '97 - p17 [501+]
> HB Guide - v8 - Fall '97 - p377 [51-250]
> KR - v65 - Ap 15 '97 - p642 [51-250]
> SLJ - v43 - Ap '97 - p151 [51-250]

Festivals (Illus. by Leonard Everett Fisher)
> SE - v61 - Ap '97 - p12* [1-50]

I Am Writing a Poem About...a Game of Poetry
> BL - v94 - S 1 '97 - p113+ [51-250]
> KR - v65 - Ag 1 '97 - p1224 [51-250]
> y VOYA - v20 - F '98 - p402 [251-500]

Llamas, Andreu
Birds Conquer the Sky (Illus. by Miriam Ferron)
> SB - v32 - D '96 - p274 [51-250]

The First Amphibians (Illus. by Luis Rizo)
> SB - v32 - D '96 - p274 [51-250]

Fleas: Bloodsucking Parasites (Illus. by Gabriel Casadevall)
> Ch BWatch - v7 - Jl '97 - p4 [1-50]

Frogs: Living in Two Worlds (Illus. by Gabriel Casadevall)
> Ch BWatch - v7 - Jl '97 - p4 [1-50]

The Great Marine Reptiles (Illus. by Albert Martinez)
> SB - v32 - D '96 - p274 [51-250]

Kangaroos: Animals with a Pouch
> Ch BWatch - v7 - Jl '97 - p4 [1-50]

Llamas Ruiz, Andres
The Fight for Survival
> Ch BWatch - v7 - N '97 - p6 [1-50]

The Life of a Cell
> y BL - v94 - D 1 '97 - p622 [51-250]

The Life of a Cell (Illus. by Luis Rizo)
> Ch BWatch - v7 - N '97 - p6 [1-50]

Metamorphosis (Illus. by Francisco Arredondo)
> KR - v65 - Ap 15 '97 - p642+ [51-250]
> SLJ - v43 - Je '97 - p111 [51-250]

The Origin of the Universe (Illus. by Luis Rizo)
> Ch BWatch - v7 - N '97 - p6 [1-50]

Volcanos and Earthquakes (Illus. by Ali Garousi)
> BL - v94 - D 1 '97 - p622 [51-250]
> Ch BWatch - v7 - N '97 - p6 [1-50]

Llewellyn, Claire
The Best Book of Bugs (Illus. by Chris Forsey)
> KR - v66 - Mr 15 '98 - p406+ [51-250]

Children's Picture Encyclopedia
> r Books - v11 - Je '97 - p21 [51-250]

Deserts and Rainforests (Illus. by Anthony Lewis)
> SLJ - v43 - S '97 - p204 [51-250]

Dorling Kindersley Children's Picture Encyclopedia
> r Sch Lib - v45 - N '97 - p205 [51-250]

I Didn't Know That Some Bugs Glow in the Dark
> Am Sci - v85 - N '97 - p559 [1-50]

Our Planet Earth
> r SLJ - v44 - F '98 - p138 [51-250]

Some Birds Hang Upside Down (Illus. by Chris Shields)
> Ch BWatch - v7 - N '97 - p6 [1-50]

Some Bugs Glow in the Dark (Illus. by Myke Taylor)
> CBRS - v25 - Jl '97 - p155 [51-250]
> Ch BWatch - v7 - My '97 - p7 [1-50]
> HB Guide - v8 - Fall '97 - p350 [51-250]
> Sch Lib - v45 - N '97 - p205 [51-250]

SLJ - v43 - S '97 - p204 [51-250]

Some Snakes Spit Poison (Illus. by Francis Phillipps)
> CBRS - v25 - Jl '97 - p155 [51-250]
> Ch BWatch - v7 - My '97 - p7 [1-50]
> KR - v65 - Je 1 '97 - p876 [51-250]
> SB - v33 - O '97 - p210 [51-250]
> Sch Lib - v45 - N '97 - p205 [51-250]

Spiders Have Fangs (Illus. by Myke Taylor)
> Ch BWatch - v7 - N '97 - p6 [1-50]
> SLJ - v44 - Mr '98 - p197 [251-500]

Wild, Wet and Windy (Illus. by Robin Budden)
> Ch BWatch - v7 - D '97 - p7 [1-50]
> KR - v65 - Ag 15 '97 - p1308 [51-250]

Lloyd, Bryant
Baseball: Batting
> SLJ - v44 - Ap '98 - p119+ [51-250]

Baseball: Field and Equipment
> SLJ - v44 - Ap '98 - p119+ [51-250]

Baseball: Pitching
> SLJ - v44 - Ap '98 - p119+ [51-250]

Baseball: Rules of the Game
> SLJ - v44 - Ap '98 - p119+ [51-250]

Baseball: Run, Throw and Catch
> SLJ - v44 - Ap '98 - p119+ [51-250]

Baseball: The Positions
> SLJ - v44 - Ap '98 - p119+ [51-250]

Football: Equipment
> SLJ - v44 - Mr '98 - p197 [51-250]

Football: Pass, Punt, and Kick
> SLJ - v44 - Mr '98 - p197 [51-250]

Football: Rules of the Game
> SLJ - v44 - Mr '98 - p197 [51-250]

Football: The Defense
> SLJ - v44 - Mr '98 - p197 [51-250]

Football: The Fundamentals
> SLJ - v44 - Mr '98 - p197 [51-250]

Football: The Offense
> SLJ - v44 - Mr '98 - p197 [51-250]

Lloyd, Emily
Forest Slump
> BL - v94 - F 15 '98 - p1012 [51-250]
> PW - v244 - S 22 '97 - p83 [51-250]
> SLJ - v44 - Ap '98 - p134 [51-250]

Lloyd, Gary G
The Lloyd (Loyd) Families of Putnam County, Missouri
> EGH - v51 - Ja '97 - p201+ [51-250]

Locker, Thomas
Water Dance
> HB Guide - v8 - Fall '97 - p272 [51-250]
> SLJ - v43 - Ap '97 - p128 [51-250]

Lockyer, John
Harry and the Anzac Poppy
> Magpies - v12 - Mr '97 - p31 [51-250]

Lodge, Bernard
Tanglebird (Illus. by Bernard Lodge)
> HB Guide - v8 - Fall '97 - p272+ [51-250]
> NYTBR - v102 - Ag 31 '97 - p13 [51-250]
> Sch Lib - v45 - Ag '97 - p131 [51-250]
> SLJ - v43 - Ap '97 - p113 [51-250]
> TES - Jl 18 '97 - p35 [251-500]

Lodge, Jo
Patch's House
> PW - v244 - S 29 '97 - p91 [51-250]

Play and Count in Patch's House
> Par - v72 - D '97 - p202 [1-50]

Loebl, Suzanne
The Wish Ring
> Ch BWatch - v8 - Ja '98 - p2 [1-50]

Loeschnig, Louis V
Simple Chemistry Experiments with Everyday Materials (Illus. by Frances Zweifel)
> ASBYP - v29 - Sum '96 - p22 [251-500]

Loewer, H Peter
Pond Water Zoo (Illus. by Jean Jenkins)
 SB - v33 - Ag '97 - p186 [1-50]

Loftis, Chris
The Boy Who Sat by the Window (Illus. by Catharine Gallagher)
 BL - v93 - Je 1 '97 - p1704 [51-250]
 SLJ - v43 - Ag '97 - p158 [51-250]

Logue, Mary
Forgiveness: The Story of Mahatma Gandhi (Illus. by Robin Lawrie)
 SLJ - v44 - Mr '98 - p198 [51-250]

Lohans, Alison
Nathaniel's Violin (Illus. by Marlene Watson)
 CBRA - '96 - p448+ [51-250]

Lomas Garza, Carmen
In My Family (Illus. by Carmen Lomas Garza)
 HMR - Sum '97 - p28 [51-250]
 RT - v51 - N '97 - p251 [51-250]
 RT - v51 - D '97 - p308 [51-250]

London, Jonathan
Ali, Child of the Desert (Illus. by Ted Lewin)
 CBRS - v25 - My '97 - p116 [51-250]
 CCB-B - v50 - Je '97 - p365 [51-250]
 Ch BWatch - v7 - My '97 - p2 [1-50]
 HB Guide - v8 - Fall '97 - p273 [51-250]
 KR - v65 - Ap 15 '97 - p643 [51-250]
 Par Ch - Awards '97 - p5 [51-250]
 SLJ - v43 - My '97 - p104 [51-250]

Dream Weaver (Illus. by Rocco Baviera)
 KR - v66 - Ap 1 '98 - p497 [51-250]

Fireflies, Fireflies, Light My Way (Illus. by Linda Messier)
 RT - v51 - O '97 - p152 [51-250]

Froggy Gets Dressed (Illus. by Frank Remkiewicz)
 PW - v244 - S 22 '97 - p82+ [51-250]

Froggy Goes to School (Illus. by Frank Remkiewicz)
 RT - v51 - O '97 - p131 [1-50]

Froggy Se Viste (Illus. by Frank Remkiewicz)
 HB Guide - v8 - Fall '97 - p339 [1-50]
 SLJ - v43 - My '97 - p154 [51-250]

Froggy's First Kiss (Illus. by Frank Remkiewicz)
 CCB-B - v51 - Ap '98 - p286+ [51-250]
 SLJ - v44 - Mr '98 - p182+ [51-250]

If I Had a Horse (Illus. by Brooke Scudder)
 BL - v94 - S 15 '97 - p242 [51-250]
 Ch BWatch - v7 - O '97 - p6 [1-50]
 PW - v244 - Ag 11 '97 - p400 [51-250]
 SLJ - v43 - S '97 - p186 [51-250]

Liplap's Wish (Illus. by Sylvia Long)
 PW - v244 - S 22 '97 - p83 [1-50]

Little Red Monkey (Illus. by Frank Remkiewicz)
 BL - v94 - D 1 '97 - p642 [51-250]
 SLJ - v43 - N '97 - p91 [51-250]

Master Elk and the Mountain Lion (Illus. by Wayne McLoughlin)
 ASBYP - v29 - Sum '96 - p22+ [251-500]

Puddles (Illus. by G Brian Karas)
 CCB-B - v51 - S '97 - p17 [51-250]
 HB Guide - v8 - Fall '97 - p273 [51-250]
 KR - v65 - Ap 15 '97 - p643 [51-250]
 SLJ - v43 - My '97 - p104 [51-250]

Red Wolf Country (Illus. by Daniel San Souci)
 SLJ - v43 - My '97 - p57 [1-50]

The Village Basket Weaver (Illus. by George Crespo)
 SE - v61 - Ap '97 - p14* [1-50]

Voices of the Wild (Illus. by Wayne McLoughlin)
 SB - v33 - O '97 - p219 [51-250]

London, Sara
Firehorse Max (Illus. by Ann Arnold)
 BL - v94 - O 1 '97 - p336+ [51-250]
 CBRS - v26 - D '97 - p39 [51-250]
 CCB-B - v51 - D '97 - p132 [51-250]

Ch BWatch - v8 - Ja '98 - p3 [1-50]
HB - v74 - Ja '98 - p65+ [51-250]
KR - v65 - S 1 '97 - p1392 [51-250]

Long, Barbara
Jim Thorpe: Legendary Athlete
BL - v93 - Je 1 '97 - p1689 [51-250]
HB Guide - v8 - Fall '97 - p371 [51-250]

Long, Jan Freeman
The Bee and the Dream (Illus. by Kaoru Ono)
RT - v51 - O '97 - p137 [1-50]

Long, John
Mystery of Devil's Roost
Ch BWatch - v7 - N '97 - p2 [51-250]
Magpies - v12 - Jl '97 - p34 [251-500]

Long, Jonathan
The Cat That Scratched
Bks Keeps - Jl '97 - p21 [51-250]

Long, Lynette
Domino Addition Book and Game Set
PW - v244 - Ag 4 '97 - p77 [51-250]

Long, Matthew
Any Bear Can Wear Glasses (Illus. by Sylvia Long)
ASBYP - v29 - Sum '96 - p23 [251-500]

Long, Sylvia
Hush Little Baby (Illus. by Sylvia Long)
BL - v93 - Je 1 '97 - p1708+ [51-250]
Bloom Rev - v17 - My '97 - p27 [51-250]
Ch BWatch - v7 - My '97 - p4 [1-50]
Ch BWatch - v7 - Je '97 - p6 [1-50]
HB Guide - v8 - Fall '97 - p253 [51-250]

Longfellow, Layne
Imaginary Menagerie (Illus. by Woodleigh Marx Hubbard)
BL - v94 - Ja 1 '98 - p824 [51-250]
KR - v65 - N 1 '97 - p1646 [51-250]
PW - v244 - N 10 '97 - p72 [51-250]
SLJ - v44 - F '98 - p86+ [51-250]

Loomis, Christine
Cowboy Bunnies (Illus. by Ora Eitan)
BL - v94 - F 15 '98 - p1020 [51-250]
HB - v73 - N '97 - p670+ [51-250]
KR - v65 - N 15 '97 - p1709 [51-250]
NYTBR - v103 - Mr 15 '98 - p23 [1-50]
PW - v244 - N 17 '97 - p60 [51-250]
SLJ - v43 - S '97 - p186 [51-250]

Loomis, Jennifer A
A Duck in a Tree
Ch BWatch - v7 - S '97 - p6 [1-50]

The Loose Caboose and Other Math Mysteries
Cur R - v37 - N '97 - p12 [51-250]

Lope, Manuel De
El Libro De Piel De Tiburon
SLJ - v43 - My '97 - p152 [51-250]

Lopez, Donald S, 1923-
Flight
ASBYP - v29 - Sum '96 - p54+ [501+]

Lopez, Gary
Air Pollution
Ch BWatch - v7 - '92 - p8 [51-250]

Lopez, Loretta
The Birthday Swap (Illus. by Loretta Lopez)
CBRS - v26 - S '97 - p8+ [51-250]
CCB-B - v50 - Je '97 - p365 [51-250]
HB Guide - v8 - Fall '97 - p273 [51-250]
SLJ - v43 - Je '97 - p97 [51-250]

Lorbiecki, Marybeth
Children of Vietnam (Illus. by Paul P Rome)
BL - v94 - Mr 15 '98 - p1238 [51-250]
SLJ - v44 - F '98 - p120 [51-250]

Just One Flick of a Finger (Illus. by David Diaz)
y   BL - v93 - Je 1 '97 - p1675 [1-50]
y   JAAL - v40 - Ap '97 - p585+ [51-250]
     RT - v51 - O '97 - p138 [1-50]
     RT - v51 - D '97 - p333 [51-250]
y   VOYA - v20 - Je '97 - p110 [51-250]

*My Palace of Leaves in Sarajevo
(Illus. by Herbert Tauss)*

y   CBRS - v25 - Jl '97 - p155+ [51-250]
     HB Guide - v8 - Fall '97 - p304 [51-250]
     SLJ - v43 - Je '97 - p122 [51-250]

Lord, Richard
Germany
     Ch BWatch - v7 - O '97 - p4+ [51-250]
     SLJ - v44 - Ja '98 - p99 [51-250]

Loredo, Elizabeth
*Boogie Bones (Illus. by Kevin
Hawkes)*
     BL - v94 - S 1 '97 - p133+ [51-250]
     CBRS - v26 - S '97 - p4 [51-250]
     CCB-B - v51 - S '97 - p17+ [51-250]
     KR - v65 - Jl 1 '97 - p1031 [51-250]
     Learning - v26 - S '97 - p45 [1-50]
     SLJ - v43 - S '97 - p186 [51-250]

Lorenz Books
A Child's Book of Prayer
     CM:CanRev - v4 - Ap 10 '98 - pONL
     [51-250]

Losi, Carol A
*The 512 Ants on Sullivan Street (Illus.
by Patrick Merrell)*
     SLJ - v44 - Ja '98 - p88+ [51-250]

Lottridge, Celia Barker
Letters to the Wind
     Can CL - v23 - Sum '97 - p74+ [501+]

*Wings to Fly (Illus. by Mary Jane
Gerber)*
     Ch BWatch - v7 - N '97 - p2 [1-50]
     CM:CanRev - v4 - Ja 16 '98 - pONL
     [251-500]
y   JAAL - v41 - N '97 - p244 [251-500]
     Quill & Q - v63 - Je '97 - p66 [251-500]
y   Ren Q - v50 - Aut '97 - p26 [501+]

Lotz, Jim
Nova Scotia. Rev. Ed.
     CBRA - '96 - p512+ [501+]

Lotz, Karen E
*Can't Sit Still (Illus. by Colleen
Browning)*
     PW - v245 - F 2 '98 - p92 [1-50]

*Snowsong Whistling (Illus. by Elisa
Kleven)*
     PW - v244 - O 13 '97 - p77 [1-50]

Lourie, Peter
Erie Canal
     SLJ - v43 - S '97 - p204 [51-250]

In the Path of Lewis and Clark
     HB Guide - v8 - Fall '97 - p385 [51-250]
y   SLJ - v43 - Ap '97 - p151+ [51-250]

Louw, Gideon
*Why Elephants and Fleas Don't Sweat
(Illus. by Dirk Van Wyk)*
     CBRA - '96 - p397 [51-250]

Love, Ann
Farming (Illus. by Pat Cupples)
     CBRA - '96 - p535 [51-250]

Love, John
Penguins
     KR - v65 - Je 1 '97 - p876+ [51-250]
y   SLJ - v44 - Ja '98 - p120 [251-500]

Loveday, John
Goodbye, Buffalo Sky
     Bks Keeps - My '97 - p16 [51-250]
     BL - v94 - Ja 1 '98 - p813+ [51-250]
     Books - v10 - S '96 - p24 [51-250]
y   CBRS - v26 - Win '98 - p71 [51-250]
     CCB-B - v51 - D '97 - p132 [51-250]
y   KR - v65 - S 1 '97 - p1392 [51-250]
y   PW - v244 - O 20 '97 - p77 [251-500]
y   SLJ - v43 - N '97 - p120 [51-250]

Lovejoy, R B
*The Golden Dog Book of Fairy Tales
and Animal Stories*
     CBRA - '96 - p502 [51-250]

Loveridge, Emma
Egypt
     HB Guide - v8 - Fall '97 - p393 [51-250]
     Magpies - v12 - Jl '97 - p42 [251-500]

SLJ - v43 - S '97 - p233 [51-250]

Loves, June
My Guardian Angel (Illus. by Tohby Riddle)
Magpies - v12 - S '97 - p34 [51-250]

Low, Robert
Arctic
Sch Lib - v45 - N '97 - p205 [51-250]

Desert
Sch Lib - v45 - N '97 - p205 [51-250]

Rainforest
Sch Lib - v45 - N '97 - p205 [51-250]

Low, William
Chinatown (Illus. by William Low)
BL - v94 - S 15 '97 - p242 [51-250]
CBRS - v26 - N '97 - p27 [51-250]
KR - v65 - Jl 1 '97 - p1031 [51-250]
SLJ - v43 - S '97 - p186 [51-250]

Lowell, Susan
The Bootmaker and the Elves (Illus. by Tom Curry)
BL - v94 - S 15 '97 - p242 [51-250]
Bloom Rev - v17 - N '97 - p33 [1-50]
CBRS - v26 - F '98 - p77 [51-250]
CCB-B - v51 - D '97 - p132+ [251-500]
HB - v73 - N '97 - p691 [51-250]
KR - v65 - Jl 1 '97 - p1032 [51-250]
PW - v244 - S 22 '97 - p80 [51-250]
SLJ - v43 - N '97 - p91 [51-250]

I Am Lavina Cumming (Caruso). Audio Version
HB - v73 - N '97 - p702+ [251-500]

Little Red Cowboy Hat (Illus. by Randy Cecil)
AB - v100 - N 17 '97 - p1271 [51-250]
CCB-B - v50 - Je '97 - p365+ [51-250]
HB Guide - v8 - Fall '97 - p273 [51-250]
Inst - v107 - Ag '97 - p21 [1-50]
SLJ - v43 - My '97 - p104+ [51-250]

The Three Little Javelinas (Illus. by Jim Harris)
ECEJ - v25 - Fall '97 - p48 [1-50]

Los Tres Pequenos Jabalies (Illus. by Jim Harris)
HB Guide - v8 - Fall '97 - p339 [51-250]
SLJ - v43 - N '97 - p136+ [51-250]

Lowry, Lois
The Giver
y   Bkbird - v35 - Sum '97 - p29+ [251-500]
NYTBR - v102 - N 16 '97 - p26 [1-50]

Number the Stars
Bkbird - v35 - Sum '97 - p29+ [251-500]
y   Emerg Lib - v24 - My '97 - p10 [1-50]
SLJ - v43 - S '97 - p131 [1-50]

See You Around, Sam! (Illus. by Diane De Groat)
Inst - v106 - My '97 - p21 [51-250]
RT - v51 - O '97 - p139 [1-50]

Stay! Keeper's Story (Illus. by True Kelley)
BL - v94 - N 1 '97 - p472 [51-250]
CBRS - v26 - N '97 - p31 [51-250]
CCB-B - v51 - Ja '98 - p165 [251-500]
HB - v74 - Ja '98 - p76+ [51-250]
KR - v65 - O 15 '97 - p1584 [51-250]
NYTBR - v103 - Mr 15 '98 - p23 [51-250]
Par Ch - Awards '97 - p6 [51-250]
PW - v244 - Jl 28 '97 - p75 [51-250]

Loyd, Luli
My Uncle Jack's a Logger (Illus. by Rebecca Davies)
CBRA - '96 - p449 [51-250]

Lubar, David
The Unwilling Witch
PW - v244 - O 6 '97 - p50 [1-50]

The Vanishing Vampire
PW - v244 - O 6 '97 - p50 [1-50]

Lucas, Daryl J
The Baker Bible Dictionary for Kids
r   SLJ - v43 - N '97 - p140 [51-250]

Lucas, Eileen
Contemporary Human Rights Activists
y   BL - v93 - Ag '97 - p1890 [51-250]
Ch BWatch - v7 - Je '97 - p5 [1-50]

y   HB Guide - v8 - Fall '97 - p384 [51-250]

Cracking the Wall (Illus. by Mark Anthony)
> BL - v94 - F 15 '98 - p1005 [51-250]
> CCB-B - v51 - Mr '98 - p249 [51-250]

Vincent Van Gogh (Illus. by Rochelle Draper)
> BL - v94 - S 1 '97 - p119 [51-250]
> SLJ - v43 - S '97 - p204 [51-250]

Lucas, Gail
Trevor, the Travelling Tree (Illus. by Gail Lucas)
> Ch BWatch - v7 - Je '97 - p3 [51-250]
> SLJ - v43 - D '97 - p96 [51-250]

Lucas, George
The Empire Strikes Back. Book and Audio Version
> TES - D 19 '97 - p23 [51-250]

Return of the Jedi. Book and Audio Version
> TES - D 19 '97 - p23 [51-250]

Star Wars. Book and Audio Version
> TES - D 19 '97 - p23 [51-250]

Lucas, Judy
Wangkangurru of the Desert
> Magpies - v12 - Jl '97 - p41+ [501+]

Lucile S. Packard Children's Hospital at Stanford
Family First Aid
> PW - v244 - O 27 '97 - p78 [1-50]

Luenn, Nancy
The Miser on the Mountain (Illus. by Pierr Morgan)
> BL - v94 - S 15 '97 - p232 [51-250]
> PW - v244 - S 1 '97 - p104 [51-250]
> SLJ - v44 - Ja '98 - p102 [51-250]

Nessa's Fish (Illus. by Neil Waldman)
> PW - v244 - N 10 '97 - p76 [1-50]

Otter Play (Illus. by Anna Vojtech)
> BL - v94 - Mr 15 '98 - p1250 [51-250]
> KR - v66 - Ja 15 '98 - p114 [51-250]
> PW - v245 - F 9 '98 - p95 [51-250]

La Pesca De Nessa (Illus. by Neil Waldman)
> PW - v244 - N 10 '97 - p76 [1-50]

Lullabies: An Illustrated Songbook
> BL - v94 - D 15 '97 - p701 [51-250]
> HMR - Win '97 - p46 [51-250]
> Par Ch - Awards '97 - p4 [1-50]
> PW - v244 - O 13 '97 - p77 [51-250]
> SLJ - v44 - Ja '98 - p101 [51-250]

Lumpkin, Susan
Dangerous Animals
> ASBYP - v29 - Sum '96 - p54+ [501+]

Lund, Jillian
Way out West Lives a Coyote Named Frank
> PW - v244 - Je 30 '97 - p77 [1-50]

Lundgren, Mary Beth
We Sing the City (Illus. by Donna Perrone)
> CBRS - v25 - Je '97 - p123 [51-250]
> HB Guide - v8 - Fall '97 - p273 [51-250]
> SLJ - v43 - Je '97 - p97+ [51-250]

Lunis, Natalie
Life in Your Backyard
> SB - v33 - Ag '97 - p177+ [51-250]

Lunn, Janet
Come to the Fair (Illus. by Gilles Pelletier)
> PW - v244 - N 10 '97 - p74 [51-250]
> Quill & Q - v63 - D '97 - p37 [251-500]
> SLJ - v44 - F '98 - p88 [51-250]

The Story of Canada. Rev. Ed. (Illus. by Alan Daniel)
> CBRA - '96 - p507+ [51-250]

Lutkenhoff, Marlene
SPINAbilities: A Young Person's Guide to Spina Bifida (Illus. by Eric Lutkenhoff)
> SLJ - v43 - Ap '97 - p153 [51-250]

Lutzeier, Elizabeth
Lost for Words
> Bks Keeps - My '97 - p25 [51-250]

Lychack, William
Russia
> HB Guide - v8 - Fall '97 - p370 [51-250]
> SLJ - v43 - My '97 - p148 [51-250]

Lye, Keith
Cold Climates
> HB Guide - v8 - Fall '97 - p386 [51-250]

Dry Climates
> HB Guide - v8 - Fall '97 - p386 [51-250]
> SLJ - v43 - Ag '97 - p171 [51-250]

The Earth in Three Dimensions World Atlas
> r   ASBYP - v29 - Sum '96 - p23+ [251-500]

Equatorial Climates
> HB Guide - v8 - Fall '97 - p386 [51-250]
> SLJ - v43 - Ag '97 - p171 [51-250]

Temperate Climates
> HB Guide - v8 - Fall '97 - p386 [51-250]
> SLJ - v43 - Ag '97 - p171 [51-250]

Lynch, Anne
Great Buildings
> ASBYP - v29 - Fall '96 - p57 [251-500]
> SB - v32 - D '96 - p276 [51-250]

Lynch, Chris
Babes in the Woods
> Emerg Lib - v25 - Ja '98 - p50 [1-50]
> HB Guide - v8 - Fall '97 - p304 [51-250]

Johnny Chesthair
> Emerg Lib - v25 - Ja '98 - p50 [51-250]
> HB Guide - v8 - Fall '97 - p304 [51-250]

Ladies' Choice
> BL - v94 - D 15 '97 - p697 [51-250]
> Emerg Lib - v25 - Ja '98 - p50 [1-50]
> SLJ - v43 - N '97 - p120 [51-250]

Scratch and the Sniffs
> Emerg Lib - v25 - Ja '98 - p50 [1-50]
> HB Guide - v8 - Fall '97 - p304 [51-250]
> y   JAAL - v41 - O '97 - p161 [51-250]
> SLJ - v43 - Ag '97 - p158 [51-250]

Slot Machine
> BL - v94 - Ja 1 '98 - p795 [1-50]
> y   JAAL - v41 - N '97 - p214 [51-250]

Wolfgang
> Emerg Lib - v25 - Ja '98 - p50 [1-50]

Lyne, Alice
A My Name Is... (Illus. by Lynne Woodcock Cravath)
> CBRS - v25 - My '97 - p111+ [51-250]
> HB Guide - v8 - Fall '97 - p273+ [51-250]
> SLJ - v43 - My '97 - p106 [51-250]

Lyon, George Ella
Counting on the Woods (Illus. by Ann W Olson)
> BL - v94 - Mr 1 '98 - p1130 [51-250]
> KR - v66 - Ja 15 '98 - p115 [51-250]
> PW - v245 - F 23 '98 - p75 [51-250]
> SLJ - v44 - Ap '98 - p120 [51-250]

Dreamplace (Illus. by Peter Catalanotto)
> BL - v93 - Je 1 '97 - p1701 [1-50]

A Sign (Illus. by Chris K Soentpiet)
> BL - v94 - F 15 '98 - p1014 [51-250]
> CCB-B - v51 - Ap '98 - p287 [51-250]
> KR - v66 - F 1 '98 - p198 [51-250]
> PW - v245 - F 2 '98 - p90 [51-250]
> SLJ - v44 - Mr '98 - p198 [51-250]

Who Came Down That Road? (Illus. by Peter Catalanotto)
> ECEJ - v25 - Fall '97 - p48 [1-50]

Lyons, Mary E
Catching the Fire (Illus. by Mannie Garcia)
> BL - v94 - S 1 '97 - p117 [51-250]
> BL - v94 - Ja 1 '98 - p734 [1-50]
> CCB-B - v51 - O '97 - p57 [51-250]
> HB - v73 - S '97 - p592 [51-250]
> KR - v65 - Jl 1 '97 - p1032 [51-250]
> SLJ - v43 - S '97 - p233+ [51-250]

The Poison Place (Illus. by Mary E Lyons)
> y   BL - v94 - D 1 '97 - p616 [51-250]
> y   CBRS - v26 - Ja '98 - p59 [51-250]
> y   CCB-B - v51 - Ja '98 - p166 [251-500]
> y   KR - v65 - O 1 '97 - p1535 [51-250]
> SLJ - v43 - N '97 - p120+ [51-250]

y   VOYA - v20 - D '97 - p318 [51-250]

M

Maar, Paul
*Ein Sams Fur Martin Taschenbier
(Illus. by Paul Maar)*
    Bkbird - v35 - Spr '97 - p49 [51-250]

Maartens, Marita
Paperbird
    BL - v93 - Je 1 '97 - p1724 [1-50]
    JOYS - v11 - Win '98 - p140 [1-50]

Maass, Robert
Garden (Illus. by Robert Maass)
    SLJ - v44 - Ap '98 - p120 [51-250]

Tugboats (Illus. by Robert Maass)
    HB Guide - v8 - Fall '97 - p358 [51-250]
    KR - v65 - Ap 15 '97 - p643 [51-250]
    SLJ - v43 - My '97 - p122 [51-250]

Macaulay, David
*Rome Antics (Illus. by David
Macaulay)*
    BL - v94 - S 15 '97 - p235 [51-250]
    BW - v28 - Ja 4 '98 - p11 [251-500]
    CBRS - v26 - D '97 - p46 [51-250]
    CCB-B - v51 - D '97 - p133 [51-250]
    Emerg Lib - v25 - Ja '98 - p52 [51-250]
    HB - v74 - Ja '98 - p66 [51-250]
    KR - v65 - S 1 '97 - p1392 [51-250]
    NYTBR - v102 - N 16 '97 - p48 [501+]
    PW - v244 - N 3 '97 - p60 [1-50]
    SLJ - v43 - N '97 - p121 [51-250]

*The Way Things Work. Electronic
Media Version*
    r   JOYS - v11 - Fall '97 - p78 [1-50]

*The Way Things Work (Illus. by David
Macaulay)*
    r   JOYS - v11 - Fall '97 - p78 [1-50]
        NYTBR - v102 - N 16 '97 - p26 [1-50]
        SB - v32 - D '96 - p259 [1-50]

MacBride, Roger Lea
New Dawn on Rocky Ridge
    BL - v94 - N 1 '97 - p472+ [51-250]
    SLJ - v44 - F '98 - p109 [51-250]

Maccarone, Grace
*Monster Math School Time (Illus. by
Marge Hartelius)*
    SLJ - v44 - Ja '98 - p88+ [51-250]

*Sharing Time Troubles (Illus. by Betsy
Lewin)*
    SLJ - v43 - Jl '97 - p70 [51-250]

MacDonald, Amy
*Cousin Ruth's Tooth (Illus. by
Marjorie Priceman)*
    RT - v51 - O '97 - p133 [1-50]

MacDonald, Betty
*Mrs. Piggle-Wiggle (Illus. by Hilary
Knight)*
    NYTBR - v102 - N 16 '97 - p26 [1-50]

*Mrs. Piggle-Wiggle's Won't-Take-a-
Bath Cure (Illus. by Bruce Whatley)*
    CBRS - v26 - N '97 - p28 [51-250]

*The Won't-Pick-Up-Toys Cure (Illus.
by Bruce Whatley)*
    CBRS - v26 - N '97 - p28 [51-250]

Macdonald, Caroline
Through the Witch's Window (Illus. by Mark Wilson)
> Aust Bk R - Ap '97 - p63 [501+]
> Magpies - v12 - Mr '97 - p10 [501+]

MacDonald, Elizabeth
The Wolf Is Coming! (Illus. by Ken Brown)
> KR - v65 - D 15 '97 - p1836 [51-250]
> SLJ - v44 - Mr '98 - p184 [51-250]

The Wolf Is Coming (Illus. by Ken Brown)
> Spec - v279 - D 6 '97 - p43 [1-50]

Macdonald, Fiona
A 16th Century Mosque (Illus. by Mark Bergin)
> Bks Keeps - N '97 - p26 [51-250]

Alexander the Great
> Sch Lib - v45 - Ag '97 - p152 [51-250]

Castle Siege (Illus. by Mark Bergin)
> PW - v244 - Je 2 '97 - p73 [51-250]

Exploring the World
> CLW - v68 - D '97 - p86 [51-250]

First Facts about the American Frontier (Illus. by Mark Bergin)
> HB Guide - v8 - Fall '97 - p396 [51-250]

First Facts about the Ancient Greeks
> Class Out - v75 - Fall '97 - p29 [1-50]

First Facts about the Ancient Romans
> Class Out - v75 - Fall '97 - p29 [1-50]
> HB Guide - v8 - Fall '97 - p388 [51-250]

A History of Ships from Log Rafts to Luxury Liners
> Bks Keeps - S '97 - p29 [51-250]

I Wonder Why Greeks Built Temples and Other Questions about Ancient Greece
> CLW - v68 - D '97 - p84+ [51-250]
> SLJ - v43 - S '97 - p204 [51-250]

I Wonder Why Romans Wore Togas and Other Questions about Ancient Rome
> CLW - v68 - D '97 - p84+ [51-250]
> SLJ - v43 - S '97 - p204 [51-250]

The Roman Colosseum (Illus. by Mark Bergin)
> HB Guide - v8 - Fall '97 - p388 [51-250]
> Magpies - v12 - Mr '97 - p41+ [51-250]

MacDonald, Jake
Juliana and the Medicine Fish
> y   CM:CanRev - v4 - F 13 '98 - pONL [251-500]
> Quill & Q - v63 - Ag '97 - p40 [251-500]

MacDonald, Margaret Read
Slop! A Welsh Folktale (Illus. by Yvonne LeBrun Davis)
> AB - v100 - N 17 '97 - p1266 [51-250]
> BL - v94 - N 1 '97 - p477 [51-250]
> SLJ - v43 - N '97 - p109+ [51-250]

Macdonald, Maryann
Hedgehog Bakes a Cake (Illus. by Lynn Munsinger)
> Ch BWatch - v7 - My '97 - p6 [1-50]

MacDonald, Suse
Peck, Slither, and Slide (Illus. by Suse MacDonald)
> CCB-B - v50 - Je '97 - p366+ [51-250]
> HB Guide - v8 - Fall '97 - p347 [51-250]
> KR - v65 - Ap 15 '97 - p643+ [51-250]
> SLJ - v43 - Ap '97 - p128 [51-250]

MacGill-Callahan, Sheila
The Children of Lir (Illus. by Gennady Spirin)
> Bks Keeps - Jl '97 - p21 [51-250]

To Capture the Wind (Illus. by Gregory Manchess)
> BL - v94 - S 1 '97 - p125 [51-250]
> CBRS - v26 - Win '98 - p66+ [51-250]
> KR - v65 - Jl 15 '97 - p1113 [51-250]
> PW - v244 - Je 23 '97 - p91 [51-250]
> SLJ - v43 - Ag '97 - p137+ [51-250]

MacGregor, Roy
Kidnapped in Sweden
> Ch BWatch - v7 - N '97 - p2 [51-250]

Mystery at Lake Placid
  Can CL - v23 - Fall '97 - p73+ [501+]

The Screech Owls' Northern Adventure
  CBRA - '96 - p483 [51-250]

Machado, Ana Maria
La Abuelita Aventurera (Illus. by Pablo Nunez)
  SLJ - v43 - Ag '97 - p181 [51-250]

Besos Magicos (Illus. by Federico Delicado)
  SLJ - v43 - N '97 - p137 [51-250]

El Domador De Monstruos (Illus. by Maria Luisa Torcida)
  SLJ - v44 - F '98 - p130 [51-250]

Macht, Norman L
Greg Maddux
  Ch BWatch - v7 - Je '97 - p2 [1-50]
  HB Guide - v8 - Fall '97 - p368 [51-250]

Mackay, Claire
Laughs: Funny Stories
  BIC - v26 - Je '97 - p35+ [501+]
  Can CL - v23 - Sum '97 - p83+ [501+]
  Ch Bk News - v20 - Sum '97 - p29 [51-250]
  Quill & Q - v63 - My '97 - p40 [251-500]
  SLJ - v43 - S '97 - p219 [51-250]

MacKay, Kathryn
Ontario. Rev. Ed.
  CBRA - '96 - p512+ [501+]

MacKay, Margaret
Jurassic Jungle
  CBRA - '96 - p532 [51-250]

Mackel, Kathy
A Season of Comebacks
  BL - v93 - Ag '97 - p1902 [51-250]
  CBRS - v25 - Spr '97 - p143 [51-250]
  HB Guide - v8 - Fall '97 - p304 [51-250]
  SLJ - v43 - Jl '97 - p70 [51-250]

Macken, JoAnn Early
Cats on Judy (Illus. by Judith DuFour Love)
  Ch BWatch - v7 - O '97 - p6 [1-50]
  SLJ - v43 - D '97 - p96 [51-250]

MacKinnon, Debbie
Daniel's Duck (Illus. by Anthea Sieveking)
  HB Guide - v8 - Fall '97 - p253 [51-250]
  Par - v72 - S '97 - p205 [51-250]

Pippa's Puppy (Illus. by Anthea Sieveking)
  HB Guide - v8 - Fall '97 - p253 [51-250]
  Par - v72 - S '97 - p205 [51-250]

Sarah's Shovel (Illus. by Anthea Sieveking)
  HB Guide - v8 - Fall '97 - p253 [51-250]
  Par - v72 - S '97 - p205 [51-250]

The Seasons (Illus. by Anthea Sieveking)
  Bks Keeps - N '97 - p20 [51-250]

Tom's Train (Illus. by Anthea Sieveking)
  HB Guide - v8 - Fall '97 - p253 [51-250]
  Par - v72 - S '97 - p205 [51-250]

MacLachlan, Patricia
Journey (Illus. by Barry Moser)
  SLJ - v44 - Ja '98 - p43 [1-50]

Sarah, Plain and Tall
  BL - v93 - Je 1 '97 - p1701 [1-50]
  HB - v74 - Ja '98 - p26+ [501+]
  NYTBR - v102 - N 16 '97 - p26 [1-50]

What You Know First (Illus. by Barry Moser)
  PW - v245 - Mr 23 '98 - p102 [1-50]

MacLaughlin, Robert
Cthulhu Live
  r Ch BWatch - v7 - Jl '97 - p5 [51-250]

MacLeod, Elizabeth
Get Started (Illus. by Esperanca Melo)
  CBRA - '96 - p520 [51-250]

MacMahon, Bryan
Jackomoora and the King of Ireland's Son (Illus. by Finbarr O'Connor)
Bks Keeps - S '97 - p23 [51-250]

MacMillan, Dianne
Destination Los Angeles
SLJ - v44 - Mr '98 - p236 [51-250]

MacMillan, Dianne M
Cheetahs
BL - v94 - F 15 '98 - p1005 [51-250]

Diwali: Hindu Festival of Lights
HB Guide - v8 - Fall '97 - p321 [51-250]
SLJ - v43 - Ag '97 - p171+ [51-250]

Japanese Children's Day and the Obon Festival
CLW - v68 - D '97 - p84 [51-250]
SLJ - v43 - Ag '97 - p149 [51-250]

Mardi Gras
CLW - v68 - D '97 - p84 [51-250]
SLJ - v43 - Ag '97 - p149 [51-250]

Mexican Independence Day and Cinco De Mayo
CLW - v68 - D '97 - p84 [51-250]
SLJ - v43 - Ag '97 - p149 [51-250]

President's Day
CLW - v68 - D '97 - p84 [51-250]
HB Guide - v8 - Fall '97 - p330 [51-250]

Thanksgiving Day
CLW - v68 - D '97 - p84 [51-250]
HB Guide - v8 - Fall '97 - p330 [51-250]
SLJ - v43 - Ag '97 - p171+ [51-250]

Macmillan Dictionary for Children. 3rd Rev. Ed.
r   BL - v94 - D 1 '97 - p650+ [501+]
r   Bloom Rev - v17 - N '97 - p31 [51-250]
r   Par Ch - Awards '97 - p29 [51-250]
r   SLJ - v43 - N '97 - p140 [51-250]

Macmillan Dictionary for Children. Newly Rev. Ed., 2nd Rev. Ed.
r   JOYS - v11 - Fall '97 - p75 [1-50]

Macmillan Encyclopedia of Science. Rev. Ed., Vols. 1-12
r   BL - v93 - Ag '97 - p1926+ [501+]
r   SLJ - v43 - Ag '97 - p185+ [51-250]

Macmillan Encyclopedia of the Environment. Vols. 1-6
r   BL - v93 - Ag '97 - p1926+ [501+]
yr   LJ - v122 - Jl '97 - p78 [51-250]
r   SLJ - v43 - Ag '97 - p186 [51-250]

The Macmillan Treasury of Poetry for Children (Illus. by Diz Wallis)
Bks Keeps - N '97 - p4+ [51-250]
NS - v126 - D 5 '97 - p63 [51-250]

MacQuarrie, Bob
The Northern Circumpolar World (Illus. by Wendy Johnson)
CBRA - '96 - p514 [51-250]

MacQuitty, Miranda
Amazing Bugs
SB - v33 - Ap '97 - p85+ [51-250]
SB - v33 - Ag '97 - p187 [1-50]

Ocean (Illus. by Frank Greenaway)
ASBYP - v29 - Sum '96 - p46+ [501+]
Emerg Lib - v25 - Ja '98 - p52 [51-250]

Macy, Sue
A Whole New Ball Game
SLJ - v44 - Mr '98 - p120 [1-50]

Winning Ways
y   Kliatt - v32 - Mr '98 - p32 [51-250]
      PW - v245 - Ja 19 '98 - p380 [1-50]
y   SLJ - v44 - Mr '98 - p120 [1-50]

Maddox, Tony
Spike's Best Nest (Illus. by Tony Maddox)
Books - v11 - Je '97 - p21 [1-50]

Madeleine-Perdrillat, Alain
Un Dimanche Avec Cezanne
Bkbird - v34 - Win '96 - p57 [51-250]

Madrigal, Antonio Hernandez
The Eagle and the Rainbow (Illus. by Tomie De Paola)

> AB - v100 - N 17 '97 - p1264+ [51-250]
> HB Guide - v8 - Fall '97 - p334 [51-250]

Madsen, Ross Martin
Perrywinkle's Magic Match (Illus. by Dirk Zimmer)

> HB - v73 - S '97 - p575 [51-250]
> SLJ - v43 - D '97 - p96+ [51-250]

Maestro, Betsy
Coming to America (Illus. by Susannah Ryan)

> Emerg Lib - v24 - My '97 - p66 [51-250]
> SE - v61 - Ap '97 - p9* [1-50]

Exploration and Conquest

> PW - v244 - Ag 18 '97 - p95 [1-50]

The New Americans (Illus. by Giulio Maestro)

> KR - v66 - Mr 1 '98 - p341 [51-250]
> PW - v245 - Mr 16 '98 - p66 [51-250]
> SLJ - v44 - Mr '98 - p198 [51-250]

The Story of Religion (Illus. by Giulio Maestro)

> SE - v61 - Ap '97 - p15* [1-50]

Maganzini, Christy
Cool Math

> BL - v94 - N 1 '97 - p464 [51-250]
> Ch BWatch - v7 - O '97 - p1 [1-50]
> Emerg Lib - v25 - Ja '98 - p56 [51-250]
> PW - v244 - Jl 28 '97 - p76 [51-250]

Maginnis, Peter
The Desert (Illus. by Kim Gamble)

> Magpies - v12 - Mr '97 - p22 [51-250]

Maguire, Gregory
Six Haunted Hairdos (Illus. by Elaine Clayton)

> BL - v94 - N 1 '97 - p473 [51-250]
> CCB-B - v51 - Ja '98 - p167 [51-250]
> KR - v65 - Je 15 '97 - p953 [51-250]
> SLJ - v43 - S '97 - p187 [51-250]

Mahy, Margaret
Beaten by a Balloon (Illus. by Jonathan Allen)

> BL - v94 - Mr 15 '98 - p1250 [51-250]
> CCB-B - v51 - Mr '98 - p250 [51-250]
> KR - v66 - Ja 1 '98 - p58+ [51-250]
> SLJ - v44 - Mr '98 - p184 [51-250]
> Spec - v279 - D 6 '97 - p43 [51-250]

Boom, Baby, Boom, Boom! (Illus. by Patricia MacCarthy)

> NYTBR - v102 - Jl 6 '97 - p16 [501+]
> Par - v72 - Je '97 - p189 [51-250]
> SLJ - v43 - My '97 - p106 [51-250]

The Five Sisters (Illus. by Patricia MacCarthy)

> CBRS - v25 - Spr '97 - p139+ [51-250]
> Cur R - v36 - Mr '97 - p12 [51-250]
> HB Guide - v8 - Fall '97 - p304 [51-250]
> Magpies - v12 - Mr '97 - p34 [51-250]
> TES - N 7 '97 - p7* [51-250]

The Greatest Show on Earth

> TES - Ap 18 '97 - p12* [51-250]

The Horribly Haunted School

> Obs - D 7 '97 - p17* [51-250]

Tingleberries, Tuckertubs and Telephones (Illus. by Robert Staermose)

> PW - v245 - Ja 12 '98 - p61 [1-50]

Maiecek, Tomaaes
Andalusian Horses

> ASBYP - v29 - Sum '96 - p52 [251-500]

Arabian Horses

> ASBYP - v29 - Sum '96 - p52 [251-500]

Friesian Horses

> ASBYP - v29 - Sum '96 - p52 [251-500]

Icelandic Ponies

> ASBYP - v29 - Sum '96 - p52 [251-500]

Lipizzaner Horses

> ASBYP - v29 - Sum '96 - p52 [251-500]

Palomino Horses

> ASBYP - v29 - Sum '96 - p52 [251-500]

Maisner, Heather
The Magic Stopwatch (Illus. by Peter Joyce)
> KR - v65 - N 1 '97 - p1647 [51-250]
> TES - N 21 '97 - p12* [51-250]

Maitland, Barbara
The Bear Who Didn't Like Honey (Illus. by Odilon Moraes)
> Ch BWatch - v7 - Je '97 - p6 [1-50]
> HB Guide - v8 - Fall '97 - p273 [1-50]
> SLJ - v43 - My '97 - p106 [51-250]

Maizlish, Lisa
The Ring (Illus. by Lisa Maizlish)
> LA - v73 - N '96 - p525 [51-250]

Majewski, Stephen
Sports Great Jerome Bettis
> CLW - v68 - S '97 - p69 [51-250]
> HB Guide - v8 - Fall '97 - p369 [51-250]
> y VOYA - v20 - Je '97 - p129 [251-500]

Major, Kevin
The House of Wooden Santas (Illus. by Imelda George)
> CM:CanRev - v4 - Mr 13 '98 - pONL [251-500]
> Quill & Q - v63 - O '97 - p40 [501+]

No Man's Land
> Can CL - v22 - Win '96 - p115+ [501+]

Make It
> Ch BWatch - v7 - Je '97 - p4 [51-250]

Malcolm, Jahnna N
Spirit of the West (Illus. by Sandy Rabinowitz)
> PW - v244 - N 17 '97 - p63 [1-50]

Mallat, Kathy
The Picture That Mom Drew (Illus. by Kathy Mallat)
> HB Guide - v8 - Fall '97 - p364 [51-250]
> SLJ - v43 - Ap '97 - p128 [51-250]

Mallory, Laura
Mother Nature's Magic Seed (Illus. by Chad Anderson)
> CBRA - '96 - p449 [51-250]

Malone, Geoffrey
Torn Ear
> Sch Lib - v45 - Ag '97 - p147 [51-250]

Malone, Mary
James Madison
> BL - v94 - S 15 '97 - p232 [51-250]
> y CLW - v68 - D '97 - p81 [51-250]
> y SLJ - v43 - S '97 - p234 [51-250]

Malone, Peter, 1953-
Star Shapes (Illus. by Peter Malone)
> BL - v94 - O 1 '97 - p337 [51-250]
> CBRS - v26 - S '97 - p4 [51-250]
> PW - v244 - Ag 4 '97 - p74 [51-250]
> SLJ - v43 - N '97 - p92+ [51-250]

Maloney, Peter, 1955-
Redbird at Rockefeller Center (Illus. by Peter Maloney)
> BL - v94 - N 1 '97 - p483 [51-250]
> CBRS - v26 - D '97 - p40 [51-250]
> KR - v65 - O 15 '97 - p1584 [51-250]
> PW - v244 - O 6 '97 - p55 [51-250]
> SLJ - v43 - D '97 - p97 [51-250]

Mama, Raouf
Why Goats Smell Bad and Other Stories from Benin (Illus. by Imna Arroyo)
> BL - v94 - F 15 '98 - p1005 [51-250]
> KR - v66 - Ja 1 '98 - p59 [51-250]
> PW - v245 - F 9 '98 - p97 [51-250]
> SLJ - v44 - Ap '98 - p149 [51-250]

Mammals: Whales, Panthers, Rats and Bats (Voyages of Discovery)
> Ch BWatch - v7 - Ap '97 - p4 [1-50]

Mammano, Julie
Rhinos Who Snowboard (Illus. by Julie Mammano)
> SLJ - v44 - Mr '98 - p184 [51-250]

Mandell, Muriel
*Simple Experiments in Time with
Everyday Materials*
  BL - v94 - D 1 '97 - p622 [51-250]

Mangan, Anne
*Little Teddy Left Behind (Illus. by
Joanne Moss)*
  CBRS - v26 - Win '98 - p63 [1-50]

Mangone, Luigi
*The Enchanted Toy Playhouse and the
Pirate*
  CBRA - '96 - p483 [51-250]

Mania, Robert C
A Forest's Life
  BL - v94 - D 15 '97 - p694 [51-250]

Mann, Elizabeth
*The Brooklyn Bridge (Illus. by Alan
Witschonke)*
  HB Guide - v8 - Fall '97 - p358 [51-
250]
  SLJ - v43 - Je '97 - p140 [51-250]

*The Great Pyramid (Illus. by Laura
Lo Turco)*
  SLJ - v43 - Je '97 - p140 [51-250]

*The Great Wall (Illus. by Alan
Witschonke)*
  BL - v94 - Ja 1 '98 - p806 [51-250]
  KR - v65 - N 1 '97 - p1647 [51-250]
  PW - v244 - D 1 '97 - p53 [51-250]
  SLJ - v43 - D '97 - p140+ [51-250]

Mann, Kenny
Egypt, Kush, Aksum
  HB Guide - v8 - Fall '97 - p393 [51-
250]
  SLJ - v43 - S '97 - p234 [51-250]

Monomotapa, Zulu, Basuto
  SE - v61 - Ap '97 - p6* [1-50]

Zenj, Buganda
  HB Guide - v8 - Fall '97 - p393 [51-
250]
  SLJ - v43 - S '97 - p234 [51-250]

Manna, Anthony L
*Mr. Semolina-Semolinus (Illus. by
Giselle Potter)*
  BL - v94 - Mr 15 '98 - p1219 [1-50]
  CBRS - v25 - Spr '97 - p136 [51-250]
  CCB-B - v50 - Jl '97 - p385+ [501+]
  Ch BWatch - v7 - My '97 - p3 [1-50]
  HB Guide - v8 - Fall '97 - p334 [51-
250]
  NYTBR - v102 - Ag 31 '97 - p13 [1-50]
  SLJ - v43 - Ap '97 - p128 [51-250]

Manning, Karen
AIDS, Can This Epidemic Be Stopped?
  ASBYP - v29 - Sum '96 - p24+ [501+]

Manning, Mick
Art School
  Books - v11 - Ag '97 - p15 [51-250]

*Honk! Honk! (Illus. by Brita
Granstrom)*
  KR - v65 - Ag 15 '97 - p1309 [51-250]
  SLJ - v43 - N '97 - p93 [51-250]

How Did I Begin?
  Bks Keeps - S '97 - p21 [51-250]
  Sch Lib - v45 - Ag '97 - p131 [51-250]

*Splish, Splash, Splosh! (Illus. by Mick
Manning)*
  Bks Keeps - Jl '97 - p22+ [51-250]
  Sch Lib - v45 - Ag '97 - p131 [51-250]
  SLJ - v44 - Ap '98 - p120 [51-250]

The World Is Full of Babies!
  Bks Keeps - Jl '97 - p22+ [51-250]
  ECEJ - v24 - Sum '97 - p249+ [51-250]

Manson, Ainslie
*Just like New (Illus. by Karen
Reczuch)*
  Can CL - v22 - Win '96 - p121+ [501+]
  Ch Bk News - v20 - Spr '97 - p34 [251-
500]
y JAAL - v40 - O '96 - p159 [51-250]

Manuel, Lynn
*Fifty-Five Grandmas and a Llama
(Illus. by Carolyn Fisher)*
  CCB-B - v50 - Jl '97 - p402+ [51-250]
  SLJ - v43 - Ap '97 - p113+ [51-250]

Lucy Maud and the Cavendish Cat (Illus. by Janet Wilson)
CM:CanRev - v4 - Ap 10 '98 - pONL [251-500]
HB - v73 - N '97 - p706+ [501+]
Quill & Q - v63 - S '97 - p74 [501+]

The Princess Who Laughed in Colours (Illus. by J O Pennanen)
CBRA - '96 - p449+ [51-250]

Manushkin, Fran
Miriam's Cup (Illus. by Bob Dacey)
PW - v244 - D 22 '97 - p54+ [51-250]
SLJ - v44 - F '98 - p88 [51-250]

Maples in the Mist (Illus. by Jean Tseng)
HMR - Sum '97 - p28 [51-250]
RT - v51 - O '97 - p150 [51-250]
RT - v51 - D '97 - p306+ [51-250]

Marc Brown's, Arthur's Teacher Trouble. Electronic Media Version
BW - v27 - D 7 '97 - p23 [51-250]
ChLAQ - v22 - Spr '97 - p30+ [501+]

Marchant, Kerena
Id-Ul-Fitr
Bks Keeps - N '97 - p24+ [51-250]

Marcus, Leonard S
The Making of Goodnight Moon
NY - v73 - O 6 '97 - p116 [51-250]

Marcuse, Aida E
Mi Diccionario De Juguete (Illus. by Maximo Sagredo Sagudo)
r　BL - v93 - Ag '97 - p1913 [1-50]

Margoshes, Dave
Saskatchewan. Rev. Ed.
CBRA - '96 - p512+ [501+]

Mariconda, Barbara
Turn the Cup Around
CBRS - v26 - D '97 - p46 [51-250]
CCB-B - v51 - N '97 - p92 [51-250]
Ch BWatch - v7 - O '97 - p3 [1-50]
KR - v65 - Je 1 '97 - p878 [51-250]
PW - v244 - Je 23 '97 - p92 [51-250]

SLJ - v43 - S '97 - p220 [51-250]

Witch Way to the Beach (Illus. by Jon McIntosh)
HB Guide - v8 - Fall '97 - p292 [51-250]
SLJ - v43 - N '97 - p93 [51-250]

Marino, Dan
First and Goal
HB Guide - v8 - Fall '97 - p371 [51-250]

Mark, Jan
A Fine Summer Knight (Illus. by Bob Harvey)
Bks Keeps - My '97 - p25+ [51-250]

Fur (Illus. by Charlotte Voake)
Bks Keeps - Jl '97 - p20 [51-250]

God's Story (Illus. by David Parkins)
y　BL - v94 - O 1 '97 - p321+ [51-250]
　HB - v74 - Ja '98 - p92+ [51-250]
y　PW - v245 - F 23 '98 - p67 [51-250]
　SLJ - v44 - Ja '98 - p127 [51-250]
　TES - D 5 '97 - p17* [1-50]
　TES - Ja 9 '98 - p17* [501+]

A Worm's Eye View (Illus. by Bethan Matthews)
Bks Keeps - My '97 - p22 [51-250]

Market, Jenny
Clouds
Ch BWatch - v7 - '92 - p8 [51-250]

Ocean Resources
Ch BWatch - v7 - '94 - p8 [51-250]

Water
Ch BWatch - v7 - '92 - p8 [51-250]

Markham, Lois
Colombia: The Gateway to South America
Ch BWatch - v7 - My '97 - p7 [1-50]
HB Guide - v8 - Fall '97 - p400 [51-250]
SLJ - v44 - Ap '98 - p149 [51-250]

Markle, Sandra
Creepy, Crawly Baby Bugs
SLJ - v43 - Ap '97 - p128+ [51-250]

Discovering Graph Secrets
> BL - v94 - F 15 '98 - p1005 [51-250]
> SLJ - v44 - Mr '98 - p236 [51-250]

Gone Forever! (Illus. by Felipe Davalos)
> KR - v66 - Ja 15 '98 - p115 [51-250]

Icky, Squishy Science
> Am Sci - v85 - N '97 - p557 [51-250]

Outside and Inside Bats
> BL - v94 - O 1 '97 - p320 [51-250]
> HB - v74 - Ja '98 - p93+ [51-250]
> SLJ - v43 - N '97 - p130+ [51-250]

Science Surprises (Illus. by June Otani)
> SLJ - v43 - Jl '97 - p85 [51-250]

Super Cool Science (Illus. by Sandra Markle)
> BL - v94 - Mr 15 '98 - p1238+ [51-250]
> CCB-B - v51 - Ap '98 - p288 [51-250]
> SLJ - v44 - Ap '98 - p120 [51-250]

Super Science Secrets
> SLJ - v43 - S '97 - p206 [51-250]

Marks, Anthony
Learn to Play Keyboard
> Ch BWatch - v7 - Ap '97 - p1 [1-50]

Marks, Diana F
Glues, Brews, and Goos
> ASBYP - v29 - Fall '96 - p22+ [501+]
> SB - v32 - D '96 - p272 [51-250]

Markun, P
The Little Painter of Sabana Grande (Illus. by Robert Casilla)
> ECEJ - v25 - Fall '97 - p48 [1-50]

Marlow, Herb
Twisters, Bronc Riders, and Cherry Pie (Illus. by Julie Caffee)
> SLJ - v43 - Jl '97 - p96 [51-250]

Marrin, Albert
Empires Lost and Won
> CBRS - v25 - Spr '97 - p143+ [51-250]
> y HB Guide - v8 - Fall '97 - p396 [51-250]
> KR - v65 - Ap 15 '97 - p644 [51-250]
> NYTBR - v102 - Ag 17 '97 - p19 [1-50]

> y SLJ - v43 - Je '97 - p141 [51-250]
> y VOYA - v20 - Je '97 - p134 [51-250]
> y VOYA - v20 - F '98 - p365+ [51-250]

Marsch, Carole
Asteroids, Comets, and Meteors
> SB - v33 - Ag '97 - p187 [1-50]

Marschall, Ken
Inside the Titanic (Illus. by Ken Marschall)
> y BL - v94 - Mr 15 '98 - p1225 [1-50]
> BL - v94 - Mr 15 '98 - p1244 [1-50]
> NYTBR - v103 - Ja 4 '98 - p20 [1-50]
> NYTLa - v147 - D 4 '97 - pE8 [51-250]
> Par Ch - Awards '97 - p4 [51-250]
> y VOYA - v21 - Ap '98 - p39 [1-50]

Marsh, Carole
Unidentified Flying Objects and Extraterrestrial Life
> SB - v33 - Ag '97 - p187 [1-50]

Marsh, T J
Way Out in the Desert (Illus. by Kenneth J Spengler)
> KR - v66 - Mr 15 '98 - p408 [51-250]

Marshall, Elizabeth L
The Human Genome Project
> y Kliatt - v31 - S '97 - p42 [251-500]
> SB - v33 - Ag '97 - p186 [1-50]
> y SLJ - v43 - Ag '97 - p172 [51-250]

A Student's Guide to the Internet
> Ch BWatch - v7 - Je '97 - p4 [51-250]

Marshall, James
George and Martha: The Complete Stories of Two Best Friends (Illus. by James Marshall)
> BW - v27 - O 5 '97 - p11 [51-250]
> Inst - v107 - Ja '98 - p27 [1-50]
> NW - v130 - D 1 '97 - p78 [1-50]
> NYTBR - v102 - N 16 '97 - p26 [1-50]
> Par - v73 - F '98 - p185 [1-50]
> PW - v244 - O 27 '97 - p78 [1-50]

Goldilocks and the Three Bears
> PW - v244 - D 15 '97 - p60 [1-50]

Hansel and Gretel
> SLJ - v44 - Ja '98 - p42+ [1-50]

Ricitos Dorados Y Los Tres Osos
HB Guide - v8 - Fall '97 - p339 [51-250]

Marshall, Janet
Banana Moon (Illus. by Janet Marshall)
CCB-B - v51 - Mr '98 - p250 [51-250]

Look Once Look Twice (Illus. by Janet Marshall)
LA - v73 - N '96 - p523 [51-250]

Martell, Hazel
The Ancient World
Ch BWatch - v7 - D '97 - p3 [1-50]

Exploring Africa (Illus. by Gerald Woods)
Ch BWatch - v7 - D '97 - p2 [1-50]
KR - v65 - D 1 '97 - p1777 [51-250]
SLJ - v44 - Ap '98 - p146 [51-250]

The Great Pyramid (Illus. by Gerald Woods)
Sch Lib - v45 - Ag '97 - p153 [51-250]

Marti, Jose
Los Zapaticos De Rosa (Illus. by Lulu Delacre)
SLJ - v43 - N '97 - p137 [51-250]

Martin, Ann M, 1955-
The Baby-Sitters Club
NYTBR - v102 - N 16 '97 - p26 [1-50]

Holiday Time
PW - v244 - O 6 '97 - p59 [1-50]

Leo the Magnificat (Illus. by Emily Arnold McCully)
SE - v61 - Ap '97 - p13* [1-50]

Martin, Bill, 1916-
Chicka Chicka Boom Boom (Illus. by Lois Ehlert)
Par - v72 - Je '97 - p189 [1-50]

The Maestro Plays (Illus. by Vladimir Radunsky)
Comw - v124 - D 5 '97 - p14 [1-50]

Swish! (Illus. by Michael Chesworth)
BL - v94 - D 15 '97 - p704 [51-250]
CBRS - v26 - S '97 - p4 [51-250]

PW - v244 - Jl 21 '97 - p200+ [51-250]
SLJ - v43 - N '97 - p93+ [51-250]

The Wizard (Illus. by Alex Schaefer)
PW - v244 - Jl 21 '97 - p203 [1-50]

Martin, Carol
Martha Black: Gold Rush Pioneer (Illus. by Jack McMaster)
CBRA - '96 - p508 [51-250]
y   Ch Bk News - v20 - Sum '97 - p30 [51-250]

Martin, David, 1944-
Five Little Piggies (Illus. by Susan Meddaugh)
HB - v74 - Mr '98 - p216 [51-250]

Little Chicken Chicken (Illus. by Sue Heap)
ECEJ - v25 - Fall '97 - p41 [51-250]
RT - v51 - S '97 - p52 [51-250]

Martin, Jacqueline Briggs
Grandmother Bryant's Pocket (Illus. by Petra Mathers)
HMR - Sum '97 - p28 [51-250]
NYTBR - v102 - Ap 27 '97 - p29 [501+]

The Green Truck Garden Giveaway (Illus. by Alec Gillman)
CBRS - v25 - Spr '97 - p140 [51-250]
HB Guide - v8 - Fall '97 - p274 [51-250]
SLJ - v43 - Je '97 - p98 [51-250]

Higgins Bend Song and Dance (Illus. by Brad Sneed)
CBRS - v26 - D '97 - p40 [51-250]
KR - v65 - Jl 1 '97 - p1032+ [51-250]
NYTLa - v147 - D 4 '97 - pE8 [51-250]
PW - v244 - Ag 18 '97 - p92 [51-250]
SLJ - v43 - S '97 - p187+ [51-250]

Martin, James, 1950-
Frogs (Illus. by Art Wolfe)
BL - v94 - D 15 '97 - p694 [51-250]
CCB-B - v51 - Mr '98 - p250+ [51-250]
KR - v65 - N 1 '97 - p1647 [51-250]
SLJ - v44 - Mr '98 - p236 [51-250]

Living Fossils (Illus. by Janet Hamlin)
BL - v93 - Je 1 '97 - p1693 [51-250]
Ch BWatch - v7 - Jl '97 - p3 [1-50]

HB Guide - v8 - Fall '97 - p347 [51-250]

y   SLJ - v43 - Je '97 - p141 [51-250]

Martin, Mary
Adam and Eve (Illus. by Bryn Barnard)

HB Guide - v8 - Fall '97 - p319 [51-250]

Martin, Nora
The Eagle's Shadow

y   BL - v93 - Ag '97 - p1891 [51-250]
     CBRS - v26 - Ja '98 - p59+ [51-250]
     CCB-B - v51 - O '97 - p59+ [51-250]
     KR - v65 - Je 15 '97 - p953 [51-250]

y   VOYA - v21 - Ap '98 - p48 [51-250]

Martin, Patricia
Travels with Rainie Marie

CBRS - v25 - Ag '97 - p167 [51-250]
HB Guide - v8 - Fall '97 - p304 [51-250]
SLJ - v43 - Jl '97 - p96 [51-250]

Martin, Patricia A Fink, 1955-
Animals That Walk on Water

BL - v94 - D 1 '97 - p632 [51-250]

Martin, Rafe
The Brave Little Parrot (Illus. by Susan Gaber)

BL - v94 - F 15 '98 - p1014+ [51-250]
CCB-B - v51 - Mr '98 - p251 [51-250]
KR - v65 - D 1 '97 - p1777 [51-250]
PW - v244 - D 1 '97 - p52+ [51-250]

The Eagle's Gift (Illus. by Tatsuro Kiuchi)

BL - v94 - S 15 '97 - p238 [51-250]
Ch BWatch - v7 - N '97 - p5 [1-50]
KR - v65 - Ag 1 '97 - p1226 [51-250]
PW - v244 - Ag 18 '97 - p92 [51-250]
SLJ - v44 - F '98 - p102 [51-250]

The Monkey Bridge (Illus. by Fahimeh Amiri)

Ch BWatch - v7 - My '97 - p2 [1-50]
HB Guide - v8 - Fall '97 - p319 [51-250]
SLJ - v43 - Jl '97 - p85+ [51-250]

Mysterious Tales of Japan (Illus. by Tatsuro Kiuchi)

CAY - v18 - Spr '97 - p5 [51-250]

RT - v51 - D '97 - p307 [51-250]

Martin, S R
Swampland

y   Aust Bk R - v279 - My '97 - p61+ [501+]
     Magpies - v12 - Jl '97 - p38 [51-250]

Martin, Terry
Why Are Zebras Black and White?

SB - v33 - Ap '97 - p82+ [251-500]
SB - v33 - Ag '97 - p187 [1-50]

Why Do Sunflowers Face the Sun?

SB - v33 - Ap '97 - p82+ [251-500]
SB - v33 - Ag '97 - p187 [1-50]

Why Do We Laugh?

SB - v33 - Ap '97 - p82+ [251-500]
SB - v33 - Ag '97 - p187 [1-50]

Why Does Lightning Strike?

SB - v33 - Ap '97 - p82+ [251-500]
SB - v33 - Ag '97 - p187 [1-50]

Martinez, Floyd
Spirits of the High Sea

CBRS - v26 - Win '98 - p67 [1-50]

Martinez, Raul
Los Cuentos Bobos (Illus. by Raul Martinez)

Bkbird - v35 - Sum '97 - p57 [1-50]

Marvis, Barbara J
Famous People of Hispanic Heritage. Vols. 5-6

SLJ - v43 - Jl '97 - p109 [51-250]

Raphael Palmeiro

Ch BWatch - v7 - O '97 - p5 [51-250]

Robert Rodriguez

Ch BWatch - v7 - O '97 - p5 [51-250]
SLJ - v44 - F '98 - p114 [51-250]

Selena

Ch BWatch - v7 - O '97 - p5 [51-250]
SLJ - v44 - F '98 - p114 [51-250]

Marzollo, Jean
Do You Know New? (Illus. by Mari Takabayashi)

KR - v66 - F 15 '98 - p276 [51-250]

Football Friends (Illus. by True Kelley)
SLJ - v44 - Mr '98 - p184 [51-250]

Home Sweet Home (Illus. by Ashley Wolff)
HB Guide - v8 - Fall '97 - p319 [51-250]
Par - v72 - D '97 - p204 [1-50]
SLJ - v43 - Ap '97 - p129 [51-250]

I Am an Apple (Illus. by Judith Moffatt)
SLJ - v44 - Ja '98 - p102 [51-250]

I Spy: Little Book (Illus. by Walter Wick)
PW - v244 - S 29 '97 - p91 [51-250]

I Spy Spooky Night
Emerg Lib - v24 - My '97 - p50+ [51-250]

I Spy Super Challenger! (Illus. by Walter Wick)
BL - v94 - O 1 '97 - p334 [51-250]
PW - v244 - S 29 '97 - p91 [51-250]

I'm a Caterpillar (Illus. by Judith Moffatt)
SLJ - v43 - N '97 - p110 [51-250]

Masefield, John
The Box of Delights
TES - Ja 2 '98 - p22* [1-50]

The Box of Delights (Illus. by Judith Masefield)
Bks Keeps - N '97 - p5 [51-250]

The Midnight Folk (Illus. by Rowland Hilder)
Bks Keeps - N '97 - p5 [51-250]
TES - Ja 2 '98 - p22* [1-50]

Masoff, Joy
Fire! (Illus. by Jack Reznicki)
CCB-B - v51 - Ap '98 - p289 [51-250]
HB - v74 - Mr '98 - p236 [51-250]
KR - v65 - D 15 '97 - p1836+ [51-250]
PW - v245 - F 9 '98 - p97 [51-250]
SLJ - v44 - Mr '98 - p198+ [51-250]

Mason, Antony
Aztec Times (Illus. by Michael White)
SLJ - v43 - D '97 - p141 [51-250]

Biblical Times
Ch BWatch - v7 - Mr '97 - p5 [51-250]

Medieval Times
Ch BWatch - v7 - Mr '97 - p5 [51-250]

Monet
Emerg Lib - v25 - N '97 - p60 [51-250]

Viking Times (Illus. by Michael Welply)
SLJ - v43 - D '97 - p141 [51-250]

Mason, Lesley
Inky Little Fingers (Illus. by Bettina Paterson)
Sch Lib - v45 - N '97 - p205 [51-250]

Mason, Paul
Atlas of Threatened Cultures
r	Ch BWatch - v7 - S '97 - p7 [51-250]
r	HB Guide - v8 - Fall '97 - p385 [51-250]

Massie, Elizabeth
Patsy and the Declaration
SLJ - v43 - Ag '97 - p138 [51-250]

Patsy's Discovery
BL - v94 - D 1 '97 - p637 [51-250]
PW - v244 - Je 2 '97 - p72 [51-250]
SLJ - v43 - Ag '97 - p138 [51-250]

Masson, Sophie
The Troublemaker
Magpies - v12 - S '97 - p35 [51-250]

The Year the Star Fell
Magpies - v12 - S '97 - p35 [51-250]

Masters, Anthony
Biker (Illus. by Gary Rees)
Bks Keeps - S '97 - p25 [51-250]
Sch Lib - v45 - Ag '97 - p146 [51-250]
TES - Jl 4 '97 - p10* [501+]

The Haunted Lighthouse (Illus. by Alan Marks)
Sch Lib - v45 - N '97 - p192 [51-250]

Wicked
y	Sch Lib - v45 - N '97 - p214 [51-250]
TES - Je 20 '97 - p7* [501+]

Mastin, Colleayn O
Canadian Ocean Creatures (Illus. by Jan Sovak)
> CBRA - '96 - p532 [51-250]

Canadian Wild Animals (Illus. by Jan Sovak)
> CM:CanRev - v4 - S 19 '97 - pONL [51-250]

Canadian Wild Flowers and Emblems (Illus. by Jan Sovak)
> CM:CanRev - v4 - S 19 '97 - pONL [51-250]

The Magic of Mythical Creatures
> Ch BWatch - v7 - D '97 - p5 [51-250]

Masurel, Claire
No, No, Titus! (Illus. by Shari Halpern)
> BL - v93 - Je 1 '97 - p1720 [51-250]
> CBRS - v25 - Jl '97 - p149 [1-50]
> HB Guide - v8 - Fall '97 - p253 [51-250]

Ten Dogs in the Window (Illus. by Pamela Paparone)
> Ch BWatch - v8 - Ja '98 - p3 [1-50]
> Emerg Lib - v25 - Ja '98 - p56 [51-250]
> PW - v244 - O 6 '97 - p82 [51-250]
> SLJ - v43 - D '97 - p97 [51-250]

Matas, Carol
After the War
> CBRA - '96 - p483 [51-250]
> CM:CanRev - v4 - F 13 '98 - pONL [251-500]
> y   Kliatt - v32 - Ja '98 - p10 [51-250]
> y   PW - v244 - S 1 '97 - p107 [1-50]
> y   SE - v61 - Ap '97 - p15* [1-50]
> y   VOYA - v20 - Je '97 - p86 [51-250]

The Garden
> CM:CanRev - v4 - F 27 '98 - pONL [251-500]
> y   HB Guide - v8 - Fall '97 - p315 [51-250]
> y   Quill & Q - v63 - S '97 - p75 [251-500]
> y   SLJ - v43 - My '97 - p137+ [51-250]
> y   VOYA - v20 - Je '97 - p110+ [251-500]

The Lost Locket
> Can CL - v23 - Sum '97 - p56+ [51-250]

Matheson, Shirlee Smith
The Gambler's Daughter
> CM:CanRev - v4 - Ap 24 '98 - pONL [501+]

Mathews, S
The Sad Night
> ECEJ - v25 - Fall '97 - p48 [1-50]

Mathis, Sharon Bell
Running Girl (Illus. by Sharon Bell Mathis)
> Am Vis - v12 - D '97 - p34 [1-50]
> BL - v94 - S 1 '97 - p126 [51-250]
> CBRS - v26 - O '97 - p23 [51-250]
> CCB-B - v51 - O '97 - p60 [51-250]

Matthews, Andrew
Marduk the Mighty and Other Stories of Creation (Illus. by Sheila Moxley)
> BL - v93 - Je 1 '97 - p1693+ [51-250]
> CCB-B - v50 - Je '97 - p367 [51-250]
> Ch BWatch - v7 - My '97 - p5 [1-50]
> HB Guide - v8 - Fall '97 - p334 [51-250]
> SLJ - v43 - Jl '97 - p86 [51-250]

Mouse Flute (Illus. by Vanessa Julian-Ottie)
> Bks Keeps - S '97 - p24 [51-250]
> Sch Lib - v45 - N '97 - p192 [51-250]

Matthews, Downs
Harp Seal Pups (Illus. by Dan Guravich)
> HB Guide - v8 - Fall '97 - p354 [51-250]

Matthews, Jenny
Potato Baby
> Magpies - v12 - S '97 - p34 [51-250]

Maurer, Richard
Airborne: The Search for the Secret of Flight
> SB - v32 - D '96 - p257 [1-50]

Mavor, Salley
You and Me (Illus. by Salley Mavor)
> KR - v65 - Jl 1 '97 - p1033 [51-250]
> PW - v244 - Ag 18 '97 - p95 [51-250]
> SLJ - v43 - S '97 - p206 [51-250]

Maw, Taylor
The Incredible Jelly Bean Day (Illus.
by Taylor Maw)
  Ch BWatch - v7 - O '97 - p5 [1-50]

Max, Jill
Spider Spins a Story (Illus. by Robert
Annesley)
  BL - v94 - D 15 '97 - p694+ [51-250]
  CBRS - v26 - S '97 - p11 [1-50]
  PW - v244 - Je 23 '97 - p92 [51-250]
  SLJ - v44 - Ja '98 - p103 [51-250]

May, Kara
Big Puss, Little Mouse (Illus. by Susie
Jenkin-Pearce)
  Bks Keeps - Jl '97 - p23 [51-250]

May, Steve
How's Harry? (Illus. by Philip
Hopman)
  Bks Keeps - S '97 - p23 [51-250]

May, Stuart
Forward in Geography
  TES - D 12 '97 - p38 [251-500]

Mayer, Marianna
Baba Yaga and Vasilisa the Brave
  ECEJ - v25 - Fall '97 - p48 [1-50]

The Mother Goose Cookbook (Illus. by
Carol Schwartz)
  SLJ - v44 - Ap '98 - p120 [51-250]

Pegasus (Illus. by Kinuko Craft)
  BL - v94 - Mr 15 '98 - p1241 [51-250]
  KR - v66 - Ap 1 '98 - p498 [51-250]
  SLJ - v44 - Ap '98 - p149+ [51-250]

Mayes, Susan
The Usborne Book of Drawing,
Painting and Lettering (Illus. by Susan
Mayes)
  Ch BWatch - v7 - Ap '97 - p1 [1-50]

Mayfield, Thomas Jefferson
Adopted by Indians (Illus. by Hilair
Chism)
  BL - v94 - Mr 1 '98 - p1128 [51-250]
  Ch BWatch - v7 - N '97 - p1 [51-250]
  KR - v65 - N 15 '97 - p1710 [51-250]

Maynard, Bill
Incredible Ned (Illus. by Frank
Remkiewicz)
  CBRS - v26 - O '97 - p16 [51-250]
  CCB-B - v51 - N '97 - p93 [51-250]
  PW - v244 - Ag 11 '97 - p401 [51-250]
  SLJ - v43 - N '97 - p94 [51-250]

Santa's Time Off (Illus. by Tom
Browning)
  CBRS - v26 - N '97 - p32 [51-250]
  PW - v244 - O 6 '97 - p59 [1-50]

Maynard, Caitlin
Rain Forests and Reefs (Illus. by Stan
Rullman)
  HB Guide - v8 - Fall '97 - p347 [51-
  250]
  SB - v33 - Ag '97 - p186 [1-50]

Maynard, Christopher
Jobs People Do
  BL - v93 - Je 1 '97 - p1711 [51-250]
  CBRS - v25 - Ag '97 - p161 [51-250]
  Ch BWatch - v7 - Jl '97 - p8 [1-50]
  CLW - v68 - S '97 - p63 [51-250]
  HB Guide - v8 - Fall '97 - p322 [51-
  250]
  Sch Lib - v45 - Ag '97 - p131 [51-250]

Sharks
  Obs - D 7 '97 - p18* [51-250]
  PW - v244 - O 6 '97 - p85 [51-250]
  SLJ - v44 - Ja '98 - p127 [51-250]

Why Are Pineapples Prickly?
  CLW - v68 - S '97 - p63+ [51-250]
  HB Guide - v8 - Fall '97 - p340 [51-
  250]
  SB - v33 - Ag '97 - p187 [1-50]
  SLJ - v43 - Ag '97 - p149 [51-250]

Why Do Volcanoes Erupt?
  CLW - v68 - S '97 - p64 [51-250]
  HB Guide - v8 - Fall '97 - p340 [51-
  250]
  SB - v33 - Ag '97 - p187 [1-50]
  Sch Lib - v45 - Ag '97 - p152 [51-250]

Maynard, Meredy
Blue True Dream of Sky
  CCB-B - v51 - O '97 - p60 [51-250]
  Quill & Q - v63 - My '97 - p30 [251-
  500]
  y VOYA - v20 - O '97 - p245 [51-250]

Maynard, Thane
Ostriches
> SLJ - v43 - My '97 - p122 [51-250]

Mayne, William
The Book of Hob Stories (Illus. by Patrick Benson)
> BL - v94 - N 1 '97 - p473 [51-250]
> PW - v244 - Ag 25 '97 - p74 [1-50]
> SLJ - v43 - N '97 - p94 [51-250]

Hob and the Peddler
> BL - v94 - Ja 1 '98 - p814 [51-250]
> CCB-B - v51 - D '97 - p134+ [51-250]
> HB - v74 - Ja '98 - p77 [51-250]
> SLJ - v43 - D '97 - p126 [51-250]

Hob and the Pedlar
> TES - N 7 '97 - p7* [51-250]

Lady Muck (Illus. by Jonathan Heale)
> BL - v94 - Ja 1 '98 - p736 [1-50]
> BW - v27 - O 5 '97 - p11 [51-250]
> HB Guide - v8 - Fall '97 - p274 [51-250]
> NYTBR - v102 - O 26 '97 - p47 [1-50]
> Sch Lib - v45 - Ag '97 - p147 [51-250]
> SLJ - v43 - My '97 - p106+ [51-250]
> TES - My 16 '97 - p14* [501+]

Mayo, Edith
The Smithsonian Book of the First Ladies
> RT - v51 - D '97 - p335 [51-250]

Mayo, Gretchen
Meet Tricky Coyote!
> ECEJ - v25 - Fall '97 - p48 [1-50]

Mayo, Margaret
Mythical Birds and Beasts from Many Lands (Illus. by Jane Ray)
> CCB-B - v50 - Jl '97 - p403 [51-250]
> HB Guide - v8 - Fall '97 - p334 [51-250]
> SLJ - v43 - Je '97 - p110 [51-250]
> Trib Bks - Jl 13 '97 - p7 [51-250]

When the World Was Young (Illus. by Louise Brierley)
> Emerg Lib - v24 - My '97 - p57 [51-250]

Maze, Stephanie
I Want to Be--a Dancer
> SLJ - v43 - D '97 - p112+ [51-250]

I Want to Be--a Veterinarian
> HB Guide - v8 - Fall '97 - p323 [51-250]
> SB - v33 - Ag '97 - p186 [1-50]

I Want to Be a Veterinarian
> SLJ - v43 - Ap '97 - p153 [51-250]

I Want to Be--an Astronaut
> A & S Sm - v12 - Je '97 - p85 [51-250]
> HB Guide - v8 - Fall '97 - p323 [51-250]
> SB - v33 - Ag '97 - p186 [1-50]
> SLJ - v43 - Ap '97 - p153 [51-250]

Mazer, Anne
Working Days
> y   BL - v94 - Mr 15 '98 - p1218 [1-50]
> y   Ch BWatch - v7 - S '97 - p6 [51-250]
> y   HB - v73 - N '97 - p682 [51-250]
> y   HMR - Fall '97 - p36 [501+]
> y   JAAL - v41 - S '97 - p82 [51-250]
> y   Kliatt - v31 - S '97 - p24 [51-250]
> y   KR - v65 - Je 15 '97 - p953+ [51-250]
>   PW - v244 - My 26 '97 - p86 [51-250]
> y   SLJ - v43 - S '97 - p220+ [51-250]
> y   VOYA - v20 - D '97 - p318 [251-500]
> y   VOYA - v21 - Ap '98 - p39 [1-50]

Mazer, Harry
The Dog in the Freezer
> y   Emerg Lib - v25 - N '97 - p51+ [51-250]
>   NYTBR - v102 - Je 1 '97 - p36 [1-50]
> y   SLJ - v43 - Jl '97 - p96 [51-250]

Mazer, Norma Fox
When She Was Good
> y   BL - v94 - S 1 '97 - p118 [51-250]
> y   BL - v94 - Ja 1 '98 - p733 [1-50]
> y   BL - v94 - Mr 15 '98 - p1218 [51-250]
> y   CBRS - v26 - N '97 - p36 [51-250]
> y   CCB-B - v51 - O '97 - p61 [251-500]
>   Ch BWatch - v7 - N '97 - p2 [1-50]
> y   Emerg Lib - v25 - Ja '98 - p50 [51-250]
> y   HB - v73 - N '97 - p682+ [51-250]
> y   JAAL - v41 - D '97 - p323 [51-250]
> y   NYTBR - v102 - N 16 '97 - p32 [501+]
> y   PW - v244 - Jl 21 '97 - p202 [51-250]
> y   SLJ - v43 - S '97 - p221 [51-250]
> y   SLJ - v43 - D '97 - p26 [1-50]

y   SLJ - v44 - Ja '98 - p43 [1-50]
y   VOYA - v20 - O '97 - p245+ [51-250]
y   VOYA - v21 - Ap '98 - p38 [1-50]

Mazzola, Frank, Jr.

Counting Is for the Birds (Illus. by Frank Mazzola Jr.)
    HB Guide - v8 - Fall '97 - p352 [51-250]
    SB - v33 - O '97 - p210 [51-250]
    SLJ - v43 - My '97 - p122 [51-250]

McAfee, Annalena

Why Do Stars Come Out at Night? (Illus. by Anthony Lewis)
    Sch Lib - v45 - N '97 - p187 [51-250]
    TES - N 7 '97 - p4* [1-50]

McAllister, Margaret

A Friend for Rachel
    Bks Keeps - My '97 - p24 [51-250]
    Magpies - v12 - Jl '97 - p34 [51-250]
y   Sch Lib - v45 - Ag '97 - p158 [51-250]

McArthur, Nancy

The Plant That Ate Dirty Socks (Adamson). Audio Version
y   BL - v94 - N 1 '97 - p495 [51-250]
    Ch BWatch - v8 - Ja '98 - p5 [51-250]
    SLJ - v43 - N '97 - p69 [51-250]

McBratney, Sam

Daisy Dare (Illus. by Jill Barton)
    Bks Keeps - Jl '97 - p21 [51-250]

The Dark at the Top of the Stairs (Illus. by Ivan Bates)
    PW - v245 - Ja 19 '98 - p380 [1-50]

Just One! (Illus. by Ivan Bates)
    BL - v94 - O 15 '97 - p416 [51-250]

Just You and Me (Illus. by Ivan Bates)
    PW - v245 - F 23 '98 - p75 [51-250]

McCann, Joseph T

Forensic Assessment with the Millon Inventories
    SB - v32 - D '96 - p265 [251-500]

McCaughrean, Geraldine

Daedalus and Icarus (Illus. by Tony Ross)
    Bks Keeps - N '97 - p22+ [51-250]
    Sch Lib - v45 - N '97 - p192 [51-250]

Forever X
    Bks Keeps - N '97 - p25 [51-250]
y   Sch Lib - v45 - N '97 - p213 [51-250]
    TES - Ag 29 '97 - p28 [51-250]

God's People (Illus. by Anna C Leplar)
    BL - v94 - Mr 1 '98 - p1130 [51-250]
    SLJ - v44 - Mr '98 - p198 [51-250]
    TES - O 17 '97 - p12* [51-250]

King Arthur and the Round Table (Illus. by Alan Marks)
    Bks Keeps - Jl '97 - p4 [51-250]

Moby Dick (Illus. by Victor G Ambrus)
    AB - v100 - N 17 '97 - p1266 [51-250]
    Bks Keeps - Jl '97 - p4 [51-250]
    Ch BWatch - v7 - My '97 - p4 [1-50]
    HB Guide - v8 - Fall '97 - p305 [51-250]
    NYTBR - v103 - F 1 '98 - p24 [501+]
    SLJ - v43 - My '97 - p136 [51-250]

Myths and Legends of the World (Illus. by Bee Willey)
    Magpies - v12 - Mr '97 - p18+ [501+]
    TES - N 7 '97 - p8* [51-250]

The Orchard Book of Greek Gods and Goddesses (Illus. by Emma Chichester Clark)
    TES - N 7 '97 - p11* [51-250]

Perseus and the Gorgon Medusa (Illus. by Tony Ross)
    Bks Keeps - N '97 - p22+ [51-250]
    Sch Lib - v45 - N '97 - p192 [51-250]

The Silver Treasure (Illus. by Bee Willey)
    CCB-B - v50 - Je '97 - p366 [51-250]
    SLJ - v43 - Ap '97 - p153 [51-250]
y   VOYA - v20 - Ag '97 - p204 [251-500]

Unicorns! Unicorns! (Illus. by Sophie Windham)
    CCB-B - v51 - D '97 - p133+ [51-250]
    Ch BWatch - v8 - Ja '98 - p2 [1-50]

CM:CanRev - v4 - Mr 13 '98 - pONL [51-250]
KR - v65 - Ag 1 '97 - p1225 [51-250]
PW - v244 - Ag 25 '97 - p71+ [51-250]
Sch Lib - v45 - N '97 - p192 [51-250]
TES - D 26 '97 - p22 [251-500]

The Wooden Horse (Illus. by Tony Ross)

Bks Keeps - N '97 - p22+ [51-250]
Sch Lib - v45 - N '97 - p192 [51-250]

McClellan, Doris
Baxter Badger's Home (Illus. by Vicki Diggs)

ASBYP - v29 - Sum '96 - p24 [251-500]

McClintock, Barbara
The Fantastic Drawings of Danielle (Illus. by Barbara McClintock)

Magpies - v12 - S '97 - p7 [51-250]

McClintock, Norah
Mistaken Identity

Can CL - v23 - Fall '97 - p73+ [501+]

McClung, Robert M
Last of the Wild (Illus. by Bob Hines)

    CCB-B - v51 - S '97 - p18 [51-250]
y   KR - v65 - Je 1 '97 - p877 [51-250]
y   SLJ - v43 - N '97 - p130 [51-250]
y   VOYA - v20 - O '97 - p265 [51-250]

McConduit, Denise Walter
D.J. and the Jazz Fest (Illus. by Emile F Henriquez)

Ch BWatch - v7 - My '97 - p4 [1-50]
HB Guide - v8 - Fall '97 - p273 [51-250]

McCormick, Rosie
All Kinds of Animals (Illus. by Anthony Lewis)

PW - v244 - O 27 '97 - p79 [51-250]

Things That Go (Illus. by Anthony Lewis)

PW - v244 - O 27 '97 - p79 [51-250]

World of the Rainforest

Sch Lib - v45 - N '97 - p203 [51-250]

McCourt, Lisa
The Best Night Out with Dad (Illus. by Bert Dodson)

SLJ - v44 - Ja '98 - p80 [251-500]

The Braids Girl (Illus. by Tim Ladwig)

PW - v245 - Mr 16 '98 - p67 [1-50]

A Dog of My Own (Illus. by Katya Krenina)

PW - v245 - Mr 16 '98 - p67 [1-50]

The Goodness Gorillas (Illus. by Pat Grant Porter)

SLJ - v44 - Ja '98 - p80 [251-500]

I Love You, Stinky Face (Illus. by Cyd Moore)

BL - v94 - O 15 '97 - p403 [51-250]
PW - v244 - Ag 25 '97 - p70 [51-250]

The Never-Forgotten Doll (Illus. by Mary O'Keefe Young)

SLJ - v44 - Ja '98 - p80 [251-500]

The Rain Forest Counts! (Illus. by Cheryl Nathan)

BL - v94 - D 15 '97 - p704 [51-250]
Ch BWatch - v7 - S '97 - p3 [51-250]

The Rain Forest Counts (Illus. by Cheryl Nathan)

SLJ - v43 - N '97 - p91+ [51-250]

McCuen, Gary E
Abortion Violence and Extremism

Ch BWatch - v7 - Je '97 - p5 [1-50]

The Death Penalty and the Disadvantaged

Ch BWatch - v7 - Je '97 - p5 [1-50]

Immigration

Ch BWatch - v7 - Je '97 - p5 [1-50]

Tobacco

Ch BWatch - v7 - Je '97 - p5 [51-250]

McCulloch, Jane
The Story of Peter Pan (Jacobi). Audio Version

Ch BWatch - v7 - D '97 - p4 [1-50]
SLJ - v44 - Mr '98 - p158 [51-250]

McCullough, L E
Plays of the Wild West: Grades 4-6
> BL - v94 - N 1 '97 - p464 [51-250]
> y   SLJ - v44 - Ja '98 - p127 [51-250]

Plays of the Wild West: Grades K-3
> BL - v94 - N 1 '97 - p464 [51-250]
> SLJ - v44 - Ja '98 - p126+ [51-250]

Stories of the Songs of Christmas (Illus. by Irene Kelly Nelson)
> PW - v244 - O 6 '97 - p58 [1-50]

McCully, Emily Arnold
The Ballot Box Battle (Illus. by Emily Arnold McCully)
> SE - v61 - Ap '97 - p11* [1-50]

Beautiful Warrior (Illus. by Emily Arnold McCully)
> CCB-B - v51 - Mr '98 - p233+ [501+]
> KR - v65 - D 15 '97 - p1836 [51-250]
> PW - v244 - N 24 '97 - p73 [51-250]
> SLJ - v44 - F '98 - p88 [51-250]

The Bobbin Girl (Illus. by Emily Arnold McCully)
> Emerg Lib - v24 - My '97 - p64 [51-250]
> RT - v51 - N '97 - p242 [51-250]
> SE - v61 - Ap '97 - p11* [1-50]

Pirate Queen
> Emerg Lib - v25 - N '97 - p46+ [51-250]

Popcorn at the Palace (Illus. by Emily Arnold McCully)
> BL - v94 - S 15 '97 - p242+ [51-250]
> CBRS - v26 - O '97 - p16 [51-250]
> CCB-B - v51 - O '97 - p57 [51-250]
> KR - v65 - Ag 1 '97 - p1225 [51-250]
> PW - v244 - Je 30 '97 - p76 [51-250]

Starring Mirette and Bellini (Illus. by Emily Arnold McCully)
> CCB-B - v50 - Jl '97 - p401 [51-250]
> CLW - v68 - D '97 - p85 [51-250]
> HB Guide - v8 - Fall '97 - p273 [51-250]
> Magpies - v12 - Jl '97 - p31 [51-250]
> SLJ - v43 - My '97 - p106 [51-250]

McCunney, Michelle
Mario's Mayan Journey (Illus. by Michelle McCunney)
> CBRS - v26 - O '97 - p20+ [51-250]
> SLJ - v43 - N '97 - p92 [51-250]

McCurdy, Michael
The Sailor's Alphabet (Illus. by Michael McCurdy)
> BW - v28 - Mr 1 '98 - p11 [51-250]
> KR - v66 - Mr 15 '98 - p407 [51-250]

Trapped by the Ice! (Illus. by Michael McCurdy)
> BL - v94 - S 15 '97 - p232+ [51-250]
> CCB-B - v51 - S '97 - p18+ [251-500]
> KR - v65 - Je 15 '97 - p952 [51-250]
> NYTBR - v103 - F 15 '98 - p25 [501+]
> PW - v244 - Jl 7 '97 - p68 [51-250]

McCutcheon, Marc
Grandfather's Christmas Camp (Illus. by Kate Kiesler)
> PW - v244 - O 6 '97 - p59 [1-50]

McDaniel, Lurlene
Lifted Up by Angels
> Ch BWatch - v7 - D '97 - p4 [1-50]

McDaniel, Melissa
South Dakota
> Ch BWatch - v8 - Ja '98 - p7 [1-50]

McDermott, Gerald
Musicians of the Sun (Illus. by Gerald McDermott)
> BL - v94 - N 1 '97 - p467 [51-250]
> CBRS - v26 - N '97 - p27+ [51-250]
> Ch BWatch - v7 - O '97 - p6 [1-50]
> NY - v73 - O 6 '97 - p115 [1-50]
> PW - v244 - S 29 '97 - p88 [51-250]
> SLJ - v43 - D '97 - p111+ [51-250]

McDonald, Joyce
Swallowing Stones
> y   BL - v94 - O 15 '97 - p397+ [51-250]
> y   BL - v94 - Mr 15 '98 - p1218 [1-50]
> y   CBRS - v26 - Win '98 - p71 [51-250]
> y   CCB-B - v51 - N '97 - p91 [51-250]
> y   KR - v65 - Jl 1 '97 - p1032 [51-250]
> y   PW - v244 - S 22 '97 - p82 [51-250]
> SLJ - v43 - S '97 - p29 [51-250]

y   VOYA - v20 - D '97 - p319 [51-250]
y   VOYA - v20 - F '98 - p366 [51-250]
y   VOYA - v21 - Ap '98 - p38 [1-50]

McDonald, Margaret Read
Tuck-Me-In Tales (McDonald). Audio Version
SLJ - v44 - Ja '98 - p68 [251-500]

McDonald, Mary Ann
Chickens
SLJ - v44 - F '98 - p102 [51-250]

Horses
SLJ - v44 - F '98 - p102 [51-250]

Jupiter
SLJ - v44 - F '98 - p98 [51-250]

McDonald, Megan
Beezy (Illus. by Nancy Poydar)
BL - v94 - S 15 '97 - p235 [51-250]
CCB-B - v51 - N '97 - p91 [51-250]
KR - v65 - Ag 1 '97 - p1225 [51-250]
PW - v244 - S 29 '97 - p89 [51-250]
SLJ - v43 - N '97 - p92 [51-250]

Beezy Magic (Illus. by Nancy Poydar)
SLJ - v44 - Ap '98 - p104 [51-250]

Insects Are My Life (Illus. by Paul Brett Johnson)
SB - v33 - O '97 - p219 [1-50]

My House Has Stars (Illus. by Peter Catalanotto)
RT - v51 - N '97 - p241 [51-250]
SE - v61 - Ap '97 - p7* [1-50]

Tundra Mouse (Illus. by S D Schindler)
BL - v94 - Ja 1 '98 - p824 [51-250]
Ch BWatch - v7 - N '97 - p4 [1-50]
KR - v65 - Ag 1 '97 - p1225 [51-250]
PW - v244 - O 6 '97 - p55 [51-250]

McDonald, Meme
The Way of the Birds (Illus. by Shane Nagle)
Sch Lib - v45 - Ag '97 - p147 [51-250]
TES - My 16 '97 - p14* [501+]

McDonnell, Flora
Flora McDonnell's ABC (Illus. by Flora McDonnell)
CCB-B - v50 - Jl '97 - p402 [51-250]
Ch BWatch - v7 - My '97 - p3 [1-50]
HB Guide - v8 - Fall '97 - p253 [51-250]
Magpies - v12 - My '97 - p22 [251-500]
Par Ch - Awards '97 - p3 [51-250]
Sch Lib - v45 - Ag '97 - p131 [51-250]

Flora McDonnell's ABC (Illus. by Flora McDonnell)
CBRS - v25 - Je '97 - p123 [51-250]
TES - Je 27 '97 - p12* [51-250]

McDonnell, Janet
Animal Camouflage
SLJ - v44 - F '98 - p102 [51-250]

Animal Communication
SLJ - v44 - F '98 - p102 [51-250]

McDonough, Yona Zeldis
Anne Frank (Illus. by Malcah Zeldis)
BL - v94 - O 1 '97 - p335 [51-250]
CCB-B - v51 - Ja '98 - p166 [51-250]
Emerg Lib - v25 - Ja '98 - p57 [51-250]
PW - v244 - Jl 28 '97 - p73+ [51-250]

McEvoy, Greg
Alfie's Long Winter
CBRA - '96 - p450 [51-250]

McFarlane, Peter
Soula the Ruler (Illus. by Stephen Axelsen)
Magpies - v12 - My '97 - p35 [51-250]

McFarlane, Sheryl
Going to the Fair (Illus. by Sheena Lott)
Can CL - v23 - Sum '97 - p94+ [251-500]
CBRA - '96 - p450 [51-250]

Moonsnail Song (Illus. by Sheena Lott)
Can CL - v23 - Fall '97 - p67+ [501+]

McGeorge, Constance W
Boomer's Big Day
Par - v72 - Je '97 - p126 [1-50]

McGill, Nancy L
Disney's The Hunchback of Notre Dame (Esmeralda and Djali) (Illus. by DiCicco Digital Arts)
Ch BWatch - v7 - Ap '97 - p2 [1-50]

McGough, Roger
Bad Bad Cats
TES - S 12 '97 - p15U [51-250]

The Kingfisher Book of Poems about Love
NS - v126 - D 5 '97 - p63 [1-50]
TES - N 7 '97 - p2* [51-250]

Until I Met Dudley (Illus. by Chris Riddell)
CBRS - v26 - S '97 - p9 [1-50]
CCB-B - v51 - Ja '98 - p166+ [51-250]
Obs - Jl 20 '97 - p18* [51-250]
SLJ - v43 - N '97 - p110 [51-250]

McGovern, Ann
The Lady in the Box (Illus. by Marni Backer)
BL - v94 - S 1 '97 - p138 [251-500]
CBRS - v26 - N '97 - p28 [51-250]
KR - v65 - S 15 '97 - p1459 [51-250]

Nicholas Bentley Stoningpot III (Illus. by Tomie De Paola)
PW - v244 - O 6 '97 - p85 [1-50]

La Senora De La Caja De Carton (Illus. by Marni Backer)
SLJ - v43 - N '97 - p137 [51-250]

McGowan, Christopher
Make Your Own Dinosaur out of Chicken Bones
New Sci - v156 - D 20 '97 - p69 [51-250]
Quill & Q - v63 - Ag '97 - p38+ [251-500]

McGowan, Diane
Math Play! (Illus. by Loretta Braren)
PW - v244 - Jl 28 '97 - p76+ [51-250]
SLJ - v44 - Ap '98 - p120 [51-250]

McGowan, Tom
1900-1919
ASBYP - v29 - Sum '96 - p64+ [51-250]

1960-1969
ASBYP - v29 - Sum '96 - p64+ [51-250]

McGraw, Eloise
The Moorchild
BL - v94 - N 1 '97 - p475 [1-50]
HMR - Sum '97 - p29 [51-250]
RT - v51 - S '97 - p58 [51-250]

McGuffee, Michael
The Day the Earth Was Silent (Illus. by Edward Sullivan)
Ch BWatch - v7 - Je '97 - p3 [51-250]

McGugan, Jim
Josepha: A Prairie Boy's Story (Illus. by Murray Kimber)
Ch Bk News - v20 - Spr '97 - p34+ [251-500]

McGuigan, Mary Ann
Where You Belong
BL - v93 - Je 1 '97 - p1695 [51-250]
CBRS - v25 - Spr '97 - p143 [51-250]
y HB Guide - v8 - Fall '97 - p315 [51-250]
SLJ - v43 - Jl '97 - p96 [51-250]
y VOYA - v20 - Ag '97 - p187+ [251-500]

McGuire, J Victor
Takiya and Thunderheart's Life Garden (Illus. by Gershom Griffith)
Ch BWatch - v7 - Jl '97 - p5 [51-250]

McGuire, Leslie
A Busy Day at Jack's Garage
PW - v244 - D 1 '97 - p55 [1-50]

McGuire, Richard
Night Becomes Day (Illus. by Richard McGuire)
PW - v244 - D 15 '97 - p60 [1-50]

What's Wrong with This Book? (Illus. by Richard McGuire)
BW - v27 - My 4 '97 - p18 [51-250]
HB Guide - v8 - Fall '97 - p292 [51-250]
NYTBR - v102 - Ag 31 '97 - p13 [1-50]

McHale, Gillian
Don't Bug Me! (Illus. by Gillian McHale)
Ch BWatch - v7 - O '97 - p5 [1-50]

McKay, Fiona
The Legs Book (Illus. by Reece Scannell)
Magpies - v12 - Mr '97 - p28 [51-250]

War-Torn: Ordinary Lives Behind the Battle Zone (Illus. by George Gittoes)
Magpies - v12 - S '97 - p42 [51-250]

McKay, George
Mammals
ASBYP - v29 - Fall '96 - p57 [251-500]

McKay, Hilary
The Amber Cat
BL - v94 - Ja 1 '98 - p734 [1-50]
CCB-B - v51 - N '97 - p91+ [51-250]
HB - v73 - N '97 - p680+ [251-500]
KR - v65 - O 1 '97 - p1535 [51-250]
SLJ - v43 - N '97 - p121+ [51-250]
SLJ - v43 - D '97 - p26 [1-50]

Dog Friday (Lambert). Audio Version
Par Ch - Awards '97 - p19 [51-250]

The Exiles in Love
CCB-B - v51 - Ap '98 - p287+ [51-250]
KR - v66 - Mr 15 '98 - p407 [51-250]
PW - v245 - F 23 '98 - p78 [1-50]

McKay, Sharon E
Pat-a-Cake Dough Book and Kit (Illus. by Marilyn Mets)
CBRA - '96 - p520 [51-250]

McKean, Thomas
My Evil Twin
y   KR - v65 - N 15 '97 - p1710 [51-250]
     PW - v244 - N 24 '97 - p75 [51-250]
     SLJ - v44 - F '98 - p109 [51-250]
y   VOYA - v21 - Ap '98 - p48 [51-250]

McKee, David
Elmer and the Snow
TES - D 5 '97 - p17* [1-50]

Elmer and Wilbur (Illus. by David McKee)
RT - v51 - O '97 - p133 [1-50]

The Elmer Pop-Up Book (Illus. by David McKee)
Magpies - v12 - Mr '97 - p20+ [501+]

I Can Too! (Illus. by David McKee)
SLJ - v44 - Ja '98 - p89 [51-250]

The Monster and the Teddy Bear (Illus. by David McKee)
Bks Keeps - N '97 - p20 [51-250]

Prince Peter and the Teddy Bear (Illus. by David McKee)
CBRS - v26 - S '97 - p4 [51-250]
KR - v65 - Je 1 '97 - p877 [51-250]
PW - v244 - Je 16 '97 - p58 [51-250]
Sch Lib - v45 - Ag '97 - p131 [51-250]
SLJ - v43 - Ag '97 - p138 [51-250]

McKellar, Shona
A Child's Book of Lullabies (Illus. by Mary Cassatt)
BL - v93 - Je 1 '97 - p1708 [51-250]
Emerg Lib - v25 - N '97 - p59 [51-250]
HB Guide - v8 - Fall '97 - p366 [51-250]

McKenna, Virginia
Back to the Blue (Illus. by Ian Andrew)
KR - v66 - F 1 '98 - p198 [51-250]
SLJ - v44 - Mr '98 - p184 [51-250]

Journey to Freedom (Illus. by Nick Mountain)
Sch Lib - v45 - Ag '97 - p152 [51-250]

McKenzie, Ellen Kindt
The Golden Band of Eddris
y   BL - v94 - F 15 '98 - p1000 [51-250]
     KR - v66 - Ja 1 '98 - p58 [51-250]
     PW - v244 - D 1 '97 - p53+ [51-250]
     SLJ - v44 - Mr '98 - p216 [251-500]
y   VOYA - v21 - Ap '98 - p56 [51-250]

McKibbon, Hugh William
The Token Gift (Illus. by Scott Cameron)
CBRA - '96 - p450+ [51-250]
Sch Lib - v45 - Ag '97 - p131 [51-250]

TCMath - v4 - S '97 - p54 [51-250]

McKinlay, Penny
Elephants Don't Do Ballet (Illus. by Graham Percy)

    CM:CanRev - v4 - Ap 24 '98 - pONL [51-250]

    Sch Lib - v45 - Ag '97 - p131 [51-250]

McKinley, Robin
Rose Daughter

y   BL - v93 - Ag '97 - p1898 [251-500]
y   BL - v94 - N 1 '97 - p475 [1-50]
y   BL - v94 - Ja 1 '98 - p733 [1-50]
y   BL - v94 - Mr 15 '98 - p1218 [1-50]
    BW - v27 - D 7 '97 - p21+ [251-500]
y   CBRS - v26 - O '97 - p23 [51-250]
y   CCB-B - v51 - O '97 - p58 [251-500]
y   HB - v73 - S '97 - p574+ [251-500]
y   KR - v65 - Je 1 '97 - p877 [51-250]
y   MFSF - v94 - Ja '98 - p28+ [501+]
    PW - v244 - Je 16 '97 - p60 [51-250]
y   SLJ - v43 - S '97 - p219+ [51-250]
y   VOYA - v20 - F '98 - p366 [51-250]
y   VOYA - v20 - F '98 - p394 [501+]
y   VOYA - v21 - Ap '98 - p13 [1-50]
y   VOYA - v21 - Ap '98 - p38 [1-50]

McKissack, Pat
The Big Bug Alphabet Book.
Electronic Media Version

    Ch BWatch - v7 - Ap '97 - p7 [51-250]

Can You Imagine?

    BL - v93 - Je 1 '97 - p1696 [51-250]
    SLJ - v43 - S '97 - p199 [51-250]

The Civil Rights Movement in America from 1865 to the Present. 2nd Ed.

    BL - v94 - F 15 '98 - p998+ [1-50]

Dear America

    Bl S - v27 - Spr '97 - p79 [1-50]

Ma Dear's Aprons (Illus. by Floyd Cooper)

    CBRS - v25 - Je '97 - p123 [51-250]
    CCB-B - v50 - Je '97 - p367 [51-250]
    HB Guide - v8 - Fall '97 - p292 [51-250]
    NYTBR - v102 - Ag 3 '97 - p14 [51-250]
    SLJ - v43 - Je '97 - p98 [51-250]

A Picture of Freedom

    Emerg Lib - v24 - My '97 - p67 [1-50]

    HB Guide - v8 - Fall '97 - p300 [51-250]
    SLJ - v43 - S '97 - p220 [51-250]

Rebels against Slavery

    PW - v245 - F 9 '98 - p98 [1-50]

Red-Tail Angels

    ABR - v19 - N '97 - p9+ [501+]
    SE - v61 - Ap '97 - p217 [51-250]

Run Away Home

    BL - v94 - O 1 '97 - p329+ [51-250]
    CBRS - v26 - N '97 - p36 [51-250]
    Ch BWatch - v8 - Ja '98 - p4 [51-250]
    HB - v73 - N '97 - p681+ [51-250]
    PW - v244 - Ag 18 '97 - p93 [51-250]
    SLJ - v43 - N '97 - p122 [51-250]

Young, Black, and Determined

y   BL - v94 - F 15 '98 - p995 [51-250]
    KR - v66 - F 15 '98 - p271 [51-250]
    SLJ - v44 - Ap '98 - p148+ [501+]

McLean, Andrew
Josh (Illus. by Andrew McLean)

    Magpies - v12 - S '97 - p26 [51-250]

Josh and Thumper (Illus. by Andrew McLean)

    Magpies - v12 - S '97 - p26 [51-250]

McLean, Dirk
Steel Drums and Ice Skates (Illus. by Ho Che Anderson)

    BIC - v26 - My '97 - p34 [501+]
    CBRA - '96 - p451 [51-250]

McLean, Virginia
Pastatively Italy

    Ch BWatch - v7 - O '97 - p7 [51-250]
    PW - v244 - N 24 '97 - p74 [51-250]

McLeish, Ewan
Europe

    HB Guide - v8 - Fall '97 - p391 [51-250]
    Magpies - v12 - Mr '97 - p40+ [251-500]

South America

    HB Guide - v8 - Fall '97 - p400 [51-250]
    Magpies - v12 - Mr '97 - p40+ [251-500]
    SLJ - v44 - F '98 - p97 [51-250]

McLerran, Alice
The Year of the Ranch (Illus. by Kimberly Bulcken Root)
SE - v61 - Ap '97 - p11* [1-50]

McMahen, Chris
Buddy Concrackle's Amazing Adventure
CBRA - '96 - p483+ [51-250]

McMahon, Patricia
Chi-Hoon: A Korean Girl (Illus. by Michael O'Brien)
PW - v245 - Ja 26 '98 - p93 [1-50]

Six Words, Many Turtles, and Three Days in Hong Kong (Illus. by Susan G Drinker)
CCB-B - v51 - O '97 - p58 [51-250]
KR - v65 - Je 15 '97 - p952+ [51-250]
PW - v244 - Je 16 '97 - p59 [51-250]
SLJ - v43 - D '97 - p112 [51-250]

McMane, Fred
Hakeem Olajuwon
Ch BWatch - v7 - S '97 - p8 [1-50]
HB Guide - v8 - Fall '97 - p368 [51-250]

McManners, Hugh
Water Sports
Sch Lib - v45 - Ag '97 - p152+ [51-250]

McMillan, Bruce
Jelly Beans for Sale (Illus. by Bruce McMillan)
RT - v51 - N '97 - p240+ [51-250]

My Horse of the North (Illus. by Bruce McMillan)
BL - v94 - S 1 '97 - p129 [51-250]
CCB-B - v51 - O '97 - p58+ [251-500]
HB - v73 - S '97 - p592+ [51-250]
SLJ - v43 - S '97 - p204 [51-250]

Nights of the Pufflings (Illus. by Bruce McMillan)
SLJ - v43 - My '97 - p57 [1-50]

Wild Flamingos (Illus. by Bruce McMillan)
HB - v73 - S '97 - p593+ [51-250]
SLJ - v43 - Ag '97 - p148+ [51-250]

McMullan, Kate
If You Were My Bunny (Illus. by David McPhail)
PW - v245 - Ja 5 '98 - p69 [1-50]

The New Kid at School (Illus. by Bill Basso)
BL - v94 - D 1 '97 - p637 [51-250]
KR - v65 - S 15 '97 - p1460 [51-250]
PW - v244 - O 6 '97 - p84 [51-250]

McNair, Joseph
Commander Coatrack Returns
SLJ - v44 - Ja '98 - p43 [1-50]

McNaughton, Colin
Boo! (Illus. by Colin McNaughton)
RT - v51 - O '97 - p130 [1-50]

Goal!
Books - v11 - Ag '97 - p15 [1-50]

Here Come the Aliens!
PW - v244 - N 10 '97 - p76 [1-50]

Making Friends with Frankenstein
Par Ch - Awards '97 - p9 [51-250]

Oops! (Illus. by Colin McNaughton)
BL - v94 - O 1 '97 - p337+ [51-250]
Books - v10 - S '96 - p24 [51-250]
CCB-B - v51 - O '97 - p59 [51-250]
HB - v74 - Ja '98 - p66+ [51-250]
Par - v72 - D '97 - p202 [1-50]
PW - v244 - Je 23 '97 - p91 [51-250]
SLJ - v43 - S '97 - p186+ [51-250]

There's an Awful Lot of Weirdos in Our Neighborhood and other Wickedly Funny Verse
Ch BWatch - v7 - N '97 - p3 [1-50]
PW - v244 - O 6 '97 - p85 [1-50]

McNaughton, Iona
Summer of Shadows
Magpies - v12 - S '97 - p1* [251-500]

McNaughton, Janel
Catch Me Once, Catch Me Twice
Can CL - v22 - Win '96 - p113+ [501+]

McNaughton, Janet
To Dance at the Palais Royale
y   BIC - v26 - My '97 - p33 [251-500]

y　CBRA - '96 - p484 [51-250]
　　Ch Bk News - v20 - Spr '97 - p33 [51-250]
y　JAAL - v40 - My '97 - p676+ [251-500]

McNaughton-Stuart, Candace
The Last Chance Dance and Other Adventures
　　CBRA - '96 - p499 [51-250]

McNeese, Tim
The New York Subway System
y　BL - v94 - D 1 '97 - p622 [51-250]
　　SLJ - v43 - N '97 - p130 [51-250]

The Panama Canal
　　BL - v93 - Ag '97 - p1895 [51-250]
　　SLJ - v43 - Jl '97 - p108+ [51-250]

McNeill, Sarah
Ancient Egyptian People
y　Ch BWatch - v7 - O '97 - p7 [1-50]
　　HB Guide - v8 - Fall '97 - p388 [51-250]

Ancient Egyptian Places
y　Ch BWatch - v7 - O '97 - p7 [1-50]
　　HB Guide - v8 - Fall '97 - p388 [51-250]

Ancient Romans
　　KR - v66 - Mr 15 '98 - p407 [51-250]

McNicoll, Sylvia
The Big Race (Illus. by Susan Gardos)
　　CBRA - '96 - p484 [51-250]

Project Disaster
　　CM:CanRev - v4 - S 19 '97 - pONL [251-500]

McNutt, Nan
The Bentwood Box (Illus. by Yasu Osawa)
　　CM:CanRev - v4 - Mr 27 '98 - pONL [501+]

The Button Blanket (Illus. by Yasu Osawa)
　　CM:CanRev - v4 - Mr 27 '98 - pONL [501+]

The Cedar Plank Mask (Illus. by Yasu Osawa)
　　CM:CanRev - v4 - Mr 27 '98 - pONL [501+]

The Spindle Whorl (Illus. by Roger Fernandes)
　　CM:CanRev - v4 - Mr 27 '98 - pONL [501+]

McPhail, David
Edward and the Pirates (Illus. by David McPhail)
　　CCB-B - v50 - Jl '97 - p402 [51-250]
　　Ch BWatch - v7 - Je '97 - p6 [51-250]
　　Emerg Lib - v25 - N '97 - p46 [51-250]
　　HB Guide - v8 - Fall '97 - p273 [51-250]
　　Inst - v107 - S '97 - p20+ [51-250]
　　NYTBR - v102 - My 18 '97 - p23+ [501+]
　　NYTBR - v102 - D 7 '97 - p78 [1-50]
　　SLJ - v43 - My '97 - p106 [51-250]

In Flight with David McPhail (Illus. by David McPhail)
　　Inst - v106 - Ap '97 - p27 [51-250]

Pigs Aplenty, Pigs Galore!
　　Bks Keeps - S '97 - p20 [51-250]

The Puddle (Illus. by David McPhail)
　　KR - v66 - Ja 1 '98 - p58 [51-250]
　　PW - v244 - D 15 '97 - p57 [51-250]
　　SLJ - v44 - Mr '98 - p184 [51-250]

Santa's Book of Names (Illus. by David McPhail)
　　Inst - v107 - S '97 - p21 [1-50]
　　PW - v244 - O 6 '97 - p59 [1-50]

Tinker and Tom and the Star Baby (Illus. by David McPhail)
　　KR - v66 - Ap 1 '98 - p498 [51-250]
　　PW - v245 - Mr 9 '98 - p67 [51-250]
　　SLJ - v44 - Ap '98 - p104 [51-250]

McPhee, Peter
A Way with Horses
　　CBRA - '96 - p484 [51-250]

McPherson, Stephanie Sammartino
TV's Forgotten Hero
　　SB - v32 - D '96 - p272+ [51-250]

McQuade, Jacqueline
Cosy Moments with Teddy Bear (Illus. by Jacqueline McQuade)
　　Bks Keeps - Jl '97 - p19 [51-250]

Good Times with Teddy Bear (Illus. by Jacqueline McQuade)
> BL - v94 - O 15 '97 - p416 [51-250]
> KR - v65 - S 15 '97 - p1460 [51-250]
> PW - v244 - O 20 '97 - p78 [51-250]
> SLJ - v43 - D '97 - p96 [51-250]

Meacham, Margaret
Oyster Moon
> Ch BWatch - v7 - Ap '97 - p5 [51-250]

Mead, Alice
Junebug
> SE - v61 - S '97 - p271 [1-50]

Mead, Katherine
Why the Leopard Has Spots (Illus. by Barry Rockwell)
> SLJ - v44 - F '98 - p88 [51-250]

Mebane, Robert C
Adventures with Atoms and Molecules
> ASBYP - v29 - Sum '96 - p26 [251-500]

Meddaugh, Susan
Cinderella's Rat (Illus. by Susan Meddaugh)
> BL - v94 - O 1 '97 - p337 [51-250]
> CBRS - v26 - O '97 - p16 [51-250]
> HB - v73 - S '97 - p560+ [51-250]
> KR - v65 - Jl 15 '97 - p1113 [51-250]
> NYTLa - v147 - D 4 '97 - pE8 [51-250]
> PW - v244 - Je 2 '97 - p70+ [51-250]

Martha Blah Blah
> Inst - v106 - My '97 - p20 [1-50]
> PW - v245 - Mr 23 '98 - p102 [1-50]

Medearis, Angela Shelf
Cooking
> BL - v94 - F 15 '98 - p1006 [51-250]
> Ch BWatch - v7 - D '97 - p7 [1-50]
> y   SLJ - v43 - N '97 - p132 [51-250]

Dance
> Ch BWatch - v7 - My '97 - p7 [51-250]
> SLJ - v43 - Jl '97 - p109 [51-250]

Dancing with the Indians
> ECEJ - v25 - Fall '97 - p48 [1-50]

The Ghost of Sifty-Sifty Sam (Illus. by Jacqueline Rogers)
> Am Vis - v12 - D '97 - p34 [1-50]
> BL - v94 - D 1 '97 - p642 [51-250]
> CCB-B - v51 - Ja '98 - p168 [51-250]
> PW - v244 - O 6 '97 - p49 [51-250]
> SLJ - v43 - N '97 - p94+ [51-250]

Haunts (Illus. by Trina Schart Hyman)
> SLJ - v43 - Ap '97 - p138 [51-250]

Music
> Ch BWatch - v7 - My '97 - p7 [51-250]
> SLJ - v43 - Jl '97 - p109 [51-250]

Princess of the Press
> y   Am Vis - v12 - D '97 - p36 [1-50]
> BL - v94 - D 1 '97 - p634 [51-250]
> Ch BWatch - v7 - N '97 - p7 [1-50]
> KR - v65 - S 15 '97 - p1460 [51-250]
> SLJ - v43 - D '97 - p113 [51-250]

Rum-A-Tum-Tum (Illus. by James Ransome)
> CBRS - v25 - My '97 - p112 [51-250]
> CCB-B - v50 - Jl '97 - p403+ [51-250]
> HB Guide - v8 - Fall '97 - p274 [51-250]
> KR - v65 - Ap 15 '97 - p644 [51-250]
> Learning - v26 - S '97 - p45 [1-50]
> SLJ - v43 - Jl '97 - p71 [51-250]

The Spray-Paint Mystery (Illus. by Richard Williams)
> SLJ - v43 - Ap '97 - p114 [51-250]

Meek, Margaret
Information and Book Learning
> Magpies - v12 - My '97 - p43 [251-500]

Meeuwissen, Tony
Remarkable Animals (Illus. by Tony Meeuwissen)
> KR - v66 - Ja 1 '98 - p59 [51-250]
> SLJ - v44 - Ap '98 - p106 [51-250]
> TES - D 5 '97 - p17* [51-250]

Megamaths: Tables
> TES - My 23 '97 - pR10 [51-250]

Meisel, Jacqueline Drobis
Australia: The Land Down Under
> Ch BWatch - v7 - My '97 - p7 [1-50]
> HB Guide - v8 - Fall '97 - p400 [51-250]

SLJ - v44 - Ap '98 - p149 [51-250]

Mele, Michael
A Gift for the Contessa (Illus. by Ronald G Paolillo)
CBRS - v26 - S '97 - p4+ [51-250]

Melendez, Francisco
Aventuras De Mr. Boisset
Bkbird - v34 - Win '96 - p57 [51-250]

Mello, Roger
Uma Historia Do Boto Vermelho (Illus. by Roger Mello)
Bkbird - v34 - Win '96 - p57 [51-250]

Melmed, Laura Krauss
Little Oh (Illus. by Jim LaMarche)
BL - v94 - S 1 '97 - p134 [51-250]
BL - v94 - Mr 15 '98 - p1219 [1-50]
CBRS - v26 - Ja '98 - p51 [51-250]
CCB-B - v51 - O '97 - p61+ [251-500]
Ch BWatch - v8 - Ja '98 - p3 [1-50]
HB - v73 - S '97 - p561+ [51-250]
KR - v65 - Ag 1 '97 - p1226 [51-250]
SLJ - v43 - N '97 - p95 [51-250]

The Marvelous Market on Mermaid (Illus. by Maryann Kovalski)
RT - v51 - O '97 - p134 [1-50]

Meltzer, Milton
Weapons and Warfare (Illus. by Sergio Martinez)
HB Guide - v8 - Fall '97 - p326 [51-250]

Menard, Valerie
Trent Dimas: Gold Medal Olympic Gymnast
Ch BWatch - v7 - O '97 - p5 [51-250]
SLJ - v44 - Ap '98 - p120+ [51-250]

Mendiguren, Xabier
Por Que No Canta El Petirrojo? (Illus. by Elena Odriozola)
SLJ - v44 - F '98 - p130+ [51-250]

Menk, James
Lillian's Fish (Illus. by Louisa Bauer)
CBRS - v26 - Win '98 - p71+ [51-250]
SLJ - v44 - Ja '98 - p89+ [51-250]

Mennel, Wolfgang
Henry and Horace Clean Up (Illus. by Gesela Durr)
RT - v51 - F '98 - p428 [51-250]

Mennen, Ingrid
Somewhere in Africa (Illus. by Nicolaas Maritz)
BL - v93 - Je 1 '97 - p1724 [1-50]
JOYS - v11 - Win '98 - p141 [1-50]

Mercier, Carrie
Christianity for Today
Sch Lib - v45 - N '97 - p205+ [51-250]
y   TES - N 28 '97 - p17* [501+]

Mercredi, Morningstar
Fort Chipewyan Homecoming (Illus. by Darren McNally)
HB Guide - v8 - Fall '97 - p399 [51-250]
SLJ - v43 - S '97 - p206 [51-250]

Merriam, Eve
The Inner City Mother Goose (Illus. by David Diaz)
y   LA - v73 - N '96 - p527 [51-250]
SE - v61 - Ap '97 - p12* [1-50]

What in the World? (Illus. by Barbara J Phillips-Duke)
KR - v66 - F 15 '98 - p271 [51-250]

Merrians, Deborah
Earthquakes and Volcanoes (Illus. by Greg Harris)
ASBYP - v29 - Fall '96 - p48+ [501+]

Merrick, Anne
Hannah's Ghost
Obs - D 7 '97 - p17* [1-50]

Merrick, Patrick
Caterpillars
SLJ - v44 - Mr '98 - p199 [51-250]

Ticks
SLJ - v44 - Mr '98 - p199 [51-250]

Walkingsticks
SLJ - v44 - Mr '98 - p199 [51-250]

Merrill, Yvonne Y
Hands-On Celebrations
　　Quill & Q - v63 - D '97 - p39 [51-250]

Hands-On Rocky Mountains (Illus. by Mary Simpson)
　　SLJ - v43 - Ap '97 - p154 [51-250]

Merritt, Susan E
The Stone Orchard
　　Beav - v77 - Je '97 - p44 [51-250]
　　CBRA - '96 - p485 [51-250]
　y　Ch Bk News - v20 - Spr '97 - p32+ [251-500]
　y　JAAL - v40 - My '97 - p678 [251-500]

Mertins, Lisa
Ginkgo and Moon
　　RT - v51 - O '97 - p152 [51-250]

Metaxas, Eric
The Fool and the Flying Ship (Williams). Audio Version
　　BL - v94 - N 1 '97 - p494 [51-250]

Jack and the Beanstalk (Palin) (Illus. by Edward Sorel). Audio Version
　　BL - v94 - N 1 '97 - p494 [51-250]

Meter, Leo
Letters to Barbara
　　TES - N 7 '97 - p7* [51-250]

The Metropolitan Museum of Art: Masks
　　BL - v94 - D 15 '97 - p700 [1-50]
　　TES - D 5 '97 - p18* [51-250]

Metzenthen, David
Finn and the Big Guy
　y　Aust Bk R - v279 - My '97 - p60+ [501+]
　　Magpies - v12 - My '97 - p36 [251-500]

Meuse, Christopher
Does Hockey Love Kids? (Illus. by Jeannine Meuse)
　　CBRA - '96 - p485 [51-250]

Meyer, Carolyn
In a Different Light (Illus. by John McDonald)
　　SE - v61 - Ap '97 - p8* [1-50]

Jubilee Journey
　　BL - v94 - S 1 '97 - p126 [51-250]
　y　BL - v94 - Mr 15 '98 - p1218 [1-50]
　　CCB-B - v51 - S '97 - p19 [51-250]
　　Ch BWatch - v7 - D '97 - p3 [51-250]
　y　JAAL - v41 - F '98 - p409 [51-250]
　y　Kliatt - v31 - N '97 - p9+ [51-250]
　y　KR - v65 - Jl 15 '97 - p1113+ [51-250]
　　SLJ - v44 - Ja '98 - p114 [251-500]
　y　VOYA - v20 - D '97 - p319 [251-500]
　y　VOYA - v21 - Ap '98 - p38 [1-50]

Meyer, Donald
Views from Our Shoes (Illus. by Cary Pillo)
　　BL - v94 - Ja 1 '98 - p808 [51-250]
　　SLJ - v44 - Ap '98 - p150 [51-250]

Micklem, Niel
The Nature of Hysteria
　　Choice - v34 - Je '97 - p1746 [51-250]
　　R&R Bk N - v12 - My '97 - p146 [51-250]

Micklethwait, Lucy
A Child's Book of Art
　　Inst - v106 - My '97 - p4* [1-50]
　　Magpies - v12 - S '97 - p7 [251-500]

A Child's Book of Play in Art
　　Emerg Lib - v25 - N '97 - p59 [51-250]
　　Inst - v106 - Ap '97 - p25+ [51-250]
　　SE - v61 - Ap '97 - p14* [1-50]
　　TES - N 7 '97 - p10* [51-250]

I Spy a Freight Train
　　RT - v51 - S '97 - p54 [51-250]
　　RT - v51 - O '97 - p138 [1-50]
　　SE - v61 - Ap '97 - p14* [1-50]

I Spy: An Alphabet in Art
　　Par Ch - Awards '97 - p8* [51-250]

The Microsoft Encarta 97 Encyclopedia. Deluxe Ed.
　r　SLMQ - v25 - Spr '97 - p180 [51-250]

Micucci, Charles
The Life and Times of the Peanut
(Illus. by Charles Micucci)
> HB Guide - v8 - Fall '97 - p361 [51-250]
> SLJ - v43 - My '97 - p122 [51-250]

Middleton, Haydn
Cleopatra (Illus. by Gary Wilkinson)
> Sch Lib - v45 - N '97 - p205 [51-250]
> TES - S 19 '97 - p16* [51-250]

Henry Ford
> TES - S 19 '97 - p16* [51-250]

Thomas Edison
> TES - S 19 '97 - p16* [51-250]

Mikaelsen, Ben
Sparrow Hawk Red (Ramirez). Audio Version
> BL - v94 - S 15 '97 - p250 [51-250]

Mike, Jan
Clever Karlis (Mike). Book and Audio Version
> SLJ - v43 - S '97 - p165 [51-250]

Mike, Jan M
The Bird Maiden (Mike). Book and Audio Version
> SLJ - v43 - S '97 - p165 [51-250]

Miles, Betty
The Sky Is Falling! (Illus. by Cynthia Fisher)
> KR - v66 - Ja 15 '98 - p115 [51-250]

The Tortoise and the Hare (Illus. by Paul Meisel)
> KR - v66 - Ja 15 '98 - p115 [51-250]

Miles, Lisa
Atlas of the 20th Century
> r TES - Jl 4 '97 - p11* [501+]
> r TES - N 7 '97 - p9* [51-250]

Rocks and Minerals
> Ch BWatch - v7 - Ap '97 - p2 [1-50]

The Usborne Illustrated Atlas of the 20th Century
> r Bks Keeps - My '97 - p26 [51-250]

World History Dates
> Ch BWatch - v7 - Ap '97 - p1 [51-250]

Milgrim, David
Here in Space (Illus. by David Milgrim)
> BL - v94 - N 1 '97 - p467 [51-250]
> BL - v94 - Ja 1 '98 - p736 [1-50]
> NYTBR - v103 - Ja 4 '98 - p20 [501+]

Milich, Melissa
Miz Fannie Mae's Fine New Easter Hat (Illus. by Yong Chen)
> HB Guide - v8 - Fall '97 - p292 [51-250]
> KR - v65 - Ap 15 '97 - p644 [51-250]
> SLJ - v43 - Je '97 - p98 [51-250]

Millard, Anne
Mysteries of Lost Civilizations (Illus. by Francis Phillipps)
> Ch BWatch - v7 - My '97 - p7 [1-50]

Pyramids
> SE - v61 - Ap '97 - p14* [1-50]

Millen, C M
A Symphony for the Sheep
> SE - v61 - Ap '97 - p12* [1-50]

Millender, Dharathula
Louis Armstrong
> Ch BWatch - v7 - Je '97 - p7 [1-50]

Miller, Angela
Dinosaurs
> ASBYP - v29 - Sum '96 - p54+ [501+]

Miller, Brandon Marie
Buffalo Gals
> BL - v93 - Je 1 '97 - p1700 [1-50]

Just What the Doctor Ordered
> SLJ - v43 - My '97 - p148 [51-250]

Miller, David, 1943-
What's for Lunch? (Illus. by David Miller)
> Magpies - v12 - S '97 - p26+ [51-250]

Miller, Debbie S
Disappearing Lake (Illus. by Jon Van Zyle)

> HB Guide - v8 - Fall '97 - p347 [51-250]
> SLJ - v43 - Ap '97 - p129 [51-250]

A Polar Bear Journey (Illus. by Jon Van Zyle)

> BL - v94 - D 15 '97 - p701 [51-250]

Miller, Dorothy Reynolds
Home Wars

> BL - v94 - S 1 '97 - p126 [51-250]
> CBRS - v26 - O '97 - p23+ [51-250]
> CCB-B - v51 - O '97 - p62 [251-500]

Miller, Jay
American Indian Families

> HB Guide - v8 - Fall '97 - p321 [51-250]
> SLJ - v43 - Ag '97 - p149 [51-250]

American Indian Festivals

> HB Guide - v8 - Fall '97 - p330 [51-250]
> SLJ - v43 - Ag '97 - p149 [51-250]

American Indian Foods

> HB Guide - v8 - Fall '97 - p361 [51-250]
> SLJ - v43 - Ag '97 - p149 [51-250]

American Indian Games

> HB Guide - v8 - Fall '97 - p330 [51-250]

Miller, Judi
Purple Is My Game, Morgan Is My Name

> PW - v245 - Ja 5 '98 - p68 [51-250]

Miller, Louise R
Turkey: Between East and West

> Ch BWatch - v8 - Ja '98 - p7 [1-50]

Miller, Michaela
Guinea Pigs

> SLJ - v44 - Ap '98 - p121 [51-250]

Miller, Nelson
Little Lake Saga (Illus. by Kathy Bedard)

> CBRA - '96 - p451 [51-250]

Miller, Robert
The Story of Nat Love

> JOYS - v10 - Sum '97 - p429 [1-50]

Miller, Sara Swan
Three Stories You Can Read to Your Cat (Illus. by True Kelley)

> HB Guide - v8 - Fall '97 - p292 [51-250]
> Inst - v107 - S '97 - p24 [1-50]
> NYTBR - v102 - O 12 '97 - p26 [1-50]
> SLJ - v43 - My '97 - p108 [51-250]

Miller, Tom
Can a Coal Scuttle Fly?

> Ch BWatch - v7 - Jl '97 - p6 [51-250]

Miller, Virginia
Be Gentle! (Illus. by Virginia Miller)

> BL - v93 - Ag '97 - p1906+ [51-250]
> CCB-B - v51 - O '97 - p62 [51-250]
> Ch BWatch - v7 - S '97 - p1 [1-50]
> KR - v65 - Jl 15 '97 - p1114 [51-250]
> Obs - Jl 20 '97 - p18* [51-250]
> Par - v72 - D '97 - p202 [1-50]
> Sch Lib - v45 - N '97 - p187 [51-250]

Miller, William
The Conjure Woman (Illus. by Terea D Shaffer)

> ECEJ - v25 - Fall '97 - p42 [51-250]

A House by the River (Illus. by Cornelius Van Wright)

> Am Vis - v12 - D '97 - p34 [51-250]
> CBRS - v25 - Ag '97 - p165 [51-250]
> Ch BWatch - v7 - Jl '97 - p6 [51-250]
> HB - v73 - Jl '97 - p445 [51-250]
> HB Guide - v8 - Fall '97 - p274 [51-250]
> KR - v65 - My 15 '97 - p803 [51-250]
> SLJ - v43 - Jl '97 - p71 [51-250]

Richard Wright and the Library Card (Illus. by Gregory Christie)

> Am Vis - v12 - D '97 - p34 [1-50]
> BL - v94 - D 1 '97 - p642 [51-250]
> CCB-B - v51 - Mr '98 - p252 [251-500]
> HMR - Win '97 - p39+ [501+]
> KR - v65 - N 15 '97 - p1710 [51-250]
> PW - v244 - N 17 '97 - p61 [51-250]
> SLJ - v44 - F '98 - p88+ [51-250]

Miller-Schroeder, Patricia
Gorillas (Illus. by Warren Clark)
> BIC - v26 - S '97 - p33+ [251-500]
> CBRA - '96 - p529 [51-250]
> HB Guide - v8 - Fall '97 - p353 [51-250]
> SB - v33 - O '97 - p209+ [51-250]

Millman, Isaac
Moses Goes to a Concert (Illus. by Isaac Millman)
> KR - v66 - Ja 1 '98 - p59 [51-250]
> PW - v245 - F 23 '98 - p76 [51-250]
> SLJ - v44 - Ap '98 - p106 [51-250]

Mills, Claudia
Gus and Grandpa (Illus. by Catherine Stock)
> HB Guide - v8 - Fall '97 - p287 [51-250]
> SLJ - v43 - Ap '97 - p114 [51-250]

Gus and Grandpa and the Christmas Cookies (Illus. by Catherine Stock)
> BL - v94 - S 15 '97 - p235+ [51-250]
> PW - v244 - O 6 '97 - p58 [1-50]

Gus and Grandpa Ride the Train (Illus. by Catherine Stock)
> KR - v66 - Ja 15 '98 - p115 [51-250]

Losers, Inc.
> HB Guide - v8 - Fall '97 - p305 [51-250]
> NYTBR - v102 - Je 8 '97 - p27 [501+]
> SLJ - v43 - Ap '97 - p138+ [51-250]

One Small Lost Sheep (Illus. by Walter Lyon Krudop)
> BL - v94 - S 1 '97 - p140 [51-250]
> CBRS - v26 - N '97 - p28 [1-50]
> CM:CanRev - v4 - F 27 '98 - pONL [251-500]
> KR - v65 - O 15 '97 - p1584 [51-250]
> PW - v244 - O 6 '97 - p59 [1-50]

Mills, Judith Christine
The Stonehook Schooner (Illus. by Judith Christine Mills)
> Can CL - v22 - Win '96 - p121+ [501+]
> SLJ - v43 - Ag '97 - p138 [51-250]

Mills, Lauren A
The Book of Little Folk (Illus. by Lauren A Mills)
> BL - v93 - Ag '97 - p1895 [51-250]

Book of Little Folk (Illus. by Lauren A Mills)
> Ch BWatch - v7 - Jl '97 - p6 [1-50]

The Book of Little Folk (Illus. by Lauren A Mills)
> SLJ - v43 - N '97 - p110 [51-250]

Milne, A A
The Best of Winnie-the-Pooh (Illus. by Ernest H Shepard)
> PW - v244 - N 10 '97 - p76 [51-250]

The House at Pooh Corner (Kuralt). Audio Version
> Ch BWatch - v7 - O '97 - p3 [1-50]
> PW - v244 - Jl 28 '97 - p29 [51-250]
> SLJ - v44 - Ja '98 - p68 [51-250]
> SLJ - v44 - Ap '98 - p39 [1-50]

Now We Are Six (Kuralt). Audio Version
> PW - v244 - Jl 28 '97 - p29 [51-250]
> SLJ - v44 - Ja '98 - p68 [51-250]

Pooh to the Rescue (Illus. by Ernest H Shepard)
> PW - v244 - Je 2 '97 - p73 [1-50]

Pooh's Enchanted Place (Illus. by Ernest H Shepard)
> PW - v244 - S 22 '97 - p83 [51-250]

Pooh's Little Instruction Book
> CLW - v68 - S '97 - p65 [51-250]

Pooh's Touch and Feel Visit
> PW - v245 - F 23 '98 - p78 [1-50]

When We Were Very Young (Kuralt). Audio Version
> PW - v244 - Jl 28 '97 - p29 [51-250]
> SLJ - v44 - Ja '98 - p68 [51-250]

Winnie-the-Pooh. Audio Version
> TES - D 19 '97 - p23 [51-250]

Winnie-the-Pooh (Kuralt). Audio Version
> Ch BWatch - v7 - O '97 - p3 [1-50]
> PW - v244 - Jl 28 '97 - p29 [51-250]
> SLJ - v44 - Ja '98 - p68 [51-250]

SLJ - v44 - Ap '98 - p39 [1-50]

Winnie-the-Pooh Tells Time (Illus. by Ernest H Shepard)
HB Guide - v8 - Fall '97 - p285 [51-250]

Milne, Lyndsay
Nature Crafts
r　Par Ch - Awards '97 - p29 [51-250]

Milner, Angela M
Geography through Play
TES - N 21 '97 - pR6 [51-250]

Milord, Susan
Adventures in Art. Rev. Ed.
Ch BWatch - v8 - Ja '98 - p6 [1-50]

Milton, Joyce
Gorillas: Gentle Giants of the Forest (Illus. by Bryn Barnard)
SLJ - v43 - Ag '97 - p149 [51-250]

Mummies (Illus. by Susan Swan)
Ch BWatch - v7 - S '97 - p1 [1-50]
SLJ - v43 - Je '97 - p110 [51-250]

The Story of George Washington (Illus. by Tom LaPadula)
Ch BWatch - v7 - Mr '97 - p4 [1-50]

Milton, Steve
Super Skaters
CBRA - '96 - p525 [51-250]
CM:CanRev - v4 - S 5 '97 - pONL [251-500]

Minarik, Else Holmelund
Little Bear (Illus. by Maurice Sendak)
NYTBR - v102 - N 16 '97 - p26 [1-50]

Minnow: The Children's Story Annual 1996 (Illus. by Margaret Kyle)
CBRA - '96 - p499 [51-250]

Miranda, Anne
To Market, to Market (Illus. by Janet Stevens)
BL - v94 - N 1 '97 - p477 [51-250]
BL - v94 - Mr 15 '98 - p1219 [1-50]
CBRS - v26 - Ja '98 - p51 [51-250]

CCB-B - v51 - N '97 - p93 [51-250]
HB - v73 - N '97 - p671+ [51-250]
KR - v65 - O 15 '97 - p1584+ [51-250]
PW - v244 - S 29 '97 - p88+ [51-250]
SLJ - v44 - Ja '98 - p90+ [51-250]

Vroom, Chugga, Vroom-Vroom (Illus. by David Murphy)
KR - v66 - Mr 1 '98 - p342 [51-250]

Miranker, Cathy
Great Software for Kids and Parents
r　Quill & Q - v63 - Ag '97 - p23 [251-500]

Mitchell, Adrian
Balloon Lagoon (Illus. by Tony Ross)
TES - N 7 '97 - p2* [51-250]

Mitchell, Barbara
Down Buttermilk Lane (Illus. by John Sandford)
ECEJ - v25 - Fall '97 - p48 [1-50]

Red Bird (Illus. by Todd L W Doney)
SE - v61 - Ap '97 - p10* [1-50]

Waterman's Child (Illus. by Daniel San Souci)
BL - v93 - Je 1 '97 - p1720 [51-250]
CBRS - v25 - Spr '97 - p136+ [51-250]
Ch BWatch - v7 - My '97 - p2+ [1-50]
HB Guide - v8 - Fall '97 - p274 [51-250]
KR - v65 - Ap 15 '97 - p645 [51-250]
SLJ - v43 - My '97 - p108 [51-250]
Trib Bks - Jl 13 '97 - p7 [51-250]

Mitchell, David
The Young Martial Arts Enthusiast (Illus. by Andy Crawford)
Ch BWatch - v7 - Jl '97 - p8 [1-50]
HB Guide - v8 - Fall '97 - p371 [51-250]
Sch Lib - v45 - Ag '97 - p153 [51-250]
SLJ - v43 - Jl '97 - p109 [51-250]

Mitchell, Margaree King
Granddaddy's Gift (Illus. by Larry Johnson)
BL - v94 - F 15 '98 - p999 [1-50]
HB Guide - v8 - Fall '97 - p274 [51-250]
SLJ - v43 - Jl '97 - p71 [51-250]

Uncle Jed's Barbershop (Illus. by James Ransome)
    ECEJ - v25 - Fall '97 - p48 [1-50]
    PW - v245 - Ja 5 '98 - p69 [1-50]

Mitchell, Rhonda
The Talking Cloth (Illus. by Rhonda Mitchell)
    CCB-B - v50 - Je '97 - p367+ [51-250]
    HB Guide - v8 - Fall '97 - p274 [51-250]
    SLJ - v43 - Jl '97 - p71+ [51-250]

Mitter, Matt
Andy the Shy Giraffe
    PW - v244 - D 1 '97 - p55 [1-50]

Emma Speaks Up!
    PW - v244 - D 1 '97 - p55 [1-50]

Mitton, Jacqueline
Galileo (Illus. by Gerry Ball)
    Sch Lib - v45 - N '97 - p205 [51-250]
    TES - S 19 '97 - p16* [51-250]

Mitton, Tony
Dazzling Diggers (Illus. by Ant Parker)
    PW - v244 - Ag 25 '97 - p74 [1-50]

Roaring Rockets (Illus. by Ant Parker)
    PW - v244 - Ag 25 '97 - p74 [1-50]

Rosie Rabbit Goes to Preschool (Illus. by Patrick Yee)
    SLJ - v43 - My '97 - p108+ [51-250]

Rosie Rabbit's Birthday Party (Illus. by Patrick Yee)
    SLJ - v43 - My '97 - p108+ [51-250]

Where's My Egg?
    Magpies - v12 - Jl '97 - p28 [1-50]

Mochizuki, Ken
Baseball Saved Us (Illus. by Dom Lee)
    ABR - v19 - N '97 - p9+ [501+]
    ECEJ - v25 - Fall '97 - p48 [1-50]

Heroes (Illus. by Dom Lee)
    ABR - v19 - N '97 - p9+ [501+]
    ECEJ - v25 - Fall '97 - p48 [1-50]

Passage to Freedom (Illus. by Dom Lee)
    ABR - v19 - N '97 - p9+ [501+]
    BL - v94 - Mr 15 '98 - p1219 [1-50]
    BW - v27 - Je 8 '97 - p8 [251-500]
    CCB-B - v51 - S '97 - p19+ [51-250]
    Ch BWatch - v7 - S '97 - p7 [51-250]
    HB - v73 - N '97 - p698+ [251-500]
    Learning - v26 - Ag '97 - p26 [51-250]
    SLJ - v43 - Jl '97 - p86 [51-250]

Models (Art House)
    Ch BWatch - v7 - N '97 - p5 [51-250]

Modern Stories (Genre Library)
    Sch Lib - v45 - Ag '97 - p147 [51-250]

Moers, Hermann
Evie to the Rescue! (Illus. by Gusti)
    KR - v65 - N 1 '97 - p1647 [51-250]
    SLJ - v43 - D '97 - p98 [51-250]

Moffatt, Judith
City Lights
    PW - v244 - S 1 '97 - p107 [1-50]

Starry Nights
    PW - v244 - S 1 '97 - p107 [1-50]

Mohr, Nicholasa
La Vieja Letivia Y El Monte De Los Pesares (Illus. by Rudy Gutierrez)
    HB Guide - v8 - Fall '97 - p339 [51-250]

Mohta, Viraf
The World Wide Web for Kids and Parents
    Quill & Q - v63 - Ag '97 - p23 [251-500]

Mole, John
Copy Cat (Illus. by Bee Willey)
    KR - v65 - Ag 1 '97 - p1226 [51-250]
    PW - v244 - S 1 '97 - p103 [51-250]
    SLJ - v43 - S '97 - p188 [51-250]

Molesworth, M L S
The Carved Lions
    TES - Ja 2 '98 - p22* [1-50]

The Cuckoo Clock
    TES - Ja 2 '98 - p22* [1-50]

Mollel, Tololwa M
Ananse's Feast (Illus. by Andrew Glass)
> HB Guide - v8 - Fall '97 - p334 [51-250]
> Inst - v107 - Ag '97 - p20 [51-250]
> SLJ - v43 - My '97 - p122+ [51-250]

Dume's Roar (Illus. by Kathy Blankley Roman)
> CCB-B - v51 - Ap '98 - p289 [51-250]
> PW - v245 - Ja 19 '98 - p377 [51-250]
> Quill & Q - v64 - F '98 - p48 [251-500]

Kele's Secret (Illus. by Catherine Stock)
> BL - v93 - Je 1 '97 - p1720 [51-250]
> Can CL - v23 - Sum '97 - p59+ [501+]
> CCB-B - v50 - Jl '97 - p404 [51-250]
> Ch Bk News - v20 - Spr '97 - p29 [51-250]
> HB Guide - v8 - Fall '97 - p274 [1-50]
> SLJ - v43 - Je '97 - p98 [51-250]
> Trib Bks - Jl 13 '97 - p7 [51-250]

Molnar, Gwen
Animal Rap and Far-Out Fables (Illus. by Jeff Wiebe)
> CBRA - '96 - p499+ [51-250]

Molnar-Fenton, Stephan
An Mei's Strange and Wondrous Journey (Illus. by Vivienne Flesher)
> KR - v66 - Ja 15 '98 - p116 [51-250]
> PW - v245 - Ja 12 '98 - p58 [51-250]
> SLJ - v44 - Ap '98 - p106 [51-250]

Moloney, Norah
The Young Oxford Book of Archaeology
> KR - v65 - D 15 '97 - p1837 [51-250]
> y   SLJ - v44 - Ap '98 - p150 [51-250]

Monfredo, Miriam Grace
Through a Gold Eagle
> Kliatt - v31 - S '97 - p12+ [51-250]

Monsell, Mary Elise
Mr. Pin: The Chocolate Files (McDonough). Audio Version
> BL - v94 - F 15 '98 - p1027 [51-250]

The Mysterious Cases of Mr. Pin (McDonough). Audio Version
> SLJ - v43 - D '97 - p70 [51-250]

The Spy Who Came North from the Pole (McDonough). Audio Version
> SLJ - v44 - Ap '98 - p82 [51-250]

Monson, A M
Wanted: Best Friend (Illus. by Lynn Munsinger)
> Ch BWatch - v7 - Mr '97 - p7 [51-250]
> HB Guide - v8 - Fall '97 - p274 [51-250]
> NYTBR - v102 - Ag 17 '97 - p19 [1-50]

Montanari, Massimo
Il Pentolino Magico (Illus. by Emanuele Luzzati)
> Bkbird - v34 - Win '96 - p57 [51-250]

Montgomery, L M
The Annotated Anne of Green Gables
> y   BL - v94 - Ja 1 '98 - p822 [1-50]
> y   HB - v74 - Mr '98 - p238 [251-500]
> y   KR - v65 - O 15 '97 - p1585 [51-250]
>   Quill & Q - v63 - S '97 - p74 [501+]
> y   SLJ - v44 - Mr '98 - p246 [51-250]

At the Altar
> Can CL - v23 - Fall '97 - p78+ [501+]

Christmas with Anne and Other Holiday Stories
> Can CL - v23 - Fall '97 - p78+ [501+]

Mood, Susan
Max's Train Ride
> PW - v244 - D 1 '97 - p55 [1-50]

Moodie, Fiona
Nabulela: A South African Folk Tale (Illus. by Fiona Moodie)
> CBRS - v25 - Jl '97 - p149 [1-50]
> CCB-B - v50 - Jl '97 - p404 [51-250]
> Ch BWatch - v7 - My '97 - p3 [1-50]
> HB Guide - v8 - Fall '97 - p334 [51-250]
> RT - v51 - F '98 - p424 [51-250]

Moon, Nicola
*Something Special (Illus. by Alex
Ayliffe)*
> BL - v93 - Je 1 '97 - p1720+ [51-250]
> HB Guide - v8 - Fall '97 - p274 [51-250]
> SLJ - v43 - Je '97 - p98+ [51-250]

Moon, Pat
The Stare (Illus. by Greg Gormley)
> Sch Lib - v45 - N '97 - p192 [51-250]

Mooney, Bel
Joining the Rainbow
> y   Sch Lib - v45 - Ag '97 - p160 [51-250]
> TES - v43 - Ag 15 '97 - p23 [251-500]

The Voices of Silence
> Ch BWatch - v7 - O '97 - p3 [1-50]
> HB Guide - v8 - Fall '97 - p305 [51-250]
> Par Ch - Awards '97 - p6+ [51-250]

Mooney, Martin
Brett Favre
> BL - v94 - Ja 1 '98 - p806 [51-250]
> Ch BWatch - v7 - N '97 - p7 [1-50]

Moore, C J
*Ishtar and Tammuz (Illus. by
Christina Balit)*
> Bks Keeps - N '97 - p21 [51-250]

Moore, Clement Clarke
*The Night before Christmas (Illus. by
Christian Birmingham)*
> NS - v126 - D 5 '97 - p62 [1-50]

*The Night before Christmas (Illus. by
Ruth Sanderson)*
> BL - v94 - S 15 '97 - p238 [51-250]
> NYTBR - v102 - D 21 '97 - p18 [1-50]
> PW - v244 - O 6 '97 - p56 [51-250]

*The Night before Christmas (Illus. by
Lis Toft)*
> PW - v244 - O 6 '97 - p58 [1-50]

*The Night before Christmas (Illus. by
Tasha Tudor)*
> Ch BWatch - v7 - D '97 - p2 [1-50]
> PW - v244 - O 6 '97 - p58 [1-50]

Moore, Dorothy D
*Mischievous Molly (Illus. by Sheila
Morrell)*
> Ch BWatch - v7 - N '97 - p3 [1-50]

Moore, Elaine
*Grandma's Garden (Illus. by Dan
Andreasen)*
> SB - v33 - O '97 - p219 [1-50]

Moore, Helen H
Beavers (Illus. by Terri Talas)
> Ch BWatch - v7 - Ap '97 - p3 [51-250]

Moore, Inga
Six Dinner Sid
> Bks Keeps - N '97 - p21 [51-250]

Moore, Ishbel
Branch of the Talking Teeth
> CBRA - '96 - p485+ [51-250]

Moore, Jo Ellen
*All about Animals (Illus. by Kelly
McMahon)*
> SB - v33 - O '97 - p207+ [251-500]

*All about My Body (Illus. by Jo
Supancich)*
> SB - v33 - O '97 - p207+ [251-500]

Dinosaurs (Illus. by Eric Jepson)
> SB - v33 - O '97 - p207+ [251-500]

Habitats (Illus. by Don Robison)
> SB - v33 - Je '97 - p141+ [251-500]

*How Your Body Works (Illus. by Jo
Supancich)*
> SB - v33 - O '97 - p207+ [251-500]

*Our Solar System (Illus. by Eric
Jepson)*
> SB - v33 - Je '97 - p142 [251-500]

*Science Experiments at Home (Illus.
by Kelly McMahon)*
> SB - v33 - Je '97 - p141+ [251-500]

Science Fun (Illus. by Jo Supancich)
> SB - v33 - Je '97 - p141+ [251-500]

*What Happens Next? (Illus. by Rick
Law)*
> SB - v33 - Je '97 - p141+ [251-500]

Moore, Lilian
Poems Have Roots (Illus. by Tad Hills)
BL - v94 - S 1 '97 - p119 [51-250]
CCB-B - v51 - N '97 - p93+ [51-250]
HMR - Win '97 - p44+ [501+]
KR - v65 - Jl 15 '97 - p1114 [51-250]
PW - v244 - Ag 18 '97 - p95 [51-250]
SLJ - v43 - D '97 - p141 [51-250]

Moore, Robin
Hercules (Illus. by Alexa Rutherford)
BL - v93 - Je 1 '97 - p1696 [51-250]
CCB-B - v51 - S '97 - p20 [51-250]
KR - v65 - My 15 '97 - p803 [51-250]
SLJ - v43 - Jl '97 - p86 [51-250]

Moores, Eldridge M
Volcanoes and Earthquakes
ASBYP - v29 - Sum '96 - p54+ [501+]

Mooser, Stephen
Young Marian's Adventures in Sherwood Forest
Ch BWatch - v7 - N '97 - p3 [51-250]

Mora, Pat
A Birthday Basket for Tia (Illus. by Cecily Lang)
ECEJ - v25 - Fall '97 - p48 [1-50]

Una Canasta De Cumpleanos Para Tia (Illus. by Cecily Lang)
BL - v94 - D 15 '97 - p707 [51-250]

Confetti: Poems for Children (Illus. by Enrique O Sanchez)
RT - v51 - D '97 - p311 [51-250]

This Big Sky (Illus. by Steve Jenkins)
BL - v94 - F 15 '98 - p1016 [51-250]
CCB-B - v51 - Ap '98 - p290 [51-250]
KR - v66 - Ja 1 '98 - p59+ [51-250]
PW - v245 - Mr 23 '98 - p99 [51-250]

Tomas and the Library Lady (Illus. by Raul Colon)
BL - v93 - Ag '97 - p1906 [51-250]
CCB-B - v51 - O '97 - p63 [51-250]
HMR - Win '97 - p39+ [501+]
Inst - v107 - Ja '98 - p26 [1-50]
KR - v65 - Ag 1 '97 - p1226 [51-250]
PW - v244 - Jl 21 '97 - p201 [51-250]

Uno, Dos, Tres (Illus. by Barbara Lavallee)
RT - v51 - N '97 - p251 [51-250]

Morck, Irene
Tiger's New Cowboy Boots (Illus. by Georgia Graham)
CBRA - '96 - p451 [51-250]

Moreillon, Judi
Sing Down the Rain (Illus. by Michael Chiago)
Ch BWatch - v7 - N '97 - p5 [51-250]
SLJ - v44 - Ja '98 - p103 [51-250]

Moreton, Daniel
La Cucaracha Martina (Illus. by Daniel Moreton)
BL - v94 - Ja 1 '98 - p818 [51-250]
CBRS - v26 - D '97 - p40 [51-250]
SLJ - v43 - N '97 - p110 [51-250]
SLJ - v43 - N '97 - p137 [51-250]

Morey, Walt
Gentle Ben (Illus. by John Schoenherr)
HB Guide - v8 - Fall '97 - p305 [51-250]

Kavik the Wolf Dog (Illus. by Peter Parnall)
HB Guide - v8 - Fall '97 - p305 [51-250]

Morgan, Allen
Matthew and the Midnight Ball Game (Illus. by Michael Martchenko)
CBRS - v25 - Jl '97 - p149 [51-250]
Quill & Q - v63 - Je '97 - p63 [251-500]

Matthew and the Midnight Pilot (Illus. by Michael Martchenko)
CBRS - v25 - Jl '97 - p149 [51-250]

Morgan, George M
Alcock and Brown and the Boy in the Middle (Illus. by Jennifer Morgan)
Can CL - v22 - Win '96 - p118+ [501+]

Morgan, Michaela

Colour Jets

    TES - N 14 '97 - p14* [51-250]

Sick as a Parrot

    Sch Lib - v45 - Ag '97 - p136 [51-250]
    TES - N 14 '97 - p14* [51-250]

Morgan, Nina

The Caribbean and the Gulf of Mexico

    ASBYP - v29 - Fall '96 - p64 [251-500]
    HB Guide - v8 - Fall '97 - p385 [51-250]

Lasers

    BL - v93 - Je 1 '97 - p1696 [51-250]
    HB Guide - v8 - Fall '97 - p358+ [51-250]
    SB - v33 - O '97 - p211 [51-250]

The North Sea and the Baltic Sea

    ASBYP - v29 - Fall '96 - p64 [251-500]
    HB Guide - v8 - Fall '97 - p385 [51-250]

Morgan, Rowland

In the Next Three Seconds (Illus. by Rod Josey)

y   BL - v94 - Mr 15 '98 - p1225 [1-50]
    Books - v11 - O '97 - p21 [51-250]
    CBRS - v25 - Ag '97 - p167 [51-250]
    HB Guide - v8 - Fall '97 - p341 [51-250]
    KR - v65 - My 15 '97 - p803+ [51-250]
    SLJ - v43 - S '97 - p206 [51-250]
y   VOYA - v21 - Ap '98 - p39 [1-50]

Morgan, Sally

In Your Dreams (Illus. by Bronwyn Bancroft)

    Aust Bk R - N '97 - p62+ [501+]

Just a Little Brown Dog (Illus. by Bronwyn Bancroft)

    Ch BWatch - v7 - Jl '97 - p6 [51-250]
    Magpies - v12 - My '97 - p28 [51-250]

Weather

    ASBYP - v29 - Fall '96 - p57 [251-500]
    SB - v32 - D '96 - p274 [251-500]

The World's Wild Places

    ASBYP - v29 - Fall '96 - p63+ [501+]
    HB Guide - v8 - Fall '97 - p385 [51-250]

Morgan, Stacy Towle

Escape from Egypt (Illus. by Pamela Querin)

    H-Net - Ja '98 - pONL [501+]

Morimoto, Junko

The Two Bullies (Illus. by Junko Morimoto)

    Aust Bk R - Ag '97 - p62+ [501+]
    Magpies - v12 - Mr '97 - p26 [51-250]

Morin, Paul

Animal Dreaming (Illus. by Paul Morin)

    BL - v94 - Mr 15 '98 - p1242 [51-250]
    KR - v66 - Mr 1 '98 - p342 [51-250]
    SLJ - v44 - Mr '98 - p236 [51-250]

Morley, Jacqueline

Exploring North America

    CLW - v68 - D '97 - p86 [51-250]

First Facts about the Ancient Egyptians (Illus. by Mark Bergin)

    HB Guide - v8 - Fall '97 - p388 [51-250]

First Facts about the Vikings (Illus. by Mark Bergin)

    CLW - v68 - S '97 - p63 [51-250]
    HB Guide - v8 - Fall '97 - p388 [51-250]

A Renaissance Town (Illus. by Mark Peppe)

    HB Guide - v8 - Fall '97 - p391 [51-250]

Morozumi, Atsuko

My Friend Gorilla (Illus. by Atsuko Morozumi)

    KR - v66 - Ja 1 '98 - p60 [51-250]
    PW - v244 - D 22 '97 - p58 [51-250]
    SLJ - v44 - Mr '98 - p185 [51-250]

Morpurgo, Michael

Beyond the Rainbow Warrior

    Books - v10 - S '06 - p25 [51-250]
    Can CL - v23 - Sum '97 - p83+ [501+]
    Magpies - v12 - Jl '97 - p34 [51-250]
    SLJ - v43 - Je '97 - p122 [51-250]
    TES - N 7 '97 - p6* [51-250]

The Butterfly Lion
> BL - v93 - Je 1 '97 - p1704 [51-250]
> CBRS - v25 - Jl '97 - p156 [51-250]
> HB Guide - v8 - Fall '97 - p305 [51-250]
> KR - v65 - Ap 15 '97 - p645 [51-250]
> SLJ - v43 - Ag '97 - p158 [51-250]

Ghost of Grania O'Malley
> Emerg Lib - v25 - N '97 - p46 [51-250]
> NS - v126 - D 5 '97 - p64 [1-50]

Robin of Sherwood (Illus. by Michael Foreman)
> Bks Keeps - Jl '97 - p4 [51-250]
> BL - v94 - Mr 1 '98 - p1125 [51-250]
> Magpies - v12 - Mr '97 - p18+ [501+]

Sam's Duck (Illus. by Keith Bowen)
> Bks Keeps - S '97 - p23 [51-250]

Waiting for Anya
> y   Kliatt - v31 - Jl '97 - p10 [51-250]
> SLJ - v43 - S '97 - p131 [1-50]

The Wreck of the Zanzibar (Morpurgo). Audio Version
> SLJ - v44 - Ap '98 - p82 [51-250]

Morris, Ann
The Baby Book (Illus. by Ken Heyman)
> ECEJ - v24 - Sum '97 - p250 [51-250]

El Chico Karateka (Illus. by David Katzenstein)
> HB Guide - v8 - Fall '97 - p339 [51-250]
> SLJ - v43 - My '97 - p154 [51-250]

I Am Six (Illus. by Nancy Sheehan)
> ECEJ - v25 - Fall '97 - p48 [1-50]

Light the Candle! Bang the Drum! (Illus. by Peter Linenthal)
> CBRS - v26 - Ja '98 - p51 [51-250]
> Ch BWatch - v7 - N '97 - p1 [1-50]
> SLJ - v44 - F '98 - p102 [51-250]

Loving (Illus. by Ken Heyman)
> Bks Keeps - S '97 - p20 [51-250]

The Mommy Book (Illus. by Ken Heyman)
> SE - v61 - Ap '97 - p13* [1-50]

Play (Illus. by Ken Heyman)
> SLJ - v44 - Mr '98 - p199 [51-250]

Work (Illus. by Ann Morris)
> SLJ - v44 - Mr '98 - p199 [51-250]

Morris, Dave
The Chronicles of the Magi. Vols. 1-3
> TES - Ag 8 '97 - p23 [251-500]

Morris, Jeffrey
The FDR Way
> SE - v61 - Ap '97 - p3* [1-50]

Morris, Jill
The Wombat Who Talked to the Stars (Illus. by Sharon Dye)
> Aust Bk R - Jl '97 - p62+ [501+]
> Magpies - v12 - Mr '97 - p23 [51-250]

Morris, Juddi
The Harvey Girls
> y   Kliatt - v31 - S '97 - p38 [51-250]
> PW - v244 - My 19 '97 - p77 [1-50]

Tending the Fire
> BL - v94 - D 1 '97 - p634 [51-250]
> Ceram Mo - v45 - O '97 - p28+ [251-500]
> SLJ - v44 - Ja '98 - p127 [51-250]

Morris, Neil
Caves (Illus. by Vanessa Card)
> SB - v33 - Ag '97 - p176+ [251-500]

Cities (Illus. by Vanessa Card)
> Emerg Lib - v25 - N '97 - p54 [1-50]
> HB Guide - v8 - Fall '97 - p386 [51-250]
> SB - v33 - Ag '97 - p176+ [251-500]

Deserts (Illus. by Martin Camm)
> CM:CanRev - v4 - S 5 '97 - pONL [51-250]

Lakes (Illus. by Vanessa Card)
> SB - v33 - Ag '97 - p176+ [251-500]

Mountains (Illus. by Martin Camm)
> CM:CanRev - v4 - S 5 '97 - pONL [51-250]

Oceans (Illus. by Martin Camm)
> CM:CanRev - v4 - S 5 '97 - pONL [51-250]

Oceans and Seas (Illus. by Vanessa Card)
>   HB Guide - v8 - Fall '97 - p386 [51-250]
>   SB - v33 - Ag '97 - p176+ [251-500]

Trains
>   Sch Lib - v45 - N '97 - p206 [51-250]

Volcanoes (Illus. by Martin Camm)
>   CM:CanRev - v4 - S 5 '97 - pONL [51-250]

Morrison, Gordon
Bald Eagle (Illus. by Gordon Morrison)
>   KR - v66 - Ap 1 '98 - p498 [51-250]

Morrison, James H
Alfred Fitzpatrick: Founder of Frontier College
>   CBRA - '96 - p508 [51-250]

Morrison, Lillian
I Scream, You Scream (Illus. by Nancy Dunaway)
>   PW - v244 - O 6 '97 - p85 [1-50]
>   SLJ - v43 - N '97 - p95 [51-250]

Morrison, Marion
Brazil
>   Ch BWatch - v7 - D '97 - p7 [51-250]
>   HB Guide - v8 - Fall '97 - p400 [51-250]
>   SLJ - v43 - Ag '97 - p163 [51-250]

Morrison, Taylor
Antonio's Apprenticeship (Illus. by Taylor Morrison)
>   RT - v51 - O '97 - p149 [51-250]

Cheetah (Illus. by Taylor Morrison)
>   KR - v66 - Mr 15 '98 - p408 [51-250]
>   SLJ - v44 - Ap '98 - p121 [51-250]

The Neptune Fountain (Illus. by Taylor Morrison)
>   BL - v93 - Je 1 '97 - p1704+ [51-250]
>   CLW - v68 - S '97 - p71 [51-250]
>   Emerg Lib - v25 - N '97 - p60 [51-250]
>   HB Guide - v8 - Fall '97 - p275 [51-250]
>   SLJ - v43 - Je '97 - p99 [51-250]

Morrison, Terry
The Great Explorer (Illus. by Len Walbourne)
>   CBRA - '96 - p509 [51-250]

Morrissey, Dean
The Great Kettles (Illus. by Dean Morrissey)
>   KR - v65 - O 15 '97 - p1585 [51-250]
>   PW - v244 - N 24 '97 - p72 [51-250]
>   SLJ - v43 - D '97 - p98 [51-250]

Morrow, Robin
Beetle Soup (Illus. by Stephen Michael King)
>   Magpies - v12 - Mr '97 - p8 [51-250]

Morton, Christine
Picnic Farm (Illus. by Sarah Barringer)
>   BL - v94 - Mr 15 '98 - p1250 [51-250]
>   KR - v66 - F 15 '98 - p271 [51-250]
>   PW - v245 - F 16 '98 - p209 [51-250]
>   SLJ - v44 - Mr '98 - p185 [51-250]

Mosel, Arlene
Tikki Tikki Tembo (Illus. by Blair Lent)
>   NYTBR - v102 - N 16 '97 - p26 [1-50]

Moser, Barry
Fly! A Brief History of Flight Illustrated
>   SB - v32 - D '96 - p257+ [1-50]

Good and Perfect Gifts (Illus. by Barry Moser)
>   BL - v94 - S 1 '97 - p140 [51-250]
>   Ch BWatch - v7 - D '97 - p1 [1-50]
>   KR - v65 - S 1 '97 - p1392+ [51-250]
>   NYTBR - v102 - D 7 '97 - p66 [1-50]

Tucker Pfeffercorn
>   Inst - v107 - Ag '97 - p24 [1-50]

Moser, Madeline
Ever Heard of an Aardwolf? (Illus. by Barry Moser)
>   Am Sci - v85 - N '97 - p561 [51-250]
>   RT - v51 - S '97 - p55+ [51-250]
>   SB - v33 - Ap '97 - p86 [51-250]
>   SB - v33 - Ag '97 - p186 [1-50]

Moses, Amy
At the Hospital (Illus. by Penny Dann)
  SLJ - v44 - Ap '98 - p116+ [51-250]
At the Zoo (Illus. by Phil Martin)
  SLJ - v44 - F '98 - p98 [51-250]

Moses, Brian
Excuse Me (Illus. by Mike Gordon)
  Sch Lib - v45 - N '97 - p187 [51-250]
I'll Do It! (Illus. by Mike Gordon)
  Sch Lib - v45 - N '97 - p187 [51-250]
It Wasn't Me! (Illus. by Mike Gordon)
  Sch Lib - v45 - N '97 - p187 [51-250]
*Look Inside a Tudor Medicine Chest
(Illus. by Adam Hook)*
  Magpies - v12 - S '97 - p42 [51-250]
  Sch Lib - v45 - Ag '97 - p153 [51-250]
*Look Inside a Victorian Schoolroom
(Illus. by Adam Hook)*
  Magpies - v12 - S '97 - p42 [51-250]
  Sch Lib - v45 - Ag '97 - p153 [51-250]
Look Inside a Victorian Toyshop
  Magpies - v12 - S '97 - p42 [51-250]
Look Inside an Egyptian Tomb
  Magpies - v12 - S '97 - p42 [51-250]
*Parent-Free Zone (Illus. by Lucy
Maddison)*
  Bks Keeps - My '97 - p25 [51-250]

Moses, Will
Silent Night (Illus. by Will Moses)
  BL - v94 - S 1 '97 - p141 [51-250]
  PW - v244 - O 6 '97 - p56 [51-250]

Mosher, Richard
The Taxi Navigator
  NYTBR - v102 - Ap 27 '97 - p29 [1-50]

Mosionier, Beatrice
*Christopher's Folly (Illus. by Terry
Gallagher)*
  CBRA - '96 - p451+ [51-250]

Moss, Jeff
Bone Poems (Illus. by Tom Leigh)
  CBRS - v26 - N '97 - p32 [51-250]
  SLJ - v43 - D '97 - p113 [51-250]

*The Dad of the Dad of the Dad of
Your Dad (Illus. by Chris L Demarest)*
  PW - v244 - Je 2 '97 - p71+ [51-250]
  SLJ - v43 - Jl '97 - p109 [51-250]

Moss, Marissa
*Amelia Hits the Road (Illus. by
Marissa Moss)*
  Ch BWatch - v7 - O '97 - p5 [1-50]
  PW - v244 - Jl 28 '97 - p77 [51-250]
  SLJ - v43 - N '97 - p95+ [51-250]
My Notebook with Help from Amelia
  PW - v244 - Je 16 '97 - p61 [51-250]
*The Ugly Menorah (Illus. by Marissa
Moss)*
  ECEJ - v25 - Fall '97 - p49 [1-50]
  RT - v51 - N '97 - p255 [51-250]

Moss, Miriam
Jigsaw (Illus. by Tony Smith)
  BL - v94 - S 15 '97 - p243 [51-250]
  CBRS - v26 - F '98 - p77 [51-250]
  KR - v65 - Jl 1 '97 - p1033 [51-250]
  PW - v244 - S 1 '97 - p107 [51-250]
  SLJ - v43 - D '97 - p98 [51-250]
  TES - N 7 '97 - p5* [51-250]

Moss, Thylias
I Want to Be (Illus. by Jerry Pinkney)
  PW - v245 - F 9 '98 - p98 [1-50]

Most, Bernard
*A Pair of Protoceratops (Illus. by
Bernard Most)*
  KR - v66 - Mr 1 '98 - p342 [51-250]
  PW - v245 - Mr 23 '98 - p97 [51-250]
*A Trio of Triceratops (Illus. by
Bernard Most)*
  PW - v245 - Mr 23 '98 - p97 [51-250]

***The Most Incredible, Outrageous,
Packed-to-the-Gills, Bulging-at-
the-Seams Sticker Book You've
Ever Seen***
  PW - v244 - S 22 '97 - p82 [51-250]

Mother Goose
*The Arnold Lobel Book of Mother
Goose (Illus. by Arnold Lobel)*
  Comw - v124 - D 5 '97 - p14 [51-250]

Mould, Chris
Frankenstein (Illus. by Chris Mould)
  NS - v126 - D 5 '97 - p64 [1-50]

Mowat, Farley
A Farley Mowat Reader (Illus. by Richard Row)
  y   CM:CanRev - v4 - O 31 '97 - pONL [251-500]
      Quill & Q - v63 - N '97 - p45 [251-500]

Mrs. Piggle-Wiggle's Won't-Take-a-Bath Cure (Illus. by Bruce Whatley)
  PW - v244 - Ag 25 '97 - p74 [51-250]

Mueller, Virginia
Monster's Birthday Hiccups (Illus. by Lynn Munsinger)
  HB Guide - v8 - Fall '97 - p275 [51-250]

Mugford, Simon
Fantastic Cutaway Book of Rescue! (Illus. by Alex Pang)
  Ch BWatch - v8 - Ja '98 - p6 [1-50]

Muir, Helen
Wonderwitch and the Spooks
  TES - O 31 '97 - p8* [51-250]

Muir, Stephen
Albert's Old Shoes (Illus. by Mary Jane Muir)
  CBRA - '96 - p452 [51-250]

Mulcahy, Robert
Medical Technology
  CCB-B - v50 - Jl '97 - p404+ [51-250]
  Ch BWatch - v7 - Ap '97 - p8 [51-250]
  y   HB Guide - v8 - Fall '97 - p359 [51-250]
      SLJ - v43 - Jl '97 - p109+ [51-250]

Muldoon, Paul
The Noctuary of Narcissus Batt (Illus. by Marketa Prachaticka)
  Bks Keeps - Jl '97 - p25+ [51-250]
  Sch Lib - v45 - N '97 - p209+ [51-250]
  TES - N 7 '97 - p2* [51-250]

Muleiro, Pepe
Chistes Para Chicos
  BL - v93 - Ag '97 - p1913 [1-50]

Mulford, Philippa Greene
The Holly Sisters on Their Own
  PW - v245 - Mr 9 '98 - p69 [51-250]
  SLJ - v44 - Ap '98 - p134 [51-250]

Mullane, R Mike
Do Your Ears Pop in Space?
  S&T - v94 - N '97 - p74+ [501+]

Muller, Gerda
Around the Oak
  SB - v33 - O '97 - p219 [51-250]

Muller, Jorg
Der Standhafte Zinnsoldat (Illus. by Jorg Muller)
  Bkbird - v35 - Sum '97 - p56 [51-250]

Muller, Robin
The Angel Tree (Illus. by Robin Muller)
  BIC - v26 - D '97 - p35 [51-250]
  Ch Bk News - v20 - Sum '97 - p28 [51-250]
  CM:CanRev - v4 - D 12 '97 - pONL [251-500]
  Quill & Q - v63 - O '97 - p43 [251-500]
  Quill & Q - v64 - F '98 - p42 [1-50]

Row, Row, Row Your Boat
  Can CL - v23 - Fall '97 - p93 [51-250]

Mullins, Patricia
One Horse Waiting for Me (Illus. by Patricia Mullins)
  BL - v94 - Mr 1 '98 - p1130 [51-250]
  CCB-B - v51 - Mr '98 - p252+ [51-250]
  KR - v66 - F 1 '98 - p199 [51-250]

Munsch, Robert
Alligator Baby (Illus. by Michael Martchenko)
  CBRS - v26 - Ja '98 - p51 [51-250]
  CCB-B - v51 - O '97 - p63+ [51-250]
  PW - v244 - Je 23 '97 - p90+ [51-250]
  Quill & Q - v63 - S '97 - p72+ [251-500]
  SLJ - v43 - N '97 - p96 [51-250]

*Andrew's Loose Tooth (Illus. by
Michael Martchenko)*
> BL - v94 - Mr 15 '98 - p1252 [51-250]
> PW - v245 - F 16 '98 - p209 [51-250]

*The Dark (Illus. by Michael
Martchenko)*
> CM:CanRev - v4 - O 31 '97 - pONL
> [251-500]
> PW - v244 - N 17 '97 - p63 [51-250]

*Love You Forever (Illus. by Sheila
McGraw)*
> NYTBR - v102 - N 16 '97 - p26 [1-50]

*Mud Puddle. Rev. Ed. (Illus. by Sami
Suomalainen)*
> CBRA - '96 - p452 [51-250]

*Stephanie's Ponytail (Illus. by Michael
Martchenko)*
> CBRA - '96 - p452+ [51-250]

*Where Is Gah-Ning? (Illus. by Helene
Desputeaux)*
> Can CL - v23 - Fall '97 - p69+ [501+]

Munson, Sammy
Los Vaqueros: Our First Cowboys
> HB Guide - v8 - Fall '97 - p396 [51-
> 250]

Munsterberg, Peggy
*Beastly Banquet (Illus. by Tracy
Gallup)*
> CBRS - v25 - Je '97 - p123 [1-50]
> HB Guide - v8 - Fall '97 - p377 [51-
> 250]

Murphy, Chuck
*Chuck Murphy's Alphabet Magic
(Illus. by Chuck Murphy)*
> HB Guide - v8 - Fall '97 - p253 [51-
> 250]
> KR - v65 - Je 1 '97 - p878 [51-250]
> PW - v244 - Je 2 '97 - p73 [51-250]

Color Surprises
> BL - v94 - D 15 '97 - p700 [1-50]
> Bloom Rev - v17 - N '97 - p33 [51-250]
> PW - v244 - S 1 '97 - p106 [1-50]

Colors (Illus. by Chuck Murphy)
> KR - v65 - My 15 '97 - p804 [51-250]

Razzle Dazzle
> PW - v244 - Je 2 '97 - p73 [1-50]

Murphy, Claire Rudolf
Caribou Girl (Illus. by Linda Russell)
> KR - v66 - Mr 15 '98 - p408 [51-250]

Murphy, Frank
Lockie and Dadge
> Bkbird - v35 - Sum '97 - p58 [51-250]

Murphy, Jim
Across America on an Emigrant Train
> SLJ - v43 - Jl '97 - p35 [1-50]

Gone A-Whaling
> y   BL - v94 - Mr 15 '98 - p1233 [51-250]
> CCB-B - v51 - Ap '98 - p290 [51-250]

West to a Land of Plenty
> CCB-B - v51 - Mr '98 - p253 [51-250]
> SLJ - v44 - Ap '98 - p134 [51-250]

Murphy, Mary, 1961-
*I Like It When... (Illus. by Mary
Murphy)*
> Bks Keeps - My '97 - p19 [51-250]
> Ch BWatch - v7 - S '97 - p4 [1-50]
> HB Guide - v8 - Fall '97 - p254 [51-
> 250]
> SLJ - v43 - My '97 - p109 [51-250]

You Smell (Illus. by Mary Murphy)
> BL - v94 - D 1 '97 - p642+ [51-250]
> PW - v244 - O 6 '97 - p82 [51-250]
> SLJ - v44 - Ja '98 - p90 [51-250]

Murphy, Nora
A Hmong Family
> Bloom Rev - v17 - S '97 - p23 [51-250]
> Ch BWatch - v7 - My '97 - p6 [1-50]
> SLJ - v43 - Ag '97 - p162 [51-250]

Murphy, Pat
*The Science Explorer (Illus. by Jason
Gorski)*
> SB - v33 - Ag '97 - p187 [1-50]

The Science Explorer Out and About
> SLJ - v44 - F '98 - p120+ [51-250]

Murphy, Stuart J
*The Best Vacation Ever (Illus. by
Nadine Bernard Westcott)*
> HB Guide - v8 - Fall '97 - p275 [51-
> 250]

Betcha! (Illus. by S D Schindler)
  BL - v94 - O 1 '97 - p336 [51-250]
  KR - v65 - S 15 '97 - p1460 [51-250]
  SLJ - v44 - Ja '98 - p103 [51-250]

Circus Shapes (Illus. by Edward Miller)
  BL - v94 - Mr 1 '98 - p1142 [51-250]
  CCB-B - v51 - Ja '98 - p169 [51-250]
  KR - v65 - N 15 '97 - p1710 [51-250]
  PW - v245 - Ja 19 '98 - p379+ [51-250]
  SLJ - v44 - Ap '98 - p121+ [51-250]

Divide and Ride (Illus. by George Ulrich)
  HB Guide - v8 - Fall '97 - p341 [51-250]

Elevator Magic (Illus. by G Brian Karas)
  BL - v94 - O 1 '97 - p336 [51-250]
  SLJ - v43 - N '97 - p110 [51-250]

Every Buddy Counts (Illus. by Fiona Dunbar)
  Emerg Lib - v25 - Ja '98 - p56 [51-250]
  HB Guide - v8 - Fall '97 - p254 [51-250]

A Fair Bear Share (Illus. by John Speirs)
  BL - v94 - Mr 1 '98 - p1142 [51-250]
  PW - v245 - Ja 19 '98 - p379+ [51-250]

Get Up and Go! (Illus. by Diane Greenseid)
  SB - v32 - D '96 - p273 [51-250]
  TCMath - v4 - S '97 - p52 [51-250]

Just Enough Carrots (Illus. by Frank Remkiewicz)
  BL - v94 - O 1 '97 - p336 [51-250]
  SLJ - v43 - D '97 - p113 [51-250]

Lemonade for Sale (Illus. by Tricia Tusa)
  BL - v94 - Mr 1 '98 - p1142 [51-250]
  KR - v65 - N 15 '97 - p1711 [51-250]
  PW - v245 - Ja 19 '98 - p379+ [51-250]

A Pair of Socks (Illus. by Lois Ehlert)
  SB - v32 - D '96 - p273 [51-250]
  TCMath - v4 - S '97 - p52 [51-250]

Too Many Kangaroo Things to Do! (Illus. by Kevin O'Malley)
  SB - v32 - D '96 - p273 [51-250]
  TCMath - v4 - S '97 - p52 [51-250]

Murray, Jerome T
The Year 2000 Computing Crisis
  SB - v32 - D '96 - p260 [51-250]

Murray, Marjorie Dennis
The Stars Are Waiting (Illus. by Jacqueline Rogers)
  PW - v245 - Mr 9 '98 - p66 [51-250]

Murray, Peter, 1952, Sep., 9-
Bravery: The Story of Sitting Bull (Illus. by Robin Lawrie)
  SLJ - v44 - Mr '98 - p198 [51-250]

Floods
  SLJ - v43 - Jl '97 - p86 [51-250]

Pigs
  SLJ - v44 - F '98 - p102 [51-250]

Saturn
  SLJ - v44 - F '98 - p98 [51-250]

Snails
  SLJ - v44 - Mr '98 - p199 [51-250]

Music of the Bells (Little Play a Sound)
  Ch BWatch - v7 - Ap '97 - p2 [1-50]

Muskat, Carrie
Barry Bonds
  Ch BWatch - v7 - Je '97 - p2 [1-50]
  HB Guide - v8 - Fall '97 - p368 [51-250]

Frank Thomas
  Ch BWatch - v7 - Je '97 - p2 [1-50]
  HB Guide - v8 - Fall '97 - p368 [51-250]

Musleah, Rahel
Sharing Blessings (Illus. by Mary O'Keefe Young)
  BL - v94 - O 1 '97 - p322+ [51-250]
  PW - v244 - Jl 28 '97 - p69 [51-250]
  SLJ - v43 - S '97 - p206 [51-250]

Mutchnick, Brenda
A Noteworthy Tale (Illus. by Ian Penney)
  PW - v244 - N 17 '97 - p61+ [51-250]
  SLJ - v44 - Ja '98 - p90 [51-250]

**My Amazing Human Body.
Electronic Media Version**
> SLJ - v44 - Mr '98 - p140 [251-500]

My Home (Star Bright)
> PW - v244 - D 15 '97 - p60 [51-250]

**My Little Animals Board Book
(Dorling Kindersley)**
> PW - v245 - Mr 23 '98 - p102 [51-250]

**My Little House Christmas Sticker
Book (Illus. by Renee Graef)**
> PW - v244 - O 6 '97 - p57 [1-50]

My Very First Oxford Atlas
> r Sch Lib - v45 - Ag '97 - p132 [51-250]

Myers, Anna
The Keeping Room
> BL - v94 - N 1 '97 - p473 [51-250]
> CCB-B - v51 - Ja '98 - p169 [51-250]
> KR - v65 - S 1 '97 - p1393 [51-250]
> SLJ - v43 - D '97 - p126+ [51-250]

Red-Dirt Jessie
> PW - v244 - D 22 '97 - p61 [1-50]
> y SS - v88 - N '97 - p279 [51-250]

Spotting the Leopard
> PW - v244 - D 22 '97 - p61 [1-50]

Myers, Walter Dean
Angel to Angel
> BL - v94 - F 15 '98 - p1006 [51-250]
> KR - v66 - Ap 1 '98 - p498 [51-250]
> PW - v245 - Mr 23 '98 - p97 [51-250]

*Harlem: A Poem (Illus. by
Christopher Myers)*
> y BL - v94 - Ja 1 '98 - p733 [1-50]
> y BL - v94 - Mr 15 '98 - p1211 [1-50]
> BL - v94 - Mr 15 '98 - p1224 [1-50]
> y BL - v94 - Mr 15 '98 - p1225 [1-50]
> Ch BWatch - v7 - My '97 - p3 [1-50]
> HB Guide - v8 - Fall '97 - p377 [51-250]
> NYTBR - v102 - Jl 20 '97 - p22 [501+]
> y VOYA - v20 - O '97 - p266+ [51-250]
> y VOYA - v20 - F '98 - p366 [51-250]
> y VOYA - v21 - Ap '98 - p38 [1-50]
> y VOYA - v21 - Ap '98 - p39 [1-50]

*Harlem: A Poem (Dee) (Illus. by
Christopher Myers). Book and Audio
Version*
> SLJ - v44 - Ap '98 - p38 [1-50]

*How Mr. Monkey Saw the Whole
World (Illus. by Synthia Saint James)*
> PW - v244 - S 22 '97 - p83 [1-50]

A Long Road to Freedom
> BL - v94 - F 15 '98 - p1003 [51-250]

Malcolm X: By Any Means Necessary
> y Kliatt - v32 - Mr '98 - p32 [51-250]
> PW - v245 - Ja 12 '98 - p61 [1-50]

*The Righteous Revenge of Artemis
Bonner*
> BL - v93 - Je 1 '97 - p1701 [1-50]

Somewhere in the Darkness
> PW - v244 - S 1 '97 - p107 [1-50]
> y SLJ - v43 - Jl '97 - p35 [1-50]

N

Naden, C J
Sharks (Illus. by Paul Lopez)
    ASBYP - v29 - Fall '96 - p48+ [501+]

Nagda, Ann Whitehead
Bamboo Valley (Kaye) (Illus. by Jim Effler). Book and Audio Version
    SLJ - v44 - Ap '98 - p84+ [51-250]

Canopy Crossing. Book and Audio Version
    SLJ - v43 - D '97 - p72 [51-250]

Naidoo, Beverley
No Turning Back
    Bks Keeps - My '97 - p4+ [501+]
    Bks Keeps - My '97 - p16 [51-250]
    BL - v93 - Je 1 '97 - p1724 [1-50]
    Ch BWatch - v7 - Ap '97 - p4 [51-250]
    HB Guide - v8 - Fall '97 - p305 [51-250]
    JOYS - v11 - Win '98 - p140 [1-50]
    NYTBR - v102 - My 11 '97 - p24 [1-50]
    RT - v51 - F '98 - p431 [51-250]
    TES - Je 6 '97 - p8* [51-250]
y   VOYA - v20 - O '97 - p246 [51-250]

Naik, Anita
Drugs
    Books - v11 - O '97 - p21 [1-50]

Nakawatari, H
The Sea and I
    ECEJ - v25 - Fall '97 - p48+ [1-50]

Namioka, Lensey
Den of the White Fox
y   BL - v93 - Je 1 '97 - p1686 [51-250]

HB Guide - v8 - Fall '97 - p305 [51-250]
y   Kliatt - v31 - S '97 - p13 [251-500]
y   SLJ - v43 - Je '97 - p122 [51-250]
y   VOYA - v20 - Ag '97 - p188 [251-500]

Nanji, Shenaaz
The Old Fisherman of Lamu (Illus. by Shahd Shaker)
    CBRA - '96 - p503 [51-250]

Nanton, Isabel
British Columbia. Rev. Ed.
    CBRA - '96 - p512+ [501+]

Napoli, Donna Jo
Jimmy, the Pickpocket of the Palace (Illus. by Judith Byron Schachner)
    PW - v244 - N 24 '97 - p76 [1-50]

On Guard
    HB Guide - v8 - Fall '97 - p305 [51-250]
    SLJ - v43 - My '97 - p138 [51-250]

Stones in Water
    BL - v94 - O 1 '97 - p333 [51-250]
y   BL - v94 - Mr 15 '98 - p1218 [1-50]
    BL - v94 - Mr 15 '98 - p1224 [1-50]
    CBRS - v26 - Ja '98 - p60 [51-250]
    HB - v74 - Ja '98 - p77+ [51-250]
y   KR - v65 - O 15 '97 - p1585 [51-250]
    PW - v244 - S 1 '97 - p106 [51-250]
    PW - v244 - N 3 '97 - p60 [1-50]
    SLJ - v43 - N '97 - p122 [51-250]
y   VOYA - v20 - F '98 - p387+ [251-500]
y   VOYA - v21 - Ap '98 - p38 [1-50]

Trouble on the Tracks
    HB Guide - v8 - Fall '97 - p305 [51-250]

Nardo, Don
Age of Augustus
   Ch BWatch - v7 - My '97 - p6 [1-50]

The Fall of the Roman Empire
y   BL - v94 - Mr 1 '98 - p1124 [51-250]
    Ch BWatch - v8 - Ja '98 - p7 [51-250]
y   Kliatt - v32 - Ja '98 - p31 [51-250]

Nasu, Masamoto
*E De Yomu Hiroshima No Gembaku
(Illus. by Shigeo Nishimura)*
   Bkbird - v34 - Win '96 - p57 [51-250]

Nathan, Amy
*Surviving Homework (Illus. by Anne
Canevari Green)*
   BL - v93 - Je 1 '97 - p1696 [51-250]
   SLJ - v43 - Jl '97 - p110 [51-250]

National Geographic World
p   Par Ch - Awards '97 - p27 [1-50]

*National Storytelling Directory
1997*
r   CAY - v18 - Spr '97 - p6 [51-250]

Nature Facts (DK)
   Ch BWatch - v7 - Je '97 - p4 [1-50]

Nayer, Judy
How Many?
   TCMath - v4 - S '97 - p52 [51-250]

Who Wears Shoes?
   TCMath - v4 - S '97 - p52 [51-250]

Naylor, Phyllis Reynolds
*Ducks Disappearing (Illus. by Tony
Maddox)*
   HB Guide - v8 - Fall '97 - p275 [1-50]

*The Healing of Texas Jake (Illus. by
Alan Daniel)*
   HB Guide - v8 - Fall '97 - p306 [51-
   250]
   SLJ - v43 - Ap '97 - p140 [51-250]

*I Can't Take You Anywhere! (Illus. by
Jef Kaminsky)*
   BL - v94 - O 1 '97 - p338 [51-250]
   CBRS - v26 - N '97 - p28 [51-250]
   CCB-B - v51 - Ja '98 - p169+ [51-250]

KR - v65 - S 1 '97 - p1393 [51-250]
PW - v244 - O 20 '97 - p76 [51-250]

Outrageously Alice
y   BL - v94 - Mr 15 '98 - p1218 [1-50]
    CCB-B - v50 - Jl '97 - p405 [51-250]
    HB - v73 - Jl '97 - p460+ [51-250]
y   HB Guide - v8 - Fall '97 - p306 [51-
    250]
y   JAAL - v41 - F '98 - p409 [51-250]
    KR - v65 - Ap 15 '97 - p645+ [51-250]
    NYTBR - v102 - Jl 6 '97 - p16 [1-50]
    SLJ - v43 - Je '97 - p122+ [51-250]
y   VOYA - v20 - O '97 - p246 [51-250]
y   VOYA - v21 - Ap '98 - p38 [1-50]

Saving Shiloh (Illus. by Barry Moser)
   BL - v94 - S 1 '97 - p118 [51-250]
y   CCB-B - v51 - S '97 - p20 [251-500]
   Ch BWatch - v7 - O '97 - p2 [51-250]
   HB - v73 - S '97 - p576 [51-250]
   KR - v65 - Jl 15 '97 - p1114 [51-250]
   NYTBR - v103 - F 15 '98 - p25 [1-50]
   PW - v244 - Je 30 '97 - p77 [51-250]
   SLJ - v43 - S '97 - p222 [51-250]

Shiloh
   BL - v94 - S 1 '97 - p119 [1-50]

*Shiloh Season (Moriarty). Audio
Version*
   Ch BWatch - v7 - D '97 - p4 [1-50]

The Treasure of Bessledorf Hill
   BL - v94 - Ja 1 '98 - p814 [51-250]
   SLJ - v44 - Mr '98 - p216 [51-250]

Neff, Rena
The Junior Chef
   Ch BWatch - v7 - O '97 - p7 [51-250]

Neitzel, Shirley
*From the Land of the White Birch
(Illus. by Daniel Powers)*
   SLJ - v44 - F '98 - p102+ [51-250]

*The House I'll Build for the Wrens
(Illus. by Nancy Winslow Parker)*
   BL - v93 - Ag '97 - p1899 [51-250]
   HB - v73 - S '97 - p562 [51-250]
   SLJ - v43 - S '97 - p188 [51-250]

*We're Making Breakfast for Mother
(Illus. by Nancy Winslow Parker)*
   Ch BWatch - v7 - Je '97 - p7 [1-50]
   HB Guide - v8 - Fall '97 - p275 [51-
   250]

SLJ - v43 - Ap '97 - p114 [51-250]

Nelisi, Lino
Tane Steals the Show (Illus. by Gus Hunter)
Magpies - v12 - S '97 - p5* [51-250]

Tane Te Whetu O Te Ra (Illus. by Gus Hunter)
Magpies - v12 - S '97 - p5* [51-250]

Nelles, Ann
Alice of Wonderfarm Goes to the Races (Illus. by Ann Nelles)
Can CL - v23 - Sum '97 - p63+ [501+]
CBRA - '96 - p453 [51-250]

Alice of Wonderfarm Saves the Drumlin (Illus. by Ann Nelles)
CBRA - '96 - p453 [51-250]

Nelson, Rosemary
The Golden Grasshopper
CBRA - '96 - p486 [51-250]
CM:CanRev - v30 - Ja 30 '98 - pONL [251-500]

Nelson English Dictionary
r   TES - S 19 '97 - p19* [501+]

Nelson First English Dictionary
r   TES - S 19 '97 - p19* [501+]

Nerlove, Miriam
Flowers on the Wall (Illus. by Miriam Nerlove)
SE - v61 - Ap '97 - p15* [1-50]

Nesbit, E
The Best of Shakespeare
BL - v94 - O 15 '97 - p401 [51-250]
y   Emerg Lib - v25 - Ja '98 - p51 [51-250]
y   PW - v244 - Je 16 '97 - p61 [51-250]

Five Children and It
TES - Ja 2 '98 - p22* [51-250]

The Magic City
Ch BWatch - v7 - My '97 - p5 [51-250]
TES - Ja 2 '98 - p22* [1-50]

The Phoenix and the Carpet
TES - Ja 2 '98 - p22* [51-250]

The Railway Children (Illus. by George Buchanan)
HB Guide - v8 - Fall '97 - p288 [51-250]

Wet Magic
Ch BWatch - v7 - My '97 - p5 [51-250]

Ness, Evaline
Tom Tit Tot (Illus. by Evaline Ness)
PW - v244 - Ag 4 '97 - p77 [1-50]

Nettell, Stephanie
A Christmas Treasury (Illus. by Ian Penney)
BL - v94 - S 1 '97 - p137 [51-250]
PW - v244 - O 6 '97 - p57 [1-50]

Neufeldt, Victoria
Webster's New World Children's Dictionary. Rev. Ed.
r   SLJ - v44 - F '98 - p138 [51-250]

Neuschwander, Cindy
Sir Circumference and the First Round Table (Illus. by Wayne Geehan)
CBRS - v26 - Win '98 - p67 [51-250]

New Baby's Cloth Bible
PW - v245 - Mr 23 '98 - p95+ [51-250]

The New Book of Knowledge 97. Vols. 1-21
r   BL - v94 - S 15 '97 - p258+ [251-500]

New English Dictionary
r   TES - S 19 '97 - p19* [501+]

New Moon: The Magazine for Girls and Their Dreams
p   Par Ch - Awards '97 - p27 [1-50]

Newberry, Clare Turlay
April's Kittens (Caruso). Audio Version
BL - v94 - F 15 '98 - p1027 [51-250]
SLJ - v44 - Mr '98 - p156 [51-250]

Barkis (Illus. by Clare Turlay Newberry)
PW - v245 - F 2 '98 - p91 [51-250]

Herbert the Lion (Illus. by Clare Turlay Newberry)
PW - v245 - F 2 '98 - p91 [51-250]

Mittens (Illus. by Clare Turlay Newberry)
PW - v245 - F 2 '98 - p91 [51-250]

Smudge (Illus. by Clare Turlay Newberry)
PW - v245 - F 2 '98 - p91 [51-250]

Newlands, Anne
Emily Carr: An Introduction to Her Life and Art
Quill & Q - v63 - Jl '97 - p51 [251-500]

Newman, Barbara
The Illustrated Book of Ballet Stories (Illus. by Gil Tomblin)
BL - v94 - D 15 '97 - p694 [51-250]
PW - v244 - O 13 '97 - p77 [51-250]

Newman, Leslea
Fat Chance
BL - v94 - Ja 1 '98 - p795 [1-50]

Matzo Ball Moon (Illus. by Elaine Greenstein)
PW - v245 - F 23 '98 - p76 [51-250]

Too Far Away to Touch (Illus. by Catherine Stock)
PW - v245 - Mr 9 '98 - p70 [1-50]

Newman, Shirlee P
Isabella: A Wish for Miguel, Peru 1820 (Illus. by Laurie Harden)
SLJ - v44 - Ap '98 - p106 [51-250]

Newton, David E
Black Holes and Supernovae
Ch BWatch - v7 - My '97 - p8 [1-50]
SLJ - v43 - Je '97 - p132 [51-250]

NgCheong-Lum, Roseline
Tahiti
Ch BWatch - v7 - Je '97 - p5 [251-250]

Nichelason, Margery G
Shoes
BL - v94 - Ja 1 '98 - p796 [51-250]
Ch BWatch - v7 - D '97 - p8 [1-50]

Nichol, Barbara
Biscuits in the Cupboard (Illus. by Philippe Beha)
PW - v245 - F 2 '98 - p91 [51-250]
Quill & Q - v63 - D '97 - p36 [251-500]
SLJ - v44 - Mr '98 - p199 [51-250]

Dippers (Illus. by Barry Moser)
Ch Bk News - v20 - Spr '97 - p35 [251-500]
Ch BWatch - v7 - My '97 - p1 [51-250]
CM:CanRev - v4 - O 3 '97 - pONL [251-500]
HB Guide - v8 - Fall '97 - p293 [51-250]
Quill & Q - v63 - Ap '97 - p35 [251-500]
Quill & Q - v64 - F '98 - p42 [51-250]
SLJ - v43 - S '97 - p188+ [51-250]

Nichols, Grace
Asana and the Animals (Illus. by Sarah Adams)
Bks Keeps - Jl '97 - p21 [51-250]
BL - v93 - Je 1 '97 - p1711 [51-250]
HB Guide - v8 - Fall '97 - p377 [1-50]
Sch Lib - v45 - Ag '97 - p132 [51-250]
SLJ - v43 - Jl '97 - p86 [51-250]

Nicholson, John
Explorers of Australia (Illus. by John Nicholson)
Magpies - v12 - Mr '97 - p43 [251-500]

A Home among the Gum Trees (Illus. by John Nicholson)
Magpies - v12 - S '97 - p41 [251-500]

Nicholson, Libby
Creating with Fimo Acrylic Clay (Illus. by Tracy Walker)
CBRA - '96 - p521 [51-250]

Nicholson, Lois
Booker T. Washington
Ch BWatch - v7 - Je '97 - p2 [1-50]
HB Guide - v8 - Fall '97 - p381 [51-250]

Ken Griffey, Jr.
Ch BWatch - v7 - Je '97 - p2 [1-50]
HB Guide - v8 - Fall '97 - p368 [51-250]

Oprah Winfrey
> HB Guide - v8 - Fall '97 - p381 [51-250]
> SLJ - v43 - Ag '97 - p173 [51-250]

Nicholson, Nicholas B A
Little Girl in a Red Dress with Cat and Dog (Illus. by Cynthia Von Buhler)
> PW - v244 - D 15 '97 - p57 [51-250]
> SLJ - v44 - F '98 - p89 [51-250]
> BL - v94 - D 15 '97 - p704 [51-250]
> HB - v74 - Mr '98 - p216+ [51-250]
> KR - v65 - N 15 '97 - p1711 [51-250]

Nickel, Barbara Kathleen
The Secret Wish of Nannerl Mozart
> CBRA - '96 - p486+ [51-250]

Nickles, Greg
Pirates
> Ch BWatch - v7 - D '97 - p2 [1-50]
> Emerg Lib - v25 - N '97 - p47 [51-250]
> HB Guide - v8 - Fall '97 - p386 [51-250]

Nicolle, David
Medieval Knights
> SLJ - v44 - Ja '98 - p128 [51-250]

Nicolson, Cynthia Pratt
The Earth (Illus. by Bill Slavin)
> BL - v94 - S 1 '97 - p108 [51-250]
> CBRA - '96 - p532+ [51-250]
> CBRS - v26 - O '97 - p19+ [51-250]
> PW - v244 - S 1 '97 - p106 [1-50]
> SLJ - v43 - S '97 - p200 [51-250]

Niderost, Heather I
The Light World
> CBRA - '96 - p487 [51-250]

Nies, Judith
Native American History
> yr   Kliatt - v31 - Jl '97 - p31 [251-500]
> r   SLJ - v43 - My '97 - p160 [51-250]

Nightingale, Hugh
I Can Make Magic (Illus. by John Freeman)
> SLJ - v43 - Ap '97 - p129+ [51-250]

Nikola-Lisa, W
America: My Land, Your Land, Our Land (Illus. by Yvonne Buchanan)
> BL - v94 - S 1 '97 - p134 [51-250]
> HB Guide - v8 - Fall '97 - p275 [51-250]
> KR - v65 - My 15 '97 - p804 [51-250]
> SLJ - v43 - Jl '97 - p72 [51-250]

Shake Dem Halloween Bones (Illus. by Mike Reed)
> BL - v94 - O 1 '97 - p338 [51-250]
> CBRS - v26 - N '97 - p29 [1-50]
> CCB-B - v51 - D '97 - p135 [51-250]
> PW - v244 - O 6 '97 - p49 [51-250]

Tangletalk (Illus. by Jessica Clerk)
> CBRS - v25 - Ag '97 - p161 [1-50]
> HB Guide - v8 - Fall '97 - p275 [1-50]
> Inst - v107 - S '97 - p22 [1-50]
> KR - v65 - Ap 15 '97 - p646 [51-250]
> NYTBR - v102 - S 14 '97 - p30 [1-50]
> SLJ - v43 - Jl '97 - p72 [51-250]

Till Year's Good End (Illus. by Christopher Manson)
> BL - v94 - O 15 '97 - p409+ [51-250]
> CCB-B - v51 - Ja '98 - p170 [51-250]
> KR - v65 - S 1 '97 - p1393+ [51-250]
> PW - v244 - O 13 '97 - p75 [51-250]
> SLJ - v43 - D '97 - p142+ [51-250]

Niland, Kilmeny
Feathers, Fur and Frills
> Magpies - v12 - Jl '97 - p40 [51-250]

Nilsson, Eleanor
Outside Permission
> TES - Ag 29 '97 - p28 [51-250]
> y   TES - N 7 '97 - p13* [51-250]

Nimmo, Jenny
Delilah Alone (Illus. by Georgien Overwater)
> Bks Keeps - S '97 - p25 [51-250]
> Sch Lib - v45 - Ag '97 - p147 [51-250]

The Dragon's Child (Illus. by Alan Marks)
> Bks Keeps - N '97 - p23 [51-250]
> Sch Lib - v45 - N '97 - p192 [51-250]
> TES - S 19 '97 - p13* [501+]

Griffin's Castle
> HB Guide - v8 - Fall '97 - p306 [51-250]
> SLJ - v43 - Je '97 - p124 [51-250]
> y VOYA - v20 - Ag '97 - p188 [251-500]

Hot Dog Cool Cat (Illus. by David Wynn Millward)
> Sch Lib - v45 - N '97 - p192+ [51-250]

The Owl Tree (Illus. by Anthony Lewis)
> Bks Keeps - Jl '97 - p23 [51-250]
> Magpies - v12 - My '97 - p30 [51-250]
> Sch Lib - v45 - Ag '97 - p147 [51-250]

Seth and the Strangers (Illus. by Peter Melnyczuk)
> Sch Lib - v45 - N '97 - p201 [51-250]

Nirgiotis, Nicholas
No More Dodos
> HB Guide - v8 - Fall '97 - p328 [51-250]

Nivola, Claire A
Elisabeth (Illus. by Claire A Nivola)
> CLW - v68 - D '97 - p85 [51-250]
> HB Guide - v8 - Fall '97 - p293 [51-250]
> SLJ - v43 - Ap '97 - p114 [51-250]

Nix, Garth
Sabriel
> Ch BWatch - v7 - Mr '97 - p2 [51-250]
> y Kliatt - v32 - Ja '98 - p17+ [51-250]
> y PW - v244 - Ag 25 '97 - p74 [1-50]
> y VOYA - v20 - Ap '97 - p12 [1-50]
> y VOYA - v20 - Ap '97 - p44+ [251-500]
> y VOYA - v20 - Je '97 - p86 [51-250]

Shade's Children
> y BL - v94 - O 1 '97 - p320 [51-250]
> y BL - v94 - Mr 15 '98 - p1218 [1-50]
> BW - v27 - D 7 '97 - p22 [51-250]
> y CBRS - v26 - Ja '98 - p60 [51-250]
> y CCB-B - v51 - N '97 - p94 [51-250]
> y Emerg Lib - v25 - Ja '98 - p50 [51-250]
> y HB - v73 - S '97 - p576+ [251-500]
> y KR - v65 - Ag 15 '97 - p1309+ [51-250]
> y Magpies - v12 - S '97 - p39 [51-250]
> y PW - v244 - Je 16 '97 - p60 [51-250]
> y SLJ - v43 - Ag '97 - p158 [51-250]
> y VOYA - v20 - F '98 - p366 [51-250]
> y VOYA - v21 - Ap '98 - p38 [1-50]

Nixon, Carl
Guardians of Mother Earth
> Magpies - v12 - Mr '97 - p8* [51-250]

Nixon, Joan Lowery
Circle of Love
> Ch BWatch - v7 - Ap '97 - p4+ [1-50]
> CLW - v68 - S '97 - p65 [51-250]
> HB Guide - v8 - Fall '97 - p306 [51-250]
> SLJ - v43 - My '97 - p138 [51-250]

The Deadman's Mine Mystery
> Sch Lib - v45 - N '97 - p201 [51-250]

Lucy's Wish
> BL - v94 - D 15 '97 - p697+ [51-250]

The Walking Statue Mystery
> Sch Lib - v45 - N '97 - p201 [51-250]

Noble, Trinka Hakes
El Dia Que La Boa De Jimmy Se Comio La Ropa (Illus. by Steven Kellogg)
> SLJ - v43 - Ag '97 - p181 [51-250]

Nodelman, Perry
Alice Falls Apart (Illus. by Stuart Duncan)
> CBRA - '96 - p453+ [51-250]

A Completely Different Place
> y CBRA - '96 - p487 [51-250]
> y CCB-B - v51 - S '97 - p21 [51-250]
> HB Guide - v8 - Fall '97 - p306 [51-250]
> KR - v65 - My 15 '97 - p804 [51-250]
> SLJ - v43 - Je '97 - p124+ [51-250]
> y VOYA - v20 - Ag '97 - p195 [251-500]

Nodset, Joan L
Go Away, Dog (Illus. by Paul Meisel)
> BL - v93 - Ag '97 - p1909 [51-250]

Nolan, Dennis
Androcles and the Lion (Illus. by Dennis Nolan)
> BL - v94 - O 15 '97 - p410 [51-250]
> CCB-B - v51 - Mr '98 - p253+ [51-250]
> SLJ - v43 - N '97 - p110 [51-250]

Nolen, Jerdine
Raising Dragons (Illus. by Elise Primavera)
> HB - v74 - Mr '98 - p217 [251-500]
> KR - v66 - Mr 1 '98 - p343 [51-250]
> PW - v245 - Mr 9 '98 - p67+ [51-250]
> SLJ - v44 - Ap '98 - p106 [51-250]

Noll, Sally
Surprise! (Illus. by Sally Noll)
> BL - v94 - O 1 '97 - p338 [51-250]
> CCB-B - v51 - S '97 - p21 [51-250]

Norac, Carl
I Love You so Much (Illus. by Claude K Dubois)
> KR - v65 - N 15 '97 - p1711 [51-250]
> PW - v245 - Ja 5 '98 - p66 [51-250]
> SLJ - v44 - F '98 - p89 [51-250]

Norman, David
The Humongous Book of Dinosaurs
> KR - v65 - My 15 '97 - p805 [51-250]

Norman, Howard
The Girl Who Dreamed Only Geese and Other Tales of the Far North (Illus. by Leo Dillon)
> BL - v94 - S 15 '97 - p233 [51-250]
> BW - v28 - Ja 4 '98 - p11 [251-500]
> Ch BWatch - v8 - Ja '98 - p3 [1-50]
> KR - v65 - S 1 '97 - p1394 [51-250]
> NYTBR - v102 - N 16 '97 - p30 [501+]
> Quill & Q - v63 - D '97 - p36+ [251-500]
> SLJ - v43 - N '97 - p132 [51-250]
> SLJ - v43 - D '97 - p26+ [1-50]
> y   VOYA - v20 - F '98 - p366 [51-250]

Norman, Lilith
The Paddock: A Story in Praise of the Earth (Illus. by Robert Roennfeldt)
> SB - v33 - O '97 - p219 [1-50]

Norman, Roger
Treetime
> Obs - D 7 '97 - p17* [51-250]

Norris, Jill
Keeping Healthy
> SB - v33 - O '97 - p207+ [251-500]

What Is in the Sky?
> SB - v33 - Je '97 - p142 [51-250]

Norriss, Andrew
Aquila
> Obs - D 7 '97 - p17* [51-250]

North American Birds. Electronic Media Version
> r   Choice - v35 - Ja '98 - p846 [251-500]
> r   SB - v32 - D '96 - p280 [251-500]

Northeast, Brenda V
For the Love of Vincent
> Magpies - v12 - S '97 - p6 [51-250]

Norton, Mary
The Borrowers (Illus. by Beth Krush)
> NYTBR - v102 - N 16 '97 - p26 [1-50]

Magic Bedknob
> TES - Ja 2 '98 - p22* [1-50]

Norworth, Jack
Take Me Out to the Ballgame (Illus. by Alec Gillman)
> Inst - v107 - O '97 - p49 [1-50]

Nostlinger, Christine
Mini, Detective
> BL - v93 - Ag '97 - p1913 [1-50]

Notrog, Bryna
The Little Wooden Table (Illus. by Marilyn Smith Romeiser)
> Ch BWatch - v7 - Je '97 - p1 [51-250]
> Ch BWatch - v7 - S '97 - p5 [51-250]

Novac, Ana
The Beautiful Days of My Youth
> y   CCB-B - v51 - O '97 - p64 [51-250]
> y   PW - v244 - Jl 7 '97 - p69 [251-500]
> PW - v244 - N 3 '97 - p60 [51-250]
> y   SLJ - v43 - N '97 - p132+ [51-250]
> y   VOYA - v21 - Ap '98 - p70 [51-250]

Novak, Matt
Mouse TV (Illus. by Matt Novak)
> SLJ - v44 - Mr '98 - p120 [51-250]

Newt (Illus. by Matt Novak)
> RT - v51 - O '97 - p135 [1-50]

The Pillow War (Illus. by Matt Novak)
   BL - v94 - F 15 '98 - p1020 [51-250]
   KR - v66 - F 1 '98 - p199 [51-250]
   PW - v245 - F 9 '98 - p94 [51-250]
   SLJ - v44 - Mr '98 - p185 [51-250]

Numbers, an Australian Board Book
   Magpies - v12 - Mr '97 - p29 [51-250]

Numeroff, Laura
What Mommies Do Best/What Daddies Do Best (Illus. by Lynn Munsinger)
   PW - v245 - F 2 '98 - p89 [51-250]
   SLJ - v44 - Ap '98 - p106 [51-250]

Numeroff, Laura Joffe
The Chicken Sisters (Illus. by Sharleen Collicott)
   CBRS - v25 - Jl '97 - p149 [51-250]
   Ch BWatch - v7 - Je '97 - p7 [1-50]
   HB Guide - v8 - Fall '97 - p275 [1-50]
   NYTBR - v102 - S 14 '97 - p30 [1-50]
   Par - v72 - S '97 - p205 [51-250]
   SLJ - v43 - My '97 - p109 [51-250]

If You Give a Moose a Muffin (Benson). Book and Audio Version
   SLJ - v44 - Mr '98 - p157+ [51-250]

If You Give a Mouse a Cookie (Illus. by Felicia Bond)
   NYTBR - v102 - N 16 '97 - p26 [1-50]

If You Give a Pig a Pancake (Illus. by Felicia Bond)
   PW - v245 - Mr 16 '98 - p62 [51-250]

Nunes, S
The Last Dragon (Illus. by Chris K Soentpiet)
   ECEJ - v25 - Fall '97 - p49 [1-50]

Nuttall, Neil
Thoughts like an Ocean
   TES - N 7 '97 - p2* [1-50]

Nwanunobi, Onyeka
Soninke
   Cur R - v36 - Mr '97 - p12+ [51-250]

Nye, Naomi Shihab
Habibi
  y BL - v94 - S 15 '97 - p224 [51-250]
  y BL - v94 - Mr 15 '98 - p1218 [1-50]
     BL - v94 - Mr 15 '98 - p1224 [1-50]
  y CBRS - v26 - F '98 - p81 [51-250]
     CCB-B - v51 - N '97 - p94+ [51-250]
     HB - v73 - N '97 - p683+ [51-250]
  y KR - v65 - Ag 15 '97 - p1310 [51-250]
     NYTBR - v102 - N 16 '97 - p50 [501+]
     SLJ - v43 - S '97 - p223+ [51-250]
  y VOYA - v20 - F '98 - p388 [251-500]
  y VOYA - v21 - Ap '98 - p38 [1-50]

Lullaby Raft (Illus. by Vivienne Flesher)
   BL - v94 - N 1 '97 - p483 [51-250]
   CBRS - v26 - Win '98 - p63 [1-50]
   CCB-B - v51 - O '97 - p64+ [51-250]
   NYTBR - v102 - N 23 '97 - p32 [1-50]
   PW - v244 - Je 23 '97 - p90 [51-250]
   SLJ - v43 - S '97 - p189 [51-250]

Sitti's Secrets (Illus. by Nancy Carpenter)
   SLJ - v43 - Jl '97 - p35 [1-50]

The Space between Our Footsteps
  y BL - v94 - Mr 1 '98 - p1131 [51-250]
  y HB - v74 - Mr '98 - p229+ [251-500]
     KR - v66 - Ap 1 '98 - p499 [51-250]

This Same Sky
   Comw - v124 - D 5 '97 - p15 [1-50]

O

Ober, H
How Music Came to the World (Illus. by Carol Ober)
ECEJ - v25 - Fall '97 - p49 [1-50]

Oberman, Sheldon
The Always Prayer Shawl (Illus. by Ted Lewin)
Can CL - v23 - Fall '97 - p80+ [501+]
ECEJ - v25 - Fall '97 - p49 [1-50]

By the Hanukkah Light (Illus. by Neil Waldman)
BL - v94 - S 1 '97 - p139 [51-250]
CLW - v68 - D '97 - p85 [51-250]
CM:CanRev - v4 - O 3 '97 - pONL [251-500]
NYTBR - v102 - D 21 '97 - p18 [1-50]
PW - v244 - O 6 '97 - p52 [51-250]

The White Stone in the Castle Wall (Illus. by Les Tait)
Can CL - v22 - Win '96 - p121+ [501+]

Oborne, Martine
Juice the Pig (Illus. by Axel Scheffler)
HB Guide - v8 - Fall '97 - p276 [51-250]
SLJ - v43 - Jl '97 - p72 [51-250]

O'Brien, Claire
Sam's Sneaker Search (Illus. by Charles Fuge)
CBRS - v25 - Ag '97 - p161 [1-50]
CCB-B - v51 - S '97 - p21+ [51-250]
HB Guide - v8 - Fall '97 - p276 [1-50]
SLJ - v43 - Jl '97 - p72 [51-250]

O'Brien, John, 1953-
Mother Hubbard's Christmas (Illus. by John O'Brien)
RT - v51 - O '97 - p134 [1-50]

O'Brien, Robert C
Mrs. Frisby and the Rats of Nimh
BL - v94 - D 15 '97 - p695 [1-50]

O'Connor, Barbara
Beethoven in Paradise
y   CBRS - v25 - Jl '97 - p156+ [1-50]
    HB Guide - v8 - Fall '97 - p306 [51-250]
y   JAAL - v41 - F '98 - p410 [51-250]
    SLJ - v43 - Ap '97 - p140 [51-250]

O'Connor, Jane
Dragon Breath (Illus. by Jeff Spackman)
HB Guide - v8 - Fall '97 - p288 [51-250]

Nina, Nina, Star Ballerina (Illus. by DyAnne DiSalvo-Ryan)
BL - v93 - Ag '97 - p1909 [51-250]
HB Guide - v8 - Fall '97 - p287 [51-250]

O'Dell, Scott
Island of the Blue Dolphins
NYTBR - v102 - N 16 '97 - p26 [1-50]

O'Donnell, Elizabeth Lee
Winter Visitors (Illus. by Carol Schwartz)
BL - v94 - S 15 '97 - p243 [51-250]
CBRS - v26 - N '97 - p29 [51-250]
Ch BWatch - v8 - Ja '98 - p8 [1-50]

KR - v65 - O 1 '97 - p1536 [51-250]

O'Faolain, Eileen
Irish Sagas and Folk Tales
Bks Keeps - Jl '97 - p24 [51-250]

Offen, Hilda
The Bad Day ABC
TES - Je 27 '97 - p12* [51-250]

Good Girl, Gracie Growler!
Ch BWatch - v7 - S '97 - p3 [1-50]

There Might Be Giants
Bks Keeps - S '97 - p20 [51-250]
Sch Lib - v45 - Ag '97 - p132 [51-250]
TES - Jl 18 '97 - p35 [251-500]

Ogawa, Brian
To Tell the Truth
Ch BWatch - v7 - O '97 - p1 [51-250]

Ogburn, Jacqueline K
The Reptile Ball (Illus. by John O'Brien)
BL - v94 - O 15 '97 - p410 [51-250]
CCB-B - v50 - Jl '97 - p406 [51-250]
Ch BWatch - v7 - O '97 - p6+ [51-250]
Learning - v26 - S '97 - p45 [1-50]
PW - v244 - Ag 18 '97 - p95 [51-250]

Ogden, David
Dreambirds (Illus. by Jody Bergsma)
Ch BWatch - v7 - Jl '97 - p6 [51-250]

O'Grady, Kathleen
Sweet Secrets
Quill & Q - v63 - D '97 - p38 [251-500]

O'Grady, Scott
Basher Five-Two
y   BL - v94 - Mr 15 '98 - p1225 [1-50]
CCB-B - v50 - Jl '97 - p405 [51-250]
HB - v73 - Jl '97 - p476+ [51-250]
HB Guide - v8 - Fall '97 - p381 [51-250]
SLJ - v43 - Jl '97 - p110 [51-250]
y   VOYA - v21 - Ap '98 - p39+ [1-50]

O'Keefe, Frank
If It Rains Again Tomorrow, Can We Go Home?
CBRA - '96 - p488 [51-250]

Oktober, Tricia
Drought
Magpies - v12 - Jl '97 - p30 [51-250]

Old, Wendie C
George Washington
BL - v94 - S 15 '97 - p233 [51-250]
HB Guide - v8 - Fall '97 - p395 [51-250]
y   SLJ - v43 - D '97 - p144 [51-250]

Thomas Jefferson
SLJ - v44 - Mr '98 - p236+ [51-250]

Older, Effin
Randi's Missing Skates
Ch BWatch - v7 - Je '97 - p7 [1-50]

Older, Jules
Cow (Illus. by Lyn Severance)
PW - v244 - Ag 11 '97 - p400 [51-250]
SB - v33 - Ag '97 - p186 [1-50]

Oldfield, Jenny
Abandoned
Books - v11 - O '97 - p21 [1-50]

Intensive Care
Books - v11 - O '97 - p21 [1-50]

O'Leary, Patsy Baker
With Wings as Eagles
y   BL - v94 - O 15 '97 - p398 [51-250]
y   CBRS - v26 - D '97 - p47 [51-250]
CCB-B - v51 - D '97 - p136 [51-250]
y   KR - v65 - S 1 '97 - p1394 [51-250]
y   PW - v244 - O 13 '97 - p76 [51-250]
y   SLJ - v43 - D '97 - p127 [51-250]

Olesky, Walter
Business and Industry
ASBYP - v29 - Fall '96 - p50 [501+]

Entertainment
ASBYP - v29 - Fall '96 - p50 [501+]

Olien, Rebecca
Exploring Plants
SB - v33 - Je '97 - p144 [51-250]

Olney, Ross R

Lyn St. James: Driven to Be First

HB Guide - v8 - Fall '97 - p371 [51-250]

Olson, Gretchen

Joyride

y   BL - v94 - Mr 1 '98 - p1124 [51-250]
    KR - v66 - F 1 '98 - p199 [51-250]
y   PW - v245 - Ja 19 '98 - p379 [51-250]
y   SLJ - v44 - Ap '98 - p134+ [51-250]
y   VOYA - v21 - Ap '98 - p48 [51-250]

Oluikpe, Benson O

Swazi

SLJ - v43 - D '97 - p144 [51-250]

O'Malley, Kevin

Velcome (Illus. by Kevin O'Malley)

BL - v94 - S 1 '97 - p137 [51-250]
CBRS - v26 - O '97 - p16 [1-50]
CCB-B - v51 - N '97 - p79+ [501+]
KR - v65 - Jl 15 '97 - p1115 [51-250]
PW - v244 - Ag 18 '97 - p92 [51-250]
SLJ - v43 - S '97 - p189 [51-250]

O'Mara, Carmel

Good Morning, Good Night

Magpies - v12 - Jl '97 - p26 [51-250]

On the Farm (Balloon)

PW - v244 - N 10 '97 - p76 [1-50]

On the Farm (Star Bright)

PW - v244 - D 15 '97 - p60 [51-250]

One Small Square: Seashore. Electronic Media Version

y   BL - v94 - N 1 '97 - p492 [51-250]
    Emerg Lib - v24 - My '97 - p52 [51-250]

O'Neill, Judith

Hearing Voices

Magpies - v12 - Mr '97 - p34+ [251-500]

Ontario Science Centre

Plants (Illus. by Ray Boudreau)

Am Sci - v85 - N '97 - p560+ [51-250]

Onyefulu, Ifeoma

A Is for Africa

PW - v244 - Je 23 '97 - p93 [1-50]

Chidi Only Likes Blue (Illus. by Ifeoma Onyefulu)

Bks Keeps - N '97 - p23 [51-250]
BL - v94 - S 15 '97 - p243 [51-250]
Bloom Rev - v17 - N '97 - p32 [1-50]
CCB-B - v51 - N '97 - p95 [51-250]
HB - v73 - Jl '97 - p477 [51-250]
Sch Lib - v45 - N '97 - p187 [51-250]
SLJ - v43 - Ag '97 - p149+ [51-250]
TES - Ag 22 '97 - p25 [51-250]
TES - N 7 '97 - p9* [501+]

Emeka's Gift

TCMath - v4 - N '97 - p184 [51-250]

Ogbo: Sharing Life in an African Village (Illus. by Ifeoma Onyefulu)

RT - v51 - D '97 - p308 [51-250]
RT - v51 - F '98 - p431 [51-250]
SE - v61 - Ap '97 - p6* [1-50]

Opie, Iona

Humpty Dumpty and Other Rhymes (Illus. by Rosemary Wells)

BL - v94 - Mr 1 '98 - p1141 [51-250]
PW - v244 - N 10 '97 - p76 [51-250]
SLJ - v43 - D '97 - p98 [51-250]

Little Boy Blue and Other Rhymes (Illus. by Rosemary Wells)

BL - v94 - Mr 1 '98 - p1141 [51-250]
PW - v244 - N 10 '97 - p76 [51-250]
SLJ - v43 - D '97 - p98+ [51-250]

My Very First Mother Goose (Illus. by Rosemary Wells)

CM:CanRev - v4 - S 5 '97 - pONL [51-250]
Comw - v124 - D 5 '97 - p14 [51-250]
Inst - v106 - My '97 - p20+ [51-250]
Par - v72 - Je '97 - p189 [51-250]
TES - N 7 '97 - p2* [1-50]

The Opie Book of Nursery Rhymes (Illus. by Pauline Baynes)

PW - v244 - Jl 7 '97 - p70 [1-50]

Pussycat Pussycat and Other Rhymes (Illus. by Rosemary Wells)

BL - v94 - Mr 1 '98 - p1141 [51-250]
PW - v244 - N 10 '97 - p76 [51-250]
SLJ - v43 - D '97 - p98 [51-250]

Wee Willie Winkie and Other Rhymes (Illus. by Rosemary Wells)

    BL - v94 - Mr 1 '98 - p1141 [51-250]
    PW - v244 - N 10 '97 - p76 [51-250]
    SLJ - v43 - D '97 - p98+ [51-250]

Oppel, Kenneth

Follow That Star (Illus. by Kim LaFave)

    Can CL - v23 - Fall '97 - p85+ [501+]

Silverwing

    Can CL - v23 - Sum '97 - p52+ [501+]
    CBRS - v26 - D '97 - p47 [51-250]
    CCB-B - v51 - Ja '98 - p170 [251-500]
    HB - v73 - N '97 - p684 [251-500]
y   JAAL - v40 - My '97 - p677+ [501+]
y   KR - v65 - S 1 '97 - p1394 [51-250]
    PW - v244 - O 20 '97 - p76 [51-250]
    Quill & Q - v63 - Ap '97 - p37 [51-250]
y   VOYA - v21 - Ap '98 - p14 [1-50]
y   VOYA - v21 - Ap '98 - p58 [51-250]

Oppenheim, Joanne

Have You Seen Bugs? (Illus. by Ron Broda)

    CBRA - '96 - p533 [51-250]

Oppenheim, Shulamith Levey

The Hundredth Name (Illus. by Michael Hays)

    PW - v244 - S 1 '97 - p107 [1-50]

What Is the Full Moon Full Of? (Illus. by Cyd Moore)

    BL - v94 - D 1 '97 - p643 [51-250]
    CBRS - v26 - Win '98 - p63 [51-250]
    SLJ - v43 - D '97 - p99 [51-250]

Opposites (Fit-a-Shape)

    Magpies - v12 - Mr '97 - p29 [51-250]

Oram, Hiawyn

Baba Yaga and the Wise Doll (Illus. by Ruth Brown)

    BL - v94 - Ja 1 '98 - p818+ [51-250]
    HB - v74 - Mr '98 - p227 [51-250]
    KR - v66 - Ja 1 '98 - p60 [51-250]
    PW - v245 - Ja 12 '98 - p58 [51-250]
    SLJ - v44 - Mr '98 - p199+ [51-250]

Cat in a Corner (Illus. by Judith Lawton)

    TES - Jl 11 '97 - p14* [51-250]

Dog in Danger (Illus. by Judith Lawton)

    TES - Jl 11 '97 - p14* [51-250]

Dolphin SOS (Illus. by Judith Lawton)

    TES - Jl 11 '97 - p14* [51-250]

Mole's Moon (Illus. by Susan Varley)

    Sch Lib - v45 - Ag '97 - p132 [51-250]

Monkey in Space (Illus. by Judith Lawton)

    TES - Jl 11 '97 - p14* [51-250]

Wise Doll (Illus. by Ruth Brown)

    Obs - D 7 '97 - p17* [51-250]

O'Rear, Sybil J

Jesse Chisholm: The Story of a Trailblazer and Peacemaker in Early Texas and Oklahoma

    HB Guide - v8 - Fall '97 - p396 [51-250]
    SLJ - v43 - Ag '97 - p173 [51-250]

Orgel, Doris

The Princess and the God

y   Kliatt - v32 - Mr '98 - p20 [51-250]
    PW - v244 - D 1 '97 - p55 [1-50]

Two Crows Counting

    Ch BWatch - v7 - My '97 - p6 [1-50]

Orgill, Roxane

If I Only Had a Horn (Illus. by Leonard Jenkins)

    BL - v94 - N 1 '97 - p476 [251-500]
    CBRS - v26 - N '97 - p29 [51-250]
    CCB-B - v51 - S '97 - p22 [251-500]
    KR - v65 - Ag 15 '97 - p1310 [51-250]
    NW - v130 - D 1 '97 - p77+ [51-250]
    SLJ - v43 - S '97 - p206+ [51-250]

Orlev, Uri

The Lady with the Hat

y   Kliatt - v32 - Mr '98 - p14 [51-250]
    PW - v244 - D 1 '97 - p55 [1-50]
    SS - v88 - My '97 - p139+ [501+]

Orme, David
We Was Robbed (Illus. by Marc Vyvyan-Jones)
    Bks Keeps - Jl '97 - p23 [51-250]
    Sch Lib - v45 - Ag '97 - p156 [51-250]

Ormerod, Jan
Peek-A-Boo! (Illus. by Jan Ormerod)
    KR - v66 - Ja 1 '98 - p60 [51-250]

Who's Whose? (Illus. by Jan Ormerod)
    BL - v94 - Mr 15 '98 - p1241 [51-250]
    KR - v66 - Mr 1 '98 - p343 [51-250]
    PW - v245 - Ja 19 '98 - p377+ [51-250]
    SLJ - v44 - Ap '98 - p106+ [51-250]

Orna-Ornstein, John
The Story of Money
    Sch Lib - v45 - Ag '97 - p153 [51-250]

Orozco, Jose-Luis
Diez Deditos (Illus. by Elisa Kleven)
    BL - v94 - Ja 1 '98 - p819 [51-250]
    CCB-B - v51 - Mr '98 - p254 [51-250]
    HB - v74 - Mr '98 - p231 [251-500]
    KR - v65 - D 15 '97 - p1837 [51-250]
    PW - v244 - D 8 '97 - p74 [51-250]
    SLJ - v44 - F '98 - p132 [51-250]

Orr, Richard
The Burrow Book (Illus. by Richard Orr)
    SLJ - v43 - D '97 - p104 [51-250]

Nature Cross-Sections
    ASBYP - v29 - Sum '96 - p26+ [251-500]

Orr, Wendy
Paradise Palace (Illus. by David Mackintosh)
    Magpies - v12 - S '97 - p32 [51-250]

Sally's Painting Room (Illus. by Janice Bowles)
    Magpies - v12 - S '97 - p31 [51-250]

Ortiz, Simon J
The People Shall Continue
    BL - v93 - Je 1 '97 - p1700 [1-50]

Orwin, Joanna
The Tar Dragon (Illus. by Wendy Hodder)
    Magpies - v12 - S '97 - p5*+ [51-250]

Osborne, Mary Pope
American Tall Tales (Illus. by Michael McCurdy)
    SLJ - v43 - N '97 - p41 [1-50]

The Magic Tree House Series
    Par - v72 - Je '97 - p190 [51-250]

One World, Many Religions
    RT - v51 - O '97 - p150 [51-250]
    SE - v61 - Ap '97 - p15* [1-50]

Rocking Horse Christmas (Illus. by Ned Bittinger)
    BL - v94 - O 1 '97 - p338 [51-250]
    CBRS - v26 - N '97 - p29 [51-250]
    CCB-B - v51 - D '97 - p136+ [51-250]
    Ch BWatch - v7 - D '97 - p1 [1-50]
    CM:CanRev - v4 - Ja 2 '98 - pONL [251-500]
    PW - v244 - O 6 '97 - p55 [51-250]

Osborne, Rick
I Want to Know about the Bible
    PW - v245 - F 23 '98 - p67 [51-250]

Osofsky, Audrey
Dreamcatcher (Illus. by Ed Young)
    ECEJ - v25 - Fall '97 - p49 [1-50]

Free to Dream
    RT - v51 - S '97 - p54 [51-250]
 y RT - v51 - D '97 - p308 [51-250]

Ostheeren, Ingrid
Jonathan Mouse (Illus. by Agnes Mathieu)
    PW - v244 - N 10 '97 - p76 [1-50]

Osuchowska, Isia
The Gift: A Magical Story about Caring for the Earth
    HB Guide - v8 - Fall '97 - p276 [51-250]

Otfinoski, Steven
Around the Track
    Ch BWatch - v7 - D '97 - p7 [1-50]
    SLJ - v44 - Ap '98 - p122 [51-250]

On the High Seas
  Ch BWatch - v7 - D '97 - p7 [1-50]

On the Road
  Ch BWatch - v7 - D '97 - p7 [1-50]

Pedaling Along
  SLJ - v43 - Je '97 - p110 [51-250]

Riding the Rails
  SLJ - v43 - Je '97 - p110 [51-250]

To the Rescue
  SLJ - v43 - Je '97 - p110 [51-250]

Wild on Wheels
  Ch BWatch - v7 - D '97 - p7 [1-50]

Otis, James, 1848-1912
Toby Tyler, or, Ten Weeks with a Circus (Purinton). Audio Version
  y   Kliatt - v31 - Jl '97 - p52 [51-250]
      SLJ - v44 - Ja '98 - p68 [51-250]

Otten, Charlotte F
January Rides the Wind (Illus. by Todd L W Doney)
      BL - v94 - O 15 '97 - p403 [51-250]
      BL - v94 - Ja 1 '98 - p736 [1-50]
      CBRS - v26 - D '97 - p44 [1-50]
      CCB-B - v51 - Ja '98 - p171 [51-250]
      KR - v65 - S 15 '97 - p1461 [51-250]

Otteson, Paul
Kids Who Walk on Volcanoes
  Ch BWatch - v7 - S '97 - p4 [1-50]

Ouellet, Danielle
Quebec. Rev. Ed.
  CBRA - '96 - p512+ [501+]

Oughton, Jerrie
The War in Georgia
  y   BL - v94 - Mr 15 '98 - p1218 [1-50]
  y   CCB-B - v50 - Je '97 - p368+ [51-250]
      HB Guide - v8 - Fall '97 - p306 [51-250]
      SLJ - v43 - My '97 - p138+ [51-250]
  y   VOYA - v21 - Ap '98 - p38 [1-50]

Our Amazing Bodies
  ASBYP - v29 - Sum '96 - p41+ [501+]

Our World in Danger
  ASBYP - v29 - Sum '96 - p65+ [501+]

Ovenell-Carter, Julie
Adam's Daycare (Illus. by Ruth Ohi)
  BL - v94 - Ja 1 '98 - p824+ [51-250]
  SLJ - v44 - Ja '98 - p90 [51-250]

Owen, Annie
From Snowflakes to Sandcastles
  Bks Keeps - My '97 - p20 [51-250]

Owen, Roy
My Night Forest (Illus. by Amy Cordova)
  SB - v33 - O '97 - p219 [1-50]

Owens, Ann-Maureen
Forts of Canada (Illus. by Don Kilby)
  Beav - v77 - Je '97 - p44 [51-250]
  Can CL - v22 - Win '96 - p101+ [501+]
  CBRA - '96 - p509 [51-250]

Owens, Thomas S
The Chicago Bulls Basketball Team
  BL - v94 - O 15 '97 - p400 [51-250]

Owens, Yvonne
The Cup of Mari Anu (Illus. by Kevan Jane Miller)
  CBRA - '96 - p488 [51-250]

Owomoyela, Oyekan
Yoruba Trickster Tales
  y   CAY - v18 - Win '97 - p6 [51-250]
  y   Choice - v35 - F '98 - p987 [51-250]
  y   Kliatt - v32 - Ja '98 - p21+ [51-250]
  y   LJ - v122 - Jl '97 - p92 [51-250]
      PW - v244 - Ag 4 '97 - p76 [1-50]

Oxenbury, Helen
Tom and Pippo in the Garden
  Par - v73 - F '98 - p185 [1-50]

Oxford Children's Encyclopedia on CD-ROM. Electronic Media Version
  r   HT - v47 - D '97 - p53 [51-250]
  r   Magpies - v12 - My '97 - p44+ [501+]
  r   PW - v244 - O 13 '97 - p77 [51-250]

Oxlade, Chris

Crime Detection

   SLJ - v43 - N '97 - p111 [51-250]

Electronic Communication (Illus. by Colin Mier)

   BL - v94 - Ja 1 '98 - p806 [51-250]
   SB - v34 - Ap '98 - p78 [51-250]
   SLJ - v44 - F '98 - p103 [51-250]

Movies

   SLJ - v43 - N '97 - p111 [51-250]

Telecommunications

   BL - v93 - Je 1 '97 - p1696 [51-250]
   HB Guide - v8 - Fall '97 - p358+ [51-250]
   SB - v33 - O '97 - p207 [251-500]

P

Pachai, Bridglal
William Hall: Winner of the Victoria Cross
CBRA - '96 - p509+ [51-250]

Pacheco, Gumersindo
Maria Virginia Esta De Vacaciones (Illus. by Nelson Dominguez)
Bkbird - v35 - Sum '97 - p57 [1-50]

Padowicz, Julian
Runaway Horses, Chickens, and Other Upset People (Padowicz). Audio Version
SLJ - v44 - Ap '98 - p82 [51-250]

Page, Debra
Orcas around Me (Illus. by Leslie W Bowman)
BL - v93 - Ag '97 - p1903 [51-250]
CCB-B - v51 - S '97 - p22+ [51-250]
CLW - v68 - D '97 - p84 [51-250]
HB - v74 - Ja '98 - p94 [51-250]
KR - v65 - Je 15 '97 - p954+ [51-250]
Par Ch - Awards '97 - p4 [51-250]
PW - v244 - Je 23 '97 - p92 [51-250]
SLJ - v43 - S '97 - p207 [51-250]

Page, Jan
Dog on a Broomstick (Illus. by Nick Price)
Bks Keeps - S '97 - p23 [51-250]
Sch Lib - v45 - Ag '97 - p147 [51-250]

Page, Katherine Hall
Christie and Company Down East
SLJ - v43 - Jl '97 - p96 [51-250]

Page, Robin
The Alphabet Sticker Book
Par - v72 - Je '97 - p189 [1-50]

Paget, Campbell
Kaspar's Greatest Discovery (Illus. by Reg Cartwright)
Sch Lib - v45 - N '97 - p187 [51-250]

Paint (Art House)
Ch BWatch - v7 - N '97 - p5 [51-250]

Painter, Mike
Satellite Fever (Illus. by Mic Rolph)
Bks Keeps - N '97 - p25 [51-250]

Palatini, Margie
Elf Help (Illus. by Mike Reed)
KR - v65 - D 1 '97 - p1777+ [51-250]
PW - v244 - O 6 '97 - p59 [1-50]

Moosetache (Illus. by Henry Cole)
CBRS - v25 - Jl '97 - p149 [1-50]
Ch BWatch - v7 - My '97 - p4 [1-50]
HB Guide - v8 - Fall '97 - p276 [51-250]
Inst - v107 - Ja '98 - p26 [51-250]
SLJ - v43 - My '97 - p109 [51-250]

Piggie Pie! (Illus. by Howard Fine)
Inst - v107 - Ja '98 - p26+ [1-50]
Learning - v26 - Ag '97 - p22 [51-250]
PW - v244 - Ag 18 '97 - p95 [1-50]

The Wonder Worm Wars
BL - v94 - O 1 '97 - p333 [51-250]
KR - v65 - Ag 15 '97 - p1310 [51-250]
SLJ - v43 - D '97 - p99 [51-250]

Zak's Lunch (Illus. by Howard Fine)
KR - v66 - Ap 15 '98 - p585 [51-250]

Paley, Vivian Gussin
The Girl with the Brown Crayon
  LATBR - Ap 27 '97 - p7 [501+]
  NY - v73 - O 6 '97 - p114 [1-50]

Pallotta, Jerry
The Airplane Alphabet Book (Illus. by Rob Bolster)
  CBRS - v25 - My '97 - p112 [1-50]
  HB Guide - v8 - Fall '97 - p359 [51-250]
  SLJ - v43 - Jl '97 - p86 [51-250]

Palmer, Edward
T-Ball Coloring Book
  Ch BWatch - v7 - S '97 - p1 [51-250]

Panagopoulos, Janie Lynn
Little Ship under Full Sail
  CCB-B - v51 - Mr '98 - p254 [51-250]

Pandit, Maneesha S
It's I Can Do Anything Day! (Illus. by Lynn Torola)
  Ch BWatch - v7 - Je '97 - p1 [51-250]

Pank, Rachel
Delilah Digs for Treasure
  Bks Keeps - S '97 - p24 [51-250]
  Sch Lib - v45 - N '97 - p201 [51-250]
  TES - N 14 '97 - p14* [51-250]

Paparone, Pamela
Los Cinco Patitos (Illus. by Pamela Paparone)
  BL - v94 - D 15 '97 - p707 [1-50]
  SLJ - v43 - Ag '97 - p181 [51-250]

Paper (Art House)
  Ch BWatch - v7 - N '97 - p5 [51-250]

Paraskevas, Betty
The Tangerine Bear (Illus. by Michael Paraskevas)
  BL - v94 - N 1 '97 - p483+ [51-250]
  CBRS - v26 - Ja '98 - p51+ [51-250]
  CCB-B - v51 - N '97 - p95+ [51-250]
  Ch BWatch - v8 - Ja '98 - p3 [1-50]
  KR - v65 - Jl 15 '97 - p1119 [51-250]
  PW - v244 - Jl 28 '97 - p73 [51-250]

Pare, Michael A
Sports Stars Series 1. Vols. 1-2
  r   BL - v94 - S 1 '97 - p158 [51-250]

Sports Stars Series 2. Vols. 1-2
  r   BL - v94 - S 1 '97 - p158 [51-250]

Sports Stars Series 3
  r   BL - v94 - S 1 '97 - p158 [51-250]
  r   SLJ - v44 - F '98 - p138+ [51-250]

Pare, Roger
On the Go (Illus. by Roger Pare)
  CBRA - '96 - p454 [51-250]

Parish, Herman
Bravo, Amelia Bedelia! (Illus. by Lynn Sweat)
  HB Guide - v8 - Fall '97 - p276 [51-250]
  SLJ - v43 - Ap '97 - p114 [51-250]

Parish, Peggy
Amelia Bedelia (Illus. by Fritz Siebel)
  HB Guide - v8 - Fall '97 - p339 [1-50]
  SLJ - v43 - Ag '97 - p181 [51-250]

Park, Barbara
Junie B. Jones and That Meanie Jim's Birthday (Illus. by Denise Brunkus)
  RT - v51 - O '97 - p133 [1-50]

Junie B. Jones Has a Monster Under Her Bed (Illus. by Denise Brunkus)
  SLJ - v43 - N '97 - p96 [51-250]

Junie B. Jones Is a Party Animal (Illus. by Denise Brunkus)
  SLJ - v44 - F '98 - p89 [51-250]

Junie B. Jones Is Not a Crook (Illus. by Denise Brunkus)
  SLJ - v43 - N '97 - p96 [51-250]

Mick Harte Was Here
  y   JAAL - v41 - N '97 - p212 [51-250]
  SLJ - v44 - Ja '98 - p43 [1-50]

Mick Harte Was Here (Lubotsky). Audio Version
  y   BL - v94 - N 1 '97 - p495 [51-250]
  HB - v73 - N '97 - p704+ [51-250]
  SLJ - v44 - Ja '98 - p67+ [51-250]
  SLJ - v44 - Ap '98 - p38+ [1-50]

Parker, Barry
Chaos in the Cosmos
SB - v32 - D '96 - p263 [51-250]

Parker, David L
Stolen Dreams (Illus. by David L Parker)
y   BL - v94 - N 1 '97 - p459 [51-250]
y   HB - v74 - Mr '98 - p236+ [251-500]
     PW - v244 - N 10 '97 - p75 [51-250]
y   VOYA - v20 - F '98 - p403 [51-250]

Parker, Jane
The Fantastic Book of Horses
Ch BWatch - v7 - My '97 - p7 [1-50]
HB Guide - v8 - Fall '97 - p354 [51-250]
SLJ - v43 - Ag '97 - p170 [51-250]

Rainforests
KR - v65 - N 1 '97 - p1648 [51-250]
SLJ - v44 - Ja '98 - p104 [51-250]

Parker, Janice
Great African Americans in Film
BL - v94 - S 15 '97 - p228 [51-250]
Ch BWatch - v7 - Je '97 - p4 [51-250]
HB Guide - v8 - Fall '97 - p384 [51-250]
SLJ - v43 - D '97 - p138 [51-250]

Grizzly Bears (Illus. by Warren Clark)
CBRA - '96 - p529 [51-250]
HB Guide - v8 - Fall '97 - p353 [51-250]
Quill & Q - v63 - My '97 - p42 [51-250]

Parker, John
Not Nice Stories
Magpies - v12 - Mr '97 - p7* [51-250]

Parker, Steve
Airplanes (Illus. by Peter Wilks)
ASBYP - v29 - Sum '96 - p62+ [501+]

Beginner's Guide to Animal Autopsy (Illus. by Rob Stone)
CBRS - v26 - Ja '98 - p60 [51-250]

Blood (Illus. by Ian Thompson)
SLJ - v44 - Ap '98 - p122 [51-250]

The Brain and Nervous System
BL - v93 - Je 1 '97 - p1696 [51-250]

Ch BWatch - v7 - N '97 - p7 [1-50]
y   HB Guide - v8 - Fall '97 - p355 [51-250]
Magpies - v12 - Jl '97 - p43+ [251-500]
SB - v33 - Ag '97 - p180 [51-250]
SLJ - v43 - Ag '97 - p162 [51-250]

Computers
HB Guide - v8 - Fall '97 - p358+ [51-250]
SB - v33 - O '97 - p207 [51-250]

The Earth (Illus. by Tony Kenyon)
ASBYP - v29 - Sum '96 - p62+ [501+]

Flight and Flying Machines
SB - v32 - D '96 - p259 [1-50]

High in the Sky
Ch BWatch - v7 - D '97 - p7 [1-50]
HB Guide - v8 - Fall '97 - p359 [51-250]
Sch Lib - v45 - N '97 - p206 [51-250]
SLJ - v44 - Ja '98 - p104 [51-250]

The Human Body (Discoveries)
Bks Keeps - Jl '97 - p26 [51-250]
Magpies - v12 - Jl '97 - p43+ [251-500]
TES - My 9 '97 - pR16 [51-250]

The Human Body (What If) (Illus. by Tony Kenyon)
ASBYP - v29 - Sum '96 - p62+ [501+]

The Human Body: An Amazing Inside Look at You
HB Guide - v8 - Fall '97 - p356 [51-250]

The Lungs and Respiratory System
y   HB Guide - v8 - Fall '97 - p355 [51-250]
Magpies - v12 - Jl '97 - p43+ [251-500]
SB - v33 - Ag '97 - p180 [51-250]
SLJ - v43 - Ag '97 - p162 [51-250]

Making Tracks
Ch BWatch - v7 - D '97 - p7 [1-50]
HB Guide - v8 - Fall '97 - p359 [51-250]
Sch Lib - v45 - N '97 - p206 [51-250]
SLJ - v44 - Ja '98 - p104 [51-250]

Professor Protein's Fitness, Health, Hygiene, and Relaxation Tonic (Illus. by Rob Shone)
SB - v32 - D '96 - p276 [51-250]
SB - v33 - Ag '97 - p186 [1-50]

The Reproductive System
    Ch BWatch - v7 - N '97 - p7 [1-50]
y SB - v34 - Ap '98 - p76 [51-250]
    SLJ - v44 - F '98 - p111 [51-250]

Rocks and Minerals
    CLW - v68 - S '97 - p63 [51-250]

Satellites
    HB Guide - v8 - Fall '97 - p358+ [51-250]
    SB - v33 - N '97 - p244 [51-250]

Sharks
    ASBYP - v29 - Fall '96 - p24 [251-500]
    SB - v32 - D '96 - p275+ [51-250]

Space (Illus. by Tony Kenyon)
    ASBYP - v29 - Sum '96 - p62+ [501+]

What If...Giraffes (Illus. by John Lobban)
    RT - v51 - S '97 - p55 [51-250]

What's Inside Airplanes? (Illus. by K Madison)
    ASBYP - v29 - Sum '96 - p63+ [501+]

What's Inside Buildings? (Illus. by B Watson)
    ASBYP - v29 - Sum '96 - p63+ [501+]

Parker, Vic

Bearobics: A Hip-Hop Counting Story (Illus. by Emily Bolam)
    CBRS - v25 - Je '97 - p124 [51-250]
    HB Guide - v8 - Fall '97 - p276 [51-250]

Parkinson, David

Pinkerton Inks (Illus. by Guy Parker-Rees)
    Magpies - v12 - My '97 - p5 [51-250]

The Young Oxford Book of the Movies
r   KR - v65 - D 15 '97 - p1837 [51-250]
r   PW - v244 - D 15 '97 - p60 [51-250]
yr SLJ - v44 - Mr '98 - p238 [51-250]
yr VOYA - v21 - Ap '98 - p71 [51-250]

Parkison, Jami

Amazing Mallika (Illus. by Itoko Maeno)
    CBRS - v25 - My '97 - p116 [51-250]
    HB Guide - v8 - Fall '97 - p276 [51-250]
    SLJ - v43 - Jl '97 - p72 [51-250]

Parks, Rosa

Dear Mrs. Parks
y RT - v51 - N '97 - p244 [51-250]
    RT - v51 - D '97 - p334 [51-250]
    SE - v61 - Ap '97 - p4* [1-50]

I Am Rosa Parks (Illus. by Wil Clay)
    CCB-B - v50 - Je '97 - p369 [51-250]
    Ch BWatch - v7 - S '97 - p8 [1-50]
    HB Guide - v8 - Fall '97 - p326 [51-250]
    SLJ - v43 - My '97 - p123 [51-250]

Parks, Van Dyke

Jump Again! (Illus. by Barry Moser)
    PW - v244 - S 29 '97 - p91 [1-50]

Jump on Over (Illus. by Barry Moser)
    PW - v245 - Mr 9 '98 - p70 [1-50]

Parmiani, Floria N

Classic Italian Tales
    Ch BWatch - v7 - Jl '97 - p1 [51-250]

San Francisco in Colors
    Ch BWatch - v7 - Jl '97 - p1 [51-250]

Parry-Jones, Jemima

Eagle
    Sch Lib - v45 - N '97 - p206 [51-250]

Eagle and Birds of Prey (Illus. by Frank Greenaway)
    Ch BWatch - v7 - Jl '97 - p3 [51-250]
    HB Guide - v8 - Fall '97 - p352 [51-250]

Parsons, Alexandra

I Am Special (Illus. by Ann Johns)
    HB Guide - v8 - Fall '97 - p317 [51-250]

I'm Happy, I'm Healthy! (Illus. by Ann Johns)
    HB Guide - v8 - Fall '97 - p356 [51-250]

My Wonderful Body (Illus. by Ann Johns)
    HB Guide - v8 - Fall '97 - p356 [51-250]

You're Special, Too (Illus. by Ann Johns)
    HB Guide - v8 - Fall '97 - p317 [51-250]

Parsons, Martin
*The History Detective Investigates
Local History*
> Bks Keeps - Jl '97 - p26 [51-250]
> Sch Lib - v45 - Ag '97 - p153 [51-250]

Partridge, Elizabeth
Clara and the HooDoo Man
> RT - v51 - S '97 - p55 [51-250]

Paschkis, Julie
Play All Day (Illus. by Julie Paschkis)
> KR - v66 - Mr 1 '98 - p346 [51-250]

Pascoe, Elaine
Animal Intelligence
> Ch BWatch - v7 - N '97 - p7 [1-50]
> KR - v65 - S 15 '97 - p1461 [51-250]
> SLJ - v43 - D '97 - p144+ [51-250]

*Butterflies and Moths (Illus. by
Dwight Kuhn)*
> Ch BWatch - v7 - Ap '97 - p3 [1-50]
> SB - v33 - Ag '97 - p186 [1-50]
> SLJ - v43 - Ap '97 - p130 [51-250]
> SLMQ - v25 - Win '97 - p118 [1-50]

Earthworms (Illus. by Dwight Kuhn)
> SB - v33 - Ag '97 - p186 [1-50]

Mysteries of the Rain Forest
> Ch BWatch - v7 - N '97 - p7 [1-50]
> SLJ - v44 - F '98 - p121 [51-250]

New Dinosaurs
> Ch BWatch - v7 - N '97 - p7 [1-50]
> SLJ - v44 - F '98 - p121 [51-250]

The Right to Vote
> Ch BWatch - v7 - Je '97 - p4 [1-50]
> HB Guide - v8 - Fall '97 - p325 [51-250]
> SLJ - v43 - My '97 - p148 [51-250]

*Seeds and Seedlings (Illus. by Dwight
Kuhn)*
> SB - v33 - Ag '97 - p186 [1-50]
> SB - v34 - Ap '98 - p80 [51-250]

Tadpoles (Illus. by Dwight Kuhn)
> Ch BWatch - v7 - Ap '97 - p3 [1-50]
> SB - v33 - Ag '97 - p186 [1-50]

Virtual Reality
> Ch BWatch - v7 - N '97 - p7 [1-50]

Pastuchiv, Olga
*Minas and the Fish (Illus. by Olga
Pastuchiv)*
> HB Guide - v8 - Fall '97 - p276 [51-250]
> SLJ - v43 - My '97 - p109+ [51-250]

Patent, Dorothy Hinshaw
Apple Trees (Illus. by William Munoz)
> KR - v66 - F 1 '98 - p199+ [51-250]
> SLJ - v44 - Ap '98 - p122 [51-250]

*Back to the Wild (Illus. by William
Munoz)*
> CCB-B - v51 - S '97 - p23 [51-250]
> HB Guide - v8 - Fall '97 - p328 [51-250]
> KR - v65 - Ap 15 '97 - p646 [51-250]
> NH - v106 - D '97 - p10 [51-250]
> SB - v33 - D '97 - p276 [251-500]
> SLJ - v43 - Ap '97 - p155 [51-250]

Biodiversity (Illus. by William Munoz)
> y   Am Sci - v85 - N '97 - p559 [51-250]
> SB - v32 - D '96 - p272 [51-250]
> SB - v33 - Ag '97 - p186 [1-50]
> y   VOYA - v20 - Ag '97 - p165 [51-250]

Children Save the Rain Forest
> BL - v94 - D 1 '97 - p629 [1-50]

*Eagles of America (Illus. by William
Munoz)*
> ASBYP - v29 - Sum '96 - p27+ [251-500]

Feathers (Illus. by William Munoz)
> SLJ - v43 - My '97 - p57 [1-50]

*Flashy Fantastic Rain Forest Frogs
(Illus. by Kendahl Jan Jubb)*
> BL - v94 - D 1 '97 - p629 [1-50]
> HB Guide - v8 - Fall '97 - p351 [51-250]

Pigeons (Illus. by William Munoz)
> BL - v94 - S 1 '97 - p120 [51-250]

Paterson, Cynthia
The Foxwood Treasury
> Books - v11 - D '97 - p21 [51-250]
> Obs - D 7 '97 - p18* [51-250]

Paterson, John
Images of God (Illus. by Alexander Koshkin)
>   PW - v245 - Mr 23 '98 - p95 [51-250]
>   SLJ - v44 - Ap '98 - p152 [51-250]

Paterson, Katherine
Bridge to Terabithia (Illus. by Donna Diamond)
>   NYTBR - v102 - N 16 '97 - p26 [1-50]

The Great Gilly Hopkins (Bresnahan). Audio Version
>   BL - v94 - S 15 '97 - p250 [51-250]
>   SLJ - v44 - Ap '98 - p38 [1-50]

Jip: His Story
>   RT - v51 - S '97 - p59 [51-250]
> y   VOYA - v20 - Ap '97 - p32 [51-250]

Lyddie
> y   BL - v93 - Ag '97 - p1913 [1-50]
>   SLJ - v43 - S '97 - p131 [1-50]
> y   VOYA - v21 - Ap '98 - p43 [1-50]

Marvin's Best Christmas Present Ever (Illus. by Jane Clark Brown)
>   BL - v94 - S 1 '97 - p140 [51-250]
>   HB - v73 - N '97 - p684+ [51-250]
>   KR - v65 - S 15 '97 - p1461 [51-250]
>   PW - v244 - O 6 '97 - p55 [51-250]
>   SLJ - v43 - D '97 - p27 [1-50]

Parzival: The Quest of the Grail Knight
>   BL - v94 - Mr 1 '98 - p1123 [51-250]
>   BW - v28 - Mr 1 '98 - p11 [251-500]
> y   Kliatt - v32 - Mr '98 - p5 [51-250]
> y   KR - v66 - Ja 1 '98 - p60+ [51-250]
>   PW - v245 - F 9 '98 - p96 [51-250]
>   SLJ - v44 - F '98 - p109 [51-250]

Patilla, Peter
Mental Maths Daily Workout. Bks. 1-5
>   TES - My 23 '97 - pR10 [251-500]

Paton Walsh, Jill
Connie Came to Play (Illus. by Stephen Lambert)
>   Bks Keeps - S '97 - p20 [51-250]

When I Was Little Like You (Illus. by Stephen Lambert)
>   KR - v65 - O 15 '97 - p1585+ [51-250]
>   PW - v244 - N 17 '97 - p60 [51-250]

>   SLJ - v43 - D '97 - p102+ [51-250]
>   Spec - v279 - D 6 '97 - p43 [1-50]

Patrick, Denise Lewis
The Adventures of Midnight Son
>   BL - v94 - D 15 '97 - p698 [51-250]
>   CBRS - v26 - F '98 - p81 [51-250]
>   CCB-B - v51 - Ja '98 - p171 [51-250]
>   KR - v65 - O 15 '97 - p1586 [51-250]
>   SLJ - v43 - D '97 - p127+ [51-250]

Car Washing Street (Illus. by John Ward)
>   ECEJ - v25 - Fall '97 - p49 [1-50]

Red Dancing Shoes (Illus. by James E Ransome)
>   ECEJ - v25 - Fall '97 - p49 [1-50]
>   PW - v245 - Ja 26 '98 - p93 [1-50]

Patrick, Diane
The New York Public Library Amazing African American History
>   BL - v94 - F 15 '98 - p996 [51-250]
>   KR - v65 - D 15 '97 - p1838 [51-250]
>   PW - v245 - Ja 5 '98 - p69 [51-250]
> y   SLJ - v44 - Ap '98 - p152 [51-250]

Patrick-Wexler, Diane
Toni Morrison
>   HB Guide - v8 - Fall '97 - p379 [51-250]
>   SLJ - v44 - F '98 - p114 [51-250]

Patron, Susan
Maybe Yes, Maybe No, Maybe Maybe (Illus. by Dorothy Donahue)
>   SLJ - v44 - Ja '98 - p43 [1-50]

Patterson, Elizabeth Burman
Whose Eyes Are These?
>   BL - v94 - S 1 '97 - p129 [51-250]

Patterson, Geoffrey
The Naughty Boy and the Strawberry Horse (Illus. by Geoffrey Patterson)
>   SLJ - v43 - Jl '97 - p72+ [51-250]

Patterson, Jose
Israel
>   Bks Keeps - S '97 - p28 [51-250]
>   HB Guide - v8 - Fall '97 - p392 [51-250]

Magpies - v12 - Jl '97 - p42 [251-500]

Patterson, Paul
Anastasia: A Princess in Paris
Ch BWatch - v7 - D '97 - p2 [51-250]

Paul, Ann Whitford
Hello Toes! Hello Feet! (Illus. by Nadine Bernard Westcott)
BL - v94 - Mr 1 '98 - p1141 [51-250]
KR - v66 - Ja 15 '98 - p116 [51-250]
PW - v245 - F 9 '98 - p94 [51-250]
SLJ - v44 - Mr '98 - p186 [51-250]

The Seasons Sewn (Illus. by Michael McCurdy)
SE - v61 - Ap '97 - p11* [1-50]

Paul, Tessa
By Lakes and Rivers
Ch BWatch - v7 - Jl '97 - p3 [1-50]
Quill & Q - v63 - Je '97 - p64 [251-500]

By the Seashore
Ch BWatch - v7 - Jl '97 - p3 [1-50]
Quill & Q - v63 - Je '97 - p64 [251-500]

In Fields and Meadows
Ch BWatch - v7 - Jl '97 - p3 [1-50]
Quill & Q - v63 - Je '97 - p64 [251-500]

In Woods and Forests
Ch BWatch - v7 - Jl '97 - p3 [1-50]
Quill & Q - v63 - Je '97 - p64 [251-500]

Paulsen, Gary
Amos Binder, Secret Agent
SLJ - v43 - Ap '97 - p114 [51-250]

Captive! Gary Paulsen World of Adventure (Woodman). Audio Version
y   Kliatt - v31 - N '97 - p38 [51-250]
SLJ - v43 - N '97 - p68 [51-250]

A Christmas Sonata (Illus. by Leslie W Bowman)
PW - v244 - O 6 '97 - p58 [1-50]

Danger on Midnight River (Woodman). Audio Version
y   Kliatt - v31 - N '97 - p38 [51-250]
SLJ - v43 - N '97 - p68 [51-250]

Hatchet
NYTBR - v102 - N 16 '97 - p26 [1-50]
y   VOYA - v21 - Ap '98 - p42 [1-50]

Hook 'Em, Snotty (Woodman). Audio Version
SLJ - v43 - N '97 - p68 [51-250]

Ice Race
Magpies - v12 - My '97 - p38 [51-250]

My Life in Dog Years (Illus. by Ruth Wright Paulsen)
BL - v94 - Ja 1 '98 - p799 [51-250]
y   CCB-B - v51 - Mr '98 - p254+ [51-250]
KR - v65 - N 15 '97 - p1711 [51-250]
PW - v244 - D 1 '97 - p55 [51-250]
SLJ - v44 - Mr '98 - p238 [51-250]
y   VOYA - v21 - Ap '98 - p71+ [51-250]

The Rifle
Ch BWatch - v7 - Je '97 - p7 [1-50]

Sarny, a Life Remembered
Ch BWatch - v7 - D '97 - p3 [1-50]
y   JAAL - v41 - O '97 - p161 [51-250]

The Schernoff Discoveries
y   Bks Keeps - N '97 - p27 [51-250]
BL - v93 - Je 1 '97 - p1705 [51-250]
y   BL - v94 - Mr 15 '98 - p1218 [1-50]
y   BL - v94 - Mr 15 '98 - p1226 [1-50]
y   CCB-B - v50 - Jl '97 - p406+ [51-250]
y   Ch BWatch - v7 - Jl '97 - p3 [1-50]
HB Guide - v8 - Fall '97 - p306 [51-250]
y   JAAL - v41 - O '97 - p159 [51-250]
KR - v65 - My 15 '97 - p805 [51-250]
PW - v244 - My 19 '97 - p77 [51-250]
y   Sch Lib - v45 - N '97 - p214 [51-250]
SLJ - v43 - Jl '97 - p96+ [51-250]
TES - Je 20 '97 - p7* [501+]
y   VOYA - v20 - O '97 - p247 [51-250]
y   VOYA - v21 - Ap '98 - p38 [1-50]
y   VOYA - v21 - Ap '98 - p40 [1-50]

Tucket's Ride
Ch BWatch - v7 - Ap '97 - p4 [1-50]
y   HB Guide - v8 - Fall '97 - p315 [51-250]
NYTBR - v102 - Je 8 '97 - p29 [1-50]
Roundup M - v4 - Je '97 - p34 [51-250]

Tucket's Ride (Jones). Audio Version
y   BL - v94 - D 15 '97 - p711 [1-50]
SLJ - v43 - N '97 - p68 [51-250]

Worksong (Illus. by Ruth Wright Paulsen)

> ABR - v19 - N '97 - p12+ [501+]
> HB Guide - v8 - Fall '97 - p277 [51-250]
> SLJ - v43 - My '97 - p123 [51-250]

Pausewang, Gudrun

The Final Journey

> y RT - v51 - D '97 - p309+ [51-250]
>   RT - v51 - D '97 - p333+ [51-250]
> y SE - v61 - Ap '97 - p15* [1-50]
> y VOYA - v20 - Ap '97 - p32 [51-250]

Paxton, Tom

Engelbert Joins the Circus (Illus. by Roberta Wilson)

> HB Guide - v8 - Fall '97 - p27 [51-250]

The Marvelous Toy (Illus. by Elizabeth Sayles)

> RT - v51 - O '97 - p131 [1-50]

The Story of Santa Claus (Illus. by Michael Dooling)

> PW - v244 - O 6 '97 - p59 [1-50]

Payne, Lauren Murphy

We Can Get Along (Illus. by Claudia Rohling)

> BL - v93 - Ag '97 - p1903+ [51-250]
> Ch BWatch - v7 - My '97 - p8 [51-250]
> SLJ - v43 - Ap '97 - p130 [51-250]

Peake, Mervyn Laurence

Boy in Darkness

> Books - v10 - S '96 - p24 [51-250]
> y NS - v126 - D 5 '97 - p66 [51-250]

Pearce, Philippa

A Century of Children's Ghost Stories

> BW - v27 - My 18 '97 - p12 [1-50]

Tom's Midnight Garden

> Bks Keeps - S '97 - p32 [501+]
> TES - Ja 2 '98 - p22* [1-50]

Who's Afraid and Other Strange Stories (Rodska). Audio Version

> BL - v93 - Je 1 '97 - p1733 [51-250]

Pearce, Q L

Even More Scary Stories for Sleep-Overs (Gaines). Audio Version

> Ch BWatch - v7 - D '97 - p4 [1-50]

Pearson, Debora

Cookie Count and Bake (Illus. by Jane Kurisu)

> CBRA - '96 - p521 [51-250]

Cookie Critters (Illus. by Vlasta Van Kampen)

> PW - v244 - O 27 '97 - p79 [51-250]

The Meadow Mouse Treasury

> Can CL - v23 - Sum '97 - p74+ [501+]

Pearson, Gayle

The Secret Box

> BL - v93 - Ag '97 - p1902 [51-250]
> CCB-B - v50 - Jl '97 - p407 [51-250]
> KR - v65 - Ap 15 '97 - p646 [51-250]
> SLJ - v43 - Je '97 - p125 [51-250]

Pearson, Kit

Awake and Dreaming

> BL - v93 - Je 1 '97 - p1705 [51-250]
> Can CL - v23 - Sum '97 - p77+ [251-500]
> CBRA - '96 - p488+ [51-250]
> CBRS - v25 - Je '97 - p131 [51-250]
> Ch BWatch - v7 - My '97 - p5 [51-250]
> HB Guide - v8 - Fall '97 - p306 [51-250]
> KR - v65 - Ap 15 '97 - p647 [51-250]
> y SLJ - v43 - Je '97 - p125 [51-250]

The Lights Go on Again

> Can CL - v22 - Win '96 - p113+ [501+]
> y Sch Lib - v45 - Ag '97 - p161 [51-250]
>   TES - My 9 '97 - p19U [501+]

Looking at the Moon

> y Sch Lib - v45 - Ag '97 - p161 [51-250]
>   TES - My 9 '97 - p19U [501+]

The Sky Is Falling

> y Sch Lib - v45 - Ag '97 - p161 [51-250]
>   TES - My 9 '97 - p19U [501+]

Pearson, Maggie, 1941-

The Fox and the Rooster and Other Tales (Illus. by Joanne Moss)

> BL - v94 - F 15 '98 - p1016 [51-250]
> CCB-B - v51 - Mr '98 - p255 [51-250]

Pearson, Susan
Silver Morning (Illus. by David Christiana)
> BL - v94 - Mr 15 '98 - p1250+ [51-250]
> KR - v66 - F 15 '98 - p271 [51-250]
> SLJ - v44 - Ap '98 - p108 [51-250]

Pearson, Tracey Campbell
The Purple Hat (Illus. by Tracey Campbell Pearson)
> Bloom Rev - v17 - Mr '97 - p20 [51-250]
> HB Guide - v8 - Fall '97 - p277 [51-250]
> SLJ - v43 - Ap '97 - p114 [51-250]

Peat, Anne
Easy Guide to the 20th Century
> r   TES - Jl 4 '97 - p11* [501+]

Peck, Jan
The Giant Carrot (Illus. by Barry Root)
> BL - v94 - Mr 15 '98 - p1246 [51-250]
> CCB-B - v51 - Mr '98 - p255+ [51-250]
> KR - v65 - D 1 '97 - p1778 [51-250]
> PW - v245 - F 16 '98 - p210 [51-250]
> SLJ - v44 - F '98 - p103 [51-250]

Peck, Richard, 1934-
Lost in Cyberspace
> PW - v244 - S 1 '97 - p107 [1-50]

Peck, Robert Newton
A Part of the Sky
> y   Kliatt - v32 - Mr '98 - p14 [51-250]
> PW - v244 - Jl 21 '97 - p203 [1-50]

Pedersen, Ted
True Fright
> RT - v51 - O '97 - p143 [1-50]

Peduzzi, Kelli
Shaping a President (Illus. by Diane Smook)
> BL - v94 - D 1 '97 - p634+ [51-250]
> SLJ - v44 - Mr '98 - p238+ [51-250]

Peguero, Leone
What a Goose! (Illus. by Simone Kennedy)
> Magpies - v12 - My '97 - p27+ [51-250]
> Sch Lib - v45 - Ag '97 - p132 [51-250]

Pelham, David
ABC Fun
> Par - v72 - D '97 - p202 [1-50]
> PW - v244 - S 1 '97 - p106 [1-50]

Pelletier, David
The Graphic Alphabet (Illus. by David Pelletier)
> ABR - v19 - N '97 - p5+ [501+]

Pellowski, Michael
The Art of Making Comic Books
> JOYS - v10 - Sum '97 - p429 [1-50]

Pelta, Kathy
Cattle Trails
> Ch BWatch - v8 - Ja '98 - p7 [51-250]
> HB Guide - v8 - Fall '97 - p396 [51-250]
> y   SLJ - v43 - D '97 - p145 [51-250]

The Royal Roads
> HB Guide - v8 - Fall '97 - p396 [51-250]
> y   SLJ - v43 - D '97 - p145 [51-250]

Trails to the West
> Ch BWatch - v8 - Ja '98 - p7 [51-250]
> y   Cur R - v37 - D '97 - p13 [51-250]

Pemberton, N
The Child's World of Responsibility. Rev. Ed. (Illus. by Mechelle Ann)
> SLJ - v44 - Ap '98 - p122 [51-250]

Pencheva, Stanka
Mili Bate! (Illus. by Tonya Goranova)
> Bkbird - v35 - Sum '97 - p56+ [1-50]

Pendleton, Scott
The Ultimate Guide to Student Contests, Grades K-6
> r   BL - v94 - Mr 15 '98 - p1242 [51-250]

Pendragon: Lordly Domains
> r   Ch BWatch - v7 - Jl '97 - p5 [1-50]

Penner, Fred
Proud (Illus. by Vickey Bolling)
 Quill & Q - v63 - O '97 - p39 [251-500]

Penner, Lucille Recht
The Teddy Bear Book (Illus. by Jody Wheeler)
 HB Guide - v8 - Fall '97 - p362 [51-250]

Westward Ho! (Illus. by Bryn Barnard)
 SLJ - v44 - Mr '98 - p200 [251-500]

Penny, Malcolm
The Indian Ocean
 Ch BWatch - v7 - D '97 - p7 [1-50]
 HB Guide - v8 - Fall '97 - p385 [51-250]

The Polar Seas
 Ch BWatch - v7 - D '97 - p7 [1-50]
 HB Guide - v8 - Fall '97 - p385 [51-250]
 SB - v33 - Je '97 - p143 [51-250]

Pepper, Dennis
The Young Oxford Book of Ghost Stories
 PW - v244 - O 27 '97 - p79 [51-250]

Perera, Hilda
Froggie Froggette (Illus. by Vivi Escriva)
 PW - v244 - My 26 '97 - p85+ [51-250]
 SLJ - v44 - F '98 - p89+ [51-250]

Perez, Olga Marta
Las Sombras Andan Solas (Illus. by Ariel Baro)
 Bkbird - v35 - Fall '97 - p50 [1-50]

Perez Diaz, Enrique
Se Jubilan Las Hadas (Illus. by Daniel Zorrilla)
 Bkbird - v35 - Sum '97 - p57 [1-50]

Perham, Molly
Aladdin and Ali Baba (Illus. by Francesca Pelizzoli)
 HB Guide - v8 - Fall '97 - p334+ [51-250]

Resources (Illus. by Sallie Alane Reason)
 HB Guide - v8 - Fall '97 - p326 [51-250]
 SB - v33 - Je '97 - p141 [51-250]

Wildlife (Illus. by Sallie Alane Reason)
 HB Guide - v8 - Fall '97 - p347 [51-250]

Perkal, Stephanie
Midnight: A Cinderella Alphabet (Illus. by Spencer Alston Bartsch)
 PW - v244 - Je 2 '97 - p71 [51-250]
 SLJ - v43 - S '97 - p207 [51-250]

Perkins, Lynne Rae
Clouds for Dinner (Illus. by Lynne Rae Perkins)
 CBRS - v26 - Ja '98 - p52 [51-250]
 HB - v73 - S '97 - p562+ [51-250]
 KR - v65 - Je 15 '97 - p955 [51-250]
 SLJ - v43 - S '97 - p189+ [51-250]

Perkyns, Dorothy
The Mastodon Mystery
 BIC - v26 - Ap '97 - p35+ [251-500]
y CBRA - '96 - p489 [51-250]

Signal across the Sea
 Can CL - v22 - Win '96 - p111+ [501+]

Perl, Lila
Four Perfect Pebbles
 SE - v61 - Ap '97 - p15* [1-50]

Pernoud, Regine
A Miller (Illus. by Giorgio Bacchin)
 Ch BWatch - v7 - O '97 - p7 [1-50]
 SLJ - v44 - Mr '98 - p240 [51-250]

A Noblewoman (Illus. by Giorgio Bacchin)
 BL - v94 - Ja 1 '98 - p806+ [51-250]
 Ch BWatch - v7 - O '97 - p7 [1-50]
 KR - v65 - O 15 '97 - p1586 [51-250]
 SLJ - v44 - F '98 - p122 [51-250]

A Stonecutter (Illus. by Giorgio Bacchin)
 BL - v94 - N 1 '97 - p464+ [51-250]
 Bloom Rev - v17 - N '97 - p32 [51-250]
 Ch BWatch - v7 - O '97 - p7 [1-50]
 SLJ - v44 - Ja '98 - p128 [51-250]

A Troubador (Illus. by Giorgio Bacchin)
> Ch BWatch - v7 - O '97 - p7 [1-50]

Perrault, Charles
Tales from Perrault (Illus. by Tony Chance)
> AB - v100 - N 17 '97 - p1260 [251-500]

Perrin, Randy
Time like a River
> CM:CanRev - v4 - F 13 '98 - pONL [251-500]
> SLJ - v44 - Mr '98 - p216 [251-500]

Perry, Phyllis J
Armor to Venom
> SLJ - v43 - D '97 - p113+ [51-250]

Ballooning
> HB Guide - v8 - Fall '97 - p359 [51-250]

The Crocodilians: Reminders of the Age of Dinosaurs
> y SB - v33 - O '97 - p205+ [251-500]
> SLJ - v43 - Ag '97 - p173+ [51-250]

Hide and Seek
> SLJ - v44 - F '98 - p103+ [51-250]

The Snow Cats
> HB Guide - v8 - Fall '97 - p354 [51-250]
> SLJ - v43 - Ag '97 - p173+ [51-250]

Soaring
> HB Guide - v8 - Fall '97 - p368 [51-250]

Perry, Sarah
If...
> Magpies - v12 - S '97 - p8 [51-250]

Perversi, Margaret
Henry's Bath (Illus. by Ron Brooks)
> Aust Bk R - Ag '97 - p62+ [501+]
> Magpies - v12 - Jl '97 - p26 [51-250]

Henry's Bed (Illus. by Ron Brooks)
> Aust Bk R - Ag '97 - p62+ [501+]
> Magpies - v12 - Jl '97 - p26 [51-250]
> TES - N 7 '97 - p5* [1-50]

Peters, Andrew
Strange and Spooky Stories (Illus. by Zdenka Kabatova-Taborska)
> CBRS - v26 - F '98 - p78+ [51-250]

Petersen, David, 1946-
Bryce Canyon National Park
> SLJ - v43 - My '97 - p123 [51-250]

Death Valley National Park
> SLJ - v43 - My '97 - p123 [51-250]

Petersen, P J
Can You Keep a Secret? (Illus. by Meredith Johnson)
> BL - v94 - O 1 '97 - p333 [51-250]
> CCB-B - v51 - N '97 - p96+ [51-250]
> KR - v65 - O 15 '97 - p1586 [51-250]
> SLJ - v44 - Ja '98 - p90 [51-250]

White Water
> BL - v93 - Je 1 '97 - p1705 [51-250]
> y BL - v94 - Mr 15 '98 - p1226 [1-50]
> CCB-B - v50 - Je '97 - p369 [51-250]
> HB Guide - v8 - Fall '97 - p306 [51-250]
> y JAAL - v41 - F '98 - p410+ [51-250]
> KR - v65 - My 15 '97 - p805 [51-250]
> SLJ - v43 - My '97 - p139 [51-250]
> y VOYA - v21 - Ap '98 - p40 [1-50]

Peterson, Cassandra
Bad Dog, Andy
> Ch BWatch - v8 - Ja '98 - p1 [51-250]

Peterson, Cris
Harvest Year (Illus. by Alvis Upitis)
> RT - v51 - N '97 - p256+ [51-250]
> SB - v33 - Ag '97 - p186 [1-50]

Horsepower: The Wonder of Draft Horses (Illus. by Alvis Upitis)
> HB Guide - v8 - Fall '97 - p354 [51-250]
> SLJ - v43 - Ap '97 - p130 [51-250]

Peterson, Shelley
Dancer
> BIC - v26 - O '97 - p35+ [501+]
> CBRA - '96 - p489 [51-250]
> y JAAL - v41 - N '97 - p245 [251-500]

Petrie, Glen
Lucy and the Pirates
Emerg Lib - v25 - N '97 - p46 [51-250]

Petry, Ann
Tituba of Salem Village
NYTBR - v102 - N 16 '97 - p26 [1-50]

Pets (A Child's First Library of Learning)
SLJ - v43 - Ap '97 - p122 [51-250]

Petty, Kate
Build Your Own Space Station
SB - v32 - D '96 - p259 [1-50]

Dinosaurs Laid Eggs (Illus. by James Field)
Ch BWatch - v7 - N '97 - p6 [1-50]

The Great Grammer Book
Books - v10 - S '96 - p24 [51-250]

Rosie Plants a Radish (Illus. by Axel Scheffler)
TES - Je 13 '97 - pR7 [51-250]

Sam Plants a Sunflower (Illus. by Axel Scheffler)
TES - Je 13 '97 - pR7 [51-250]

Some Trains Run on Water (Illus. by Ross Walton)
Ch BWatch - v7 - N '97 - p6 [1-50]
SLJ - v44 - Mr '98 - p197 [51-250]

The Sun Is a Star (Illus. by Francis Phillipps)
CBRS - v25 - Jl '97 - p155 [51-250]
HB Guide - v8 - Fall '97 - p341 [51-250]
SB - v33 - N '97 - p240 [251-500]
Sch Lib - v45 - Ag '97 - p153 [51-250]
SLJ - v43 - S '97 - p204 [51-250]

You Can Jump Higher on the Moon (Illus. by Francis Phillipps)
CBRS - v25 - Jl '97 - p155 [51-250]
Ch BWatch - v7 - My '97 - p7 [1-50]
HB Guide - v8 - Fall '97 - p360 [51-250]
SB - v33 - N '97 - p240 [251-500]
Sch Lib - v45 - Ag '97 - p153 [51-250]

Pevsner, Stella
Sing for Your Father, Su Phan
BL - v94 - Ja 1 '98 - p814 [51-250]
y   CBRS - v26 - Win '98 - p72 [51-250]
CCB-B - v51 - Ja '98 - p171+ [51-250]
y   Ch BWatch - v8 - Ja '98 - p4 [1-50]
KR - v65 - O 1 '97 - p1536 [51-250]
SLJ - v43 - D '97 - p128 [51-250]

Peyton, K M
Windy Webley (Illus. by Nick Price)
Sch Lib - v45 - N '97 - p201 [51-250]

Pfeffer, Susan Beth
Devil's Den
KR - v66 - Mr 15 '98 - p408 [51-250]

Justice for Emily
Ch BWatch - v7 - My '97 - p5 [51-250]
HB Guide - v8 - Fall '97 - p307 [51-250]

Portrait's of Little Women: Amy's Story
CBRS - v26 - F '98 - p81+ [51-250]

Portraits of Little Women: Amy's Story
Ch BWatch - v7 - D '97 - p3+ [1-50]
PW - v244 - N 24 '97 - p75+ [1-50]

Portraits of Little Women: Beth's Story
CBRS - v26 - F '98 - p81+ [51-250]
Ch BWatch - v7 - D '97 - p3+ [1-50]
PW - v244 - N 24 '97 - p75+ [1-50]

Portraits of Little Women: Jo's Story
CBRS - v26 - F '98 - p81+ [51-250]
Ch BWatch - v7 - D '97 - p3+ [1-50]
PW - v244 - N 24 '97 - p75+ [1-50]
SLJ - v44 - Ja '98 - p90 [251-500]

Portraits of Little Women: Meg's Story
CBRS - v26 - F '98 - p81+ [51-250]
Ch BWatch - v7 - D '97 - p3+ [1-50]
PW - v244 - N 24 '97 - p75+ [1-50]

Pfeffer, Wendy
From Tadpole to Frog (Illus. by Holly Keller)
ASBYP - v29 - Fall '96 - p52 [501+]

A Log's Life (Illus. by Robin Brickman)
> BL - v94 - S 15 '97 - p238 [51-250]
> Inst - v107 - N '97 - p19 [1-50]
> SLJ - v43 - S '97 - p207 [51-250]

What's It like to Be a Fish? (Illus. by Holly Keller)
> ASBYP - v29 - Fall '96 - p52+ [501+]

Pfiffner, George
Earth-Friendly Outdoor Fun
> ASBYP - v29 - Fall '96 - p24+ [251-500]

Pfister, Marcus
The Christmas Star Mini Book
> PW - v244 - O 6 '97 - p57 [1-50]

Hopper's Treetop Adventure
> Ch BWatch - v7 - Je '97 - p7 [1-50]
> HB Guide - v8 - Fall '97 - p277 [1-50]

How Leo Learned to Be King (Illus. by Marcus Pfister)
> BL - v94 - Mr 1 '98 - p1141 [51-250]
> KR - v66 - Mr 1 '98 - p343 [51-250]
> PW - v245 - Mr 16 '98 - p63 [51-250]

Milo and the Magical Stones (Illus. by Marcus Pfister)
> AB - v100 - N 17 '97 - p1264 [251-500]
> BL - v94 - O 1 '97 - p338 [51-250]
> CBRS - v26 - D '97 - p40 [51-250]
> CCB-B - v51 - N '97 - p97 [51-250]
> KR - v65 - Je 15 '97 - p955 [51-250]
> PW - v244 - Je 2 '97 - p71 [51-250]
> RT - v51 - F '98 - p429 [51-250]
> SLJ - v43 - S '97 - p190 [51-250]

Penguin Pete, Ahoy!
> PW - v245 - Mr 9 '98 - p70 [1-50]

El Pinguino Pedro Y Sus Nuevos Amigos
> HB Guide - v8 - Fall '97 - p339 [1-50]

Rainbow Fish
> Par - v73 - F '98 - p185 [1-50]

The Rainbow Fish Board Book (Illus. by Marcus Pfister)
> RT - v51 - O '97 - p131 [1-50]

Rainbow Fish to the Rescue!
> Par - v72 - My '97 - p92 [1-50]

Saltarin (Illus. by Marcus Pfister)
> BL - v94 - D 15 '97 - p707 [1-50]

The Sleepy Owl
> PW - v245 - Mr 9 '98 - p70 [1-50]

Pfitsch, Patricia Curtis
Keeper of the Light
> y   BL - v94 - N 1 '97 - p462 [51-250]
>   CCB-B - v51 - Ja '98 - p172 [51-250]
>   KR - v65 - N 15 '97 - p1711 [51-250]
>   PW - v244 - N 17 '97 - p62 [51-250]
> y   VOYA - v20 - F '98 - p389 [51-250]

Pflueger, Lynda
Stonewall Jackson: Confederate General
>   BL - v94 - O 1 '97 - p326 [51-250]
> y   CLW - v68 - D '97 - p81 [51-250]
> y   HB Guide - v8 - Fall '97 - p378 [51-250]

Philabaum, Dabney Miller
Desert Buddies
> Bloom Rev - v17 - S '97 - p23 [51-250]

Philbrick, Rodman
Max the Mighty
> y   CCB-B - v51 - Ap '98 - p291+ [51-250]
>   KR - v66 - F 15 '98 - p272 [51-250]
>   PW - v245 - Ja 26 '98 - p91+ [51-250]
>   SLJ - v44 - Ap '98 - p136 [51-250]

Philip, Neil
The Adventures of Odysseus (Illus. by Peter Malone)
> Bks Keeps - Jl '97 - p4 [51-250]
> HB Guide - v8 - Fall '97 - p373 [51-250]
> Magpies - v12 - Mr '97 - p18+ [501+]
> NS - v126 - D 5 '97 - p62 [1-50]
> SLJ - v43 - My '97 - p148 [51-250]

Earth Always Endures (Illus. by Edward S Curtis)
> RT - v51 - O '97 - p149 [51-250]
> SE - v61 - Ap '97 - p11* [1-50]
> y   VOYA - v20 - Je '97 - p126+ [251-500]

Fairy Tales of the Brothers Grimm (Illus. by Isabelle Brent)
> BL - v94 - O 15 '97 - p401 [51-250]
> KR - v65 - N 1 '97 - p1648 [51-250]
> PW - v244 - Ag 4 '97 - p76 [51-250]

SLJ - v44 - F '98 - p116+ [51-250]

The Illustrated Book of Fairy Tales (Illus. by Nilesh Mistry)
SLJ - v44 - Ap '98 - p122 [51-250]

In a Sacred Manner I Live
y   BL - v94 - Mr 15 '98 - p1211 [1-50]
     CBRS - v26 - S '97 - p11 [1-50]
     KR - v65 - Jl 1 '97 - p1034 [51-250]
     NYTBR - v102 - N 16 '97 - p42 [501+]
     NYTBR - v102 - D 7 '97 - p80 [1-50]
y   SLJ - v43 - D '97 - p145 [51-250]
y   VOYA - v20 - F '98 - p365 [51-250]
y   VOYA - v21 - Ap '98 - p37 [1-50]

The New Oxford Book of Children's Verse
TLS - O 10 '97 - p27 [501+]

A New Treasury of Poetry (Illus. by John Lawrence)
Comw - v124 - D 5 '97 - p14 [1-50]

Robin Hood (Illus. by Nick Harris)
CLW - v68 - D '97 - p86 [51-250]
HB Guide - v8 - Fall '97 - p335 [51-250]
SLJ - v43 - S '97 - p207 [51-250]
TES - Je 6 '97 - p8* [501+]

Phillips, Dave
Donkey Kong Country (Illus. by Dave Phillips)
PW - v244 - O 27 '97 - p78 [51-250]

Super Mario's Adventures (Illus. by Dave Phillips)
PW - v244 - O 27 '97 - p78 [51-250]

Phillips, David
Light Up Your Life (Illus. by Mic Rolph)
Bks Keeps - N '97 - p25 [51-250]
New Sci - v154 - Je 28 '97 - p44 [51-250]

Phillips, Tom
Aspects of Art
Spec - v279 - Ag 16 '97 - p35 [501+]
TES - My 16 '97 - pR4+ [251-500]
TES - N 7 '97 - p10* [1-50]

Philpot, Don K
The Moons of Goose Island (Illus. by Margaret Hessian)
Quill & Q - v63 - Ap '97 - p35+ [251-500]

Philpot, Graham
The Troglobytes
Books - v11 - O '97 - p21 [51-250]

Piasecki, Jerry
Ketchup Power and the Starship Meatloaf
PW - v244 - S 29 '97 - p90 [51-250]

Pichon, Joelle
The Sea Lion (Illus. by Sophie De Wilde)
SB - v33 - Ag '97 - p179 [51-250]

Pickering, David
Bible Questions and Answers
Sch Lib - v45 - Ag '97 - p153 [51-250]

Pienkowski, Jan
Big Machines (Illus. by Jan Pienkowski)
BL - v94 - D 15 '97 - p700 [1-50]
Par - v72 - D '97 - p201 [1-50]
PW - v244 - Je 23 '97 - p93 [51-250]
SLJ - v43 - Ag '97 - p138 [51-250]

Boats (Illus. by Jan Pienkowski)
Bks Keeps - My '97 - p19+ [51-250]
Par - v72 - D '97 - p201 [1-50]
PW - v244 - Je 23 '97 - p93 [51-250]
SLJ - v43 - Ag '97 - p138 [51-250]

Planes and Other Things That Fly (Illus. by Jan Pienkowski)
Bks Keeps - My '97 - p19+ [51-250]
Par - v72 - D '97 - p201 [1-50]
PW - v244 - Je 23 '97 - p93 [51-250]
SLJ - v43 - Ag '97 - p138 [51-250]

Trucks and Other Working Wheels (Illus. by Jan Pienkowski)
Bks Keeps - My '97 - p19+ [51-250]
Par - v72 - D '97 - p201 [1-50]
PW - v244 - Je 23 '97 - p93 [51-250]
SLJ - v43 - Ag '97 - p138 [51-250]

Pierce, Tamora
Circle of Magic
y   BL - v94 - S 1 '97 - p106+ [51-250]
y   CBRS - v26 - Ja '98 - p60 [51-250]
y   CCB-B - v51 - N '97 - p97+ [51-250]
y   CCB-B - v51 - Ap '98 - p292 [51-250]
y   KR - v65 - Jl 15 '97 - p1115 [51-250]
    PW - v244 - Je 23 '97 - p93 [51-250]
y   VOYA - v20 - D '97 - p327 [251-500]
y   VOYA - v21 - Ap '98 - p14 [1-50]

Sandry's Book
y   BW - v27 - D 7 '97 - p22 [51-250]
    SLJ - v43 - S '97 - p224 [51-250]

Tris's Book
    SLJ - v44 - Ap '98 - p134 [51-250]

Pietrusza, David
Smoking
    BL - v93 - Ag '97 - p1895 [51-250]
y   HB Guide - v8 - Fall '97 - p327 [51-250]
y   SLJ - v43 - Jl '97 - p110 [51-250]
y   VOYA - v20 - Ag '97 - p206 [251-500]

Piglet (DK)
    Ch BWatch - v7 - Je '97 - p4 [1-50]

Pikering, Robert
The People (Illus. by Ted Finger)
    ASBYP - v29 - Fall '96 - p61+ [501+]

Pilger, Mary Anne
Science Experiments Index for Young People. 2nd Ed.
r   SLMQ - v25 - Win '97 - p116 [1-50]

Pilkey, Dav
The Adventures of Captain Underpants (Illus. by Dav Pilkey)
    CBRS - v26 - O '97 - p21 [51-250]
    KR - v65 - Je 1 '97 - p878 [51-250]
    NW - v130 - D 1 '97 - p77 [1-50]
    SLJ - v43 - D '97 - p99 [51-250]

Big Dog and Little Dog Getting in Trouble (Illus. by Dav Pilkey)
    Par - v72 - D '97 - p202 [1-50]
    PW - v244 - S 29 '97 - p91 [51-250]

God Bless the Gargoyles (Illus. by Dav Pilkey)
    RT - v51 - O '97 - p137 [1-50]

The Paperboy (Illus. by Dav Pilkey)
    Inst - v106 - My '97 - p20 [51-250]
    SE - v61 - Ap '97 - p14* [1-50]

The Silly Gooses (Illus. by Dav Pilkey)
    CCB-B - v51 - Ap '98 - p292 [51-250]
    KR - v65 - D 15 '97 - p1838 [51-250]
    PW - v244 - D 8 '97 - p72 [51-250]
    SLJ - v44 - F '98 - p90 [51-250]

Pilling, Ann
Creation: Read-Aloud Stories from Many Lands (Illus. by Michael Foreman)
    BL - v94 - S 1 '97 - p120 [51-250]
    KR - v65 - Jl 15 '97 - p1115 [51-250]
    PW - v244 - Ag 4 '97 - p76 [51-250]
    Sch Lib - v45 - N '97 - p201 [51-250]

Creation Stories from Around the World (Illus. by Michael Foreman)
    Magpies - v12 - S '97 - p31 [51-250]

Love Stories (Illus. by Aafke Brouwer)
    SLJ - v43 - D '97 - p128 [51-250]

The Year of the Worm (Copley). Audio Version
    BL - v93 - Je 1 '97 - p1733 [51-250]

Pinkney, Andrea Davis
Bill Pickett: Rodeo-Ridin' Cowboy (Illus. by J Brian Pinkney)
    BL - v93 - Je 1 '97 - p1701 [1-50]
    Emerg Lib - v24 - My '97 - p66 [51-250]
    Inst - v107 - O '97 - p24 [1-50]
    RT - v51 - N '97 - p240 [51-250]
    RT - v51 - D '97 - p334+ [51-250]
    SE - v61 - Ap '97 - p3* [1-50]

Duke Ellington (Illus. by J Brian Pinkney)
    KR - v66 - Ap 1 '98 - p499 [51-250]

I Smell Honey
    Am Vis - v12 - D '97 - p34 [1-50]

Pretty Brown Face
    Am Vis - v12 - D '97 - p34 [1-50]

Shake, Shake, Shake
    Am Vis - v12 - D '97 - p34 [1-50]

Pinkney, J Brian

The Adventures of Sparrowboy (Illus. by J Brian Pinkney)

    CBRS - v25 - My '97 - p112 [51-250]
    CCB-B - v50 - Je '97 - p369+ [51-250]
    HB - v73 - Jl '97 - p445+ [51-250]
    HB Guide - v8 - Fall '97 - p277 [51-250]
    Inst - v107 - S '97 - p24 [1-50]
    NYTBR - v102 - Je 8 '97 - p27 [1-50]
    SLJ - v43 - Ap '97 - p115 [51-250]

Max Found Two Sticks (Illus. by J Brian Pinkney)

    PW - v244 - Je 2 '97 - p73 [1-50]

Pinkney, Jerry

Rikki-Tikki-Tavi (Illus. by Jerry Pinkney)

    BL - v94 - S 1 '97 - p117 [51-250]
    BL - v94 - Ja 1 '98 - p734 [1-50]
    CCB-B - v51 - Ja '98 - p163 [51-250]
    KR - v65 - Jl 1 '97 - p1030 [51-250]
    PW - v244 - Je 2 '97 - p70 [51-250]
    PW - v244 - N 3 '97 - p59 [51-250]
    SLJ - v43 - Ag '97 - p136+ [51-250]

Pinkwater, Daniel Manus

5 Novels

    BW - v27 - S 7 '97 - p11 [501+]
  y CM:CanRev - v4 - F 27 '98 - pONL [251-500]
    PW - v244 - Jl 7 '97 - p70 [51-250]

At the Hotel Larry (Illus. by Jill Pinkwater)

    BL - v94 - S 1 '97 - p134 [51-250]
    CBRS - v26 - D '97 - p41 [51-250]
    CCB-B - v51 - S '97 - p23 [251-500]
    PW - v244 - Jl 7 '97 - p67 [51-250]

Author's Day

    Inst - v107 - S '97 - p20 [1-50]

The Big Orange Splot

    Emerg Lib - v24 - My '97 - p9+ [1-50]
    Emerg Lib - v24 - My '97 - p9+ [501+]

Young Larry (Illus. by Jill Pinkwater)

    BL - v94 - S 1 '97 - p134 [51-250]
    CBRS - v26 - D '97 - p41 [51-250]
    CCB-B - v51 - S '97 - p23 [251-500]
    KR - v65 - Ag 15 '97 - p1311 [51-250]
    NYTBR - v103 - F 1 '98 - p24 [1-50]
    PW - v244 - Jl 7 '97 - p67 [51-250]

Pipe, Jim

Aliens

    Ch BWatch - v7 - My '97 - p7 [1-50]
    Sch Lib - v45 - N '97 - p206 [51-250]

The Giant Book of Bugs and Creepy Crawlies

  r PW - v245 - Mr 16 '98 - p67 [51-250]

In the Footsteps of the Werewolf

    RT - v51 - O '97 - p142 [1-50]

Mystery History of a Medieval Castle (Illus. by Dave Burroughs)

    Ch BWatch - v7 - Mr '97 - p5 [1-50]
    SLJ - v43 - Jl '97 - p110 [51-250]

Mystery History of a Pharaoh's Tomb (Illus. by Mike Bell)

    Ch BWatch - v7 - My '97 - p7 [1-50]
    SLJ - v43 - Ag '97 - p166 [51-250]

Mystery History of a Pharaoh's Tomb (Illus. by Roger Hutchins)

    HB Guide - v8 - Fall '97 - p387 [51-250]

Trojan Horse (Illus. by Roger Hutchins)

    Ch BWatch - v8 - Ja '98 - p6 [1-50]
    SLJ - v44 - Ap '98 - p112+ [51-250]

Witches (Illus. by Richard Rockwood)

    CBRS - v26 - Win '98 - p67 [51-250]
    Ch BWatch - v8 - Ja '98 - p6 [1-50]

Pippen, Scottie

Reach Higher (Illus. by Doug Keith)

    BL - v94 - O 1 '97 - p326 [51-250]

Piquemal, Michel

Paroles De Fraternite (Illus. by Mireille Vautier)

    Bkbird - v34 - Win '96 - p57 [51-250]

Pirotta, Saviour

Fossils and Bones

    HB Guide - v8 - Fall '97 - p343 [51-250]

Turtle Bay (Illus. by Nilesh Mistry)

    CBRS - v26 - S '97 - p5 [51-250]
    Ch BWatch - v7 - N '97 - p4 [1-50]
    KR - v65 - Ag 1 '97 - p1227 [51-250]
    NH - v106 - D '97 - p8 [51-250]
    Sch Lib - v45 - N '97 - p187 [51-250]

SLJ - v43 - N '97 - p96+ [51-250]

The Wild, Wild West
HB Guide - v8 - Fall '97 - p396 [51-250]

Plain, Ferguson
Rolly's Bear
CBRA - '96 - p454 [51-250]

Platt, Chris
Willow King
KR - v66 - Mr 15 '98 - p409 [51-250]
PW - v245 - Mr 23 '98 - p100 [51-250]

Platt, Richard
Inventions Explained
BL - v94 - Mr 1 '98 - p1126 [51-250]
KR - v65 - D 15 '97 - p1838 [51-250]
SLJ - v44 - F '98 - p115 [51-250]

Pirate
Emerg Lib - v25 - N '97 - p46 [51-250]

Shipwreck (Illus. by Alex Wilson)
Ch BWatch - v7 - D '97 - p8 [1-50]

Spy
SLJ - v43 - Je '97 - p142 [51-250]

Play Farm: An Interactive Book
PW - v244 - N 10 '97 - p76 [51-250]

Play Shop: An Interactive Book
PW - v244 - N 10 '97 - p76 [51-250]

Playtime Rhymes (Illus. by Priscilla Lamont)
PW - v245 - Mr 9 '98 - p70 [51-250]

Pledger, Maurice
The Adventure of Charlie Chick (Illus. by Maurice Pledger)
TES - Je 13 '97 - pR7 [51-250]

An Adventure with Billy Bunny
Bks Keeps - Jl '97 - p19 [51-250]

Plessix, Michel
A Wind in the Willows (Illus. by Michel Plessix)
Ch BWatch - v8 - Ja '98 - p3 [51-250]
PW - v245 - Ja 19 '98 - p380 [51-250]

Plourde, Lynn
Pigs in the Mud in the Middle of the Rud (Illus. by John Schoenherr)
Ch BWatch - v7 - My '97 - p3 [1-50]
Emerg Lib - v24 - My '97 - p57 [1-50]
Emerg Lib - v25 - Ja '98 - p46 [51-250]
HB Guide - v8 - Fall '97 - p277 [1-50]
SLJ - v43 - D '97 - p27 [1-50]

Plummer, David
Counting Kittens (Illus. by Liisa Chauncy Guida)
HB Guide - v8 - Fall '97 - p277 [1-50]
KR - v65 - Ap 15 '97 - p652 [51-250]
SLJ - v43 - Jl '97 - p73 [51-250]

Pochocki, Ethel
The Wind Harp and Other Angel Tales
CLW - v68 - S '97 - p65 [51-250]

Pocket School Dictionary
r   TES - S 19 '97 - p19* [501+]

Pockets English Dictionary
r   CLW - v68 - D '97 - p82+ [51-250]

Poe, Edgar Allan
Tales of Mystery and Imagination (Illus. by Gary Kelley)
HB Guide - v8 - Fall '97 - p307 [51-250]

Poems Go Clang! (Illus. by Debi Gliori)
Ch BWatch - v7 - S '97 - p1 [1-50]
SLJ - v44 - Mr '98 - p200 [51-250]

Poffenberger, Nancy
Instant Piano Fun with Nursery Rhymes
Ch BWatch - v7 - S '97 - p2 [51-250]

Pohrt, Tom
Coyote Goes Walking
PW - v244 - S 1 '97 - p107 [1-50]

Polacco, Patricia
Chicken Sunday
ECEJ - v25 - Fall '97 - p49 [1-50]

I Can Hear the Sun (Illus. by Patricia Polacco)
RT - v51 - O '97 - p146 [1-50]

In Enzo's Splendid Gardens (Illus. by Patricia Polacco)
BL - v93 - Ag '97 - p1907 [51-250]
CBRS - v25 - Jl '97 - p150 [1-50]
Ch BWatch - v7 - Je '97 - p6 [1-50]
HB Guide - v8 - Fall '97 - p277 [51-250]
KR - v65 - Ap 15 '97 - p647 [51-250]
SLJ - v43 - My '97 - p110 [51-250]

Just Plain Fancy
ECEJ - v25 - Fall '97 - p49 [1-50]

Mrs. Katz and Tush
ECEJ - v25 - Fall '97 - p49 [1-50]

My Rotten Redheaded Older Brother (Illus. by Patricia Polacco)
SLJ - v44 - Ja '98 - p43 [1-50]

Pink and Say (Illus. by Patricia Polacco)
y   BL - v93 - Je 1 '97 - p1675 [1-50]
ECEJ - v25 - Fall '97 - p49 [1-50]
SLJ - v43 - S '97 - p131 [1-50]

Pink Y Say (Illus. by Patricia Polacco)
SLJ - v44 - F '98 - p132 [51-250]

El Pollo De Los Domingos
BL - v94 - D 15 '97 - p707 [1-50]

Thank You, Mr. Falker (Illus. by Patricia Polacco)
KR - v66 - Ap 1 '98 - p499+ [51-250]

The Trees of the Dancing Goats
Ch BWatch - v7 - D '97 - p2 [1-50]

Poling-Kempes, Lesley
The Golden Era (Illus. by Lynette C Ross)
Bloom Rev - v17 - S '97 - p23 [51-250]

Polk, Milbry
Egyptian Mummies (Illus. by Roger Stewart)
BL - v94 - D 15 '97 - p700 [1-50]
y   BL - v94 - Mr 15 '98 - p1225 [1-50]
Books - v11 - O '97 - p21 [51-250]
PW - v244 - N 24 '97 - p76 [51-250]
SLJ - v44 - Ja '98 - p104 [51-250]
TES - D 5 '97 - p18* [51-250]

y   VOYA - v21 - Ap '98 - p40 [1-50]

Pollard, Michael
The Ganges
SLJ - v44 - Ap '98 - p152 [51-250]

The Mississippi
SLJ - v44 - Mr '98 - p241 [51-250]

The Rhine
SLJ - v44 - Mr '98 - p241 [51-250]

The Yangtze
SLJ - v44 - Ap '98 - p152 [51-250]

Pollock, Steve
Animals
PW - v244 - Jl 21 '97 - p203 [51-250]

Polly, Jean Armour
The Internet Kids and Family Yellow Pages. 2nd Ed.
CBR - v15 - Fall '97 - p29 [51-250]
r   LJ - v122 - S 1 '97 - p212 [51-250]

Poluck, Kathy
Too Much Snow (Illus. by Nella Zaccaria)
CBRA - '96 - p454+ [51-250]

Pomeranc, Marion Hess
The American Wei (Illus. by DyAnne DiSalvo-Ryan)
BL - v94 - Mr 15 '98 - p1252 [51-250]
CCB-B - v51 - Ap '98 - p292+ [51-250]
KR - v66 - F 15 '98 - p272 [51-250]
PW - v245 - Mr 9 '98 - p68 [51-250]

The Hand-Me-Down Horse (Illus. by Joanna Yardley)
SE - v61 - Ap '97 - p9* [1-50]

Pomerantz, Charlotte
Mangaboom (Illus. by Anita Lobel)
CBRS - v25 - My '97 - p112 [51-250]
HB Guide - v8 - Fall '97 - p277 [51-250]
KR - v65 - Ap 15 '97 - p647 [51-250]
NYTBR - v102 - Je 22 '97 - p22 [1-50]
SLJ - v43 - Ap '97 - p115 [51-250]

Pomeroy, Diana
Wildflower ABC (Illus. by Diana Pomeroy)

    HB Guide - v8 - Fall '97 - p349 [51-250]

    SB - v33 - Ag '97 - p186 [1-50]

    SLJ - v43 - N '97 - p111 [51-250]

Poole, Josephine
Hero

    Sch Lib - v45 - N '97 - p201 [51-250]

Jack and the Beanstalk (Illus. by Paul Hess)

    Bks Keeps - S '97 - p20 [51-250]

The Water Babies (Illus. by Jan Ormerod)

    Bks Keeps - Jl '97 - p5 [51-250]

Pooley, Sarah
Jump the World (Illus. by Sarah Pooley)

    CBRS - v25 - Spr '97 - p140 [51-250]

    CCB-B - v50 - Jl '97 - p407 [51-250]

    HB Guide - v8 - Fall '97 - p373 [51-250]

    Quill & Q - v63 - D '97 - p39 [51-250]

    SLJ - v43 - Je '97 - p142+ [51-250]

Pope, Joyce
The Children's Atlas of Natural Wonders

    r   ASBYP - v29 - Sum '96 - p28 [251-500]

Poploff, Michelle
Tea Party for Two (Illus. by Maryann Cocca-Leffler)

    KR - v65 - N 15 '97 - p1712 [51-250]

    SLJ - v44 - F '98 - p90 [51-250]

Popov, Nikolai
Why? (Illus. by Nikolai Popov)

    SE - v61 - Ap '97 - p4* [1-50]

Porte, Barbara Ann
Harry's Pony (Illus. by Yossi Abolafia)

    BL - v93 - Ag '97 - p1910 [51-250]

    CCB-B - v51 - O '97 - p65 [51-250]

    HB - v73 - S '97 - p577+ [51-250]

    KR - v65 - Je 15 '97 - p956 [51-250]

    SLJ - v43 - Ag '97 - p138 [51-250]

Surprise! Surprise! It's Grandfather's Birthday (Illus. by Bo Jia)

    CBRS - v25 - Jl '97 - p150 [51-250]

    HB Guide - v8 - Fall '97 - p277 [51-250]

    SLJ - v43 - My '97 - p110 [51-250]

Tale of a Tadpole (Illus. by Annie Cannon)

    BL - v93 - Ag '97 - p1907 [51-250]

    KR - v65 - Jl 15 '97 - p1115 [51-250]

    PW - v244 - S 1 '97 - p103+ [51-250]

    SLJ - v43 - S '97 - p190 [51-250]

Porter, Sue
Parsnip (Illus. by Sue Porter)

    SLJ - v44 - Ap '98 - p108 [51-250]

Porter, Tracey
Treasures in the Dust

    BL - v93 - Ag '97 - p1902 [51-250]

    CBRS - v26 - D '97 - p47 [51-250]

    CCB-B - v51 - N '97 - p98 [51-250]

    HB - v73 - S '97 - p578 [51-250]

    KR - v65 - Jl 1 '97 - p1034 [51-250]

    SLJ - v43 - D '97 - p128+ [51-250]

Poskitt, Kjartan
The Gobsmacking Galaxy

    New Sci - v155 - Ag 16 '97 - p42 [51-250]

Murderous Maths

    Books - v11 - Je '97 - p21 [51-250]

    New Sci - v156 - N 22 '97 - p62 [51-250]

Poteet, Lewis J
Hockey Talk

    CBRA - '96 - p525 [51-250]

Potter, Beatrix
The Adventures of Peter Rabbit (Illus. by Stephanie Britt)

    Ch BWatch - v7 - Je '97 - p3 [51-250]

The Adventures of Tom Kitten. Audio Version

    Ch BWatch - v7 - My '97 - p5 [51-250]

A First Peter Rabbit Book (Illus. by Beatrix Potter)
 HB Guide - v8 - Fall '97 - p254 [51-250]

Mrs. Tiggy-Winkle and Friends. Audio Version
 Ch BWatch - v7 - My '97 - p5 [51-250]

Peter Rabbit. Audio Version
 Ch BWatch - v7 - My '97 - p5 [51-250]

The Tailor of Gloucester
 Bks Keeps - N '97 - p5 [51-250]

The Tale of Two Bad Mice. Deluxe Ed.
 HB Guide - v8 - Fall '97 - p277 [1-50]

The World of Peter Rabbit and Friends Bedtime Story Book. Vol. 2
 HB Guide - v8 - Fall '97 - p278 [51-250]

Potter, Giselle
Lucy's Eyes and Margaret's Dragon (Illus. by Giselle Potter)
 CLW - v68 - D '97 - p62 [51-250]
 SLJ - v44 - F '98 - p122 [51-250]

Potter, Jean
Science in Seconds with Toys
 SLJ - v44 - Ap '98 - p122 [51-250]

Potter, Joan
African Americans Who Were First
 BL - v94 - S 1 '97 - p120 [51-250]
 BL - v94 - S 15 '97 - p233 [51-250]
 y Ch BWatch - v7 - O '97 - p5 [51-250]
 KR - v65 - Jl 1 '97 - p1034 [51-250]
 SLJ - v43 - S '97 - p236 [51-250]

Potter, Tessa
Digger: The Story of a Mole in the Fall (Illus. by Ken Lilly)
 HB Guide - v8 - Fall '97 - p278 [51-250]
 SB - v33 - D '97 - p277 [251-500]

Fang: The Story of a Fox in Winter (Illus. by Ken Lilly)
 HB Guide - v8 - Fall '97 - p278 [51-250]
 SB - v33 - D '97 - p277 [251-500]

Grayfur: The Story of a Rabbit in Summer (Illus. by Ken Lilly)
 BL - v93 - Je 1 '97 - p1721 [51-250]
 HB Guide - v8 - Fall '97 - p278 [51-250]
 SB - v33 - D '97 - p277 [251-500]

Sarn: The Story of an Otter in Spring (Illus. by Ken Lilly)
 BL - v93 - Je 1 '97 - p1721 [51-250]
 HB Guide - v8 - Fall '97 - p278 [51-250]
 SB - v33 - D '97 - p277 [251-500]

Poulsen, David A
Ride the High Country
 CBRA - '96 - p489+ [51-250]

The Vampire's Visit
 CBRA - '96 - p490 [51-250]

Powell, Anton
The Greek News
 Bks Keeps - My '97 - p26 [51-250]
 Emerg Lib - v24 - My '97 - p57 [1-50]
 RT - v51 - O '97 - p150+ [51-250]

Powell, Jillian
Artists
 Magpies - v12 - S '97 - p6 [51-250]
 TES - S 19 '97 - p16* [51-250]

Bread
 HB Guide - v8 - Fall '97 - p361 [51-250]
 SB - v33 - N '97 - p245 [51-250]
 TES - Jl 4 '97 - p16* [51-250]

Caring for Others
 Sch Lib - v45 - Ag '97 - p153 [51-250]

Caring for Yourself
 Sch Lib - v45 - Ag '97 - p153 [51-250]

Drug Trafficking
 y Bks Keeps - My '97 - p27 [51-250]
 Ch BWatch - v7 - My '97 - p7 [1-50]
 HB Guide - v8 - Fall '97 - p328 [1-50]
 SLJ - v43 - S '97 - p236 [51-250]

Eggs
 HB Guide - v8 - Fall '97 - p361 [51-250]
 SB - v33 - N '97 - p245 [51-250]
 SLJ - v43 - Ag '97 - p150 [51-250]
 TES - Jl 4 '97 - p16* [51-250]

Exercise and Your Health

SLJ - v44 - F '98 - p104 [51-250]

Fish

HB Guide - v8 - Fall '97 - p361 [51-250]

SB - v33 - D '97 - p276+ [51-250]

TES - Jl 4 '97 - p16* [51-250]

Food and Your Health

Sch Lib - v45 - N '97 - p206 [51-250]

SLJ - v44 - F '98 - p104 [51-250]

Fruit

HB Guide - v8 - Fall '97 - p361 [51-250]

SB - v33 - D '97 - p276+ [51-250]

SLJ - v43 - Jl '97 - p86+ [51-250]

TES - Jl 4 '97 - p16* [51-250]

Hygiene and Your Health

Sch Lib - v45 - N '97 - p206 [51-250]

Milk

HB Guide - v8 - Fall '97 - p361 [51-250]

SB - v33 - D '97 - p276+ [51-250]

SLJ - v43 - Ag '97 - p150 [51-250]

TES - Jl 4 '97 - p16* [51-250]

Pasta

HB Guide - v8 - Fall '97 - p361 [51-250]

SB - v33 - N '97 - p245 [51-250]

SLJ - v43 - Jl '97 - p86+ [51-250]

TES - Jl 4 '97 - p16* [51-250]

Potatoes

HB Guide - v8 - Fall '97 - p361 [51-250]

SB - v33 - N '97 - p245 [51-250]

TES - Jl 4 '97 - p16* [51-250]

Poultry

HB Guide - v8 - Fall '97 - p361 [51-250]

SB - v33 - D '97 - p276+ [51-250]

Rice

HB Guide - v8 - Fall '97 - p361 [51-250]

SB - v33 - N '97 - p245 [51-250]

TES - Jl 4 '97 - p16* [51-250]

The Supernatural

ASBYP - v29 - Fall '96 - p56+ [251-500]

Vegetables

HB Guide - v8 - Fall '97 - p361 [51-250]

SB - v33 - D '97 - p276+ [51-250]

Powell, Polly

Just Dessert (Illus. by Polly Powell)

RT - v51 - O '97 - p133+ [1-50]

Powers, Daniel

Jiro's Pearl (Illus. by Daniel Powers)

BL - v94 - O 1 '97 - p338 [51-250]

CBRS - v25 - Ag '97 - p161+ [1-50]

Ch BWatch - v7 - Je '97 - p6 [1-50]

HB Guide - v8 - Fall '97 - p278 [51-250]

Magpies - v12 - My '97 - p28+ [51-250]

PW - v244 - My 19 '97 - p76 [51-250]

Sch Lib - v45 - Ag '97 - p132 [51-250]

SLJ - v43 - Jl '97 - p73 [51-250]

Powers, Tom

Steven Spielberg: Master Storyteller

BL - v93 - Je 1 '97 - p1696+ [51-250]

y   Ch BWatch - v7 - Ap '97 - p6 [1-50]

HB Guide - v8 - Fall '97 - p382 [51-250]

LATBR - Jl 13 '97 - p8 [501+]

Powling, Chris

Famous with Smokey Joe (Illus. by Alan Marks)

Bks Keeps - My '97 - p23 [51-250]

Poydar, Nancy

Snip, Snip...Snow! (Illus. by Nancy Poydar)

BL - v94 - N 1 '97 - p484 [51-250]

CBRS - v26 - O '97 - p16+ [51-250]

KR - v65 - Ag 15 '97 - p1311 [51-250]

NYTBR - v103 - F 15 '98 - p25 [1-50]

Poynter, Margaret

The Leakeys: Uncovering the Origins of Humankind

BL - v94 - D 1 '97 - p630+ [51-250]

SLJ - v44 - Ja '98 - p128 [251-500]

Pozzi, Gianni

Chagall (Illus. by Claudia Saraceni)

y   BL - v94 - Mr 1 '98 - p1123 [51-250]

KR - v65 - N 15 '97 - p1712 [51-250]

y   SLJ - v43 - D '97 - p145 [51-250]

Prado, Miguelanxo
Peter and the Wolf (Illus. by Miguelanxo Prado)
    KR - v66 - Ap 1 '98 - p500 [51-250]
    PW - v245 - Ja 19 '98 - p380 [51-250]

Pratchett, Terry
Johnny and the Bomb
    TES - v135 - My 2 '97 - p8* [1-50]

Prater, John
Bear's Bad Mood
    Bks Keeps - My '97 - p21 [51-250]
    TES - N 14 '97 - p14* [51-250]

Once upon a Time
    Bks Keeps - N '97 - p21 [51-250]

Pratt, Kristin Joy
Fly in the Sky
    RT - v51 - O '97 - p152 [51-250]

Pratt, Pierre
Hippo Beach
    CBRS - v26 - D '97 - p41 [51-250]

Pratt, T K
Gage Canadian School Thesaurus
  r   Quill & Q - v63 - O '97 - p21 [251-500]

Preller, James
Cardinal and Sunflower (Illus. by Huy Voun Lee)
    KR - v66 - Ap 1 '98 - p500 [51-250]

NBA Game Day
    BL - v94 - Ja 1 '98 - p807 [51-250]

Preller, Martie
Anderkantland
    Bkbird - v35 - Spr '97 - p50 [51-250]

Prelutsky, Jack
The Beauty of the Beast (Illus. by Meilo So)
  y BL - v94 - S 15 '97 - p223 [1-50]
    BL - v94 - Mr 15 '98 - p1224 [1-50]
    BW - v27 - D 7 '97 - p22 [51-250]
    CCB-B - v51 - Ja '98 - p151+ [501+]
    Ch BWatch - v8 - Ja '98 - p2 [1-50]
    Emerg Lib - v25 - Ja '98 - p51 [51-250]
    NYTBR - v102 - N 16 '97 - p36 [501+]

    PW - v244 - O 6 '97 - p85 [1-50]
    SLJ - v44 - Ja '98 - p104 [51-250]

Monday's Troll (Illus. by Peter Sis)
    RT - v51 - N '97 - p252 [51-250]

Monday's Troll (Prelutsky). Audio Version
    BL - v94 - Ja 1 '98 - p740 [1-50]
    SLJ - v43 - Ap '97 - p82 [51-250]

A Pizza the Size of the Sun (Illus. by James Stevenson)
    Inst - v106 - My '97 - p21 [1-50]

Ride a Purple Pelican (Illus. by Garth Williams)
    PW - v244 - Ag 25 '97 - p74 [1-50]

Presilla, Maricel E
Life around the Lake
    RT - v51 - F '98 - p430 [51-250]
    SE - v61 - Ap '97 - p6* [1-50]

Presnall, Judith Janda
Artificial Organs
    ASBYP - v29 - Fall '96 - p60+ [501+]

Press, Judy
Alphabet Art (Illus. by Sue Dennen)
    Ch BWatch - v8 - Ja '98 - p8 [51-250]
    SLJ - v44 - Mr '98 - p202 [51-250]

Vroom! Vroom! (Illus. by Michael Kline)
    Ch BWatch - v8 - Ja '98 - p6 [1-50]
    Cur R - v37 - N '97 - p13 [51-250]
    SLJ - v43 - Ag '97 - p150 [51-250]

Price, L
Aida (Illus. by Leo Dillon)
    ECEJ - v25 - Fall '97 - p49 [1-50]

Price, Marilyn
More Australian Dinosaurs
    Magpies - v12 - S '97 - p44+ [51-250]

Price, Mathew
Lift-the-Flap Chick (Illus. by Moira Kemp)
    SLJ - v44 - Mr '98 - p186 [51-250]

Lift-the-Flap Kitten (Illus. by Moira Kemp)
SLJ - v44 - Mr '98 - p186 [51-250]

Lift-the-Flap Mouse (Illus. by Moira Kemp)
SLJ - v44 - Mr '98 - p186 [51-250]

Lift-the-Flap Puppy (Illus. by Moira Kemp)
SLJ - v44 - Mr '98 - p186 [51-250]

Price, Susan
The Saga of Aslak (Illus. by Barry Wilkinson)
Bks Keeps - N '97 - p24 [51-250]

Price, Susanna
Click! Fun with Photography
SLJ - v43 - Ag '97 - p174 [51-250]

Prieto, Iliana
Querido Diario (Illus. by David Rodriguez Hernandez)
Bkbird - v35 - Sum '97 - p57 [1-50]

Prince, Alison
Magic Dad (Illus. by Magda Van Tilburg)
Sch Lib - v45 - N '97 - p201 [51-250]

Pringle, Laurence
Animal Monsters
BL - v94 - S 1 '97 - p120 [51-250]

Drinking: A Risky Business
y   BL - v94 - D 15 '97 - p690 [51-250]
Ch BWatch - v7 - N '97 - p1 [1-50]
SLJ - v44 - Ja '98 - p128+ [51-250]

Elephant Woman (Illus. by Cynthia Moss)
CCB-B - v51 - Mr '98 - p256 [51-250]
HB - v74 - Ja '98 - p95 [51-250]
KR - v65 - N 1 '97 - p1648 [51-250]
SLJ - v43 - D '97 - p145+ [51-250]

Everybody Has a Bellybutton (Illus. by Clare Wood)
BL - v94 - S 15 '97 - p238 [51-250]
CBRS - v26 - O '97 - p17 [51-250]
KR - v65 - Ag 1 '97 - p1227 [51-250]

An Extraordinary Life (Illus. by Bob Marstall)
BL - v94 - Mr 15 '98 - p1219 [1-50]
Ch BWatch - v7 - D '97 - p6 [51-250]
HB Guide - v8 - Fall '97 - p350 [51-250]
SLJ - v43 - My '97 - p148+ [51-250]

Naming the Cat (Illus. by Katherine Potter)
BL - v94 - O 1 '97 - p338 [51-250]
CBRS - v26 - S '97 - p5 [1-50]
CCB-B - v51 - O '97 - p65 [51-250]
KR - v65 - Jl 1 '97 - p1035 [51-250]
PW - v244 - Je 16 '97 - p59 [51-250]
SLJ - v43 - N '97 - p97 [51-250]

Nature! Wild and Wonderful (Illus. by Tim Holmstrom)
BL - v93 - Je 1 '97 - p1696 [51-250]
SLJ - v43 - S '97 - p199 [51-250]

One Room School (Illus. by Barbara Garrison)
BL - v94 - Mr 1 '98 - p1138 [51-250]
CCB-B - v51 - Ap '98 - p293 [51-250]
KR - v66 - Ja 15 '98 - p116 [51-250]
PW - v245 - Ja 5 '98 - p67 [51-250]
SLJ - v44 - Ap '98 - p122+ [51-250]

Smoking: A Risky Business
SLMQ - v25 - Spr '97 - p185 [51-250]
y   VOYA - v20 - Ap '97 - p60 [251-500]

Taking Care of the Earth (Illus. by Bobbie Moore)
ASBYP - v29 - Fall '96 - p26 [51-250]

Prior, Katherine
The History of Emigration from China and Southeast Asia
SLJ - v44 - F '98 - p118 [51-250]
TES - S 19 '97 - p16* [501+]

The History of Emigration from Ireland
Bks Keeps - My '97 - p26 [51-250]
HB Guide - v8 - Fall '97 - p391 [51-250]
Sch Lib - v45 - Ag '97 - p153+ [51-250]
TES - S 19 '97 - p16* [501+]

The History of Emigration from the Indian Subcontinent
Bks Keeps - My '97 - p26 [51-250]

HB Guide - v8 - Fall '97 - p392 [51-250]
Sch Lib - v45 - Ag '97 - p153+ [51-250]
SLJ - v43 - Jl '97 - p100+ [51-250]
TES - S 19 '97 - p16* [501+]

Workers' Rights

Bks Keeps - S '97 - p29 [51-250]
y   Sch Lib - v45 - N '97 - p218 [51-250]
SLJ - v44 - Ja '98 - p129 [51-250]
TES - O 17 '97 - pR7 [51-250]

Prose, Francine
The Angel's Mistake (Illus. by Mark Podwal)

CCB-B - v50 - Jl '97 - p408 [51-250]
HB - v73 - Jl '97 - p468 [51-250]
HB Guide - v8 - Fall '97 - p335 [51-250]
KR - v65 - Ap 15 '97 - p648 [51-250]
NYTBR - v102 - S 28 '97 - p28 [1-50]
SLJ - v43 - Ap '97 - p130 [51-250]
Trib Bks - Je 8 '97 - p7 [51-250]

Pruneti, Luigi
Viking Explorers

CLW - v68 - D '97 - p86 [51-250]

Pryor, Bonnie
The Dream Jar (Illus. by Mark Graham)

RT - v51 - N '97 - p257 [51-250]
SE - v61 - Ap '97 - p13* [1-50]

Louie and Dan Are Friends (Illus. by Elizabeth Miles)

BL - v94 - O 1 '97 - p338+ [51-250]
CBRS - v26 - S '97 - p5 [1-50]
SLJ - v43 - S '97 - p190+ [51-250]

Toenails, Tonsils, and Tornadoes (Illus. by Helen Cogancherry)

CCB-B - v50 - Je '97 - p370 [51-250]
HB Guide - v8 - Fall '97 - p307 [51-250]
SLJ - v43 - My '97 - p110+ [51-250]

Puerto, Carlos
Hala, Vamos A Alabama! (Illus. by Javier Vazquez)

SLJ - v44 - F '98 - p132 [51-250]

The Puffin Treasury of Australian Children's Stories

Aust Bk R - N '97 - p61+ [501+]

The Puffin Treasury of Children's Stories

Magpies - v12 - Mr '97 - p8+ [251-500]

The Puffin Treasury of Classics

TES - N 7 '97 - p16* [51-250]
TES - N 21 '97 - p8* [251-500]

Pulford, Elizabeth
The Memory Tree

Magpies - v12 - Mr '97 - p2* [1-50]

Pullman, Philip
Clockwork, or, All Wound Up

y   Bks Keeps - N '97 - p6 [51-250]
NS - v126 - D 5 '97 - p64 [51-250]
TES - v135 - My 2 '97 - p8* [1-50]

The Firework-Maker's Daughter

Magpies - v12 - My '97 - p35 [51-250]

The Golden Compass

y   BL - v94 - N 1 '97 - p475 [1-50]
y   Kliatt - v31 - Jl '97 - p18+ [51-250]
NY - v73 - O 6 '97 - p118+ [251-500]
y   VOYA - v20 - Je '97 - p86 [51-250]

The Subtle Knife

y   BL - v94 - Ja 1 '98 - p733 [1-50]
y   BL - v94 - Mr 15 '98 - p1218 [1-50]
y   BW - v27 - Ag 3 '97 - p1+ [501+]
y   CCB-B - v51 - N '97 - p98 [51-250]
y   Ch BWatch - v7 - O '97 - p3 [51-250]
y   HB - v73 - S '97 - p578+ [51-250]
y   KR - v65 - Jl 15 '97 - p1116 [51-250]
y   MFSF - v93 - D '97 - p28+ [251-500]
y   NS - v126 - S 26 '97 - p66 [501+]
NY - v73 - O 6 '97 - p118+ [251-500]
y   Par Ch - Awards '97 - p7 [51-250]
PW - v244 - Je 30 '97 - p77 [51-250]
PW - v244 - N 3 '97 - p60 [51-250]
TES - S 19 '97 - p7* [501+]
y   TES - N 7 '97 - p12* [51-250]
TES - D 5 '97 - p17* [1-50]
y   TES - D 26 '97 - p14 [51-250]
y   VOYA - v20 - F '98 - p366 [51-250]
y   VOYA - v21 - Ap '98 - p38 [1-50]

Pulver, Robin
Alicia's Tutu (Illus. by Mark Graham)
> BL - v94 - S 1 '97 - p134+ [51-250]
> Ch BWatch - v7 - O '97 - p6 [51-250]

Purkis, Christine
Dark beneath the Moon
> Sch Lib - v45 - N '97 - p201 [51-250]

Paddlefeet
> Obs - D 7 '97 - p17* [51-250]

Pushkin, Alexand Sergeevich
The Tale of Tsar Saltan (Illus. by Gennady Spirin)
> RT - v51 - F '98 - p429 [51-250]

Putt-Putt's Night before Christmas
> Cur R - v37 - D '97 - p13 [51-250]

Pyle, Howard
Bearskin (Illus. by Trina Schart Hyman)
> BL - v94 - N 1 '97 - p468 [51-250]
> BL - v94 - Ja 1 '98 - p734+ [51-250]
> BW - v27 - N 2 '97 - p6 [51-250]
> CCB-B - v51 - N '97 - p98+ [51-250]
> HB - v73 - S '97 - p588 [51-250]
> Inst - v107 - Ja '98 - p29+ [1-50]
> PW - v244 - Jl 7 '97 - p67 [51-250]
> SLJ - v43 - Ag '97 - p139 [51-250]
> SLJ - v43 - D '97 - p27 [1-50]

Q R

Quackenbush, Robert
Batbaby (Illus. by Robert Quackenbush)
> SLJ - v43 - D '97 - p100 [51-250]

Quattlebaum, Mary
The Magic Squad and the Dog of Great Potential (Illus. by Frank Remkiewicz)
> HB Guide - v8 - Fall '97 - p293 [51-250]
> SLJ - v43 - My '97 - p111 [51-250]

Underground Train (Illus. by Cat Bowman Smith)
> BL - v94 - D 1 '97 - p643 [51-250]
> CCB-B - v51 - D '97 - p137 [51-250]
> KR - v65 - N 1 '97 - p1648 [51-250]
> PW - v244 - N 24 '97 - p73 [51-250]
> SLJ - v43 - N '97 - p97 [51-250]

Quigley, James
Johnny Germ Head (Illus. by JoAnn Adinolfi)
> BL - v94 - D 1 '97 - p637+ [51-250]
> SLJ - v43 - D '97 - p100 [51-250]

Quindlen, Anna
Happily Ever After (Illus. by James Stevenson)
> CBRS - v25 - Ag '97 - p165 [51-250]
> Cur R - v36 - Mr '97 - p13 [51-250]
> ECEJ - v25 - Fall '97 - p42+ [51-250]
> HB Guide - v8 - Fall '97 - p307 [51-250]
> NYTBR - v102 - My 18 '97 - p28 [501+]

The Tree That Came to Stay (Illus. by Nancy Carpenter)
> PW - v244 - O 6 '97 - p58 [1-50]

Quinlan, Alexis
Junior Astrologer Series
> PW - v244 - Jl 28 '97 - p76 [51-250]

Quinlan, Patricia
Baby's Feet (Illus. by Linda Hendry)
> Can CL - v23 - Fall '97 - p93 [51-250]
> CBRA - '96 - p455 [51-250]

Baby's Hands (Illus. by Linda Hendry)
> Can CL - v23 - Fall '97 - p93 [51-250]
> CBRA - '96 - p455 [51-250]

Night Fun (Illus. by Ron Berg)
> CBRS - v26 - Ja '98 - p52 [51-250]
> CM:CanRev - v4 - Ap 10 '98 - pONL [51-250]
> Quill & Q - v63 - S '97 - p74 [251-500]

Quirk, Anne
Dancing with Great-Aunt Cornelia
> BL - v93 - Je 1 '97 - p1705+ [51-250]
> CBRS - v25 - Je '97 - p131 [51-250]
> CCB-B - v50 - Je '97 - p370 [51-250]
> HB Guide - v8 - Fall '97 - p307 [51-250]
> KR - v65 - My 15 '97 - p806 [51-250]
> SLJ - v43 - My '97 - p139 [51-250]

Rabe, Berniece
Hiding Mr. McMulty
> y Am Vis - v12 - D '97 - p36 [51-250]
> BL - v94 - O 15 '97 - p406 [51-250]
> y CBRS - v26 - F '98 - p82 [51-250]
> HB - v74 - Ja '98 - p79+ [51-250]
> KR - v65 - O 15 '97 - p1587 [51-250]

SLJ - v43 - D '97 - p129 [51-250]
y VOYA - v20 - F '98 - p390 [251-500]

Rabe, Tish
*The Song of the Zubble-Wump (Illus.
by Tom Brannon)*
Ch BWatch - v7 - My '97 - p1 [1-50]
HB Guide - v8 - Fall '97 - p278 [51-250]

Raber, Thomas
Michael Jordan. Rev. Ed.
Ch BWatch - v7 - S '97 - p7 [1-50]

Radcliffe, Theresa
*Bashi, Elephant Baby (Illus. by John
Butler)*
CCB-B - v51 - Mr '98 - p257 [51-250]
HB - v74 - Ja '98 - p67 [51-250]
KR - v65 - D 15 '97 - p1838 [51-250]
PW - v244 - D 8 '97 - p71+ [51-250]
SLJ - v44 - F '98 - p90 [51-250]

Radford, Derek
Harry at the Garage
ASBYP - v29 - Sum '96 - p28+ [251-500]

Radunsky, Vladimir
*Yucka Drucka Droni (Illus. by
Vladimir Radunsky)*
KR - v65 - D 15 '97 - p1839 [51-250]
PW - v245 - Ja 19 '98 - p376 [51-250]
SLJ - v44 - Mr '98 - p186 [51-250]

Rae, Jennifer
*Gilbert De La Frogponde (Illus. by
Rose Cowles)*
CBRS - v26 - Win '98 - p67+ [51-250]
Quill & Q - v63 - O '97 - p43 [251-500]
Quill & Q - v63 - N '97 - p43+ [501+]

Rael, Elsa Okon
*When Zaydeh Danced on Eldridge
Street (Illus. by Marjorie Priceman)*
BL - v94 - O 1 '97 - p324 [51-250]
CCB-B - v51 - O '97 - p65+ [251-500]
Ch BWatch - v7 - D '97 - p2 [1-50]
HB - v73 - N '97 - p672+ [251-500]
NYTBR - v102 - S 28 '97 - p28 [501+]
PW - v244 - Je 16 '97 - p59 [51-250]

Raeside, Adrian
*Dennis and the Fantastic Forest (Illus.
by Adrian Raeside)*
CM:CanRev - v4 - N 28 '97 - pONL [51-250]
Quill & Q - v63 - Ag '97 - p38 [51-250]

Raezek, L
*The Night the Grandfathers Danced
(Illus. by Katalin Olah Ehling)*
ECEJ - v25 - Fall '97 - p49 [1-50]

Raffi
Baby Beluga (Illus. by Ashley Wolff)
PW - v244 - Jl 7 '97 - p70 [1-50]

*Rise and Shine (Illus. by Eugenie
Fernandes)*
CBRA - '96 - p517 [51-250]

*Wheels on the Bus (Illus. by Sylvie
Kantorovitz Wickstrom)*
PW - v245 - Ja 5 '98 - p69 [1-50]

Rafkin, Louise
*The Tiger's Eye, the Bird's Fist (Illus.
by Leslie McGrath)*
BL - v93 - Je 1 '97 - p1697 [51-250]
CCB-B - v51 - S '97 - p24 [51-250]
SLJ - v43 - Jl '97 - p110 [51-250]
y VOYA - v20 - O '97 - p268+ [51-250]

Raftery, Kevin
KidsGardening
WER - Sum '97 - p66 [51-250]

Rahaman, Vashanti
*A Little Salmon for Witness (Illus. by
Sandra Speidel)*
CBRS - v25 - Spr '97 - p137 [51-250]
HB Guide - v8 - Fall '97 - p278 [51-250]

*O Christmas Tree (Illus. by Frane
Lessac)*
ECEJ - v25 - Fall '97 - p49 [1-50]
RT - v51 - N '97 - p256 [51-250]
SE - v61 - Ap '97 - p7* [1-50]

*Read for Me, Mama (Illus. by Lori
McElrath-Eslick)*
HB Guide - v8 - Fall '97 - p278 [1-50]
NYTBR - v102 - My 18 '97 - p23+ [501+]

SLJ - v43 - Ap '97 - p115+ [51-250]

Raimondo, L
The Little Lama of Tibet
ECEJ - v25 - Fall '97 - p49 [1-50]

Rainbow Tales. Audio Version
BL - v94 - N 1 '97 - p494 [51-250]

Rainbow Tales, Too. Audio Version
BL - v94 - N 1 '97 - p494 [51-250]

Rainis, Kenneth G
A Guide to Microlife
   SB - v33 - Ag '97 - p186 [1-50]
yr SLJ - v43 - My '97 - p150 [51-250]

Raintree Steck-Vaughn Illustrated Science Encyclopedia. Vols. 1-24
yr SB - v33 - Je '97 - p138 [51-250]
r   SLJ - v43 - My '97 - p162 [51-250]
yr VOYA - v20 - Ap '97 - p68 [251-500]

Rambeck, Richard
Kristi Yamaguchi
SLJ - v44 - Mr '98 - p202 [51-250]

Michelle Kwan
SLJ - v44 - Mr '98 - p202 [51-250]

Monica Seles
SLJ - v43 - Je '97 - p110 [51-250]

Pete Sampras
SLJ - v43 - Je '97 - p110 [51-250]

Tiger Woods
SLJ - v44 - Mr '98 - p202 [51-250]

Ramirez, Michael Rose
Hola, California!
PW - v244 - Ag 11 '97 - p402 [51-250]
SLJ - v44 - Ja '98 - p90+ [51-250]

Hoppin' Halloween!
SLJ - v44 - Ja '98 - p90+ [51-250]

Ramsay, Helena
Rivers and Lakes (Illus. by Roger Stewart)
HB Guide - v8 - Fall '97 - p342 [51-250]
Sch Lib - v45 - Ag '97 - p150 [51-250]

Rand, Gloria
Baby in a Basket (Illus. by Ted Rand)
KR - v65 - S 15 '97 - p1461 [51-250]
PW - v244 - O 27 '97 - p75 [51-250]
SLJ - v43 - N '97 - p97+ [51-250]

A Home for Spooky (Illus. by Ted Rand)
KR - v66 - F 15 '98 - p272 [51-250]

Rand McNally and Company
World Contemporary Atlas with CD-Rom. Book and Electronic Media Version
r CG - v117 - S '97 - p86 [51-250]

Randall, Ronne P
The Little Red Hen (Illus. by Stephen Holmes)
HB Guide - v8 - Fall '97 - p331 [51-250]

Randall, Ronnie
Big Book of Rhymes and Stories (Illus. by Peter Stevenson)
TES - O 31 '97 - p16* [51-250]

Rankin, Joan
Scaredy Cat (Illus. by Joan Rankin)
NYTBR - v102 - Ap 27 '97 - p29 [501+]

Wow! It's Great Being a Duck (Illus. by Joan Rankin)
KR - v65 - D 1 '97 - p1778 [51-250]
PW - v244 - D 22 '97 - p59 [51-250]
Sch Lib - v45 - N '97 - p187+ [51-250]
SLJ - v44 - Mr '98 - p186 [51-250]

Rankin, Laura
Merl and Jasper's Supper Caper (Illus. by Laura Rankin)
CCB-B - v50 - Je '97 - p370+ [51-250]
HB Guide - v8 - Fall '97 - p278 [51-250]
KR - v65 - My 15 '97 - p806 [51-250]
PW - v244 - My 19 '97 - p75 [51-250]
SLJ - v43 - Jl '97 - p73 [51-250]

Ransom, Candice F
Fire in the Sky (Illus. by Shelly O Haas)
SLJ - v43 - Ag '97 - p139 [51-250]

One Christmas Dawn (Illus. by Peter Fiore)
SE - v61 - Ap '97 - p14 * [1-50]

Rappaport, Doreen
The Flight of Red Bird
KR - v65 - My 15 '97 - p806+ [51-250]
SLJ - v43 - Jl '97 - p111 [51-250]

The Lizzie Borden Trial
JOYS - v10 - Sum '97 - p429 [1-50]

Rappoport, Ken
Grant Hill
Ch BWatch - v7 - Ap '97 - p5 [1-50]
y   VOYA - v20 - Ag '97 - p165 [51-250]
y   VOYA - v20 - Ag '97 - p201+ [251-500]

Guts and Glory
BL - v93 - Ag '97 - p1895+ [51-250]
y   HB Guide - v8 - Fall '97 - p371 [51-250]
SLJ - v43 - Jl '97 - p111 [51-250]

Sports Great Eric Lindros
HB Guide - v8 - Fall '97 - p369 [51-250]

Rapunzel: A Fairy Tale (Illus. by Maja Dusikova)
BL - v93 - Ag '97 - p1903 [51-250]
HB Guide - v8 - Fall '97 - p333 [51-250]
NYTBR - v102 - N 16 '97 - p54+ [501+]

Raschka, Chris
Mysterious Thelonious (Illus. by Chris Raschka)
BL - v94 - N 1 '97 - p476 [251-500]
BL - v94 - Mr 15 '98 - p1224 [1-50]
CBRS - v26 - F '98 - p77 [51-250]
CCB-B - v51 - O '97 - p66 [51-250]
Emerg Lib - v25 - Ja '98 - p57 [51-250]
HB - v74 - Ja '98 - p68 [51-250]
KR - v65 - Jl 15 '97 - p1116 [51-250]
NYTBR - v102 - N 16 '97 - p28 [251-500]
NYTBR - v102 - D 7 '97 - p80 [1-50]
PW - v244 - Jl 28 '97 - p74 [51-250]
PW - v244 - N 3 '97 - p59 [1-50]
SLJ - v43 - S '97 - p207+ [51-250]

Simple Gifts (Illus. by Chris Raschka)
BL - v94 - Mr 1 '98 - p1131 [51-250]

HB - v74 - Mr '98 - p217 [51-250]
KR - v66 - F 15 '98 - p273 [51-250]
PW - v245 - F 16 '98 - p210 [51-250]
SLJ - v44 - Ap '98 - p125 [51-250]

Raskin, Ellen
The Westing Game
PW - v244 - Je 16 '97 - p61 [1-50]

Rassmus, Jens
Farmer Enno and His Cow (Illus. by Jens Rassmus)
KR - v66 - Ja 1 '98 - p61 [51-250]
PW - v245 - Ja 19 '98 - p378 [51-250]
SLJ - v44 - Ap '98 - p108 [51-250]

Rathmann, Peggy
Officer Buckle and Gloria (Lithgow). Book and Audio Version
SLJ - v44 - Ap '98 - p39 [1-50]

Ratnett, Michael
Horrible Holly's Pet Raptor (Illus. by Nate Evans)
PW - v244 - S 1 '97 - p104 [51-250]
SLJ - v43 - N '97 - p98 [51-250]

Rau, Dana Meachen
A Box Can Be Many Things (Illus. by Paige Billin-Frye)
HB Guide - v8 - Fall '97 - p278 [1-50]

Undersea City. Book and Audio Version
SLJ - v43 - D '97 - p72+ [51-250]

Rauzon, Mark J
Hummingbirds
HB Guide - v8 - Fall '97 - p352 [51-250]
SB - v33 - O '97 - p210 [51-250]
SLJ - v43 - Ag '97 - p174 [51-250]

Parrots
SLJ - v43 - Ap '97 - p155 [51-250]

Seabirds
SLJ - v43 - Ap '97 - p155 [51-250]

Vultures
HB Guide - v8 - Fall '97 - p352 [51-250]
SB - v33 - O '97 - p210 [51-250]

Water, Water Everywhere
    ASBYP - v29 - Sum '96 - p29 [251-500]

Ravage, Barbara
Rachel Carson: Protecting Our Environment
    HB Guide - v8 - Fall '97 - p379 [51-250]

Raven, Margot
Angels in the Dust (Illus. by Roger Essley)
    HB Guide - v8 - Fall '97 - p278 [51-250]
    SLJ - v43 - Je '97 - p99+ [51-250]

Rawls, Wilson
Where the Red Fern Grows
    NYTBR - v102 - N 16 '97 - p26 [1-50]

Ray, Jane
Hansel and Gretel (Illus. by Jane Ray)
    BL - v94 - D 1 '97 - p635 [51-250]
    Ch BWatch - v8 - Ja '98 - p3 [51-250]
    KR - v65 - O 15 '97 - p1587 [51-250]
    SLJ - v43 - N '97 - p111 [51-250]

The Twelve Dancing Princesses
    CBRA - '96 - p503 [51-250]
    RT - v51 - D '97 - p331+ [51-250]

Ray, Mary Lyn
Mud (Illus. by Lauren Stringer)
    RT - v51 - O '97 - p135 [1-50]

Rayban, Chloe
Love in Cyberia
    TES - v135 - My 2 '97 - p8* [1-50]

Rayner, Mary
The Small Good Wolf (Illus. by Mary Rayner)
    Bks Keeps - Jl '97 - p21 [51-250]
    Sch Lib - v45 - Ag '97 - p132 [51-250]

Rayner, Shoo
Hey Diddle Diddle and Other Mother Goose Rhymes
    Bks Keeps - Jl '97 - p19+ [51-250]
    Magpies - v12 - S '97 - p28+ [51-250]

Razzell, Mary
White Wave
    Can CL - v22 - Win '96 - p117+ [501+]

Read, Nicholas
One in a Million
    CBRA - '96 - p490 [51-250]

Readhead, Lloyd
Gymnastics
    BL - v94 - Mr 15 '98 - p1242 [51-250]

Rearick, John
Greek Myths
    Cur R - v37 - N '97 - p14 [51-250]

Reasoner, Charles
Who's Bugging You?
    Ch BWatch - v7 - Je '97 - p4 [51-250]

Whose Daddy Does This?
    Ch BWatch - v7 - Je '97 - p4 [1-50]
    NYTBR - v102 - S 14 '97 - p30 [501+]

Recheis, Kathe
Lisa Y El Gato Sin Nombre (Illus. by Claudia De Weck)
    SLJ - v44 - F '98 - p132 [51-250]

Rediger, Pat
Great African Americans in Business
    Ch BWatch - v7 - Mr '97 - p5 [51-250]

Great African Americans in Civil Rights
    Ch BWatch - v7 - Mr '97 - p5 [51-250]

Redmond, Ian
Gorilla (Illus. by Peter Anderson)
    ASBYP - v29 - Sum '96 - p46+ [501+]

Reeder, Carolyn
Across the Lines
    CCB-B - v50 - Je '97 - p371 [51-250]
    HB Guide - v8 - Fall '97 - p307 [51-250]
y   SLJ - v43 - Je '97 - p126 [51-250]
y   VOYA - v20 - Ag '97 - p188+ [251-500]

Foster's War
    BW - v28 - Mr 1 '98 - p11 [51-250]
    KR - v66 - Ja 1 '98 - p61 [51-250]

PW - v245 - F 9 '98 - p96 [51-250]
SLJ - v44 - Mr '98 - p216 [51-250]

Reeder, Stephanie Owen
The Flaming Witch (Illus. by Dadang Christanto)

Aust Bk R - S '97 - p64+ [51-250]
Magpies - v12 - S '97 - p19 [251-500]

Rees, Douglas
Lightning Time

y   BL - v94 - Ja 1 '98 - p794+ [51-250]
CBRS - v26 - Win '98 - p72 [51-250]
y   CCB-B - v51 - Ja '98 - p173 [251-500]
HB - v74 - Ja '98 - p80 [51-250]
KR - v65 - O 15 '97 - p1587 [51-250]
y   SLJ - v43 - D '97 - p129 [51-250]
y   VOYA - v21 - Ap '98 - p48+ [51-250]

Rees, Rosemary
The Ancient Egyptians

SLJ - v43 - S '97 - p208 [51-250]

The Ancient Greeks

SLJ - v43 - S '97 - p208 [51-250]

Regan, Colm
Africa

HB Guide - v8 - Fall '97 - p393 [51-250]
Magpies - v12 - Mr '97 - p40+ [251-500]

Regan, Dian Curtis
Dear Dr. Sillybear (Illus. by Randy Cecil)

CBRS - v26 - S '97 - p5 [1-50]
SLJ - v43 - S '97 - p191 [51-250]

Monsters in Cyberspace (Illus. by Melissa Sweet)

BL - v93 - Je 1 '97 - p1706 [51-250]
CCB-B - v50 - Jl '97 - p408+ [51-250]
HB Guide - v8 - Fall '97 - p307 [51-250]
SLJ - v43 - S '97 - p224+ [51-250]

Reid, Barbara
The Party (Illus. by Barbara Reid)

CM:CanRev - v4 - D 12 '97 - pONL [251-500]
Quill & Q - v63 - N '97 - p46 [251-500]
Quill & Q - v64 - F '98 - p42 [51-250]

Reid, Margarette S
A String of Beads (Illus. by Ashley Wolff)

BL - v93 - Ag '97 - p1899 [51-250]
CBRS - v26 - Win '98 - p68 [51-250]
SLJ - v43 - N '97 - p111+ [51-250]

Reid, Struan
The Children's Atlas of Lost Treasures

Ch BWatch - v8 - Ja '98 - p6 [1-50]
r   SLJ - v44 - Mr '98 - p241 [51-250]

Reid, Susan
Aliens in the Basement (Illus. by Susan Gardos)

CM:CanRev - v4 - Mr 13 '98 - pONL [251-500]

Reid, Thomas
My Manitoba Friends, A-Z (Illus. by Thomas Reid)

CBRA - '96 - p514+ [51-250]

Reider, Katja
Snail Started It! (Illus. by Angela Von Roehl)

Ch BWatch - v7 - Mr '97 - p6 [51-250]
HB Guide - v8 - Fall '97 - p278+ [51-250]
Learning - v26 - Ag '97 - p22 [51-250]
Par Ch - Awards '97 - p3 [51-250]
RT - v51 - F '98 - p427 [51-250]
SLJ - v43 - Je '97 - p100 [51-250]
Ch BWatch - v7 - Je '97 - p7 [1-50]

Reidy, Hannah
Crazy Creatures Counting

TES - Je 13 '97 - pR7 [51-250]

Reilly, DeeDee
Tibby (Illus. by Betsy Walker)

SB - v33 - Ag '97 - p186 [1-50]

Reinagle, Damon
Draw Sports Figures

BWatch - v18 - D '97 - p2 [1-50]

Reinhard, Johan
Discovering the Inca Ice Maiden

KR - v66 - F 15 '98 - p273 [51-250]

Reiser, Lynn
Beach Feet (Illus. by Lynn Reiser)
> LA - v73 - N '96 - p522 [51-250]
> SB - v32 - D '96 - p275 [51-250]

· *Best Friends Think Alike (Illus. by Lynn Reiser)*
> BL - v93 - Je 1 '97 - p1721 [51-250]
> HB Guide - v8 - Fall '97 - p254 [51-250]
> SLJ - v43 - My '97 - p111+ [51-250]

Cherry Pies and Lullabies (Illus. by Lynn Reiser)
> BL - v94 - Mr 1 '98 - p1141 [51-250]
> KR - v66 - Ap 1 '98 - p500 [51-250]
> PW - v245 - F 2 '98 - p90 [51-250]

Tortillas and Lullabies (Illus. by Corazones Valientes (Organization))
> KR - v66 - Ap 1 '98 - p501 [51-250]
> PW - v245 - F 23 '98 - p78 [51-250]
> SLJ - v44 - Ap '98 - p108 [51-250]

Reiss, Kathryn
Paperquake: A Puzzle
> y   KR - v66 - F 15 '98 - p273 [51-250]
> PW - v245 - Ja 26 '98 - p92 [51-250]

Rekela, George
Sports Great Muggsy Bogues
> HB Guide - v8 - Fall '97 - p369 [51-250]

Rendon, Marcie R
Powwow Summer (Illus. by Cheryl Walsh Bellville)
> SE - v61 - Ap '97 - p10* [1-50]

Renee
I Have to Go Home
> Magpies - v12 - My '97 - p7* [51-250]

Repchuk, Caroline
The Christmas Bears (Illus. by Stephanie Boey)
> Ch BWatch - v7 - D '97 - p1 [1-50]
> PW - v244 - O 6 '97 - p57 [1-50]

The Forgotten Garden (Illus. by Ian Andrew)
> CBRS - v25 - Je '97 - p128 [51-250]
> SLJ - v43 - S '97 - p191 [51-250]

My Little Supermarket (Illus. by Claire Henley)
> Bks Keeps - Jl '97 - p20 [51-250]

The Snow Tree (Illus. by Josephine Martin)
> BL - v94 - S 1 '97 - p140 [51-250]
> Bloom Rev - v17 - N '97 - p33 [51-250]
> CBRS - v26 - D '97 - p41 [51-250]
> Ch BWatch - v7 - D '97 - p2 [1-50]

Rescue (Machines)
> Ch BWatch - v7 - Je '97 - p4 [1-50]

Reviere, Susan L
Memory of Childhood Trauma
> SB - v32 - D '96 - p265 [51-250]

Rex, Michael
The Painting Gorilla (Illus. by Michael Rex)
> BL - v94 - D 1 '97 - p643 [51-250]
> CBRS - v26 - F '98 - p77+ [1-50]
> KR - v65 - Jl 1 '97 - p1035 [51-250]
> Par - v73 - F '98 - p185 [51-250]
> SLJ - v43 - S '97 - p191+ [51-250]

Rey, H A
Find the Constellations
> Par - v72 - Ag '97 - p170 [1-50]

Rey, Margret
Spotty (Illus. by H A Rey)
> HB Guide - v8 - Fall '97 - p279 [51-250]

Reynolds, Marilynn, 1940-
The New Land (Illus. by Stephen McCallum)
> BL - v94 - O 15 '97 - p416+ [51-250]
> HB Guide - v8 - Fall '97 - p279 [51-250]
> Quill & Q - v63 - Ap '97 - p36 [251-500]
> SLJ - v43 - Jl '97 - p73+ [51-250]

Rhodes, Vicki
Pumpkin Decorating
> SLJ - v44 - Ja '98 - p130 [51-250]

Riccio, Nina
Five Kids and a Monkey Banish the Stinkies
> Ch BWatch - v7 - Jl '97 - p1 [51-250]

Five Kids and a Monkey Investigate a Vicious Virus
> Ch BWatch - v7 - Jl '97 - p1 [51-250]

Five Kids and a Monkey Solve the Great Cupcake Caper
> Ch BWatch - v7 - Jl '97 - p1 [51-250]

Ricciuti, Edward R
America's Top 10 Bridges
> BL - v94 - Ja 1 '98 - p807 [51-250]
> r   Ch BWatch - v7 - O '97 - p1 [1-50]
> SLJ - v44 - F '98 - p122 [51-250]

America's Top 10 Natural Wonders
> r   Ch BWatch - v7 - O '97 - p1 [1-50]

America's Top 10 Skyscrapers
> r   Ch BWatch - v7 - O '97 - p1 [1-50]

Chaparral
> SB - v32 - D '96 - p275 [51-250]

Desert
> SB - v32 - D '96 - p275 [51-250]

Grassland
> SB - v32 - D '96 - p275 [51-250]

What on Earth Is a Hydrax?
> ASBYP - v29 - Fall '96 - p68 [251-500]

What on Earth Is a Pout?
> ASBYP - v29 - Fall '96 - p68 [251-500]
> SLMQ - v25 - Win '97 - p118 [1-50]

Rice, Chris
My First Body Book
> ASBYP - v29 - Sum '96 - p29+ [251-500]

Rice, David L
Lifetimes (Illus. by Michael S Maydak)
> BL - v93 - Je 1 '97 - p1697 [51-250]
> KR - v65 - Ap 15 '97 - p648 [51-250]
> Quill & Q - v63 - O '97 - p38 [251-500]
> SB - v33 - D '97 - p274 [51-250]
> SLJ - v44 - F '98 - p104 [51-250]

Richards, David, 1953-
Soldier Boys
> Can CL - v22 - Win '96 - p111 [51-250]

Richards, Jon
The Fantastic Cutaway Book of Speed (Illus. by Alex Pang)
> y   BL - v94 - Mr 15 '98 - p1225 [1-50]
> Ch BWatch - v7 - My '97 - p7 [51-250]
> HB Guide - v8 - Fall '97 - p359 [51-250]
> y   VOYA - v21 - Ap '98 - p40 [1-50]

The Young People's Atlas of the World (Illus. by Stephen Sweet)
> r   Ch BWatch - v7 - My '97 - p7 [1-50]
> r   KR - v65 - Je 15 '97 - p956 [51-250]
> r   PW - v244 - Je 23 '97 - p93 [51-250]
> r   SLJ - v44 - F '98 - p104 [51-250]

Richards, Nancy Wilcox
Farmer Joe Baby-Sits (Illus. by Werner Zimmermann)
> CM:CanRev - v4 - S 5 '97 - pONL [251-500]

Richardson, Joy
In the Distance
> Sch Lib - v45 - Ag '97 - p155 [51-250]

Looking at Pictures (Illus. by Charlotte Voake)
> Bks Keeps - My '97 - p26 [51-250]
> CCB-B - v50 - Jl '97 - p409 [251-500]
> HB Guide - v8 - Fall '97 - p364 [51-250]
> Magpies - v12 - S '97 - p4+ [51-250]
> SLJ - v43 - Je '97 - p143 [51-250]
> TES - N 7 '97 - p10* [1-50]

Making Faces
> Sch Lib - v45 - Ag '97 - p155 [51-250]

Richardson, Judith Benet
First Came the Owl
> PW - v245 - Ja 12 '98 - p61 [1-50]

Richardson, Sandy
The Girl Who Ate Chicken Feet
> BL - v94 - Mr 1 '98 - p1134+ [51-250]
> KR - v66 - Ja 1 '98 - p61 [51-250]
> SLJ - v44 - Mr '98 - p218 [51-250]

Richler, Mordecai
Jacob Two-Two's First Spy Case (Illus. by Michael Chesworth)
> BL - v93 - Ag '97 - p1902 [51-250]
> Bloom Rev - v17 - Jl '97 - p21 [51-250]
> HB - v73 - Jl '97 - p462 [51-250]
> HB Guide - v8 - Fall '97 - p307 [51-250]
> NYTBR - v102 - My 18 '97 - p29 [501+]
> SLJ - v43 - Ag '97 - p139+ [51-250]

Jacob Two-Two's First Spy Case (Illus. by Norman Eyolfson)
> Can CL - v23 - Sum '97 - p79+ [501+]

Richter, Konrad
Wipe Your Feet, Santa Claus! (Illus. by Jozef Wilkon)
> PW - v244 - O 6 '97 - p59 [1-50]

Rickard, Lisa
My Kindy
> Magpies - v12 - My '97 - p28 [51-250]

Riddle, Tohby
The Great Escape from City Zoo (Illus. by Tohby Riddle)
> Aust Bk R - Ag '97 - p62+ [501+]

Ridley, Philip
Kasper in the Glitter (Illus. by Chris Riddell)
> CBRS - v26 - S '97 - p12 [51-250]
> y   KR - v65 - Jl 15 '97 - p1116 [51-250]
> SLJ - v43 - D '97 - p129+ [51-250]

Scribbleboy (Illus. by Chris Riddell)
> Bks Keeps - N '97 - p26 [51-250]
> Magpies - v12 - Jl '97 - p34+ [51-250]
> Sch Lib - v45 - Ag '97 - p147 [51-250]
> TES - N 7 '97 - p8* [1-50]

Ridpath, Ian
Facts on File Stars and Planets Atlas. 2nd Ed.
> r   BL - v94 - Mr 15 '98 - p1258 [51-250]

Riggio, Anita
Beware the Brindlebeast
> PW - v244 - O 6 '97 - p50 [1-50]

Secret Signs (Illus. by Anita Riggio)
> Emerg Lib - v24 - My '97 - p64 [51-250]
> HB Guide - v8 - Fall '97 - p279 [51-250]

Riley, Linnea Asplind
Mouse Mess (Illus. by Linnea Asplind Riley)
> BL - v94 - O 1 '97 - p339 [51-250]
> CBRS - v26 - Ja '98 - p52 [1-50]
> CCB-B - v51 - D '97 - p137 [51-250]
> KR - v65 - S 15 '97 - p1462 [51-250]
> Par - v72 - D '97 - p204 [1-50]
> PW - v244 - S 29 '97 - p88 [51-250]
> SLJ - v43 - N '97 - p98 [51-250]
> SLJ - v43 - D '97 - p27 [1-50]

Rinaldi, Ann
An Acquaintance with Darkness
> y   BL - v94 - S 15 '97 - p231 [51-250]
> y   BL - v94 - Mr 15 '98 - p1218 [1-50]
> y   CCB-B - v51 - O '97 - p66+ [51-250]
> Ch BWatch - v7 - N '97 - p2 [51-250]
> y   PW - v244 - Jl 7 '97 - p69 [51-250]
> y   VOYA - v20 - F '98 - p390 [251-500]
> y   VOYA - v21 - Ap '98 - p38 [1-50]

Hang a Thousand Trees with Ribbons
> RT - v51 - S '97 - p54+ [51-250]
> y   RT - v51 - N '97 - p244+ [51-250]
> y   RT - v51 - D '97 - p307 [51-250]

Keep Smiling Through
> SE - v61 - Ap '97 - p13* [1-50]
> y   SE - v61 - S '97 - p271 [1-50]

The Second Bend in the River
> SLJ - v43 - Je '97 - p126 [51-250]

Rinder, Lenore
A Big Mistake
> Inst - v106 - My '97 - p4* [1-50]

Ring, Elizabeth
What Rot! (Illus. by Dwight Kuhn)
> ASBYP - v29 - Fall '96 - p26+ [251-500]
> SB - v33 - Ag '97 - p186 [1-50]

Ringgold, Faith
Bonjour, Lonnie (Illus. by Faith Ringgold)
> ABR - v19 - N '97 - p9+ [501+]

RT - v51 - O '97 - p153 [51-250]
SE - v61 - Ap '97 - p13* [1-50]

My Dream of Martin Luther King
BL - v94 - F 15 '98 - p999 [1-50]

Riordan, James
The Songs My Paddle Sings (Illus. by Michael Foreman)
BL - v94 - Mr 15 '98 - p1242 [51-250]
KR - v66 - F 15 '98 - p273 [51-250]

The Twelve Labors of Hercules (Illus. by Christina Balit)
BL - v94 - Ja 1 '98 - p807 [51-250]
CCB-B - v51 - D '97 - p138 [51-250]
SLJ - v44 - F '98 - p122+ [51-250]

The Twelve Labours of Hercules (Illus. by Christina Balit)
Bks Keeps - N '97 - p22 [51-250]
Spec - v279 - D 6 '97 - p44 [1-50]

Ripken, Cal, Jr.
The Only Way I Know (Fontana). Audio Version
y   Kliatt - v31 - S '97 - p59 [251-500]
y   Kliatt - v31 - N '97 - p48 [51-250]
LJ - v122 - Je 15 '97 - p115 [51-250]

Ripley, Catherine
Do the Doors Open by Magic? and Other Supermarket Questions (Illus. by Scot Ritchie)
Can CL - v23 - Fall '97 - p94 [51-250]

Why Do Stars Twinkle? and Other Nighttime Questions (Illus. by Scot Ritchie)
Can CL - v23 - Sum '97 - p72+ [501+]
CBRA - '96 - p533 [51-250]

Why Does Popcorn Pop? and Other Kitchen Questions (Illus. by Scot Ritchie)
BL - v94 - D 1 '97 - p633 [51-250]
SLJ - v44 - F '98 - p104 [51-250]

Why Is Soap So Slippery? and Other Bathtime Questions (Illus. by Scot Ritchie)
Can CL - v23 - Fall '97 - p94 [51-250]

Why Is the Sky Blue? and Other Outdoor Questions (Illus. by Scot Ritchie)
SB - v33 - Je '97 - p142 [251-500]

Rivard, Ken
Mom, the School Flooded! (Illus. by Jacques Laplante)
CBRA - '96 - p455 [51-250]

Rix, Jamie
Free the Whales
TES - N 14 '97 - p14* [51-250]

Robb, Jackie
Bat (Illus. by Karen Duncan)
BL - v93 - Je 1 '97 - p1706 [51-250]
CBRS - v25 - Jl '97 - p150 [1-50]
HB Guide - v8 - Fall '97 - p279 [51-250]

Brain Cell (Illus. by Karen Duncan)
BL - v93 - Je 1 '97 - p1706 [51-250]
CBRS - v25 - Jl '97 - p150 [1-50]
HB Guide - v8 - Fall '97 - p279 [51-250]

Slug (Illus. by Karen Duncan)
BL - v93 - Je 1 '97 - p1706 [51-250]
CBRS - v25 - Jl '97 - p150 [1-50]
HB Guide - v8 - Fall '97 - p279 [51-250]

Spider (Illus. by Karen Duncan)
BL - v93 - Je 1 '97 - p1706 [51-250]
CBRS - v25 - Jl '97 - p150 [1-50]
HB Guide - v8 - Fall '97 - p279 [51-250]

Robb, Laura
Music and Drum (Illus. by Debra Lill)
CBRS - v25 - Je '97 - p131 [1-50]
Ch BWatch - v7 - My '97 - p4 [1-50]
CLW - v68 - S '97 - p67 [51-250]
HB Guide - v8 - Fall '97 - p374+ [51-250]
NYTBR - v102 - My 18 '97 - p25 [501+]
SLJ - v43 - My '97 - p150 [51-250]

Robbennolt, Roger L
The Unicorn at the Manger
Ch BWatch - v7 - Mr '97 - p8 [51-250]
Ch BWatch - v7 - My '97 - p1 [51-250]
Ch BWatch - v7 - Je '97 - p1 [51-250]

Robbins, Deri
Great Pirate Activity Book
Emerg Lib - v25 - N '97 - p46 [51-250]

Robbins, Glenn
Uncle Arthur's Bedtime Stories: Cinderella (Illus. by Mitch Vane)
Magpies - v12 - S '97 - p34+ [51-250]

Robbins, Ken
Fire
ASBYP - v29 - Fall '96 - p27 [51-250]

Roberts, Bethany
Halloween Mice (Illus. by Doug Cushman)
PW - v244 - O 6 '97 - p50 [1-50]

A Mouse Told His Mother (Illus. by Maryjane Begin)
CBRS - v25 - My '97 - p112+ [51-250]
Ch BWatch - v7 - Je '97 - p6 [1-50]
HB Guide - v8 - Fall '97 - p279 [51-250]
SLJ - v43 - My '97 - p112 [51-250]

Valentine Mice! (Illus. by Doug Cushman)
BL - v94 - D 15 '97 - p704 [51-250]
KR - v65 - D 1 '97 - p1778 [51-250]
PW - v244 - D 1 '97 - p52 [51-250]
SLJ - v44 - Ja '98 - p91 [51-250]

Roberts, Jack L
The Importance of Oskar Schindler
RT - v51 - O '97 - p151 [51-250]

Roberts, M L
Bugs and Other Creepy Creatures
ASBYP - v29 - Sum '96 - p64 [251-500]

Sea Creatures
ASBYP - v29 - Sum '96 - p64 [251-500]

Roberts, Willo Davis
The Kidnappers: A Mystery
CCB-B - v51 - Mr '98 - p257 [51-250]
KR - v65 - D 15 '97 - p1839 [51-250]
SLJ - v44 - Mr '98 - p218 [51-250]

Secrets at Hidden Valley
HB Guide - v8 - Fall '97 - p308 [51-250]
SLJ - v43 - Je '97 - p126+ [51-250]

Robertshaw, Andrew
A Soldier's Life
BL - v93 - Je 1 '97 - p1697+ [51-250]
CBRS - v25 - Ag '97 - p167+ [51-250]
y CCB-B - v50 - Je '97 - p371+ [51-250]
Ch BWatch - v7 - O '97 - p1 [1-50]
HB Guide - v8 - Fall '97 - p326 [51-250]
PW - v244 - Je 16 '97 - p61 [51-250]
SLJ - v43 - Je '97 - p143 [51-250]

Robertson, Joanne
The Harvest Queen (Illus. by Karen Reczuch)
CBRA - '96 - p455+ [51-250]

Robinet, Harriette Gillem
Mississippi Chariot
Ch BWatch - v7 - Je '97 - p7 [1-50]

The Twins, the Pirates, and the Battle of New Orleans
KR - v65 - O 1 '97 - p1536 [51-250]
SLJ - v43 - D '97 - p130 [51-250]

Robinson, Aminah Brenda Lynn
A Street Called Home
Am Vis - v12 - D '97 - p34 [1-50]
BL - v94 - D 15 '97 - p700 [1-50]
CCB-B - v51 - N '97 - p99 [251-500]
KR - v65 - S 15 '97 - p1462 [51-250]
NY - v73 - O 6 '97 - p116 [51-250]
PW - v244 - O 27 '97 - p78+ [51-250]
SLJ - v44 - F '98 - p104 [51-250]

Robinson, Barbara
The Best Christmas Pageant Ever (Illus. by Judith Gwyn Brown)
NYTBR - v102 - N 16 '97 - p26 [1-50]

Robinson, Claire
Crocodiles
SLJ - v44 - Ap '98 - p124 [51-250]

Penguins
SLJ - v44 - Ap '98 - p124 [51-250]

Robinson, Fay
Pilots Fly Planes
SLJ - v43 - Ap '97 - p126 [51-250]

Robinson, Marc
Cock-a-Doodle-Doo! What Does It Sound Like to You? (Illus. by Steve Jenkins)
ECEJ - v25 - Fall '97 - p49 [1-50]

Robshaw, Brandon
The Boy with the Eggshell Skull
Sch Lib - v45 - Ag '97 - p147 [51-250]

Robson, Pam
Air, Wind and Flight
SB - v32 - D '96 - p259 [1-50]

Body Language (Illus. by Colin Mier)
BL - v94 - Ja 1 '98 - p806 [51-250]
SB - v34 - Ap '98 - p78 [51-250]
SLJ - v44 - Mr '98 - p202 [51-250]

Roc, Margaret
Little Koala Finds a Friend (Illus. by Deborah Brown)
Magpies - v12 - Jl '97 - p27 [51-250]

Roca, Nuria
Aparato Respiratorio (Illus. by Antonio Munoz Tenllado)
JAAL - v40 - Ap '97 - p591 [51-250]

El Sistema Nervioso (Illus. by Antonio Munoz Tenllado)
JAAL - v40 - Ap '97 - p591 [51-250]

Roche, Denis
Art around the World (Illus. by Denis Roche)
KR - v66 - F 15 '98 - p274 [51-250]

Brave Georgie Goat (Illus. by Denis Roche)
CCB-B - v51 - Mr '98 - p257+ [251-500]
PW - v244 - O 27 '97 - p74+ [51-250]
SLJ - v44 - Ja '98 - p91+ [51-250]

Ollie All Over (Illus. by Denis Roche)
CCB-B - v50 - Je '97 - p372 [51-250]
HB Guide - v8 - Fall '97 - p254 [51-250]

SLJ - v43 - Ag '97 - p140 [51-250]

Only One Ollie (Illus. by Denis Roche)
CCB-B - v50 - Je '97 - p372 [51-250]
HB Guide - v8 - Fall '97 - p254 [51-250]
SLJ - v43 - Ag '97 - p140 [51-250]

Roche, Hannah
My Dad's a Wizard (Illus. by Chris Fisher)
SB - v33 - Ag '97 - p186 [1-50]

My Mom Is Magic (Illus. by Chris Fisher)
SB - v33 - Ag '97 - p186 [1-50]

My Sister Is Super (Illus. by Chris Fisher)
SB - v33 - Ag '97 - p186 [1-50]

Rochelle, Belinda
Jewels (Illus. by Cornelius Van Wright)
BL - v94 - F 15 '98 - p1020 [51-250]
CCB-B - v51 - Mr '98 - p258 [251-500]
KR - v65 - D 15 '97 - p1839 [51-250]
PW - v244 - D 22 '97 - p59 [51-250]
SLJ - v44 - Mr '98 - p186 [51-250]

Rochford, Deirdre
Rights for Animals?
Bks Keeps - My '97 - p26+ [51-250]
HB Guide - v8 - Fall '97 - p318 [51-250]
y   SB - v33 - Je '97 - p138 [51-250]
SLJ - v43 - My '97 - p145+ [51-250]

Rock, Lois
Best Loved Prayers (Illus. by Alison Wissenfeld)
PW - v245 - Ja 26 '98 - p86 [51-250]

Glimpses of Heaven (Illus. by Gabrielle Izen)
Sch Lib - v45 - Ag '97 - p132 [51-250]

Rock 'n Learn Solar System. Book and Audio Version
SLJ - v44 - Ja '98 - p70 [51-250]

Rocklin, Joanne

The Case of the Missing Birthday Party (Illus. by John Speirs)
> SLJ - v43 - My '97 - p112 [51-250]

For Your Eyes Only! (Illus. by Mark Todd)
> CBRS - v25 - Spr '97 - p144 [51-250]
> Ch BWatch - v7 - Je '97 - p1 [51-250]
> y   JAAL - v41 - O '97 - p158 [51-250]
> SLJ - v43 - D '97 - p27 [1-50]

One Hungry Cat (Illus. by Rowan Barnes-Murphy)
> SLJ - v43 - Jl '97 - p74 [51-250]

Rockwell, Anne

Halloween Day (Illus. by Lizzy Rockwell)
> BL - v94 - S 1 '97 - p140 [51-250]
> Emerg Lib - v25 - N '97 - p55 [1-50]
> KR - v65 - Je 15 '97 - p956 [51-250]
> PW - v244 - O 6 '97 - p48 [51-250]
> SLJ - v43 - S '97 - p192 [51-250]

I Fly (Illus. by Annette Cable)
> BL - v93 - Ag '97 - p1907 [51-250]
> HB Guide - v8 - Fall '97 - p279 [51-250]
> SLJ - v43 - Jl '97 - p74 [51-250]

Once upon a Time This Morning (Illus. by Sucie Stevenson)
> HB Guide - v8 - Fall '97 - p293 [51-250]

One Bean (Illus. by Megan Halsey)
> KR - v66 - Ap 1 '98 - p501 [51-250]

The One-Eyed Giant (Illus. by Anne Rockwell)
> SE - v61 - Ap '97 - p5* [1-50]

Show and Tell Day (Illus. by Lizzy Rockwell)
> HB Guide - v8 - Fall '97 - p254 [51-250]
> SLJ - v43 - My '97 - p112+ [51-250]

The Story Snail (Illus. by Theresa Smith)
> HB Guide - v8 - Fall '97 - p293 [51-250]
> SLJ - v43 - S '97 - p192 [51-250]

Rockwell, Thomas

How to Get Fabulously Rich (Illus. by Nick Sharratt)
> Sch Lib - v45 - N '97 - p201 [51-250]

Rodda, Emily

Power and Glory (Illus. by Geoff Kelly)
> Inst - v106 - My '97 - p20 [1-50]

Rowan and the Keeper of the Crystal
> Magpies - v12 - Mr '97 - p35 [51-250]

Yay! (Illus. by Craig Smith)
> BL - v94 - S 1 '97 - p135 [51-250]
> CBRS - v26 - S '97 - p6 [1-50]
> Magpies - v12 - Mr '97 - p28 [51-250]
> SLJ - v43 - Ag '97 - p140 [51-250]

Roddie, Shen

Best of Friends! (Illus. by Sally Anne Lambert)
> Sch Lib - v45 - N '97 - p188 [51-250]

Toes Are to Tickle (Illus. by Kady MacDonald Denton)
> Bks Keeps - Jl '97 - p19 [51-250]
> BL - v93 - Je 1 '97 - p1721 [51-250]
> CCB-B - v51 - S '97 - p24 [51-250]
> HB Guide - v8 - Fall '97 - p254 [51-250]
> KR - v65 - Je 1 '97 - p879 [51-250]
> PW - v244 - My 26 '97 - p84 [51-250]
> Quill & Q - v63 - My '97 - p44 [51-250]
> Sch Lib - v45 - Ag '97 - p132 [51-250]
> SLJ - v43 - S '97 - p192 [51-250]

Too Close Friends (Illus. by Sally Anne Lambert)
> KR - v65 - D 15 '97 - p1840 [51-250]
> PW - v245 - Mr 16 '98 - p63 [51-250]
> SLJ - v44 - Mr '98 - p186+ [51-250]

Roden, Katie

Farming
> Ch BWatch - v7 - Mr '97 - p5 [1-50]

Plague
> Ch BWatch - v7 - My '97 - p7 [1-50]
> Sch Lib - v45 - N '97 - p206 [51-250]

Solving International Crime
> Ch BWatch - v7 - My '97 - p7 [1-50]

Terrorism
> Ch BWatch - v7 - My '97 - p7 [1-50]
> HB Guide - v8 - Fall '97 - p328 [1-50]
y Sch Lib - v45 - Ag '97 - p165 [51-250]
> SLJ - v43 - S '97 - p236 [51-250]

Rodgers, Frank
Gorilla Granny
> Sch Lib - v45 - N '97 - p201+ [51-250]

Rodowsky, Colby
The Turnabout Shop
> KR - v66 - Ja 15 '98 - p117 [51-250]
> PW - v245 - Ja 5 '98 - p68 [51-250]
> SLJ - v44 - Mr '98 - p218 [51-250]

Rodriguez, Antonio Orlando
El Sueno
> Bkbird - v35 - Sum '97 - p24 [51-250]

Rodriguez, Janel
Nely Galan
> HB Guide - v8 - Fall '97 - p379 [51-250]

Roehm, Michelle
Girls Know Best
> Ch BWatch - v7 - N '97 - p1 [51-250]
> PW - v244 - Ag 18 '97 - p95 [51-250]
> SLJ - v43 - D '97 - p146 [51-250]

Roessel, Monty
Songs from the Loom
> SE - v61 - Ap '97 - p216 [51-250]

Rogasky, Barbara
Winter Poems (Illus. by Trina Schart Hyman)
> Comw - v124 - D 5 '97 - p15 [1-50]

Rogers, Alan
Blue Tortoise
> CBRS - v26 - D '97 - p41 [1-50]

Yellow Hippo
> CBRS - v26 - D '97 - p41 [1-50]

Rogers, Fred
Let's Talk about It (Illus. by Jim Judkis)
> BL - v94 - O 15 '97 - p410 [51-250]

Stepfamilies (Illus. by Jim Judkis)
> CCB-B - v51 - Ja '98 - p174 [51-250]

Rogers, Linda
Molly Brown Is Not a Clown (Illus. by Rick Van Krugel)
> CBRA - '96 - p490+ [51-250]

Rogers, Paul
Cat's Kittens (Illus. by Sophy Williams)
> Ch BWatch - v7 - Mr '97 - p6 [1-50]

Nearly, but Not Quite (Illus. by John Prater)
> Bks Keeps - S '97 - p20 [51-250]
> Sch Lib - v45 - Ag '97 - p132 [51-250]
> TES - Jl 18 '97 - p35 [251-500]

Rogers, Sally
Earthsong (Illus. by Melissa Bay Mathis)
> BL - v94 - Mr 1 '98 - p1138 [51-250]
> KR - v66 - Ja 1 '98 - p62 [51-250]
> PW - v245 - Mr 9 '98 - p66 [51-250]
> SLJ - v44 - Mr '98 - p202 [51-250]

Rohmann, Eric
The Cinder-Eyed Cats (Illus. by Eric Rohmann)
> CCB-B - v51 - Ja '98 - p174 [51-250]
> Ch BWatch - v8 - Ja '98 - p1 [1-50]
> NYTBR - v102 - N 23 '97 - p32 [1-50]
> NYTLa - v147 - D 4 '97 - pE8 [51-250]
> PW - v244 - S 22 '97 - p80 [51-250]
> SLJ - v43 - N '97 - p98+ [51-250]

Rohmer, Harriet
Just like Me
> BL - v94 - S 1 '97 - p114 [51-250]
> CBRS - v26 - N '97 - p32 [51-250]
> Ch BWatch - v7 - O '97 - p6 [1-50]
> SLJ - v43 - D '97 - p114 [51-250]

Roland-Entwistle, Theodore
More Errata (Illus. by Hemesh Alles)
> LA - v73 - N '96 - p524 [51-250]

Romain, Joseph
The Wagner Whacker
> CBRA - '96 - p491 [51-250]

Romain, Trevor

Bullies Are a Pain in the Brain (Illus. by Trevor Romain)

> SLJ - v44 - F '98 - p124 [51-250]

How to Do Homework without Throwing Up (Illus. by Trevor Romain)

> SLJ - v43 - My '97 - p123 [51-250]

Romanelli, Serena

Little Bobo Saves the Day (Illus. by Hans De Beer)

> KR - v65 - N 1 '97 - p1649 [51-250]
> SLJ - v43 - D '97 - p100+ [51-250]

Roop, Connie

Walk on the Wild Side! (Illus. by Anne Canevari Green)

> HB Guide - v8 - Fall '97 - p347 [51-250]
> SLJ - v43 - Je '97 - p143 [51-250]

Roop, Peter

Let's Celebrate Christmas (Illus. by Katy Keck Arnsteen)

> BL - v94 - S 1 '97 - p137 [51-250]
> Ch BWatch - v8 - Ja '98 - p8 [1-50]
> PW - v244 - O 6 '97 - p58 [1-50]

Let's Celebrate Halloween (Illus. by Katy Keck Arnsteen)

> BL - v94 - S 1 '97 - p137 [51-250]
> PW - v244 - O 6 '97 - p52 [1-50]
> SLJ - v43 - Ag '97 - p150 [51-250]

Root, Phyllis

The Hungry Monster (Illus. by Sue Heap)

> HB Guide - v8 - Fall '97 - p255 [51-250]
> SLJ - v43 - My '97 - p113 [51-250]

Mrs. Potter's Pig (Illus. by Russell Ayto)

> PW - v244 - Jl 21 '97 - p203 [1-50]
> RT - v51 - O '97 - p134+ [1-50]

Rosie's Fiddle (Illus. by Kevin O'Malley)

> HB Guide - v8 - Fall '97 - p279 [51-250]
> SLJ - v43 - Ap '97 - p116 [51-250]

Rosa-Casanova, Sylvia

Mama Provi and the Pot of Rice (Illus. by Robert Roth)

> CBRS - v25 - Ag '97 - p162 [1-50]
> CCB-B - v51 - S '97 - p24+ [51-250]
> HB Guide - v8 - Fall '97 - p280 [51-250]
> NYTBR - v102 - Jl 6 '97 - p16 [501+]
> SLJ - v43 - Jl '97 - p74 [51-250]

Rosales, Melodye

'Twas the Night B'Fore Christmas (Illus. by Melodye Rosales)

> SE - v61 - Ap '97 - p12* [1-50]

Rose, David

Passover

> HB Guide - v8 - Fall '97 - p320 [51-250]

Rose, Emma

Pumpkin Faces (Illus. by Judith Moffatt)

> PW - v244 - O 6 '97 - p50 [1-50]
> SLJ - v43 - N '97 - p99 [51-250]

Rose, Marie

The Human Body

> SB - v33 - O '97 - p211 [51-250]

Rosen, Michael

Tea in the Sugar Bowl, Potato in My Shoe (Illus. by Quentin Blake)

> NS - v126 - D 5 '97 - p63 [51-250]
> TES - O 31 '97 - p16* [51-250]
> TES - N 7 '97 - p2* [1-50]

Rosen, Michael, 1946-

The Hypnotiser

> NS - v126 - D 5 '97 - p63 [1-50]

Michael Rosen's ABC (Illus. by Bee Willey)

> BL - v93 - Je 1 '97 - p1712 [51-250]

We're Going on a Bear Hunt (Illus. by Helen Oxenbury)

> PW - v244 - Ag 11 '97 - p403 [1-50]

Rosen, Michael J
Home: A Collaboration of Thirty Distinguished Authors and Illustrators of Children's Books to Aid the Homeless
   Par Ch - Awards '97 - p9 [51-250]

Rosen, Michael J, 1954-
The Dog Who Walked with God (Illus. by Stan Fellows)
   BL - v94 - Mr 15 '98 - p1246 [51-250]
   CCB-B - v51 - Ap '98 - p294 [51-250]

Down to Earth
   SLJ - v44 - Ap '98 - p153 [51-250]

Elijah's Angel (Illus. by Aminah Brenda Lynn Robinson)
   ECEJ - v25 - Fall '97 - p49 [1-50]
   PW - v244 - O 6 '97 - p53 [1-50]

Food Fight (Illus. by Michael J Rosen)
   HMR - Sum '97 - p28 [51-250]
   SLJ - v43 - Ap '97 - p156 [51-250]

The Heart Is Big Enough (Illus. by Matthew Valiquette)
 y CBRS - v25 - My '97 - p120 [51-250]
   HB Guide - v8 - Fall '97 - p308 [51-250]
   KR - v65 - Ap 15 '97 - p648 [51-250]
   SLJ - v43 - Jl '97 - p97 [51-250]

Rosen, Sidney
Can You Catch a Falling Star? (Illus. by Dean Lindberg)
   ASBYP - v29 - Fall '96 - p62 [251-500]

Where's the Big Dipper? (Illus. by Dean Lindberg)
   ASBYP - v29 - Fall '96 - p62 [251-500]

Rosenberg, Doris
The Talking Lady Presents--Having a Brain Tumor (Illus. by Tom Mortensen)
   CBRA -   '96 - p527 [51-250]

Rosenberg, John
William Parker: Rebel Without Rights
   RT - v51 - D '97 - p334 [51-250]

Rosenberg, Laurie
Jewish Synagogue
   Sch Lib - v45 - N '97 - p206 [51-250]

Rosenberg, Liz
A Big and Little Alphabet (Illus. by Vera Rosenberry)
   BL - v94 - N 1 '97 - p484 [51-250]
   Emerg Lib - v25 - Ja '98 - p56 [51-250]
   NYTBR - v103 - F 1 '98 - p24 [1-50]
   Par - v73 - F '98 - p185 [1-50]

Earth-Shattering Poems
 y BL - v94 - D 15 '97 - p688 [51-250]
 y HB - v74 - Ja '98 - p88 [51-250]
   PW - v244 - O 6 '97 - p85 [51-250]
 y SLJ - v44 - F '98 - p124 [51-250]
 y VOYA - v20 - F '98 - p400 [251-500]

Eli and Uncle Dawn (Illus. by Susan Gaber)
   CCB-B - v50 - Je '97 - p372 [51-250]
   HB Guide - v8 - Fall '97 - p280 [51-250]
   SLJ - v43 - Je '97 - p100 [51-250]

Grandmother and the Runaway Shadow (Illus. by Beth Peck)
   NYTBR - v102 - My 11 '97 - p24 [1-50]
   RT - v51 - D '97 - p332 [51-250]

The Invisible Ladder
 y ABR - v19 - N '97 - p1+ [501+]
 y BL - v94 - S 15 '97 - p223 [1-50]
   HMR - Sum '97 - p28 [51-250]

Rosenberg, Maxine B
Hiding to Survive
   SS - v88 - My '97 - p139+ [501+]

Mommy's in the Hospital Having a Baby (Illus. by Robert Maass)
   CBRS - v25 - Spr '97 - p137 [1-50]
   HB Guide - v8 - Fall '97 - p356 [51-250]
   SLJ - v43 - My '97 - p123+ [51-250]

Rosenblatt, Richard
Michael Irvin
   Ch BWatch - v7 - Je '97 - p2 [1-50]
   HB Guide - v8 - Fall '97 - p369 [51-250]

Rosenburg, John
Young George Washington
> Ch BWatch - v7 - Jl '97 - p3 [51-250]
> HB Guide - v8 - Fall '97 - p308 [51-250]
> SLJ - v43 - Ap '97 - p140 [51-250]
> y   VOYA - v20 - Ag '97 - p189 [251-500]

Rosenfeld, Diana
The Very Best Book (Illus. by Vitalii Romanenko)
> Ch BWatch - v7 - My '97 - p4 [51-250]

Rosenfeld, Dina
Peanut Butter and Jelly for Snabbos (Illus. by Norman Nodel)
> Ch BWatch - v7 - Je '97 - p1 [51-250]

Rosenthal, Paul
Yo, Aesop! (Illus. by Marc Rosenthal)
> KR - v66 - Mr 15 '98 - p409 [51-250]
> PW - v245 - Mr 23 '98 - p99 [51-250]

Rosner, Ruth
I Hate My Best Friend (Illus. by Ruth Rosner)
> SLJ - v43 - Ag '97 - p140 [51-250]

Ross, Alice
The Copper Lady (Illus. by Leslie W Bowman)
> BL - v93 - Ag '97 - p1910 [51-250]
> CCB-B - v50 - Jl '97 - p409+ [51-250]
> HB Guide - v8 - Fall '97 - p293 [51-250]
> SLJ - v43 - S '97 - p192+ [51-250]

Ross, Anna
Cookie Monster! (Illus. by Norman Gorbaty)
> PW - v244 - O 27 '97 - p78 [51-250]

Elmo! (Illus. by Norman Gorbaty)
> PW - v244 - O 27 '97 - p78 [51-250]

Ernie! (Illus. by Norman Gorbaty)
> PW - v244 - O 27 '97 - p78 [51-250]

Grover! (Illus. by Norman Gorbaty)
> PW - v244 - O 27 '97 - p78 [51-250]

Ross, Calvin
The Frugal Youth Cybrarian
> y   BL - v93 - Ag '97 - p1912 [51-250]
> Emerg Lib - v25 - Ja '98 - p40 [51-250]
> JOYS - v11 - Win '98 - p186+ [251-500]
> Quill & Q - v63 - My '97 - p42 [251-500]
> SLJ - v44 - Mr '98 - p123 [51-250]
> VOYA - v20 - Ag '97 - p211 [51-250]

Ross, Catherine Sheldrick
The Amazing Milk Book (Illus. by Linda Hendry)
> Can CL - v23 - Fall '97 - p93+ [51-250]

Squares (Illus. by Bill Slavin)
> CBRA - '96 - p536 [51-250]

Ross, Jim
Dear Oklahoma City, Get Well Soon
> LA - v73 - N '96 - p526 [51-250]
> SE - v61 - Ap '97 - p4* [1-50]
> y   SE - v61 - S '97 - p271 [1-50]

Ross, Kathy
Crafts for Kids Who Are Wild about Dinosaurs (Illus. by Sharon Lane Holm)
> HB Guide - v8 - Fall '97 - p362 [51-250]
> SB - v33 - O '97 - p212 [51-250]
> SLJ - v43 - Je '97 - p110+ [51-250]

Crafts for Kids Who Are Wild about Insects (Illus. by Sharon Lane Holm)
> PW - v244 - Jl 28 '97 - p77 [51-250]
> SLJ - v43 - S '97 - p208 [51-250]

Crafts for Kids Who Are Wild about Outer Space (Illus. by Sharon Lane Holm)
> HB Guide - v8 - Fall '97 - p362 [51-250]
> SB - v33 - O '97 - p212 [251-500]
> SLJ - v43 - Je '97 - p110+ [51-250]

Crafts for Kids Who Are Wild about Rainforests (Illus. by Sharon Lane Holm)
> BL - v94 - D 1 '97 - p629 [1-50]
> PW - v244 - Jl 28 '97 - p77 [51-250]
> SLJ - v43 - S '97 - p208 [51-250]

*Crafts from Your Favorite Fairy Tales
(Illus. by Vicky Enright)*
> SLJ - v43 - D '97 - p114 [51-250]

*The Jewish Holiday Craft Book (Illus.
by Melinda Levine)*
> Ch BWatch - v7 - My '97 - p4 [1-50]
> HB Guide - v8 - Fall '97 - p362 [51-250]
> SLJ - v43 - Ap '97 - p130 [51-250]

Ross, Mandy
Joke Book
> Ch BWatch - v7 - Ap '97 - p1 [51-250]

Ross, Michael Elsohn
*Bird Watching with Margaret Morse
Nice (Illus. by Laurie A Caple)*
> Ch BWatch - v7 - D '97 - p8 [51-250]
> SB - v34 - Ap '98 - p83 [501+]
> SLJ - v44 - Mr '98 - p241 [51-250]

*Bug Watching with Charles Henry
Turner (Illus. by Laurie A Caple)*
> BL - v94 - Mr 1 '98 - p1132 [51-250]
> Ch BWatch - v7 - D '97 - p8 [51-250]
> KR - v65 - D 1 '97 - p1778+ [51-250]
> SB - v34 - Ap '98 - p83 [501+]
> SLJ - v44 - Mr '98 - p241+ [51-250]

*Caterpillarology (Illus. by Brian
Grogan)*
> SLJ - v44 - Mr '98 - p202+ [51-250]

*Flower Watching with Alice Eastwood
(Illus. by Laurie A Caple)*
> BL - v94 - Mr 1 '98 - p1132 [51-250]
> Ch BWatch - v7 - D '97 - p8 [51-250]
> KR - v65 - N 15 '97 - p1712 [51-250]
> SB - v34 - Ap '98 - p83 [501+]
> SLJ - v44 - Mr '98 - p241+ [51-250]

*Ladybugology (Illus. by Brian
Grogan)*
> KR - v66 - Ja 15 '98 - p117 [51-250]
> SLJ - v44 - Mr '98 - p202+ [51-250]

*Wildlife Watching with Charles
Eastman (Illus. by Laurie A Caple)*
> Ch BWatch - v7 - D '97 - p8 [51-250]
> SB - v34 - Ap '98 - p83 [501+]
> SLJ - v44 - Mr '98 - p241 [51-250]

Ross, Pat
*Creepy Cafeteria (Illus. by Patrick
Girouard)*
> SLJ - v43 - Ag '97 - p141 [51-250]

*Welcome to Chillsville Elementary
(Illus. by Patrick Girouard)*
> SLJ - v43 - Ag '97 - p141 [51-250]

Ross, Stewart
And Then...History of the World
> Ch BWatch - v7 - Mr '97 - p5 [51-250]

Beasts (Illus. by Francis Phillipps)
> Ch BWatch - v8 - Ja '98 - p6 [1-50]

*Charlotte Bronte and Jane Eyre (Illus.
by Robert Van Nutt)*
> BL - v94 - Ja 1 '98 - p807 [51-250]
> CBRS - v26 - D '97 - p47 [51-250]
> CCB-B - v51 - Ja '98 - p174+ [51-250]
> Ch BWatch - v7 - N '97 - p7 [51-250]
> KR - v65 - S 15 '97 - p1462 [51-250]
> PW - v244 - N 3 '97 - p86 [51-250]
> SLJ - v44 - Ja '98 - p130 [51-250]

*Conquerors and Explorers (Illus. by
McRae Books)*
> Ch BWatch - v7 - Mr '97 - p5 [1-50]
> SLJ - v43 - Ap '97 - p156 [51-250]

*Gods and Giants (Illus. by Francis
Phillipps)*
> Ch BWatch - v8 - Ja '98 - p6 [1-50]
> SLJ - v44 - Ap '98 - p124 [51-250]

*Monsters of the Deep (Illus. by
Francis Phillipps)*
> Ch BWatch - v7 - N '97 - p6 [1-50]

Pirates
> Emerg Lib - v25 - N '97 - p47 [51-250]

*Secret Societies (Illus. by McRae
Books)*
> Ch BWatch - v7 - Mr '97 - p5 [1-50]
> SLJ - v43 - Ap '97 - p156 [51-250]

*Warriors and Witches (Illus. by
Francis Phillipps)*
> Ch BWatch - v8 - Ja '98 - p6 [1-50]

Ross, Tony
Nicky (Illus. by Tony Ross)
> Sch Lib - v45 - Ag '97 - p132+ [51-250]
> TES - My 30 '97 - p8* [501+]

Rossiter, Nan Parson
Rugby and Rosie
> CBRS - v25 - Spr '97 - p137 [51-250]
> HB Guide - v8 - Fall '97 - p280 [51-250]

Rossiter, Sean
Hockey the NHL Way: Goal Scoring
> Quill & Q - v63 - D '97 - p39 [51-250]

Hockey the NHL Way: Goaltending
> Quill & Q - v63 - D '97 - p39 [51-250]

Roth, Susan L
My Love for You
> HB Guide - v8 - Fall '97 - p255 [51-250]

Rothman, Cynthia
Think about the Weather
> SB - v33 - Ap '97 - p84+ [51-250]

Rotner, Shelley
Close, Closer, Closest (Illus. by Shelley Rotner)
> HB Guide - v8 - Fall '97 - p255 [51-250]
> SLJ - v43 - Jl '97 - p87 [51-250]

Lots of Dads (Illus. by Shelley Rotner)
> BL - v93 - Ag '97 - p1904 [51-250]
> HB Guide - v8 - Fall '97 - p322 [51-250]
> NYTBR - v102 - S 14 '97 - p30 [501+]
> SLJ - v43 - D '97 - p114 [51-250]

Rotter, Charles
Fungi
> Ch BWatch - v7 - '94 - p8 [51-250]

Hurricanes
> Ch BWatch - v7 - '94 - p8 [51-250]

Mountains
> Ch BWatch - v7 - '95 - p8 [51-250]

The Prairie
> Ch BWatch - v7 - '94 - p8 [51-250]

Rottman, S L
Hero
> BL - v94 - D 1 '97 - p638 [51-250]
> y CCB-B - v51 - Ja '98 - p175 [51-250]
> y KR - v65 - S 15 '97 - p1462 [51-250]
> y PW - v244 - Ag 18 '97 - p93 [51-250]

> y SLJ - v43 - D '97 - p130+ [51-250]
> y VOYA - v20 - D '97 - p320+ [51-250]

Rounds, Glen
Sod Houses on the Great Plains (Illus. by Glen Rounds)
> BL - v93 - Je 1 '97 - p1701 [1-50]

Rouse, Jeff
The Young Swimmer
> BL - v93 - Ag '97 - p1896 [51-250]
> Ch BWatch - v7 - Jl '97 - p8 [1-50]
> HB Guide - v8 - Fall '97 - p371 [51-250]
> Magpies - v12 - S '97 - p44 [51-250]
> Sch Lib - v45 - Ag '97 - p155 [51-250]
> SLJ - v44 - F '98 - p124 [51-250]

Rouss, Sylvia A
Sammy Spider's First Rosh Hashanah (Illus. by Katherine Janus Kahn)
> SLJ - v43 - My '97 - p113 [51-250]

Sammy Spider's First Shabbat (Illus. by Katherine Janus Kahn)
> PW - v244 - D 22 '97 - p55 [1-50]
> PW - v245 - F 23 '98 - p66 [51-250]

Rowe, John
Can You Spot the Spotted Dog?
> Emerg Lib - v24 - My '97 - p50 [51-250]
> RT - v51 - S '97 - p52 [51-250]

Rowe, John A
Smudge (Illus. by John A Rowe)
> BL - v94 - D 1 '97 - p643+ [51-250]
> Bloom Rev - v17 - N '97 - p33 [51-250]
> KR - v65 - O 1 '97 - p1536 [51-250]
> SLJ - v44 - F '98 - p90 [51-250]

Rowell, Jonathan
Malaysia
> HB Guide - v8 - Fall '97 - p392 [51-250]

Rowland-Entwistle, Theodore
Eureka! A Puzzle Book of Inventions
> Emerg Lib - v24 - My '97 - p50 [51-250]

Rowley, John
Harriet Tubman
BL - v94 - Mr 15 '98 - p1245 [51-250]

Rowling, J K
Harry Potter and the Philosopher's Stone
Bks Keeps - S '97 - p27 [51-250]
NS - v126 - D 5 '97 - p64 [51-250]
Sch Lib - v45 - Ag '97 - p147 [51-250]

Roy, Ron
The Bald Bandit (Illus. by John Steven Gurney)
SLJ - v44 - Ja '98 - p92 [51-250]

Royston, Angela
Where Do Babies Come From?
ASBYP - v29 - Fall '96 - p27 [251-500]

Rubalcaba, Jill
A Place in the Sun
HB Guide - v8 - Fall '97 - p308 [51-250]
SLJ - v43 - Ap '97 - p140 [51-250]

Rubel, David
Scholastic Encyclopedia of the Presidents and Their Times. Updated 1997 Ed.
yr   Ch BWatch - v7 - Jl '97 - p5 [51-250]
r   JOYS - v11 - Fall '97 - p78 [1-50]
r   SLJ - v43 - My '97 - p162 [51-250]

Rubin, Susan Goldman
Emily in Love
HB Guide - v8 - Fall '97 - p308 [51-250]
y   SLJ - v43 - My '97 - p139 [51-250]
y   VOYA - v20 - Je '97 - p113 [251-500]

Rubinstein, Gillian
Jake and Pete and the Stray Dogs (Illus. by Terry Denton)
Magpies - v12 - S '97 - p29 [51-250]

Shinkei
Bks Keeps - N '97 - p26 [51-250]
y   Sch Lib - v45 - Ag '97 - p161 [51-250]

Skymaze
Bks Keeps - N '97 - p26 [51-250]
y   Sch Lib - v45 - Ag '97 - p161 [51-250]

Space Demons
Bks Keeps - N '97 - p26 [51-250]
y   Sch Lib - v45 - Ag '97 - p161 [51-250]
TES - Ag 8 '97 - p23 [251-500]

Under the Cat's Eye
Aust Bk R - O '97 - p57+ [501+]

Rucki, Ani
When the Earth Wakes (Illus. by Ani Rucki)
BL - v94 - Mr 1 '98 - p1141 [51-250]
KR - v65 - D 15 '97 - p1840 [51-250]
PW - v245 - Ja 5 '98 - p67 [51-250]
SLJ - v44 - Mr '98 - p187 [51-250]

Ruddell, Nancy
Mystery of the Maya (Illus. by Douglas Brant Spencer)
CBRA - '96 - p353 [51-250]

Ruediger, Beth
The Barber of Bingo (Illus. by John McPherson)
AB - v100 - N 17 '97 - p1264 [51-250]
Ch BWatch - v7 - Jl '97 - p6 [51-250]

Ruelle, Karen Gray
The Book of Baths (Illus. by Lizi Boyd)
PW - v244 - O 27 '97 - p78 [51-250]

The Book of Bedtimes (Illus. by Lizi Boyd)
PW - v244 - O 27 '97 - p78 [51-250]

The Book of Breakfasts (Illus. by Lizi Boyd)
PW - v244 - O 27 '97 - p78 [51-250]

Ruffell, Ann
The Pirate Band (Illus. by Philip Hopman)
Sch Lib - v45 - Ag '97 - p147 [51-250]

Ruiz, Andres Llamas
Evolution (Illus. by Ferron-Retana)
SLJ - v43 - Je '97 - p111 [51-250]

Rumford, James
*The Island-below-the-Star (Illus. by
James Rumford)*
> BL - v94 - Mr 15 '98 - p1252 [51-250]
> KR - v66 - Mr 1 '98 - p343 [51-250]

Russell, Barbara T
Blue Lightning
> CBRS - v25 - Ag '97 - p168 [51-250]
> Ch BWatch - v7 - Ap '97 - p4 [51-250]
> HB Guide - v8 - Fall '97 - p308 [51-250]

Last Left Standing
> PW - v245 - Mr 23 '98 - p102 [51-250]

Russell, Ching Yeung
*Lichee Tree (Illus. by Christopher
Zhong-Yuan Zhang)*
> CLW - v68 - S '97 - p71 [251-500]
> HB Guide - v8 - Fall '97 - p308 [51-250]
> SLJ - v43 - Je '97 - p127+ [51-250]

*Moon Festival (Illus. by Christopher
Zhong-Yuan Zhang)*
> BL - v94 - S 15 '97 - p236 [51-250]
> CBRS - v26 - O '97 - p21 [1-50]

Russell, Ginny
Step by Step
> y   Can CL - v23 - Sum '97 - p78+ [251-500]
>   CBRA - '96 - p491 [51-250]

Russell, Janice
Goldilocks (Illus. by Janice Russell)
> CLW - v68 - S '97 - p65 [51-250]
> HB Guide - v8 - Fall '97 - p335 [1-50]

Russell, P Craig
*Rudy Kipling's Jungle Book (Illus. by
P Craig Russell)*
> PW - v245 - Ja 19 '98 - p380 [51-250]

Rudyard Kipling's Jungle Book Stories
> Ch BWatch - v7 - O '97 - p1 [51-250]

Russell, Tom
Magic Step-by-Step
> SLJ - v43 - Ag '97 - p150 [51-250]

Russo, Marisabina
*Under the Table (Illus. by Marisabina
Russo)*
> CBRS - v25 - My '97 - p113 [51-250]
> HB Guide - v8 - Fall '97 - p255 [51-250]
> NYTBR - v102 - S 14 '97 - p30 [1-50]
> SLJ - v43 - Ap '97 - p116 [51-250]

*When Mama Gets Home (Illus. by
Marisabina Russo)*
> BL - v94 - Mr 1 '98 - p1141+ [51-250]
> KR - v66 - F 15 '98 - p274 [51-250]
> SLJ - v44 - Ap '98 - p108 [51-250]

Russon, Jacqueline
Face Painting (Illus. by Steve Shott)
> SLJ - v44 - Ap '98 - p113 [51-250]

Rutter, Jill
Jewish Migrations
> SS - v88 - My '97 - p139+ [501+]

Ruurs, Margriet
*Emma's Eggs (Illus. by Barbara
Spurll)*
> CBRA - '96 - p456 [51-250]

*A Mountain Alphabet (Illus. by
Andrew Kiss)*
> BIC - v26 - Ap '97 - p35 [251-500]
> CBRA - '96 - p456 [51-250]

Ryan, Margaret
Queen Lizzie Rules OK!
> TES - Je 20 '97 - p12* [501+]

Ryan, Mary E
Alias
>   CBRS - v25 - Jl '97 - p157 [51-250]
> y   CBRS - v25 - Jl '97 - p157 [51-250]
> y   CCB-B - v50 - Jl '97 - p410 [51-250]
> y   HB Guide - v8 - Fall '97 - p315 [51-250]
> y   JAAL - v41 - F '98 - p409 [51-250]
> y   KR - v65 - Ap 15 '97 - p648+ [51-250]
> y   SLJ - v43 - Jl '97 - p97 [51-250]
> y   VOYA - v20 - Ag '97 - p189 [51-250]

Ryan, Pam Munoz

Armadillos Sleep in Dugouts and Other Places Animals Live (Illus. by Diane DeGroat)
> KR - v65 - O 1 '97 - p1537 [51-250]
> SLJ - v43 - D '97 - p114+ [51-250]

The Crayon Counting Board Book (Illus. by Frank Mazzola Jr.)
> PW - v244 - Ag 11 '97 - p403 [1-50]

The Crayon Counting Book (Illus. by Frank Mazzola Jr.)
> RT - v51 - O '97 - p130 [1-50]
> TCMath - v4 - N '97 - p184+ [51-250]

The Flag We Love (Illus. by Ralph Masiello)
> SE - v61 - Ap '97 - p9* [1-50]

A Pinky Is a Baby Mouse and Other Baby Animal Names (Illus. by Diane De Groat)
> BL - v93 - Je 1 '97 - p1712 [51-250]
> CBRS - v25 - My '97 - p113 [51-250]
> HB Guide - v8 - Fall '97 - p347 [51-250]
> Inst - v107 - N '97 - p18 [1-50]
> SLJ - v43 - Jl '97 - p87 [51-250]

Riding Freedom (Illus. by Brian Selznick)
> BL - v94 - Ja 1 '98 - p814+ [51-250]
> BW - v28 - Mr 1 '98 - p11 [51-250]
> KR - v65 - D 1 '97 - p1779 [51-250]
> PW - v245 - F 2 '98 - p91 [51-250]
> SLJ - v44 - Mr '98 - p218 [51-250]

Ryan-Lush, Geraldine

Jeremy Jeckles Hates Freckles (Illus. by Kathy Kaulbach)
> Can CL - v23 - Sum '97 - p65+ [501+]

Ryden, Hope

ABC of Crawlers and Flyers
> SB - v33 - Ag '97 - p186 [1-50]

Wild Horse Summer (Illus. by Paul Casale)
> BL - v93 - Ag '97 - p1902 [51-250]
> CCB-B - v51 - N '97 - p99+ [51-250]
> Ch BWatch - v8 - Ja '98 - p4 [51-250]
> KR - v65 - Ag 15 '97 - p1311+ [51-250]
> SLJ - v43 - S '97 - p225 [51-250]

Ryder, Joanne

Jaguar in the Rain Forest
> BL - v94 - D 1 '97 - p629 [1-50]

Shark in the Sea (Illus. by Michael Rothman)
> HB Guide - v8 - Fall '97 - p280 [51-250]
> SB - v33 - Ag '97 - p187 [1-50]
> SLJ - v43 - Ap '97 - p116 [51-250]

Where Butterflies Grow
> Inst - v106 - Ap '97 - p4* [1-50]

Winter White (Illus. by Carol Lacey)
> BL - v94 - D 1 '97 - p644 [51-250]
> Ch BWatch - v8 - Ja '98 - p8 [1-50]

Ryder, Nora Leigh

In the Wild
> BL - v94 - D 15 '97 - p700 [1-50]
> Ch BWatch - v7 - S '97 - p4 [1-50]
> HB Guide - v8 - Fall '97 - p348 [51-250]
> SLJ - v43 - My '97 - p124 [51-250]

Rylant, Cynthia

Appalachia, the Voices of Singing Birds (Illus. by Barry Moser)
> ECEJ - v25 - Fall '97 - p50 [1-50]

The Blue Hill Meadows (Illus. by Ellen Beier)
> BL - v94 - S 1 '97 - p126+ [51-250]
> CBRS - v26 - S '97 - p12 [51-250]
> Ch BWatch - v8 - Ja '98 - p3 [1-50]
> KR - v65 - Ag 1 '97 - p1227 [51-250]
> Par - v72 - D '97 - p206 [1-50]
> PW - v244 - Je 16 '97 - p59+ [51-250]
> PW - v244 - N 3 '97 - p59 [1-50]

Cat Heaven (Illus. by Cynthia Rylant)
> BL - v94 - S 1 '97 - p135 [51-250]
> CCB-B - v51 - N '97 - p100 [51-250]
> Emerg Lib - v25 - N '97 - p54 [1-50]
> Emerg Lib - v25 - Ja '98 - p51 [51-250]
> KR - v65 - Jl 1 '97 - p1035 [51-250]
> PW - v244 - Je 16 '97 - p58 [51-250]

An Everyday Book
> HB Guide - v8 - Fall '97 - p255 [51-250]

A Fine White Dust
> BL - v94 - O 1 '97 - p323 [51-250]

*Henry and Mudge and the Bedtime
Thumps (Guidall). Audio Version*
SLJ - v44 - Mr '98 - p157 [51-250]

*Henry and Mudge and the Sneaky
Crackers (Illus. by Sucie Stevenson)*
CCB-B - v51 - Mr '98 - p258 [51-250]
KR - v65 - N 15 '97 - p1712 [51-250]

*Henry and Mudge and the Starry
Night (Illus. by Sucie Stevenson)*
KR - v66 - F 1 '98 - p200 [51-250]
SLJ - v44 - Ap '98 - p108+ [51-250]

*Henry and Mudge in the Family Trees
(Illus. by Sucie Stevenson)*
BL - v93 - Ag '97 - p1910 [51-250]

*Henry and Mudge: The First Book
(Guidall). Audio Version*
SLJ - v43 - N '97 - p69 [51-250]

The Islander
y　KR - v66 - F 1 '98 - p200 [51-250]
y　PW - v245 - Ja 19 '98 - p378+ [51-250]
　　SLJ - v44 - Mr '98 - p218+ [51-250]

Margaret, Frank, and Andy
　　RT - v51 - O '97 - p146 [1-50]
y　VOYA - v20 - Ap '97 - p60 [51-250]

*Mr. Putter and Tabby Fly the Plane
(Illus. by Arthur Howard)*
HB Guide - v8 - Fall '97 - p293 [51-250]
SLJ - v43 - Ap '97 - p116 [51-250]

*Mr. Putter and Tabby Row the Boat
(Illus. by Arthur Howard)*
HB Guide - v8 - Fall '97 - p293 [51-250]
KR - v65 - Ap 15 '97 - p649 [51-250]
NYTBR - v102 - S 14 '97 - p30 [1-50]
SLJ - v43 - Ap '97 - p116 [51-250]

*Mr. Putter and Tabby Toot the Horn
(Illus. by Arthur Howard)*
SLJ - v44 - Ap '98 - p109 [51-250]

Poppleton (Illus. by Mark Teague)
Ch BWatch - v7 - My '97 - p3+ [1-50]
CM:CanRev - v4 - N 14 '97 - pONL
[51-250]
HB Guide - v8 - Fall '97 - p294 [51-250]
Magpies - v12 - Jl '97 - p29 [51-250]
Par - v72 - D '97 - p204 [1-50]

*Poppleton and Friends (Illus. by Mark
Teague)*
BL - v93 - Ag '97 - p1910+ [51-250]
KR - v65 - Ag 1 '97 - p1228 [51-250]
Par - v72 - D '97 - p204 [1-50]
SLJ - v43 - S '97 - p193 [51-250]

*Poppleton Everyday (Illus. by Mark
Teague)*
CCB-B - v51 - Ap '98 - p294+ [51-250]

Scarecrow (Illus. by Lauren Stringer)
KR - v66 - Ap 15 '98 - p585 [51-250]
PW - v245 - Mr 9 '98 - p68 [51-250]
SLJ - v44 - Ap '98 - p109 [51-250]

*Silver Packages (Illus. by Chris K
Soentpiet)*
BL - v94 - S 1 '97 - p140+ [51-250]
Bloom Rev - v17 - N '97 - p33 [1-50]
CBRS - v26 - O '97 - p17 [51-250]
CCB-B - v51 - D '97 - p138 [51-250]
Ch BWatch - v7 - N '97 - p4 [1-50]
NYTBR - v102 - D 7 '97 - p66 [501+]
PW - v244 - O 6 '97 - p59 [1-50]

*Tulip Sees America (Illus. by Lisa
Desimini)*
BL - v94 - Mr 15 '98 - p1252 [51-250]
SLJ - v44 - Ap '98 - p109 [51-250]

The Van Gogh Cafe
PW - v245 - F 9 '98 - p98 [1-50]

Rymill, Linda R
Good Knight (Illus. by G Brian Karas)
CCB-B - v51 - Ap '98 - p295 [51-250]
KR - v66 - F 15 '98 - p274 [51-250]
SLJ - v44 - Mr '98 - p187 [51-250]

Ryskamp, George R
*A Student's Guide to Mexican
American Genealogy*
Ch BWatch - v7 - Ap '97 - p1 [51-250]

S

Saari, Peggy
Scientists. Vols. 1-3
yr BL - v94 - Ja 1 '98 - p738 [1-50]
r   SLJ - v43 - My '97 - p162 [51-250]
yr SLMQ - v25 - Spr '97 - p182 [51-250]
yr VOYA - v20 - Ag '97 - p213+ [51-250]

Sabbeth, Alex
Rubber-Band Banjos and a Java Jive Bass
New Sci - v155 - Ag 23 '97 - p44 [251-500]
SLJ - v43 - Je '97 - p144 [51-250]

Sabuda, Robert
The 12 Days of Christmas
Inst - v106 - My '97 - p18 [1-50]

Cookie Count (Illus. by Robert Sabuda)
BL - v94 - D 15 '97 - p700 [1-50]
CCB-B - v51 - Mr '98 - p259 [51-250]
PW - v244 - D 1 '97 - p55 [51-250]

Sachs, Marilyn
Another Day
y   BL - v93 - Je 1 '97 - p1686 [51-250]
y   CBRS - v25 - Jl '97 - p157 [51-250]
    CCB-B - v50 - Jl '97 - p410 [51-250]
    HB Guide - v8 - Fall '97 - p308 [51-250]
    KR - v65 - My 15 '97 - p807 [51-250]
    SLJ - v43 - Je '97 - p128 [51-250]
y   VOYA - v20 - D '97 - p321 [251-500]

Surprise Party
KR - v66 - F 15 '98 - p274 [51-250]

Sadler, Judy Ann
Beading: Bracelets, Earrings, Necklaces and More (Illus. by Tracy Walker)
CBRA - '96 - p521 [51-250]

Beads
BL - v94 - D 1 '97 - p638+ [51-250]

Easy Braids, Barrettes and Bows (Illus. by Sarah Jane English)
BL - v94 - O 15 '97 - p400+ [51-250]
SLJ - v43 - N '97 - p134 [51-250]

The Kids Can Press Jumbo Book of Crafts (Illus. by Caroline Price)
CM:CanRev - v4 - N 14 '97 - pONL [251-500]

Prints (Illus. by Marilyn Mets)
BL - v94 - O 15 '97 - p400+ [51-250]
SLJ - v44 - Ja '98 - p104 [51-250]

Sewing
BL - v94 - D 1 '97 - p638+ [51-250]

Sadler, Marilyn
Elizabeth and Larry (Illus. by Roger Bollen)
ECEJ - v25 - Fall '97 - p50 [1-50]

Honey Bunny Funnybunny (Illus. by Roger Bollen)
HB Guide - v8 - Fall '97 - p280 [51-250]

The Parakeet Girl (Illus. by Roger Bollen)
CCB-B - v50 - Jl '97 - p411 [51-250]
HB Guide - v8 - Fall '97 - p287 [51-250]
SLJ - v43 - S '97 - p193 [51-250]

Sadu, Itah
Christopher Changes His Name (Illus. by Roy Condy)
    CBRA - '96 - p456+ [51-250]

Christopher, Please Clean Up Your Room (Illus. by Roy Condy)
    Can CL - v23 - Sum '97 - p65+ [501+]

Saenz, Benjamin Alire
A Gift from Papa Diego (Illus. by Geronimo Garcia)
    KR - v66 - Ap 15 '98 - p585 [51-250]
    PW - v245 - Ja 19 '98 - p378 [51-250]

St. George, Judith
Betsy Ross: Patriot of Philadelphia (Illus. by Sasha Meret)
    BL - v94 - Ja 1 '98 - p807+ [51-250]
    CCB-B - v51 - Ja '98 - p178 [51-250]
    SLJ - v44 - F '98 - p124 [51-250]

Sacagawea
    BL - v93 - Ag '97 - p1896 [51-250]
    CCB-B - v51 - N '97 - p103 [51-250]
    Ch BWatch - v7 - N '97 - p7 [51-250]
  y KR - v65 - Je 15 '97 - p956 [51-250]
    PW - v244 - Je 30 '97 - p77 [51-250]
    SLJ - v44 - Mr '98 - p242 [51-250]

Saint James, Synthia
The Gifts of Kwanzaa
    PW - v244 - O 6 '97 - p53 [51-250]

Sakurai, Gail
The Jamestown Colony
    Ch BWatch - v7 - O '97 - p8 [1-50]
    HB Guide - v8 - Fall '97 - p397 [51-250]

Salisbury, Graham
Shark Bait
  y BL - v94 - S 1 '97 - p107 [51-250]
    CBRS - v26 - F '98 - p82 [51-250]
  y CCB-B - v51 - D '97 - p138+ [51-250]
  y HB - v73 - S '97 - p579 [51-250]
  y KR - v65 - Jl 1 '97 - p1035 [51-250]
  y SLJ - v43 - S '97 - p225 [51-250]

Saller, Carol
Florence Kelley (Illus. by Ken Green)
    BL - v93 - Je 1 '97 - p1712 [51-250]
    CCB-B - v50 - Jl '97 - p411 [51-250]

HB Guide - v8 - Fall '97 - p382 [51-250]
SLJ - v43 - N '97 - p112 [51-250]

Sallnow, John
Russia
    Ch BWatch - v7 - D '97 - p7 [51-250]
    HB Guide - v8 - Fall '97 - p390 [51-250]
    SLJ - v43 - Ag '97 - p164 [51-250]

Saltzberg, Barney
Phoebe and the Spelling Bee
    BL - v94 - O 1 '97 - p339 [51-250]
    PW - v244 - O 13 '97 - p74+ [51-250]

Salwi, Dilip
Fire on the Moon and Other Stories
    Bkbird - v34 - Win '96 - p33+ [51-250]

Sammis, Fran
Cities and Towns (Illus. by Richard Maccabe)
    Ch BWatch - v7 - D '97 - p7 [1-50]
    SLJ - v44 - Ap '98 - p124+ [51-250]

Measurements
    Ch BWatch - v7 - D '97 - p7 [1-50]
    SB - v34 - Ap '98 - p82+ [501+]

Samoyault, Tiphaine
Give Me a Sign!
    BL - v94 - O 15 '97 - p401+ [51-250]
    CBRS - v26 - F '98 - p82+ [51-250]
    KR - v65 - N 1 '97 - p1649 [51-250]
    SLJ - v44 - Ja '98 - p130 [51-250]

Sampson, Michael
Star of the Circus (Illus. by Jose Aruego)
    AB - v100 - N 17 '97 - p1268 [51-250]
    HB Guide - v8 - Fall '97 - p280 [51-250]

Samson, Suzanne
Tumblebugs and Hairy Bears (Illus. by Preston Neel)
    SB - v33 - O '97 - p219 [51-250]

Samton, Sheila White
Ten Tiny Monsters (Illus. by Sheila White Samton)
    SLJ - v43 - D '97 - p101 [51-250]

Sanchez Sanchez, Isidro
Bears: Animals That Hibernate (Illus. by Gabriel Casadevall)
Ch BWatch - v7 - Jl '97 - p4 [1-50]

Fish: Swimming and Floating (Illus. by Gabriel Casadevall)
Ch BWatch - v7 - Jl '97 - p4 [1-50]

Sandak, Cass R
The United States
SLJ - v43 - Ag '97 - p166 [51-250]

Sandburg, Carl
Grassroots (Illus. by Wendell Minor)
BL - v94 - Mr 15 '98 - p1242 [51-250]
KR - v66 - Mr 1 '98 - p344 [51-250]
PW - v245 - F 23 '98 - p75 [51-250]

More Rootabagas (Illus. by Paul O Zelinsky)
SLJ - v43 - N '97 - p41 [1-50]

Not Everyday an Aurora Borealis for Your Birthday (Illus. by Anita Lobel)
KR - v65 - D 15 '97 - p1840 [51-250]
PW - v244 - D 1 '97 - p52 [51-250]
SLJ - v44 - Ap '98 - p110 [51-250]

Sandeman, Anna
Babies
SB - v33 - Ag '97 - p187 [1-50]

Blood
SB - v33 - Ag '97 - p187 [1-50]

Bones
SB - v33 - Ag '97 - p187 [1-50]

Brain (Illus. by Ian Thompson)
SB - v32 - D '96 - p276 [51-250]
SB - v33 - Ag '97 - p187 [1-50]

Breathing
SB - v33 - Ag '97 - p187 [1-50]

Eating
SB - v33 - Ag '97 - p187 [1-50]

Senses
SB - v33 - Ag '97 - p187 [1-50]

Skin, Teeth, and Hair
SB - v33 - Ag '97 - p187 [1-50]

Sandemose, Iben
Englepels (Illus. by Iben Sandermose)
Bkbird - v34 - Win '96 - p57+ [51-250]

Sanders, Pete
Bodyworks (Illus. by Derek Matthews)
SLJ - v44 - Mr '98 - p242 [51-250]

Divorce and Separation
HB Guide - v8 - Fall '97 - p322 [51-250]

Drinking Alcohol
HB Guide - v8 - Fall '97 - p329 [51-250]
y   TES - D 26 '97 - p23 [501+]

Drugs
ASBYP - v29 - Fall '96 - p27+ [251-500]
SB - v33 - N '97 - p226 [51-250]

Feeling Violent (Illus. by Mike Lacey)
SLJ - v44 - Ap '98 - p125 [51-250]

It's My Life (Illus. by Kevin Faerber)
SLJ - v44 - Ja '98 - p120 [51-250]

Sanders, Scott R, 1945-
The Floating House (Illus. by Helen Cogancherry)
ECEJ - v25 - Fall '97 - p50 [1-50]

Meeting Trees (Illus. by Robert Hynes)
CBRS - v25 - Jl '97 - p152 [51-250]
HB Guide - v8 - Fall '97 - p349 [51-250]
SLJ - v43 - Jl '97 - p74 [51-250]

A Place Called Freedom (Illus. by Thomas B Allen)
BL - v93 - Je 1 '97 - p1721+ [51-250]
CBRS - v25 - Ag '97 - p165 [51-250]
CCB-B - v50 - Jl '97 - p412 [51-250]
HB Guide - v8 - Fall '97 - p280 [51-250]
KR - v65 - Je 1 '97 - p879 [51-250]
NYTBR - v102 - Je 22 '97 - p22 [51-250]
PW - v244 - My 19 '97 - p76 [51-250]
SLJ - v43 - Ag '97 - p141 [51-250]

Sanderson, Ruth
Rose Red and Snow White (Illus. by Ruth Sanderson)
Ch BWatch - v7 - Je '97 - p6 [1-50]

HB Guide - v8 - Fall '97 - p335 [51-250]

SLJ - v43 - My '97 - p124+ [51-250]

Sandler, Martin W

Civil War

SE - v61 - Ap '97 - p9* [1-50]

Inventors

ASBYP - v29 - Fall '96 - p28+ [251-500]

Sandved, Kjell B

The Butterfly Alphabet (Illus. by Kjell B Sandved)

RT - v51 - O '97 - p132 [1-50]

Sanfield, Steve

The Girl Who Wanted a Song (Illus. by Stephen T Johnson)

SLJ - v43 - Jl '97 - p74 [51-250]

Sanford, William R

Bill Pickett: African-American Rodeo Star

HB Guide - v8 - Fall '97 - p397 [51-250]

Daniel Boone: Wilderness Pioneer

HB Guide - v8 - Fall '97 - p397 [51-250]

SLJ - v43 - Ap '97 - p157 [51-250]

Richard King: Texas Cattle Rancher

HB Guide - v8 - Fall '97 - p397 [51-250]

SLJ - v43 - Ap '97 - p157 [51-250]

Sacagawea: Native American Hero

HB Guide - v8 - Fall '97 - p397 [51-250]

San Jose, Christine

The Emperor's New Clothes (Illus. by Anastassija Archipowa)

KR - v66 - F 1 '98 - p202 [51-250]

SLJ - v44 - Ap '98 - p112 [51-250]

Sleeping Beauty (Illus. by Dominic Catalano)

BL - v94 - O 15 '97 - p410+ [51-250]

SLJ - v43 - S '97 - p208 [51-250]

Sansome, Rosemary

The Oxford Young Reader's Dictionary. Large Print Ed.

r   Sch Lib - v45 - Ag '97 - p134 [51-250]

San Souci, Robert D

Even More Short and Shivery (Illus. by Jacqueline Rogers)

BW - v27 - O 5 '97 - p11 [51-250]

Ch BWatch - v7 - O '97 - p3 [1-50]

y   JAAL - v41 - S '97 - p80 [51-250]

PW - v244 - O 6 '97 - p50 [1-50]

The Hired Hand (Illus. by Jerry Pinkney)

Am Vis - v12 - D '97 - p34 [51-250]

BW - v27 - My 4 '97 - p18 [251-500]

CBRS - v25 - Jl '97 - p152 [51-250]

Ch BWatch - v7 - My '97 - p3 [51-250]

HB Guide - v8 - Fall '97 - p335 [51-250]

KR - v65 - Ap 15 '97 - p649 [51-250]

NYTBR - v102 - N 9 '97 - p24 [1-50]

SLJ - v43 - My '97 - p124 [51-250]

Los Huevos Parlantes (Illus. by Jerry Pinkney)

HB Guide - v8 - Fall '97 - p339 [1-50]

Nicholas Pipe (Illus. by David Shannon)

BL - v93 - Je 1 '97 - p1712 [51-250]

CCB-B - v50 - Jl '97 - p411+ [251-500]

Ch BWatch - v7 - Jl '97 - p6 [51-250]

HB Guide - v8 - Fall '97 - p335 [51-250]

KR - v65 - My 15 '97 - p807 [51-250]

SLJ - v43 - My '97 - p124 [51-250]

The Samurai's Daughter (Illus. by Stephen T Johnson)

PW - v244 - D 22 '97 - p61 [1-50]

Two Bear Cubs (Illus. by Daniel San Souci)

BL - v94 - Ja 1 '98 - p819 [51-250]

CCB-B - v51 - Mr '98 - p259 [51-250]

PW - v244 - N 10 '97 - p74 [51-250]

SLJ - v44 - Ap '98 - p125 [51-250]

A Weave of Words (Illus. by Raul Colon)

BL - v94 - Mr 15 '98 - p1241 [51-250]

CCB-B - v51 - Ap '98 - p295 [251-500]

KR - v66 - Ja 15 '98 - p117 [51-250]

PW - v245 - Ja 26 '98 - p91 [51-250]

SLJ - v44 - Mr '98 - p206 [51-250]

Young Arthur (Illus. by Jamichael Henterly)
BL - v94 - N 1 '97 - p477 [51-250]
Ch BWatch - v8 - Ja '98 - p2 [1-50]
PW - v244 - N 24 '97 - p75 [1-50]

Santella, Andrew
The Battle of the Alamo
CCB-B - v51 - S '97 - p25 [51-250]
HB Guide - v8 - Fall '97 - p397 [51-250]

Santore, Charles
William the Curious (Illus. by Charles Santore)
BL - v94 - D 15 '97 - p704 [51-250]
CCB-B - v51 - D '97 - p139 [51-250]
Ch BWatch - v8 - Ja '98 - p2 [1-50]
SLJ - v44 - F '98 - p90+ [51-250]

Sarfati, Sonia
Comme Une Peau De Chagrin
Bkbird - v34 - Win '96 - p58 [1-50]

Sargent, Pat L
The Black Panther (Illus. by Jane Lenoir)
SLJ - v43 - Jl '97 - p98 [51-250]

Sarmonpal, Paulette
Where Are My Onions? (Illus. by Silvia Vignale)
CM:CanRev - v4 - D 12 '97 - pONL [251-500]

Sasso, Sandy Eisenberg
A Prayer for the Earth (Illus. by Bethanne Andersen)
Bloom Rev - v17 - My '97 - p27 [51-250]
CCB-B - v50 - Jl '97 - p412 [51-250]
Ch BWatch - v7 - Mr '97 - p7 [51-250]
HB Guide - v8 - Fall '97 - p319 [51-250]
PW - v244 - N 3 '97 - p58 [51-250]
SLJ - v43 - Je '97 - p111 [51-250]

Sateren, Shelley Swanson
Canada: Star of the North
SLJ - v43 - Je '97 - p139 [51-250]

The Humane Societies
RT - v51 - O '97 - p142 [1-50]

Sathre, Vivian
Leroy Potts Meets the McCrooks (Illus. by Rowan Barnes-Murphy)
HB Guide - v8 - Fall '97 - p294 [51-250]
SLJ - v43 - S '97 - p193+ [51-250]

On Grandpa's Farm (Illus. by Anne Hunter)
CBRS - v26 - D '97 - p41 [1-50]
KR - v65 - Jl 15 '97 - p1117 [51-250]
SLJ - v43 - S '97 - p194 [51-250]

Three Kind Mice (Illus. by Rodger Wilson)
HB Guide - v8 - Fall '97 - p280 [51-250]
Par - v72 - Je '97 - p189 [51-250]

Satterfield, Barbara
The Story Dance (Illus. by Fran Gregory)
Ch BWatch - v7 - Mr '97 - p1 [51-250]
HB Guide - v8 - Fall '97 - p280 [51-250]

Sattler, Helen Roney
Giraffes, the Sentinels of the Savannahs (Illus. by Christopher Santoro)
SLJ - v43 - My '97 - p57 [1-50]

Saul, Carol P
Someplace Else (Illus. by Barry Root)
PW - v244 - D 22 '97 - p61 [1-50]

Sauvain, Philip
Kings and Queens
TES - S 19 '97 - p16* [51-250]

Oceans
Ch BWatch - v7 - D '97 - p8 [1-50]
HB Guide - v8 - Fall '97 - p386 [51-250]
SLJ - v44 - Ja '98 - p130 [51-250]

Rain Forests
HB Guide - v8 - Fall '97 - p386 [51-250]

Saints
TES - S 19 '97 - p16* [51-250]

Savage, Jeff

Andre Agassi
Ch BWatch - v7 - S '97 - p7 [1-50]

Barry Bonds: Mr. Excitement
HB Guide - v8 - Fall '97 - p371 [51-250]

Drag Racing
RT - v51 - O '97 - p137 [1-50]

Grant Hill: Humble Hotshot
Cur R - v36 - Mr '97 - p12 [1-50]
HB Guide - v8 - Fall '97 - p371 [51-250]
SLJ - v43 - Je '97 - p144 [51-250]
y   VOYA - v20 - Ag '97 - p201+ [251-500]

Junior Seau: Star Linebacker
CLW - v68 - S '97 - p68 [51-250]
HB Guide - v8 - Fall '97 - p371 [51-250]

Mike Piazza: Hard-Hitting Catcher
Ch BWatch - v7 - S '97 - p7 [1-50]

Monster Trucks
RT - v51 - O '97 - p142 [1-50]

Supercross Motorcycle Racing
RT - v51 - O '97 - p142 [1-50]

Top 10 Basketball Point Guards
CLW - v68 - S '97 - p69 [51-250]
HB Guide - v8 - Fall '97 - p372 [51-250]
y   VOYA - v20 - O '97 - p270 [51-250]

Top 10 Basketball Power Forwards
CLW - v68 - S '97 - p69 [1-50]
HB Guide - v8 - Fall '97 - p372 [51-250]
y   VOYA - v20 - O '97 - p270 [51-250]

Top 10 Football Sackers
CLW - v68 - S '97 - p69 [51-250]
HB Guide - v8 - Fall '97 - p372 [51-250]

Savage, Stephen

Animals of the Desert
HB Guide - v8 - Fall '97 - p348 [51-250]
SB - v33 - Ag '97 - p179 [251-500]
SLJ - v43 - Ag '97 - p150 [51-250]

Animals of the Grasslands
HB Guide - v8 - Fall '97 - p348 [51-250]

SB - v33 - Ag '97 - p179 [251-500]

Animals of the Oceans
HB Guide - v8 - Fall '97 - p348 [51-250]
SB - v33 - Ag '97 - p179 [251-500]
SLJ - v43 - Ag '97 - p150 [51-250]

Animals of the Rain Forest
HB Guide - v8 - Fall '97 - p348 [51-250]
SB - v33 - Ag '97 - p179 [251-500]

Sawyer, Kem Knapp

The Underground Railroad in American History
CLW - v68 - S '97 - p71 [51-250]
HB Guide - v8 - Fall '97 - p397 [51-250]

Sawyer, Ruth

The Remarkable Christmas of the Cobbler's Sons (Illus. by Barbara Cooney)
PW - v244 - O 6 '97 - p59 [1-50]

Sawyers, June Skinner

Famous Firsts of Scottish-Americans
BL - v93 - Je 1 '97 - p1698 [51-250]
y   HB Guide - v8 - Fall '97 - p384 [51-250]

Say, Allen

Allison (Illus. by Allen Say)
BL - v94 - D 15 '97 - p693 [51-250]
CBRS - v26 - N '97 - p29+ [51-250]
CCB-B - v51 - Ja '98 - p175 [51-250]
HB - v74 - Ja '98 - p69 [51-250]
KR - v65 - O 1 '97 - p1537 [51-250]
PW - v244 - Ag 4 '97 - p74 [51-250]

Emma's Rug (Illus. by Allen Say)
RT - v51 - S '97 - p53 [51-250]

Grandfather's Journey
BL - v93 - Je 1 '97 - p1701 [1-50]
ECEJ - v25 - Fall '97 - p50 [1-50]
SLJ - v43 - Jl '97 - p35 [1-50]

Under the Cherry Blossom Tree
BW - v27 - My 4 '97 - p17 [501+]
CBRS - v25 - Je '97 - p124 [51-250]
HB Guide - v8 - Fall '97 - p335 [51-250]

Sayre, April Pulley
Coral Reef
> ASBYP - v29 - Fall '96 - p45 [501+]
> y VOYA - v20 - Ap '97 - p60 [251-500]

Endangered Birds of North America
> BL - v94 - D 1 '97 - p632 [51-250]
> SLJ - v44 - Ja '98 - p130+ [51-250]

If You Should Hear a Honey Guide (Illus. by S D Schindler)
> SLJ - v43 - My '97 - p57 [1-50]

Ocean
> ASBYP - v29 - Fall '96 - p45 [501+]
> y VOYA - v20 - Ap '97 - p60 [251-500]

Put on Some Antlers and Walk Like a Moose
> BL - v94 - D 1 '97 - p632 [51-250]
> SLJ - v44 - F '98 - p124+ [51-250]
> y VOYA - v20 - F '98 - p404 [51-250]

Seashore
> ASBYP - v29 - Fall '96 - p45 [501+]

Tropical Rain Forest
> BL - v94 - D 1 '97 - p629 [1-50]

Scarborough, Kate
My First Canadian Science Encyclopedia (Illus. by Teresa Foster)
> r CBRA - '96 - p536+ [51-250]

Watch It Grow: Spider's Nest
> New Sci - v155 - Ag 23 '97 - p44 [51-250]

Scarborough, Ken
Doug's Secret Christmas (Illus. by Matthew Peters)
> PW - v244 - O 6 '97 - p58 [1-50]

Scarry, Richard
Mr. Fixit's Mix-Ups
> PW - v245 - Ja 5 '98 - p69 [1-50]

Mr. Frumble's Pickle Car
> PW - v245 - Ja 5 '98 - p69 [1-50]

Richard Scarry's The Ginger Bread Man
> Ch BWatch - v7 - D '97 - p2 [51-250]

Schade, Susan
Snow Bugs
> HB Guide - v8 - Fall '97 - p287 [51-250]

Toad Takes Off (Illus. by Susan Schade)
> SLJ - v43 - Ag '97 - p141+ [51-250]

Schanzer, Rosalyn
How We Crossed the West (Illus. by Rosalyn Schanzer)
> BL - v94 - S 15 '97 - p233 [51-250]
> CBRS - v25 - Ag '97 - p168 [51-250]
> CCB-B - v51 - N '97 - p100 [51-250]
> Inst - v107 - O '97 - p25+ [51-250]
> KR - v65 - O 15 '97 - p1588 [51-250]
> PW - v244 - S 29 '97 - p89+ [51-250]

Schar, Brigitte
Das Geht Doch Nicht!
> Bkbird - v34 - Win '96 - p58 [51-250]

Schecter, Darrow
Planets (Illus. by Tom LaPadula)
> ASBYP - v29 - Fall '96 - p48+ [501+]

Schecter, Ellen
Real Live Monsters!
> Ch BWatch - v7 - My '97 - p6 [51-250]

Town Mouse and Country Mouse
> Ch BWatch - v7 - My '97 - p6 [1-50]

Scheffler, Ursel
Grandpa's Amazing Computer (Illus. by Ruth Scholte Van Mast)
> BL - v94 - F 15 '98 - p1012 [51-250]
> KR - v65 - N 1 '97 - p1649 [51-250]

The Spy in the Attic (Illus. by Christa Unzner)
> BL - v93 - Je 1 '97 - p1706 [51-250]
> CBRS - v25 - My '97 - p116 [51-250]
> HB Guide - v8 - Fall '97 - p294 [51-250]
> Sch Lib - v45 - Ag '97 - p147+ [51-250]
> SLJ - v43 - Ap '97 - p116 [51-250]

Schenk de Regniers, Beatrice
David and Goliath (Illus. by Scott Cameron)
> SE - v61 - Ap '97 - p15* [1-50]

Schermbrucker, Reviva
Charlie's House (Illus. by Niki Daly)
> BL - v93 - Je 1 '97 - p1724 [1-50]
> JOYS - v11 - Win '98 - p141 [51-250]

Schertle, Alice
Keepers (Illus. by Ted Rand)
> RT - v51 - D '97 - p330 [51-250]

Schiller, Pam
Count on Math (Illus. by Cheryl Kirk Noll)
> SB - v33 - D '97 - p272+ [51-250]

Schisgall, Jim
The Sand Witch (Illus. by John Timmins)
> Ch BWatch - v7 - N '97 - p1 [51-250]

Schleichert, Elizabeth
Sitting Bull: Sioux Leader
> CLW - v68 - S '97 - p68 [51-250]
> HB Guide - v8 - Fall '97 - p399 [51-250]
> y   SLJ - v43 - Je '97 - p138 [51-250]

Schlein, Miriam
More than One
> TCMath - v4 - O '97 - p122 [51-250]

The Puzzle of the Dinosaur-Bird (Illus. by Mark Hallett)
> SB - v33 - Ap '97 - p85 [51-250]

Sleep Safe, Little Whale (Illus. by Peter Sis)
> CCB-B - v51 - Ja '98 - p176 [51-250]
> KR - v65 - Jl 1 '97 - p1036 [51-250]
> Par - v73 - F '98 - p185 [1-50]
> Par Ch - Awards '97 - p3 [51-250]
> PW - v244 - Ag 25 '97 - p73 [51-250]

What's a Penguin Doing in a Place Like This?
> Am Sci - v85 - N '97 - p560 [51-250]
> BL - v93 - Je 1 '97 - p1698 [51-250]
> HB Guide - v8 - Fall '97 - p352 [51-250]
> SB - v33 - Ag '97 - p187 [1-50]
> SB - v33 - N '97 - p243 [51-250]
> SLJ - v43 - Jl '97 - p87 [51-250]

Schlissel, Lillian
Black Frontiers
> BL - v93 - Je 1 '97 - p1700 [1-50]

Schmidt, Gary D
The Blessing of the Lord (Illus. by Dennis Nolan)
> BL - v94 - N 1 '97 - p469 [51-250]
> PW - v244 - Ag 25 '97 - p66 [51-250]

Schmidt, Norman
Paper Birds That Fly (Illus. by Jerry Grajewski)
> CBRA - '96 - p521+ [51-250]
> y   Ch BWatch - v7 - S '97 - p6 [1-50]
> SLJ - v43 - Jl '97 - p111 [51-250]

Schnakenberg, Robert
Scottie Pippen
> Ch BWatch - v7 - S '97 - p7 [1-50]

Schnapper, LaDena
Teenage Refugees from Ethiopia Speak Out
> SLJ - v44 - F '98 - p126 [51-250]

Schneider, Mical
Between the Dragon and the Eagle
> y   Ch BWatch - v7 - Jl '97 - p2 [51-250]
> HB Guide - v8 - Fall '97 - p308 [51-250]
> SLJ - v43 - Ap '97 - p140 [51-250]

Schnur, Steven
Autumn: An Alphabet Acrostic (Illus. by Leslie Evans)
> BL - v94 - S 1 '97 - p129+ [51-250]
> CBRS - v26 - S '97 - p6 [51-250]
> CCB-B - v51 - S '97 - p25 [51-250]
> Emerg Lib - v25 - Ja '98 - p51 [1-50]
> KR - v65 - Jl 1 '97 - p1036 [51-250]
> NYTBR - v102 - O 26 '97 - p47 [1-50]
> SLJ - v43 - S '97 - p194 [51-250]

The Koufax Dilemma (Illus. by Meryl Treatner)
> HB Guide - v8 - Fall '97 - p308 [51-250]
> NYTBR - v102 - Je 8 '97 - p27 [501+]
> SLJ - v43 - My '97 - p140 [51-250]

Scholastic's the Magic School Bus Explores in the Age of Dinosaurs. Electronic Media Version

SLJ - v43 - D '97 - p57+ [51-250]

Schomp, Virginia

If You Were a...Ballet Dancer
BL - v94 - F 15 '98 - p1006 [51-250]
SLJ - v44 - F '98 - p104+ [51-250]

If You Were a...Construction Worker
BL - v94 - F 15 '98 - p1006 [51-250]

If You Were an...Astronaut
SLJ - v44 - F '98 - p104+ [51-250]

If You Were a...Veterinarian
SB - v34 - Ap '98 - p82 [251-500]
SLJ - v44 - F '98 - p104+ [51-250]

School Bus (Box Cars)

PW - v245 - Mr 23 '98 - p102 [1-50]

Schotter, Roni

Nothing Ever Happens on 90th Street (Illus. by Kyrsten Brooker)
CBRS - v25 - My '97 - p116 [51-250]
HB Guide - v8 - Fall '97 - p280 [51-250]
Inst - v107 - S '97 - p23+ [51-250]
NYTBR - v102 - Ag 3 '97 - p14 [501+]

Passover Magic (Illus. by Marylin Hafner)
PW - v244 - D 22 '97 - p55 [1-50]

Purim Play (Illus. by Marylin Hafner)
KR - v66 - Ja 1 '98 - p62 [51-250]
PW - v245 - F 23 '98 - p67 [51-250]
SLJ - v44 - Ap '98 - p110 [51-250]

Schraff, Anne

Are We Moving to Mars?
Ch BWatch - v7 - S '97 - p4 [1-50]

Coretta Scott King: Striving for Civil Rights
CLW - v68 - S '97 - p67 [51-250]
HB Guide - v8 - Fall '97 - p381 [1-50]

Jimmy Carter
KR - v66 - F 1 '98 - p200 [51-250]
y   VOYA - v21 - Ap '98 - p74 [51-250]

Schrecengost, Maity

Researching People
Emerg Lib - v24 - My '97 - p42 [51-250]
yr   SLMQ - v25 - Spr '97 - p183 [51-250]

Schroeder, Alan

Carolina Shout! (Illus. by Bernie Fuchs)
Inst - v106 - Ap '97 - p24 [1-50]

Charlie Chaplin: The Beauty of Silence
y   BL - v93 - Je 1 '97 - p1680 [51-250]
y   HB Guide - v8 - Fall '97 - p382 [51-250]
SLJ - v43 - Je '97 - p144 [51-250]

Minty: A Story of Young Harriet Tubman (Illus. by Jerry Pinkney)
Emerg Lib - v24 - My '97 - p64 [51-250]
RT - v51 - N '97 - p243 [51-250]
RT - v51 - D '97 - p308+ [51-250]
TES - My 2 '97 - p8* [501+]

Satchmo's Blues (Illus. by Floyd Cooper)
CCB-B - v51 - S '97 - p22 [251-500]
y   JAAL - v40 - Ap '97 - p588 [51-250]
RT - v51 - S '97 - p54 [51-250]
RT - v51 - N '97 - p243+ [51-250]

Smoky Mountain Rose (Illus. by Brad Sneed)
CBRS - v25 - Jl '97 - p153 [1-50]
CCB-B - v50 - Jl '97 - p413 [51-250]
HB Guide - v8 - Fall '97 - p336 [51-250]
Inst - v107 - Ag '97 - p23 [1-50]
KR - v65 - Ap 15 '97 - p649 [51-250]
SLJ - v43 - Je '97 - p111+ [51-250]
Trib Bks - Jl 13 '97 - p7 [51-250]

Schroeder, Russell

Mickey Mouse: My Life in Pictures
y   BL - v94 - Mr 15 '98 - p1225 [1-50]
SLJ - v44 - F '98 - p126 [51-250]
y   VOYA - v21 - Ap '98 - p40 [1-50]

Walt Disney: His Life in Pictures
RT - v51 - D '97 - p328 [51-250]

Schubert, Ingrid
Abracadabra (Illus. by Dieter Schubert)
> HB Guide - v8 - Fall '97 - p281 [51-250]
> KR - v65 - Ap 15 '97 - p650 [51-250]

Schuett, Stacey
Somewhere in the World Right Now
> PW - v244 - N 17 '97 - p63 [1-50]

Schulman, Arlene
Carmine's Story (Illus. by Arlene Schulman)
> BL - v94 - Mr 15 '98 - p1236 [51-250]
> KR - v65 - N 15 '97 - p1713 [51-250]

Schulson, Rachel
Guns: What You Should Know (Illus. by Mary Jones)
> BL - v94 - O 15 '97 - p411 [51-250]
> CCB-B - v51 - D '97 - p139 [51-250]
> SLJ - v43 - D '97 - p115 [51-250]

Schultz, Ellen
Birds (Illus. by Lisa Bonforte)
> ASBYP - v29 - Fall '96 - p48+ [501+]

Schumaker, Ward
Sing a Song of Circus (Illus. by Ward Schumaker)
> CBRS - v25 - Spr '97 - p137+ [51-250]
> HB Guide - v8 - Fall '97 - p281 [51-250]
> SLJ - v43 - Je '97 - p100+ [51-250]

Schuman, Michael A
Harry S. Truman
> HB Guide - v8 - Fall '97 - p395 [51-250]
> y   SLJ - v43 - Ag '97 - p174+ [51-250]

Theodore Roosevelt
> SLJ - v44 - F '98 - p126 [51-250]

Schur, Maxine
When I Left My Village (Illus. by J Brian Pinkney)
> RT - v51 - D '97 - p310+ [51-250]
> SE - v61 - Ap '97 - p15* [1-50]

Schwabacher, Martin
Superstars of Women's Tennis
> Ch BWatch - v7 - S '97 - p8 [1-50]
> HB Guide - v8 - Fall '97 - p369 [51-250]
> SLJ - v43 - Ag '97 - p175 [51-250]

Schwartz, Ellen
Starshine on TV
> CBRA - '96 - p491+ [51-250]

Schwartz, Gary
Hieronymus Bosch
> y   BL - v94 - D 15 '97 - p690 [51-250]
> y   KR - v65 - O 1 '97 - p1537 [51-250]
> PW - v244 - D 22 '97 - p61 [1-50]

Schwartz, Howard
The Diamond Tree
> PW - v245 - F 2 '98 - p92 [1-50]

Schwartz, Michael
LaDonna Harris
> BL - v93 - Je 1 '97 - p1698 [51-250]
> HB Guide - v8 - Fall '97 - p382 [51-250]

Luis Rodriguez
> HB Guide - v8 - Fall '97 - p379 [51-250]
> SLJ - v43 - Je '97 - p144 [51-250]

Schwartz, Noa
Crazy for Canada (Illus. by Mick Beaumont)
> Quill & Q - v63 - Je '97 - p64 [251-500]

Schwartz, Perry
Carolyn's Story (Illus. by Perry Schwartz)
> SLJ - v43 - Ap '97 - p130 [51-250]

Scieszka, Jon
The Book That Jack Wrote (Illus. by Daniel Adel)
> JAAL - v40 - My '97 - p669 [51-250]

Knights of the Kitchen Table (Illus. by Lane Smith)
> SLJ - v43 - Jl '97 - p35 [1-50]

Math Curse
>   ASBYP - v29 - Sum '96 - p30+ [251-500]
>   Emerg Lib - v24 - My '97 - p51 [51-250]

The Stinky Cheese Man and Other Fairly Stupid Tales (Illus. by Lane Smith)
>   NYTBR - v102 - N 16 '97 - p26 [1-50]
>   SLJ - v43 - N '97 - p41 [1-50]

The True Story of the 3 Little Pigs (Illus. by Lane Smith)
>   NYTBR - v102 - N 16 '97 - p26 [1-50]

Tut Tut (Illus. by Lane Smith)
>   Magpies - v12 - Mr '97 - p35 [51-250]

La Verdadera Historia De Los Tres Cerditos. Book and Audio Version
>   Ch BWatch - v7 - My '97 - p5 [1-50]
>   SLJ - v44 - Ap '98 - p81+ [51-250]

Scott, A
One Good Horse (Illus. by Lynn Sweat)
>   ECEJ - v25 - Fall '97 - p50 [1-50]

Scott, Carey
Kittens
>   CLW - v68 - D '97 - p84 [51-250]
>   SLJ - v44 - F '98 - p105 [51-250]

Puppies
>   BL - v94 - O 15 '97 - p401 [51-250]
>   CLW - v68 - D '97 - p84 [51-250]
>   SLJ - v44 - F '98 - p105 [51-250]

Scott, Deborah
The Kid Who Got Zapped through Time
>   BL - v94 - N 1 '97 - p473+ [51-250]
>   CBRS - v26 - O '97 - p24 [1-50]
>   SLJ - v43 - S '97 - p225+ [51-250]

Scott, Elaine
Close Encounters
>   KR - v66 - Ap 15 '98 - p586 [51-250]

Twins! (Illus. by Margaret Miller)
>   KR - v66 - Ja 15 '98 - p117 [51-250]

Scott, Hugh
The Ghosts of Ravens Crag
>   Magpies - v12 - Jl '97 - p39 [51-250]

Scott, Julie
Sleepy Kitten
>   Sch Lib - v45 - N '97 - p188 [51-250]

Screenivasan, Jyotsna
Aruna's Journeys
>   CBRS - v25 - Je '97 - p131 [51-250]

Scudamore, Beverly
Worm Pie
>   CM:CanRev - v4 - O 3 '97 - pONL [251-500]

Scuderi, Lucia
To Fly (Illus. by Lucia Scuderi)
>   KR - v66 - Mr 1 '98 - p344 [51-250]
>   PW - v245 - Mr 9 '98 - p66 [51-250]

Seabrook, Elizabeth
Cabbages and Kings (Illus. by Jamie Wyeth)
>   BL - v93 - Ag '97 - p1907 [51-250]
>   CBRS - v25 - Ag '97 - p162 [51-250]
>   KR - v65 - Je 15 '97 - p957 [51-250]
>   NYTBR - v102 - O 12 '97 - p26 [1-50]
>   PW - v244 - Je 16 '97 - p58 [51-250]
>   SLJ - v43 - N '97 - p99 [51-250]

Seabrooke, Brenda
The Care and Feeding of Dragons
>   KR - v65 - N 15 '97 - p1713 [51-250]
>   SLJ - v44 - F '98 - p91 [51-250]

The Haunting of Holroyd Hill
>   y   Kliatt - v31 - N '97 - p16+ [51-250]
>   LA - v73 - N '96 - p528+ [51-250]

Under the Pear Tree (Illus. by Roger Essley)
>   BL - v93 - Ag '97 - p1896 [51-250]
>   HB - v73 - Jl '97 - p471 [51-250]
>   KR - v65 - Je 1 '97 - p879 [51-250]
>   SLJ - v43 - S '97 - p236 [51-250]

Seago, Kate
Matthew Unstrung
>   y   CCB-B - v51 - Mr '98 - p259+ [51-250]
>   y   Kliatt - v32 - Mr '98 - p6 [51-250]
>   y   KR - v65 - D 15 '97 - p1840 [51-250]

SLJ - v44 - Mr '98 - p224 [51-250]

y   VOYA - v20 - F '98 - p390 [251-500]

Seary, Michael
So You Love to Draw (Illus. by Michel Bisson)

CBRA - '96 - p522 [51-250]

Sebba, Jane
Ring-a-Ding-Ding

Sch Lib - v45 - Ag '97 - p155 [51-250]

Seese, Wendy
The Ambitious Baker's Batter

Ch BWatch - v7 - D '97 - p5 [51-250]

Sefton, Catherine
The Pocket Elephant (Illus. by Andy Ellis)

Obs - D 7 '97 - p17* [51-250]

Sehnert, Chris W
Top 10 Sluggers

BL - v94 - Ja 1 '98 - p807 [51-250]

Seibert, Patricia
Toad Overload (Illus. by Jan Davey Ellis)

ASBYP - v29 - Fall '96 - p29 [251-500]

SB - v33 - Ag '97 - p187 [1-50]

Seibold, J Otto
Free Lunch (Illus. by J Otto Seibold)

ABR - v19 - N '97 - p5+ [501+]

Going to the Getty (Illus. by J Otto Seibold)

BL - v94 - F 15 '98 - p1006 [51-250]

PW - v244 - D 22 '97 - p61 [51-250]

Mr. Lunch Borrows a Canoe (Illus. by J Otto Seibold)

PW - v244 - Ag 25 '97 - p74 [1-50]

Olive, the Other Reindeer (Illus. by J Otto Seibold)

BL - v94 - O 15 '97 - p417 [51-250]

CCB-B - v51 - Ja '98 - p176 [51-250]

Ch BWatch - v7 - D '97 - p1 [51-250]

CM:CanRev - v4 - Ja 2 '98 - pONL [251-500]

KR - v65 - N 1 '97 - p1649 [51-250]

NW - v130 - D 1 '97 - p78 [1-50]

NYTBR - v102 - D 21 '97 - p18 [1-50]

PW - v244 - O 6 '97 - p54 [51-250]

Seidler, Tor
Mean Margaret (Illus. by Jon Agee)

BL - v94 - D 1 '97 - p619 [51-250]

CBRS - v26 - O '97 - p21 [51-250]

HB - v74 - Ja '98 - p80+ [51-250]

KR - v65 - S 1 '97 - p1395 [51-250]

NYTBR - v102 - N 16 '97 - p34 [501+]

PW - v244 - Ag 18 '97 - p93 [51-250]

PW - v244 - N 3 '97 - p60 [51-250]

SLJ - v43 - N '97 - p99+ [51-250]

SLJ - v43 - D '97 - p27 [1-50]

Selby, Jennifer
The Seed Bunny (Illus. by Jennifer Selby)

BL - v93 - Je 1 '97 - p1722 [51-250]

HB Guide - v8 - Fall '97 - p255 [51-250]

SLJ - v43 - Ap '97 - p116 [51-250]

Selby, Rick
HO Railroad from Set to Scenery

LJ - v122 - N 15 '97 - p56 [1-50]

Selden, Bernice
The Story of Walt Disney (Illus. by David Rickman)

Ch BWatch - v7 - Mr '97 - p4 [1-50]

Selden, George
The Cricket in Times Square (Illus. by Garth Williams)

NYTBR - v102 - N 16 '97 - p26 [1-50]

Sellier, Marie
Bonnard from A to Z

KR - v65 - D 15 '97 - p1841 [51-250]

Chagall from A to Z (Illus. by Marie Sellier)

RT - v51 - F '98 - p429 [51-250]

Seltzer, Eric
4 Pups and a Worm (Illus. by Eric Seltzer)

RT - v51 - O '97 - p133 [1-50]

Selway, Martina
What Can I Write? (Illus. by Martina Selway)
  Obs - Jl 20 '97 - p18* [51-250]
  Sch Lib - v45 - N '97 - p188 [51-250]
  TES - Je 20 '97 - p12* [1-50]

Sendak, Maurice
Alligators All Around
  Par - v72 - Je '97 - p189 [1-50]

Donde Viven Los Monstros (Illus. by Maurice Sendak)
  SLJ - v43 - My '97 - p154 [51-250]

Where the Wild Things Are (Illus. by Maurice Sendak)
  NYTBR - v102 - N 16 '97 - p26 [1-50]

Senisi, Ellen B
Just Kids (Illus. by Ellen B Senisi)
  KR - v65 - D 15 '97 - p1841 [51-250]
  SLJ - v44 - Ap '98 - p110 [51-250]

A Sense of Purpose
  r   Magpies - v12 - Mr '97 - p43 [51-250]

Sensier, Danielle
Inner Cities
  Sch Lib - v45 - Ag '97 - p155 [251-500]

Villages
  Sch Lib - v45 - Ag '97 - p155 [251-500]

Service, Pamela F
The Ancient African Kingdom of Kush
  Ch BWatch - v8 - Ja '98 - p7 [51-250]

SETI Institute
How Might Life Evolve on Other Planets?
  ASBYP - v29 - Sum '96 - p31+ [501+]

Seuling, Barbara
To Be a Writer (Illus. by Anna DiVito)
  BL - v93 - Je 1 '97 - p1698 [51-250]
  Ch BWatch - v7 - My '97 - p7 [1-50]
  SLJ - v43 - Ag '97 - p175 [51-250]
  y   VOYA - v20 - O '97 - p270 [51-250]

Seuss, Dr.
The Butter Battle Book
  SE - v61 - S '97 - p271 [1-50]

The Cat in the Hat (Illus. by Dr. Seuss)
  Bks Keeps - N '97 - p28 [501+]
  Books - v11 - D '97 - p21 [51-250]
  NY - v73 - O 6 '97 - p112+ [501+]
  NYTBR - v102 - N 16 '97 - p26 [1-50]
  Spec - v279 - D 6 '97 - p43 [51-250]
  TES - N 7 '97 - p12* [501+]
  TES - N 7 '97 - p16* [51-250]

The Cat in the Hat Comes Back
  TES - N 7 '97 - p12* [501+]

Dr. Seuss's ABC. 40th-Anniversary Ed.
  TES - N 7 '97 - p12* [501+]

The Foot Book. 40th-Anniversary Ed.
  TES - N 7 '97 - p12* [501+]

Fox in Socks. 40th-Anniversary Ed.
  TES - N 7 '97 - p12* [501+]

Green Eggs and Ham. 40th-Anniversary Ed.
  TES - N 7 '97 - p12* [501+]

Green Eggs and Ham. Electronic Media Version
  BL - v94 - D 1 '97 - p646+ [51-250]
  Emerg Lib - v25 - N '97 - p48 [51-250]

The Grinch's Song
  Ch BWatch - v7 - Je '97 - p1 [1-50]

A Hatful of Seuss
  Ch BWatch - v7 - Mr '97 - p1 [51-250]
  HB Guide - v8 - Fall '97 - p281 [51-250]

Hooray for Diffendoofer Day! (Illus. by Lane Smith)
  KR - v66 - Ap 1 '98 - p501 [51-250]
  PW - v245 - F 16 '98 - p211 [51-250]

How the Grinch Stole Christmas (Illus. by Dr. Seuss)
  NYTBR - v102 - N 16 '97 - p26 [1-50]

The Lorax
  PW - v245 - Ja 26 '98 - p93 [1-50]

Mr. Brown Can Moo! Can You?. 40th-Anniversary Ed.
  TES - N 7 '97 - p12* [501+]

One Fish Two Fish Red Fish Blue Fish
TES - N 7 '97 - p12* [501+]

There's a Wocket in My Pocket!
TES - N 7 '97 - p12* [501+]

The Cat in the Hat. Electronic Media Version
LJ - v123 - Ja '98 - p157 [51-250]
SLJ - v44 - Ap '98 - p40 [1-50]

The Shape of Me and Other Stuff
PW - v244 - Ag 4 '97 - p77 [51-250]

What Was I Scared Of?
PW - v244 - Ag 4 '97 - p77 [1-50]

Severance, John B
Gandhi, Great Soul
y   CCB-B - v50 - Je '97 - p373 [51-250]
    Ch BWatch - v7 - Je '97 - p2 [51-250]
    HB Guide - v8 - Fall '97 - p382 [51-250]
    NYTBR - v102 - Ag 17 '97 - p19 [1-50]
y   SLJ - v43 - Ap '97 - p157 [51-250]

Sewell, Anna
Black Beauty (Illus. by Victor G Ambrus)
CLW - v68 - D '97 - p86 [51-250]
HB Guide - v8 - Fall '97 - p302 [51-250]
SLJ - v43 - Jl '97 - p98 [51-250]
TES - Je 6 '97 - p8* [501+]

Black Beauty (Illus. by Lucy Kemp-Welch)
HB Guide - v8 - Fall '97 - p309 [51-250]

Sexton, Margot
The Twelve Tales of Christmas (Illus. by Janis Jones)
Can CL - v23 - Fall '97 - p92 [51-250]

Seymour, Tres
Too Quiet for These Old Bones (Illus. by Paul Brett Johnson)
CBRS - v26 - Win '98 - p63+ [51-250]
KR - v65 - Ag 1 '97 - p1228 [51-250]
PW - v244 - Ag 11 '97 - p401 [51-250]

We Played Marbles (Illus. by Dan Andreasen)
BL - v94 - F 15 '98 - p1020 [51-250]
KR - v66 - Ja 15 '98 - p118 [51-250]
PW - v245 - F 2 '98 - p88+ [51-250]
SLJ - v44 - Mr '98 - p187 [51-250]

Sgouros, Charissa
A Pillow for My Mom (Illus. by Christine Ross)
KR - v66 - Ap 1 '98 - p501 [51-250]

Shahan, Sherry
Barnacles Eat with Their Feet (Illus. by Sherry Shahan)
ASBYP - v29 - Fall '96 - p29+ [251-500]

Dashing through the Snow (Illus. by Sherry Shahan)
HB Guide - v8 - Fall '97 - p372 [51-250]
SLJ - v43 - Ap '97 - p132 [51-250]

, Shahrukh Husain
What Do We Know about Islam?
HB Guide - v8 - Fall '97 - p318+ [51-250]

Shaik, Fatima
The Jazz of Our Street (Illus. by E B Lewis)
KR - v66 - Ap 15 '98 - p586 [51-250]

Melitte
y   BL - v94 - O 15 '97 - p398+ [51-250]
    CBRS - v26 - F '98 - p83 [51-250]
    CCB-B - v51 - Ja '98 - p176+ [51-250]
    HB - v73 - N '97 - p685 [51-250]
    KR - v65 - O 15 '97 - p1588 [51-250]
    PW - v244 - O 27 '97 - p76+ [51-250]
y   VOYA - v20 - F '98 - p390+ [251-500]

Shakespeare, William
Romeo and Juliet (Acclaim)
LATBR - Mr 2 '97 - p13 [501+]

Shange, Ntozake
Whitewash (Illus. by Michael Sporn)
CBRS - v26 - N '97 - p32 [51-250]
KR - v65 - O 1 '97 - p1537+ [51-250]
PW - v244 - N 3 '97 - p85 [51-250]

Shank, Jackie
Happily Ever After and All That (Illus. by Linda Alexander)
Ch BWatch - v7 - S '97 - p2 [51-250]

Shannon, David
A Bad Case of Stripes (Illus. by David Shannon)
BL - v94 - Ja 1 '98 - p825 [51-250]
CCB-B - v51 - Mr '98 - p260 [51-250]
KR - v65 - D 15 '97 - p1841 [51-250]
PW - v245 - Ja 12 '98 - p59+ [51-250]
SLJ - v44 - Mr '98 - p188 [51-250]

Shannon, George
This Is the Bird (Illus. by David Soman)
HB Guide - v8 - Fall '97 - p281 [51-250]
SLJ - v43 - Ap '97 - p117 [51-250]

Tomorrow's Alphabet (Illus. by Donald Crews)
Emerg Lib - v25 - Ja '98 - p52 [1-50]
Inst - v106 - My '97 - p18 [1-50]
LA - v73 - N '96 - p523 [51-250]
RT - v51 - O '97 - p150 [51-250]
RT - v51 - N '97 - p241 [51-250]
SE - v61 - Ap '97 - p7* [1-50]

True Lies (Illus. by John O'Brien)
CCB-B - v51 - S '97 - p26 [51-250]
HB - v73 - Jl '97 - p469 [51-250]
HB Guide - v8 - Fall '97 - p336 [51-250]
KR - v65 - My 15 '97 - p807 [51-250]
SLJ - v43 - Je '97 - p112 [51-250]

Shannon, Margaret
Gullible's Troubles (Illus. by Margaret Shannon)
KR - v66 - F 15 '98 - p274+ [51-250]
PW - v245 - Mr 23 '98 - p98 [51-250]

Shapes (Fit-a-Shape)
Magpies - v12 - Mr '97 - p29 [51-250]

Shapiro, Arnold
The Day before Christmas (Illus. by Reg Sandland)
Ch BWatch - v7 - D '97 - p2 [1-50]
PW - v244 - O 6 '97 - p57 [1-50]

The First Christmas (Illus. by Reg Sandland)
Ch BWatch - v7 - D '97 - p2 [1-50]
PW - v244 - O 6 '97 - p57 [1-50]

Mice Squeak, We Speak (Illus. by Tomie De Paola)
BL - v94 - S 15 '97 - p231 [51-250]
BL - v94 - Ja 1 '98 - p736 [51-250]
CBRS - v26 - S '97 - p2 [51-250]
Ch BWatch - v7 - O '97 - p6 [1-50]
Emerg Lib - v25 - N '97 - p55 [1-50]
Emerg Lib - v25 - Ja '98 - p52 [1-50]
Inst - v107 - N '97 - p18 [1-50]
KR - v65 - Ag 1 '97 - p1228 [51-250]
PW - v244 - Ag 18 '97 - p91 [51-250]

Trouble at the Haunted House (Illus. by Reg Sandland)
PW - v244 - O 6 '97 - p49 [1-50]

Wanda Witch's Bad Day (Illus. by Reg Sandland)
PW - v244 - O 6 '97 - p49 [1-50]

Shapiro, Colin
Who Needs to Sleep Anyway? (Illus. by Sari O'Sullivan)
Can CL - v23 - Sum '97 - p72+ [501+]
CBRA - '96 - p533+ [51-250]

Sharman, Helen
The Space Place (Illus. by Mic Rolph)
Bks Keeps - N '97 - p25 [51-250]
New Sci - v155 - Ag 23 '97 - p44 [51-250]

Sharmat, Marjorie Weinman
Nate the Great and the Crunchy Christmas (Illus. by Marc Simont)
PW - v244 - O 6 '97 - p59 [1-50]

Sharratt, Nick
The Animal Orchestra
PW - v244 - Ag 4 '97 - p76 [1-50]

Ketchup on Your Cornflakes? (Illus. by Nick Sharratt)
CCB-B - v50 - Je '97 - p373+ [51-250]
HB Guide - v8 - Fall '97 - p255 [51-250]

Rocket Countdown
ASBYP - v29 - Sum '96 - p32 [251-500]

Shaw, Eve
Grandmother's Alphabet (Illus. by Eve Shaw)
    SLJ - v43 - My '97 - p113 [51-250]

Shaw, Nancy
Sheep in a Jeep (Illus. by Margot Apple)
    PW - v244 - Jl 7 '97 - p70 [1-50]

Sheep in a Shop (Illus. by Margot Apple)
    PW - v244 - Jl 7 '97 - p70 [1-50]

Sheep Trick or Treat (Illus. by Margot Apple)
    BL - v94 - S 1 '97 - p141 [51-250]
    HB - v73 - S '97 - p563+ [51-250]
    NYTBR - v102 - N 23 '97 - p32 [501+]
    PW - v244 - O 6 '97 - p50 [1-50]
    SLJ - v43 - S '97 - p194 [51-250]

Shaw, Sarah
Favourite Christmas Carols
    CM:CanRev - v4 - F 13 '98 - pONL [51-250]

Shaw-MacKinnon, Margaret
Tiktala (Illus. by Laszlo Gal)
    CBRA - '96 - p457 [51-250]
    SE - v61 - Ap '97 - p8* [1-50]

Shea, George
First Flight (Illus. by Don Bolognese)
    HB Guide - v8 - Fall '97 - p359 [51-250]

Shearer, Alex
Professor Sniff and the Lost Spring Breezes (Illus. by Tony Kenyon)
    SLJ - v44 - Ap '98 - p110 [51-250]

The Summer Sisters and the Dance Disaster (Illus. by Tony Kenyon)
    KR - v66 - Mr 15 '98 - p409 [51-250]

Sheehan, Patricia
Luxembourg
    Ch BWatch - v7 - Je '97 - p5 [51-250]
    HB Guide - v8 - Fall '97 - p390 [51-250]

Sheehan, Sean
Lebanon
    HB Guide - v8 - Fall '97 - p392 [51-250]
    SLJ - v43 - Je '97 - p144 [51-250]

Shefelman, J
A Peddler's Dream (Illus. by Tom Shefelman)
    ECEJ - v25 - Fall '97 - p50 [1-50]

Sheldon, Dyan
Elena the Frog (Illus. by Sue Heap)
    Bks Keeps - Jl '97 - p22 [51-250]
    Magpies - v12 - S '97 - p31 [51-250]
    Sch Lib - v45 - Ag '97 - p134 [51-250]

Unicorn City (Illus. by Neil Reed)
    Sch Lib - v45 - N '97 - p188 [51-250]
    TES - D 26 '97 - p22 [251-500]

Unicorn Dreams (Illus. by Neil Reed)
    CBRS - v26 - Win '98 - p64 [51-250]
    PW - v244 - O 27 '97 - p75 [51-250]
    SLJ - v44 - Ja '98 - p92 [51-250]

Shemie, Bonnie
Houses of Adobe
    Can CL - v23 - Sum '97 - p71+ [501+]

Houses of China (Illus. by Bonnie Shemie)
    CBRA - '96 - p537 [51-250]

Mounds of Earth and Shell
    Can CL - v23 - Sum '97 - p71+ [501+]

Shepard, Aaron
The Gifts of Wali Dad (Illus. by Daniel San Souci)
    ECEJ - v25 - Fall '97 - p50 [1-50]

Master Maid (Illus. by Pauline Ellison)
    BL - v93 - Je 1 '97 - p1714 [51-250]
    CBRS - v25 - Ag '97 - p162 [51-250]
    CCB-B - v51 - S '97 - p26+ [51-250]
    Ch BWatch - v7 - Jl '97 - p6 [1-50]
    HB Guide - v8 - Fall '97 - p336 [51-250]
    KR - v65 - Je 1 '97 - p880 [51-250]
    SLJ - v43 - Je '97 - p112+ [51-250]

The Sea King's Daughter (Illus. by Gennady Spirin)

    BL - v94 - Mr 15 '98 - p1219 [1-50]
    NYTBR - v102 - O 26 '97 - p47 [1-50]
    PW - v244 - Ag 25 '97 - p72 [51-250]
    SLJ - v43 - D '97 - p115 [51-250]

Shepherd, Donna Walsh

Tundra

    SLJ - v43 - Ap '97 - p157+ [51-250]

Sherman, Eileen B

Independence Avenue

    BL - v93 - Je 1 '97 - p1701 [1-50]

Sherrow, Victoria

American Indian Children of the Past

    HB Guide - v8 - Fall '97 - p399 [51-250]
    SLJ - v43 - Jl '97 - p111 [51-250]

The Blaze Engulfs January 1939 to December 1941

 y BL - v94 - O 15 '97 - p396 [51-250]
    CCB-B - v51 - Ja '98 - p162+ [51-250]
 y SLJ - v44 - F '98 - p134 [51-250]

Connecticut

    Ch BWatch - v8 - Ja '98 - p7 [1-50]

Freedom of Worship

    Ch BWatch - v7 - My '97 - p5 [1-50]
    HB Guide - v8 - Fall '97 - p325 [51-250]
    SLJ - v43 - My '97 - p148 [51-250]

Hardship and Hope

 y BL - v93 - Je 1 '97 - p1680 [51-250]
    Ch BWatch - v7 - My '97 - p7 [1-50]
 y SLJ - v43 - Ag '97 - p175+ [51-250]

Linus Pauling: Investigating the Magic Within

    HB Guide - v8 - Fall '97 - p379 [51-250]

Smoke to Flame September 1935 to December 1938

 y BL - v94 - O 15 '97 - p396 [51-250]
    CCB-B - v51 - Ja '98 - p162+ [51-250]
 yr SLJ - v44 - F '98 - p134 [51-250]

Shields, Carol Diggory

I Wish My Brother Was a Dog (Illus. by Paul Meisel)

    BL - v93 - Je 1 '97 - p1722 [51-250]

    CBRS - v25 - Ag '97 - p162 [51-250]
    HB Guide - v8 - Fall '97 - p281 [51-250]
    Par - v72 - S '97 - p205 [51-250]
    PW - v244 - My 19 '97 - p76 [51-250]
    SLJ - v43 - Jl '97 - p74+ [51-250]

Saturday Night at the Dinosaur Stomp (Illus. by Scott Nash)

    CBRS - v26 - N '97 - p32+ [51-250]
    CCB-B - v51 - Ja '98 - p177+ [51-250]
    Ch BWatch - v7 - N '97 - p4 [1-50]
    KR - v65 - O 15 '97 - p1588 [51-250]
    PW - v244 - S 29 '97 - p88 [51-250]
    SLJ - v43 - N '97 - p100 [51-250]

Shipton, Paul

The Mighty Skink

    Magpies - v12 - Mr '97 - p35 [251-500]

Short, Joan

Platypus (Illus. by Andrew Wichlinski)

    SLJ - v43 - Ag '97 - p150 [51-250]

Whales (Illus. by Deborah Savin)

    SLJ - v43 - S '97 - p208 [51-250]

Shortt, Tim

The Babe Ruth Ballet School (Illus. by Tim Shortt)

    CBRA - '96 - p457 [51-250]

Showell, Ellen H

From Indian Corn to Outer Space

    ASBYP - v29 - Sum '96 - p32+ [251-500]

Showers, Paul

Sleep Is for Everyone (Illus. by Wendy Watson)

    BL - v93 - Ag '97 - p1904 [51-250]
    CCB-B - v51 - S '97 - p27 [51-250]
    HB Guide - v8 - Fall '97 - p356 [1-50]
    SLJ - v43 - Ag '97 - p150+ [51-250]

Shrestha, Kavita Ram

From the Mango Tree and Other Folktales from Nepal

    CAY - v18 - Win '97 - p9 [51-250]
    CLW - v68 - S '97 - p71+ [51-250]

Shreve, Susan Richards
The Flunking of Joshua T. Bates
PW - v244 - O 6 '97 - p85 [1-50]

The Goalie (Bresnahan). Audio Version
SLJ - v43 - N '97 - p68+ [51-250]

Jonah, the Whale
CCB-B - v51 - Ap '98 - p296 [51-250]
SLJ - v44 - Ap '98 - p138 [51-250]

Joshua T. Bates in Trouble Again (Illus. by Roberta Smith)
SLJ - v44 - Ja '98 - p92+ [51-250]

Joshua T. Bates Takes Charge
PW - v244 - O 6 '97 - p85 [1-50]

Shulevitz, Uri
The Golden Goose (Illus. by Uri Shulevitz)
PW - v245 - F 16 '98 - p213 [1-50]

The Secret Room
ECEJ - v25 - Fall '97 - p50 [1-50]

Shulman, William L
Resource Guide
y   BL - v94 - O 15 '97 - p396 [51-250]
r   CCB-B - v51 - Ja '98 - p162+ [51-250]
yr   SLJ - v44 - F '98 - p134 [51-250]

Voices and Visions
y   BL - v94 - O 15 '97 - p396 [51-250]
     CCB-B - v51 - Ja '98 - p162 [51-250]
yr   SLJ - v44 - F '98 - p134 [51-250]

Shuter, Jane
The Ancient Egyptians
SLJ - v43 - N '97 - p112 [51-250]

Siamon, Sharon
A Fine Day for Drool
Can CL - v23 - Sum '97 - p56+ [51-250]

Sibley, Brian
A Close Shave
TES - D 5 '97 - p17* [51-250]

Siburt, Ruth
Dragon Charmer
Ch BWatch - v7 - O '97 - p2 [51-250]

Siddals, Mary McKenna
Tell Me a Season (Illus. by Petra Mathers)
CCB-B - v50 - Jl '97 - p413 [51-250]
HB Guide - v8 - Fall '97 - p255 [51-250]
SLJ - v43 - My '97 - p114 [51-250]

Siebert, Diane
Train Song (Illus. by Mike Wimmer)
SLJ - v43 - Jl '97 - p35 [1-50]

Siebold, J Otto
Free Lunch (Illus. by J Otto Siebold)
Magpies - v12 - My '97 - p30 [51-250]

Siegal, Aranka
Upon the Head of the Goat (Moore). Audio Version
HB - v73 - N '97 - p704 [251-500]

Sierra, Judy
Antarctic Antics (Illus. by Jose Aruego)
KR - v66 - Mr 1 '98 - p344 [51-250]
PW - v245 - Mr 9 '98 - p70 [1-50]

Counting Crocodiles (Illus. by Will Hillenbrand)
BL - v94 - S 1 '97 - p135 [51-250]
CBRS - v26 - Ja '98 - p52 [51-250]
Ch BWatch - v8 - Ja '98 - p3 [1-50]
Emerg Lib - v25 - Ja '98 - p56 [51-250]
Inst - v107 - N '97 - p22 [1-50]
PW - v244 - Je 30 '97 - p75 [51-250]

The Mean Hyena (Illus. by Michael Bryant)
BL - v94 - S 1 '97 - p120+ [51-250]
KR - v65 - Ag 1 '97 - p1228 [51-250]

Siff, Lowell
Love (Illus. by Vanni)
PW - v244 - N 3 '97 - p87 [51-250]

Signals: An Anthology of Poetry and Prose
TES - Ja 9 '98 - p17* [51-250]

Silent Night (Illus. by Laura Rader)
Ch BWatch - v7 - N '97 - p6 [1-50]

Sill, Cathryn

About Mammals (Illus. by John Sill)

    BL - v93 - Je 1 '97 - p1714 [51-250]
    HB Guide - v8 - Fall '97 - p354 [51-250]
    SB - v33 - O '97 - p210+ [51-250]
    SLJ - v43 - Je '97 - p113 [51-250]

The Silly Sheep

    PW - v245 - F 9 '98 - p97 [1-50]

Silox-Jarrett, Diane

Heroines of the American Revolution

    BL - v94 - F 15 '98 - p1006 [51-250]
    Ch BWatch - v8 - Ja '98 - p5 [51-250]

Silsbe, Brenda

The Watcher (Illus. by Alice Priestley)

    Can CL - v23 - Sum '97 - p65+ [501+]

Silton, Faye

Of Heroes, Hooks and Heirlooms

    BL - v94 - O 1 '97 - p333 [51-250]
    CBRS - v25 - Ag '97 - p168+ [51-250]

Silver, Maggie

Who Lives Here?

    ASBYP - v29 - Sum '96 - p33 [251-500]

Silverman, Erica

The Halloween House (Illus. by Jon Agee)

    BL - v94 - S 1 '97 - p141 [51-250]
    CBRS - v26 - O '97 - p17 [51-250]
    CCB-B - v51 - N '97 - p101 [51-250]
    HB - v73 - S '97 - p564 [51-250]
    KR - v65 - Jl 1 '97 - p1036 [51-250]
    NYTBR - v102 - O 26 '97 - p47 [1-50]
    Par - v72 - S '97 - p205 [51-250]
    PW - v244 - O 6 '97 - p49 [51-250]
    SLJ - v43 - N '97 - p100 [51-250]

Silverman, Jerry

Just Listen to This Song I'm Singing

    SE - v61 - Ap '97 - p8* [1-50]

Silverman, Robin Landew

A Bosnian Family

    Bloom Rev - v17 - S '97 - p23 [51-250]
    Ch BWatch - v7 - My '97 - p6 [1-50]
    SLJ - v43 - Jl '97 - p99 [51-250]

Silverstein, Alvin

The Florida Panther

    HB Guide - v8 - Fall '97 - p354 [51-250]
    SLJ - v43 - Je '97 - p146 [51-250]

Fungi

    ASBYP - v29 - Fall '96 - p50+ [251-500]

Invertebrates

    ASBYP - v29 - Fall '96 - p50+ [251-500]

The Mustang

    HB Guide - v8 - Fall '97 - p354 [51-250]
    SLJ - v43 - Je '97 - p146 [51-250]

Plants

    SB - v32 - D '96 - p275 [51-250]

Vertebrates

    ASBYP - v29 - Fall '96 - p50+ [251-500]

Silverstein, Ruth

Spanish Now!. 5th Ed.

    Ch BWatch - v7 - Jl '97 - p3 [51-250]

Silverstein, Shel

Falling Up (Illus. by Shel Silverstein)

    Emerg Lib - v24 - My '97 - p57 [1-50]
    RT - v51 - O '97 - p137 [1-50]

Silverthorne, Judith

The Secret of Sentinel Rock

    CBRA - '96 - p492 [51-250]
    Emerg Lib - v25 - Ja '98 - p46 [51-250]

Silvey, Anita

Help Wanted

    y   BL - v94 - N 1 '97 - p461+ [51-250]
    y   HB - v73 - N '97 - p682 [51-250]
          HMR - Fall '97 - p36 [501+]
    y   PW - v244 - Ag 4 '97 - p76 [51-250]
    y   SLJ - v43 - N '97 - p123 [51-250]
    y   VOYA - v20 - D '97 - p318 [251-500]

Sim, Dorrith M

In My Pocket (Illus. by Gerald Fitzgerald)

    CBRS - v25 - Je '97 - p124 [51-250]
    CCB-B - v50 - Je '97 - p374 [51-250]
    HB Guide - v8 - Fall '97 - p281 [51-250]

KR - v65 - Ap 15 '97 - p650 [51-250]
SLJ - v43 - My '97 - p114 [51-250]

Simmie, Lois

Mister Got to Go (Illus. by Cynthia Nugent)

Can CL - v23 - Sum '97 - p93 [51-250]

No Cats Allowed (Illus. by Cynthia Nugent)

SLJ - v43 - Ap '97 - p117+ [51-250]

Simmons, Al

Counting Feathers (Illus. by Brian Floca)

KR - v65 - O 15 '97 - p1589 [51-250]
PW - v244 - O 20 '97 - p75 [51-250]
Quill & Q - v63 - O '97 - p39 [251-500]

Simmons, Alex

Denzel Washington

HB Guide - v8 - Fall '97 - p379 [51-250]
SLJ - v44 - F '98 - p114 [51-250]

Simmons, Jane

Come Along, Daisy! (Illus. by Jane Simmons)

PW - v245 - Mr 16 '98 - p62 [51-250]

Simmons, Steven J

Alice and Greta (Illus. by Cyd Moore)

KR - v65 - Ag 15 '97 - p1312 [51-250]
PW - v244 - Ag 18 '97 - p91 [51-250]
SLJ - v44 - Ja '98 - p93 [51-250]

Simms, Laura

The Bone Man (Illus. by Michael McCurdy)

BL - v94 - N 1 '97 - p469 [51-250]
BL - v94 - Mr 15 '98 - p1219 [1-50]
CCB-B - v51 - D '97 - p140 [51-250]
HB - v74 - Ja '98 - p84 [51-250]
SLJ - v43 - N '97 - p112 [51-250]

Simon, Carly

Midnight Farm (Illus. by David Delamare)

CBRS - v26 - S '97 - p6 [1-50]
Ch BWatch - v7 - S '97 - p3 [51-250]
PW - v244 - Je 16 '97 - p58+ [51-250]
SLJ - v43 - S '97 - p194+ [51-250]

Simon, Charnan

Bill Gates: Helping People Use Computers

SLJ - v44 - Ja '98 - p105 [51-250]

Come! Sit! Speak! (Illus. by Bari Weissman)

SLJ - v44 - F '98 - p91 [51-250]

Jesse Jackson: I Am Somebody!

SLJ - v44 - Ja '98 - p105 [51-250]

One Happy Classroom (Illus. by Rebecca McKillip Thornburgh)

HB Guide - v8 - Fall '97 - p255 [51-250]

Simon, Dominique

The Dog: Faithful Friend

PW - v245 - Mr 23 '98 - p102 [51-250]

Simon, Francesca

Spider School (Illus. by Peta Coplans)

RT - v51 - O '97 - p136 [1-50]

The Topsy Turvies (Illus. by Keren Ludlow)

Bks Keeps - S '97 - p20 [51-250]
RT - v51 - O '97 - p136 [1-50]

Simon, Norma

The Story of Hanukkah (Illus. by Leonid Gore)

BL - v94 - S 1 '97 - p141 [51-250]
PW - v244 - O 6 '97 - p53 [51-250]

The Story of Passover (Illus. by Erika Weihs)

Ch BWatch - v7 - My '97 - p4 [1-50]
HB Guide - v8 - Fall '97 - p321 [51-250]
PW - v245 - F 23 '98 - p68 [1-50]

Simon, Seymour

The Brain: Our Nervous System

BL - v93 - Ag '97 - p1896 [51-250]
CCB-B - v51 - N '97 - p101 [51-250]
Ch BWatch - v7 - S '97 - p4 [1-50]
HB - v73 - S '97 - p594 [51-250]
KR - v65 - Jl 1 '97 - p1036 [51-250]
SLJ - v43 - Ag '97 - p152 [51-250]

Destination: Jupiter

KR - v66 - F 15 '98 - p275 [51-250]

The Halloween Horror and Other Cases (Illus. by S D Schindler)
> PW - v244 - O 6 '97 - p50 [1-50]

Lightning
> HB Guide - v8 - Fall '97 - p343 [51-250]
> NH - v106 - D '97 - p10 [51-250]
> SLJ - v43 - My '97 - p126 [51-250]

The On-Line Spaceman and Other Cases (Illus. by S D Schindler)
> HB Guide - v8 - Fall '97 - p309 [51-250]
> SLJ - v43 - Ap '97 - p140+ [51-250]

Ride the Wind (Illus. by Elsa Warnick)
> Am Sci - v85 - N '97 - p560 [51-250]
> CBRS - v25 - Spr '97 - p140 [51-250]
> HB Guide - v8 - Fall '97 - p348 [51-250]
> SLJ - v43 - My '97 - p150 [51-250]

Strange Mysteries from Around the World
> HB Guide - v8 - Fall '97 - p340 [51-250]
> SB - v33 - Ag '97 - p187 [1-50]
> SLJ - v43 - Ap '97 - p158+ [51-250]

Wild Babies
> HB Guide - v8 - Fall '97 - p348 [51-250]
> SB - v33 - Je '97 - p145 [51-250]
> SB - v33 - Ag '97 - p187 [1-50]

Wildfires
> ASBYP - v29 - Fall '96 - p30+ [51-250]
> RT - v51 - N '97 - p257 [51-250]

Simons, Moya
Dead Worried!
> TES - N 7 '97 - p7* [1-50]

Hatty's Hotline
> Magpies - v12 - My '97 - p35 [51-250]

Simont, Marc
The Goose Who Almost Got Cooked (Illus. by Marc Simont)
> BL - v94 - N 1 '97 - p468 [51-250]
> CBRS - v26 - O '97 - p17 [51-250]
> Inst - v107 - N '97 - p22 [1-50]
> KR - v65 - Jl 15 '97 - p1117 [51-250]
> PW - v244 - Je 23 '97 - p91 [51-250]
> SLJ - v43 - Ag '97 - p142 [51-250]
> SLJ - v43 - D '97 - p27 [1-50]

Simpson, Carolyn
Methadone
> SLJ - v43 - N '97 - p134 [51-250]

Simpson, Judith
Ancient Greece
> Bks Keeps - Jl '97 - p26 [51-250]
> KR - v65 - Je 1 '97 - p879 [51-250]
> Magpies - v12 - Mr '97 - p41 [51-250]
> SLJ - v43 - D '97 - p146 [51-250]

Ancient Rome
> KR - v65 - Jl 1 '97 - p1037 [51-250]
> Magpies - v12 - S '97 - p43 [51-250]
> SLJ - v43 - D '97 - p146 [51-250]

Mighty Dinosaurs
> SB - v32 - D '96 - p274+ [51-250]

Sinclair, Thomas R
Investigating Plants
> SB - v33 - Ag '97 - p178 [51-250]

Singer, Marilyn
Bottoms Up! (Illus. by Patrick O'Brien)
> BL - v94 - Mr 15 '98 - p1242+ [51-250]

Singer, Muff
Baby's First Nativity (Illus. by Peter Stevenson)
> PW - v244 - O 6 '97 - p57 [1-50]

Bedtime for Tiny Mouse
> Books - v11 - O '97 - p21 [1-50]
> PW - v244 - D 1 '97 - p55 [1-50]

Buster Has the Hiccups!
> PW - v244 - D 1 '97 - p55 [1-50]

Coco's Trip around the World
> PW - v244 - D 1 '97 - p55 [1-50]

Tiny Monkey
> Books - v11 - O '97 - p21 [1-50]

Tiny Monkey Can, Too!
> PW - v244 - D 1 '97 - p55 [1-50]

Tiny Penguin's Flying Lesson
> Books - v11 - O '97 - p21 [1-50]
> PW - v244 - D 1 '97 - p55 [1-50]

Tiny Pig's Big Adventure
> Books - v11 - O '97 - p21 [1-50]
> PW - v244 - D 1 '97 - p55 [1-50]

Sinha, Nilima
The Chandipur Jewels
>   Bkbird - v34 - Win '96 - p33 [51-250]

Sinykin, Sheri Cooper
A Matter of Time
>   PW - v245 - F 23 '98 - p77 [51-250]

Siomades, Lorianne
A Place to Bloom (Illus. by Lorianne Siomades)
>   CBRS - v26 - Win '98 - p64 [51-250]
>   CCB-B - v51 - N '97 - p101+ [51-250]
>   CLW - v68 - D '97 - p83 [51-250]
>   KR - v65 - Ag 1 '97 - p1229 [51-250]
>   SLJ - v43 - S '97 - p195 [51-250]

Sipiera, Diane M
Constellations
>   HB Guide - v8 - Fall '97 - p341 [51-250]
>   SB - v33 - N '97 - p240 [51-250]

The Hubble Space Telescope
>   BL - v94 - D 1 '97 - p632 [51-250]

Project Apollo
>   BL - v94 - D 1 '97 - p632 [51-250]

Project Gemini
>   BL - v94 - D 1 '97 - p632 [51-250]
>   SLJ - v44 - Ja '98 - p105 [51-250]

Project Mercury
>   BL - v94 - D 1 '97 - p632 [51-250]
>   SLJ - v44 - Ja '98 - p105 [51-250]

Sipiera, Paul P
Black Holes
>   HB Guide - v8 - Fall '97 - p341 [51-250]
>   SB - v33 - N '97 - p240+ [51-250]

Comets and Meteor Showers
>   BL - v94 - S 15 '97 - p233 [51-250]
>   HB Guide - v8 - Fall '97 - p341 [51-250]
>   SB - v33 - N '97 - p241 [51-250]

Galaxies
>   HB Guide - v8 - Fall '97 - p341 [51-250]
>   SB - v33 - N '97 - p241 [51-250]

The Solar System
>   BL - v94 - S 15 '97 - p233 [51-250]

>   HB Guide - v8 - Fall '97 - p341 [51-250]
>   SB - v33 - N '97 - p241 [51-250]

Stars
>   HB Guide - v8 - Fall '97 - p341 [51-250]
>   SB - v33 - N '97 - p241 [51-250]

Siriwardena, Denagama
Friends (Illus. by Sybil Wettasinghe)
>   Bkbird - v35 - Fall '97 - p52 [51-250]

Sis, Peter
Follow the Dream (Illus. by Peter Sis)
>   Par Ch - Awards '97 - p9 [51-250]

Starry Messenger (Illus. by Peter Sis)
>   HMR - Sum '97 - p28 [51-250]
>   RT - v51 - O '97 - p148 [51-250]
>   SE - v61 - Ap '97 - p4* [1-50]

Starry Messenger (Caruso). Audio Version
>   SLJ - v43 - D '97 - p72 [51-250]

Sisnett, Ana
Grannie Jus' Come! (Illus. by Karen Lusebrink)
>   CBRS - v26 - O '97 - p21 [51-250]
>   Ch BWatch - v7 - O '97 - p6 [1-50]
>   PW - v244 - S 29 '97 - p89 [51-250]

Sisulu, Elinor
The Day Gogo Went to Vote (Illus. by Sharon Wilson)
>   BL - v93 - Je 1 '97 - p1724 [1-50]
>   ECEJ - v25 - Fall '97 - p50 [1-50]
>   JOYS - v11 - Win '98 - p141+ [1-50]
>   RT - v51 - N '97 - p240 [51-250]
>   RT - v51 - D '97 - p311 [51-250]
>   SE - v61 - Ap '97 - p6* [1-50]

Skelton, Mora
The Baritone Cat (Illus. by Janet Wilson)
>   Can CL - v23 - Sum '97 - p94 [51-250]

Skelton, Olivia
Vietnam: Still Struggling, Still Spirited
>   Ch BWatch - v8 - Ja '98 - p7 [1-50]

Skelton, Robin
*Long, Long Ago (Illus. by Pamela
Breeze Currie)*
    CBRA - '96 - p492 [51-250]

Skofield, James
*Detective Dinosaur: Lost and Found
(Illus. by R W Alley)*
    SLJ - v44 - Mr '98 - p188 [51-250]

Skolsky, Mindy Warshaw
Love from Your Friend, Hannah
    CCB-B - v51 - Ap '98 - p296 [51-250]
    KR - v66 - Ja 15 '98 - p118 [51-250]
    PW - v245 - F 16 '98 - p211+ [51-250]
    SLJ - v44 - Ap '98 - p138 [51-250]

Skrypuch, Marsha Forchuk
*Silver Threads (Illus. by Michael
Martchenko)*
    Can CL - v22 - Win '96 - p119 [501+]
    CBRA - '96 - p457 [51-250]

Skurzynski, Gloria
*Caitlin's Big Idea (Illus. by Cathy
Diefendorf)*
    ASBYP - v29 - Fall '96 - p31 [251-500]

Good-Bye, Billy Radish
    SLJ - v43 - S '97 - p131 [1-50]

Virtual War
y   BL - v93 - Ag '97 - p1891 [51-250]
y   BL - v94 - Mr 15 '98 - p1218 [1-50]
y   BL - v94 - Mr 15 '98 - p1226 [1-50]
y   CCB-B - v50 - Jl '97 - p413+ [51-250]
y   Emerg Lib - v25 - Ja '98 - p49+ [51-250]
    HB Guide - v8 - Fall '97 - p309 [51-250]
    KR - v65 - My 15 '97 - p808 [51-250]
    PW - v244 - My 19 '97 - p76+ [51-250]
    SLJ - v43 - Jl '97 - p98 [51-250]
y   VOYA - v20 - Ag '97 - p196 [251-500]
y   VOYA - v20 - F '98 - p366 [51-250]
y   VOYA - v21 - Ap '98 - p14 [1-50]
y   VOYA - v21 - Ap '98 - p38 [1-50]
y   VOYA - v21 - Ap '98 - p40 [1-50]

Wolf Stalker
    BL - v94 - D 15 '97 - p698 [51-250]
y   CBRS - v26 - F '98 - p83 [51-250]
    Ch BWatch - v7 - D '97 - p3 [51-250]
    SLJ - v44 - Ja '98 - p114 [51-250]

Slade, Arthur G
Draugr
y   CM:CanRev - v4 - N 14 '97 - pONL [251-500]
    Quill & Q - v64 - Ja '98 - p38 [251-500]

Slate, Joseph
*Miss Bindergarten Gets Ready for
Kindergarten (Illus. by Ashley Wolff)*
    Inst - v106 - My '97 - p18 [1-50]

Slater, Pat
*Amazing Facts about Australian
Insects and Spiders (Illus. by Steve
Parish)*
    Magpies - v12 - Jl '97 - p43 [51-250]

Slavin, Bill
The Stone Lion (Illus. by Bill Slavin)
    CBRA - '96 - p457+ [51-250]

Slawski, Wolfgang
*Captain Jonathan Sails the Sea (Illus.
by Wolfgang Slawski)*
    KR - v65 - N 1 '97 - p1650 [51-250]
    SLJ - v44 - Ja '98 - p93 [51-250]

Sleator, William
The Beasties
    BL - v94 - O 1 '97 - p333 [51-250]
y   BL - v94 - Mr 15 '98 - p1226 [1-50]
    CBRS - v26 - D '97 - p48 [51-250]
    CCB-B - v51 - N '97 - p102 [51-250]
    HB - v73 - S '97 - p580 [51-250]
y   KR - v65 - O 15 '97 - p1589 [51-250]
    SLJ - v43 - D '97 - p131 [51-250]
y   VOYA - v21 - Ap '98 - p14 [1-50]
y   VOYA - v21 - Ap '98 - p40 [1-50]
y   VOYA - v21 - Ap '98 - p61 [51-250]

The Boxes
    KR - v66 - Ap 15 '98 - p586+ [51-250]

The Boy Who Reversed Himself
    PW - v245 - F 9 '98 - p98 [1-50]

Slepian, Jan
The Broccoli Tapes
    SLJ - v43 - Jl '97 - p35 [1-50]

Emily Just in Time (Illus. by Glo Coalson)

KR - v66 - Ap 1 '98 - p502 [51-250]

The Mind Reader

BL - v94 - S 15 '97 - p236 [51-250]
CBRS - v26 - D '97 - p48 [51-250]
CCB-B - v51 - D '97 - p140+ [51-250]
HB - v73 - S '97 - p580+ [51-250]
y KR - v65 - Jl 15 '97 - p1117 [51-250]
PW - v244 - Ag 4 '97 - p75 [51-250]
SLJ - v43 - S '97 - p226 [51-250]

Sloat, Teri
Sody Sallyratus

HB Guide - v8 - Fall '97 - p281 [51-250]
Inst - v107 - Ag '97 - p20 [1-50]

Slobodkina, Esphyr
Caps for Sale (Illus. by Esphyr Slobodkina)

NYTBR - v102 - N 16 '97 - p25 [1-50]

Slotboom, Wendy
King Snake (Illus. by John Manders)

HB Guide - v8 - Fall '97 - p281 [51-250]
SLJ - v43 - My '97 - p114 [51-250]

Slyder, Ingrid
The Fabulous Flying Fandinis (Illus. by Ingrid Slyder)

RT - v51 - O '97 - p133 [1-50]

Small, David
George Washington's Cows (Illus. by David Small)

Par Ch - Awards '97 - p8 [51-250]

Hoover's Bride

Inst - v107 - Ja '98 - p31 [1-50]

A Small Treasury of Christmas (Illus. by Susan Spellman)

PW - v244 - O 6 '97 - p57 [1-50]

A Small Treasury of Easter Poems and Prayers (Illus. by Susan Spellman)

CLW - v68 - S '97 - p67 [51-250]
HB Guide - v8 - Fall '97 - p374 [51-250]

SLJ - v43 - Jl '97 - p87 [51-250]

Smalls-Hector, Irene
Because You're Lucky (Illus. by Michael Hays)

Am Vis - v12 - D '97 - p33 [1-50]
BL - v94 - S 1 '97 - p135+ [51-250]
CCB-B - v51 - N '97 - p102 [51-250]
KR - v65 - Ag 1 '97 - p1229 [51-250]

Irene Jennie and the Christmas Masquerade (Illus. by Melodye Rosales)

RT - v51 - N '97 - p256 [51-250]
RT - v51 - D '97 - p311+ [51-250]

Louise's Gift (Illus. by Colin Bootman)

LA - v73 - N '96 - p526 [51-250]

Smith, Alastair
Picture Puzzles

Ch BWatch - v7 - Ap '97 - p1+ [1-50]

Smith, Albert Gray
Where Am I?

BL - v94 - S 1 '97 - p121 [51-250]
Quill & Q - v63 - S '97 - p72 [251-500]

Smith, Arahia
He Ingoa Ngarara (Illus. by Denise Durkin)

Magpies - v12 - Jl '97 - p8* [51-250]

Smith, Christine
How to Draw Dinosaurs

Ch BWatch - v8 - Ja '98 - p8 [1-50]

How to Draw Pets

Ch BWatch - v8 - Ja '98 - p8 [1-50]

How to Draw Trucks and Cars

Ch BWatch - v8 - Ja '98 - p8 [1-50]

How to Draw Wild Animals

Ch BWatch - v8 - Ja '98 - p8 [1-50]

Smith, Claudia
When the Sugar Bird Sings

CM:CanRev - v4 - O 3 '97 - pONL [51-250]

Smith, Debbie
Activities
Quill & Q - v63 - D '97 - p39 [1-50]

Smith, Dodie
The Starlight Barking (Illus. by Janet Grahame-Johnstone)
PW - v244 - Ag 25 '97 - p74 [1-50]

Smith, Kelvin
Chess for Kids
Quill & Q - v64 - F '98 - p45 [251-500]

Smith, Lane
Disney's James and the Giant Peach (Illus. by Lane Smith)
RT - v51 - O '97 - p138 [1-50]

The Happy Hocky Family
Par Ch - Awards '97 - p9 [51-250]

Smith, Linda Wasmer
Louis Pasteur: Disease Fighter
BL - v94 - D 1 '97 - p632 [51-250]
SLJ - v43 - D '97 - p139+ [51-250]

Smith, Maggie
This Is Your Garden (Illus. by Maggie Smith)
KR - v66 - Ap 1 '98 - p502 [51-250]

Smith, Marisa
The Seattle Children's Theatre
y   BL - v93 - Je 1 '97 - p1680 [51-250]
     SLJ - v43 - Je '97 - p146 [51-250]

Smith, Mark
Pay Attention, Slosh! (Illus. by Gail Piazza)
BL - v94 - D 1 '97 - p638 [51-250]

Smith, Miranda
Living Earth
SB - v32 - D '96 - p275 [51-250]

Smith, Nigel, 1947-
Sports (Illus. by James Field)
Ch BWatch - v7 - Ap '97 - p5 [1-50]

Transport
r   Sch Lib - v45 - N '97 - p206 [51-250]

Transportation Then and Now
Ch BWatch - v8 - Ja '98 - p6 [1-50]

Smith, Patricia T
The Miracle of the Loaves and Fishes (Illus. by Kirsten Soderlind)
HB Guide - v8 - Fall '97 - p319 [51-250]

Smith, Peter, 1924-
Nelson Handwriting. New Ed.
TES - S 12 '97 - p16* [251-500]

Smith, Pohla
Superstars of Women's Figure Skating
Ch BWatch - v7 - S '97 - p8 [1-50]
HB Guide - v8 - Fall '97 - p369 [51-250]
SLJ - v43 - Ag '97 - p175 [51-250]

Smith, Roland
In the Forest with Elephants (Illus. by Roland Smith)
HB - v74 - Mr '98 - p237+ [51-250]
KR - v66 - Mr 1 '98 - p344 [51-250]
SLJ - v44 - Ap '98 - p154 [51-250]

Jaguar
CBRS - v25 - Ag '97 - p169 [51-250]
y   Emerg Lib - v25 - Ja '98 - p49 [51-250]
     HB Guide - v8 - Fall '97 - p309 [51-250]
y   KR - v65 - My 15 '97 - p808 [51-250]
     NYTBR - v102 - Je 8 '97 - p27 [1-50]
y   SLJ - v43 - Je '97 - p128 [51-250]

Journey of the Red Wolf (Illus. by Roland Smith)
RT - v51 - O '97 - p142 [1-50]

Vultures (Illus. by Lynn M Stone)
SLJ - v44 - Mr '98 - p191+ [51-250]

Smith, Rose Marie
Kid-Etiquette (Illus. by Anthea Waterfield)
CBRA - '96 - p516 [51-250]

Smith, Sherwood
Court Duel
BL - v94 - Mr 1 '98 - p1136 [51-250]
y   PW - v245 - F 23 '98 - p78 [1-50]
y   SLJ - v44 - Ap '98 - p138+ [51-250]

Crown Duel
    BL - v94 - N 1 '97 - p475 [1-50]
y CBRS - v25 - Spr '97 - p144 [51-250]
y CCB-B - v50 - Jl '97 - p414 [51-250]
y HB Guide - v8 - Fall '97 - p316 [51-250]
y KR - v65 - Ap 15 '97 - p650 [51-250]
y SLJ - v43 - Ag '97 - p158+ [51-250]
y VOYA - v20 - Je '97 - p121 [51-250]
y VOYA - v21 - Ap '98 - p14 [1-50]

Smith, Timothy R
Buck Wilder's Small Twig Hiking and Camping Guide (Illus. by Mark J Herrick)
    SLJ - v43 - D '97 - p115+ [51-250]

Smith-Ayala, Emilie
Clouds on the Mountain (Illus. by Alice Priestley)
    CBRA - '96 - p458 [51-250]

Smucker, Barbara
Selina and the Bear Paw Quilt (Illus. by Janet Wilson)
    Can CL - v22 - Win '96 - p121+ [501+]
y JAAL - v40 - O '96 - p158+ [51-250]

Snape, Juliet
The Classic Tales Maze Book
    PW - v244 - D 15 '97 - p60 [51-250]

Snedden, Robert
Explor-a-Maze (Illus. by Tim Oliver)
    BL - v94 - Mr 15 '98 - p1243 [51-250]
    KR - v66 - Ja 15 '98 - p118 [51-250]
    PW - v245 - F 2 '98 - p92 [51-250]
    SLJ - v44 - Mr '98 - p206 [51-250]

The Internet
    Sch Lib - v45 - N '97 - p206 [51-250]

Yuck! A Big Book of Little Horrors
    SB - v33 - Ag '97 - p187 [1-50]

Sneve, Virginia Driving Hawk
The Apaches (Illus. by Ronald Himler)
    HB Guide - v8 - Fall '97 - p399 [51-250]
    SLJ - v43 - Jl '97 - p87+ [51-250]

The Trickster and the Troll
    BL - v94 - S 15 '97 - p236 [51-250]
    LJ - v122 - Jl '97 - p92 [51-250]

    PW - v244 - Ag 4 '97 - p76 [1-50]
    SLJ - v43 - D '97 - p146 [51-250]

Snihura, Ulana
I Miss Franklin P. Shuckles (Illus. by Leanne Franson)
    Quill & Q - v64 - F '98 - p46 [251-500]

Snyder, Zilpha Keatley
Cat Running
    SLJ - v44 - Mr '98 - p120 [1-50]

Gib Rides Home
    BL - v94 - Ja 1 '98 - p816 [51-250]
    HB - v74 - Mr '98 - p224 [51-250]
    KR - v65 - D 1 '97 - p1779 [51-250]
    PW - v244 - D 15 '97 - p59 [51-250]
    SLJ - v44 - Ja '98 - p114 [251-500]

The Gypsy Game
    Ch BWatch - v7 - My '97 - p5 [51-250]
    HB Guide - v8 - Fall '97 - p309 [51-250]

So, Sungwan
C Is for China (Illus. by Sungwan So)
    Bks Keeps - N '97 - p23 [51-250]
    CM:CanRev - v4 - Ja 2 '98 - pONL [251-500]
    Sch Lib - v45 - N '97 - p188 [51-250]
    TES - Ag 22 '97 - p25 [51-250]

Sobey, Edwin J C
Car Smarts
    Ch BWatch - v7 - O '97 - p3 [1-50]
    SLJ - v44 - Ap '98 - p125 [51-250]

Wrapper Rockets and Trombone Straws (Illus. by Carol Chapin)
    SLJ - v43 - Je '97 - p146 [51-250]

Sobol, Donald J
Encyclopedia Brown (Illus. by Leonard Shortall)
    NYTBR - v102 - N 16 '97 - p26 [1-50]

Sohi, Morteza E
Look What I Did with a Leaf!
    ASBYP - v29 - Sum '96 - p34 [51-250]

Sola, Michele
Angela Weaves a Dream (Illus. by Jeffrey Jay Foxx)

CCB-B - v50 - Je '97 - p375 [51-250]
HB Guide - v8 - Fall '97 - p364 [51-250]
SLJ - v43 - Jl '97 - p111+ [51-250]

Solga, Kim
Art Fun! (Illus. by Pamela Monfort)

SLJ - v44 - Ja '98 - p105 [51-250]

Craft Fun! (Illus. by Pamela Monfort)

SLJ - v44 - Ja '98 - p105 [51-250]

Solheim, James
It's Disgusting--and We Ate It! (Illus. by Eric Brace)

CCB-B - v51 - Ap '98 - p296+ [51-250]

Solis, Valerie
Pink for Polar Bear

TES - Jl 11 '97 - p14* [51-250]

Somerville, Louisa
Animals in Art

Ch BWatch - v7 - Ap '97 - p8 [1-50]

Sommer, Carl
Can You Help Me Find My Smile? (Illus. by Greg Budwine)

SLJ - v43 - Jl '97 - p75 [51-250]

No Longer a Dilly Dally (Illus. by Kennon James)

SLJ - v43 - Jl '97 - p75 [51-250]

No One Will Ever Know (Illus. by Dick Westbrook)

SLJ - v43 - Jl '97 - p75 [51-250]

Tied Up in Knots (Illus. by Greg Budwine)

SLJ - v43 - Jl '97 - p75+ [51-250]

Sonenklar, Carol
Bug Boy (Illus. by Betsy Lewin)

HB Guide - v8 - Fall '97 - p309 [51-250]
SLJ - v43 - Jl '97 - p76 [51-250]

Soto, Gary
Off and Running (Illus. by Eric Velasquez)

PW - v244 - D 8 '97 - p74 [1-50]

The Old Man and His Door (Illus. by Joe Cepeda)

RT - v51 - O '97 - p148 [51-250]

Petty Crimes

BL - v94 - Mr 15 '98 - p1245 [51-250]
y   KR - v66 - Mr 1 '98 - p345 [51-250]

Snapshots from the Wedding (Illus. by Stephanie Garcia)

BL - v94 - Ja 1 '98 - p736 [1-50]
CBRS - v25 - My '97 - p113 [51-250]
HB Guide - v8 - Fall '97 - p282 [51-250]
Inst - v107 - Ja '98 - p27 [1-50]
SLJ - v43 - My '97 - p114 [51-250]

Too Many Tamales (Illus. by Ed Martinez)

ECEJ - v25 - Fall '97 - p50 [1-50]

Sotzek, Hannelore
A Koala Is not a Bear! (Illus. by Barbara Bedell)

Ch BWatch - v7 - Jl '97 - p3 [1-50]

A Koala Is Not a Bear! (Illus. by Barbara Bedell)

HB Guide - v8 - Fall '97 - p353 [51-250]
SLJ - v43 - S '97 - p208 [51-250]

Souhami, Jessica
Rama and the Demon King (Illus. by Jessica Souhami)

Bks Keeps - N '97 - p22 [51-250]
KR - v65 - Ag 15 '97 - p1312 [51-250]
Sch Lib - v45 - N '97 - p188 [51-250]
SLJ - v43 - S '97 - p208+ [51-250]
TES - N 7 '97 - p8* [51-250]

South, Coleman
Jordan

HB Guide - v8 - Fall '97 - p392 [51-250]
SLJ - v43 - Je '97 - p144 [51-250]

Space Technology (Illus. by Hemesh Alles)

ASBYP - v29 - Sum '96 - p65+ [501+]

Spaulding, Dean T
Housing Our Feathered Friends
> BL - v94 - O 15 '97 - p404 [51-250]
> Ch BWatch - v7 - D '97 - p8 [51-250]
> SB - v33 - D '97 - p275 [51-250]
> SLJ - v43 - S '97 - p236+ [51-250]

Protecting Our Feathered Friends
> BL - v94 - O 15 '97 - p404 [51-250]
> Ch BWatch - v7 - D '97 - p8 [51-250]
> SB - v33 - D '97 - p275 [51-250]
> SLJ - v43 - S '97 - p236+ [51-250]

*Watching Our Feathered Friends
(Illus. by Dean T Spaulding)*
> KR - v65 - D 1 '97 - p1779 [51-250]

Spedden, Daisy Corning Stone
*Polar the Titanic Bear (Illus. by
Laurie McGaw)*
> BL - v94 - Mr 15 '98 - p1244 [51-250]
> Can CL - v22 - Win '96 - p120 [501+]

Speed, Toby
Two Cool Cows (Illus. by Barry Root)
> PW - v244 - D 8 '97 - p74 [1-50]

Water Voices (Illus. by Julie Downing)
> KR - v65 - D 1 '97 - p1779 [51-250]
> PW - v244 - D 15 '97 - p57 [51-250]
> SLJ - v44 - Ap '98 - p110 [51-250]

*Whoosh! Went the Wish (Illus. by
Barry Root)*
> CBRS - v25 - Ag '97 - p162+ [51-250]
> CCB-B - v51 - S '97 - p27+ [51-250]
> HB Guide - v8 - Fall '97 - p282 [51-250]
> NYTBR - v102 - Je 22 '97 - p22 [1-50]
> SLJ - v43 - S '97 - p195 [51-250]

Speedy (Machines)
> Ch BWatch - v7 - Je '97 - p4 [1-50]

Speir, Peter
People
> Emerg Lib - v24 - My '97 - p9+ [1-50]

Spelman, Cornelia
*Your Body Belongs to You (Illus. by
Teri Weidner)*
> BL - v94 - S 1 '97 - p130 [51-250]
> SLJ - v43 - S '97 - p195+ [51-250]

Spence, David
Pirates!
> HB Guide - v8 - Fall '97 - p387 [51-250]

Spencer, Anne
*The Memory Book (Illus. by Malcolm
Cullen)*
> CBRA - '96 - p458 [51-250]

Sperry, Armstrong
*Call It Courage (Phillips). Audio
Version*
> Ch BWatch - v7 - D '97 - p4 [1-50]
> y   Kliatt - v32 - Mr '98 - p42 [51-250]

*Esto Es Coraje (Illus. by Armstrong
Sperry)*
> SLJ - v43 - Ag '97 - p181 [51-250]

Spewock, Theodosia
Just for Babies
> Ch BWatch - v7 - Mr '97 - p1 [51-250]

Just for Fives
> Ch BWatch - v7 - Mr '97 - p1 [51-250]

Just for Four's
> Ch BWatch - v7 - Mr '97 - p1 [51-250]

Just for One's
> Ch BWatch - v7 - Mr '97 - p1 [51-250]

Just for Three's
> Ch BWatch - v7 - Mr '97 - p1 [51-250]

Just for Two's
> Ch BWatch - v7 - Mr '97 - p1 [51-250]

Spider, the Magazine for Children
> p   LA - v73 - N '96 - p538+ [501+]
> p   Par Ch - Awards '97 - p27 [1-50]

Spiegelman, Art
*Open Me...I'm a Dog! (Illus. by Art
Spiegelman)*
> CCB-B - v51 - S '97 - p28 [51-250]
> KR - v65 - Je 1 '97 - p880 [51-250]
> LATBR - S 14 '97 - p7 [501+]
> NY - v73 - O 6 '97 - p116 [51-250]
> NYTBR - v102 - D 21 '97 - p18 [501+]
> Par - v72 - D '97 - p202 [1-50]
> PW - v244 - My 26 '97 - p84 [51-250]
> SLJ - v43 - N '97 - p100+ [51-250]

Spinelli, Eileen
Boy, Can He Dance! (Illus. by Paul Yalowitz)

 PW - v244 - Je 16 '97 - p61 [1-50]

Lizzie Logan Gets Married

 BL - v93 - Ag '97 - p1902 [51-250]
 CCB-B - v51 - S '97 - p28 [51-250]
 KR - v65 - My 15 '97 - p809 [51-250]
 Learning - v26 - N '97 - p30 [51-250]
 SLJ - v43 - Je '97 - p101 [51-250]

Lizzie Logan Wears Purple Sunglasses

 PW - v245 - Ja 19 '98 - p380 [1-50]

Spinelli, Jerry
Crash

y Kliatt - v31 - Jl '97 - p11 [51-250]
 RT - v51 - O '97 - p141 [1-50]
y Sch Lib - v45 - N '97 - p214 [51-250]
 TES - Je 20 '97 - p7* [501+]
 TES - N 7 '97 - p7* [1-50]
y VOYA - v20 - Je '97 - p87 [51-250]
y VOYA - v21 - Ap '98 - p42 [1-50]

Crash (Woodman). Audio Version

y Kliatt - v31 - Jl '97 - p43 [51-250]
 SLJ - v44 - Ap '98 - p38 [1-50]

The Library Card

 Ch BWatch - v7 - Je '97 - p1 [51-250]
y Emerg Lib - v25 - N '97 - p52 [51-250]
 HB Guide - v8 - Fall '97 - p309 [51-250]
 HMR - Win '97 - p39+ [501+]
y JAAL - v41 - S '97 - p81 [51-250]
 KR - v65 - Ap 15 '97 - p650+ [51-250]
 NYTBR - v102 - Ag 17 '97 - p19 [1-50]
y VOYA - v20 - O '97 - p248 [51-250]

Wringer

 BL - v94 - S 1 '97 - p118 [51-250]
 BL - v94 - Ja 1 '98 - p735 [1-50]
 BL - v94 - Mr 15 '98 - p1224 [1-50]
 CBRS - v26 - D '97 - p48 [51-250]
 CCB-B - v51 - O '97 - p67+ [251-500]
y Emerg Lib - v25 - Ja '98 - p50 [51-250]
 HB - v73 - S '97 - p581 [51-250]
y JAAL - v41 - D '97 - p323 [51-250]
 KR - v65 - Je 15 '97 - p957 [51-250]
 NYTBR - v102 - N 16 '97 - p52 [501+]
 PW - v244 - Je 2 '97 - p72 [51-250]
 SLJ - v43 - S '97 - p226 [51-250]
 SLJ - v43 - D '97 - p27 [1-50]
y VOYA - v20 - F '98 - p366+ [51-250]

Spinner, Stephanie
Born to Be Wild (Illus. by Steve Bjorkman)

 HB Guide - v8 - Fall '97 - p294 [51-250]

Bright Lights, Little Gerbil (Illus. by Steve Bjorkman)

 HB Guide - v8 - Fall '97 - p294 [51-250]
 SLJ - v43 - Jl '97 - p76 [51-250]

Spires, Elizabeth
With One White Wing (Illus. by Eric Blegvad)

 Emerg Lib - v24 - My '97 - p51 [51-250]

Spirn, Michele Sobel
A Know-Nothing Birthday (Illus. by R W Alley)

 HB Guide - v8 - Fall '97 - p287 [51-250]
 SLJ - v43 - Je '97 - p101 [51-250]

Spivak, Dawnine
Grass Sandals (Illus. by Demi)

 BW - v27 - My 4 '97 - p17 [501+]
 CBRS - v25 - My '97 - p116+ [51-250]
 CCB-B - v50 - Jl '97 - p414 [51-250]
 Ch BWatch - v7 - My '97 - p3 [1-50]
 HMR - Sum '97 - p26+ [501+]
 SLJ - v43 - Ap '97 - p132 [51-250]

Spohn, Kate
Chick's Daddy

 PW - v245 - Ja 5 '98 - p69 [1-50]

Dog and Cat Make a Splash (Illus. by Kate Spohn)

 HB Guide - v8 - Fall '97 - p287 [51-250]
 KR - v65 - Ap 15 '97 - p651 [51-250]
 SLJ - v43 - Je '97 - p101 [51-250]

Kitten's Nap (Illus. by Kate Spohn)

 KR - v66 - Ja 1 '98 - p62 [51-250]
 PW - v245 - Ja 5 '98 - p69 [1-50]

Piglet's Bath

 PW - v245 - Ja 5 '98 - p69 [1-50]

Puppy's Games

 PW - v245 - Ja 5 '98 - p69 [1-50]

Spooner, Alan
Concise Oxford School Thesaurus
r   Sch Lib - v45 - N '97 - p205 [51-250]
r   TES - S 19 '97 - p19* [501+]

Sports Illustrated for Kids
p   Par Ch - Awards '97 - p27 [1-50]

Springer, Nancy
I Am Mordred
    HB - v74 - Mr '98 - p219 [251-500]
y   KR - v66 - Ja 1 '98 - p62+ [51-250]
y   PW - v245 - Mr 16 '98 - p65 [51-250]
y   VOYA - v21 - Ap '98 - p61+ [51-250]

Secret Star
y   CBRS - v25 - Jl '97 - p157 [51-250]
y   CCB-B - v50 - Je '97 - p375+ [51-250]
y   HB Guide - v8 - Fall '97 - p316 [51-250]
    SLJ - v43 - My '97 - p140 [51-250]
y   VOYA - v20 - D '97 - p321+ [251-500]

Spyri, Johanna
Heidi (Illus. by Rozier Gaudriault)
    Sch Lib - v45 - Ag '97 - p145 [51-250]

Spyru, Demetres
O Psyllos
    Bkbird - v34 - Win '96 - p58 [51-250]

Srivastav, Sigrun
The Ghost Rider of Darbhanga
    Bkbird - v34 - Win '96 - p34 [51-250]

Staake, Bob
My Little 123 Book (Illus. by Bob Staake)
    KR - v65 - D 15 '97 - p1842 [51-250]
    PW - v245 - Mr 23 '98 - p101+ [51-250]
    SLJ - v44 - Mr '98 - p188 [51-250]

My Little ABC Book (Illus. by Bob Staake)
    PW - v245 - Mr 23 '98 - p101+ [51-250]
    SLJ - v44 - Mr '98 - p188 [51-250]

Stacey, Cherylyn
How Do You Spell Abducted?
y   Can CL - v23 - Sum '97 - p76+ [251-500]

CBRA - '96 - p492+ [51-250]

Stadler, John
The Cats of Mrs. Calamari (Illus. by John Stadler)
    BL - v94 - Ja 1 '98 - p736 [1-50]
    HB Guide - v8 - Fall '97 - p282 [51-250]
    SLJ - v43 - My '97 - p114+ [51-250]

Stadtler, Bea
The Holocaust: A History of Courage and Resistance
    Ch BWatch - v7 - Jl '97 - p7 [51-250]

Stamper, Judith Bauer
Five Goofy Ghosts (Illus. by Tim Raglin)
    PW - v244 - O 6 '97 - p50 [1-50]

Stanbridge, Joanne
The Leftover Kid
    CM:CanRev - v4 - S 5 '97 - pONL [251-500]

Stanfield, Jeff
Homes
    Sch Lib - v45 - Ag '97 - p155 [51-250]

The Street
    Sch Lib - v45 - Ag '97 - p155 [51-250]

Stanley, Diane
Cleopatra (Illus. by Diane Stanley)
    PW - v244 - Ag 18 '97 - p95 [1-50]

Elena
    ECEJ - v25 - Fall '97 - p50 [1-50]

The Gentleman and the Kitchen Maid (Illus. by Dennis Nolan)
y   BL - v93 - Je 1 '97 - p1674 [1-50]
    PW - v244 - Jl 7 '97 - p70 [1-50]

Leonardo Da Vinci (Illus. by Diane Stanley)
    Emerg Lib - v25 - N '97 - p59 [51-250]
    HMR - Sum '97 - p29 [51-250]
y   JAAL - v40 - Ap '97 - p587+ [251-500]
    Magpies - v12 - S '97 - p5+ [251-500]
    RT - v51 - S '97 - p56 [51-250]
    SE - v61 - Ap '97 - p3* [1-50]

Petrosinella: A Neapolitan Rapunzel
PW - v244 - D 8 '97 - p74 [1-50]

Rumpelstiltskin's Daughter (Illus. by Diane Stanley)
BL - v94 - Ja 1 '98 - p736 [1-50]
BL - v94 - Mr 15 '98 - p1219 [1-50]
CBRS - v25 - My '97 - p117 [51-250]
CCB-B - v50 - Jl '97 - p414+ [51-250]
HB Guide - v8 - Fall '97 - p282 [51-250]
Inst - v107 - Ag '97 - p23+ [51-250]
NYTBR - v102 - My 18 '97 - p28 [501+]
Par Ch - Awards '97 - p7 [1-50]
SLJ - v43 - D '97 - p27 [1-50]

Saving Sweetness (Illus. by G Brian Karas)
BL - v93 - Je 1 '97 - p1701 [1-50]

Stanley, George Edward
Who Invited Aliens to My Slumber Party? (Illus. by Sal Murdocca)
SLJ - v43 - Je '97 - p101 [51-250]

Stanley, Jerry
Big Annie of Calumet
y   JAAL - v40 - O '96 - p150 [51-250]
SE - v61 - Ap '97 - p11* [1-50]

Stanley, Loren
San Francisco 49ers
HB Guide - v8 - Fall '97 - p370 [51-250]

Stanley, Sanna
Monkey Sunday (Illus. by Sanna Stanley)
CCB-B - v51 - Ap '98 - p297 [51-250]
KR - v66 - Ja 1 '98 - p63 [51-250]
SLJ - v44 - Ap '98 - p110 [51-250]

Stannard, Russell
More Letters to Uncle Albert
Bks Keeps - Jl '97 - p26 [51-250]

Stanton, Mary
My Aunt, The Monster
PW - v244 - Je 2 '97 - p72 [51-250]

Staples, Suzanne Fisher
Dangerous Skies
y   Ch BWatch - v7 - Ap '97 - p4 [51-250]
RT - v51 - S '97 - p59 [51-250]
y   RT - v51 - D '97 - p309 [51-250]

Starkey, Dinah
Scholastic Atlas of Exploration
r   JOYS - v11 - Fall '97 - p75 [1-50]

Staub, Frank
Children of Belize (Illus. by Frank Staub)
KR - v65 - D 15 '97 - p1842 [51-250]
SLJ - v44 - Mr '98 - p195 [51-250]

Children of Cuba
Ch BWatch - v7 - My '97 - p6 [1-50]

Children of Yucatan
Ch BWatch - v7 - My '97 - p6 [1-50]

Herons (Illus. by Frank Staub)
Bloom Rev - v17 - Jl '97 - p21 [51-250]
Ch BWatch - v7 - Jl '97 - p3 [1-50]
HB Guide - v8 - Fall '97 - p352 [51-250]
KR - v65 - Je 15 '97 - p957 [51-250]
SLJ - v43 - Ag '97 - p176 [51-250]

Staunton, Ted
Morgan Makes Magic (Illus. by Bill Slavin)
CM:CanRev - v4 - N 28 '97 - pONL [251-500]

Stavish, Corinne
I'd Rather Be Me! (Stavish). Audio Version
SLJ - v43 - My '97 - p87+ [51-250]

Stavreva, Kirilka
Bulgaria
HB Guide - v8 - Fall '97 - p390 [51-250]

Stearman, Kaye
Gender Issues
y   HB Guide - v8 - Fall '97 - p327 [51-250]
y   SB - v33 - Ap '97 - p76 [251-500]
TES - O 17 '97 - pR7 [51-250]
y   VOYA - v20 - Je '97 - p138 [51-250]

Stearns, Michael
A Nightmare's Dozen
> SF Chr - v19 - O '97 - p50 [1-50]

Steckman, Elizabeth
Silk Peony, Parade Dragon (Illus. by Carol Inouye)
> HB Guide - v8 - Fall '97 - p282 [51-250]

Steedman, Scott
The Egyptian News
> Bks Keeps - My '97 - p26 [51-250]
> Ch BWatch - v7 - Ap '97 - p7 [1-50]
> HB Guide - v8 - Fall '97 - p389 [51-250]
> SLJ - v43 - S '97 - p237 [51-250]

Writing and Printing (Illus. by David Antram)
> HB Guide - v8 - Fall '97 - p359 [51-250]
> SLJ - v43 - Jl '97 - p84 [51-250]

Steele, Philip
The Aztec News
> Bks Keeps - My '97 - p26 [51-250]
> Ch BWatch - v7 - Ap '97 - p7 [1-50]
> HB Guide - v8 - Fall '97 - p389 [51-250]
> SLJ - v43 - S '97 - p237 [51-250]

Freedom of Speech
> Bks Keeps - S '97 - p29 [51-250]
> y Sch Lib - v45 - N '97 - p218 [51-250]
> TES - O 17 '97 - pR7 [51-250]

Grasslands
> HB Guide - v8 - Fall '97 - p386 [51-250]

The Kingfisher Young People's Atlas of the World
> r Ch BWatch - v7 - D '97 - p3 [1-50]
> r SLJ - v43 - N '97 - p142+ [51-250]

Pirates
> CLW - v68 - S '97 - p63 [51-250]
> Emerg Lib - v25 - N '97 - p47 [51-250]
> SLJ - v43 - My '97 - p126 [51-250]

Rocking and Rolling
> SLJ - v44 - Mr '98 - p206 [51-250]

Tundra
> Ch BWatch - v7 - D '97 - p8 [1-50]

> HB Guide - v8 - Fall '97 - p386 [51-250]
> SLJ - v44 - Ja '98 - p130 [51-250]

Stefoff, Rebecca
Alaska
> Ch BWatch - v8 - Ja '98 - p7 [1-50]

Ant
> Ch BWatch - v7 - D '97 - p7 [1-50]
> SB - v34 - Ap '98 - p81 [51-250]
> SLJ - v44 - Mr '98 - p206 [51-250]

Beetle
> Ch BWatch - v7 - Jl '97 - p3 [51-250]
> HB Guide - v8 - Fall '97 - p350 [51-250]

Butterfly
> HB Guide - v8 - Fall '97 - p350 [51-250]

Chameleon
> ASBYP - v29 - Fall '96 - p55 [251-500]

Crab
> Ch BWatch - v7 - D '97 - p7 [1-50]

Frog
> Ch BWatch - v7 - Jl '97 - p3 [51-250]

Giant Turtle
> ASBYP - v29 - Fall '96 - p55 [251-500]

Hummingbird
> Ch BWatch - v7 - Jl '97 - p3 [51-250]
> HB Guide - v8 - Fall '97 - p352 [51-250]

Jellyfish
> Ch BWatch - v7 - Jl '97 - p3 [51-250]
> HB Guide - v8 - Fall '97 - p350 [51-250]
> SB - v33 - D '97 - p275+ [51-250]

Octopus
> ASBYP - v29 - Fall '96 - p55 [251-500]

Oregon
> Ch BWatch - v7 - My '97 - p7 [51-250]
> HB Guide - v8 - Fall '97 - p394 [51-250]
> SLJ - v43 - Jl '97 - p108 [51-250]

The Oregon Trail in American History
> SLJ - v44 - F '98 - p127 [51-250]

Owl
> Ch BWatch - v7 - D '97 - p7 [1-50]
> SB - v34 - Ap '98 - p81+ [51-250]

Penguin
Ch BWatch - v7 - D '97 - p7 [1-50]

Praying Mantis
ASBYP - v29 - Fall '96 - p55 [251-500]

Sea Horse
ASBYP - v29 - Fall '96 - p55 [251-500]

Snake
Ch BWatch - v7 - Jl '97 - p3 [51-250]

Starfish
ASBYP - v29 - Fall '96 - p55 [251-500]

Steger, Will
Over the Top of the World
y   BL - v94 - Mr 15 '98 - p1211 [1-50]
      HB Guide - v8 - Fall '97 - p386 [51-250]
      NYTBR - v103 - F 15 '98 - p25 [501+]
      SLJ - v43 - Ap '97 - p160 [51-250]
y   VOYA - v20 - F '98 - p371 [51-250]
y   VOYA - v21 - Ap '98 - p39 [1-50]

Steig, William
La Isla De Abel (Illus. by William Steig)
      SLJ - v43 - My '97 - p154 [51-250]

Toby, Where Are You? (Illus. by Teryl Euvremer)
      ECEJ - v25 - Fall '97 - p40 [51-250]
      HB Guide - v8 - Fall '97 - p256 [51-250]
      SLJ - v43 - D '97 - p28 [1-50]

Stein, R Conrad
The Assassination of Martin Luther King Jr.
      SLJ - v43 - Ap '97 - p132 [51-250]

Athens
      HB Guide - v8 - Fall '97 - p391 [51-250]

The Battle of the Little Bighorn
      HB Guide - v8 - Fall '97 - p397 [51-250]

The Boston Tea Party
      SLJ - v43 - My '97 - p126 [51-250]

Chicago
      HB Guide - v8 - Fall '97 - p395 [51-250]
      SLJ - v44 - F '98 - p119 [51-250]

Chuck Yeager Breaks the Sound Barrier
      HB Guide - v8 - Fall '97 - p359 [51-250]

The Transcontinental Railroad in American History
      SLJ - v44 - Ja '98 - p132 [251-500]

The Underground Railroad
      Ch BWatch - v7 - O '97 - p8 [1-50]
      HB Guide - v8 - Fall '97 - p397 [51-250]

Steiner, Barbara
Desert Trip (Illus. by Ronald Himler)
      RT - v51 - O '97 - p152 [51-250]

Spring Break
      Bks Keeps - S '97 - p28 [51-250]

Steinhauser, Peggy
Mousetracks: A Kid's Computer Idea Book
      PW - v244 - Je 16 '97 - p61 [51-250]
      SLJ - v43 - Ag '97 - p152 [51-250]

Steins, Richard
Hungary: Crossroads of Europe
      Ch BWatch - v7 - My '97 - p7 [1-50]
      HB Guide - v8 - Fall '97 - p390 [51-250]
      SLJ - v44 - Ja '98 - p97+ [51-250]

Shiloh
      SLJ - v44 - Ja '98 - p132 [51-250]

Stelzig, Christine
Can You Spot the Leopard?
      PW - v244 - D 15 '97 - p60 [51-250]

Stem, Jacqueline
The Cellar in the Woods
      SLJ - v44 - Ja '98 - p116 [51-250]

Stephens, Clark
More Is in You. Book and Audio Version
      Sch Lib - v45 - N '97 - p208 [51-250]

Stephens, Jack
The Ballerina and the Gargoyle (Illus. by Niki Leopold)
      AB - v100 - N 17 '97 - p1268 [51-250]

Stephens, Michael

King Coker's Sword

y   Aust Bk R - S '97 - p61+ [501+]

      Magpies - v12 - S '97 - p35 [51-250]

Steptoe, John

Creativity (Illus. by E B Lewis)

      Am Vis - v12 - D '97 - p33 [1-50]

      HB Guide - v8 - Fall '97 - p282 [51-250]

      SLJ - v43 - Ap '97 - p118 [51-250]

Sterling, Shirley

My Name Is Seepeetza

      BL - v94 - O 1 '97 - p323 [1-50]

      HB Guide - v8 - Fall '97 - p309 [51-250]

Sterman, Betsy

Backyard Dragon

      BL - v94 - N 1 '97 - p475 [1-50]

Stern, Maggie

The Missing Sunflowers (Illus. by Donna Ruff)

      HB Guide - v8 - Fall '97 - p282 [51-250]

      Par - v73 - F '98 - p186 [51-250]

      SLJ - v43 - Ap '97 - p118 [51-250]

Stern, Zoe

Divorce Is Not the End of the World

y   Kliatt - v31 - N '97 - p23 [51-250]

      PW - v244 - S 22 '97 - p83 [51-250]

y   VOYA - v21 - Ap '98 - p76 [51-250]

Stevens, Diane

Liza's Star Wish

y   BL - v94 - S 15 '97 - p224 [51-250]

      CCB-B - v51 - N '97 - p103+ [51-250]

      KR - v65 - O 1 '97 - p1538 [51-250]

Stevens, Janet

Coyote Steals the Blanket (Illus. by Janet Stevens)

      SLJ - v43 - N '97 - p41 [1-50]

Old Bag of Bones

      PW - v244 - Ag 25 '97 - p74 [1-50]

Stevenson, Harvey

Big, Scary Wolf (Illus. by Harvey Stevenson)

      BL - v94 - S 1 '97 - p136 [51-250]

      CBRS - v26 - S '97 - p6 [1-50]

      CCB-B - v51 - S '97 - p28+ [51-250]

      KR - v65 - Je 15 '97 - p958 [51-250]

      SLJ - v43 - Ag '97 - p142 [51-250]

Stevenson, James

Heat Wave at Mud Flat (Illus. by James Stevenson)

      HB - v73 - Jl '97 - p463+ [51-250]

      HB Guide - v8 - Fall '97 - p294 [51-250]

      SLJ - v43 - My '97 - p115 [51-250]

      SLJ - v43 - D '97 - p28 [1-50]

Mud Flat April Fool (Illus. by James Stevenson)

      BL - v94 - F 15 '98 - p1012 [51-250]

      KR - v66 - F 15 '98 - p275 [51-250]

      SLJ - v44 - Mr '98 - p188 [51-250]

The Mud Flat Mystery (Illus. by James Stevenson)

      BL - v94 - S 15 '97 - p236 [51-250]

      HB - v73 - S '97 - p581 [51-250]

      KR - v65 - Jl 1 '97 - p1037 [51-250]

      Par Ch - Awards '97 - p5 [51-250]

      SLJ - v43 - Ag '97 - p142 [51-250]

Popcorn (Illus. by James Stevenson)

      CCB-B - v51 - Ap '98 - p297 [51-250]

      KR - v66 - Mr 15 '98 - p410 [51-250]

Sam the Zamboni Man (Illus. by Harvey Stevenson)

      CCB-B - v51 - Ap '98 - p298 [51-250]

      HB - v74 - Mr '98 - p218 [51-250]

      KR - v66 - Ja 1 '98 - p64 [51-250]

      NYTBR - v103 - F 15 '98 - p26 [251-500]

      PW - v244 - D 15 '97 - p58 [51-250]

      SLJ - v44 - Mr '98 - p188 [51-250]

The Unprotected Witness

      BL - v94 - O 1 '97 - p332 [51-250]

      CCB-B - v51 - Ja '98 - p178 [51-250]

      HB - v73 - N '97 - p686 [51-250]

      Learning - v26 - N '97 - p28 [51-250]

      PW - v244 - O 20 '97 - p77 [51-250]

      SLJ - v43 - S '97 - p226 [51-250]

A Village Full of Valentines

      PW - v245 - Ja 19 '98 - p380 [1-50]

Stevenson, Jane Byrne
*Make-a-Face: Book and Body
Painting Kit for Kids of All Ages
(Illus. by Toni Hafkenscheid)*
CBRA - '96 - p522 [51-250]

Stevenson, Robert Louis, 1850-1894
A Child's Garden of Verses
TES - O 31 '97 - p16* [51-250]

Stewart, David Evelyn, 1950-
*From Tadpole to Frog (Illus. by
Carolyn Scrace)*
SLJ - v44 - Mr '98 - p197 [51-250]

Stewart, Dianne
The Dove (Illus. by Jude Daly)
JOYS - v11 - Win '98 - p142 [1-50]

Gift of the Sun (Illus. by Jude Daly)
SE - v61 - Ap '97 - p6* [1-50]

Stewart, Elisabeth J
*Bimmi Finds a Cat (Illus. by James
Ransome)*
SLJ - v43 - Ag '97 - p143 [51-250]

Stewart, Maureen
Easy Meat
Aust Bk R - Je '97 - p58+ [501+]

Easy Meat (Keith)
Magpies - v12 - Jl '97 - p39 [51-250]

Stewart, Sarah
The Gardener (Illus. by David Small)
BL - v93 - Je 1 '97 - p1722 [51-250]
BL - v94 - Mr 15 '98 - p1219 [1-50]
BW - v27 - D 7 '97 - p21 [51-250]
CCB-B - v51 - O '97 - p39+ [501+]
CM:CanRev - v4 - Ap 10 '98 - pONL
[251-500]
HB - v73 - N '97 - p673+ [251-500]
KR - v65 - Je 15 '97 - p958 [51-250]
NY - v73 - O 6 '97 - p116+ [51-250]
NYTBR - v102 - N 16 '97 - p53 [501+]
NYTBR - v102 - D 7 '97 - p80 [1-50]
PW - v244 - Je 2 '97 - p70 [51-250]
PW - v244 - N 3 '97 - p59 [1-50]
SLJ - v43 - Ag '97 - p143 [51-250]
SLJ - v43 - D '97 - p28 [1-50]

Stibane
L'Arbre Aux Corbeaux
Bkbird - v34 - Win '96 - p58 [51-250]

Stickland, Henrietta
The Christmas Bear
PW - v244 - O 6 '97 - p57 [51-250]

Stickland, Paul
*Dinosaur Roar! (Illus. by Paul
Stickland)*
Bks Keeps - S '97 - p20 [51-250]
HB Guide - v8 - Fall '97 - p256 [51-250]

*Dinosaur Stomp! (Illus. by Paul
Stickland)*
RT - v51 - O '97 - p130 [1-50]

*One Bear, One Dog (Illus. by Paul
Stickland)*
Bks Keeps - N '97 - p19 [51-250]
BL - v93 - Ag '97 - p1907 [51-250]
CBRS - v26 - S '97 - p6 [51-250]
HB Guide - v8 - Fall '97 - p256 [1-50]
KR - v65 - Je 1 '97 - p880 [51-250]
Magpies - v12 - S '97 - p26 [51-250]
PW - v244 - Je 2 '97 - p70 [51-250]
Sch Lib - v45 - N '97 - p188 [51-250]
SLJ - v43 - S '97 - p196 [51-250]

Ten Terrible Dinosaurs
Par - v72 - D '97 - p201 [51-250]
TES - N 7 '97 - p5* [1-50]

Stiefer, Sandy
A Risky Prescription
y   BL - v94 - D 1 '97 - p614 [51-250]
SLJ - v44 - Mr '98 - p243 [51-250]

Stienecker, David
Countries (Illus. by Richard Maccabe)
Ch BWatch - v7 - D '97 - p7 [1-50]

Maps (Illus. by Richard Maccabe)
Ch BWatch - v7 - D '97 - p7 [1-50]
SLJ - v44 - Ap '98 - p124+ [51-250]

States
Ch BWatch - v7 - D '97 - p7 [1-50]

The World
Ch BWatch - v7 - D '97 - p7 [1-50]

Stille, Darlene R
Airplanes
> BL - v94 - S 15 '97 - p233 [51-250]
> HB Guide - v8 - Fall '97 - p360 [51-250]

Blimps
> HB Guide - v8 - Fall '97 - p360 [51-250]

The Circulatory System
> BL - v94 - D 1 '97 - p632 [51-250]
> SLJ - v44 - F '98 - p105 [51-250]

The Digestive System
> SLJ - v44 - F '98 - p105 [51-250]

Extraordinary Women of Medicine
> y   BL - v94 - O 1 '97 - p316 [51-250]
> SB - v33 - D '97 - p277 [51-250]

Helicopters
> HB Guide - v8 - Fall '97 - p360 [51-250]

The Nervous System
> BL - v94 - F 15 '98 - p1006 [51-250]

The Respiratory System
> SLJ - v44 - F '98 - p105 [51-250]

Trains
> BL - v94 - S 15 '97 - p233 [51-250]
> HB Guide - v8 - Fall '97 - p360 [51-250]

Trucks
> HB Guide - v8 - Fall '97 - p360 [51-250]

Stine, Megan
The Story of Laura Ingalls Wilder (Illus. by Marcy Dunn Ramsey)
> Ch BWatch - v7 - Mr '97 - p4 [1-50]

Stine, R L
Fear Street Series
> NYTBR - v102 - N 16 '97 - p26 [1-50]

Goosebumps Series
> NYTBR - v102 - N 16 '97 - p26 [1-50]

It Came from Ohio!
> BL - v93 - Ag '97 - p1896 [51-250]
> y   BL - v94 - Mr 15 '98 - p1225 [1-50]
> CCB-B - v50 - Je '97 - p376 [51-250]
> HB - v73 - Jl '97 - p478 [51-250]
> HB Guide - v8 - Fall '97 - p382 [51-250]

> SLJ - v43 - Jl '97 - p112 [51-250]
> y   VOYA - v21 - Ap '98 - p40 [1-50]

R.L. Stine's Ghosts of Fear Street (Weiner). Audio Version
> SLJ - v43 - S '97 - p166 [51-250]
> SLJ - v43 - D '97 - p70 [51-250]

Stinson, Kathy
One Year Commencing
> y   Ch Bk News - v20 - Sum '97 - p29 [51-250]
> Quill & Q - v63 - Jl '97 - p49 [251-500]

Stock, Catherine
Armien's Fishing Trip
> BL - v93 - Je 1 '97 - p1724 [1-50]
> JOYS - v11 - Win '98 - p142 [51-250]

Stodart, Eleanor
The Adventures of Softbill the Strong
> Magpies - v12 - S '97 - p35 [51-250]

Stoeke, Janet Morgan
A Friend for Minerva Louise (Illus. by Janet Morgan Stoeke)
> CCB-B - v51 - Ja '98 - p179 [51-250]
> KR - v65 - Jl 1 '97 - p1037 [51-250]
> NYTBR - v102 - D 7 '97 - p78+ [1-50]
> PW - v244 - Ag 25 '97 - p73 [1-50]
> SLJ - v43 - N '97 - p101 [51-250]
> SLJ - v43 - D '97 - p28 [1-50]

Minerva Louise at School (Illus. by Janet Morgan Stoeke)
> RT - v51 - O '97 - p131 [1-50]

Stoker, Bram
Dracula
> LJ - v123 - Ja '98 - p150 [51-250]

Dracula. Audio Version
> BWatch - v18 - O '97 - p10 [1-50]

Dracula (Illus. by Tudor Humphries)
> y   BL - v94 - Mr 15 '98 - p1226 [1-50]
> CLW - v68 - D '97 - p86 [51-250]
> HB Guide - v8 - Fall '97 - p302 [51-250]
> y   LJ - v122 - S 15 '97 - p108 [51-250]
> Sch Lib - v45 - Ag '97 - p145 [51-250]
> y   SLJ - v43 - S '97 - p217+ [51-250]
> TES - Je 6 '97 - p8* [501+]
> y   VOYA - v21 - Ap '98 - p40 [1-50]

Stokes, Deidre
Desert Dreamings
Magpies - v12 - My '97 - p20+ [51-250]

Stolz, Mary
A Ballad of the Civil War (Illus. by Sergio Martinez)
BL - v94 - O 1 '97 - p333 [51-250]
KR - v65 - N 1 '97 - p1650 [51-250]
PW - v244 - N 10 '97 - p74 [51-250]
SLJ - v44 - F '98 - p110 [51-250]

Stone, Lynn M
Cougars (Illus. by Lynn M Stone)
Bloom Rev - v17 - Jl '97 - p21 [51-250]
Ch BWatch - v7 - Jl '97 - p3 [1-50]
HB Guide - v8 - Fall '97 - p354 [51-250]

Swans (Illus. by Lynn M Stone)
Bloom Rev - v17 - Jl '97 - p21 [51-250]
Ch BWatch - v7 - Jl '97 - p3 [1-50]
HB Guide - v8 - Fall '97 - p352 [51-250]
KR - v65 - Je 1 '97 - p880 [51-250]

Stone, Phoebe
When the Wind Bears Go Dancing (Illus. by Phoebe Stone)
BL - v94 - Ja 1 '98 - p825 [51-250]
CBRS - v26 - D '97 - p42 [51-250]
Ch BWatch - v7 - N '97 - p4 [1-50]
KR - v65 - Ag 15 '97 - p1312 [51-250]
SLJ - v44 - Ja '98 - p93+ [51-250]

Stone, Tanya Lee
America's Top 10 Construction Wonders
r   Ch BWatch - v7 - O '97 - p1 [1-50]
SLJ - v44 - F '98 - p122 [51-250]

America's Top 10 National Monuments
r   Ch BWatch - v7 - O '97 - p1 [1-50]
SLJ - v44 - Ja '98 - p132 [51-250]

Medical Causes
SLJ - v44 - Ja '98 - p120+ [251-500]

Stone, Walter N
Group Psychotherapy for People with Chronic Mental Illness
SB - v32 - D '96 - p266 [51-250]

Stoner, John
Makonde
Ch BWatch - v8 - Ja '98 - p7 [51-250]

Stones, Rosemary
Where Babies Come From (Illus. by Nick Sharratt)
TES - S 19 '97 - p13* [501+]

Stoops, Erik D
Dolphins
SLJ - v43 - Jl '97 - p88 [51-250]

Whales
ASBYP - v29 - Sum '96 - p35 [251-500]

Wolves and Their Relatives
BL - v94 - N 1 '97 - p469 [51-250]
SLJ - v44 - Ja '98 - p132+ [51-250]

Storer, Pat
Your Puppy, Your Dog
BL - v94 - D 15 '97 - p695 [51-250]

Stories (Artists' Workshop)
Emerg Lib - v25 - N '97 - p60 [51-250]

Storyworks
p   Par Ch - Awards '97 - p27 [1-50]

Stott, Carole
Fly the Space Shuttle
Obs - D 7 '97 - p18* [1-50]

Space Exploration (Illus. by Steve Gorton)
Ch BWatch - v7 - D '97 - p8 [1-50]
SB - v34 - Ap '98 - p82 [51-250]
SLJ - v44 - Ja '98 - p134 [51-250]
TES - N 7 '97 - p13* [501+]

Stotter, Mike
Wild West
Ch BWatch - v7 - D '97 - p3 [1-50]
SLJ - v44 - Ja '98 - p134 [51-250]

Stow, Jenny
Following the Sun (Illus. by Jenny Stow)
KR - v65 - N 1 '97 - p1650 [51-250]

Strachan, Ian

Dan's Den (Illus. by Lucy Su)

Sch Lib - v45 - N '97 - p202 [51-250]

The Iliad (Illus. by Victor G Ambrus)

BL - v94 - Ja 1 '98 - p816 [51-250]
KR - v65 - S 1 '97 - p1395 [51-250]
PW - v244 - O 20 '97 - p77 [1-50]
SLJ - v43 - N '97 - p124 [51-250]

The Joke Shop (Illus. by Ron Tiner)

Sch Lib - v45 - N '97 - p202 [51-250]

Throwaways

TES - Je 6 '97 - p8* [51-250]

Strasser, Todd

Hey, Dad, Get a Life!

HB Guide - v8 - Fall '97 - p309 [51-250]

Kidnap Kids

BL - v94 - Ja 1 '98 - p816 [51-250]
CCB-B - v51 - Mr '98 - p260+ [51-250]
KR - v65 - D 15 '97 - p1842 [51-250]
PW - v244 - D 22 '97 - p60 [51-250]
SLJ - v44 - Mr '98 - p224 [51-250]

Straub, Deborah Gillan

Hispanic American Voices

r   SLJ - v43 - N '97 - p144 [51-250]
yr   VOYA - v20 - D '97 - p340 [251-500]

Native North American Voices

r   SLJ - v43 - N '97 - p144+ [51-250]

Strauss, Michael

Where Puddles Go (Illus. by Lynn Jeffery)

ASBYP - v29 - Fall '96 - p31+ [251-500]

Strazzabosco, Jeanne M

Choosing a Career in Cosmetology

SLJ - v43 - Ag '97 - p168 [51-250]

Learning about Responsibility from the Life of Colin Powell

SLJ - v43 - My '97 - p126 [51-250]

Streissguth, Thomas

Communications: Sending the Message

Ch BWatch - v7 - N '97 - p6 [1-50]
SLJ - v44 - F '98 - p127 [51-250]

France (Globe-Trotters Club)

Ch BWatch - v8 - Ja '98 - p6+ [1-50]

France (A Ticket To)

Ch BWatch - v8 - Ja '98 - p6 [1-50]

Japan (A Ticket To)

Ch BWatch - v8 - Ja '98 - p6 [1-50]

Japan (Globe-Trotters Club)

Ch BWatch - v8 - Ja '98 - p6+ [1-50]

Mexico (A Ticket To)

Ch BWatch - v8 - Ja '98 - p6 [1-50]

Russia (Globe-Trotters Club)

Ch BWatch - v8 - Ja '98 - p6+ [1-50]

Russia (A Ticket To)

Ch BWatch - v8 - Ja '98 - p6 [1-50]

Streissguth, Tom

Writer of the Plains (Illus. by Karen Ritz)

BL - v93 - Je 1 '97 - p1698 [51-250]
Ch BWatch - v7 - S '97 - p7 [1-50]
HB Guide - v8 - Fall '97 - p382 [51-250]

Strete, Craig

Little Coyote Runs Away (Illus. by Harvey Stevenson)

CBRS - v26 - Win '98 - p64 [51-250]
Ch BWatch - v7 - N '97 - p5 [1-50]
SLJ - v43 - S '97 - p196 [51-250]

They Thought They Saw Him (Illus. by Jose Aruego)

ASBYP - v29 - Fall '96 - p32 [251-500]
RT - v51 - N '97 - p254 [51-250]

Strickland, Brad

Be a Wolf! (Illus. by Don Punchatz)

SLJ - v44 - Ja '98 - p116 [251-500]

The Bell, the Book, and the Spellbinder

BL - v94 - S 1 '97 - p127 [51-250]
Ch BWatch - v7 - N '97 - p2 [51-250]
SLJ - v43 - Ag '97 - p160 [51-250]

Strickland, Charlene

Dogs, Cats, and Horses

r   JOYS - v10 - Spr '97 - p263 [1-50]

Strickland, Michael R
My Own Song and Other Poems to Groove To (Illus. by Eric Sabee)
y BL - v94 - O 15 '97 - p394+ [51-250]
   KR - v65 - S 15 '97 - p1463 [51-250]
   SLJ - v43 - D '97 - p148 [51-250]

Strickland, Tessa
One Earth, One Spirit
   BL - v94 - N 1 '97 - p477 [51-250]
   PW - v244 - O 27 '97 - p71 [51-250]
   SLJ - v43 - N '97 - p112 [51-250]

Strong, Jeremy
Giant Jim and the Hurricane (Illus. by Nick Sharratt)
   Bks Keeps - N '97 - p23+ [51-250]
   Sch Lib - v45 - N '97 - p202 [51-250]

The Indoor Pirates (Illus. by Nick Sharratt)
   Bks Keeps - N '97 - p23+ [51-250]

My Granny's Great Escape (Illus. by Nick Sharratt)
   Sch Lib - v45 - N '97 - p202 [51-250]

Otherworld (Illus. by Anthony Morris)
   Bks Keeps - S '97 - p25 [51-250]
   Sch Lib - v45 - Ag '97 - p135 [51-250]
   TES - Jl 4 '97 - p10* [501+]

Pirate Pandemonium (Illus. by Judy Brown)
   Bks Keeps - S '97 - p24+ [51-250]

There's a Pharaoh in Our Bath! (Illus. by Nick Sharratt)
   Bks Keeps - My '97 - p23 [51-250]
   TES - Ap 18 '97 - p12* [51-250]

Viking at School (Illus. by John Levers)
   Bks Keeps - S '97 - p24+ [51-250]

Stroud, Bettye
Down Home at Miss Dessa's (Illus. by Felicia Marshall)
   RT - v51 - D '97 - p328+ [51-250]

Stroud, Jonathan
The Lost Treasure of Captain Blood (Illus. by Cathy Gale)
   Emerg Lib - v24 - My '97 - p51 [51-250]

   Magpies - v12 - Mr '97 - p30 [251-500]
   TES - N 21 '97 - p12* [51-250]

The Viking Saga of Harri Bristlebeard (Illus. by Cathy Gale)
   Sch Lib - v45 - N '97 - p202 [51-250]
   TES - N 21 '97 - p12* [51-250]

Strug, Kerri
Heart of Gold (Illus. by Doug Keith)
   HB Guide - v8 - Fall '97 - p372 [51-250]

Stubbs, Lisa
Sonny's Wonderful Wellies
   Bks Keeps - S '97 - p20 [51-250]
   Sch Lib - v45 - Ag '97 - p134 [51-250]

Stynes, Barbara White
Walking with Mama (Illus. by Barbara White Stynes)
   BL - v94 - S 15 '97 - p243 [51-250]
   Ch BWatch - v7 - My '97 - p2 [51-250]
   CLW - v68 - S '97 - p66 [51-250]

Suarez, Maribel
Las Frutas (Illus. by Maribel Suarez)
   SLJ - v44 - F '98 - p132 [51-250]

Suen, Anastasia
Man on the Moon (Illus. by Benrei Huang)
   BL - v94 - N 1 '97 - p477 [51-250]
   CBRS - v26 - Win '98 - p64 [1-50]
   CCB-B - v51 - Mr '98 - p261 [51-250]
   KR - v65 - S 15 '97 - p1463 [51-250]
   NYTBR - v103 - Ja 4 '98 - p20 [501+]
   PW - v244 - N 10 '97 - p73 [51-250]
   SLJ - v43 - N '97 - p112 [51-250]

Sugar, Bert Randolph
The Great Baseball Players
   Ch BWatch - v7 - S '97 - p8 [51-250]

Sullivan, Charles
Imaginary Animals
y BL - v94 - Mr 15 '98 - p1211 [1-50]
   HB Guide - v8 - Fall '97 - p375 [51-250]
y VOYA - v21 - Ap '98 - p37 [1-50]

Sullivan, George
Alamo!
CCB-B - v51 - S '97 - p25 [51-250]

Snowboarding: A Complete Guide for Beginners
HB Guide - v8 - Fall '97 - p372 [51-250]

Sullivan, Missy
The Native American Look Book
Ch BWatch - v7 - My '97 - p5 [1-50]

Sullivan, Otha Richard
African American Inventors
KR - v66 - Ap 15 '98 - p587 [51-250]

Sullivan, Robert
Maui: Legends of the Outcast
Magpies - v12 - My '97 - p8* [51-250]

Sumemos Con El Domino
PW - v244 - Ag 4 '97 - p77 [1-50]

Summers, Kate
Milly and Tilly (Illus. by Maggie Kneen)
BL - v93 - Ag '97 - p1907+ [251-500]
CBRS - v26 - S '97 - p6+ [1-50]
KR - v65 - Je 1 '97 - p881 [51-250]
PW - v244 - My 26 '97 - p85 [51-250]
SLJ - v43 - Jl '97 - p76 [51-250]

Summers, Susan
The Greatest Gift
TES - D 5 '97 - p17* [51-250]

Sumners, Carolyn
Toys in Space (Illus. by Chris Meister)
SB - v33 - D '97 - p273 [251-500]

Sun, Chyng Feng
On a White Pebble Hill (Illus. by Chyng Feng Sun)
RT - v51 - F '98 - p429 [51-250]

Supermachines. Reference Ed.
r   SB - v32 - D '96 - p259 [1-50]

Supraner, Robyn
Sam Sunday and the Mystery at the Ocean Beach Hotel (Illus. by Will Hillenbrand)
RT - v51 - O '97 - p136 [1-50]

Sussex, Lucy
The Penguin Friend (Illus. by Margaret Power)
Magpies - v12 - My '97 - p30 [51-250]

Sutcliff, Rosemary
Sword Song
y   Sch Lib - v45 - N '97 - p214+ [51-250]
TES - Jl 4 '97 - p11* [251-500]

Suzuki, David
The Backyard Time Detectives (Illus. by Eugenie Fernandes)
Can CL - v23 - Fall '97 - p94 [51-250]

Swann, Brian
Touching the Distance (Illus. by Maria Rendon)
KR - v66 - Mr 1 '98 - p345 [51-250]
PW - v245 - Mr 9 '98 - p70 [51-250]
SLJ - v44 - Ap '98 - p154+ [51-250]

Swanson, Diane
Buffalo Sunrise
ASBYP - v29 - Fall '96 - p32+ [251-500]
CBRA - '96 - p534 [51-250]
CM:CanRev - v4 - S 19 '97 - pONL [51-250]
SE - v61 - Ap '97 - p8* [1-50]

Bug Bites
Quill & Q - v63 - S '97 - p72 [251-500]

The Day of the Twelve-Story Wave (Illus. by Laura Cook)
CM:CanRev - v4 - D 12 '97 - pONL [51-250]

Welcome to the World of Bears
CM:CanRev - v4 - O 31 '97 - pONL [251-500]
Quill & Q - v63 - Je '97 - p64 [251-500]

Welcome to the World of Otters
CM:CanRev - v4 - O 31 '97 - pONL [251-500]

Quill & Q - v63 - Je '97 - p64 [251-500]

Welcome to the World of Whales
CBRA - '96 - p534 [51-250]

Welcome to the World of Wolves
CBRA - '96 - p534 [51-250]
Ch BWatch - v7 - Je '97 - p4 [51-250]

Swanson, Susan Marie
Getting Used to the Dark (Illus. by Peter Catalanotto)
Ch BWatch - v8 - Ja '98 - p4 [51-250]
HMR - Win '97 - p44+ [501+]
KR - v65 - O 15 '97 - p1589 [51-250]
PW - v244 - O 6 '97 - p85 [1-50]
SLJ - v44 - Ja '98 - p105+ [251-500]

Letter to the Lake (Illus. by Peter Catalanotto)
KR - v66 - Ja 15 '98 - p118+ [51-250]

Sweasey, Penny
Studying Contrasting UK Localities
TES - N 21 '97 - pR6 [51-250]

Sweeney, Joan
Bijou, Bonbon and Beau (Illus. by Leslie Wu)
KR - v66 - Ap 15 '98 - p587 [51-250]

Swinburne, Stephen R
Moon in Bear's Eyes (Illus. by Crista Forest)
KR - v66 - Mr 1 '98 - p345 [51-250]

Swindells, Robert
The Ghosts of Givenham Keep. Audio Version
Ch BWatch - v7 - D '97 - p4 [1-50]

Hurricane Summer (Illus. by Kim Palmer)
Sch Lib - v45 - N '97 - p202 [51-250]
TES - Ja 2 '98 - p22* [51-250]

Jacqueline Hyde
Bks Keeps - N '97 - p24 [51-250]

Nightmare Stairs
Bks Keeps - N '97 - p24 [51-250]
Sch Lib - v45 - Ag '97 - p148 [51-250]

Swinden, Liz
Look Good, Feel Good (Illus. by Kevin Faerber)
SLJ - v44 - Mr '98 - p242 [51-250]

Swoopes, Sheryl
Bounce Back (Illus. by Doug Keith)
HB Guide - v8 - Fall '97 - p372 [51-250]

Swope, Sam
The Krazees (Illus. by Eric Brace)
CBRS - v26 - Ja '98 - p52+ [51-250]
CM:CanRev - v4 - Ap 10 '98 - pONL [251-500]
KR - v65 - Ag 15 '97 - p1313 [51-250]
NYTBR - v103 - Mr 15 '98 - p24 [51-250]
PW - v244 - Je 23 '97 - p90 [51-250]
SLJ - v43 - D '97 - p101 [51-250]

Sykes, Julie
Dora's Eggs (Illus. by Jane Chapman)
CBRS - v25 - Ag '97 - p163 [51-250]
PW - v244 - My 19 '97 - p75 [51-250]
Sch Lib - v45 - Ag '97 - p134 [51-250]
SLJ - v43 - D '97 - p101 [51-250]

I Don't Want to Have a Bath! (Illus. by Tim Warnes)
Sch Lib - v45 - N '97 - p188 [51-250]

I Don't Want to Take a Bath (Illus. by Tim Warnes)
BL - v94 - D 1 '97 - p644 [51-250]

Sylloge Pruse, Kosta
To Basilopullon Tes Benedias (Illus. by Champes Tsangares)
Bkbird - v34 - Win '96 - p58 [51-250]

Symonds, Jimmy
The Hunchback of Notre Dame (Illus. by Tony Smith)
CLW - v68 - D '97 - p86 [51-250]
HB Guide - v8 - Fall '97 - p302 [51-250]
Sch Lib - v45 - Ag '97 - p145 [51-250]
y   SLJ - v43 - S '97 - p217+ [51-250]
TES - Je 6 '97 - p8* [501+]

Szabo, Corinne
Sky Pioneer
>BL - v94 - Mr 15 '98 - p1219 [1-50]
>HB Guide - v8 - Fall '97 - p382 [51-250]
>SLJ - v43 - Ap '97 - p160 [51-250]

Szekeres, Cyndy
The Deep Blue Sky Twinkles with Stars (Illus. by Cyndy Szekeres)
>BL - v94 - F 15 '98 - p1020+ [51-250]
>PW - v245 - Ja 12 '98 - p58 [51-250]
>SLJ - v44 - Mr '98 - p188 [51-250]

I Love My Busy Book (Illus. by Cyndy Szekeres)
>Ch BWatch - v7 - S '97 - p4 [1-50]
>HB Guide - v8 - Fall '97 - p256 [51-250]
>SLJ - v43 - Ap '97 - p118 [51-250]

The Mouse That Jack Built (Illus. by Cyndy Szekeres)
>CCB-B - v51 - Ja '98 - p179 [51-250]
>CM:CanRev - v30 - Ja 30 '98 - pONL [51-250]
>CM:CanRev - v4 - F 13 '98 - pONL [51-250]
>PW - v244 - N 24 '97 - p72 [51-250]
>SLJ - v43 - N '97 - p101 [51-250]

Yes, Virginia, There Is a Santa Claus (Illus. by Cyndy Szekeres)
>Ch BWatch - v7 - D '97 - p1 [1-50]
>CM:CanRev - v4 - Ja 2 '98 - pONL [51-250]
>PW - v244 - O 6 '97 - p54 [51-250]

Szirtes, George
The Red-All-Over Riddle Book (Illus. by Andrew Stooke)
>Bks Keeps - Jl '97 - p25+ [51-250]
>TES - N 7 '97 - p2* [1-50]

T

Taback, Simms
There Was an Old Lady Who Swallowed a Fly (Illus. by Simms Taback)
>BL - v94 - Mr 15 '98 - p1219 [1-50]
>CBRS - v26 - Ja '98 - p53 [51-250]
>CCB-B - v51 - Mr '98 - p261 [51-250]
>KR - v65 - S 15 '97 - p1463 [51-250]
>NYTBR - v102 - N 16 '97 - p56 [501+]
>Par Ch - Awards '97 - p3 [51-250]
>PW - v244 - Ag 18 '97 - p91 [51-250]
>SLJ - v43 - D '97 - p101 [51-250]

Tabor, Nancy
We Are a Rainbow (Illus. by Nancy Tabor)
>CCB-B - v51 - Ja '98 - p179+ [51-250]

Tafuri, Nancy
I Love You, Little One (Illus. by Nancy Tafuri)
>KR - v66 - Ja 15 '98 - p119 [51-250]
>PW - v245 - Ja 5 '98 - p67 [51-250]
>SLJ - v44 - Mr '98 - p188 [51-250]

What the Sun Sees, What the Moon Sees (Illus. by Nancy Tafuri)
>CBRS - v26 - O '97 - p18 [51-250]
>KR - v65 - Jl 15 '97 - p1117 [51-250]
>PW - v244 - S 1 '97 - p103 [51-250]

Takamado, Princess
Katie and the Dream-Eater (Illus. by Brian Wildsmith)
>CBRS - v26 - O '97 - p18 [51-250]
>PW - v245 - Ja 5 '98 - p67+ [51-250]
>SLJ - v43 - D '97 - p99+ [51-250]

Takao, Yuko
A Winter Concert (Illus. by Yuko Takao)
>CBRS - v26 - Ja '98 - p53 [51-250]
>SLJ - v44 - Ja '98 - p94 [51-250]

Takashima, Shizuye
A Child in Prison Camp (Illus. by Shizuye Takashima)
>Ch Bk News - v20 - Spr '97 - p34 [251-500]

Talbert, Marc
A Sunburned Prayer
>Emerg Lib - v25 - Ja '98 - p46 [51-250]

Talbot, Frank H
Under the Sea
>ASBYP - v29 - Sum '96 - p55+ [501+]

Talbott, Hudson
Amazon Diary (Illus. by Mark Greenberg)
>Books - v11 - O '97 - p21 [1-50]
>y JAAL - v40 - Ap '97 - p587 [251-500]
>RT - v51 - D '97 - p332 [51-250]

Talley, Linda
Bea's Own Good (Illus. by Andra Chase)
>CBRS - v25 - Ag '97 - p165+ [51-250]
>HB Guide - v8 - Fall '97 - p282 [51-250]
>SLJ - v43 - Ag '97 - p143+ [51-250]

Plato's Journey (Illus. by Itoko Maeno)
>KR - v65 - D 1 '97 - p1780 [51-250]
>PW - v244 - D 8 '97 - p72 [51-250]

Tamar, Erika
Alphabet City Ballet
> Ch BWatch - v7 - Ap '97 - p4 [1-50]
> JAAL - v41 - O '97 - p166+ [51-250]
> y   Kliatt - v32 - Ja '98 - p12 [51-250]

The Garden of Happiness (Illus. by Barbara Lambase)
> RT - v51 - S '97 - p58 [51-250]
> RT - v51 - D '97 - p311 [51-250]
> SE - v61 - Ap '97 - p13* [1-50]

The Junkyard Dog
> PW - v244 - N 24 '97 - p76 [1-50]

Tan, Sheri
Seiji Ozawa
> HB Guide - v8 - Fall '97 - p382+ [51-250]
> SLJ - v43 - S '97 - p209 [51-250]

Tanaka, Shelley
The Buried City of Pompeii (Illus. by Greg Ruhl)
> BL - v94 - D 1 '97 - p635 [51-250]
> CM:CanRev - v4 - Ap 10 '98 - pONL [51-250]
> Quill & Q - v63 - S '97 - p72 [251-500]
> SLJ - v44 - Mr '98 - p243 [51-250]

Discovering the Iceman (Illus. by Laurie McGaw)
> y   BL - v94 - Mr 15 '98 - p1225 [1-50]
> Can CL - v22 - Win '96 - p104 [251-500]
> CBRA - '96 - p510 [51-250]
> Ch Bk News - v20 - Sum '97 - p29 [51-250]
> CM:CanRev - v4 - Mr 27 '98 - pONL [501+]
> HB Guide - v8 - Fall '97 - p343 [51-250]
> NYTBR - v102 - Jl 6 '97 - p16 [51-250]
> SLJ - v43 - Je '97 - p148 [51-250]
> y   VOYA - v21 - Ap '98 - p40 [1-50]

On Board the Titanic (Illus. by Ken Marschall)
> Can CL - v22 - Win '96 - p102+ [501+]
> CBRA - '96 - p510 [51-250]
> RT - v51 - D '97 - p332 [51-250]
> SE - v61 - Ap '97 - p7* [1-50]
> y   VOYA - v20 - Je '97 - p87 [51-250]

Taris, James Robert
Curious Creatures: Bats
> SB - v33 - D '97 - p276 [251-500]

Curious Creatures: Owls
> SB - v33 - D '97 - p276 [251-500]

Curious Creatures: Snakes
> SB - v33 - D '97 - p276 [251-500]

Curious Creatures: Spiders
> SB - v33 - D '97 - p276 [251-500]

Curious Creatures: Wolves
> SB - v33 - D '97 - p276 [251-500]

Tarpley, Natasha Anastasia
I Love My Hair! (Illus. by E B Lewis)
> BL - v94 - F 15 '98 - p1021 [51-250]
> CCB-B - v51 - Ap '98 - p298 [51-250]
> KR - v65 - D 1 '97 - p1780 [51-250]
> PW - v244 - D 1 '97 - p52 [51-250]
> SLJ - v44 - F '98 - p91+ [51-250]

Tarsky, Sue
The Busy Building Book (Illus. by Alex Ayliffe)
> BL - v94 - Ja 1 '98 - p819 [51-250]
> CCB-B - v51 - Mr '98 - p261+ [51-250]
> KR - v65 - D 1 '97 - p1780 [51-250]
> SLJ - v44 - Mr '98 - p206 [51-250]

Tashjian, Janet
Tru Confessions
> BL - v94 - Ja 1 '98 - p816+ [51-250]
> CBRS - v26 - F '98 - p83+ [51-250]
> CCB-B - v51 - Ja '98 - p180 [51-250]
> KR - v65 - O 1 '97 - p1538 [51-250]
> PW - v244 - O 20 '97 - p77 [51-250]
> SLJ - v43 - D '97 - p131+ [51-250]
> y   VOYA - v20 - D '97 - p322 [51-250]

Tate, Eleanora E
Don't Split the Pole (Illus. by Cornelius Van Wright)
> BL - v94 - N 1 '97 - p474 [51-250]
> CBRS - v26 - Ja '98 - p56 [1-50]
> y   Ch BWatch - v7 - N '97 - p2 [1-50]
> KR - v65 - O 15 '97 - p1589 [51-250]
> PW - v244 - O 6 '97 - p84 [51-250]
> SLJ - v43 - N '97 - p124 [51-250]

Tate, Nikki
Rebel of Dark Creek
Quill & Q - v64 - F '98 - p49 [251-500]

Taylor, Barbara
About the Weather
Bks Keeps - Jl '97 - p24 [51-250]

Animal Homes
SB - v33 - Ap '97 - p86 [51-250]
SB - v33 - Ag '97 - p187 [1-50]

Earth Explained
AB - v100 - N 17 '97 - p1270 [51-250]
BL - v93 - Ag '97 - p1896+ [51-250]
Ch BWatch - v7 - N '97 - p7 [1-50]
r   HB Guide - v8 - Fall '97 - p343 [51-250]
SLJ - v43 - Je '97 - p148 [51-250]

Incredible Plants
Bks Keeps - S '97 - p26 [51-250]
HB Guide - v8 - Fall '97 - p349 [51-250]
New Sci - v154 - Je 28 '97 - p44 [51-250]
SB - v33 - D '97 - p274+ [51-250]
Sch Lib - v45 - N '97 - p208 [51-250]
SLJ - v43 - Ag '97 - p176 [51-250]

Incredible Plants (Inside Guides)
Ch BWatch - v7 - Jl '97 - p8 [1-50]
SB - v33 - Ag '97 - p187 [1-50]

The Really Deadly and Dangerous Dinosaur and Other Monsters of the Prehistoric World
SLJ - v43 - D '97 - p116 [51-250]

The Really Sinister Savage Shark and Other Creatures of the Deep
SLJ - v43 - D '97 - p116 [51-250]

Taylor, C J
How We Saw the World (Illus. by C J Taylor)
Ch BWatch - v7 - Ap '97 - p3 [51-250]

The Messenger of Spring (Illus. by C J Taylor)
Ch BWatch - v7 - O '97 - p6 [51-250]
Quill & Q - v63 - N '97 - p46 [251-500]

Taylor, Cora
Vanishing Act
CM:CanRev - v4 - Mr 13 '98 - pONL [251-500]

Taylor, David, 1934-
The Big and Little Body Book (Illus. by Peter Massey)
ASBYP - v29 - Sum '96 - p44+ [251-500]

Dogs
Ch BWatch - v7 - Je '97 - p4 [1-50]
r   TES - My 2 '97 - pR2 [501+]

The Fast and Slow Animal Book (Illus. by Peter Massey)
ASBYP - v29 - Sum '96 - p44+ [251-500]

The Heavy and Light Animal Book (Illus. by Peter Massey)
ASBYP - v29 - Sum '96 - p44+ [251-500]

The Long and Short Lived Animal Book (Illus. by Peter Massey)
ASBYP - v29 - Sum '96 - p44+ [251-500]

Taylor, George
Imagination in Art
Ch BWatch - v7 - Ap '97 - p8 [1-50]

Taylor, Harriet Peck
When Bear Stole the Chinook (Illus. by Harriet Peck Taylor)
BL - v94 - Ja 1 '98 - p819 [51-250]
CBRS - v26 - Ja '98 - p53 [1-50]
Ch BWatch - v7 - N '97 - p4 [1-50]
CM:CanRev - v30 - Ja 30 '98 - pONL [251-500]
KR - v65 - S 1 '97 - p1395 [51-250]

Taylor, L R
Creeps from the Deep (Illus. by Norbert Wu)
BL - v94 - D 15 '97 - p695 [51-250]
PW - v244 - N 3 '97 - p87 [1-50]
SLJ - v44 - Ap '98 - p155 [51-250]

Taylor, Livingston
Can I Be Good? (Illus. by Ted Rand)
PW - v244 - Jl 7 '97 - p70 [1-50]

Taylor, Margaret
Three against Time
CM:CanRev - v4 - O 3 '97 - pONL [501+]
Quill & Q - v63 - Ap '97 - p39 [51-250]

Taylor, Mildred D
The Friendship
PW - v245 - F 2 '98 - p92 [1-50]

The Gold Cadillac
PW - v245 - F 2 '98 - p92 [1-50]

Roll of Thunder, Hear My Cry
NYTBR - v102 - N 16 '97 - p26 [1-50]

Taylor, Pat
The Ancient Greeks
SLJ - v43 - N '97 - p112 [51-250]

Taylor, Paul
How to Hide an Elephant in Your Room
Ch BWatch - v7 - S '97 - p4 [1-50]

Taylor, Theodore
The Trouble with Tuck (Moore). Audio Version
SLJ - v43 - N '97 - p70 [51-250]

Tazewell, Charles
The Littlest Tree (Illus. by Karen Jerome)
PW - v244 - O 6 '97 - p58 [1-50]

Tchana, Katrin Hyman
Oh, No, Toto! (Illus. by Colin Bootman)
CBRS - v25 - Je '97 - p124 [51-250]
HB Guide - v8 - Fall '97 - p282 [51-250]

Teague, Mark
Baby Tamer (Illus. by Mark Teague)
BL - v93 - Ag '97 - p1908 [51-250]
CBRS - v26 - O '97 - p18 [51-250]
CCB-B - v51 - N '97 - p104 [51-250]
KR - v65 - Ag 15 '97 - p1313 [51-250]
PW - v244 - Ag 11 '97 - p401 [51-250]

The Field beyond the Outfield
SLJ - v44 - Mr '98 - p120 [1-50]

How I Spent My Summer Vacation
PW - v244 - Ag 11 '97 - p403 [1-50]

The Secret Shortcut
RT - v51 - O '97 - p146 [1-50]

Technology (Marshall Cavendish Library of Science)
SB - v32 - D '96 - p259 [1-50]

Teckentrup, Britta
Rumble in the Jungle (Illus. by Britta Teckentrup)
BL - v93 - Je 1 '97 - p1722 [51-250]
CBRS - v26 - S '97 - p7 [51-250]
HB Guide - v8 - Fall '97 - p256 [51-250]
KR - v65 - Je 1 '97 - p881 [51-250]

Te Kanawa, Kiri
Land of the Long White Cloud (Illus. by Michael Foreman)
y   BL - v94 - S 1 '97 - p104+ [51-250]
Magpies - v12 - S '97 - p8* [251-500]

Telford, Carole
Through a Termite City
SLJ - v44 - Ap '98 - p126 [51-250]

Up a Rainforest Tree
SLJ - v44 - Ap '98 - p126 [51-250]

Temko, Florence
Paper Gifts and Jewelry (Illus. by John Walls)
SLJ - v43 - S '97 - p209 [51-250]

Paper Tags and Cards (Illus. by John Walls)
SLJ - v43 - S '97 - p209 [51-250]

Traditional Crafts from Mexico and Central America
Ch BWatch - v7 - My '97 - p6 [51-250]

Traditional Crafts from Native North America
BL - v94 - O 1 '97 - p326 [51-250]
Ch BWatch - v7 - My '97 - p6 [51-250]
SLJ - v43 - Jl '97 - p113 [51-250]

Tempelman-Kluit, Anne
Yukon. Rev. Ed.
CBRA - '96 - p512+ [501+]

Temperley, Alan
Harry and the Wrinklies
> Sch Lib - v45 - Ag '97 - p148 [51-250]
> TES - My 16 '97 - p14* [51-250]

Temple, Frances
The Beduins' Gazelle
>   H-Net - D '97 - pONL [501+]
> y JAAL - v40 - O '96 - p152 [51-250]
> y PW - v245 - F 9 '98 - p98 [1-50]
>   RT - v51 - S '97 - p55 [51-250]

The Ramsay Scallop
> RT - v51 - S '97 - p55 [1-50]

Tenquist, Alasdair
Nigeria
> SLJ - v43 - S '97 - p237+ [51-250]

Terban, Marvin
Scholastic Dictionary of Idioms
> yr Kliatt - v32 - Mr '98 - p22 [51-250]
> r PW - v245 - F 9 '98 - p98 [1-50]

Tesar, Jenny E
America's Top 10 Cities
> r Ch BWatch - v7 - O '97 - p1 [1-50]
>   SLJ - v44 - F '98 - p122 [51-250]

America's Top 10 Curiosities
>   BL - v94 - Ja 1 '98 - p807 [51-250]
> r Ch BWatch - v7 - O '97 - p1 [1-50]
>   Cur R - v37 - D '97 - p12 [1-50]

America's Top 10 Mountains
> r Ch BWatch - v7 - O '97 - p1 [1-50]
>   SLJ - v44 - F '98 - p127 [51-250]

America's Top 10 National Parks
> r Ch BWatch - v7 - O '97 - p1 [1-50]
>   SLJ - v44 - Ja '98 - p132 [51-250]

America's Top 10 Rivers
> r Ch BWatch - v7 - O '97 - p1 [1-50]
>   SLJ - v44 - Ja '98 - p132 [51-250]

What on Earth Is a Quokka?
> ASBYP - v29 - Fall '96 - p68 [251-500]

Testa, Fulvio
A Long Trip to Z (Illus. by Fulvio Testa)
> BL - v94 - O 1 '97 - p339 [51-250]
> CBRS - v26 - O '97 - p18 [51-250]
> PW - v244 - Jl 28 '97 - p77 [1-50]

> Sch Lib - v45 - Ag '97 - p134 [51-250]
> TES - Je 27 '97 - p12* [251-500]

Testa, Maria
Nine Candles (Illus. by Amanda Schaffer)
> RT - v51 - O '97 - p135 [1-50]

Tetro, Marc
Monty Goes South (Illus. by Marc Tetro)
> Quill & Q - v64 - F '98 - p47+ [251-500]

Tews, Susan
Lizard Sees the World (Illus. by George Crespo)
> BL - v94 - N 1 '97 - p484+ [51-250]
> CBRS - v26 - Win '98 - p68 [51-250]
> CCB-B - v51 - D '97 - p141 [51-250]
> SLJ - v43 - S '97 - p196 [51-250]

Thaler, Mike
The Librarian from the Black Lagoon (Illus. by Jared Lee)
> Bloom Rev - v17 - N '97 - p30 [51-250]

Theobalds, Prue
Daisy and Jack and the Surprise Pie (Illus. by Prue Theobalds)
> Bks Keeps - My '97 - p19 [51-250]

Theodorou, Rod
Bat and Bird
> SLJ - v43 - Jl '97 - p88 [51-250]

Big and Small (Illus. by Gwen Tourret)
> SLJ - v43 - Ap '97 - p132 [51-250]

Hard and Soft (Illus. by Sheila Townsend)
> SLJ - v43 - Ap '97 - p132 [51-250]

Polar Bear and Grizzly Bear
> SLJ - v43 - Jl '97 - p88 [51-250]

Prickly and Smooth (Illus. by Sheila Townsend)
> SLJ - v43 - Ap '97 - p132 [51-250]

Shark and Dolphin
> SLJ - v43 - Jl '97 - p88 [51-250]

Short and Tall (Illus. by Sheila Townsend)

    SLJ - v43 - Ap '97 - p132 [51-250]

Snake and Lizard

    SLJ - v43 - Jl '97 - p88 [51-250]

Spider and Scorpion

    SLJ - v43 - Jl '97 - p88 [51-250]

Theriault, Luc F

Confused? A Kid's Guide to the Internet's World Wide Web

  r   CBRA - '96 - p537 [51-250]

Thesman, Jean

The Storyteller's Daughter

  y   BL - v94 - N 1 '97 - p462 [51-250]
        HB - v73 - N '97 - p686+ [51-250]
        KR - v65 - Ag 1 '97 - p1229+ [51-250]
        PW - v244 - Je 30 '97 - p76+ [51-250]
        SLJ - v43 - S '97 - p226 [51-250]
  y   VOYA - v20 - F '98 - p391 [251-500]

Thibeaux, Tamara

When Heaven Smiled on Our World

    Can CL - v22 - Win '96 - p121+ [501+]

Thiele, Colin

With Dew on My Boots

    Magpies - v12 - Jl '97 - p19 [501+]

Thomas, Abigail

Lily (Illus. by William Low)

    PW - v244 - S 22 '97 - p83 [1-50]

Thomas, Bill

Big and Noisy

    PW - v244 - D 15 '97 - p60 [51-250]

Thomas, Frances

Mr. Bear and the Bear (Illus. by Ruth Brown)

    Bks Keeps - S '97 - p23 [51-250]

Thomas, Jane Resh

Celebration! (Illus. by Raul Colon)

    CBRS - v25 - Ag '97 - p163 [51-250]
    HB Guide - v8 - Fall '97 - p283 [51-250]
    KR - v65 - My 15 '97 - p809 [51-250]

    NYTBR - v102 - Je 22 '97 - p22 [251-500]
    PW - v244 - My 19 '97 - p75 [51-250]
    SLJ - v43 - Jl '97 - p76 [51-250]
    Trib Bks - Je 8 '97 - p7 [51-250]

Thomas, John E

The Ultimate Book of Kid Concoctions (Illus. by Robb Durr)

    SLJ - v44 - Mr '98 - p206+ [51-250]

Thomas, Joyce Carol

Brown Honey in Broomwheat Tea (Illus. by Floyd Cooper)

    SB - v33 - O '97 - p219 [51-250]

I Have Heard of a Land (Illus. by Floyd Cooper)

    BL - v94 - F 15 '98 - p1009 [51-250]

Thomas, Marlo

Free to Be...You and Me. Free to Be...a Family

    PW - v245 - Mr 16 '98 - p66 [51-250]

Thomas, Naturi

Uh-Oh! It's Mama's Birthday (Illus. by Keinyo White)

    CBRS - v25 - Spr '97 - p136 [51-250]
    HB Guide - v8 - Fall '97 - p283 [51-250]
    SLJ - v43 - My '97 - p115 [51-250]

Thomas, Paul

Revolutionaries

    Bks Keeps - My '97 - p26 [51-250]

Thomas, Peggy

Medicines from Nature

  y   BL - v94 - S 15 '97 - p231 [51-250]
        Ch BWatch - v7 - Je '97 - p5 [51-250]
  y   SB - v33 - N '97 - p238+ [51-250]
  y   SLJ - v43 - Ag '97 - p176 [51-250]

Thomas, Rob

Rats Saw God (Heller). Audio Version

    BL - v94 - S 15 '97 - p250 [51-250]
    BL - v94 - Ja 1 '98 - p740 [1-50]
  y   Kliatt - v31 - Jl '97 - p50 [51-250]

Thomas, Valerie
Winnie in Winter (Illus. by Korky Paul)
    SLJ - v43 - D '97 - p101+ [51-250]

Thomas, Velma Maia
Lest We Forget
    BL - v94 - D 15 '97 - p700 [1-50]
y BL - v94 - Mr 15 '98 - p1225 [1-50]
y BW - v27 - D 7 '97 - p15 [251-500]
y VOYA - v21 - Ap '98 - p40 [1-50]

Thomassie, Tynia
Feliciana Meets D'Loup Garou (Illus. by Cat Bowman Smith)
    SLJ - v44 - Ap '98 - p110+ [51-250]

Mimi's Tutu (Illus. by Jan Spivey Gilchrist)
    SE - v61 - Ap '97 - p13* [1-50]

Thompson, Colin
The Last Circus (Illus. by Kim Gamble)
    Aust Bk R - N '97 - p62+ [501+]
    Magpies - v12 - S '97 - p30 [251-500]

The Paradise Garden (Illus. by Colin Thompson)
    KR - v66 - Mr 1 '98 - p345+ [51-250]
    PW - v245 - Mr 16 '98 - p64 [51-250]

Sailing Home (Illus. by Matt Ottley)
    Magpies - v12 - Mr '97 - p28+ [51-250]

The Tower to the Sun (Illus. by Colin Thompson)
    HB Guide - v8 - Fall '97 - p283 [51-250]
    Magpies - v12 - Mr '97 - p30 [51-250]
    SLJ - v43 - Jl '97 - p76 [51-250]

Thompson, Gare
Cities: The Building of America
    HB Guide - v8 - Fall '97 - p397 [51-250]

Immigrants: Coming to America
    HB Guide - v8 - Fall '97 - p322 [51-250]

Leaders: People Who Make a Difference
    HB Guide - v8 - Fall '97 - p384 [51-250]

Transportation: From Cars to Planes
    HB Guide - v8 - Fall '97 - p360 [51-250]

Thompson, Jan
Christian Festivals
    BL - v93 - Ag '97 - p1897 [51-250]
    SLJ - v43 - D '97 - p140 [51-250]

Thompson, Julian F
Ghost Story
    HB Guide - v8 - Fall '97 - p310 [51-250]
y JAAL - v41 - O '97 - p159 [51-250]
y SLJ - v43 - Ap '97 - p142 [51-250]
y VOYA - v20 - Ag '97 - p190 [251-500]

Thompson, Kate
Switchers
    Bks Keeps - N '97 - p26 [51-250]
    BL - v94 - Mr 15 '98 - p1245 [51-250]
y KR - v66 - Mr 15 '98 - p410 [51-250]
    TES - O 3 '97 - p9* [251-500]

Thompson, Kim Mitzo
I'd Like to Be a Marine Biologist (Illus. by Mark Paskiet)
    SB - v33 - Ag '97 - p178 [51-250]

I'd Like to Be a Meteorologist (Illus. by Mark Paskiet)
    SB - v33 - Ag '97 - p177 [251-500]

I'd Like to Be a Physicist (Illus. by Mark Paskiet)
    SB - v33 - O '97 - p208 [51-250]

I'd Like to Be an Entomologist (Illus. by Mark Paskiet)
    SB - v33 - Ag '97 - p179 [51-250]

Thompson, Liz
The Bhil of India
    Magpies - v12 - Mr '97 - p40 [251-500]

The Dani of Irian Jaya
    Magpies - v12 - Mr '97 - p40 [251-500]

The Trobriand Islanders of Papua New Guinea
    Magpies - v12 - Mr '97 - p40 [251-500]

Thompson, Mary
Gran's Bees (Illus. by Donna Peterson)

> ASBYP - v29 - Fall '96 - p34 [251-500]
> RT - v51 - D '97 - p330 [51-250]
> SB - v32 - D '96 - p276 [51-250]
> SB - v33 - O '97 - p219 [1-50]

Thompson, Richard
Cold Night, Brittle Light (Illus. by Henry Fernandes)

> Can CL - v23 - Fall '97 - p66+ [251-500]

Thompson, Ruth Plumly
Captain Salt in Oz (Illus. by John R Neill)

> SF Chr - v18 - Ap '97 - p69 [51-250]

Handy Mandy in Oz (Illus. by John R Neill)

> SF Chr - v18 - Ap '97 - p69+ [51-250]

Thomson, Pat
A Box of Stories for Six Year Olds (Illus. by Phillip Norman)

> Bks Keeps - Jl '97 - p21+ [51-250]
> Sch Lib - v45 - Ag '97 - p134 [51-250]

A Ghost-Light in the Attic (Illus. by Annabel Large)

> Bks Keeps - N '97 - p24 [51-250]

Thomson, Peggy
The Nine-Ton Cat

> BL - v94 - Ja 1 '98 - p735 [1-50]
> BW - v27 - My 4 '97 - p17 [251-500]
> HB Guide - v8 - Fall '97 - p365 [51-250]
> Magpies - v12 - S '97 - p5 [51-250]
> y SLJ - v43 - Ap '97 - p160 [51-250]
> y VOYA - v20 - F '98 - p371 [51-250]

Take Me Out to the Bat and Ball Factory (Illus. by Gloria Kamen)

> KR - v66 - Ap 1 '98 - p502 [51-250]

Thomson, Ruth
Have You Started Yet? (Illus. by Jane Eccles)

> BL - v94 - N 1 '97 - p469 [51-250]
> y Kliatt - v31 - N '97 - p23 [51-250]
> SLJ - v44 - Ja '98 - p134 [51-250]

Thorn, John
Total Baseball. 5th Ed.

> r BL - v94 - S 1 '97 - p159 [51-250]

Thornhill, Jan
Before and After (Illus. by Jan Thornhill)

> BL - v94 - O 1 '97 - p335 [51-250]
> KR - v65 - S 15 '97 - p1463+ [51-250]
> PW - v244 - O 20 '97 - p78 [51-250]
> Quill & Q - v63 - N '97 - p47 [251-500]
> SLJ - v43 - S '97 - p209 [51-250]

Wild in the City

> Ch BWatch - v7 - Mr '97 - p5 [51-250]

Thornley, Stew
Emmitt Smith: Relentless Rusher

> Cur R - v36 - Mr '97 - p12 [1-50]
> HB Guide - v8 - Fall '97 - p372 [51-250]
> SLJ - v43 - Ag '97 - p176+ [51-250]

Frank Thomas

> Ch BWatch - v7 - S '97 - p7 [1-50]

Sports Great Greg Maddux

> y CLW - v68 - S '97 - p69 [51-250]
> HB Guide - v8 - Fall '97 - p369 [51-250]
> y VOYA - v20 - Je '97 - p129 [251-500]

Threadgall, Colin
Animal Families

> ASBYP - v29 - Fall '96 - p34+ [251-500]

Animal Homes

> ASBYP - v29 - '96 - p34+ [251-500]

Thurman, Mark
One Two Many (Illus. by Mark Thurman)

> Can CL - v23 - Sum '97 - p65+ [501+]

Tibo, Gilles
Simon Finds a Treasure (Illus. by Gilles Tibo)

> BIC - v26 - My '97 - p33+ [251-500]
> CBRA - '96 - p458+ [51-250]

Tierney, Tom
Modern Dance

> BW - v27 - D 7 '97 - p20 [1-50]

Tildes, Phyllis Limbacher
*Animals: Black and White (Illus. by
Phyllis Limbacher Tildes)*
RT - v51 - O '97 - p130 [1-50]

Animals: Brightly Colored
PW - v245 - Mr 23 '98 - p102 [1-50]

Counting on Calico
TCMath - v4 - N '97 - p184 [51-250]

*Gifts (Illus. by Phyllis Limbacher
Tildes)*
Ch BWatch - v7 - D '97 - p5 [51-250]

Tillage, Leon
Leon's Story (Illus. by Susan L Roth)
BL - v94 - O 1 '97 - p332 [51-250]
BL - v94 - Ja 1 '98 - p735 [51-250]
BL - v94 - F 15 '98 - p999 [1-50]
y   BL - v94 - Mr 15 '98 - p1211 [1-50]
BL - v94 - Mr 15 '98 - p1219 [1-50]
BW - v27 - N 2 '97 - p6 [501+]
CBRS - v26 - F '98 - p84 [51-250]
CCB-B - v51 - D '97 - p142 [51-250]
HB - v73 - N '97 - p699+ [251-500]
KR - v65 - O 15 '97 - p1590 [51-250]
NYTBR - v103 - F 15 '98 - p25 [51-250]
PW - v244 - N 3 '97 - p60 [1-50]
SLJ - v43 - D '97 - p148 [51-250]
y   VOYA - v21 - Ap '98 - p39 [1-50]

Tocci, Salvatore
*How to Do a Science Fair Project.
Rev. Ed.*
y   BL - v94 - D 1 '97 - p621 [51-250]
SLJ - v43 - D '97 - p148 [51-250]

Toksvig, Sandi
*If I Didn't Have Elbows (Illus. by
David Melling)*
ASBYP - v29 - Fall '96 - p35 [251-500]
SB - v33 - Ag '97 - p180 [51-250]
SB - v33 - Ag '97 - p187 [1-50]

*Unusual Day (Illus. by Georgien
Overwater)*
Sch Lib - v45 - Ag '97 - p148 [51-250]

Tolan, Stephanie S
Save Halloween!
PW - v244 - O 6 '97 - p52 [1-50]

Welcome to the Ark
Ch BWatch - v7 - Mr '97 - p2 [51-250]
y   VOYA - v20 - Ap '97 - p34 [251-500]

Toles, Tom
*My School Is Worse than Yours (Illus.
by Tom Toles)*
CBRS - v26 - S '97 - p12 [1-50]
KR - v65 - Je 1 '97 - p881 [51-250]
SLJ - v43 - S '97 - p196+ [51-250]

Tolkien, J R R
The Hobbit
TES - Ja 2 '98 - p22* [51-250]

Tolstoy, Leo, Graf
*Shoemaker Martin (Illus. by
Bernadette Watts)*
PW - v244 - S 1 '97 - p107 [1-50]

Tomacek, Steve
*Simple Attractions (Illus. by Arnie
Ten)*
ASBYP - v29 - Sum '96 - p36 [251-500]

Tomaselli, Doris
*Adventures in Ponyland (Illus. by
Holly Jones)*
PW - v244 - Je 2 '97 - p73 [51-250]

*My Little People School Bus (Illus. by
Carolyn Bracken)*
PW - v244 - D 1 '97 - p55 [1-50]

*Tomie De Paolas'The Art Lesson.
Version 1.0l for Windows/
Macintosh. Electronic Media
Version*
BL - v94 - D 1 '97 - p648 [51-250]

Tomlinson, Theresa
Dancing through the Shadows
Bks Keeps - Jl '97 - p25 [51-250]
y   BL - v94 - N 1 '97 - p463 [51-250]
y   CBRS - v26 - F '98 - p84 [51-250]
KR - v65 - S 15 '97 - p1464 [51-250]
PW - v244 - N 3 '97 - p86 [51-250]
y   SLJ - v43 - N '97 - p124 [51-250]
TES - My 23 '97 - p7* [501+]
y   VOYA - v20 - F '98 - p391+ [51-250]

The Forestwife
y   BL - v94 - Mr 1 '98 - p1125 [51-250]
     Ch BWatch - v7 - Je '97 - p7 [1-50]
y   Kliatt - v31 - S '97 - p15 [51-250]

*The Little Stowaway (Illus. by Jane
Browne)*
     Spec - v279 - D 6 '97 - p43 [51-250]

*Meet Me by the Steelmen (Illus. by
Anthony Lewis)*
     Sch Lib - v45 - N '97 - p202 [51-250]

Tompert, Ann
*How Rabbit Lost His Tail (Illus. by
Jacqueline Chwast)*
     HB Guide - v8 - Fall '97 - p283 [51-
     250]
     KR - v65 - Ap 15 '97 - p651 [51-250]
     SLJ - v43 - My '97 - p115+ [51-250]

*The Jade Horse, the Cricket and the
Peach Stone (Illus. by Winson Trang)*
     Ch BWatch - v7 - Ap '97 - p6 [51-250]

*Saint Patrick (Illus. by Michael
Garland)*
     CCB-B - v51 - Ap '98 - p298+ [51-250]
     KR - v66 - F 1 '98 - p201 [51-250]
     PW - v245 - Ja 26 '98 - p86 [51-250]
     SLJ - v44 - Mr '98 - p207 [51-250]

Tong, Willabel
*A Three-Dimensional Medieval Castle
(Illus. by Phil Wilson)*
     PW - v244 - O 27 '97 - p79 [1-50]

Tonkin, Rachel
*When I Was a Kid (Illus. by Rachel
Tonkin)*
     Aust Bk R - Jl '97 - p62+ [501+]
     Magpies - v12 - Jl '97 - p19 [51-250]

Topsy Turvy (Little Play a Sound)
     Ch BWatch - v7 - Ap '97 - p2 [1-50]

Torres, Daniel
Tom (Illus. by Daniel Torres)
     RT - v51 - S '97 - p57 [51-250]

Torres, John
Greg Maddux: Ace!
     Ch BWatch - v7 - S '97 - p7+ [1-50]

Toten, Teresa
The Onlyhouse
     Can CL - v23 - Sum '97 - p54+ [501+]

Tougas, Chris
The Dizzy Duck
     PW - v245 - F 9 '98 - p97 [1-50]

Tough (Machines)
     Ch BWatch - v7 - Je '97 - p4 [1-50]

Tournier, Michel
Amandine, Ou, Les Deux Jardins
     Bkbird - v35 - Sum '97 - p12+ [501+]

Towne, M
Dive through the Wave
     SS - v88 - N '97 - p281 [51-250]

Townsend, Brad
Anfernee Hardaway
     Ch BWatch - v7 - S '97 - p7 [1-50]

Townson, Hazel
*Tale of the Terrible Teeth (Illus. by
Russell Ayto)*
     TES - Ap 18 '97 - p12* [51-250]

Tracqui, Valerie
*The Brown Bear (Illus. by BIOS
Agency)*
     PW - v245 - Mr 23 '98 - p102 [1-50]

Funny Faces
     SLJ - v43 - Ag '97 - p144 [51-250]

*My Home Is Africa (Illus. by M Denis-
Hout)*
     SLJ - v43 - Ag '97 - p144 [51-250]

The Whale
     ASBYP - v29 - Fall '96 - p39 [251-500]

Traditional Stories (Genre Library)
     Sch Lib - v45 - Ag '97 - p147 [51-250]

Trapani, Iza
*How Much Is That Doggie in the
Window? (Illus. by Iza Trapani)*
     Ch BWatch - v7 - O '97 - p6 [1-50]
     SLJ - v44 - Mr '98 - p207 [51-250]

Trapani, Margi
Inside a Support Group
y   BL - v94 - D 15 '97 - p690+ [51-250]
    SLJ - v44 - Ja '98 - p134+ [51-250]

Traub, Carol G
Philanthropists and Their Legacies
y   BL - v94 - F 15 '98 - p996+ [51-250]
    Ch BWatch - v7 - N '97 - p6+ [1-50]
    SLJ - v44 - F '98 - p127 [51-250]

Travers, Bridget
Medical Discoveries. Vols. 1-3
r   SLJ - v43 - Ag '97 - p187 [51-250]
yr   VOYA - v20 - F '98 - p407+ [251-500]

Travers, P L
Mary Poppins
    TES - Ja 2 '98 - p22* [1-50]

Travers, Will
The Elephant Truck (Illus. by Lawrie Taylor)
    KR - v66 - F 1 '98 - p201 [51-250]
    SLJ - v44 - Mr '98 - p184 [51-250]

Travolta, John
Propeller One-Way Night Coach
    Ent W - N 7 '97 - p80 [51-250]

Propeller One-Way Night Coach (Travolta). Audio Version
    PW - v244 - D 1 '97 - p22 [51-250]

Trease, Geoffrey
Danger in the Wings
    Sch Lib - v45 - Ag '97 - p148 [51-250]
y   TES - Je 13 '97 - p9* [251-500]

Mission to Marathon (Illus. by Paul Fisher-Johnson)
    Bks Keeps - N '97 - p24 [51-250]

Tregebov, Rhea
Sasha and the Wind (Illus. by Helene Desputeaux)
    CBRA - '96 - p459 [51-250]

Trevelyan, Kathy
Don't Be Surprised! (Illus. by Haydn Cornner)
    KR - v65 - Jl 1 '97 - p1037 [51-250]

Trevino, Elizabeth Borton De
Yo, Juan De Pareja
    SLJ - v43 - My '97 - p154 [51-250]

Trezise, Percy
Land of the Dingo People (Illus. by Percy Trezise)
    Magpies - v12 - My '97 - p20+ [51-250]

Triggs, Tony D
Fishbourne: A Day in a Roman Palace
    Bks Keeps - S '97 - p27 [51-250]
    Sch Lib - v45 - Ag '97 - p155 [51-250]

Tripp, Valerie
Josefina Learns a Lesson (Illus. by Jean-Paul Tibbles)
    BL - v94 - O 1 '97 - p333 [51-250]
    SLJ - v43 - D '97 - p102 [51-250]

Meet Josefina (Illus. by Jean-Paul Tibbles)
    BL - v94 - O 1 '97 - p333 [51-250]
    KR - v65 - Ag 15 '97 - p1313 [51-250]
    SLJ - v43 - D '97 - p102 [51-250]

Trivizas, Eugene
The Three Little Wolves and the Big Bad Pig (Illus. by Helen Oxenbury)
    Ch BWatch - v7 - O '97 - p6 [1-50]
    Par Ch - Awards '97 - p9 [51-250]
    SLJ - v43 - N '97 - p41 [1-50]

Trottier, Maxine
Loon Rock (Illus. by Dozay Christmas)
    CBRA - '96 - p459 [51-250]

Pavlova's Gift (Illus. by Victoria Berdichevsky)
    CBRA - '96 - p459+ [51-250]
    CLW - v68 - D '97 - p81+ [51-250]

A Safe Place (Illus. by Judith Friedman)
    BL - v93 - Je 1 '97 - p1723 [51-250]
    CBRS - v25 - Je '97 - p124+ [51-250]
    HB Guide - v8 - Fall '97 - p283 [51-250]
    SLJ - v43 - My '97 - p116 [51-250]

The Voyage of Wood Duck (Illus. by Patsy MacAulay-MacKinnon)
    CBRA - '96 - p460 [51-250]

Trudel, Sylvain
Max the Hero (Illus. by Suzanne Langlois)
    CBRA - '96 - p493+ [51-250]

Max the Superhero (Illus. by Suzanne Langlois)
    BIC - v26 - My '97 - p35+ [501+]

Trullols, Anna Gasol
Takao, Yo Soy Del Japon (Illus. by Domenec)
    SLJ - v44 - F '98 - p132 [51-250]

Trumbauer, Lisa
Balance and Motion
    SB - v33 - Je '97 - p141 [51-250]

Sink or Float?
    SB - v33 - D '97 - p273 [501+]

Sound
    SB - v33 - D '97 - p273 [501+]

What Is Matter?
    SB - v33 - D '97 - p273 [501+]

Trumble, Kelly
Cat Mummies (Illus. by Laszlo Kubinyi)
    NYTBR - v102 - Ag 17 '97 - p19 [501+]
    RT - v51 - O '97 - p150 [51-250]

Tryon, Leslie
Albert's Christmas
    Ch BWatch - v7 - D '97 - p2 [1-50]
    PW - v244 - O 6 '97 - p58+ [1-50]

Tucker, Kathy
Do Cowboys Ride Bikes? (Illus. by Nadine Bernard Westcott)
    CCB-B - v50 - Je '97 - p376 [51-250]
    SLJ - v43 - Je '97 - p101+ [51-250]

Do Pirates Take Baths? (Illus. by Nadine Bernard Westcott)
    PW - v244 - S 1 '97 - p107 [1-50]

Tudor, Tasha
The Great Corgiville Kidnapping (Illus. by Tasha Tudor)
    BL - v94 - O 15 '97 - p406 [51-250]
    CBRS - v26 - S '97 - p9 [51-250]

    CCB-B - v51 - O '97 - p68+ [51-250]
    Ch BWatch - v7 - N '97 - p4 [1-50]
    KR - v65 - Ag 15 '97 - p1313 [51-250]
    PW - v244 - Ag 25 '97 - p70 [51-250]
    SLJ - v43 - D '97 - p102 [51-250]

The Springs of Joy (Illus. by Tasha Tudor)
    PW - v245 - Ja 26 '98 - p90 [51-250]

Tuft, Lynne
The Grapes Grow Sweet
    Ch BWatch - v7 - S '97 - p1 [51-250]

Tulloch, Richard
Adventures with Bananas in Pajamas (Illus. by Nick Watson)
    HB Guide - v8 - Fall '97 - p283 [51-250]

Mr. Biffy's Battle (Illus. by Andrew McLean)
    Aust Bk R - v279 - My '97 - p62+ [501+]
    Magpies - v12 - Mr '97 - p27 [51-250]

Tunnell, Michael O
The Children of Topaz
    RT - v51 - S '97 - p56+ [51-250]
    RT - v51 - D '97 - p310 [51-250]
    SE - v61 - Ap '97 - p15* [1-50]
   y   VOYA - v20 - Ag '97 - p167 [51-250]

Mailing May (Illus. by Ted Rand)
    BL - v93 - Ag '97 - p1908 [51-250]
    BL - v94 - Mr 15 '98 - p1219 [1-50]
    BW - v27 - D 7 '97 - p21 [51-250]
    CBRS - v26 - Ja '98 - p53+ [51-250]
    CCB-B - v51 - O '97 - p69 [51-250]
    HB - v73 - S '97 - p564 [51-250]
    Inst - v107 - O '97 - p26 [51-250]
    KR - v65 - Je 15 '97 - p958 [51-250]
    NYTBR - v103 - Mr 15 '98 - p24 [51-250]
    Par Ch - Awards '97 - p5 [51-250]
    SLJ - v43 - S '97 - p197 [51-250]

School Spirits
    BL - v94 - F 15 '98 - p1012 [51-250]
    CCB-B - v51 - Mr '98 - p262 [51-250]
    KR - v65 - D 15 '97 - p1843 [51-250]
    PW - v244 - D 8 '97 - p72+ [51-250]
    SLJ - v44 - Mr '98 - p224 [51-250]

Turk, Ruth
Rosalynn Carter: Steel Magnolia
>   BL - v94 - D 1 '97 - p618 [51-250]

Turner, Ann
Finding Walter
>   BL - v94 - O 15 '97 - p406+ [51-250]
>   CBRS - v26 - N '97 - p36 [51-250]
>   CCB-B - v51 - O '97 - p69 [51-250]
>   HB - v74 - Ja '98 - p82 [51-250]
>   KR - v65 - Ag 1 '97 - p1230 [51-250]

Katie's Trunk (Illus. by Ronald Himler)
>   PW - v244 - D 22 '97 - p61 [1-50]

Mississippi Mud (Illus. by Robert J Blake)
>   CBRS - v25 - Jl '97 - p153 [51-250]
>   CCB-B - v50 - Je '97 - p376+ [51-250]
>   HB Guide - v8 - Fall '97 - p377 [51-250]
>   NYTBR - v102 - Je 8 '97 - p27 [1-50]
>   SLJ - v43 - Je '97 - p113 [51-250]

Shaker Hearts (Illus. by Wendell Minor)
>   HB Guide - v8 - Fall '97 - p320 [51-250]
>   NYTBR - v102 - Je 1 '97 - p36 [1-50]

Turner, Barrie Carson
The Living Clarinet
>   SLJ - v43 - Ap '97 - p160+ [51-250]

The Living Flute
>   SLJ - v43 - Ap '97 - p160+ [51-250]

The Living Piano
>   SLJ - v43 - Ap '97 - p160+ [51-250]

Turner, Glennette Tilley
Follow in Their Footsteps
> y HB Guide - v8 - Fall '97 - p384 [51-250]
>   SLJ - v43 - Ap '97 - p162 [51-250]
> y VOYA - v20 - O '97 - p272 [51-250]

Turner, Gwenda
The Ballet Class (Illus. by Gwenda Turner)
>   Magpies - v12 - S '97 - p28 [51-250]

Turner, Megan Whalen
The Thief
>   BL - v94 - N 1 '97 - p475 [1-50]
>   PW - v245 - Ja 12 '98 - p61 [1-50]
>   RT - v51 - F '98 - p427 [51-250]
> y VOYA - v20 - Je '97 - p114 [251-500]

Turner, Philip
The Bible Story (Illus. by Brian Wildsmith)
>   PW - v244 - D 22 '97 - p55 [1-50]

Turner, Robyn Montana
Texas Traditions
>   SE - v61 - Ap '97 - p9* [1-50]
>   SLJ - v43 - Ap '97 - p162 [51-250]

Turner, Steven
In the Beginning (Illus. by Jill Newton)
>   TES - O 17 '97 - p12* [51-250]

Tuttle, Dennis R
Albert Belle
>   Ch BWatch - v7 - Je '97 - p2 [1-50]
>   HB Guide - v8 - Fall '97 - p368 [51-250]

Tuxworth, Nicola
Baby Animals: A Very First Picture Book
>   CM:CanRev - v30 - Ja 30 '98 - pONL [51-250]

Twagilimana, Aimable
Hutu and Tutsi
>   Ch BWatch - v8 - Ja '98 - p7 [51-250]
>   SLJ - v44 - Mr '98 - p243 [51-250]

Teenage Refugees from Rwanda Speak Out
>   SLJ - v44 - F '98 - p126 [51-250]

Twain, Mark
The Adventures of Tom Sawyer. Electronic Media Version
>   BW - v27 - D 7 '97 - p23 [51-250]
>   Econ - v343 - My 17 '97 - p12* [501+]
> y JAAL - v41 - N '97 - p240+ [501+]
> y SLJ - v43 - Ag '97 - p48 [51-250]

The Adventures of Tom Sawyer (Illus. by Claude Lapointe)
    Sch Lib - v45 - Ag '97 - p145 [51-250]
y   SE - v61 - Ap '97 - p7* [1-50]

Tom Sawyer (Acclaim)
    LATBR - Mr 2 '97 - p13 [501+]

The Twelve Days of Christmas (Illus. by Emily Bolam)
    BL - v94 - S 1 '97 - p141 [51-250]
    Ch BWatch - v7 - D '97 - p2 [1-50]
    NYTBR - v102 - D 7 '97 - p66 [1-50]
    PW - v244 - O 6 '97 - p58 [1-50]

Twigg, Aeres
Where the Owl Hunts
    Sch Lib - v45 - N '97 - p216 [51-250]

Twinem, Neecy
In the Air (Illus. by Neecy Twinem)
    KR - v65 - Je 1 '97 - p881 [51-250]

In the Ocean
    PW - v245 - Mr 23 '98 - p102 [1-50]

Twinkle, Twinkle (Illus. by Bobbi Fabian)
    PW - v244 - O 20 '97 - p74 [51-250]

Twinkle, Twinkle, an Animal Lover's Mother Goose (Illus. by Bobbi Fabian)
    BL - v94 - D 1 '97 - p639 [51-250]
    CBRS - v26 - Win '98 - p61 [51-250]
    KR - v65 - O 15 '97 - p1578 [51-250]

Twinn, Michael
Bunny (Illus. by Pam Adams)
    Bks Keeps - N '97 - p21 [51-250]

Kitten (Illus. by Pam Adams)
    Bks Keeps - N '97 - p21 [51-250]

Tyler, Jenny
There's a Dragon at My School (Illus. by Stephen Cartwright)
    Bks Keeps - My '97 - p20 [51-250]

There's a Monster in My House (Illus. by Stephen Cartwright)
    Bks Keeps - My '97 - p20 [51-250]

Tyrrell, Frances
Woodland Christmas (Illus. by Frances Tyrrell)
    Can CL - v23 - Fall '97 - p85+ [501+]

U

Uchida, Yoskiko
The Bracelet
ABR - v19 - N '97 - p9+ [501+]

Uderzo, Albert
Asterix--The New Album
Books - v10 - S '96 - p24+ [51-250]

Uglow, Loyd
Abraham Lincoln, Will You Ever Give Up? (Illus. by Kennon James)
SLJ - v43 - Jl '97 - p88 [51-250]

Ugly Bugs
New Sci - v154 - Je 7 '97 - p48 [51-250]

Ugolini, Lydia
The Story of a Rich Dog and a Poor Dog
Ch BWatch - v7 - Jl '97 - p1 [51-250]

Ulitzka, Irene
Das Land Der Ecken (Illus. by Gerhard Gepp)
Bkbird - v35 - Spr '97 - p6+ [501+]

Ulmer, Wendy K
A Campfire for Cowboy Billy (Illus. by Kenneth J Spengler)
BL - v94 - D 1 '97 - p644 [51-250]
CBRS - v26 - O '97 - p18 [51-250]
PW - v244 - S 1 '97 - p105 [51-250]
SLJ - v44 - Ja '98 - p94 [51-250]

The Ultimate 3D Skeleton.
Electronic Media Version
SB - v32 - D '96 - p281 [251-500]

The Ultimate Book of Cross-Sections
RQ - v36 - Sum '97 - p610 [251-500]
y   SB - v33 - Ap '97 - p80 [51-250]
SE - v61 - Ap '97 - p12* [1-50]
y   VOYA - v20 - Je '97 - p126 [51-250]

The Ultimate Human Body.
Electronic Media Version
r   JOYS - v11 - Fall '97 - p78 [1-50]

The Ultimate Show-Me-How Activity Book (Illus. by John Freeman)
SLJ - v43 - Ag '97 - p152 [51-250]

Umansky, Kaye
You Can Swim, Jim (Illus. by Margaret Chamberlain)
Sch Lib - v45 - Ag '97 - p134 [51-250]
TES - Jl 18 '97 - p35 [251-500]

Unbelievable Gardening Playbook
Magpies - v12 - Mr '97 - p20+ [501+]

Unwin, David
Mysteries of Prehistoric Life (Illus. by Francis Phillipps)
Ch BWatch - v7 - My '97 - p7 [1-50]

The New Book of Dinosaurs (Illus. by Richard Rockwood)
BL - v94 - S 15 '97 - p233+ [51-250]
Ch BWatch - v7 - My '97 - p7 [1-50]
HB Guide - v8 - Fall '97 - p343 [51-250]
SLJ - v43 - S '97 - p238 [51-250]

Unwin, Pippa
Tomcat Takes a Walk
Bks Keeps - Jl '97 - p19 [51-250]

Updike, John
A Helpful Alphabet of Friendly Objects (Illus. by David Updike)
PW - v245 - F 16 '98 - p213 [51-250]

Ure, Jean
Beck Bananas--This Is Your Life! (Illus. by Mick Brownfield)
Bks Keeps - Jl '97 - p25 [51-250]

The Girl in the Blue Tunic
Bks Keeps - My '97 - p24 [51-250]

Whistle and I'll Come
Bks Keeps - N '97 - p24 [51-250]

Uribe, Veronica
Tres Buches De Agua Salada
Bkbird - v35 - Sum '97 - p22+ [51-250]

Urrutia, Maria Cristina
La Batalla Del 5 De Mayo
SLJ - v43 - N '97 - p137 [51-250]

V

Vaega, Akarana
Kuia (Illus. by Akarana Vaega)
  Magpies - v12 - S '97 - p5* [251-500]

Nana (Illus. by Akarana Vaega)
  Magpies - v12 - S '97 - p5* [251-500]

Te Wiki (Illus. by Akarana Vaega)
  Magpies - v12 - S '97 - p5* [251-500]

The Week (Illus. by Akarana Vaega)
  Magpies - v12 - S '97 - p5* [251-500]

Vagin, Vladimir
The Enormous Carrot (Illus. by Vladimir Vagin)
  BL - v94 - Mr 1 '98 - p1138 [51-250]
  KR - v66 - Ja 15 '98 - p119 [51-250]
  PW - v245 - Mr 9 '98 - p66 [51-250]
  SLJ - v44 - Mr '98 - p189 [51-250]

Vail, Rachel
Daring to Be Abigail
  PW - v244 - Jl 28 '97 - p77 [1-50]
  SLJ - v44 - Mr '98 - p120 [1-50]

Vainio, Pirkko
The Christmas Angel
  PW - v244 - O 6 '97 - p59 [1-50]

The Dream House (Illus. by Pirkko Vainio)
  SLJ - v44 - Ja '98 - p94 [51-250]

Valenta, Barbara
Pop-o-Mania: How to Create Your Own Pop-Ups (Illus. by Barbara Valenta)
  Bks Keeps - S '97 - p26 [51-250]
  BL - v94 - D 15 '97 - p700 [1-50]

HB Guide - v8 - Fall '97 - p363 [51-250]
KR - v65 - Ap 15 '97 - p651 [51-250]
SLJ - v43 - Je '97 - p113 [51-250]

Valfre, Edward
Vacationers from Outer Space (Illus. by Edward Valfre)
  PW - v245 - Ja 12 '98 - p59 [51-250]

Valgardson, W D
Garbage Creek and Other Stories (Illus. by Michel Bisson)
  BL - v94 - Ja 1 '98 - p817 [51-250]
  CM:CanRev - v4 - Ja 16 '98 - pONL [251-500]
  KR - v65 - O 1 '97 - p1538 [51-250]
  Quill & Q - v63 - O '97 - p35 [251-500]

Sarah and the People of Sand River (Illus. by Ian Wallace)
  CBRA - '96 - p460 [51-250]
  Ch Bk News - v20 - Spr '97 - p34+ [251-500]

Van Allsburg, Chris
Los Misterios Del Senor Burdick (Illus. by Chris Van Allsburg)
  BL - v93 - Ag '97 - p1913 [1-50]

The Polar Express (Illus. by Chris Van Allsburg)
  NYTBR - v102 - N 16 '97 - p26 [1-50]

The Widow's Broom (Illus. by Chris Van Allsburg)
  SLJ - v43 - N '97 - p41 [1-50]

Vanasse, Deb
A Distant Enemy
  y   CBRS - v25 - Spr '97 - p144+ [51-250]

HB Guide - v8 - Fall '97 - p310 [51-250]

Van Camp, Richard
A Man Called Raven (Illus. by George Littlechild)
Bloom Rev - v17 - My '97 - p27 [51-250]
Ch BWatch - v7 - Mr '97 - p6 [51-250]
HB Guide - v8 - Fall '97 - p283 [51-250]
SLJ - v43 - Je '97 - p102 [51-250]

VanCleave, Janice Pratt
Janice VanCleave's 202 Oozing, Bubbling, Dripping, and Bouncing Experiments
SB - v33 - Ap '97 - p83 [51-250]

Janice VanCleave's Constellations for Every Kid
y   BL - v94 - D 1 '97 - p622+ [51-250]
PW - v244 - Jl 21 '97 - p203 [51-250]

Janice VanCleave's Ecology for Every Kid
ASBYP - v29 - Fall '96 - p36 [251-500]

Janice VanCleave's Guide to the Best Science Fair Projects
Emerg Lib - v24 - My '97 - p57 [1-50]

Janice VanCleave's Guide to the Best Science Fair Projects
New Sci - v156 - N 22 '97 - p62 [51-250]

Janice VanCleave's Guide to the Best Science Fair Projects
y   SB - v33 - Ap '97 - p77 [51-250]
SLJ - v43 - Ap '97 - p162 [51-250]

Janice VanCleave's Oceans for Every Kid
Am Sci - v85 - N '97 - p557 [51-250]

Janice VanCleave's Plants
SB - v33 - N '97 - p243 [51-250]

Janice VanCleave's Play and Find Out about Math (Illus. by Michelle Nidenoff)
BL - v94 - D 1 '97 - p633 [51-250]
PW - v244 - Jl 28 '97 - p76 [51-250]
SLJ - v44 - Ja '98 - p106 [51-250]

Janice VanCleave's Play and Find Out about Nature (Illus. by Michelle Nidenoff)
BL - v93 - Je 1 '97 - p1714 [51-250]
SB - v33 - N '97 - p242 [251-500]
SLJ - v43 - Jl '97 - p88 [51-250]

Janice VanCleave's Play and Find Out about Science
Ch BWatch - v7 - Ap '97 - p7 [51-250]

Janice VanCleave's Rocks and Minerals
ASBYP - v29 - Fall '96 - p36+ [501+]

Van Der Meer, Ron
The Ultimate 3-D Pop-Up Art Book
Obs - D 7 '97 - p18* [51-250]
y   TES - D 5 '97 - p18* [51-250]

Vande Velde, Vivian
Tales from the Brothers Grimm and the Sisters Weird
Ch BWatch - v7 - Jl '97 - p5 [1-50]
y   JAAL - v41 - N '97 - p214+ [1-50]

Van Draanen, Wendelin
Sammy Keyes and the Hotel Thief
KR - v66 - Ap 1 '98 - p502 [51-250]

Van Dyck, Sara
Insect Wars
HB Guide - v8 - Fall '97 - p350 [51-250]
SB - v33 - N '97 - p243+ [51-250]
SLJ - v43 - Ag '97 - p152 [51-250]

Van El, Alannah
Aran's Medley
CBRA - '96 - p493+ [51-250]

Van Fleet, Matthew
Fuzzy Yellow Ducklings
Magpies - v12 - Mr '97 - p29 [51-250]

Van Hage, Mary An
Little Green Fingers
New Sci - v155 - Ag 23 '97 - p44 [51-250]

Van Kampen, Vlasta
Beetle Bedlam (Illus. by Vlasta Van Kampen)

Ch BWatch - v7 - S '97 - p3 [51-250]
KR - v65 - Je 1 '97 - p882 [51-250]
PW - v244 - Je 23 '97 - p90 [51-250]
Quill & Q - v63 - Ap '97 - p37 [251-500]
SLJ - v44 - F '98 - p92 [51-250]

Van Laan, Nancy
Little Baby Bobby (Illus. by Laura Cornell)

BL - v94 - O 1 '97 - p339 [51-250]
PW - v244 - Ag 11 '97 - p400 [51-250]
SLJ - v43 - N '97 - p101 [51-250]

Little Fish, Lost (Illus. by Jane Conteh-Morgan)

KR - v66 - Ja 15 '98 - p119 [51-250]
PW - v245 - Ja 5 '98 - p66 [51-250]
SLJ - v44 - Ap '98 - p111 [51-250]

Shingebiss: An Ojibwe Legend (Illus. by Betsy Bowen)

CCB-B - v51 - S '97 - p29 [51-250]
HB - v73 - N '97 - p691+ [51-250]
KR - v65 - Jl 1 '97 - p1037+ [51-250]

With a Whoop and a Holler (Illus. by Scott Cook)

BL - v94 - Mr 1 '98 - p1131 [51-250]
KR - v66 - Ja 15 '98 - p119+ [51-250]
PW - v245 - Ja 26 '98 - p92 [51-250]
SLJ - v44 - Ap '98 - p126 [51-250]

Van Leeuwen, Jean
Amanda Pig, Schoolgirl (Illus. by Ann Schweninger)

Par - v72 - D '97 - p206 [1-50]
SLJ - v43 - Jl '97 - p77 [51-250]
SLJ - v43 - D '97 - p28+ [1-50]

Blue Sky, Butterfly

RT - v51 - O '97 - p141 [1-50]

A Fourth of July on the Plains (Illus. by Henri Sorensen)

BL - v93 - Je 1 '97 - p1701 [1-50]
CCB-B - v50 - Jl '97 - p415 [51-250]
HB Guide - v8 - Fall '97 - p283 [51-250]
KR - v65 - My 15 '97 - p809 [51-250]
PW - v244 - My 19 '97 - p75+ [51-250]
SLJ - v43 - My '97 - p116 [51-250]

Going West (Illus. by Thomas B Allen)

PW - v244 - Ag 4 '97 - p77 [1-50]

Oliver and Amanda's Halloween (Illus. by Ann Schweninger)

PW - v244 - O 6 '97 - p50 [1-50]

The Tickle Stories (Illus. by Mary Whyte)

KR - v66 - Ap 15 '98 - p588 [51-250]

Touch the Sky Summer (Illus. by Dan Andreasen)

BL - v93 - Je 1 '97 - p1723 [51-250]
HB Guide - v8 - Fall '97 - p283 [51-250]
KR - v65 - My 15 '97 - p809 [51-250]
SLJ - v43 - Jl '97 - p77 [51-250]

Van Metre, Susan
Haunted House (Illus. by Nan Brooks)

PW - v244 - O 6 '97 - p49 [1-50]

Van Nutt, Robert
The Legend of Sleepy Hollow (Close) (Illus. by Robert Van Nutt). Book and Audio Version

Ch BWatch - v7 - D '97 - p4 [51-250]

VanOosting, James
The Last Payback

BL - v93 - Je 1 '97 - p1706+ [51-250]
CBRS - v25 - Ag '97 - p169 [51-250]
CCB-B - v50 - Je '97 - p377 [51-250]
HB - v73 - Jl '97 - p465 [51-250]
HB Guide - v8 - Fall '97 - p310 [51-250]
KR - v65 - My 15 '97 - p810 [51-250]
SLJ - v43 - Jl '97 - p98 [51-250]

Van Rynbach, Iris
Captain Cook's Christmas Pudding

CBRS - v26 - N '97 - p33 [51-250]
PW - v244 - O 6 '97 - p56 [51-250]

Van Steenwyk, Elizabeth
Frontier Fever

ASBYP - v29 - Sum '96 - p36+ [501+]

Mathew Brady: Civil War Photographer

BL - v94 - S 1 '97 - p121 [51-250]

My Name Is York (Illus. by Bill Farnsworth)
CBRS - v25 - Ag '97 - p166 [51-250]
CCB-B - v51 - S '97 - p29+ [51-250]

Varma, Nishu
I Bastoni Dello Yeti E Altre Favole Del Nepal (Illus. by Yacopo Camagni)
Bkbird - v35 - Fall '97 - p51 [1-50]

Il Lago Della Luna E Altre Favole Dell'India (Illus. by Pulak Biswas)
Bkbird - v35 - Fall '97 - p51 [51-250]

Vaughn, Mo
Follow Your Dreams (Illus. by Christopher Paluso)
HB Guide - v8 - Fall '97 - p372 [51-250]

Vecchione, Glen
Magnet Science (Illus. by Glen Vecchione)
ASBYP - v29 - Sum '96 - p37+ [251-500]

Vecere, Joel
A Story about Courage (Illus. by Benton Mahan)
SB - v33 - Ap '97 - p91 [51-250]

Velthuijs, Max
Frog Is Frog
Books - v11 - D '97 - p21 [51-250]

Venezia, Mike
The Beatles
HB Guide - v8 - Fall '97 - p366 [51-250]

Getting to Know the World's Greatest Artists Series
Inst - v106 - My '97 - p4* [1-50]

Henri De Toulouse-Lautrec
Emerg Lib - v25 - N '97 - p60 [51-250]

Henri Matisse
HB Guide - v8 - Fall '97 - p365 [51-250]

Verboven, Agnes
Ducks like to Swim (Illus. by Anne Westerduin)
BL - v94 - S 1 '97 - p136 [51-250]
CBRS - v26 - F '98 - p78 [51-250]
KR - v65 - Je 15 '97 - p958 [51-250]
SLJ - v43 - S '97 - p197+ [51-250]

Verdy, Violette
Of Swans, Sugarplums, and Satin Slippers
BW - v27 - D 7 '97 - p19 [1-50]

Verne, Jules
Michael Strogoff (Illus. by N C Wyeth)
PW - v244 - O 13 '97 - p77 [51-250]

Vezza, Diane Simone
Passport on a Plate (Illus. by Susan Greenstein)
y   BL - v94 - N 1 '97 - p461 [51-250]
HMR - Win '97 - p46 [51-250]
NYTBR - v102 - N 16 '97 - p38 [51-250]
PW - v244 - S 22 '97 - p83 [51-250]

Vieira, Linda
Grand Canyon: A Trail through Time (Illus. by Christopher Canyon)
KR - v65 - N 15 '97 - p1713 [51-250]
PW - v244 - N 17 '97 - p62 [51-250]

Viesti, Joe
Celebrate! In Central America (Illus. by Joe Viesti)
BL - v94 - S 15 '97 - p234 [51-250]
SLJ - v43 - Ag '97 - p152 [51-250]

Vigna, Judith
I Live with Daddy
HB Guide - v8 - Fall '97 - p283 [51-250]

The Viking Treasury of Children's Stories
BL - v93 - Je 1 '97 - p1707 [51-250]
HB Guide - v8 - Fall '97 - p374 [51-250]
SLJ - v43 - Jl '97 - p77 [51-250]

The Viking Treasury of Classics
PW - v245 - Ja 12 '98 - p61 [51-250]

Vila Roca, Roser
Fatima Vanessa, Yo Soy De El Salvador
SLJ - v43 - N '97 - p137 [51-250]

Viola, Herman J
North American Indians (Illus. by Bryn Barnard)
BWatch - v18 - Je '97 - p10 [51-250]
SE - v61 - Ap '97 - p9* [1-50]

Viorst, Judith
Absolutely Positively Alexander (Illus. by Ray Cruz)
PW - v244 - O 20 '97 - p78 [51-250]

Alexander and the Terrible, Horrible, No Good, Very Bad Day (Illus. by Ray Cruz)
NYTBR - v102 - N 16 '97 - p26 [1-50]

Rosie and Michael (Illus. by Lorna Tomei)
PW - v245 - Ja 12 '98 - p61 [51-250]

Viswanath, R
Teenage Refugees and Immigrants from India Speak Out
SLJ - v44 - Ap '98 - p155 [51-250]

Vitberg, Alan K
Marketing Health Care into the Twenty-First Century
SB - v32 - D '96 - p262 [51-250]

Vivelo, Jackie
Chills in the Night
BL - v94 - Ja 1 '98 - p795 [51-250]
Ch BWatch - v8 - Ja '98 - p4 [51-250]
SLJ - v44 - Ja '98 - p116 [51-250]

Vizurraga, Susan
Our Old House (Illus. by Leslie Baker)
BL - v94 - D 1 '97 - p644 [51-250]
CBRS - v26 - Ja '98 - p54 [51-250]
KR - v65 - Jl 15 '97 - p1118 [51-250]
PW - v244 - Ag 18 '97 - p92 [51-250]

Voake, Charlotte
Ginger (Illus. by Charlotte Voake)
BL - v94 - Mr 15 '98 - p1219 [1-50]

BW - v27 - My 4 '97 - p15+ [51-250]
CBRS - v25 - My '97 - p113 [51-250]
Ch BWatch - v7 - My '97 - p3 [51-250]
HB Guide - v8 - Fall '97 - p284 [51-250]
Magpies - v12 - My '97 - p27 [51-250]
NYTBR - v102 - Jl 6 '97 - p16 [51-250]
SLJ - v43 - Ap '97 - p118 [51-250]
TES - N 7 '97 - p5* [51-250]

Over the Moon (Illus. by Charlotte Voake)
Comw - v124 - D 5 '97 - p14 [51-250]

Vogel, Carole Garbuny
The Great Midwest Flood
ASBYP - v29 - Sum '96 - p38 [251-500]

Vogt, Gregory L
Asteroids, Comets and Meteors
ASBYP - v29 - Fall '96 - p46+ [501+]

Earth
ASBYP - v29 - Fall '96 - p46+ [501+]

The Sun
ASBYP - v29 - Fall '96 - p46+ [501+]

Voigt, Cynthia
Bad, Badder, Baddest
BL - v94 - N 1 '97 - p472 [51-250]
CCB-B - v51 - D '97 - p142 [51-250]
HB - v74 - Ja '98 - p82+ [51-250]
y   KR - v65 - N 1 '97 - p1650 [51-250]
PW - v244 - S 22 '97 - p81 [51-250]
SLJ - v43 - N '97 - p124 [51-250]

Bad Girls
y   JAAL - v40 - O '96 - p152 [51-250]
PW - v244 - S 1 '97 - p107 [1-50]

Vojtech, Anna
Marushka and the Month Brothers (Illus. by Anna Vojtech)
HB Guide - v8 - Fall '97 - p336 [51-250]
RT - v51 - F '98 - p424+ [51-250]
SE - v61 - Ap '97 - p5* [1-50]

Vos, Ida
Dancing on the Bridge of Avignon
SS - v88 - My '97 - p139+ [501+]

Vozar, David
*Rapunzel: A Happenin' Rap (Illus. by
Betsy Lewin)*
>BL - v94 - Ja 1 '98 - p821 [51-250]
>KR - v65 - D 1 '97 - p1780+ [51-250]
>PW - v244 - D 8 '97 - p71 [51-250]

Vries, Anke De
*Happy Birthday to Me (Illus. by Jung-
Hee Spetter)*
>CBRS - v26 - S '97 - p2 [51-250]

*Piggy's Birthday Dream (Illus. by
Jung-Hee Spetter)*
>PW - v244 - Ag 4 '97 - p74 [51-250]
>SLJ - v43 - N '97 - p101+ [51-250]

Vulliamy, Clara
Ellen and Penguin and the New Baby
>ECEJ - v24 - Sum '97 - p251 [51-250]

W

Waber, Bernard

Bearsie Bear and the Surprise Sleepover Party (Illus. by Bernard Waber)

    BL - v94 - O 1 '97 - p339 [51-250]
    HB - v73 - S '97 - p565 [51-250]
    KR - v65 - S 15 '97 - p1464 [51-250]

Waboose, Jan Bourdeau

Morning on the Lake (Illus. by Karen Reczuch)

    BL - v94 - Mr 15 '98 - p1252 [51-250]
    CM:CanRev - v4 - O 17 '97 - pONL [251-500]
    KR - v66 - Mr 1 '98 - p346 [51-250]
    PW - v245 - F 2 '98 - p90 [51-250]
    Quill & Q - v63 - Jl '97 - p50 [251-500]

Waddell, Martin

The Big Big Sea (Illus. by Jennifer Eachus)

    PW - v245 - Ja 12 '98 - p61 [1-50]

The Hidden House (Illus. by Angela Barrett)

    CBRS - v26 - D '97 - p44+ [1-50]
    Ch BWatch - v7 - N '97 - p3 [1-50]

John Joe and the Big Hen (Illus. by Paul Howard)

    Bks Keeps - S '97 - p21 [51-250]

The Life and Loves of Zoe T. Curley

    Magpies - v12 - My '97 - p35 [51-250]
y   NS - v126 - D 5 '97 - p66 [51-250]
y   Sch Lib - v45 - Ag '97 - p161+ [51-250]

Mimi's Christmas (Illus. by Leo Hartas)

    PW - v244 - O 6 '97 - p58 [1-50]

Owl Babies (Illus. by Patrick Benson)

    Books - v10 - S '96 - p24 [1-50]

What Use Is a Moose? (Illus. by Arthur Robins)

    PW - v245 - Mr 16 '98 - p67 [1-50]

When the Teddy Bears Came (Illus. by Penny Dale)

    ECEJ - v24 - Sum '97 - p251 [51-250]

Yum, Yum, Yummy (Illus. by John Bendall-Brunello)

    CCB-B - v51 - Ap '98 - p299 [51-250]

Wade, Mary Dodson

I'm Going to California (Illus. by Virginia Marsh Roeder)

    SLJ - v43 - Jl '97 - p77+ [51-250]

Wadsworth, Ginger

Desert Discoveries (Illus. by John Carrozza)

    HB Guide - v8 - Fall '97 - p348 [51-250]
    SB - v33 - N '97 - p244 [51-250]

John Burroughs: The Sage of Slabsides

    HB - v73 - Jl '97 - p478+ [51-250]
    HB Guide - v8 - Fall '97 - p383 [51-250]
    NYTBR - v102 - Ag 31 '97 - p13 [1-50]
    SLJ - v43 - My '97 - p151 [51-250]

Laura Ingalls Wilder: Storyteller of the Prairie

    CCB-B - v51 - S '97 - p30 [51-250]
y   Ch BWatch - v7 - Ap '97 - p5+ [1-50]
    HB Guide - v8 - Fall '97 - p383 [51-250]
    SLJ - v43 - Ap '97 - p162 [51-250]

One on a Web (Illus. by James M Needham)
>PW - v244 - Jl 21 '97 - p203 [1-50]

Wagener, Gerda
The Ghost in the Classroom (Illus. by Uli Waas)
>BL - v94 - Ja 1 '98 - p817 [51-250]
>KR - v65 - N 1 '97 - p1651 [51-250]

A Mouse in the House! (Illus. by Uli Waas)
>TES - Ap 18 '97 - p12* [51-250]

Wagner, Jenny
John Brown, Rose, and the Midnight Cat
>TES - D 26 '97 - p14 [1-50]

Wahl, Jan
I Met a Dinosaur (Illus. by Chris Sheban)
>BL - v94 - N 1 '97 - p485 [51-250]
>CBRS - v26 - D '97 - p45 [51-250]
>KR - v65 - S 1 '97 - p1396 [51-250]
>PW - v244 - S 22 '97 - p80 [51-250]
>SLJ - v43 - N '97 - p102 [51-250]

Little Eight John (Illus. by Wil Clay)
>PW - v245 - F 9 '98 - p97+ [1-50]

The Singing Geese (Illus. by Sterling Brown)
>BL - v94 - F 15 '98 - p1016 [51-250]
>KR - v65 - N 15 '97 - p1714 [51-250]
>PW - v244 - D 1 '97 - p53 [51-250]
>SLJ - v44 - F '98 - p105 [51-250]

Waite, Michael P
Jojofu (Illus. by Yoriko Ito)
>Emerg Lib - v24 - My '97 - p57 [1-50]

Waitt, Andrea
Pinocchio (Illus. by Peter Stevenson)
>HB Guide - v8 - Fall '97 - p294 [1-50]

Wakefield, Kerry
Shooting Stars
>Magpies - v12 - Jl '97 - p35 [51-250]

Young Bloods
>y   Aust Bk R - Ag '97 - p60 [501+]
>Magpies - v12 - Jl '97 - p35 [51-250]

Waldman, Neil
The Never-Ending Greenness (Illus. by Neil Waldman)
>CCB-B - v50 - Je '97 - p347+ [501+]
>Ch BWatch - v7 - Je '97 - p7 [1-50]
>HB Guide - v8 - Fall '97 - p284 [51-250]
>SLJ - v43 - Ap '97 - p142 [51-250]

The Two Brothers (Illus. by Neil Waldman)
>BL - v94 - O 1 '97 - p324 [51-250]
>CCB-B - v51 - O '97 - p69+ [51-250]
>NYTBR - v102 - S 28 '97 - p28 [1-50]
>SLJ - v43 - S '97 - p209 [51-250]

Waldron, Jan L
Angel Pig and the Hidden Christmas (Illus. by David McPhail)
>BL - v94 - S 1 '97 - p140 [51-250]
>CBRS - v26 - F '98 - p78 [51-250]
>CCB-B - v51 - D '97 - p142+ [51-250]
>Ch BWatch - v7 - D '97 - p2 [1-50]
>PW - v244 - O 6 '97 - p54+ [51-250]

Waldron, Kathleen Cook
A Wilderness Passover (Illus. by Leslie Gould)
>Can CL - v23 - Fall '97 - p81+ [501+]

Walker, Gladys
Molly Meets Mona and Friends (Illus. by Denise Bennet Minner)
>Ch BWatch - v7 - N '97 - p5 [51-250]

Walker, Niki
Sharks
>Ch BWatch - v7 - Jl '97 - p3 [1-50]
>HB Guide - v8 - Fall '97 - p351 [51-250]

Walker, Paul Robert
Bigfoot and Other Legendary Creatures (Illus. by William Noonan)
>PW - v244 - S 22 '97 - p83 [1-50]

Little Folk (Illus. by James Bernardin)
>CCB-B - v50 - Jl '97 - p415 [51-250]
>SLJ - v43 - Ap '97 - p132 [51-250]

Walker, Richard
A Right to Die?
>Bks Keeps - My '97 - p26+ [51-250]

HB Guide - v8 - Fall '97 - p318 [51-250]
SB - v33 - Ag '97 - p176 [51-250]
SLJ - v43 - My '97 - p145+ [51-250]

The Visual Dictionary of the Skeleton
r   ASBYP - v29 - Sum '96 - p38+ [251-500]

Walker, Sally M
The 18 Penny Goose (Illus. by Ellen Beier)
KR - v65 - D 1 '97 - p1781 [51-250]
SLJ - v44 - Mr '98 - p189 [51-250]

Hippos (Illus. by Gerry Ellis)
SLJ - v44 - Ap '98 - p126 [51-250]

Rhinos (Illus. by Gerry Ellis)
Cur R - v36 - Mr '97 - p13 [51-250]

The Walker Treasury of First Stories
Obs - D 7 '97 - p18* [51-250]

Wallace, Barbara Brooks
Sparrows in the Scullery
BL - v94 - S 15 '97 - p236 [51-250]
CCB-B - v51 - Ja '98 - p180 [51-250]
KR - v65 - O 15 '97 - p1590 [51-250]
SLJ - v43 - N '97 - p124 [51-250]

Wallace, Bill
A Dog Called Kitty (Ganser). Audio Version
SLJ - v43 - My '97 - p87 [51-250]

The Final Freedom
SLJ - v43 - Ag '97 - p160 [51-250]
y   VOYA - v20 - O '97 - p248 [51-250]

Upchuck and the Rotten Willy (Illus. by David Slonim)
KR - v66 - F 1 '98 - p201 [51-250]
PW - v244 - D 22 '97 - p60 [51-250]
SLJ - v44 - Mr '98 - p189 [51-250]

Wallace, Ian
A Winter's Tale (Illus. by Ian Wallace)
BL - v94 - O 15 '97 - p417 [51-250]
CCB-B - v51 - Já '98 - p180+ [51-250]
CM:CanRev - v4 - Ja 2 '98 - pONL [251-500]
Emerg Lib - v25 - Ja '98 - p52 [51-250]

Quill & Q - v63 - D '97 - p36 [251-500]
SLJ - v43 - D '97 - p102 [51-250]

Wallace, John
Building a House with Mr. Bumble
HB Guide - v8 - Fall '97 - p256 [51-250]

Dressing Up with Mr. Bumble
HB Guide - v8 - Fall '97 - p256 [51-250]

Little Bean's Friend (Illus. by John Wallace)
BL - v93 - Je 1 '97 - p1723 [51-250]
HB - v73 - S '97 - p566 [51-250]
HB Guide - v8 - Fall '97 - p256 [51-250]

Wallace, Karen
All Aboard for the Milky Way
TES - N 14 '97 - p14* [51-250]

Imagine You Are a Crocodile (Illus. by Mike Bostock)
BL - v94 - Ja 1 '98 - p736 [1-50]
HB Guide - v8 - Fall '97 - p284 [51-250]
SLJ - v43 - Jl '97 - p78 [51-250]

Imagine You Are a Tiger (Illus. by Peter Melnyczuk)
Ch BWatch - v7 - Ap '97 - p3 [51-250]

It Takes Two
Bks Keeps - S '97 - p21 [51-250]
Sch Lib - v45 - Ag '97 - p131 [1-50]

Louis Pasteur
TES - S 19 '97 - p16* [51-250]

Never Say No to a Martian! (Illus. by Tony Blundell)
Sch Lib - v45 - Ag '97 - p148 [51-250]

Roller-Blading Royals
Sch Lib - v45 - N '97 - p202 [51-250]

Thomas Edison
TES - S 19 '97 - p16* [51-250]

Wallace, Mary
I Can Make Art (Illus. by Mary Wallace)
Quill & Q - v63 - N '97 - p48 [251-500]
SLJ - v43 - D '97 - p148 [51-250]

I Can Make Costumes
   CBRA - '96 - p522 [51-250]

I Can Make Jewelry (Illus. by Mary Wallace)
   BL - v93 - Ag '97 - p1904 [51-250]
   Bloom Rev - v17 - My '97 - p27 [1-50]
   Ch BWatch - v7 - O '97 - p3 [1-50]

I Can Make Nature Crafts
   CBRA - '96 - p522+ [51-250]

Wallace, Rich
Shots on Goal
   y   BL - v94 - S 15 '97 - p224 [51-250]
   y   CCB-B - v51 - D '97 - p143+ [51-250]
   y   HB - v73 - N '97 - p687 [51-250]
   y   KR - v65 - Jl 15 '97 - p1118 [51-250]
       SLJ - v43 - N '97 - p124+ [51-250]

Wallace, Shelagh
The TV Book (Illus. by Lorraine Tuson)
   CBRA - '96 - p537+ [51-250]

Wallace and Gromit: A Close Shave
   Books - v11 - O '97 - p21 [1-50]

Wallner, Alexandra
An Alcott Family Christmas (Illus. by Alexandra Wallner)
   RT - v51 - N '97 - p255 [51-250]

Laura Ingalls Wilder (Illus. by Alexandra Wallner)
   BL - v94 - O 1 '97 - p335 [51-250]
   CCB-B - v51 - Ja '98 - p181 [51-250]
   HB - v73 - N '97 - p700 [51-250]
   KR - v65 - S 1 '97 - p1396 [51-250]
   SLJ - v43 - N '97 - p112 [51-250]

Wallwork, Amanda
Find the Fish
   PW - v245 - Ja 5 '98 - p69 [1-50]

Golden Slumbers
   HB Guide - v8 - Fall '97 - p337 [51-250]

Twinkle, Twinkle Little Star
   Bloom Rev - v17 - My '97 - p27 [1-50]
   HB Guide - v8 - Fall '97 - p337 [51-250]

Walpole, Brenda
Counting
   ASBYP - v29 - Sum '96 - p52+ [501+]

Distance
   ASBYP - v29 - Sum '96 - p52+ [501+]

Hearing
   ASBYP - v29 - Fall '96 - p65+ [251-500]

Seeing
   ASBYP - v29 - Fall '96 - p65+ [251-500]

Size
   ASBYP - v29 - Sum '96 - p54+ [501+]

Smell and Taste
   ASBYP - v29 - Fall '96 - p65+ [251-500]

Speed
   ASBYP - v29 - Sum '96 - p52+ [501+]

Temperature
   ASBYP - v29 - Sum '96 - p52+ [501+]

Time
   ASBYP - v29 - Sum '96 - p52+ [501+]

Touch
   ASBYP - v29 - Fall '96 - p65+ [251-500]

Walsh, Ellen Stoll
Jack's Tale (Illus. by Ellen Stoll Walsh)
   BL - v94 - D 1 '97 - p644 [51-250]
   KR - v65 - O 1 '97 - p1539 [51-250]
   PW - v244 - O 20 '97 - p75 [51-250]
   SLJ - v43 - N '97 - p102 [51-250]

Walsh, Melanie
Do Monkeys Tweet? (Illus. by Melanie Walsh)
   BL - v94 - S 1 '97 - p130 [51-250]
   CCB-B - v51 - O '97 - p70 [51-250]
   HB - v73 - N '97 - p674 [51-250]
   KR - v65 - Jl 1 '97 - p1038 [51-250]
   PW - v244 - S 1 '97 - p103 [51-250]

Do Pigs Have Stripes? (Illus. by Melanie Walsh)
   RT - v51 - O '97 - p130 [1-50]

Walsh, Mike
Martha Counts Her Kittens
    PW - v244 - S 1 '97 - p106 [1-50]

Walter, Virginia
Making Up Megaboy (Illus. by Katrina Roeckelein)
y BL - v94 - F 15 '98 - p1009 [251-500]
y KR - v66 - Ja 15 '98 - p120 [51-250]
y PW - v245 - F 16 '98 - p212 [51-250]
    SLJ - v44 - Ap '98 - p139 [51-250]

Walters, Catherine
When Will It Be Spring? (Illus. by Catherine Walters)
    BL - v94 - Ja 1 '98 - p825 [51-250]
    KR - v65 - N 15 '97 - p1714 [51-250]
    SLJ - v44 - Ap '98 - p111 [51-250]

Walters, Eric
Trapped in Ice
    CM:CanRev - v4 - Ap 10 '98 - pONL [251-500]
    Quill & Q - v63 - D '97 - p37+ [251-500]

Walton, Rick
Dance, Pioneer, Dance! (Illus. by Brad Teare)
    Ch BWatch - v7 - D '97 - p5 [51-250]

Pig Pigger Piggest (Illus. by Jimmy Holder)
    CBRS - v26 - D '97 - p42 [51-250]
    CCB-B - v51 - N '97 - p104 [51-250]
    SLJ - v43 - N '97 - p102 [51-250]

So Many Bunnies (Illus. by Paige Miglio)
    BL - v94 - Mr 15 '98 - p1252+ [51-250]
    KR - v66 - F 15 '98 - p275 [51-250]
    PW - v245 - Ja 26 '98 - p90 [51-250]
    SLJ - v44 - Mr '98 - p189 [51-250]

Wangberg, James K
Do Bees Sneeze? and Other Questions Kids Ask about Insects (Illus. by Ellen Parker)
    AB - v100 - N 17 '97 - p1270 [51-250]
    BL - v94 - Ja 1 '98 - p808 [51-250]
y SLJ - v44 - Ap '98 - p155 [51-250]

Warabe, Kimika
Baby Animals (Illus. by Kimika Warabe)
    CM:CanRev - v30 - Ja 30 '98 - pONL [51-250]
    PW - v244 - S 29 '97 - p91 [51-250]

Zoom Zoom (Illus. by Kimika Warabe)
    CM:CanRev - v30 - Ja 30 '98 - pONL [51-250]
    PW - v244 - S 29 '97 - p91 [51-250]

Ward, Heather P
I Promise I'll Find You (Illus. by Sheila McGraw)
    CBRS - v25 - Spr '97 - p138 [51-250]

Ward, Helen
The King of the Birds (Illus. by Helen Ward)
    BL - v94 - O 15 '97 - p411 [51-250]
    CBRS - v26 - Win '98 - p65 [51-250]
    CCB-B - v51 - N '97 - p105 [51-250]
    Magpies - v12 - S '97 - p30 [51-250]
    PW - v244 - Jl 7 '97 - p67 [51-250]
    SB - v33 - Ag '97 - p187 [1-50]
    Sch Lib - v45 - N '97 - p188 [51-250]
    SLJ - v44 - Ja '98 - p106 [251-500]

Ward, Jon
Howard Wise and the Monster Mop
    Ch BWatch - v8 - Ja '98 - p3 [51-250]

Ward, Rebecca
Time to Go Downtown (Illus. by Tony Linsell)
    PW - v245 - F 9 '98 - p97 [1-50]

Wardlaw, Lee
Bow-Wow Birthday (Illus. by Arden Johnson-Petrov)
    BL - v94 - Mr 1 '98 - p1142 [51-250]
    CCB-B - v51 - Ap '98 - p299+ [51-250]
    KR - v66 - F 1 '98 - p202 [51-250]

Bubblemania (Illus. by Sandra Forrest)
    BL - v94 - O 1 '97 - p326 [51-250]
    KR - v65 - S 1 '97 - p1396 [51-250]
    SLJ - v44 - Ja '98 - p135 [51-250]

*Punia and the King of Sharks (Illus.
by Felipe Davalos)*
> HB Guide - v8 - Fall '97 - p336 [51-250]
> Inst - v107 - Ag '97 - p21 [1-50]

Wardley, Rachel
*The Usborne First Dictionary (Illus.
by Teri Gower)*
> r   SLJ - v44 - F '98 - p139 [51-250]

Ware, Cheryl
*Catty-Cornered (Illus. by Paul
Yalowitz)*
> KR - v66 - F 1 '98 - p202 [51-250]
> PW - v245 - F 23 '98 - p78 [1-50]
> SLJ - v44 - Mr '98 - p224 [51-250]

Warner, Gertrude Chandler
*The Lighthouse Mystery (Newman).
Book and Audio Version*
> Ch BWatch - v7 - Ap '97 - p2 [51-250]

*Mystery of the Secret Message (Illus.
by Charles Tang)*
> Ch BWatch - v7 - Je '97 - p7 [51-250]

Warner, J A
One Norse Town
> SLJ - v44 - Ap '98 - p139 [51-250]

Warner, Penny
The Kids'Pick-a-Party Book
> PW - v245 - F 2 '98 - p92 [51-250]

Warner, Rachel
Refugees
> HB Guide - v8 - Fall '97 - p327 [51-250]
> TES - O 17 '97 - pR7 [51-250]

Warner, Sally
Ellie and the Bunheads
> BL - v93 - Je 1 '97 - p1707 [51-250]
> CCB-B - v51 - S '97 - p30 [51-250]
> Ch BWatch - v7 - O '97 - p3 [51-250]
> HB Guide - v8 - Fall '97 - p310 [51-250]
> y   KR - v65 - Ap 15 '97 - p651+ [51-250]
> SLJ - v43 - S '97 - p226+ [51-250]

Sort of Forever
> KR - v66 - Mr 1 '98 - p346 [51-250]

Warner, Sunny
*The Magic Sewing Machine (Illus. by
Sunny Warner)*
> BL - v94 - S 15 '97 - p243 [51-250]
> CBRS - v26 - Win '98 - p65 [51-250]
> KR - v65 - Jl 15 '97 - p1118 [51-250]
> PW - v244 - Je 23 '97 - p91 [51-250]
> SLJ - v43 - S '97 - p198 [51-250]

Warren, Andrea
Orphan Train Rider
> HMR - Sum '97 - p29 [51-250]
> SE - v61 - Ap '97 - p10* [1-50]
> y   VOYA - v20 - Je '97 - p87 [51-250]

Warren, Elizabeth
Baby Animals (Illus. by Peter Barrett)
> ASBYP - v29 - Fall '96 - p48+ [501+]

Warren, Jean
Super Snacks
> Ch BWatch - v7 - S '97 - p5 [1-50]

Warren, Scott S
Desert Dwellers
> BL - v94 - S 1 '97 - p121 [51-250]

Wassiljewa, Tatjana
Hostage to War
> BW - v27 - Je 8 '97 - p8 [251-500]
> CBRS - v25 - Ag '97 - p169 [51-250]
> y   HB Guide - v8 - Fall '97 - p390 [51-250]
> PW - v244 - My 19 '97 - p77 [51-250]
> y   SLJ - v43 - Je '97 - p150 [51-250]

Waterlow, Julia
The Atlantic Ocean
> ASBYP - v29 - Fall '96 - p64 [251-500]
> HB Guide - v8 - Fall '97 - p385 [51-250]

China
> HB Guide - v8 - Fall '97 - p392 [51-250]
> SB - v33 - O '97 - p212 [51-250]
> SLJ - v43 - Ag '97 - p166 [51-250]

A Family from Bosnia
> Bks Keeps - S '97 - p27 [51-250]
> BL - v94 - D 15 '97 - p695+ [51-250]
> Sch Lib - v45 - Ag '97 - p155 [51-250]

A Family from Ethiopia
Bks Keeps - S '97 - p27 [51-250]
Sch Lib - v45 - Ag '97 - p155 [51-250]

A Family from Guatemala
SLJ - v44 - Mr '98 - p207 [51-250]

The Red Sea and the Arabian Gulf
Ch BWatch - v7 - D '97 - p7 [1-50]
HB Guide - v8 - Fall '97 - p385 [51-250]

Waters, John F
Night Raiders along the Cape
BL - v94 - F 15 '98 - p1012+ [51-250]

Waters, Kate
On the Mayflower (Illus. by Russ Kendall)
Ch BWatch - v7 - Mr '97 - p5 [51-250]

Tapenum's Day (Illus. by Russ Kendall)
RT - v51 - N '97 - p251 [51-250]
SE - v61 - Ap '97 - p10* [1-50]

Waterton, Betty
The Lighthouse Dog (Illus. by Dean Griffiths)
Quill & Q - v63 - S '97 - p73 [251-500]

Quincy Rumpel and the All-Day Breakfast
Can CL - v23 - Sum '97 - p93 [51-250]
CBRA - '96 - p494 [51-250]

A Salmon for Simon (Illus. by Ann Blades)
CBRA - '96 - p460 [51-250]

Watkins, Richard Ross
Gladiator (Illus. by Richard Ross Watkins)
BL - v94 - N 1 '97 - p468 [51-250]
CBRS - v26 - S '97 - p12 [51-250]
CCB-B - v51 - O '97 - p70+ [251-500]
HB - v74 - Ja '98 - p95 [51-250]
KR - v65 - Ag 15 '97 - p1314 [51-250]

Watson, Carol
Bus Driver
Sch Lib - v45 - N '97 - p208 [51-250]

Christian
HB Guide - v8 - Fall '97 - p319 [51-250]

Dentist
Sch Lib - v45 - N '97 - p208 [51-250]

Watson, Lyall
Warriors, Warthogs, and Wisdom (Illus. by Keith West)
BL - v94 - O 1 '97 - p326+ [51-250]
y   Ch BWatch - v7 - S '97 - p7 [51-250]
SLJ - v43 - Ag '97 - p178 [51-250]
TES - My 16 '97 - p9* [251-500]

Watt, E Melanie
Black Rhinos (Illus. by Warren Clark)
CM:CanRev - v4 - F 13 '98 - pONL [251-500]

Jaguars (Illus. by Warren Clark)
CM:CanRev - v4 - F 13 '98 - pONL [251-500]

Watt, Fiona
Starting Lettering
Ch BWatch - v7 - Ap '97 - p1 [1-50]
Ch BWatch - v7 - O '97 - p4 [1-50]

The Usborne Book of Hair Braiding (Illus. by Chris Chaisty)
Ch BWatch - v7 - Ap '97 - p1 [1-50]

Usborne Cookery School
Books - v11 - D '97 - p21 [51-250]

Watts, Barrie
Butterfly and Caterpillar Storybook
Inst - v106 - Ap '97 - p4* [1-50]

Watts, Bernadette
The Elves and the Shoemaker (Illus. by Bernadette Watts)
PW - v244 - S 1 '97 - p107 [1-50]

Harvey Hare, Postman Extraordinaire (Illus. by Bernadette Watts)
CBRS - v25 - Spr '97 - p138 [1-50]
Ch BWatch - v7 - Je '97 - p7 [1-50]
HB Guide - v8 - Fall '97 - p284 [51-250]
Sch Lib - v45 - Ag '97 - p134 [51-250]

Watts, Irene N
The Fish Princess (Illus. by Steve Mennie)
> CBRA - '96 - p460+ [51-250]
> Sch Lib - v45 - Ag '97 - p148 [51-250]

Watts, Jeri Hanel
Keepers (Illus. by Felicia Marshall)
> BL - v94 - Ja 1 '98 - p825 [51-250]
> CBRS - v26 - F '98 - p79 [51-250]
> KR - v65 - N 1 '97 - p1651 [51-250]
> PW - v244 - N 24 '97 - p73 [51-250]
> SLJ - v44 - Ja '98 - p94+ [51-250]

Watts, Leslie Elizabeth
Princess Stinky-Toes and the Brave Frog Robert (Illus. by Leslie Elizabeth Watts)
> CBRA - '96 - p461 [51-250]

Watts, Nigel
Professor Blabbermouth on the Moon (Illus. by Jamie Smith)
> Sch Lib - v45 - Ag '97 - p148 [51-250]

Waugh, Sylvia
Mennyms Alive
> BL - v94 - S 15 '97 - p236 [51-250]
> CCB-B - v51 - N '97 - p105 [51-250]
> HB - v73 - N '97 - p687 [51-250]
> PW - v244 - O 20 '97 - p78 [1-50]
> SLJ - v43 - S '97 - p227 [51-250]

Waxman, Sydell
Changing the Pattern (Illus. by Linda Potts)
> CBRA - '96 - p511 [51-250]

The Wayland Atlas of Threatened Cultures
> r   Magpies - v12 - My '97 - p42+ [251-500]

Wayne-Von-Konigslow, Andrea
Would You Love Me?
> Ch Bk News - v20 - Spr '97 - p31 [51-250]

We Three Kings (Illus. by Laura Rader)
> Ch BWatch - v7 - N '97 - p6 [1-50]

Wear, Terri
Horse Stories
> r   JOYS - v10 - Spr '97 - p263 [1-50]

Weatherall, Peter
Beyond the Pale
> Magpies - v12 - My '97 - p8* [51-250]

Weatherby, Mark Alan
My Dinosaur (Illus. by Mark Alan Weatherby)
> CM:CanRev - v4 - S 19 '97 - pONL [251-500]
> HB Guide - v8 - Fall '97 - p284 [51-250]

Weatherly, Myra
Women Pirates
> CCB-B - v51 - Ap '98 - p300 [51-250]
> y   KR - v65 - D 15 '97 - p1843 [51-250]
> y   PW - v244 - D 22 '97 - p60+ [51-250]

Weber, Michael
Yorktown
> SLJ - v44 - Ja '98 - p132 [51-250]

Webster's World Encyclopedia. Electronic Media Version
> r   Sch Lib - v45 - Ag '97 - p140 [251-500]

Wegman, William
ABC
> Par - v72 - Je '97 - p189 [1-50]

Puppies (Illus. by William Wegman)
> CCB-B - v51 - Ja '98 - p181 [51-250]
> Ent W - O 10 '97 - p86 [51-250]
> Ent W - Ja 16 '98 - p64 [1-50]
> PW - v244 - S 22 '97 - p79 [51-250]

William Wegman's Farm Days (Illus. by William Wegman)
> HB Guide - v8 - Fall '97 - p284 [51-250]
> SLJ - v43 - Jl '97 - p78 [51-250]

Weidt, Maryann N
Revolutionary Poet (Illus. by Mary O'Keefe Young)
> BL - v94 - F 15 '98 - p1006 [51-250]
> KR - v65 - N 1 '97 - p1651 [51-250]

Weigant, Chris
Choosing a Career in Computers
 SLJ - v43 - Ag '97 - p168 [51-250]

Weil, Ann
Michael Dorris
 BL - v93 - Je 1 '97 - p1698 [51-250]
 HB Guide - v8 - Fall '97 - p382 [51-250]

Weil, Kelly
Zink the Zebra (Illus. by Jay Jocham)
 Ch BWatch - v7 - S '97 - p3 [1-50]

Weiss, M Jerry
From One Experience to Another
 y JAAL - v41 - D '97 - p320 [51-250]
  PW - v244 - Ag 18 '97 - p94 [51-250]
 y SLJ - v43 - N '97 - p125 [51-250]
 y VOYA - v20 - D '97 - p316 [251-500]

Weitzman, David
Old Ironsides (Illus. by David Weitzman)
 CCB-B - v50 - Je '97 - p377+ [51-250]
 HB Guide - v8 - Fall '97 - p310 [51-250]
 SLJ - v43 - Ap '97 - p142 [51-250]

Welch, Catherine A
Margaret Bourke-White (Illus. by Jennifer Hagerman)
 BL - v94 - S 1 '97 - p119 [51-250]
 SLJ - v43 - Ag '97 - p152 [51-250]

Welch, Leona Nicholas
Kai: The Lost Statue, Africa 1440 (Illus. by Elaine Arnold)
 SLJ - v44 - Ap '98 - p102 [51-250]

Welch, R C
Scary Stories for Sleep-Overs. Audio Version
 Ch BWatch - v7 - D '97 - p4 [1-50]

Welch, Ronald
Bowmen of Crecy (Illus. by Ian Ribbons)
 Spec - v279 - D 6 '97 - p44 [1-50]

Weldon, Fay
Nobody Likes Me! (Illus. by Claudio Munoz)
 KR - v65 - N 15 '97 - p1714 [51-250]
 Obs - Jl 20 '97 - p18* [251-500]
 PW - v244 - N 17 '97 - p61 [51-250]
 SLJ - v44 - F '98 - p92 [51-250]
 TES - Jl 4 '97 - p7* [501+]

Weldon, Maureen
Studying Distant Places
 TES - N 21 '97 - pR6 [51-250]

Weller, Dave
Arctic and Antarctic
 Emerg Lib - v25 - N '97 - p54 [1-50]

Weller, Frances Ward
Madaket Millie (Illus. by Marcia Sewall)
 HB Guide - v8 - Fall '97 - p284 [51-250]
 NYTBR - v102 - Ag 3 '97 - p14 [1-50]
 SLJ - v43 - Ap '97 - p118 [51-250]

Wellington, Monica
Baby at Home (Illus. by Monica Wellington)
 BL - v94 - S 1 '97 - p136 [51-250]
 HB Guide - v8 - Fall '97 - p256 [51-250]
 PW - v244 - Je 2 '97 - p73 [51-250]
 SLJ - v43 - Je '97 - p102 [51-250]

Baby Goes Shopping (Illus. by Monica Wellington)
 BL - v94 - S 1 '97 - p136 [51-250]
 HB Guide - v8 - Fall '97 - p256 [51-250]
 KR - v65 - My 15 '97 - p810 [51-250]
 PW - v244 - Je 2 '97 - p73 [51-250]
 SLJ - v43 - Je '97 - p102 [51-250]

Night House, Bright House (Illus. by Monica Wellington)
 CBRS - v25 - Je '97 - p125 [51-250]
 HB Guide - v8 - Fall '97 - p256 [51-250]
 SLJ - v43 - Ap '97 - p118 [51-250]

Wells, Donna
Biotechnology
 SB - v33 - Ap '97 - p67 [1-50]

Wells, Duncan

Duncan Back-to-Back (Illus. by Alison R Grapes)

CBRA - '96 - p494+ [251-500]

Wells, Robert E

Is a Blue Whale the Biggest Thing There Is?

Bks Keeps - N '97 - p23 [51-250]

What's Faster than a Speeding Cheetah? (Illus. by Robert E Wells)

BL - v94 - O 1 '97 - p335 [51-250]
KR - v65 - Ag 15 '97 - p1314 [51-250]
SLJ - v44 - Ja '98 - p106 [51-250]

Wells, Rosemary

Bunny Cakes (Illus. by Rosemary Wells)

BL - v94 - Ja 1 '98 - p736 [1-50]
BW - v27 - My 4 '97 - p18 [51-250]
Ch BWatch - v7 - Mr '97 - p7 [1-50]
HB Guide - v8 - Fall '97 - p284 [51-250]
Inst - v107 - Ja '98 - p30 [51-250]
Par - v72 - D '97 - p202 [1-50]
Sch Lib - v45 - N '97 - p188 [51-250]
SLJ - v43 - D '97 - p29 [1-50]

Bunny Money (Illus. by Rosemary Wells)

CCB-B - v51 - O '97 - p71 [51-250]
Ch BWatch - v7 - O '97 - p6 [51-250]
Inst - v107 - Ja '98 - p30 [1-50]
KR - v65 - Jl 15 '97 - p1119 [51-250]
Learning - v26 - N '97 - p29 [51-250]
Par - v72 - D '97 - p202 [1-50]
PW - v244 - My 26 '97 - p85 [51-250]
SLJ - v43 - Jl '97 - p78 [51-250]

Edward's First Day at School

Magpies - v12 - Jl '97 - p28 [51-250]

Edward's First Night Away

Magpies - v12 - Jl '97 - p28 [51-250]

Edward's First Swimming Party

Magpies - v12 - Jl '97 - p28 [51-250]

Jack and the Beanstalk (Illus. by Norman Messenger)

BL - v94 - N 1 '97 - p476 [51-250]
Sch Lib - v45 - N '97 - p188 [51-250]
SLJ - v43 - D '97 - p103 [51-250]

The Language of Doves (Illus. by Greg Shed)

RT - v51 - D '97 - p335 [51-250]
SE - v61 - Ap '97 - p13* [1-50]

Max and Ruby's First Greek Myth (Illus. by Rosemary Wells)

SLJ - v43 - N '97 - p41 [1-50]
SLJ - v44 - Ja '98 - p43 [1-50]

Max's Birthday

PW - v245 - F 16 '98 - p213 [1-50]

Max's Breakfast

PW - v245 - F 16 '98 - p213 [1-50]

Max's First Word

PW - v245 - F 16 '98 - p213 [1-50]

Max's New Suit

PW - v245 - F 16 '98 - p213 [1-50]

McDuff and the Baby (Illus. by Susan Jeffers)

BL - v94 - S 15 '97 - p243 [51-250]
Ch BWatch - v8 - Ja '98 - p1+ [1-50]
HB - v74 - Ja '98 - p65 [51-250]
Inst - v107 - Ja '98 - p30 [1-50]
NYTBR - v102 - D 21 '97 - p18 [501+]
Par - v72 - D '97 - p204 [1-50]
PW - v244 - Ag 25 '97 - p73 [1-50]
PW - v244 - N 3 '97 - p59 [1-50]

McDuff Comes Home (Illus. by Susan Jeffers)

BL - v93 - Je 1 '97 - p1723 [51-250]
CBRS - v25 - Je '97 - p125 [51-250]
HB - v73 - Jl '97 - p446+ [51-250]
HB Guide - v8 - Fall '97 - p284 [51-250]
Inst - v107 - Ja '98 - p30 [1-50]
NYTBR - v102 - D 21 '97 - p18 [501+]
Par - v72 - D '97 - p204 [1-50]
PW - v244 - N 3 '97 - p59 [1-50]
SLJ - v43 - Jl '97 - p78 [51-250]

McDuff Moves In (Illus. by Susan Jeffers)

CBRS - v25 - Je '97 - p125 [51-250]
Ch BWatch - v7 - Je '97 - p6 [1-50]
HB - v73 - Jl '97 - p446+ [51-250]
HB Guide - v8 - Fall '97 - p284 [51-250]
Inst - v107 - Ja '98 - p30 [1-50]
NYTBR - v102 - D 21 '97 - p18 [501+]
Par - v72 - D '97 - p204 [1-50]
PW - v244 - N 3 '97 - p59 [1-50]
SLJ - v43 - My '97 - p116 [51-250]

SLJ - v43 - D '97 - p29 [1-50]

Noisy Nora (Illus. by Rosemary Wells)
BL - v93 - Ag '97 - p1908 [51-250]
HB Guide - v8 - Fall '97 - p285 [51-250]
SLJ - v43 - My '97 - p116+ [51-250]

Nora La Revoltosa (Illus. by Rosemary Wells)
BL - v94 - D 15 '97 - p707 [51-250]
SLJ - v43 - Ag '97 - p181 [51-250]

Old MacDonald (Illus. by Rosemary Wells)
PW - v245 - Mr 23 '98 - p101 [1-50]

Read to Your Bunny (Illus. by Rosemary Wells)
CCB-B - v51 - Ap '98 - p300 [51-250]
PW - v245 - Ja 26 '98 - p90 [51-250]
SLJ - v44 - Mr '98 - p189+ [51-250]

Welsh, Renate
Disteltage
Bkbird - v35 - Fall '97 - p50 [51-250]

Weninger, Brigitte
Lumina (Illus. by Julie Wintz-Litty)
BL - v94 - O 15 '97 - p417 [51-250]
Ch BWatch - v8 - Ja '98 - p3 [1-50]
KR - v65 - Ag 15 '97 - p1314 [51-250]
SLJ - v43 - N '97 - p102 [51-250]

Ragged Bear (Illus. by Alan Marks)
RT - v51 - F '98 - p429 [51-250]

What's the Matter, Davy? (Illus. by Eve Tharlet)
BL - v94 - Mr 15 '98 - p1253 [51-250]

Will You Mind the Baby, Davy? (Illus. by Eve Tharlet)
HB Guide - v8 - Fall '97 - p285 [51-250]
SLJ - v43 - Jl '97 - p78 [51-250]

Wesley, Valerie Wilson
Freedom's Gifts (Illus. by Sharon Wilson)
Am Vis - v12 - D '97 - p33+ [1-50]
CBRS - v25 - Spr '97 - p145 [51-250]
CCB-B - v50 - Je '97 - p378 [51-250]
HB Guide - v8 - Fall '97 - p285 [51-250]
NYTBR - v102 - Je 22 '97 - p22 [51-250]

SLJ - v43 - Je '97 - p102+ [51-250]

West, Colin
The Caterpillow Fight
Bks Keeps - Jl '97 - p21 [51-250]

One Day in the Jungle
Bks Keeps - Jl '97 - p21 [51-250]

West, Tracey
Five Senses
SB - v33 - Je '97 - p142+ [51-250]

Westall, Robert
Demons and Shadows
y   Kliatt - v31 - N '97 - p17 [51-250]
PW - v244 - S 1 '97 - p107 [1-50]

Time of Fire
y   BL - v93 - Ag '97 - p1893 [51-250]
CBRS - v26 - O '97 - p24 [51-250]
CCB-B - v50 - Jl '97 - p415+ [51-250]
HB - v73 - S '97 - p582 [51-250]
y   KR - v65 - Je 1 '97 - p882 [51-250]
y   SLJ - v43 - Jl '97 - p98+ [51-250]

Westheimer, Ruth K
Dr. Ruth Talks about Grandparents (Illus. by Tracey Campbell Pearson)
BL - v93 - Ag '97 - p1897 [51-250]
CM:CanRev - v4 - Ap 10 '98 - pONL [251-500]
KR - v65 - Je 15 '97 - p959 [51-250]
PW - v244 - Jl 7 '97 - p70 [51-250]
SLJ - v43 - S '97 - p238 [51-250]

Weston, Martha
Bad Baby Brother (Illus. by Martha Weston)
CBRS - v25 - Je '97 - p125 [1-50]
HB Guide - v8 - Fall '97 - p256 [51-250]
SLJ - v43 - Je '97 - p103 [51-250]

Westrup, Hugh
The Mammals (Illus. by Ted Finger)
ASBYP - v29 - Fall '96 - p61+ [501+]

Wetterer, Margaret K
Clyde Tombaugh and the Search for Planet X (Illus. by Laurie A Caple)
Cur R - v36 - Mr '97 - p12 [51-250]
SB - v33 - Ap '97 - p83+ [51-250]

The Snow Walker (Illus. by Mary O'Keefe Young)
Inst - v107 - O '97 - p26+ [1-50]

Wexler, Jerome
Everyday Mysteries (Illus. by Jerome Wexler)
ASBYP - v29 - Sum '96 - p39+ [251-500]

Sundew Strangers
JOYS - v10 - Sum '97 - p429 [1-50]

Whalley, Paul
Butterfly and Moth
Inst - v106 - Ap '97 - p4* [1-50]

What Happens When...?
New Sci - v154 - Je 7 '97 - p48 [51-250]

What Makes the World Go Round?
r   HB Guide - v8 - Fall '97 - p340 [51-250]

Whatley, Bruce
Detective Donut and the Wild Goose Chase (Illus. by Bruce Whatley)
CBRS - v25 - Ag '97 - p163 [51-250]
HB Guide - v8 - Fall '97 - p285 [51-250]
Magpies - v12 - My '97 - p4+ [251-500]
SLJ - v43 - D '97 - p103 [51-250]

Whatley's Quest (Illus. by Bruce Whatley)
LA - v73 - N '96 - p524 [51-250]

Wheatley, Jonathan
Real Canadian Mysteries and Monsters (Illus. by Karena Kozol)
CBRA - '96 - p503+ [51-250]

Wheatley, Nadia
The Greatest Treasure of Charlemagne the King (Illus. by Deborah Klein)
Aust Bk R - D '97 - p64+ [501+]

Wheaton, Elizabeth
Myra Bradwell: First Woman Lawyer
Ch BWatch - v7 - Ap '97 - p6 [1-50]

y   HB Guide - v8 - Fall '97 - p383 [51-250]
y   SLJ - v43 - Ap '97 - p162 [51-250]

Wheeler, Cindy
More Simple Signs (Illus. by Cindy Wheeler)
BL - v94 - Ja 1 '98 - p821 [51-250]
KR - v65 - D 15 '97 - p1843 [51-250]
PW - v245 - F 9 '98 - p97 [51-250]
SLJ - v44 - Ja '98 - p107 [51-250]

Wheeler, Jill
Tiger Woods
Ch BWatch - v7 - S '97 - p7 [1-50]

Wheeler, Sara
Dear Daniel
Books - v11 - O '97 - p21 [1-50]

Whelan, Gloria
Forgive the River, Forgive the Sky
KR - v66 - Ap 15 '98 - p588 [51-250]

The Indian School (Illus. by Gabriela Dellosso)
PW - v244 - S 1 '97 - p107 [1-50]
RT - v51 - D '97 - p333 [51-250]

The Miracle of Saint Nicholas (Illus. by Judith Brown)
BL - v94 - N 1 '97 - p485 [51-250]
PW - v244 - O 6 '97 - p56 [51-250]

Shadow of the Wolf (Illus. by Tony Meers)
HB Guide - v8 - Fall '97 - p294 [51-250]

Whelehan, Dennis
The Dad Library (Illus. by Tim Archbold)
Bks Keeps - S '97 - p25 [51-250]
Sch Lib - v45 - Ag '97 - p148 [51-250]

Whetung, James
The Vision Seeker (Illus. by Paul Morin)
CBRA - '96 - p504 [51-250]

Whitaker, David L
Games, Games, Games
Ch BWatch - v8 - Ja '98 - p4 [51-250]

Whitcher, Susan
The Key to the Cupboard (Illus. by Andrew Glass)
> BL - v94 - S 1 '97 - p136 [51-250]
> CBRS - v26 - Ja '98 - p54 [51-250]
> NYTBR - v102 - O 26 '97 - p47 [501+]
> SLJ - v43 - S '97 - p198 [51-250]

White, Alana J
Sacagawea: Westward with Lewis and Clark
> HB Guide - v8 - Fall '97 - p399 [51-250]
> SLJ - v43 - Ag '97 - p178 [51-250]
> y   VOYA - v20 - Ag '97 - p209+ [251-500]

White, Carolyn
Whuppity Stoorie (Illus. by S D Schindler)
> BL - v94 - S 1 '97 - p130+ [51-250]
> CBRS - v25 - Ag '97 - p163 [51-250]
> CCB-B - v50 - Jl '97 - p416 [51-250]
> Ch BWatch - v7 - Jl '97 - p5 [51-250]
> HB Guide - v8 - Fall '97 - p336 [51-250]
> Inst - v107 - Ag '97 - p24 [1-50]
> NYTBR - v102 - O 26 '97 - p47 [501+]
> SLJ - v43 - Jl '97 - p88+ [51-250]

White, E B
Charlotte's Web (Illus. by Garth Williams)
> NYTBR - v102 - N 16 '97 - p25 [1-50]

White, Linda
Too Many Pumpkins (Illus. by Megan Lloyd)
> PW - v244 - O 6 '97 - p50+ [1-50]
> RT - v51 - O '97 - p136 [1-50]

White, Ruth
Belle Prater's Boy
> y   Kliatt - v32 - Mr '98 - p15 [51-250]
> PW - v245 - F 9 '98 - p98 [1-50]
> RT - v51 - S '97 - p56 [51-250]
> y   RT - v51 - N '97 - p244 [51-250]
> RT - v51 - D '97 - p309 [51-250]
> SE - v61 - Ap '97 - p13* [1-50]
> y   VOYA - v20 - Je '97 - p87 [51-250]

Whitelaw, Nancy
Clara Barton: Civil War Nurse
> BL - v94 - Mr 15 '98 - p1243 [51-250]
> SLJ - v44 - F '98 - p127+ [51-250]

More Perfect Union
> Ch BWatch - v7 - N '97 - p7 [51-250]
> y   HB Guide - v8 - Fall '97 - p383 [51-250]
> y   KR - v65 - My 15 '97 - p810 [51-250]

Whitfield, Susan
The Animals of the Chinese Zodiac (Illus. by Philippa-Alys Browne)
> Ch BWatch - v8 - Ja '98 - p2 [51-250]
> KR - v65 - D 15 '97 - p1844 [51-250]
> SLJ - v44 - F '98 - p105 [51-250]

The Legend of the Chinese Zodiac (Illus. by Philippa-Alys Browne)
> PW - v244 - D 1 '97 - p53 [51-250]

Whitman, Candace
The Night Is like an Animal
> PW - v244 - S 1 '97 - p107 [1-50]

Whitman, John
Eaten Alive
> Ch BWatch - v7 - Je '97 - p7 [1-50]

Star Wars: A Droid's Tale (Illus. by Steven D Anderson)
> Ch BWatch - v7 - D '97 - p2 [51-250]

Star Wars: The Death Star (Illus. by Barbara Gibson)
> BL - v94 - D 15 '97 - p700 [1-50]

Whitman, Walt
Walt Whitman (Illus. by Jim Burke)
> PW - v244 - O 6 '97 - p85 [51-250]
> SLJ - v43 - N '97 - p130 [51-250]

Whitney, Alexandra
First Place (Illus. by Alexandra Whitney)
> Ch BWatch - v7 - O '97 - p5 [1-50]

Whitney, Brooks
Super Slumber Parties (Illus. by Nadine Bernard Westcott)
> PW - v244 - S 22 '97 - p82 [51-250]

Why Are There Waves?

CLW - v68 - S '97 - p63+ [51-250]
HB Guide - v8 - Fall '97 - p340 [51-250]
SB - v33 - Ag '97 - p187 [1-50]
SLJ - v43 - Ag '97 - p149 [51-250]

Why Do Seasons Change?

CLW - v68 - S '97 - p63+ [51-250]
HB Guide - v8 - Fall '97 - p340 [51-250]
SB - v33 - Ag '97 - p187 [1-50]

Whybrow, Ian

Little Wolf's Diary of Daring Deeds (Illus. by Tony Ross)

Books - v11 - O '97 - p21 [1-50]

Parcel for Stanley (Illus. by Sally Hobson)

Books - v11 - Ag '97 - p15 [1-50]
Sch Lib - v45 - N '97 - p188 [51-250]

Wick, Walter

A Drop of Water (Illus. by Walter Wick)

BL - v94 - Ja 1 '98 - p735 [51-250]
BL - v94 - Mr 15 '98 - p1219 [1-50]
CBRS - v25 - My '97 - p117 [51-250]
HB Guide - v8 - Fall '97 - p342 [51-250]
NYTBR - v102 - My 18 '97 - p27 [501+]
SB - v33 - Ag '97 - p187 [1-50]
y   VOYA - v20 - F '98 - p371 [51-250]

Wickham, Martha

A Golden Age. Book and Audio Version

SLJ - v43 - Jl '97 - p57+ [51-250]

Superstars of Women's Track and Field

Ch BWatch - v7 - S '97 - p8 [1-50]
HB Guide - v8 - Fall '97 - p369 [51-250]
SLJ - v44 - Ap '98 - p147 [51-250]
y   VOYA - v20 - O '97 - p260 [251-500]

Wicks, Ben

Dear Canada

CBRA - '96 - p497 [51-250]

Wieler, Diana

To the Mountains by Morning (Illus. by Ange Zhang)

Can CL - v23 - Sum '97 - p63+ [501+]

Wiese, Jim

Cosmic Science (Illus. by Tina Cash-Walsh)

Ch BWatch - v7 - My '97 - p8 [51-250]
SLJ - v43 - Jl '97 - p89 [51-250]
S&T - v95 - Ap '98 - p69 [1-50]

Detective Science (Illus. by Ed Shems)

ASBYP - v29 - Fall '96 - p38+ [251-500]
CBRA - '96 - p538 [51-250]

Spy Science (Illus. by Ed Shems)

BIC - v26 - Ap '97 - p36 [251-500]
CBRA - '96 - p538 [51-250]
Emerg Lib - v24 - My '97 - p51 [51-250]
New Sci - v156 - N 22 '97 - p62 [51-250]

Wiesner, David

Hurricane (Illus. by David Wiesner)

SLJ - v44 - Ja '98 - p43 [51-250]

Tuesday

PW - v244 - Jl 28 '97 - p77 [1-50]

Wiggin, Kate Douglas

The Birds' Christmas Carol (Illus. by Jessie Gillespie)

PW - v244 - O 6 '97 - p58 [1-50]

Wilbur, C Keith

Early Explorers of North America

Ch BWatch - v7 - My '97 - p7 [1-50]
y   HB Guide - v8 - Fall '97 - p386 [51-250]

Indian Handcrafts

y   CAY - v18 - Fall '97 - p13 [51-250]
Ch BWatch - v7 - My '97 - p7 [1-50]
y   HB Guide - v8 - Fall '97 - p363 [51-250]

Pirates and Patriots of the Revolution

Ch BWatch - v7 - My '97 - p7 [1-50]
yr   HB Guide - v8 - Fall '97 - p387 [51-250]

Revolutionary Medicine 1700-1800

BL - v93 - Je 1 '97 - p1698+ [51-250]

Ch BWatch - v7 - My '97 - p7 [1-50]
y HB Guide - v8 - Fall '97 - p397 [51-250]
SB - v33 - O '97 - p211+ [51-250]
y SLJ - v43 - Jl '97 - p113 [51-250]

Revolutionary Medicine 1700-1800. 2nd Ed.
y CAY - v18 - Win '97 - p8 [51-250]

The Revolutionary Soldier 1775-1783
BL - v93 - Je 1 '97 - p1698+ [51-250]
Ch BWatch - v7 - My '97 - p7 [1-50]
y HB Guide - v8 - Fall '97 - p397 [51-250]
y SLJ - v43 - Jl '97 - p113 [51-250]

Tall Ships of the World
Ch BWatch - v7 - My '97 - p7 [1-50]
y HB Guide - v8 - Fall '97 - p360 [51-250]

Wilcox, Jane
Why Do We Celebrate That?
SLJ - v43 - Ag '97 - p170 [51-250]

Wild, Margaret
Big Cat Dreaming (Illus. by Anne Spudvilas)
BIC - v26 - D '97 - p35 [251-500]
CBRS - v26 - Win '98 - p65 [51-250]
Ch BWatch - v7 - N '97 - p4 [1-50]
KR - v65 - N 15 '97 - p1714 [51-250]
SLJ - v44 - F '98 - p92 [51-250]

Let the Celebrations Begin
Emerg Lib - v24 - My '97 - p9+ [1-50]
y Emerg Lib - v24 - My '97 - p10 [1-50]

Old Pig (Illus. by Ron Brooks)
Bks Keeps - Jl '97 - p6+ [501+]
SE - v61 - Ap '97 - p14* [1-50]

Our Granny (Illus. by Julie Vivas)
Emerg Lib - v25 - Ja '98 - p46 [51-250]

Wild Outdoor World
p Par Ch - Awards '97 - p27 [1-50]

Wilde, Oscar
Canterville Ghost
Ch BWatch - v7 - N '97 - p3 [1-50]

Wilder, Laura Ingalls
The Adventures of Laura and Jack (Illus. by Renee Graef)
HB Guide - v8 - Fall '97 - p295 [51-250]

Animal Adventures (Illus. by Renee Graef)
HB Guide - v8 - Fall '97 - p295 [51-250]

The Laura Ingalls Wilder Country Cookbook (Illus. by Leslie A Kelly)
NYTBR - v102 - N 16 '97 - p38 [51-250]
PW - v244 - S 22 '97 - p83 [51-250]

The Little House Books
CSM - v90 - F 24 '98 - p16 [1-50]

A Little House Reader
KR - v65 - D 15 '97 - p1832 [51-250]
PW - v245 - F 16 '98 - p213 [51-250]

Little House Sisters (Illus. by Garth Williams)
HB Guide - v8 - Fall '97 - p295 [51-250]

My Little House 1 2 3 (Illus. by Renee Graef)
HB Guide - v8 - Fall '97 - p256+ [51-250]

My Little House A B C (Illus. by Renee Graef)
HB Guide - v8 - Fall '97 - p256+ [51-250]

Pioneer Sisters (Illus. by Renee Graef)
HB Guide - v8 - Fall '97 - p295 [51-250]

Prairie Day (Illus. by Renee Graef)
HB Guide - v8 - Fall '97 - p285 [51-250]

Wildlife of the Town
New Sci - v154 - Ap 26 '97 - p46 [51-250]

Wildsmith, Brian
Amazing World of Words (Illus. by Brian Wildsmith)
Emerg Lib - v25 - Ja '98 - p51 [51-250]

Brian Wildsmith's Amazing World of Words (Illus. by Brian Wildsmith)
> HB Guide - v8 - Fall '97 - p337 [51-250]
> Magpies - v12 - My '97 - p22+ [251-500]
> SLJ - v43 - My '97 - p126 [51-250]

Jack and the Meanstalk
> Magpies - v12 - Jl '97 - p28 [51-250]

Joseph (Illus. by Brian Wildsmith)
> BW - v28 - Ja 4 '98 - p11 [251-500]
> PW - v245 - Ja 26 '98 - p86 [51-250]
> Spec - v279 - D 6 '97 - p44 [51-250]

Wilkes, Angela
Children's Quick and Easy Cookbook
> BL - v94 - D 15 '97 - p696 [51-250]
> Obs - D 7 '97 - p18* [1-50]
> PW - v244 - O 27 '97 - p79 [1-50]
> SLJ - v44 - Ja '98 - p135 [51-250]

My First Word Board Book
> HB Guide - v8 - Fall '97 - p257 [51-250]
> SLJ - v43 - Jl '97 - p79 [51-250]

Wilkes, Maria D
Little Clearing in the Woods (Illus. by Dan Andreasen)
> KR - v66 - Ap 1 '98 - p503 [51-250]

Little Town at the Crossroads (Illus. by Dan Andreasen)
> HB Guide - v8 - Fall '97 - p310 [51-250]
> SLJ - v43 - Jl '97 - p99 [51-250]

Wilkinson, Beth
Papermaking for Kids (Illus. by Albert Molnar)
> PW - v244 - D 15 '97 - p60 [51-250]

Wilks, Mike
Metamorphosis
> Ch BWatch - v8 - Ja '98 - p1 [51-250]

Willard, Nancy
Beauty and the Beast (Illus. by Barry Moser)
> SLJ - v43 - N '97 - p41 [1-50]

Cracked Corn and Snow Ice Cream (Illus. by Jane Dyer)
> BL - v94 - N 1 '97 - p469 [51-250]
> CBRS - v26 - S '97 - p9 [51-250]
> KR - v65 - Jl 15 '97 - p1120 [51-250]
> PW - v244 - Jl 28 '97 - p73 [51-250]

The Magic Cornfield (Illus. by Nancy Willard)
> CBRS - v25 - My '97 - p114 [51-250]
> CCB-B - v50 - Je '97 - p378+ [51-250]
> HB Guide - v8 - Fall '97 - p285 [51-250]
> SLJ - v43 - Ap '97 - p118+ [51-250]

The Tortilla Cat (Illus. by Jeanette Winter)
> BL - v94 - Mr 1 '98 - p1136 [51-250]
> KR - v66 - F 15 '98 - p275 [51-250]
> SLJ - v44 - Mr '98 - p190 [51-250]

Williams, Arlene
Dragon Soup (Illus. by Sally J Smith)
> RT - v51 - O '97 - p133 [1-50]

Williams, Brian
Ancient China
> Emerg Lib - v24 - My '97 - p57 [1-50]
> SE - v61 - Ap '97 - p14* [1-50]

World Book Looks at the Sea and Its Marvels
> SB - v33 - O '97 - p209 [251-500]

Williams, Carol Lynch
If I Forget, You Remember
> KR - v65 - D 15 '97 - p1844 [51-250]
> PW - v245 - Ja 5 '98 - p68 [51-250]
> SLJ - v44 - Mr '98 - p226 [51-250]

The True Colors of Caitlynne Jackson
> y BL - v94 - Mr 15 '98 - p1218 [1-50]
> y BL - v94 - Mr 15 '98 - p1226 [1-50]
> y HB Guide - v8 - Fall '97 - p316 [51-250]
> y JAAL - v41 - O '97 - p160 [51-250]
> PW - v245 - Mr 16 '98 - p67 [1-50]
> y VOYA - v21 - Ap '98 - p39 [1-50]
> y VOYA - v21 - Ap '98 - p41 [1-50]

Williams, Frances
Human Body
> Ch BWatch - v7 - Jl '97 - p8 [1-50]
> HB Guide - v8 - Fall '97 - p356+ [51-250]

SB - v33 - Ag '97 - p187 [1-50]
SLJ - v43 - Ag '97 - p176 [51-250]

Williams, Jeanne
The Confederate Fiddle
y   BL - v94 - Mr 15 '98 - p1236 [51-250]
     Ch BWatch - v8 - Ja '98 - p4 [51-250]

Williams, John, 1905, Mar., 3-
Projects with Flight
     SB - v32 - D '96 - p259 [1-50]

Williams, John, 1936-
Water Projects
     SLJ - v44 - Ap '98 - p157 [51-250]

Williams, John, 1939-
Houses and Homes
     Sch Lib - v45 - Ag '97 - p155 [51-250]

Toys and Games
     Sch Lib - v45 - Ag '97 - p155 [51-250]

Williams, Laura E
Behind the Bedroom Wall
     Ch BWatch - v7 - N '97 - p3 [51-250]

Williams, Linda
La Viejecita Que No Le Tenia Miedo A Nada (Illus. by Megan Lloyd)
     HB Guide - v8 - Fall '97 - p339 [51-250]

Williams, Marcia
The Adventures of Robin Hood (Illus. by Marcia Williams)
     BL - v94 - Mr 1 '98 - p1125 [51-250]

The Iliad and the Odyssey (Illus. by Marcia Williams)
     SLJ - v43 - My '97 - p126 [51-250]

King Arthur and the Knights of the Round Table
     PW - v244 - Je 2 '97 - p73 [1-50]

Williams, Margery
The Velveteen Rabbit (Illus. by Loretta Krupinski)
     HB Guide - v8 - Fall '97 - p295 [51-250]
     SLJ - v43 - Jl '97 - p79 [51-250]

Williams, Melanie
Fabric Painting
     Ch BWatch - v7 - Je '97 - p4 [51-250]

Williams, Rose
The Barefoot Book of Fairies (Illus. by Robin T Barrett)
     TES - D 26 '97 - p22 [51-250]

The Book of Fairies (Illus. by Robin T Barrett)
     AB - v100 - N 17 '97 - p1260+ [251-500]
     BL - v94 - Ja 1 '98 - p808 [51-250]
     Ch BWatch - v7 - D '97 - p2 [1-50]
     KR - v65 - N 1 '97 - p1651 [51-250]
     PW - v244 - O 27 '97 - p79 [51-250]
     SLJ - v44 - Ja '98 - p135 [51-250]
     SLJ - v44 - F '98 - p128 [51-250]

Williams, Suzanne
Library Lil (Illus. by Steven Kellogg)
     BL - v94 - O 15 '97 - p417+ [51-250]
     BW - v28 - Ja 4 '98 - p11 [251-500]
     Inst - v107 - Ja '98 - p26 [51-250]
     KR - v65 - O 1 '97 - p1539 [51-250]
     PW - v244 - O 6 '97 - p82+ [51-250]
     SLJ - v43 - N '97 - p102+ [51-250]

Made in China (Illus. by Andrea Fong)
     Ch BWatch - v7 - Mr '97 - p5 [51-250]
     Ch BWatch - v8 - Ja '98 - p7+ [51-250]
     HB Guide - v8 - Fall '97 - p389 [51-250]
     SLJ - v43 - Jl '97 - p113 [51-250]

My Dog Never Says Please (Illus. by Tedd Arnold)
     CBRS - v25 - Jl '97 - p150 [51-250]
     HB Guide - v8 - Fall '97 - p285 [51-250]
     SLJ - v43 - Je '97 - p103 [51-250]

Williams, Sylvia
Alex Haley: I Have a Dream
     Ch BWatch - v7 - S '97 - p7 [1-50]

Williams, Tony
Fizz, the Wildest Boy in the Universe
     Magpies - v12 - My '97 - p8* [51-250]

Williams, Vera B
Lucky Song (Illus. by Vera B Williams)
> BL - v94 - O 1 '97 - p332 [51-250]
> BW - v27 - D 7 '97 - p21 [51-250]
> CBRS - v26 - N '97 - p30 [1-50]
> HB - v73 - S '97 - p566+ [51-250]
> KR - v65 - Je 15 '97 - p959 [51-250]
> PW - v244 - Je 23 '97 - p91 [51-250]
> SLJ - v43 - Ag '97 - p144 [51-250]

More More More, Said the Baby (Illus. by Vera B Williams)
> PW - v244 - Ag 25 '97 - p73 [51-250]

Williamson, Julie
The Melding
> Magpies - v12 - S '97 - p7* [51-250]

Williamson, Sarah
Kids Cook!
> Ch BWatch - v7 - S '97 - p5 [51-250]

Willing, Karen Bates
Fabric Fun for Kids
> SLJ - v44 - Ap '98 - p157 [51-250]

Willis, Jeanne
The Rascally Cake (Illus. by Korky Paul)
> NS - v126 - D 5 '97 - p62 [1-50]

Sloth's Shoes (Illus. by Tony Ross)
> KR - v66 - Mr 1 '98 - p346 [51-250]
> Obs - D 7 '97 - p17* [51-250]
> PW - v245 - F 23 '98 - p76 [51-250]
> TES - N 7 '97 - p5* [51-250]

Willis, Meredith Sue
Marco's Monster
> Inst - v106 - Ap '97 - p27 [51-250]
> Inst - v106 - My '97 - p21 [1-50]

Willis, Nancy Carol
The Robins in Your Backyard (Illus. by Nancy Carol Willis)
> CCB-B - v50 - Je '97 - p379 [51-250]
> SLJ - v43 - Jl '97 - p89 [51-250]

Willis, Patricia
Danger along the Ohio
> HB Guide - v8 - Fall '97 - p310 [51-250]
> SLJ - v43 - My '97 - p140 [51-250]

Willner-Pardo, Gina
Daphne Eloise Slater, Who's Tall for Her Age (Illus. by Glo Coalson)
> BL - v93 - Ag '97 - p1902+ [51-250]
> CBRS - v26 - N '97 - p33 [51-250]
> CCB-B - v51 - N '97 - p106 [51-250]
> HB - v73 - S '97 - p582+ [51-250]

Spider Storch's Carpool Catastrophe (Illus. by Nick Sharratt)
> SLJ - v43 - N '97 - p103 [51-250]

Spider Storch's Teacher Torture (Illus. by Nick Sharratt)
> BL - v94 - Ja 1 '98 - p817 [51-250]
> KR - v65 - O 15 '97 - p1590 [51-250]
> SLJ - v43 - N '97 - p103 [51-250]

Wills, Jeanne
What Do You Want to Be, Brian? (Illus. by Mary Rees)
> TES - My 30 '97 - p8* [501+]

Wills, Steven R
Mind-Boggling Astronomy
> ASBYP - v29 - Sum '96 - p40 [501+]

Willson, Sarah
The Rugrats' Book of Chanukah (Illus. by Barry Goldberg)
> PW - v244 - O 6 '97 - p53 [51-250]

Wilmink, Willem
Ali Baba En De Veertig Tekenaars
> Bkbird - v34 - Win '96 - p58 [1-50]

Wilner, Barry
Reggie Miller
> Ch BWatch - v7 - S '97 - p8 [1-50]

Superstars of Women's Golf
> Ch BWatch - v7 - S '97 - p8 [1-50]
> HB Guide - v8 - Fall '97 - p369 [51-250]

Wilson, A N
Hazel the Guinea-Pig (Illus. by Jonathan Heale)
>Bks Keeps - Jl '97 - p23 [51-250]

Wilson, April
The Christmas Deer
>Ch BWatch - v7 - N '97 - p6 [51-250]

Wilson, Bob
Bing Bang Boogie, It's a Boy Scout
>Sch Lib - v45 - N '97 - p202 [51-250]

Wilson, Budge
Duff the Giant Killer (Illus. by Kim LaFave)
>CM:CanRev - v4 - S 19 '97 - pONL [251-500]
>Quill & Q - v63 - Jl '97 - p50 [51-250]

The Long Wait (Illus. by Eugenie Fernandes)
>CBRS - v25 - Jl '97 - p150+ [51-250]
>Ren Q - v50 - Aut '97 - p27 [51-250]

Wilson, Clive
The Kingfisher Young People's Book of Music
>r SE - v61 - Ap '97 - p12* [1-50]

Wilson, Colin
Mysteries of the Universe
>SLJ - v44 - F '98 - p128 [51-250]

UFOs and Aliens
>SLJ - v44 - F '98 - p128 [51-250]
>TES - N 7 '97 - p13* [501+]

Wilson, Eric
The Case of the Golden Boy
>Can CL - v23 - Fall '97 - p73+ [501+]

Escape from Big Muddy
>Quill & Q - v64 - F '98 - p49 [251-500]

Wilson, Etta
A Child's Story of Easter (Illus. by Mary Ann Utt)
>HB Guide - v8 - Fall '97 - p321 [51-250]

Wilson, Forrest
What It Feels like to Be a Building
>SB - v32 - D '96 - p259 [1-50]

Wilson, Jacqueline
Bad Girls
>TES - My 2 '97 - p8* [1-50]

The Bed and Breakfast Star
>Bks Keeps - My '97 - p4+ [501+]

Double Act (Illus. by Nick Sharratt)
>BL - v94 - Ja 1 '98 - p799 [51-250]
>KR - v66 - Ja 1 '98 - p63 [51-250]
>PW - v245 - Ja 12 '98 - p60 [51-250]
>SLJ - v44 - Mr '98 - p226 [51-250]

The Lottie Project (Illus. by Nick Sharratt)
>Bks Keeps - S '97 - p27 [51-250]
>Sch Lib - v45 - Ag '97 - p148 [51-250]
>y TES - Jl 4 '97 - p11* [251-500]

The Monster Story-Teller (Illus. by Nick Sharratt)
>Bks Keeps - My '97 - p22 [51-250]

The Suitcase Kid
>BL - v94 - O 15 '97 - p407 [51-250]
>CBRS - v26 - O '97 - p24 [51-250]
>CCB-B - v50 - Jl '97 - p416+ [51-250]
>Ch BWatch - v8 - Ja '98 - p4 [51-250]
>KR - v65 - Ag 1 '97 - p1230 [51-250]
>SLJ - v43 - S '97 - p227 [51-250]
>TES - N 14 '97 - p11* [51-250]

Wilson, John, 1951-
Across Frozen Seas
>Quill & Q - v63 - O '97 - p37 [251-500]

Weet's Quest
>CM:CanRev - v4 - F 13 '98 - pONL [251-500]

Wilson, Lois Miriam
Miriam, Mary and Me
>CBRA - '96 - p511 [51-250]

Wilson, Lori Lee
The Salem Witch Trials
>y BL - v94 - S 1 '97 - p105 [51-250]
>CCB-B - v51 - S '97 - p31 [51-250]
>Cur R - v37 - N '97 - p12 [51-250]
>y SLJ - v43 - Ag '97 - p178 [51-250]
>y SLJ - v43 - D '97 - p29 [1-50]

Wilson, Nancy Hope
Old People, Frogs, and Albert (Illus. by Marcy Dunn Ramsey)
> BL - v94 - S 15 '97 - p236 [51-250]
> CBRS - v26 - Ja '98 - p56+ [51-250]
> KR - v65 - Je 15 '97 - p959 [51-250]
> SLJ - v43 - N '97 - p103 [51-250]

Wilson, Sarah
Good Zap, Little Grog (Illus. by Susan Meddaugh)
> PW - v244 - O 13 '97 - p77 [1-50]

What Do People Do? (Illus. by Josie Yee)
> PW - v244 - D 1 '97 - p55 [1-50]

Wilson-Max, Ken
Big Blue Engine
> Books - v10 - S '96 - p24 [51-250]

Big Red Fire Truck
> PW - v244 - S 29 '97 - p91 [51-250]
> SLJ - v44 - F '98 - p93 [51-250]

Big Silver Space Shuttle
> PW - v245 - Ja 26 '98 - p93 [51-250]

Little Green Tow Truck
> BL - v94 - D 15 '97 - p700 [1-50]
> HB Guide - v8 - Fall '97 - p257 [51-250]

Winch, Gordon
The Grammar Handbook for Word-Wise Kids (Illus. by Jane Wade)
> CBRA - '96 - p516 [51-250]

Winch, John
The Old Woman Who Loved to Read (Illus. by John Winch)
> Ch BWatch - v7 - Ap '97 - p6 [1-50]
> HB Guide - v8 - Fall '97 - p285 [51-250]
> Inst - v107 - S '97 - p21 [1-50]
> PW - v245 - Mr 16 '98 - p67 [1-50]
> SLJ - v43 - My '97 - p117 [51-250]

Winer, Yvonne
Nanangka (Illus. by Marianne Yamaguchi)
> Magpies - v12 - Mr '97 - p35 [251-500]

Spiders Spin Webs (Illus. by Karen Lloyd-Jones)
> Magpies - v12 - Mr '97 - p24 [251-500]

Wing, Natasha
Jalapeno Bagels (Illus. by Robert Casilla)
> SE - v61 - Ap '97 - p13* [1-50]

Wingate, Philippa
The Internet for Beginners
> Sch Lib - v45 - Ag '97 - p156 [51-250]

Winkelaar, Peter R
Your First Horse Book
> SLJ - v43 - Jl '97 - p113 [51-250]

Winner, Cherie
Coyotes
> ASBYP - v29 - Sum '96 - p40+ [251-500]

The Sunflower Family
> Am Sci - v85 - N '97 - p560 [51-250]

Winnick, Karen B
Mr. Lincoln's Whiskers (Illus. by Karen B Winnick)
> Emerg Lib - v24 - My '97 - p64 [51-250]
> RT - v51 - O '97 - p149+ [51-250]

Winslow, Vicki
Follow the Leader (Illus. by Colin Bootman)
> BL - v94 - N 1 '97 - p474 [51-250]
> KR - v65 - N 1 '97 - p1652 [51-250]
> PW - v244 - N 24 '97 - p74 [51-250]
> SLJ - v43 - D '97 - p132 [51-250]

Winters, Kay
The Teeny Tiny Ghost (Illus. by Lynn Munsinger)
> BL - v94 - S 1 '97 - p141 [51-250]
> CBRS - v26 - N '97 - p30 [51-250]
> CCB-B - v51 - N '97 - p106+ [51-250]
> PW - v244 - O 6 '97 - p48 [51-250]
> SLJ - v43 - N '97 - p103+ [51-250]

Wolf Watch (Illus. by Laura Regan)
> BL - v94 - N 1 '97 - p485 [51-250]
> CBRS - v26 - F '98 - p78 [1-50]
> Ch BWatch - v8 - Ja '98 - p3 [1-50]

KR - v65 - O 1 '97 - p1539 [51-250]
NYTBR - v102 - N 16 '97 - p58+
[501+]
PW - v244 - O 27 '97 - p75 [51-250]
SLJ - v43 - N '97 - p104 [51-250]

Winthrop, Elizabeth
As the Crow Flies (Illus. by Joan Sandin)
KR - v66 - Ap 15 '98 - p588 [51-250]

The Battle for the Castle
BL - v94 - N 1 '97 - p475 [1-50]

The Battle for the Castle (Winthrop). Audio Version
BL - v94 - N 1 '97 - p495 [51-250]
SLJ - v43 - S '97 - p164 [51-250]

The Castle in the Attic. Audio Version
SLJ - v43 - Ap '97 - p80+ [51-250]

The Little Humpbacked Horse (Illus. by Alexander Koshkin)
Ch BWatch - v7 - My '97 - p4 [1-50]
Ch BWatch - v7 - Jl '97 - p6 [1-50]
HB Guide - v8 - Fall '97 - p336 [51-250]
SLJ - v43 - Ap '97 - p132 [51-250]

Wise, Noreen
America the Beautiful
Ch BWatch - v7 - Ap '97 - p1 [1-50]

Dog Named Zog (Illus. by Susan Tait Porcaro)
Ch BWatch - v7 - Ap '97 - p1 [1-50]

Muffin Huff 'N Puff
Ch BWatch - v7 - Ap '97 - p1 [1-50]

Wise, William
Perfect Pancakes, if You Please (Illus. by Richard Egielski)
BW - v27 - Jl 6 '97 - p11 [251-500]
CBRS - v25 - Je '97 - p125 [51-250]
HB Guide - Fall '97 - p285 [51-250]

Wiseman, Ann Sayre
Making Things. Rev. Ed. (Illus. by Ann Sayre Wiseman)
SLJ - v43 - Ag '97 - p178 [51-250]

Wiseman, Eva
A Place Not Home
CBRA - '96 - p495 [51-250]

Wisler, G Clifton
The Drummer Boy of Vicksburg
HB Guide - v8 - Fall '97 - p310 [51-250]

Mustang Flats
BL - v93 - Ag '97 - p1903 [51-250]
CCB-B - v51 - S '97 - p31 [51-250]
KR - v65 - Je 1 '97 - p882 [51-250]
SLJ - v43 - Jl '97 - p99 [51-250]

Wisniewski, David
Golem (Illus. by David Wisniewski)
RT - v51 - S '97 - p58 [51-250]
RT - v51 - D '97 - p307 [51-250]

Rain Player (Illus. by David Wisniewski)
CLW - v68 - D '97 - p82 [51-250]

The Secret Knowledge of Grown-Ups (Illus. by David Wisniewski)
BL - v94 - Mr 1 '98 - p1132 [51-250]
KR - v66 - Ap 1 '98 - p503 [51-250]
PW - v245 - F 9 '98 - p95 [51-250]
SLJ - v44 - Mr '98 - p207 [51-250]

Sundiata, Lion King of Mali (Illus. by David Wisniewski)
CLW - v68 - D '97 - p82 [51-250]

Witanachchi, Lalitha K
The Paddy Bird
Bkbird - v35 - Fall '97 - p52 [51-250]

Witkowski, Dan
The Funhouse Mirrors
ASBYP - v29 - Sum '96 - p41 [251-500]

Wittmann, Patricia
Buffalo Thunder (Illus. by Bert Dodson)
BL - v94 - S 15 '97 - p243+ [51-250]
CBRS - v26 - Win '98 - p65 [51-250]
SLJ - v43 - S '97 - p198 [51-250]

Woelfle, Gretchen
The Wind at Work
BL - v94 - S 1 '97 - p121 [51-250]

y   Kliatt - v31 - N '97 - p30 [51-250]

Wojciechowska, Maia
Shadow of a Bull (Rivela). Audio Version
BL - v94 - F 15 '98 - p1027 [51-250]
SLJ - v43 - D '97 - p70 [51-250]
SLJ - v44 - Ap '98 - p39 [1-50]

Wojciechowski, Susan
Beany (Not Beanhead) and the Magic Crystal (Illus. by Susanna Natti)
CCB-B - v50 - Jl '97 - p417 [51-250]
KR - v65 - Je 1 '97 - p882 [51-250]
Par Ch - Awards '97 - p5 [51-250]
SLJ - v43 - Jl '97 - p79 [51-250]

Beany (Not Beanhead) and the Magic Crystal (Illus. by Susanna Natti)
Magpies - v12 - My '97 - p32 [51-250]

Wolf, Bernard
HIV Positive
BL - v94 - Ja 1 '98 - p735 [1-50]
CBRS - v25 - Jl '97 - p153 [51-250]
HB Guide - v8 - Fall '97 - p357 [51-250]
SLJ - v43 - Je '97 - p150 [51-250]

Wolf, Ema
Maruja (Illus. by Jorge Sanzol)
SLJ - v44 - F '98 - p132 [51-250]

Wolf, Gita
Mala: A Women's Folktale (Illus. by Annouchka Gravel Galouchko)
CBRA - '96 - p504 [51-250]

The Very Hungry Lion (Illus. by Indrapramit Roy)
CBRA - '96 - p504+ [51-250]
ECEJ - v25 - Fall '97 - p42 [51-250]

Wolf, Jake
Daddy, Could I Have an Elephant? (Illus. by Marylin Hafner)
NYTBR - v102 - Ap 27 '97 - p29 [1-50]

Wolfe, Gillian
Dulwich Picture Gallery Children's Art Book (Illus. by David Teniers)
Obs - Jl 20 '97 - p18* [51-250]
TES - My 16 '97 - pR4+ [251-500]

Wolff, Ashley
Stella and Roy (Illus. by Ashley Wolff)
SLJ - v44 - Ja '98 - p43 [1-50]

Wolff, Ferida
Halloween Fun for Everyone (Illus. by Judy Lanfredi)
PW - v244 - O 6 '97 - p50 [1-50]
SLJ - v44 - Ja '98 - p107 [51-250]

On Halloween Night (Illus. by Dolores Avendano)
PW - v244 - O 6 '97 - p50 [1-50]

Pink Slippers, Bat Mitzvah Blues
BW - v27 - D 7 '97 - p20 [1-50]

A Year for Kiko (Illus. by Joung Un Kim)
BL - v94 - D 15 '97 - p704 [51-250]
CBRS - v26 - Win '98 - p65+ [51-250]
CCB-B - v51 - N '97 - p107 [51-250]
KR - v65 - Jl 15 '97 - p1119 [51-250]

Wolkstein, Diane
Bouki Dances the Kokioko (Illus. by Jesse Sweetwater)
BL - v94 - S 15 '97 - p238+ [51-250]
CBRS - v26 - D '97 - p42 [1-50]
CCB-B - v51 - S '97 - p31+ [51-250]
KR - v65 - O 1 '97 - p1539 [51-250]
PW - v244 - O 20 '97 - p76 [51-250]
SLJ - v43 - N '97 - p112+ [51-250]

Esther's Story (Illus. by Juan Wijngaard)
PW - v245 - Ja 26 '98 - p87 [1-50]

The White Wave (Illus. by Ed Young)
RT - v51 - D '97 - p332 [51-250]

Wong, Janet S
A Suitcase of Seaweed and Other Poems (Illus. by Janet S Wong)
SE - v61 - Ap '97 - p12* [1-50]

The Won't-Pick-Up-Toys Cure (Illus. by Bruce Whatley)
PW - v244 - Ag 25 '97 - p74 [51-250]

Wood, A J
Search for the Lost City (Illus. by Maggie Downer)
Sch Lib - v45 - Ag '97 - p134 [51-250]

Wood, Angela
Jewish Festivals
SLJ - v43 - D '97 - p136 [51-250]

Passover
Sch Lib - v45 - Ag '97 - p149 [51-250]

Wood, Audrey
Birdsong (Illus. by Robert Florczak)
BL - v94 - O 1 '97 - p339 [51-250]
CCB-B - v51 - O '97 - p71 [51-250]
KR - v65 - Ag 15 '97 - p1315 [51-250]
PW - v244 - Jl 7 '97 - p68 [51-250]

Bright and Early Thursday Evening (Illus. by Don Wood)
NY - v73 - O 6 '97 - p115 [51-250]
RT - v51 - S '97 - p52 [51-250]
RT - v51 - O '97 - p132 [1-50]

The Bunyans (Illus. by David Shannon)
RT - v51 - O '97 - p146 [1-50]
SLJ - v43 - N '97 - p41 [1-50]

The Flying Dragon Room (Illus. by Mark Teague)
Inst - v106 - My '97 - p19 [1-50]

Sweet Dream Pie (Illus. by Mark Teague)
BL - v94 - F 15 '98 - p1021 [51-250]
CCB-B - v51 - Mr '98 - p262+ [51-250]
KR - v66 - Ja 15 '98 - p120 [51-250]
PW - v245 - F 2 '98 - p89 [51-250]
SLJ - v44 - Mr '98 - p190 [51-250]

Wood, Brian
The Cramp Twins: Swamp Fever
Books - v11 - Ag '97 - p15 [51-250]

Wood, Douglas
Rabbit and the Moon (Illus. by Leslie Baker)
BL - v94 - F 15 '98 - p1016 [51-250]
KR - v66 - Ja 15 '98 - p120 [51-250]
PW - v245 - F 23 '98 - p75 [51-250]

Wood, Frances M
Becoming Rosemary
HB Guide - v8 - Fall '97 - p310 [51-250]
y   VOYA - v20 - Ap '97 - p34+ [251-500]

Wood, Jakki
Across the Big Blue Sea (Illus. by Jakki Wood)
KR - v66 - Ap 1 '98 - p503 [51-250]
SLJ - v44 - Ap '98 - p111 [51-250]

Moo Moo, Brown Cow (Illus. by Rog Bonner)
HB Guide - v8 - Fall '97 - p257 [51-250]

Wood, June Rae
Turtle on a Fence Post
y   KR - v65 - S 1 '97 - p1396 [51-250]
SLJ - v43 - S '97 - p227+ [51-250]

Wood, Marion
The World of Native Americans
BL - v94 - Mr 15 '98 - p1243 [51-250]

Wood, Michele
Going Back Home (Illus. by Michele Wood)
RT - v51 - S '97 - p53 [51-250]
RT - v51 - D '97 - p307+ [51-250]
SLJ - v43 - Jl '97 - p106 [51-250]

Wood, Nancy
The Serpent's Tongue
y   BL - v94 - D 1 '97 - p619 [51-250]
y   BL - v94 - D 15 '97 - p684 [1-50]
y   BL - v94 - Ja 1 '98 - p733 [1-50]
y   HMR - Win '97 - p46 [51-250]
y   PW - v244 - O 13 '97 - p76 [51-250]
SLJ - v43 - D '97 - p150 [51-250]

Wood, Richard
Great Inventions
ASBYP - v29 - Sum '96 - p55+ [501+]

Kitchens through the Ages
Bks Keeps - N '97 - p27 [51-250]
Sch Lib - v45 - N '97 - p208 [51-250]

Loos through the Ages
Bks Keeps - N '97 - p27 [51-250]
Sch Lib - v45 - N '97 - p208 [51-250]

Wood, Ted
Ghosts of the Southwest (Illus. by Ted Wood)
HB Guide - v8 - Fall '97 - p318 [51-250]

SLJ - v43 - Ap '97 - p162+ [51-250]

Iditarod Dream (Illus. by Ted Wood)
RT - v51 - N '97 - p243 [51-250]
y   VOYA - v20 - Ag '97 - p167 [51-250]

Wood, Tim
Ancient Wonders
SLJ - v44 - Ja '98 - p135 [251-500]

Woodbury, Mary
A Gift for Johnny Know-It-All (Illus. by Barbara Hartmann)
CBRA - '96 - p495 [51-250]

The Invisible Polly McDoodle
Can CL - v23 - Fall '97 - p73+ [501+]

Jess and the Runaway Grandpa
y   BIC - v26 - My '97 - p33 [251-500]
Ch Bk News - v20 - Sum '97 - p30 [51-250]
y   JAAL - v41 - N '97 - p246 [51-250]
Quill & Q - v63 - My '97 - p40 [251-500]

Woodruff, Elvira
Dear Levi (Illus. by Beth Peck)
PW - v245 - F 9 '98 - p98 [1-50]

The Orphan of Ellis Island
BL - v93 - Je 1 '97 - p1707 [51-250]
CBRS - v25 - Je '97 - p132 [51-250]
HB Guide - v8 - Fall '97 - p311 [51-250]
SLJ - v43 - My '97 - p140 [51-250]

Woodruff, John
Magnetism
BL - v94 - Mr 15 '98 - p1237 [51-250]

Woods, Tim
Houses and Homes
SLJ - v44 - Ap '98 - p157 [51-250]

Woodson, Marion
The Amazon Influence
Can CL - v23 - Fall '97 - p73+ [501+]

Woodward, Richard
The Pillow King
CBRA - '96 - p461 [51-250]

Woodworth, Deborah
Compassion: The Story of Clara Barton (Illus. by Leon Baxter)
SLJ - v44 - Mr '98 - p198 [51-250]

Woodworth, Viki
Do Pencils Grow in the Summer? (Illus. by Viki Woodworth)
SLJ - v44 - Mr '98 - p190 [51-250]

Do Zebras Bloom in the Spring? (Illus. by Viki Woodworth)
SLJ - v44 - Mr '98 - p190 [51-250]

Woog, Adam
The Beatles
SLJ - v43 - D '97 - p150 [51-250]

Wooldridge, Connie Nordhielm
Wicked Jack (Illus. by Will Hillenbrand)
SLJ - v43 - N '97 - p41 [1-50]

Woollam, Ray
Twelve Polar Bears and a Dog (Illus. by Kathleen Lanier)
CBRA - '96 - p500 [51-250]

Word Dance
p   Inst - v106 - My '97 - p8 [1-50]

Working in Airports
TES - O 17 '97 - p19* [51-250]

Working in Buildings and Property
TES - O 17 '97 - p19* [51-250]

Working in Enviromental Services
TES - O 17 '97 - p19* [51-250]

Working in Local Government
TES - O 17 '97 - p19* [51-250]

Working in Manufacturing
TES - O 17 '97 - p19* [51-250]

Working in Teaching
TES - O 17 '97 - p19* [51-250]

Working in Transport and Distribution
>TES - O 17 '97 - p19* [51-250]

Working in TV, Film and Radio
>TES - O 17 '97 - p19* [51-250]

The World Almanac and Book of Facts 1923-
>r   JOYS - v11 - Fall '97 - p78 [1-50]

The World Almanac for Kids 1998
>r   Ch BWatch - v7 - S '97 - p5 [51-250]

The World Book 1998 Multimedia Encyclopedia. Deluxe Ed. Electronic Media Version
>yr   BL - v94 - Ja 1 '98 - p844+ [501+]
>yr   LJ - v123 - F 15 '98 - p179 [51-250]
>r   PW - v244 - N 3 '97 - p87 [51-250]

The World Book Encyclopedia. 1997 Ed., Vols. 1-22
>r   BL - v94 - S 15 '97 - p260 [251-500]

The World Book Encyclopedia 1997. Electronic Media Version
>r   TES - My 2 '97 - pR3 [251-500]

World Book Encyclopedia, Inc.
Papier Mache
>Ch BWatch - v7 - N '97 - p5 [51-250]

The World Book Encyclopedia of Science. 1997 Ed., Vols. 1-8
>r   BL - v93 - Ag '97 - p1924 [51-250]
>r   SLJ - v43 - N '97 - p145 [51-250]

The World Book Multimedia Encyclopedia 1997. Electronic Media Version
>r   Magpies - v12 - S '97 - p20+ [501+]
>r   Sch Lib - v45 - N '97 - p197 [501+]

The World Book of Math Power. Vols. 1-2
>Math T - v90 - O '97 - p606 [51-250]

World Book's Young Scientist. Vols. 1-10
>r   BL - v94 - D 1 '97 - p662 [251-500]

World Wildlife Fund (U.S.)
Colors
>BL - v94 - O 15 '97 - p412 [51-250]
>PW - v244 - Ag 25 '97 - p74 [1-50]

Mothers and Babies
>PW - v244 - Ag 25 '97 - p74 [1-50]

Spots
>BL - v94 - O 15 '97 - p412 [51-250]
>PW - v244 - Ag 25 '97 - p74 [1-50]

Stripes
>BL - v94 - O 15 '97 - p412 [51-250]
>PW - v244 - Ag 25 '97 - p74 [1-50]

Worldlife Fund (U.S.)
Animal ABC's
>PW - v244 - Ag 25 '97 - p74 [1-50]

Wormell, Mary
Hilda Hen's Scary Night
>PW - v244 - Jl 21 '97 - p203 [1-50]

Wormser, Richard
American Childhoods
>RT - v51 - D '97 - p333 [51-250]

Wright, Alexandra
Alice in Pastaland (Illus. by Reagan Word)
>CBRS - v26 - Win '98 - p67 [51-250]

Wright, Betty Ren
The Ghost in Room 11 (Illus. by Jacqueline Rogers)
>BL - v94 - Mr 1 '98 - p1136+ [51-250]
>CCB-B - v51 - Ap '98 - p300+ [51-250]
>PW - v245 - Ja 5 '98 - p68 [51-250]
>SLJ - v44 - Mr '98 - p190 [51-250]

Too Many Secrets
>BL - v94 - O 1 '97 - p333 [51-250]
>CCB-B - v51 - O '97 - p72 [51-250]
>HB - v73 - Jl '97 - p465+ [51-250]
>KR - v65 - Je 15 '97 - p959 [51-250]
>SLJ - v43 - Ag '97 - p144 [51-250]

Wright, Chris
Buddhism for Today
> Sch Lib - v45 - N '97 - p205+ [51-250]
> y   TES - N 28 '97 - p17* [501+]

Wright, Cliff
Santa's Ark
> BL - v94 - D 15 '97 - p704 [51-250]
> CBRS - v26 - N '97 - p30 [51-250]
> Ch BWatch - v8 - Ja '98 - p8 [1-50]
> PW - v244 - O 6 '97 - p57 [1-50]

Wright, Courtni C
Wagon Train (Illus. by Gershom Griffith)
> BL - v93 - Je 1 '97 - p1701 [1-50]

Wright, David, 1943-
Computers
> ASBYP - v29 - Sum '96 - p50+ [251-500]

Wright, David K
Arthur Ashe: Breaking the Color Barrier in Tennis
> RT - v51 - O '97 - p139 [1-50]

P.T. Barnum (Illus. by Mike White)
> HB Guide - v8 - Fall '97 - p380 [1-50]

Wright, David R
Facts on File Environment Atlas
> r   BL - v94 - Mr 15 '98 - p1260 [251-500]

Wright, Lynn Floyd
Flick the Hero! (Illus. by Tony Waters)
> SLJ - v43 - Ag '97 - p144 [51-250]

Wroble, Lisa A
Kids in Colonial Times
> SLJ - v44 - Ap '98 - p126 [51-250]
> SLJ - v44 - Ap '98 - p127 [51-250]

Kids in the Middle Ages
> SLJ - v44 - Mr '98 - p207 [51-250]

Wu, Norbert
A City under the Sea
> SB - v33 - Ag '97 - p187 [1-50]
> SB - v33 - N '97 - p251 [501+]

Wukovits, John F
Annie Oakley
> HB Guide - v8 - Fall '97 - p398 [51-250]

The Black Cowboys
> Ch BWatch - v7 - D '97 - p4 [51-250]

Butch Cassidy
> SLJ - v44 - Ap '98 - p157 [51-250]

The Gunslingers
> HB Guide - v8 - Fall '97 - p398 [51-250]

Jesse James
> HB Guide - v8 - Fall '97 - p398 [51-250]
> SLJ - v43 - Ap '97 - p164 [51-250]

Vince Lombardi
> Ch BWatch - v7 - Je '97 - p2 [1-50]
> HB Guide - v8 - Fall '97 - p369 [51-250]

Wyatt Earp
> Ch BWatch - v7 - S '97 - p8 [1-50]
> HB Guide - v8 - Fall '97 - p398 [51-250]

Wulffson, Don L
The Kid Who Invented the Popsicle and Other Surprising Stories about Inventions
> BW - v27 - S 7 '97 - p11 [51-250]
> HB Guide - v8 - Fall '97 - p360 [51-250]

Wunderlich, Gooloo S
Nursing Staff in Hospitals and Nursing Homes
> SB - v32 - D '96 - p262 [51-250]

Wyatt, Isabel
Thorkill of Iceland
> Sch Lib - v45 - Ag '97 - p148+ [51-250]

Wyatt, Valerie
The Science Book for Girls and Other Intelligent Beings (Illus. by Pat Cupples)
> KR - v65 - Ag 15 '97 - p1315 [51-250]
> PW - v244 - S 1 '97 - p106 [1-50]

Wyeth, Sharon Dennis
Always My Dad (Illus. by Raul Colon)
>>> ECEJ - v25 - Fall '97 - p50 [1-50]
>>> PW - v244 - D 15 '97 - p60 [1-50]

Once on This River
> y   BL - v94 - D 15 '97 - p691+ [51-250]
>>> CCB-B - v51 - Ap '98 - p301 [51-250]
>>> KR - v65 - D 1 '97 - p1781 [51-250]
>>> PW - v244 - D 8 '97 - p73 [51-250]
>>> SLJ - v44 - Ap '98 - p139+ [51-250]

Wynne-Jones, Tim
The Book of Changes
>>> PW - v244 - Ag 11 '97 - p403 [1-50]

Dracula (Illus. by Laszlo Gal)
>>> CM:CanRev - v4 - Ja 16 '98 - pONL [251-500]
>>> Quill & Q - v63 - D '97 - p38 [501+]

The Hunchback of Notre Dame (Illus. by Bill Slavin)
>>> Bloom Rev - v17 - N '97 - p33 [51-250]
>>> KR - v65 - Jl 1 '97 - p1038 [51-250]
>>> PW - v244 - O 13 '97 - p75 [51-250]
>>> SLJ - v44 - Ap '98 - p132 [51-250]

The Maestro
>>> Ch BWatch - v7 - My '97 - p5+ [1-50]
> y   Emerg Lib - v24 - My '97 - p56 [51-250]
>>> PW - v245 - Mr 16 '98 - p67 [1-50]
> y   VOYA - v20 - Ap '97 - p35 [251-500]

Mouse in the Manger (Illus. by Elaine Blier)
>>> Can CL - v23 - Fall '97 - p85+ [501+]

Y

Yablonsky, Buster
*Class Trip to the Spooky Museum
(Illus. by Margeaux Lucas)*
>   PW - v244 - Ag 18 '97 - p94 [51-250]

Yaccarino, Dan
*Good Night, Mr. Night (Illus. by Dan
Yaccarino)*
>   BL - v94 - N 1 '97 - p485 [51-250]
>   CBRS - v26 - Win '98 - p66 [1-50]
>   CCB-B - v51 - Ja '98 - p182 [51-250]
>   KR - v65 - Ag 15 '97 - p1315 [51-250]
>   Par - v72 - D '97 - p202+ [1-50]
>   PW - v244 - Jl 21 '97 - p200 [51-250]

*If I Had a Robot (Illus. by Dan
Yaccarino)*
>   NYTBR - v102 - My 11 '97 - p24
>   [501+]
>   RT - v51 - O '97 - p133 [1-50]

*An Octopus Followed Me Home (Illus.
by Dan Yaccarino)*
>   BL - v93 - Ag '97 - p1908 [51-250]
>   Ch BWatch - v8 - Ja '98 - p3 [51-250]
>   KR - v65 - Ag 15 '97 - p1315 [51-250]
>   NW - v130 - D 1 '97 - p78 [1-50]
>   PW - v244 - O 20 '97 - p74+ [51-250]
>   SLJ - v44 - Ja '98 - p95 [51-250]

*Zoom! Zoom! Zoom! I'm Off to the
Moon! (Illus. by Dan Yaccarino)*
>   CBRS - v26 - Ja '98 - p54 [51-250]
>   HB - v73 - S '97 - p567 [51-250]
>   KR - v65 - Jl 15 '97 - p1119 [51-250]
>   NYTBR - v103 - Mr 15 '98 - p23 [1-50]
>   PW - v244 - Jl 21 '97 - p200 [51-250]
>   SLJ - v43 - D '97 - p103 [51-250]

Yagyu, Genichiro
The Soles of Your Feet
>   HB Guide - v8 - Fall '97 - p348 [51-250]

Yamamoto, Thoru
*Pickle's Book. Book and Electronic
Media Version*
>   PW - v245 - Ja 26 '98 - p93 [51-250]

Yanez, Alberto
*Este Libro Horroroso Sin Remedio
(Illus. by Raul Castillo)*
>   Bkbird - v35 - Fall '97 - p50 [1-50]

Yarbro, Chelsea Quinn
*Monet's Ghost (Illus. by Pat
Morrissey)*
>   y   BL - v93 - Je 1 '97 - p1687 [51-250]
>   y   BL - v94 - N 1 '97 - p475 [1-50]
>   y   CBRS - v25 - Ag '97 - p169 [51-250]
>   HB Guide - v8 - Fall '97 - p311 [51-250]
>   y   KR - v65 - Je 15 '97 - p960 [51-250]
>   y   SLJ - v43 - Je '97 - p129 [51-250]
>   y   VOYA - v20 - Ag '97 - p197+ [251-500]

Yashinsky, Dan
*Ghostwise: A Book of Midnight
Stories*
>   y   CCB-B - v51 - Mr '98 - p263 [51-250]
>   y   Kliatt - v31 - N '97 - p17 [51-250]
>   Quill & Q - v63 - Jl '97 - p48 [251-500]
>   y   VOYA - v20 - F '98 - p392 [251-500]

Yates, Irene
All about Color (Illus. by Jill Newton)
>   SLJ - v44 - Ap '98 - p127 [51-250]

SLJ - v44 - Ap '98 - p127 [51-250]

*All about Pattern (Illus. by Jill
Newton)*
SLJ - v44 - Ap '98 - p127 [51-250]
SLJ - v44 - Ap '98 - p127 [51-250]

All about Shape (Illus. by Jill Newton)
SLJ - v44 - F '98 - p105 [51-250]

All about Touch (Illus. by Jill Newton)
SLJ - v44 - F '98 - p105 [51-250]

*From Birth to Death (Illus. by
Graham Austin)*
BL - v94 - D 1 '97 - p630 [51-250]
CBRS - v26 - D '97 - p43 [1-50]
Ch BWatch - v7 - N '97 - p6 [1-50]
SLJ - v44 - Ja '98 - p99 [51-250]

Yates, Phillip
World's Silliest Jokes
Ch BWatch - v8 - Ja '98 - p8 [1-50]

Ye, Ting-Xing
*Three Monks, No Water (Illus. by
Harvey Chan)*
CM:CanRev - v4 - F 27 '98 - pONL
[51-250]
Quill & Q - v63 - O '97 - p43 [251-500]
SLJ - v43 - D '97 - p103+ [51-250]

Yee, Patrick
*Rosie Rabbit's Colors (Illus. by
Patrick Yee)*
PW - v245 - Ja 26 '98 - p93 [1-50]
SLJ - v44 - F '98 - p93 [51-250]

*Rosie Rabbit's Numbers (Illus. by
Patrick Yee)*
PW - v245 - Ja 26 '98 - p93 [1-50]
SLJ - v44 - F '98 - p93 [51-250]

*Rosie Rabbit's Opposites (Illus. by
Patrick Yee)*
KR - v66 - Ja 1 '98 - p64 [51-250]
PW - v245 - Ja 26 '98 - p93 [1-50]
SLJ - v44 - F '98 - p93 [51-250]

*Rosie Rabbit's Shapes (Illus. by
Patrick Yee)*
PW - v245 - Ja 26 '98 - p93 [1-50]
SLJ - v44 - F '98 - p93 [51-250]

Yee, Paul
Ghost Train (Illus. by Harvey Chan)
CBRA - '96 - p461+ [51-250]
Ch Bk News - v20 - Spr '97 - p35+
[251-500]
TES - Jl 25 '97 - p29 [51-250]

*Tales from Gold Mountain (Illus. by
Simon Ng)*
y   BL - v93 - Je 1 '97 - p1701 [1-50]
Ch Bk News - v20 - Spr '97 - p34 [251-
500]

Yee, Tammy
*Wildlife Coloring and Activity Books
(Illus. by Tammy Yee)*
Ch BWatch - v7 - O '97 - p3+ [51-250]

Yee, Wong Herbert
*Fireman Small to the Rescue (Illus. by
Wong Herbert Yee)*
KR - v66 - F 15 '98 - p276 [51-250]
PW - v245 - Mr 23 '98 - p101 [1-50]

*Mrs. Brown Went to Town (Illus. by
Wong Herbert Yee)*
RT - v51 - O '97 - p134 [1-50]

*The Officers' Ball (Illus. by Wong
Herbert Yee)*
HB Guide - v8 - Fall '97 - p286 [51-
250]
SLJ - v43 - My '97 - p117+ [51-250]
Trib Bks - Jl 13 '97 - p7 [51-250]

Sergeant Hippo's Busy Week
PW - v245 - Mr 23 '98 - p101 [1-50]

Yektai, Niki
*Bears at the Beach (Illus. by Niki
Yektai)*
RT - v51 - O '97 - p130 [1-50]

Yeoman, John
Mr. Nodd's Ark
Bks Keeps - N '97 - p22 [51-250]

*The Seven Voyages of Sinbad the
Sailor (Illus. by Quentin Blake)*
BL - v94 - Ja 1 '98 - p808+ [51-250]
HB - v74 - Mr '98 - p228 [51-250]
KR - v65 - O 1 '97 - p1540 [51-250]
PW - v244 - O 20 '97 - p77 [1-50]
SLJ - v43 - D '97 - p150 [51-250]

Yep, Laurence

The Case of the Goblin Pearls
    Ch BWatch - v7 - O '97 - p2 [1-50]
    HB Guide - v8 - Fall '97 - p311 [51-250]

The Cook's Family
    BL - v94 - Ja 1 '98 - p817 [51-250]
    KR - v65 - D 15 '97 - p1844 [51-250]
    PW - v245 - F 23 '98 - p78 [1-50]
    SLJ - v44 - Ap '98 - p140 [51-250]

Dragon Prince (Illus. by Kam Mak)
    CBRS - v26 - S '97 - p7 [1-50]
    CCB-B - v51 - D '97 - p144 [51-250]
    Ch BWatch - v7 - N '97 - p5 [1-50]
    Inst - v107 - Ja '98 - p29 [1-50]
    KR - v65 - Ag 15 '97 - p1316 [51-250]
    PW - v244 - Ag 25 '97 - p71 [51-250]

Dragonwings
    BL - v93 - Je 1 '97 - p1701 [1-50]

*The Imp That Ate My Homework
(Illus. by Benrei Huang)*
    BL - v94 - D 15 '97 - p698 [51-250]
    CCB-B - v51 - Ap '98 - p302 [251-500]
    KR - v65 - D 1 '97 - p1782 [51-250]
    PW - v244 - N 24 '97 - p74+ [51-250]
    SLJ - v44 - Mr '98 - p190 [51-250]

*The Khan's Daughter (Illus. by Jean
Tseng)*
    Ch BWatch - v7 - My '97 - p4 [1-50]
    Emerg Lib - v24 - My '97 - p57 [1-50]
    HB Guide - v8 - Fall '97 - p336 [51-250]
    Inst - v107 - Ag '97 - p22 [51-250]
    NY - v73 - O 6 '97 - p115 [1-50]

Ribbons
  y Kliatt - v32 - Ja '98 - p12 [51-250]
    Learning - v26 - S '97 - p45 [1-50]
    PW - v244 - O 13 '97 - p77 [51-250]
    RT - v51 - D '97 - p309 [51-250]
  y SE - v61 - Ap '97 - p14* [1-50]

Yerxa, Leo

*Last Leaf First Snowflake to Fall
(Illus. by Leo Yerxa)*
    Sch Lib - v45 - N '97 - p202 [51-250]

Yezerski, Thomas

*Together in Pinecone Patch (Illus. by
Thomas Yezerski)*
    KR - v66 - Ja 1 '98 - p64 [51-250]

PW - v245 - Ja 12 '98 - p59 [51-250]
SLJ - v44 - Mr '98 - p190+ [51-250]

Yildirim, Eljay

*Aunty Dot's Incredible Adventure
Atlas (Illus. by Brigitte McDonald)*
    PW - v245 - Ja 19 '98 - p380 [51-250]

Yolen, Jane

*The Ballad of the Pirate Queens (Illus.
by David Shannon)*
    Emerg Lib - v25 - N '97 - p46 [51-250]
    SLJ - v43 - N '97 - p41 [1-50]

*Child of Faerie, Child of Earth (Illus.
by Jane Dyer)*
    BL - v94 - Ja 1 '98 - p825 [51-250]
    PW - v244 - O 20 '97 - p75 [51-250]
    SLJ - v44 - Ja '98 - p95 [51-250]

*Elfabet: An ABC of Elves (Illus. by
Lauren A Mills)*
    PW - v244 - Jl 28 '97 - p77 [1-50]

*Good Griselle (McDonough). Audio
Version*
    SLJ - v44 - Mr '98 - p157 [51-250]

Here There Be Angels
    MFSF - v92 - My '97 - p128 [251-500]
  y VOYA - v20 - Ap '97 - p11 [1-50]
  y VOYA - v20 - Ap '97 - p49 [251-500]

*King Long Shanks (Illus. by Victoria
Chess)*
    PW - v245 - Mr 9 '98 - p67 [51-250]

Merlin
    BL - v94 - N 1 '97 - p475 [1-50]
    CLW - v68 - S '97 - p64 [51-250]
    HB Guide - v8 - Fall '97 - p311 [51-250]
    SLJ - v43 - My '97 - p140+ [51-250]

*Milk and Honey (Illus. by Louise
August)*
    SE - v61 - Ap '97 - p15* [1-50]

Miz Berlin (Illus. by Floyd Cooper)
    Ch BWatch - v7 - N '97 - p5 [1-50]

*Miz Berlin Walks (Illus. by Floyd
Cooper)*
    BL - v94 - S 15 '97 - p243 [51-250]
    CBRS - v26 - O '97 - p19 [1-50]
    PW - v244 - Je 2 '97 - p71 [51-250]

Nocturne (Illus. by Anne Hunter)
    BL - v94 - O 1 '97 - p339 [51-250]
    CBRS - v26 - N '97 - p30 [51-250]
    PW - v244 - O 13 '97 - p74 [51-250]
    SLJ - v43 - N '97 - p104 [51-250]

Once upon a Bedtime Story (Illus. by Ruth Tietjen Councell)
    Ch BWatch - v7 - S '97 - p2 [1-50]
    SLJ - v43 - S '97 - p198 [51-250]

Once upon Ice and Other Frozen Poems (Illus. by Jason Stemple)
    CLW - v68 - S '97 - p66+ [51-250]
    HB Guide - v8 - Fall '97 - p375 [51-250]

The Originals: Animals That Time Forgot (Illus. by Ted Lewin)
    PW - v245 - Mr 23 '98 - p102 [1-50]
    SLJ - v44 - Mr '98 - p243 [51-250]

Sacred Places (Illus. by David Shannon)
    RT - v51 - S '97 - p56 [51-250]
    SE - v61 - Ap '97 - p128 [1-50]

The Three Bears Rhyme Book (Illus. by Jane Dyer)
    PW - v244 - S 29 '97 - p91 [1-50]

Twelve Impossible Things before Breakfast
y   BL - v94 - N 1 '97 - p463 [51-250]
    Ch BWatch - v7 - D '97 - p3 [1-50]
    SLJ - v43 - D '97 - p132 [51-250]
y   VOYA - v20 - D '97 - p328 [51-250]
y   VOYA - v21 - Ap '98 - p15 [1-50]

Welcome to the Green House
    BL - v94 - D 1 '97 - p629 [1-50]

Welcome to the Ice House (Illus. by Laura Regan)
    BL - v94 - F 15 '98 - p1016 [51-250]
    PW - v245 - Mr 23 '98 - p102 [1-50]
    SLJ - v44 - Mr '98 - p207 [51-250]

Welcome to the Sea of Sand (Illus. by Laura Regan)
    SLJ - v43 - My '97 - p57 [1-50]

Wings (Illus. by Dennis Nolan)
    PW - v244 - Ag 25 '97 - p74 [1-50]

Yorinks, Arthur
Oh, Brother (Illus. by Richard Egielski)
    SLJ - v43 - Jl '97 - p35 [1-50]
    SLJ - v44 - Ja '98 - p43 [1-50]

York, Sarah Mountbatten-Windsor, Duchess of
Bright Lights
    PW - v244 - O 13 '97 - p77 [51-250]

The Royal Switch
    PW - v244 - O 13 '97 - p77 [51-250]

Yoshida, Toshi
Young Lions (Illus. by Toshi Yoshida)
    SLJ - v43 - My '97 - p57 [1-50]

Youd, Pauline
I Wonder Why Did Elijah Hide? (Illus. by Elaine Garvin)
    CLW - v68 - S '97 - p55 [51-250]

I Wonder Why Was Andrew Surprised? (Illus. by Elaine Garvin)
    CLW - v68 - S '97 - p55 [51-250]

I Wonder Why Was Deborah Mad? (Illus. by Elaine Garvin)
    CLW - v68 - S '97 - p55 [51-250]

I Wonder Why Was Gideon Worried? (Illus. by Elaine Garvin)
    CLW - v68 - S '97 - p55 [51-250]

I Wonder Why Was Jeremiah Sad? (Illus. by Elaine Garvin)
    CLW - v68 - S '97 - p55 [51-250]

I Wonder Why Was Mary Embarrassed? (Illus. by Elaine Garvin)
    CLW - v68 - S '97 - p55 [51-250]

Young, Allen M
Lives Intertwined
    SLJ - v43 - Ap '97 - p164 [51-250]

Young, Caroline
The Big Bug Search
    New Sci - v154 - Je 7 '97 - p48 [51-250]

Young, Ed
The Lost Horse (Illus. by Ed Young)
> BL - v94 - Mr 15 '98 - p1246 [51-250]
> KR - v66 - Ap 1 '98 - p504 [51-250]
> SLJ - v44 - Ap '98 - p127 [51-250]

Mouse Match (Illus. by Ed Young)
> BL - v94 - O 15 '97 - p403 [51-250]
> BL - v94 - Ja 1 '98 - p736 [1-50]
> CCB-B - v51 - D '97 - p144 [51-250]
> HB - v73 - N '97 - p674+ [251-500]
> Inst - v107 - Ja '98 - p27+ [51-250]
> KR - v65 - O 1 '97 - p1540 [51-250]

Voices of the Heart (Illus. by Ed Young)
> HB Guide - v8 - Fall '97 - p317 [51-250]
> HMR - Sum '97 - p27 [501+]
> SLJ - v43 - Je '97 - p150 [51-250]

Young, Jay
Beyond Amazing
> PW - v244 - O 6 '97 - p84 [51-250]

The Even More Amazing Science Pop-Up Book
> Magpies - v12 - Jl '97 - p44+ [251-500]
> TES - N 7 '97 - p10* [51-250]
> TES - Ja 9 '98 - p34* [501+]

Young, Karen Romano
Guinness Record Breakers
> Ch BWatch - v7 - N '97 - p1 [51-250]
> PW - v244 - D 15 '97 - p60 [51-250]

Young, Richard, 1946-
Scary Story Reader
> CAY - v18 - Sum '97 - p13 [51-250]

Young, Robert, 1951-
Money
> KR - v66 - Ap 15 '98 - p589 [51-250]

The Real Patriots of the American Revolution
> BL - v94 - S 15 '97 - p234 [51-250]
> HB Guide - v8 - Fall '97 - p398 [51-250]
> y   Kliatt - v31 - S '97 - p37 [51-250]

The Transcontinental Railroad
> BL - v94 - S 15 '97 - p234 [51-250]
> HB Guide - v8 - Fall '97 - p398 [51-250]

> y   Kliatt - v31 - S '97 - p37 [51-250]

Young, Ronder Thomas
Moving Mama to Town
> BL - v93 - Je 1 '97 - p1695 [51-250]
> CCB-B - v51 - S '97 - p32 [51-250]
> HB - v73 - Jl '97 - p466 [51-250]
> HB Guide - v8 - Fall '97 - p311 [51-250]
> NYTBR - v102 - Je 1 '97 - p36 [1-50]
> y   SLJ - v43 - Je '97 - p129+ [51-250]

Young, Ruth
Who Says Moo? (Illus. by Lisa Campbell Ernst)
> Bks Keeps - N '97 - p19 [51-250]

Young, Selina
Big Dog and Little Dog Visit the Moon
> Magpies - v12 - My '97 - p31 [51-250]

Young, Sue
The Scholastic Rhyming Dictionary
> r   JOYS - v11 - Fall '97 - p75 [1-50]

Writing with Style
> SLJ - v43 - My '97 - p151 [51-250]

Young Rider
> p   JOYS - v10 - Spr '97 - p263 [1-50]

Yount, Lisa
Antoine Lavoisier: Founder of Modern Chemistry
> HB Guide - v8 - Fall '97 - p380 [51-250]
> SB - v33 - O '97 - p212 [51-250]

Anton Van Leeuwenhoek: First to See Microscopic Life
> ASBYP - v29 - Fall '96 - p47+ [501+]

Yue, Charlotte
Shoes: Their History in Words and Pictures (Illus. by Charlotte Yue)
> CCB-B - v50 - Je '97 - p379 [51-250]
> HB Guide - v8 - Fall '97 - p330 [51-250]
> y   SLJ - v43 - Ap '97 - p164 [51-250]

Yumoto, Kazumi
The Friends
    CLW - v68 - S '97 - p71 [51-250]
    HMR - Sum '97 - p29 [51-250]
    RT - v51 - F '98 - p427 [51-250]
    SE - v61 - Ap '97 - p13* [1-50]
y   VOYA - v20 - Ap '97 - p35+ [251-500]

*The Friends (Woodman). Audio
Version*
y   BL - v94 - D 15 '97 - p711 [1-50]
    HB - v73 - N '97 - p703 [251-500]

Z

Zagwyn, Deborah Turney
The Pumpkin Blanket
PW - v244 - O 6 '97 - p52 [1-50]

Turtle Spring (Illus. by Deborah Turney Zagwyn)
KR - v66 - Mr 15 '98 - p410 [51-250]

Zakarin, Debra Mostow
The Ultimate Baby-Sitter's Handbook (Illus. by Ruta Daugavietis)
BL - v94 - S 15 '97 - p234 [51-250]
y Kliatt - v31 - N '97 - p23 [51-250]
SLJ - v43 - D '97 - p150+ [51-250]

Zakowski, Connie
The Insect Book (Illus. by Connie Zakowski)
SB - v33 - O '97 - p211 [51-250]
SLJ - v43 - My '97 - p126 [51-250]

Zalben, Jane Breskin
Pearl's Marigolds for Grandpa (Illus. by Jane Breskin Zalben)
BL - v94 - N 1 '97 - p485 [51-250]
PW - v244 - Ag 25 '97 - p70 [51-250]
SLJ - v43 - S '97 - p198 [51-250]

Zambreno, Mary Frances
Journeyman Wizard
BL - v94 - N 1 '97 - p475 [1-50]

Zamorano, Ana
Let's Eat! (Illus. by Julie Vivas)
CBRS - v25 - Ag '97 - p163+ [51-250]
HB Guide - v8 - Fall '97 - p286 [51-250]
NYTBR - v102 - Jl 6 '97 - p15 [501+]
SLJ - v43 - Ap '97 - p119 [51-250]

Zanzarella, Marianne
The Good Housekeeping Illustrated Children's Cookbook (Illus. by Tom Eckerle)
BL - v94 - D 15 '97 - p696 [51-250]
NYTBR - v102 - N 16 '97 - p38 [51-250]
PW - v244 - S 22 '97 - p83 [51-250]
SLJ - v44 - Ja '98 - p135 [51-250]

Zarin, Cynthia
Rose and Sebastian (Illus. by Sarah Durham)
CCB-B - v51 - O '97 - p73 [51-250]
HB - v73 - S '97 - p567 [51-250]
KR - v65 - Ag 15 '97 - p1316 [51-250]
NY - v73 - O 6 '97 - p116 [51-250]
PW - v244 - Je 30 '97 - p76 [51-250]
SLJ - v43 - S '97 - p198 [51-250]

Zeinert, Karen
The Amistad Slave Revolt and American Abolition
HB Guide - v8 - Fall '97 - p398 [51-250]
y Kliatt - v32 - Ja '98 - p32 [251-500]
NYTBR - v102 - Ag 31 '97 - p13 [501+]
y SLJ - v43 - Je '97 - p150 [51-250]

Wisconsin
Ch BWatch - v8 - Ja '98 - p7 [1-50]

Zelinsky, Paul O
Rapunzel (Illus. by Paul O Zelinsky)
BL - v94 - Mr 15 '98 - p1224 [1-50]
BW - v27 - N 2 '97 - p6 [51-250]
CCB-B - v51 - Ja '98 - p182 [51-250]
HB - v74 - Ja '98 - p85+ [51-250]
KR - v65 - O 1 '97 - p1540 [51-250]

454

NW - v130 - D 1 '97 - p77 [1-50]
NYTBR - v102 - N 16 '97 - p54+
[501+]
PW - v244 - S 29 '97 - p89 [51-250]
PW - v244 - N 3 '97 - p59 [51-250]
SLJ - v43 - N '97 - p113 [51-250]
SLJ - v43 - D '97 - p29 [1-50]

Zemach, Kaethe
The Character in the Book (Illus. by Kaethe Zemach)
BL - v94 - F 15 '98 - p1021 [51-250]
KR - v65 - D 1 '97 - p1782 [51-250]
PW - v244 - D 8 '97 - p71 [51-250]
SLJ - v44 - Ap '98 - p111+ [51-250]

Zeman, Anne
Everything You Need to Know about Geography Homework
CM:CanRev - v4 - S 5 '97 - pONL
[251-500]

Everything You Need to Know about Geography Homework (Illus. by Moffit Cecil)
r   SLJ - v43 - My '97 - p151 [51-250]

Zeman, Ludmila
The First Red Maple Leaf (Illus. by Ludmila Zeman)
Can CL - v23 - Sum '97 - p51+ [501+]
Ch Bk News - v20 - Sum '97 - p28 [51-250]
CM:CanRev - v4 - F 27 '98 - pONL
[251-500]
HB Guide - v8 - Fall '97 - p286 [51-250]
Quill & Q - v63 - Je '97 - p63+ [251-500]
SLJ - v43 - S '97 - p209 [51-250]

Zevy, Aaron
No Nuts for Me! (Illus. by Susan Tebbutt)
CBRA - '96 - p462 [51-250]

Zhang, Song Nan
The Children of China
Ch BWatch - v7 - Mr '97 - p6 [51-250]

Cowboy on the Steppes (Illus. by Song Nan Zhang)
BL - v94 - F 15 '98 - p1006+ [51-250]
CM:CanRev - v4 - F 27 '98 - pONL
[251-500]

Quill & Q - v63 - N '97 - p46 [251-500]
SLJ - v44 - F '98 - p128 [51-250]

Ziefert, Harriet
Baby Buggy, Buggy Baby (Illus. by Richard Brown)
HB Guide - v8 - Fall '97 - p338 [51-250]
SLJ - v43 - Jl '97 - p89 [51-250]

Bears Odd, Bears Even (Illus. by Andrea Baruffi)
SLJ - v43 - N '97 - p113 [51-250]

The Best Smelling Christmas Book Ever (Illus. by Laura Rader)
PW - v244 - O 6 '97 - p57 [1-50]

The Cow in the House (Illus. by Emily Bolam)
BL - v93 - Ag '97 - p1911 [51-250]

A Dozen Dozens (Illus. by Chris L Demarest)
SLJ - v44 - F '98 - p93+ [51-250]

Eight Days of Hanukkah (Illus. by Melinda Levine)
BL - v94 - S 15 '97 - p244 [51-250]
PW - v244 - O 6 '97 - p52 [51-250]

Henny-Penny (Illus. by Emily Bolam)
HB Guide - v8 - Fall '97 - p337 [51-250]

I Swapped My Dog (Illus. by Emily Bolam)
PW - v245 - Mr 9 '98 - p67 [51-250]

The Magic Porridge Pot (Illus. by Emily Bolam)
HB Guide - v8 - Fall '97 - p337 [51-250]

Math Riddles (Illus. by Andrea Baruffi)
BL - v93 - Ag '97 - p1911 [51-250]
SLJ - v43 - D '97 - p116 [51-250]

Mother Goose Math (Illus. by Emily Bolam)
BL - v93 - Je 1 '97 - p1711 [51-250]
CCB-B - v50 - Jl '97 - p417 [51-250]
SLJ - v44 - F '98 - p94 [51-250]

Night, Knight (Illus. by Richard Brown)
HB Guide - v8 - Fall '97 - p338 [51-250]
SLJ - v43 - Jl '97 - p89 [51-250]

Pushkin Meets the Bundle (Illus. by Donald Saaf)
KR - v66 - F 1 '98 - p202 [51-250]
PW - v245 - F 16 '98 - p209+ [51-250]

Rabbit and Hare Divide an Apple (Illus. by Emily Bolam)
SLJ - v44 - F '98 - p94 [51-250]

Sleepy-O! (Illus. by Laura Rader)
BL - v94 - S 1 '97 - p131 [51-250]
CBRS - v26 - O '97 - p19 [51-250]
CCB-B - v51 - O '97 - p73 [51-250]
SLJ - v44 - Ja '98 - p107 [51-250]

Swapped My Dog (Illus. by Emily Bolam)
BL - v94 - Mr 1 '98 - p1142 [51-250]

Wee G. (Illus. by Donald Saaf)
CBRS - v25 - Spr '97 - p138 [51-250]
HB Guide - v8 - Fall '97 - p286 [51-250]
SLJ - v43 - Je '97 - p103 [51-250]

Ziegler, Sandra
The Child's World of Manners (Illus. by Mechelle Ann)
SLJ - v44 - Ap '98 - p122 [51-250]

Zim, Herbert Spencer
Birds: A Guide to Familiar American Birds. Rev. and Updated Ed.
r   JOYS - v11 - Fall '97 - p76 [1-50]

Flowers: A Guide to Familiar American Wildflowers. Rev. Ed.
r   JOYS - v11 - Fall '97 - p76 [1-50]

Insects: A Guide to Familiar American Insects. Rev. Ed.
r   JOYS - v11 - Fall '97 - p76 [1-50]

Mammals: A Guide to Familiar American Species. Rev. Ed.
r   JOYS - v11 - Fall '97 - p76 [1-50]

Trees: A Guide to Familiar American Trees. Rev. Ed.
r   JOYS - v11 - Fall '97 - p76 [1-50]

Zinovieff, Sofka
The History of Emigration from Greece
Bks Keeps - My '97 - p26 [51-250]
HB Guide - v8 - Fall '97 - p391 [51-250]
Sch Lib - v45 - Ag '97 - p153+ [51-250]
TES - S 19 '97 - p16* [501+]

Zoehfeld, Kathleen Weidner
Cactus Cafe. Book and Audio Version
SLJ - v43 - D '97 - p72 [51-250]

What's Alive (Illus. by Nadine Bernard Westcott)
ASBYP - v29 - Sum '96 - p43 [51-250]

Zolotow, Charlotte
The Bunny Who Found Easter (Illus. by Helen Craig)
BL - v94 - Mr 1 '98 - p1142 [51-250]
KR - v66 - F 15 '98 - p276 [51-250]
PW - v245 - F 2 '98 - p89 [51-250]

Wake Up and Goodnight (Illus. by Pamela Paparone)
KR - v66 - F 15 '98 - p276 [51-250]

When the Wind Stops (Illus. by Stefano Vitale)
SLJ - v43 - My '97 - p57 [1-50]

Who Is Ben? (Illus. by Kathryn Jacobi)
BL - v93 - Je 1 '97 - p1695 [51-250]
CBRS - v25 - My '97 - p114 [51-250]
HB Guide - v8 - Fall '97 - p286 [51-250]
Par - v72 - Je '97 - p190 [51-250]
SLJ - v43 - Je '97 - p103+ [51-250]

Zoo Books
p   Par Ch - Awards '97 - p27 [1-50]

Zubrowski, Bernie
Soda Science (Illus. by Roy Doty)
BL - v93 - Ag '97 - p1897 [51-250]
CCB-B - v51 - S '97 - p32 [51-250]
HB Guide - v8 - Fall '97 - p340 [51-250]

Zuehlke, Mark
*Fun B.C. Facts for Kids (Illus. by
Sean Sharpe)*
  CBRA - '96 - p515 [51-250]

Zurbo, Matt
*I Got a Rocket! (Illus. by Dean
Gorrissen)*
  Aust Bk R - S '97 - p64+ [51-250]

Zweifel, Frances
*The Make-Something Club Is Back!
(Illus. by Ann Schweninger)*
  HB Guide - v8 - Fall '97 - p363 [51-250]

Zytman, Leah
*The Bravest Fireman (Illus. by Leah
Malka Diskind)*
  PW - v245 - Mr 23 '98 - p95 [51-250]

Illustrator Index

Illustrator's names appear in bold face followed by titles and authors of the books each has illustrated. In some cases, the illustrator and author are the same person. To find the review citations for the titles listed, search under the author's name in the main section of *CBRI*.

A

Abolafia, Yossi
Harry's Pony - Porte, Barbara Ann

Adams, Pam
Bunny - Twinn, Michael
Kitten - Twinn, Michael

Adams, Sarah
Asana and the Animals - Nichols, Grace

Adams, Susi
I'm Scared - Davies, Gill

Adel, Daniel
The Book That Jack Wrote - Scieszka, Jon

Adinolfi, JoAnn
Johnny Germ Head - Quigley, James
Liar, Liar, Pants on Fire - Korman, Gordon
Tina's Diner - Adinolfi, JoAnn

Adlerman, Kimberly M
Africa Calling, Nighttime Falling - Adlerman, Daniel

Agee, Jon
The Halloween House - Silverman, Erica
Mean Margaret - Seidler, Tor
The Return of Freddy LeGrand - Agee, Jon

Aiello, Laurel
Kids Are Cookin' - Brown, Karen
Science around the World - Levine, Shar

Aitchison, Martin
Rapunzel - Baxter, Nicola

Alborough, Jez
Martin's Mice - King-Smith, Dick
Watch Out! Big Bro's Coming! - Alborough, Jez

Alexander, Linda
Happily Ever After and All That - Shank, Jackie

Ali, Abira
The Big Bazoohley - Carey, Peter

Ali, Hemlata Farida
Storyteller: A Collection of 17 Stories for Children - Ali, Hemlata Farida

Aliki
My Visit to the Zoo - Aliki

Allan, Nicholas
The Bird - Allan, Nicholas

Allen, Joe
Four Seasons of Corn - Hunter, Sally M

Allen, Jonathan
The Bear Whose Bones Were Jezebel Jones - Grossman, Bill
Beaten by a Balloon - Mahy, Margaret
Wake Up, Sleeping Beauty - Allen, Jonathan
Wolf Academy - Allen, Jonathan

Allen, Pamela
The Bear's Lunch - Allen, Pamela
Ordinary Albert - Antle, Nancy

Allen, Thomas B
Going West - Van Leeuwen, Jean
Good-Bye, Charles Lindbergh - Borden, Louise
A Green Horn Blowing - Birchman, David F
El Jugar Mas Bonito Del Mundo - Cameron, Ann
Littlejim's Dreams - Houston, Gloria
A Place Called Freedom - Sanders, Scott R

459

Alles, Hemesh
More Errata - Roland-Entwistle, Theodore
Space Technology -
Alley, R W
Detective Dinosaur: Lost and Found -
  Skofield, James
A Know-Nothing Birthday - Spirn, Michele
  Sobel
The New Dog - Hazen, Barbara Shook
*Paddington Bear and the Christmas
  Surprise* - Bond, Michael
Sheepish Riddles - Hall, Katy
Alphin, Elaine Marie
Toasters - Alphin, Elaine Marie
Ambrus, Victor G
Black Beauty - Sewell, Anna
The Iliad - Strachan, Ian
Amiri, Fahimeh
The Monkey Bridge - Martin, Rafe
Amoss, John
How to Rock Your Baby - Fleming, Sibley
Amstutz, Andre
Master Track's Train - Ahlberg, Allan
Monkey Do! - Ahlberg, Allan
Ancona, George
Fiesta Fireworks - Ancona, George
Mayeros: A Yucatec Maya Family -
  Ancona, George
Andersen, Bethanne
A Prayer for the Earth - Sasso, Sandy
  Eisenberg
Seven Brave Women - Hearne, Betsy
Anderson, C W
Blaze and the Gray Spotted Pony -
  Anderson, C W
Anderson, Chad
Mother Nature's Magic Seed - Mallory,
  Laura
Anderson, Ho Che
Steel Drums and Ice Skates - McLean,
  Dirk
Anderson, Lena
Tick-Tock - Anderson, Lena
Anderson, Peggy Perry
Out to Lunch - Anderson, Peggy Perry
Anderson, Peter
Fearsome Hunters - Donnelly, Jane
Gorilla - Redmond, Ian
Anderson, Scoular
The Most Brilliant Trick Ever - Allen,
  Judy
Anderson, Steven D
Star Wars: A Droid's Tale - Whitman,
  John

Anderson, Susan
Flowers for Mommy - Anderson, Susan
Andreasen, Dan
Eagle Song - Bruchac, Joseph
Grandma's Garden - Moore, Elaine
Little Clearing in the Woods - Wilkes,
  Maria D
Little Town at the Crossroads - Wilkes,
  Maria D
Pioneer Girl - Anderson, William
Pony Express! - Kroll, Steven
Touch the Sky Summer - Van Leeuwen,
  Jean
We Played Marbles - Seymour, Tres
Andrew, Ian
Back to the Blue - McKenna, Virginia
The Forgotten Garden - Repchuk,
  Caroline
Premlata and the Festival of Lights -
  Godden, Rumer
Andrews, Benny
I Am the Darker Brother - Adoff, Arnold
Sky Sash So Blue - Hathorn, Libby
Anholt, Catherine
Billy and the Big New School - Anholt,
  Laurence
Anita
Beware the Brindlebeast - Riggio, Anita
Ann, Mechelle
The Child's World of Manners - Ziegler,
  Sandra
The Child's World of Responsibility -
  Pemberton, N
Annesley, Robert
Spider Spins a Story - Max, Jill
Anthony, Mark
Cracking the Wall - Lucas, Eileen
Antram, David
Exploring the Polar Regions - Green, Jen
Radio and Television - Lafferty, Peter
Writing and Printing - Steedman, Scott
Apple, Margot
Casey's New Hat - Gardella, Tricia
Sheep in a Jeep - Shaw, Nancy
Sheep in a Shop - Shaw, Nancy
Sheep Trick or Treat - Shaw, Nancy
Appleby, Ellen
Elmo Saves Christmas - Ferraro, Christine
*Hanukkah Chubby Board Book and
  Dreidels* - Benjamin, Alan
Arai, Kazuyoshi
*Konnichiwa! I Am a Japanese-American
  Girl* - Brown, Tricia

Araten, Harry
Seven Animal Stories for Children - Bogot, Howard I
Arbuckle, Scott
Zeb, the Cow's on the Roof Again! and Other Tales of Early Texas Dwellings - Arbuckle, Scott
Archbold, Tim
The Dad Library - Whelehan, Dennis
Arcouette, Evelyne
Discovering the Heavens - Brillon, Gilles
Ardizzone, Edward
A Likely Place - Fox, Paula
Arenson, Roberta
A Caribbean Counting Book - Charles, Faustin
Argent, Kerry
Gotcha! - Jorgensen, Gail
Armitage, David
Flora and the Strawberry Red Birthday Party - Armitage, Ronda
Armour-Chudu, Louise
Pest Friends - Goodhart, Pippa
Armstrong, Robb
Drew and the Bub Daddy Showdown - Armstrong, Robb
Drew and the Homeboy Question - Armstrong, Robb
Arnold, Ann
Firehorse Max - London, Sara
Arnold, Arthur P
Stone Age Farmers Beside the Sea - Arnold, Caroline
Arnold, Elaine
Kai: The Lost Statue, Africa 1440 - Welch, Leona Nicholas
Arnold, Katya
Duck, Duck, Goose? - Arnold, Katya
Katya's Book of Mushrooms - Arnold, Katya
Meow! - Arnold, Katya
Arnold, Tedd
Help! I'm Falling Apart - Arnold, Tedd
My Dog Never Says Please - Williams, Suzanne
Parts - Arnold, Tedd
Arnosky, Jim
All about Alligators - Arnosky, Jim
All about Deer - Arnosky, Jim
All about Rattlesnakes - Arnosky, Jim
Bring 'Em Back Alive! - Arnosky, Jim
Crinkleroot's Guide to Knowing Animal Habitats - Arnosky, Jim
Little Lions - Arnosky, Jim
Watching Water Birds - Arnosky, Jim

Arnsteen, Katy Keck
Let's Celebrate Christmas - Roop, Peter
Let's Celebrate Halloween - Roop, Peter
Putting on a Play - Bentley, Nancy
Arredondo, Francisco
Metamorphosis - Llamas Ruiz, Andres
Arroyo, Andrea
In Rosa's Mexico - Geeslin, Campell
Arroyo, Imna
Why Goats Smell Bad and Other Stories from Benin - Mama, Raouf
Aruego, Jose
Alligators and Others All Year Long - Dragonwagon, Crescent
Antarctic Antics - Sierra, Judy
Leo the Late Bloomer - Kraus, Robert
Little Louie the Baby Bloomer - Kraus, Robert
Star of the Circus - Sampson, Michael
They Thought They Saw Him - Strete, Craig
Asbury, Kelly
Bonnie's Blue House - Asbury, Kelly
Rusty's Red Vacation - Asbury, Kelly
Yolanda's Yellow School - Asbury, Kelly
Asch, Frank
Barnyard Lullaby - Asch, Frank
Moonbear's Pet - Asch, Frank
Asch, Jan
One Man Show - Asch, Frank
Atkin, S Beth
Voices from the Streets - Atkin, S Beth
Auch, Herm
I Was a Third Grade Science Project - Auch, Mary Jane
Auch, Mary Jane
Bantam of the Opera - Auch, Mary Jane
Eggs Mark the Spot - Auch, Mary Jane
August, Louise
Milk and Honey - Yolen, Jane
Austin, Graham
From Birth to Death - Yates, Irene
The Hunt for Food - Ganeri, Anita
Austin, Virginia
Kate's Giants - Gregory, Valiska
Avendano, Dolores
On Halloween Night - Wolff, Ferida
Avishai, Susan
When the Big Dog Barks - Curtis, Munzee
Axelsen, Stephen
Soula the Ruler - McFarlane, Peter
Axtell, David
Fruits: A Caribbean Counting Poem - Bloom, Valerie

Beier, Ellen
The 18 Penny Goose - Walker, Sally M
The Blue Hill Meadows - Rylant, Cynthia

Bell, Leslie
Estelle and the Self-Esteem Machine -
Bannatyne-Cugnet, Jo

Bell, Mike
Mystery History of a Pharaoh's Tomb -
Pipe, Jim
Roman Colosseum - Ash, Rhiannon
Viking Longboat - Finney, Fred

Bell, Simon M
Insects and Spiders - Bell, Simon M
Snakes and Lizards - Bell, Simon M

Belton, Robyn
The Bantam and the Soldier - Beck,
Jennifer

Ben-Ami, Doron
Tornado - Byars, Betsy Cromer

Bendall-Brunello, John
Into the Castle - Crebbin, June
Yum, Yum, Yummy - Waddell, Martin

Bender, Robert
The A to Z Beastly Jamboree - Bender,
Robert
Barnyard Song - Greene, Rhonda Gowler
The Chizzywink and the Alamagoozlum -
Johnston, Tony

Benedict, Judith Ann
When Dawn Stole the Dark - Joerg, Donna

Benenfeld, Rikki
I Go to School - Benenfeld, Rikki

Bennett, Jill
Harry's Mad - King-Smith, Dick

Benson, Patrick
The Book of Hob Stories - Mayne, William
*The Last of the Wallendas and Other
Poems* - Hoban, Russell
The Lord Fish - De La Mare, Walter
Owl Babies - Waddell, Martin

Berdichevsky, Victoria
Pavlova's Gift - Trottier, Maxine

Berenzy, Alix
A Frog Prince - Berenzy, Alix
Into the Sea - Guiberson, Brenda Z

Berg, Ron
Night Fun - Quinlan, Patricia

Berger, Barbara Helen
A Lot of Otters - Berger, Barbara Helen

Bergin, Mark
A 16th Century Mosque - Macdonald,
Fiona
Castle Siege - Macdonald, Fiona
First Facts about the American Frontier -
Macdonald, Fiona
First Facts about the Ancient Egyptians -
Morley, Jacqueline
First Facts about the Vikings - Morley,
Jacqueline
Knights and Armor - Kerr, Daisy
The Roman Colosseum - Macdonald, Fiona

Bergsma, Jody
Dreambirds - Ogden, David

Bernal, Richard
Smasher - King-Smith, Dick

Bernardin, James
Little Folk - Walker, Paul Robert

Bernhard, Durga
Prairie Dogs - Bernhard, Emery
Trouble - Kurtz, Jane

Berridge, Richard
The World of the Pirate - Garwood, Val

Betteridge, Deirdre
The Boy Who Wouldn't Speak - Berry,
Steve

Bial, Raymond
Cajun Home - Bial, Raymond
Mist over the Mountains - Bial, Raymond
The Strength of These Arms - Bial,
Raymond
Where Lincoln Walked - Bial, Raymond

Bianchi, John
The Lab Rats of Doctor Eclair - Bianchi,
John
Melody Mooner Takes Lessons - Edwards,
Frank B

Biard, Philippe
Construction - Delafosse, Claude

Biesty, Stephen
*Stephen Biesty's Cross-Sections: Man-of-
War* - Biesty, Stephen
Stephen Biesty's Incredible Everything -
Biesty, Stephen
Stephen Biesty's Incredible Explosions -
Biesty, Stephen

Billin-Frye, Paige
A Box Can Be Many Things - Rau, Dana
Meachen
Mystery of the Tooth Gremlin - Graves,
Bonnie
This Is the Pumpkin - Levine, Abby

Binch, Caroline
Boundless Grace - Hoffman, Mary
Grace and Family - Hoffman, Mary
Gregory Cool - Binch, Caroline
Since Dad Left - Binch, Caroline

Birmingham, Christian
The Night before Christmas - Moore,
   Clement Clarke
Oliver Twist - Baxter, Lesley
The Sea of Tranquillity - Haddon, Mark
The Windhover - Brown, Alan

Birt, Hazel
*Flikka and the Prince Edward Island
   Mystery* - Birt, Hazel

Bishop, Gavin
Little Rabbit and the Sea - Bishop, Gavin
Maui and the Sun - Bishop, Gavin

Bishop, Nic
The Secrets of Animal Flight - Bishop, Nic

Bisseker, Lesley
The Lost Treasure - Hooper, Mary
Poppy's Secret - Hooper, Mary

Bisson, Michel
Garbage Creek and Other Stories -
   Valgardson, W D
So You Love to Draw - Seary, Michael

Biswas, Pulak
*Il Lago Della Luna E Altre Favole
   Dell'India* - Varma, Nishu

Bittinger, Ned
The Blue and the Gray - Bunting, Eve
Rocking Horse Christmas - Osborne, Mary
   Pope

Bjorkman, Steve
Born to Be Wild - Spinner, Stephanie
Bright Lights, Little Gerbil - Spinner,
   Stephanie
Thanksgiving Is. . . - Borden, Louise

Black, Trevor
Bounce Me, Tickle Me, Hug Me -
   Carpenter-Davis, Sandra

Blades, Ann
Back to the Cabin - Blades, Ann
Pond Seasons - Alderson, Sue Ann
A Salmon for Simon - Waterton, Betty

Blake, Quentin
Clown - Blake, Quentin
Mrs. Armitage and the Big Wave - Blake,
   Quentin
The Penguin Book of Nonsense Verse -
   Blake, Quentin
The Roald Dahl Treasury - Dahl, Roald
Roald Dahl's Revolting Recipes - Fison,
   Josie
The Seven Voyages of Sinbad the Sailor -
   Yeoman, John
Tea in the Sugar Bowl, Potato in My Shoe
   - Rosen, Michael

Blake, Robert J
Akiak: A Tale from the Iditarod - Blake,
   Robert J
Mississippi Mud - Turner, Ann

Blathwayt, Benedict
Little Red Train to the Rescue - Blathwayt,
   Benedict

Blatt, Christina C
Earthquake Games - Levy, Matthys

Blau, Aljoscha
The Five Fingers and the Moon - Kurt,
   Kemal

Blegvad, Eric
With One White Wing - Spires, Elizabeth

Blier, Elaine
Mouse in the Manger - Wynne-Jones, Tim

Bloch, Alex
Let's Celebrate Our Jewish Holidays -
   Kolatch, Alfred J

Blommaert, Gerard
Buckskin, the Brave - Clancy, Dorothy

Bloom, Lloyd
Treehouse Tales - Isaacs, Anne

Blundell, Tony
Never Say No to a Martian! - Wallace,
   Karen

Bluthenthal, Diana Cain
Hot Fudge Hero - Brisson, Pat
The La-Di-Da Hare - Lewis, J Patrick
Matilda the Moocher - Bluthenthal, Diana
   Cain

Blythe, Gary
This Is the Star - Dunbar, Joyce

Bobak, Cathy
The Big Monkey Mix-Up - Jane, Pamela

Bochak, Grayce
The Gamemaster - Bochak, John

Bodal, Susi
1,2,3 What Do You See? - Bohdal, Susi

Boddy, Joe
The Mystery of the Fallen Tree - Christian,
   Mary Blount

Boey, Stephanie
  The Christmas Bears - Repchuk, Caroline
Bogacki, Tomasz
  Cat and Mouse - Bogacki, Tomasz
  Cat and Mouse in the Rain - Bogacki,
    Tomasz
  I Hate You! I Like You! - Bogacki,
    Tomasz
  The Story of a Blue Bird - Bogacki,
    Tomasz
Bogan, Paulette
  Spike - Bogan, Paulette
Bolam, Emily
  Bearobics: A Hip-Hop Counting Story -
    Parker, Vic
  The Cow in the House - Ziefert, Harriet
  Henny-Penny - Ziefert, Harriet
  I Swapped My Dog - Ziefert, Harriet
  The Magic Porridge Pot - Ziefert, Harriet
  Mother Goose Math - Ziefert, Harriet
  Rabbit and Hare Divide an Apple -
    Ziefert, Harriet
  Swapped My Dog - Ziefert, Harriet
  The Twelve Days of Christmas -
Bollen, Roger
  Elizabeth and Larry - Sadler, Marilyn
  Honey Bunny Funnybunny - Sadler,
    Marilyn
  The Parakeet Girl - Sadler, Marilyn
Bolling, Vickey
  Proud - Penner, Fred
Bollinger, Peter
  Hercules the Strong Man - Geringer,
    Laura
  Ulysses the Soldier King - Geringer, Laura
Bolognese, Don
  First Flight - Shea, George
Bolster, Rob
  The Airplane Alphabet Book - Pallotta,
    Jerry
Bond, Denny
  Sleepy Little Owl - Goldsmith, Howard
Bond, Felicia
  If You Give a Mouse a Cookie - Numeroff,
    Laura Joffe
  If You Give a Pig a Pancake - Numeroff,
    Laura Joffe
Bonner, Rog
  Moo Moo, Brown Cow - Wood, Jakki
Bonners, Susan
  Hunter in the Snow - Bonners, Susan
  The Silver Balloon - Bonners, Susan
Bonson, Richard
  Disaster! - Bonson, Richard

Boomer, Beverley
  My Dad Never Had a Paper Route -
    Graham, Julie
Boon, Debbie
  My Gran - Boon, Debbie
Bootman, Colin
  Follow the Leader - Winslow, Vicki
  Louise's Gift - Smalls-Hector, Irene
  Oh, No, Toto! - Tchana, Katrin Hyman
Bornstein, Ruth
  That's How It Is When We Draw -
    Bornstein, Ruth
Bostock, Mike
  Imagine You Are a Crocodile - Wallace,
    Karen
Boudreau, Ray
  Simple Machines - Hodge, Deborah
  Wake Up to Your Dreams - Collier, Sandra
    L
Bourgeau, Vincent
  I'm Sick of It! A Fishy Melodrama -
    Bourgeau, Vincent
  I'm Sick of It! A Mouse's Reality Check -
    Bourgeau, Vincent
Bowen, Betsy
  Shingebiss: An Ojibwe Legend - Van
    Laan, Nancy
Bowen, Keith
  Sam's Duck - Morpurgo, Michael
Bowles, Janice
  Sally's Painting Room - Orr, Wendy
Bowman, Leslie W
  A Christmas Sonata - Paulsen, Gary
  The Copper Lady - Ross, Alice
  The Fiddler of the Northern Lights -
    Kinsey-Warnock, Natalie
  Orcas around Me - Page, Debra
Boyd, Lizi
  The Book of Baths - Ruelle, Karen Gray
  The Book of Bedtimes - Ruelle, Karen
    Gray
  The Book of Breakfasts - Ruelle, Karen
    Gray
  Lulu Crow's Garden - Boyd, Lizi
Boynton, Sandra
  Snoozers: 7 Short Short Bedtime Stories
    for Lively Little Kids - Boynton, Sandra
Brace, Eric
  6 Wild Adventures - Albee, Sarah
  9 Puzzle Mysteries - Gutelle, Andrew
  It's Disgusting--and We Ate It! - Solheim,
    James
  The Krazees - Swope, Sam
  Virtual Fred - Courtney, Vincent

Bracken, Carolyn
My Little People School Bus - Tomaselli, Doris
Bradford, June
Paper Airplanes and Other Super Flyers - Francis, Neil
Your Own ABC - Baron, Marcie
Braginetz, Donna
Ornithomimids: The Fastest Dinosaur - Lessem, Don
Troodon: The Smartest Dinosaur - Lessem, Don
Utahraptor: The Deadliest Dinosaur - Lessem, Don
Brammer, Erin McGonigle
Babes in Toyland -
The Sea Maidens of Japan - Bell, Lili
Branch, Willis
Juneteenth: Freedom Day - Branch, Muriel Miller
Brandenberg, Alexa
Chop, Simmer, Season - Brandenberg, Alexa
We Love the Dirt - Johnston, Tony
Brandenburg, Jim
To the Top of the World - Brandenburg, Jim
Brannon, Tom
Qh, That Nuzzle! - Johnson, David
The Song of the Zubble-Wump - Rabe, Tish
Braren, Loretta
Math Play! - McGowan, Diane
Bratton, Heidi
Imagine: A Story about the Beginning - Bratton, Heidi
Spirit! - Bratton, Heidi
Where Is God? - Bratton, Heidi
Yes, I Can! - Bratton, Heidi
Brazell, Derek
Cleversticks - Ashley, Bernard
Breathed, Berkeley
Red Ranger Came Calling - Breathed, Berkeley
Breckon, Brett
The World of the Medieval Knight - Gravett, Christopher
Breeze, Lynn
Billy and the Baby - Bradman, Tony
Brender A Brandis, G
Rebellion: A Novel of Upper Canada - Brandis, Marianne
Brenner, Fred
The Tremendous Tree Book - Brenner, Barbara

Brent, Isabelle
Fairy Tales of the Brothers Grimm - Philip, Neil
Brett, Jan
The Hat - Brett, Jan
Noelle of the Nutcracker - Jane, Pamela
Brickman, Robin
A Log's Life - Pfeffer, Wendy
Brierley, Louise
When the World Was Young - Mayo, Margaret
Briggs, Raymond
The Snowman Storybook - Briggs, Raymond
Brighton, Catherine
My Napoleon - Brighton, Catherine
Brillhart, Julie
When Daddy Took Us Camping - Brillhart, Julie
Britt, Stephanie
The Adventures of Peter Rabbit - Potter, Beatrix
Broda, Ron
Have You Seen Bugs? - Oppenheim, Joanne
Broeck, Fabricio Vanden
Under the Breadfruit Tree - Gunning, Monica
Bronson, Linda
Crookjaw - Cohen, Caron Lee
Brooker, Kyrsten
Nothing Ever Happens on 90th Street - Schotter, Roni
Brooks, Donna
The Rabbit and the Promise Sign - Day-Bivins, Pat
Brooks, Joe
Oh, Freedom! - King, Casey
Brooks, Nan
Haunted House - Van Metre, Susan
Brooks, Ron
Henry's Bath - Perversi, Margaret
Henry's Bed - Perversi, Margaret
Old Pig - Wild, Margaret
Brouwer, Aafke
Ginny's Egg - Goodhart, Pippa
Love Stories - Pilling, Ann
Brown, Calef
Polkabats and Octopus Slacks - Brown, Calef
Brown, Deborah
Little Koala Finds a Friend - Roc, Margaret

Brown, Don
Alice Ramsey's Grand Adventure - Brown, Don

Brown, Doreen
And I Always Been Moving! - Lennon, Jessie

Brown, Jane Clark
Marvin's Best Christmas Present Ever - Paterson, Katherine

Brown, Judith
The Miracle of Saint Nicholas - Whelan, Gloria

Brown, Judith Gwyn
The Best Christmas Pageant Ever - Robinson, Barbara
Bless All Creatures Here Below - Brown, Judith Gwyn

Brown, Judy
Anna's Birthday Adventure - Jones, Allan Frewin
Pirate Pandemonium - Strong, Jeremy

Brown, Kathryn
From Lullaby to Lullaby - Geras, Adele

Brown, Ken
Mucky Pup - Brown, Ken
The Wolf Is Coming - MacDonald, Elizabeth
The Wolf Is Coming! - MacDonald, Elizabeth

Brown, Lisa M
Outrageous Women of Ancient Times - Leon, Vicki

Brown, M K
Selby Speaks - Ball, Duncan

Brown, Marc
Arthur Writes a Story - Brown, Marc
Arthur's Computer Disaster - Brown, Marc
Arthur's Family Vacation (Brown) - Brown, Marc
Arthur's Halloween (Brown) - Brown, Marc
Arthur's Nose - Brown, Marc
Arthur's Really Helpful Word Book - Brown, Marc
D.W. All Wet - Brown, Marc
D.W. Flips - Brown, Marc
Rex and Lilly Schooltime - Brown, Laurene Krasny
What's the Big Secret? - Brown, Laurene Krasny
When Dinosaurs Die - Brown, Laurene Krasny

Brown, Martin
The Groovy Greeks - Deary, Terry
The Rotten Romans - Deary, Terry

Brown, Richard
Baby Buggy, Buggy Baby - Ziefert, Harriet
Night, Knight - Ziefert, Harriet
The Thanksgiving Monster - Inches, Alison

Brown, Rick
Put a Fan in Your Hat! - Carrow, Robert
Turn on the Lights--from Bed! - Carrow, Robert

Brown, Rod
From Slave Ship to Freedom Road - Lester, Julius

Brown, Ruth
Baba - Brown, Ruth
Baba Yaga and the Wise Doll - Oram, Hiawyn
Cry Baby - Brown, Ruth
Mr. Bear and the Bear - Thomas, Frances
Wise Doll - Oram, Hiawyn

Brown, Sterling
The Singing Geese - Wahl, Jan

Browne, Anthony
Willy the Dreamer - Browne, Anthony
Willy the Wizard - Browne, Anthony

Browne, Eileen
La Sorpresa De Nandi - Browne, Eileen

Browne, Jane
The Little Stowaway - Tomlinson, Theresa

Browne, Philippa-Alys
The Animals of the Chinese Zodiac - Whitfield, Susan
The Legend of the Chinese Zodiac - Whitfield, Susan

Brownfield, Mick
Beck Bananas--This Is Your Life! - Ure, Jean

Browning, Colleen
Can't Sit Still - Lotz, Karen E

Browning, Tom
Santa's Time Off - Maynard, Bill

Brownlie, Betty
Under My Bed There Lives a Tiger - Gardner, Rosalind

Brownridge, William Roy
The Final Game - Brownridge, William Roy

C

Cable, Annette
I Fly - Rockwell, Anne

Cabrera, Jane
Cat's Colors - Cabrera, Jane
Cat's Colours - Cabrera, Jane

Caffee, Julie
Twisters, Bronc Riders, and Cherry Pie -
Marlow, Herb

Caldwell, Chris
Alsek's ABC Adventure - Caldwell, Chris

Camagni, Yacopo
*I Bastoni Dello Yeti E Altre Favole Del
Nepal* - Varma, Nishu

Cameron, Marie
*The Wisdom of the Crows and Other
Buddhist Tales* - Chodzin, Sherab

Cameron, Scott
David and Goliath - Schenk de Regniers,
Beatrice
Maple Moon - Crook, Connie Brummel
The Token Gift - McKibbon, Hugh
William

Camm, Martin
Deserts - Morris, Neil
Mountains - Morris, Neil
Oceans - Morris, Neil

Campbell, Ken
River, My Friend - Bell, William

Campbell, Peter A
Launch Day - Campbell, Peter A

Campbell, Rod
Little Bird - Campbell, Rod

Cann, Helen
A Child's Book of Celtic Prayers -
Denham, Joyce
Father and Daughter Tales -
Evetts-Secker, Josephine
Mother and Daughter Tales -
Evetts-Secker, Josephine

Cannon, Annie
Tale of a Tadpole - Porte, Barbara Ann

Cannon, Janell
Stellaluna: A Pop-up Book and Mobile -
Cannon, Janell
Verdi - Cannon, Janell

Canyon, Christopher
Grand Canyon: A Trail through Time -
Vieira, Linda
Wonderful Nature, Wonderful You -
Ireland, Karen

Caple, Laurie A
Bird Watching with Margaret Morse Nice
- Ross, Michael Elsohn
Bug Watching with Charles Henry Turner
- Ross, Michael Elsohn
*Clyde Tombaugh and the Search for
Planet X* - Wetterer, Margaret K
Flower Watching with Alice Eastwood -
Ross, Michael Elsohn
Wildlife Watching with Charles Eastman -
Ross, Michael Elsohn

Caras, Roger A
A Most Dangerous Journey - Caras, Roger
A

Card, Vanessa
Caves - Morris, Neil
Cities - Morris, Neil
The History News: Medicine - Gates, Phil
Lakes - Morris, Neil
Oceans and Seas - Morris, Neil

Carla Dijs
The Tortoise and the Hare - Dijs, Carla

Carle, Eric
Catch the Ball - Carle, Eric
Flora and Tiger - Carle, Eric
From Head to Toe - Carle, Eric
Hello, Red Fox - Carle, Eric
A House for Hermit Crab - Carle, Eric
Let's Paint a Rainbow - Carle, Eric
Today Is Monday - Carle, Eric
The Very Hungry Caterpillar - Carle, Eric
The Very Quiet Cricket - Carle, Eric
What's for Lunch - Carle, Eric

Carlson, Nancy L
ABC, I Like Me! - Carlson, Nancy L
I Like Me! (Weeks) - Carlson, Nancy L
Me Gusto Como Soy! - Carlson, Nancy L

Carmichael, Clay
Used-Up Bear - Carmichael, Clay

Caron, Romi
Side by Side - Baillie, Marilyn
Wild Talk - Baillie, Marilyn

Carpenter, Nancy
Masai and I - Kroll, Virginia L
Sitti's Secrets - Nye, Naomi Shihab
The Tree That Came to Stay - Quindlen,
Anna
Twinnies - Bunting, Eve

Carpenter, Stephen
No More Homework! No More Tests! -
Lansky, Bruce

Carreiro, Carolyn
Hand-Print Animal Art - Carreiro, Carolyn

Carrozza, John
Desert Discoveries - Wadsworth, Ginger

Carter, Abby
Annie Bananie - Komaiko, Leah
Annie Bananie and the People's Court - Komaiko, Leah
Annie Bananie--Best Friends to the End - Komaiko, Leah
Flashlight Games - Keller, Ellen
The Invisible Day - Jocelyn, Marthe

Carter, Penny
A Big Trip for the Morrisons - Carter, Penny

Cartlidge, Michelle
The Mice of Mousehole - Cartlidge, Michelle

Cartwright, Reg
The Band over the Hill - Isherwood, Shirley
The Boat of Many Rooms - Lewis, J Patrick
Kaspar's Greatest Discovery - Paget, Campbell
Mouse Creeps - Harris, Peter

Cartwright, Stephen
There's a Dragon at My School - Tyler, Jenny
There's a Monster in My House - Tyler, Jenny

Casadevall, Gabriel
Baby Birds - Garcia, Eulalia
Bears: Animals That Hibernate - Sanchez Sanchez, Isidro
Fish: Swimming and Floating - Sanchez Sanchez, Isidro
Fleas: Bloodsucking Parasites - Llamas, Andreu
Frogs: Living in Two Worlds - Llamas, Andreu
Giant Squid - Garcia, Eulalia
Jellyfish: Animals with a Deadly Touch - Garcia, Eulalia

Casale, Paul
Wild Horse Summer - Ryden, Hope

Caseley, Judith
Dorothy's Darkest Days - Caseley, Judith
Jorah's Journal - Caseley, Judith

Casey, Patricia
Beep! Beep! Oink! Oink! Animals in the City - Casey, Patricia

Cash-Walsh, Tina
Cosmic Science - Wiese, Jim
The Math Chef - D'Amico, Joan
The Science Chef Travels around the World - D'Amico, Joan

Casilla, Robert
Jalapeno Bagels - Wing, Natasha
The Legend of Mexicatl - Harper, Jo
The Little Painter of Sabana Grande - Markun, P
A Picture Book of Thurgood Marshall - Adler, David A

Cassatt, Mary
A Child's Book of Lullabies - McKellar, Shona

Cassels, Jean
Swift as the Wind - Esbensen, Barbara Juster

Castillo, Raul
Este Libro Horroroso Sin Remedio - Yanez, Alberto

Catalano, Dominic
Merry Christmas, Old Armadillo - Brimner, Larry Dane

Catalanotto, Peter
Dreamplace - Lyon, George Ella
Getting Used to the Dark - Swanson, Susan Marie
Letter to the Lake - Swanson, Susan Marie
My House Has Stars - McDonald, Megan
The Rolling Store - Johnson, Angela
Who Came Down That Road? - Lyon, George Ella

Cathcart, Yvonne
Shoot for the Moon, Robyn - Hutchins, H J

Catrow, David
Who Said That? - Burleigh, Robert
Why Lapin's Ears Are Long and Other Tales from the Louisiana Bayou - Doucet, Sharon Arms

Cavanaugh, Matthew
Batboy: An Inside Look at Spring Training - Anderson, Joan

Cazet, Denys
Night Lights - Cazet, Denys

Cecil, Randy
Dear Dr. Sillybear - Regan, Dian Curtis
Little Red Cowboy Hat - Lowell, Susan

Cencetti, Greta
Play Me a Story - Adler, Naomi

Cepeda, Joe
The Old Man and His Door - Soto, Gary

Cha, Chu
Dia's Story Cloth - Cha, Dia

Chagall, Marc
Fables of La Fontaine - La Fontaine, Jean De

Chaisty, Chris
The Usborne Book of Hair Braiding - Watt, Fiona

Chamberlain, Margaret
You Can Swim, Jim - Umansky, Kaye
Chambers, Mary
55 Waverly Street - Black, Thom
Chambliss, Maxie
I'm a Big Brother - Cole, Joanna
I'm a Big Sister - Cole, Joanna
I'm Going to the Doctor -
Chan, Harvey
The Charlotte Stories - Jam, Teddy
Ghost Train - Yee, Paul
Three Monks, No Water - Ye, Ting-Xing
Chance, Tony
Tales from Perrault - Perrault, Charles
Chanell, Jim
The Alligator - Crewe, Sabrina
Chang, Gui Fong
Happy Birthday to You - Fang, Su Chen
Chang, Shih-Ming
Emperor and the Nightingale - Hao,
Kuang-Ts'
Chang, Warren
Ola Shakes It Up - Hyppolite, Joanne
Chapin, Carol
Wrapper Rockets and Trombone Straws -
Sobey, Edwin J C
Chapman, Jane
Dora's Eggs - Sykes, Julie
Penny and Pup - Jennings, Linda
Charko, Kasia
The Princess Who Danced with Cranes -
LeBox, Annette
Snow Story - Hundal, Nancy
Charles, Veronika Martenova
Necklace of Stars - Charles, Veronika
Martenova
Charlot, Jean
Secret of the Andes - Clark, Ann Nolan
Charlton, Michael
Across the Roman Wall - Breslin, Theresa
Charteris, Jamie
A Bad Start for Santa Claus - Hayes,
Sarah
Chase, Andra
Bea's Own Good - Talley, Linda
Chatterjee, Khitish
La Pulga Cecilia - Carreno, Mada
Chatterton, Martin
The Magnificent Mummies - Bradman,
Tony
Chayka, Doug
Beekeepers - High, Linda Oatman
Cheese, Chloe
The Babies Are Coming! - Hest, Amy

Chen, Ju-Hong
*The Tale of Aladdin and the Wonderful
Lamp* - Kimmel, Eric A
Chen, Yong
Miz Fannie Mae's Fine New Easter Hat -
Milich, Melissa
Cherry, Lynne
The Armadillo from Amarillo - Cherry,
Lynne
Flute's Journey - Cherry, Lynne
Chesi, Matteo
The Atlas of the Classical World - Bardi,
Piero
Chess, Victoria
King Long Shanks - Yolen, Jane
This for That - Aardema, Verna
Chester, Jonathan
Splash! A Penguin Counting Book -
Chester, Jonathan
Chesworth, Michael
The Adventures of Pippi Longstocking -
Lindgren, Astrid
Jacob Two-Two's First Spy Case -
Richler, Mordecai
Swish! - Martin, Bill
Chiago, Michael
Sing Down the Rain - Moreillon, Judi
Chichester Clark, Emma
The Frog Princess - Cecil, Laura
Little Miss Muffet Counts to Ten -
Chichester Clark, Emma
Little Miss Muffet's Count-Along Surprise
- Chichester Clark, Emma
Mrs. Vole the Vet - Ahlberg, Allan
*The Orchard Book of Greek Gods and
Goddesses* - McCaughrean, Geraldine
Chicoine, Stephen
A Liberian Family - Chicoine, Stephen
Chism, Hilair
Adopted by Indians - Mayfield, Thomas
Jefferson
Choi, Yangsook
Nim and the War Effort - Lee, Milly
The Sun Girl and the Moon Boy - Choi,
Yangsook
Chorao, Kay
Jumpety-Bumpety Hop - Chorao, Kay
Little Farm by the Sea - Chorao, Kay
Mother Goose Magic - Chorao, Kay
Christanto, Dadang
The Flaming Witch - Reeder, Stephanie
Owen

Cole, Henry
Barefoot: Escape on the Underground Railroad - Edwards, Pamela Duncan
Dinorella: A Prehistoric Fairy Tale - Edwards, Pamela Duncan
I Took a Walk - Cole, Henry
Livingstone Mouse - Edwards, Pamela Duncan
Moosetache - Palatini, Margie
Warthogs in the Kitchen - Edwards, Pamela Duncan

Colle, Gisela
The Star Tree - Colle, Gisela

Collicott, Sharleen
The Chicken Sisters - Numeroff, Laura Joffe

Collier, Mary
My Little House Christmas Crafts Book - Collins, Carolyn

Collington, Peter
The Angel and the Soldier Boy - Collington, Peter
The Coming of the Surfman - Collington, Peter
Little Pickle - Collington, Peter
On Christmas Eve - Collington, Peter
A Small Miracle - Collington, Peter
The Tooth Fairy - Collington, Peter

Collins, Heather
Frankie on the Run - Holeman, Linda
Hungry Animals - Hickman, Pamela
The Kids Campfire Book - Drake, Jane
The Kids Canadian Bug Book - Hickman, Pamela
The Kids Canadian Plant Book - Hickman, Pamela
A New Butterfly - Hickman, Pamela
Pioneer Crafts - Greenwood, Barbara
A Seed Grows - Hickman, Pamela

Collins, Jim
Big Whiskers Saves the Cove - Carolan, Trevor

Colon, Raul
Always My Dad - Wyeth, Sharon Dennis
Celebration! - Thomas, Jane Resh
Tomas and the Library Lady - Mora, Pat
A Weave of Words - San Souci, Robert D

Colston, Fifi
Get Real Paddy Manson - Corrin, Ruth

Condy, Roy
Christopher Changes His Name - Sadu, Itah
Christopher, Please Clean Up Your Room - Sadu, Itah
Shark Attacks and Spider Snacks - Condy, Roy

Conklin, Paul
To Seek a Better World - Ashabranner, Brent

Connolly, Peter
Oxford Children's Ancient History - Burrell, Roy E C

Conteh-Morgan, Jane
Little Fish, Lost - Van Laan, Nancy

Cony, Sue
Eric's Elephant Goes Camping - Gatehouse, John
Puss-in-Boots - Butterfield, Moira
Sleeping Beauty - Butterfield, Moira

Cook, Donald
Washington Irving's Rip Van Winkle - Bergen, Lara

Cook, Laura
The Day of the Twelve-Story Wave - Swanson, Diane

Cook, Scott
With a Whoop and a Holler - Van Laan, Nancy

Cooney, Barbara
Eleanor - Cooney, Barbara
Only Opal - Boulton, Jane
The Remarkable Christmas of the Cobbler's Sons - Sawyer, Ruth

Cooper, Deborah
People of Salmon and Cedar - Hirschi, Ron

Cooper, Elisha
Ballpark - Cooper, Elisha
Country Fair - Cooper, Elisha

Dann, Geoff
Baby's World--At Home -
Baby's World--Outdoors -
Dann, Penny
At the Hospital - Moses, Amy
What Are Friends For? - Grindley, Sally
D'Antonio, Nancy
Our Baby from China - D'Antonio, Nancy
Darling, Tara
ABC Dogs - Darling, Kathy
Amazon ABC - Darling, Kathy
Chameleons: On Location - Darling,
Kathy
Desert Babies - Darling, Kathy
Komodo Dragon - Darling, Kathy
Seashore Babies - Darling, Kathy
Darrach, Susan
Beauty and the Beast Rap - Dunn, Sonja
Daugavietis, Ruta
The Ultimate Baby-Sitter's Handbook -
Zakarin, Debra Mostow
D'Aulaire, Ingri
D'Aulaires' Book of Greek Myths -
D'Aulaire, Ingri
Davalos, Felipe
Gone Forever! - Markle, Sandra
The Lizard and the Sun - Ada, Alma Flor
Punia and the King of Sharks - Wardlaw,
Lee
Davenier, Christine
Leon and Albertine - Davenier, Christine
David, Mark
Fantastic Plastic - Ingram, Anne
Davidson, Andrew
Godhanger - King-Smith, Dick
Davidson, Dennis
The Sun and Other Stars - Harris, Richard
Davie, Helen
Animals in Winter - Bancroft, Henrietta
Davie, Helen K
Echoes for the Eye - Esbensen, Barbara
Juster
Davies, Jo
Bertie's Big Blue Binoculars - Faulkner,
Keith
Davies, Kate
What's That Noise - Davies, Gill
Davies, Rebecca
My Uncle Jack's a Logger - Loyd, Luli
Davies, Sally J K
Why Did We Have to Move Here? -
Davies, Sally J K

Davis, Jack E
Dr. Jekyll, Orthodontist - Greenburg, Dan
A Ghost Named Wanda - Greenburg, Dan
Great-Grandpa's in the Litter Box -
Greenburg, Dan
*I'm Out of My Body--Please Leave a
Message* - Greenburg, Dan
My Son, the Time Traveler - Greenburg,
Dan
Never Trust a Cat Who Wears Earrings -
Greenburg, Dan
Through the Medicine Cabinet -
Greenburg, Dan
Zap! I'm a Mind Reader - Greenburg, Dan
Davis, John
The Scarecrows of Necum Teuch - Geddes,
Angella
Davis, Lambert
The Bells of Christmas - Hamilton,
Virginia
Davis, Wendy
From Metal to Music - Davis, Wendy
Davis, Yvonne LeBrun
Slop! A Welsh Folktale - MacDonald,
Margaret Read
Daviz, Paul
Not More Poems to Shout Out Loud -
Henry, Ernest
DaVolls, Andy
Tano and Binti - DaVolls, Andy
The Wolf Watchers - Hood, Alison
Dawson, Blair
Mary Margaret's Tree - Dawson, Blair
Day, Alexandra
The Christmas We Moved to the Barn -
Day, Alexandra
Mirror - Darling, Christina
Day, Bruce
The Case of the Dognapped Cat - Howard,
Milly
De Beer, Hans
Little Bobo Saves the Day - Romanelli,
Serena
Ollie the Elephant - Bos, Burny
De Groat, Diane
Bug in a Rug - Gilson, Jamie
*A Pinky Is a Baby Mouse and Other Baby
Animal Names* - Ryan, Pam Munoz
See You Around, Sam! - Lowry, Lois

Doolittle, Michael J
Stones, Bones, and Petroglyphs -
Goodman, Susan E

Dose, Jo
Rocking Chair Love - Gibson, Kathleen

Doty, Roy
Soda Science - Zubrowski, Bernie

Douzou, Olivier
The Wolf's Lunch - Douzou, Olivier

Downer, Maggie
Search for the Lost City - Wood, A J

Downes, Belinda
Every Little Angel's Handbook - Downes,
Belinda

Downing, Julie
Baby Jesus - Downing, Julie
A First Bible Story Book - Hoffman, Mary
Jonah and the Whale - Downing, Julie
Joseph's Colorful Coat - Downing, Julie
The Magpie's Nest - Foster, Joanna
Water Voices - Speed, Toby

Draper, Rochelle
Vincent Van Gogh - Lucas, Eileen

Drawson, Blair
Flying Dimitri - Drawson, Blair

Drescher, Henrik
The Boy Who Ate Around - Drescher,
Henrik
*Brer Rabbit and the Wonderful Tar Baby
(Lover)* - Harris, Joel Chandler

Drinker, Susan G
*Six Words, Many Turtles, and Three Days
in Hong Kong* - McMahon, Patricia

Drummond, Allan
Moby Dick - Drummond, Allan

Du Bois, William Pene
A Certain Small Shepherd - Caudill,
Rebecca

Dubois, Claude K
I Love You so Much - Norac, Carl

Dubowski, Mark
Pirate School - Dubowski, Cathy East

Dubrowski, Ken
Up and Away! - Davis, Meredith

Duffy, Daniel Mark
Bite Makes Right - Calhoun, B B
The Competition - Calhoun, B B
Fair Play - Calhoun, B B
On the Right Track - Calhoun, B B
Out of Place - Calhoun, B B
Theodoric's Rainbow - Kramer, Stephen

Dugan, Karen
Bicycle Riding and Other Poems - Liatsos,
Sandra Olson
Dominoes around the World - Lankford,
Mary D
Halmoni and the Picnic - Choi, Sook Nyul
Spring Break - Hurwitz, Johanna
Yunmi and Halmoni's Trip - Choi, Sook
Nyul

Duke, Kate
One Guinea Pig Is Not Enough - Duke,
Kate

Dunaway, Nancy
I Scream, You Scream - Morrison, Lillian

Dunbar, Fiona
The Camp Knock Knock Mystery - Duffey,
Betsy
Every Buddy Counts - Murphy, Stuart J

Duncan, Karen
Bat - Robb, Jackie
Brain Cell - Robb, Jackie
Slug - Robb, Jackie
Spider - Robb, Jackie

Duncan, Stuart
Alice Falls Apart - Nodelman, Perry

Dunfield, Robb Terrence
If Sarah Will Take Me - Bouchard, Dave

Dunrea, Olivier
The Trow-Wife's Treasure - Dunrea,
Olivier

Dupasquier, Philippe
Fizzy in the Spotlight - Coleman, Michael

Dupre, Rick
Give Me Bach My Schubert - Cleary,
Brian P

Durham, Lyn
*Marie: Mystery at the Paris Ballet, Paris
1775* - Greene, Jacqueline D
Marie: Summer in the Country, Paris 1775
- Greene, Jacqueline D

Durham, Sarah
Rose and Sebastian - Zarin, Cynthia

Durkin, Denise
He Ingoa Ngarara - Smith, Arahia

Durr, Gesela
Henry and Horace Clean Up - Mennel,
Wolfgang

Durr, Robb
The Ultimate Book of Kid Concoctions -
Thomas, John E

Durrell, Julie
  A Glass Slipper for Rosie - Giff, Patricia
    Reilly
  Halloween Hide-and-Seek - Jane, Pamela
  Mermaid Island - Frith, Margaret
  Not-So-Perfect Rosie - Giff, Patricia Reilly
  Starring Rosie - Giff, Patricia Reilly

Dusikova, Maja
  Rapunzel: A Fairy Tale -

Duvall, Lili
  Chef Ki Is Serving Dinner! - Duvall, Jill
  *Meet Rory Hohenstein, a Professional
    Dancer* - Duvall, Jill
  Mr. Duvall Reports the News - Duvall, Jill
  Ms. Moja Makes Beautiful Clothes -
    Duvall, Jill
  *Who Keeps the Water Clean? Ms.
    Schindler!* - Duvall, Jill

Dwyer, Mindy
  Aurora: A Tale of the Northern Lights -
    Dwyer, Mindy
  Coyote in Love - Dwyer, Mindy

Dye, Sharon
  The Wombat Who Talked to the Stars -
    Morris, Jill

Dyer, Jane
  Child of Faerie, Child of Earth - Yolen,
    Jane
  Cracked Corn and Snow Ice Cream -
    Willard, Nancy
  My Father - Collins, Judy
  Talking like the Rain - Kennedy, X J
  The Three Bears Rhyme Book - Yolen,
    Jane
  Time for Bed - Fox, Mem

E

Eachus, Jennifer
  The Big Big Sea - Waddell, Martin
  Goodbye Pappa - Leavy, Una

Eagle Walking Turtle
  Full Moon Stories - Eagle Walking Turtle

Early, Margaret
  Robin Hood - Early, Margaret
  Romeo and Juliet - Early, Margaret

Eastman, P D
  *The Cat in the Hat Beginner Book
    Dictionary* - Eastman, P D

Eastwood, John
  All Because of Jackson - King-Smith, Dick

Eccles, Jane
  Have You Started Yet? - Thomson, Ruth
  Tongue Twisters and Tonsil Twizzlers -
    Cookson, Paul

Eckerle, Tom
  *The Good Housekeeping Illustrated
    Children's Cookbook* - Zanzarella,
    Marianne

Eduar, Gilles
  Jooka Saves the Day - Eduar, Gilles

Effler, Jim
  Bamboo Valley (Kaye) - Nagda, Ann
    Whitehead

Egan, Robert
  From Wheat to Pasta - Egan, Robert

Egan, Tim
  Burnt Toast on Davenport Street - Egan,
    Tim
  Distant Feathers - Egan, Tim

Egielski, Richard
  Call Me Ahnighito - Conrad, Pam
  The Gingerbread Boy - Egielski, Richard
  Oh, Brother - Yorinks, Arthur
  Perfect Pancakes, if You Please - Wise,
    William
  The Tub Grandfather - Conrad, Pam

Ehlert, Lois
  Chicka Chicka Boom Boom - Martin, Bill
  Cuckoo: A Mexican Folktale - Ehlert, Lois
  Hands - Ehlert, Lois
  A Pair of Socks - Murphy, Stuart J

Ehling, Katalin Olah
  The Night the Grandfathers Danced -
    Raezek, L

Eisenburger, Doris
  *Franz Schubert--Ein Musikalisches
    Bilderbuch* - Ekker, Ernst A

Eitan, Ora
  Cowboy Bunnies - Loomis, Christine

Eitzen, Allan
  Cherry Tree - Bond, Ruskin

Elgar, Rebecca
  Jack: Happy Birthday - Elgar, Rebecca

Elizabeth Enright
  Spider-Web for Two - Enright, Elizabeth

Ellis, Andy
  The Pocket Elephant - Sefton, Catherine

Ellis, Gerry
  Hippos - Walker, Sally M
  Rhinos - Walker, Sally M

Ellis, Jan Davey
  The Book of Slime - Jackson, Ellen
  Toad Overload - Seibert, Patricia

Ellis, Tim
  The Gooch Machine - Bagert, Brod

Ellison, Pauline
Master Maid - Shepard, Aaron
Ellwand, David
Emma's Elephant and Other Favorite Animal Friends - Ellwand, David
Emberley, Ed
Drummer Hoff - Emberley, Barbara
Glad Monster, Sad Monster - Emberley, Ed
Emberley, Michael
Happy Birth Day! - Harris, Robie H
It's Perfectly Normal - Harris, Robie H
Emberley, Rebecca
My Mother's Secret Life - Emberley, Rebecca
Emerling, Dorothy
Along the Seashore - Cooper, Ann C
Engel, Diana
Holding On - Engel, Diana
Engelbreit, Mary
My Symphony - Channing, William Henry
English, Sarah Jane
Easy Braids, Barrettes and Bows - Sadler, Judy Ann
Enright, Elizabeth
Then There Were Five - Enright, Elizabeth
Enright, Vicky
Crafts from Your Favorite Fairy Tales - Ross, Kathy
Epanya, Christian
Konte Chameleon, Fine, Fine, Fine! - Kessler, Cristina
Konte Chameleon, Fine, Fine, Fine - Kessler, Cristina
Erlbruch, Wolf
Mrs. Meyer the Bird - Erlbruch, Wolf
Vom Kleinen Maulwurf, Der Wissen Wollte, Wer Ihm Auf Den Kopf Gemacht Hat - Holzwarth, Werner
Ernst, Barbara
Song of the Kalahari - Ernst, Barbara
Ernst, Lisa Campbell
Bubba and Trixie - Ernst, Lisa Campbell
The Letters Are Lost - Ernst, Lisa Campbell
Potato: A Tale from the Great Depression - Lied, Kate
Who Says Moo? - Young, Ruth
Escriva, Vivi
Froggie Froggette - Perera, Hilda
Tainos - Dorris, Michael
Espinosa, Alain
El Rey Que Se Equivoco De Cuento - Granados, Antonio

Essley, Roger
Angels in the Dust - Raven, Margot
Under the Pear Tree - Seabrooke, Brenda
Euvremer, Teryl
Toby, Where Are You? - Steig, William
Evans, Leslie
Autumn: An Alphabet Acrostic - Schnur, Steven
Evans, Nate
Horrible Holly's Pet Raptor - Ratnett, Michael
Everitt, Betsy
Up the Ladder, down the Slide - Everitt, Betsy
Ewart, Claire
The Biggest Horse I Ever Did See - Couture, Susan Arkin
Time Train - Fleischman, Paul
Ewers, Joe
The Bunny Slipper Mystery - Dussling, Jennifer
Ewing, Carolyn
Dear Timothy Tibbitts - Enderle, Judith Ross

F

Fabian, Bobbi
Twinkle, Twinkle -
Twinkle, Twinkle, an Animal Lover's Mother Goose -
Fabrick, Harriett
Furello - Fabrick, Harriett
Facklam, Paul
The Biggest Bug Book - Facklam, Margery
Fadden, John Kahionhes
The Native Stories from Keepers of the Animals - Bruchac, Joseph
Faerber, Kevin
Look Good, Feel Good - Swinden, Liz
Faidley, Warren
Eye of the Storm - Kramer, Stephen P
Falwell, Cathryn
Hands! - Kroll, Virginia L
Fanelli, Sara
Dibby Dubby Dhu - Barker, George
Wolf - Fanelli, Sara
Farman, John
Egyptians - Farman, John
Tudors - Farman, John
Victorians - Farman, John
Vikings - Farman, John
Farmer, Andrew
Hills and Mountains - Crewe, Sabrina

Fisher-Johnson, Paul
Mission to Marathon - Trease, Geoffrey
Fitzgerald, Gerald
In My Pocket - Sim, Dorrith M
Fitzgerald, Joanne
Jacob's Best Sisters - Jam, Teddy
Fitzpatrick, Marie-Louise
The Long March - Fitzpatrick, Marie-Louise
Flavin, Teresa
The Old Cotton Blues - England, Linda
Fleming, Denise
Time to Sleep - Fleming, Denise
Flesher, Vivienne
Lullaby Raft - Nye, Naomi Shihab
An Mei's Strange and Wondrous Journey - Molnar-Fenton, Stephan
Floca, Brian
Counting Feathers - Simmons, Al
Where Are You, Little Zack? - Enderle, Judith Ross
Flook, Helen
The Town That Floated Away - Birdsel, Sandra
Florczak, Robert
Birdsong - Wood, Audrey
Florian, Douglas
In the Swim - Florian, Douglas
Insectlopedia - Florian, Douglas
Fong, Andrea
Made in China - Williams, Suzanne
Ford, George
The Story of Ruby Bridges - Coles, Robert
Wild, Wild Hair - Grimes, Nikki
Ford, Miela
Watch Us Play - Ford, Miela
Ford, Wayne
Big and Bulky - Butterfield, Moira
Big, Rough, and Wrinkly - Butterfield, Moira
Brown, Fierce, and Furry - Butterfield, Moira
Colourful and Bright - Butterfield, Moira
Fast, Strong, and Striped - Butterfield, Moira
Quick, Quiet, and Feathered - Butterfield, Moira
Scaly and Snappy - Butterfield, Moira
Strong and Stripy - Butterfield, Moira
Swift and Silent - Butterfield, Moira
Foreman, Mark
Mark Foreman's Great Race - Foreman, Mark

Foreman, Michael
After the War Was Over - Foreman, Michael
Angel and the Box of Time - Foreman, Michael
The Brothers Grimm: Popular Folk Tales - Grimm, Jacob
Creation: Read-Aloud Stories from Many Lands - Pilling, Ann
Creation Stories from Around the World - Pilling, Ann
The Knight and the Squire - Jones, Terry
Land of the Long White Cloud - Te Kanawa, Kiri
The Little Reindeer - Foreman, Michael
The Little Ships - Borden, Louise
Look! Look! - Foreman, Michael
Peter Pan and Wendy - Barrie, J M
Peter's Place - Grindley, Sally
Robin of Sherwood - Morpurgo, Michael
Seal Surfer - Foreman, Michael
The Songs My Paddle Sings - Riordan, James
Forest, Crista
Moon in Bear's Eyes - Swinburne, Stephen R
Formby, Caroline
Tristan's Temper Tantrum - Formby, Caroline
Forrest, Sandra
Bubblemania - Wardlaw, Lee
Forsey, Chris
The Best Book of Bugs - Llewellyn, Claire
Creatures of the Past - Fitzsimons, Cecilia
Fosberg, John
Cookie Shapes - Fosberg, John
Ice Cream Colors - Fosberg, John
Foster, Karen Sharp
Good Night My Little Chicks - Foster, Karen Sharp
Foster, Mike
The World of Architectural Wonders - Corbishley, Mike
Foster, Teresa
My First Canadian Science Encyclopedia - Scarborough, Kate
Fox-Davies, Sarah
Walk with a Wolf - Howker, Janni
Foxx, Jeffrey Jay
Angela Weaves a Dream - Sola, Michele
Frampton, David
Clouds of Glory - Chaikin, Miriam
Miro in the Kingdom of the Sun - Kurtz, Jane
When Plague Strikes - Giblin, James Cross

Garcia, Alejandro Campos
El Alma En Una Nube - Artiles Perez,
   Emma
Garcia, Fatima
Mao Tiang Pelos Tiesos - Amo,
   Montserrat Del
Garcia, Geronimo
A Gift from Papa Diego - Saenz, Benjamin
   Alire
Garcia, Mannie
Catching the Fire - Lyons, Mary E
Garcia, Stephanie
Snapshots from the Wedding - Soto, Gary
Gardner, Sally
Hello? Is Anybody There? - Gaarder,
   Jostein
Gardos, Susan
Aliens in the Basement - Reid, Susan
The Big Race - McNicoll, Sylvia
School Campout - Citra, Becky
Garland, Michael
Diary of a Drummer Boy - Brill, Marlene
   Targ
Electra and the Charlotte Russe - Bliss,
   Corinne Demas
Leah's Pony - Friedrich, Elizabeth
The Mouse before Christmas - Garland,
   Michael
Saint Patrick - Tompert, Ann
Garland, Sarah
Tex the Cowboy - Garland, Sarah
Garlick, Jackie
Mama Bessie's Nest - Garlick, Jackie
Garousi, Ali
Volcanos and Earthquakes - Llamas Ruiz,
   Andres
Garrison, Barbara
One Room School - Pringle, Laurence
Garvin, Elaine
I Wonder Why Did Elijah Hide? - Youd,
   Pauline
I Wonder Why Was Andrew Surprised? -
   Youd, Pauline
I Wonder Why Was Deborah Mad? -
   Youd, Pauline
I Wonder Why Was Gideon Worried? -
   Youd, Pauline
I Wonder Why Was Jeremiah Sad? -
   Youd, Pauline
I Wonder Why Was Mary Embarrassed? -
   Youd, Pauline
Gates, Donald
The Summer of Stanley - Kinsey-Warnock,
   Natalie

Gaudriault, Rozier
Heidi - Spyri, Johanna
Gay, Marie-Louise
The Fabulous Song - Gillmor, Don
Fat Charlie's Circus - Gay, Marie-Louise
Rumpelstiltskin - Gay, Marie-Louise
Gazsi, Edward S
*Hans Christian Andersen's The Snow
   Queen* - Kennedy, Richard
Geehan, Wayne
*Sir Circumference and the First Round
   Table* - Neuschwander, Cindy
Geisert, Arthur
The Etcher's Studio - Geisert, Arthur
Prairie Town - Geisert, Bonnie
Genaille, Velma
Grampa's Cat - Ferguson, John
George, Cliff
Newfoundland Pony Tales - Fraser,
   Andrew F
George, Imelda
The House of Wooden Santas - Major,
   Kevin
Georgeson, Peter
Creatures - Colombo, Luann
Germs - Colombo, Luann
Gepp, Gerhard
Das Land Der Ecken - Ulitzka, Irene
Gerard, Elena
Even a Little Is Something - Glass, Tom
Gerber, Mary Jane
Wings to Fly - Lottridge, Celia Barker
Germain, Philippe
Un Crocodile Dans La Baignoire - Hebert,
   Marie-Francine
Dr. Ah Chu and Jonah's Egg - Allan, Ted
Poppy's Whale - Hebert, Marie-Francine
Gerrard, Roy
Wagons West! - Gerrard, Roy
Gerstein, Mordicai
Jonah and the Two Great Fish - Gerstein,
   Mordicai
Something Queer in the Wild West - Levy,
   Elizabeth
Geter, Tyrone
White Socks Only - Coleman, Evelyn

Gibbons, Gail
Cats - Gibbons, Gail
Click! A Book about Cameras and Taking Pictures - Gibbons, Gail
Dogs - Gibbons, Gail
Gulls--Gulls--Gulls - Gibbons, Gail
The Honey Makers - Gibbons, Gail
Marshes and Swamps - Gibbons, Gail
The Moon Book - Gibbons, Gail
Sea Turtles - Gibbons, Gail
Soaring with the Wind - Gibbons, Gail
Yippee-Yay! A Book about Cowboys and Cowgirls - Gibbons, Gail

Gibbons, Tony
Chasmosaurus - Amery, Heather
Green, Tamara, Muttaburrasaurus - Amery, Heather
Oviraptor - Amery, Heather
Psittacosaurus - Amery, Heather
Spinosaurus - Amery, Heather
Vulcanodon - Amery, Heather

Gibson, Barbara
Star Wars: The Death Star - Whitman, John

Gilbert, Anne Yvonne
A Christmas Star Called Hannah - French, Vivian

Gilbert, Rob
Hey, Diddle Diddle - Eagle, Kin

Gilbert, Yvonne
Per and the Dala Horse - Hickox, Rebecca

Gilchrist, Jan Spivey
For the Love of the Game - Greenfield, Eloise
Kia Tanisha Drives Her Car - Greenfield, Eloise
Lemonade Sun and Other Summer Poems - Dotlich, Rebecca Kai
Madelia - Gilchrist, Jan Spivey
Mimi's Tutu - Thomassie, Tynia
Singing Down the Rain - Cowley, Joy
Waiting for Christmas - Greenfield, Monica

Gillespie, Jessie
The Birds' Christmas Carol - Wiggin, Kate Douglas

Gillman, Alec
The Green Truck Garden Giveaway - Martin, Jacqueline Briggs
Take Me Out to the Ballgame - Norworth, Jack

Gilman, Phoebe
Jillian Jiggs to the Rescue - Gilman, Phoebe

Gilson, Jamie
Can't Catch Me, I'm the Gingerbread Man - Gilson, Jamie

Girouard, Patrick
Creepy Cafeteria - Ross, Pat
Welcome to Chillsville Elementary - Ross, Pat

Gisbert, Joan Manuel
La Aventura Inmortal De Max Urkhaus - Gisbert, Joan Manuel

Gittoes, George
War-Torn: Ordinary Lives Behind the Battle Zone - McKay, Fiona

Glanzman, Louis S
Pippi Longstocking - Lindgren, Astrid

Glass, Andrew
Ananse's Feast - Mollel, Tololwa M
The Key to the Cupboard - Whitcher, Susan
A Right Fine Life - Glass, Andrew
The Sweetwater Run - Glass, Andrew

Glen, Maggie
The Midnight Doll - Glen, Maggie

Gliori, Debi
Poems Go Clang! -

Gloeckner, Phoebe
Weird but True - Goldenberg, Janet

Goble, Paul
The Legend of the White Buffalo Woman - Goble, Paul
Remaking the Earth - Goble, Paul
The Return of the Buffaloes - Goble, Paul

Godkin, Celia
Sea Otter Inlet - Godkin, Celia

Godon, Ingrid
Curious Kids Go on Vacation - Antoine, Heloise

Goetzl, Robert F
Many Nations - Bruchac, Joseph

Goffe, Toni
Miss Fannie's Hat - Karon, Jan

Goldberg, Barry
The Rugrats' Book of Chanukah - Willson, Sarah

Goldin, David
Lost Cat - Hardy, Tad

Goldman, Dara
Let's Play Hide and Seek! - Birney, Betty

Golembe, Carla
Dog Magic - Golembe, Carla

Goloshapov, Sergei
The Brave Little Tailor - Grimm, Jacob

Gonzales, Edward
The Farolitos of Christmas - Anaya, Rudolfo

Gonzalez, Maya Christina
Laughing Tomatoes and Other Spring Poems - Alarcon, Francisco X
Goode, Diane
Diane Goode's American Christmas - Goode, Diane
Diane Goode's Book of Giants and Little People - Goode, Diane
The House Gobbaleen - Alexander, Lloyd
Mama's Perfect Present - Goode, Diane
Goodell, Jon
A Mouse Called Wolf - King-Smith, Dick
Goodman, Vivienne
Where the Whales Sing - Kelleher, Victor
Goor, Ron
Insect Metamorphosis - Goor, Ron
Goranova, Tonya
Mili Bate! - Pencheva, Stanka
Gorbachev, Valeri
Nicky and the Big, Bad Wolves - Gorbachev, Valeri
Red, Blue, and Yellow Yarn - Kosman, Miriam R
Young Mouse and Elephant - Farris, Pamela J
Gorbaty, Norman
Cookie Monster! - Ross, Anna
Elmo! - Ross, Anna
Ernie! - Ross, Anna
Grover! - Ross, Anna
Gordon, Gus
The Case of the Smelly Armpit - Bond, Royce
Gordon, Mike
Excuse Me - Moses, Brian
Fun with Materials - Gordon, Maria
I'll Do It! - Moses, Brian
It Wasn't Me! - Moses, Brian
Rocks and Soil - Gordon, Maria
Gore, Leonid
The Malachite Palace - Ada, Alma Flor
The Story of Hanukkah - Simon, Norma
Gormley, Greg
The Stare - Moon, Pat
Gorrissen, Dean
I Got a Rocket! - Zurbo, Matt
Gorski, Jason
The Science Explorer - Murphy, Pat
Gorton, Julia
Riddle Rhymes - Ghigna, Charles
Gosling, Brett
Peggy Goes Cod Fishing - Bath, Linda H
Peggy's Scrawny Green Lobster - Bath, Linda H

Goto, Scott
Heat Wave! - Ketteman, Helen
Gottlieb, Dale
Busy Little Hands Books - Gottlieb, Dale
I Got a Family - Cooper, Melrose
Ms. Sneed's Guide to Hygiene - Gottlieb, Dale
Gould, Leslie
A Wilderness Passover - Waldron, Kathleen Cook
Gould, Philip
The World of William Joyce Scrapbook - Joyce, William
Gould, Roberta
Making Cool Crafts and Awesome Art - Gould, Roberta
Gouldthorpe, Peter
First Light - Crew, Gary
The Wonder Thing - Hawthorn, Libby
Gower, Teri
The Usborne First Dictionary - Wardley, Rachel
Goyallon, Jerome
Drawing Prehistoric Animals - Goyallon, Jerome
Graber, Susan
The Woman Who Flummoxed the Fairies - Forest, Heather
Graef, Renee
The Adventures of Laura and Jack - Wilder, Laura Ingalls
Animal Adventures - Wilder, Laura Ingalls
My Little House 1 2 3 - Wilder, Laura Ingalls
My Little House A B C - Wilder, Laura Ingalls
My Little House Christmas Sticker Book - Pioneer Sisters - Wilder, Laura Ingalls
Prairie Day - Wilder, Laura Ingalls
Graham, Bob
Greetings from Sandy Beach - Graham, Bob
Queenie, One of the Family - Graham, Bob
Queenie the Bantam - Graham, Bob
Graham, Georgia
Tiger's New Cowboy Boots - Morck, Irene
Graham, Jenny
Get Out of the Alphabet, Number 2! - Dakos, Kalli
Graham, Mark
Alicia's Tutu - Pulver, Robin
The Dream Jar - Pryor, Bonnie
If I Were Queen of the World - Hiatt, Fred
Wilderness Cat - Kinsey-Warnock, Natalie

Grahame-Johnstone, Janet
The Starlight Barking - Smith, Dodie

Grajewski, Jerry
Candy Making for Beginners - Fryatt,
Evelyn Howe
Paper Birds That Fly - Schmidt, Norman

GrandPre, Mary
Batwings and the Curtain of Night -
Davol, Marguerite W
Chin Yu Min and the Ginger Cat -
Armstrong, Jennifer

Granstrom, Brita
Honk! Honk! - Manning, Mick

Grapes, Alison R
Duncan Back-to-Back - Wells, Duncan
God and Me - Green, Sheila

Graston, Arlene
Thumbelina - Andersen, Hans Christian

Graves, Linda
The Enchanted Gardening Book - Herck,
Alice

Green, Andy
Jenny Giraffe's Mardi Gras Ride - Dartez,
Cecilia Casrill

Green, Anne Canevari
*Becoming Best Friends with Your
Hamster, Guinea Pig, or Rabbit* -
Gutman, Bill
Becoming Your Cat's Best Friend -
Gutman, Bill
Surviving Homework - Nathan, Amy
Walk on the Wild Side! - Roop, Connie

Green, Gwen
Honest - Amos, Janine
Kind - Amos, Janine
Reliable - Amos, Janine

Green, Ken
Florence Kelley - Saller, Carol

Greenaway, Frank
Eagle and Birds of Prey - Parry-Jones,
Jemima
Ocean - MacQuitty, Miranda
The Snake Book - Ling, Mary

Greenaway, Kate
The Pied Piper of Hamelin - Greenaway,
Kate

Greenberg, Mark
Amazon Diary - Talbott, Hudson

Greenberg, Sheldon
Flood Fish - Eversole, Robyn

Greene, Jeffrey
The Rain - Laser, Michael

Greenseid, Diane
Get Up and Go! - Murphy, Stuart J
When Aunt Lena Did the Rhumba -
Kurtis-Kleinman, Eileen

Greenstein, Elaine
Matzo Ball Moon - Newman, Leslea
The Mitten Tree - Christiansen, Candace
While the Candles Burn - Goldin, Barbara
Diamond

Greenstein, Susan
A Big Quiet House - Forest, Heather
Passport on a Plate - Vezza, Diane
Simone

Greenwald, Sheila
Rosy Cole: She Grows and Graduates -
Greenwald, Sheila

Gregory, Fran
The Story Dance - Satterfield, Barbara

Grifalconi, Ann
Tio Armando - Heide, Florence Parry

Griffin, Molly Dwyer
Snakes in Question - Ernst, Carl H

Griffith, Gershom
Off to School - Battle-Lavert, G
Takiya and Thunderheart's Life Garden -
McGuire, J Victor
Wagon Train - Wright, Courtni C

Griffiths, Dean
The Lighthouse Dog - Waterton, Betty
The Patchwork House - Fitz-Gibbon, Sally

Grogan, Brian
Caterpillarology - Ross, Michael Elsohn
Ladybugology - Ross, Michael Elsohn

Groome, Helen
The Ikho of Laos - Holloway, Tracey

Grover, Max
Max's Wacky Taxi Day - Grover, Max

Guida, Liisa Chauncy
Counting Kittens - Plummer, David

Gukova, Julia
The Mole's Daughter - Gukova, Julia
The Other Side - Aura, Alejandro

Gunson, Christopher
Over on the Farm - Gunson, Christopher

Guravich, Dan
Harp Seal Pups - Matthews, Downs

Gurney, John Steven
The Bald Bandit - Roy, Ron
Mrs. Jeepers Is Missing! - Dadey, Debbie

Gusti
Evie to the Rescue! - Moers, Hermann

Gutierrez, Rudy
*La Vieja Letivia Y El Monte De Los
Pesares* - Mohr, Nicholasa

Harker, Lesley
Jack and Me and the Ball - Gowar, Mick
Jack and Me and the Pizza - Gowar, Mick
Jack and Me and the Snowman - Gowar, Mick
Jack and Me at the Seaside - Gowar, Mick
Kelly and the Crime Club - French, Vivian
Peter and the Ghost - French, Vivian
Tilly Beany Saves the World - Dalton, Annie

Harley, Kim
Roller Madonnas - Ashley, Bernard

Harness, Cheryl
Abe Lincoln Goes to Washington 1837-1865 - Harness, Cheryl
Ghosts of the White House - Harness, Cheryl
Young Abe Lincoln - Harness, Cheryl
Young Teddy Roosevelt - Harness, Cheryl

Harper, Peter
The Fantastic Book of Car Racing - Kirkwood, Jon

Harper, Piers
Snakes and Ladders and Hundreds of Mice - Harper, Piers

Harris, Greg
Earthquakes and Volcanoes - Merrians, Deborah

Harris, Jim
Jack and the Giant - Harris, Jim
The Three Little Javelinas - Lowell, Susan
Los Tres Pequenos Jabalies - Lowell, Susan

Harris, Nick
Dragon Quest - Dixon, Andy

Harris, Pamela
Hot, Cold, Shy, Bold - Harris, Pamela

Hartas, Leo
Haunted Castle - Hartas, Leo
Mimi's Christmas - Waddell, Martin

Hartelius, Marge
Monster Math School Time - Maccarone, Grace

Harter, Debbie
Walking through the Jungle - Harter, Debbie

Hartmann, Barbara
A Gift for Johnny Know-It-All - Woodbury, Mary

Harvey, Bob
A Fine Summer Knight - Mark, Jan

Harvey, Lisa
A Head Full of Notions - Bowen, Andy Russell

Harvey, Roland
Burke and Wills - Harvey, Roland
Eureka Stockade - Boardman, Alan
The First Fleet - Boardman, Alan

Harvill, Kitty
Sitting Down to Eat - Harley, Bill

Hassett, John
Charles of the Wild - Hassett, John

Hawken, Stephanie
The Silkie - Horn, Sandra Ann

Hawkes, Kevin
Boogie Bones - Loredo, Elizabeth
Marven of the Great North Woods - Lasky, Kathryn
My Little Sister Ate One Hare - Grossman, Bill
Painting the Wind - Dionetti, Michelle
The Poombah of Badoombah - Lillegard, Dee

Hawksley, Gerry
Surprise Spell - Davies, Gill
Whizzer Bat - Davies, Gill

Haynes, Max
In the Driver's Seat - Haynes, Max

Hays, Michael
Because You're Lucky - Smalls-Hector, Irene
The Hundredth Name - Oppenheim, Shulamith Levey

Hazell, Rebecca
Heroes: Great Men through the Ages - Hazell, Rebecca

Hazelwood, Pauline
Matthew's Goals - Hardcastle, Michael

Heal, Gillian
Grandpa Bear's Fantastic Scarf - Heal, Gillian

Heale, Jonathan
Hazel the Guinea-Pig - Wilson, A N
Lady Muck - Mayne, William

Heap, Sue
Cowboy Baby - Heap, Sue
Elena the Frog - Sheldon, Dyan
The Hungry Monster - Root, Phyllis
Little Chicken Chicken - Martin, David

Hearn, Diane Dawson
Anna in the Garden - Hearn, Diane Dawson
Turtle Dreams - Bauer, Marion Dane

Heatwole, Marsha
Primary Cats - Heatwole, Marsha

Hedderwick, Mairi
Katie Morag and the Grand Concert - Hedderwick, Mairi
Katie Morag and the New Pier - Hedderwick, Mairi
Katie Morag and the Two Grandmothers - Hedderwick, Mairi
Katie Morag and the Wedding - Hedderwick, Mairi
Katie Morag Delivers the Mail - Hedderwick, Mairi
Oh No, Peedie Peebles! - Hedderwick, Mairi

Hedlund, Carey
Night Fell at Harry's Farm - Hedlund, Carey

Heliadore
Butterflies -

Hellard, Susan
Dilly and the Goody Goody - Bradman, Tony
Harvey Goes to School - Dicks, Terrance

Heller, Ruth
The Korean Cinderella - Climo, Shirley
Mine, All Mine - Heller, Ruth

Hemmant, Lynette
Zucchini Out West - Dana, Barbara

Henderson, Douglas
Dinosaur Ghosts - Gillette, J Lynett
Living with Dinosaurs - Lauber, Patricia

Hendry, Linda
The Amazing Milk Book - Ross, Catherine Sheldrick
Baby's Feet - Quinlan, Patricia
Baby's Hands - Quinlan, Patricia
Erik the Viking Sheep - Creith, Elizabeth

Henkes, Kevin
Bailey Goes Camping - Henkes, Kevin
Lilly's Purple Plastic Purse - Henkes, Kevin

Henley, Claire
My Little Supermarket - Repchuk, Caroline

Henriquez, Emile F
D.J. and the Jazz Fest - McConduit, Denise Walter

Henterly, Jamichael
Young Arthur - San Souci, Robert D

Heo, Yumi
A Is for Asia - Chin-Lee, Cynthia
Pets! - Cooper, Melrose
The Rabbit's Escape - Han, Suzanne Crowder

Hermes, Jules
Children of Guatemala - Hermes, Jules

Hernandez, David Rodriguez
Querido Diario - Prieto, Iliana

Herrick, Mark J
Buck Wilder's Small Twig Hiking and Camping Guide - Smith, Timothy R

Hess, Mark
Hercules: The Man, the Myth, the Hero - Lasky, Kathryn

Hess, Paul
Jack and the Beanstalk - Poole, Josephine

Hessian, Margaret
The Moons of Goose Island - Philpot, Don K

Hewetson, Nicholas
Photography and Film - Graham, Ian

Hewetson, Sarah
Silly Heads - Hewetson, Sarah

Hewett, Richard
Bobcats - Arnold, Caroline
Peacocks - Berman, Ruth
Stories in Stone - Arnold, Caroline

Hewitson, Jennifer
Brother Rabbit - Ho, Minfong

Hewitt, Kathryn
Flower Garden - Bunting, Eve
Lives of the Athletes - Krull, Kathleen

Heyer, Carol
Here Come the Brides - Jackson, Ellen

Heyman, Ken
The Baby Book - Morris, Ann
Loving - Morris, Ann
The Mommy Book - Morris, Ann
Play - Morris, Ann

Hilder, Rowland
The Midnight Folk - Masefield, John

Hill, Eric
Where's Spot? - Hill, Eric

Hillenbrand, Will
Counting Crocodiles - Sierra, Judy
The Golden Sandal - Hickox, Rebecca
Sam Sunday and the Mystery at the Ocean Beach Hotel - Supraner, Robyn
The Tale of Ali Baba and the Forty Thieves - Kimmel, Eric A
Wicked Jack - Wooldridge, Connie Nordhielm

Hills, Ruth
Away in a Manger -
Deck the Halls -

Hills, Tad
Poems Have Roots - Moore, Lilian

Himler, Ronald
The Apaches - Sneve, Virginia Driving
  Hawk
A Christmas Star - High, Linda Oatman
A Day's Work - Bunting, Eve
Desert Trip - Steiner, Barbara
Fly Away Home - Bunting, Eve
Hook Moon Night - Gibbons, Faye
Katie's Trunk - Turner, Ann
The Log Cabin Quilt - Howard, Ellen
Sadako Y Las Mil Grullas De Papel -
  Coerr, Eleanor
Train to Somewhere - Bunting, Eve
Himmelman, John
Honest Tulio - Himmelman, John
Hine, Lewis W
The Empire State Building - Doherty,
  Craig A
Hines, Anna Grossnickle
Bean - Hines-Stephens, Sarah
Bean's Games - Hines-Stephens, Sarah
Bean's Night - Hines-Stephens, Sarah
Miss Emma's Wild Garden - Hines, Anna
  Grossnickle
Hines, Bob
Last of the Wild - McClung, Robert M
Hiscock, Bruce
The Big Rivers - Hiscock, Bruce
Hissey, Jane
Hoot - Hissey, Jane
Hitchcock-Pratt, Sue
Emily's Wonderful Pie - Cornish, Jane
Hoban, Lillian
A Bargain for Frances - Hoban, Russell
The Big Seed - Howard, Ellen
Ever-Clever Elisa - Hurwitz, Johanna
La Nueva Hermanita De Francisca -
  Hoban, Russell
Silly Tilly's Valentine - Hoban, Lillian
Hoban, Tana
Just Look - Hoban, Tana
Look Book - Hoban, Tana
So Many Circles, So Many Squares -
  Hoban, Tana
Hobbie, Holly
Toot and Puddle - Hobbie, Holly
Hobbs, Leigh
Old Tom Goes to Mars - Hobbs, Leigh
Hobson, Sally
Parcel for Stanley - Whybrow, Ian
Hochstatter, Daniel J
*Just Look 'n' Learn Spanish Picture
  Dictionary* -
Hodder, Wendy
The Tar Dragon - Orwin, Joanna

Hoff, Syd
Danny and the Dinosaur Go to Camp -
  Hoff, Syd
Where's Prancer? - Hoff, Syd
Holbrook, Heather
Miss Rafferty's Rainbow Socks - LeBox,
  Annette
Holder, Jimmy
Pig Pigger Piggest - Walton, Rick
Holling, Holling C
Minn of the Mississippi - Holling, Holling
  C
Holm, Sharon Lane
Beautiful Bats - Glaser, Linda
*Crafts for Kids Who Are Wild about
  Dinosaurs* - Ross, Kathy
*Crafts for Kids Who Are Wild about
  Insects* - Ross, Kathy
*Crafts for Kids Who Are Wild about Outer
  Space* - Ross, Kathy
*Crafts for Kids Who Are Wild about
  Rainforests* - Ross, Kathy
Happy Birthday, Everywhere! - Erlbach,
  Arlene
Sidewalk Games around the World -
  Erlbach, Arlene
Holman, Karlyn
Christmas Song of the North - Bonicatto,
  Marsha
Little Brother Moose - Kasperson, James
Holmes, Gerald L
The Case of the Vampire Vacuum Sweeper
  - Erickson, John R
*The Original Adventures of Hank the
  Cowdog* - Erickson, John R
Holmes, Sally
Ballet Stories - Castor, Harriet
Holmstrom, Tim
Nature! Wild and Wonderful - Pringle,
  Laurence
Holstien, Elisabeth
A Duck So Small - Benjamin, A H
Holub, Joan
No Fair! - Holtzman, Caren
Pen Pals - Holub, Joan
Homer, Winslow
The Eventful History of Three Blind Mice -
Honeywood, Varnette P
The Best Way to Play - Cosby, Bill
The Meanest Thing to Say - Cosby, Bill
Shipwreck Saturday - Cosby, Bill
The Treasure Hunt - Cosby, Bill

Hook, Adam
Animal Habitats - Fitzsimons, Cecilia
Look Inside a Tudor Medicine Chest -
Moses, Brian
Look Inside a Victorian Schoolroom -
Moses, Brian
Hook, Jeff
Harry the Honkerzoid - Hook, Brendan
Hopcraft, Xan
How It Was with Dooms - Hopcraft, Xan
Hopman, Philip
The Chocolate Touch II - Catling, Patrick
Skene
The Ghost of Able Mabel - Dolan, Penny
How's Harry? - May, Steve
The Pirate Band - Ruffell, Ann
Horenstein, Henry
Baseball in the Barrios - Horenstein,
Henry
Beisbol En Los Barrios - Horenstein,
Henry
Hornsby, Christopher
Take a Look, It's in a Book - Krauss,
Ronnie
Hoskin, Brian
The Day Miss Francie Got Skunked -
DeFord, Diane
Hosking, Joe
Physics Lab in a Hardware Store -
Friedhoffer, Bob
Physics Lab in a Housewares Store -
Friedhoffer, Bob
Howard, Arthur
Mr. Putter and Tabby Fly the Plane -
Rylant, Cynthia
Mr. Putter and Tabby Row the Boat -
Rylant, Cynthia
Mr. Putter and Tabby Toot the Horn -
Rylant, Cynthia
When I Was Five - Howard, Arthur
Howard, Kim
Where Does God Live? - Bea, Holly
Zorro and Quwi - Hickox, Rebecca
Howard, Paul
Care of Henry - Fine, Anne
The Invisible Dog - King-Smith, Dick
John Joe and the Big Hen - Waddell,
Martin
Staying with Grandpa - Lively, Penelope
Huang, Benrei
The Imp That Ate My Homework - Yep,
Laurence
Man on the Moon - Suen, Anastasia
Mr. Pak Buys a Story - Farley, Carol J

Hubbard, Woodleigh Marx
Imaginary Menagerie - Longfellow, Layne
Huff, Jean Lirley
The Black Kettle Ride - Brown, Cinita
Hughes, Rian
The Lie Spider - Goodhart, Pippa
Hughes, Shirley
Alfie and the Birthday Surprise - Hughes,
Shirley
Being Together - Hughes, Shirley
Enchantment in the Garden - Hughes,
Shirley
Playing - Hughes, Shirley
Huling, Phil
Moses in Egypt - Kessler, Brad
Humphries, Tudor
Dracula - Stoker, Bram
Hiding - Humphries, Tudor
Hunt, Judith
The Timbertoes 1 2 3 Counting Book -
The Timbertoes A B C Alphabet Book -
Hunter, Anne
Nocturne - Yolen, Jane
On Grandpa's Farm - Sathre, Vivian
Possum and the Peeper - Hunter, Anne
Hunter, Gus
Tane Steals the Show - Nelisi, Lino
Tane Te Whetu O Te Ra - Nelisi, Lino
Hurd, Clement
Goodnight Moon - Brown, Margaret Wise
Hurd, Thacher
Art Dog - Hurd, Thacher
Zoom City - Hurd, Thacher
Husted, Marty
Hush! A Gaelic Lullaby - Gerber, Carole
Huszar, Susan
Grandma - Bailey, Debbie
Grandpa - Bailey, Debbie
Meet Matt and Roxy - Huszar, Karen
Hutchins, Pat
Shrinking Mouse - Hutchins, Pat
Titch and Daisy - Hutchins, Pat
Hutchins, Roger
Trojan Horse - Pipe, Jim
Hutton, Warwick
Theseus and the Minotaur - Hutton,
Warwick
Hyman, Trina Schart
Bearskin - Pyle, Howard
The Fortune-Tellers - Alexander, Lloyd
Haunts - Medearis, Angela Shelf
Winter Poems - Rogasky, Barbara
Hynes, Robert
Meeting Trees - Sanders, Scott R

I

Ichikawa, Satomi
Tanya and the Magic Wardrobe - Gauch,
   Patricia Lee
Illiffe, Emma
Happy Birthday - Bednarczyk, Angela
Opposites: A Beginner's Book of Signs -
   Bednarczyk, Angela
Ingman, Bruce
Lost Property - Ingman, Bruce
Ingpen, Robert
The Drover's Boy - Egan, Ted
Ingraham, Erick
Flood - Calhoun, Mary
Inkpen, Mick
Bear - Inkpen, Mick
Everyone Hide from Wibbly Pig - Inkpen,
   Mick
Nothing - Inkpen, Mick
Innocenti, Roberto
Nutcracker - Hoffmann, E T A
Inouye, Carol
Silk Peony, Parade Dragon - Steckman,
   Elizabeth
Intrater, Roberta Grobel
Smile! - Intrater, Roberta Grobel
Isadora, Rachel
At the Crossroads - Isadora, Rachel
Isadora Dances - Isadora, Rachel
Lili Backstage - Isadora, Rachel
The Little Mermaid - Isadora, Rachel
A South African Night - Isadora, Rachel
Young Mozart - Isadora, Rachel
Isles, Joanna
The Nutcracker - Freeman, David
Ito, Yoriko
Jojofu - Waite, Michael P
Izen, Gabrielle
Glimpses of Heaven - Rock, Lois

J

Jabar, Cynthia
The Frog Who Wanted to Be a Singer -
   Goss, Linda
The Girls' Guide to Life - Dee, Catherine
Snow Dance - Evans, Lezlie
Won't You Come and Play with Me? -
   Donovan, Mary Lee
Jackson, Chris
Edmund for Short - Jackson, Chris

Jackson, Julian
The Drummer Boy's Battle - Jackson,
   Dave
Jackson, Shelley
The Old Woman and the Wave - Jackson,
   Shelley
Willy's Silly Grandma - DeFelice, Cynthia
Jacob, Murv
Dog People - Bruchac, Joseph
Jacobi, Kathryn
Who Is Ben? - Zolotow, Charlotte
Jahn-Clough, Lisa
ABC Yummy - Jahn-Clough, Lisa
James, Ann
After Dusk - Greenwood, Ted
Dog Star - Brian, Janeen
Hannah Plus One - Gleeson, Libby
Pidge - Bell, Krista
James, Kennon
Abraham Lincoln, Will You Ever Give Up?
   - Uglow, Loyd
*George Washington Carver, What Do You
   See?* - Benge, Janet
No Longer a Dilly Dally - Sommer, Carl
James, Simon
Leon and Bob - James, Simon
Jarecka, Danuta
Joseph and His Coat of Many Colors -
   Kassirer, Sue
Jeffers, Susan
McDuff and the Baby - Wells, Rosemary
McDuff Comes Home - Wells, Rosemary
McDuff Moves In - Wells, Rosemary
Jeffery, Lynn
Where Puddles Go - Strauss, Michael
Jeffery, Megan
The Dog Ate My Homework - Caserta,
   Carmen
Jeffrey, Lynn
*If Peas Could Taste Like Candy and Other
   Funny Poems for Kids* - Bowman,
   Crystal
Jenkin-Pearce, Susie
Big Puss, Little Mouse - May, Kara
Phoebe and the Monster Maze - Castle,
   Caroline
Jenkins, Debra Reid
I See the Moon - Appelt, Kathi
Jenkins, Jean
Pond Water Zoo - Loewer, H Peter
Jenkins, Leonard
If I Only Had a Horn - Orgill, Roxane

Lafrance, Marie
Mind Me Good Now! - Comissiong,
Lynette
LaMarche, Jim
Grandmother's Pigeon - Erdrich, Louise
Little Oh - Melmed, Laura Krauss
Lambase, Barbara
The Garden of Happiness - Tamar, Erika
Lambert, Jonathan
Gizmos Galore - Faulkner, Keith
The Long-Nosed Pig - Faulkner, Keith
The Wide-Mouthed Frog - Faulkner, Keith
Lambert, Sally Anne
Best of Friends! - Roddie, Shen
Too Close Friends - Roddie, Shen
Lambert, Stephen
Bedtime! - Blos, Joan W
Connie Came to Play - Paton Walsh, Jill
Row, Row, Row Your Boat - Goodhart,
Pippa
The Train Ride - Crebbin, June
When I Was Little Like You - Paton Walsh,
Jill
Lambson, Elizabeth
Socks - Gill, Janie Spaht
Lamont, Priscilla
Playtime Rhymes -
Lamut, Sonja
Alex and the Cat - Griffith, Helen V
Dinosaur Habitat - Griffith, Helen V
Landon, Lucinda
*Meg Mackintosh and the Mystery at the
Soccer Match* - Landon, Lucinda
Landstrom, Olof
Boo and Baa at Sea - Landstrom, Olof
Boo and Baa on a Cleaning Spree -
Landstrom, Olof
Lanfredi, Judy
Halloween Fun for Everyone - Wolff,
Ferida
Lang, Cecily
Annie's Shabbat - Lamstein, Sarah Marwil
A Birthday Basket for Tia - Mora, Pat
Una Canasta De Cumpleanos Para Tia -
Mora, Pat
Langevin, Isabelle
The Mystery of Eagle Lake - Gaetz, Dayle
Campbell
Langley, Jonathan
Baby's Bedtime -
Langlois, Florence
The Extraordinary Gift - Langlois,
Florence

Langlois, Suzanne
Max the Hero - Trudel, Sylvain
Max the Superhero - Trudel, Sylvain
Lanier, Kathleen
Twelve Polar Bears and a Dog - Woollam,
Ray
LaPadula, Tom
Planets - Schecter, Darrow
The Story of George Washington - Milton,
Joyce
Laplante, Jacques
Mom, the School Flooded! - Rivard, Ken
Lapointe, Claude
The Adventures of Tom Sawyer - Twain,
Mark
Large, Annabel
A Ghost-Light in the Attic - Thomson, Pat
Larson, Chris
The Best of Holy Days and Holidays -
Cronin, Gaynell Bordes
Lattimore, Deborah Nourse
Cinderhazel: The Cinderella of Halloween
- Lattimore, Deborah Nourse
The Fool and the Phoenix - Lattimore,
Deborah Nourse
Lavallee, Barbara
Mama, Do You Love Me? - Joosse,
Barbara M
Uno, Dos, Tres - Mora, Pat
Lavies, Bianca
Compost Critters - Lavies, Bianca
Lavis, Steve
Jump! - Lavis, Steve
Law, Rick
What Happens Next? - Moore, Jo Ellen
Lawrence, Jacob
Aesop's Fables -
Harriet and the Promised Land (Dee) -
Lawrence, Jacob
Lawrence, John
The Mysteries of Zigomar - Ahlberg, Allan
A New Treasury of Poetry - Philip, Neil
The Old Stories - Crossley-Holland, Kevin
Selected Poems for Children - Causley,
Charles
Lawrie, Robin
Bravery: The Story of Sitting Bull -
Murray, Peter
*Forgiveness: The Story of Mahatma
Gandhi* - Logue, Mary
Song of the Morning - Alexander, Pat

Lawton, Judith
Cat in a Corner - Oram, Hiawyn
Dog in Danger - Oram, Hiawyn
Dolphin SOS - Oram, Hiawyn
Monkey in Space - Oram, Hiawyn
Le Tord, Bijou
Sing a New Song -
Lear, Edward
A Book of Nonsense - Lear, Edward
Lee, Dom
Baseball Saved Us - Mochizuki, Ken
Heroes - Mochizuki, Ken
Passage to Freedom - Mochizuki, Ken
Lee, Hector Viveros
Get Set! Swim! - Atkins, Jeannine
Yo Tenia Un Hipopotamo - Lee, Hector
Viveros
Lee, Huy Voun
Cardinal and Sunflower - Preller, James
In the Park - Lee, Huy Voun
Lee, Ileana C
Kneeling Carabao and Dancing Giants -
Krasno, Rena
Lee, Jared
The Librarian from the Black Lagoon -
Thaler, Mike
Lee, Jeanne M
The Ch'i-Lin Purse - Fang, Linda
Lee, Paul
Amistad Rising - Chambers, Veronica
Leedy, Loreen
Measuring Penny - Leedy, Loreen
Mission--Addition - Leedy, Loreen
Lefebvre, Yolaine
Secret Dawn - Chase, Edith Newlin
LeGlatin Keis, Marie
Children of Summer - Anderson, Margaret
Jean
Leigh, Tom
Bone Poems - Moss, Jeff
Lelooska
Echoes of the Elders - Lelooska
Lember, Barbara Hirsch
The Shell Book - Lember, Barbara Hirsch
Lenoir, Jane
The Black Panther - Sargent, Pat L
Lent, Blair
Tikki Tikki Tembo - Mosel, Arlene
Leopold, Niki
The Ballerina and the Gargoyle -
Stephens, Jack
Leplar, Anna C
God's People - McCaughrean, Geraldine
Lerner, Carol
My Backyard Garden - Lerner, Carol

Lessac, Frane
O Christmas Tree - Rahaman, Vashanti
Queen Esther Saves Her People - Gelman,
Rita Golden
Lester, Alison
Alice and Aldo - Lester, Alison
The Quicksand Pony - Lester, Alison
Lester, Helen
Author: A True Story - Lester, Helen
Lesynski, Loris
Ogre Fun - Lesynski, Loris
Letourneau, Tony
Korean Games - Koh, Frances M
Letzig, Michael
The Crayon Box That Talked - DeRolf,
Shane
Lev
The Lion Is No Longer King - Bofane, In
Koli
Leveille, Michael
Fearless Fergie - Cocks, Nancy
Fergie Feels Left Out - Cocks, Nancy
Fergie Goes Moose Hunting - Cocks,
Nancy
Fergie Hogs the Lily Pad - Cocks, Nancy
Levers, John
Viking at School - Strong, Jeremy
Levert, Mireille
Molly's Bath - Levert, Mireille
Molly's Breakfast - Levert, Mireille
Molly's Clothes - Levert, Mireille
Molly's Toys - Levert, Mireille
Levin, Ted
Cactus Poems - Asch, Frank
Sawgrass Poems - Asch, Frank
Up River - Asch, Frank
Levine, Melinda
Eight Days of Hanukkah - Ziefert, Harriet
The Jewish Holiday Craft Book - Ross,
Kathy
Lewin, Betsy
Booby Hatch - Lewin, Betsy
Bug Boy - Sonenklar, Carol
No Such Thing - Koller, Jackie French
Rapunzel: A Happenin' Rap - Vozar,
David
Sharing Time Troubles - Maccarone,
Grace
A Thousand Cousins - Harrison, David L
What's the Matter, Habibi? - Lewin, Betsy

Lewin, Ted
Ali, Child of the Desert - London, Jonathan
The Always Prayer Shawl - Oberman, Sheldon
American Too - Bartone, Elisa
Fair! - Lewin, Ted
I Was a Teenage Professional Wrestler - Lewin, Ted
Market! - Lewin, Ted
The Originals: Animals That Time Forgot - Yolen, Jane
The Storytellers - Lewin, Ted

Lewis, Anthony
All Kinds of Animals - McCormick, Rosie
Deserts and Rainforests - Llewellyn, Claire
Meet Me by the Steelmen - Tomlinson, Theresa
The Owl Tree - Nimmo, Jenny
Things That Go - McCormick, Rosie
Why Do Stars Come Out at Night? - McAfee, Annalena

Lewis, E B
Creativity - Steptoe, John
Fire on the Mountain - Kurtz, Jane
I Love My Hair! - Tarpley, Natasha Anastasia
The Jazz of Our Street - Shaik, Fatima
The Magic Moonberry Jump Ropes - Hru, Dakari
Only a Pigeon - Kurtz, Jane
Staying Cool - Antle, Nancy

Lewis, Kim
The Last Train - Lewis, Kim

Lewis, Paul Owen
Frog Girl - Lewis, Paul Owen

Lewis, Rob
Grandpa Comes to Stay - Lewis, Rob
Hide-and-Seek with Grandpa - Lewis, Rob

Lia, Simone
Allie's Apples - Dunmore, Helen

Lidz, Jane
Zak: The One-of-a-Kind Dog - Lidz, Jane

Lies, Brian
Flatfoot Fox and the Case of the Missing Schoolhouse - Clifford, Eth

Lightburn, Ron
How Smudge Came - Gregory, Nan

Lill, Debra
Music and Drum - Robb, Laura

Lilly, Ken
Digger: The Story of a Mole in the Fall - Potter, Tessa
Fang: The Story of a Fox in Winter - Potter, Tessa
Grayfur: The Story of a Rabbit in Summer - Potter, Tessa
Sarn: The Story of an Otter in Spring - Potter, Tessa

Linch, Tanya
Easy Peasy! - Jennings, Linda
Kitty's Fishy Dinner - Jennings, Linda

Lindberg, Dean
Can You Catch a Falling Star? - Rosen, Sidney
Where's the Big Dipper? - Rosen, Sidney

Lindstrom, Jack
The Great Tooth Fairy - Butler, Dori Hillestad

Linenthal, Peter
Light the Candle! Bang the Drum! - Morris, Ann

Linsell, Tony
Time to Go Downtown - Ward, Rebecca

Lionni, Leo
A Color of His Own - Lionni, Leo

Lippincott, Gary A
The Skull of Truth - Coville, Bruce

Lipscomb, Sascha
Wasim in the Deep End - Ashley, Chris

Lisi, Victoria
If I Were the Wind - Evans, Lezlie

Lisker, Emily
Sol A Sol - Carlson, Lori M

Little, Mimi Otey
Yoshiko and the Foreigner - Little, Mimi Otey

Little, Susan
Adventures in Cranberry Forest - Coburn, Brian

Littlechild, George
A Man Called Raven - Van Camp, Richard

Litzinger, Rosanne
Leprechaun Gold - Bateman, Teresa
Louella Mae, She's Run Away! - Alarcon, Karen Beaumont
Sing, Sophie! - Dodds, Dayle Ann
You Can't Catch Me - Doyle, Charlotte

Liu, Lesley
The Mouse Bride - Chang, Monica

Liu, Zonghui
Yuanyuan De Facai Meng - Ceng, Yangqing

Lloyd, Gita
  Disney's Hercules: The Heart of a Hero - Caughill, Michael
Lloyd, Megan
  Dance with Me - Esbensen, Barbara Juster
  Spoonbill Swamp - Guiberson, Brenda Z
  Too Many Pumpkins - White, Linda
  La Viejecita Que No Le Tenia Miedo A Nada - Williams, Linda
Lloyd-Jones, Karen
  Spiders Spin Webs - Winer, Yvonne
Lobban, John
  What If. . .Giraffes - Parker, Steve
Lobel, Anita
  Mangaboom - Pomerantz, Charlotte
  Not Everyday an Aurora Borealis for Your Birthday - Sandburg, Carl
  Toads and Diamonds - Huck, Charlotte S
Lobel, Arnold
  The Arnold Lobel Book of Mother Goose -
Locker, Thomas
  Between Earth and Sky - Bruchac, Joseph
Locoste, Nathalie
  How Does Your Garden Grow? - Joly, Dominique
Lodge, Bernard
  Noah Makes a Boat - Goodhart, Pippa
  Tanglebird - Lodge, Bernard
Lofting, Hugh
  Story of Dr. Dolittle - Kleinbaum, N H
  Voyages of Dr. Dolittle - Kleinbaum, N H
Lohstoeter, Lori
  Iguana Beach - Franklin, Kristine L
Lomas Garza, Carmen
  In My Family - Lomas Garza, Carmen
Long, Sylvia
  Any Bear Can Wear Glasses - Long, Matthew
  Hush Little Baby - Long, Sylvia
  Liplap's Wish - London, Jonathan
Long, Teddy Cameron
  Terrific Stencils and Stamps - Kelly, Jo'Anne
Lopez, Ernesto
  Princesa and Friskie. . . - Johnson, Diana F
Lopez, Loretta
  The Birthday Swap - Lopez, Loretta
  Say Hola to Spanish - Erya, Susan Middleton
  Say Hola to Spanish, Otra Vez (Again!) - Elya, Susan Middleton
Lorseyedi, Barbara
  Simple Science Experiments - Bentley, Joan

Lott, Sheena
  Going to the Fair - McFarlane, Sheryl
  Moonsnail Song - McFarlane, Sheryl
Love, Judith DuFour
  Cats on Judy - Macken, JoAnn Early
Loverock, Faye
  Sunflower Mountain - Foster-Morgan, Kathleen
Low, William
  Chinatown - Low, William
  Lily - Thomas, Abigail
Lowry, Miles
  The Emperor's Body - Jenoff, Marvyne
Lucas, Cedric
  What's in Aunt Mary's Room? - Howard, Elizabeth Fitzgerald
Lucas, David
  Shaggy and Spotty - Hughes, Ted
Lucas, Gail
  Harry, the Happy Snake of Happy Hollow - Birchmore, Daniel A
  The Reluctant Santa - Birchmore, Daniel A
  Trevor, the Travelling Tree - Lucas, Gail
  The White Curtain - Birchmore, Daniel A
Lucas, Margeaux
  Class Trip to the Spooky Museum - Yablonsky, Buster
Ludlow, Keren
  The Topsy Turvies - Simon, Francesca
Lund, Jillian
  Tortoise Brings the Mail - Lillegard, Dee
Lusebrink, Karen
  Grannie Jus' Come! - Sisnett, Ana
Lutkenhoff, Eric
  SPINAbilities: A Young Person's Guide to Spina Bifida - Lutkenhoff, Marlene
Luzzati, Emanuele
  Il Pentolino Magico - Montanari, Massimo
Lynch, P J
  The Candlewick Book of Fairy Tales - Hayes, Sarah
  Catkin - Barber, Antonia
  The King of Ireland's Son - Behan, Brendan
  When Jessie Came across the Sea - Hest, Amy
Lyon, Carol
  Shark Attack Almanac - Batten, Mary
Lyons, Mary E
  The Poison Place - Lyons, Mary E

M

Ma, Wenhai
Older Brother, Younger Brother - Jaffe, Nina
Maar, Paul
Ein Sams Fur Martin Taschenbier - Maar, Paul
Maass, Robert
Garden - Maass, Robert
Mommy's in the Hospital Having a Baby - Rosenberg, Maxine B
Tugboats - Maass, Robert
Macaulay, David
Rome Antics - Macaulay, David
The Way Things Work - Macaulay, David
MacAulay-MacKinnon, Patsy
The Voyage of Wood Duck - Trottier, Maxine
Maccabe, Richard
Cities and Towns - Sammis, Fran
Countries - Stienecker, David
MacCarter, Don
Wildlife Rescue - Dewey, Jennifer Owings
MacCarthy, Patricia
Boom, Baby, Boom, Boom! - Mahy, Margaret
The Five Sisters - Mahy, Margaret
MacDonald, Suse
Peck, Slither, and Slide - MacDonald, Suse
Mackintosh, David
The Midwife's Daughters - Halligan, Marion
Paradise Palace - Orr, Wendy
MacRae, Jock
The Kids Book of Canada - Greenwood, Barbara
Maday, Jane
Itty Bitty Kitty - Keeshan, Bob
Maddison, Lucy
Parent-Free Zone - Moses, Brian
Maddox, Tony
Ducks Disappearing - Naylor, Phyllis Reynolds
Spike's Best Nest - Maddox, Tony
Madin, Larry
Beneath Blue Waters - Kovacs, Deborah
Madison, K
What's Inside Airplanes? - Parker, Steve
Maeno, Itoko
Amazing Mallika - Parkison, Jami
Plato's Journey - Talley, Linda

Maestro, Giulio
The New Americans - Maestro, Betsy
The Story of Religion - Maestro, Betsy
Mahan, Benton
A Story about Courage - Vecere, Joel
Maione, Heather Harms
Princess Lulu Goes to Camp - Cristaldi, Kathryn
Maizlish, Lisa
The Ring - Maizlish, Lisa
Mak, Kam
Dragon Prince - Yep, Laurence
Makowski, Robin Lee
The Saving of Valiant Blue Heron - Harms, John
Maland, Nick
Big Blue Whale - Davies, Nicola
Mallat, Kathy
The Picture That Mom Drew - Mallat, Kathy
Malone, Peter
The Adventures of Odysseus - Philip, Neil
The Magic Flute - Gatti, Anne
Star Shapes - Malone, Peter
Maloney, Peter
Redbird at Rockefeller Center - Maloney, Peter
Mammano, Julie
Rhinos Who Snowboard - Mammano, Julie
Manahan, Rosita
It Isn't Easy - Connolly, Margaret
Manchess, Gregory
To Capture the Wind - MacGill-Callahan, Sheila
Manders, John
King Snake - Slotboom, Wendy
Mangalika, Kusum
Somapura Weerayo - Fonseka, Kulasena
Mangelsen, Thomas D
Faces in the Forest - Hirschi, Ron
Faces in the Mountains - Hirschi, Ron
Manning, Mick
Splish, Splash, Splosh! - Manning, Mick
Manson, Christopher
Till Year's Good End - Nikola-Lisa, W
Marcellino, Fred
The Story of Little Babaji - Bannerman, Helen
Marchesi, Stephen
Terror Below! - Del Prado, Dana
Maritz, Nicolaas
Somewhere in Africa - Mennen, Ingrid
Markle, Sandra
Super Cool Science - Markle, Sandra

Marks, Alan
  Alexander the Great - Langley, Andrew
  Amelia Earhart - Langley, Andrew
  The Dragon's Child - Nimmo, Jenny
  Famous with Smokey Joe - Powling, Chris
  The Haunted Lighthouse - Masters,
    Anthony
  King Arthur and the Round Table -
    McCaughrean, Geraldine
  Ragged Bear - Weninger, Brigitte
  With Love - Goodall, Jane
Marquis, Huguette
  The Magdalen Islands Mystery - Guillet,
    Jean-Pierre
Marschall, Ken
  Inside the Titanic - Marschall, Ken
  On Board the Titanic - Tanaka, Shelley
Marsh, James
  Making Faces - Forward, Toby
Marshall, Felicia
  Down Home at Miss Dessa's - Stroud,
    Bettye
Marshall, James
  *George and Martha: The Complete Stories
    of Two Best Friends* - Marshall, James
  There's a Party at Mona's Tonight -
    Allard, Harry
Marshall, Janet
  Banana Moon - Marshall, Janet
  Forest Tracks - Duffyall, Dee Dee
  Look Once Look Twice - Marshall, Janet
Marshall, Lynne
  *Juliet: Midsummer at Greenchapel,
    England 1340* - Kirwan, Anna
  *Juliet: Rescue at Marlehead Manor,
    England 1340* - Kirwan, Anna
Marstall, Bob
  An Extraordinary Life - Pringle, Laurence
Martchenko, Michael
  Alligator Baby - Munsch, Robert
  Andrew's Loose Tooth - Munsch, Robert
  The Dark - Munsch, Robert
  Matthew and the Midnight Ball Game -
    Morgan, Allen
  Matthew and the Midnight Pilot - Morgan,
    Allen
  Silver Threads - Skrypuch, Marsha
    Forchuk
  Stephanie's Ponytail - Munsch, Robert
Martin, Barbara
  Smallest Rabbit - Barkhouse, Joyce
Martin, Josephine
  The Snow Tree - Repchuk, Caroline

Martin, Phil
  At the Animal Hospital - Greene, Carol
  At the Fire Station - Greene, Carol
  At the Zoo - Moses, Amy
  Teachers Help Us Learn - Greene, Carol
Martinez, Albert
  The Great Marine Reptiles - Llamas,
    Andreu
Martinez, Ed
  Maria De Sautuola: The Bulls in the Cave
    - Fradin, Dennis B
  Too Many Tamales - Soto, Gary
Martinez, Leovigildo
  Los Veinticinco Gatos Mixtecos - Gollub,
    Matthew
Martinez, Raul
  Los Cuentos Bobos - Martinez, Raul
Martinez, Sergio
  A Ballad of the Civil War - Stolz, Mary
  Weapons and Warfare - Meltzer, Milton
Martino, Val
  Lights Out - Gordon, Lynn
  The Witch's Revenge - Gordon, Lynn
Marton, Jirina
  Lady Kaguya's Secret -
Martyr, Paula
  No More Time for Paisley - Dyrbye, Helen
Masiello, Ralph
  The Flag We Love - Ryan, Pam Munoz
Mason-Fry, Douglas L
  I Like Being Me - Lalli, Judy
Massey, Peter
  The Big and Little Body Book - Taylor,
    David
  The Fast and Slow Animal Book - Taylor,
    David
  The Heavy and Light Animal Book -
    Taylor, David
  The Long and Short Lived Animal Book -
    Taylor, David
Mathers, Petra
  Borreguita and the Coyote - Aardema,
    Verna
  Grandmother Bryant's Pocket - Martin,
    Jacqueline Briggs
  I Need a Snake - Jonell, Lynne
  Mommy Go Away! - Jonell, Lynne
  Tell Me a Season - Siddals, Mary
    McKenna
Mathieu, Agnes
  Jonathan Mouse - Ostheeren, Ingrid
Mathis, Melissa Bay
  Earthsong - Rogers, Sally
Mathis, Sharon Bell
  Running Girl - Mathis, Sharon Bell

Matthews, Bethan
A Worm's Eye View - Mark, Jan

Matthews, Derek
Bodyworks - Sanders, Pete
Living in the World - Cann, Kate

Matysiak, Janek
Captain Hawk and the Stone of Destiny -
Eldridge, Jim

Mauterer, Erin Marie
Molly - Bonsall, Joseph S

Mavor, Salley
You and Me - Mavor, Salley

Maw, Taylor
The Incredible Jelly Bean Day - Maw,
Taylor

Maydak, Michael S
Lifetimes - Rice, David L

Mayer, Danuta
Rikki Tikki Tavi - Kipling, Rudyard

Mayes, Susan
*The Usborne Book of Drawing, Painting
and Lettering* - Mayes, Susan

Mayhew, James
Classic Poems to Read Aloud - Berry,
James

Mayo, Diana
Fabulous Beasts - Bevan, Finn
Mighty Mountains - Bevan, Finn
Sacred Skies - Bevan, Finn
The Waters of Life - Bevan, Finn

Maze, Deborah
Edmund and the White Witch - Lewis, C S
Lucy Steps through the Wardrobe - Lewis,
C S

Mazzola, Frank Jr.
Counting Is for the Birds - Mazzola, Frank
Jr.
The Crayon Counting Board Book - Ryan,
Pam Munoz
The Crayon Counting Book - Ryan, Pam
Munoz

McAllister-Stammen, Jo Ellen
If You Were Born a Kitten - Bauer, Marion
Dane
Teddy Bear Tears - Aylesworth, Jim

McCallum, Stephen
The New Land - Reynolds, Marilynn

McCarty, Peter
Life on Mars - Getz, David
Sons of Liberty - Griffin, Adele

McClelland, Linda
Why, Nana? - Geissler, Carol

McClintock, Barbara
The Fantastic Drawings of Danielle -
McClintock, Barbara
The Gingerbread Man - Aylesworth, Jim

McCue, Lisa
Corduroy's Birthday - Hennessy, B G

McCully, Emily Arnold
The Ballot Box Battle - McCully, Emily
Arnold
Beautiful Warrior - McCully, Emily
Arnold
The Bobbin Girl - McCully, Emily Arnold
The Divide - Bedard, Michael
Leo the Magnificat - Martin, Ann M
Old Home Day - Hall, Donald
One Very Best Valentine's Day - Blos,
Joan W
Popcorn at the Palace - McCully, Emily
Arnold
Starring Mirette and Bellini - McCully,
Emily Arnold

McCunney, Michelle
Mario's Mayan Journey - McCunney,
Michelle

McCurdy, Michael
American Tall Tales - Osborne, Mary
Pope
The Bone Man - Simms, Laura
The Sailor's Alphabet - McCurdy, Michael
The Seasons Sewn - Paul, Ann Whitford
Trapped by the Ice! - McCurdy, Michael

McDermott, Gerald
Musicians of the Sun - McDermott, Gerald

McDonald, Brigitte
Aunty Dot's Incredible Adventure Atlas -
Yildirim, Eljay

McDonald, John
In a Different Light - Meyer, Carolyn

McDonnell, Flora
Flora McDonnell's ABC - McDonnell,
Flora

McElrath-Eslick, Lori
Read for Me, Mama - Rahaman, Vashanti

McGaw, Laurie
Discovering the Iceman - Tanaka, Shelley
Polar the Titanic Bear - Spedden, Daisy
Corning Stone
Something to Remember Me By - Bosak,
Susan V

McGinley-Nally, Sharon
My Grandmother's Journey - Cech, John
Pigs Go to Market - Axelrod, Amy
Pigs in the Pantry - Axelrod, Amy

McGrath, Leslie
   The Tiger's Eye, the Bird's Fist - Rafkin,
   Louise
McGraw, Sheila
   I Promise I'll Find You - Ward, Heather P
   Love You Forever - Munsch, Robert
McGuire, Richard
   Night Becomes Day - McGuire, Richard
   What's Wrong with This Book? - McGuire,
   Richard
McHale, Gillian
   Don't Bug Me! - McHale, Gillian
McIntosh, Jon
   Witch Way to the Beach - Mariconda,
   Barbara
McKean, Dave
   *The Day I Swapped My Dad for Two
   Goldfish* - Gaiman, Neil
McKee, David
   Elmer and Wilbur - McKee, David
   The Elmer Pop-Up Book - McKee, David
   I Can Too! - McKee, David
   The Monster and the Teddy Bear - McKee,
   David
   Prince Peter and the Teddy Bear - McKee,
   David
McLean, Andrew
   Josh - McLean, Andrew
   Josh and Thumper - McLean, Andrew
   Mr. Biffy's Battle - Tulloch, Richard
McLoughlin, Wayne
   Fireflies - Hoffman, Alice
   Master Elk and the Mountain Lion -
   London, Jonathan
   Voices of the Wild - London, Jonathan
McMahon, Kelly
   All about Animals - Moore, Jo Ellen
   Science Experiments at Home - Moore, Jo
   Ellen
McMaster, Jack
   Martha Black: Gold Rush Pioneer -
   Martin, Carol
McMillan, Bruce
   Jelly Beans for Sale - McMillan, Bruce
   My Horse of the North - McMillan, Bruce
   Nights of the Pufflings - McMillan, Bruce
   Wild Flamingos - McMillan, Bruce
McNally, Darren
   Fort Chipewyan Homecoming - Mercredi,
   Morningstar

McNaughton, Colin
   *Another Day on Your Foot and I Would
   Have Died* - Agard, John
   Boo! - McNaughton, Colin
   Oops! - McNaughton, Colin
   We Couldn't Provide Fish Thumbs -
   Berry, James
McNeill, Shannon
   Albert Goes to Town - Jordan, Jennifer
McPhail, David
   Angel Pig and the Hidden Christmas -
   Waldron, Jan L
   Edward and the Pirates - McPhail, David
   If You Were My Bunny - McMullan, Kate
   In Flight with David McPhail - McPhail,
   David
   The Puddle - McPhail, David
   Santa's Book of Names - McPhail, David
   Tinker and Tom and the Star Baby -
   McPhail, David
McPherson, John
   The Barber of Bingo - Ruediger, Beth
McQuade, Jacqueline
   Cosy Moments with Teddy Bear -
   McQuade, Jacqueline
   Good Times with Teddy Bear - McQuade,
   Jacqueline
Meade, Holly
   Boss of the Plains - Carlson, Laurie
   Cocoa Ice - Appelbaum, Diana Karter
   Hush! A Thai Lullaby - Ho, Minfong
Meddaugh, Susan
   Cinderella's Rat - Meddaugh, Susan
   Five Little Piggies - Martin, David
   Good Zap, Little Grog - Wilson, Sarah
Medlock, Scott
   Opening Days - Hopkins, Lee Bennett
Meers, Tony
   Shadow of the Wolf - Whelan, Gloria
Meeuwissen, Tony
   Remarkable Animals - Meeuwissen, Tony
Meisel, Paul
   Engine, Engine, Number Nine -
   Calmenson, Stephanie
   Go Away, Dog - Nodset, Joan L
   I Wish My Brother Was a Dog - Shields,
   Carol Diggory
Meister, Chris
   Toys in Space - Sumners, Carolyn
Melendez, Francisco
   El Valle De Los Cocuyos - Diaz, Gloria
   Cecilia
Melling, David
   If I Didn't Have Elbows - Toksvig, Sandi

Mello, Roger
Uma Historia Do Boto Vermelho - Mello, Roger

Melnyczuk, Peter
Imagine You Are a Tiger - Wallace, Karen
Seth and the Strangers - Nimmo, Jenny

Melo, Esperanca
Get Started - MacLeod, Elizabeth
Lettering: Make Your Own Cards, Signs, Gifts and More - Lewis, Amanda

Menchin, Scott
The Day the Whale Came - Bunting, Eve

Mennie, Steve
The Fish Princess - Watts, Irene N

Menzel, Peter
I Want to Be--an Engineer - Grace, Catherine O'Neill

Meret, Sasha
Betsy Ross: Patriot of Philadelphia - St. George, Judith
Make Things Fly - Kennedy, Dorothy

Merino, Jose Luis
El Gato Con Botas - Boada, Francesc

Merrell, Patrick
The 512 Ants on Sullivan Street - Losi, Carol A

Messier, Linda
Fireflies, Fireflies, Light My Way - London, Jonathan

Mets, Marilyn
Cameron and Me - Harris, Dorothy Joan
November Boots - Hundal, Nancy
Pat-a-Cake Dough Book and Kit - McKay, Sharon E
Prints - Sadler, Judy Ann

Meuse, Jeannine
Does Hockey Love Kids? - Meuse, Christopher

Michaels, Michael
Fun Food - Bastyra, Judy

Micucci, Charles
The Life and Times of the Peanut - Micucci, Charles

Middleton, Phoebe
Big Bad Bruce - Bates, Dianne

Mier, Colin
Body Language - Robson, Pam
Electronic Communication - Oxlade, Chris
Space Race - Blackman, Malorie

Migdale, Lawrence
Buffalo Days - Hoyt-Goldsmith, Diane
Celebrating Hanukkah - Hoyt-Goldsmith, Diane
Day of the Dead - Hoyt-Goldsmith, Diane
Lacrosse: The National Game of the Iroquois - Hoyt-Goldsmith, Diane
Migrant Worker - Hoyt-Goldsmith, Diane
Potlatch: A Tsimshian Celebration - Hoyt-Goldsmith, Diane

Miglio, Paige
So Many Bunnies - Walton, Rick

Miles, Elizabeth
Louie and Dan Are Friends - Pryor, Bonnie

Milgrim, David
Here in Space - Milgrim, David

Miller, David
Boo to a Goose - Fox, Mem
What's for Lunch? - Miller, David

Miller, Edward
Circus Shapes - Murphy, Stuart J
Cross a Bridge - Hunter, Ryan Ann

Miller, Kevan Jane
The Cup of Mari Anu - Owens, Yvonne

Miller, Margaret
The New Baby at Your House - Cole, Joanna
Twins! - Scott, Elaine

Miller, Myron
Fantastic Lateral Thinking Puzzles - Harsham, Edward

Miller, Virginia
Be Gentle! - Miller, Virginia

Millman, Isaac
Moses Goes to a Concert - Millman, Isaac

Mills, Judith Christine
The Stonehook Schooner - Mills, Judith Christine

Mills, Lauren A
The Book of Little Folk - Mills, Lauren A
Book of Little Folk - Mills, Lauren A
Elfabet: An ABC of Elves - Yolen, Jane

Millward, David Wynn
Hot Dog Cool Cat - Nimmo, Jenny

Miner, Julia
The Unbreakable Code - Hunter, Sara Hoagland

Minner, Denise Bennet
Molly Meets Mona and Friends - Walker, Gladys

Minor, Wendell
Arctic Son - George, Jean Craighead
Grassroots - Sandburg, Carl
Julie's Wolf Pack - George, Jean
   Craighead
Shaker Hearts - Turner, Ann
Minton, Barbara
Texas Star - Cole, Barbara Hancock
Mirocha, Paul
Acorn Pancakes, Dandelion Salad and 38
   Other Wild Recipes - George, Jean
   Craighead
How Do Birds Find Their Way? - Gans,
   Roma
Mistry, Nilesh
The Illustrated Book of Fairy Tales -
   Philip, Neil
Turtle Bay - Pirotta, Saviour
Mitchell, David
Tricky Tricky Twins - Ernest, Kate
   Elizabeth
Mitchell, Rhonda
Daddy Calls Me Man - Johnson, Angela
The Talking Cloth - Mitchell, Rhonda
Mitchell, Roger
A Breeze in the Willows - Johnson, Allen
   Jr.
Mitchell, Tracy
What Do Fish Have to Do with Anything?
   and Other Stories - Avi
Moffatt, Judith
I Am an Apple - Marzollo, Jean
I'm a Caterpillar - Marzollo, Jean
Pumpkin Faces - Rose, Emma
Mogensen, Suzanne
Jenny and the Hanukkah Queen - Little,
   Jean
The Night Book - Hickman, Pamela
Moignot, Daniel
Frogs -
Molina-Sy, George
Hurley and the Bone - Dahab, Farida
   Elizabeth
Molnar, Albert
Papermaking for Kids - Wilkinson, Beth
Mombourquette, Paul
Emma and the Silk Train - Lawson, Julie
Mones, Isidre
The Twelve Labors of Hercules - Cerasini,
   Marc
Monfort, Pamela
Art Fun! - Solga, Kim
Craft Fun! - Solga, Kim
Montanez, Nivea Ortiz
Mediopollito - Izcoa, Carmen Rivera

Montgomery, Mary
The Secret under the Whirlpool -
   Hammond, Elaine Breault
Montgomery, Michael
Johnny Appleseed - Demuth, Patricia
Montserrat, Pep
El Regalo - Keselman, Gabriela
Moodie, Fiona
Nabulela: A South African Folk Tale -
   Moodie, Fiona
Moore, Andrew
Buried Alive - Fletcher, Ralph
Moore, Bobbie
Pioneer Days - King, David C
Taking Care of the Earth - Pringle,
   Laurence
Moore, Cyd
Alice and Greta - Simmons, Steven J
I Love You, Stinky Face - McCourt, Lisa
What Is the Full Moon Full Of? -
   Oppenheim, Shulamith Levey
Moore, Inga
The River Bank and Other Stories from
   The Wind in the Willows - Grahame,
   Kenneth
Moore, Robin
Real - Holman, Felice
Moore, Yvette
A Prairie Year - Bannatyne-Cugnet, Jo
Mora, Francisco
Pablo and Pimienta - Covault, R
Moraes, Odilon
The Bear Who Didn't Like Honey -
   Maitland, Barbara
Moreno, Rene King
Fiesta! - Guy, Ginger Foglesong
Moreton, Daniel
La Cucaracha Martina - Moreton, Daniel
Morgan, Jennifer
Alcock and Brown and the Boy in the
   Middle - Morgan, George M
Morgan, Pierr
The Miser on the Mountain - Luenn,
   Nancy
Moriarty, William
Jonathan Goes to the Doctor - Baggette,
   Susan
Jonathan Goes to the Grocery Store -
   Baggette, Susan
Jonathan Goes to the Library - Baggette,
   Susan
Morimoto, Junko
The Two Bullies - Morimoto, Junko

Newberry, Clare Turlay
Barkis - Newberry, Clare Turlay
Herbert the Lion - Newberry, Clare Turlay
Mittens - Newberry, Clare Turlay
Smudge - Newberry, Clare Turlay
Newbigging, Martha
Crime Science - Bowers, Vivien
Newsham, Ian
Baby Bear Comes Home - Lishak, Antony
Newsome, Donna
The Adventures of Jason Jackrabbit - Dee, M M
Newton, Jill
All about Color - Yates, Irene
All about Pattern - Yates, Irene
All about Shape - Yates, Irene
All about Touch - Yates, Irene
In the Beginning - Turner, Steven
Newton-White, Muriel E
Mystery on Grandma's Farm - Gilmour, Nancy
Ng, Simon
Tales from Gold Mountain - Yee, Paul
Nicholson, John
Explorers of Australia - Nicholson, John
A Home among the Gum Trees - Nicholson, John
Nickle, John
Things That Are Most in the World - Barrett, Judi
Nidenoff, Michelle
Janice VanCleave's Play and Find Out about Math - VanCleave, Janice Pratt
Janice VanCleave's Play and Find Out about Nature - VanCleave, Janice Pratt
Nishimura, Shigeo
E De Yomu Hiroshima No Gembaku - Nasu, Masamoto
Nivola, Claire A
Elisabeth - Nivola, Claire A
Nodel, Norman
Peanut Butter and Jelly for Snabbos - Rosenfeld, Dina
Nolan, Dennis
Androcles and the Lion - Nolan, Dennis
The Blessing of the Lord - Schmidt, Gary D
The Gentleman and the Kitchen Maid - Stanley, Diane
William Shakespeare's A Midsummer Night's Dream - Coville, Bruce
Wings - Yolen, Jane
Noll, Cheryl Kirk
Count on Math - Schiller, Pam

Noll, Sally
Surprise! - Noll, Sally
What Color Was the Sky Today? - Ford, Miela
Noonan, William
Bigfoot and Other Legendary Creatures - Walker, Paul Robert
Great Crystal Bear - Lesser, Carolyn
Norman, Phillip
A Box of Stories for Six Year Olds - Thomson, Pat
Norton, Lindy
Myths and Legends - King, Penny
Novak, Matt
Mouse TV - Novak, Matt
Newt - Novak, Matt
The Pillow War - Novak, Matt
Twelve Snails to One Lizard - Hightower, Susan
Nugent, Cynthia
Mister Got to Go - Simmie, Lois
No Cats Allowed - Simmie, Lois
Nunez, Pablo
La Abuelita Aventurera - Machado, Ana Maria

O

Ober, Carol
How Music Came to the World - Ober, H
O'Brien, Anne Sibley
Talking Walls - Knight, Margy Burns
O'Brien, John
Mother Hubbard's Christmas - O'Brien, John
The Reptile Ball - Ogburn, Jacqueline K
Six Sandy Sheep - Enderle, Judith Ross
True Lies - Shannon, George
Uncle Switch - Kennedy, X J
O'Brien, Michael
Chi-Hoon: A Korean Girl - McMahon, Patricia
O'Brien, Patrick
Bottoms Up! - Singer, Marilyn
Teddy Roosevelt's Elk - Guiberson, Brenda Z
Ochoa, Ana
Una Vaca Querida - Antillano, Laura
O'Connor, Finbarr
Jackomoora and the King of Ireland's Son - MacMahon, Bryan
Odriozola, Elena
Por Que No Canta El Petirrojo? - Mendiguren, Xabier

Palen, Debbie
Girl Talk - Harlan, Judith
Palmer, Kim
Hurricane Summer - Swindells, Robert
Paluso, Christopher
Follow Your Dreams - Vaughn, Mo
Pang, Alex
101 Amazing Optical Illusions - Jennings, Terry
Fantastic Cutaway Book of Rescue! - Mugford, Simon
The Fantastic Cutaway Book of Speed - Richards, Jon
Science Fair Projects: Energy - Bonnet, Robert L
Paolillo, Ronald G
A Gift for the Contessa - Mele, Michael
Paparone, Pamela
Los Cinco Patitos - Paparone, Pamela
Nobody Owns the Sky - Lindbergh, Reeve
Ten Dogs in the Window - Masurel, Claire
Wake Up and Goodnight - Zolotow, Charlotte
Paradise, Susan
Brass Button - Dragonwagon, Crescent
Paraskevas, Michael
The Tangerine Bear - Paraskevas, Betty
Pare, Roger
On the Go - Pare, Roger
Parish, Steve
Amazing Facts about Australian Insects and Spiders - Slater, Pat
Amazing Facts about Australian Landscapes - Fox, Allan
Parker, Ant
Charlie the Chicken - Denchfield, Nick
Dazzling Diggers - Mitton, Tony
Roaring Rockets - Mitton, Tony
Parker, David L
Stolen Dreams - Parker, David L
Parker, Ellen
Do Bees Sneeze? and Other Questions Kids Ask about Insects - Wangberg, James K
Parker, Nancy Winslow
The House I'll Build for the Wrens - Neitzel, Shirley
We're Making Breakfast for Mother - Neitzel, Shirley
Parker, Robert Andrew
The Hatmaker's Sign - Fleming, Candace
Parker, Ron
Voices from the Wild - Bouchard, Dave
Parker-Rees, Guy
Pinkerton Inks - Parkinson, David

Parkins, David
Fly Traps! - Jenkins, Martin
God's Story - Mark, Jan
Parkinson, Kathy
Little Bunny's Cool Tool Set - Boelts, Maribeth
My Sister Rose Has Diabetes - Beatty, Monica Driscoll
Parnall, Peter
Kavik the Wolf Dog - Morey, Walt
Paschkis, Julie
Play All Day - Paschkis, Julie
Paskiet, Mark
I'd Like to Be a Marine Biologist - Thompson, Kim Mitzo
I'd Like to Be a Meteorologist - Thompson, Kim Mitzo
I'd Like to Be a Physicist - Thompson, Kim Mitzo
I'd Like to Be an Entomologist - Thompson, Kim Mitzo
Pastuchiv, Olga
Minas and the Fish - Pastuchiv, Olga
Paterson, Bettina
Inky Little Fingers - Mason, Lesley
Sticky Little Fingers - Frere, Jane
Paterson, Diane
Marmee's Surprise - Kulling, Monica
Patrick, Pamela
An Amish Christmas - Ammon, Richard
Through the Night - Aylesworth, Jim
Patterson, Geoffrey
The Naughty Boy and the Strawberry Horse - Patterson, Geoffrey
Paul, Korky
Aesop's Funky Fables - French, Vivian
Magic Poems - Foster, John
The Rascally Cake - Willis, Jeanne
Winnie in Winter - Thomas, Valerie
Paul, Ruth
The Penguins' Day Out - Joseph, Vivienne
Paulsen, Ruth Wright
My Life in Dog Years - Paulsen, Gary
Worksong - Paulsen, Gary
Payne, Mark
A Brat Called Annie - Fowler, Thurley
Pearson, Tracey Campbell
The Awful Aardvarks Go to School - Lindbergh, Reeve
Dr. Ruth Talks about Grandparents - Westheimer, Ruth K
The Purple Hat - Pearson, Tracey Campbell

Peck, Beth
   Dear Levi - Woodruff, Elvira
   Grandmother and the Runaway Shadow -
      Rosenberg, Liz
Pedersen, Judy
   Gather Up, Gather In - Helldorfer, M C
   Seedfolks - Fleischman, Paul
Pelizzoli, Francesca
   Aladdin and Ali Baba - Perham, Molly
   Lao Lao of Dragon Mountain -
      Bateson-Hill, Margaret
Pelletier, David
   The Graphic Alphabet - Pelletier, David
Pelletier, Gilles
   Come to the Fair - Lunn, Janet
Pennanen, J O
   The Princess Who Laughed in Colours -
      Manuel, Lynn
Penney, Ian
   A Christmas Treasury - Nettell, Stephanie
   A Noteworthy Tale - Mutchnick, Brenda
Peppe, Mark
   A Renaissance Town - Morley, Jacqueline
Pepworth, Andrew
   The Beaver - Crewe, Sabrina
Percy, Graham
   Elephants Don't Do Ballet - McKinlay,
      Penny
Pere, Joan
   Los Tres Cerditos - Escardo I Bas, Merce
Perkins, Lynne Rae
   Clouds for Dinner - Perkins, Lynne Rae
Perko, Peter
   The Gift - Kertes, Joseph
   The Red Corduroy Shirt - Kertes, Joseph
Perrone, Donna
   The Rajah's Rice - Barry, David
   We Sing the City - Lundgren, Mary Beth
Peters, David
   Supergiants! The Biggest Dinosaurs -
      Lessem, Don
Peters, Matthew
   Doug's Secret Christmas - Scarborough,
      Ken
Peterson, Donna
   Gran's Bees - Thompson, Mary
Petricic, Dusan
   Bone Button Borscht - Davis, Aubrey
   The Enormous Potato - Davis, Aubrey
   Let's Play - Gryski, Camilla
   Scary Science - Funston, Sylvia
Petruzzi, Rosemary
   Eric VanNoodle - Cohn, Arlen

Pfister, Marcus
   How Leo Learned to Be King - Pfister,
      Marcus
   Milo and the Magical Stones - Pfister,
      Marcus
   The Rainbow Fish Board Book - Pfister,
      Marcus
   Saltarin - Pfister, Marcus
Pham, Leuyen
   *Sugarcane House and Other Stories about
      Mr. Fat* - Bond, Adrienne Moore
Phillipps, Francis
   Beasts - Ross, Stewart
   Gods and Giants - Ross, Stewart
   Monsters of the Deep - Ross, Stewart
   Mysteries of Lost Civilizations - Millard,
      Anne
   Mysteries of Prehistoric Life - Unwin,
      David
   Some Snakes Spit Poison - Llewellyn,
      Claire
   The Sun Is a Star - Petty, Kate
   Warriors and Witches - Ross, Stewart
   You Can Jump Higher on the Moon -
      Petty, Kate
Phillips, Dave
   Donkey Kong Country - Phillips, Dave
   Super Mario's Adventures - Phillips, Dave
Phillips, Louise
   Wormworld - Levine, Shar
Phillips-Duke, Barbara J
   Digby - Hazen, Barbara Shook
   What in the World? - Merriam, Eve
Piazza, Gail
   Pay Attention, Slosh! - Smith, Mark
Pickett, Robert
   Rain - Davies, Kay
Pienkowski, Jan
   Big Machines - Pienkowski, Jan
   Boats - Pienkowski, Jan
   Planes and Other Things That Fly -
      Pienkowski, Jan
   Trucks and Other Working Wheels -
      Pienkowski, Jan
Pignataro, Anna
   I'm in the Sky and I Can't Come Back -
      Huth, Holly Young
   Quicksilver - Broome, Errol

Poydar, Nancy
Beezy - McDonald, Megan
Beezy Magic - McDonald, Megan
Snip, Snip. . .Snow! - Poydar, Nancy
Prachaticka, Marketa
The Noctuary of Narcissus Batt -
Muldoon, Paul
Prado, Miguelanxo
Peter and the Wolf - Prado, Miguelanxo
Prater, John
Nearly, but Not Quite - Rogers, Paul
Price, Caroline
The Kids Can Press Jumbo Book of Crafts
- Sadler, Judy Ann
Price, David
Rosa Parks - Holland, Gini
Price, Nick
Dog on a Broomstick - Page, Jan
Windy Webley - Peyton, K M
Priceman, Marjorie
Cousin Ruth's Tooth - MacDonald, Amy
One of Each - Hoberman, Mary Ann
When Zaydeh Danced on Eldridge Street -
Rael, Elsa Okon
Priestley, Alice
Clouds on the Mountain - Smith-Ayala,
Emilie
A Friend like Zilla - Gilmore, Rachna
Lights for Gita - Gilmore, Rachna
Roses for Gita - Gilmore, Rachna
The Watcher - Silsbe, Brenda
Primavera, Elise
Moonlight Kite - Buckley, Helen Elizabeth
Raising Dragons - Nolen, Jerdine
Prunier, James
Little Women - Alcott, Louisa May
Punchatz, Don
Be a Wolf! - Strickland, Brad

Q

Quackenbush, Robert
Batbaby - Quackenbush, Robert
Querin, Pamela
Escape from Egypt - Morgan, Stacy Towle

R

Rabinowitz, Sandy
Ride of Courage - Felder, Deborah
Spirit of the West - Malcolm, Jahnna N

Rader, Laura
Away in a Manger (Little Angels Series) -
The Best Smelling Christmas Book Ever -
Ziefert, Harriet
Come All Ye Faithful -
The First Noel (Angel Wings) -
Joy to the World -
Scamper's Year - Kindley, Jeff
Silent Night -
Sleepy-O! - Ziefert, Harriet
We Three Kings -
Radunsky, Vladimir
The Maestro Plays - Martin, Bill
Telephone - Gambrell, Jamey
Yucka Drucka Droni - Radunsky, Vladimir
Raeside, Adrian
Dennis and the Fantastic Forest - Raeside,
Adrian
Rafferty, Trisha
I Wouldn't Thank You for a Valentine -
Duffy, Carol Ann
Raglin, Tim
Five Goofy Ghosts - Stamper, Judith Bauer
Ramsey, Marcy Dunn
Dare to Be, M.E.! - LeMieux, Anne C
Old People, Frogs, and Albert - Wilson,
Nancy Hope
The Story of Laura Ingalls Wilder - Stine,
Megan
Ramstad, Ralph L
The Back of Beyond - Bowen, Andy
Russell
Rand, Ted
Baby in a Basket - Rand, Gloria
The Bear Who Heard Crying -
Kinsey-Warnock, Natalie
Can I Be Good? - Taylor, Livingston
A Home for Spooky - Rand, Gloria
The Hullabaloo ABC - Cleary, Beverly
Keepers - Schertle, Alice
Mailing May - Tunnell, Michael O
Secret Place - Bunting, Eve
Storm on the Desert - Lesser, Carolyn
Randall, Wally
3-D Paper Crafts - Broda, Ron
Christmas Crafts with Crayola Model
Magic - Fernandes, Kim
Gifts to Make with Crayola Model Magic -
Fernandes, Kim
Rankin, Joan
Scaredy Cat - Rankin, Joan
Wow! It's Great Being a Duck - Rankin,
Joan

Reznicki, Jack
Fire! - Masoff, Joy
Ribbons, Ian
Bowmen of Crecy - Welch, Ronald
Rice, James
A Leprechaun's St. Patrick's Day -
Blazek, Sarah Kirwan
Rich, Anna
Joshua's Masai Mask - Hru, Dakari
Just Right Stew - English, Karen
Rickman, David
The Story of Sitting Bull - Eisenberg, Lisa
The Story of Walt Disney - Selden, Bernice
Riddell, Chris
Kasper in the Glitter - Ridley, Philip
Scribbleboy - Ridley, Philip
Something Else - Cave, Kathryn
The Swan's Stories - Andersen, Hans
Christian
The Tall Story - Hughes, Frieda
Until I Met Dudley - McGough, Roger
Riddle, Tohby
The Great Escape from City Zoo - Riddle,
Tohby
My Guardian Angel - Loves, June
Rieger, Birgit
Hexe Lilli Zaubert Hausaufgaben - Knister
Riggio, Anita
Coal Mine Peaches - Dionetti, Michelle
Noah's Wife - Figley, Marty Rhodes
Secret Signs - Riggio, Anita
Rigol, Francese
If I Went on Safari - Hood, Susan
Riley, Linnea Asplind
Mouse Mess - Riley, Linnea Asplind
Ringgold, Faith
Bonjour, Lonnie - Ringgold, Faith
Ripplinger, Henry
If You're Not from the Prairie. . . -
Bouchard, Dave
Ritchie, Scot
Do the Doors Open by Magic? and Other
Supermarket Questions - Ripley,
Catherine
Eenie Meenie Manitoba - Heidbreder,
Robert
Why Do Stars Twinkle? and Other
Nighttime Questions - Ripley, Catherine
Why Does Popcorn Pop? and Other
Kitchen Questions - Ripley, Catherine
Why Is Soap So Slippery? and Other
Bathtime Questions - Ripley, Catherine
Why Is the Sky Blue? and Other Outdoor
Questions - Ripley, Catherine

Ritz, Karen
Hiding from the Nazis - Adler, David A
Hilde and Eli - Adler, David A
Writer of the Plains - Streissguth, Tom
Rizo, Luis
The First Amphibians - Llamas, Andreu
The Life of a Cell - Llamas Ruiz, Andres
The Origin of the Universe - Llamas Ruiz,
Andres
Robar-DeCoste, Twila
At the Seashore - Hickman, Pamela
Roberts, Richard Samuel
All around Town - Johnson, Dinah
Robertson, Mark
A Treasury of Dragon Stories - Clark,
Margaret
Robins, Arthur
Daft Jack and the Bean Stack - Anholt,
Laurence
The Rather Small Turnip - Anholt,
Laurence
There's a Monster Who Eats Books in Our
House - Grindley, Sally
What Use Is a Moose? - Waddell, Martin
Robinson, Aminah Brenda Lynn
Elijah's Angel - Rosen, Michael J
Sophie - Fox, Mem
To Be a Drum - Coleman, Evelyn
Robison, Don
Habitats - Moore, Jo Ellen
Rocco, Joe
Snow Inside the House - Diviny, Sean
Roche, Denis
Art around the World - Roche, Denis
Brave Georgie Goat - Roche, Denis
Ollie All Over - Roche, Denis
Only One Ollie - Roche, Denis
Rockwell, Anne
The One-Eyed Giant - Rockwell, Anne
Rockwell, Barry
Why the Leopard Has Spots - Mead,
Katherine
Rockwell, Lizzy
Halloween Day - Rockwell, Anne
On the Move - Heiligman, Deborah
Show and Tell Day - Rockwell, Anne
Rockwood, Richard
The New Book of Dinosaurs - Unwin,
David
Witches - Pipe, Jim
Rodgers, Frank
The Huge Bag of Worries - Ironside,
Virginia
The Jolly Witch - King-Smith, Dick

Illustrator Index

Ross, Tony
Amber Brown Sees Red - Danziger, Paula
Balloon Lagoon - Mitchell, Adrian
Daedalus and Icarus - McCaughrean,
    Geraldine
Forever Amber Brown - Danziger, Paula
Harry the Poisonous Centipede - Banks,
    Lynne Reid
Little Wolf's Diary of Daring Deeds -
    Whybrow, Ian
Michael - Bradman, Tony
Miss Dirt the Dustman's Daughter -
    Ahlberg, Allan
Ms. Wiz Supermodel - Blacker, Terence
Nicky - Ross, Tony
Perseus and the Gorgon Medusa -
    McCaughrean, Geraldine
Seeing Red - Garland, Sarah
Sloth's Shoes - Willis, Jeanne
The Wooden Horse - McCaughrean,
    Geraldine
Roth, Robert
Journey of the Nightly Jaguar - Albert,
    Burton
Mama Provi and the Pot of Rice -
    Rosa-Casanova, Sylvia
Pearl Moscowitz's Last Stand - Levine,
    Arthur A
Roth, Roger
Billy the Ghost and Me - Greer, Gery
Mr. Ape - King-Smith, Dick
Roth, Susan L
Leon's Story - Tillage, Leon
Rothman, Michael
Here Is the Tropical Rain Forest -
    Dunphy, Madeleine
Shark in the Sea - Ryder, Joanne
Rotman, Jeffrey L
The Octopus: Phantom of the Sea -
    Cerullo, Mary M
Sharks: Challengers of the Deep - Cerullo,
    Mary M
Rotner, Shelley
Close, Closer, Closest - Rotner, Shelley
Lots of Dads - Rotner, Shelley
Rounds, Glen
Sod Houses on the Great Plains - Rounds,
    Glen
Three Billy Goats Gruff - Asbjornsen,
    Peter Christen
Row, Richard
A Farley Mowat Reader - Mowat, Farley
Rowe, Gavin
The Frightened Little Owl - Ezra, Mark
The Hungry Otter - Ezra, Mark

Roy, Indrapramit
The Very Hungry Lion - Wolf, Gita
Rubel, Nicole
Bunny Riddles - Hall, Katy
Mummy Riddles - Hall, Katy
Rotten Ralph's Rotten Romance - Gantos,
    Jack
*When Someone in the Family Drinks Too
    Much* - Langsen, Richard C
Rubenstein, Len
The Big Book of Nature Projects -
Rucki, Ani
When the Earth Wakes - Rucki, Ani
Ruff, Donna
The Missing Sunflowers - Stern, Maggie
Ruffins, Reynold
Everywhere Faces Everywhere - Berry,
    James
Ruhl, Greg
The Buried City of Pompeii - Tanaka,
    Shelley
Rullman, Stan
Rain Forests and Reefs - Maynard, Caitlin
Rumford, James
The Island-below-the-Star - Rumford,
    James
Russell, Janice
Goldilocks - Russell, Janice
Russell, Linda
Caribou Girl - Murphy, Claire Rudolf
Russell, Lynne
One Smiling Grandma - Linden, Ann
    Marie
Russell, P Craig
Rudy Kipling's Jungle Book - Russell, P
    Craig
Russo, Marisabina
Under the Table - Russo, Marisabina
When Mama Gets Home - Russo,
    Marisabina
Rutherford, Alexa
Hercules - Moore, Robin
Ryan, Susannah
Coming to America - Maestro, Betsy
Darcy and Gran Don't Like Babies -
    Cutler, Jane
*Sparky and Eddie: The First Day of
    School* - Johnston, Tony
Sparky and Eddie: Wild, Wild Rodeo! -
    Johnston, Tony
Rylant, Cynthia
Cat Heaven - Rylant, Cynthia

S

Saaf, Donald
Pushkin Meets the Bundle - Ziefert,
Harriet
Wee G. - Ziefert, Harriet
Sabee, Eric
*My Own Song and Other Poems to Groove
To* - Strickland, Michael R
Sabuda, Robert
Cookie Count - Sabuda, Robert
The Paper Dragon - Davol, Marguerite W
Sagredo Sagudo, Maximo
Mi Diccionario De Juguete - Marcuse,
Aida E
Saillard, Remi
Mr. Fine, Porcupine - Joly, Fanny
St.-Aubin, Bruno
Fred and the Stinky Cheese - Croteau,
Marie-Danielle
Saint James, Synthia
Greetings, Sun - Gershator, Phillis
How Mr. Monkey Saw the Whole World -
Myers, Walter Dean
Neeny Coming, Neeny Going - English,
Karen
Salgado, Rosa
Barco De Suenos - Espino Ortega, Jose
Manuel
Samton, Sheila White
Jamaica Louise James - Hest, Amy
Ten Tiny Monsters - Samton, Sheila White
San Souci, Daniel
The Gifts of Wali Dad - Shepard, Aaron
Red Wolf Country - London, Jonathan
Two Bear Cubs - San Souci, Robert D
Waterman's Child - Mitchell, Barbara
Sanchez, Enrique O
Amelia's Road - Altman, Linda Jacobs
Confetti: Poems for Children - Mora, Pat
Palampam Day - Gershator, David
Sandermose, Iben
Englepels - Sandemose, Iben
Sanderson, Ruth
Rose Red and Snow White - Sanderson,
Ruth
A Treasury of Princesses - Climo, Shirley
Sandford, John
Down Buttermilk Lane - Mitchell, Barbara
Moonstick: The Seasons of the Sioux -
Bunting, Eve
Sandin, Joan
As the Crow Flies - Winthrop, Elizabeth
La Montana De Fuego - Lewis, Thomas P

Sandland, Reg
The Day before Christmas - Shapiro,
Arnold
The First Christmas - Shapiro, Arnold
Trouble at the Haunted House - Shapiro,
Arnold
Wanda Witch's Bad Day - Shapiro, Arnold
Sandved, Kjell B
The Butterfly Alphabet - Sandved, Kjell B
Sansevero, Tony
The Secret Admirer - Guthrie, Donna W
Sing, Henrietta! Sing! - Downey, Lynn
Santore, Charles
William the Curious - Santore, Charles
Santoro, Christopher
Dinosaurs - Howard, John
Dom DeLuise's Hansel and Gretel -
DeLuise, Dom
Giraffes, the Sentinels of the Savannahs -
Sattler, Helen Roney
Sanz, Araceli
Ulrico Y Las Puertas Que Hablan -
Frabetti, Carlo
Sanzol, Jorge
Maruja - Wolf, Ema
Saport, Linda
The Face at the Window - Hanson, Regina
Saraceni, Claudia
Chagall - Pozzi, Gianni
Sarecky, Melody
Quincy's Clubhouse - Glenchur, Paul
Sarmo, Tom
The Crimson Elf - Caduto, Michael J
Sasaki, Goro
Me, Dad and Number 6 - Jennings, Dana
Andrew
Sauber, Robert
Florence Robinson - Hoobler, Dorothy
*Louis Braille: The Blind Boy Who Wanted
to Read* - Fradin, Dennis B
Sirko and the Wolf - Kimmel, Eric A
Savadier, Elivia
A Bedtime Story - Fox, Mem
I Swim an Ocean in My Sleep - Farber,
Norma
The Mysterious Visitor - Jaffe, Nina
Save, Ken
Genesis for Kids - Lambier, Doug
Savin, Deborah
Whales - Short, Joan
Say, Allen
Allison - Say, Allen
Emma's Rug - Say, Allen

Shefelman, Tom
  A Peddler's Dream - Shefelman, J
Shelton, Daniel
  Rosemary for Remembrance - Craddock,
  Sonia
Shemie, Bonnie
  Houses of China - Shemie, Bonnie
Shems, Ed
  Detective Science - Wiese, Jim
  Spy Science - Wiese, Jim
Shepard, Ernest H
  The Best of Winnie-the-Pooh - Milne, A A
  Pooh to the Rescue - Milne, A A
  Pooh's Enchanted Place - Milne, A A
  Winnie-the-Pooh Tells Time - Milne, A A
El Sherbini, Riham
  Egyptology - Ikram, Salima
Shields, Chris
  Some Birds Hang Upside Down -
  Llewellyn, Claire
Shields, Sue
  Chameleons Are Cool - Jenkins, Martin
Shine, Andrea
  Big Band Sound - Diller, Harriett
  The Faraway Drawer - Diller, Harriett
  The Summer My Father Was Ten -
  Brisson, Pat
Shinn, Everett
  A Christmas Carol - Dickens, Charles
Shipman, Ronnie Walter
  I'll Go to School If. . . - Flood, Nancy Bo
Shone, Rob
  Face Painting - Lincoln, Margaret
  The Most Excellent Book of Dress Up -
  Casey, Moe
  *Professor Protein's Fitness, Health,
  Hygiene, and Relaxation Tonic* - Parker,
  Steve
Shore, Judie
  The Jumbo Book of Nature Science -
  Hickman, Pamela
Shortall, Leonard
  Encyclopedia Brown - Sobol, Donald J
Shortt, Tim
  The Babe Ruth Ballet School - Shortt, Tim
Shostak, Peter
  Prairie Born - Bouchard, Dave
Shulevitz, Uri
  The Golden Goose - Shulevitz, Uri
  Hosni the Dreamer - Ben-Ezer, Ehud
Shupe, Bobbi
  Storytelling Adventures - Dubrovin, Vivian
Siebel, Fritz
  Amelia Bedelia - Parish, Peggy

Siegl, Helen
  *The Lion's Whiskers and Other Ethiopian
  Tales* - Ashabranner, Brent
Sierra, F John
  My Mexico - Johnston, Tony
Sieveking, Anthea
  Daniel's Duck - MacKinnon, Debbie
  Pippa's Puppy - MacKinnon, Debbie
  Sarah's Shovel - MacKinnon, Debbie
  The Seasons - MacKinnon, Debbie
  Tom's Train - MacKinnon, Debbie
Sill, John
  About Mammals - Sill, Cathryn
Silva, Simon
  Gathering the Sun - Ada, Alma Flor
Silverstein, Shel
  Falling Up - Silverstein, Shel
Silvestro, Loui
  You Little Monster - Bowring, Jane
Simmons, Jane
  Come Along, Daisy! - Simmons, Jane
Simont, Marc
  Ant Plays Bear - Byars, Betsy Cromer
  The Goose Who Almost Got Cooked -
  Simont, Marc
  Nate the Great and the Crunchy Christmas
  - Sharmat, Marjorie Weinman
Simpson, Kate
  Kitten Tales - Grindley, Sally
Simpson, Mary
  Hands-On Rocky Mountains - Merrill,
  Yvonne Y
Sims, Blanche
  *Living with My Stepfather Is Like Living
  with a Moose* - Bowdish, Lynea
  Marvin and the Mean Words - Kline, Suzy
  What's the Matter with Kelly Beans? -
  Enderle, Judith Ross
Sinclair, Jeff
  Classic Brainteasers - Gardener, Martin
  Mathamusements - Blum, Raymond
Siomades, Lorianne
  A Place to Bloom - Siomades, Lorianne
Sis, Peter
  The 13th Floor - Fleischman, Sid
  Follow the Dream - Sis, Peter
  Monday's Troll - Prelutsky, Jack
  Sleep Safe, Little Whale - Schlein, Miriam
  Starry Messenger - Sis, Peter
Sivertson, Liz
  North Country Spring - Lindbergh, Reeve
Skiles, Pat
  Elizabeth's Beauty - Alberts, Nancy
  Markham

Slavin, Bill
1984: The Year I Was Born - Granfield, Linda
1985: The Year I Was Born - Hancock, Pat
The Earth - Nicolson, Cynthia Pratt
The Hunchback of Notre Dame - Hugo, Victor
The Moon - Bourgeois, Paulette
Morgan Makes Magic - Staunton, Ted
Squares - Ross, Catherine Sheldrick
The Stone Lion - Slavin, Bill
The Sun - Bourgeois, Paulette

Slawski, Wolfgang
Captain Jonathan Sails the Sea - Slawski, Wolfgang

Slobodkina, Esphyr
Caps for Sale - Slobodkina, Esphyr

Slocum, Katherine Rose
Magical Chango - Lewis, Diana

Slonim, David
Upchuck and the Rotten Willy - Wallace, Bill

Slyder, Ingrid
The Fabulous Flying Fandinis - Slyder, Ingrid

Small, David
The Gardener - Stewart, Sarah
George Washington's Cows - Small, David

Smedley, Chris
Nark the Mysterious Crocodile - Girling, Brough

Smith, Cat Bowman
Boom Town - Levitin, Sonia
Feliciana Meets D'Loup Garou - Thomassie, Tynia
Nine for California - Levitin, Sonia
Underground Train - Quattlebaum, Mary

Smith, Craig
Yay! - Rodda, Emily

Smith, Duncan
More Jessame Stories - Jarman, Julia

Smith, A G
The Railways - Livesey, Robert

Smith, Jamie
Professor Blabbermouth on the Moon - Watts, Nigel

Smith, Jan
Monster in Love - Jungman, Ann
Monster in Trouble - Jungman, Ann

Smith, Jos. A
Clay Boy - Ginsburg, Mirra
The Giant - Heller, Nicholas
How Do You Spell God? - Gellman, Marc
Jim Ugly - Fleischman, Sid
Sugaring - Haas, Jessie

Smith, Lane
Disney's James and the Giant Peach - Smith, Lane
Hooray for Diffendoofer Day! - Seuss
Knights of the Kitchen Table - Scieszka, Jon
The Stinky Cheese Man and Other Fairly Stupid Tales - Scieszka, Jon
The True Story of the 3 Little Pigs - Scieszka, Jon
Tut Tut - Scieszka, Jon

Smith, Maggie
Achoo! All about Colds - Demuth, Patricia
This Is Your Garden - Smith, Maggie

Smith, Roberta
Joshua T. Bates in Trouble Again - Shreve, Susan Richards

Smith, Roland
In the Forest with Elephants - Smith, Roland
Journey of the Red Wolf - Smith, Roland

Smith, Sally J
Dragon Soup - Williams, Arlene

Smith, Theresa
The Story Snail - Rockwell, Anne

Smith, Tony
Jigsaw - Moss, Miriam

Smith-Moore, J J
The Babysitter's Handbook - Kuch, K D

Smook, Diane
Shaping a President - Peduzzi, Kelli

Sneed, Brad
Higgins Bend Song and Dance - Martin, Jacqueline Briggs
Smoky Mountain Rose - Schroeder, Alan

Snider, Jackie
Petula, Who Wouldn't Take a Bath - Bailey, Linda

So, Meilo
The Beauty of the Beast - Prelutsky, Jack

So, Sungwan
C Is for China - So, Sungwan

Sobat, Vera
Little Bear Brushes His Teeth - Langreuter, Jutta
Little Bear Goes to Kindergarten - Langreuter, Jutta

Soderlind, Kirsten
  The Miracle of the Loaves and Fishes -
    Smith, Patricia T
Soentpiet, Chris K
  The Last Dragon - Nunes, S
  More than Anything Else - Bradby, Marie
  Peacebound Trains - Balgassi, Haemi
  A Sign - Lyon, George Ella
  Silver Packages - Rylant, Cynthia
  So Far from the Sea - Bunting, Eve
Sofilas, Mark
  The Burnt Stick - Hill, Anthony
Soman, David
  This Is the Bird - Shannon, George
  When I Am Old with You - Johnson,
    Angela
Somers, Greg
  Nanna - Freeman, Pamela
Somerville, Charles C
  Bubble Monster and Other Science Fun -
    Falk, John H
Sopko, Eugen
  Look Out, Cinder! - Lachner, Dorothea
Sorel, Edward
  Jack and the Beanstalk (Palin) - Metaxas,
    Eric
Sorensen, Henri
  A Fourth of July on the Plains - Van
    Leeuwen, Jean
  Mommy's Lap - Horowitz, Ruth
Souhami, Jessica
  Rama and the Demon King - Souhami,
    Jessica
Sovak, Jan
  Canadian Ocean Creatures - Mastin,
    Colleayn O
  Canadian Wild Animals - Mastin, Colleayn
    O
  Canadian Wild Flowers and Emblems -
    Mastin, Colleayn O
Sovka, David
  The Microscope Book - Levine, Shar
Spackman, Jeff
  Dragon Breath - O'Connor, Jane
  Fly Trap - Anastasio, Dina
Spaulding, Dean T
  Watching Our Feathered Friends -
    Spaulding, Dean T
Spears, Rick
  Dino-Trekking - Halls, Kelly Milner
Speidel, Sandra
  A Little Salmon for Witness - Rahaman,
    Vashanti

Speirs, John
  The Case of the Missing Birthday Party -
    Rocklin, Joanne
  A Fair Bear Share - Murphy, Stuart J
Spellman, Susan
  A Small Treasury of Christmas -
  *A Small Treasury of Easter Poems and
    Prayers* -
Spence, Annora
  W.D. the Wonder Dog - Boggs, Cary
Spence, Jim
  No One Told the Aardvark - Eaton,
    Deborah
Spencer, Douglas Brant
  Mystery of the Maya - Ruddell, Nancy
Spencer, Laurie
  Alison's Fierce and Ugly Halloween -
    Bauer, Marion Dane
  Alison's Puppy - Bauer, Marion Dane
Spengler, Kenneth J
  A Campfire for Cowboy Billy - Ulmer,
    Wendy K
  Way Out in the Desert - Marsh, T J
Sperry, Armstrong
  Esto Es Coraje - Sperry, Armstrong
Spetter, Jung-Hee
  Happy Birthday to Me - Vries, Anke De
  Just a Minute! - Kranendonk, Anke
  Piggy's Birthday Dream - Vries, Anke De
Spiegelman, Art
  Open Me. . .I'm a Dog! - Spiegelman, Art
Spirin, Gennady
  The Children of Lir - MacGill-Callahan,
    Sheila
  The Sea King's Daughter - Shepard,
    Aaron
  Snow White and Rose Red - Grimm, Jacob
  The Tale of Tsar Saltan - Pushkin,
    Alexand Sergeevich
Spohn, Kate
  Dog and Cat Make a Splash - Spohn, Kate
  Kitten's Nap - Spohn, Kate
Sporn, Michael
  Whitewash - Shange, Ntozake
Springett, Martin
  Too Many Suns - Lawson, Julie
Spudvilas, Anne
  Big Cat Dreaming - Wild, Margaret
  Bright Star - Crew, Gary
Spurll, Barbara
  Emma's Eggs - Ruurs, Margriet
Staake, Bob
  My Little 123 Book - Staake, Bob
  My Little ABC Book - Staake, Bob

Stone, Lynn M
Cougars - Stone, Lynn M
Swans - Stone, Lynn M
Tigers - DuTemples, Leslie
Stone, Peter
Condor Magic - Hoopes, Lyn Littlefield
Stone, Phoebe
When the Wind Bears Go Dancing - Stone, Phoebe
Stone, Rob
Beginner's Guide to Animal Autopsy - Parker, Steve
Stooke, Andrew
The Red-All-Over Riddle Book - Szirtes, George
Stott, Dorothy
Make It a Merry Christmas! - Jensen, Nancy
Stow, Jenny
Following the Sun - Stow, Jenny
Strassburg, Brian
What's Up with You, Taquandra Fu? - Cibula, Matt
Stringer, Lauren
Mud - Ray, Mary Lyn
Scarecrow - Rylant, Cynthia
Stryker, Jane
Growing Up - Homan, Beulah
Stynes, Barbara White
Walking with Mama - Stynes, Barbara White
Su, Lucy
Dan's Den - Strachan, Ian
Suarez, Maribel
Las Frutas - Suarez, Maribel
Sullivan, Edward
The Day the Earth Was Silent - McGuffee, Michael
Sun, Chyng Feng
On a White Pebble Hill - Sun, Chyng Feng
Suomalainen, Sami
Mud Puddle - Munsch, Robert
Supancich, Jo
All about My Body - Moore, Jo Ellen
How Your Body Works - Moore, Jo Ellen
Science Fun - Moore, Jo Ellen
Susie Poole
The Lion Storyteller Bible - Hartman, Bob
Suzan, Gerardo
Butterfly Boy - Kroll, Virginia L
Sweat, Lynn
Bravo, Amelia Bedelia! - Parish, Herman
One Good Horse - Scott, A

Sweet, Melissa
Monsters in Cyberspace - Regan, Dian Curtis
Pinky and Rex and the New Neighbors - Howe, James
Pinky and Rex and the School Play - Howe, James
Sweet, Stephen
The Young People's Atlas of the World - Richards, Jon
Sweetwater, Jesse
Bouki Dances the Kokioko - Wolkstein, Diane
Synarski, Susan
Bright Ideas -
Syrette, Ken
The Star Man and Other Tales - Johnston, Basil
Szekeres, Cyndy
The Deep Blue Sky Twinkles with Stars - Szekeres, Cyndy
I Love My Busy Book - Szekeres, Cyndy
The Mouse That Jack Built - Szekeres, Cyndy
Yes, Virginia, There Is a Santa Claus - Szekeres, Cyndy

T

Taback, Simms
There Was an Old Lady Who Swallowed a Fly - Taback, Simms
Tabor, Nancy
We Are a Rainbow - Tabor, Nancy
Tafuri, Nancy
The Biggest Boy - Henkes, Kevin
I Love You, Little One - Tafuri, Nancy
What the Sun Sees, What the Moon Sees - Tafuri, Nancy
Tait, Les
The White Stone in the Castle Wall - Oberman, Sheldon
Takabayashi, Mari
Do You Know New? - Marzollo, Jean
Flannel Kisses - Brennan, Linda Crotta
Takao, Yuko
A Winter Concert - Takao, Yuko
Takashima, Shizuye
A Child in Prison Camp - Takashima, Shizuye
Talas, Terri
Beavers - Moore, Helen H

Twinem, Neecy
In the Air - Twinem, Neecy
Tyner-Keating, Susie
I Wish I Had an Elegant Elephant -
Bedell, Sean
Tyrol, Adelaide Murphy
Earth Tales from around the World -
Caduto, Michael J
Tyrrell, Frances
The Dragon's Egg - Baird, Alison
Woodland Christmas - Tyrrell, Frances

U

Ulrich, George
Divide and Ride - Murphy, Stuart J
Things That Go Eek on Halloween -
Clements, Andrew
Unzner, Christa
Meredith, the Witch Who Wasn't -
Lachner, Dorothea
The Spy in the Attic - Scheffler, Ursel
Updike, David
A Helpful Alphabet of Friendly Objects -
Updike, John
Upitis, Alvis
Harvest Year - Peterson, Cris
Horsepower: The Wonder of Draft Horses
- Peterson, Cris
Urberuaga, Emilio
La Bruja De La Montana - Diaz, Gloria
Cecilia
Utt, Mary Ann
A Child's Story of Easter - Wilson, Etta
Utton, Peter
Billy and the Barglebogle - Camp, Lindsay

V

Vaega, Akarana
Kuia - Vaega, Akarana
Nana - Vaega, Akarana
Te Wiki - Vaega, Akarana
The Week - Vaega, Akarana
Vagin, Vladimir
The Enormous Carrot - Vagin, Vladimir
Vainio, Pirkko
The Dream House - Vainio, Pirkko
Valenta, Barbara
*Pop-o-Mania: How to Create Your Own
Pop-Ups* - Valenta, Barbara

Valentine
Dina the Deaf Dinosaur - Addabbo,
Carole
Valfre, Edward
Vacationers from Outer Space - Valfre,
Edward
Valiquette, Matthew
The Heart Is Big Enough - Rosen, Michael
J
Valverde, Mikel
Shola Y Los Jabalies - Atxaga, Bernardo
Van Allsburg, Chris
A City in Winter - Helprin, Mark
Los Misterios Del Senor Burdick - Van
Allsburg, Chris
The Polar Express - Van Allsburg, Chris
The Veil of Snows - Helprin, Mark
The Widow's Broom - Van Allsburg, Chris
Van Der Merwe, Anita
Ndito Runs - Anderson, Laurie Halse
Van Kampen, Vlasta
Beetle Bedlam - Van Kampen, Vlasta
Cookie Critters - Pearson, Debora
Van Krugel, Rick
Molly Brown Is Not a Clown - Rogers,
Linda
Van Nutt, Robert
Charlotte Bronte and Jane Eyre - Ross,
Stewart
The Legend of Sleepy Hollow (Close) -
Van Nutt, Robert
Van Tilburg, Magda
Magic Dad - Prince, Alison
Van Wright, Cornelius
An Angel Just like Me - Hoffman, Mary
The Best Older Sister - Choi, Sook Nyul
Don't Split the Pole - Tate, Eleanora E
A House by the River - Miller, William
Jewels - Rochelle, Belinda
Sam and the Lucky Money - Chinn, Karen
Van Wyk, Dirk
Why Elephants and Fleas Don't Sweat -
Louw, Gideon
Van Zyle, Jon
Disappearing Lake - Miller, Debbie S
Kayuktuk: An Arctic Quest - Heinz, Brian
A Polar Bear Journey - Miller, Debbie S
Raven and River - Carlstrom, Nancy
White
Vane, Mitch
Uncle Arthur's Bedtime Stories: Cinderella
- Robbins, Glenn
Vanni
Love - Siff, Lowell

Children's Book Review Index 1998

Wallace, John
Little Bean's Friend - Wallace, John
Wallace, Mary
I Can Make Art - Wallace, Mary
I Can Make Jewelry - Wallace, Mary
Wallis, Diz
The Macmillan Treasury of Poetry for Children -
The Puffin Book of Classic Children's Stories - Carpenter, Humphrey
Wallner, Alexandra
An Alcott Family Christmas - Wallner, Alexandra
Laura Ingalls Wilder - Wallner, Alexandra
Wallner, John
A Picture Book of Louis Braille - Adler, David A
A Picture Book of Thomas Alva Edison - Adler, David A
Walls, John
Paper Gifts and Jewelry - Temko, Florence
Paper Tags and Cards - Temko, Florence
Walsh, Ellen Stoll
Jack's Tale - Walsh, Ellen Stoll
Walsh, Melanie
Do Monkeys Tweet? - Walsh, Melanie
Do Pigs Have Stripes? - Walsh, Melanie
Walsh Bellville, Cheryl
Powwow Summer - Rendon, Marcie R
Walters, Catherine
When Will It Be Spring? - Walters, Catherine
Walton, Ross
Some Trains Run on Water - Petty, Kate
Wang, Eva
The Giant and the Spring - Hao, Kuang-Ts'ai
Seven Magic Brothers - Hao, Kuang-Ts'ai
Warabe, Kimika
Zoom Zoom - Warabe, Kimika
Ward, Helen
The King of the Birds - Ward, Helen
Water Life - Fitzsimons, Cecilia
Ward, John
Car Washing Street - Patrick, Denise Lewis
Kente Colors - Chocolate, Deborah M Newton
Seven Days of Kwanzaa - Grier, Ella
Ward, Tom
Where the Wind Sleeps - Langille, Carole Glasser

Warhola, James
Bubba the Cowboy Prince - Ketteman, Helen
Warner, Sunny
The Magic Sewing Machine - Warner, Sunny
Warnes, Tim
Davy's Scary Journey - Leeson, Christine
I Don't Want to Have a Bath! - Sykes, Julie
I Don't Want to Take a Bath - Sykes, Julie
Warnick, Elsa
Ride the Wind - Simon, Seymour
Washburn, Lucia
Look to the North - George, Jean Craighead
Sunshine, Moonshine - Armstrong, Jennifer
Waterfield, Anthea
Kid-Etiquette - Smith, Rose Marie
Waters, Tony
Flick the Hero! - Wright, Lynn Floyd
Watkins, Richard Ross
Gladiator - Watkins, Richard Ross
Watling, James
The Arrow over the Door - Bruchac, Joseph
Finding Providence - Avi
The Hessian's Secret Diary - Banim, Lisa
Watson, B
Everyday Things - Lafferty, Peter
What's Inside Buildings? - Parker, Steve
Watson, Marlene
Nathaniel's Violin - Lohans, Alison
Watson, Nick
Adventures with Bananas in Pajamas - Tulloch, Richard
Watson, Wendy
Sleep Is for Everyone - Showers, Paul
Watts, Bernadette
The Elves and the Shoemaker - Watts, Bernadette
Harvey Hare, Postman Extraordinaire - Watts, Bernadette
Shoemaker Martin - Tolstoy, Leo
Watts, Leslie Elizabeth
Princess Stinky-Toes and the Brave Frog Robert - Watts, Leslie Elizabeth
There's a Mouse in My House! - Fitch, Sheree
Weatherby, Mark Alan
My Dinosaur - Weatherby, Mark Alan
Webb, Philip
The Great Bamboozle - Cowley, Joy

Weck, Claudia De
Lisa Y El Gato Sin Nombre - Recheis,
    Kathe
Wegman, William
William Wegman's Farm Days - Wegman,
    William
Wegner, Fritz
Ms. Cliff the Climber - Ahlberg, Allan
Weidner, Teri
Your Body Belongs to You - Spelman,
    Cornelia
Weihs, Erika
The Story of Passover - Simon, Norma
Weir, Doffy
*There's a Troll at the Bottom of Our
    Street* - Jungman, Ann
Weisgard, Leonard
The Quiet Noisy Book - Brown, Margaret
    Wise
Weissman, Bari
Come! Sit! Speak! - Simon, Charnan
The Disease Book - Hyde, Margaret O
From Caterpillar to Butterfly - Heiligman,
    Deborah
Weitzman, David
Old Ironsides - Weitzman, David
Wellington, Monica
Baby at Home - Wellington, Monica
Baby Goes Shopping - Wellington, Monica
Night House, Bright House - Wellington,
    Monica
Wells, Robert E
What's Faster than a Speeding Cheetah? -
    Wells, Robert E
Wells, Rosemary
Bunny Cakes - Wells, Rosemary
Bunny Money - Wells, Rosemary
Humpty Dumpty and Other Rhymes -
    Opie, Iona
Little Boy Blue and Other Rhymes - Opie,
    Iona
Max and Ruby's First Greek Myth - Wells,
    Rosemary
My Very First Mother Goose - Opie, Iona
Noisy Nora - Wells, Rosemary
Nora La Revoltosa - Wells, Rosemary
Old MacDonald - Wells, Rosemary
Pussycat Pussycat and Other Rhymes -
    Opie, Iona
Read to Your Bunny - Wells, Rosemary
Wee Willie Winkie and Other Rhymes -
    Opie, Iona
Welply, Michael
Viking Times - Mason, Antony

Werner, Thomas
The Sky Is Not So Far Away - Hiller,
    Margaret
West, Keith
Warriors, Warthogs, and Wisdom -
    Watson, Lyall
Westbrook, Dick
No One Will Ever Know - Sommer, Carl
Westcott, Nadine Bernard
The Best Vacation Ever - Murphy, Stuart J
Do Cowboys Ride Bikes? - Tucker, Kathy
Do Pirates Take Baths? - Tucker, Kathy
Hello Toes! Hello Feet! - Paul, Ann
    Whitford
Is There Room on the Feather Bed? -
    Gray, Libba Moore
Miss Mary Mack - Hoberman, Mary Ann
Oh, Cats! - Buck, Nola
Super Slumber Parties - Whitney, Brooks
What's Alive - Zoehfeld, Kathleen
    Weidner
Westerduin, Anne
Ducks like to Swim - Verboven, Agnes
Weston, Martha
Bad Baby Brother - Weston, Martha
Owen Foote, Soccer Star - Greene,
    Stephanie
Wettasinghe, Sybil
Friends - Siriwardena, Denagama
Wexler, Jerome
Everyday Mysteries - Wexler, Jerome
Whatley, Bruce
*Detective Donut and the Wild Goose
    Chase* - Whatley, Bruce
*Mrs. Piggle-Wiggle's Won't-Take-a-Bath
    Cure* -
Whatley's Quest - Whatley, Bruce
The Won't-Pick-Up-Toys Cure -
Wheeler, Cindy
More Simple Signs - Wheeler, Cindy
Wheeler, Jean
Rojo - Bryant-Mole, Karen
Wheeler, Jody
The Teddy Bear Book - Penner, Lucille
    Recht
White, Keinyo
Uh-Oh! It's Mama's Birthday - Thomas,
    Naturi
White, Michael
Aztec Times - Mason, Antony
White, Michael P
The Secret of Old Zeb - Deedy, Carmen
    Agra

White, Mike
Nelson Mandela - Holland, Gini
P.T. Barnum - Wright, David K
Wilma Mankiller - Holland, Gini
Whitesell, Rae
A Friend for Cyril - Lines, Patricia
Whitman, Candace
Zoo-Looking - Fox, Mem
Whitney, Alexandra
First Place - Whitney, Alexandra
Whyte, Mary
I Love You the Purplest - Joosse, Barbara
M
The Tickle Stories - Van Leeuwen, Jean
Wichlinski, Andrew
Platypus - Short, Joan
Wick, Walter
A Drop of Water - Wick, Walter
I Spy: Little Book - Marzollo, Jean
I Spy Super Challenger! - Marzollo, Jean
Wickstrom, Sylvie Kantorovitz
Wheels on the Bus - Raffi
Wickstrom, Thor
The Brothers' Promise - Harber, Frances
Chickie Riddles - Hall, Katy
Widener, Terry
Lou Gehrig: The Luckiest Man - Adler,
David A
Wiebe, Jeff
Animal Rap and Far-Out Fables - Molnar,
Gwen
Wiese, Kurt
La Historia De Ping - Flack, Marjorie
Wiesner, David
Hurricane - Wiesner, David
Wijngaard, Juan
Esther's Story - Wolkstein, Diane
A Piece of Home - Levitin, Sonia
Wilde, Sophie De
The Sea Lion - Pichon, Joelle
Wildsmith, Brian
Amazing World of Words - Wildsmith,
Brian
The Bible Story - Turner, Philip
*Brian Wildsmith's Amazing World of
Words* - Wildsmith, Brian
Joseph - Wildsmith, Brian
Katie and the Dream-Eater - Takamado
Wilkinson, Barry
The Saga of Aslak - Price, Susan
Wilkinson, Gary
Cleopatra - Middleton, Haydn
Wilkon, Jozef
Wipe Your Feet, Santa Claus! - Richter,
Konrad

Willard, Nancy
The Magic Cornfield - Willard, Nancy
Willey, Bee
Copy Cat - Mole, John
Michael Rosen's ABC - Rosen, Michael
Myths and Legends of the World -
McCaughrean, Geraldine
Nonsense Songs - Lear, Edward
The Silver Treasure - McCaughrean,
Geraldine
Spider Pie - Cassidy, Anne
Williams, Dan
The Gargoyle - Kilworth, Garry
Williams, Garth
Charlotte's Web - White, E B
The Cricket in Times Square - Selden,
George
Little House Sisters - Wilder, Laura Ingalls
Ride a Purple Pelican - Prelutsky, Jack
Williams, Jared T
Mischief, Mad Mary, and Me - Knight,
Dawn
Williams, Marcia
The Adventures of Robin Hood - Williams,
Marcia
The Iliad and the Odyssey - Williams,
Marcia
Williams, Richard
The Spray-Paint Mystery - Medearis,
Angela Shelf
Williams, Sophy
Cat's Kittens - Rogers, Paul
You're Safe Now, Waterdog - Edwards,
Richard
Williams, Vera B
Lucky Song - Williams, Vera B
More More More, Said the Baby -
Williams, Vera B
Willis, Nancy Carol
The Robins in Your Backyard - Willis,
Nancy Carol
The Rock - Birchmore, Daniel A
Wilsdorf, Anne
The Old Man Who Loved Cheese - Keillor,
Garrison
Wilson, Alex
Shipwreck - Platt, Richard
Witches and Magic-Makers - Hill, Douglas

Wilson, Janet
Amazing Grace - Granfield, Linda
At Grandpa's Sugar Bush - Carney,
Margaret
The Baritone Cat - Skelton, Mora
In Flanders Fields - Granfield, Linda
Lucy Maud and the Cavendish Cat -
Manuel, Lynn
Selina and the Bear Paw Quilt - Smucker,
Barbara
What's He Doing Now? - Farmer, Patti
Wilson, Mark
Through the Witch's Window - Macdonald,
Caroline
Wilson, Phil
A Three-Dimensional Medieval Castle -
Tong, Willabel
Wilson, Roberta
Engelbert Joins the Circus - Paxton, Tom
Wilson, Rodger
Three Kind Mice - Sathre, Vivian
Wilson, Sharon
The Day Gogo Went to Vote - Sisulu,
Elinor
Freedom's Gifts - Wesley, Valerie Wilson
Wilson-Max, Ken
K Is for Kwanzaa - Ford, Juwanda G
Wimmer, Mike
Train Song - Siebert, Diane
Winborn, Marsha
Digby and Kate and the Beautiful Day -
Baker, Barbara
Winch, John
The Old Woman Who Loved to Read -
Winch, John
Windham, Sophie
Unicorns! Unicorns! - McCaughrean,
Geraldine
Wing, Lori Anderson
Circles - Gill, Janie Spaht
Winnick, Karen B
Mr. Lincoln's Whiskers - Winnick, Karen
B
Winter, Jeanette
The Tortilla Cat - Willard, Nancy
Winter, Susan
Henry's Baby - Hoffman, Mary
Wintz-Litty, Julie
Lumina - Weninger, Brigitte
Wise, Nicki
Racing Clouds - Jackson, Tandi
Wiseman, Ann Sayre
Making Things - Wiseman, Ann Sayre

Wisniewski, David
Ducky - Bunting, Eve
Golem - Wisniewski, David
Rain Player - Wisniewski, David
The Secret Knowledge of Grown-Ups -
Wisniewski, David
Sundiata, Lion King of Mali - Wisniewski,
David
Wissenfeld, Alison
Best Loved Prayers - Rock, Lois
Witschonke, Alan
The Brooklyn Bridge - Mann, Elizabeth
The Great Wall - Mann, Elizabeth
Wojtowycz, David
The Lion Who Wanted to Love - Andreae,
Giles
Rumble in the Jungle - Andreae, Giles
Wolf, Alex De
Alice's Birthday Pig - Kennemore, Tim
Alice's World Record - Kennemore, Tim
Wolff, Ashley
Baby Beluga - Raffi
Home Sweet Home - Marzollo, Jean
*Miss Bindergarten Gets Ready for
Kindergarten* - Slate, Joseph
Stella and Roy - Wolff, Ashley
A String of Beads - Reid, Margarette S
Wolk-Stanley, Jessica
*The New York Public Library Amazing
Space* - Campbell, Ann
*The New York Public Library Incredible
Earth* - Campbell, Ann
Wong, Janet S
A Suitcase of Seaweed and Other Poems -
Wong, Janet S
Wood, Clare
Everybody Has a Bellybutton - Pringle,
Laurence
Wood, Don
Bright and Early Thursday Evening -
Wood, Audrey
Wood, Gerald
Medieval Town - Kerr, Daisy
Wood, Jakki
Across the Big Blue Sea - Wood, Jakki
Wood, Michele
Going Back Home - Wood, Michele
I See the Rhythm - Igus, Toyomi
Wood, Ted
Ghosts of the Southwest - Wood, Ted
Iditarod Dream - Wood, Ted
Woodroffe, David
Elements - Knapp, Brian J
Woods, Gerald
Exploring Africa - Martell, Hazel

Yue, Charlotte
Shoes: Their History in Words and Pictures - Yue, Charlotte

Z

Zaccaria, Nella
Too Much Snow - Poluck, Kathy
Zagwyn, Deborah Turney
Turtle Spring - Zagwyn, Deborah Turney
Zakowski, Connie
The Insect Book - Zakowski, Connie
Zalben, Jane Breskin
Pearl's Marigolds for Grandpa - Zalben, Jane Breskin
Zallinger, Jean Day
The Journey of English - Brook, Donna
Zawadzki, Marek
Ahaiyute and Cloud Eater - Hulpach, Vladimir
Zeldis, Malcah
Honest Abe - Kunhardt, Edith
Martin Luther King - Bray, Rosemary L
Zelinsky, Paul O
More Rootabagas - Sandburg, Carl
Swamp Angel - Isaacs, Anne
Zemach, Kaethe
The Character in the Book - Zemach, Kaethe
Zeman, Ludmila
The First Red Maple Leaf - Zeman, Ludmila
Zhang, Ange
The Fishing Summer - Jam, Teddy
To the Mountains by Morning - Wieler, Diana
Zhang, Christopher Zhong-Yuan
Lichee Tree - Russell, Ching Yeung
Moon Festival - Russell, Ching Yeung
Zhang, Song Nan
Cowboy on the Steppes - Zhang, Song Nan
Zimmer, Dirk
Perrywinkle's Magic Match - Madsen, Ross Martin
Zimmermann, Werner
Farmer Joe Baby-Sits - Richards, Nancy Wilcox
Whatever You Do, Don't Go Near That Canoe! - Lawson, Julie
Zinn, David
Business as Usual - Haynes, David
The Gumma Wars - Haynes, David

Zorrilla, Daniel
Se Jubilan Las Hadas - Perez Diaz, Enrique
Zweifel, Frances
Science Fair Projects: Flight, Space and Astronomy - Bonnet, Robert L
Science Fair Projects: The Environment - Bonnet, Robert L
Simple Chemistry Experiments with Everyday Materials - Loeschnig, Louis V
Zwerger, Lisbeth
The Wizard of Oz - Baum, L Frank
Der Zauberer Von Oz - Baum, L Frank

Title Index

A

1 2 3 Yippie (Illus. by Lisa
Jahn-Clough) — *Jahn-Clough, Lisa*
2 X 2 = BOO! — *Leedy, Loreen*
3-D Paper Crafts (Illus. by Wally
Randall) — *Broda, Ron*
3 Kids Dreamin' (Illus. by Dena
Schutzer) — *England, Linda*
4 Pups and a Worm (Illus. by Eric
Seltzer) — *Seltzer, Eric*
5 Novels — *Pinkwater, Daniel Manus*
6 Wild Adventures (Illus. by Eric Brace)
— *Albee, Sarah*
9 Puzzle Mysteries (Illus. by Eric Brace)
— *Gutelle, Andrew*
The 12 Circus Rings. Electronic Media
Version
The 12 Days of Christmas — *Sabuda,
Robert*
The 13th Floor (Illus. by Peter Sis)
— *Fleischman, Sid*
A 16th Century Mosque (Illus. by Mark
Bergin) — *Macdonald, Fiona*
The 17th Century — *Halliwell, Sarah*
The 18 Penny Goose (Illus. by Ellen
Beier) — *Walker, Sally M*
The 18th Century — *Halliwell, Sarah*
19th Century Girls and Women
— *Kalman, Bobbie*
r 20th Century: A Visual History
— *Adams, Simon*
45 and 47 Stella Street — *Honey,
Elizabeth*
55 Waverly Street (Illus. by Mary
Chambers) — *Black, Thom*
r 100 Greatest. Vols. 1-12

101 Amazing Optical Illusions (Illus. by
Alex Pang) — *Jennings, Terry*
101 Amazing Things to Do with Your
Computer
r 101 Great Science Experiments
— *Ardley, Neil*
1,2,3 What Do You See? (Illus. by Susi
Bodal) — *Bohdal, Susi*
The 512 Ants on Sullivan Street (Illus.
by Patrick Merrell) — *Losi, Carol A*
1900-1919 — *McGowan, Tom*
1930-1939 — *Aaseng, Nathan*
1940-1949 — *Aaseng, Nathan*
1960-1969 — *McGowan, Tom*
1970-1979 — *Gutfreund, Geraldine
Marshall*
1984: The Year I Was Born (Illus. by
Bill Slavin) — *Granfield, Linda*
1985: The Year I Was Born (Illus. by
Bill Slavin) — *Hancock, Pat*
A Is for Africa — *Onyefulu, Ifeoma*
A Is for Artist — *J. Paul Getty Museum*
A Is for Asia (Illus. by Yumi Heo)
— *Chin-Lee, Cynthia*
A My Name Is... (Illus. by Lynne
Woodcock Cravath) — *Lyne, Alice*
A.N.T.I.D.O.T.E. — *Blackman, Malorie*
The A to Z Beastly Jamboree (Illus. by
Robert Bender) — *Bender, Robert*
Aaron's Awful Allergies (Illus. by
Eugenie Fernandes) — *Harrison,
Troon*
Abandoned — *Oldfield, Jenny*
ABC — *Wegman, William*
ABC Dogs (Illus. by Tara Darling)
— *Darling, Kathy*
ABC Fun — *Pelham, David*

ABC, I Like Me! (Illus. by Nancy L
Carlson) — *Carlson, Nancy L*
ABC of Crawlers and Flyers — *Ryden,
Hope*
ABC Yummy (Illus. by Lisa
Jahn-Clough) — *Jahn-Clough, Lisa*
Abe Lincoln Goes to Washington 1837-
1865 (Illus. by Cheryl Harness)
— *Harness, Cheryl*
Abortion Violence and Extremism
— *McCuen, Gary E*
About Mammals (Illus. by John Sill)
— *Sill, Cathryn*
About the Weather — *Taylor, Barbara*
Abracadabra (Illus. by Dieter Schubert)
— *Schubert, Ingrid*
The Abracadabra Kid — *Fleischman,
Sid*
Abraham Lincoln — *Ito, Tom*
Abraham Lincoln, Will You Ever Give
Up? (Illus. by Kennon James)
— *Uglow, Loyd*
Absolutely Positively Alexander (Illus.
by Ray Cruz) — *Viorst, Judith*
Abuela (Illus. by Elisa Kleven)
— *Dorros, Arthur*
Abuela's Weave — *Casteneda, Omar*
La Abuelita Aventurera (Illus. by Pablo
Nunez) — *Machado, Ana Maria*
Abuelita's Heart (Illus. by Amy
Cordova) — *Cordova, Amy*
r Academic American Encyclopedia. Vols.
1-21
Achoo! All about Colds (Illus. by
Maggie Smith) — *Demuth, Patricia*
Acid Rain — *Edmonds, Alex*
Acorn Pancakes, Dandelion Salad and
38 Other Wild Recipes (Illus. by Paul
Mirocha) — *George, Jean Craighead*
An Acquaintance with Darkness
— *Rinaldi, Ann*
Across America on an Emigrant Train
— *Murphy, Jim*
Across Frozen Seas — *Wilson, John,
1951-*
Across the Big Blue Sea (Illus. by Jakki
Wood) — *Wood, Jakki*
Across the Lines — *Reeder, Carolyn*
Across the Roman Wall (Illus. by
Michael Charlton) — *Breslin, Theresa*
Across the Wide and Lonesome Prairies
— *Gregory, Kristiana*
The Acting Bug — *Ellis, Kathryn*
Action Rhymes (Illus. by Carol
Thompson) — *Foster, John*

Activities — *Smith, Debbie*
Adam and Eve (Illus. by Bryn Barnard)
— *Martin, Mary*
Adam's Daycare (Illus. by Ruth Ohi)
— *Ovenell-Carter, Julie*
Adam's War — *Levitin, Sonia*
Addie's Forever Friend (Illus. by Helen
Cogancherry) — *Lawlor, Laurie*
Adopted by Indians (Illus. by Hilair
Chism) — *Mayfield, Thomas Jefferson*
Adoption — *Currie, Stephen*
The Adventure of Charlie Chick (Illus.
by Maurice Pledger) — *Pledger,
Maurice*
An Adventure with Billy Bunny
— *Pledger, Maurice*
Adventures in Art. Rev. Ed. — *Milord,
Susan*
Adventures in Cranberry Forest (Illus.
by Susan Little) — *Coburn, Brian*
Adventures in Ponyland (Illus. by Holly
Jones) — *Tomaselli, Doris*
The Adventures of Captain Underpants
(Illus. by Dav Pilkey) — *Pilkey, Dav*
The Adventures of Inch Worm Willie
— *Lidgold, Carole M*
The Adventures of Jason Jackrabbit
(Illus. by Donna Newsome) — *Dee, M
M*
The Adventures of Laura and Jack
(Illus. by Renee Graef) — *Wilder,
Laura Ingalls*
The Adventures of Midnight Son
— *Patrick, Denise Lewis*
The Adventures of Odysseus (Illus. by
Peter Malone) — *Philip, Neil*
The Adventures of Peter Rabbit (Illus.
by Stephanie Britt) — *Potter, Beatrix*
The Adventures of Pippi Longstocking
(Illus. by Michael Chesworth)
— *Lindgren, Astrid*
The Adventures of Robin Hood (Illus.
by Marcia Williams) — *Williams,
Marcia*
The Adventures of Softbill the Strong
— *Stodart, Eleanor*
The Adventures of Sparrowboy (Illus.
by J Brian Pinkney) — *Pinkney, J
Brian*
The Adventures of Tintin. Vol. 6
— *Herge*
The Adventures of Tom Kitten. Audio
Version — *Potter, Beatrix*

Alice in Pastaland (Illus. by Reagan Word) — *Wright, Alexandra*
Alice of Wonderfarm Goes to the Races (Illus. by Ann Nelles) — *Nelles, Ann*
Alice of Wonderfarm Saves the Drumlin (Illus. by Ann Nelles) — *Nelles, Ann*
Alice Ramsey's Grand Adventure (Illus. by Don Brown) — *Brown, Don*
Alice Rose and Sam — *Lasky, Kathryn*
Alice: The Musical. Book and Audio Version — *Johnson, Mark*
Alice's Birthday Pig (Illus. by Alex De Wolf) — *Kennemore, Tim*
Alice's World Record (Illus. by Alex De Wolf) — *Kennemore, Tim*
Alicia's Tutu (Illus. by Mark Graham) — *Pulver, Robin*
Alien Blood — *Archer, Chris*
Alien Terror — *Archer, Chris*
Aliens — *Hawkins, Colin*
Aliens in the Basement (Illus. by Susan Gardos) — *Reid, Susan*
Aliens to Earth — *Cooling, Wendy*
Alison's Fierce and Ugly Halloween (Illus. by Laurie Spencer) — *Bauer, Marion Dane*
Alison's Puppy (Illus. by Laurie Spencer) — *Bauer, Marion Dane*
All Aboard! — *Demarest, Chris L*
All Aboard for the Milky Way — *Wallace, Karen*
All about Alfie — *Hughes, Shirley*
All about Alligators (Illus. by Jim Arnosky) — *Arnosky, Jim*
All about Animals (Illus. by Kelly McMahon) — *Moore, Jo Ellen*
All about Color (Illus. by Jill Newton) — *Yates, Irene*
All about Deer (Illus. by Jim Arnosky) — *Arnosky, Jim*
All about My Body (Illus. by Jo Supancich) — *Moore, Jo Ellen*
All about Pattern (Illus. by Jill Newton) — *Yates, Irene*
All about Rattlesnakes (Illus. by Jim Arnosky) — *Arnosky, Jim*
All about Shape (Illus. by Jill Newton) — *Yates, Irene*
All about Touch (Illus. by Jill Newton) — *Yates, Irene*
All around Town (Illus. by Richard Samuel Roberts) — *Johnson, Dinah*
All Because of Jackson (Illus. by John Eastwood) — *King-Smith, Dick*

All God's Children (Illus. by Amanda Schaffer) — *Hopkins, Lee Bennett*
All Kinds of Animals (Illus. by Anthony Lewis) — *McCormick, Rosie*
All Saints, All Souls, and Halloween — *Chambers, Catherine*
All Year Round — *Desimini, Lisa*
Allie's Apples (Illus. by Simone Lia) — *Dunmore, Helen*
Allie's Basketball Dream — *Barber, Barbara*
The Alligator (Illus. by Jim Chanell) — *Crewe, Sabrina*
Alligator Baby (Illus. by Michael Martchenko) — *Munsch, Robert*
Alligators All Around — *Sendak, Maurice*
Alligators Always Dress for Dinner — *Donigan, Linda*
Alligators and Crocodiles (Illus. by Warren Clark) — *Dudley, Karen*
Alligators and Others All Year Long (Illus. by Jose Aruego) — *Dragonwagon, Crescent*
Allison (Illus. by Allen Say) — *Say, Allen*
El Alma En Una Nube (Illus. by Alejandro Campos Garcia) — *Artiles Perez, Emma*
Almost Famous Daisy! — *Kidd, Richard*
Along the Seashore (Illus. by Dorothy Emerling) — *Cooper, Ann C*
Alonzo Mourning: Center of Attention — *Gutman, Bill*
Alpha Bugs — *Carter, David A*
Alphabet Art (Illus. by Sue Dennen) — *Press, Judy*
Alphabet City Ballet — *Tamar, Erika*
The Alphabet Sticker Book — *Page, Robin*
Alsek's ABC Adventure (Illus. by Chris Caldwell) — *Caldwell, Chris*
Alternative Energy Sources — *Chandler, Gary*
Always My Dad (Illus. by Raul Colon) — *Wyeth, Sharon Dennis*
The Always Prayer Shawl (Illus. by Ted Lewin) — *Oberman, Sheldon*
Always Wear Clean Underwear! and Other Ways Parents Say I Love You (Illus. by Debbie Tilley) — *Gellman, Marc*
Am I Naturally This Crazy? — *Holbrook, Sara*

Antonio's Apprenticeship (Illus. by Taylor Morrison) — *Morrison, Taylor*

Antonio's Rain Forest — *Lewington, Anna*

Any Bear Can Wear Glasses (Illus. by Sylvia Long) — *Long, Matthew*

The Anyday Book (Illus. by Alan Tiegreen) — *Cole, Joanna*

Anywhere but Here — *Dueck, Adele*

The Apaches (Illus. by Ronald Himler) — *Sneve, Virginia Driving Hawk*

Aparato Respiratorio (Illus. by Antonio Munoz Tenllado) — *Roca, Nuria*

Appalachia, the Voices of Singing Birds (Illus. by Barry Moser) — *Rylant, Cynthia*

Apple Pie Tree (Illus. by Shari Halpern) — *Hall, Zoe*

Apple Trees (Illus. by William Munoz) — *Patent, Dorothy Hinshaw*

The Apprenticeship of Lucas Whitaker — *DeFelice, Cynthia*

The Apprenticeship of Lucas Whitaker (McDonough). Audio Version — *DeFelice, Cynthia*

April's Kittens (Caruso). Audio Version — *Newberry, Clare Turlay*

Aquila — *Norriss, Andrew*

Arabian Horses — *Maiecek, Tomaaes*

Aran's Medley — *Van El, Alannah*

L'Arbre Aux Corbeaux — *Stibane*

Archaeologists Dig for Clues — *Duke, Kate*

Archway Arrow — *Beames, Margaret*

Arctic — *Low, Robert*

Arctic and Antarctic — *Weller, Dave*

Arctic Son (Illus. by Wendell Minor) — *George, Jean Craighead*

Arctic Tundra — *Forman, Michael H*

Are We Moving to Mars? — *Schraff, Anne*

Are You There, God? It's Me, Margaret — *Blume, Judy*

Are You There God? It's Me, Margaret (Hamilton). Audio Version — *Blume, Judy*

Arm in Arm — *Charlip, Remy*

The Armadillo from Amarillo (Illus. by Lynne Cherry) — *Cherry, Lynne*

Armadillos Sleep in Dugouts and Other Places Animals Live (Illus. by Diane DeGroat) — *Ryan, Pam Munoz*

An Armenian Family (Illus. by Carol Halebian) — *Greenberg, Keith Elliot*

Armien's Fishing Trip — *Stock, Catherine*

Armor to Venom — *Perry, Phyllis J*

Armored Animals — *Brown, Andrew*

r Arms and Armor (Illus. by James Field) — *Gilbert, Adrian*

r Arms and Armour — *Gilbert, Adrian*

Arms Control — *Gold, Susan Dudley*

Arms Law

The Arnold Lobel Book of Mother Goose (Illus. by Arnold Lobel) — *Mother Goose*

Around the Oak — *Muller, Gerda*

Around the Track — *Otfinoski, Steven*

Around the World with Phineas Frog — *Adshead, Paul*

The Arrow over the Door (Illus. by James Watling) — *Bruchac, Joseph*

Art around the World (Illus. by Denis Roche) — *Roche, Denis*

Art Dog (Illus. by Thacher Hurd) — *Hurd, Thacher*

Art Fun! (Illus. by Pamela Monfort) — *Solga, Kim*

The Art Lesson — *De Paola, Tomie*

The Art of Making Comic Books — *Pellowski, Michael*

The Art of the Renaissance (Illus. by L R Galante) — *Corrain, Lucia*

Art School — *Manning, Mick*

Arthur Ashe: Breaking the Color Barrier in Tennis — *Wright, David K*

Arthur Babysits — *Brown, Marc*

Arthur Writes a Story (Illus. by Marc Brown) — *Brown, Marc*

Arthur's Chicken Pox — *Brown, Marc*

Arthur's Computer Disaster (Illus. by Marc Brown) — *Brown, Marc*

Arthur's Family Vacation (Brown) (Illus. by Marc Brown). Book and Audio Version — *Brown, Marc*

Arthur's First Sleepover — *Brown, Marc*

Arthur's Halloween (Brown) (Illus. by Marc Brown). Book and Audio Version — *Brown, Marc*

Arthur's New Puppy — *Brown, Marc*

Arthur's Nose (Illus. by Marc Brown) — *Brown, Marc*

Arthur's Reading Race. Electronic Media Version — *Brown, Marc*

Arthur's Really Helpful Word Book (Illus. by Marc Brown) — *Brown, Marc*

Away in a Manger (Little Angels Series)
(Illus. by Laura Rader)
The Awful Aardvarks Go to School
(Illus. by Tracey Campbell Pearson)
— *Lindbergh, Reeve*
The Aztec News — *Steele, Philip*
Aztec Times (Illus. by Michael White)
— *Mason, Antony*
The Aztecs — *Chapman, Gillian*

B

Baba (Illus. by Ruth Brown) — *Brown,
Ruth*
Baba Yaga and the Wise Doll (Illus. by
Ruth Brown) — *Oram, Hiawyn*
Baba Yaga and Vasilisa the Brave
— *Mayer, Marianna*
Babe and Other Stories (Illus. by
Michael Terry) — *King-Smith, Dick*
The Babe Ruth Ballet School (Illus. by
Tim Shortt) — *Shortt, Tim*
Babes in the Woods — *Lynch, Chris*
Babes in Toyland (Illus. by Erin
McGonigle Brammer)
Babies — *Sandeman, Anna*
The Babies Are Coming! (Illus. by
Chloe Cheese) — *Hest, Amy*
Baboon (Illus. by Georg Hallensleben)
— *Banks, Kate*
Baby Angels (Illus. by Jane
Cowen-Fletcher) — *Cowen-Fletcher,
Jane*
Baby Animals — *Brown, Andrew*
Baby Animals (Balloon)
Baby Animals: A Very First Picture
Book — *Tuxworth, Nicola*
Baby at Home (Illus. by Monica
Wellington) — *Wellington, Monica*
Baby Bear Comes Home (Illus. by Ian
Newsham) — *Lishak, Antony*
Baby Beluga (Illus. by Ashley Wolff)
— *Raffi*
Baby Birds (Illus. by Gabriel
Casadevall) — *Garcia, Eulalia*
Baby Boo! — *Hawkins, Colin*
The Baby Book (Illus. by Ken Heyman)
— *Morris, Ann*
Baby Buggy, Buggy Baby (Illus. by
Richard Brown) — *Ziefert, Harriet*
Baby Goes Shopping (Illus. by Monica
Wellington) — *Wellington, Monica*
Baby in a Basket (Illus. by Ted Rand)
— *Rand, Gloria*

Baby Jesus (Illus. by Julie Downing)
— *Downing, Julie*
Baby-O (Illus. by Sucie Stevenson)
— *Carlstrom, Nancy White*
Baby Rock, Baby Roll (Illus. by Denise
Fernando) — *Blackstone, Stella*
The Baby Sister (Illus. by Tomie De
Paola) — *De Paola, Tomie*
The Baby-Sitters Club — *Martin, Ann
M, 1955-*
Baby Tamer (Illus. by Mark Teague)
— *Teague, Mark*
Baby Tweety's Flying Machine
The Baby Who Wouldn't Go to Bed
(Illus. by Helen Cooper) — *Cooper,
Helen, 1963-*
p Babybug
The Babylonians — *Landau, Elaine*
Baby's Bedtime (Illus. by Jonathan
Langley)
Baby's Feet (Illus. by Linda Hendry)
— *Quinlan, Patricia*
Baby's First Nativity (Illus. by Peter
Stevenson) — *Singer, Muff*
Baby's First Prayers
Baby's Hands (Illus. by Linda Hendry)
— *Quinlan, Patricia*
Baby's World--At Home (Illus. by Geoff
Dann)
Baby's World--Outdoors (Illus. by Geoff
Dann)
The Babysitter's Handbook (Illus. by J
J Smith-Moore) — *Kuch, K D*
The Back of Beyond (Illus. by Ralph L
Ramstad) — *Bowen, Andy Russell*
Back of Beyond — *Ellis, Sarah*
Back to the Blue (Illus. by Ian Andrew)
— *McKenna, Virginia*
Back to the Cabin (Illus. by Ann
Blades) — *Blades, Ann*
Back to the Wild (Illus. by William
Munoz) — *Patent, Dorothy Hinshaw*
Backyard Bird Watching for Kids
— *Harrison, George H*
Backyard Birds of Summer — *Lerner,
Carol*
Backyard Dragon — *Sterman, Betsy*
The Backyard Time Detectives (Illus. by
Eugenie Fernandes) — *Suzuki, David*
Bad Baby Brother (Illus. by Martha
Weston) — *Weston, Martha*
Bad Bad Cats — *McGough, Roger*
Bad, Badder, Baddest — *Voigt, Cynthia*
A Bad Case of Stripes (Illus. by David
Shannon) — *Shannon, David*

Baseball: Run, Throw and Catch
— *Lloyd, Bryant*
Baseball Saved Us (Illus. by Dom Lee)
— *Mochizuki, Ken*
Baseball: The Positions — *Lloyd, Bryant*
Baseball Turnaround — *Christopher, Matt*
Basher Five-Two — *O'Grady, Scott*
Bashi, Elephant Baby (Illus. by John Butler) — *Radcliffe, Theresa*
r The Basic Oxford Picture Dictionary To Basilopullon Tes Benedias (Illus. by Champes Tsangares) — *Sylloge Pruse, Kosta*
The Basketball Player (Illus. by Sheldon Cohen) — *Carrier, Roch*
Basketball Stars — *Dolin, Nick*
I Bastoni Dello Yeti E Altre Favole Del Nepal (Illus. by Yacopo Camagni) — *Varma, Nishu*
Bat (Illus. by Karen Duncan) — *Robb, Jackie*
Bat and Bird — *Theodorou, Rod*
Bat in the Dining Room (Illus. by S D Schindler) — *Dragonwagon, Crescent*
Bat Jamboree — *Appelt, Kathi*
La Batalla Del 5 De Mayo — *Urrutia, Maria Cristina*
Batbaby (Illus. by Robert Quackenbush) — *Quackenbush, Robert*
Batboy: An Inside Look at Spring Training (Illus. by Matthew Cavanaugh) — *Anderson, Joan*
Bath-Time Boots (Illus. by Satoshi Kitamura) — *Kitamura, Satoshi*
Bats! — *Cole, Ron*
Bats about Baseball (Illus. by Kim LaFave) — *Little, Jean*
Bats, Bugs, and Biodiversity — *Goodman, Susan E*
Bats: Shadows in the Night (Illus. by Merlin Tuttle) — *Ackerman, Diane*
Batswana — *Bolaane, Maitseo*
The Battle for the Castle — *Winthrop, Elizabeth*
The Battle for the Castle (Winthrop). Audio Version — *Winthrop, Elizabeth*
The Battle of Pook Island — *Lasenby, Jack*
The Battle of the Alamo — *Bredeson, Carmen*
The Battle of the Little Bighorn — *Stein, R Conrad*

The Battle of the Little Bighorn in American History — *Ferrell, Nancy Warren*
Batwings and the Curtain of Night (Illus. by Mary GrandPre) — *Davol, Marguerite W*
Baxter Badger's Home (Illus. by Vicki Diggs) — *McClellan, Doris*
Bayard Rustin: Behind the Scenes of the Civil Rights Movement — *Haskins, James*
Be a Wolf! (Illus. by Don Punchatz) — *Strickland, Brad*
Be Aware of Danger — *Gutman, Bill*
Be Gentle! (Illus. by Virginia Miller) — *Miller, Virginia*
Be Good to Eddie Lee (Illus. by Floyd Cooper) — *Fleming, Virginia*
Be Not Far from Me (Illus. by David Diaz) — *Kimmel, Eric A*
Be Smart, Stay Safe — *Elliott, Michele*
Beach Day (Illus. by Catarina Kruusval) — *Kruusval, Catarina*
Beach Feet (Illus. by Lynn Reiser) — *Reiser, Lynn*
The Beaded Moccasins — *Durrant, Lynda*
Beading: Bracelets, Earrings, Necklaces and More (Illus. by Tracy Walker) — *Sadler, Judy Ann*
Beads — *Sadler, Judy Ann*
Bean (Illus. by Anna Grossnickle Hines) — *Hines-Stephens, Sarah*
Bean's Games (Illus. by Anna Grossnickle Hines) — *Hines-Stephens, Sarah*
Bean's Night (Illus. by Anna Grossnickle Hines) — *Hines-Stephens, Sarah*
Beany (Not Beanhead) and the Magic Crystal (Illus. by Susanna Natti) — *Wojciechowski, Susan*
Beany (Not Beanhead) and the Magic Crystal (Illus. by Susanna Natti) — *Wojciechowski, Susan*
The Bear (Illus. by Robert Morton) — *Crewe, Sabrina*
Bear (Illus. by Mick Inkpen) — *Inkpen, Mick*
The Bear Who Didn't Like Honey (Illus. by Odilon Moraes) — *Maitland, Barbara*
The Bear Who Heard Crying (Illus. by Ted Rand) — *Kinsey-Warnock, Natalie*

Big Whiskers Saves the Cove (Illus. by Jim Collins) — *Carolan, Trevor*

Bigfoot and Other Legendary Creatures (Illus. by William Noonan) — *Walker, Paul Robert*

Bigger (Illus. by Daniel Kirk) — *Kirk, Daniel*

Bigger than T. Rex — *Lessem, Don*

The Biggest Boy (Illus. by Nancy Tafuri) — *Henkes, Kevin*

The Biggest Bug Book (Illus. by Paul Facklam) — *Facklam, Margery*

The Biggest Horse I Ever Did See (Illus. by Claire Ewart) — *Couture, Susan Arkin*

The Biggest Pest on Eighth Avenue (Illus. by Cynthia Fisher) — *Lawlor, Laurie*

Biggest, Strongest, Fastest — *Jenkins, Steve*

Bigmama's — *Crews, Donald*

Bijou, Bonbon and Beau (Illus. by Leslie Wu) — *Sweeney, Joan*

Biker (Illus. by Gary Rees) — *Masters, Anthony*

Bikes, Cars, Trucks and Trains

Bill and Pete to the Rescue (Illus. by Tomie De Paola) — *De Paola, Tomie*

Bill Clinton and His Presidency — *Landau, Elaine*

Bill Clinton: President of the 90s — *Cwiklik, Robert*

Bill Gates: Billionaire Computer Genius — *Dickinson, Joan D*

Bill Gates: Helping People Use Computers — *Simon, Charnan*

Bill Pickett: African-American Rodeo Star — *Sanford, William R*

Bill Pickett: Rodeo-Ridin' Cowboy (Illus. by J Brian Pinkney) — *Pinkney, Andrea Davis*

Billy and the Baby (Illus. by Lynn Breeze) — *Bradman, Tony*

Billy and the Barglebogle (Illus. by Peter Utton) — *Camp, Lindsay*

Billy and the Big New School (Illus. by Catherine Anholt) — *Anholt, Laurence*

Billy the Ghost and Me (Illus. by Roger Roth) — *Greer, Gery*

Billygoat Goes Wild (Illus. by Robert Roennfeldt) — *Horniman, Joanne*

Bimmi Finds a Cat (Illus. by James Ransome) — *Stewart, Elisabeth J*

Bing Bang Boogie, It's a Boy Scout — *Wilson, Bob*

Bingo Brown, Gypsy Lover — *Byars, Betsy Cromer*

Biodiversity (Illus. by William Munoz) — *Patent, Dorothy Hinshaw*

r Biography Today: Artists Series. Vol. 1 — *Harris, Lurie Lanzen*

r Biography Today: Profiles of People of Interest to Young Readers. Vol. 2 — *Harris, Laurie Lanzen*

r Biography Today Sport Series. Vol. 1-

r Biography Today Sports Series. Vol. 2

Biotechnology — *Wells, Donna*

The Bird (Illus. by Nicholas Allan) — *Allan, Nicholas*

The Bird Maiden (Mike). Book and Audio Version — *Mike, Jan M*

Bird Watcher — *Arnosky, Jim*

Bird Watching with Margaret Morse Nice (Illus. by Laurie A Caple) — *Ross, Michael Elsohn*

Birdie's Lighthouse (Illus. by Kimberly Bulcken Root) — *Hopkinson, Deborah*

Birds (Illus. by L R Galante) — *Alderton, David*

r Birds: A Guide to Familiar American Birds. Rev. and Updated Ed. — *Zim, Herbert Spencer*

The Birds' Christmas Carol (Illus. by Jessie Gillespie) — *Wiggin, Kate Douglas*

Birds Conquer the Sky (Illus. by Miriam Ferron) — *Llamas, Andreu*

The Birds Keep on Singing — *Cockett, Stephen*

Birds of the Countryside

Birdsong (Illus. by Robert Florczak) — *Wood, Audrey*

A Birthday Basket for Tia (Illus. by Cecily Lang) — *Mora, Pat*

Birthday Cake and I Scream — *Katz, Fred E*

Birthday Flowers (Illus. by Catarina Kruusval) — *Kruusval, Catarina*

A Birthday for Frances — *Hoban, Russell*

The Birthday Swap (Illus. by Loretta Lopez) — *Lopez, Loretta*

Biscuit Finds a Friend (Illus. by Pat Schories) — *Capucilli, Alyssa*

Biscuits in the Cupboard (Illus. by Philippe Beha) — *Nichol, Barbara*

Bit Scream — *Gunther, Richard*

Boo and Baa on a Cleaning Spree (Illus. by Olof Landstrom) — *Landstrom, Olof*

Boo to a Goose (Illus. by David Miller) — *Fox, Mem*

Boo Who — *Holub, Joan*

Booby Hatch (Illus. by Betsy Lewin) — *Lewin, Betsy*

Boogie Bones (Illus. by Kevin Hawkes) — *Loredo, Elizabeth*

The Book of Baths (Illus. by Lizi Boyd) — *Ruelle, Karen Gray*

The Book of Bedtimes (Illus. by Lizi Boyd) — *Ruelle, Karen Gray*

The Book of Breakfasts (Illus. by Lizi Boyd) — *Ruelle, Karen Gray*

The Book of Changes — *Wynne-Jones, Tim*

The Book of Fairies (Illus. by Robin T Barrett) — *Williams, Rose*

The Book of Hob Stories (Illus. by Patrick Benson) — *Mayne, William*

The Book of Little Folk (Illus. by Lauren A Mills) — *Mills, Lauren A*

The Book of Miracles (Illus. by Lawrence Kushner) — *Kushner, Lawrence*

A Book of Nonsense (Illus. by Edward Lear) — *Lear, Edward*

The Book of Slime (Illus. by Jan Davey Ellis) — *Jackson, Ellen*

The Book of Unicorns — *French, Jackie*

The Book That Jack Wrote (Illus. by Daniel Adel) — *Scieszka, Jon*

Booker T. Washington — *Nicholson, Lois*

Boom, Baby, Boom, Boom! (Illus. by Patricia MacCarthy) — *Mahy, Margaret*

Boom Town (Illus. by Cat Bowman Smith) — *Levitin, Sonia*

Boomer's Big Day — *McGeorge, Constance W*

Boot — *Brooks, Bruce*

The Bootmaker and the Elves (Illus. by Tom Curry) — *Lowell, Susan*

Bootsie Barker, Ballerina (Illus. by G Brian Karas) — *Bottner, Barbara*

Boredom Busters — *Hart, Avery*

Born in the Gravy — *Cazet, Denys*

Born to Be Wild (Illus. by Steve Bjorkman) — *Spinner, Stephanie*

Borreguita and the Coyote (Illus. by Petra Mathers) — *Aardema, Verna*

The Borrowed Hanukkah Latkes (Illus. by Nancy Cote) — *Glaser, Linda*

The Borrowers (Illus. by Beth Krush) — *Norton, Mary*

A Bosnian Family — *Silverman, Robin Landew*

Boss of the Plains (Illus. by Holly Meade) — *Carlson, Laurie*

The Boston Tea Party — *Stein, R Conrad*

Bottoms Up! (Illus. by Patrick O'Brien) — *Singer, Marilyn*

Bouki Dances the Kokioko (Illus. by Jesse Sweetwater) — *Wolkstein, Diane*

Bounce Back (Illus. by Doug Keith) — *Swoopes, Sheryl*

Bounce Me, Tickle Me, Hug Me (Illus. by Trevor Black) — *Carpenter-Davis, Sandra*

Boundless Grace (Illus. by Caroline Binch) — *Hoffman, Mary*

Bow-Wow Birthday (Illus. by Arden Johnson-Petrov) — *Wardlaw, Lee*

Bowl Patrol — *Janovitz, Marilyn*

Bowmen of Crecy (Illus. by Ian Ribbons) — *Welch, Ronald*

A Box Can Be Many Things (Illus. by Paige Billin-Frye) — *Rau, Dana Meachen*

The Box of Delights — *Masefield, John*

A Box of Silver Birch — *Hesketh, Phoebe*

A Box of Stories for Six Year Olds (Illus. by Phillip Norman) — *Thomson, Pat*

Box Top Dreams — *Glassman, Miriam*

The Boxes — *Sleator, William*

Boy, Can He Dance! (Illus. by Paul Yalowitz) — *Spinelli, Eileen*

Boy in Darkness — *Peake, Mervyn Laurence*

Boy Soup or When Giant Caught Cold — *Lesynski, Loris*

The Boy, the Dollar and the Wonderful Hat (Illus. by San Murata) — *Helmer, Marilyn*

The Boy Who Ate Around (Illus. by Henrik Drescher) — *Drescher, Henrik*

The Boy Who Ate Words (Illus. by Thierry Dedieu) — *Dedieu, Thierry*

The Boy Who Cried Wolf (Illus. by Carla Dijs) — *Dijs, Carla*

The Boy Who Longed for a Lift (Illus. by Brian Selznick) — *Farber, Norma*

The Boy Who Reversed Himself
— *Sleator, William*
The Boy Who Sat by the Window (Illus.
by Catharine Gallagher) — *Loftis,
Chris*
The Boy Who Wouldn't Go to Bed
(Illus. by Helen Cooper) — *Cooper,
Helen, 1963-*
The Boy Who Wouldn't Speak (Illus. by
Deirdre Betteridge) — *Berry, Steve*
The Boy with the Eggshell Skull
— *Robshaw, Brandon*
Boys in the Well — *Beeler, Cecil
Freeman*
The Bracelet — *Uchida, Yoskiko*
Bradley and the Billboard — *Farrell,
Mame*
The Braids Girl (Illus. by Tim Ladwig)
— *McCourt, Lisa*
The Brain — *Barmeir, Jim*
Brain (Illus. by Ian Thompson)
— *Sandeman, Anna*
The Brain and Nervous System
— *Parker, Steve*
Brain Cell (Illus. by Karen Duncan)
— *Robb, Jackie*
The Brain: Our Nervous System
— *Simon, Seymour*
Brainteasers from Jewish Folklore
— *Kaye, Rosalind Charney*
Brambly Hedge Spring and Summer
Stories (Moffat). Audio Version
— *Barklem, Jill*
Branch of the Talking Teeth — *Moore,
Ishbel*
The Brand New Creature — *Beeke,
Jemma*
Brass Button (Illus. by Susan Paradise)
— *Dragonwagon, Crescent*
A Brat Called Annie (Illus. by Mark
Payne) — *Fowler, Thurley*
Brave Bessie Flying Free — *Fisher,
Lilian M*
Brave Georgie Goat (Illus. by Denis
Roche) — *Roche, Denis*
Brave Horace (Illus. by Holly Keller)
— *Keller, Holly*
The Brave Little Parrot (Illus. by Susan
Gaber) — *Martin, Rafe*
The Brave Little Tailor (Illus. by Sergei
Goloshapov) — *Grimm, Jacob*
The Brave Ones — *Kerins, Tony*
Bravery: The Story of Sitting Bull (Illus.
by Robin Lawrie) — *Murray, Peter,
1952, Sep., 9-*

The Bravest Cat! (Illus. by DyAnne
DiSalvo-Ryan) — *Driscoll, Laura*
The Bravest Fireman (Illus. by Leah
Malka Diskind) — *Zytman, Leah*
Braving the Frozen Frontier
— *Johnson, Rebecca L*
Bravo, Amelia Bedelia! (Illus. by Lynn
Sweat) — *Parish, Herman*
Brazil — *Morrison, Marion*
Bread — *Powell, Jillian*
Breakaway — *Little, Kimberley Griffiths*
Breakfast at the Liberty Diner (Illus. by
Daniel Kirk) — *Kirk, Daniel*
Breaking Ground, Breaking Silence
— *Hansen, Joyce*
Breaking into Print (Illus. by Bonnie
Christensen) — *Krensky, Stephen*
Breaking the Chains — *Katz, William
Loren*
Breaking the Spell (Illus. by Susan
Field) — *Grindley, Sally*
Breath of a Ghost — *Horrocks, Anita*
Breath of the Dragon (Illus. by June
Otani) — *Giles, Gail*
Breathing — *Sandeman, Anna*
A Breeze in the Willows (Illus. by Roger
Mitchell) — *Johnson, Allen, Jr.*
The Bremen Town Musicians (Illus. by
David Johnson) — *Johnson, David,
1951-*
Brenda and Edward (Illus. by Maryann
Kovalski) — *Kovalski, Maryann*
Brer Rabbit and the Wonderful Tar
Baby (Lover) (Illus. by Henrik
Drescher). Book and Audio Version
— *Harris, Joel Chandler*
Brett Favre — *Mooney, Martin*
Brian Wildsmith's Amazing World of
Words (Illus. by Brian Wildsmith)
— *Wildsmith, Brian*
Bridge to Terabithia (Illus. by Donna
Diamond) — *Paterson, Katherine*
Bridges Connect — *Hill, Lee Sullivan*
Bright and Early Thursday Evening
(Illus. by Don Wood) — *Wood,
Audrey*
Bright Ideas (Illus. by Susan Synarski)
Bright Lights — *York, Sarah
Mountbatten-Windsor, Duchess of*
Bright Lights, Little Gerbil (Illus. by
Steve Bjorkman) — *Spinner,
Stephanie*
Bright Star (Illus. by Anne Spudvilas)
— *Crew, Gary*

Calico the Wonder Horse — *Burton, Virginia Lee*

The California Gold Rush in American History — *Altman, Linda Jacobs*

Call It Courage (Phillips). Audio Version — *Sperry, Armstrong*

Call Me Ahnighito (Illus. by Richard Egielski) — *Conrad, Pam*

Call Me Consuelo — *Lachtman, Ofelia Dumas*

r Call of Cthulhu: Dreamlands. 4th Ed.

A Call to Character — *Greer, Colin*

Callie Shaw, Stable Boy — *Alter, Judy*

Cam Jansen and the Scary Snake Mystery (Illus. by Susanna Natti) — *Adler, David A*

Camaros — *Ethan, Eric*

Cameron and Me (Illus. by Marilyn Mets) — *Harris, Dorothy Joan*

Camp All-Star — *Coldwell, Michael*

Camp Ghost-Away (Moore). Audio Version — *Delton, Judy*

The Camp Knock Knock Mystery (Illus. by Fiona Dunbar) — *Duffey, Betsy*

A Campfire for Cowboy Billy (Illus. by Kenneth J Spengler) — *Ulmer, Wendy K*

Can a Coal Scuttle Fly? — *Miller, Tom*

Can I Be Good? (Illus. by Ted Rand) — *Taylor, Livingston*

Can It Really Rain Frogs? — *Christian, Spencer*

Can Kids Save the Earth? — *Berger, Melvin*

Can We Save Them? (Illus. by James M Needham) — *Dobson, David*

Can You Catch a Falling Star? (Illus. by Dean Lindberg) — *Rosen, Sidney*

Can You Help Me Find My Smile? (Illus. by Greg Budwine) — *Sommer, Carl*

Can You Imagine? — *McKissack, Pat*

Can You Keep a Secret? (Illus. by Meredith Johnson) — *Petersen, P J*

Can You Spot the Leopard? — *Stelzig, Christine*

Can You Spot the Spotted Dog? — *Rowe, John*

Canada — *Barlas, Robert*

Canada: Star of the North — *Sateren, Shelley Swanson*

Canadian Ocean Creatures (Illus. by Jan Sovak) — *Mastin, Colleayn O*

Canadian Wild Animals (Illus. by Jan Sovak) — *Mastin, Colleayn O*

Canadian Wild Flowers and Emblems (Illus. by Jan Sovak) — *Mastin, Colleayn O*

Canals Are Water Roads — *Hill, Lee Sullivan*

Una Canasta De Cumpleanos Para Tia (Illus. by Cecily Lang) — *Mora, Pat*

The Candlewick Book of Fairy Tales (Illus. by P J Lynch) — *Hayes, Sarah*

Candy Making for Beginners (Illus. by Jerry Grajewski) — *Fryatt, Evelyn Howe*

Canopy Crossing. Book and Audio Version — *Nagda, Ann Whitehead*

Can't Catch Me, I'm the Gingerbread Man (Illus. by Jamie Gilson) — *Gilson, Jamie*

Can't Sit Still (Illus. by Colleen Browning) — *Lotz, Karen E*

Canterville Ghost — *Wilde, Oscar*

Caps for Sale (Illus. by Esphyr Slobodkina) — *Slobodkina, Esphyr*

Captain Blackheart's Gold — *Lister, Jan*

Captain Cook's Christmas Pudding — *Van Rynbach, Iris*

Captain Hawk and the Stone of Destiny (Illus. by Janek Matysiak) — *Eldridge, Jim*

Captain Jonathan Sails the Sea (Illus. by Wolfgang Slawski) — *Slawski, Wolfgang*

Captain Salt in Oz (Illus. by John R Neill) — *Thompson, Ruth Plumly*

Captain Scott — *Fischel, Emma*

Captive! Gary Paulsen World of Adventure (Woodman). Audio Version — *Paulsen, Gary*

Car Smarts — *Sobey, Edwin J C*

Car Washing Street (Illus. by John Ward) — *Patrick, Denise Lewis*

Cardboard Boxes (Illus. by Sarah-Jane Neaves) — *Connor, Nikki*

Cardboard Tubes (Illus. by Sarah-Jane Neaves) — *Connor, Nikki*

Cardinal and Sunflower (Illus. by Huy Voun Lee) — *Preller, James*

The Care and Feeding of Dragons — *Seabrooke, Brenda*

Care of Henry (Illus. by Paul Howard) — *Fine, Anne*

r Career Discovery Encyclopedia. 3rd Ed., Vols. 1-6

The Caribbean and the Gulf of Mexico — *Morgan, Nina*

D

Daisy and Jack and the Surprise Pie
(Illus. by Prue Theobalds)
— *Theobalds, Prue*
Daisy Dare (Illus. by Jill Barton)
— *McBratney, Sam*
Daisy Is a Mommy — *Kopper, Lisa*
Daisy Is a Mummy (Illus. by Lisa
Kopper) — *Kopper, Lisa*
The Dalai Lama: A Biography of the
Tibetan Spiritual and Political Leader
(Illus. by Demi) — *Demi*
The Dallas Cowboys Football Team
— *Lace, William W*
Dams Give Us Power — *Hill, Lee
Sullivan*
Dance — *Medearis, Angela Shelf*
Dance, Pioneer, Dance! (Illus. by Brad
Teare) — *Walton, Rick*
Dance with Me (Illus. by Megan Lloyd)
— *Esbensen, Barbara Juster*
Dancer — *Peterson, Shelley*
The Dancing Fox (Illus. by Mary K
Okheena) — *Bierhorst, John*
Dancing on the Bridge of Avignon
— *Vos, Ida*
Dancing through the Shadows
— *Tomlinson, Theresa*
Dancing with Ben Hall and Other Yarns
— *French, Jackie*
Dancing with Dziadziu (Illus. by Annika
Nelson) — *Bartoletti, Susan Campbell*
Dancing with Great-Aunt Cornelia
— *Quirk, Anne*
Dancing with the Indians — *Medearis,
Angela Shelf*
Dandelion Adventures (Illus. by Anca
Hariton) — *Kite, L Patricia*
Dandelions (Illus. by Greg Shed)
— *Bunting, Eve*
Danger along the Ohio — *Willis,
Patricia*
Danger in the Desert — *Fields, Terri*
Danger in the Wings — *Trease, Geoffrey*
Danger on Midnight River (Woodman).
Audio Version — *Paulsen, Gary*
Dangerous Animals
Dangerous Ghosts — *Cohen, Daniel,
1936-*
Dangerous Skies — *Staples, Suzanne
Fisher*
The Dani of Irian Jaya — *Thompson,
Liz*
Daniel Boone: Wilderness Pioneer
— *Sanford, William R*

Daniel's Duck (Illus. by Anthea
Sieveking) — *MacKinnon, Debbie*
Danny and the Dinosaur Go to Camp
(Illus. by Syd Hoff) — *Hoff, Syd*
Dan's Den (Illus. by Lucy Su)
— *Strachan, Ian*
Daphne Eloise Slater, Who's Tall for
Her Age (Illus. by Glo Coalson)
— *Willner-Pardo, Gina*
Darcy and Gran Don't Like Babies
(Illus. by Susannah Ryan) — *Cutler,
Jane*
Dare to Be, M.E.! (Illus. by Marcy
Dunn Ramsey) — *LeMieux, Anne C*
Daredevil Specialist — *Greenberg, Keith
Elliot*
Daring to Be Abigail — *Vail, Rachel*
The Dark (Illus. by Michael
Martchenko) — *Munsch, Robert*
The Dark at the Top of the Stairs (Illus.
by Ivan Bates) — *McBratney, Sam*
Dark beneath the Moon — *Purkis,
Christine*
The Dark Is Rising — *Cooper, Susan*
Dark of the Moon — *Haworth-Attard,
Barbara*
Dashing through the Snow (Illus. by
Sherry Shahan) — *Shahan, Sherry*
Dateline: Troy — *Fleischman, Paul*
Daughter, Have I Told You? (Illus. by
Virginia Halstead) — *Coyne, Rachel*
Daughter of Suqua — *Hamm, Diane
Johnston*
Daughter of the Sea (Illus. by Sian
Bailey) — *Doherty, Berlie*
D'Aulaires' Book of Greek Myths (Illus.
by Ingri D'Aulaire) — *D'Aulaire,
Ingri*
David and Goliath (Illus. by Scott
Cameron) — *Schenk de Regniers,
Beatrice*
David, Donny, and Darren — *Aldape,
Virginia Totorica*
David Robinson — *Bock, Hal*
Davin — *Gordon, Dan, 1947-*
Davy's Scary Journey (Illus. by Tim
Warnes) — *Leeson, Christine*
The Day before Christmas (Illus. by Reg
Sandland) — *Shapiro, Arnold*
The Day Gogo Went to Vote (Illus. by
Sharon Wilson) — *Sisulu, Elinor*
The Day I Swapped My Dad for Two
Goldfish (Illus. by Dave McKean)
— *Gaiman, Neil*

Desert Discoveries (Illus. by John
Carrozza) — *Wadsworth, Ginger*
Desert Dreamings — *Stokes, Deidre*
Desert Dwellers — *Warren, Scott S*
Desert Mammals — *Landau, Elaine*
Desert Trip (Illus. by Ronald Himler)
— *Steiner, Barbara*
Deserts (Illus. by Martin Camm)
— *Morris, Neil*
Deserts and Rainforests (Illus. by
Anthony Lewis) — *Llewellyn, Claire*
Destination: Jupiter — *Simon, Seymour*
Destination Los Angeles — *MacMillan,
Dianne*
Destination: Rain Forest — *Grupper,
Jonathan*
Detective Dinosaur: Lost and Found
(Illus. by R W Alley) — *Skofield,
James*
Detective Donut and the Wild Goose
Chase (Illus. by Bruce Whatley)
— *Whatley, Bruce*
Detective Science (Illus. by Ed Shems)
— *Wiese, Jim*
Devil Sticks for the Complete Klutz
— *Cassidy, John*
Devil's Den — *Pfeffer, Susan Beth*
The Dewey Decimal System — *Fowler,
Allan*
El Dia Que La Boa De Jimmy Se Comio
La Ropa (Illus. by Steven Kellogg)
— *Noble, Trinka Hakes*
Diabetes — *Ferber, Elizabeth*
The Diamond Tree — *Schwartz, Howard*
Diana: Queen of Hearts — *Cerasini,
Marc*
Diane Goode's American Christmas
(Illus. by Diane Goode) — *Goode,
Diane*
Diane Goode's Book of Giants and
Little People (Illus. by Diane Goode)
— *Goode, Diane*
Diary of a Drummer Boy (Illus. by
Michael Garland) — *Brill, Marlene
Targ*
The Diary of a Young Girl: The
Definitive Edition — *Frank, Anne*
Dia's Story Cloth (Illus. by Chu Cha)
— *Cha, Dia*
Dibby Dubby Dhu (Illus. by Sara
Fanelli) — *Barker, George*
r Diccionario Escolar De La Lengua
Espanola
Diego Rivera (Illus. by Gary Rees)
— *Holland, Gini*

Diez Deditos (Illus. by Elisa Kleven)
— *Orozco, Jose-Luis*
A Different Kind of Hero — *Blakeslee,
Ann R*
A Different Life — *Keith, Lois*
Digby (Illus. by Barbara J
Phillips-Duke) — *Hazen, Barbara
Shook*
Digby and Kate and the Beautiful Day
(Illus. by Marsha Winborn) — *Baker,
Barbara*
The Digestive System — *Stille, Darlene
R*
Digger: The Story of a Mole in the Fall
(Illus. by Ken Lilly) — *Potter, Tessa*
Digging for Dinosaurs — *Berger, Melvin*
Dilly and the Cup Final — *Bradman,
Tony*
Dilly and the Goody Goody (Illus. by
Susan Hellard) — *Bradman, Tony*
Un Dimanche Avec Cezanne
— *Madeleine-Perdrillat, Alain*
Dina the Deaf Dinosaur (Illus. by
Valentine) — *Addabbo, Carole*
Ding Dong! Merrily on High (Illus. by
Francesca Crespi) — *Crespi,
Francesca*
Dinner at Magritte's — *Garland,
Michael*
Dino-Trekking (Illus. by Rick Spears)
— *Halls, Kelly Milner*
Dinorella: A Prehistoric Fairy Tale
(Illus. by Henry Cole) — *Edwards,
Pamela Duncan*
Dinosaur Dinner with a Slice of
Alligator Pie (Illus. by Debbie Tilley)
— *Lee, Dennis, 1939-*
Dinosaur Ghosts (Illus. by Douglas
Henderson) — *Gillette, J Lynett*
Dinosaur Habitat (Illus. by Sonja
Lamut) — *Griffith, Helen V*
Dinosaur Roar! (Illus. by Paul
Stickland) — *Stickland, Paul*
Dinosaur Stomp! (Illus. by Paul
Stickland) — *Stickland, Paul*
Dinosaur with an Attitude — *Johansen,
Hanna*
Dinosaurs (Illus. by Christopher
Santoro) — *Howard, John*
The Dinosaurs (Illus. by Ted Finger)
— *Krueger, Richard*
Dinosaurs — *Miller, Angela*
The Dinosaurs Are Back and It's All
Your Fault, Edward! (Illus. by Niki
Daly) — *Hartmann, Wendy*

Dr. Ruth Talks about Grandparents
(Illus. by Tracey Campbell Pearson)
— *Westheimer, Ruth K*

Dr. Seuss's ABC. 40th-Anniversary Ed.
— *Seuss, Dr.*

Does God Know How to Tie Shoes?.
Book and Audio Version
— *Carlstrom, Nancy White*

Does Hockey Love Kids? (Illus. by
Jeannine Meuse) — *Meuse,
Christopher*

Dog and Cat Make a Splash (Illus. by
Kate Spohn) — *Spohn, Kate*

The Dog Ate My Homework (Illus. by
Megan Jeffery) — *Caserta, Carmen*

A Dog Called Kitty (Ganser). Audio
Version — *Wallace, Bill*

The Dog: Faithful Friend — *Simon,
Dominique*

Dog Friday (Lambert). Audio Version
— *McKay, Hilary*

Dog in Danger (Illus. by Judith Lawton)
— *Oram, Hiawyn*

The Dog in the Freezer — *Mazer, Harry*

Dog Magic (Illus. by Carla Golembe)
— *Golembe, Carla*

Dog Named Zog (Illus. by Susan Tait
Porcaro) — *Wise, Noreen*

A Dog of My Own (Illus. by Katya
Krenina) — *McCourt, Lisa*

Dog on a Broomstick (Illus. by Nick
Price) — *Page, Jan*

Dog People (Illus. by Murv Jacob)
— *Bruchac, Joseph*

Dog Star (Illus. by Ann James)
— *Brian, Janeen*

The Dog Who Walked with God (Illus.
by Stan Fellows) — *Rosen, Michael J,
1954-*

Doggerel (Illus. by Kim LaFave)
— *Dalton, Sheila*

Dogs (Illus. by Gail Gibbons)
— *Gibbons, Gail*

r Dogs, Cats, and Horses — *Strickland,
Charlene*

Dolls — *Ansary, Mir Tamim*

p Dolphin Log

Dolphin SOS (Illus. by Judith Lawton)
— *Oram, Hiawyn*

Dolphins — *Stoops, Erik D*

Dom DeLuise's Hansel and Gretel (Illus.
by Christopher Santoro) — *DeLuise,
Dom*

El Domador De Monstruos (Illus. by
Maria Luisa Torcida) — *Machado,
Ana Maria*

Domino Addition Book and Game Set
— *Long, Lynette*

Dominoes around the World (Illus. by
Karen Dugan) — *Lankford, Mary D*

Donde Viven Los Monstros (Illus. by
Maurice Sendak) — *Sendak, Maurice*

Donkey Dust — *Buxton, Jane*

Donkey Kong Country (Illus. by Dave
Phillips) — *Phillips, Dave*

Don't Be Surprised! (Illus. by Haydn
Cornner) — *Trevelyan, Kathy*

Don't Bug Me! (Illus. by Gillian
McHale) — *McHale, Gillian*

Don't Dig So Deep, Nicholas
— *Harrison, Troon*

Don't Laugh, Joe! (Illus. by Keiko
Kasza) — *Kasza, Keiko*

Don't Pat the Wombat! — *Honey,
Elizabeth*

Don't Split the Pole (Illus. by Cornelius
Van Wright) — *Tate, Eleanora E*

Don't Try This at Home! (Illus. by True
Kelley) — *Cobb, Vicki*

The Door in the Lake — *Butts, Nancy*

Dora's Eggs (Illus. by Jane Chapman)
— *Sykes, Julie*

r Dorling Kindersley Children's Picture
Encyclopedia

r The Dorling Kindersley Science
Encyclopedia. 2nd Ed., Rev. and
Updated

Dorothy's Darkest Days (Illus. by Judith
Caseley) — *Caseley, Judith*

Double Act (Illus. by Nick Sharratt)
— *Wilson, Jacqueline*

Double Trouble — *DeClements, Barthe*

Double Trouble in Walla Walla (Illus.
by Sal Murdocca) — *Clements,
Andrew*

Dougal Dixon's Dinosaurs Updated
— *Dixon, Dougal*

Douglas Fir — *Davis, Wendy*

Doug's Secret Christmas (Illus. by
Matthew Peters) — *Scarborough, Ken*

The Dove (Illus. by Jude Daly)
— *Stewart, Dianne*

Down Buttermilk Lane (Illus. by John
Sandford) — *Mitchell, Barbara*

Down Comes the Rain (Illus. by James
Graham Hale) — *Branley, Franklyn
Mansfield*

A Duck in a Tree — *Loomis, Jennifer A*
A Duck So Small (Illus. by Elisabeth
    Holstien) — *Benjamin, A H*
Ducks Disappearing (Illus. by Tony
    Maddox) — *Naylor, Phyllis Reynolds*
Ducks like to Swim (Illus. by Anne
    Westerduin) — *Verboven, Agnes*
Ducky (Illus. by David Wisniewski)
    — *Bunting, Eve*
Duff the Giant Killer (Illus. by Kim
    LaFave) — *Wilson, Budge*
Duffy: Everyone's Dog (Illus. by Cathy
    Netherwood) — *Bernard, Patricia*
The Duke and the Peasant — *Beckett,*
    Wendy
Duke Ellington (Illus. by J Brian
    Pinkney) — *Pinkney, Andrea Davis*
Dulwich Picture Gallery Children's Art
    Book (Illus. by David Teniers)
    — *Wolfe, Gillian*
The Dumb Bunnies (Illus. by Dav
    Pilkey) — *Denim, Sue*
The Dumb Bunnies' Easter (Illus. by
    Dav Pilkey) — *Denim, Sue*
The Dumb Bunnies Go to the Zoo (Illus.
    by Dav Pilkey) — *Denim, Sue*
Dume's Roar (Illus. by Kathy Blankley
    Roman) — *Mollel, Tololwa M*
Dump Truck (Box Cars)
Dump Trucks and Diggers (Illus. by
    Robert Crowther) — *Crowther,*
    Robert
Duncan Back-to-Back (Illus. by Alison
    R Grapes) — *Wells, Duncan*
A Dune Buggy Ride with Baby Taz
The Dust Bowl (Illus. by Karen
    Reczuch) — *Booth, David*

E

E De Yomu Hiroshima No Gembaku
    (Illus. by Shigeo Nishimura) — *Nasu,*
    Masamoto
E-Mail — *Brimner, Larry Dane*
Eagle — *Parry-Jones, Jemima*
Eagle and Birds of Prey (Illus. by Frank
    Greenaway) — *Parry-Jones, Jemima*
The Eagle and the Rainbow (Illus. by
    Tomie De Paola) — *Madrigal, Antonio*
    Hernandez
The Eagle and the River — *Craighead,*
    Charles
The Eagle as Wide as the World
    — *Kennedy, X J*

Eagle Boy (Illus. by Cara Moser)
    — *Hausman, Gerald*
Eagle Song (Illus. by Dan Andreasen)
    — *Bruchac, Joseph*
The Eagle's Gift (Illus. by Tatsuro
    Kiuchi) — *Martin, Rafe*
Eagles of America (Illus. by William
    Munoz) — *Patent, Dorothy Hinshaw*
The Eagle's Shadow — *Martin, Nora*
Early Explorers of North America
    — *Wilbur, C Keith*
The Earth (Illus. by Bill Slavin)
    — *Nicolson, Cynthia Pratt*
Earth — *Vogt, Gregory L*
Earth Always Endures (Illus. by
    Edward S Curtis) — *Philip, Neil*
Earth Explained — *Taylor, Barbara*
Earth-Friendly Outdoor Fun — *Pfiffner,*
    George
The Earth Giant (Illus. by Melvin
    Burgess) — *Burgess, Melvin*
r The Earth in Three Dimensions World
    Atlas — *Lye, Keith*
Earth-Shattering Poems — *Rosenberg,*
    Liz
Earth Tales from around the World
    (Illus. by Adelaide Murphy Tyrol)
    — *Caduto, Michael J*
Earthquake — *Duey, Kathleen*
Earthquake Games (Illus. by Christina
    C Blatt) — *Levy, Matthys*
Earthquake Terror — *Kehret, Peg*
Earthquakes and Volcanoes (Illus. by
    Greg Harris) — *Merrians, Deborah*
r Earth's Natural Resources CD-ROM.
    Electronic Media Version
Earthsong (Illus. by Melissa Bay
    Mathis) — *Rogers, Sally*
Earthworms (Illus. by Dwight Kuhn)
    — *Pascoe, Elaine*
Eastern Europe — *Burke, Patrick*
Easy Braids, Barrettes and Bows (Illus.
    by Sarah Jane English) — *Sadler,*
    Judy Ann
r Easy Guide to the 20th Century
    — *Peat, Anne*
Easy Math Puzzles (Illus. by Cynthia
    Fisher) — *Adler, David A*
Easy Meat — *Stewart, Maureen*
Easy Peasy! (Illus. by Tanya Linch)
    — *Jennings, Linda*
Easy to See Why — *Gwynne, Fred*
The Easy Way to Draw Animals
    — *Angelo, Sandra McFall*
Eaten Alive — *Whitman, John*

Flight and Flying Machines — *Parker, Steve*

The Flight of Burl Crow — *Jones, Tim Wynne*

The Flight of Red Bird — *Rappaport, Doreen*

Flikka and the Prince Edward Island Mystery (Illus. by Hazel Birt) — *Birt, Hazel*

The Flimflam Man (Illus. by Eileen Christelow) — *Beard, Darleen Bailey*

Flip-Flops (Illus. by Nancy Cote) — *Cote, Nancy*

Floating Home (Illus. by Michael Rex) — *Getz, David*

The Floating House (Illus. by Helen Cogancherry) — *Sanders, Scott R, 1945-*

Floating in Space (Illus. by True Kelley) — *Branley, Franklyn Mansfield*

Flood (Illus. by Erick Ingraham) — *Calhoun, Mary*

Flood Fish (Illus. by Sheldon Greenberg) — *Eversole, Robyn*

Floods — *Armbruster, Ann*

Flora and the Strawberry Red Birthday Party (Illus. by David Armitage) — *Armitage, Ronda*

Flora and Tiger (Illus. by Eric Carle) — *Carle, Eric*

Flora McDonnell's ABC (Illus. by Flora McDonnell) — *McDonnell, Flora*

Flora McDonnell's ABC (Illus. by Flora McDonnell) — *McDonnell, Flora*

Florence Kelley (Illus. by Ken Green) — *Saller, Carol*

Florence Nightingale — *Fischel, Emma*

Florence Robinson (Illus. by Robert Sauber) — *Hoobler, Dorothy*

The Florida Panther — *Silverstein, Alvin*

Flour Babies — *Fine, Anne*

The Flower Fairies Sticker Activity Book

Flower Garden (Illus. by Kathryn Hewitt) — *Bunting, Eve*

Flower Watching with Alice Eastwood (Illus. by Laurie A Caple) — *Ross, Michael Elsohn*

Flowers — *Bryant-Mole, Karen*

r Flowers: A Guide to Familiar American Wildflowers. Rev. Ed. — *Zim, Herbert Spencer*

Flowers for Mommy (Illus. by Susan Anderson) — *Anderson, Susan*

Flowers Grow — *Butler, Daphne*

Flowers on the Wall (Illus. by Miriam Nerlove) — *Nerlove, Miriam*

The Flunking of Joshua T. Bates — *Shreve, Susan Richards*

Flute's Journey (Illus. by Lynne Cherry) — *Cherry, Lynne*

Fly! A Brief History of Flight Illustrated — *Moser, Barry*

Fly Away Home (Illus. by Ronald Himler) — *Bunting, Eve*

Fly in the Sky — *Pratt, Kristin Joy*

Fly the Space Shuttle — *Stott, Carole*

Fly the Unfriendly Skies — *Engle, Marty M*

Fly Trap (Illus. by Jeff Spackman) — *Anastasio, Dina*

Fly Traps! (Illus. by David Parkins) — *Jenkins, Martin*

Fly with the Birds (Illus. by Satoshi Kitamura) — *Edwards, Richard, 1949-*

Flying Dimitri (Illus. by Blair Drawson) — *Drawson, Blair*

The Flying Dragon Room (Illus. by Mark Teague) — *Wood, Audrey*

Fog Hounds, Wind Cat, Sea Mice (Illus. by Peter Bailey) — *Aiken, Joan*

The Folks in the Valley (Illus. by Stefano Vitale) — *Aylesworth, Jim*

Follow in Their Footsteps — *Turner, Glennette Tilley*

Follow That Star (Illus. by Kim LaFave) — *Oppel, Kenneth*

Follow That Trash! — *Jacobs, Francine*

Follow the Dream (Illus. by Peter Sis) — *Sis, Peter*

Follow the Drinking Gourd (Illus. by Yvonne Buchanan) — *Connelly, Bernardine*

Follow the Leader (Illus. by Colin Bootman) — *Winslow, Vicki*

Follow the Star — *Elmer, Robert*

Follow Your Dreams (Illus. by Christopher Paluso) — *Vaughn, Mo*

Following the Sun (Illus. by Jenny Stow) — *Stow, Jenny*

Food (First Words Series)

Food — *Bryant-Mole, Karen*

Food and Your Health — *Powell, Jillian*

Food Cooks — *Butler, Daphne*

Food Fight — *Bode, Janet*

The Fool and the Flying Ship (Williams). Audio Version — *Metaxas, Eric*

Title Index

Franz Schubert—Ein Musikalisches Bilderbuch (Illus. by Doris Eisenburger) — *Ekker, Ernst A*

Fred and the Stinky Cheese (Illus. by Bruno St.-Aubin) — *Croteau, Marie-Danielle*

Frederick's Fables — *Lionni, Leo*

Free Lunch (Illus. by J Otto Seibold) — *Seibold, J Otto*

Free the Whales — *Rix, Jamie*

Free to Be...You and Me. Free to Be...a Family — *Thomas, Marlo*

Free to Dream — *Osofsky, Audrey*

Freedom of Assembly — *King, David C*

Freedom of Belief — *Hirst, Mike*

Freedom of Movement — *Bradley, Christine*

Freedom of Speech — *Steele, Philip*

Freedom of Worship — *Sherrow, Victoria*

Freedom Rides — *Haskins, James*

Freedom's Gifts (Illus. by Sharon Wilson) — *Wesley, Valerie Wilson*

Freedom's Sons — *Jurmain, Suzanne*

The Fresh Grave and Other Ghostly Stories — *Bial, Raymond*

A Friend for Boots — *Kitamura, Satoshi*

A Friend for Cyril (Illus. by Rae Whitesell) — *Lines, Patricia*

A Friend for Minerva Louise (Illus. by Janet Morgan Stoeke) — *Stoeke, Janet Morgan*

A Friend for Rachel — *McAllister, Margaret*

A Friend like Zilla (Illus. by Alice Priestley) — *Gilmore, Rachna*

Friends (Illus. by Sybil Wettasinghe) — *Siriwardena, Denagama*

The Friends — *Yumoto, Kazumi*

The Friends (Woodman). Audio Version — *Yumoto, Kazumi*

Friends in High Places (Little Play a Sound)

Friends to Die For — *Giberga, Jane Sughrue*

The Friendship — *Taylor, Mildred D*

Friesian Horses — *Maiecek, Tomaaes*

The Frightened Little Owl (Illus. by Gavin Rowe) — *Ezra, Mark*

The Frightful Story of Harry Walfish — *Floca, Brian*

Frindle (Illus. by Brian Selznick) — *Clements, Andrew*

The Frog — *Crewe, Sabrina*

Frog — *Stefoff, Rebecca*

Frog Girl (Illus. by Paul Owen Lewis) — *Lewis, Paul Owen*

Frog Is Frog — *Velthuijs, Max*

A Frog Prince (Illus. by Alix Berenzy) — *Berenzy, Alix*

The Frog Princess (Illus. by Emma Chichester Clark) — *Cecil, Laura*

The Frog Princess of Pelham — *Conford, Ellen*

The Frog Who Wanted to Be a Singer (Illus. by Cynthia Jabar) — *Goss, Linda*

Froggie Froggette (Illus. by Vivi Escriva) — *Perera, Hilda*

Froggy Gets Dressed (Illus. by Frank Remkiewicz) — *London, Jonathan*

Froggy Goes to School (Illus. by Frank Remkiewicz) — *London, Jonathan*

Froggy Se Viste (Illus. by Frank Remkiewicz) — *London, Jonathan*

Froggy's First Kiss (Illus. by Frank Remkiewicz) — *London, Jonathan*

Frogs (Illus. by Daniel Moignot)

Frogs and the Ballet — *Elliott, Donald*

Frogs Jump (Illus. by Steven Kellogg) — *Brooks, Alan*

Frogs: Living in Two Worlds (Illus. by Gabriel Casadevall) — *Llamas, Andreu*

Frogs, Toads and Turtles — *Burns, Diane L*

From Birth to Death (Illus. by Graham Austin) — *Yates, Irene*

From Blood Two Brothers — *Gray, Keith*

From Caterpillar to Butterfly (Illus. by Bari Weissman) — *Heiligman, Deborah*

From Cow to Ice Cream (Illus. by Bertram T Knight) — *Knight, Bertram T*

From Egg to Chicken (Illus. by Carolyn Scrace) — *Legg, Gerald*

From Head to Toe (Illus. by Eric Carle) — *Carle, Eric*

From Indian Corn to Outer Space — *Showell, Ellen H*

From Lullaby to Lullaby (Illus. by Kathryn Brown) — *Geras, Adele*

From Metal to Music (Illus. by Wendy Davis) — *Davis, Wendy*

From Miss Ida's Porch (Illus. by Floyd Cooper) — *Belton, Sandra*

From Mud to House — *Knight, Bertram T*

The Gardener (Illus. by David Small)
— *Stewart, Sarah*
The Gargoyle (Illus. by Dan Williams)
— *Kilworth, Garry*
Gary Chalk's Hide and Seek in History
— *Chalk, Gary*
Gather Up, Gather In (Illus. by Judy
Pedersen) — *Helldorfer, M C*
Gathering Food — *Butler, Daphne*
A Gathering of Garter Snakes
— *Lavies, Bianca*
Gathering the Sun (Illus. by Simon
Silva) — *Ada, Alma Flor*
El Gato Con Botas (Illus. by Jose Luis
Merino) — *Boada, Francesc*
Gator's Out, Said the Trout (Illus. by
Bob Reese) — *Gill, Janie Spaht*
Gauguin — *Boutan, Mila*
Das Geht Doch Nicht! — *Schar, Brigitte*
Gemini7 — *Cray, Jordan*
Gender Issues — *Stearman, Kaye*
General Lee and Santa Claus
— *Bedwell, Randall*
The General Store (Illus. by Barbara
Bedell) — *Kalman, Bobbie*
Genesis — *Bible. O.T. Genesis. English.
Young. 1995*
Genesis for Kids (Illus. by Ken Save)
— *Lambier, Doug*
The Genius Academy — *Apps, Roy*
Gentle Ben (Illus. by John Schoenherr)
— *Morey, Walt*
The Gentleman and the Kitchen Maid
(Illus. by Dennis Nolan) — *Stanley,
Diane*
The Gentleman Outlaw and Me, Eli
— *Hahn, Mary Downing*
The Geography of the Earth — *Brooks,
Susan*
r Geography of the World
Geography through Play — *Milner,
Angela M*
Geography Wizardry for Kids
— *Kenda, Margaret*
George and Martha: The Complete
Stories of Two Best Friends (Illus. by
James Marshall) — *Marshall, James*
George Washington — *Old, Wendie C*
George Washington: A Picture Book
Biography (Illus. by Michael Dooling)
— *Giblin, James Cross*
George Washington Carver, What Do
You See? (Illus. by Kennon James)
— *Benge, Janet*

George Washington's Cows (Illus. by
David Small) — *Small, David*
George Washington's World. Expanded
Ed. — *Foster, Genevieve*
George's Store at the Shore (Illus. by
Francine Bassede) — *Bassede,
Francine*
Germany — *Lord, Richard*
Germs (Illus. by Peter Georgeson)
— *Colombo, Luann*
Geronimo: Apache Freedom Fighter
— *Hermann, Spring*
Gertie's Not Alone — *Chartier,
Normand*
Gertrude Chandler Warner and the
Boxcar Children (Illus. by Marie
DeJohn) — *Ellsworth, Mary Ellen*
Gespensterjager Im Feuerspuk (Illus. by
Cornelia Funke) — *Funke, Cornelia*
Get Off Our Train — *Burningham, John*
Get Out of the Alphabet, Number 2!
(Illus. by Jenny Graham) — *Dakos,
Kalli*
Get Real Paddy Manson (Illus. by Fifi
Colston) — *Corrin, Ruth*
Get Set! Swim! (Illus. by Hector Viveros
Lee) — *Atkins, Jeannine*
Get Started (Illus. by Esperanca Melo)
— *MacLeod, Elizabeth*
Get Up and Go! (Illus. by Diane
Greenseid) — *Murphy, Stuart J*
Getting Around — *Butler, Daphne*
Getting to Know the World's Greatest
Artists Series — *Venezia, Mike*
Getting Used to the Dark (Illus. by
Peter Catalanotto) — *Swanson, Susan
Marie*
Geysers: When Earth Roars — *Gallant,
Roy A*
The Ghost by the Sea — *Dunlop, Eileen*
Ghost Canoe — *Hobbs, Will*
The Ghost Followed Us Home
(Montbertrand). Audio Version
— *Kehret, Peg*
The Ghost in Room 11 (Illus. by
Jacqueline Rogers) — *Wright, Betty
Ren*
The Ghost in the Classroom (Illus. by
Uli Waas) — *Wagener, Gerda*
Ghost Knight — *Cascone, A G*
A Ghost-Light in the Attic (Illus. by
Annabel Large) — *Thomson, Pat*
A Ghost Named Wanda (Illus. by Jack
E Davis) — *Greenburg, Dan*

The Girl Who Lived with the Bears
(Illus. by Andrew Plewes) — *Goldin,*
Barbara Diamond
The Girl Who Wanted a Song (Illus. by
Stephen T Johnson) — *Sanfield, Steve*
The Girl with the Brown Crayon
— *Paley, Vivian Gussin*
The Girls' Guide to Life (Illus. by
Cynthia Jabar) — *Dee, Catherine*
Girls Know Best — *Roehm, Michelle*
Girls Speak Out — *Johnston, Andrea*
Give Me a Sign! — *Samoyault, Tiphaine*
Give Me Bach My Schubert (Illus. by
Rick Dupre) — *Cleary, Brian P*
The Giver — *Lowry, Lois*
Gizmos Galore (Illus. by Jonathan
Lambert) — *Faulkner, Keith*
Glacial Geology — *Erickson, Jon*
Glaciers — *George, Michael*
Glad Monster, Sad Monster (Illus. by
Ed Emberley) — *Emberley, Ed*
Gladiator (Illus. by Richard Ross
Watkins) — *Watkins, Richard Ross*
A Glass Slipper for Rosie (Illus. by Julie
Durrell) — *Giff, Patricia Reilly*
Glass Town (Illus. by Laura Fernandez)
— *Bedard, Michael*
Glimpses of Heaven (Illus. by Gabrielle
Izen) — *Rock, Lois*
Gloria's Gramophone — *Agbami,*
Akulah
The Glow-in-the-Dark Night Sky Book
— *Hatchett, Clint*
Glues, Brews, and Goos — *Marks,*
Diana F
Go Away, Dog (Illus. by Paul Meisel)
— *Nodset, Joan L*
Go, Dog, Go! — *Eastman, P D*
Go for Goal — *Cooling, Wendy*
Go for It, Carrie (Illus. by Mark
Thurman) — *Choyce, Lesley*
Go to Jail! (Illus. by Peter Kent)
— *Kent, Peter*
Goal! — *McNaughton, Colin*
The Goalie (Bresnahan). Audio Version
— *Shreve, Susan Richards*
The Gobsmacking Galaxy — *Poskitt,*
Kjartan
God and Me (Illus. by Alison R Grapes)
— *Green, Sheila*
God Bless the Gargoyles (Illus. by Dav
Pilkey) — *Pilkey, Dav*
Goddesses, Heroes, and Shamans
Godhanger (Illus. by Andrew Davidson)
— *King-Smith, Dick*

Gods and Giants (Illus. by Francis
Phillipps) — *Ross, Stewart*
The Gods and Goddesses of Ancient
Egypt (Illus. by Leonard Everett
Fisher) — *Fisher, Leonard Everett*
God's Best Gift (Illus. by Kathy Rogers)
— *Conan, Sally Anne*
God's People (Illus. by Anna C Leplar)
— *McCaughrean, Geraldine*
God's Story (Illus. by David Parkins)
— *Mark, Jan*
Godzilla on Monster Island — *Dwyer,*
Jacqueline
Godzilla vs. Gigan and the Smog
Monster — *Alfonsi, Alice*
Going Back Home (Illus. by Michele
Wood) — *Wood, Michele*
Going Home (Illus. by David Diaz)
— *Bunting, Eve*
Going Places. Bks. 1-2 — *Burton, Eric*
Going through the Gate — *Anderson,*
Janet S
Going to the Fair (Illus. by Sheena Lott)
— *McFarlane, Sheryl*
Going to the Getty (Illus. by J Otto
Seibold) — *Seibold, J Otto*
Going West (Illus. by Thomas B Allen)
— *Van Leeuwen, Jean*
Gold and Silver Water — *Arnold,*
Elizabeth
The Gold at the End of the Rainbow
(Illus. by Loek Koopmans) — *Hanel,*
Wolfram
The Gold Cadillac — *Taylor, Mildred D*
Gold Rush! (Illus. by Michael Rohani)
— *Klein, James*
A Golden Age. Book and Audio Version
— *Wickham, Martha*
Golden Age of Islam — *George, Linda*
The Golden Band of Eddris
— *McKenzie, Ellen Kindt*
The Golden Compass — *Pullman, Philip*
The Golden Dog Book of Fairy Tales
and Animal Stories — *Lovejoy, R B*
The Golden Era (Illus. by Lynette C
Ross) — *Poling-Kempes, Lesley*
Golden Girl and Other Stories — *Chan,*
Gillian
The Golden Glove — *Bowen, Fred*
The Golden Goose (Illus. by Uri
Shulevitz) — *Shulevitz, Uri*
The Golden Grasshopper — *Nelson,*
Rosemary
The Golden Pine Cone (Illus. by Greta
Guzek) — *Clark, Catherine Anthony*

The Great Escape from City Zoo (Illus.
by Tohby Riddle) — *Riddle, Tohby*
Great Expectations (Schofield). Audio
Version — *Dickens, Charles*
Great Experiments with H2O
— *Fiarotta, Noel*
The Great Explorer (Illus. by Len
Walbourne) — *Morrison, Terry*
The Great Frog Race and Other Poems
(Illus. by Kate Kiesler) — *George,
Kristine O'Connell*
The Great Gilly Hopkins (Bresnahan).
Audio Version — *Paterson, Katherine*
The Great Grammer Book — *Petty,
Kate*
Great-Grandpa's in the Litter Box
(Illus. by Jack E Davis) — *Greenburg,
Dan*
Great History Search — *Khanduri,
Kamini*
Great Inventions — *Wood, Richard*
Great Journeys — *Chrisp, Peter*
The Great Kapok Tree — *Cherry,
Lynne*
The Great Kettles (Illus. by Dean
Morrissey) — *Morrissey, Dean*
Great Lives: The American Frontier
— *Calvert, Patricia*
Great Map Mysteries — *Julio, Susan*
The Great Marine Reptiles (Illus. by
Albert Martinez) — *Llamas, Andreu*
The Great Midwest Flood — *Vogel,
Carole Garbuny*
Great Moments in Science — *Haven,
Kendall*
Great Pirate Activity Book — *Robbins,
Deri*
The Great Pyramid (Illus. by Carolyn
Croll) — *Cooper, Stephen R*
The Great Race (Illus. by Huang-Zhong
Yang) — *Bouchard, Dave*
r Great Software for Kids and Parents
— *Miranker, Cathy*
The Great Tooth Fairy (Illus. by Jack
Lindstrom) — *Butler, Dori Hillestad*
The Great Turkey Walk — *Karr,
Kathleen*
The Great Wall (Illus. by Alan
Witschonke) — *Mann, Elizabeth*
The Great Wonder. Book and Audio
Version — *Howard, Annabelle*
The Great World Tour — *Khanduri,
Kamini*
The Greatest Gift — *Summers, Susan*

The Greatest Show on Earth — *Mahy,
Margaret*
The Greatest Treasure of Charlemagne
the King (Illus. by Deborah Klein)
— *Wheatley, Nadia*
Greek Gazette — *Fleming, Fergus*
Greek Myths — *Rearick, John*
The Greek News — *Powell, Anton*
Green Eggs and Ham. Electronic Media
Version — *Seuss, Dr.*
Green-Eyed Ghost — *Blankman, Lynn*
Green Fun — *Gjersvik, Marianne Haug*
A Green Horn Blowing (Illus. by
Thomas B Allen) — *Birchman, David*
F
Green, Tamara, Muttaburrasaurus
(Illus. by Tony Gibbons) — *Amery,
Heather*
The Green Truck Garden Giveaway
(Illus. by Alec Gillman) — *Martin,
Jacqueline Briggs*
Green Wilma — *Arnold, Tedd*
Greetings from Sandy Beach (Illus. by
Bob Graham) — *Graham, Bob*
Greetings, Sun (Illus. by Synthia Saint
James) — *Gershator, Phillis*
Greg Maddux — *Macht, Norman L*
Greg Maddux: Ace! — *Torres, John*
Gregor Mendel: Father of Genetics
— *Klare, Roger*
Gregory Cool (Illus. by Caroline Binch)
— *Binch, Caroline*
Greylands — *Carmody, Isobelle*
Griffin's Castle — *Nimmo, Jenny*
Grimm's Grimmest (Illus. by Tracy
Dockray)
The Grinch's Song — *Seuss, Dr.*
Grizzlies — *Lepthien, Emilie U*
Grizzly Bear — *Cherry, Lynne*
Grizzly Bears (Illus. by Warren Clark)
— *Parker, Janice*
r The Grolier Library of Women's
Biographies. Vols. 1-10
r Grolier Multimedia Encyclopedia 1997.
Electronic Media Version
r Grolier Multimedia Encyclopedia 1998.
Electronic Media Version
Groom Your Room (Illus. by Michael
Walker)
The Groovy Greeks (Illus. by Martin
Brown) — *Deary, Terry*
Grossology Begins at Home (Illus. by
Jack Keely) — *Branzei, Sylvia*

Grossology: The Science of Really Gross
Things. Electronic Media Version
— *Branzei, Sylvia*
Group Psychotherapy for People with
Chronic Mental Illness — *Stone,
Walter N*
Grover! (Illus. by Norman Gorbaty)
— *Ross, Anna*
Growing Up (Illus. by Jane Stryker)
— *Homan, Beulah*
The Growing-Up Feet (Illus. by DyAnne
DiSalvo-Ryan) — *Cleary, Beverly*
Growing Up in a Holler in the
Mountains — *Gravelle, Karen*
Growing Up in Coal Country
— *Bartoletti, Susan Campbell*
Growing Up in the People's Century
— *Clare, John D*
Growing Up Where the Partridge
Drums Its Wings — *Gravelle, Karen*
The Grumpy Morning (Illus. by Darcia
Labrosse) — *Edwards, Pamela
Duncan*
Gruntle Piggle Takes Off (Illus. by
Johnny Wales) — *Little, Jean*
GTOs — *Ethan, Eric*
Guardians of Mother Earth — *Nixon,
Carl*
Guardians of Wildlife — *Chandler,
Gary*
Guess Who's Coming, Jesse Bear (Illus.
by Bruce Degen) — *Carlstrom, Nancy
White*
A Guide to Microlife — *Rainis, Kenneth
G*
Guinea Pigs — *Miller, Michaela*
Guinness Record Breakers — *Young,
Karen Romano*
Gullible's Troubles (Illus. by Margaret
Shannon) — *Shannon, Margaret*
Gulliverzone — *Baxter, Stephen*
Gulls--Gulls--Gulls (Illus. by Gail
Gibbons) — *Gibbons, Gail*
The Gumma Wars (Illus. by David
Zinn) — *Haynes, David, 1955-*
Guns: What You Should Know (Illus.
by Mary Jones) — *Schulson, Rachel*
The Gunslingers — *Wukovits, John F*
Gus and Grandpa (Illus. by Catherine
Stock) — *Mills, Claudia*
Gus and Grandpa and the Christmas
Cookies (Illus. by Catherine Stock)
— *Mills, Claudia*
Gus and Grandpa Ride the Train (Illus.
by Catherine Stock) — *Mills, Claudia*

Gus Grissom: A Space Biography
— *Bredeson, Carmen*
Guts and Glory — *Rappoport, Ken*
Gymnastics — *Kalman, Bobbie*
The Gypsy Game — *Snyder, Zilpha
Keatley*
The Gypsy Princess — *Gilman, Phoebe*

H

Habibi — *Nye, Naomi Shihab*
Habitats (Illus. by Don Robison)
— *Moore, Jo Ellen*
Hairy Maclary, — *Dodd, Lynley*
A Haitian Family (Illus. by Carol
Halebian) — *Greenberg, Keith Elliot*
Hakeem Olajuwon — *McMane, Fred*
Hala, Vamos A Alabama! (Illus. by
Javier Vazquez) — *Puerto, Carlos*
The Halfmen of O — *Gee, Maurice*
p The Halifax Explosion (Illus. by Michael
Dixon) — *Hawkins, Peter*
Halloween Day (Illus. by Lizzy
Rockwell) — *Rockwell, Anne*
Halloween Fun for Everyone (Illus. by
Judy Lanfredi) — *Wolff, Ferida*
Halloween Helpers (Illus. by Alan
Tiegreen) — *Delton, Judy*
Halloween Hide-and-Seek (Illus. by Julie
Durrell) — *Jane, Pamela*
The Halloween Horror and Other Cases
(Illus. by S D Schindler) — *Simon,
Seymour*
The Halloween House (Illus. by Jon
Agee) — *Silverman, Erica*
Halloween Mice (Illus. by Doug
Cushman) — *Roberts, Bethany*
Halmoni and the Picnic (Illus. by Karen
Dugan) — *Choi, Sook Nyul*
The Hand-Me-Down Horse (Illus. by
Joanna Yardley) — *Pomeranc,
Marion Hess*
Hand-Print Animal Art (Illus. by
Carolyn Carreiro) — *Carreiro,
Carolyn*
Handa's Surprise — *Browne, Eileen*
A Handful of Gold — *Aiken, Joan*
A Handful of Seeds (Illus. by Luis
Garay) — *Hughes, Monica*
Hands (Illus. by Lois Ehlert) — *Ehlert,
Lois*
Hands! (Illus. by Cathryn Falwell)
— *Kroll, Virginia L*

The History News: Medicine (Illus. by Vanessa Card) — *Gates, Phil*
The History of Emigration from Africa — *Chambers, Catherine*
The History of Emigration from China and Southeast Asia — *Prior, Katherine*
The History of Emigration from Greece — *Zinovieff, Sofka*
The History of Emigration from Ireland — *Prior, Katherine*
The History of Emigration from Scotland — *Hurst, Mike*
The History of Emigration from the Indian Subcontinent — *Prior, Katherine*
The History of Health and Medicine — *Bryan, Jenny*
A History of Inventions — *Lafferty, Peter*
The History of Printmaking (Voyages of Discovery)
A History of Ships from Log Rafts to Luxury Liners — *Macdonald, Fiona*
HIV Positive — *Wolf, Bernard*
A Hmong Family — *Murphy, Nora*
HO Railroad from Set to Scenery — *Selby, Rick*
Hob and the Peddler — *Mayne, William*
Hob and the Pedlar — *Mayne, William*
The Hobbit — *Tolkien, J R R*
Hockey Goaltending for Young Players — *Allaire, Francois*
Hockey Superstars 1996-1997
The Hockey Sweater (Illus. by Sheldon Cohen) — *Carrier, Roch*
Hockey Talk — *Poteet, Lewis J*
Hockey the NHL Way: Goal Scoring — *Rossiter, Sean*
Hockey the NHL Way: Goaltending — *Rossiter, Sean*
The Hokey Pokey (Illus. by Sheila Hamanaka) — *La Prise, Larry*
Hola, California! — *Ramirez, Michael Rose*
Hold On, McGinty (Illus. by Don Kilby) — *Hartry, Nancy*
Holding On (Illus. by Diana Engel) — *Engel, Diana*
Holi — *Kadodwala, Dilip*
Holiday Time — *Martin, Ann M, 1955-*
The Holly Sisters on Their Own — *Mulford, Philippa Greene*
The Holocaust: A History of Courage and Resistance — *Stadtler, Bea*

Home: A Collaboration of Thirty Distinguished Authors and Illustrators of Children's Books to Aid the Homeless — *Rosen, Michael J*
A Home among the Gum Trees (Illus. by John Nicholson) — *Nicholson, John*
Home Child — *Haworth-Attard, Barbara*
A Home for Spooky (Illus. by Ted Rand) — *Rand, Gloria*
Home on the Range (Illus. by Bernie Fuchs) — *Janeczko, Paul B*
Home Page — *Lampton, Christopher*
Home Sweet Home (Illus. by Ashley Wolff) — *Marzollo, Jean*
Home Wars — *Miller, Dorothy Reynolds*
Homes — *Stanfield, Jeff*
Homes around the World — *Kalman, Bobbie*
Homes Discovered through Art and Technology — *Bryant-Mole, Karen*
The Homes We Live In — *Hewitt, Sally*
Honest (Illus. by Gwen Green) — *Amos, Janine*
Honest Abe (Illus. by Malcah Zeldis) — *Kunhardt, Edith*
Honest Tulio (Illus. by John Himmelman) — *Himmelman, John*
Honey Biscuits (Illus. by Alison Bartlett) — *Hooper, Meredith*
Honey Bunny Funnybunny (Illus. by Roger Bollen) — *Sadler, Marilyn*
The Honey Makers (Illus. by Gail Gibbons) — *Gibbons, Gail*
Honk! Honk! (Illus. by Brita Granstrom) — *Manning, Mick*
Honus and Me — *Gutman, Dan*
Hook 'Em, Snotty (Woodman). Audio Version — *Paulsen, Gary*
Hook Moon Night (Illus. by Ronald Himler) — *Gibbons, Faye*
Hoops (Illus. by Stephen T Johnson) — *Burleigh, Robert*
Hooray for Dairy Farming — *Kalman, Bobbie*
Hooray for Diffendoofer Day! (Illus. by Lane Smith) — *Seuss, Dr.*
Hooray for Sheep Farming! — *Kalman, Bobbie*
Hoot (Illus. by Jane Hissey) — *Hissey, Jane*
Hoover's Bride — *Small, David*
Hope's Crossing — *Goodman, Joan Elizabeth*

How the Grinch Stole Christmas (Illus. by Dr. Seuss) — *Seuss, Dr.*

How Things Work — *Graham, Ian, 1953-*

How to Do a Science Fair Project. Rev. Ed. — *Tocci, Salvatore*

How to Do Homework without Throwing Up (Illus. by Trevor Romain) — *Romain, Trevor*

How to Draw Dinosaurs — *Smith, Christine*

How to Draw Pets — *Smith, Christine*

How to Draw Trucks and Cars — *Smith, Christine*

How to Draw Wild Animals — *Smith, Christine*

How to Get Fabulously Rich (Illus. by Nick Sharratt) — *Rockwell, Thomas*

How to Hide an Elephant in Your Room — *Taylor, Paul*

How to Make a Mummy Talk (Illus. by True Kelley) — *Deem, James M*

How to Make Holiday Pop-Ups — *Irvine, Joan*

How to Rock Your Baby (Illus. by John Amoss) — *Fleming, Sibley*

How to Study (Butler). Audio Version — *Fry, Ron*

How We Crossed the West (Illus. by Rosalyn Schanzer) — *Schanzer, Rosalyn*

How We Know about the Romans — *James, John*

How We Saw the World (Illus. by C J Taylor) — *Taylor, C J*

How Your Body Works (Illus. by Jo Supancich) — *Moore, Jo Ellen*

Howard Wise and the Monster Mop — *Ward, Jon*

How's Harry? (Illus. by Philip Hopman) — *May, Steve*

The Hubble Space Telescope — *Sipiera, Diane M*

Los Huevos Parlantes (Illus. by Jerry Pinkney) — *San Souci, Robert D*

The Huge Bag of Worries (Illus. by Frank Rodgers) — *Ironside, Virginia*

The Hullabaloo ABC (Illus. by Ted Rand) — *Cleary, Beverly*

The Human Body — *Berger, Melvin*

Human Body — *Williams, Frances*

The Human Body (Discoveries) — *Parker, Steve*

The Human Body (What If) (Illus. by Tony Kenyon) — *Parker, Steve*

The Human Body: An Amazing Inside Look at You — *Parker, Steve*

The Human Genome Project — *Marshall, Elizabeth L*

The Human Machine

Human Rights — *Gold, Susan Dudley*

The Humane Societies — *Sateren, Shelley Swanson*

Hummingbird — *Stefoff, Rebecca*

Hummingbirds — *Rauzon, Mark J*

The Humongous Book of Dinosaurs — *Norman, David*

Humpty Dumpty and Other Rhymes (Illus. by Rosemary Wells) — *Opie, Iona*

The Hunchback of Notre Dame (Play a Sound)

The Hunchback of Notre Dame (Illus. by Bill Slavin) — *Hugo, Victor*

The Hundredth Name (Illus. by Michael Hays) — *Oppenheim, Shulamith Levey*

Hungary: Crossroads of Europe — *Steins, Richard*

Hungry Animals (Illus. by Heather Collins) — *Hickman, Pamela*

The Hungry Monster (Illus. by Sue Heap) — *Root, Phyllis*

The Hungry Otter (Illus. by Gavin Rowe) — *Ezra, Mark*

The Hungry Pig

The Hunt for Food (Illus. by Graham Austin) — *Ganeri, Anita*

Hunter in the Snow (Illus. by Susan Bonners) — *Bonners, Susan*

The Hunterman and the Crocodile (Illus. by Baba Wague Diakite) — *Diakite, Baba Wague*

Hurley and the Bone (Illus. by George Molina-Sy) — *Dahab, Farida Elizabeth*

Hurricane (Illus. by David Wiesner) — *Wiesner, David*

Hurricane Summer (Illus. by Kim Palmer) — *Swindells, Robert*

Hurricanes — *Rotter, Charles*

Hurricanes: Earth's Mightiest Storms — *Lauber, Patricia*

Hush! A Gaelic Lullaby (Illus. by Marty Husted) — *Gerber, Carole*

Hush! A Thai Lullaby (Illus. by Holly Meade) — *Ho, Minfong*

Hush, Little Baby (Illus. by Shari Halpern)

Hush Little Baby (Illus. by Sylvia Long) — *Long, Sylvia*

r Interactive Science Encyclopedia on CD-
ROM. Electronic Media Version
The Internet — *Jortberg, Charles A*
The Internet for Beginners — *Wingate,*
Philippa
The Internet for Kids — *Kazunas,*
Charnan
Internet for Kids. 2nd Ed. — *Frazier,*
Deneen
The Internet Kids and Family Yellow
Pages. 2nd Ed. — *Polly, Jean Armour*
Into the Castle (Illus. by John
Bendall-Brunello) — *Crebbin, June*
Into the Ice (Illus. by Lynn Curlee)
— *Curlee, Lynn*
Into the Land of the Unicorns
— *Coville, Bruce*
Into the Sea (Illus. by Alix Berenzy)
— *Guiberson, Brenda Z*
Into the Woods (Illus. by Loretta
Krupinski) — *Krupinski, Loretta*
An Introduction to Claude Monet
— *Harrison, Peter*
An Introduction to Vincent Van Gogh
— *Harrison, Peter*
Inventions Explained — *Platt, Richard*
Inventors — *Burns, Peggy*
Inventors and Inventions — *Egan,*
Lorraine Hopping
Invertebrates — *Silverstein, Alvin*
Investigating Plants — *Sinclair, Thomas*
R
The Investigation of Murder — *Lane,*
Brian
The Invisible Day (Illus. by Abby
Carter) — *Jocelyn, Marthe*
The Invisible Dog (Illus. by Paul
Howard) — *King-Smith, Dick*
The Invisible Ladder — *Rosenberg, Liz*
The Invisible Polly McDoodle
— *Woodbury, Mary*
Invitations to Cells — *Camp, Carole*
Ann
Invitations to Evolving — *Camp, Carole*
Ann
Invitations to Heredity — *Camp, Carole*
Ann
Irene Jennie and the Christmas
Masquerade (Illus. by Melodye
Rosales) — *Smalls-Hector, Irene*
Irish Fairy Tales and Legends (Illus. by
Susan Field) — *Leavy, Una*
Irish Sagas and Folk Tales
— *O'Faolain, Eileen*

Iron Man (Hughes). Audio Version
— *Hughes, Ted*
The Iron Ring — *Alexander, Lloyd*
The Iron Way — *Cross, Gillian*
Is a Blue Whale the Biggest Thing
There Is? — *Wells, Robert E*
Is That You, Winter? (Illus. by Stephen
Gammell) — *Gammell, Stephen*
Is There Room on the Feather Bed?
(Illus. by Nadine Bernard Westcott)
— *Gray, Libba Moore*
Is Your Mama a Llama? (Illus. by
Steven Kellogg) — *Guarino, Deborah*
Isaac Newton: The Greatest Scientist of
All Time — *Anderson, Margaret J*
Isabella: A Wish for Miguel, Peru 1820
(Illus. by Laurie Harden) — *Newman,*
Shirlee P
Isadora Dances (Illus. by Rachel
Isadora) — *Isadora, Rachel*
Ishtar and Tammuz (Illus. by Christina
Balit) — *Moore, C J*
La Isla De Abel (Illus. by William Steig)
— *Steig, William*
Islamic Festivals — *Knight, Khadijah*
The Island-below-the-Star (Illus. by
James Rumford) — *Rumford, James*
Island Bound — *Levin, Betty*
Island of the Blue Dolphins — *O'Dell,*
Scott
Island of Trees — *Bond, Ruskin*
The Islander — *Rylant, Cynthia*
Israel — *Foy, Don*
It Came from Ohio! — *Stine, R L*
It Came from the Deep — *Cascone, A G*
It Could Still Be a Desert — *Fowler,*
Allan
It Could Still Be a Robot — *Fowler,*
Allan
It Could Still Be Coral — *Fowler, Allan*
It Isn't Easy (Illus. by Rosita Manahan)
— *Connolly, Margaret*
It Takes Two — *Wallace, Karen*
It Wasn't Me! (Illus. by Mike Gordon)
— *Moses, Brian*
Italy — *Harvey, Miles*
Italy: Gem of the Mediterranean
— *King, David C*
Italy--in Pictures — *Lerner Publications*
Company. Geography Dept.
It's a Spoon, Not a Shovel (Illus. by
Mark Buehner) — *Buehner, Caralyn*
It's about Time, Jesse Bear (Illus. by
Bruce Degen) — *Carlstrom, Nancy*
White

It's Disgusting--and We Ate It! (Illus. by Eric Brace) — *Solheim, James*

It's I Can Do Anything Day! (Illus. by Lynn Torola) — *Pandit, Maneesha S*

It's My Life — *Harrison, Michael*

It's Not Your Fault, Koko Bear — *Lansky, Vicki*

r It's Perfectly Normal (Illus. by Michael Emberley) — *Harris, Robie H*

It's Raining Laughter (Illus. by Myles C Pinkney) — *Grimes, Nikki*

Itty Bitty Kitty (Illus. by Jane Maday) — *Keeshan, Bob*

Ivan and the Dynamos — *Bowman, Crystal*

I've Lost My Yellow Zebra — *Brooksbank, Angela*

J

Jack and Me and the Ball (Illus. by Lesley Harker) — *Gowar, Mick*

Jack and Me and the Pizza (Illus. by Lesley Harker) — *Gowar, Mick*

Jack and Me and the Snowman (Illus. by Lesley Harker) — *Gowar, Mick*

Jack and Me at the Seaside (Illus. by Lesley Harker) — *Gowar, Mick*

Jack and the Beanstalk (Illus. by Paul Hess) — *Poole, Josephine*

Jack and the Beanstalk (Palin) (Illus. by Edward Sorel). Audio Version — *Metaxas, Eric*

Jack and the Giant (Illus. by Jim Harris) — *Harris, Jim*

Jack and the Meanstalk — *Wildsmith, Brian*

Jack Black and the Ship of Thieves — *Hughes, Carol*

Jack: Happy Birthday (Illus. by Rebecca Elgar) — *Elgar, Rebecca*

Jackie Robinson: Baseball's Civil Rights Legend — *Coombs, Karen Mueller*

Jackomoora and the King of Ireland's Son (Illus. by Finbarr O'Connor) — *MacMahon, Bryan*

Jack's Black Book — *Gantos, Jack*

Jack's Garden — *Cole, Henry*

Jack's Tale (Illus. by Ellen Stoll Walsh) — *Walsh, Ellen Stoll*

Jacob Two-Two's First Spy Case (Illus. by Michael Chesworth) — *Richler, Mordecai*

Jacob's Best Sisters (Illus. by Joanne Fitzgerald) — *Jam, Teddy*

Jacqueline Hyde — *Swindells, Robert*

Jade and Iron (Illus. by Luis Garay) — *Aldana, Patricia*

The Jade Horse, the Cricket and the Peach Stone (Illus. by Winson Trang) — *Tompert, Ann*

Jade McKade (Illus. by Virginia Barrett) — *Carroll, Jane*

Jafta: The Homecoming (Illus. by Lisa Kopper) — *Lewin, Hugh*

Jaguar (Illus. by Helen Cowcher) — *Cowcher, Helen*

Jaguar in the Rain Forest — *Ryder, Joanne*

Jaguars (Illus. by Warren Clark) — *Watt, E Melanie*

Jake and Pete and the Stray Dogs (Illus. by Terry Denton) — *Rubinstein, Gillian*

Jalapeno Bagels (Illus. by Robert Casilla) — *Wing, Natasha*

Jamaica — *Brownlie, Alison*

Jamaica Louise James (Illus. by Sheila White Samton) — *Hest, Amy*

Jamaica's Find — *Havill, Juanita*

James Madison — *Malone, Mary*

James Printer — *Jacobs, Paul Samuel*

The Jamestown Colony — *Sakurai, Gail*

Janet's Last Book — *Ahlberg, Allan*

Janey Crane. Book and Audio Version — *DeRubertis, Barbara*

Janice VanCleave's 202 Oozing, Bubbling, Dripping, and Bouncing Experiments — *VanCleave, Janice Pratt*

Janice VanCleave's Constellations for Every Kid — *VanCleave, Janice Pratt*

Janice VanCleave's Ecology for Every Kid — *VanCleave, Janice Pratt*

Janice VanCleave's Guide to the Best Science Fair Projects — *VanCleave, Janice Pratt*

Janice VanCleave's Oceans for Every Kid — *VanCleave, Janice Pratt*

Janice VanCleave's Plants — *VanCleave, Janice Pratt*

Janice VanCleave's Play and Find Out about Math (Illus. by Michelle Nidenoff) — *VanCleave, Janice Pratt*

Janice VanCleave's Play and Find Out about Nature (Illus. by Michelle Nidenoff) — *VanCleave, Janice Pratt*

Title Index

Junie B. Jones Has a Monster Under
Her Bed (Illus. by Denise Brunkus)
— *Park, Barbara*
Junie B. Jones Is a Party Animal (Illus.
by Denise Brunkus) — *Park, Barbara*
Junie B. Jones Is Not a Crook (Illus. by
Denise Brunkus) — *Park, Barbara*
Junior Astrologer Series — *Quinlan,*
Alexis
The Junior Chef — *Neff, Rena*
r Junior Chronicle of the 20th Century
r Junior Environmental Activities on File
— *Chapman, Victoria*
Junior Seau: Star Linebacker
— *Savage, Jeff*
Junk — *Burgess, Melvin*
Junk Pile! (Illus. by Kimberly Bulcken
Root) — *Borton, Lady*
The Junkyard Dog — *Tamar, Erika*
Jupiter — *McDonald, Mary Ann*
Jurassic Jungle — *MacKay, Margaret*
Just a Little Brown Dog (Illus. by
Bronwyn Bancroft) — *Morgan, Sally*
Just a Minute! (Illus. by Jung-Hee
Spetter) — *Kranendonk, Anke*
p Just about Horses
Just Another Ordinary Day (Illus. by
Rod Clement) — *Clement, Rod*
Just Dessert (Illus. by Polly Powell)
— *Powell, Polly*
Just Enough Carrots (Illus. by Frank
Remkiewicz) — *Murphy, Stuart J*
Just for Babies — *Spewock, Theodosia*
Just for Fives — *Spewock, Theodosia*
Just for Four's — *Spewock, Theodosia*
Just for One's — *Spewock, Theodosia*
Just for Three's — *Spewock, Theodosia*
Just for Two's — *Spewock, Theodosia*
Just Kids (Illus. by Ellen B Senisi)
— *Senisi, Ellen B*
Just like Me — *Rohmer, Harriet*
Just like New (Illus. by Karen Reczuch)
— *Manson, Ainslie*
Just Listen to This Song I'm Singing
— *Silverman, Jerry*
Just Look (Illus. by Tana Hoban)
— *Hoban, Tana*
r Just Look 'n' Learn Spanish Picture
Dictionary (Illus. by Daniel J
Hochstatter)
Just One! (Illus. by Ivan Bates)
— *McBratney, Sam*
Just One Flick of a Finger (Illus. by
David Diaz) — *Lorbiecki, Marybeth*
Just Plain Fancy — *Polacco, Patricia*

Just Right Stew (Illus. by Anna Rich)
— *English, Karen*
Just Tricking (Illus. by Terry Denton)
— *Griffiths, Andy*
Just What the Doctor Ordered
— *Miller, Brandon Marie*
Just You and Me (Illus. by Ivan Bates)
— *McBratney, Sam*
Justice for Emily — *Pfeffer, Susan Beth*
Justin Morgan Had a Horse
(McDonough). Audio Version
— *Henry, Marguerite*

K

K Is for Kwanzaa (Illus. by Ken
Wilson-Max) — *Ford, Juwanda G*
Kai: The Lost Statue, Africa 1440 (Illus.
by Elaine Arnold) — *Welch, Leona*
Nicholas
Kaj, Smukke Kaj — *Leten, Mats*
The Kalahari — *Inserra, Rose*
The Kangaroo — *Crewe, Sabrina*
Kangaroos: Animals with a Pouch
— *Llamas, Andreu*
Kangaroos Have Joeys — *Browne,*
Philippa-Alys
Kaspar's Greatest Discovery (Illus. by
Reg Cartwright) — *Paget, Campbell*
Kasper in the Glitter (Illus. by Chris
Riddell) — *Ridley, Philip*
Kate's Giants (Illus. by Virginia Austin)
— *Gregory, Valiska*
Katherine Paterson — *Cary, Alice*
Katie and the Dream-Eater (Illus. by
Brian Wildsmith) — *Takamado,*
Princess
Katie Morag and the Grand Concert
(Illus. by Mairi Hedderwick)
— *Hedderwick, Mairi*
Katie Morag and the New Pier (Illus. by
Mairi Hedderwick) — *Hedderwick,*
Mairi
Katie Morag and the Two
Grandmothers (Illus. by Mairi
Hedderwick) — *Hedderwick, Mairi*
Katie Morag and the Wedding (Illus. by
Mairi Hedderwick) — *Hedderwick,*
Mairi
Katie Morag Delivers the Mail (Illus. by
Mairi Hedderwick) — *Hedderwick,*
Mairi
Katie's Trunk (Illus. by Ronald Himler)
— *Turner, Ann*

King Arthur and the Round Table
(Illus. by Alan Marks)
— *McCaughrean, Geraldine*
King Coker's Sword — *Stephens,
Michael*
King George III — *Green, Robert*
King Long Shanks (Illus. by Victoria
Chess) — *Yolen, Jane*
King of Another Country (Illus. by
Fiona French) — *French, Fiona*
The King of Ireland's Son (Illus. by P J
Lynch) — *Behan, Brendan*
The King of the Birds (Illus. by Helen
Ward) — *Ward, Helen*
King Snake (Illus. by John Manders)
— *Slotboom, Wendy*
r The Kingfisher Beano Book of Amazing
Facts
The Kingfisher Book of Poems about
Love — *McGough, Roger*
r The Kingfisher First Encyclopedia
— *Civardi, Anne*
r The Kingfisher First Science
Encyclopedia — *Ganeri, Anita*
r The Kingfisher Illustrated Junior
Dictionary — *Grisewood, John*
r The Kingfisher Young People's Atlas of
the World — *Steele, Philip*
r The Kingfisher Young People's Book of
Music — *Wilson, Clive*
The Kingfisher Young People's Book of
Oceans — *Lambert, David*
Kings and Queens — *Sauvain, Philip*
The King's Giraffe (Illus. by Stephane
Poulin) — *Collier, Mary Jo*
Kipper's Snowy Day (French). Book
and Audio Version — *Inkpen, Mick*
A Kiss Like This — *Anholt, Catherine*
Kiss the Dust — *Laird, Elizabeth*
Kissing the Witch — *Donoghue, Emma*
Kitchen (First Words Series)
Kitchens through the Ages — *Wood,
Richard*
Kite — *Burgess, Melvin*
Kitten (Illus. by Pam Adams) — *Twinn,
Michael*
Kitten Tales (Illus. by Kate Simpson)
— *Grindley, Sally*
Kittens — *Scott, Carey*
Kitten's Nap (Illus. by Kate Spohn)
— *Spohn, Kate*
Kitten's Spell (Illus. by Caroline Jayne
Church) — *Golsack, Gaby*
Kitty's Fishy Dinner (Illus. by Tanya
Linch) — *Jennings, Linda*

Knee Knock Rise (Toren). Audio
Version — *Babbitt, Natalie*
Kneeling Carabao and Dancing Giants
(Illus. by Ileana C Lee) — *Krasno,
Rena*
The Knight and the Squire (Illus. by
Michael Foreman) — *Jones, Terry*
The Knight with the Lion — *Howe,
John*
Knightmare — *Barnes, Johnny Ray*
Knights and Armor (Illus. by Mark
Bergin) — *Kerr, Daisy*
The Knight's Handbook — *Gravett,
Christopher*
Knights of the Kitchen Table (Illus. by
Lane Smith) — *Scieszka, Jon*
Know about Smoking. 3rd Ed. — *Hyde,
Margaret O*
A Know-Nothing Birthday (Illus. by R
W Alley) — *Spirn, Michele Sobel*
A Koala Is not a Bear! (Illus. by
Barbara Bedell) — *Sotzek, Hannelore*
Kofi and His Magic (Illus. by Margaret
Courtney-Clarke) — *Angelou, Maya*
Koi and the Kola Nuts (Gobbege).
Audio Version — *Brian, Gleeson*
Kombumerri--Saltwater People — *Best,
Ysola*
Komodo Dragon (Illus. by Tara
Darling) — *Darling, Kathy*
Konnichiwa! I Am a Japanese-American
Girl (Illus. by Kazuyoshi Arai)
— *Brown, Tricia*
Konte Chameleon, Fine, Fine, Fine!
(Illus. by Christian Epanya)
— *Kessler, Cristina*
The Korean Cinderella (Illus. by Ruth
Heller) — *Climo, Shirley*
Korean Games (Illus. by Tony
Letourneau) — *Koh, Frances M*
The Koufax Dilemma (Illus. by Meryl
Treatner) — *Schnur, Steven*
The Krazees (Illus. by Eric Brace)
— *Swope, Sam*
Kristi Yamaguchi — *Rambeck, Richard*
Kuia (Illus. by Akarana Vaega)
— *Vaega, Akarana*
A Kwanzaa Fable (Daniel). Audio
Version — *Copage, Eric V*

L

The La-Di-Da Hare (Illus. by Diana
Cain Bluthenthal) — *Lewis, J Patrick*

The Lab Rats of Doctor Eclair (Illus. by John Bianchi) — *Bianchi, John*
Lacrosse: The National Game of the Iroquois (Illus. by Lawrence Migdale) — *Hoyt-Goldsmith, Diane*
Laddie of the Light — *Briggs-Bunting, Jane*
Ladies' Choice — *Lynch, Chris*
LaDonna Harris — *Schwartz, Michael*
The Lady in the Box (Illus. by Marni Backer) — *McGovern, Ann*
Lady Kaguya's Secret (Illus. by Jirina Marton)
Lady Muck (Illus. by Jonathan Heale) — *Mayne, William*
The Lady with the Hat — *Orlev, Uri*
The Ladybird Guide to the Presidents of the United States
r The Ladybird Thesaurus
p Ladybug
The Ladybug — *Crewe, Sabrina*
Ladybug Garden — *Godkin, Celia*
Ladybugology (Illus. by Brian Grogan) — *Ross, Michael Elsohn*
La Lagartija Y El Sol — *Ada, Alma Flor*
El Lago De La Luna — *Gantschev, Ivan*
Il Lago Della Luna E Altre Favole Dell'India (Illus. by Pulak Biswas) — *Varma, Nishu*
Lake Erie — *Armbruster, Ann*
Lake Huron — *Armbruster, Ann*
Lake Michigan — *Armbruster, Ann*
Lake Ontario — *Armbruster, Ann*
Lake Superior — *Armbruster, Ann*
Lakes (Illus. by Vanessa Card) — *Morris, Neil*
Lamb (Snapshot)
Lamb Chop's Special Chanukah — *Lewis, Shari*
Das Land Der Ecken (Illus. by Gerhard Gepp) — *Ulitzka, Irene*
Land of the Dingo People (Illus. by Percy Trezise) — *Trezise, Percy*
Land of the Long White Cloud (Illus. by Michael Foreman) — *Te Kanawa, Kiri*
Landscapes — *Delafosse, Claude*
Landslides, Slumps, and Creep — *Goodwin, Peter*
The Language of Doves (Illus. by Greg Shed) — *Wells, Rosemary*
A Lantern in Her Hand — *Aldrich, Bess Streeter*

Lao Lao of Dragon Mountain (Illus. by Francesca Pelizzoli) — *Bateson-Hill, Margaret*
Laos--in Pictures — *Lerner Publications Company. Geography Dept.*
The Lapsnatcher (Illus. by Marissa Moss) — *Coville, Bruce*
Lasers — *Fox, Mary Virginia*
Lassie: A Christmas Story (Illus. by Kevin Burke) — *Hamner, Earl*
The Last Algonquin — *Kazimiroff, Theodore*
The Last Chance Dance and Other Adventures — *McNaughton-Stuart, Candace*
The Last Circus (Illus. by Kim Gamble) — *Thompson, Colin*
The Last Dragon (Illus. by Chris K Soentpiet) — *Nunes, S*
Last Leaf First Snowflake to Fall (Illus. by Leo Yerxa) — *Yerxa, Leo*
Last Left Standing — *Russell, Barbara T*
The Last of the Wallendas and Other Poems (Illus. by Patrick Benson) — *Hoban, Russell*
Last of the Wild (Illus. by Bob Hines) — *McClung, Robert M*
The Last One In — *Engle, Marty M*
The Last Payback — *VanOosting, James*
The Last-Place Sports Poems of Jeremy Bloom — *Korman, Gordon*
The Last Rail (Illus. by Bill Farnsworth). Book and Audio Version — *Bailer, Darice*
The Last Rainmaker — *Garland, Sherry*
The Last Shot — *Baillie, Allan*
The Last Train (Illus. by Kim Lewis) — *Lewis, Kim*
Lasting Echoes (Illus. by Paul Morin) — *Bruchac, Joseph*
Laughing Tomatoes and Other Spring Poems (Illus. by Maya Christina Gonzalez) — *Alarcon, Francisco X*
Laughs: Funny Stories — *Mackay, Claire*
Launch Day (Illus. by Peter A Campbell) — *Campbell, Peter A*
Laura Ingalls Wilder (Illus. by Alexandra Wallner) — *Wallner, Alexandra*
The Laura Ingalls Wilder Country Cookbook (Illus. by Leslie A Kelly) — *Wilder, Laura Ingalls*

Lily's Crossing (Moore). Audio Version
— *Giff, Patricia Reilly*
Link across America — *Anderson, Mary Elizabeth*
Linnea in Monet's Garden (Moore).
Audio Version — *Bjork, Christina*
Linus Pauling: Investigating the Magic Within — *Sherrow, Victoria*
The Lion and the Mouse (Illus. by Carla Dijs) — *Dijs, Carla*
The Lion First Bible (Illus. by Leon Baxter) — *Alexander, Pat*
The Lion Is No Longer King (Illus. by Lev) — *Bofane, In Koli*
The Lion Storyteller Bible — *Hartman, Bob*
The Lion, the Witch and the Wardrobe (Illus. by Pauline Baynes) — *Lewis, C S*
The Lion Who Wanted to Love (Illus. by David Wojtowycz) — *Andreae, Giles*
The Lion's Whiskers and Other Ethiopian Tales (Illus. by Helen Siegl) — *Ashabranner, Brent*
Lipizzaner Horses — *Maiecek, Tomaaes*
Liplap's Wish (Illus. by Sylvia Long) — *London, Jonathan*
Lisa Y El Gato Sin Nombre (Illus. by Claudia De Weck) — *Recheis, Kathe*
Listen to This — *Freeman, Marcia S*
The Listener — *Laird, Elizabeth*
Lithuania — *Kagda, Sakina*
Little Angels' Book of Christmas — *Anglund, Joan Walsh*
Little Baby Bobby (Illus. by Laura Cornell) — *Van Laan, Nancy*
Little Bean's Friend (Illus. by John Wallace) — *Wallace, John*
Little Bear (Illus. by Maurice Sendak) — *Minarik, Else Holmelund*
Little Bear Brushes His Teeth (Illus. by Vera Sobat) — *Langreuter, Jutta*
Little Bear Goes to Kindergarten (Illus. by Vera Sobat) — *Langreuter, Jutta*
Little Bighorn — *Krehbiel, Randy*
Little Bird (Illus. by Rod Campbell) — *Campbell, Rod*
Little Bobo Saves the Day (Illus. by Hans De Beer) — *Romanelli, Serena*
Little Boy Blue and Other Rhymes (Illus. by Rosemary Wells) — *Opie, Iona*
Little Brother Moose (Illus. by Karlyn Holman) — *Kasperson, James*

Little Bunny's Cool Tool Set (Illus. by Kathy Parkinson) — *Boelts, Maribeth*
Little Chicken Chicken (Illus. by Sue Heap) — *Martin, David, 1944-*
Little Clearing in the Woods (Illus. by Dan Andreasen) — *Wilkes, Maria D*
Little Cloud — *Carle, Eric*
Little Coyote Runs Away (Illus. by Harvey Stevenson) — *Strete, Craig*
Little Eight John (Illus. by Wil Clay) — *Wahl, Jan*
Little Farm by the Sea (Illus. by Kay Chorao) — *Chorao, Kay*
Little Fish, Lost (Illus. by Jane Conteh-Morgan) — *Van Laan, Nancy*
Little Folk (Illus. by James Bernardin) — *Walker, Paul Robert*
Little Girl in a Red Dress with Cat and Dog (Illus. by Cynthia Von Buhler) — *Nicholson, Nicholas B A*
Little Green Fingers — *Van Hage, Mary An*
Little Green Tow Truck — *Wilson-Max, Ken*
The Little House Books — *Wilder, Laura Ingalls*
A Little House Reader — *Wilder, Laura Ingalls*
Little House Sisters (Illus. by Garth Williams) — *Wilder, Laura Ingalls*
The Little Humpbacked Horse (Illus. by Alexander Koshkin) — *Winthrop, Elizabeth*
Little Koala Finds a Friend (Illus. by Deborah Brown) — *Roc, Margaret*
Little Lake Saga (Illus. by Kathy Bedard) — *Miller, Nelson*
The Little Lama of Tibet — *Raimondo, L*
Little Lil and the Swing-Singing Sax (Illus. by Lisa Cohen) — *Gray, Libba Moore*
Little Lions (Illus. by Jim Arnosky) — *Arnosky, Jim*
Little Long-Nose (Illus. by Laura Stoddart) — *Hauff, Wilhelm*
Little Louie the Baby Bloomer (Illus. by Jose Aruego) — *Kraus, Robert*
The Little Mermaid (Illus. by Rachel Isadora) — *Isadora, Rachel*
Little Miss Muffet Counts to Ten (Illus. by Emma Chichester Clark) — *Chichester Clark, Emma*

M

The Magdalen Islands Mystery (Illus. by Huguette Marquis) — *Guillet, Jean-Pierre*

Magic Bedknob — *Norton, Mary*

Magic Betsey (Illus. by Lis Toft) — *Blackman, Malorie*

The Magic Bicycle — *Hill, William*

The Magic City — *Nesbit, E*

The Magic Cornfield (Illus. by Nancy Willard) — *Willard, Nancy*

Magic Dad (Illus. by Magda Van Tilburg) — *Prince, Alison*

The Magic Dreidels (Illus. by Katya Krenina) — *Kimmel, Eric A*

The Magic Flute (Illus. by Peter Malone) — *Gatti, Anne*

The Magic Maguey (Illus. by Elisa Kleven) — *Johnston, Tony*

Magic Money — *Adler, David A*

The Magic Moonberry Jump Ropes (Illus. by E B Lewis) — *Hru, Dakari*

The Magic of Mythical Creatures — *Mastin, Colleayn O*

The Magic of Spider Woman (Illus. by Shonto Begay) — *Duncan, Lois*

Magic Poems (Illus. by Korky Paul) — *Foster, John*

The Magic Porridge Pot (Illus. by Emily Bolam) — *Ziefert, Harriet*

The Magic School Bus and the Electric Field Trip (Illus. by Bruce Degen) — *Cole, Joanna*

The Magic School Bus at the Waterworks (Illus. by Bruce Degen) — *Cole, Joanna*

The Magic School Bus Blows Its Top (Illus. by Bruce Degen) — *Cole, Joanna*

The Magic School Bus Inside a Beehive (Illus. by Bruce Degen) — *Cole, Joanna*

The Magic Sewing Machine (Illus. by Sunny Warner) — *Warner, Sunny*

The Magic Sleigh Bell — *Elliott, W Peter*

The Magic Squad and the Dog of Great Potential (Illus. by Frank Remkiewicz) — *Quattlebaum, Mary*

Magic Step-by-Step — *Russell, Tom*

The Magic Stopwatch (Illus. by Peter Joyce) — *Maisner, Heather*

The Magic Tree House Series — *Osborne, Mary Pope*

Magical Chango (Illus. by Katherine Rose Slocum) — *Lewis, Diana*

Magical Objects from around the World — *Dolphin, Laurie*

Magnet Science (Illus. by Glen Vecchione) — *Vecchione, Glen*

Magnetism — *Woodruff, John*

The Magnificent Mummies (Illus. by Martin Chatterton) — *Bradman, Tony*

The Magpie's Nest (Illus. by Julie Downing) — *Foster, Joanna*

Mailing May (Illus. by Ted Rand) — *Tunnell, Michael O*

Maisy's Colors — *Cousins, Lucy*

Maisy's House — *Cousins, Lucy*

Make-a-Face: Book and Body Painting Kit for Kids of All Ages (Illus. by Toni Hafkenscheid) — *Stevenson, Jane Byrne*

Make a Joyful Noise — *Crespi, Francesca*

Make It

Make It a Merry Christmas! (Illus. by Dorothy Stott) — *Jensen, Nancy*

The Make-Something Club Is Back! (Illus. by Ann Schweninger) — *Zweifel, Frances*

Make Things Fly (Illus. by Sasha Meret) — *Kennedy, Dorothy*

Make Your Own Dinosaur out of Chicken Bones — *McGowan, Christopher*

Make Your Own Megillah (Illus. by Katherine Janus Kahn) — *Groner, Judyth*

Makiawisug: The Gift of the Little People (Illus. by David Wagner) — *Fawcett, Melissa Jayne*

Making Cool Crafts and Awesome Art (Illus. by Roberta Gould) — *Gould, Roberta*

Making Faces (Illus. by James Marsh) — *Forward, Toby*

Making Friends with Frankenstein — *McNaughton, Colin*

The Making of Goodnight Moon — *Marcus, Leonard S*

Making Pictures — *James, Ann*

Making Shapes — *Gibson, Gary*

Making Things. Rev. Ed. (Illus. by Ann Sayre Wiseman) — *Wiseman, Ann Sayre*

Making Things Change — *Gibson, Gary*

Making Tracks — *Parker, Steve*

Making Up Megaboy (Illus. by Katrina Roeckelein) — *Walter, Virginia*

Makonde — *Stoner, John*

Title Index

Marmee's Surprise (Illus. by Diane
Paterson) — *Kulling, Monica*
Mars — *George, Michael*
Marshes and Swamps (Illus. by Gail
Gibbons) — *Gibbons, Gail*
Martha Black: Gold Rush Pioneer
(Illus. by Jack McMaster) — *Martin,
Carol*
Martha Blah Blah — *Meddaugh, Susan*
Martha Counts Her Kittens — *Walsh,
Mike*
Martha Graham: A Dancer's Life
— *Freedman, Russell*
Martian Fossils on Earth? — *Bortz,
Fred*
Martin Luther King (Illus. by Malcah
Zeldis) — *Bray, Rosemary L*
Martin's Mice (Illus. by Jez Alborough)
— *King-Smith, Dick*
Maruja (Illus. by Jorge Sanzol) — *Wolf,
Ema*
Marushka and the Month Brothers
(Illus. by Anna Vojtech) — *Vojtech,
Anna*
The Marvelous Market on Mermaid
(Illus. by Maryann Kovalski)
— *Melmed, Laura Krauss*
Marvelous Math (Illus. by Karen
Barbour) — *Hopkins, Lee Bennett*
The Marvelous Mix-Up and Other Tales
of Reb Shalom (Illus. by Vitaliy
Romanenko) — *Feuerman, Ruchama
King*
The Marvelous Toy (Illus. by Elizabeth
Sayles) — *Paxton, Tom*
Marven of the Great North Woods
(Illus. by Kevin Hawkes) — *Lasky,
Kathryn*
Marvin and the Mean Words (Illus. by
Blanche Sims) — *Kline, Suzy*
Marvin's Best Christmas Present Ever
(Illus. by Jane Clark Brown)
— *Paterson, Katherine*
Mary Margaret's Tree (Illus. by Blair
Dawson) — *Dawson, Blair*
Mary Mclean and the St. Patrick's Day
Parade (Illus. by Michael Dooling)
— *Kroll, S*
Mary Mehan Awake — *Armstrong,
Jennifer*
Mary Poppins — *Travers, P L*
Masai and I (Illus. by Nancy Carpenter)
— *Kroll, Virginia L*

The Mash and Smash Cookbook (Illus.
by Ralph Butler) — *Buck-Murray,
Marian*
Masks — *Hatrick, Gloria*
Master Elk and the Mountain Lion
(Illus. by Wayne McLoughlin)
— *London, Jonathan*
Master Maid (Illus. by Pauline Ellison)
— *Shepard, Aaron*
Master Track's Train (Illus. by Andre
Amstutz) — *Ahlberg, Allan*
The Mastodon Mystery — *Perkyns,
Dorothy*
The Math Chef (Illus. by Tina
Cash-Walsh) — *D'Amico, Joan*
Math Curse — *Scieszka, Jon*
Math Play! (Illus. by Loretta Braren)
— *McGowan, Diane*
Math Riddles (Illus. by Andrea Baruffi)
— *Ziefert, Harriet*
Mathamusements (Illus. by Jeff Sinclair)
— *Blum, Raymond*
The Mathematical Olympiad Handbook
— *Gardiner, Tony*
Mathematics Now!. Bk. 1 — *Bell, Tony*
Mathew Brady: Civil War Photographer
— *Van Steenwyk, Elizabeth*
Matilda (Hanley). Audio Version
— *Dahl, Roald*
Matilda the Moocher (Illus. by Diana
Cain Bluthenthal) — *Bluthenthal,
Diana Cain*
Matter and Materials (Illus. by Terry
Hadler) — *Kerrod, Robin*
A Matter of Time — *Sinykin, Sheri
Cooper*
Matthew and the Midnight Ball Game
(Illus. by Michael Martchenko)
— *Morgan, Allen*
Matthew and the Midnight Pilot (Illus.
by Michael Martchenko) — *Morgan,
Allen*
Matthew Unstrung — *Seago, Kate*
Matthew's Dream — *Lionni, Leo*
Matthew's Goals (Illus. by Pauline
Hazelwood) — *Hardcastle, Michael*
Mattie's Hats Won't Wear That!
— *Greenstein, Elaine*
Matzo Ball Moon (Illus. by Elaine
Greenstein) — *Newman, Leslea*
Maui and the Sun (Illus. by Gavin
Bishop) — *Bishop, Gavin*
Maui: Legends of the Outcast
— *Sullivan, Robert*
Max — *Isadora, Rachel*

Title Index

Mental Maths Daily Workout. Bks. 1-5
— *Patilla, Peter*
Meow! (Illus. by Katya Arnold)
— *Arnold, Katya*
Meredith, the Witch Who Wasn't (Illus.
by Christa Unzner) — *Lachner,
Dorothea*
Merl and Jasper's Supper Caper (Illus.
by Laura Rankin) — *Rankin, Laura*
Merlin — *Yolen, Jane*
Merlin's Castle (Illus. by Laszlo Gal)
— *Gal, Laszlo*
Mermaid Island (Illus. by Julie Durrell)
— *Frith, Margaret*
Merry Christmas, Geraldine (Illus. by
Holly Keller) — *Keller, Holly*
Merry Christmas, Old Armadillo (Illus.
by Dominic Catalano) — *Brimner,
Larry Dane*
Merrywinkle: The Adventures of
Santa's Big Brother — *Fewell, Anne*
The Message — *Applegate, Katherine*
The Messenger of Spring (Illus. by C J
Taylor) — *Taylor, C J*
Metamorphosis (Illus. by Francisco
Arredondo) — *Llamas Ruiz, Andres*
Methadone — *Simpson, Carolyn*
The Metropolitan Museum of Art:
Masks
Mexican Independence Day and Cinco
De Mayo — *MacMillan, Dianne M*
Mexico — *Berendes, Mary*
Mexico (A Ticket To) — *Streissguth,
Thomas*
r Mi Diccionario De Juguete (Illus. by
Maximo Sagredo Sagudo)
— *Marcuse, Aida E*
The Mice of Mousehole (Illus. by
Michelle Cartlidge) — *Cartlidge,
Michelle*
Mice Squeak, We Speak (Illus. by
Tomie De Paola) — *Shapiro, Arnold*
Michael (Illus. by Tony Ross)
— *Bradman, Tony*
Michael Dorris — *Weil, Ann*
Michael Irvin — *Rosenblatt, Richard*
Michael Jordan. Rev. Ed. — *Raber,
Thomas*
Michael Rosen's ABC (Illus. by Bee
Willey) — *Rosen, Michael, 1946-*
Michael Strogoff (Illus. by N C Wyeth)
— *Verne, Jules*
Michelle Kwan — *Rambeck, Richard*
Michelle Kwan, Heart of a Champion
— *Kwan, Michelle*

Mick Harte Was Here — *Park, Barbara*
Mick Harte Was Here (Lubotsky).
Audio Version — *Park, Barbara*
Mickey Mouse: My Life in Pictures
— *Schroeder, Russell*
Microlife — *Burnie, David*
The Microscope Book (Illus. by David
Sovka) — *Levine, Shar*
r The Microsoft Encarta 97 Encyclopedia.
Deluxe Ed.
The Middle Passage (Illus. by Tom
Feelings) — *Feelings, Tom*
Midnight: A Cinderella Alphabet (Illus.
by Spencer Alston Bartsch) — *Perkal,
Stephanie*
Midnight Dance of the Snowshoe Hare
(Illus. by Ken Kuroi) — *Carlstrom,
Nancy White*
The Midnight Doll (Illus. by Maggie
Glen) — *Glen, Maggie*
Midnight Farm (Illus. by David
Delamare) — *Simon, Carly*
The Midnight Folk (Illus. by Rowland
Hilder) — *Masefield, John*
The Midnight Game — *Barnes, Johnny
Ray*
A Midsummer Night's Dream for Kids
— *Burdett, Lois*
The Midwife's Apprentice — *Cushman,
Karen*
The Midwife's Daughters (Illus. by
David Mackintosh) — *Halligan,
Marion*
Midwinter — *Henry, Maeve*
Miffy Goes Outside — *Bruna, Dick*
Miffy Likes to... — *Bruna, Dick*
Mighty Dinosaurs — *Simpson, Judith*
Mighty Giants — *Donnelly, Jane*
Mighty Mountains (Illus. by Diana
Mayo) — *Bevan, Finn*
The Mighty Skink — *Shipton, Paul*
Migrant Worker (Illus. by Lawrence
Migdale) — *Hoyt-Goldsmith, Diane*
Mike Piazza — *James, Brant*
Mike Piazza: Hard-Hitting Catcher
— *Savage, Jeff*
Mili Bate! (Illus. by Tonya Goranova)
— *Pencheva, Stanka*
Milk — *Powell, Jillian*
Milk and Honey (Illus. by Louise
August) — *Yolen, Jane*
The Milkman's Boy (Illus. by Greg
Shed) — *Hall, Donald, 1928-*
A Miller (Illus. by Giorgio Bacchin)
— *Pernoud, Regine*

Mittens (Illus. by Clare Turlay
  Newberry) — *Newberry, Clare Turlay*
Mitzi, Molly and Max the Kittens
  — *Buck, Gisela*
Miz Berlin (Illus. by Floyd Cooper)
  — *Yolen, Jane*
Miz Berlin Walks (Illus. by Floyd
  Cooper) — *Yolen, Jane*
Miz Fannie Mae's Fine New Easter Hat
  (Illus. by Yong Chen) — *Milich,
  Melissa*
Moby Dick (Illus. by Allan Drummond)
  — *Drummond, Allan*
The Moccasin Goalie — *Brownridge,
  William Roy*
Model Cars — *Ansary, Mir Tamim*
Models (Art House)
Modern Dance — *Tierney, Tom*
Modern Stories (Genre Library)
Mohandas Gandhi — *Barraclough, John*
The Mole's Daughter (Illus. by Julia
  Gukova) — *Gukova, Julia*
Mole's Moon (Illus. by Susan Varley)
  — *Oram, Hiawyn*
Molly (Illus. by Erin Marie Mauterer)
  — *Bonsall, Joseph S*
Molly Brown Is Not a Clown (Illus. by
  Rick Van Krugel) — *Rogers, Linda*
Molly Meets Mona and Friends (Illus.
  by Denise Bennet Minner) — *Walker,
  Gladys*
Molly's Bath (Illus. by Mireille Levert)
  — *Levert, Mireille*
Molly's Breakfast (Illus. by Mireille
  Levert) — *Levert, Mireille*
Molly's Clothes (Illus. by Mireille
  Levert) — *Levert, Mireille*
Molly's Pilgrim (Moore). Audio Version
  — *Cohen, Barbara*
Molly's Toys (Illus. by Mireille Levert)
  — *Levert, Mireille*
Mom, the School Flooded! (Illus. by
  Jacques Laplante) — *Rivard, Ken*
Mommies Don't Get Sick! — *Hafner,
  Marylin*
The Mommy Book (Illus. by Ken
  Heyman) — *Morris, Ann*
Mommy Go Away! (Illus. by Petra
  Mathers) — *Jonell, Lynne*
Mommy's in the Hospital Having a
  Baby (Illus. by Robert Maass)
  — *Rosenberg, Maxine B*
Mommy's Lap (Illus. by Henri
  Sorensen) — *Horowitz, Ruth*
Monarch Butterfly — *Gibbons, Gail*

The Monday Horses — *Doty, Jean
  Slaughter*
Monday's Troll (Illus. by Peter Sis)
  — *Prelutsky, Jack*
Monday's Troll (Prelutsky). Audio
  Version — *Prelutsky, Jack*
Monet — *Boutan, Mila*
Monet's Ghost (Illus. by Pat Morrissey)
  — *Yarbro, Chelsea Quinn*
Money — *Young, Robert, 1951-*
Monica Seles — *Rambeck, Richard*
Monica Seles: Returning Champion
  — *Fehr, Kristin Smith*
The Monkey Bridge (Illus. by Fahimeh
  Amiri) — *Martin, Rafe*
Monkey Do! (Illus. by Andre Amstutz)
  — *Ahlberg, Allan*
Monkey in Space (Illus. by Judith
  Lawton) — *Oram, Hiawyn*
Monkey See, Monkey Do (Illus. by Leo
  Timmers) — *Holsonback, Anita*
Monkey Sunday (Illus. by Sanna
  Stanley) — *Stanley, Sanna*
The Monkey Thief — *Henderson, Aileen
  Kilgore*
Monomotapa, Zulu, Basuto — *Mann,
  Kenny*
Monsieur Thermidor (Illus. by Lindsey
  Kidd) — *Kidd, Richard*
The Monster and the Teddy Bear (Illus.
  by David McKee) — *McKee, David*
Monster in Love (Illus. by Jan Smith)
  — *Jungman, Ann*
Monster in Trouble (Illus. by Jan
  Smith) — *Jungman, Ann*
r Monster Machines — *Bingham,
  Caroline, 1962-*
Monster Math School Time (Illus. by
  Marge Hartelius) — *Maccarone,
  Grace*
Monster Stew (Illus. by Bob Reese)
  — *Gill, Janie Spaht*
The Monster Story-Teller (Illus. by Nick
  Sharratt) — *Wilson, Jacqueline*
Monster Trucks — *Savage, Jeff*
Monster Vision — *Leroe, E W*
Monster's Birthday Hiccups (Illus. by
  Lynn Munsinger) — *Mueller, Virginia*
Monsters in Cyberspace (Illus. by
  Melissa Sweet) — *Regan, Dian Curtis*
Monsters of the Deep (Illus. by Francis
  Phillipps) — *Ross, Stewart*
The Monsters' Test (Illus. by Sal
  Murdocca) — *Heinz, Brian*

Mother Goose Math (Illus. by Emily Bolam) — *Ziefert, Harriet*

Mother Hubbard's Christmas (Illus. by John O'Brien) — *O'Brien, John, 1953-*

Mother Nature's Magic Seed (Illus. by Chad Anderson) — *Mallory, Laura*

Mothers and Babies — *World Wildlife Fund (U.S.)*

Motherstone — *Gee, Maurice*

Motley the Cat — *Amoore, Susannah*

Mounds of Earth and Shell — *Shemie, Bonnie*

A Mountain Alphabet (Illus. by Andrew Kiss) — *Ruurs, Margriet*

Mountain Biking — *Brimner, Larry Dane*

Mountain Mammals — *Landau, Elaine*

Mountains (Illus. by Martin Camm) — *Morris, Neil*

Mouse and Mole and the All Weather Train Ride (Illus. by Doug Cushman) — *Cushman, Doug*

Mouse and Mole and the Year-Round Garden (Illus. by Doug Cushman) — *Cushman, Doug*

The Mouse before Christmas (Illus. by Michael Garland) — *Garland, Michael*

The Mouse Bride (Illus. by Lesley Liu) — *Chang, Monica*

A Mouse Called Wolf (Illus. by Jon Goodell) — *King-Smith, Dick*

Mouse Creeps (Illus. by Reg Cartwright) — *Harris, Peter*

Mouse Flute (Illus. by Vanessa Julian-Ottie) — *Matthews, Andrew*

A Mouse in the House! (Illus. by Uli Waas) — *Wagener, Gerda*

Mouse in the Manger (Illus. by Elaine Blier) — *Wynne-Jones, Tim*

Mouse Match (Illus. by Ed Young) — *Young, Ed*

Mouse Mess (Illus. by Linnea Asplind Riley) — *Riley, Linnea Asplind*

The Mouse That Jack Built (Illus. by Cyndy Szekeres) — *Szekeres, Cyndy*

A Mouse Told His Mother (Illus. by Maryjane Begin) — *Roberts, Bethany*

Mouse TV (Illus. by Matt Novak) — *Novak, Matt*

Mouse's Halloween (Illus. by Alan Baker) — *Baker, Alan*

Mousetracks: A Kid's Computer Idea Book — *Steinhauser, Peggy*

Movies — *Oxlade, Chris*

Moving Days — *Harshman, Marc*

Moving Mama to Town — *Young, Ronder Thomas*

Mr. Ape (Illus. by Roger Roth) — *King-Smith, Dick*

Mr. Bear and the Bear (Illus. by Ruth Brown) — *Thomas, Frances*

Mr. Bear Says a Spoonful for You — *Gliori, Debi*

Mr. Bear Says Goodnight — *Gliori, Debi*

Mr. Bear Says I Love You — *Gliori, Debi*

Mr. Bear Says Peek-a-boo — *Gliori, Debi*

Mr. Biffy's Battle (Illus. by Andrew McLean) — *Tulloch, Richard*

Mr. Brown Can Moo! Can You?. 40th-Anniversary Ed. — *Seuss, Dr.*

Mr. Bumble (Illus. by Doug Kennedy) — *Kennedy, Kim*

Mr. Duvall Reports the News (Illus. by Lili Duvall) — *Duvall, Jill*

Mr. Fine, Porcupine (Illus. by Remi Saillard) — *Joly, Fanny*

Mr. Fixit's Mix-Ups — *Scarry, Richard*

Mr. Frumble's Pickle Car — *Scarry, Richard*

Mr. Lincoln's Whiskers (Illus. by Karen B Winnick) — *Winnick, Karen B*

Mr. Lunch Borrows a Canoe (Illus. by J Otto Seibold) — *Seibold, J Otto*

Mr. Merlin and the Turtle (Illus. by Seymour Chwast) — *Chwast, Seymour*

Mr. Mysterious and Company (Illus. by Eric Von Schmidt) — *Fleischman, Sid*

Mr. Nodd's Ark — *Yeoman, John*

Mr. Pak Buys a Story (Illus. by Benrei Huang) — *Farley, Carol J*

Mr. Pin: The Chocolate Files (McDonough). Audio Version — *Monsell, Mary Elise*

Mr. Putter and Tabby Fly the Plane (Illus. by Arthur Howard) — *Rylant, Cynthia*

Mr. Putter and Tabby Row the Boat (Illus. by Arthur Howard) — *Rylant, Cynthia*

Mr. Putter and Tabby Toot the Horn (Illus. by Arthur Howard) — *Rylant, Cynthia*

Mr. Semolina-Semolinus (Illus. by Giselle Potter) — *Manna, Anthony L*

My Favourite Monsters — *James, Vincent*

My First Body Book — *Rice, Chris*

r My First Canadian Science Encyclopedia (Illus. by Teresa Foster) — *Scarborough, Kate*

My First Flashlight (Illus. by Jeff Cummins) — *Bentley, Dawn*

My First Word Board Book — *Wilkes, Angela*

My Friend Gorilla (Illus. by Atsuko Morozumi) — *Morozumi, Atsuko*

My Friend's a Werewolf — *Johnson, Pete*

My Gran (Illus. by Debbie Boon) — *Boon, Debbie*

My Grandmother's Journey (Illus. by Sharon McGinley-Nally) — *Cech, John*

My Granny's Great Escape (Illus. by Nick Sharratt) — *Strong, Jeremy*

My Guardian Angel (Illus. by Tohby Riddle) — *Loves, June*

My Home (Star Bright)

My Home Is Africa (Illus. by M Denis-Hout) — *Tracqui, Valerie*

My Home Is over Jordan — *Forrester, Sandra*

My Horse of the North (Illus. by Bruce McMillan) — *McMillan, Bruce*

My House Has Stars (Illus. by Peter Catalanotto) — *McDonald, Megan*

My Journey through Art — *Cave, Kathryn*

My Kindy — *Rickard, Lisa*

My Life as a Fifth-Grade Comedian — *Levy, Elizabeth*

My Life in Dog Years (Illus. by Ruth Wright Paulsen) — *Paulsen, Gary*

My Life with the Wave (Illus. by Mark Buehner) — *Cowan, Catherine*

My Little 123 Book (Illus. by Bob Staake) — *Staake, Bob*

My Little ABC Board Book — *Bunting, Jane*

My Little ABC Book (Illus. by Bob Staake) — *Staake, Bob*

My Little Animals Board Book (Dorling Kindersley)

My Little House 1 2 3 (Illus. by Renee Graef) — *Wilder, Laura Ingalls*

My Little House A B C (Illus. by Renee Graef) — *Wilder, Laura Ingalls*

My Little House Christmas Crafts Book (Illus. by Mary Collier) — *Collins, Carolyn*

My Little House Christmas Sticker Book (Illus. by Renee Graef)

My Little House Cookbook and Apron (Illus. by Holly Jones) — *Cotler, Amy*

My Little People School Bus (Illus. by Carolyn Bracken) — *Tomaselli, Doris*

My Little Sister Ate One Hare (Illus. by Kevin Hawkes) — *Grossman, Bill*

My Little Supermarket (Illus. by Claire Henley) — *Repchuk, Caroline*

My Love for You — *Roth, Susan L*

My Manitoba Friends, A-Z (Illus. by Thomas Reid) — *Reid, Thomas*

My Mexico (Illus. by F John Sierra) — *Johnston, Tony*

My Mom Is Magic (Illus. by Chris Fisher) — *Roche, Hannah*

My Mom Married the Principal — *Bechard, Margaret*

My Mother's Secret Life (Illus. by Rebecca Emberley) — *Emberley, Rebecca*

My Muslim Life — *El Droubie, Riadh*

My Name Is Seepeetza — *Sterling, Shirley*

My Name Is York (Illus. by Bill Farnsworth) — *Van Steenwyk, Elizabeth*

My Napoleon (Illus. by Catherine Brighton) — *Brighton, Catherine*

My Night Forest (Illus. by Amy Cordova) — *Owen, Roy*

My Notebook with Help from Amelia — *Moss, Marissa*

My Own Song and Other Poems to Groove To (Illus. by Eric Sabee) — *Strickland, Michael R*

My Palace of Leaves in Sarajevo (Illus. by Herbert Tauss) — *Lorbiecki, Marybeth*

My Pet Cats (Illus. by Andy King) — *Engfer, LeeAnne*

My Pet Hamster and Gerbils (Illus. by Andy King) — *Engfer, LeeAnne*

My Pony Ride — *Kopper, Lisa*

My Pop-Up Surprise 123 (Illus. by Robert Crowther) — *Crowther, Robert*

My Pop-Up Surprise ABC (Illus. by Robert Crowther) — *Crowther, Robert*

N

Ordinary Albert (Illus. by Pamela Allen) — Antle, Nancy

Ordinary Things (Illus. by Walter Lyon Krudop) — Fletcher, Ralph

Oregon — Stefoff, Rebecca

The Oregon Trail in American History — Stefoff, Rebecca

The Origin of the Universe (Illus. by Luis Rizo) — Llamas Ruiz, Andres

The Original Adventures of Hank the Cowdog (Illus. by Gerald L Holmes) — Erickson, John R

The Originals: Animals That Time Forgot (Illus. by Ted Lewin) — Yolen, Jane

The Orion Book of Princesses — Gardner, Sally

Ornithomimids: The Fastest Dinosaur (Illus. by Donna Braginetz) — Lessem, Don

The Orphan of Ellis Island — Woodruff, Elvira

Orphan Runaways — Gregory, Kristiana

Orphan Train Rider — Warren, Andrea

Ostriches — Maynard, Thane

The Other Side (Illus. by Julia Gukova) — Aura, Alejandro

The Other Side of the Bridge — Hanel, Wolfram

The Other Way to Listen — Baylor, Byrd

Otherwise Known as Sheila the Great (Blume). Audio Version — Blume, Judy

Otherworld (Illus. by Anthony Morris) — Strong, Jeremy

Otter Play (Illus. by Anna Vojtech) — Luenn, Nancy

Our Amazing Bodies

Our Baby from China (Illus. by Nancy D'Antonio) — D'Antonio, Nancy

Our Beckoning Borders — Ashabranner, Brent

Our Favorite Stories (Illus. by Amanda Hall) — Gavin, Jamila

Our Granny (Illus. by Julie Vivas) — Wild, Margaret

Our Journey from Tibet (Illus. by Nancy Jo Johnson) — Dolphin, Laurie

Our Oceans (Illus. by Patricia Keeler) — Fleisher, Paul

Our Old House (Illus. by Leslie Baker) — Vizurraga, Susan

Our Planet — Hannaford, Priscilla

r Our Planet Earth — Llewellyn, Claire

Our Solar System (Illus. by Eric Jepson) — Moore, Jo Ellen

Our Wonderful Earth — Baxter, Nicola

Our World in Danger

Our World, Our Rights — Brown, Margot

Out of Darkness (Illus. by Kate Kiesler) — Freedman, Russell

Out of Place (Illus. by Daniel Mark Duffy) — Calhoun, B B

Out of the Ark (Illus. by Jackie Morris) — Ganeri, Anita

Out of the Dump — Franklin, Kristine L

Out of the Dust — Hesse, Karen

Out of the Ocean (Illus. by Debra Frasier) — Frasier, Debra

Out of This World — King, Penny

Out to Lunch (Illus. by Peggy Perry Anderson) — Anderson, Peggy Perry

The Outcast — Bernard, Patricia

Outrageous Women of Ancient Times (Illus. by Lisa M Brown) — Leon, Vicki

Outrageous Women of the Middle Ages — Leon, Vicki

Outrageously Alice — Naylor, Phyllis Reynolds

Outside and Inside Bats — Markle, Sandra

Outside Permission — Nilsson, Eleanor

The Outsiders — Hinton, S E

Over on the Farm (Illus. by Christopher Gunson) — Gunson, Christopher

Over the Moon (Illus. by Karen Katz) — Katz, Karen

Over the Top of the World — Steger, Will

Oviraptor (Illus. by Tony Gibbons) — Amery, Heather

Owen Foote, Soccer Star (Illus. by Martha Weston) — Greene, Stephanie

Owl — Stefoff, Rebecca

Owl Babies (Illus. by Patrick Benson) — Waddell, Martin

Owl in Love — Kindl, Patrice

Owl in the House (Illus. by Peter Bailey) — Evans, Gregory

The Owl Service — Garner, Alan

The Owl, the Two and the Medlar — Brooke, Agnes-Mary

The Owl Tree (Illus. by Anthony Lewis) — Nimmo, Jenny

Parsnip (Illus. by Sue Porter) — *Porter, Sue*

A Part of the Sky — *Peck, Robert Newton*

The Parthenon — *Chrisp, Peter*

Parts (Illus. by Tedd Arnold) — *Arnold, Tedd*

The Party (Illus. by Barbara Reid) — *Reid, Barbara*

Parzival: The Quest of the Grail Knight — *Paterson, Katherine*

Passage to Freedom (Illus. by Dom Lee) — *Mochizuki, Ken*

Passover — *Rose, David*

Passover Magic (Illus. by Marylin Hafner) — *Schotter, Roni*

Passport on a Plate (Illus. by Susan Greenstein) — *Vezza, Diane Simone*

Pasta — *Powell, Jillian*

Pastatively Italy — *McLean, Virginia*

The Pasteboard Bandit (Illus. by Peggy Turley) — *Bontemps, Arna Wendell*

Pat-a-Cake Dough Book and Kit (Illus. by Marilyn Mets) — *McKay, Sharon E*

Patch's House — *Lodge, Jo*

The Patchwork House (Illus. by Dean Griffiths) — *Fitz-Gibbon, Sally*

Pateando Lunas — *Berocay, Roy*

Patsy and the Declaration — *Massie, Elizabeth*

Patsy's Discovery — *Massie, Elizabeth*

Patterns Everywhere — *Gold, Kari Jenson*

Patterns of Software — *Gabriel, Richard P*

Pavlova's Gift (Illus. by Victoria Berdichevsky) — *Trottier, Maxine*

Pay Attention, Slosh! (Illus. by Gail Piazza) — *Smith, Mark*

Peacebound Trains (Illus. by Chris K Soentpiet) — *Balgassi, Haemi*

Peach Boy — *Hooks, William*

Peacocks (Illus. by Richard Hewett) — *Berman, Ruth*

The Peacock's Pride (Illus. by Jo'Anne Kelly) — *Kajpust, Melissa*

Peanut Butter and Jelly for Snabbos (Illus. by Norman Nodel) — *Rosenfeld, Dina*

Pearl Moscowitz's Last Stand (Illus. by Robert Roth) — *Levine, Arthur A*

Pearl's First Prize Plant (Illus. by A Delaney) — *Delaney, A*

Pearl's Marigolds for Grandpa (Illus. by Jane Breskin Zalben) — *Zalben, Jane Breskin*

Pearls of Lutra (Illus. by Allan Curless) — *Jacques, Brian*

The Pebble in My Pocket (Illus. by Chris Coady) — *Hooper, Meredith*

Peck, Slither, and Slide (Illus. by Suse MacDonald) — *MacDonald, Suse*

Pedaling Along — *Otfinoski, Steven*

A Peddler's Dream (Illus. by Tom Shefelman) — *Shefelman, J*

Pedrito's Day (Illus. by Luis Garay) — *Garay, Luis*

Pee Wee Scouts (Illus. by Alan Tiegreen) — *Delton, Judy*

Peek-a-Boo! — *Ahlberg, Janet*

Peek-A-Boo! (Illus. by Jan Ormerod) — *Ormerod, Jan*

Peekaboo Babies — *Lionel*

Peepo! — *Ahlberg, Janet*

Pegasus (Illus. by Kinuko Craft) — *Mayer, Marianna*

Peggy Goes Cod Fishing (Illus. by Brett Gosling) — *Bath, Linda H*

Peggy's Scrawny Green Lobster (Illus. by Brett Gosling) — *Bath, Linda H*

Pen Pals (Illus. by Joan Holub) — *Holub, Joan*

Penalty Shot — *Christopher, Matt*

r Pendragon: Lordly Domains

Penguin — *Stefoff, Rebecca*

The Penguin Book of Nonsense Verse (Illus. by Quentin Blake) — *Blake, Quentin*

The Penguin Friend (Illus. by Margaret Power) — *Sussex, Lucy*

Penguin Pete, Ahoy! — *Pfister, Marcus*

Penguins — *Love, John*

The Penguins' Day Out (Illus. by Ruth Paul) — *Joseph, Vivienne*

Pennies to Dollars — *Branch, Muriel Miller*

Penny and Pup (Illus. by Jane Chapman) — *Jennings, Linda*

Penny Wishes — *Burke-Weiner, Kimberly*

Il Pentolino Magico (Illus. by Emanuele Luzzati) — *Montanari, Massimo*

The People (Illus. by Ted Finger) — *Pikering, Robert*

People — *Speir, Peter*

People and Plants — *Carpenter, Zelma V*

r The People Atlas — *Chiarelli, Brunetto*

A Picture Book of Louis Braille (Illus. by John Wallner) — *Adler, David A*

A Picture Book of Rosa Parks. Book and Audio Version — *Adler, David A*

A Picture Book of Thomas Alva Edison (Illus. by John Wallner) — *Adler, David A*

A Picture Book of Thurgood Marshall (Illus. by Robert Casilla) — *Adler, David A*

r The Picture History of Great Inventors — *Clements, Gillian*

A Picture of Freedom — *McKissack, Pat*

Picture Poems — *Benton, Michael*

Picture Puzzles — *Smith, Alastair*

The Picture That Mom Drew (Illus. by Kathy Mallat) — *Mallat, Kathy*

Pictures in the Dark — *Cross, Gillian*

A Picture's Worth — *Balan, Bruce*

Pidge (Illus. by Ann James) — *Bell, Krista*

A Piece of Home (Illus. by Juan Wijngaard) — *Levitin, Sonia*

The Pied Piper of Hamelin (Illus. by Kate Greenaway) — *Greenaway, Kate*

Pig-Heart Boy — *Blackman, Malorie*

Pig Out! — *Aborio, Portia*

Pig Pigger Piggest (Illus. by Jimmy Holder) — *Walton, Rick*

Pigen Der Var God Til Mange Ting (Illus. by Dorte Karrebaek) — *Karrebaek, Dorte*

Pigeons (Illus. by William Munoz) — *Patent, Dorothy Hinshaw*

Piggie Pie! (Illus. by Howard Fine) — *Palatini, Margie*

Piggy's Birthday Dream (Illus. by Jung-Hee Spetter) — *Vries, Anke De*

Piglet (DK)

Piglet's Bath — *Spohn, Kate*

Pigouts (Illus. by Bob Reese) — *Gill, Janie Spaht*

Pigs — *Murray, Peter, 1952, Sep., 9-*

Pigs Aplenty, Pigs Galore! — *McPhail, David*

A Pig's Book of Manners — *Allan, Nicholas*

Pigs Go to Market (Illus. by Sharon McGinley-Nally) — *Axelrod, Amy*

Pigs in the Mud in the Middle of the Rud (Illus. by John Schoenherr) — *Plourde, Lynn*

Pigs in the Pantry (Illus. by Sharon McGinley-Nally) — *Axelrod, Amy*

A Pillow for My Mom (Illus. by Christine Ross) — *Sgouros, Charissa*

The Pillow King — *Woodward, Richard*

The Pillow War (Illus. by Matt Novak) — *Novak, Matt*

Pilots Fly Planes — *Robinson, Fay*

The Pinatas Maker — *Ancona, George*

El Pinguino Pedro Y Sus Nuevos Amigos — *Pfister, Marcus*

Pink and Say (Illus. by Patricia Polacco) — *Polacco, Patricia*

Pink for Polar Bear — *Solis, Valerie*

Pink Slippers, Bat Mitzvah Blues — *Wolff, Ferida*

Pink Y Say (Illus. by Patricia Polacco) — *Polacco, Patricia*

Pinkerton Inks (Illus. by Guy Parker-Rees) — *Parkinson, David*

Pinky and Rex (Moore). Audio Version — *Howe, James*

Pinky and Rex and the Mean Old Witch (Moore). Audio Version — *Howe, James*

Pinky and Rex and the New Neighbors (Illus. by Melissa Sweet) — *Howe, James*

Pinky and Rex and the School Play (Illus. by Melissa Sweet) — *Howe, James*

Pinky and Rex and the Spelling Bee (Moore). Audio Version — *Howe, James*

Pinky and Rex Get Married (Moore). Audio Version — *Howe, James*

Pinky and Rex Go to Camp (Moore). Audio Version — *Howe, James*

A Pinky Is a Baby Mouse and Other Baby Animal Names (Illus. by Diane De Groat) — *Ryan, Pam Munoz*

Pinocchio (Illus. by Peter Stevenson) — *Waitt, Andrea*

Pinocchio (Sessions). Book and Audio Version — *Collodi, Carlo*

Pioneer Crafts (Illus. by Heather Collins) — *Greenwood, Barbara*

Pioneer Days (Illus. by Bobbie Moore) — *King, David C*

Pioneer Girl (Illus. by Dan Andreasen) — *Anderson, William, 1952-*

Pioneer Projects (Illus. by Barbara Bedell) — *Kalman, Bobbie*

Pioneer Sisters (Illus. by Renee Graef) — *Wilder, Laura Ingalls*

Pippa's Puppy (Illus. by Anthea Sieveking) — *MacKinnon, Debbie*

The Polar Bear Son (Illus. by Lydia
Dabcovich) — *Dabcovich, Lydia*
The Polar Express (Illus. by Chris Van
Allsburg) — *Van Allsburg, Chris*
Polar Mammals — *Brimner, Larry Dane*
The Polar Seas — *Penny, Malcolm*
Polar the Titanic Bear (Illus. by Laurie
McGaw) — *Spedden, Daisy Corning
Stone*
Polkabats and Octopus Slacks (Illus. by
Calef Brown) — *Brown, Calef*
El Pollo De Los Domingos — *Polacco,
Patricia*
Pompeii — *Connolly, Peter*
Pond Seasons (Illus. by Ann Blades)
— *Alderson, Sue Ann*
Pond Water Zoo (Illus. by Jean Jenkins)
— *Loewer, H Peter*
Pony Express! (Illus. by Dan
Andreasen) — *Kroll, Steven*
Pooh to the Rescue (Illus. by Ernest H
Shepard) — *Milne, A A*
Pooh's Enchanted Place (Illus. by
Ernest H Shepard) — *Milne, A A*
Pooh's Little Instruction Book — *Milne,
A A*
Pooh's Touch and Feel Visit — *Milne, A
A*
The Poombah of Badoombah (Illus. by
Kevin Hawkes) — *Lillegard, Dee*
Pop-o-Mania: How to Create Your Own
Pop-Ups (Illus. by Barbara Valenta)
— *Valenta, Barbara*
Popcorn (Illus. by James Stevenson)
— *Stevenson, James*
Popcorn at the Palace (Illus. by Emily
Arnold McCully) — *McCully, Emily
Arnold*
Poppleton (Illus. by Mark Teague)
— *Rylant, Cynthia*
Poppleton and Friends (Illus. by Mark
Teague) — *Rylant, Cynthia*
Poppleton Everyday (Illus. by Mark
Teague) — *Rylant, Cynthia*
Poppy — *Avi*
Poppy's Secret (Illus. by Lesley
Bisseker) — *Hooper, Mary*
Poppy's Whale (Illus. by Philippe
Germain) — *Hebert, Marie-Francine*
Por Que No Canta El Petirrojo? (Illus.
by Elena Odriozola) — *Mendiguren,
Xabier*
Pork and Beef's Great Adventure (Illus.
by Damon Burnard) — *Burnard,
Damon*

A Portrait of Spotted Deer's
Grandfather (Illus. by Marlowe
DeChristopher) — *Littlesugar, Amy*
Portrait's of Little Women: Amy's Story
— *Pfeffer, Susan Beth*
Portraits of Little Women: Beth's Story
— *Pfeffer, Susan Beth*
Portraits of Little Women: Jo's Story
— *Pfeffer, Susan Beth*
Portraits of Little Women: Meg's Story
— *Pfeffer, Susan Beth*
Portraits of Pioneers in Psychology. Vol.
2 — *Kimble, Gregory A*
Possum and the Peeper (Illus. by Anne
Hunter) — *Hunter, Anne*
Postcards Talk (Illus. by Mark
Thurman) — *Granfield, Linda*
Postman Pat and the Hole in the Road
(Barrie). Book and Audio Version
— *Cunliffe, John*
Potato: A Tale from the Great
Depression (Illus. by Lisa Campbell
Ernst) — *Lied, Kate*
Potato Baby — *Matthews, Jenny*
Potatoes — *Powell, Jillian*
Potbelly and the Haunted House (Illus.
by Keith Brunton) — *Impey, Rose*
Potbelly in Love (Illus. by Keith
Brunton) — *Impey, Rose*
Potbelly Needs a Job (Illus. by Keith
Brunton) — *Impey, Rose*
Potbelly's Lost His Bike (Illus. by Keith
Brunton) — *Impey, Rose*
Potlatch: A Tsimshian Celebration
(Illus. by Lawrence Migdale)
— *Hoyt-Goldsmith, Diane*
Poultry — *Powell, Jillian*
Power and Glory (Illus. by Geoff Kelly)
— *Rodda, Emily*
Powerful Beasts of the Wild
— *Greenaway, Theresa*
The Powerhouse — *Halam, Ann*
Powwow Summer (Illus. by Cheryl
Walsh Bellville) — *Rendon, Marcie R*
The Prairie — *Rotter, Charles*
Prairie Born (Illus. by Peter Shostak)
— *Bouchard, Dave*
A Prairie Boy's Summer (Illus. by
William Kurelek) — *Kurelek, William*
A Prairie Boy's Winter (Illus. by
William Kurelek) — *Kurelek, William*
Prairie Day (Illus. by Renee Graef)
— *Wilder, Laura Ingalls*
The Prairie Dog — *Crewe, Sabrina*

The Puffin Book of Classic Children's Stories (Illus. by Diz Wallis) — *Carpenter, Humphrey*

The Puffin Treasury of Australian Children's Stories

The Puffin Treasury of Children's Stories

The Puffin Treasury of Classics

La Pulga Cecilia (Illus. by Khitish Chatterjee) — *Carreno, Mada*

The Pumpkin Blanket — *Zagwyn, Deborah Turney*

Pumpkin Decorating — *Rhodes, Vicki*

Pumpkin Faces (Illus. by Judith Moffatt) — *Rose, Emma*

The Pumpkin Fair (Illus. by Eileen Christelow) — *Bunting, Eve*

Pumpkin Ted (Illus. by Caroline Jayne Church) — *Golsack, Gaby*

Un Punado De Semillas (Illus. by Luis Garay) — *Hughes, Monica*

Punia and the King of Sharks (Illus. by Felipe Davalos) — *Wardlaw, Lee*

A Punishment to Fit the Crime? — *Cooper, Alison*

Puppies — *Scott, Carey*

Puppy Love (Illus. by Anita Jeram) — *King-Smith, Dick*

The Puppy Sister (Illus. by Jacqueline Rogers) — *Hinton, S E*

Puppy's Games — *Spohn, Kate*

Purely Rosie Pearl — *Cochrane, Patricia A*

Purim Play (Illus. by Marylin Hafner) — *Schotter, Roni*

The Purloined Corn Popper — *Hildick, E W*

The Purple Hat (Illus. by Tracey Campbell Pearson) — *Pearson, Tracey Campbell*

Purple Is My Game, Morgan Is My Name — *Miller, Judi*

Push and Pull — *Freeman, Marcia*

Pushing and Pulling — *Gibson, Gary*

Pushkin Meets the Bundle (Illus. by Donald Saaf) — *Ziefert, Harriet*

Puss-in-Boots (Illus. by Sue Cony) — *Butterfield, Moira*

Pussycat Pussycat and Other Rhymes (Illus. by Rosemary Wells) — *Opie, Iona*

Pussywillows and Other Things. 3rd Ed. — *Lister, Jan*

Put a Fan in Your Hat! (Illus. by Rick Brown) — *Carrow, Robert*

Put on Some Antlers and Walk Like a Moose — *Sayre, April Pulley*

Putt-Putt's Night before Christmas

Putting on a Play (Illus. by Katy Keck Arnsteen) — *Bentley, Nancy*

The Puzzle of the Dinosaur-Bird (Illus. by Mark Hallett) — *Schlein, Miriam*

Puzzles — *Hewitt, Sally*

Puzzling Day in the Land of the Pharaohs — *Anderson, Scoular*

Pyramids — *Millard, Anne*

Pyramids! 50 Hands-On Activities to Experience Ancient Egypt (Illus. by Michael Kline) — *Hart, Avery*

Q R

Quack! Said the Billy-Goat (Illus. by Barbara Firth) — *Causley, Charles*

Quantum Squeak — *Hoffman, Mary*

Quebec. Rev. Ed. — *Ouellet, Danielle*

Queen Elizabeth I — *Green, Robert*

Queen Elizabeth II — *Green, Robert*

Queen Esther Saves Her People (Illus. by Frane Lessac) — *Gelman, Rita Golden*

Queen Lizzie Rules OK! — *Ryan, Margaret*

Queen of the Sixth Grade — *Cooper, Ilene*

Queen of the Universe (Illus. by David Cox) — *Gleeson, Libby*

Queen Victoria — *Castor, Harriet*

Queenie, One of the Family (Illus. by Bob Graham) — *Graham, Bob*

Queenie the Bantam (Illus. by Bob Graham) — *Graham, Bob*

The Quentin Blake Book of Nonsense Stories — *Blake, Quentin*

Querido Diario (Illus. by David Rodriguez Hernandez) — *Prieto, Iliana*

Quest for the West — *Kent, Peter*

A Question of Trust — *Bauer, Marion Dane*

Quick, Quiet, and Feathered (Illus. by Wayne Ford) — *Butterfield, Moira*

The Quicksand Pony (Illus. by Alison Lester) — *Lester, Alison*

Quicksilver (Illus. by Anna Pignataro) — *Broome, Errol*

The Quiet Noisy Book (Illus. by Leonard Weisgard) — *Brown, Margaret Wise*

Title Index

Reach Higher (Illus. by Doug Keith)
— *Pippen, Scottie*
Reaching Dustin — *Grove, Vicki*
Read for Me, Mama (Illus. by Lori
McElrath-Eslick) — *Rahaman,
Vashanti*
Read to Your Bunny (Illus. by
Rosemary Wells) — *Wells, Rosemary*
Real (Illus. by Robin Moore)
— *Holman, Felice*
Real Canadian Mysteries and Monsters
(Illus. by Karena Kozol) — *Wheatley,
Jonathan*
Real Live Monsters! — *Schecter, Ellen*
The Real Patriots of the American
Revolution — *Young, Robert, 1951-*
The Really Deadly and Dangerous
Dinosaur and Other Monsters of the
Prehistoric World — *Taylor, Barbara*
The Really Fearsome Blood-Loving
Vampire Bat and Other Creatures
with Strange Eating Habits
— *Greenaway, Theresa*
The Really Fearsome Bloodloving
Vampire Bat and Other Creatures
with Curious Eating Habits
— *Greenaway, Theresa*
The Really Hairy Scary Spider and
Other Creatures with Lots of Legs
— *Greenaway, Theresa*
The Really Horrible Horned Toad and
Other Cold, Clammy Creatures
— *Greenaway, Theresa*
The Really Horrible Horny Toad and
Other Cold, Clammy Creatures
— *Greenaway, Theresa*
The Really Sinister Savage Shark and
Other Creatures of the Deep
— *Taylor, Barbara*
The Really Wicked Droning Wasp and
Other Things That Bite and Sting
— *Greenaway, Theresa*
Rebel of Dark Creek — *Tate, Nikki*
Rebel Rebel — *Kemp, Gene*
Rebellion: A Novel of Upper Canada
(Illus. by G Brender A Brandis)
— *Brandis, Marianne*
Rebels against Slavery — *McKissack,
Pat*
Rebus Riot — *Christensen, Bonnie*
Recreation Can Be Risky — *Gutman,
Bill*
Recycling — *Chandler, Gary*
The Red-All-Over Riddle Book (Illus. by
Andrew Stooke) — *Szirtes, George*

Red Bird (Illus. by Todd L W Doney)
— *Mitchell, Barbara*
Red, Blue, and Yellow Yarn (Illus. by
Valeri Gorbachev) — *Kosman,
Miriam R*
The Red Corduroy Shirt (Illus. by Peter
Perko) — *Kertes, Joseph*
Red Dancing Shoes (Illus. by James E
Ransome) — *Patrick, Denise Lewis*
Red-Dirt Jessie — *Myers, Anna*
The Red-Eared Ghosts — *Alcock, Vivien*
Red Fox and the Baby Bunnies
— *Baron, Alan*
Red Light, Green Light, Mama and Me
(Illus. by Niki Daly) — *Best, Cari*
Red Parka Mary (Illus. by Rhian
Brynjolson) — *Eyvindson, Peter*
Red Ranger Came Calling (Illus. by
Berkeley Breathed) — *Breathed,
Berkeley*
Red Scarf Girl — *Jiang, Ji-Li*
The Red Sea and the Arabian Gulf
— *Waterlow, Julia*
The Red Shoes — *Bazilian, Barbara*
Red-Tail Angels — *McKissack, Pat*
Red Wolf Country (Illus. by Daniel San
Souci) — *London, Jonathan*
Redbird at Rockefeller Center (Illus. by
Peter Maloney) — *Maloney, Peter,
1955-*
Redoute: The Man Who Painted
Flowers (Illus. by Carolyn Croll)
— *Croll, Carolyn*
Redwall — *Jacques, Brian*
Redwall (Jacques). Audio Version
— *Jacques, Brian*
Refugees — *Warner, Rachel*
El Regalo (Illus. by Pep Montserrat)
— *Keselman, Gabriela*
Regarding the Fountain (Illus. by M
Sarah Klise) — *Klise, Kate*
Reggie Miller — *Wilner, Barry*
Relationships (Illus. by Teco G
Rodrigues) — *Campbell, Judith*
Relax Max! — *Caswell, Brian*
Reliable (Illus. by Gwen Green)
— *Amos, Janine*
Religions Explained — *Ganeri, Anita*
The Reluctant Santa (Illus. by Gail
Lucas) — *Birchmore, Daniel A*
REM--Rapid Eye Movement (Illus. by
Istvan Banyai) — *Banyai, Istvan*
Remaking the Earth (Illus. by Paul
Goble) — *Goble, Paul*

S

Sabriel — *Nix, Garth*
Sacagawea — *St. George, Judith*
Sacagawea: Native American Hero
— *Sanford, William R*
Sacagawea: Westward with Lewis and
Clark — *White, Alana J*
Sacred Places (Illus. by David Shannon)
— *Yolen, Jane*
Sacred Skies (Illus. by Diana Mayo)
— *Bevan, Finn*
The Sad Night — *Mathews, S*
Sadako Y Las Mil Grullas De Papel
(Illus. by Ronald Himler) — *Coerr,
Eleanor*
r Saddlery. Rev. Ed. — *Edwards, Elwyn
Hartley*
A Safe Home for Manatees (Illus. by
Martin Classen) — *Jenkins, Priscilla
Belz*
Safe Horse, Safe Rider — *Haas, Jessie*
A Safe Place (Illus. by Judith Friedman)
— *Trottier, Maxine*
The Saga of Aslak (Illus. by Barry
Wilkinson) — *Price, Susan*
Saguaro Cactus — *Berquist, Paul*
Sailaway Home (Illus. by Bruce Degen)
— *Degen, Bruce*
Sailing Home (Illus. by Matt Ottley)
— *Thompson, Colin*
The Sailor's Alphabet (Illus. by Michael
McCurdy) — *McCurdy, Michael*
St. Lawrence Seaway — *Armbruster,
Ann*
Saint Patrick (Illus. by Michael
Garland) — *Tompert, Ann*
Saints — *Sauvain, Philip*
The Salem Witch Trials — *Wilson, Lori
Lee*
Sallie the Shrew — *Buck, Gisela*
Sally Bradford (Illus. by Robert Gantt
Steele) — *Hoobler, Dorothy*
Sally Ride: First American Woman in
Space — *Camp, Carole Ann*
Sally's Painting Room (Illus. by Janice
Bowles) — *Orr, Wendy*
The Salmon — *Crewe, Sabrina*
A Salmon for Simon (Illus. by Ann
Blades) — *Waterton, Betty*
Saltarin (Illus. by Marcus Pfister)
— *Pfister, Marcus*
Sam and the Lucky Money (Illus. by
Cornelius Van Wright) — *Chinn,
Karen*

Sam and the Tigers (Illus. by Jerry
Pinkney) — *Lester, Julius*
Sam Plants a Sunflower (Illus. by Axel
Scheffler) — *Petty, Kate*
Sam Sunday and the Mystery at the
Ocean Beach Hotel (Illus. by Will
Hillenbrand) — *Supraner, Robyn*
Sam the Zamboni Man (Illus. by
Harvey Stevenson) — *Stevenson,
James*
Sammy, Dog Detective (Illus. by Colleen
Stanley Bare) — *Bare, Colleen Stanley*
Sammy Keyes and the Hotel Thief
— *Van Draanen, Wendelin*
Sammy Spider's First Rosh Hashanah
(Illus. by Katherine Janus Kahn)
— *Rouss, Sylvia A*
Sammy Spider's First Shabbat (Illus. by
Katherine Janus Kahn) — *Rouss,
Sylvia A*
Sammy's Story (Illus. by David
Kooharian) — *Kooharian, David*
Sam's Duck (Illus. by Keith Bowen)
— *Morpurgo, Michael*
Sam's Sneaker Search (Illus. by Charles
Fuge) — *O'Brien, Claire*
The Samurai's Daughter (Illus. by
Stephen T Johnson) — *San Souci,
Robert D*
San Francisco 49ers — *Stanley, Loren*
San Francisco in Colors — *Parmiani,
Floria N*
Sand on the Move — *Gallant, Roy A*
The Sand Witch (Illus. by John
Timmins) — *Schisgall, Jim*
Sandra Day O'Connor (Illus. by Gary
Rees) — *Holland, Gini*
Sandry's Book — *Pierce, Tamora*
The Sandy Bottom Orchestra
— *Keillor, Garrison*
Santa's Ark — *Wright, Cliff*
Santa's Book of Names (Illus. by David
McPhail) — *McPhail, David*
Santa's Favorite Story (Illus. by Ivan
Gantschev) — *Aoki, Hisako*
Santa's Short Suit Shrunk and Other
Christmas Tongue Twisters (Illus. by
Sue Truesdell) — *Buck, Nola*
Santa's Time Off (Illus. by Tom
Browning) — *Maynard, Bill*
The Santee Sioux Indians — *Dolan,
Terrance*
Sarah and the People of Sand River
(Illus. by Ian Wallace) — *Valgardson,
W D*

Sarah, Plain and Tall — *MacLachlan, Patricia*

Sarah's Shovel (Illus. by Anthea Sieveking) — *MacKinnon, Debbie*

Sarn: The Story of an Otter in Spring (Illus. by Ken Lilly) — *Potter, Tessa*

Sarny, a Life Remembered — *Paulsen, Gary*

Sasha and the Wind (Illus. by Helene Desputeaux) — *Tregebov, Rhea*

Saskatchewan. Rev. Ed. — *Margoshes, Dave*

Satchmo's Blues (Illus. by Floyd Cooper) — *Schroeder, Alan*

Satellite Fever (Illus. by Mic Rolph) — *Painter, Mike*

Satellites — *Parker, Steve*

Saturday Night at the Dinosaur Stomp (Illus. by Scott Nash) — *Shields, Carol Diggory*

Saturn — *Murray, Peter, 1952, Sep., 9-*

Save Halloween! — *Tolan, Stephanie S*

Save the Florida Key Deer — *Clark, Margaret Goff*

Saving Energy — *Dineen, Jacqueline*

The Saving of Valiant Blue Heron (Illus. by Robin Lee Makowski) — *Harms, John*

Saving Shiloh (Illus. by Barry Moser) — *Naylor, Phyllis Reynolds*

Saving Sweetness (Illus. by G Brian Karas) — *Stanley, Diane*

Sawgrass Poems (Illus. by Ted Levin) — *Asch, Frank*

r Say Hola to Spanish (Illus. by Loretta Lopez) — *Erya, Susan Middleton*

Say Hola to Spanish, Otra Vez (Again!) (Illus. by Loretta Lopez) — *Elya, Susan Middleton*

Scaly and Snappy (Illus. by Wayne Ford) — *Butterfield, Moira*

Scamper's Year (Illus. by Laura Rader) — *Kindley, Jeff*

The Scandinavian American Family Album — *Hoobler, Dorothy*

Scarecrow (Illus. by Lauren Stringer) — *Rylant, Cynthia*

The Scarecrow of Oz (Illus. by John R Neill) — *Baum, L Frank*

The Scarecrows of Necum Teuch (Illus. by John Davis) — *Geddes, Angella*

Scared in School — *Brown, Roberta Simpson*

Scaredy Cat (Illus. by Joan Rankin) — *Rankin, Joan*

Scary Science (Illus. by Dusan Petricic) — *Funston, Sylvia*

Scary Stories for Sleep-Overs. Audio Version — *Welch, R C*

Scary Story Reader — *Young, Richard, 1946-*

The Schernoff Discoveries — *Paulsen, Gary*

Schnitzel Von Krumm Forget-Me-Not (Illus. by Lynley Dodd) — *Dodd, Lynley*

r Scholastic Atlas of Exploration — *Starkey, Dinah*

r Scholastic Dictionary of Idioms — *Terban, Marvin*

r Scholastic Encyclopedia of the Presidents and Their Times. Updated 1997 Ed. — *Rubel, David*

r Scholastic Encyclopedia of Women in the United States — *Keenan, Sheila*

r The Scholastic Rhyming Dictionary — *Young, Sue*

Scholastic's the Magic School Bus Explores in the Age of Dinosaurs. Electronic Media Version

The School Bag — *Heaney, Seamus*

School Bus (Box Cars)

The School Bus Adventure — *Jango-Cohen, Judith*

School Campout (Illus. by Susan Gardos) — *Citra, Becky*

School Spirits — *Tunnell, Michael O*

Schools Help Us Learn — *Hill, Lee Sullivan*

r Science and Technology Breakthroughs. Vols. 1-2 — *Bruno, Leonard C*

Science around the World (Illus. by Laurel Aiello) — *Levine, Shar*

The Science Book for Girls and Other Intelligent Beings (Illus. by Pat Cupples) — *Wyatt, Valerie*

The Science Chef Travels around the World (Illus. by Tina Cash-Walsh) — *D'Amico, Joan*

Science Experiments at Home (Illus. by Kelly McMahon) — *Moore, Jo Ellen*

r Science Experiments Index for Young People. 2nd Ed. — *Pilger, Mary Anne*

The Science Explorer (Illus. by Jason Gorski) — *Murphy, Pat*

The Science Explorer Out and About — *Murphy, Pat*

Science Fair Projects: Energy (Illus. by Alex Pang) — *Bonnet, Robert L*

Science Fair Projects: Flight, Space and Astronomy (Illus. by Frances Zweifel) — *Bonnet, Robert L*

Science Fair Projects: The Environment (Illus. by Frances Zweifel) — *Bonnet, Robert L*

Science for Fun Experiments — *Gibson, Gary*

Science Fun (Illus. by Jo Supanich) — *Moore, Jo Ellen*

Science in Seconds with Toys — *Potter, Jean*

Science Project Ideas about Air — *Gardner, Robert*

Science Project Ideas about Animal Behavior (Illus. by Jacob Katari) — *Gardner, Robert*

Science Project Ideas about Rain — *Gardner, Robert*

Science Project Ideas about the Moon — *Gardner, Robert*

Science Project Ideas about the Sun — *Gardner, Robert*

Science Project Ideas about Trees (Illus. by Jacob Katari) — *Gardner, Robert*

Science Surprises (Illus. by June Otani) — *Markle, Sandra*

r Scientists. Vols. 1-3 — *Saari, Peggy*

Scientists and Doctors — *Lindop, Laurie*

Scotland — *Hirst, Mike*

Scottie Pippen — *Schnakenberg, Robert*

Scratch and the Sniffs — *Lynch, Chris*

The Screech Owls' Northern Adventure — *MacGregor, Roy*

Screen Test — *Klass, David*

Scribbleboy (Illus. by Chris Riddell) — *Ridley, Philip*

Se Ilama Cuerpo — *Formiguera, Pere*

Se Jubilan Las Hadas (Illus. by Daniel Zorrilla) — *Perez Diaz, Enrique*

The Sea and I — *Nakawatari, H*

Sea Creatures — *Roberts, M L*

The Sea Hole — *Collins, Ross*

Sea Horse — *Stefoff, Rebecca*

Sea Jellies — *Gowell, Elizabeth Tayntor*

The Sea King's Daughter (Illus. by Gennady Spirin) — *Shepard, Aaron*

The Sea Lion (Illus. by Sophie De Wilde) — *Pichon, Joelle*

Sea Lion Roars. Book and Audio Version — *Lamm, C Drew*

The Sea Maidens of Japan (Illus. by Erin McGonigle Brammer) — *Bell, Lili*

The Sea of Tranquillity (Illus. by Christian Birmingham) — *Haddon, Mark*

Sea Otter Inlet (Illus. by Celia Godkin) — *Godkin, Celia*

Sea Otters — *Kalman, Bobbie*

The Sea Piper (Illus. by Jason Cockcroft) — *Cresswell, Helen*

The Sea Serpent — *Calvert, Frankie*

Sea Turtles (Illus. by Gail Gibbons) — *Gibbons, Gail*

Seabirds — *Rauzon, Mark J*

Seal — *Cherry, Lynne*

The Seal Singer — *Dinan, Carolyn*

Seal Surfer (Illus. by Michael Foreman) — *Foreman, Michael*

The Search for Gold — *Barber, Nicola*

The Search for Lost Cities — *Barber, Nicola*

The Search for Riches — *Langley, Andrew*

The Search for Sunken Treasure — *Barber, Nicola*

Search for the Lost City (Illus. by Maggie Downer) — *Wood, A J*

The Search for the Right Whale — *Kraus, Scott*

The Search for Tombs — *Ganeri, Anita*

Searching for Alien Life — *Fradin, Dennis B*

Searching for Candlestick Park — *Kehret, Peg*

Seashore — *Burnie, David*

Seashore Babies (Illus. by Tara Darling) — *Darling, Kathy*

A Season of Comebacks — *Mackel, Kathy*

The Seasons (Illus. by Anthea Sieveking) — *MacKinnon, Debbie*

The Seasons Sewn (Illus. by Michael McCurdy) — *Paul, Ann Whitford*

The Seattle Children's Theatre — *Smith, Marisa*

The Second Bend in the River — *Rinaldi, Ann*

Second Best — *Hill, David J*

The Secret Admirer (Illus. by Tony Sansevero) — *Guthrie, Donna W*

The Secret Birthday — *Carle, Eric*

The Secret Box — *Pearson, Gayle*

Secret Dawn (Illus. by Yolaine Lefebvre) — *Chase, Edith Newlin*

The Secret Fairy Handbook — *Dann, Penny*

The Secret Family — *Bodanis, David*

The Seven Voyages of Sinbad the Sailor (Illus. by Quentin Blake) — *Yeoman, John*

Sewing — *Sadler, Judy Ann*

Shade's Children — *Nix, Garth*

The Shadow Jumper and the Monster — *Bydlinski, Georg*

Shadow of a Bull (Rivela). Audio Version — *Wojciechowska, Maia*

Shadow of the Wolf (Illus. by Tony Meers) — *Whelan, Gloria*

Shadows of Night (Illus. by Barbara Bash) — *Bash, Barbara*

Shaggy and Spotty (Illus. by David Lucas) — *Hughes, Ted*

Shake Dem Halloween Bones (Illus. by Mike Reed) — *Nikola-Lisa, W*

Shake, Rattle, and Roll — *Christian, Spencer*

Shake, Shake, Shake — *Pinkney, Andrea Davis*

Shaker Hearts (Illus. by Wendell Minor) — *Turner, Ann*

The Shakespeare Stealer — *Blackwood, Gary L*

Shannon: The Schoolmarm Mysteries, San Francisco 1880 (Illus. by Bill Farnsworth) — *Kudlinski, Kathleen V*

The Shape of Me and Other Stuff — *Seuss, Dr.*

Shapes — *Hewitt, Sally*

Shapes (Fit-a-Shape)

Shapes for Lunch (Illus. by Charles Reasoner) — *Lilly, Melinda*

Shaping a President (Illus. by Diane Smook) — *Peduzzi, Kelli*

Sharing Blessings (Illus. by Mary O'Keefe Young) — *Musleah, Rahel*

Sharing Time Troubles (Illus. by Betsy Lewin) — *Maccarone, Grace*

Shark — *Brooks, Bruce*

Shark and Dolphin — *Theodorou, Rod*

Shark Attack Almanac (Illus. by Carol Lyon) — *Batten, Mary*

Shark Attacks and Spider Snacks (Illus. by Roy Condy) — *Condy, Roy*

Shark Bait — *Salisbury, Graham*

Shark in the Sea (Illus. by Michael Rothman) — *Ryder, Joanne*

Sharks — *Maynard, Christopher*

Sharks: Challengers of the Deep (Illus. by Jeffrey L Rotman) — *Cerullo, Mary M*

Sharks! True Stories and Legends — *Gourley, Catherine*

Sharp Horns on the Moon — *Crowe, Carole*

The Shawnee — *Landau, Elaine*

She Dared to Fly — *Johnson, Dolores*

The Shearwater Bell — *Beames, Margaret*

Sheep in a Jeep (Illus. by Margot Apple) — *Shaw, Nancy*

Sheep in a Shop (Illus. by Margot Apple) — *Shaw, Nancy*

Sheep in Wolves' Clothing (McDonough). Audio Version — *Kitamura, Satoshi*

The Sheep-Pig — *King-Smith, Dick*

The Sheep-Pig (Thorne). Audio Version — *King-Smith, Dick*

A Sheep Tale — *Friesen, Peter*

Sheep Trick or Treat (Illus. by Margot Apple) — *Shaw, Nancy*

Sheepish Riddles (Illus. by R W Alley) — *Hall, Katy*

The Shell Book (Illus. by Barbara Hirsch Lember) — *Lember, Barbara Hirsch*

Shells — *Chambers, Catherine*

The Sherlock Holmes Collection (Rathbone). Audio Version — *Doyle, Arthur Conan, Sir*

She's Been Working on the Railroad (Illus. by Shirley Burman) — *Levinson, Nancy Smiler*

Shiloh — *Naylor, Phyllis Reynolds*

Shiloh Season (Moriarty). Audio Version — *Naylor, Phyllis Reynolds*

Shingebiss: An Ojibwe Legend (Illus. by Betsy Bowen) — *Van Laan, Nancy*

Shinkei — *Rubinstein, Gillian*

Shinto — *Hartz, Paula*

Shipwreck (Illus. by Alex Wilson) — *Platt, Richard*

Shipwreck Saturday (Illus. by Varnette P Honeywood) — *Cosby, Bill*

Shoemaker Martin (Illus. by Bernadette Watts) — *Tolstoy, Leo, Graf*

Shoes — *Nichelason, Margery G*

Shoes Like Miss Alice's (Illus. by Ken Page) — *Johnson, Angela*

Shoes: Their History in Words and Pictures (Illus. by Charlotte Yue) — *Yue, Charlotte*

Shola Y Los Jabalies (Illus. by Mikel Valverde) — *Atxaga, Bernardo*

Shoot for the Moon, Robyn (Illus. by Yvonne Cathcart) — *Hutchins, H J*

Shooting Star — *Blacker, Terence*

Sing, like a Hermit Thrush — *Green, Richard G*

Sing 'n Learn Korean. Book and Audio Version — *Kim, Bo-Kyang*

Sing, Sophie! (Illus. by Rosanne Litzinger) — *Dodds, Dayle Ann*

Singing Down the Rain (Illus. by Jan Spivey Gilchrist) — *Cowley, Joy*

The Singing Geese (Illus. by Sterling Brown) — *Wahl, Jan*

Sing'n Learn Chinese. Book and Audio Version — *Jeng, Trio Jan*

Sink or Float? — *Trumbauer, Lisa*

Sip, Slurp, Soup (Illus. by Alex Pardo DeLange) — *Bertrand, Diane Gonzales*

Sir Cedric Rides Again — *Gerrard, Roy*

Sir Circumference and the First Round Table (Illus. by Wayne Geehan) — *Neuschwander, Cindy*

Sir Galahad, Mr. Longfellow, and Me — *Horvath, Betty*

Sirko and the Wolf (Illus. by Robert Sauber) — *Kimmel, Eric A*

El Sistema Nervioso (Illus. by Antonio Munoz Tenllado) — *Roca, Nuria*

Sitting Bull: Sioux Leader — *Schleichert, Elizabeth*

Sitting Down to Eat (Illus. by Kitty Harvill) — *Harley, Bill*

Sitti's Secrets (Illus. by Nancy Carpenter) — *Nye, Naomi Shihab*

Six Dinner Sid — *Moore, Inga*

Six Haunted Hairdos (Illus. by Elaine Clayton) — *Maguire, Gregory*

Six Sandy Sheep (Illus. by John O'Brien) — *Enderle, Judith Ross*

Six Words, Many Turtles, and Three Days in Hong Kong (Illus. by Susan G Drinker) — *McMahon, Patricia*

Size — *Walpole, Brenda*

Skating Out of the House — *Crowe, Anna*

The Skeleton and Muscular System — *Ballard, Carol*

Skin, Teeth, and Hair — *Sandeman, Anna*

Skitterfoot Leaper — *Else, Barbara*

The Skull of Truth (Illus. by Gary A Lippincott) — *Coville, Bruce*

The Skull of Truth (Coville). Audio Version — *Coville, Bruce*

The Sky Is Falling! (Illus. by Cynthia Fisher) — *Miles, Betty*

The Sky Is Falling — *Pearson, Kit*

The Sky Is Not So Far Away (Illus. by Thomas Werner) — *Hiller, Margaret*

Sky Pioneer — *Szabo, Corinne*

Sky Sash So Blue (Illus. by Benny Andrews) — *Hathorn, Libby*

Skymaze — *Rubinstein, Gillian*

Slavery from Africa to the Americas — *Hatt, Christine*

Sleep Is for Everyone (Illus. by Wendy Watson) — *Showers, Paul*

Sleep Safe, Little Whale (Illus. by Peter Sis) — *Schlein, Miriam*

Sleeping Beauty (Illus. by Sue Cony) — *Butterfield, Moira*

The Sleeping Beauty in the Wood — *Heyer, Carol*

Sleepy Kitten — *Scott, Julie*

Sleepy Little Owl (Illus. by Denny Bond) — *Goldsmith, Howard*

Sleepy-O! (Illus. by Laura Rader) — *Ziefert, Harriet*

The Sleepy Owl — *Pfister, Marcus*

Slippery Babies — *Johnston, Ginny*

Slop! A Welsh Folktale (Illus. by Yvonne LeBrun Davis) — *MacDonald, Margaret Read*

Slot Machine — *Lynch, Chris*

Sloth's Shoes (Illus. by Tony Ross) — *Willis, Jeanne*

Slug (Illus. by Karen Duncan) — *Robb, Jackie*

Slugs, Bugs, and Salamanders — *Kniedel, Sally*

The Small Good Wolf (Illus. by Mary Rayner) — *Rayner, Mary*

A Small Miracle (Illus. by Peter Collington) — *Collington, Peter*

Small Steps — *Kehret, Peg*

A Small Treasury of Christmas (Illus. by Susan Spellman)

A Small Treasury of Easter Poems and Prayers (Illus. by Susan Spellman)

Smallest Rabbit (Illus. by Barbara Martin) — *Barkhouse, Joyce*

Smart Dad — *Graham, Amanda*

Smart Girls Forever (Illus. by Axel Scheffler) — *Leeson, Robert*

Smasher (Illus. by Richard Bernal) — *King-Smith, Dick*

Smell and Taste — *Walpole, Brenda*

Smile! (Illus. by Roberta Grobel Intrater) — *Intrater, Roberta Grobel*

The Smithsonian Book of the First Ladies — *Mayo, Edith*

Title Index

Title Index

The Top and Bottom of the World
— *Fowler, Allan*
Top Banana (Illus. by Erika Oller)
— *Best, Cari*
Top Secret — *Cooling, Wendy*
The Top-Secret Journal of Fiona Claire
Jardin — *Cruise, Robin*
The Topsy Turvies (Illus. by Keren
Ludlow) — *Simon, Francesca*
Topsy Turvy (Little Play a Sound)
Torn Ear — *Malone, Geoffrey*
Tornado (Illus. by Doron Ben-Ami)
— *Byars, Betsy Cromer*
Tornado Warning — *Givens, Steven J*
The Tortilla Cat (Illus. by Jeanette
Winter) — *Willard, Nancy*
Tortillas and Lullabies (Illus. by
Corazones Valientes (Organization))
— *Reiser, Lynn*
The Tortoise and the Hare — *Dijs,
Carla*
Tortoise Brings the Mail (Illus. by
Jillian Lund) — *Lillegard, Dee*
Tot Shabbat (Illus. by Camille Kress)
— *Kress, Camille*
r Total Baseball. 5th Ed. — *Thorn, John*
The Totally Awesome Money Book for
Kids and Their Parents — *Berg,
Adriane*
Touch — *Walpole, Brenda*
Touch the Sky — *Elmer, Robert*
Touch the Sky Summer (Illus. by Dan
Andreasen) — *Van Leeuwen, Jean*
Touching the Distance (Illus. by Maria
Rendon) — *Swann, Brian*
Tough (Machines)
The Tower to the Sun (Illus. by Colin
Thompson) — *Thompson, Colin*
Towers Reach High — *Hill, Lee Sullivan*
Town Mouse and Country Mouse
— *Schecter, Ellen*
The Town That Floated Away (Illus. by
Helen Flook) — *Birdsel, Sandra*
Toys — *Bryant-Mole, Karen*
Toys and Games — *Williams, John,
1939-*
Toys Discovered through Art and
Technology — *Bryant-Mole, Karen*
Toys in Space (Illus. by Chris Meister)
— *Sumners, Carolyn*
The Toys We Play With — *Hewitt, Sally*
Tracking Dinosaurs in the Gobi
— *Facklam, Margery*
Tracks in the Snow — *Bledsoe, Lucy
Jane*

Tractors and Trucks (Illus. by Robert
Crowther) — *Crowther, Robert*
Traditional Crafts from Mexico and
Central America — *Temko, Florence*
Traditional Crafts from Native North
America — *Temko, Florence*
Traditional Stories (Genre Library)
Traditional Stories for Children of All
Ages (Bulla). Audio Version — *Bulla,
Dale*
Trails to the West — *Pelta, Kathy*
The Train Ride (Illus. by Stephen
Lambert) — *Crebbin, June*
Train Song (Illus. by Mike Wimmer)
— *Siebert, Diane*
Train to Somewhere (Illus. by Ronald
Himler) — *Bunting, Eve*
Trains — *Morris, Neil*
The Transcontinental Railroad
— *Young, Robert, 1951-*
The Transcontinental Railroad in
American History — *Stein, R Conrad*
r Transport — *Smith, Nigel, 1947-*
r Transportation: Automobiles to
Zeppelins — *English, June*
Transportation: From Cars to Planes
— *Thompson, Gare*
Transportation Then and Now — *Smith,
Nigel, 1947-*
Trapped by Coal — *Horne, Constance*
Trapped by the Ice! (Illus. by Michael
McCurdy) — *McCurdy, Michael*
Trapped in Ice — *Walters, Eric*
Trash Trucks! — *Kirk, Daniel*
Die Traume Von Jonathan Jabbok
(Illus. by Claudia Seeger) — *Isau,
Ralf*
The Traveler: A Magical Journey (Illus.
by Daniel Page Schallau) — *Keller,
James*
Travelling on Land — *Chancellor,
Deborah*
Travels with Rainie Marie — *Martin,
Patricia*
Treacherous Traitors — *Aaseng, Nathan*
The Treasure Hunt (Illus. by Varnette P
Honeywood) — *Cosby, Bill*
The Treasure Hunt (Briers). Book and
Audio Version — *Butterworth, Nick*
The Treasure of Bessledorf Hill
— *Naylor, Phyllis Reynolds*
Treasures in the Dust — *Porter, Tracey*
A Treasury of Dragon Stories (Illus. by
Mark Robertson) — *Clark, Margaret*

Title Index

The Unicorn at the Manger
— *Robbennolt, Roger L*
Unicorn City (Illus. by Neil Reed)
— *Sheldon, Dyan*
Unicorn Dreams (Illus. by Neil Reed)
— *Sheldon, Dyan*
Unicorns! Unicorns! (Illus. by Sophie
Windham) — *McCaughrean,
Geraldine*
Unidentified Flying Objects and
Extraterrestrial Life — *Marsh, Carole*
The United States — *Sandak, Cass R*
The Universe — *Hawkes, Nigel*
Uno, Dos, Tres (Illus. by Barbara
Lavallee) — *Mora, Pat*
The Unprotected Witness — *Stevenson,
James*
Unreal! (Mitchley). Audio Version
— *Jennings, Paul*
Until I Met Dudley (Illus. by Chris
Riddell) — *McGough, Roger*
Unusual Day (Illus. by Georgien
Overwater) — *Toksvig, Sandi*
The Unwilling Witch — *Lubar, David*
Up a Rainforest Tree — *Telford, Carole*
Up and Away! (Illus. by Ken
Dubrowski) — *Davis, Meredith*
Up River (Illus. by Ted Levin) — *Asch,
Frank*
Up the Ladder, down the Slide (Illus. by
Betsy Everitt) — *Everitt, Betsy*
Upchuck and the Rotten Willy (Illus. by
David Slonim) — *Wallace, Bill*
Upon the Head of the Goat (Moore).
Audio Version — *Siegal, Aranka*
The Upstairs Cat (Illus. by Howard
Fine) — *Kuskin, Karla*
USA from Space — *Fallen, Anne-
Catherine*
The Usborne Book of Drawing, Painting
and Lettering (Illus. by Susan Mayes)
— *Mayes, Susan*
The Usborne Book of Hair Braiding
(Illus. by Chris Chaisty) — *Watt,
Fiona*
Usborne Cookery School — *Watt, Fiona*
r The Usborne First Dictionary (Illus. by
Teri Gower) — *Wardley, Rachel*
r The Usborne Illustrated Atlas of the
20th Century — *Miles, Lisa*
r The Usborne Illustrated Thesaurus
— *Bingham, Jane*
Usborne Soccer School — *Harvey, Gill*
Used-Up Bear (Illus. by Clay
Carmichael) — *Carmichael, Clay*

Utahraptor: The Deadliest Dinosaur
(Illus. by Donna Braginetz)
— *Lessem, Don*
The Utterly Nutty History of Football
— *Chatterton, Martin*

V

Una Vaca Querida (Illus. by Ana
Ochoa) — *Antillano, Laura*
Vacationers from Outer Space (Illus. by
Edward Valfre) — *Valfre, Edward*
Vacuum Cleaners — *Alphin, Elaine
Marie*
Valentine Mice! (Illus. by Doug
Cushman) — *Roberts, Bethany*
El Valle De Los Cocuyos (Illus. by
Francisco Melendez) — *Diaz, Gloria
Cecilia*
The Vampire Vanishes (Glover). Audio
Version — *Hall, Willis*
The Vampire's Visit — *Poulsen, David
A*
The Van Gogh Cafe — *Rylant, Cynthia*
Vanishing Act — *Taylor, Cora*
The Vanishing Vampire — *Lubar,
David*
Los Vaqueros: Our First Cowboys
— *Munson, Sammy*
Vegetables — *Powell, Jillian*
The Veil of Snows (Illus. by Chris Van
Allsburg) — *Helprin, Mark*
Los Veinticinco Gatos Mixtecos (Illus.
by Leovigildo Martinez) — *Gollub,
Matthew*
Velcome (Illus. by Kevin O'Malley)
— *O'Malley, Kevin*
Velociraptor (Illus. by Ely Kish)
— *Glossop, Jennifer*
The Velveteen Rabbit (Illus. by Loretta
Krupinski) — *Williams, Margery*
La Verdadera Historia De Los Tres
Cerditos. Book and Audio Version
— *Scieszka, Jon*
Verdi (Illus. by Janell Cannon)
— *Cannon, Janell*
Vermont — *Elish, Dan*
Vertebrates — *Silverstein, Alvin*
The Very Best Book (Illus. by Vitalii
Romanenko) — *Rosenfeld, Diana*
The Very Hungry Caterpillar (Illus. by
Eric Carle) — *Carle, Eric*
The Very Hungry Lion (Illus. by
Indrapramit Roy) — *Wolf, Gita*

Title Index

When I Was a Kid (Illus. by Rachel
Tonkin) — *Tonkin, Rachel*
When I Was Five (Illus. by Arthur
Howard) — *Howard, Arthur*
When I Was Little Like You (Illus. by
Stephen Lambert) — *Paton Walsh,
Jill*
When I Was Your Age — *Ehrlich, Amy*
When Jessie Came across the Sea (Illus.
by P J Lynch) — *Hest, Amy*
When Mama Gets Home (Illus. by
Marisabina Russo) — *Russo,
Marisabina*
When Mom Turned into a Monster
— *Harrison, Joanna*
When Plague Strikes (Illus. by David
Frampton) — *Giblin, James Cross*
When She Was Good — *Mazer, Norma
Fox*
When Someone in the Family Drinks
Too Much (Illus. by Nicole Rubel)
— *Langsen, Richard C*
When the Big Dog Barks (Illus. by
Susan Avishai) — *Curtis, Munzee*
When the Earth Wakes (Illus. by Ani
Rucki) — *Rucki, Ani*
When the Sugar Bird Sings — *Smith,
Claudia*
When the Teddy Bears Came (Illus. by
Penny Dale) — *Waddell, Martin*
When the Wind Bears Go Dancing
(Illus. by Phoebe Stone) — *Stone,
Phoebe*
When the Wind Stops (Illus. by Stefano
Vitale) — *Zolotow, Charlotte*
When the World Was Young (Illus. by
Louise Brierley) — *Mayo, Margaret*
When We Were Very Young (Kuralt).
Audio Version — *Milne, A A*
When Will It Be Spring? (Illus. by
Catherine Walters) — *Walters,
Catherine*
When Willard Met Babe Ruth (Illus. by
Barry Moser) — *Hall, Donald, 1928-*
When Zaydeh Danced on Eldridge
Street (Illus. by Marjorie Priceman)
— *Rael, Elsa Okon*
Where Am I? — *Smith, Albert Gray*
Where Are My Onions? (Illus. by Silvia
Vignale) — *Sarmonpal, Paulette*
Where Are You, Little Zack? (Illus. by
Brian Floca) — *Enderle, Judith Ross*
Where Babies Come From (Illus. by
Nick Sharratt) — *Stones, Rosemary*

Where Butterflies Grow — *Ryder,
Joanne*
Where Do Babies Come From?
— *Royston, Angela*
Where Does God Live? (Illus. by Kim
Howard) — *Bea, Holly*
Where Fireflies Dance (Illus. by Mira
Reisberg) — *Corpi, Lucha*
Where Is Gah-Ning? (Illus. by Helene
Desputeaux) — *Munsch, Robert*
Where Is God? (Illus. by Heidi Bratton)
— *Bratton, Heidi*
Where Land Meets Sea — *Fowler, Allan*
Where Lincoln Walked (Illus. by
Raymond Bial) — *Bial, Raymond*
Where on Earth Am I? — *Gardner,
Robert*
Where Once There Was a Wood
— *Fleming, Denise*
Where Puddles Go (Illus. by Lynn
Jeffery) — *Strauss, Michael*
Where the Moon Lives (Illus. by Ivan
Gantschev) — *Gantschev, Ivan*
Where the Owl Hunts — *Twigg, Aeres*
Where the Red Fern Grows — *Rawls,
Wilson*
Where the Whales Sing (Illus. by
Vivienne Goodman) — *Kelleher,
Victor*
Where the Wild Things Are (Illus. by
Maurice Sendak) — *Sendak, Maurice*
Where the Wind Sleeps (Illus. by Tom
Ward) — *Langille, Carole Glasser*
Where Will This Shoe Take You?
— *Lawlor, Laurie*
Where You Belong — *McGuigan, Mary
Ann*
Where's My Egg? — *Mitton, Tony*
Where's Prancer? (Illus. by Syd Hoff)
— *Hoff, Syd*
Where's Spot? (Illus. by Eric Hill)
— *Hill, Eric*
Where's the Bear? — *Brueghel, Jan*
Where's the Big Dipper? (Illus. by Dean
Lindberg) — *Rosen, Sidney*
Where's Wally? — *Handford, Martin*
Where's Wally in Hollywood?
— *Handford, Martin*
Where's Wally Now? — *Handford,
Martin*
Where's Wally: The Fantastic Journey
— *Handford, Martin*
Where's Wally: The Wonder Book
— *Handford, Martin*

The Wizard (Illus. by Alex Schaefer)
— Martin, Bill, 1916-
A Wizard Abroad — Duane, Diane
The Wizard in the Tree (Illus. by Laszlo
Kubinyi) — Alexander, Lloyd
The Wizard of Oz (Illus. by Lisbeth
Zwerger) — Baum, L Frank
Wolf (Illus. by Sara Fanelli) — Fanelli,
Sara
The Wolf — Havard, Christian
Wolf Academy (Illus. by Jonathan
Allen) — Allen, Jonathan
The Wolf Is Coming! (Illus. by Ken
Brown) — MacDonald, Elizabeth
Wolf Shadows — Casanova, Mary
Wolf Stalker — Skurzynski, Gloria
Wolf Watch (Illus. by Laura Regan)
— Winters, Kay
The Wolf Watchers (Illus. by Andy
DaVolls) — Hood, Alison
Wolfgang — Lynch, Chris
Wolfgang Amadeus Mozart — Castor,
Harriet
The Wolfhound (Illus. by Kris
Waldherr) — Franklin, Kristine L
Wolfman Sam (Illus. by Bill Basso)
— Levy, Elizabeth
The Wolf's Lunch (Illus. by Olivier
Douzou) — Douzou, Olivier
Wolves (Illus. by Warren Clark)
— Dudley, Karen
Wolves and Their Relatives — Stoops,
Erik D
The Woman in the Wall — Kindl,
Patrice
The Woman Who Flummoxed the
Fairies (Illus. by Susan Graber)
— Forest, Heather
The Wombat Who Talked to the Stars
(Illus. by Sharon Dye) — Morris, Jill
Wombats Can't Fly (Illus. by Jane
Burrell) — Dugan, Michael
Women at the Front — Blashfield, Jean
F
Women Invent — Casey, Susan
Women of the Bible — Armstrong,
Carole
Women Pirates — Weatherly, Myra
A Wonder Book for Girls and Boys
(Illus. by Walter Crane)
— Hawthorne, Nathaniel
The Wonder Thing (Illus. by Peter
Gouldthorpe) — Hawthorn, Libby
The Wonder Worm Wars — Palatini,
Margie

Wonderful Nature, Wonderful You
(Illus. by Christopher Canyon)
— Ireland, Karen
The Wonders of Me from A to Z
— Kalman, Bobbie
Wonderwitch and the Spooks — Muir,
Helen
The Won't-Pick-Up-Toys Cure (Illus. by
Bruce Whatley)
Won't You Come and Play with Me?
(Illus. by Cynthia Jabar) — Donovan,
Mary Lee
Wood — Chambers, Catherine
The Wooden Horse (Illus. by Tony
Ross) — McCaughrean, Geraldine
Woodland Christmas (Illus. by Frances
Tyrrell) — Tyrrell, Frances
Woodsie (Illus. by Erik Butler)
— Brooks, Bruce
p Word Dance
Work (Illus. by Ann Morris) — Morris,
Ann
Workers' Rights — Prior, Katherine
Working Days — Mazer, Anne
Working in Airports
Working in Buildings and Property
Working in Enviromental Services
Working in Local Government
Working in Manufacturing
Working in Teaching
Working in Transport and Distribution
Working in TV, Film and Radio
Working Trot — Haas, Jessie
Worksong (Illus. by Ruth Wright
Paulsen) — Paulsen, Gary
The World — Stienecker, David
r The World Almanac and Book of Facts
1923-
r The World Almanac for Kids 1998
r The World Book 1998 Multimedia
Encyclopedia. Deluxe Ed. Electronic
Media Version
r The World Book Dictionary. 1996 Ed.,
Vols. 1-2 — Barnhart, Robert K
r The World Book Encyclopedia. 1997
Ed., Vols. 1-22
r The World Book Encyclopedia 1997.
Electronic Media Version
r The World Book Encyclopedia of
Science. 1997 Ed., Vols. 1-8
World Book Looks at the Sea and Its
Marvels — Williams, Brian
r The World Book Multimedia
Encyclopedia 1997. Electronic Media
Version

X Y Z